4th Edition

SOCIAL PSYCHOLOGY AND HUMAN NATURE

ROY F. BAUMEISTER

Florida State University, USA

BRAD J. BUSHMAN

*The Ohio State University, USA
& VU University
Amsterdam, The Netherlands*

CENGAGE
Learning®

Australia · Brazil · Canada · Mexico · Singapore · Spain · United Kingdom · United States

CENGAGE
Learning®

Social Psychology and Human Nature,
Fourth Edition
Roy F. Baumeister and Brad J. Bushman

Product Director: Jon-David Hague

Product Manager: Melissa Gena

Content Developer: Tangelique Williams-Grayer

Product Assistant: Kimiya Hojjat

Marketing Manager: Melissa Larmon

Content Project Manager: Michelle Clark

Art Director: Vernon Boes

Manufacturing Planner: Karen Hunt

Production Service: Megan Knight,
 Graphic World, Inc.

Text and Photo Researcher: Lumina Datamatics

Copy Editor: Mary Rosewood

Illustrator: Graphic World, Inc.

Text and Cover Designer: Terri Wright

Cover Image: Anna Omelchenko / Masterfile

Compositor: Graphic World, Inc.

For product information and technology assistance, contact us at
Cengage Learning Customer & Sales Support, 1-800-354-9706.

For permission to use material from this text or product, submit all requests online at **www.cengage.com/permissions.**
Further permissions questions can be e-mailed to
permissionrequest@cengage.com.

Library of Congress Control Number: 2015946816

Student Edition: ISBN: 978-1-305-49791-7

Student Edition (Brief): ISBN: 978-1-305-67354-0

Instructor Edition: ISBN: 978-1-305-67351-9

Instructor Edition (Brief): ISBN: 978-1-305-67352-6

Loose-leaf Edition: ISBN: 978-1-305-67353-3

Loose-leaf Edition (Brief): ISBN: 978-1-305-67467-7

Cengage Learning
20 Channel Center Street
Boston, MA 02210
USA

Cengage Learning is a leading provider of customized learning solutions with employees residing in nearly 40 different countries and sales in more than 125 countries around the world. Find your local representative at **www.cengage.com**.

Cengage Learning products are represented in Canada by Nelson Education, Ltd.

To learn more about Cengage Learning Solutions, visit **www.cengage.com**.

Purchase any of our products at your local college store or at our preferred online store **www.cengagebrain.com**.

Printed in Canada
Print Number: 01 Print Year: 2015

SOCIAL PSYCHOLOGY
AND
HUMAN NATURE

About the Cover

For the cover of the fourth edition, we selected a progressive rock music theme. Progressive rock is a form of rock music that evolved in the late 1960s and early 1970s as part of a "mostly British attempt to elevate rock music to new levels of artistic credibility,"[1] in such bands such as *Genesis, Yes, King Crimson, Pink Floyd, Jethro Tull*, and *Emerson, Lake, and Palmer*. One distinguishing feature of progressive rock is "concept albums that made unified statements, usually telling an epic story or tackling a grand overarching theme."[2] Rather than a collection of individual songs, the concept album used a unifying theme to weave the individual songs together. That is exactly what we try to do in our textbook *Social Psychology and Human Nature*. The unifying theme is that humans are cultural animals, and this underlying theme weaves the chapters of our textbook together.

Progressive rock bands also pushed "rock's technical and compositional boundaries by going beyond the standard rock or popular verse-chorus-based song structures."[3] In our textbook, we also try to push the boundaries of typical introductory social psychology textbooks. For example, most textbooks talk about how humans are similar to other animals, whereas we talk about how humans are different from other animals. Likewise, most textbooks talk about how different people from different cultures are, whereas we talk about how similar people from different cultures are. In addition, most textbooks consider obedience to authority to be destructive. Of course, blind obedience to malevolent authority figures is destructive, but most obedience to authority is constructive rather than destructive, such as when people obey traffic laws. That is why we include obedience in our chapter on prosocial behavior.

Two progressive rock musicians, Steve Hackett and Patrick Moraz (friends of Bushman), have both received copies of earlier editions of our textbook. Both have written concept albums, not only in the progressive rock groups they were part of but also in their individual solo albums. Both have also pushed the technical and compositional boundaries of music. In addition, both are compassionate and kind human beings. It is an honor to have both of these progressive rock musicians endorse our textbook.

Steve Hackett was born in London, England. He played lead guitar for *Quiet World* (1969, with his younger brother John Hackett on flute), *Genesis* (1970–1977), and *GTR* (1985–1987; co-founded with guitarist Steve Howe from *Yes* and *Asia*). Hackett perfected the tapping technique, which has been copied by many other guitarists (e.g., Eddie van Halen). He also plays classical guitar on several solo albums.

Patrick Moraz was born in Morges, Switzerland. He played keyboards for progressive rock groups *Mainhorse* (1968–1972), *Refugee* (1973–1974; with former members of *The Nice*—Lee Jackson and Brian Davison), *Yes* (1974–1976), and *The Moody Blues* (1978–1990). He also recorded several solo albums in which he plays his own jazz piano compositions or classical piano compositions. In 1976 he received the "Best Keyboard Album of the Year" award from Contemporary Keyboard Magazine for his album "I" (a.k.a. "The Story of I").

In addition, Steve Hackett and Patrick Moraz have each been involved in numerous projects with other progressive rock musicians. Both Hackett and Moraz have recorded albums with drummer Bill Bruford (who played with progressive rock bands *Yes, King Crimson, Genesis, UK*, and *Gordian Knot* and produced several solo albums). Hackett has also played with several *Yes* musicians besides guitarist Steve Howe and drummer Bill Bruford, including bassist Christopher Squire (indeed they formed a band together—*Squackett*), guitarist Peter Banks, keyboardist Rick Wakeman, and keyboardist Geoffrey Downes (also of *Asia*). Patrick Moraz played on Christopher Squire's solo album "Fish out of Water."

This is what they had to say about our social psychology textbook *Social Psychology and Human Nature*.

Steve Hackett said: "As a musician, when I work on an album I draw ideas and music from many different genres and also from a variety of cultures. I find both the contrasts and similarities between cultures fascinating. Completely different musical forms can connect perfectly, whilst each adds something new and exciting to the whole. I also sometimes go for a theme that gives a framework and a sense of cohesiveness for all these linked ideas.

"In their textbook, Roy Baumeister and Brad Bushman tell a story using the important concept that humans are much more than social animals—they are cultural animals. They explore similarities and differences in the way I interplay contrasting and complementary musical cultures. Also, how they weave the concept through the chapters resembles the way I weave a concept through an album."

Patrick Moraz said: "This fascinating and important work by Roy Baumeister, Ph.D., and Brad Bushman, Ph.D., is constructed in the same way I would research, elaborate, and compose the different movements felt and chosen from the various and immense repository of artistic and musical ideas at my mind's disposal to create and produce a progressive rock album, or even a symphonic work.

"*Social Psychology and Human Nature*, in its entirety, will help the student analyze, understand and build a formidable knowledge to run the gamut of cultural perspectives that humans strive to acquire and assist them further in their explorations of 'cognitive resonance' to a point of utmost clarity and completeness.

"It will, most certainly, elevate its readers to the newest and highest levels of comprehension in the transcultural studies of human nature and might even help them update, enhance and modify their social media behavior.

"As a creative artist, I feel strongly that what clearly differentiates humans from animals and machines, is being inspired spontaneously by new emotional ideas, as opposed to only muscle memories, since the true emotion of the soul is at the basis of our Art."

WE DEDICATE THIS BOOK TO OUR MENTORS AND THEIR MENTORS,

in appreciation of the teaching of psychology through these relationships.

Roy F. BAUMEISTER (1953–)
Ph.D. 1978, Princeton University

Brad J. BUSHMAN (1960–)
Ph.D. 1989, University of Missouri

Edward E. JONES (1926–1993)
Ph.D. 1953, Harvard University

Russell G. GEEN (1932–)
Ph.D. 1967, University of Wisconsin

Jerome S. BRUNER (1915–)
Ph.D. 1941, Harvard University

Leonard BERKOWITZ (1926–)
Ph.D. 1951, University of Michigan

Gordon ALLPORT (1897–1967)
Ph.D. 1922, Harvard University

Daniel KATZ (1903–1998)
Ph.D. 1928, Syracuse University

Herbert S. LANGFELD (1879–1958)
Ph.D. 1909, University of Berlin

Floyd H. ALLPORT (1879–1958)
Ph.D. 1919, Harvard University

Carl STUMPF (1848–1936)
Ph.D. 1868, University of Leipzig

Hugo MÜNSTERBERG (1863–1916)
Ph.D. 1885, Leipzig University
M.D. 1887, Heidelberg University

Edwin B. HOLT (1873–1946)
Ph.D. 1901, Harvard University

Rudolf H. LOTZE (1817–1881)
M.D. 1838, University of Leipzig

Wilhelm WUNDT (1832–1920)
M.D. 1856, Harvard University

William JAMES (1840–1910)
M.D. 1869, Harvard University

About the Authors

ROY F. BAUMEISTER holds the Eppes Eminent Professorship in Psychology at Florida State University, where he is the head of the social psychology graduate program and teaches social psychology to students at all levels. He has taught introductory social psychology to thousands of undergraduate students. He received his Ph.D. from Princeton in 1978, and his teaching and research activities have included appointments at the University of California at Berkeley, Case Western Reserve University, the University of Texas at Austin, the University of Virginia, the Max Planck Institute in Munich (Germany), the VU University Amsterdam (the Netherlands), King Abdulaziz University (Saudi Arabia), and the Center for Advanced Study in the Behavioral Sciences at Stanford. Baumeister is an active researcher whose work has been funded by the National Institutes of Health and by the Templeton Foundation. He has done research on the self (including self-esteem and self-control), the need to belong, sexuality, aggression, and how people find meaning in life. In 2005, the Institute for Scientific Information concluded from a survey of published bibliographies that he was among the most influential psychologists in the world (the top 1%), and that status has been confirmed several times since then. According to Google Scholar, his works have been cited more than 90,000 times in the scientific literature. In his (very rare) spare time, he likes to ski and play jazz. In 2013 he received the William James Award, the highest honor bestowed by the Association for Psychological Science in all of psychology, as recognition of his lifetime achievements and contributions to basic scientific research in psychology.

BRAD J. BUSHMAN is a professor of communication and psychology at The Ohio State University, where he holds the Rinehart Chair of Mass Communication. He is also a professor of communication science at the VU University Amsterdam, the Netherlands, in the summer. For more than 25 years he has conducted research on the causes, consequences, and solutions to the problem of human aggression and violence. He co-chaired the National Science Foundation youth violence advisory committee that was formed in the wake of the shooting in Newtown, Connecticut. He also is a member of President Obama's committee on gun violence. He is ranked number 2 in citations among communication scholars. In 2014 he received the Distinguished Lifetime Contribution to Media Psychology and Technology, American Psychological Association. His research has challenged several myths (e.g., violent media have a trivial effect on aggression, venting anger reduces aggression, violent people suffer from low self-esteem, violence and sex on TV sell products, warning labels reduce audience size). One colleague calls him the "myth buster." His research has been published in the top scientific journals (e.g., *Science*, *Nature*, *PNAS*) and has been featured extensively in the mass media (e.g., *BBC*, *New York Times*, *NPR*). He lives in Columbus, Ohio, with his wife, Tam Stafford, and their youngest son, Branden. Their two oldest children, Becca and Nathan, are students at The Ohio State University. In his spare time, he likes to ride his bicycle (especially in Amsterdam), train in Tang Soo Do at J. Kim martial arts (where he currently is Dan 2), and listen to progressive rock (e.g., Patrick Moraz, Steve Hackett, *Yes*, *Genesis*, *Pink Floyd*) and jazz (e.g., Michiel Borstlap, Miles Davis, John Coltrane, Sonny Rollins).

Brief Contents

Contents

Preface

This textbook is simultaneously an expression of love and rebellion. The love is our feeling toward our field. We followed different paths into social psychology, but over the years we have developed an affectionate appreciation for it. We agreed to write this textbook partly because we thought we could contribute to the field by covering what we love about it. The process of writing strengthened those positive feelings, by helping us see the remarkably diverse and creative work that our fellow psychologists have produced over the past several decades. We are also both very active social psychological researchers and teachers. We love doing social psychology research, and we love teaching students about the field of social psychology.

The rebellion part begins with the title. Maybe social psychology has sold itself short by clinging to the message "it's all about situations!" We think it's partly about situations, but to us, social psychology is very much about people. We think students sign up for social psychology courses because they want to learn about people. And we think social psychologists actually have plenty to tell them about people. Hence the "human nature" part of our title.

In other words, we are rebelling against the old dogma that social psychology's truth requires treating people as blank slates who just respond to situations. Instead, we see people as highly complex, exquisitely designed, and variously inclined cultural animals who respond to situations. Our textbook will tell students plenty about the power of situations, but it also seeks to tell them about the people in those situations.

To us, the most exciting aspect of this project has been the attempt to "put the person back together," in the phrase that got us started on the book. We believe that social psychology can offer a remarkably new, coherent, and accurate vision of human nature.

In fact, this new vision of human nature was central to the story behind the book. Both of us had been approached many times by various publishers about possibly writing a social psychology textbook, and both of us had repeatedly brushed them off as quickly and thoroughly as possible. Back then we thought that writing a textbook sounded like a tedious, uncreative set of chores requiring reading and describing every part of the field, regardless of how interesting. Both of us loathe anything that is boring.

The turning point came when one of us spent a year at an interdisciplinary institute and embraced the task of trying to package what social psychology has learned that could be useful to other fields. Scholars in those fields mostly want to know about people and why they act as they do. The response to this took the form of a book for general audiences called *The Cultural Animal* (Baumeister, 2005), but the realization slowly dawned that this new, more integrated understanding of the human being might provide a powerful basis for a social psychology textbook.

We have used many different textbooks in our own social psychology courses. Many of them are quite good. One dissatisfaction with them, however, and indeed one that we have heard echoed by many other instructors and students, is that they end up being just narrative lists of findings grouped by topic, rather like a handbook or encyclopedia. We wanted more. We wanted an integrated, coherent vision. And now we had a basis in the form of a new understanding of human nature that put together the results of thousands of social psychology studies. So this time when publishers asked us about writing a textbook, we thought it over. And then we decided to do it.

Some might think that explaining human nature isn't the job of social psychology and should be left to the personality psychologists. In our view, personality's claim to that question is not naturally any stronger than social psychology's. After all, personality psychologists mainly study differences between people, and so understanding the patterns common to all people isn't any more likely to arise from those data than from social psychology's data. *Au contraire*, learning about how people in general will respond to ordinary social dilemmas and events is at least as promising as studying individual differences in terms of being able to point toward general patterns of human nature.

Most general theories about human nature agonize over the competing explanations based on evolution and cultural influence. Our synthesis is based on the question "What sort of picture of the human being emerges from the results of thousands of social psychology experiments?" The answer is novel: Nature "made" human beings for culture. That is, we think human beings evolved specifically to belong to these complicated, information-using social systems that we call culture. It is interesting that the Merriam-Webster word of the year for 2014 was "culture" (based on online searches).

Our book has many themes that are mentioned occasionally in the various chapters to tie things together, and these are mostly derived from the central theme of human beings as cultural animals. The theme of putting people first is a subtle way of conveying what is biologically unique about humans: whereas most animals get what they need from their physical environment, people get what they need from each other. This message was implicit even in the classic Asch conformity experiments, in which people would disregard the direct evidence of their physical senses in order to go along with what other people (even a collection of strangers!) were saying.

Another central theme is that inner processes serve interpersonal functions. The conventional wisdom in psychology, going back to its Freudian roots, has been more or less that what happens to people is a result of what's inside them. We think the research in social psychology points toward the need to turn that on its head. What is inside people is a result of what happens between them. Even in terms of what evolution has built into the human psyche, what is there inside the person is there to help people thrive in their social and cultural groups. People are built to relate to other people. Even the "self," much discussed and invoked throughout social psychology, is designed to cultivate social acceptance and other forms of success that are valued in human cultures.

This is not a book about evolution, nor is it a book about cultural differences. It is a book about people. Toward that end, we occasionally use insights that emerge from cultural and evolutionary studies. But those remain mostly on the sidelines. We differ from the evolutionists in that we focus more on how humans are different from other animals rather than how they are similar to other animals. We differ from the cultural psychologists in that we focus more on what cultures have in common than on how they differ. These are differences of emphasis, but they are fundamental and large ones.

The bottom line, for us, is a very positive view of human nature. Over the years, many of the major theories about people have emphasized the negative. They have depicted people as dominated by violent, destructive urges or by strivings for power, as souped-up rats in societal Skinner boxes, as spineless beings at the mercy of giant social forces or willy-nilly situational influences. We have been persuaded partly by the positive psychology movement that psychology loses much of its value when it focuses overly on the negative side. And, heck, we like people. So the integrated picture we offer is a generally positive one, though we give the dark side of human nature its due.

Hence one important feature of this book is that every chapter ends with a brief section entitled "What Makes Us Human? Putting the Cultural Animal in Perspective" that provides a quick review of what answers have emerged in that chapter. These were easy to write because we really do see that human social life is remarkably and importantly different from that of other animals. We do not shrink from discussing the flaws and biases in humanity, and we acknowledge humankind's vast capacity for petty malice and occasional capacity for great evil. But we think the final picture is mostly favorable. These end-of-chapter sections offer a brief reflection on what is special about human nature.

⫸ Concept Features

When we embarked on this book we listened long and hard to the complaints that fellow teachers of social psychology had regarding their textbooks and the way the field was taught. We also listened to the feedback from many students. Several features of our textbook are directly influenced by this feedback. We have sought to offer a new, positive alternative to existing textbooks.

The most common complaint, of course, was the lack of integration. Many instructors, and even those who liked their particular textbook, still felt that textbooks merely hopped from one finding and one phenomenon to another without any broad vision. Hence at the end of the term, as one colleague put it, the take-home message was "Social psychology is a large, interesting, and diverse field of study." Our overarching goal of putting the person back together was a direct response to this complaint and is, in our view, the defining feature of our book. The themes that run through the book help to flesh this out. These are developed in Chapter 2, "Culture and Nature," which we regard as the theoretical foundation of the book. We recommend that instructors assign this chapter early in the semester. That is why we put it early in our textbook. The subsequent chapters can be taught in almost any order. Thus, the book is not a linear sequence in which each chapter builds on the preceding one. We deliberately rejected that approach because we know many instructors like to adapt the sequence of topics to their own schedules, goals, and plans. Instead, the design of this book is like a wheel. Chapters 1 and 2 are the center, and all the other chapters are spokes.

Our chapters contain four box feature inserts. Although many textbooks have boxes, we are especially pleased with our set. In the first edition, they proved to be student favorites. We began with a fairly long list of possible boxes and gradually, based on input and feedback from students and instructors, trimmed these down to the list of four that run through the chapters. For the second edition, we kept three of the four boxes from the first edition. The fourth set, devoted to the broad theme that "Bad is stronger than good," was also well received, but reluctantly we deleted that set to make room for an even more exciting set called "Money Matters." Our readers liked this set of boxes so much that we retained them for the third and fourth editions, but we updated them, replaced some with new ones, and added some. Some of the modules also contain boxes.

 One box in every chapter has to do with eating. One of us recalls a conversation years ago with Peter Herman, who observed, "Eating is the perfect social psychology variable, because it is connected to almost every social variable or process you can think of!" As we researched the various chapters and thought about the findings, we came to see he was right, and so each chapter has a box that covers some findings showing how the chapter's topic influences or is influenced by eating. We thought this would be especially appealing to today's students, for whom college often presents a novel set of challenges and opportunities for eating, dieting, drinking, and related concerns. Eating is a microcosm of social processes. Following are the *Food for Thought* topics included in the book:

- **Does Chicken Soup Reduce Cold Symptoms?** *(Chapter 1)*
- **Virtuous Vegetarians** *(Chapter 2)*
- **Eating Binges and Escaping the Self** *(Chapter 3)*
- **Dieting as Self-Regulation** *(Chapter 4)*

- **It's the Thought That Counts (or Doesn't Count!) the Calories**   *(Chapter 5)*
- **Mood and Food**   *(Chapter 6)*
- **Would You Eat a Bug or a Worm?**   *(Chapter 7)*
- **Convert Communicators and Health Messages**   *(Chapter 8)*
- **Restaurants, Rules, and the Bad Taste of Nonconformity**   *(Chapter 9)*
- **Is There a Link Between Diet and Violence?**   *(Chapter 10)*
- **Social Rejection and the Jar of Cookies**   *(Chapter 11)*
- **Eating in Front of a Cute Guy**   *(Chapter 12)*
- **Prejudice Against the Obese**   *(Chapter 13)*
- **Is Binge Eating Socially Contagious?**   *(Chapter 14)*

The Social Side of *Sex*   The same can be said for sex, and so most chapters include a box applying social psychology to sexuality. We suspect that few people leave college with their sexual selves unchanged since arrival, and so students' natural and personal interest in sexuality can be useful for illuminating many perspectives and patterns in social psychology. Our emphasis is, of course, not on the mechanics or techniques of sex but rather on the social context and influences, which the field of sexuality has often underappreciated. It is also helpful that human sexual behavior is a vivid, dramatic example of something that shows powerful influences of both nature and culture. Following are *The Social Side of Sex* topics included in the book:

- **Sex and Culture**   *(Chapter 2)*
- **Self-Esteem and Saying No to Sex**   *(Chapter 3)*
- **Gender, Sex, and Decisions**   *(Chapter 4)*
- **Counting Sex Partners**   *(Chapter 5)*
- **Can People Be Wrong About Whether They Are Sexually Aroused?**   *(Chapter 6)*
- **A–B Inconsistency and Erotic Plasticity**   *(Chapter 7)*
- **Scared into Safe Sex?**   *(Chapter 8)*
- **Helping, Sex, and Friends**   *(Chapter 9)*
- **Sexual Aggression**   *(Chapter 10)*
- **What Is Beauty?**   *(Chapter 11)*
- **Roots of Anti-gay Prejudice**   *(Chapter 13)*
- **Is Marriage a Group?**   *(Chapter 14)*

There is no *The Social Side of Sex* box in Chapter 12 because half of that chapter is about sex.

A third box presents tradeoffs. In this box we attempt to stimulate critical thinking. Many students come to social psychology wanting to find ways to change the world and solve its problems. We applaud that idealism, but we also think that many problems have their origin in the basic truth that solving one problem sometimes creates another. Many social psychology findings highlight tradeoffs in which each gain comes with a loss. Indeed, in other writings, we apply that principle to assorted issues, not least including gender differences: if men are better than women at something, they are probably worse at something else, and the two are interlinked. We hope that students will come away from these boxes with a heightened integrative capacity to see both sides of many problems and behaviors. Following are the *Tradeoffs* topics included in the book:

We replaced the "Bad is stronger than good" boxes in the first edition of our book with a series of boxes on money for the second, third, and fourth editions. This set was stimulated in part by listening to Paul Rozin, a thoughtful contrarian who has criticized psychology for being out of step with the interests of most people. He would hold up a copy of *USA Today*, "the nation's newspaper," and note that its four sections (politics/crime, money, sports, and life/style) are presumably what American citizens are most interested in reading—yet these topics are scarcely even mentioned in the indexes of most psychology textbooks.

Money is highly relevant to our theme of humans as cultural animals. Money is often spent on getting things that nature makes us want: food, shelter, warmth, comfort, and even health and sex. Social events, such as war, can greatly influence the value of money. Yet money is undeniably a cultural phenomenon. Thus, money shows how humankind has found cultural means of satisfying natural inclinations. Social psychologists (like intellectuals across the ages) have often been skeptical and critical of money, and especially of the desire for money. Although the Bible says "the love of money is the root of all evil" (1 Timothy 6:10), money is a fact of life and an almost indispensable ingredient to the good life in modern society. We hope that this brand-new series of boxes will stimulate students to see money through the prism of social psychology's diverse interests.

Following are the *Money Matters* topics included in the book:

- **Mating, Money, and Men**   *(Chapter 12)*
- **Racial Discrimination in Sports: Paying More to Win**   *(Chapter 13)*
- **Money, Power, and Laughter**   *(Chapter 14)*

Other themes run through the book without being formally reflected in specific boxes. The "duplex mind," divided into the automatic/deliberate and the controlled/conscious sets of processes, has become a powerful theme in the field's thinking about a great many issues, and we want students to appreciate it. It is a profound insight into how the human mind is organized. "The long road to social acceptance" reflects how much work humans have to do to gain and keep their places in their social networks. "Nature says go, culture says stop" was not on our original list of themes but kept coming up as we wrote, and so we went back to revise our earlier chapters to recognize this common way that nature and culture interact to shape human behavior.

⫸ Pedagogical Features

Our book has also benefited from input and suggestions for what can help students master the material. We have kept what has worked well in other textbooks, such as including glossaries, tables, graphs, and illustrations. Each chapter begins with a set of "Learning Objectives" and ends with a "Chapter Summary," where we present lists of bullet points summarizing key content in the chapter.

A more novel feature of our textbook is the inclusion of many self-quizzes. Each major header in each chapter ends with a series of multiple-choice questions. These were wildly popular with students in the first three editions. We can understand why many books don't include them—they were an immense amount of work to prepare, and we wrote them ourselves rather than hiring them out to someone less familiar with the content—but we think the effort was worth it. Every time students finish reading a section of a chapter, they can get a quick check on how well they understood it by answering those questions and verifying whether their answers are correct. Research shows that taking quizzes is one of the best ways to learn new material,[4] far more effective than other techniques such as highlighting and underlining textbooks, rereading, and summarization.[5]

Another exciting feature of this book is the set of five application modules that can be assigned according to instructor preference. It is possible to get the book printed with or without these modules, or indeed with any combination of them. The five modules are: (Module A) Applying Social Psychology to Consumer Behavior, (Module B) Applying Social Psychology to Health, (Module C) Applying Social Psychology to the Workplace, (Module D) Applying Social Psychology to Law, and (Module E) Applying Social Psychology to the Environment. These modules enable an instructor to tailor a course that can encompass some of the most important applied fields of study that have had long, close relationships with social psychology.

For the third and the fourth editions we added six to eight learning objectives for each chapter and module. A learning objective describes what students should know at the end of the chapter that they didn't know before they read it. Learning objectives should be useful for both instructors and students. They also set our book apart from other social psychology books that do not include learning objectives.

⫸ More With Less

When we embarked on this textbook, we made "doing more with less" one of our guiding mottos. As we saw it, social psychology was approaching a turning point. The early textbooks often went into lively detail about many specific studies. That was possible because back then there wasn't a great deal of material to cover. Since then, the body of knowledge in the field has expanded year by year, with new findings being continuously documented in established journals along with new journals popping up all the time. It is no longer possible to cover all the influential studies in great detail.

Some textbooks have responded to information overload by packing more and more findings into the same amount of space. This plainly cannot go on forever. Either textbooks have to get longer and longer, or they have to become more and more selective. We chose the latter course. As things turned out, we were able to cover most of what has become standard in textbooks, but we do not claim or pretend to be exhaustive. Our model for this is introductory psychology. Once upon a time, perhaps, introductory textbooks could provide a comprehensive overview of psychology, but it has by now become standard practice for them merely to select a few topics for each chapter to illustrate rather than fully cover what that field has to offer. We think social psychology is reaching the same point and that the way forward is to accept the impossibility of covering it all.

To be sure, the review process did push us to be more thorough. One thing experts are very good at is saying, "Well, you could also cover topic *X*," and we heeded many such comments from our expert reviewers. But our goal all along has been to offer students an in-depth look at some information, with all its implications and connections highlighted, rather than to make sure to cite every relevant study. We hope instructors will add their personal favorites to the lectures, to augment what we have included. But to keep the book to a manageable length and still do justice to our goals, we had to leave out many important and worthy studies. Even some large topics ended up getting short shrift. Most notably, we devote fairly little space to the social neuroscience work that has become an important theme in the field. We don't dispute its importance. We simply think it is not what is best for introductory students. Our recommendation is that universities offer a subsequent course that can focus on brain processes and their link to social behavior. For the first course, we think students would prefer to learn about the more familiar and more readily understood questions about how people think, feel, and act in recognizable social situations.

⫸ What's New in the Fourth Edition?

We were delighted with the positive reception of the first three editions of our textbook. We are full of gratitude toward all who have used the book. We heard from many instructors and students who made suggestions for material to cover, noticed typos or other things to fix, or simply wanted to express their liking for the book. Thanks to all.

In that happy spirit we set to work on the fourth edition. Our goals were to keep it current, to retain its core vision and best features, and to make substantial, targeted improvements in a few areas where we felt there were promising opportunities or recent developments in the field.

All chapters have come in for revision, especially updating their coverage with the addition of some recent research findings. Still, some chapters underwent more sweeping changes than others. We added a *Social Side of Sex* box to Chapter 14 called **Is Marriage a Group?** We also replaced the *Tradeoffs* box in Chapter 10 with a new one called **Creativity and Cheating**. The old *Tradeoffs* box called Gun Ownership no longer seemed much like a tradeoff, because it has become increasingly obvious, based on statistical and research evidence, that most people are much safer if they do not own a gun than if they do own a gun.

We added new opening vignettes to Chapter 5 on social cognition, Chapter 9 on prosocial behavior, and Chapter 13 on prejudice. We begin Chapter 5 by talking about why some people believe that vaccinations cause autism even though numerous reputable organizations have denied a link between vaccinations and autism (e.g., Centers for Disease Control and Prevention, American Academy of Pediatrics, Institute of Medicine, U.S. National Academy of Sciences, U.K. National Health Service, Cochrane Library). We begin Chapter 9 by discussing "pay it forward," where a person does an unexpected good deed for someone, and asks the recipient to repay it to others instead of to the original benefactor. Chapter 9 also includes a new section on morality. We begin Chapter 13 by discussing human zoos, in which Africans and indigenous peoples are put on display like animals. All modules were also revised and updated.

For the fourth edition, like the third edition, we use the endnote reference style used in the top scientific journals (e.g., *Science, Nature, Proceedings of the National Academy of Science*). This is not a cosmetic change. This makes the text much more readable to students. It also changes the emphasis from *who* did the research to *what* the research found. The references in the endnotes are formatted according to the guidelines of the *Publication Manual of the American Psychological Association* (APA) so interested students can become familiar with APA formatting.

We hope you will enjoy the fourth edition of our book. If you have suggestions for improvement or discover errors in the text, please let us know by dropping us an e-mail (baumeister@psy.fsu.edu or bushman.20@osu.edu). Again, we are deeply grateful for the opportunity to share our love of social psychology with students and teachers around the world.

⁞⁞⁞▶ Content Overview

CHAPTER 1
The Mission & the Method

The opening chapter explains what social psychologists do and why students may want to learn about it. It explains social psychology's place among the different fields that study human behavior. It offers a brief introduction to the methods social psychologists use to tell the difference between right and wrong theories.

CHAPTER 2
Culture and Nature

Chapter 2 sets up the big picture. How do we explain people? Departing from the old and tired battle of nature against nurture, this book follows a newly emerging understanding: nature and culture worked together, such that nature designed the human being to be capable of culture. The stock notion of "the social animal" is shown to be correct but far too limited, whereas the "cultural animal" captures what is special about human beings.

This chapter then sets up many of the integrative themes that will run through the book to help make sense of the many facts and findings that will be covered.

CHAPTER 3
The Self

The human self is a complex and marvelous participant in the social world. This chapter provides a coherent understanding of the human self that is based on both classic and recent research in social psychology.

CHAPTER 4
Choices and Actions: The Self in Control

The self is not just an idea but also a doer. This chapter covers key social psychology topics of choice, decision-making, self-regulation, and the psychology of action. The remarkable recent progress in this work lends extra excitement to this material.

CHAPTER 5
Social Cognition

Social cognition revolutionized social psychology in the 1980s. Now it has settled into a core basis for understanding many spheres of social life. Cognition is vital to cultural animals, because cultures operate on the basis of information. This is a showcase for many of the great achievements of social psychology.

CHAPTER 6
Emotion and Affect

Studying emotion has proven much harder than studying cognition, and so Chapter 6 cannot compare with Chapter 5 in being able to point to a solid body of accepted knowledge. Despite that, much has been learned, and the "work-in-progress" flavor of the social psychology of emotion—combined with the natural human interest in emotion that students can readily share—should make this chapter an appealing read.

CHAPTER 7
Attitudes, Beliefs, and Consistency

The study of attitudes has a long and distinguished history in social psychology. This chapter brings together the influential early, classic studies with the latest advances.

CHAPTER 8
Social Influence and Persuasion

Social influence and attempted persuasion are deeply woven into the fabric of human social life, and indeed it is the rare social interaction that has absolutely none. As information-using cultural animals, humans often find themselves wanting to influence others or being the targets of influence. This chapter covers how people exert that influence, why they do—and how sometimes people manage to resist influence.

CHAPTER 9
Prosocial Behavior: Doing What's Best for Others

In this chapter, we look at what people do in order to make possible the success of their cultural and social groups. Many textbooks have a chapter on helping. We cover helping in this chapter, but the broad focus is on all prosocial behavior. The integrative focus helps resolve some long-running debates, such as whether helping is genuinely altruistic and prosocial or merely egoistic and selfish. We also break with the Milgram tradition of depicting obedience and conformity as bad, because culture and thus human social life would collapse without them. This chapter also discusses morality.

CHAPTER 10
Aggression & Antisocial Behavior

Just as Chapter 9 replaced the traditional, narrow focus on helping with a broader focus on prosocial behavior, this chapter replaces the traditional focus on aggression with a broader treatment of antisocial behavior. Aggression is treated here as a holdover from the social animal stage—which is why cultures mainly struggle to reduce and prevent aggression, favoring nonviolent means of resolving conflicts. Other antisocial behaviors covered include cheating, lying, stealing, and littering.

CHAPTER 11
Interpersonal Attraction and Rejection

This chapter combines two very different but complementary sets of findings. The study of interpersonal attraction has a long history and, despite the occasional new finding, is a fairly well-established body of knowledge. The study of interpersonal rejection is far more recent but has become a thriving, fast-moving area. Together they constitute the two sides of the coin of people trying to connect with each other.

CHAPTER 12
Close Relationships: Passion, Intimacy, and Sexuality

In its first decades, social psychology mainly studied interactions among strangers—but most social life involves ongoing relationships. The study of close, intimate relationships blossomed in the 1980s from a small, underappreciated corner into a profound and exciting enterprise that changed the field. This chapter covers this work, much of it quite recent. It emphasizes romantic and sexual relationships, showcasing what social psychology has contributed to understanding of these grand, perennial human dramas. Human romance and sex are eternal problems that reveal our evolutionary background but also highlight the many striking ways in which humans are unique.

CHAPTER 13
Prejudice and Intergroup Relations

Prejudice occurs all over the world, often contributing to violence and oppression and other forms of misery. This chapter examines the many forms and faces of prejudice, ranging from the standard topics of racism and sexism to the less remarked prejudices against obese people, Arabs and Muslims, atheists, and homosexuals. Special emphasis is given to the emerging and uplifting work on how people overcome prejudice.

CHAPTER 14
Groups

All over the world, human beings live in small groups. This chapter takes a fresh and exciting look at the social psychology of groups. The first part addresses one often overlooked but basic question, namely why are some groups more and others less than the sum of their parts? Classic material on group processes is mixed with new and exciting research.

 # MindTap for Baumeister and Bushman's *Social Psychology and Human Nature*

MindTap is a personalized teaching experience with relevant assignments that guide students to analyze, apply, and improve thinking, allowing you to measure skills and outcomes with ease.

- **Personalized Teaching:** Becomes yours with a learning path that is built with key student objectives. Control what students see and when they see it. Use it as-is or match to your syllabus exactly—hide, rearrange, add, and create your own content.

- **Guide Students:** A unique learning path of relevant readings, multimedia, and activities that move students up the learning taxonomy from basic knowledge and comprehension to analysis and application.

- **Promote Better Outcomes:** Empower instructors and motivate students with analytics and reports that provide a snapshot of class progress, time in course, engagement and completion rates.

In addition to the benefits of the platform, MindTap for Baumeister and Bushman's *Social Psychology and Human Nature* features:

- **Videos, animations, and survey-type activities,** all based on key social psychology topics and concepts.

- **Chapter-opening activities that include** "choose-your-own-activity style exercises in which students progress through by answering questions and to indicate their next steps. At the end, their decision-based outcome is presented, along with related social psych research.

- **Quizzing for every** chapter, including multiple choice, true-false, and short response reflection questions to encourage application and critical thinking
- **Cerego Mastery Training** lessons to reinforce and help student learning of important topics

ⅢⅢ➡ Supplements

Instructor's Resource Manual The Online Instructor's Research Manual includes the following tools for each chapter:

- **Chapter outline.** Detailed review of the chapter with key terms underlined and defined.
- **Lecture/discussion ideas.** Helpful ways to address topics in text, cover topics tangential to what is in text, or provide alternative examples to what are presented in the text.
- **Class activity/demonstration ideas.** Ideas and prompts for in-class activities.
- **Student projects/homework.** Short- and longer-term assignments, as well as substantial prompts for projects that students can do on their own as out-of-class assignments or short-term projects.
- **Video clip suggestions** our *Research in Action* video collection, YouTube, and other videoclip suggestions.
- **Handouts.** Each chapter includes helpful handouts correlated with suggested activities and homework.

ISBN: 9781305873902

Cognero Cengage Learning Testing Powered by Cognero is a flexible, online system that allows you to author, edit, and manage test bank content from multiple Cengage Learning solutions, create multiple test versions in an instant, and deliver tests from your Learning Management System (LMS), your classroom, or wherever you want. **ISBN:** 9781305856974

PowerPoint The Online PowerPoint features lecture outlines and key images from the text. **ISBN:** 9781305873919

Acknowledgments

MANUSCRIPT REVIEWERS

We thank our colleagues for their diligent and thoughtful fourth edition pre-revision surveys, as well as to those who reviewed earlier editions of *Social Psychology and Human Nature*. Their suggestions pointed the way to make this a better book.

FOURTH EDITION

Anila Putcha-Bhagavatula,
California State University, Fullerton

Kathleen Schiaffino,
Fordham University

Mary Shuttlesworth,
Mt. Aloysius College

Heidi Dempsey,
Jacksonville State University

Stephanie Afful,
Fontbonne University

Lindsey Rodriguez,
University of Houston

Corey Cook,
Skidmore College

Nao Hagiwara,
Virginia Commonwealth U

Ashlee Lien,
SUNY College at Old Westbury

Ken Cheung,
Brooklyn College

Julie Blaskewicz Boron,
Youngstown State

Carrie V. Smith,
University of Mississippi

Fionnuala Butler,
Carthage College

Erin Ward Sparks,
Purdue University

Melanie Covert,
Brenau University

Alisa Aston,
University of North Florida

Luis Vega,
California State University, Bakersfield

THIRD EDITION

Keith Davis,
University of South Carolina, Columbia

Philip Mazzocco,
The Ohio State University at Mansfield

Michael Dudley,
Southern Illinois University

Eirini Papafratzeskakou,
Virginia Tech, Blacksburg

Lisa Finkelstein,
Northern Illinois University

Randall Renstrom,
Loyola University, Chicago

Evan Kleiman,
George Mason University

SECOND EDITION

Gordon Bear,
Ramapo College of New Jersey

Kathleen McKinley,
Cabrini College

Khanh Bui,
Pepperdine University

Mark Muraven,
University at Albany

Nilanjana Dasgupta,
University of Massachusetts—Amherst

Ernest Park,
Cleveland State University

Kimberly Fairchild,
Manhattan College

Ludmila Praslova,
Vanguard University of Southern California

Jennifer Feenstra,
Northwestern College

Christopher Robinson,
University of Alabama, Birmingham

Joseph R. Ferrari,
Vincent DePaul University

Heidi Wayment,
Northern Arizona University

FIRST EDITION

Nancy L. Ashton,
The Richard Stockton College of New Jersey

Kurt Boniecki,
University of Central Arkansas

Melissa Atkins,
Marshall University

Thomas Britt,
Clemson University

Kevin Bennett,
Pennsylvania State University–Beaver

Jonathan Brown,
University of Washington

John Bickford,
University of Massachusetts–Amherst

Jeff Bryson,
San Diego State University

Shawn Burn,
California Polytechnic State University

Jennifer L. Butler,
Wittenberg University

Keith Campbell,
University of Georgia

Laurie Couch,
Morehead State University

Traci Y. Craig,
University of Idaho

Janet Crawford,
Rutgers University

Layton Curl,
Metropolitan State College of Denver

Deborah Davis,
University of Nevada–Reno

John Davis,
Texas State University–San Marcos

Dorothee Dietrich,
Hamline University

Nancy Dye,
Humboldt State University

Sarah Estow,
Dartmouth College

Jennifer Feenstra,
Northwestern College

Joe R. Ferrari,
DePaul University

Lisa Finkelstein,
Northern Illinois University

Phil Finney,
Southeast Missouri State University

Wendi Gardner,
Northwestern University

Bryan Gibson
Central Michigan University

Tom Gilovich,
Cornell University

Traci Giuliano,
Southwestern University

Wind Goodfriend,
Buena Vista University

Elizabeth Gray,
Northpark University

Jeffrey D. Green,
Soka University

Hillary Haley,
Santa Monica College

Darlene Hannah,
Wheaton College

Judith Harackiewicz,
University of Wisconsin

Lora Harpster,
Salt Lake City Community College

Helen C. Harton,
University of Northern Iowa

Sandra Hoyt,
Ohio University

Jon Iuzzini,
University of Tennessee–Knoxville

Norine Jalbert,
Western Connecticut State University

Robert Johnson,
Arkansas State University

Deana Julka,
University of Portland

Patrice Karn,
University of Ottawa

Benjamin R. Karney,
University of Florida

Timothy Ketelaar,
New Mexico State University

Charles Kimble,
University of Dayton

Linda Kline,
California State University–Chico

Elisha Klirs,
George Mason University

C. Raymond Knee,
University of Houston

Susan Kraus,
Fort Lewis College

Neil Kressel,
William Patterson University

Joachim Kreuger,
Brown University

Roger Kreuz,
University of Memphis

Douglas Krull,
Northern Kentucky University

Barry Kuhle,
Dickinson College

Paul Kwon,
Washington State University

Benjamin Le,
Haverford College

Jean Twenge,
San Diego State University

Kathleen Vohs,
University of Minnesota

CONTENT AREA EXPERT REVIEWERS

We thank our colleagues for providing their expertise on specific chapters. Their comments sharpened and improved these chapters.

Craig A. Anderson,
Iowa State University James R. Averill, University of Massachusetts–Amherst

Donal E. Carlston,
Purdue University

Eddie M. Clark,
St. Louis University

William D. Crano,
Claremont Graduate University

Wind Goodfriend,
Buena Vista University

Anne K. Gordon,
Bowling Green State University

Michael Hogg,
University of Queensland

Lee Jussim,
Rutgers University

Marc Kiviniemi,
University of Nebraska–Lincoln

Mark K. Leary,
Duke University

George Levinger,
University of Massachusetts–Amherst

Norman Miller,
University of Southern California

Todd D. Nelson,
California State University–Stanislaus

Laurie O'Brien,
University of California–Santa Barbara

B. Keith Payne,
University of North Carolina–Chapel Hill

Louis A. Penner,
Wayne State University

Cynthia L. Pickett,
University of California–Davis

Deborah Richardson,
Augusta State University

Brandon J. Schmeichel,
Texas A&M University

Peter B. Smith,
University of Sussex

Jeff Stone,
University of Arizona

Duane T. Wegener,
The Ohio State University

Kipling D. Williams,
Purdue University

CONTRIBUTORS OF APPLYING SOCIAL PSYCHOLOGY MODULES

Special thanks go to our colleagues who wrote the application modules. These are specialized topics outside our own expertise, and we could not have done these ourselves even half as well. These modules add to the breadth and flexibility of what can be taught with this textbook.

Module A: Applying Social Psychology to Consumer Behavior
Curtis Haugtvedt,
The Ohio State University

Module B: Applying Social Psychology to Health
Regan A. R. Gurung,
University of Wisconsin–Green Bay

Module C: Applying Social Psychology to the Workplace
Kathy Hanisch,
Iowa State University

Module D: Applying Social Psychology to the Law
Margaret Bull Kovera,
John Jay College of Criminal Justice, City University of New York

Module E: Applying Social Psychology to the Environment
Richard L. Miller,
University of Nebraska at Kearney

CENGAGE TEAM

This book would not have been possible without the excellent in-house team at Cengage. Thanks to the following people for your belief in our vision for this book: Melissa Gena, Product Manager; Jon-David Hague, Publisher; Tangelique Williams-Grayer, Sr. Content Developer; Kimiya Hojjat, Product Assistant; Michelle Clark, Content Project Manager; Vernon Boes, Senior Art Director; and Megan Knight, Project Manager for Graphic World Publishing Services.

We acknowledge our appreciation and debt to this full team, but we must single out one person who has had the most direct contact with us and who, at least from where we have sat for these several years, has made the most difference. Jeremy Judson was a patient, thoughtful, intelligent, and diplomatic editor who was remarkably effective at steering the manuscript through the nuts and bolts of the revision process. Often he would manage to sort through a dozen or more reviews, boiling the chaotic mass of suggestions down into the key targets for improvement and managing the process with reason and good humor.

THE MISSION & THE METHOD

1

LEARNING OBJECTIVES

1 Define social psychology.

2 Name the early influences and key ideas that had a lasting influence on the field.

3 Describe the ABC triad of social psychology.

4 Explain how social psychology relates to other fields of study.

5 Assess the different methods of data collection in social psychology.

Christian Mueller/Shutterstock.com

1

YOU are a member of a social world on a planet containing more than seven billion people. This social world is filled with paradox, mystery, suspense, and outright absurdity. Recently, one man spent $70,000 in an auction for eight stuffed squirrels wearing boxing gloves.[1] In many parts of the world less than $50 can feed a person for a year, which means 1,400 people could be fed for an entire year for the price paid for just eight dead squirrels.

Or consider that a homeless man in Kansas City, Missouri, went from having no money to having $145,000 after he returned an engagement ring that a woman accidentally dropped in his panhandling cup along with some spare change. He returned it to her the next day when she returned to see if he had it. The woman was so happy to get her ring back that she set up a website seeking donations for him, and over 6,000 people responded.[2]

Another ironic case involved a U.S. Air Force officer who oversaw the Air Force Sexual Assault Prevention and Response unit. He was charged with groping a woman in a parking lot.[3] The Air Force website states, "Sexual assault is criminal conduct. It falls well short of the standards America expects of its men and women in uniform."

Can social psychology help us make sense of the baffling diversity of human behavior? The answer to this question is a resounding "Yes!" **Social psychology** is the scientific study of how people affect and are affected by others. Whether you know it or not, social psychology can help you make sense of your own social world. The material discussed in this book is intensely relevant to your life. For example, have you ever asked yourself questions such as these: "How can I get him to go along with my plan?" "Should I ask her right up front to do this big favor, or is there a better way to get her to say yes?" "How can I bring them around to my way of thinking?" Social psychology can also help you understand simpler things, such as taking a coffee break. If your boss told you to make 10,000 decisions before you got your first cup of coffee, you'd probably think you had a cruel boss! The Starbucks chain of coffee shops, however, has advertised that they offer 19,000 beverage options, if you count the different coffees, teas, cold drinks, and all the things you could add to them. In a sense, therefore, the customer who walks into a Starbucks shop for a morning drink is confronted with more than 19,000 choices. After making 19,000 decisions, you can end up with a cup of coffee that costs over $50! It is called the Sexagintuple Vanilla Bean Mocha Frappuccino. It has 60 shots and comes in a 128-ounce (3.79-liter) glass. Isn't having so many choices just a way to frustrate people? How does Starbucks make money? Why don't their customers protest? More to the point (at least for a social psychologist), how do people get by in a world that offers them thousands of options at every turn, even for the simplest decisions? In Chapter 5 we discuss some of the heuristics people use to manage such information overload.

Chances are, something in this book will prove helpful to you in the future. This is not to say that social psychology is a cookbook for how to influence and manipulate others. Social psychology, however, can help you understand basic principles of social influence, as well as many other principles of social behavior. It is also just plain interesting to learn how and why people act the way they do.

The point is that there are plenty of reasons why you ought to be interested in social psychology. As you learn more, you can profit more and get more enjoyment from what social psychology has to offer. Let's begin by looking at how social psychology became the field it is. ●

After making 19,000 decisions, you can end up with a cup of coffee that costs over $50! The Sexagintuple Vanilla Bean Mocha Frappuccino has 60 shots and comes in a 128-ounce (3.75 liter) glass.

A Brief History of Social Psychology

It is hard to know what the first social psychology experiment was, but consider a few of the earliest ones we know about. Indiana University professor Norman Triplett conducted one of the first social psychology experiments in 1897.[4] While examining the cycling records for the 1897 season, he noticed that bicycle riders who competed against others performed better than those who competed against the clock. Triplett proposed that the presence of another rider releases a competitive instinct, which increases "nervous energy" and thereby enhances individual performance. Triplett tested his hypothesis by building a "competition machine." He had 40 children wind up a reel, alternating between working alone and working parallel to each other. Winding times were faster when children worked side by side than when they worked alone. Thus, the mere presence of another person enhanced performance on this simple task.

Another early social psychological experiment was conducted in the 1880s by a French professor of agricultural engineering named Max Ringelmann.[5] He had men pull on a rope alone and as part of a group, and he measured the amount of effort exerted by each participant. He found that as group size increased, individual effort decreased. This study can explain why people tend to slack off when working on group projects.

These two seminal studies started a long chain of subsequent studies. Note, though, that the two studies pointed in opposite directions—one found that people worked harder in the presence of others, and the other found that people slacked off in the presence of others. Chapter 14 will try to resolve this seeming contradiction, but for now the point is to get used to the idea that social behavior is complicated.

social psychology the scientific study of how people affect and are affected by others

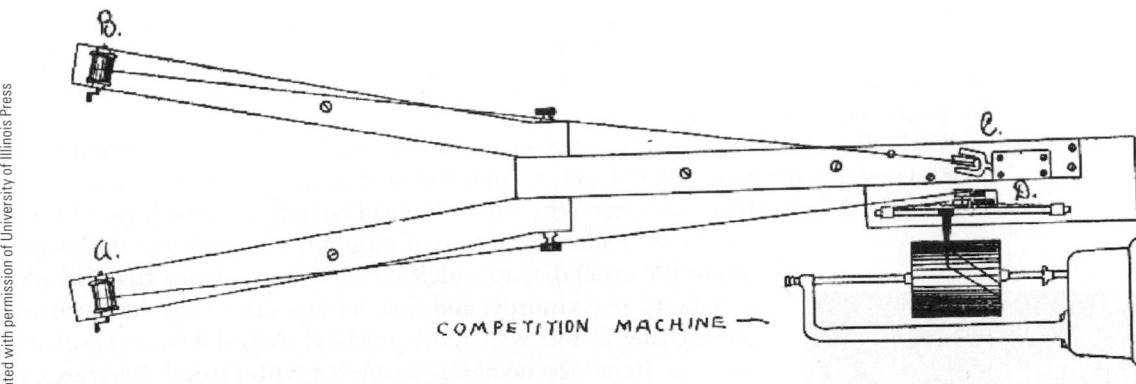

Reprinted with permission of University of Illinois Press

DGB/Alamy

The competition machine (pictured above), created by Triplett to test whether the presence of others affects individual performance, is one of the first social psychology experiments. Triplett found that children wound the fishing reel faster in the presence of other children than when they were alone. Ringelmann found that people exert less effort in groups, such as in a tug-of-war (pictured left), than as individuals.

The introduction of textbooks is an important milestone in the development of a field. In 1908, the first two books to bear the title *Social Psychology* were published, one by the psychologist William McDougall[6] and the other by the sociologist Edward Ross.[7] In 1924, Floyd Allport[8] published another early social psychology book. Your own current textbook is another in a long line of social psychology textbooks. It addresses many of the same issues as those early ones—but of course it has much more information, thanks to the toils of researchers all over the world.

During the early part of the 20th century, many thinkers began to ponder where human society was going and why it had changed so much. Two world wars, the rise of communism and fascism, the spread of automobiles, the rapid changes in sexual behavior, the rise of advertising, popular fads, the population shift from farms to cities, and shocking economic events such as the Great Depression all challenged intellectuals to wonder what were the basic laws of how people relate to each other. They began to toss about various new and big ideas, including some that would shape the thinking of early social psychologists. One idea was that modern life makes people vulnerable to alienation and exploitation by giant social systems. Another idea was that we learn who we are from other people and our interactions with them. Still another idea was that modern humans act less on the basis of firm inner moral principles than on the basis of following the crowd.

Two ideas from this period had a lasting influence on social psychology. One was Gordon Allport's observation in 1954 that attitudes were "the most distinctive and indispensable concept in contemporary American social psychology" (p. 43).[9] The study of attitudes dominated social psychology research for decades and is still centrally important today (see Chapter 7). (Gordon Allport also observed that the study of the self was going to be recognized as increasingly important in the coming years, and on that prediction he was also quite correct; see Chapter 3.)

The other key idea was Kurt Lewin's formula that behavior is a function of the person and the situation.[10] Thus, if you want to predict whether Nathan will finish his school paper on time, you need two kinds of information. First, you must know something about Nathan: Is he lazy? Does he like the topic of the paper? Is he smart enough to get the job done? Is he punctual? Second, you must know something about his situation: Is the task hard? Are other people bothering him? Is there a penalty for being late? Is his printer broken? Knowing only one kind of information without the other is an inadequate basis for predicting what will happen.

World War II stimulated a great deal of research in the social sciences, and in social psychology in particular. Several factors contributed to this rise in research. Some involved grand theoretical questions: Why did millions of citizens in a modern, civilized nation with a long tradition of religion, morality, and philosophy follow the cruel dictator Adolf Hitler in his policies that included systematic mass murder and violent invasion of neighboring countries? Other factors were more practical: Why did soldiers seem to have so many psychological problems with stress? What exactly motivates soldiers to continue doing their duty on modern battlefields where they could be killed at any moment? World War II also caused many researchers to leave Europe and migrate to the United States. The influx of influential thinkers (including Kurt Lewin, whom we already mentioned) swelled the ranks of American thinkers and helped make the United States a world leader in social psychology. This European "brain drain" helped social psychology flourish in the United States.

In fact, the terrible events during World War II in Nazi Germany were the impetus for the most well-known social psychology studies ever conducted. It was shortly after Adolf Eichmann (a high-ranking Nazi and SS officer) was captured, tried, and hanged by an Israeli court that Stanley Milgram conducted his studies on obedience. During his trial, Eichmann did not dispute the facts of the Holocaust but said he was only

Historical/Corbis

World War II stimulated a great deal of social psychological research.

"following orders." He testified that he "never did anything, great or small, without obtaining in advance express instructions from Adolf Hitler or any of my superiors." Milgram asked, "Could it be that Eichmann and his million accomplices in the Holocaust were just following orders? Could we call them all accomplices?"[11] In summarizing his findings, Milgram said, "I set up a simple experiment at Yale University to test how much pain an ordinary citizen would inflict on another person simply because he was ordered to by an experimental scientist. Stark authority was pitted against the subjects' strongest moral imperatives against hurting others, and, with the subjects' ears ringing with the screams of the victims, authority won more often than not."[12] In Chapter 9, we describe Milgram's original study and subsequent studies in detail. We point out, however, that although obedience to malevolent authority is detrimental, obedience to nonmalevolent authority is often very beneficial to society (e.g., when motorists obey traffic laws).

Social psychology began to come into its own as a field in the 1950s and 1960s. At the time, psychology was divided between two camps. One camp, known as **behaviorism** sought to explain human behavior in terms of learning principles such as reward and punishment. (Countless studies were conducted with white laboratory rats in order to establish these principles.) Behaviorists were opposed to talking about the mind, thoughts, emotions, or other inner processes, focusing instead on observable actions that could be studied experimentally using the scientific method. The other camp was **Freudian psychoanalysis** which preferred elaborate interpretations of individual experiences (especially from clinical practice) instead of experimental studies that counted behaviors. Social psychology was not really compatible with either camp. Social psychology was more congenial to the behaviorist camp, in that it favored experiments and the scientific method, but it was also sympathetic to the Freudian camp with its interest in inner states and processes. For a while it sought to steer a middle course. Eventually (by the 1970s and 1980s), social psychology found its own way, using scientific approaches to measure not only behavior but also thoughts, feelings, and other inner states.

What about the more recent past? Historians are generally uncomfortable writing about recent times because main themes are easier to see from a distance than from up close. Still, we can make a few broad statements about the recent history of social psychology. The study of simple cognitive (mental) processes, such as attribution theory (attributions are explanations people come up with to explain the behavior of others), evolved in the 1970s and 1980s into a large and sophisticated study of social cognition (how people think about people and the social world in general). This area of interest has continued up to the present.

Another huge development from the 1990s onward was a growing openness to biology. The influx of biology was boosted by evolutionary psychology, which sought to extend and apply the basic ideas of evolution to understanding human social behavior. It gained further momentum as some social psychologists began to study the brain in order to learn how its workings are related to social events. Today, social neuroscience is an interdisciplinary field of study that investigates how biological systems influence social thought and behavior. Sophisticated instruments allow researchers to directly manipulate (e.g., transcranial direct current stimulation, tDCS) and measure (e.g., functional Magnetic Resonance Imaging, fMRI) brain processes.

The study of the self has been another central theme of social psychology since the 1970s. It is hard to realize that in the 1960s people hardly ever used the term *self-esteem* or cared about it. In recent decades, social psychologists have explored many different aspects of the self—not only self-esteem but also self-control, self-concept, and self-presentation. We discuss these topics in Chapters 3 and 4.

The field continues to change and evolve. In the 1980s, the conflict between the so-called free world and communist totalitarian systems was the dominant conflict in the world and the main focus of conflict studies. When the Soviet empire abruptly collapsed in 1989, the study of conflict between groups refocused on racial and ethnic conflict, which in the United States meant a sharp rise of interest in prejudice and stereotyping. Today, the same theories have been applied to understand stereotyping, prejudice, and discrimination of other stigmatized groups.

WILL PRESS LEVER FOR FOOD

© Craig Swanson/perspicuity.com

Behavioral psychologists conducted countless studies using white rats.

behaviorism theoretical approach that seeks to explain behavior in terms of learning principles, without reference to inner states, thoughts, or feelings

Freudian psychoanalysis theoretical approach that seeks to explain behavior by looking at the deep unconscious forces inside the person

1. The earliest social psychological experiments were conducted in the late 1800s by researchers such as Max Ringelmann and Norman Triplett. What was the topic of these early studies?

ⓐ Aggression ⓑ Attitude change ⓒ Presence of others on individual performance ⓓ Prosocial behavior

2. According to Gordon Allport, what was the most central concept in social psychology?

ⓐ Aggression ⓑ Altruism ⓒ Attitudes ⓓ Attributions

3. According to Kurt Lewin's formula, behavior is a function of what two variables?

ⓐ Affect and cognition ⓑ Appraisals and attributions ⓒ Attitudes and beliefs ⓓ Person and situation

4. In the 1950s and 1960s, psychology was divided between what two camps?

ⓐ Behaviorist and cognitive camps ⓑ Behaviorist and psychoanalytical camps ⓒ Cognitive and comparative camps ⓓ Cognitive and psychoanalytical camps

answers: see pg 30

What Do Social Psychologists Do?

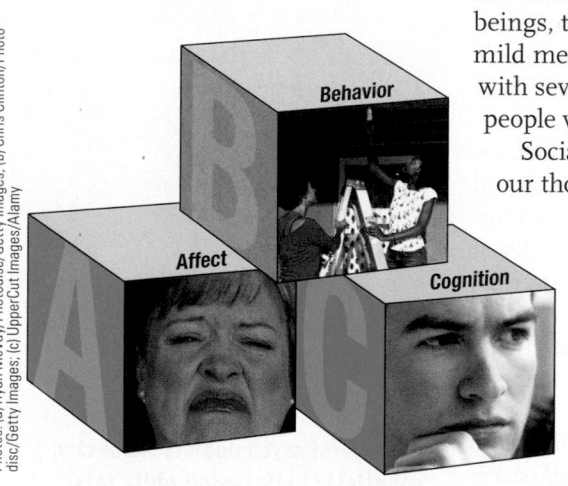

Photos: (a) Ryan McVay/Photodisc/Getty Images; (b) Chris Clinton/Photo disc/Getty Images; (c) UpperCut Images/Alamy

FIGURE 1.1

Affect, Behavior, and Cognition are the ABCs of what social psychologists study.

ABC triad Affect (how people feel inside), Behavior (what people do), Cognition (what people think about)

Social psychology aims for a broad understanding of the social factors that influence how human beings think, act, and feel. It focuses particularly on normal adult human beings, though some social psychologists do study children and people who suffer from mild mental illness (such as depression). Very little of what people do, other than those with severe mental illness, is off-limits to social psychology. Clinical psychologists study people with severe mental illness.

Social psychology is concerned with the effect of other people (real or imagined) on our thoughts, feelings, and behaviors. These three dimensions or building blocks of social psychology are known as the **ABC triad** (**FIGURE 1.1**). The **A** stands for Affect (pronounced 'AF-ekt; note that this word is a noun, not a verb, which is pronounced 'ə-'fekt)—how people feel inside. Social psychologists are interested in how people feel about themselves (e.g., self-esteem), how they feel about others (e.g., prejudice), and how they feel about various issues (e.g., attitudes). The **B** stands for Behavior—what people do, their actions. Social psychologists are interested in all the various behaviors people engage in, such as joining groups, helping others, hurting others, loving others, working, playing, praying, and relaxing. The **C** stands for Cognition—what people think about. Social psychologists are interested in what people think about themselves (e.g., self-concept), what they think about others (e.g., forming impressions), and what they think about various problems and issues in the social world (e.g., protecting the environment).

Social psychologists study the effects of personal and situational influences on these ABCs—especially the power of situations. That is, when trying to explain some pattern of behavior, the first place social psychologists generally look is to the situation. In this focus, social psychology departed from two powerful traditions in psychology. Freudian psychoanalysis sought to explain behavior by looking at the deep unconscious forces inside the person, whereas behaviorist learning theory sought to explain behavior by looking at reinforcement histories (e.g., what behaviors were previously rewarded or punished). Social psychology emphasizes how people react to the world around them, and how small changes in their immediate circumstances can produce substantial changes in behavior. Social psychologists even study the influence of situational factors that people may not even be aware of. For example, participants in one famous study[13] arranged scrambled words to form sentences. Participants were shown five words and were told to choose four of the words to make a sentence. By the flip of a coin, participants received either words associated with the elderly (e.g., A LET'S KITE FLY OLD, which can make the sentence LET'S FLY A KITE), or words not associated with the elderly (e.g., A LET'S KITE FLY COLOR, which can make the same sentence LET'S FLY A KITE). After participants completed the task, the researcher thanked them for participating and told them that the elevator was down the hall. Using a hidden stopwatch, the researchers timed how long it took participants to walk to the elevator. Participants who had unscrambled the elderly words took significantly longer to walk to the elevator than did participants who had unscrambled the neutral words. In contrast, participants in another study[14] who were subliminally exposed to entitlement words (e.g., SPECIAL, SUPERIOR) walked significantly faster when they left the study than did participants who were subliminally exposed to neutral words (e.g., WATER, NUMBER), presumably because they felt like they were very important people who had better things to do with their "precious" time.

Social psychology embraces the scientific method. Most social psychologists conduct experiments, which are careful and systematic ways of testing theories. You will learn more about how experiments are conducted later in this chapter. There are many ways to learn about people, such as reading a novel, watching people at the shopping mall, living in a foreign country, or talking with friends for hours at a time. All those approaches may yield valuable lessons, but the scientific method has important advantages over them. In particular, it is hard to know whether the insights gleaned from reading a novel or watching people are correct. The scientific method is the most rigorous way of sorting out the valid lessons from the mistaken ones. We discuss the scientific method later in this chapter.

1. Unconscious forces are to reinforcement histories as _____ is to _____.
   - (a) affect; cognition
   - (b) cognition; affect
   - (c) behaviorism; psychoanalysis
   - (d) psychoanalysis; behaviorism

2. What research methodology do most social psychologists use?
   - (a) Experimental studies
   - (b) Longitudinal studies
   - (c) Quasi-experimental studies
   - (d) Survey studies

3. What are the components of the **ABC** triad?
   - (a) Affect, Behavior, Cognition
   - (b) Affect, Beliefs, Cognition
   - (c) Attitudes, Beliefs, Compliance
   - (d) Affect, Behavior, Conformity

4. What is the primary approach that social psychologists use to uncover the truth about human social behavior?
   - (a) Reliance on authority figures
   - (b) Introspection
   - (c) Rationalism
   - (d) Scientific method

answers: see pg 30

Social Psychology's Place in the World

Social psychology is related to other social sciences and to other branches of psychology. It also differs from them in important ways.

Social Psychology's Place in the Social Sciences

Social scientists study people and the societies in which they live. Social scientists are interested in how people relate to one another. The various social sciences focus on different aspects of social life.

Anthropology is the study of human culture. Human culture consists of the shared values, beliefs, and practices of a group of people, which are passed down from one generation to another. Not only are humans social animals, they are also cultural animals. This is one of the central themes of this book (see Chapter 2). Social psychologists cannot understand human behavior fully unless they understand the cultural context in which that behavior occurs.

Economics is the study of the production, distribution, and consumption of goods and services. Social psychologists are very interested in these topics. In fact, some social psychological theories are based on economic principles. For example, social exchange theory predicts commitment to relationships by considering factors such as the costs, rewards, investments, and the number of alternatives available. Economics also calls our attention to large social systems (such as the labor market or money system) and to how these systems shape human behavior. Again, a full understanding of human behavior requires appreciating not just what goes on inside one person's head and what is happening in his or her immediate environment at the time, but also how the person's behavior fits into the larger social system.

History is the study of past events. For humans to progress, they should understand past events and learn from them. As Spanish philosopher George Santayana said, "Those who cannot remember the past are condemned to repeat it."[15] Society progresses when members can avoid repeating the same mistakes others have made. Social psychologists sometimes debate whether the behaviors they study have changed historically, but until recently little interaction has occurred between social psychologists and historians.

Political science is the study of political organizations and institutions, especially governments. Social psychologists conduct research on political behavior. They study political issues such as voting, party identification, liberal versus conservative views, and political advertising. Political leaders can have a tremendous influence on the people they govern. Social psychologists are also interested in what makes some people better leaders than others (see Chapter 14).

Sociology is the study of human societies and the groups that form those societies. Although both sociologists and social psychologists are interested in how people behave in societies and groups, they differ in what they focus on. Psychologists tend to start from inside the individual and work outward, whereas sociologists start with large units such as countries, religions, and organizations, and work from there. Some sociologists call themselves social psychologists, and the exchange of ideas and findings between the two fields has sometimes been quite fruitful because they bring different perspectives to the same problems. For example, one social psychology textbook titled *Two Social Psychologies: An Integrative Approach* tried to integrate sociological and psychological perspectives of human behavior.[16]

Social Psychology's Place Within Psychology

Psychology is the study of human behavior. Psychology is like a big tree that contains many branches. Social psychology is just one of those branches, but it is intertwined with some of the other branches (see **TABLE 1.1**).

People are biological creatures, and everything that people think, do, or feel involves some bodily processes such as brain activity or hormones. **Biological psychology** or **physiological psychology** and (more recently) **neuroscience** have focused on learning about what happens in the brain, nervous system, and other aspects of the body. Until recently, this work had little contact with social psychology, but during the 1990s (the "Decade of the Brain") many social psychologists began looking into the biological aspects of social behavior, and that interest has continued into the 21st century. Social neuroscience and social psychophysiology are now thriving fields.

---

anthropology the study of human culture—the shared values, beliefs, and practices of a group of people

economics the study of the production, distribution, and consumption of goods and services, and the study of money

history the study of past events

political science the study of political organizations and institutions, especially governments

sociology the study of human societies and the groups that form those societies

psychology the study of human behavior

biological psychology (physiological psychology, neuroscience) the study of what happens in the brain, nervous system, and other aspects of the body

---

TABLE 1.1 Descriptions of Psychology Subdisciplines

Psychology Subdiscipline	Description
Biological psychology	Biological psychologists focus on what happens in the brain, nervous system, and other aspects of the body.
Clinical psychology	Clinical psychologists focus on "abnormal" behavior.
Cognitive psychology	Cognitive psychologists focus on thought processes, such as how memory works and what people notice.
Developmental psychology	Developmental psychologists study how people change across their lives, from conception and birth to old age and death.
Personality psychology	Personality psychologists focus on important differences between individuals, as well as inner processes.
Social psychology	Social psychologists focus on how human beings think, act, and feel. Thoughts, actions, and feelings are a joint function of personal and situational influences.

Clinical psychology focuses on "abnormal" behavior, whereas social psychology focuses on "normal" behavior. Social psychological theory can shed a great deal of light on so-called normal behavior. Although abnormal and clinical cases may seem different, in fact social and clinical psychology have had a long tradition of exchanging ideas and stimulating insights into each other's fields. In particular, clinical psychologists have made good use of social psychological theories.

Cognitive psychology is the basic study of thought processes, such as how memory works and what events people notice. In recent decades, social psychology has borrowed heavily from cognitive psychology, especially by using their methods for measuring cognitive processes (e.g., reaction times to various stimuli). Under the rubric of "social cognition," social psychologists study how people think about their social lives, such as thinking about other people or solving problems in their world. Conversely, however, cognitive psychology has not borrowed much from social psychology except the occasional theory.

Developmental psychology is the study of how people change across their lives, from conception and birth to old age and death. In practice, most developmental psychologists study children. Developmental psychology has borrowed much from social psychology and built on it, such as by studying at what age children begin to show various patterns of social behavior. Developmental psychology also has often borrowed social psychology theories. Until now, social psychology has not taken much from developmental psychology, though this may be changing. Social psychologists interested in self-regulation, emotion, gender differences, helping behavior, and antisocial behavior sometimes look to the research on child development to see how these patterns get started.

Personality psychology focuses on important differences between individuals, as well as inner processes. For example, some people are introverted and avoid social contact, whereas other people are extraverted and crave social contact. Social and personality psychology have had a long and close relationship,[17] as reflected in the titles of four of the top scientific journals in the field: *Journal of Personality and Social Psychology, Personality and Social Psychology Bulletin, Personality and Social Psychology Review,* and *Social Psychological and Personality Science.* The relationship between personality and social psychology has been sometimes complementary (personality psychologists looked inside the person, whereas social psychologists looked outside at the situation) and sometimes competitive (is it more important to understand the person or the situation?). In recent years, the line between these two fields has become blurred, as social psychologists have come to

clinical psychology branch of psychology that focuses on behavior disorders and other forms of mental illness, and how to treat them

cognitive psychology the study of thought processes, such as how memory works and what people notice

developmental psychology the study of how people change across their lives, from conception and birth to old age and death

personality psychology the branch of psychology that focuses on important differences between individuals

recognize the importance of inner processes and personality psychologists have come to recognize the importance of circumstances and situations.

Of course, we did not cover all branches of psychology (e.g., community psychology, counseling psychology, educational psychology, environmental psychology, forensic psychology, health psychology, industrial/organization [I/O] psychology, media psychology). Our list is by no means exhaustive, but it should give you a feel for how social psychology differs from some other main branches of psychology in the tree we call "psychology."

QUIZ YOURSELF

Social Psychology's Place in the World

answers: see pg 30

1. **A social psychologist is usually interested in studying the _____.**
   - ⓐ community
   - ⓑ group
   - ⓒ individual
   - ⓓ institution

2. **Social psychology has most heavily borrowed methodological tools from what other psychology branch?**
   - ⓐ Cognitive
   - ⓑ Clinical
   - ⓒ Counseling
   - ⓓ Developmental

3. **A researcher is interested in studying how the annual divorce rate changes as a function of the unemployment rate. This researcher is probably a(n) _____.**
   - ⓐ anthropologist
   - ⓑ political scientist
   - ⓒ psychologist
   - ⓓ sociologist

4. **"Abnormal" behavior is to "normal" behavior as _____ psychology is to _____ psychology.**
   - ⓐ biological; cognitive
   - ⓑ clinical; cognitive
   - ⓒ clinical; social
   - ⓓ personality; social

Why People Study Social Psychology

Curiosity About People

Some social events make you wonder why people act the way they do. For example, why does the man usually pay for the date even when the woman also earns money and could pay her own way? Why do so many people fail to vote in elections yet still complain about the government? Why are actors and celebrities so admired in America, when their success depends mainly on saying words that other people write for them and pretending to have emotions they do not really have? Why did the president of Kenya tell everyone in his country to abstain from sex for two years (and do you think people obeyed him)? Why do the French live longer than people in just about any other country but also report much lower average happiness in life? Why do many people spend more than they earn?

One of the most highly respected and influential social psychologists, Edward E. Jones, was once asked how he could justify spending his entire life studying social psychology, even though his research did not translate directly into plans for how to cure human suffering or make lots of money. He looked at his questioner with genuine puzzlement and explained that he, and presumably everyone else, had a "basic curiosity about people." For most people, this curiosity is merely a personal interest, but by becoming a social psychologist, Jones was able to make it his life's work. Jones thought that understanding people was an end in itself and did not need to be justified on other grounds (such as making money, though as a successful professor he earned a comfortable living). Only careful scientific research, like that practiced by social psychologists, can ultimately lead to a more reliable and valid understanding of people.

(Reliability and validity have precise scientific meanings, which will be covered later in this chapter.)

We think curiosity about people is still an excellent reason for studying social psychology. Social psychology can teach you a great deal about how to understand people. If this book does not help you to understand people significantly better, then either you or we (or both) have failed. But more likely you will be able to see your fellow human beings in a new light once you have finished this book and course.

Experimental Philosophy

Philosophy (from the Greek *philo-sophia*) means "love of wisdom." Over the centuries philosophers have thought deeply about many of the most interesting and profound questions in the world. Most fields of study, including psychology, were originally part of philosophy. Psychology separated itself from philosophy around 1900, which in the context of Western civilization is pretty recent.

Psychology addresses many questions that pertain to the love of wisdom and that also interest philosophers: Why are human beings sometimes cruel to each other? What is knowledge, and where does it come from? Is altruism (selflessly helping others) truly possible, or are helpers merely trying to feel better about themselves? What is virtue? Why do people so often give in to temptation? What is the nature of the self and identity?

What separates philosophy from psychology is psychology's heavy reliance on the scientific method. Philosophers deal with problems by thinking carefully and systematically about them; psychologists address the same problems by systematically collecting data. Psychology, including social psychology, thus offers a marvelous opportunity to combine an interest in profound questions with the scientific method of seeking answers.

Making the World Better

Many social psychologists (and social scientists) are motivated by a wish to make the world a better place. They come to this field because they are troubled by injustice, violence, pollution, poverty, or the sufferings of some group. They want to understand the causes of these problems and perhaps begin to find ways of fixing them.

Hardly anyone thinks our society is perfect. Changing it is often a tricky business, however, because many so-called remedies do not work, and sometimes the steps one takes to fix one problem end up creating a new or different problem. For example,

philosophy "love of wisdom"; the pursuit of knowledge about fundamental matters such as life, death, meaning, reality, and truth

Philip Gould/Terra/Corbis

Ben Osborne/The Image Bank/Getty Images

With almost every decision there are tradeoffs. Drilling for oil can increase energy supplies and reduce energy costs, but it can also lead to environmental pollution, kill wildlife and destroy their habitats, and make natural areas less pristine.

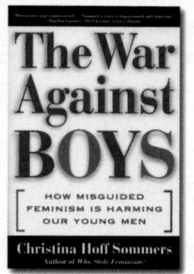

AP Images/Sipa Press/Rodin Banica/McMullan CO

Bill Aron/PhotoEdit

drilling for oil can increase energy supplies and reduce energy costs, but it can also lead to environmental pollution and make natural areas less beautiful.

Social scientists disagree among themselves as to the nature of many problems and the desired solutions, but most share a belief that better knowledge will in the long run enable society to deal with its problems more effectively. If a government passes new laws and makes new policies based on wrong information, those laws and policies are not likely to bring about the desired effects. That is why scientific research is so important, and not just to the field of psychology.

The desire to fix particular problems causes some social scientists to focus their study on the specific problem, such as the plight of welfare mothers, or why people don't wear seat belts, or how to get people to conserve electric power. These scholars conduct what is called **applied research** because the research is applied to a specific problem. There are specific journals in social psychology that focus on applied research, such as the *Journal of Applied Social Psychology*. Others, however, try to advance the cause of knowledge generally, in the hope that creating a solid knowledge base will eventually result in a general understanding of basic principles that can be applied to many different problems. These scholars conduct what is called **basic research**. When Kurt Lewin, one of the founding fathers of social psychology, was asked whether his research had sufficient practical value, he answered, "There is nothing as practical as a good theory."[18]

A passion to make the world a better place is a fine reason to study social psychology. Sometimes, however, researchers let their ideals or their political beliefs cloud their judgment, such as in how they interpret their research findings. Social psychology can only be a science if it puts the pursuit of truth above all other goals. When researchers focus on a topic that is politically charged, such as race relations or whether divorce is bad for children, it is important to be extra careful in making sure that all views (perhaps especially disagreeable ones, or ones that go against established prejudices) are considered and that the conclusions from research are truly warranted.

For example, Christina Hoff Sommers has written about pressures she faced regarding unpopular views.[19] When she had this interview, in 1994, women's rights groups were campaigning for better treatment of adolescent girls, and they cited the high rate of girls' deaths from eating disorders as one sign of urgent need for intervention. Hoff Sommers discovered a huge error in how the frequency of these eating disorder deaths had been determined, which meant that the real death toll was far less than that reported. When she began to bring this up, Hoff Sommers said, many feminists told her that she should keep silent about it, because the reported numbers—even though wildly inaccurate—were helpful to their cause. Hoff Sommers was sympathetic to the desire to make life better for teenage girls, but she decided that spreading falsehoods was not a good means toward that end. Other researchers, however, were apparently quite willing to put their political ideals above the truth.

Social Psychology Is Fun!

Another reason to study social psychology is that it is fun. Not only do social psychologists get to spend their working lives dealing with many of the most fascinating questions that occupy other people in their free time, but the process is also enjoyable.

To be good at social psychology, especially once you reach the stage of conducting research, it is helpful to be creative. The questions are exciting, but the challenge of

applied research research that focuses on solving particular practical problems

basic research research that focuses on a general understanding of basic principles that can be applied to many different problems

testing them scientifically is often difficult. Social psychologists constantly try to come up with new and clever ways to test their ideas.

1. **Who said that he spent his entire life studying social psychology because he had a "basic curiosity about people"?**

(a) Floyd Allport (b) Edward E. Jones (c) Kurt Lewin (d) Norman Triplett

2. **What term when translated means "love of wisdom"?**

(a) History (b) Philosophy (c) Psychology (d) Sociology

3. **What is the main factor that separates philosophy from psychology?**

(a) The length of time the disciplines have been around (b) The types of problems studied (c) The methods used to study problems (d) All of the above

4. **Which of the following researchers would be classified as a "basic researcher"?**

(a) Dr. Trash studies why people litter. (b) Dr. Conflict studies aggression between siblings. (c) Dr. Brain studies memory processes. (d) Comparative and psychoanalytical camps.

QUIZ YOURSELF

Why People Study Social Psychology

answers: see pg 30

How Do Social Psychologists Answer Their Own Questions?

Accumulated Common Wisdom

It turns out that world knowledge, or accumulated common wisdom, is loaded with social psychological "truths." Consider the adages your grandmother may have told you:[20]

- "Idle hands are the devil's workshop."
- "Absence makes the heart grow fonder."
- "Birds of a feather flock together."
- "Opposites attract."
- "Out of sight, out of mind."

Note that some of these adages contradict each other! For example, how can "birds of a feather flock together" and "opposites attract"? Opposites actually do not attract, but birds of a feather do flock together (see Chapter 11). People were offering adages long before your grandma's time. The problem with so-called common wisdom or common sense is that it allows us to happily and effortlessly judge adages as being true and, at the same time, judge their opposites as being true. For example, research participants rated the following actual adages and their opposites as equally true.[21]

- "Fear is stronger than love." AND "Love is stronger than fear."
- "He that is fallen cannot help him who is down." AND "He that is down cannot help him who is fallen."
- "Wise men make proverbs and fools repeat them." AND "Fools make proverbs and wise men repeat them."

Thus, human intuition is a poor method for discovering truth.

Common wisdom is probably right more often than it is wrong, but that is not good enough for science. In the long run, science can find the right answers to

Scientists aren't just "good guessers," like the people at carnivals who try to guess your age or weight. Their hypotheses are derived from theories, which are well-substantiated, well-supported, well-documented explanations for observations.

almost everything that can be measured in a reliable and valid manner. (In the short run, scientists have to be content with slowly making progress toward the truth, such as replacing a partly right and partly wrong theory with another theory that is still partly wrong but a little more right.) Hence social psychologists do not rely too heavily on common sense or accumulated wisdom. If anything, they have often had to justify their scientific studies by finding patterns that go against common sense. At most, common sense provides a good starting point for social psychologists to do their work. They can take ideas that everyone assumes to be true and find out which ones really are true, as opposed to which ones are always false. As for those that are sometimes true and sometimes false, social psychologists can study what factors determine when they are true and when they are false. For example, which absences do make the heart grow fonder, and which circumstances cause people to forget about their absent friends or lovers and refocus on the other people?

Overview of the Scientific Method

Most people think that science is chemistry or biology or physics. Science is, however, a method for discovering truth, not a discipline. So what is the scientific method? What steps does it involve? The scientific method involves five basic steps.

- The researcher states a problem for study.
- The researcher formulates a testable hypothesis as a tentative solution to the problem. The Cambridge Dictionary defines a hypothesis as "an idea or explanation for something that is based on known facts but has not yet been proved." Lay people often define a hypothesis as an "educated guess." But scientists aren't just "good guessers," like the people at carnivals who try to guess your age, weight, or birth month. Hypotheses are generally derived from theories. For example, one hypothesis is that playing violent video games increases aggressive behavior.
- The researcher designs a study to test the hypothesis and collects data. Anyone following the same data collection process should be able to get similar results if they want to replicate the study.
- A test is made of the hypothesis by confronting it with the data. Statistical methods are used to test whether the data are consistent or inconsistent with the hypothesis. No single study can prove anything beyond all doubt. There is always the possibility that the data turned out a certain way as a fluke, by random chance. Usually researchers test their hypotheses at the .05 (or 5%) significance level. If the test is significant at this level, it means that researchers are 95% confident that the results from their studies indicate a real difference and not just a random fluke. Thus, only 5% of research conclusions should be "flukes." Moreover, the pressures to replicate studies will sharply reduce the number and proportion of such false, invalid conclusions.
- The researcher reports the study results to the scientific community. The researcher submits a manuscript describing exactly what was done and what was found to the editor of a scientific journal. The editor then selects a few experts (usually 2–5) in the area to review the manuscript. The editor reads the manuscript independently, reads the reviewers' comments, and then decides whether to accept the manuscript for publication. Only about 10%–20% of manuscripts submitted to the best social psychology journals are accepted. These high standards help ensure that only the best research is published in social psychology journals. Once an article is published, it is in the public domain. If other social psychologists don't believe the results, they can replicate the study themselves to see if they obtain similar results. *Food for Thought* illustrates the various steps of the scientific method.

Scientific Theories

Social psychologists are not content to know what people do; they also want to know *why* they do it. That is why psychologists derive their hypotheses from theories.

Theories are composed of constructs (abstract ideas or concepts) that are linked together in a logical way. They are called constructs because the researcher must construct them or build them up by specifying their dimensions.[22] For example, the construct of "aggression" may have multiple dimensions such as physical versus verbal, direct versus indirect, passive versus active.[23] A theory is more than a hunch—it explains *why* something is expected to occur.

Because constructs cannot be observed directly, the researcher connects them with concrete, observable variables using operational definitions. **FIGURE 1.2** illustrates the relationship between unobservable constructs (in dashed boxes) and observable variables (in solid boxes). For example, one early theory proposed that frustration causes aggression.[24] Frustration was defined as blocking someone from obtaining a goal. Aggression was defined as intentionally harming another person.

In science, a theory is not just a guess. It's a well-substantiated, well-supported, well-documented explanation for observations. For example, just because it's called the "theory of gravity" doesn't mean that it is just a guess. The theory of gravity is based on principles in physics, has been tested many times, and has been supported by many observations. Likewise, social psychological theories are not just guesses or hunches about human behavior.

The **independent variable** is any observable event that causes the person to do something. It is independent in the sense that its values are created by the researcher and are not affected by anything else that happens in the experiment. In other words, the independent variable is *independent* of the participant's control. It is a variable because it has at least two levels, categories, types, or groups (e.g., frustration and a non-frustrated condition).

Manipulated independent variables are different from measured variables, such as measurements of naturally occurring differences among persons, in one very important way. Social psychologists have long recognized that behavior is a function of

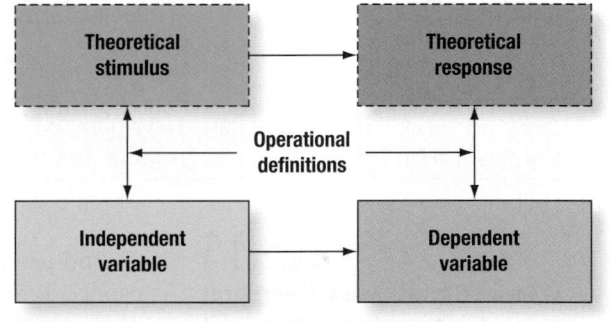

© Cengage Learning

FIGURE 1.2

Representation of a theoretical model. Unobservable constructs are represented as dashed boxes on the top level. Observable variables are in solid boxes on the bottom level.

hypothesis an idea about the possible nature of reality; a prediction tested in an experiment

within-subjects design participants are exposed to all levels of the independent variable

between-subjects design participants are exposed to only one level of the independent variable

theories unobservable constructs that are linked together in some logical way

independent variable the variable manipulated by the researcher that is assumed to lead to changes in the dependent variable

both situational and individual difference factors. Situational factors can be manipulated in experiments. Individual difference variables, such as gender, age, intelligence, ability, personality, and attitudes, can be measured but cannot be manipulated. For example, a researcher cannot manipulate whether participants will be male or female or whether they will be high or low in intelligence. Participants arrive for the experiment already possessing these attributes. A researcher can only draw cause–effect conclusions about the true independent variables that were manipulated in the experiment. This is important: We cannot ever really know that intelligence or gender *causes* a particular outcome because only experimentation can establish causality, and those variables cannot be manipulated in an experiment. Still, we can learn a great deal about what typically correlates with gender or intelligence.

The **dependent variable** is any observable behavior a person produces. It is "dependent" in the sense that the researcher assumes that its values *depend upon* the values of the independent variable. In a study of the effect of alcoholic versus nonalcoholic beer on aggression, for example, aggression is the dependent variable. (The alcoholic versus nonalcoholic beer is the independent variable.) A researcher could use different measures of aggression (e.g., hostile verbal insults or physical acts such as hitting, kicking, or choking someone).

Researchers must at some point tie their unobservable constructs to concrete representations of those constructs. This is accomplished by using operational definitions. An **operational definition** classifies theoretical constructs in terms of observable operations, procedures, and measurements. The more abstract the construct, the more difficult it is to operationally define.

An example will help illustrate these abstract concepts. In a study[25] that tested frustration–aggression theory, participants were waiting in long lines at various stores, banks, restaurants, ticket windows, and airport passenger check-in stands, when a confederate crowded in front of them in line. They didn't even realize they were in a study. (A **confederate** is somebody who is secretly working for the researcher.) By the flip of a coin, the confederate crowded in front of the 2nd person in line or in front of the 12th person in line. According to frustration–aggression theory, events are more frustrating if you are close to the goal (e.g., 2nd person in line) than if you are far from the goal (e.g., 12th person in line). It is especially frustrating if you can "almost taste it," but someone gets in your way. The confederate then recorded the participant's reaction. No response was coded 0; a somewhat aggressive response was coded 1 (e.g., participant tells confederate "Watch it!"); and a very aggressive response was coded 2 (e.g., participant pushes confederate). The results showed that participants 2nd in line responded more aggressively to the confederate who crowded in front of them than did participants 12th in line, which is consistent with frustration–aggression theory. **FIGURE 1.3** contains the theoretical stimulus, theoretical response, independent variable, and dependent variable for this study.

Other factors can influence how aggressive people become when someone crowds in front of them in line. For example, participants in a similar study were more aggressive if the confederate who crowded in front of them wore a shirt that said "Drop Dead," and they were less aggressive if the confederate used a crutch or said: "Please, I'm in a hurry."[26]

If the operational definitions of the constructs are valid, the study is said to have construct validity.[27] **Construct validity of the cause** means that the independent variable is a valid representation of the theoretical stimulus. **Construct validity of the effect** means that the dependent variable is a valid representation of the theoretical response. Consider our example in Figure 1.3. Is crowding in front of someone in line a valid way to define "frustration"? If so, the construct validity of the cause is high. Is pushing someone a valid way to define "aggression"? If so, the construct validity of the effect is high.

For a theory to be scientific, it must be testable. To test a theory, one must be able to define its theoretical constructs operationally. If the theoretical constructs cannot be operationally defined, the theory is beyond the realm of science. It might fall within the realm of philosophy or religion instead.

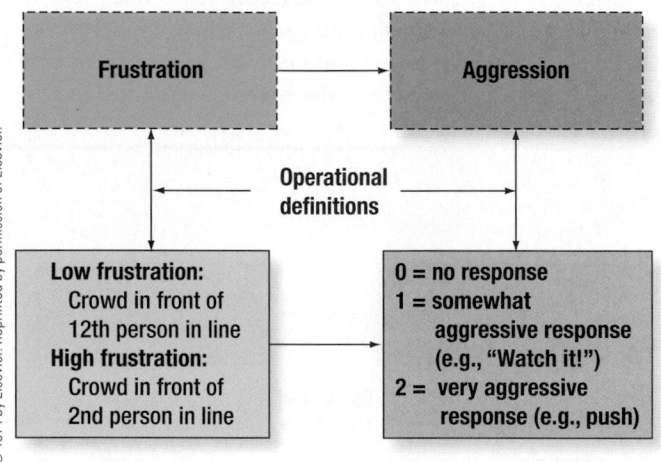

FIGURE 1.3

Theoretical stimulus, theoretical response, independent variable, and dependent variable for the study on crowding in line that was used to test frustration-aggression theory.[25]

dependent variable the variable in a study that represents the result of the events and processes

operational definitions observable operations, procedures, and measurements that are based on the independent and dependent variables

confederate a research assistant pretending to be another participant in a study

construct validity of the cause extent to which the independent variable is a valid representation of the theoretical stimulus

construct validity of the effect extent to which the dependent variable is a valid representation of the theoretical response

Lucy's theory is not scientific because it cannot be tested.

1. **A testable prediction about the conditions under which an event will occur is called a _____.**

   (a) construct (b) hypothesis (c) theory (d) variable

2. **Which of the following is an operational definition of racial prejudice?**

   (a) A negative attitude toward individuals based on their membership in a particular race.

   (b) The number of negative traits the person selects from a list of traits when doing the list for his or her own race versus another race.

   (c) The tendency to believe that people of a particular race are less deserving than are people of another race.

   (d) All of the above could be operational definitions of prejudice.

3. **With random assignment, each participant _____.**

   (a) is exposed to all levels of the dependent variable

   (b) is exposed to all levels of the independent variable

   (c) has an equal chance of being exposed to each level of the dependent variable

   (d) has an equal chance of being exposed to each level of the independent variable

4. **Which of the following correlations shows the strongest relationship between the variables?**

   (a) The correlation between alcohol consumption and traffic deaths is $r = .36$.

   (b) The correlation between height and IQ is $r = 0$.

   (c) The correlation between time spent partying and grades among college students is $r = -.80$.

   (d) The correlation between watching media violence and aggression is $r = .20$.

answers: see pg 30

> **QUIZ YOURSELF**
>
> **How Do Social Psychologists Answer Their Own Questions?**

Research Design

Social psychologists use both experimental and nonexperimental studies. In this section we describe both types of studies.

Experimental Studies

Most social psychologists favor experimental studies over nonexperimental studies, partly because a well-designed experiment can show causality. An **experiment** has two essential features. First, the researcher has control over the procedures. The researcher manipulates the independent variable and holds all other variables constant. All those who participate in an experiment are treated the same, except for the level of the independent variable they are exposed to. By exercising control, the researcher tries to make sure that any differences observed on the dependent variable were caused by the independent variable and not by other factors.

experiment a study in which the researcher manipulates an independent variable and randomly assigns people to groups (levels of the independent variable)

The following research example illustrates the tradeoff between the potential harm research can have on participants and the potential benefits research can have on society.

For men visiting public restrooms, proper etiquette is to leave at least one empty urinal between them and the next guy. If the urinals are not all being used, it seems a violation of personal space to use an adjacent urinal, which may increase stress levels. As one group of researchers noted, "At the onset of micturition, the detrusor muscles of the bladder contract, increasing intravesical pressure and forcing urine out of the bladder. At the same time, the two sphincters of the urethra relax, particularly the external sphincter, allowing urine to flow. Social stressors appear to affect both these mechanisms of micturition" (p. 542).[28]

This research group conducted two studies to test their hypothesis. In both studies, the laboratory was actually a lavatory and the participants did not know they were in a study. In the first study, 48 male university students entered a public restroom that contained two banks of five urinals. The researcher, who was at a sink pretending to groom himself, recorded the selected urinal and the placement of the next nearest user. He also timed the micturition delay (the time between when a participant unzipped his fly and when urination began)

TRADE Offs

and the micturition duration (the time between the onset and completion of urination). As you can see in **FIGURE 1.4** men had trouble urinating when their space was invaded—it took them longer to begin urinating, and they spent less time doing it.

The research group followed up this correlational study with a field

experiment. Participants were 60 men using a restroom that contained two toilet stalls next to three urinals. The men had no idea they were in a study. An observer sat in a stall and recorded measurements using a periscopic prism imbedded in a stack of books lying on the floor. The participant's face was not visible, but his penis was. Participants were forced to use the leftmost urinal (next to the stall) under one of three levels of

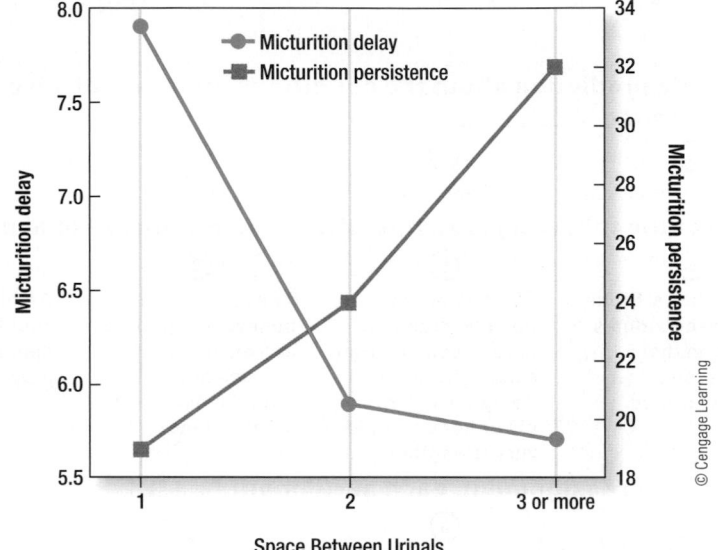

FIGURE 1.4

Effects of personal space (number of urinals between men) on micturition delay (the time between when a participant unzips his fly and when urination began) and micturition persistence (the time between the onset and completion of urination).

SOURCE: Middlemist et al. (1976).

---

random assignment procedure whereby each study participant has an equal chance of being in each treatment group

Institutional Review Board (IRB) is a committee that makes sure that a research study conducted in university settings is ethical. The board must contain at least one scientist, one nonscientist, and one person not affiliated with the university

consent form a document that participants receive before a study begins; the form contains enough information about the study procedures, including any potential harm they (or others) might experience, so participants can decide if they want to participate

Second, participants are randomly assigned to the levels of the independent variable. A different group experiences each level of the independent variable. If the independent variable has two levels (e.g., experimental group versus control group), the researcher can flip a coin to assign participants to groups. If the independent variable has more than two groups, the researcher can draw a number from a hat or roll a die to assign participants to groups. **Random assignment** means that each participant has an equal chance of being in each group. By randomly assigning participants to groups, the researcher attempts to ensure no initial differences between groups. Random assignment is the great equalizer, especially if the study includes a large number of participants. Think about flipping a coin 20 times versus 200 times. Getting 20 heads in 20 flips is much more likely than getting 200 heads in 200 flips. If participants are randomly assigned to groups, the participants in one group should be no different—no smarter, no taller, no more liberal or conservative, no more mean-tempered, no more eager for love—than the participants in another group. If differences between groups of participants do appear after the independent variable is manipulated, these differences should be due to the independent variable rather than to any initial, preexisting differences between participants.

interpersonal distance that were randomly determined. In the close distance condition (16–18 inches; 41–46 cm), a confederate stood at the middle urinal, and a "Don't use, washing urinal" sign accompanied by a bucket of water and a sponge was placed on the rightmost urinal. In the moderate distance condition (52–54 inches; 132–137 cm), a confederate stood at the rightmost urinal, and the bucket and sign were placed in the middle urinal. In the control condition, no confederate was present in the lavatory and both the middle and right urinals had signs on them with the water bucket in between them. The results replicated the first study.

Are studies like this ethical? For example, the men in the second study had no idea that an observer could see their penis (but not their face) in a periscope and was measuring how quickly and how long they urinated. Then again, do you think the men were harmed in any way, other than possibly having spending a few extra seconds standing at the toilet? And meanwhile, how much do those data contribute to advancing scientific knowledge?

Psychologists weren't the only ones conducting possibly unethical research. Partly in response to the Tuskegee syphilis study, in which medical doctors from the U.S. Public Health Service studied the natural progression of untreated syphilis in rural African American men who thought they were receiving free health care from the U.S. government from 1932 to 1972, the U.S. Congress passed the National

Research Act in 1974. This act created a National Commission for the Protection of Human Subjects of Biomedical and Behavioral Research to oversee and regulate the use of human participants in research studies. It required that all federally funded studies must first receive **Institutional Review Board (IRB)** approval. Today both funded and unfunded studies conducted at universities must first obtain IRB approval. The IRB committee makes sure the research being conducted is ethical.

Almost all studies require researchers to give participants a **consent form**. This means that participants must be given enough information about the study procedures, including any potential harm they (or others) might experience, so they can decide whether they want to participate. Willingness to participate is indicated by the participant's signature on the consent form. However, even if a participant signs a consent form, he or she can withdraw consent and discontinue participation at any time. No researcher can force any participant to remain in a study. Neither the Tuskegee study nor the urinal study would receive approval to be conducted today.

It is natural for research participants to try to figure out what a study is about. They want to know what the researcher's hypothesis is. Any cues that convey the hypothesis to participants are called **demand characteristics**,[29] and they can have a significant effect on how participants behave. For example, some participants want

to help the researcher out by confirming the hypothesis. Other participants want to do the opposite and disprove the researcher's hypothesis.

To reduce demand characteristics, researchers sometimes give participants false information about the purpose of the study. These so-called **deception studies** must include a **debriefing** at the end where participants are given a full description of the purpose of the study, including revealing any deception that was involved. One might think participants would be angered after learning they have been deceived. In actuality, they usually understand the need for deception and actually enjoy studies that use deception more than studies that employ no deception, mainly because they think the deception studies are more interesting to participate in.[30]

For a researcher to use deception, he or she must demonstrate that the potential scientific gains outweigh any potential costs to participants. This is the big tradeoff in social psychology studies that employ deception. There are other tradeoffs as well. Some researchers argue that IRBs are far too conservative and therefore limit the importance of the types of experiments that can be conducted. Thus, there is a tradeoff between potential harm to participants and potential gains to society that can accrue by conducting important, high impact research. Indeed, many important social psychological studies from the past probably would not be granted IRB approval today.

Some social psychology experiments involve deception. See the *Tradeoffs* box for a discussion of the tradeoff between potential harm to participants and potential gain to society that comes from scientific knowledge.

If a researcher can manipulate an independent variable but cannot use random assignment, the study is called a **quasi-experiment**. In a quasi-experiment, the researcher "takes people as they are." Researchers often use preexisting groups (e.g., classrooms, fraternity groups, athletic clubs) because random assignment is not possible. For example, if you wanted to learn about marriage, you would ideally like to assign people randomly to be married or single (and whom to marry), but this is clearly not feasible! So you rely on comparing people who are already married with those who happen to be single.

Suppose that a researcher is interested in determining whether a relationship exists between two variables, say X and Y. For example, a researcher might be interested in the relationship between feeling happy (X) and spending money (Y). When two variables are related in a systematic manner, three possible explanations for the relationship are possible: (a) X caused Y; (b) Y caused X; (c) some other variable (e.g., Z) caused both X and Y.

The two essential features of an experiment (control and random assignment) allow the researcher to be fairly certain that the independent variable (X) caused differences in

demand characteristics any clues in a study that suggest to participants what the researcher's hypothesis is

deception studies research studies that withhold information from participants or intentionally mislead them about the purpose of the study

debriefing an oral or written statement participants receive at the end of a psychological study; it serves two main purposes: (1) to fully inform participants about the study and answer any questions they have, and (2) to reduce or eliminate any stress or harm the participant experienced by being in the study

quasi-experiment a type of study in which the researcher can manipulate an independent variable but cannot randomly assign participants to conditions

the dependent variable (Y). Note that one cannot conclude that Y caused X in an experiment. We know what caused X, and it wasn't Y. The researcher caused X, because the researcher manipulated X. Thus, we know that X preceded Y in time. Because Y came after X, Y could not cause X. In an experiment it is also unlikely that some other variable (Z) caused both X and Y. The researcher controlled many other variables by treating groups of participants identically. Random assignment is used to spread out the effect of other variables that cannot be controlled (e.g., the mood participants are in, their personalities).

A study is said to have **internal validity** if the researcher can be relatively confident that changes in the independent variable caused changes in the dependent variable.[31] Internal validity is usually very high in experimental studies.

Consider the violent video game example again. In a true experiment, the researcher doesn't ask participants if they would rather play a violent or a nonviolent video game. If the researcher let people choose what video game they wanted to play, people choosing the violent game might be very different from those choosing the nonviolent game. For example, people choosing the violent game might be more aggressive, less intelligent, or less socially skilled to begin with. That is why the researcher flips a coin to determine what video game participants play. That way, the two groups should be similar before they play the game. If the researcher flips a coin to determine what game participants are assigned to play, it is very unlikely that all the aggressive people will end up playing the violent game, especially if the experiment involves a large number of participants. Suppose there are 200 participants in the experiment (100 in each group). There should be a 50/50 chance of an aggressive person playing a violent game. Think about flipping a fair coin 200 times. On average, you should get about 100 heads. It would be very unlikely to get 200 heads in a row, or even 150 heads out of 200 flips. Rare events are much less common when sample sizes are large. That is why researchers try to test a large number of participants in their studies, rather than just a few.

Next, one group plays a violent game, and the other group plays a nonviolent game. In all other respects, the researcher must treat the two groups of participants identically. For example, the researcher is not rude to the participants who play a violent game and nice to the participants who play a nonviolent game. Indeed, the researcher tries to avoid contact with the participant whenever possible, and to give instructions on the computer screen or via a recorded message, so as to keep everything standard and consistent. In a carefully conducted experiment, the violent and nonviolent video games would be matched on other dimensions that could increase aggression, such as how frustrating and competitive they are. For example, it is well known that frustration increases aggression.[23] If the violent video games are difficult and frustrating to play, and the nonviolent video games are easy and nonfrustrating, any differences in subsequent aggressive behavior might be due to how frustrating the games are rather than to how violent they are. In other words, the effects of video game violence and frustration cannot be separated because the two variables are **confounded** (see **FIGURE 1.5A**). In the dictionary, to confound is defined as "to mingle so that the elements cannot be distinguished or separated." In this case, frustration and violent content are mingled together in the same game, so their individual effects cannot be separated. Similarly, if the violent game is competitive (as most are), but the nonviolent game is noncompetitive, any differences in subsequent aggressive behavior might be due to how competitive the games are rather than to how violent they are (see **FIGURE 1.5B**). Of course, there are other possible confounding variables too, such as how action-packed the game is.

In addition, the researcher should use several different violent video games and several different nonviolent games. This technique is called **stimulus sampling** because the researcher samples several different versions of the stimulus of interest.[32] Otherwise, the comparison is between two particular video games (e.g., *Grand Theft Auto* versus *Sims*), not between violent and nonviolent video games in general. The results might be due to something peculiar about the particular games used rather than about violent and nonviolent games in general.

Last, the researcher measures the aggressive behavior of both groups of participants. For example, participants are given an opportunity to hurt another person, such as by administering electric shocks. The "other person" is actually a confederate of the researcher who is pretending to be another participant receiving the shock. If shock levels are higher

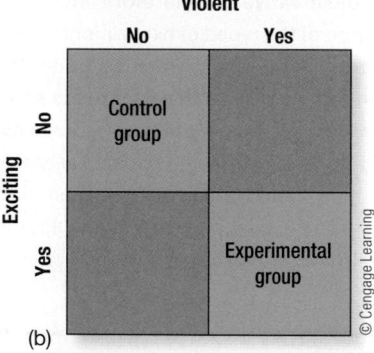

FIGURE 1.5

When two variables are confounded, their individual effects are mixed together and cannot be separated. (a) Violent content is confounded with frustration. (b) Violent content is confounded with excitement.

internal validity the extent to which changes in the independent variable caused changes in the dependent variable

confounding occurs when the two effects of variables cannot be separated

stimulus sampling using more than one exemplar of a stimulus (e.g., more than one violent video game)

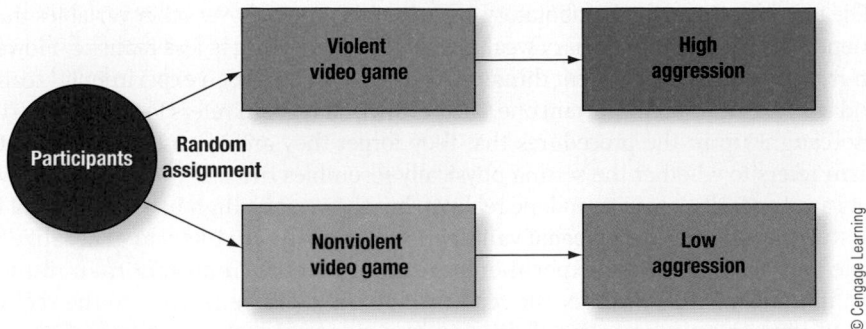

© Cengage Learning

among those who play a violent game than among those who play a nonviolent game, what else could have caused the difference except the game they played? Random assignment ensures that the two groups were equally aggressive before they played the video game. The researcher treats the two groups identically except for the type of game they played. In an experimental study, one can say that playing violent video games caused an increase in aggression. The only other possible explanation is a random fluke, but that should occur less than 5% of the time (because the researcher conducts statistical tests at the .05 significance level). This process is depicted in **FIGURE 1.6**.

Laboratory and Field Experiments

Have you ever looked for a parking spot in a very crowded parking lot? You have found no empty spots, but you see a shopper returning to her car and decide to wait to get her spot when she leaves. Unfortunately, she takes a very long time to leave. She takes her time putting bags into her car. When she gets into the car, she puts on her seat belt, adjusts the mirror, arranges her hair, and so on. At long last, she starts the car. She lets it warm up awhile before pulling out. When she finally does pull out, it seems like a snail could do it faster. After she leaves, you zoom into the parking spot before somebody else grabs it.

Perhaps you have also had the converse experience. Your car is already parked in a lot, and some obnoxious driver hovers over you waiting for you to leave. To teach the other driver a lesson, you take your sweet time leaving. After all, it is your spot and you had it first.

These common experiences illustrate how territorial humans can be. People don't want others to encroach on their territory. An intruder creates a challenge to the occupant's control over the territory. According to psychological reactance theory,[33] people respond to such threats by experiencing an unpleasant emotional response called **reactance**, which motivates them to defend their territory.

A field experiment was conducted to study territorial behavior in parking lots.[34] Most experiments are conducted in a laboratory setting, but some are conducted in a real-world setting. Experiments conducted in a real-world setting outside a laboratory are called **field experiments**. In this field experiment, participants were drivers who were leaving their parking spaces at a mall. The researchers manipulated the level of intrusion. In the high-intrusion condition, a confederate stopped four spaces from the departing driver's car, flashed his turn signal in the direction of the departing car, and honked his horn as soon as the departing driver sat behind the steering wheel. In the low-intrusion condition, the confederate stopped four spaces from the departing car, but did not flash his turn signal or honk his horn. In the control condition, the researchers simply timed how long it took drivers to leave their parking space when no intruder was present. The results showed that departing drivers took longer to leave when someone was waiting for their spot than when no one was waiting. In addition, drivers took longer to depart when the confederate flashed his turn signal and honked his horn than when he did not. The results are depicted in **FIGURE 1.7**. Another example of a field experiment is the frustration–aggression experiment described earlier, where people crowded in front of either the 2nd or 12th person standing in line.[35]

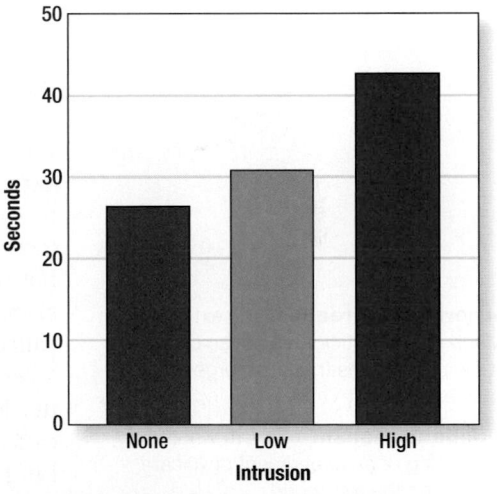

© Cengage Learning

FIGURE 1.7
Drivers took their sweet time leaving a parking spot when an intruder was waiting to get it.[34]

reactance an unpleasant emotional response that people often experience when someone is trying to restrict their freedom

field experiment an experiment conducted in a real-world setting

The primary strength of a laboratory experiment is control over other variables that might influence the results; the primary weakness is that the setting is less realistic. However, the term *realistic* can mean different things. The distinction between experimental realism and mundane realism is an important one.[36] **Experimental realism** refers to whether participants get so caught up in the procedures that they forget they are in an experiment. **Mundane realism** refers to whether the setting physically resembles the real world. Laboratory experiments are generally low in mundane realism, but they can be high in experimental realism.

A study is said to have **external validity** if the findings are likely to generalize to other people and other settings. Experimental realism is more important than mundane realism in determining whether the results of a study will generalize to the real world.[37]

Field experiments are generally high in experimental and mundane realism, but they lack the tight control that laboratory experiments have. Thus, it is more difficult to make causal statements from field experiments than from laboratory experiments. That's why some researchers prefer the lab whereas others prefer the field. No method is perfect. Scientific progress is best served by using both lab and field. Indeed, one's confidence in the reliability of the finding increases if similar effects are obtained in lab and field experiments.

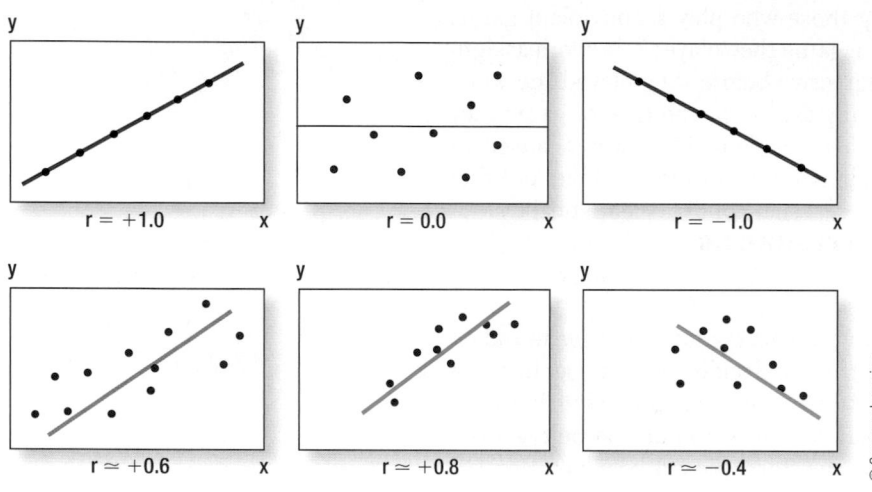

r = +1.0   x   r = 0.0   x   r = −1.0   x

r ≈ +0.6   x   r ≈ +0.8   x   r ≈ −0.4   x

© Cengage Learning

Nonexperimental Studies

Although social psychologists generally prefer experimental studies, sometimes they cannot be used. Recall that the two hallmarks of an experiment are control and random assignment. Some variables cannot be controlled and random assignment cannot be used for practical or ethical reasons, such as gender, race, ethnicity, marital status, and age. For example, suppose a researcher is interested in the relationship between combat experiences in war and post-traumatic stress disorder (PTSD). It would be unethical to control the frequency, intensity, and duration of combat war experiences, and to randomly assign participants to have or not have combat war experiences.

Faced with such difficulties, social psychologists often adopt an alternative research technique known as the **correlational approach.** In this approach, the researcher does not try to control variables or randomly assign participants to groups. Instead, the researcher merely observes whether variables go together normally. Such associations are called correlations. A **correlation** gives the relationship or association between two variables. When a correlation is positive, as one variable goes up the other variable also goes up. For example, there is a positive correlation between smoking cigarettes and lung cancer: The more cigarettes people smoke, the more likely they are (on average) to get lung cancer.[38] When a correlation is negative, as one variable goes up the other variable goes down. For example, there is a negative correlation between time spent playing video games and grades in college: The more time college students spend playing video games, the lower their grade point average is.[39] When there is no correlation, the two variables are not related in a linear fashion. For example, there is no correlation between IQ scores and shoe size.

Mathematically, correlations are computed in terms of the **correlation coefficient,** denoted by r. A correlation coefficient can range from +1.0 (a perfect positive correlation) to −1.0 (a perfect negative correlation). A correlation coefficient of 0 indicates that the two variables are not linearly related. The closer a correlation is to +1.0 or −1.0, the stronger it is (see **FIGURE 1.8**). As a general rule of thumb, a "small" correlation is $r = \pm.1$, a "medium" correlation is $r = \pm.3$, and a "large" correlation is $r = \pm.5$, in the social sciences.[40]

A correlation of 0, however, does not mean that the two variables are unrelated. Consider the graph in **FIGURE 1.9** between "Alcohol intake" (x-axis) and "Feeling of

experimental realism the extent to which study participants get so caught up in the procedures that they forget they are in an experiment

mundane realism refers to whether the setting of an experiment physically resembles the real world

external validity the extent to which the findings from a study can be generalized to other people, other settings, and other time periods

correlational approach a nonexperimental method in which the researcher merely observes whether variables are associated or related

correlation the relationship or association between two variables

correlation coefficient the statistical relationship or association between two variables

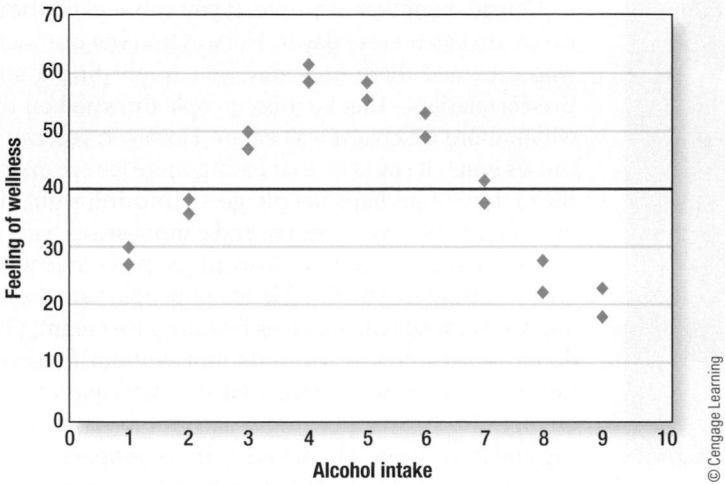

FIGURE 1.9
A situation in which a correlational approach is not appropriate. Correlation can only be applied when two variables are linearly related. In this graph, the relationship between alcohol intake and feeling well is not linear—it goes up and then down. Even though the correlation in this graph is zero (denoted by the flat red line), there is a strong relationship between alcohol intake and feelings of well-being. As alcohol consumption increases to about four drinks, mood also increases. As the number of drinks increases beyond four, peoples' mood decreases.

wellness" (y-axis). The correlation in this graph is zero (i.e., the red line is flat), but there is a strong relationship between alcohol intake and feeling well. As alcohol consumption increases, feelings of wellness also increase (e.g., people become happier). After about four drinks, however, feelings of wellness decrease (e.g., people become sick or hung over).

A **meta-analysis** is a literature review that averages the statistical results (e.g., correlations) from all studies conducted on the same topic. It is a quantitative literature review. It gives a "big picture" view of what all the studies show together.

The main weakness of the correlational approach is that it does not allow the researcher to conclude that changes in one variable caused the changes in the other variable. Recall that when two variables (say X and Y) are correlated, any combination of three explanations is possible: (1) X could cause Y, (2) Y could cause X, and/or (3) some other variable (e.g., Z) could cause both X and Y. For example, suppose a researcher finds a positive correlation between media violence (X) and violent crime (Y). At least three explanations are possible: (a) Media violence causes violent crime; (b) violent criminals are attracted to violent media; (c) some other variable (e.g., low intelligence, poverty, poor social skills) causes people to watch media violence and to commit violent crimes. The difficulty of drawing causal conclusions about media violence is reflected in the cartoon on this page. As the Calvin cartoon suggests, it is difficult to prove that media violence causes violent crime using the correlational approach. Of course, one cannot use the experimental approach either because it would not be ethical for researchers to allow violent crimes such as assaults, rapes, and murders to occur in their laboratories! In Chapter 10 we will discuss in detail the effects of violent media on aggression and violence.

meta-analysis a quantitative literature review that combines the statistical results (e.g., correlation coefficients) from all studies conducted on a topic

Even Calvin knows that correlation does not equal causation.

Image Source/Getty Images

A bogus news story had the headline, "Only Predictor Of Happy Marriage Is If Husband Ever Won Wife Big Stuffed Animal At Amusement Park." Of course, correlation does not necessarily translate to causation.

Consider another example. If you counted up the amount of ice cream eaten every day in Norway and the number of people who drowned there each day, you might find a strong positive correlation—that is, more people drowned on the days on which more ice cream was eaten. However, you can't tell what causes what. It could be that eating more ice cream causes people to drown; perhaps people go swimming right after eating lots of ice cream, get cramps, and cannot swim back from deep water. Or it could be that drownings cause an increase in ice cream eating; maybe the friends of people who drown feel sad and try to console themselves by eating ice cream. (This seems doubtful on intuitive grounds, but without further information one cannot be certain that it is wrong.) Or, most likely, changes in the weather might account for both ice cream eating and drownings. On hot days, more people swim and hence more people drown, and hot days also promote ice cream eating. On snowy or rainy days, fewer people swim and fewer people eat ice cream. That's enough to produce a correlation, even though ice cream has no direct effect on drowning.

As a joke, one recent article in *The Onion* reported that "Only Predictor Of Happy Marriage Is If Husband Ever Won Wife Big Stuffed Animal At Amusement Park."[41] The researcher of the bogus study reported, "Whether it's achieved by knocking over three milk cans with a ball or filling a clown's mouth with a jet of water, we noted a direct correlation between the quality of love two married people experience and whether or not the husband ever successfully won a carnival game and thereby earned his wife a giant plush Tweety Bird or fuzzy blue bear."

Survey Research

A recent survey reported the following result: "Over 68% of all convicted male rapists viewed pornography before the age of 17." Wow, 68% seems really high. However, 74% of non-rapist males viewed pornography before the age of 17! We actually made up these "numbers" to teach you a valuable lesson: Never trust survey conclusions from a single statistic that has no comparison statistic.

Have you ever heard of Alf Landon? The weekly news magazine *Literary Digest* predicted he would beat Franklin D. Roosevelt in a landslide in the 1936 U.S. presidential election, winning 57% of the popular vote and 370 electoral votes. The fact that you know who Roosevelt is, but probably have no idea who Landon is, tells you the *Literary Digest* was wrong in its prediction. Roosevelt actually won 60.8% of the popular vote and 523 electoral votes (98.49%), winning all but two states.

This *Literary Digest* poll forever changed polling. What went wrong? The *Literary Digest* mailed 10 million postcards, and got 2 million back! This is a massive sample size, perhaps larger than any other poll in U.S. history. Unfortunately, the 10 million postcards were not sent to a random sample of Americans. The addresses for the postcards were obtained from telephone books and automobile registrations. In 1936, America was in the midst of the Great Depression, and many Americans could not afford telephones or automobiles. Thus, the sample favored richer Americans, who were more likely to vote for the Republican candidate Landon than for the Democratic candidate Roosevelt.

Although the *Literary Digest* poll was a disaster, polls that use large random samples yield very accurate predictions. Since 1936, Gallup poll results taken just before U.S. national election days have diverged from actual election results by an average of only 2.1%.[42]

The best way to obtain a representative sample of the population is to take a **random sample.** A sample is random if each person in the population has an equal chance of being selected (see **FIGURE 1.10**). The **population** is the total number of people under consideration. One surprising fact about polls that you might not know is that a random sample of 1,200 can give results that are 95% accurate, within ±3% (called the **margin of error**), regardless of the size of the population from which the sample was drawn. Even if you want to know the attitudes of the entire U.S. population (or even the entire world

random sample a sample wherein each person in the population has an equal chance of being selected

population the total number of people under consideration

margin of error a statistic measure of the amount of random sampling error in a survey's results—for example, a 3% margin of error means that the survey's result could be 3% lower or 3% higher than the average response—the larger the sample is, the smaller the margin of error is

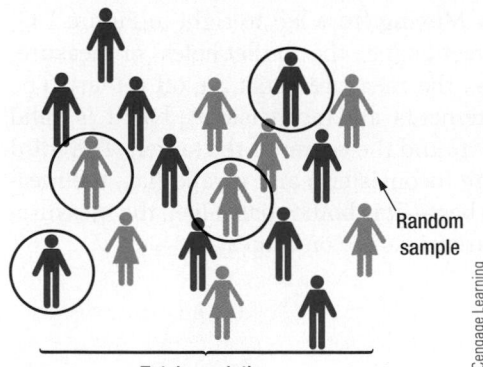

FIGURE 1.10
The best way to obtain a representative sample of the population is to take a random sample. A sample is random if each person (or object) in the population has an equal chance of being selected.

Random sample

Total population

population), a sample of 1,200 will give you a result that is accurate 95% of the time, within 3%, as long as it is random. One telephone poll found that more Americans think marijuana should be legal (55%) than think it should be illegal (44%)—the other 1% were undecided.[43] The poll used a random sample of 1,010 American adults (18 and older). The margin of error for the poll was ± 3%. Thus, one can say, with 95% confidence, that the percentage of Americans who favor legalizing marijuana ranges from 52% to 58% (i.e., 55% ±3% margin of error).

Polls that are not based on random samples tell you little or nothing about what the general population thinks. For example, a *Glamour* magazine poll asked female respondents: "Have you ever kissed a girl?" More than 63% said yes. Does that mean that about 63% of females have kissed another female? No. Does it mean that 63% of readers of *Glamour* magazine have kissed another female? No. It just means that 63% of the females who responded to this poll reported that they had kissed another female, but we do not know what population these respondents represent. (Another issue is how people interpret the question: Might some of the "yes" responses refer to nonromantic kissing?)

It may also surprise you that very subtle aspects of a survey, such as the order of questions and the number of options given, can have a tremendous impact on the results.[44,45] One clear trend is that the American public is becoming more and more negative in their attitudes about polls and surveys over time, and they are becoming less cooperative in taking them. This is due to a variety of factors, such as privacy concerns, the rise of telemarketers, biases of polling organizations, and negative attitudes about the societal benefits of survey research. Indeed, pollsters are perceived to be about as (un)trustworthy as members of the U.S. Congress.[46]

Reliability and Validity

Social psychologists often survey people, but all surveys are not public opinion polls. For example, some surveys measure peoples' personality traits or their attitudes. With regard to surveys, two aspects of measurement are especially important: reliability and validity. The term **reliability** means a survey gives consistent results; the term **validity** means a survey measures what it purports to measure. **FIGURE 1.11** provides a useful visualization of the concepts of reliability and validity. Suppose the same survey is given to the same individual 21 times. Each target contains 21 "bullet holes" with each bullet

Most Americans have never heard of Alf Landon, yet a poll predicted him to win the 1936 U.S. presidential election over Franklin D. Roosevelt in a landslide. The opposite occurred because the pollsters did not take a random sample of Americans.

reliability a measure that gives consistent results

validity refers to whether a measure actually measures what it purports to measure

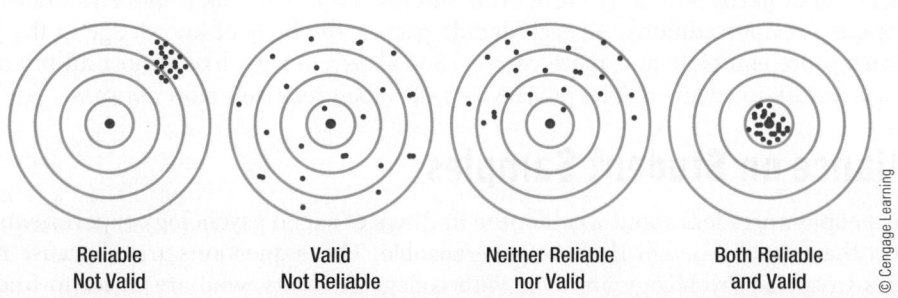

Reliable Not Valid

Valid Not Reliable

Neither Reliable nor Valid

Both Reliable and Valid

FIGURE 1.11
Illustrations of reliability and validity in a measure given to the same person 21 times. Each "bullet hole" in the target represents a time the measure was given.

hole representing a time the survey was given. Moving from left to right in Figure 1.12, the first survey is reliable—it gives consistent results (i.e., the "bullet holes" or measurements are close together), but it is invalid (i.e., the measurements are off center). The second survey is unreliable (i.e., the measurements are inconsistent), but it is valid (i.e., the measurements are evenly distributed around the center of the target). The third survey is unreliable (i.e., the measurements are inconsistent) and invalid (i.e., the measurements are off center). The fourth survey is best—it is both reliable (i.e., the measurements are consistent) and valid (i.e., the measurements are on center).

How Much of Social Psychology Is True?

Many thousands of social psychology studies are done every year. On the one hand, this volume of activity gives the impression that a great deal is being learned and great progress is being made. On the other hand, the many arguments and controversies in the field create the impression that chaos and anarchy prevail and no progress is being made. Also, many people criticize social psychology experiments as not being good ways to learn about reality. The critics argue that social psychology laboratories are artificial settings, that social psychology measures are unrealistic, and that the participants tested (mainly college students, especially ones from individualistic countries such the United States and Western Europe) are not representative of real people. In other words, the critics claim that social psychology research lacks external validity. Accordingly, let us spend a little time reflecting on how much confidence we can have in what social psychologists learn—indeed, on how much one can believe what is presented in the rest of this book!

Self-Correcting Nature of Science

As already mentioned, one source of concern about social psychology is that experts sometimes disagree. Sometimes both sides can point to experiments that seem to support their conflicting viewpoints. Moreover, some experiments can produce a wrong or misleading conclusion, possibly due to a hidden flaw in the experimental design. It is even possible that researchers occasionally fail to report their work correctly, and once in a great while researchers lie about their work, perhaps to advance their careers, by claiming to have produced some new discovery.

In the long run, these problems are corrected. Flawed experiments or misleading interpretations can arise, but in general new work builds on older work, and if the older research contains mistakes, the newer research will find them and correct them. **Replication** means repeating a study, and many studies replicate earlier ones, so if the result of the earlier one was a fluke or a fraud, the replication will produce a different result, and gradually the correct answer will emerge from multiple studies. Recently, psychological journals have started publishing more replication studies. As the title of one article states, "Rewarding Replications (is a) Sure and Simple Way to Improve Psychological Science."[47] This is one of the great advantages of the sciences (including the social sciences) as opposed to the humanities (e.g., literary criticism): It is possible, eventually, to establish that some ideas or conclusions are wrong.

Hence some of the conclusions described in this book may turn out in the long run to be wrong or partly wrong. However, this edition of our textbook is more accurate than any of our previous editions. As each decade passes, the body of knowledge in the field becomes more complete and more correct. Social psychology, like almost all scientific fields, is a work in progress. The progress is real, albeit relatively slow at times.

Reliance on Student Samples

Many people worry less about whether the findings of social psychology experiments are correct than about whether they are generalizable. These questions arise because most studies in social psychology are done with college students, who are easier to find for

> "There are many hypotheses in science which are wrong. That's perfectly all right; they're the aperture to finding out what's right. Science is a self-correcting process."
> — Carl Sagan, *astronomer*

replication repeating a study to see if the effect is reliable

research (especially because most researchers are college or university professors). Some argue that students might not be typical of everyone else, so a social psychology based on college students might not generalize to other groups, such as the elderly, middle-aged corporate executives, or homeless people.

Periodically, social psychologists seek to replicate their studies using other groups. In general, the results are quite similar. College students do not differ all that fundamentally from other people in most respects. When they do differ, it is often more a matter of degree than of behaving according to different principles. A social psychology experiment typically seeks to establish whether some causal relationship exists—such as whether frustration causes aggression. As it happens, college students do become more aggressive when frustrated, but so do most other people. It might be that some groups will respond with more extreme aggression and others with less, but the general principle is the same: Frustration causes aggression.

Social psychology is also mainly interested in normal, typical people. College students are drawn from a broad segment of normal people, and so findings based on them typically can be generalized to other typical groups. One should be careful generalizing from findings based on students (or on other normal groups) to very unusual groups.

When college students do differ from other people, these differences are probably limited to a few specific areas, and researchers interested in them should be cautious.[48,49] On average, college students may be more thoughtful than others, and more intelligent (because people of low intelligence are less likely to go to college). Their self-concepts may be less firmly established because most college students are still in the process of building their adult identities. They may have less experience with the burdens of responsibility than other adults who must cope with the demands of work and taking care of a family. They may come from slightly more affluent backgrounds and have somewhat smaller proportions of ethnic minorities than the population at large. None of these differences is likely to make students radically different from other people. Hence, social psychology's disproportionate reliance on studying college students does not represent a serious problem.

Cultural Relativity

Most social psychology research is conducted in the United States and a few other very similar Western countries (e.g., Belgium, Canada, France, Germany, Italy, the Netherlands, the United Kingdom). Some people worry that findings based in these cultures would not apply to people who live in very different cultures, such as in sub-Saharan Africa, the Middle East, or central Asia.

We do not have enough evidence to know how serious this problem may be. Because Western countries dominate social psychology research (although much work is being conducted elsewhere), we simply do not know how different people in other cultures may be. There is little evidence to suggest that people in other cultures fail to conform to certain basic patterns of social psychology—for example, that similarity promotes liking (see Chapter 11). Likewise, playing violent video games can increase aggression in players from both Western and Eastern countries (e.g., Japan).[50] It is also true that no one has tested whether these same patterns can be found everywhere.

Although we are optimistic that much of what Western social psychologists find will prove to be true of people everywhere, we think it prudent to expect that some differences may exist. At present, it seems reasonably safe to generalize what social psychology knows to the vast majority of adult citizens in Western cultures, but to be cautious and hesitant about generalizing to people who live in very different cultures. For example, people from Eastern countries tend to conform more than those from Western countries.[51]

This book is based on the assumption that human nature has some basic, universal features. In other words, we do believe that some psychological facts and principles are true for people everywhere. We know that cultural differences do exist and that some of them are quite substantial and important. People may be born the same everywhere in many respects, but different cultures can build on these same basic traits in different ways and shape them according to different values. This theme is reflected in the next chapter, where we discuss humans as cultural animals.

1. **What concept allows science to be self-correcting over time?**
   - (a) Correlation
   - (b) Generalizability
   - (c) Random assignment
   - (d) Replication

2. **Most social psychological studies use participants from which continent?**
   - (a) Asia
   - (b) Australia
   - (c) North America
   - (d) South America

3. **What type of participants do most social psychologists use in their studies?**
   - (a) Children
   - (b) College students
   - (c) Senior citizens
   - (d) White rats

4. **Compared to the general population, college students _____.**
   - (a) are more extraverted
   - (b) are more introverted
   - (c) have less crystallized self-concepts
   - (d) have more crystallized self-concepts

CHAPTER 1 SUMMARY

A Brief History of Social Psychology

- Social psychology can help you make sense of your own social world.
- The mere presence of another person enhances performance on a simple task.
- Individual effort decreases as group size increases.
- Behaviorism seeks to explain all of psychology in terms of learning principles such as reward and punishment.

What Do Social Psychologists Do?

- Social psychology features experiments and the scientific method. It studies inner states and processes as well as behavior.
- Social psychology is concerned with the effect of other people on (mainly adult) human beings' thoughts, feelings, and behaviors.
- The ABC triad in social psychology stands for
  - Affect, or how people feel inside (including emotion),
  - Behavior, or what people do, their actions,
  - Cognition, or what people think about.
- Social psychology focuses especially on the power of situations.

Social Psychology's Place in the World

- Social psychology is both similar to and different from other social sciences.
- Anthropology is the study of human culture.
- Economics is the study of the production, distribution, and consumption of goods and services.

- History is the study of past events.
- Political science is the study of political organizations and institutions, especially governments.
- Sociology is the study of human societies and the groups that form those societies.
- Psychology is the study of human behavior. Several other areas of psychology are related to social psychology.
- Biological psychology, physiological psychology, and neuroscience focus on the brain, nervous system, and other aspects of the body.
- Clinical psychology focuses on abnormal behavior and disorders.
- Cognitive psychology is the basic study of thought processes.
- Developmental psychology focuses on how people change across their lives, from conception and birth to old age and death.
- Personality psychology focuses on differences between individuals, as well as inner processes.
- What separates philosophy from psychology is psychology's heavy reliance on the scientific method.

Why People Study Social Psychology

- Social psychologists often find the topics they study to be intrinsically interesting.
- Applied researchers study a specific practical problem, usually outside the laboratory.

How Do Social Psychologists Answer Their Own Questions?

- To be a good social psychology researcher, it is helpful to be creative.
- Common sense can be mistaken.

- The scientific method involves five basic steps:
  - State a problem for study.
  - Formulate a testable hypothesis (educated guess) as a tentative solution to the problem.
  - Design a study to test the hypothesis and collect data.
  - Test the hypothesis by confronting it with the data.
  - Communicate the study's results.
- The independent variable is an observable event that causes a person in an experiment to do something. It has at least two levels, categories, types, or groups.
- In a between-subjects design, participants are exposed to only one level of the independent variable; in a within-subjects design participants are exposed to all levels of the independent variable.
- The dependent variable is an observable behavior produced by a person in an experiment.
- An operational definition classifies theoretical variables in terms of observable operations, procedures, and measurements.
- For a theory to be scientific, it must be testable, so its theoretical constructs must be operationally defined.
- Two essential features of experiments are control and random assignment:
  - By exercising experimental control, the researcher tries to make sure that any differences observed on the dependent variable were caused by the independent variable and not by other factors.
  - Participants in an experiment must be randomly assigned to levels of the independent variable (assignment to groups is random if each participant has an equal chance of being in each group).
- A confederate is someone who helps the researcher by pretending to be another participant.
- Experiments conducted in a real-world rather than a laboratory setting are called field experiments.

- Experimental realism refers to whether participants get so caught up in the procedures that they forget they are in an experiment (important for determining whether the results obtained in the experiment can be applied to the real world).
- Mundane realism refers to whether the setting and research procedures physically resemble the real world.
- In the correlational approach, the researcher does not try to control variables or randomly assign participants to groups, but merely observes whether things go together.
- A correlation gives the relationship or association between two variables.
- When a correlation is positive, as one variable goes up the other variable also goes up.
- When a correlation is negative, as one variable increases the other variable decreases.
- A correlation coefficient can range from +1.0 (a perfect positive correlation) to −1.0 (a perfect negative correlation).
- The main weakness of the correlational approach is it does not allow the researcher to conclude that changes in one variable caused the changes in the other variable.
- A sample is random if each person in the population has an equal chance of being selected.
- The population is the total number of people under consideration.
- The margin of error is how much the results of a survey can be expected to deviate by chance alone.
- A survey is reliable if it gives consistent results.
- A survey is valid if it measures what it purports to measure.

How Much of Social Psychology Is True?

- Because research builds on older research, science is self-correcting.
- Some psychological facts and principles are true for people everywhere. There are also cultural differences, and some of them are quite substantial and important.

key terms

quiz yourself ANSWERS

1. A Brief History of Social Psychology **p. 6**
   answers: 1.c 2.c 3.d 4.b

2. What Do Social Psychologists Do? **p. 7**
   answers: 1.d 2.a 3.a 4.d

3. Social Psychology's Place in the World **p. 10**
   answers: 1.c 2.a 3.d 4.c

4. Why People Study Social Psychology **p. 13**
   answers: 1.b 2.b 3.e 4.c

5. How Do Social Psychologists Answer Their Own Questions? **p. 17**
   answers: 1.b 2.b 3.d 4.c

6. How Much of Social Psychology Is True? **p. 28**
   answers: 1.d 2.c 3.b 4.c

CULTURE AND NATURE

2

LEARNING OBJECTIVES

1 Explain how and why the human brain evolved the way it did.

2 Understand how culture and nature work together to affect choices and behavior and make culture a better way of being social.

3 Summarize how the two system of the duplex mind differ and work together.

4 Describe how inner processes serve interpersonal functions.

In 1965 a Canadian woman gave birth to a pair of healthy twin boys. When the boys were eight months old, they were taken to the hospital to be circumcised. Through a series of mishaps, one of the boys had his penis practically burned off by an electric cauterizing machine. Medical technology could not repair the damage. After some long and anxious conversations, the family and medical staff decided that the best thing to do was to remove the rest of the penis and raise the boy as a girl.[1]

The decision was not taken lightly. The family consulted with leading experts on gender and sexuality. In the past, many psychologists and others had believed that men and women were innately different, but the feminist movement had challenged those beliefs as being mere rationalizations for oppressing women. Most expert opinion had come around to agree that boys and girls were not born different but were made different by how they were brought up. Many Canadian and American parents were themselves rethinking how to raise their children so as to undo the constraining stereotypes and perhaps produce more autonomous, stronger daughters and more sensitive, caring sons. If adult personality depended mainly on upbringing, then it should not matter much whether a child was born as a boy or a girl. It should therefore be possible to raise this baby boy as a girl with no untoward consequences. At most, the experts thought that the child would need some injections of female hormones around the time of puberty.

Little Brenda (as the child was named) was not told about the botched circumcision or the gender switch. She grew up wearing long hair and dresses, playing with other girls, and in other ways being introduced to the female sex role. The sex experts kept in touch and reported back to the scientific community that the experiment was working. Brenda was a normal girl.

The reports were not quite right, however. The parents were anxious to avoid displeasing the experts, and perhaps they also wanted to avoid admitting that they might have made a mistake in converting their son into a daughter. But the girl never fit in. She wanted to play rough games like the boys did. She was more interested in sports, race cars, and fighting toys than in dolls, makeup, or tea parties. Her dress was often dirty and disheveled, and her hair was tangled, unlike the other girls'. As the children approached puberty and began to play kissing games or to try dancing at parties, the tensions increased. Brenda did not know what was wrong, but she wanted no part of kissing boys or dancing with them. Her rebellious behavior increased.

Finally it came time for the hormone shots. By now Brenda was in regular therapy. She rebelled and absolutely refused to accept the injections. When her parents broke down and told her the full story of how she had been born as a boy, she finally felt as if she could understand herself. She immediately quit being a girl. She cut her hair, replaced her dresses with boys' clothes, and took a male name. He insisted on having lengthy, agonizing surgeries to remove his breasts and create a sort of penis from the muscles and skin of his legs. Although his body could not biologically father a child, the former Brenda was even able to become a father by virtue of marrying a woman who already had children. But happiness proved elusive, and at age 38 he killed himself.[2,3]

Later, investigative reporters uncovered other such cases. Each time, the person born as a boy and raised as a girl did not turn out to be a typical adult woman. One of them, for example, smoked cigars, refused to wear dresses and skirts, and worked as an auto mechanic. For another example, former Olympic Athlete Bruce Jenner is now Caitlyn Jenner.

These stories are important because they suggest limits to the power of socialization. In the 1970s and 1980s, most psychologists accepted the view that the differences between men and women were due to parental care and

As Nature Made Him: The Boy Who Was Raised as a Girl, by John Colapinto.

upbringing. Parents supposedly taught their sons to be aggressive while teaching their daughters to be passive and compliant. For a while, the early part of the "Brenda" story was reported in some textbooks as evidence that sex roles are entirely due to socialization, and Brenda was described as a normal and healthy girl. But the problems that emerged later suggested that the differences between male and female are partly innate. (*Innate* means something you are born with, as opposed to something you learned or acquired during your life. *Innate* is also understood to mean something that cannot be fully or easily changed.) There are limits to how much can be accomplished by teaching, upbringing, and other aspects of socialization.

None of this should be taken to mean that learning and culture are irrelevant. Boys and girls do learn from their culture how to act and how to understand themselves. The power of culture is, however, limited. Apparently people are predisposed to learn some things more easily than others. If gender identity were entirely a matter of learning, Brenda should have been a normal girl. Parents, teachers, psychologists, and others were all working together to raise her as a girl, and none of her peers or friends was told that she had once been a boy. At times she seemed to accept herself as a female and to act as girls were expected to act. However, the experiment failed. Apparently some parts of who you are come from biology, regardless of what your parents and teachers tell you.

Social psychology is aimed at exploring how people think, feel, and act. The ultimate explanations for human behavior lie in nature and culture, and researchers have engaged in many long, bitter debates over which of those is more important. The one clearly correct answer is that both are very important. In this chapter, we will consider the complementary influences of nature and culture. ●

Nature and Social Behavior

Explaining the Psyche

One approach to understanding how people think, feel, and act is to try to understand what the human psyche is designed for. (The **psyche** is a broader term for mind, encompassing emotions, desires, perceptions, and indeed all psychological processes.) To understand something, you have to know what it was designed to do.

Imagine someone who has grown up on a deserted island and has never met another human being or seen any human-made items. Then one day a box washes ashore containing an electric can opener. How would the person figure out what the can opener does? Having grown up on a deserted island, the person knows nothing about cans or electricity. This hypothetical person might take it apart, analyze it, observe its parts, and see what some of their properties are, but it would be almost impossible for this person to understand it properly.

Understanding the human psyche is somewhat like that. To understand and explain how it works, it is useful to know what the psyche/human mind is designed for. Hence, we turn to nature and culture because those are what made the psyche the way it is. If the psyche was designed to do something in particular, then nature and culture designed it for that purpose. Accordingly, if we can learn what the purpose is, then we can understand people much better.

Why are people the way they are? Why is the human mind set up as it is? Why do people think, want, feel, and act in certain ways? Nature and culture. The nature explanations say that people are born a certain way; their genes, hormones, brain structure, and other processes dictate how they will choose and act. In contrast, the cultural explanations focus on what people learn from their parents, from society, and from their own experiences.

Such debates have raged over many other forms of social interaction and behavior. Are people born with a natural tendency to be aggressive, or is aggression something they pick up from watching violent films, playing with toy guns, and copying other people's actions? Are some people born to be

psyche a broader term for mind, encompassing emotions, desires, perceptions, and all other psychological processes

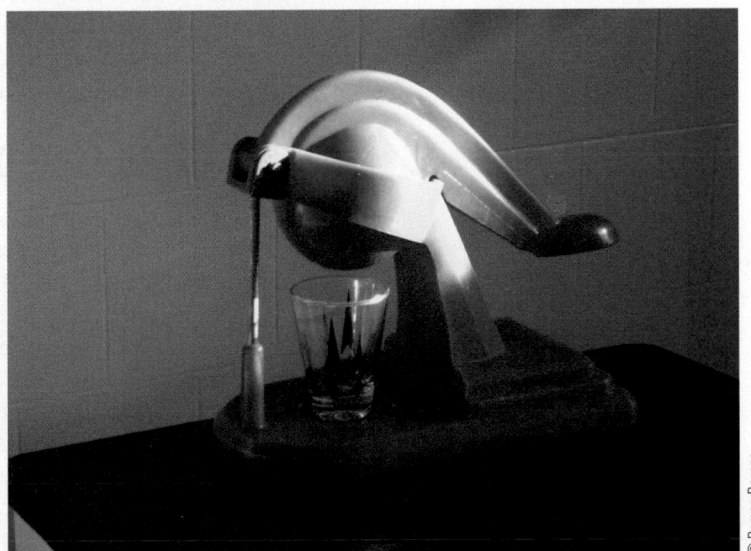

© Roman Barnes

To understand how to work this device, you have to know what it is designed to do.

homosexuals, or can people choose and change their sexual orientation? Is mental illness the result of how your parents treated you, or is it something in your genes? What about whether someone likes to drink alcohol or gamble? What about heroism, especially when people risk their own lives to protect or save others? How many of the differences between men and women reflect their innate, genetic tendencies, and how many are the product of cultural stereotypes?

Many social scientists have grown tired of nature–nurture debates and wish to put an end to them, though others continue to pursue them vigorously. In recent years, some researchers have stressed that both nature and culture have real influences. The most common resolution tends to favor nature as more important, however, because nature is indispensable. As Frans de Waal[4] argued, nature versus culture isn't a fair fight because without nature you have nothing. He proposed that the argument should be waged between whether a particular behavior is the direct result of nature or stems from a combination of nature and culture. Your body has to perceive what is happening, your brain has to understand events, and your body has to carry out your decisions (and brain and body are both created by nature). Put more simply, nature comes first, and culture builds on what nature has furnished. That is one view.

This book, however, favors the view that nature and culture have shaped each other. In particular, nature has prepared human beings specifically for culture. That is, the characteristics that set humans apart from other animals (including language, a flexible self that can hold multiple roles, and an advanced ability to understand each other's mental states) are mainly there to enable people to create and sustain culture. This interaction between nature and culture is the key to understanding how people think, act, and feel. But let's start by considering nature and culture separately.

Nature Defined

Nature is the physical world around us, including its laws and processes. It includes the entire world that would be there even if no human beings existed. Nature includes trees and grass, bugs and elephants, gravity, the weather, hunger and thirst, birth and death, atoms and molecules, and all the laws of physics and chemistry. Nature made people too. (People who believe that the original humans were created by a divine power still recognize that the natural processes of reproduction and childbirth create today's people.)

Those who explain human behavior using nature invoke the sorts of processes that natural sciences have shown. For example, neuroscientists look for explanations in terms of what happens inside the brain (chemical reactions, electrical activity). Behavior geneticists seek to understand behavior as the result of genes and show that people are born with tendencies to feel and act in certain ways. Above all, however, the advocates of nature in psychology turn to evolutionary theory to understand behavior patterns. The next section provides an introduction to this style of thinking.

Evolution, and Doing What's Natural

Over the past two decades, many social psychologists have begun looking to the theory of evolution to help explain social behavior. The **theory of evolution**, proposed by the British biologist Charles Darwin in the 1800s, focuses on how change occurs in nature. Over thousands of years, a plant or animal may evolve into a somewhat different kind of creature. Human beings and the great apes evolved from a common ancestor.

Human beings may be different from all other animals, but we are animals nonetheless. As such, we have many of the same wants, needs, and problems that most other animals have. We need food and water on a regular basis, preferably a couple of times every day. We need sleep. We need shelter and warmth. We need air. We suffer illnesses and injuries and must find ways to recover from them. Our interactions with others are sometimes characterized by sexual desire, competition, aggressive impulses, family ties, or friendly companionship. Sometimes we say that certain people are "acting like animals," but this is not surprising, because we are all animals. That phrase merely expresses the point that people can sometimes rise above their animal nature, but the animal parts are there inside all of us.

nature the physical world around us, including its laws and processes

theory of evolution a theory proposed by Charles Darwin to explain how change occurs in nature

An important feature of most living things, including animals and hence humans, is the drive to prolong life. There are two ways to do this. Obviously, one way is to go on living. (Wouldn't you like to live forever? Death has always been a disturbing threat, and beliefs that death is not the end but merely a transition into a different kind of life, whether as a ghost, a spirit in heaven, or a reincarnated person, have been found all over the earth since prehistoric times.) The other is reproduction: Life makes new life. Indeed, you might say that nature was unable to create an immortal being and therefore settled on reproduction as the only viable strategy to enable any form of life to continue into the future.

Change is another common trait of living things. Each living thing changes as it grows older, but more important forms of change occur from one generation to the next: Children are different from their parents. Nature cannot plan ahead and design a certain kind of change. Instead, nature produces changes that are essentially random. That is, the complicated processes that mix the genes of two parents to produce a unique set of genes in the baby sometimes produce novel outcomes in the form of new traits. However, powerful forces react to these random changes. As a result, some random changes will disappear, whereas others will endure. The process of **natural selection** decides which traits will disappear and which will continue.

For example, imagine that one baby was born with no ears, another with one leg longer than the other, and the third with eyes that could see farther than the average eye. Having no ears or having legs of unequal length would probably be disadvantages, and natural selection would not preserve these traits for future generations. (That's a polite way of saying that those babies would probably die before being able to pass on their genes by having offspring.) A significant improvement in vision might, however, be selected to remain because the baby who grew up seeing better than other people would be able to find more food and spot danger from a safer distance. The genes for better vision would therefore remain in the gene pool (assuming that this baby would grow up and have babies), and so in future generations more and more people would enjoy this improvement.

Natural selection has two criteria: survival and reproduction. (Remember, these are the two ways of prolonging life.) A trait that improves survival or reproduction will tend to endure for many generations and become more common. A trait that reduces one's chances for survival or reproduction will probably not become common. These are crucial themes because the biological success of any trait is measured in those terms. A novel trait that makes someone happier or gives the person higher self-esteem or fosters a weird sense of humor, will not necessarily be passed on to future generations, unless those changes can translate into better survival or better reproduction.

Survival is not hard to understand. It means living longer. Darwin's contemporary Herbert Spencer coined the phrase "survival of the fittest" to describe natural selection. Animals compete against each other to survive, as in who can get the best food or who can best escape being eaten by larger animals. In a group of zebras, for example, the ones who run the slowest are most likely to be eaten by lions, so the ones born to be fast are more likely to live long enough to pass along their genes.

Survival depends in part on the circumstances in your environment. Consider the coloring of fish. Most fish have a relatively light colored belly and a relatively dark colored top or back. Why? That coloring is adapted for survival in the water. Most fish live until a bigger fish eats them, making the ability to hide from bigger fish an important trait for survival. Some big fish swim near the surface and look downward for food. The lower (deeper) you go in the water, the darker it gets. When a big fish looks downward, therefore, it can't see dark-colored fish very well, so fish who are dark on the top side are harder to see (and therefore safer). Meanwhile, some big fish lurk in the depths and look upward for their food. Looking upward is looking into the light, so the best way for a fish to blend in is to have a light coloring on its underside. Over millions of years, the fish who were dark on top and light on the bottom survived longest because they were the hardest for the bigger fish to see, so they were less likely to be eaten and, therefore, more likely to make more baby fish with the same coloring. As a result of this selection process, most fish have this coloring today.

off the mark.com — by Mark Parisi

DO THOSE SWEET SOUNDING BELLS SEEM TO BE GETTING CLOSER OR IS IT JUST ME?

NATURAL SELECTION AT WORK

Reprinted by permission of Atlantic Feature Syndicate/Mark Parisi.

natural selection the process whereby those members of a species that survive and reproduce most effectively are the ones that pass along their genes to future generations

survival living longer

off the mark.com   by Mark Parisi

I'M HAVING THE WORST LUCK...

SURVIVAL THROUGH EVOLUTION

offthemark.com

Reprinted by permission of Atlantic Feature Syndicate/Mark Parisi.

Gradually, biologists have shifted their emphasis from survival to reproduction as the single most important factor in natural selection. Survival is important mainly as a means to achieve reproduction. **Reproduction** means producing babies—though the babies also have to survive long enough to reproduce. Reproductive success consists of creating many offspring who will in turn create many offspring. Put another way, nature judges you by how many grandchildren you produce.

For example, suppose a **mutation** (that is, a new gene or combination of genes) today could double the expected life span of a woman, from about 75 years to about 150. That is, one particular woman was born with the biological makeup to enable her to live 150 years. Would subsequent generations have more and more of this trait, and thus be more and more like this woman (and hence able to live longer)? Possibly not. If the woman was still done having babies around the age of 40, and if her longer life did not improve her quantity or quality of children and grandchildren, then her genetic traits would not spread. Now imagine another woman born with a mutation that doubled the number of children she produced, even though she would die at age 75 just like the others. Subsequent generations might well contain more and more people like her.

Much of the recent work in evolutionary theory has focused on gender differences.[5,6,7] For example, evolution would likely select men to want more sex partners than women want. A woman can only have about one baby a year no matter how many men she has sex with, but a man can father dozens of children each year if he has sex with many women. Moreover, a woman's children would be most likely to survive to adulthood if they were cared for by two parents rather than just their mother. Hence, men today are probably descended from men who desired multiple partners, whereas today's women probably descended from female ancestors who preferred long-lasting monogamous relationships. Current research suggests that this pattern is found all over the world, in many different cultures: Men desire more sex partners than women.[8]

How, exactly, does biological evolution produce changes? The causal processes depend entirely on random changes to physical entities, such as genes. The person (or other creature) is programmed to respond a certain way. Crucially, nothing has to be thought, understood, or spoken in order for these changes to occur. That is, meaning has nothing to do with it. Molecules, chemicals, electrical impulses in the body, and other physical mechanisms produce the results. Behavior changes because the physical makeup of the newborn individual is different. This is quite different from how culture works, as we shall see.

Social Animals

Psychologists study people. Many psychologists have studied other animals, especially rats. But psychologists have never shown much interest in studying trees. Why not?

Trees, like people and all other living creatures, need to get certain things (e.g., water, nutrients) from the world around them. What is inside them is there to enable them to get what they need. The inside parts of trees enable them to draw water from the soil, chemicals from sunlight, and so forth. Trees, however, do not move around in search of food or to escape from predators. They take what comes to them where they are. Facing few decisions and being therefore essentially indifferent to other trees, they do not have much psychology. They don't have much in the way of thoughts, feelings, or behavior because they don't need these things to survive and reproduce. (That's why psychologists don't find them interesting.)

Contrast this with animals that also live as loners. They have to find food, possibly kill it, and eat it. They need more food and produce more waste than trees do. They need to sleep and so must find safe places to do so. Reproduction is more complicated than it is for trees, so they may need to perform a particular set of behaviors in order to reproduce. Like trees, they need to interact with their world, but doing so is more complicated for animals, so what is inside them has to be up to the task. Psychologists start to get interested in these processes.

reproduction producing babies that survive long enough to also reproduce

mutation a new gene or combination of genes

Many animals are not loners. They discovered, or perhaps nature discovered for them, that by living and working together, they could interact with the world more effectively. For example, if an animal hunts for food by itself, it can only catch, kill, and eat animals much smaller than itself—but if animals band together in a group, they can catch and kill animals bigger than they are. A pack of wolves can kill a horse, which can feed the group very well. Thus, more food is available to the same animals in the same forest if they work together than if they work alone. Cooperation has other benefits: The animals can alert each other to danger, can find more food (if they search separately and then follow the ones who succeed in finding food), and can even provide some care to those who are sick and injured. Mating and reproduction are also easier if the animals live in a group than if they live far apart.

In short, being social provides benefits. Being social is a strategy that enables some animals to survive and reproduce effectively. That is the biological starting point of social psychology: Being social improves survival and reproduction.

The downside of being social is that it is more difficult to achieve than solitary life. As with trees, what is inside social animals is there to enable them to get what they need from the environment. But to be social, one has to have quite a bit going on inside. (Hence, psychologists can find much to study.) Social animals have to have something inside them that makes them recognize each other and want to be together. They must have something that prompts them to work together, such as automatic impulses to copy what the others are doing. (Hunting in groups doesn't happen by mere coincidence.) They must have ways to resolve the conflicts that inevitably arise in social life, as when two animals both want the same piece of food. They need something akin to self-control to enable them to adjust to group life. Social animals need complex, powerful brains.

The Social Brain

Trees don't need brains, and solitary creatures can get by with relatively simple ones. Social animals, however, require brains with additional, flexible capabilities.

The evolutionary anthropologist Robin Dunbar[9,10] compared the brain sizes of many different species to see what behavioral differences went with bigger brains. (Brain size is always adjusted for body weight because bigger animals generally have bigger brains. For example, human men have bigger brains than women, but that's mainly because men are bigger all over. Adult men and women have about the same average intelligence, despite the brain size difference.) Did big-brained species eat better foods, or more complicated foods such as fruit (which ripens and turns rotten rapidly)? Did they roam over larger territories, so that they needed a bigger brain to maintain a more complex mental map? No. Dunbar found that bigger brains were mainly linked to having larger and more complex social groups. Small-brained animals tend to live alone or in small, simple groups, whereas bigger-brained, presumably smarter animals have more relationships with each other and more complicated groups (such as those with dominance hierarchies and competing allies). More recent work has extended this to human beings: People with bigger social networks have been found to be bigger in some key brain parts, notably the orbital prefrontal cortex.[11]

Blickwinkel/Alamy

"So really, what are you like deep down inside?"

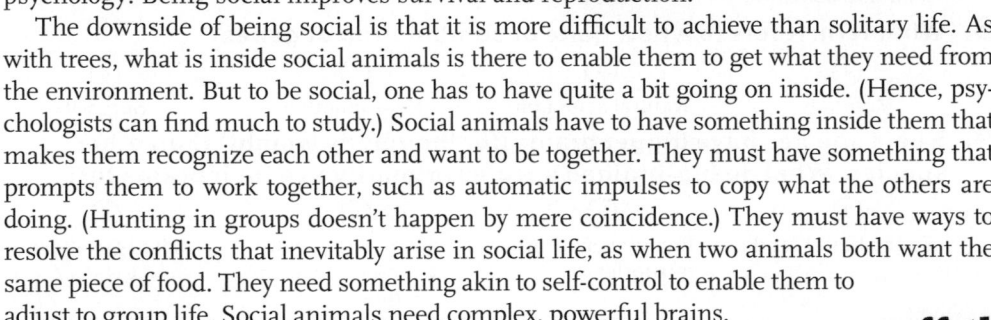

off the mark .com   by Mark Parisi

WHEN I WAS A KID, WE DIDN'T HAVE BIG JUICY BRAINS TO PROBE ...NO... WE HAD TO GET BY ABDUCTING CAVE PEOPLE WITH PUNY BRAINS... ...AND HAIRY BODIES!

offthemark.com

This conclusion is highly important. The human brain did not evolve because it helped us outsmart lions and tigers and bears or build better shelters or invent calculus. It evolved mainly to enable human beings to have rich, complex social lives. The brain is not for understanding the physical world around us so much as it is for understanding each other. It is not so much a calculating brain or a problem-solving brain as it is a social brain.

Again, what is inside enables the creature to satisfy its needs and, ultimately, to survive and reproduce. Social animals (including humans) accomplish those things by means of social interaction. Much of what goes on inside the human mind is designed to help the person relate to others. Social psychologists spend much time studying people's inner processes, including their thoughts and feelings and, recently, how their brains work. They study those things because *inner processes serve interpersonal functions*. Remember that phrase; it will be one of the themes of this book, and it is a good basis for understanding social psychology.

QUIZ YOURSELF

Nature and Social Behavior

answers: see pg 65

1. **The finding that kids who watch violent TV programs become more aggressive as adults than do kids who watch nonviolent TV programs can best be explained in terms of _____ influences.**
   - (a) biological
   - (b) genetic
   - (c) hormonal
   - (d) societal

2. **Suppose that a new baby girl was born with no teeth. Unfortunately, because she had great difficulty eating, she died of starvation before she could have any children. Thus, the trait of having no teeth was not preserved for future generations. This process is called _____ .**
   - (a) natural selection
   - (b) nurture
   - (c) praxis
   - (d) None of the above

3. **What term refers to a new gene or combination of genes?**
   - (a) Mutation
   - (b) Natural selection
   - (c) Reproduction
   - (d) Survival

4. **Some species have bigger brains (for their body weight) than other species. What do big-brained species primarily use their brains for?**
   - (a) Eating better foods
   - (b) Roaming over larger territories
   - (c) Having larger and more complex social structures
   - (d) All of the above

Culture and Human Social Life

Social Animal or Cultural Animal?

Social psychologists like to use the phrase "the social animal" to describe human nature. Many influential thinkers, from the ancient Greek philosopher Aristotle right down to the modern social psychologist Elliot Aronson,[12] have used this phrase. By calling people **social animals**, these thinkers are saying that people seek connections to others and prefer to live, work, and play together with other people.

People are indeed social animals, but using this label may miss the mark of what is special about human beings. Plenty of other animals are social, from ants to elephants (as Aronson and others acknowledge). Human beings are not the only and perhaps not even the most social animals.

Being social animals is not what is most special about human beings. What is special is being **cultural animals**. Some other animals have bits and scraps of culture, such as when a tribe of monkeys all use a certain group of stones to open nuts, or learn to rinse their potatoes in the stream to get the dirt off,[13] but none comes anywhere close to having the remarkably rich and powerful cultural systems that humans

social animals animals that seek connections to others and prefer to live, work, and play with other members of their species

cultural animal theory the view that evolution shaped the human psyche so as to enable humans to create and take part in culture

have. Moreover, human beings have culture everywhere; human life is almost impossible to imagine without it. Culture in animals is typically a bonus or a luxury, something they could live almost as well without. All humans use culture every day and depend on it for their survival.

Culture is thus the essence of what makes us human. Yes, we are social beings, but we have plenty of company in that respect. We are also deeply cultural beings, and in that respect we are unique. Let us therefore consider what culture is.

Culture Defined

Culture is harder to define than nature. (In fact, one book listed 164 different definitions of culture that different thinkers have used!)[14] The term originally referred to a system of farming (a usage one can still see in terms like *agriculture*). Then it came to refer to musical

Not a good idea.

and artistic achievements, such as paintings and symphonies. Social scientists eventually began to use the term to refer to what a large group of people have in common. French culture, for example, refers to everything that French people share: language, values, food preferences, a style of government, a place (France), and a shared sense of connection to the artistic and historical achievements of other French people.

For present purposes, the important thing about culture is that it is a kind of social system. Just as a pack of wolves or a school of fish is a social system, so is France. But there are obvious differences. France is much more complex than a pack of wolves. It is rich in symbols, meanings, and information. There are more different kinds of relationships among the French people than among the wolves.

Culture is thus an advanced way of being social. If we think of evolution as proceeding from simple creatures such as plants, to solitary animals, to social animals, then cultural animals are a further step in that same direction.

Following are some important features of culture.

Shared Ideas

Culture is the world of shared ideas. Culture enables you to interact with people you have never met before; by virtue of belonging to the same culture, you have enough in common that you can do things together. If you travel to another city and meet new people, many interactions are possible because of culture: You might talk to them about sports or politics, or you might buy something from them in a store, or you might work together to sail a boat. To say that culture consists of "shared ideas" is to say that no single person has culture by himself or herself.

People may argue about many beliefs and practices, but the arguments occur on the basis of shared underlying beliefs. In the United States, for example, Democrats and Republicans argue about how best to run the country, but they share an underlying faith in certain values such as free elections, help for the sick and needy, a prosperous economy, and good schools. They just disagree about how to provide these things and how to choose between two values when they conflict.

If culture is an important part of what humans evolved to do, then we would expect the human brain to be strongly oriented toward shared ideas. Plenty of evidence confirms this. As one sign, young human children quickly grasp the possibility of shared attention, in the sense that they emphasize looking at the same things that other people (especially their mother or primary caregiver) are looking at. (The expression "look!" is one that very young children understand: they obey it and even say it.)

Recent work in social psychology has provided remarkable evidence of the human brain's attunement to shared ideas. Emotions, for example, seem to be intensified merely by seeing something and knowing that another member of your group is sharing the experience. Participants in these studies saw images, advertisements, or a short video (e.g., the plight of homeless people, or cute puppies cavorting). They were told that other members of the group were viewing the same stimuli at the same time, or one minute earlier, or one minute later, or they were told strangers rather than group members were seeing these things, or in another control condition that they were watching alone. People had the strongest emotional reactions only in the first condition: when another group member was seeing it at exactly the same time.[15] Thus, simultaneous sharing causes the mind to react more strongly to the same information.

Likewise, people learn more quickly and pick up norms for behavior faster when they know another group member is viewing the same information than when they view it alone. If the other person is not a fellow group member, learning is slower, as it is if one's fellow group member is viewing something else.[16]

In fact, people seem especially attuned to knowing that some important information is shared. A clever series of studies required participants to make choices, some of which involved trusting each other, after hearing all the instructions and options. They showed the most trust if the information came by loudspeaker so they were sure the other person heard exactly the same thing they did.[17] Simply being told that the same information was being communicated to the other person had less of an effect. In principle it shouldn't matter whether you are informed that someone else is getting the same information versus you directly experience it together, but it did. The difference is that in one case one has direct, certain knowledge that the other has exactly the same information. In most social settings throughout history, knowing that someone else heard the same story was no guarantee that the other person had exactly the same information, because stories can be told and heard in different ways. This suggests that the brain puts special priority on information that is directly experienced as shared with someone else.

Culture as Social System

Culture exists as a network linking many different people. The idea of a network is useful because it captures the essential point that culture connects many people together and exists in what they share. The problem with the idea of a network is that it doesn't sufficiently capture the dynamic (changing) aspect of culture. Culture never sits still.

Instead of a network, therefore, it is useful to think of culture as a system consisting of many moving parts that work together. Think, for example, of how people get food nowadays: Farmers grow it, factories process it, truckers transport it, stores display it, people buy it and cook it. When a family sits down to dinner, it is likely that 50 or 100 other people have directly helped get that food there (not to mention the thousands of others who were indirectly involved, including the management of the supermarket chain, the banks that financed the farms and the trucking company, the corporations that paid the mother and father the salaries they used to buy the food, the factories that built the refrigerator and stove, the suppliers of electricity, and so on).

The food system is an initial illustration of one theme of social psychology that we will call *putting people first*. (We will talk more about this later in the chapter, and throughout the book.) Most animals get their food directly from nature, at least after a brief period of infancy. In the modern world, most people get their food from other people. Human survival and success depend more on how we deal with each other than on how we deal with the natural world around us.

Culture as Praxis

Anthropologists now argue among themselves as to whether a culture should be understood more on the basis of shared beliefs and values or shared ways of doing things. (Many use the term **praxis** to refer to practical ways of doing things.) Almost certainly, the answer is both. The culture that people in Philadelphia share involves some shared values, such as the value of money, democracy, preferences for some kinds of food, aversion to crime, support for their local sports teams, and so forth. They also share ways of

praxis practical ways of doing things

doing things: They drive on the same roads, use the same hospitals when they are sick, buy their food at local supermarkets, borrow money from the same banks, read the same newspapers, and so on. You will not live very well in Philadelphia if you refuse to shop at Philadelphia stores, or insist on driving your car on the left side of the road, or only go to a hospital to play billiards rather than to get treatment for illness.

Often the praxis depends on shared ideas. Money provides a good example: Certain round bits of metal and strips of colored paper are inherently worthless but, by virtue of shared ideas about them, acquire value and can be exchanged for all sorts of things. You can analyze the physics and chemistry of a dollar bill (e.g., its molecular structure) without gaining any clue to its value, because the value depends on shared social understandings. To learn more about the cultural significance of money, see the *Money Matters* box.

Culture, Information, and Meaning

Another crucial aspect of culture is that it is based on meaningful information. All cultures use language to encode and share information. People act as they do because they process this information. People change their behavior based on information they get from the culture, such as laws and rules, religious teachings and moral principles, historical events, symbols, what they read in books or see on television, and what they learned in school. Nonhuman animals respond to very little information of those kinds.

Human beings can think about and plan for the future, unlike squirrels. If you dig up all a squirrel's nuts and cart them off, the squirrel just goes on burying more nuts at the same pace, not even trying to compensate for the loss. But if humans lose their stores—perhaps because of a power failure that causes all the food in the refrigerator to spoil—then people quickly compensate by replacing the lost supply.

Nature, Culture, and Money

Money is such a familiar feature of human life that we take its existence and power for granted. All countries in the world today use money, so culturally it is nearly universal by now. Looked at from the perspective of nature, however, money is quite unusual. No species of plant or animal (other than humans) uses money. Money is thus a product of human culture, but it is estimated to be only about 3,000 years old,[18] which means that early civilizations did not have it. It is much too recent to have shaped human nature biologically. There is no "money instinct."

Clearly people want money, and many people work long and hard to get it. One reason is that money operates as a kind of a tool.[19] Just as animals use tools to get what they want, people use money to get what they want. Biology has programmed humans (like other animals) to want things, so people also come to want money because it enables them to get these things. As a tool, money is desired not for itself but for what can be done with it.

But the money-as-tool analogy failed to explain the widespread human concern with money. For example, some people hoard money, obviously wanting to get it and keep it but not spend it. What good is a tool you never use?

So theorists have produced a second analogy: Money is not just like a tool; it is also like a drug. People come to want it for its own sake, even though it does not confer any benefit that biology recognizes.[20]

Drugs take advantage of the body's natural capacities for pleasure. People feel happy when they do something that will ultimately lead to survival or reproduction, such as when they have sex or fall in love or find something great to eat. Drugs in a sense trick the body. When you take a drug, you might feel as good as if you had fallen in love, but whereas being in love might help you achieve survival and reproduction, being high on drugs will not normally accomplish either of these. In the same way, money comes to be desired for its own sake, rather than for the sake of the good things one gets for it. That's why people might hoard money, for example. It is as if they are addicted to money.

Although animals never develop money on their own, some of them seem capable of learning aspects of money, if humans teach them. Studies done with monkeys show this.[21] After several months of training, the monkeys learned to trade little coins for treats such as grapes. When the researchers changed the price, the monkeys adjusted their purchases accordingly. Researchers saw few signs of monkeys' using money with each other, except for one enterprising male who managed to trade a coin for sex with a female (who then spent the coin on getting a grape, her favorite treat). Still, their grasp of money remained rudimentary, and the researchers reported that they sometimes tried to use cucumber slices as if they were coins, at least when trading with humans (who did not fall for the counterfeit).

As cultural animals, humans find meaning through connecting with others. For example, researchers on consumer psychology have found that people seem to get more pleasure and value from spending money on experiences (e.g., going out to dinner or theater) than on objects (e.g., buying a new coat or power tool).[22] The reason for this difference has been much disputed. Two social psychologists found the answer: Experiences are generally shared with others, whereas objects are often used by oneself alone. They found, for example, that solitary experiences were no valued or meaningful any more than material possessions.[23]

Summary

What, then, is culture? The different components mentioned in this section can be summarized in this way: **Culture** is an information-based system, involving both shared understandings and praxis, that enables groups of people to live together in an organized fashion and to get what they need. Culture can have a significant influence even on basic human needs, such as food and sex. To learn more, read the *Food for Thought* and *Social Side of Sex* boxes.

Nature and Culture Interacting

See what sort of explanation you can think of for this: Statisticians began noticing that a large number of professional hockey players in the National Hockey League had birthdays in January and February.[29] Maybe being born in winter makes someone love winter sports more? Getting ice skates for your birthday? But November and December should also be good for that, and those months were marked by relatively few birthdays of NHL

culture an information-based system that includes shared ideas and common ways of doing things

---

FOOD FOR *Thought*

Virtuous Vegetarians

Throughout this book, we will feature research relevant to eating. We have selected eating for this treatment because human eating is relevant to both nature and culture.

On the nature side, eating is natural; all animals eat. Eating is a vital means of getting what one needs for survival, which, as we saw, was a crucial goal of biological life. Social animals are social precisely because their social interactions help them get food and thereby survive. Like other animals, humans feel bad when they do not have enough to eat, and these bad feelings motivate people to seek food. Also like other animals, humans quickly learn to dislike and avoid foods that make them sick.

Humans resemble other animals in their need to eat regularly. But eating has been transformed by culture. Unlike all other animals, humans go on diets, have elaborate systems of etiquette and table manners, cook their food, experiment endlessly with recipes, and sometimes serve meals to total strangers.

Another uniquely human trait is the tendency to reject certain categories of food based on ideas. Many religions, for example, prescribe or forbid particular foods, especially on certain days. Based on different religious views, some people will eat beef but not pork, whereas others eat pork but not beef.

Vegetarianism is a revealing example. Some animals eat only plants, but that is the way nature made them. Humans are capable of eating meat and naturally do eat meat, yet cultural reasons convince many people to refuse to eat meat. For example, some people believe that it is morally proper to refuse to eat other animals.[24,25,26,27,28] That means ideas convince them not to eat meat. These ideas include a belief that animals should have rights similar to humans, or a belief that it is better for the planet to have people eat only plant food (because land used for growing livestock is less productive than land used for growing plants).

Nothing like this has been seen in any other species. We have no evidence of any animal that naturally eats meat but sometimes decides, for moral or religious reasons, to eat only plant food. Many human beings do precisely that, however. Such behavior is not found in nature but is well documented among human beings, and it reflects the power of meaning (ideas) to change and determine how people act.

RUBES®   **By Leigh Rubin**

www.creators.com
rubes2@earthlink.net
www.egreetings.com/rubes

Early radicals of the Animal Rights Movement

By permission Leigh Rubin and Creators Syndicate, Inc.

---

players. Also, the same pattern began to emerge in other sports as well, especially soccer, where the effect has been found all over the world.[30] (So obviously it wasn't specifically about cold weather sports.) The pattern is statistically undeniable. What might cause professional athletes to have birthdays in January? Astrology? No.

The unequal birthday pattern emerges from a curious mix of nature and culture. In hockey, as in many sports, pro athletes generally got their start while they were children. Children's leagues are grouped by age, but rather than automatically moving from league to league on their birthday (which might disrupt teams), kids are grouped for each season based on a cutoff date—typically January 1. Thus, when the season starts in November, if you're already 9 or will turn 9 by the end of December, you play with the 9-year-olds, but if your birthday isn't until after January 1, you play with the 8-year-olds. Why does that matter? Nine-year-olds are usually bigger and stronger than 8-year-olds. Kids born late in the year grow up always being matched against others who are older, stronger, and faster, so they tend to drop out of the sport. Meanwhile, the lucky kids with birthdays in January will grow up being the oldest (and therefore often the biggest and strongest) children in their league, which puts them at a physical advantage. This advantage helps them be successful and makes the sport fun for them.

You might think the effect would wear off as children grow up. But many of the younger children have already dropped out. Moreover, coaching increases the problem. Coaches want to win, so they bestow their attention and more playing time on their best players—which often means their oldest (hence biggest, strongest, and most coordinated) ones. Children born after January 1 end up getting more training and more opportunities to compete, whereas those born late in the year spend more time on the bench.

The so-called relative age effect[35] is not limited to sports. It has been shown in school performance also.[36,37] Children who end up getting classified as gifted often benefited from starting school later than others, which made them older than their classmates.[38] Before you start planning to have your babies in January, however, note that school cutoff dates are different from sports ones. In many schools, it is the children born in the summer (just before school starts in September) who are destined to be always the youngest in their class and therefore suffer disadvantages in school.[39]

Sport in general is a combination of nature (innate physical abilities) and culture (practice, training, and arbitrary rules). Star pro athletes are thus neither made nor born: They need both the gifts of nature and the benefits of culture. And, it appears, the luck to be born on the right side of the cutoff date also helps!

This chapter began with the story of little Brenda. The failure to raise the boy as a girl suggests that being male has some elements of nature that are not easily overcome by culture. Yet manhood also has strong aspects of culture. Research on "precarious manhood"[40] has shown some cultural differences in beliefs about being a man versus being a woman. Many cultures require boys to prove themselves before they can claim to be men, whereas all girls grow up to be women. Even among modern American college students, manhood is regarded as more tentative and requiring of proof than womanhood. In one of their studies, students read about people who said they felt they were no longer a man, or no longer a woman. Loss of womanhood seemed difficult to fathom, and students thought it must mean that the woman had undergone a sex change operation. Loss of manhood was more readily seen as a result of social factors, such as not being able to provide for one's family.

Thus, in a sense, society regards womanhood as a biological achievement, whereas manhood requires a cultural achievement. (Note that both are cultural opinions, however!) The need for men to prove themselves is relevant to many gender differences. In laboratory studies on precarious manhood, threats to a man's masculinity caused him to feel aggressive and anxious, whereas parallel threats to a woman's femininity produced no such response.[41]

Nature and Culture Shaping Each Other

When people argue whether a behavior is a product of nature or culture, they often seem to assume the two are separate causes. Yet the separation is far from complete. Nature shapes culture, and vice versa.

The Social Side of Sex

Sex and Culture

Like eating, sexual behavior will be featured through this book as an important category of behavior that is shaped by both nature and culture. Whereas food is needed for survival, sex is needed for reproduction.

Sex has been a bitter battleground between those who explain it on the basis of nature and evolution and those who emphasize cultural construction. Is sex a matter of genes and hormones causing people to feel desires the way nature has prescribed them? Or is culture the principal cause of who wants to do what to whom in bed?

Some features of sexuality are found everywhere and may well be rooted in nature. In all cultures, for example, men seem to desire a greater number of sexual partners than women.[31] Sex is everywhere the main way (and usually the only way) to make babies. The same basic sex practices are known to most cultures. One sex historian observed that the sex manuals written thousands of years ago in ancient China covered almost all the same techniques one would find in a sex manual today, with only one major exception (sadomasochism).[32]

Some other universal aspects of sex reflect the influence of culture. All known cultures have rules about sex.[33] Cultures know that sex leads to making babies, and efforts to prevent pregnancy have been found all over the world, though the ancient means of preventing conception (except for abstaining from sex) are generally less effective than modern technologies such as the birth control pill and the IUD. Some form of prostitution, in which people pay money for sex, is found in most large cultures, although many aspects of it (such as whether it is legally tolerated and what it costs) differ substantially.

Cultural differences in sex are also evident. In Turkey, women are expected to be virgins until they marry, and until quite recently it was standard practice for many brides-to-be to have a medical examination to certify their virginity. Lebanese men who have sex with male animals are likewise subject to the death penalty, but it is perfectly legal for them to have sex with female animals. In New Guinea, some tribes regard male–male sex as normal while people are growing up, and boys are expected to perform oral sex on young men as a way of acquiring fluids that produce masculine strength, but after marriage men are supposed to stop their homosexual activities and restrict themselves to their wives.[34] Liberty Corner, New Jersey, has a law prohibiting people from beeping the horn of a parked car during sexual intercourse; one can scarcely imagine what life must have been like in that town before that law restored peace and quiet! Another curious law comes from Liverpool, England: Topless salesgirls are forbidden to work in tropical fish stores, though not in other stores.

Mar Photographics/Alamy

Last, there are plenty of differences within a culture too. In the United States today, some people reach their 30th birthdays while still virgins, whereas others have had sex with more than a dozen people by the age of 15. Millions of people go through their entire lives having sex with only one person (their spouse) and only in the missionary position (man on top, woman on bottom), whereas some people have more than a thousand sex partners without ever using the missionary position. Genghis Khan, perhaps the world's most successful lover, has more than 16 million direct male descendants alive today! Many people yearn for practices that others regard as dangerous perversions. Some people love to read about sex or watch films of people having sex, whereas others find those materials disgusting and want them to be outlawed.

Nature or culture? Human sexuality provides ample evidence of both.

The influence of nature on culture starts with very basic and simple insights. As we have said, one function of culture is to help people satisfy their biological needs. People need food, water, and shelter, and they often need a good environment for raising their children. Cultures that fail to provide these do not last long.[42,43]

Recent work has shown some surprising ways that cultures are shaped by nature. One big factor is whether the local area has plenty of viruses, bacteria, germs, and similar things, called pathogens, because they make you sick. It turns out that fairly standard differences in cultural practices arise based on whether the local environment is relatively healthy (not very many pathogens) or more risky (abundant pathogens).

In places where there are many pathogens, like southeast Asia and parts of Africa, the cultures that develop put more pressure on people to conform and obey the rules.

Nonconformists are more likely to be tolerated where there are few pathogens because the nonconformists will not spread disease so easily there. In fact, in places where abundant pathogens create a high risk of disease, society members are more similar to each other, even in their personalities.[44] Many researchers classify cultures along a continuum from individualism (everyone takes care of himself or herself and is free to choose how to act) to collectivism (maintaining relationships and getting along with others is more important than doing what you want). Collectivistic cultures tend to be found in places with many pathogens. Individualistic cultures are more common in low-disease environments with few pathogens.[45]

More diseases cause people to be more prejudiced, especially toward people who look different, as if the body automatically suspects strange-looking people of carrying illness.[46] Sexual restraint (such as having fewer sex partners) is a more common and important value when there are many diseases because the close physical contact of sex can spread disease.[47] But even beyond sex, people in such cultures tend to be less oriented toward meeting lots of people, less open to new ideas, and less interested in trying out new experiences.[48]

What about the other way around? Might culture influence nature? In general, nature comes first, but some reversals are increasingly difficult to argue. The human capacity for speech (nature), for example, probably evolved in step with along the emergence of spoken language among humans (culture). (It is hard to imagine why evolution would have favored humans who could talk well, unless they gained some benefit by talking.) Thus, some theorists have begun to speak of "co-evolution," meaning that nature and culture changed together and shaped each other.[49,50] Once the social environment began to include more and more culture, the humans with greater competence for functioning in culture would survive and reproduce better than others. That, after all, is the basic idea of seeing humans as cultural animals![51]

What Makes Cultural Animals?

The human being is a product of both nature and culture. A traditional way of thinking has been that nature provides the foundation, and then culture builds on top of that. That style of thought puts nature first, culture second. However, recent theories have looked for ways to blend the two, such that nature and culture shape each other.[52,53]

Many animals have a little bit of culture. Hence, it is likely that culture existed on earth before humans evolved. If culture was already in the environment, then it could have guided natural selection to endow humans with traits that promoted culture.

Why is culture so rare or rudimentary in nonhuman animals? The answer lies almost certainly in the advanced psychological requirements for culture. We saw earlier that animals need more inner processes to be social than to be solitary. In the same way, they need more inner processes to be cultural than to be merely social. Most animals don't have enough brainpower to sustain culture.

What are some of the main differences between being social and being cultural (or, more precisely, between being merely social and being both social and cultural)? Social animals may act together, as when a swarm of bees or a pack of wolves or a herd of zebras all move together. This mass action is social because the animals know what the others are doing and coordinate their own behavior with it. In contrast, cultural animals often have elaborate division of labor, in which each individual performs a unique function. Compare the collective work of a corporation or a football team with that of a swarm of bees, for example. Although different bees might have different roles (e.g., the queen bee is the mother of all the bees in her hive, worker bees lack reproductive capacity but carry pollen back to the hive to feed the young), the roles are far simpler, less flexible, and fewer than roles in human society.

Social animals may figure out good ways of doing things and may possibly copy something they see another doing. Cultural animals (human beings) deliberately share their knowledge throughout the group, so that it can be preserved and passed on to the next generation. Humans are the only animals to have schools, universities, and libraries, for example. The preservation of knowledge allows for progress, too. One man

Still no progress on cooked food, democracy, female liberation, social security, patent law, football, e-mail, or cosmetic surgery.

Meyers/Blickwinkel/Alamy

(Alexander Graham Bell) invented the telephone, and even though he has been dead for decades, many people have and use telephones without having to invent them all over again. Among animals without culture, each problem has to be solved anew by each generation, and in some cases by each individual.

Social creatures can often communicate, such as with grunts and barks. Their communication refers mainly to events or entities that are present at that moment. Cultural animals use language, which enables them to communicate about many things that are far removed from the here and now. Human children often study history, for example, in which they learn about events that occurred centuries before they were born. Such communication is impossible for merely social animals. No animal knows anything about what happened before it was born, including the history of its social group.

Social animals may help each other, but in general helping is limited to relatives. It is quite rare for any nonhuman animal to make some sacrifice (such as willingly giving away food) in order to benefit another, even if the two animals are related (and especially if they aren't). In contrast, cultural animals have a broader sense of community and sometimes help total strangers. Some people donate large sums of money to alleviate hunger or sickness among people they have never met, who may be of a different race and may live on a faraway continent. Others help people even when it involves great danger to themselves.

When animals live and work together, some degree of conflict is probably inevitable. Social animals have few ways of resolving these disputes other than aggression. If two animals (not related to each other) want the same piece of food, the bigger and stronger one is likely to get it, by force if necessary. In contrast, culture offers many alternative means of resolving disputes. These include moral principles, compromise, and going before a judge in a court of law. Most social animals do not have that luxury. In fact, most cultures strongly discourage people from settling their disputes by resorting to violence.

Thus, the best approach to social psychology is to assume that people are products of both nature and culture. Nature has given humans certain traits and abilities because over time those enabled some people to survive and reproduce better than others. And humans really do survive and reproduce by means of their culture. Hence, we think that natural selection has shaped the human mind to "do" culture. In that sense, it is natural for humans to share information, seek to be together, form groups with multiple roles, communicate with each other about their inner thought processes, and more.

To sum up: Culture is a better way of being social. Being social, and thus being cultural, is a biological strategy. Biology measures success in terms of survival and reproduction. By those measures, human culture has been remarkably successful, even despite its problems such as war, pollution, social inequality, and oppression. Survival has improved remarkably. Indeed, by virtue of research (an important cultural activity), humans have nearly tripled their average life span—something no other species has been able to do. Meanwhile, the human population has risen from one woman about 200,000 years ago to over 7 billion people now. Our animal relatives such as the great apes all live near the equator, but humans have been able to live in mountains, in forests, in plains, in cold and snowy places, in deserts, in rain-soaked places, and in others, thanks to cultural innovations such as clothing, heated homes, and cooked food.

Are People the Same Everywhere?

At first blush, people are very different. If you have ever visited a foreign country, you probably encountered striking differences. People speak different languages, read different books and magazines, and eat very different foods. These differences reflect the influence of culture.

What could be more natural than sleep? Yet there are important cultural differences in how people sleep. In the United States, most people sleep only at night and wake up with an alarm clock. Many consume coffee or some other substance containing a drug that wakes them up. In Mexico, it is customary for adults to take a nap (a siesta) in the middle of the day, and as a result they may not sleep as much at night. Some cultures and religions disapprove of consuming coffee and similar drugs, so people must wake up naturally.

Sleeping arrangements are also quite different, even though most people regard their own sleeping patterns as natural. For example, should small children sleep alone or with their parents? In the United States, the prevailing practice is to keep children out of their parents' bed and even in a separate bedroom. One study of white, middle-class, two-parent families in Cleveland, Ohio, found that only 3% of the babies slept in their parents' bedroom during their first year of life, and only 1% after that.[54]

In other cultures, however, sleeping arrangements are quite different. In a survey of many different non-Western, nonindustrial societies, anthropologists found that the norm everywhere was for infants to sleep with their mothers.[55] Researchers in Japan confirmed that a typical Japanese person hardly ever sleeps alone at any point in life, nor does he or she want to. Roughly half of Japanese children ages 11 to 15 sleep in the same bed with their mother or father; others sleep with siblings. The only Japanese who normally sleep alone are unmarried young adults who are living away from home and old people whose spouse has died and whose children (and grandchildren) are living elsewhere.

People who are accustomed to the middle-class American system might regard it as dangerous, immoral, or even pathological (sick) to let children sleep with their parents. However, when Japanese or people from other cultures learn about the American practice, they have a similar reaction. They think that Americans must not love their children if they put them through the terrifying ordeal of making them sleep by themselves. Some point out that in the animal kingdom, too, babies want to be with their mothers, especially at night, and so it seems "natural" to them to do the same. The American practice thus seems dangerous, immoral, or wrong to them.

In these and countless other ways, people are different, both within and between cultures. Then again, in other respects people are much more similar. Nearly everywhere, people love their children, try to get enough to eat, talk about the weather, wait their turn, make distinctions between right and wrong, compete for status, help each other (and help family and relatives more readily than strangers), worry about money, and drive their cars on the same side of the road. Usually they drive on the right, though in some countries (such as England and Australia) they drive on the left, but the important thing is that they share a rule that tells everyone to drive on the same side.

The question of whether people are the same everywhere, or differ in different cultures, is a vexing one for social psychology. By far the greatest amount of research is done in the United States, most of it at American universities with university students as participants. Some social psychologists despair that the cultural differences are so big that it is impossible to formulate any general conclusions, and some suggest that we should never generalize beyond American college students (or at least not without years of careful checking to verify what patterns are found everywhere).

Others are more optimistic. Although cultural differences are real and important, they are often merely matters of degree rather than opposites. For example, people respond more aggressively to insults and criticism than to praise, people are attracted to others similar to themselves more than to those who are different, and people get jealous when their romantic partners have sex with someone else. There are cultural differences in how these reactions are expressed and perhaps even in how strongly they are felt, but there is no known culture in which the opposite patterns (e.g., disliking similar others, or aggressing more in response to praise than insult) are found. Likewise, basic beliefs about people and the world have broadly similar consequences; for example, social cynicism (expecting that social life will often produce negative outcomes) goes with low conformity, low drive to achieve, and various negative attitudes toward leaders.[56]

DAJ/amana images inc./Alamy

In some cultures it is not only acceptable, but desirable, for children to sleep with their parents.

In this book, we will present some interesting findings of cultural differences. But our greater quest is for underlying similarities. For example, languages are very different from each other, but underneath they have great similarities, and all known human cultures have and use language. Hence, we think the use of language is part of human nature. Moreover, evolution helped install the necessary equipment (vocal cords, ears that can tell thousands of words apart, and brains that can use grammar) for people to use language. Much of social psychology can be understood by assuming that the human psyche was designed by nature (via natural selection) for culture. This means that culture is in our genes, even though cultural differences may not be.

We started with the question of what the human psyche was designed for. Culture is a large, important part of the answer. That is, the human mind, including its emotions, was designed in part to enable it to take part in the advanced kinds of social life that humans have.

answers: see pg 65

QUIZ YOURSELF

Culture and Human Social Life

1. **Humans are best described as _____ .**
   - (a) cultural animals
   - (b) social animals
   - (c) both cultural and social animals
   - (d) neither cultural animals nor social animals

2. **In social psychology, the "nature versus nurture" debate _____ .**
   - (a) is alive and well
   - (b) has largely died out; most social psychologists maintain that human behavior is shaped mostly by social forces
   - (c) has largely died out; most social psychologists maintain that human behavior is shaped mostly by genetic forces
   - (d) has been reframed; the debate now concerns how nature and nurture interact with one another and influence one another

3. **All known cultures have rules about _____ .**
   - (a) agriculture
   - (b) sex
   - (c) sleeping
   - (d) All of the above

4. **Most social psychological research has been conducted in _____ .**
   - (a) Asia
   - (b) Canada
   - (c) Europe
   - (d) the United States

Important Features of Human Social Life

In this section, we will cover several features of human social life that set humans apart from other animals and that are crucial for understanding social interaction among humans. They reflect important ways that human life was shaped by nature to cope with human social life, including culture. These themes will come up repeatedly in the chapters that follow.

The Duplex Mind

The human mind has two main systems. In a sense, this is what Freud said when he distinguished between the conscious ego and the unconscious. Most experts no longer accept Freud's account of how the mind is laid out, but there is a new and exciting version of the theory that the mind has two parts. We call this the **duplex mind**, as in a duplex house with two separate apartments.

Unfortunately, the experts don't agree about what to call these two systems or exactly what goes where. Here, our summary combines many views of the duplex mind, but you should be aware that many different variations exist and that many details are disputed.

Two Systems

We can call the two systems the automatic and the deliberate. The **automatic system** operates mainly outside of consciousness, though it is not a Freudian kind of unconscious full of repressed urges and thoughts you are afraid to think. Instead, it is like a team of little robots doing lots of simple jobs to make your life easier. You are not aware of the robots and the work they are doing. Whereas Freud thought that the unconscious often trips you up by making you say or do the wrong thing, the automatic system is usually very helpful. It handles the endless mundane tasks, such as interpreting, organizing, and categorizing all the information that comes in through your eyes and ears. For example, it might sort through the stream of babbling sounds that your ears hear in order to pick out the score of the game involving your favorite team, and it links that score with relevant information in your memory, such as how your team is doing generally and whether today's outcome will help it qualify for the playoffs.

The **deliberate system** is the other "half" of the duplex mind. (We put "half" in quotation marks because a precise comparison of sizes is not possible given the present state of knowledge. Most likely the automatic system is much bigger than the deliberate system.) The deliberate system mostly operates in consciousness, so it can also be called the conscious system. Though people sometimes think they are conscious of everything in their minds, in reality they are conscious of only one part—but that is a very important part.

The deliberate system is what seems to turn on when you wake up and turn off when you go to sleep. The automatic system continues to operate during sleep, sorting information and making simple judgments.[57] (That is presumably why you wake up if someone softly says your name.) It also moves the body around in bed, as when you bump into your sleeping partner and roll away without waking up. It processes information, too: You will wake up to the sound of your own name spoken more softly than almost any other word, which means that your mind can tell the difference in the meanings of words even when asleep.[58] Telling the difference is the job of the automatic system.

An influential article has called the two systems "impulsive" and "reflective," and these terms capture the gist of how they operate.[59] The automatic system operates by impulse; you feel something and then do it, for example. The reflective system typically involves conscious deliberation about what would be the best thing to do.

What Is Consciousness For?

Most people think their conscious minds are in charge of everything they do. They believe the conscious mind constantly directs their actions and their train of thought. These beliefs are false. The automatic system generally runs almost everything. Consider walking, for example, which is something that most people do over and over all day long. Do you consciously control the movements of your legs and feet? Does your conscious mind have to say, "Now pick up the left foot, swing it forward, hold it high enough so it doesn't bump the ground, set down the heel, roll forward, shift weight off the back foot," and so forth? Of course not. Someday watch a small child who is just learning to walk, and you may see what happens when the conscious mind tries to figure out how to make the legs walk. But after walking has been learned, the person almost never thinks about it again. Walking is done automatically, not deliberatively or reflectively.

Over the past couple of decades, there has been a huge shift in psychological theory about the role of consciousness. This change has been driven by the rise in research findings that show how much the automatic system does. Much of behavior is driven and directed by these automatic responses that occur outside of awareness. Many of these findings will be covered in subsequent chapters. The combination of them has led many experts to begin questioning what consciousness is good for—if anything! The automatic system can learn, think, choose, and respond. It has ideas and emotions, or at least simple

duplex mind the idea that the mind has two different processing systems (deliberate and automatic)

automatic system the part of the mind outside of consciousness that performs simple operations

deliberate system the part of the mind that performs complex operations

versions of them. It knows your "self" and other people. Even when people believe they are deciding something, often it can be shown that the automatic system has already decided. Their decisions are swayed by subliminal cues or other bits of information of which the person is unaware that have been processed automatically.

Many experts today believe that consciousness doesn't really do much of anything. One psychobiologist concluded from working with people whose brains had been surgically split in half (usually to control epilepsy) that consciousness is just a side effect of other processes and of thinking about the future, and that it doesn't serve any important function.[60,60] Some psychologists think consciousness is simply a kind of emotional signal to call attention to our own actions so we don't confuse them with what other people have done.[62] Others have observed that the automatic system does more than we thought and the deliberate system less, and maybe the field will soon conclude that the conscious part of the mind doesn't do anything at all.[63,64,65,66] With all due respect to these experts, we disagree. We think that the deliberate system was difficult and expensive (in terms of biological requirements) for nature to give us, so most likely some very profound advantages make consciousness worth the trouble. Yes, the automatic system does most of the work of the psyche, but the deliberate system probably does something very important too. Most likely these special jobs involve complex kinds of thought that combine information and follow explicit rules, as in logical reasoning.[67]

Differences Between the Systems

For now, it is important to know that the two systems exist and to appreciate their established differences. These are summarized in **TABLE 2.1**.[68,69]

First, there is a difference in how much each system can do at the same time. The automatic system is like many different little machines doing many unrelated or loosely related things at once. The deliberate system does one thing at a time. As you read, your automatic system converts the visual images of letters into words, converts the words into meanings, and links the information with all sorts of things that are already stored in memory. Meanwhile, you consciously have only one thought at a time. Some recent studies showed that people are less aware of the taste of food if they are distracted.[70] Thus, if they ate foods while mentally rehearsing a phone number, they rated the food as having less taste—and they ate more of it!

TABLE 2.1 The Duplex Mind: Deliberate and Automatic Systems	
Deliberate	**Automatic**
Slow	Fast
Controllable	Outside of conscious control
Guided by intention	Unintentional
Flexible	Inflexible
Good at combining information	Poor at combining information
Precise, rule-based calculations	Estimates
Can perform complex operations	Can perform simple operations
Does one thing at a time	Can do many things at once
Reasoning	Intuition
Effortful	Effortless
Features full-blown emotions	Features quick feelings of like and dislike, good and bad
Depends on automatic system	Can be independent of conscious processing
"Figure it out"	"Go with your gut feeling"

The automatic system is quick and efficient. It performs tasks quite effectively and with relatively little effort. In contrast, the deliberate system is slow and cumbersome. Return to the example of walking: Try the experiment of consciously controlling every muscle movement while you are walking. You can do it, but it is very slow and awkward. That is why the mind naturally tries to make everything automatic.

The deliberate system often requires effort, whereas the automatic system doesn't. In fact, you have to deliberately start to think consciously about something, but the automatic system starts by itself and often cannot be stopped. If we show you a word with a missing letter, you probably cannot stop yourself from filling in the blank. Try to read these letters without thinking of a word: K*SS. Probably you can't. The automatic system is too quick and efficient. It gives you the answer before your conscious mind can even think to formulate the question. The word is KISS.

All the differences mentioned so far favor the automatic system. If it were better at everything, however, we would have to conclude that the deliberate system is just a poorer, dumber, less effective system all around, which would raise the question of why we have it at all. (And that's why some experts, like the ones quoted earlier, have begun to doubt openly that it has any value.) But the deliberate system does have some advantages. First, the deliberate system is much more flexible than the automatic system. The automatic system is like a well-programmed robot or computer. It performs standard, familiar tasks according to the program, and it does them very reliably, quickly, and efficiently. But when the automatic system confronts something novel and unfamiliar, it doesn't know how to deal with it. The conscious mind, slow and cumbersome as it is, is much better at confronting novel, unfamiliar circumstances and deciding how to react.

The advantage of the deliberate system in dealing with novel circumstances is probably one crucial reason that human beings, as cultural animals, developed consciousness. Life in a cultural society is vastly more complicated, in terms of encountering new, unexpected, and unfamiliar dilemmas, than the lives of most other creatures. Imagine a robot that has been programmed to sort red beans from green beans. It will probably do this effectively and quickly, even performing much better than a human being. But then along comes a banana! The robot won't know what to do with a banana, unless it has been programmed for that eventuality too. Unlike a robot, a conscious human mind can deal with the banana even when it was expecting only red and green beans.

Another crucial advantage of the deliberate system is that it is able to combine information in complex, rule-driven ways. An automatic system that has been well trained can estimate that, say, 6 times 53 is a few hundred, but only the deliberate system can calculate that it is precisely 318. The deliberate system alone can perform complex logical reasoning.[71]

The influential social psychologist Daniel Kahneman[72,73] prefers to describe the thinking styles of the two systems as reasoning versus intuition. The automatic system is intuitive, in the sense that it is guided by gut reactions and quick feelings rather than a process of carefully thinking through all the implications of a problem. When you face a decision and someone advises you to "go with your gut feeling," that person is essentially telling you to rely on your automatic system (and its intuitions) rather than trying to reason through the problem logically, as the deliberate system will do. Often that is good advice because the automatic system does produce quick and usually good answers. But the highest achievements and advances of culture depend on the application of careful reasoning, which is the province of the deliberate system and conscious thought.

Go with your gut feeling, or figure out what is best?

Kayte Deioma/PhotoEdit

How They Work Together

The two parts of the duplex mind are not entirely independent of each other. In fact, they often work together.[74,75] The automatic system serves the deliberate system, in the sense that it operates behind the scenes to make conscious thought possible. You may think consciously that something you heard on the radio is illogical. But before that can happen, the automatic system has to have done a great deal of work: It processed the stream of sounds into comprehensible language, understood the gist of the message, and activated various other ideas in your memory that were associated with the core idea. The automatic system also works like an alarm system that signals to the deliberate system that something is wrong and that careful, conscious thinking is needed.

For example, suppose you heard on the news that someone was seriously injured at a campus party last night, and the dean was recommending that all further parties be canceled. Your automatic system understands the reasoning: Party caused injury, injury is bad, so parties are bad, so the dean cancels all parties. But the automatic system also connects this news to your feelings, and you realize: Wait! I love parties! I don't want all parties to be canceled! This is about as far as the automatic system can process, but it sends out an alarm to the deliberate system. Now you can reason through the situation consciously: One party caused an injury, but that doesn't reflect badly on all parties; there should be a way to reduce or avoid further injuries without canceling all parties. In that way, the two mental systems work together.

Conscious Override

Sometimes the two systems work against each other, however. One particularly important case is when the deliberate system overrides the automatic impulse. You feel like doing something, but you restrain yourself. For example, if you are looking forward to having a doughnut, and you see someone else take the last doughnut just before you get to the serving tray, you may have a natural impulse to protest. Hey! Give me my doughnut! You might even feel like grabbing it out of the other person's hand. After all, most other animals would act that way if someone took their food. But human beings can restrain that impulse. Rarely do human beings come to blows over the last doughnut. Indeed, the point that people restrain themselves is an important key to the psychology of aggression. We shall see that a great many factors cause aggression: violent films, hot temperatures, frustration, and insults. Given that nearly everyone occasionally experiences frustration, wounded pride, media violence, and heat, you might think that human beings would be constantly violent. But in reality people are not usually aggressive or violent. Why not? People may have many angry impulses, but they restrain them. The conscious mind is often vital for overriding the impulses that the automatic system produces. As we shall see, this pattern is found in many spheres of social behavior, from dieting to prejudice.

Conscious overriding is vital to life in culture. Culture is full of rules about how to behave—norms, guidelines, laws, morals, and expectations. You can't just do whatever you feel like at any moment. Moreover, many situations are complicated and have hidden implications, so it is best to stop and think before acting. Imagine you are driving on a highway when another driver speeds up, passes you, and then slows down to take the next exit. Your natural impulse might be to smash into the back of the other driver's car with your own car, to hold your horn down, or to make angry gestures at the other driver—but that might get you in trouble. It would be better for your conscious mind to override these impulses and exercise self-control over your anger.

The Long Road to Social Acceptance

Living in a culture offers many advantages as compared with living in a merely social group. But it also makes much greater demands.

Consider what it takes to live in a North American city. If you're a bird, maybe you can just fly into town, find an empty tree, build a nest, and then hang around with some other birds until they let you stay. As a human, you need an apartment, which may take you a week of checking advertisements and going around to different addresses. (And to do that, you need to know how to read, how to use a map, and how to get and use a newspaper or the Internet.) You'll probably need to sign a lease promising to live there for a year. You need money to pay the rent, and probably that means you will need a job. A job typically requires credentials, such as education and training, and these may take years to obtain. A better job means more money, but it probably requires more training, and you have to perform well to keep the job. Finding a romantic partner is a much more complicated process in human beings than in other animals. You need to know where to meet people, how to act on a date, how to play the games and roles that are in fashion in this particular group.

This is one of the basic jobs of the human self: to garner acceptance. You need to figure out what other people prefer and expect, and then you need to change yourself to meet those expectations. The requirements for social acceptance are different in different cultures and eras. In the Victorian era (late 1800s), people who picked their noses or said four-letter words aloud were considered socially unacceptable, so most middle- and upper-class people learned to avoid doing those things. Nowadays saying four-letter words is more acceptable in many circles, whereas picking your nose is still not cool.

Outside the lab, people have to do many things to obtain social acceptance. It is not just a matter of etiquette. As previously noted, people need to acquire skills and credentials, gain the discipline to hold down a job, attract and hold relationship partners, and so on.

Built to Relate

The long road that humans travel to social acceptance means that people have to do a great deal of work to get along with others. To do that, they must develop many skills and capabilities. One thing that sets humans apart from other animals is how many inner, psychological traits they have that help them get along. These include the understanding that other humans have inner states like theirs, the capacity for language, and the ability to imagine how others perceive them.

This brings up one very important and broadly helpful theme that we have already mentioned: What is inside people is there because of what happens between people. That is, *inner processes serve interpersonal functions*. The psychological traits people have are designed to enable humans to connect with each other.

When you first consider the matter, it seems the other way around: What is inside people determines what happens between them. Because we are capable of language, we talk to other people. Because we have emotional responses of love and affection, we become attached to others. There is some truth to this view, but only from a relatively narrow perspective. To understand human nature, it is important to recognize that evolution created humans with the capacity for language and the emotional capabilities for love and affection *because* these traits improved people's ability to connect with others.

Earlier in this chapter we discussed the social brain theory, which asserted that evolution made intelligent brains not for understanding the physical environment but rather to increase the capability for having social relations. The intelligent brain is one of the defining traits of human beings. This was a first example of the pattern of inner processes serving interpersonal functions: The inner processes and structures (in this case, the intelligent brain) evolved for the sake of improving interpersonal relations.

Increasing evidence confirms that emotions also serve social functions. When people talk, even about seemingly trivial things, they end up sharing their feelings.[76] The discovery that they have similar emotional reactions creates a bond between them that contributes to a feeling of bonding and even to a willingness to trust each other with money.

People's motivation to do well and achieve is also deeply social. People work harder when a social bond is present, even if the bond is irrelevant to the task. For example, math students worked harder on math problems after reading a brief article about math written by someone whose birthday matched their own than by someone with a different birthday.[77] These findings fit the view of humans as cultural animals, because much of culture is about working together—and the research findings show that feeling connected to others increases one's motivation to work.

Automatic processes (see the earlier section on the duplex mind) also serve interpersonal functions. When cues make people automatically think about a group of others, they respond in ways that suggest preparing to interact with that group. For example, when people think about a group they dislike, they automatically start feeling more aggressive, even if the other group is not aggressive. When they think about the elderly, they change their behavior to prepare for interacting with older people: If they have positive feelings toward the elderly, they become more similar and accommodating (e.g., they walk more slowly, enabling them to walk with old people); if their feelings toward this group are negative, they change in ways that make them less friendly to the elderly (they walk faster, as if making it harder for old folks to keep up!).[78]

Even music may be fundamentally about connecting with others. Music is an important human and cultural phenomenon (which is why we put musicians on the cover of this textbook!), and one that has posed a challenge to psychologists to explain. Recent findings have shown that people who like music and are sensitive to it are also more oriented toward working together with group members than musically indifferent people. They favor their group more, give other group members preferential treatment, and desire to belong more. In fact, the threat of being socially rejected from one's group makes people attend more carefully to music.[79] All these findings indicate that music can be partly explained as something that helps bring groups together and strengthen interpersonal ties. It seems that music is indeed the "universal language."

As with other themes, we should be careful not to overstate the case. Not all inner processes are there to serve interpersonal processes. Hunger and thirst, for example, are clearly there to prompt the animal or person to get enough food and water to sustain life. Hunger and thirst are thus inner processes that do not serve interpersonal functions. Still, many of the more advanced, complex, and interesting psychological phenomena do promote social interaction.

Thus, a social psychology approach to human nature will emphasize that many (though not all) inner processes exist for the sake of interpersonal interaction. In the next few chapters, we will see that the self, thinking, and emotion (among others) seem well designed to help people form and maintain relationships with others. Recall our discussion about trees earlier. Trees are neither social nor cultural. They do not need selves, nor the capacity to understand language, nor the knowledge that the inner states of other trees resemble their own. Trees were designed by nature to survive alone and get what they need from their physical surroundings. In contrast, humans were designed by nature to develop relationships and share information with each other. The human psyche is designed for social purposes, and especially for cultural ones, insofar as culture is a better way of being social.

Nature Says Go, Culture Says Stop

What aspects of human behavior come from nature as opposed to culture? There are many different answers, but one broad pattern is a theme that we summarize as "nature says go, culture says stop." That is, people seem naturally to have impulses, wishes, and other automatic reactions that predispose them to act in certain ways. Culture serves not so much to create new wishes and desires as to teach or preach self-control and restraint.

People may naturally feel sexual desires and aggressive urges at many points; they do not seem to need to be taught by culture to have those feelings. In that sense, sex and aggression are natural. But culture does have considerable influence on both sex and aggression. This influence mainly takes the form of restraining behaviors. Culture is full of rules that restrict sex, as by designating certain sexual acts or pairings as unacceptable. Sexual morality is mostly a matter of saying which sexual acts are wrong; likewise, laws about sex mainly prohibit sex acts. (Imagine laws that required people to have sexual intercourse on particular occasions!) Likewise, aggression is subject to a broad variety of cultural restraints, including moral prohibitions and laws that forbid many aggressive acts.

Often, culture works by ideas. Many of those ideas tell people what not to do. Most laws and moral principles say what not to do rather than what one should do. The Ten Commandments of Judeo-Christian religion, for example, mostly begin "Thou shalt not" and then mention some specific behavior. The only two that don't say "not" still imply it to some degree: Keeping the Sabbath holy is mostly a matter of not doing certain things (such as work or shopping) on the Sabbath, and honoring your parents is mostly a matter of refraining from disrespectful treatment. Thus, the most famous list of moral rules in Western culture is basically a list of ideas (rules) about what not to do, probably because people naturally sometimes feel urges to do precisely those things, but the culture (including its religion) disapproves.

To be sure, it would be a gross oversimplification to say that the role of nature is *always* to create positive desires and impulses or that culture *only* says what not to do. There are some important exceptions. Disgust reactions, for example, are quite natural and say "no" in a big way. Likewise, people may start eating because official policy and the clock (representing culture) say it is lunchtime, and they may stop eating because their inner sensations (representing nature) signal them that their bellies are full. In this case, culture says go and nature says stop. People may start engaging in aggression because their government (culture) has declared war, and they may stop aggressing because bodily states (nature) of exhaustion or injury dictate that they cannot continue.

Still, "nature says go and culture says stop" is probably right more often than it is wrong, and it provides a helpful way to understand much of the interplay between nature and culture. Throughout this book, we will see many examples in which impulses arise naturally and are restrained, with difficulty, by individuals who exert themselves to comply with cultural rules. Nature made us full of desires and impulses, and culture teaches us to restrain them for the sake of being able to live together in peace and harmony.

Self-control is one important psychological process that enables people to live in culture and follow cultural rules.[80] And most acts of self-control involve stopping oneself from thinking, feeling, or doing something.[81] With regard to spending money, eating and dieting, engaging in sexual behavior, drinking alcohol or taking drugs, and many similar behaviors, having good self-control means holding oneself back instead of acting on every impulse. Dieters need self-control to keep themselves from eating too much or eating the wrong kinds of food, for example. The desire to eat is natural; the restraints are cultural. Self-control is discussed in Chapter 4.

Selfish Impulse Versus Social Conscience

Selfishness is a particularly important instance of the principle that nature says go and culture says stop. To put the matter in overly simple terms, nature has made us selfish, but culture needs us to resist and overcome selfish impulses.

Selfishness is natural. This is not to say that selfish behavior is good or appropriate, but only that nature programmed us to be selfish. This is probably rooted in the biological processes of evolution. Natural selection favors traits that promote the survival and reproduction of the individual. Some biologists have occasionally proposed "group selection," suggesting that natural selection will promote traits that sacrifice the individual for the sake of the group, but most biologists have rejected those arguments.[82,83] (Some experts think group selection may occur when the individual and group interests are aligned.) Each animal looks out for its own welfare and perhaps that of its children. The natural tendency, reinforced by countless centuries of evolution, is to want what is best for oneself.

In contrast, culture often demands that what is best for society take precedence over the individual's wants and needs. In order to get along with others, people must take turns, respect each other's property, and stifle their anger or at least express it constructively. They may have to share their food and possessions, whether informally through acts of kindness or more systematically through taxes. Many will have to follow commands issued by authority figures.

Compared to humans, animals that live in social groups make only minimal sacrifices for the sake of the group. Culture often imposes far greater requirements in terms of restraining selfishness. All cultures have systems of morality, and one of the main thrusts of morality is to do what is best for the community rather than what is best for the self. To return to the example of the Ten Commandments, note that those rules are divided between commands to uphold the religion (such as by not having other gods) and rules against behaviors that would undermine society (murder, theft, adultery, lying, coveting other people's things, and disrespecting one's parents).

Morality is often effective in small groups. In larger groups, law begins to take the place of morality, but it has the same overarching goal of restraining selfish actions in favor of what is best for the community. The difference seems to be that morality relies on a network of social relationships and therefore works best on people who know each other. The more that social life involves contacts between strangers, the more that laws are needed instead of just morals. Even in modern societies, small groups such as families usually rely on morals and informal rules because these are sufficient in the context of the relationship. Far more people are willing to cheat, betray, or exploit a stranger than a member of their own immediate family. Guilt—an important emotion that pushes people to behave morally instead of selfishly—is far more commonly felt in connection with friends and relatives than strangers.[84,85]

Thus, self-interest is a major battleground between nature and culture. The self is filled with selfish impulses and with the means to restrain them, and many inner conflicts come down to that basic antagonism. That conflict, between selfish impulses and self-control, is probably the most basic conflict in the human psyche.

One place to understand this conflict is in how people react to someone who has a stigma—that is, a trait that others perceive as highly undesirable and that makes them want to avoid the person. Many people have an automatic reaction of wanting to avoid someone who has AIDS or cancer, or who is blind or paralyzed, even if the person is not personally responsible for his or her problem. Researchers have found that the impulse to avoid such people may be rooted in a natural fear of being contaminated by them.[86] The automatic system does not necessarily adjust for whether the person's stigma is contagious or not, so people may irrationally and unfairly avoid people whose presence poses no danger. However, many people recognize consciously that these people do not deserve to be avoided, so the social conscience may motivate them to overcome their initial tendency to avoid the stigmatized person. The automatic reaction does not disappear, but given a moment, people can act on more socially desirable feelings, such as the wish to treat the stigmatized person as a normal human being.[87]

The capacity for consciously overriding impulses, described in the earlier section on the duplex mind, is often used in connection with the battle over self-interest. The natural and selfish impulses arise automatically. Morality, conscience, legal obedience, and other pathways to proper behavior often depend on conscious efforts to know and do the right thing.

Tradeoffs: When You Can't Have It All

When no option is clearly the best in every respect, choices have tradeoffs. A **tradeoff** is a choice in which taking or maximizing one benefit requires either accepting a cost or giving up another benefit. Every option you consider has both advantages and disadvantages. With cars, for example, buying the smaller car improves your gas mileage and is better for the environment but sacrifices safety or comfort. A human being is often faced with such complicated choices, and it is necessary to find some way to add up all the pluses and minuses in order to pick one option.

Tradeoffs are an important feature of human social life. Many decisions and dilemmas involve tradeoffs, so that no one right answer will suit everyone. (In this way, tradeoffs also preserve diversity because there is more than one way to be, with none being the best.) Solving one problem will sometimes create another.

Modern culture confronts individuals with a seemingly endless array of choices, and most of these present tradeoffs. Do you want to eat something delicious or something less fattening? Do you want shoes that will be fashionable or comfortable? Should you take an extra course and thereby learn more or have a lower workload next semester? Should you follow your plan or follow your heart?

One very important set of tradeoffs concerns time. Most commonly, the tradeoff requires choosing between something that has benefits right now versus something that has benefits in the future. Our shorthand term for this sort of tradeoff is "now versus tomorrow." Studies of delay of gratification[88,89] often make the tradeoff between present

tradeoff a choice in which taking or maximizing one benefit requires either accepting a cost or sacrificing another benefit

and future explicit. In a typical study, a child is offered a choice between having one cookie right now—or three cookies if the child can wait for 20 minutes.

The ongoing controversy about drug use in sports involves a tradeoff, including a time dimension. Many athletes are tempted to try performance-enhancing drugs. Purists condemn these usages, likening drug use to cheating. But are sports different from everyday life? If you drink a cup of coffee to make yourself more alert for your psychology exam, are you cheating? Are people who use Prozac to make themselves cope better with life, or Viagra to make them perform better in bed, cheaters? And before long, gene splicing may be used to make people stronger, larger, faster, and better in other athletic realms— would those people (who benefited from events before they were born) be cheaters too?

One objection to letting athletes use performance-enhancing drugs is that these may be harmful. Some of them are. The tradeoff of now versus tomorrow is especially apparent in these cases because the so-called sports dopers trade future health problems for current athletic success. Even there, different people will decide the tradeoff differently. The man who founded the National Academy of Sports Medicine once polled 200 Olympic-caliber American athletes about this question. He asked, if you could legally take a performance-enhancing drug that would guarantee that you would win every sports competition you entered for the next five years—but that would eventually kill you—would you take it? The overwhelming majority (though not all) said yes.[90]

Natural selection has not favored caring about the distant future. Our sensory organs tell us what is here right now. Our feelings and desires focus on the immediate present. The idea of sacrificing present joy for the sake of greater joy in the future would be foreign, difficult, even incomprehensible to most animals.

A dramatic demonstration of the difference emerged from a study with chimpanzees.[91] They were fed only once a day, always at the same time, and they were allowed to have all the food they wanted. Like humans and many other animals, chimps prefer to eat multiple times during the day, so they were always very hungry in the last couple hours before their next scheduled feeding. A sensible response would have been to keep some of the available food for later, especially for the hungry hours the next morning, but the animals never learned to do this. They would rejoice over the food when it came. They would eat their fill, and then they would ignore the rest, sometimes even engaging in food fights in which they would throw the leftover food at each other. Yet, despite repeated trials, they never learned to store food for later. Even the short span of 24 hours was apparently beyond their cognitive capacity for adjusting their behavior. In contrast, humans routinely acquire and store food for days, or even weeks, months, and years.

Human beings are thus quite different from other animals. In particular, the conscious human mind can form ideas about the distant future, and current behavior can be changed on the basis of those ideas. Going to college is partly an exercise in delay of gratification for many students. A young person can earn money right away by getting a job right out of high school rather than going to college (which typically costs money rather than earning any). College students often have to live in crowded dormitories with rickety furniture and unappetizing food, whereas if they dropped out and got a job they might be able to rent a nicer apartment and eat better. In the long run, however, college pays off. The U.S. Census Bureau reported that people with advanced degrees earn, on average, four times as much as those with less than a high school diploma. If you compound that amount by a lifetime of work, the average person with an advanced degree will likely earn nearly $2 million more than a high school dropout during a 30-year career. Going to college thus sacrifices some immediate pleasures for the sake of a better future life.

The future is more important to cultural beings than to other animals, so the capacity to orient oneself toward the future rather than the present is probably a crucial skill for any cultural being to have. A person who always lived just for today, enjoying the current moment with no regard for the future, would not prosper in human society. Such a person would never pay bills, wash the laundry or dishes, or brush or floss teeth. Such a person would probably eat candy and pastries rather than vegetables. Such a person would probably not go to college or hold down a job. Such a person would make no commitments that required sacrifices, such as to sustain a close relationship. Such a person would never save any money. Such a person would probably disregard any laws that were inconvenient.

That style of life is simply not suited for human cultural life. To live for any length of time in modern society, it is necessary to pay bills, take care of things, eat reasonably healthy food, obey the laws, exercise, and the like. Many of these acts entail some sacrifice in the short run. In the long run, however, the benefits that come from living in such a society make those sacrifices well worthwhile.

Facing up to tradeoffs is not easy. In fact, some research shows that people dislike trade-offs.[92,93,94] When a decision has to be made, people prefer to think that there is one best or right answer. They like to think that what they choose will bring the best all-around outcomes, and they dislike thinking that they have really lost out on some things in order to get other things. You may find that you don't like the tradeoffs we present throughout this book because it is more comforting to think that there is always a single best answer. It is apparently normal to dislike the idea of tradeoffs, but don't let that prevent you from seeing how widespread and important they really are. The *Tradeoffs* box provides some examples of how political decisions often involve tradeoffs.

Political Tradeoffs

Tradeoffs are abundant in politics. Have you ever wondered why governments keep passing new laws, even though they hardly ever repeal any old ones? You would think that with the addition of more and more laws every year for hundreds of years, we would finally have enough. One explanation is that most laws are designed to remedy an existing problem, but sometimes they create new problems. Tradeoffs are responsible for some of the problems that arise.

As one famous example, in the 1990s the Ohio state legislature heard some sad stories about babies being born in prison (because their mothers were serving time). Taking pity on the babies, the government passed a new law to release pregnant women from prison. This solved one problem but created another, because all the women in Ohio prisons realized that they could get out of prison if they got pregnant, and many women would rather have a baby than be in prison. Female convicts began eagerly trying to have sex with male guards and lawyers. Some inmates would get a weekend pass to attend a relative's funeral—but would skip the funeral and spend the weekend having as much unprotected sex as possible. Thus, there was a tradeoff between preventing babies from being born in prison and encouraging more prisoners to get pregnant. In this case, the law was repealed.

One important political tradeoff links energy issues to environmental ones.

Should American oil companies drill for oil in our national forests, where an accident might cause an oil spill that could destroy part of a beautiful forest and kill its wildlife? Many people want to protect the environment, yet they don't want to pay more for gasoline and electricity—and these goals are in conflict. Hence, there is a tradeoff: The more you protect the environment, the more expensive power becomes. It is hard to strike exactly the right balance.

Another tradeoff connects taxes to government services. Everything the government does—maintain an army and police force, collect the garbage, operate public schools, deliver the mail, provide food for the poor—costs money, and the main method for governments to get money is to collect taxes. In general, higher taxes enable the government to provide more services. Here again is a tradeoff because people do not want to pay high taxes, but they do want their government to provide good services.

To what extent do politicians recognize these tradeoffs? Social psychologist Phillip Tetlock[95,96] analyzed the speeches of many politicians, with an eye toward whether they recognized that many problems have two sides. He noted, however, that politicians face another tradeoff in their own careers, because they have to get elected. If one politician says "Everything is expensive, and I can't give you better government services unless we raise taxes," whereas another says "I will give you better services *and* lower

taxes," the second one may be more likely to win the election.

Tetlock found that politicians seem to shuffle back and forth as to whether they acknowledge tradeoffs. When running for election, they make simple promises and ignore the political realities of tradeoffs. A successful candidate might well promise cheaper energy *and* better protection for the environment, in order to win the most votes. Once elected, however, politicians suddenly begin to recognize the complexity of tradeoffs, and their speeches often refer frankly to the difficulty of the choices, such as noting with regret that efforts to get cheaper oil may well require some sacrifices in environmental protection.

Is this change a matter of learning? After all, when one is just running for office and does not have any actual responsibilities of government, it may be possible to make all sorts of promises without fully realizing the tradeoffs involved. (Most politicians, like most people, really do want both cheaper energy and a cleaner environment.) Maybe they don't realize the tradeoffs until they actually hold office and have to face up to the difficult choices. But this is not what Tetlock concluded. He found that politicians acknowledge tradeoffs when they are in office—but only until their campaigns for reelection start. At that point, they go back to simple statements that promise all things, disregarding tradeoffs. Tetlock concluded that politicians are dealing with the tradeoff built into the election process: to win an election you must oversimplify the issues and ignore the implicit contradictions.

Putting People First

Can dogs hear better than people? If you have lived with a dog, you know they hear many things that people do not, such as very high or low tones, as well as very soft tones. One of your textbook authors is frequently teased by his wife that his dog is prone to barking at ghosts because the dog will burst into barking for no reason that any person can discern. In that sense, dogs hear better than humans. On the other hand, dogs cannot distinguish between similar sounds. If your dog's name is Fido, he will probably also respond to "buy low," "hi ho," "my dough," and "Shiloh." In that sense, dogs don't hear as well as people.

The explanation is probably rooted in a basic tradeoff in perceptual systems, but it contains an important clue about human nature. Most sense organs (even artificial ones such as cameras) have a tradeoff between detection (how much they can see) and resolution (how clearly they see it). For most animals, detection is emphasized over resolution—they perceive something and respond long before they can tell precisely what it is. Humans have more emphasis on resolution, which means perceiving things precisely. Hence, our ears cannot hear as wide a range of sounds as dogs, but we hear them much more distinctly.

More broadly, the sensory organs of most animals are aimed at detecting other species. This is crucial for survival. Animals must spot the predators who want to eat them (in order to run away in time) and the animals they eat (so they can pursue and catch them). The human sensory system is quite unusual in that it is not aimed mainly at other species. Human sense organs, especially eyes and ears, seem designed to help us perceive each other. We can pick our beloved's (or our enemy's) face out of a crowd or a choir up on stage, and we can hear tiny differences in spoken sounds.

Most likely, this unusual feature of human sense organs reflects a change in biological strategy. Nature selected humans to pursue survival and reproduction in a novel fashion. Instead of getting information from the environment, our sense organs are designed to help us get it from each other. And that's what culture is all about—humans getting information from each other in order to survive and reproduce. This is another theme of this book; we call it *putting people first*. And it doesn't stop with information. People get most of what they need from each other, instead of directly from the physical world around them.

Consider food. Many animals spend most of their waking hours looking for food and eating it. They search their environment for things to eat. Some animals search alone, and others search together, but in general they get their food directly from nature. Human food comes from nature too, but most people now get their food from other people. Over the past year, how much of what you ate did you get directly from nature, by picking it from plants or hunting and killing animals? Probably not much: most, if not all, of what you ate came either from supermarkets, where the food prepared by others is sold, or in dining establishments such as restaurants and cafeterias, where food grown by some people is cooked and served by others. If all those institutions abruptly went out of business and people had to get their food directly from nature, most of us would not know how to go about it. Many people would go hungry.

To be sure, humans evolved under conditions different from modern life, and early humans did often get their food directly from the natural environment. But the modern world probably reflects the special aspects of the human psyche better than did the circumstances of prehistoric life. Humans are heavily interdependent and are quite good at developing cultural systems that allow them to benefit from each other's work. As people have learned to make culture work effectively, it is no longer necessary for everyone to hunt, fish, or grow food. Instead, you can become good at one very narrowly specialized task, such as repairing computers or selling shoes or treating broken legs, and your work at this task gives you money with which you can buy the many different things you need and want.

What this tells us about the human psyche is that people have a natural tendency to look to each other first. When people have a problem or a need, they most often look to other people for help, relief, or satisfaction. Even when people just need information, they tend to get it from other people rather than directly from the world around them. Animals learn from their own experience. They deal with the physical world, and they are rewarded or punished depending on how things turn out. Humans, in contrast, rely much less on what they learn from their own direct experience with the physical world. People learn from each other and from the culture.

Some evidence of the importance of putting people first comes from studies pitting money against social acceptance. In one study, some participants gained money but were rejected and ostracized by others; other participants were accepted and included but lost money. The first group felt worse than the second.[97] Money is an important means of getting what you need, but apparently people are more attuned to gaining social acceptance (even from complete strangers) than money.

The culture operates as a kind of "general store" of information. When people don't know what to do, they typically ask someone else who knows the culture's information. How do you get telephone service or a new credit card? Is there sales tax on food? How early (before the scheduled start time) should one arrive for an airline flight, a bus trip, a dinner party, a baseball game, a physician's appointment? Can I get my money back for something, and if so, how? These answers are not the specific wisdom learned by specific individuals, but general rules for getting along in the culture, and any knowledgeable person can tell you the answers—after which you would be able to pass that information along to anyone else.

Putting people first builds on the earlier theme that people are "built to relate." Nature has constructed human beings to turn to each other for food, shelter, support, information, and other needs. The fact that so many inner processes serve interpersonal functions enables people to rely on each other and treat each other as vital resources.

The reliance on other people for information was shown in one of modern social psychology's first experimental investigations, the research on conformity by Solomon Asch.[98,99,100] Asch presented research participants with a line-judging task, in which they simply had to say which of three lines was the best match to a specific line that was presented. The task was easy enough that everyone could get all the answers correct simply by looking at the lines. But Asch introduced a novel twist to this task. He ran the study in groups, and sometimes almost everyone in the group was secretly working with him. Only one person in the group was a real participant. When Asch gave a prearranged signal, all the confederates (the group members who were working with him and only pretending to be real participants) would give the wrong answer. Thus, the participant suddenly had to decide whether to give the answer that his or her eyes said was correct, or instead to go along with the group and give the answer that everyone else had given. If the human brain were designed mainly to learn from one's own direct experience, participants would still have given the right answer all the time. But they didn't. In a significant number of cases, participants went along with the group, giving the answer that they could see was wrong but that conformed to what everyone else was saying. Thus, sometimes people rely on other people more than on their own direct experience. In Asch's experiment, participants felt it was more important to be accepted by the group than to be correct on the line-judging task.

Recent work has confirmed the importance of getting information from others, with the twist that the effects depend on whether the other is similar to you. Participants heard another person express liking for some music. The participant's own evaluation of that same music was influenced by the other's views. If the other person had come across as similar to the participant in other musical opinions and personal background, then the participant liked the music more. If the other person was dissimilar, however, then his liking for the music made the participant dislike it.[101] The implication is that we put people first—but especially people to whom we have some closeness or connection.

If your brain is like a computer, then culture is like the Internet. Hooking into the system greatly increases the power of what a single computer, and by analogy a single brain, can do. By belonging to culture, you can learn an immense amount of information, whereas if you had to learn from your own direct experiences, you would only have a tiny fraction of that knowledge. Our tendency to put people first enables us to take advantage of the knowledge and wisdom that accumulates in the cultural general store.

What Makes Us *Human*

Putting the Cultural Animal in Perspective

This chapter has emphasized that human social behavior results from a mixture of nature and culture. Human beings are animals and, as such, have many of the same wants, needs, and behavior patterns that other animals have. According to the theory of evolution, human beings evolved from other animals. The special traits that make us human are thus mostly a result of gradual refinements of traits that animals had. Some notable biological traits differentiate humans from other animals: We have exceptionally large and capable brains, especially in proportion to body size. We walk upright. We can talk.

What makes us human is most apparent, however, in culture. The beginnings of culture can be found in other species, but these little bits of nonhuman culture exist mostly in small, isolated patterns of behavior that make only a relatively minor difference in the animals' life. In contrast, human life is deeply enmeshed in culture; indeed, it is hard to imagine what human life would be like without culture. Culture provides us with food and housing, with languages and things to talk about, with electricity and all the appliances that use it, with all our means of travel other than walking, with our forms of work and play, with science and religion, with medicine, with art and entertainment, and with all the ideas that give our lives meaning.

Cultures are diverse, but they also have many common themes. Phenomena such as language, cooking, clothing, and money are found all over the world, but not in other species. Human life would be vastly different without language, cooking, clothing, and money, but it is only because of culture that we can have them.

Culture also creates problems that are special to humans. Crime cannot exist without laws, nor bankruptcy without money, nor nuclear waste without nuclear technology. Only humans go to war, deliberately commit suicide, or take part in genocide. Culture is not all good. Still, its benefits far outweigh its costs. Culture has enabled human beings to thrive and multiply. Indeed, nearly all of the animals most closely related to humans (apes and other primates) live near the equator in tropical climates, but human beings have spread all over the globe and live comfortably in mountains and valleys, in sunny and wintry places, in deserts and other seemingly difficult places. Culture has learned to make products (e.g., clothes, plumbing, indoor heating) that make this dispersion possible.

Perhaps most remarkably of all, culture has enabled human beings to increase their life span substantially. Advances in public health and medical care now enable many people to live 80 years, more than double what our ancestors could expect. No other animals have been able to develop knowledge that extends their life span.

Many social psychologists have used the phrase "the social animal" to describe human beings, but many other animals are also social. What makes us human is the extent to which we are cultural animals. Culture is a better way of being social. For one thing, it allows humans to accumulate knowledge over time and across generations—something almost no other animals have been able to accomplish. Most social animals start over with each new generation, which must then solve the same problems of how to live comfortably. Each new generation of human beings, however, can learn from previous generations. (Otherwise, instead of reading this textbook, you'd be trying to master how to make fire and forage for food.)

The very fact that we can think about what makes us human is itself an important part of what makes us human. Human beings can think with language and meaning in a way that no other animal can. This makes our social lives much more complicated than they would otherwise be, but it also creates the richness of human life and experience. That is, it makes our social psychology more complicated to study and learn, but it also makes it vastly more interesting!

1. The duplex mind contains what two systems?

- (a) Automatic; deliberate
- (b) Cognitive; emotional
- (c) New; old
- (d) Short-term; long-term

2. In humans, the road to social acceptance is _____ .

- (a) downhill
- (b) long
- (c) short
- (d) smooth

3. In a classic experiment with lines of different lengths, Solomon Asch found that _____ .

- (a) perceptual judgments can be influenced by others
- (b) perceptual judgments cannot be influenced by others
- (c) large groups of people tend to overestimate the lengths of lines
- (d) large groups of people tend to underestimate the lengths of lines

4. In a common analogy used by psychologists, the brain is compared to a computer. In that analogy, culture is like the _____ .

- (a) hardware
- (b) Internet
- (c) keyboard
- (d) software

answers: see pg 65

CHAPTER 2 SUMMARY

Nature and Social Behavior

- The power of socialization to change people is real, but limited.
- Nature is the physical world around us.
- Darwin's theory of evolution focuses on how change occurs in nature.
- Natural selection is a process whereby genetically based traits become more or less common in a population.
- "Survival of the fittest" means that animals compete with each other to survive.
- Reproductive success means creating offspring who will in turn create other offspring.
- A trait that increases an organism's survival rate or leads to better reproductive success is likely to become more common in a population.
- Being social helps humans and other animals survive and reproduce.
- Larger brains evolved to enable animals to function well in complex social structures.
- The human brain evolved to capitalize on culture.

Culture and Human Social Life

- Culture is an information-based system in which many people work together to help satisfy their biological and social needs.
- A culture is what a group of people have in common, including shared beliefs, meanings, and values, as well as shared ways of doing things.

- Both nature and culture are important in shaping behavior.
- Humans, unlike most other creatures, base their actions on meaning and ideas.
- Nature has prepared humans to use ideas.
- Humans and some other animals are social. Humans are far more cultural than any other animal.
- Differences between social and cultural animals include the following:
  - Social animals work together; cultural animals also use extensive division of labor.
  - Social animals may learn things from one another; cultural animals deliberately share knowledge with the group.
  - Social animals may help kin; cultural animals have a broader sense of community and often help strangers.
  - Social animals mainly use aggression to resolve conflict; cultural animals have many alternatives, including moral principles, compromise, and the rule of law.
- Although cultures differ, differences are often merely matters of degree rather than opposites.

Important Features of Human Social Life

- The human mind is a duplex mind, meaning that it has both an automatic and a deliberate system.
- The automatic system is especially useful for the simple tasks we perform, whereas the deliberate system is useful for the more complex tasks.

- The automatic system is fast and relatively effortless, whereas the deliberate system is slow and effortful.
- The automatic and deliberate systems are not independent of one another. Sometimes they work together, and sometimes they work against each other.
- Living in a culture has many advantages, but it makes many demands.
- Inner processes often serve interpersonal functions. That is, the psychological traits people have enable them to connect better with others.
- In general (though not always), nature says go and culture says stop.
- Nature makes us selfish; culture requires us to resist selfish impulses.
- Most choices in life involve tradeoffs, both benefits and costs.
- An important aspect of many tradeoffs is short-term versus long-term gain.
- Humans get most of what they need from other people.

- Culture operates as a "general store" of information.
- Asch's study demonstrated that sometimes people rely more on information from other people than on their own senses.
- If the brain is like a personal computer, then culture is like the Internet. A computer can do a lot more when it is connected to the Internet than when it is a stand-alone machine.

What Makes Us Human? Putting the Cultural Animal in Perspective

- Although human beings evolved from other animals, humans have much larger brains than other animals, especially in proportion to body size.
- Big brains may have evolved to enable more complex social relationships.
- Another main difference between humans and other animals is culture. Culture allows humans to accumulate knowledge over time and across generations.
- Although culture is not all good, its advantages outweigh its disadvantages. For example, culture has enabled modern humans to more than double the life spans of our ancestors.

key terms

automatic system 51	duplex mind 51	praxis 42	survival 37
cultural animals 40	mutation 38	psyche 35	theory of evolution 36
culture 44	natural selection 37	reproduction 38	tradeoff 58
deliberate system 51	nature 36	social animals 40	

quiz yourself ANSWERS

1. Nature and Social Behavior p. 40
   answers: 1.d 2.a 3.a 4.c

2. Culture and Human Social Life p. 50
   answers: 1.c 2.d 3.b 4.d

3. Important Features of Human Social Life p. 64
   answers: 1.a 2.b 3.a 4.b

THE SELF

3

LEARNING OBJECTIVES

1 Explain the importance of a complex self in a cultural animal.

2 Summarize the different sources and motives of self-knowledge.

3 Describe how the sources of self-knowledge lead to self-concept.

4 Analyze the benefits and drawbacks of high self-esteem and positive illusions.

5 Evaluate the different functions of self-presentation.

Sergey Nivens/Shutterstock.com

In the late 1500s, near the height of the Ottoman Turkish empire, Sultan Suleiman the Magnificent set out with a giant army to conquer as much of Europe as he could. On the way to Vienna, he took offense at some purported remark by a Hungarian nobleman, Count Miklós Zrínyi, and diverted his entire force to conquer the small castle where Zrínyi lived on his lands.[1]

The prospects for the defenders were never very good. They had only a couple of thousand men, as compared to almost 100,000 with the sultan. The castle was not impressive (Suleiman himself called it a "molehill" when he first laid eyes on it). Its best feature was that it was surrounded by a swamp and an artificial lake, which were hard for an attacking army to cross, but the summer had been dry and this natural advantage was weaker than usual. When the Turks destroyed the dam, the artificial lake drained, leaving the castle exposed. The Turks bombarded the walls with their huge cannon and drilled tunnels, which they exploded to make the walls collapse.

After days of fighting, the defenders knew their cause was hopeless. Only 300 were left alive, their castle walls had huge holes in them, and most of their ammunition was gone. Instead of waiting for the Turks to storm in upon them, Zrínyi decided to die in a blaze of glory. As he prepared for the last moments of his life, he made some curious decisions. He discarded his armor and instead put on his wedding suit of silk and velvet. He hung a heavy gold chain around his neck and stuffed his pockets with gold coins. When asked why he was doing this, he replied that he wanted whoever killed him to know that he was an important person. Thus attired, he flung open the castle doors and led his remaining troops on a suicide charge right into the heart of the Turkish army. All were killed.

The striking thing about this story is the count's concern with self-presentation, which we shall see is the task of making good impressions on other people. It is easily understandable and rational that people want to make good impressions on their bosses, or their dating partners, or their teammates. Zrínyi, however, was trying to make a good impression on someone he did not yet know and who presumably would have already killed him by the time he found the gold coins. There is no practical value to being well regarded after you are dead, especially by the person who took your life. He's not going to be your buddy nor do you any favors. But it mattered to the count anyway.

Concern with making a good impression after you are dead may seem foolish, irrational, or even bizarre, but Count Zrínyi was far from alone in this respect. In fact, news reports in the United States today indicate that more and more people are stipulating plastic surgery to prepare their bodies for their funerals. They want to look their best at their last showing, even though they will be dead and there must be better ways to spend money than for cosmetic operations on a corpse that is about to be buried or cremated!

As cultural beings, people have selves that are much more elaborate and complex than has been found anywhere else in the animal kingdom. The self is an important tool with which the human organism makes its way through human society and thereby manages to satisfy its needs. To be effective at this, the human self has taken shape in a way that it is marked by some deep, powerful drives. Among these drives is a strong concern with how one is perceived by others. This drive mostly serves the goals of survival and reproduction. However, many people care strongly about how others perceive them, even if those other people don't help them survive or reproduce. In some cases, people care about others who will kill them. We may care most about those we depend on, but the fact is that people have a deeply rooted tendency to care, broadly, about how others in general regard them. It's very hard not to care what other people think of you. ●

Zrínyi's Outburst, Krafft, Johann Peter (1780-1856) / Hungarian National Gallery, Budapest, Hungary / Bridgeman Images

The monumental work, *Zrínyi's Sortie*, dated 1825, by Peter Krafft (1780–1856). The scene is the sortie of Count Miklós Zrínyi and his men, the heroic defenders of the castle of Szigetvár, against the besieging Turks in 1566, in which Zrínyi lost his life.

What Is the Self?

The self is peculiarly difficult to define. Everyone seems to know what it is and to use the term frequently (especially if you include words like *myself*), but hardly anyone can say exactly what it is. Some brain researchers now say that the self is an illusion, mainly because they cannot find any specific spot in the brain that seems to correspond to the self, but in their everyday lives these researchers act as if they know exactly what the self is, and it is not an illusion. For example, they know the difference between what is their own and what is someone else's (wallet, apartment, feet, ideas, romantic partner). After all, if the self were merely an illusion, there would be no genuine difference between you and me, so how could we talk about whether that $20 bill in your wallet or purse is yours or mine?

Thus, nearly everyone has a basic understanding of what the self is, even if it is hard to put into words. To develop a more scientific understanding, let us begin by considering what its functions are, what its different main parts or aspects are, and where it comes from.

The Self's Main Jobs

It may sound funny to ask: "Why do we have selves?" Not having a self is not really an option! Everyone has a separate body, and selves begin with bodies, so there is no way for a human being to be completely without a self. Perhaps a more relevant question would concern the structure of the self: "Why are human selves put together the way they are?" One could also ask about their function: "What are selves for?" The structure and function questions are often related, because things are made with a given structure precisely in order to serve that function. (Handles are designed for holding things, for example.) Moreover, as we saw in Chapter 2, many inner traits of human beings serve interpersonal functions. Much of the self is designed to enable you to relate to others, including claiming and sustaining a place in a cultural system that connects you to many other people.

Another theme of this book is the conflict between selfish impulses and social conscience. The self is right in the middle of this battle. On the one hand, selves sometimes naturally feel selfish (hence the very term *self-ish!*), and in many situations they have strong impulses to do what is best for themselves. They are designed to know and do what is best for them. On the other hand, selfishness must be kept under control if society is to operate effectively, and selves often incorporate the morals and other values of the culture. Those morals mostly tell you to do what is best for the group instead of what is best for you personally or what you feel like doing. Hence, the self must be able to understand these social morals and other values—plus be able to act on them, even when that requires overriding one's natural, selfish impulses.

The self has three main parts **(FIGURE 3.1)**, which correspond to several main things that the self does. The first part consists of **self-knowledge** (sometimes called **self-concept**). Human beings have self-awareness, and this awareness enables them to develop elaborate sets of beliefs about themselves. If someone says, "Tell me something about yourself," you can probably furnish 15 or 20 specific answers without having to think very hard. Consider these experiences, all of which involve self-knowledge and self-awareness: You stop to think about what you would like to be doing in five years. You receive a grade on an exam and consider whether you are good at this particular subject. You check your hair in a mirror or your weight on a scale. You read your horoscope or the results of some medical tests. On a first date, your partner asks you about yourself, and you try to give honest answers that show the kind of person you are. You feel ashamed about something

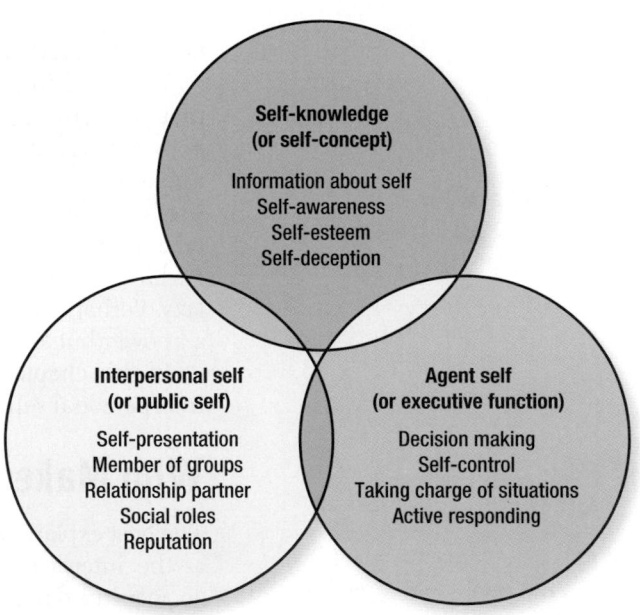

FIGURE 3.1

Three parts of the self: (1) Self-knowledge (or self-concept), (2) Interpersonal self (or public self), and (3) Agent self (or executive function).

self-knowledge (self-concept) a set of beliefs about oneself

you did last week or last year, or you feel proud about something else you did. Such moments show the self reflecting on itself and on its store of information about itself.

The **interpersonal self** or **public self** is a second part of the self that helps the person connect socially to other people. Most people have a certain image that they try to convey to others. This public self resembles the self-concept, but the two are not the same. Often, people work hard to present a particular image to others even if it is not exactly the full, precise truth as they know it. Consider some of the things people do to impress others. You dress up for a social event. You show your friends that you are easygoing and fun-loving—but meanwhile you convince your boss that you are serious, reliable, and work-oriented. You spend all day cleaning your home to get it ready for guests. You hold back from arguing for your religious or political views because you think the other people present might not approve of them. You worry about what someone thinks of you. When describing yourself on that first date, you leave out certain unflattering details, such as that nasty foot odor problem, or how you like to burp the words to "Auld Lang Syne." Furthermore, many emotions indicate concern over how one appears to others: You feel embarrassed because someone saw you do something stupid, or even just because your underwear was showing. You feel guilty if you forgot your romantic partner's birthday. You are delighted when your boss compliments you on your good work. These episodes reveal that the self is often working in complex ways to gain social acceptance and maintain good interpersonal relationships.

The third important part of the self, the **agent self** or **executive function** is the part that gets things done. It enables the self to make choices and exert control, including both self-control and control over other people (and things). Sometimes you decide not to eat something because it is unhealthy or fattening. Sometimes you make a promise and later exert yourself to keep it. Sometimes you decide what courses to take or what job to take. Perhaps you cast a vote in an election. Perhaps you sign a lease for an apartment. Perhaps you make yourself go out jogging even though the weather is bad and you feel lazy. Perhaps you place a bet on a sports event. All these actions reveal the self as not just a knower but also as a doer.

In this chapter, we focus on the first two aspects of the self: self-knowledge and the interpersonal self. The next chapter will focus on the self in action.

Who Makes the Self: The Individual or Society?

The best explanation for the origins of selfhood probably is that the self comes into being at the interface between the inner biological processes of the human body and the sociocultural network to which the person belongs (that is, the other people in the society, plus its "general store" of common beliefs and practices.[2] The importance of society is hard to deny; in fact, if you grew up on a deserted island and never met other human beings, you might hardly have a "self" at all in the usual sense. Having a name would be pointless, for example, if you never interacted with other people, nor would you have a reputation, an ethnic identity, or even a set of personal values. (At most you would have preferences, but they would not seem like your personal values if you never met anyone else who might be different.)

Then again, even without meeting other human beings, a person might still have a conception of self as a body separate from its environment. The difference between dropping a stone on your foot and dropping it on a tree root next to your foot is an important sign of self: Your foot is part of your self; the tree is not.

A True or Real Self?

Many people like to think they have an inner "true" self. Most social scientists are skeptical of such notions. If the inner self is different from the way the person acts all the time, why is the inner one the "true" one? By what criterion could we say that someone's "true" self is shy if the person doesn't act shy most of the time? The idea of an inner "true" self different from behavior may have its origins in class prejudices.[3,4,5,6] Back when social mobility began to increase, so that some aristocrats became poor while merchants became rich, the upper classes wanted to continue believing that they were inherently better

interpersonal self (public self) the image of the self that is conveyed to others

agent self (executive function) the part of the self involved in control, including both control over other people and self-control

than other people, even if the others had more money. The upper class could not point to obvious differences in behavior because in point of fact many aristocrats were drunken, conceited, stupid, lazy, sexually immoral, and in other respects deplorable. Hence, the upper class settled on the view that the superiority of the blue bloods lay in their inner traits that could not be directly seen.

Even if the inner "true" self is something of a fiction, people still believe in it, and these beliefs affect how they act. A classic article by sociologist Ralph Turner[7] noted that different cultures (and different groups or historical eras within a culture) may differ in their ideas about the true self by placing emphasis on either of two main approaches. One approach emphasizes the inner feelings as the true self. The other focuses on the way the person acts in public, especially in official roles. Many people recognize that they sometimes put on a public performance that differs from how they feel inside.[8] Turner's point was that cultures disagree as to whether the public actions or the inner feelings count as the more real or true side of the self. Suppose, for example, that a soldier is terrified in battle and wants to run and hide, but he steels himself and performs an act of heroism that helps win the battle. Which was the "real" man: the terrified coward or the brave hero?

Attitudes toward marriage may reflect different attitudes about the real self. In cultures that emphasize inner feelings as the true self, the actual wedding ceremony and its legal or religious significance are secondary. Marriage is seen as a psychological union of two persons, and what matters is how they feel about each other. If they lose their love for each other, or become attracted to someone else, they may feel justified in abandoning their spouse because to do so is to be true to themselves. A marriage is thus only as good as the current emotional state of the partners. In contrast, a culture that emphasizes public behavior and commitments downplays the inner feelings and instead places great significance on role performance. A couple may have a good marriage even if they cease to love each other, so long as they remain true to their vows and act the way spouses are supposed to act. The actual wedding ceremony counts as much more in such societies than it does among the impulse-oriented societies because it is at the wedding that the real self changes to become married in the eyes of society.

Culture and Interdependence

Selves are somewhat different across different cultures. The most studied set of such cultural differences involves independence versus interdependence. This dimension of difference entails different attitudes toward the self and different motivations as to what the self mainly tries to accomplish, and it results in different emphases about what the self is.

It is at the wedding that a couple becomes married in the eyes of society. Different cultures have different wedding traditions.

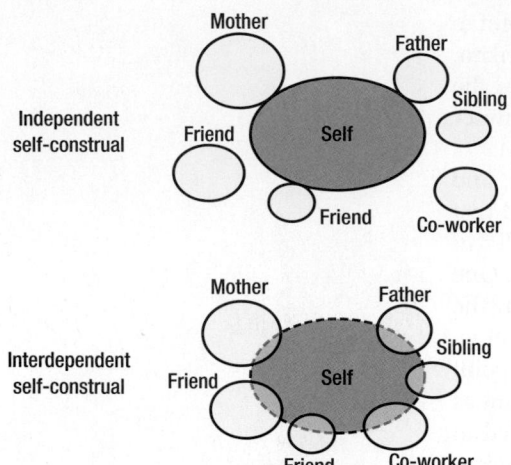

FIGURE 3.2

Depictions of independent and interdependent self-construals.

SOURCE: Markus and Kitayama (1991).[276]

The idea that cultural styles of selfhood differ along the dimension of independence was introduced by an international team of researchers.[9] They proposed that Asians differ from North Americans and Europeans in how they think of themselves and how they seek to construct the self in relation to others. To avoid the overused term *self-concept,* they introduced the term *self-construal,* which means a way of thinking about the self. An **independent self-construal** emphasizes what makes the self different and sets it apart from others. In contrast, an **interdependent self-construal** emphasizes what connects the self to other people and groups. These two types of self-construal are depicted in **FIGURE 3.2**.

To appreciate the difference, it is useful to try a simple exercise such as asking yourself "Who or what am I?" and listing a dozen or more different answers off the top of your head. When you have done this, go through the list again and see how many of your answers express something unique or special about you (such as having an unusual skill or hobby) and how many express connection to others (such as belonging to a particular family, attending a particular university, or coming from a particular place). The relative amounts of those two types of answers indicate where you stand on independence (your unique traits) and interdependence.

It is not inherently better to be either independent or interdependent. Nor is everyone in one culture independent or interdependent. Still, the general finding has been that Easterners (e.g., people from Japan, China, Korea) tend to be more interdependent, whereas Westerners (e.g., people from the United States, Canada, Western Europe) tend to be more independent. Nor are these differences merely superficial ways of talking about the self. Instead, they represent deep-seated differences in what the person strives to become. The American ideal may be the self-made man or woman, who works alone to create or achieve something, possibly overcoming obstacles or other people's resistance in the process, and who eventually becomes a true individual in the sense of a unique person with highly special traits. In contrast, the Asian ideal of selfhood may be more the consummate team player who makes valuable contributions to the group, who does not let personal egotism stand in the way of doing what is best for the group, and who remains loyal to the group and helps it overcome external threats. Asians see the self as deeply enmeshed in a web of personal, family, social, and cultural relationships, outside of which there is meaninglessness and loneliness. Americans see the self as following its own path to autonomy, self-sufficiency, and unique individuality.

A stunning story from the 1976 Olympics concerned a tight battle between the Japanese and the Soviet Russians for the men's team gymnastics medals.[10] It came down to a performance on the rings by Shun Fujimoto in the last event. His performance was nearly perfect except for a slight stutter-step by one leg when he jumped down at the end. His score was high enough that Japan won the gold medal by a very slight margin over the Russians.

What was remarkable about that story was that Shun had actually broken his leg at the knee in the previous event. He knew that the most intense pain he could imagine was waiting for him at the end of his performance, and he still managed to concentrate on what he was doing and perform perfectly.

When Americans hear Shun's story, they probably understand it in terms of the independent self. They can imagine Shun wanting the glory of the gold medal, wanting to fulfill his dreams, and wanting to complete what he had worked for years to achieve. They think he would want to be admired for his heroic effort under intensely adverse circumstances.

But Asians probably see the story differently, with a more interdependent construal. It was not personal glory but obligation to the team that pushed him to take on that suffering. If he didn't compete, his team would lose the medal, and he didn't want to let them down. In fact, Shun concealed his injury from his teammates, in case worrying about him or expecting that the team might lose would affect their performances.

Social Roles

Let us return now to the question "What are selves for?" One answer, certainly, is that the self has to gain social acceptance. People are not designed to live by themselves. They

independent self-construal a self-concept that emphasizes what makes the self different and sets it apart from others

interdependent self-construal a self-concept that emphasizes what connects the self to other people and groups

need other people to accept them in order to have a job, to have friends and lovers, to have a family. The self is one tool people use to accomplish these goals. By learning how to act properly and how to conform to social rules and norms, people can improve their chances of social acceptance. In Chapter 2 we saw that human beings follow an especially long road to social acceptance. The self is constructed to help them on that road, which includes changing and adapting themselves so as to appeal to others.

Another important purpose of the self is to play **social roles**. A long tradition in psychology and sociology considers social behavior as resembling a play or a movie, in which different people play different roles.[11,12] Indeed some theorists[13] have taken this view to an extreme and analyzed most human behavior and selfhood in terms of actors playing roles. A culture is a large system with many different roles, and everyone has to find a place in it (or several places). You cannot be a senator, or a nurse, or a parent, or a girlfriend, or a police officer unless you can reliably act in appropriate ways. Many roles, such as spouse or engineer, can only be adopted after you have taken a series of steps (such as having a wedding, or getting a college degree with a certain major); the self has to execute these steps just to get into the role. Then, after you have the role, you must perform the duties that define it. To succeed in traveling the long road to social acceptance, the person must have a self capable of all those jobs.

To be sure, humans are not the only creatures to have roles. For example, in ant colonies, ants have different roles, such as one or more fertile "queens," some fertile "drones," and many sterile "workers," "soldiers," or other specialized groups. What is special about the human self is that it is flexible enough to take on new roles and to change roles. A single human being, for example, might work at mowing lawns, writing for the school newspaper, managing the swim team, lifeguarding at several different pools, busing tables in the college dining hall, working with computers, managing others who work with computers, and so forth over the course of a lifetime. Also, a person may perform similar jobs with several different organizations, such as a professor who moves from one university to another but teaches similar courses each time. In contrast, a worker ant almost always does the same job for its entire life and within the same colony of ants; it does not need a self that can adopt and shed different roles.

Where do these roles come from? Often they are part of the social system. If you live in a small peasant farming village, as most people in the history of the world have done, then many roles are not available to you. The limited opportunities in that village's social system mean that you could not be a basketball coach, for example, or a software consultant, or a movie star because the only other people you ever meet are peasant farmers. Most roles are ways of relating to other people within a cultural system. If you lived alone in the forest, it would be silly to describe yourself as a police officer, a bartender, a schoolteacher, or vice president of telemarketing. A person's social identity thus shows the interplay of the individual organism and the larger cultural system: Society creates and defines the roles, and individual people seek them out, adopt them, and sometimes impose their own style on them. Without society, the self would not exist in full.

But let's start at the beginning. The self has its roots in the human capacity to turn attention back toward its source. Without self-awareness, selfhood and self-knowledge would be impossible. The next section will cover what social psychologists have learned about self-awareness.

Self-Awareness

Self-awareness consists of attention directed at the self. Early in the 1970s, two social psychologists began studying the difference between being and not

AP Images

The Japanese gymnast Shun Fujimoto completed the last three rotations of the 1976 men's Olympics team competition with a broken knee cap, collapsing in agony after the pain shot through his leg following his dismount from the rings.

social roles the different roles a person plays, as in a play or a movie

self-awareness attention directed at the self

The woman in this picture has at least two roles: (a) she is a soldier, and (b) she is a mother.

iStockphoto.Com/Pixdeluxe

Jutta Klee/Getty Images

I see room for improvement.

being self-aware.[14] They developed several clever procedures to increase self-awareness, such as having people work while seated in front of a mirror, or telling people that they were being videotaped.

Researchers quickly found it necessary to distinguish at least two main kinds of self-awareness: public and private.[15,16] **Private self-awareness** refers to attending to your inner states, including emotions, thoughts, desires, and traits. It is a matter of looking inward. In contrast, **public self-awareness** means attending to how you are perceived by others, including what others might think of you. Public self-awareness looks outward to understand the self. Without public self-awareness, Count Zrínyi would not have dressed as he did on the last day of his life: He wore his wedding suit and gold because he was imagining how he would look to the enemy soldiers outside. Thus, instead of attending to his inner states directly, he thought about himself as seen through other people's eyes.

One thing researchers have found is that self-awareness usually involves evaluating the self, rather than just merely being aware of it. A person looks in the mirror and compares himself or herself against various standards. It is not just "Oh, there I am in the mirror. Is that what I look like? It doesn't matter." Rather, it's "Oh, my hair is a mess. This shirt looks good on me. I should lose a little weight." The essence of self-awareness is comparing oneself against these standards (good-looking hair, good clothing, fashionable slimness, respectively) and thereby coming up with good or bad evaluations about the self.

Standards

Standards are ideas (concepts) of how things might possibly be. Standards include ideals, norms, expectations, moral principles, laws, the way things were in the past, and what other people have done. Standards are an important example of one theme of this book—namely, the power of ideas to cause and shape behavior. The self is not good or bad in a vacuum, but only when compared to certain standards. Nearly all children start talking about standards (good, bad, nice) when they are around 2 years old, which is also the age at which their self-awareness blossoms,[17] and children begin to develop a concept of themselves as separate from their parents.

Self-awareness is often unpleasant because people compare themselves to high standards such as moral ideals for good behavior or a fashion model's good looks. Researchers have found, for example, that when girls and young women watch television shows featuring especially beautiful actresses and models, they feel less positive about themselves and become more likely to develop eating disorders.[18,19,20,21,22,23,24] But people feel good when they compare themselves to the "average person" or to specific people who are not doing as well because they can usually surpass low standards (at least in their own minds!).

When people are aware that they fall short of standards, the bad feeling leads to either of two reactions: change or escape (**FIGURE 3.3**). One reaction is to try to remedy the problem, such as by improving oneself. This may be as simple as combing one's hair, or as complex as deciding to change basic aspects of one's life. Sometimes changing the standard is easier than changing the self. The other response is to try to avoid or reduce self-awareness, so as to escape from feeling bad.

private self-awareness looking inward on the private aspects of the self, including emotions, thoughts, desires, and traits

public self-awareness looking outward on the public aspects of the self that others can see and evaluate

standards ideas (concepts) of how things might possibly be

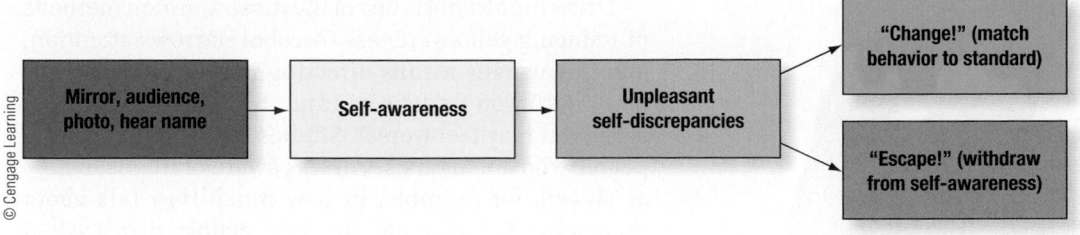

© Cengage Learning

FIGURE 3.3
Self-awareness theory suggests that some situations, such as looking in a mirror, lead to self-awareness. Self-aware people feel bad because they notice any discrepancies between who they are and standards. They can either "change" by matching the behavior to the standard, or "escape" by trying to escape the self-aware state.
SOURCE: Duval and Wicklund (1972).

Recent work suggests that a person's reactions to standards depends on how promising versus hopeless the prospect of meeting the standard seems.[25] When people think they can reach their goals or other standards in a reasonable time, self-awareness makes them try harder to do so. But if the goal looks unattainable or the person does not feel he or she is making satisfactory progress, then avoiding self-awareness looms as the more appealing solution.

Self-Awareness and Behavior

Self-awareness can make people behave better. Being self-aware makes you compare yourself to moral standards or other ideals. For example, in one study students took a test and had an opportunity to cheat on it. Students who took the test while sitting in front of a mirror were less likely to cheat than students who took the test without a mirror.[26] Another study showed that people are less likely to eat fatty food when they are sitting in front of a mirror than when there is no mirror.[27] Thus, again, self-awareness made people more attuned to societal standards and hence made them act in a more socially desirable manner. Other studies have shown that increasing self-awareness can make people behave less aggressively, conform more to their sexual morals, and stay on their diets.[28,29,30] Increased self-awareness makes people act more consistently with their attitudes about many different issues.[31] Insofar as consistency is a good thing, those findings provide more evidence that self-awareness improves behavior.

The fact that self-awareness enables people to behave better, according to cultural standards, reflects the theme that inner processes serve interpersonal functions. Humans could not get along with each other if they did not have self-awareness. Self-awareness enables people to reflect on themselves and change themselves so as to become more attractive and socially desirable—precisely what is needed to improve their ability to get along.

Does self-awareness *always* make people behave better? It does not, of course. For example, terrorists might become more fanatical and more destructive as a result of being self-aware because their standard is to terrorize their enemy. But these exceptions are just that—exceptions. The general effect of high self-awareness is to make people more aware of positive, desirable standards and make them try harder to behave in a positive manner.

One class of largely destructive behaviors, however, does stem from high self-awareness. These behaviors arise when people are aware of themselves in some bad, upsetting aspect, and they cannot solve the problem. In those cases, they may attempt to escape from self-awareness by resorting to destructive or socially undesirable methods. We'll look at this in the next section.

Escaping Self-Awareness

People seek to escape from self-awareness when it feels bad. Research participants who acted contrary to their values and attitudes were told to take a seat in a waiting room afterward. Half the seats faced mirrors (which make a person self-conscious), whereas others faced away from the mirrors. The people who had acted against their values generally chose to face away from the mirror.[32] They wanted to avoid self-awareness in order not to be reminded that they had done something wrong. Other participants, who had not done anything wrong, were happy to sit facing the mirror.

Alcohol reduces self-awareness, thereby undermining inhibitions.

Sean Murphy/Stone/Getty Images

Drinking alcohol is one of the most common methods of reducing self-awareness. Alcohol narrows attention, and this usually means directing it away from the self (although if you get drunk and just think about your problems, you may feel worse). Studies have confirmed that people who are drunk seem less aware of themselves—as shown, for example, in how much they talk about themselves.[33,34] Outside the lab, people drink when things have gone badly because the alcohol helps them stop ruminating about "What is wrong with me?" Perhaps paradoxically, people also turn to alcohol when they feel good and want to celebrate. That's because people want to let down their inhibitions in order to have a good time, and self-awareness is central to most inhibitions. (Remember, self-awareness makes you compare yourself against morals and other standards of proper behavior: that supports inhibitions.)

People use other methods to escape self-awareness. Perhaps the most extreme and destructive of these is suicide. Attempts at suicide, even when unsuccessful, are often intended as ways to escape from a sense of self as being a terrible person, or a person who is responsible for some terrible event.[35] Recent research indicates that even normal, healthy people can experience a rise in suicidal thoughts when they fail to live up to their goals, values, or other standards.[36]

Not all escapes from self-awareness are destructive, but several of them are, possibly because people who are desperate to stop thinking bad thoughts about themselves don't worry about the harm their methods might cause. *Food for Thought* discusses how escaping self-awareness can contribute to eating binges.

Why Do We Have Self-Awareness?

One explanation for human self-awareness is that it is vital for **self-regulation**—the process by which the self controls and changes itself.[37] People deliberately try to alter their responses, such as trying to get out of a bad mood, or to keep their attention and thinking focused on some problem rather than letting their mind wander, or to resist temptation. It is no accident that self-awareness usually involves comparing oneself to meaningful standards because that may be precisely what self-awareness is for. People can reflect on themselves, decide that they are not acting properly, and try to change. Understood in this way, self-awareness is part of the mechanism by which people can bring themselves into line with what other people, including their culture, want and expect. At a simple level, recognizing that your hair is a mess or your socks don't match may be an essential first step toward fixing the problem. (Chapter 4 will have more to say about self-regulation.)

Another explanation for human self-awareness is that it helps us adopt the perspective of other people and imagine how they see us. This reflects the "people first" theme that we introduced in Chapter 2: People are oriented toward other people. To get along, we look to others, and in particular we want to be accepted in social groups. Knowing how we appear to others is a great help toward making ourselves more appealing and acceptable to others. Self-awareness is helpful on the long road to social acceptance. It also indicates, again, that inner processes (in this case, self-awareness) serve interpersonal functions (to help people get along better with others).

At a more complex level, self-awareness can be an exercise in "What am I doing with my life?" Are you making progress toward your goals, such as receiving an education, getting a good job, or finding a suitable partner? People can feel good even though they have not reached their goals, as long as they are making progress toward them.[38] Self-awareness thus can help people manage their behavior over long periods of time so they can reach their goals.

self-regulation the process people use to control and change their thoughts, feelings, and behaviors

Eating Binges and Escaping the Self

Binge eating is a widespread problem, especially among adolescent and young adult females. Ironically, most of these young women are on a diet and trying to lose weight at the time, and the occasional eating binge thwarts their efforts to restrain their food consumption. Why would a woman who is on a carefully planned, calorie-counting diet suddenly one day eat most of the food in her refrigerator and cupboards?

One answer points to the importance of self-awareness. In this view, the woman may be beset with troubled thoughts and feelings that she is inadequate, unattractive, or otherwise unworthy. The process of eating enables her to escape from those thoughts and feelings.[39] She forgets herself as she becomes absorbed in the activities of chewing, eating, and swallowing food.

Many chronic dieters are preoccupied with how others perceive them. They may think that other people are whispering about how fat they are, even if they are within the normal weight range. They also tend to be people with high standards and high expectations for themselves (including being ambitious students at good universities). If something goes wrong for them—whether an academic setback, such as a bad test grade, or a personal problem, such as a romantic rejection—this tendency to focus on the self can make them miserable. They find themselves thinking about all their own possible faults and shortcomings that could have caused the problem.

At such times, eating appeals because it provides a distraction from thoughts about the self. The troubling thoughts occur at a highly meaningful level: What's wrong with me? Will I ever be a success in my career? Will people want to love me? In contrast, eating focuses the mind at a low level of meaning: take a bite, notice the taste, chew, swallow. Low levels of meaning involve little or no emotion, just sensation. The worries and anxieties about whether you are good enough are replaced by a kind of emotional calm. Eating can thus help turn off bad emotions.

Although dieters are high in **public self-consciousness** defined as thinking about how others perceive them, they are often low in private self-awareness of their inner states.[40,41] This may be because dieting involves learning to ignore one's inner feelings of hunger. Ignoring hunger may be helpful to dieting, but a common side effect is that the person also loses awareness of inner signals of satiety (that is, of being "full" and having eaten enough). This can contribute to an eating binge because the person keeps on eating even when the stomach is already full. The body sends out its usual "stop eating!" signal, but the mind has learned to ignore it along with other inner signals.

Normally, many dieters count every bite and calorie. This pattern of so-called monitoring helps keep track of food intake, so the dieter can carefully control how much she (or he) eats. This requires a watchful attitude toward the self. During an eating binge, however, self-awareness is often lost, and the person may lose track of how much she is eating. When you stop keeping track, it is hard to regulate. Even people who do not have eating disorders or dieting ambitions find that they eat more when they stop keeping track, such as when their attention is absorbed in a television show or party.

off the mark .com by Mark Parisi

IT'S ALWAYS THE SAME... I'M GOOD FOR 364 STRAIGHT DAYS, THEN IN **ONE NIGHT** I BINGE ON A HUNDRED MILLION SERVINGS OF COOKIES AND MILK...

OVEREATERS ANONYMOUS

offthemark.com

Reprinted by permission of Atlantic Feature Syndicate/Mark Parisi.

---

1. **Self-knowledge is also known as _____ .**
   - (a) self-awareness
   - (b) self-concept
   - (c) self-regulation
   - (d) self-presentation

2. **According to self-awareness theory, a self-aware state is _____ .**
   - (a) pleasant
   - (b) unpleasant
   - (c) pleasant initially, then unpleasant later
   - (d) neutral

3. **Alcohol has been shown to _____ self-awareness.**
   - (a) decrease
   - (b) increase
   - (c) not affect
   - (d) reverse

4. **The presence of a mirror has been shown to _____ self-awareness.**
   - (a) decrease
   - (b) increase
   - (c) not affect
   - (d) reverse

answers: see pg 111

Where Self-Knowledge Comes From

"Tell me something about yourself." Such openings are common, and people will generally oblige by disclosing some information. But where do they get it? How do people amass so much knowledge about themselves? Do people know themselves accurately, or are they mistaken (or do they simply lie a lot)? Humans clearly have a self-concept, or at least a stock of self-knowledge, some of which is true and some of which is distorted. Social psychologists have labored for decades to develop and test theories about how people store this information about themselves.

The next sections examine various theories about the sources of self-knowledge. When reading them, please keep a couple of things in mind: People are not passive receptacles; they actively process information that comes in. Your friend, or your mother, or society may tell you that you are not artistically talented, but you may reject that message. Then again, if all of them tell you that all the time, you may be more inclined to believe it (and they may be right!). Another thing to keep in mind is that people do not get all their self-knowledge from the same source or process. Several of these theories may be simultaneously correct, or at least partly correct.

Looking Outside: The Looking-Glass Self

One influential theory is that people learn about themselves from others. Every day people interact with others, and through these interactions they learn how others perceive them. "Wow, you are really good at sports!" "You're very attractive!" "You're a great cook!" These and many similar comments help give people information about themselves. It may seem surprising that the theme of putting people first extends even to finding out about yourself, but in fact people do learn a great deal about themselves from social interactions, from what other people tell them, and from comparing themselves to other people. These interactions also help cultivate public self-awareness, which (as noted above) is our ability to imagine how others perceive us.

The term **looking-glass self** was coined by Charles Horton Cooley[42] to refer to the idea that people learn about themselves from other people. Cooley proposed three components to the looking-glass self: (a) you imagine how you appear to others; (b) you imagine how others will judge you; (c) you develop an emotional response (such as pride or shame) as a result of imagining how others will judge you. It is as if other people hold up a mirror (a looking glass) in which you can see yourself. If you lived on a deserted island and never met anyone else, you would not know yourself nearly as well as you do growing up amid people.

The great American social philosopher George Herbert Mead[43] elaborated on this notion to suggest that most self-knowledge comes from feedback received from other people, whether particular individuals or what he called the **generalized other** (a combination of other people's views). Essentially, other people tell us who and what we are.

The notion of the looking-glass self has been tested extensively. It is partly correct and partly incorrect. Certainly there is ample evidence that people do respond to the feedback they get from others. Then again, if the looking-glass self really were the main source of self-knowledge, there ought to be a pretty good match between how everybody thinks about someone and how the person thinks about himself or herself. But there isn't. Most research suggests that a person's self-concept is often quite different from what friends, family, and coworkers think of him or her.[44]

Why doesn't the looking-glass self work better? If we were to ask you to describe yourself, and then asked all your friends and acquaintances to describe you, why would there be so many differences? Social psychologists have found that there usually is a good match between your self-concept and how you think others regard you. The gap is between what your friends really think of you and what you think they think. For example,

Failure of the sore thumbs sticking out hypothesis...

Paula Wright 2012

© Paula Wright

public self-consciousness thinking about how others perceive you

looking-glass self the idea that people learn about themselves by imagining how they appear to others

generalized other a combination of other people's views that tells you who and what you are

someone may think of herself as easy to get along with. If so, she probably thinks that everybody sees her as easy to get along with, but in reality other people may think she is a difficult, high-maintenance sort of person.

A person may be mistaken about how other people regard him or her for two reasons. The first is that people do not always tell the truth. If you ask someone, "Am I a pretty nice person, basically easy to get along with?" that person might just say "Sure!" without really meaning it. People are reluctant to communicate bad news,[45] to criticize someone, to complain, and in other ways to tell people what is wrong with them. (This generalization is subject to cultural differences. In Israel, for example, people supposedly are much more willing to communicate objections and criticisms.) It is very hard to find out if you have bad breath, for example, because almost no one will want to tell you.

The second reason is that people are not always receptive to feedback from others. People may try to tell you that you are hard to get along with, but you may not accept what they say. (You might get angry, or argue that the person is wrong, or change the subject.) As the section on self-deception will show, people are very selective in how they process incoming information about themselves. This is perhaps the biggest fallacy in the notion of the looking-glass self: It seems to depict the person as a passive recipient of information, as if people simply believed whatever other people told them about themselves. In reality, people pick and choose, and sometimes they completely reject what others tell them.

It is no wonder that many people's self-concepts do not match what others think of them. With regard to your unappealing traits, there is a sort of conspiracy of silence: Others don't want to tell you, and you don't want to hear it.

Looking Inside: Introspection

One refreshingly simple explanation of the roots of self-knowledge is that people simply have direct knowledge of what they are like. They don't need to rely on what other people tell them; they just look inward, and they know the answer. **Introspection** refers to the process by which a person examines the contents of his or her mind and mental states. People seemingly can always tell what they are thinking and feeling, probably better than anyone else. The concept of "privileged access" refers to the power of introspection; that is, I have "privileged access" to my own feelings, which I can know directly but you (or anyone else) can only infer. You only know what I am feeling if I tell you, or if you are lucky enough or sharp enough to infer my feelings from observing me.

This certainly rings true. People do know their own thoughts and feelings in ways that others cannot match. Introspection is one source of self-knowledge. It has limits, though. One is developmental. Many children think that their knowledge of their own inner states is no match for parental knowledge. Researchers asked children, "Who knows best what kind of person you really are, deep down inside?" Privileged access would mean that everyone should say, "I know myself best." But up until about the age of 11, children were more likely to say that their parents knew best.[46] The children thought that if they and their parents disagreed about some trait in the child, the parent would more likely be correct. This is remarkable: Children believe that their parents know them better than the children know themselves.

A more systematic and profound attack on introspection began with an influential article by Richard Nisbett and Timothy Wilson in 1977.[47] They proposed that people do not really have much in the way of privileged access, and hence when they look inside they simply make mistakes, guess, or give what they assume are plausible or socially desirable answers. In a series of studies, Nisbett and Wilson and their colleagues showed that people often do not realize how their minds work. For example, in one study people had to choose which stockings to buy, and by scrambling the sequence the researchers were able to show that most shoppers just chose whichever one they saw last. But the

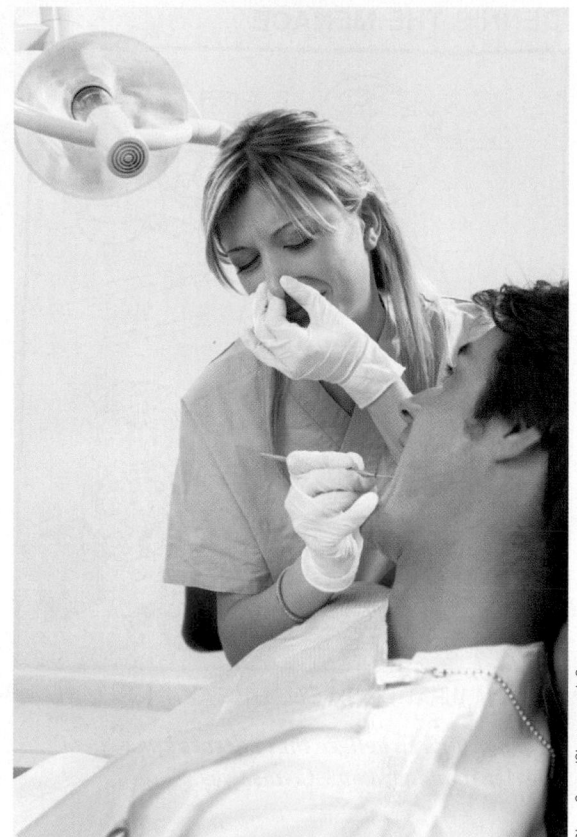

Your dental hygienist will definitely notice whether you have bad breath, but he or she probably won't tell you. Fortunately, you will probably get some mouthwash after your teeth are cleaned. Other people who notice your bad breath, however, may feel awkward offering you mouthwash or a breath mint.

introspection the process by which a person examines the contents of his or her mind and mental states

"MOM, WHAT DO I FEEL LIKE DOING?"

Young children believe that parents know them better than they know themselves.

shoppers didn't realize what they were doing. They said they chose based on color or softness instead of saying, "I just chose the last one."[48]

Another failure of introspection was shown in a study of how young men are affected by sexy car ads.[49] The different ads emphasized each car's best features: One got good gas mileage, another had a good safety record, and so forth. One of the ads also featured a pretty young woman wearing only a dark sweater and black lace panties and holding a large spear. In different sessions, the attractive model was paired with different cars. The results showed that the men tended to choose whichever car was paired with the attractive woman. But when asked to explain their choice of car, the men never invoked the scantily clad, spear-carrying young woman; instead, they explained their choice on the basis of whatever was good about that car (e.g., "A good safety record is really important to me"). Note that the experimental design allowed the researchers to establish that the woman in the ad was the true cause of preferences, but the participants were unaware that they had been thus affected. (See Chapter 1 for a discussion of how experimental designs allow researchers to make causal inferences.)

Nisbett and Wilson's[50] claim that people do not know their own minds met fierce resistance in some quarters. We noted in Chapter 1 that science tends to be self-correcting, so that the march of progress can gradually get closer and closer to the truth as new theories are tested and improved. In crucial respects, Nisbett and Wilson were right: People often do not know what goes on inside their minds. In other respects, however, they may have overstated the case. Sometimes people do know what they are thinking and feeling.

The difference lies partly in the duplex mind. As you may recall from Chapter 2, the duplex mind has two parts: one engages in automatic, nonconscious processing of information, whereas the other involves deliberate processes of which we are consciously aware. Introspection is a conscious process. The automatic system does a great deal of work that the deliberate system does not know about or understand.

Is introspection valid? People can correctly know what they think and feel. On the other hand, they may not know *why* they are thinking or feeling something. Terry may be correct when he tells you that he did not like a novel that he read. You can believe his answer (assuming he is not deliberately lying) when he tells you whether he liked it or not. But his explanation of why he liked it or disliked it is less reliable. He may have liked it for many reasons of which he is not aware.

More generally, the self has many traits, some of which are best known to the self, others more easily seen by others. A painstaking study concluded that people are the best judges of their own traits that are hard to observe, such as neuroticism (a tendency to feel unhappy and be bothered by many things). In contrast, for traits that have a strong good-bad dimension, like intelligence and creativity, people may be biased and prone to self-deception, and close acquaintances are better judges than the self.[51]

Looking at Others: Social Comparison

Sometimes self-knowledge requires looking at other people. It may seem surprising that you learn about yourself by looking to others, but other people are vital to self-knowledge. In social comparison, you learn not the facts about yourself, but what those facts mean and how they count—in the context of what other people are like. Suppose, for example, that you score 126 on a test, or you discover that you can swim a mile in half an hour. Is that good or bad? By itself, it is neither. It is only good or bad in comparison to what others do.

The theory of **social comparison**[52] laid out the power and the processes in which people learn about themselves by comparing themselves to others. Many facts about the self (such as swimming a mile in half an hour) don't carry much weight by themselves and only become meaningful in comparison to others. Social comparison is another instance (like the looking-glass self described earlier) of "putting people first"—we get the information we need, even about ourselves, by focusing on other people.

social comparison examining the difference between oneself and another person

004 ⊕⊕⊕

Olympic gold medalist Michael Phelps is an upward comparison target for swimmers. If you compare yourself as a swimmer to him, you will probably feel badly.

But to whom do you compare yourself? The most useful comparisons involve people in your same general category, whatever that might be. Comparing your swimming times to those of Michael Phelps, the legendary Olympic swimmer, isn't going to be very enlightening, especially if you are a female, middle-aged, overweight swimmer who never learned how to do flip turns.

Sometimes people deliberately compare themselves to others who are better or worse. **Upward social comparisons** involving people better than you, can inspire you to want to do better in order to reach their level. (However, they can also be discouraging.) **Downward social comparisons** against people worse off than yourself, can make you feel good.

Sometimes people compare themselves to others who are close by, such as their friends and family members. Such comparisons can be hard on the relationship, especially for the one who doesn't come out looking good. It's fine for your sister or your husband to be a swimming champ if you aren't a competitive swimmer yourself; in fact, the other's success may reflect favorably on you. But if you are a serious swimmer and your partner consistently does better than you, you may be upset by this comparison, and that can put some distance between the two of you.[53]

Self-Perception

Yet another theory about where self-knowledge comes from is that people learn about themselves in the same way they learn about others—by observing behavior and drawing conclusions. In a sense, this is the opposite of introspection theory because it dismisses the whole "privileged access" issue. There is no special route to self-knowledge. You see what you do, and you draw conclusions about what you are like. This seemed like a radical theory to many social psychologists when it was proposed in 1965. However, **self-perception theory**[54] does not really claim that people have no privileged access to knowing their inner feelings and states. In fact, the theory proposes that when people did have such information, they might not rely on self-perception processes. But sometimes looking inside is not adequate, and in those cases people are swayed by self-perception. For example, Lucy might say that she believes in God and thinks people ought to go to church, but somehow she never manages to get herself there. At some point she may notice this fact about herself and conclude that her religious convictions are perhaps somewhat weaker than she had always thought. If religion really mattered to her, she probably would manage to get to church once in a while. At a more mundane level, you may have had the experience of not having eaten for several hours and not feeling hungry

upward social comparison comparing yourself to people better than you

downward social comparison comparing yourself to people worse off than you

self-perception theory the theory that people observe their own behavior to infer what they are thinking and how they are feeling

but then noticing how eagerly you start to eat when food is available, prompting you to think, "I guess I really was hungry."

One important application of self-perception theory is the overjustification effect, described in the *Money Matters* box.

The Fluctuating Image(s) of Self

So far we have spoken about self-knowledge as the mass of information the person has and carries with him or her all the time. But social psychologists have discovered a smaller, in some ways more important, self-concept that changes much more easily and readily. Called the **phenomenal self**,[55] or the **working self-concept**,[56] it is the image of self that is currently active in the person's thoughts. Put another way, when you are self-aware, you are usually only aware of a small part of all the information you have about yourself. Each situation summons up only a few relevant aspects of the self, and these constitute the phenomenal self. The difference is comparable to that between all the

MONEY *Matters*

Doing It for Money, Not Love

One of the most important and dramatic instances of self-perception involves motivation. Early on, social psychologists learned to distinguish between intrinsic and extrinsic motivation.[57] **Intrinsic motivation** refers to wanting to perform an activity for its own sake. The activity is an end in itself. Someone might be intrinsically motivated to paint, for example, because he enjoys the process of dabbing colors onto a canvas and takes satisfaction in creating a beautiful or striking picture.

Extrinsic motivation, in contrast, refers to performing an activity because of something that results from it. The activity is a means to some other end—it is pursued for what it accomplishes or leads to, rather than for the activity itself. A person who is extrinsically motivated to paint might paint in order to make money. This painter might be very motivated and might work very hard, even if she did not really like painting much at all. One test would be whether the person would choose to spend free time doing the activity, in the absence of external rewards or incentives. An intrinsically motivated painter might well spend a free Sunday afternoon

painting, but an extrinsically motivated painter would not (unless there was money or some other incentive).

Self-perception theory led to the prediction that extrinsic motivations would gradually win out over intrinsic ones when both were relevant. This is called the **overjustification effect**—the tendency for intrinsic motivation to diminish for activities that have become associated with rewards. Essentially, overjustification means that rewards transform play into work. Mark Twain understood this concept long before psychologists did. In *The Adventures of Tom Sawyer,* Twain wrote:

> There are wealthy gentlemen in England who drive four-horse passenger coaches twenty or thirty miles on a daily line, in the summer, because the privilege costs them considerable money; but if they were offered wages for the service that would turn it into work then they would resign.

Take the intrinsically motivated painter, and suppose that someone then began to pay him to paint. The painter would gradually see himself painting away and getting paid for it. And the logical inference would be that he is painting for the money—which implies that he doesn't really love to paint for its own sake. Accordingly, over time, being paid to paint would make the painter less and less intrinsically motivated to paint.

Extrinsic rewards can create confusion in people who are engaging in an activity they love to do. People begin to wonder why they are doing the activity, for enjoyment or for pay. Reggie Jackson, a baseball player whose salary at the time was $975,000 per year, was once asked why he played baseball. He said, "A lot of it is the money, but I'd be playing if I was making [only] $150,000." Bill Russell, the former basketball star, said, "I remember that the game lost some of its magical qualities for me once I thought seriously about playing for a living."

The overjustification effect has been confirmed in many studies,[58] though there are plenty of exceptions.[59] If people get extrinsic rewards for doing something they intrinsically like to do, eventually the intrinsic motivation grows weaker and the person orients the activity more and more to its extrinsic rewards. In the first demonstrations of this pattern, students performed puzzles and were either paid or not paid for solving them. The researchers then left each student alone for a brief period and secretly observed whether the student continued to work on the puzzles (a sign of intrinsic motivation because it indicated that the person enjoyed the puzzles enough to work on them when there was no reward). Students who had been paid showed a sharp drop in their interest in doing the puzzles once the pay stopped (see **FIGURE 3.4**). In contrast, students who had done the same number of

information you have in your computer and what is currently displayed on the screen. The phenomenal self is what you see on the screen right now: It is only a small part of the total, but it is the part that you can use actively.

Different situations can call up different parts of self-knowledge into the phenomenal self. For one thing, whatever aspects of you stand out as unusual often become prominent in the phenomenal self. Thus, if you are the only woman in a roomful of men, you are probably quite aware of being a woman, whereas if you are among other women, your femaleness does not stand out so much and you may be less aware of it. Note that you are still a woman in either case, and of course you know it. The difference is merely what stands out in your mind.[68,69]

This sense of yourself as standing out is especially important when you are the only member of some category, such as a racial or ethnic group. If you are, say, the only African American on a committee, you may be acutely aware that other people think of you as African American, and you may identify more strongly than you would otherwise with being an African American. (Note that this is ironic, in a way. Some people

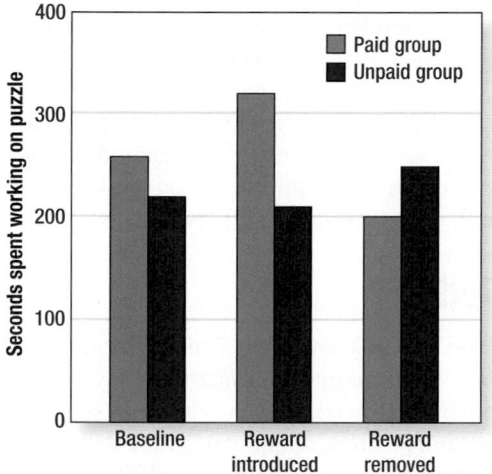

FIGURE 3.4

Average number of seconds participants in paid and unpaid groups spent working on a puzzle at baseline (before a reward was introduced to the paid group), when the reward was introduced, and after the reward was removed.[57]

puzzles but had never been paid continued to find them interesting.[60] Thus, being paid made people think, "I only do these for money," and they no longer liked to do them for their own sake. Extrinsic motivation (money) had replaced intrinsic motivation (fun). Play had become work.

A crucial and revealing factor is whether the rewards are expected during the activity, as opposed to coming as a surprise afterward. You would only infer that somebody is painting for the sake of the money if the person knew in advance that painting would bring money. If the person painted and then received some money afterward, unexpectedly, you would not conclude that money was the driving force. The same logic applies to the self. When people perform an activity and anticipate they will be paid for it, their intrinsic interest in the task diminishes. In contrast, an unexpected reward does not alter their intrinsic motivation.[61,62]

Another factor is initial liking. What if the person does not enjoy the activity? In that case, getting rewards seems to make the activity more attractive, especially if it is possible to discover some pleasure in it.[63] Some things, like swimming, require doing them for a while in order to learn to enjoy them.

You might think that people would know directly whether they desire and enjoy some activity, and that extrinsic rewards would make little difference. (Recall the earlier discussion of introspection and "privileged access.") Certainly people do know to some extent what they want and what they like. But self-perception processes still have some influence. Some experts caution against paying children money to reward them for good grades. The money may cause confusion about why they are trying to get good grades: Is it because learning is fun, or is it because they receive money for good grades? Actually, there is some evidence that when rewards convey a clear message that "you're great!" they do not undermine intrinsic motivation,[64,65] possibly because people like to be good at things. Moreover, sometimes people may say they like something but still not do it as frequently.[66]

A recent study tracked over 10,000 West Point cadets for 10 years to examine how these motives operate outside the lab.[67] Their reasons for attending West Point were sorted into intrinsic and extrinsic. Intrinsic motivation, such as the desire to become an Army officer, led to better outcomes: The higher the intrinsic motivation, the more likely the person was to become one, to get promoted, and to extend military service past the initial term. Extrinsic motivation (e.g., wanting prestige, status, officer's salary) generally reduced those good outcomes, and they greatly weakened the effects of intrinsic motivation—just like the overjustification theory predicts. But among cadets with low intrinsic motivation, having a stronger extrinsic motivation did improve their performance. Thus, again, extrinsic motivation can be good if intrinsic motivation is low, but if intrinsic is high, extrinsic undermines it.

Which ones are most aware of their own race?

blickwinkel/Alamy

might guess that you would identify yourself more as an African American if you were in a group that was composed entirely of African Americans.) Being the lone member of some category heightens self-awareness and can impair performance.[70] It can even make you feel that you are responsible for your group's reputation, which greatly increases the pressure. Worrying about how your performance may reflect on your group is called "stereotype threat" and is covered in Chapter 13.

An important aspect of the self is being the same across time. Yet people think of themselves somewhat differently when focused on the present as opposed to the future.[71] When you think about yourself as you are today, the thought tends to be full of specific and concrete facts, such as being a student in this social psychology course and reading this textbook. In contrast, when you think about yourself in the future, such as a year or two from now, your ideas will tend to be more general and abstract, such as whether you will be engaged in studying and learning in general. Future versions of self have broader categories (a man, as opposed to a tall thin man with a beard; a sports fan, as opposed to a pro football fan who favors the Kansas City Chiefs), as compared to present concept of self. In general, the future self-concept is vague, simple, broad, and general, whereas the present self-concept tends to be much more clear-cut, complex, and specific.

Why People Seek Self-Knowledge

In the last section we considered some of the roots of self-knowledge. One additional driving factor is that people want to know themselves, so in many circumstances they actively seek out information about the self. They take personality tests (even magazine self-tests that have little or no scientific validity), consult horoscopes, spend years and thousands of dollars on psychoanalysis or other therapies that promise to improve self-knowledge, learn to meditate, and above all pay close attention to what others say about them. One former mayor of New York, Ed Koch, made a standard joke out of the interest in self-knowledge by acknowledging that most people had an opinion about his performance as mayor. Whenever he met someone, instead of asking, "How are you doing?" as is customary, he would ask, "How am I doing?"

Beginnings of Self-Knowledge

Human beings have a deep thirst for self-knowledge. Some people are more eager than others to learn about themselves, but hardly anyone is indifferent to self-knowledge. The evolutionary origins of the desire for self-knowledge are hard to establish, though one can easily propose many potential benefits that might come from knowing yourself. For example, creatures might have a better idea of which potential mates to pursue if they have a more accurate understanding of their own attractiveness.[72] If you vastly overestimate your sex appeal, you might waste a great deal of time trying to hook up with people who are out of your league. Likewise, if someone challenges you, knowing your own strength and capabilities might dictate whether you choose to fight or back down, and mistakes could be costly.

The long road to social acceptance is one theme of this book, and self-knowledge can be helpful on that road. You need self-knowledge in order to fit in better with others. Will people like me? Am I similar to them? Such questions require self-knowledge. Moreover, as we have seen, cultural groups consist of different roles and different tasks, so it is valuable to know what your strengths and weaknesses are in order to know how best to fit in with the group. You don't want to demand to be the group's cook if you are terrible at cooking, for example, because your bad food might make others dislike and reject you.

Three Reasons for Wanting Self-Knowledge

People want to learn about themselves, but they'd rather learn some things than others. Three main motives shape the quest for self-knowledge. These three motives sometimes compete against each other, and different motives predominate in different people or different circumstances.

The first motive is the simple desire to learn the truth about oneself, whatever it is. This can be called the **appraisal motive**. It consists of a broad, open-minded curiosity, and its main preference is for information that is both important and reliable.[73,74] For example, the appraisal motive may motivate people to start out with tasks of medium difficulty because these offer the most information. If you start out with something that is very easy, then success does not give you much information about whether you have high or low ability because anyone might succeed at an easy task. By the same token, if you start out with something that is very difficult, then failure does not give you much information about whether you have high or low ability because anyone might fail at a difficult task.

The second motive, called the **self-enhancement motive** is the desire to learn favorable or flattering things about the self. Unlike the appraisal motive, the self-enhancement motive can exert considerable bias, driving people to dismiss or ignore criticism while exaggerating or inflating any signs of their good qualities.[75]

The third motive, the **consistency motive** is a desire to get feedback that confirms what the person already believes about himself or herself. Once people have formed ideas about themselves, they are generally reluctant to revise those opinions. In this respect, self-knowledge is no different from knowledge about many aspects of the world: Once people have formed opinions or beliefs about almost anything, they are resistant to change. The consistency motive is also sometimes called the self-verification motive, which implies that people actively seek to "verify" their self-concepts by obtaining confirmation that what they think about themselves is correct.[76,77]

To illustrate these three motives, suppose that you believe that you are not very good at sports. The appraisal motive would make you want to get more information about your sports abilities, regardless of what that information might say. The self-enhancement motive might make you want to learn that you do have some talent at sports after all. (If you can't get such feedback, then the self-enhancement motive might drive you to avoid any more information about yourself at sports, and it might also push you to compensate for your athletic deficiencies by finding out that you are good at other things, such as music or cooking.) And the consistency motive would make you prefer to gain further evidence that you are bad at sports, because that confirms what you already think.

When Motives Compete

When such conflicts arise between motives, which one wins? Logic would suggest that the answer is based on what is most useful. Accurate information is almost always more useful than false information because accurate information furnishes the best basis for making good choices. Hence, the appraisal motive should be the strongest.

It isn't, though. When the three motives were pitted against each other in a series of careful experiments, the appraisal motive emerged as the weakest of the three.[78] Self-enhancement was the strongest. People most want to hear good things about themselves. Their second preference is for confirmation of what they already think (consistency). They do also want accurate information, but the desire for the truth runs a distant third to the desires for favorable and consistent feedback. Although people may prefer positive, flattering feedback, it may not be best for them. Compared to accurate self-evaluation, inflated views of self cause multiple problems, including poor performance, defensiveness, and failing to study and prepare for upcoming challenges.[79] Students who have inflated views of themselves end up getting relatively poor grades in college and end up less

appraisal motive the simple desire to learn the truth about oneself, whatever it is

self-enhancement motive the desire to learn favorable or flattering things about the self

consistency motive a desire to get feedback that confirms what the person already believes about himself or herself

satisfied with their lives.[80] People who are prone to use self-enhancing styles of thought tend to lack resilience in the face of personal difficulties, to get poor grades, to lack social skills, and to become narcissistic.[81]

Also, people sometimes have more than one reaction to feedback, especially if feeling and thinking pull in different ways. The self-enhancement motive has an especially strong emotional appeal, whereas the consistency motive has more of a cognitive appeal. People may be more willing to believe and accept consistent feedback in terms of their cognitive reactions, but emotionally they will yearn for and prefer flattering, positive feedback. If someone tells you that you are extremely talented, for example—more talented than you had believed—you may find that your logical mind is skeptical of this news, but emotionally you are happy to hear it.[82,83,84,85]

One way of understanding this ranking of self-knowledge motives is to return to the "people first" theme. It is true that accurate knowledge would be the most useful for making decisions. But probably people want to be accepted by others more than they want a valid basis for making decisions. The human emotional system is set up to promote and reward any signs that the person is likely to be accepted by others. Hence, positive, flattering information is the most appealing because others will like you most if you have good traits.

The fact that the self-enhancement motive is stronger than the appraisal motive means that people want to think well of themselves more than they want to know the truth. One implication is that sometimes people prefer to discredit feedback, even in advance, if

self-handicapping putting obstacles in the way of one's own performance so that anticipated or possible failure can be blamed on the obstacle instead of on lack of ability

Self-Handicapping

TRADE Offs

Why would someone get drunk before an important job interview? Why do some students stay out partying all night before an important test? Are underachievers all merely too lazy to get their work done?

An intriguing theory has suggested that some people's problems stem from a strategy called **self-handicapping**.[86,87,88,89] Self-handicapping has been defined as putting obstacles in the way of one's own performance, so that anticipated or possible failure can be blamed on the obstacle instead of on lack of ability. The student who parties all night instead of studying before an exam may not get the best grade, but because that low grade can be blamed on not having studied, it does not signify that the student lacks intelligence.

Self-handicapping was first proposed as a possible explanation of alcohol abuse. Alcohol is widely (and correctly) seen as harmful to performance: Drunk people do not perform as well as sober ones. Hence, someone who fears that he or she will perform badly might find alcohol a convenient excuse.

The excuse appeals especially to someone who has already achieved a reputation for being smart or capable. (The importance of what other people think indicates that self-handicapping is primarily a self-presentational strategy, designed to control how one is perceived by others.[90]) Many people who have a big success early in their careers worry that this was just a lucky break, and they fear that they will not be able to do as well again. For example, a rock band might have a big hit with their first recording, which launches them into fame and stardom, but they are afraid that their second recording will not be as good. Fans and critics may hail them as geniuses after the first success, but the band worries that the second album may make everyone reconsider and decide that the band is only a mediocre talent after all. Instead of letting that happen, some band members may develop a drug or alcohol problem. That way, if the second album is not

as good, fans and critics can say, "They are really talented, and it's too bad that the drug problem is keeping them from producing more great music." Their reputation as geniuses remains intact. Wouldn't you rather be known as a troubled genius than an earnest mediocrity?

Moreover, if the second performance is good, then people will assign extra credit, so the self-handicapper's reputation is even improved: "Look at what a great report she gave, even though she had been on a drinking binge all week. She must really be amazingly

Do some people turn to alcohol in order to provide themselves with a handy excuse for possible failure?

they think it might make them look bad. One of social psychology's best documented patterns of avoiding feedback that could make them look bad is self-handicapping, which is described in *Tradeoffs*.

Self-Knowledge and the Duplex Mind

The duplex mind is also relevant to the interplay between these conflicting motives. The automatic system tends to favor the self-enhancement motive. When people respond automatically to questions about themselves, they lean toward "everything good is me, and everything bad is not me." Under times of stress, or when people are preoccupied or distracted, this pattern of **automatic egotism** emerges.[94]

Often a conscious override is required in order to furnish a more balanced and consistent view of self. Modesty in particular often seems to require conscious, deliberate control, because people may have a first impulse to say they are wonderful, and they must overcome this impulse in order to offer a more humble account of themselves.[95,96] It is a quick, automatic reaction to feel good about praise or to feel bad when criticized, but it takes a little more thought and effort to question the praise or to admit that the criticism may be valid. Thus, the different parts of the duplex mind may cultivate self-knowledge in different ways. The automatic system favors automatic egotism ("I'm good in general"), whereas the deliberate system can make corrections and strive toward a more balanced, accurate appraisal of the facts.

automatic egotism response by the automatic system that "everything good is me, and everything bad is not me"

smart to do great work despite her drinking problem." Some people, such as those with high self-esteem, are drawn to this advantage because it enriches one's credit for success.[91]

In one series of experiments, participants were told that the purpose was to investigate whether some new drugs had temporary side effects on intelligent performance. The experimenter explained that one drug temporarily made people smarter and the other made people temporarily less intelligent (like alcohol). Participants then took a first IQ test. On this test, some people were given unsolvable multiple-choice questions, so they had to guess, but to their surprise the experimenter kept telling them their answers were correct. These participants experienced what is called noncontingent success: They were told they did well, but at some level they had to know that they had not really earned their good rating. In another condition, people were given easier problems and accurately told which ones they got correct (thus, contingent success). All participants were then told that their score was the highest that had been seen in the study so far.

Next, the experimenter asked the participant to choose one of the drugs, in preparation for a second IQ test (which would supposedly verify whether performance improved or got worse). One of the drugs (called Actavil) was supposed to increase intellectual performance, whereas the other drug (called Pandocrin) was supposed to decrease intellectual performance. Participants who had experienced the noncontingent success overwhelmingly chose the alcohol-like drug Pandocrin that would supposedly make them perform worse (see **FIGURE 3.5**). Why? They knew the experimenter thought they were brilliant, but they privately doubted they could do as well on the second test, so they wanted the drug that would give them an excuse for poor performance.[92]

In the early 1800s, a European chess champion named M. Guillaume Le Breton Deschappelles (or Deschapelles, for short) won nearly all his matches. As he got old, however, he felt his mental powers waning, and he worried that smart young chess masters would defeat him. He used a self-handicapping strategy to preserve his reputation: He insisted that he would only play games in which his opponent got the first move (a major advantage in chess) and in which he gave up one of his pieces at the start of the game (another disadvantage for him). That way, if he lost, he would not lose respect because the loss would be attributed to his disadvantages; when he won, people

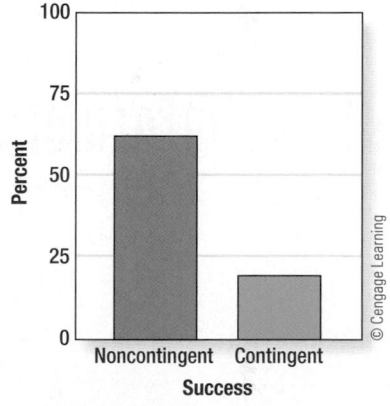

FIGURE 3.5

Percent of participants in the noncontingent and contingent success groups choosing the alcohol-like drug Pandocrin that supposedly decreased intellectual performance.

would marvel at his ability to overcome those handicaps.[93]

Self-handicapping is thus an effective strategy for good self-presentation. It discounts failure and enhances success. The downside of the tradeoff is that it makes failure more likely. Taking a test without having slept, or when hung over, may furnish a handy excuse for failure, but it also increases the odds of failure.

answers: see pg 111

QUIZ YOURSELF

Where Self-Knowledge Comes From

1. **The night before an important test, Boozer drinks all night instead of studying. This is an example of _____ .**

   (a) self-awareness (b) self-consciousness (c) self-fulfilling prophecy (d) self-handicapping

2. **"Do I like parades? Well, each year there have been several parades in town, and I haven't gone to one yet. I must not like parades." Which theory explains this internal dialogue?**

   (a) Cognitive dissonance theory (b) Psychological reactance theory (c) Psychoanalytic theory (d) Self-perception theory

3. **A teacher promises one of his preschool students a candy bar for finger painting, a task the student loves to do. The reward is likely to produce _____ .**

   (a) cognitive dissonance (b) downward social comparison (c) intrinsic motivation (d) the overjustification effect

4. **The simple desire to learn the truth about oneself is called the _____ motive.**

   (a) appraisal (b) consistency (c) extrinsic (d) self-enhancement

Self and Information Processing

Anything That Touches the Self...

Every day people process a great deal of information about their social worlds, and the self often exerts influence over how this information gets processed. For one thing, the self serves as a sign of importance: Anything that bears on the self is more likely to be important than things that do not touch the self. As a result, any link to the self makes the mind pay more attention and think more thoroughly.

One of the earliest and most basic effects of the self on information processing is the **self-reference effect**. Information bearing on the self is processed more thoroughly and more deeply, and hence remembered better, than other information. In the initial studies of this effect,[97] participants simply saw a series of words and were asked a question about each word. Sometimes these questions had nothing to do with the self, such as "Is this a long word?" and "Is it a meaningful word?" Other times, however, the question was "Does this word describe you?" Later on, the researchers gave a surprise test to the participants, asking them to remember as many words on the list as they could. The rate of correct memory depended heavily on which question had been asked, and the questions about the self elicited the best memory (see **FIGURE 3.6**). For example, participants were more likely to remember the word *friendly* if they had been asked whether they were friendly than whether *friendly* was a meaningful word or whether it was a long word.[98,99,100,101,102]

The implication was that simply thinking about a word in connection with the self led to better memory. In fact, even if participants answered "No" to the question about whether the word described them, they still remembered the word better than other words. The self apparently operates like a powerful hook, and whatever gets hung on it (even just for a moment) is more likely to be preserved.

A similar pattern has been called the **endowment effect**. Items gain in value to the person who owns them.[103] If someone asks you how much you would pay for a souvenir mug, you might offer three dollars. If someone gives you the mug and then someone

self-reference effect the finding that information bearing on the self is processed more thoroughly and more deeply, and hence remembered better, than other information

endowment effect the finding that items gain in value to the person who owns them

else wants to buy it from you, however, you might find yourself asking for four or five dollars. Somehow the mug became worth more to you during the time you owned it, even if that time was only a few minutes, and you did not have any special experiences with it that might confer sentimental value. Simply being connected to the self gave it more value. Nor does this work only with cash value: People start to like things more when they own them.[104]

Likewise, things gain in value to the self who chooses them. In one famous demonstration, people either were given a lottery ticket or chose one for themselves. Both tickets had identical chances of winning, and therefore objectively they had the same value. But when the researchers asked participants how much they would sell the ticket for, the price of the self-chosen tickets was consistently higher than the price of the randomly given tickets.[105] Somehow the process of choosing the ticket oneself made it seem more valuable to the person who chose it.

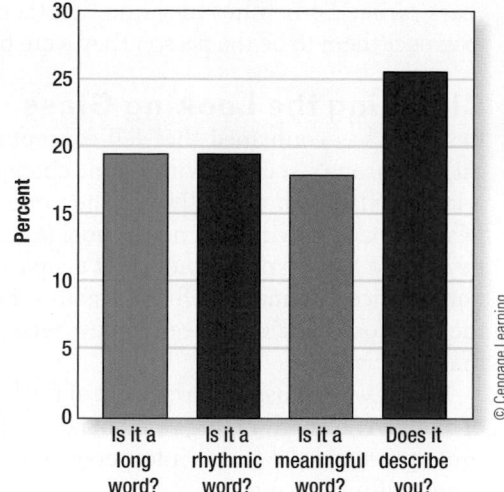

© Cengage Learning

FIGURE 3.6

The self-reference effect refers to the finding that information related to the self (e.g., Does it describe you?) is more memorable than information related to something besides the self (e.g., Is it a long word?).

Can the Self-Concept Change?

People usually believe that they have remained the same person over much of their lives. Your identity certainly changes, but it does so slowly. You have the same social security number, linked to the same tax status. Your name remains the same (even if you decide to change your last name when you marry, your first name is unaffected). You belong to the same family, though you may gradually add new members to this family (such as by marrying or having a baby). Once you start your career, you tend to stay in the same occupation for most of your life, and until recently it was common to spend one's entire career working for the same organization. Your gender remains the same in most cases, and you inhabit the same body for your entire life.

People do change, however. Children add new knowledge and skills as they grow up. Adults may take up new hobbies or break bad habits. Your body is continuous, but it changes too, first growing taller and stronger, then often growing fatter and less flexible, and finally developing wrinkles, shrinking, and acquiring other signs of old age.

Revising Self-Knowledge

When do people change so much that they also revise their self-concept? There are several plausible theories. One is that you can simply decide to change how you think about yourself, and your actions will come around to reflect the new you.[106,107] Another is the reverse: You can decide to change your behavior, and a change in self-concept will follow (see the material on cognitive dissonance in Chapter 7). Both are plausible, but neither gets at the full story.

The evidence suggests that one's social world is a powerful source of stability in the self. Other people expect you to remain pretty much the same. In part, this arises because people see other people in terms of stable traits, even though they do not see themselves that way.[108] Seeing other people in terms of their personality traits reflects the assumption that people mostly remain the same over long periods of time, and indeed there is some evidence that in many respects personality traits do remain fairly stable over long stretches, even from childhood into adulthood.[109,110,111,112]

The expectation that people stay the same can become a kind of pressure to remain constant. Many students notice this when they return home after a year or two at a university, especially if they have not stayed in regular contact with everyone back home. They feel that their parents still treat them and regard them the way they were years earlier. Sometimes they find that their old friends from high school likewise seem to expect them to be the person they were back in high school.

Changing the Looking Glass

Research has confirmed that self-concept change is most common, and possibly easiest, when one's social environment changes.[113] For example, self-esteem tends to stay relatively stable when one lives in the same social circle, and changes in self-esteem tend to accompany moving to a new school (especially going from high school to college) or a new home. One explanation is that people change gradually, but their social circle tends not to notice this and therefore pressures them to stay the same. When the person moves, the new social circle can see the new version of the person that has emerged from these gradual changes.

Earlier we discussed the concept of the looking-glass self. You know yourself by means of others. Hence, changing your social circle is a promising way to change the self. Again, inner processes are tied to interpersonal relations, so when the social circle changes, the inner self may change too.

A similar conclusion emerged from studies on brainwashing. The techniques of brainwashing first attracted research attention during the Korean War, when Chinese communists sought to change the views of captured American soldiers. The Chinese had no grand theory about how to brainwash Americans, so they just experimented with different methods. At first they tried exposing the prisoners to all-day sessions of propaganda and indoctrination, telling them how great communism was and how bad American capitalism was. This did not work very well. Then the Chinese realized that the problem was not in what happened during the day. Rather, the problem was that every night the prisoners were sent back to the barracks with the other American prisoners, where each man's American identity reasserted itself. The Chinese found that brainwashing became much more successful and effective if they kept the prisoners separate from each other. That way, the American identity and American values were not bolstered by social contacts with other Americans, and the prisoners became much more malleable.[114]

These findings about self-concept change support the view that what goes on inside the person is mainly there to serve interpersonal processes. Many people assume that the inner self is fixed, strong, and stable, and that what they do with other people is simply an expression of an inner "true" self. But that view appears to be mistaken. The important and powerful forces originate in the interactions and relationships between people, and what goes on inside the individual adapts to those interpersonal processes. This is yet another instance of our theme that inner processes serve interpersonal functions.

Promoting Change

When people want to change, therefore, it is helpful to use the social environment rather than fight against it. When people seek to change some aspect of themselves, such as trying to quit smoking or become more physically fit, they do best if they enlist the support of other people in their lives. It is hard to quit smoking if your spouse smokes and wants you to smoke with him or her. In contrast, if your spouse wants you to quit smoking, he or she will probably support your efforts to change, and your chances of success are improved.[115]

Indeed, one effective strategy for change is to persuade everyone else that you have changed. Once they expect you to act in a new and different way, you are more likely to stick to that new line of behavior. Thinking of yourself in the different way is not enough; it is more important and more powerful to get others to think of you in that way. (This also confirms our theme of putting people first: You use other people to help you to change.) In one experiment, people were induced to think of themselves in a new way, either introverted or extraverted. This was accomplished by asking people loaded questions (e.g., "What do you dislike about loud parties?"[116]). Some participants in the experiment answered these questions when sitting alone in a room, talking to a tape recorder, with a guarantee that their responses would be confidential and anonymous. These participants showed no sign of self-concept change. In contrast, other participants answered the same questions by speaking face to face with another person. These participants did change, not only in how they later saw themselves but even in how introverted or extraverted they acted with a new, different person.[117,118] The interpersonal context was necessary for changing the inner self.

Thus, one route to self-concept change involves internalizing your recent behavior. First you act in a certain way, and then gradually you come to think of yourself as being the kind of person who acts that way. Other people play a crucial role as well; acting that way by yourself, in secret, does not seem to produce much effect on the self-concept. In contrast, getting others to see you as that kind of person is helpful toward making you believe that you are that kind of person. Again, self and identity require social validation, a theme to which we will return later in the chapter in the section on self-presentation.

New Self, New Story

Once the self-concept has changed, people tend to revise their stories about their lives to fit the new version. For example, the preacher Pat Robertson published an autobiography, in which he mentioned that God had instructed him to stay away from politics. Later, Robertson decided to run for president. A new, updated version of his autobiography appeared, conveniently omitting the earlier message from God about keeping out of politics. The new version said that God wanted Robertson to run for office.

Such revisions of memory have been studied by social psychologists.[119] They have concluded that most of the time people want to believe they remain the same, but sometimes they also want to believe that they have changed, and they shuffle and edit the facts in their memory to fit whichever belief is more relevant. Thus, if people change their attitudes, they may forget what they used to believe, so that they think the new attitude does not reflect a change—rather, they say, "I thought so all along." In contrast, if they want to believe they have changed when they haven't, they may retroactively distort how they used to be. In one memorable demonstration, researchers looked at study skills enhancement programs at universities, which are designed to teach students how to study better. Most universities have such programs, but objective evidence suggests that they do not really accomplish much in the way of making people into better students or enabling them to get better grades. Students who take these programs, however, want to believe that they have improved. They persuade themselves that the program has worked by revising their memory of how bad they were before.[120] For example, if a student's study skills rated a 5 out of 10 before the program, and the program accomplished nothing, the student would rate a 5 after it as well—but she might tell herself afterward that she really had been "more like a 3" before the program, so she can believe that she really did improve.

A vivid demonstration of how memory distorts the facts to fit the self-concept involved a study of women's menstrual periods.[121] An initial survey revealed that some women thought their periods were generally quite unpleasant, whereas others thought theirs were mild and innocuous. The researchers asked the women to record their feelings and sensations on a daily basis through a couple of periods. After a month or more, the women were asked to rate how bad those periods had been. By comparing the daily ratings with the retrospective (a month later) ratings, the researchers could see how memory was distorted. Each woman's beliefs about her general reactions biased her recall. That is, the women who thought their periods were generally bad tended to recall the periods as having been worse than they had said at the time. Conversely, the women who thought their periods were generally not so bad recalled their periods as milder than they had rated them when they were occurring. We constantly revise our memories based on beliefs we hold about ourselves.

Preacher Pat Robertson experienced a self-concept change. Initially he felt that God wanted him to stay out of politics, but later he became extensively involved in politics and even campaigned for president of the United States.

1. The finding that we recall information better when it is relevant to the self is called the _____ .

- (a) distinctiveness effect
- (b) hindsight bias
- (c) self-importance bias
- (d) self-reference effect

2. When she visited San Francisco, Letitia bought several handcrafted necklaces for $10 each. When she got home, her sister offered to buy one for $10, but Letitia refused. She wanted $15 for it instead. This example illustrates the _____ effect.

- (a) distinctiveness
- (b) endowment
- (c) intrinsic
- (d) overjustification

3. During the Korean War, the Chinese found it easier to brainwash American; prisoners when _____ .

- (a) the prisoners were kept together
- (b) the prisoners were kept separate
- (c) they used one long brainwashing session
- (d) they used several short brainwashing sessions

4. When a bad event happens to a person, if it is extremely unpleasant, people remember it as being _____ , and if it was mildly unpleasant, people remember it as being _____ .

- (a) better than it was; better than it was
- (b) better than it was; worse than it was
- (c) worse than it was; better than it was
- (d) worse than it was; worse than it was

answers: see pg 111

Self-Esteem, Self-Deception, and Positive Illusions

Self-Esteem

Self-esteem refers to how favorably someone evaluates himself or herself. People with high self-esteem hold very favorable views, which usually means they consider themselves to be competent, likable, attractive, and morally good people. In principle, low self-esteem would be the opposite; that is, you might think that people with low self-esteem would regard themselves as incompetent, ugly, unlikable, and morally wicked. In practice, however, few people regard themselves in such strongly negative terms. A more common form of low self-esteem is simply the absence of strong positive views about the self. Thus, the person with high self-esteem says, "I am great," but the person with low self-esteem says, "I am so-so" rather than "I am terrible."

People with high self-esteem are not hard to understand. They think they have good traits, and they want others to share that view; they are willing to take chances and try new things because they think they will succeed. People with low self-esteem are the greater puzzle. What do they want, and what is it like to be one of them? There have been many different theories and assumptions about low self-esteem, but research is converging to show which of them are correct. Here are some of the main conclusions about people with low self-esteem:

- They do not want to fail. (This is contrary to some early theories, including those based on consistency, which assumed that people with low self-esteem would seek to confirm their bad impressions of themselves.) Indeed, people with low self-esteem have the same goals and strivings that people with high self-esteem have, such as to be successful and to get others to like them. The difference is mainly that people with low self-esteem are less confident that they can achieve these positive goals.[122]

- Their ideas about themselves are conflicted and uncertain, a pattern called "self-concept confusion." When asked questions about themselves, people with low self-esteem are more likely than other people to say they do not know or are not sure;

self-esteem how favorably someone evaluates himself or herself

more likely to give contradictory answers, such as being both "calm" and "nervous"; and more likely to describe themselves differently on different days.[123]

- They focus on self-protection instead of self-enhancement. (**Self-protection** means trying to avoid loss of esteem.) People with low self-esteem go through life looking to avoid failure, embarrassment, rejection, and other misfortunes, even if this means not taking chances or pursuing opportunities.[124]

- They are more prone to emotional highs and lows. Events affect them more strongly than other people, and so they are more vulnerable to mood swings and other emotional overreactions.[125]

In recent decades, many psychologists have turned their attention to self-esteem, both as a research area and as a practical enterprise. The practitioners' focus is on how to increase self-esteem. They believe that low self-esteem lies at the root of many social and psychological problems and that American society as a whole can benefit from widespread efforts to boost nearly everyone's self-esteem.[126]

College students today greatly value self-esteem and love to receive self-esteem boosts such as compliments. Recent research suggests that college students would rather receive a boost to their self-esteem than eat their favorite food, drink their favorite alcoholic beverage, see their best friend, get their paycheck, or engage in their favorite sexual activity.[127] In addition, college students value self-esteem boosts more than older American adults do.[128]

Is the United States really suffering from an epidemic of low self-esteem? Evidence since the 1970s suggests otherwise; in fact, average self-esteem scores have been rising.[129,130] If anything, self-esteem in the United States is unrealistically high.

One of the first illustrations came in a simple little survey that asked people to rate their driving ability as above average, average, or below average. Almost all (90%) of the people said they were above average.[131] Statistically, one would expect only about half the people to be above average (and about half below it, of course). This finding of 90% above average was at first regarded as a strange and isolated curiosity, but soon similar results began to accumulate from other studies. In a large survey of a million high school students, only 2% said they were below average in leadership ability (70% said they were above average). Even more strikingly, not one student in a million claimed to be below average in the ability to get along with others, whereas 25% claimed to be in the top 1%![132,133]

What about particular groups, such as women and African Americans, who are sometimes thought to suffer from low self-esteem? In fact, their self-esteem is often pretty healthy too, despite various alarmist claims that it is low. Women's self-esteem is only slightly below that of men's.[134] The difference is largest during adolescence, and it seems to be large not because the self-esteem of adolescent girls is especially low but because many teenage boys are very egotistical. Women and girls tend to be critical of their bodies, whereas boys and men think their bodies are just fine, and this discrepancy probably accounts for most if not all of the gender difference in self-esteem. (There is no sign that women regard themselves as less intelligent than men, for example, or less able to get along with others.) Meanwhile, African Americans actually have somewhat higher self-esteem than other Americans, though again the difference is not very large.[135,136,137] Their high self-esteem makes African Americans somewhat unusual because other minority groups average lower than European Americans in self-esteem.[138] Still, no group really scores very low in self-esteem; the differences are just a matter of whether the group regards itself as significantly above average, or closer to average.

Perhaps the most remarkable evidence of such bias was recently produced in an international study of prison inmates. People who have been convicted of a crime and sent to jail should know they are below average, at least in terms of being morally good people, right? But even these inmates rated themselves above average on a host of moral and prosocial traits.[139] They considered themselves as relatively high on kindness, honesty, trustworthiness, compassion, and self-control—both relative to other prisoners and even relative to other members of the community. The inmates rated themselves as more law-abiding than other prisoners—and although they stopped short of claiming to be more

JASON REED/Reuters/Landov

Compliments don't cost any money but are highly valued because they boost one's self-esteem. Recent research shows that college students would rather receive a boost to their self-esteem than eat their favorite food, drink their favorite alcoholic beverage, see their best friend, get their paycheck, or engage in their favorite sexual activity. In addition, college students value self-esteem boosts more than do older American adults.[274,275]

self-protection trying to avoid loss of esteem

law-abiding than the average person in the community outside the prison, they rated themselves as being about the same. The researchers thought that might be the most remarkable finding: Prisoners consider themselves to be just as law-abiding as people who aren't in prison!

Reality and Illusion

The preceding section focused on self-esteem, which entails how well a person thinks or feels about self. Whether those feelings are accurate is another matter. Are self-concepts accurate, or filled with illusion?

In the 1960s, clinical psychologists noticed that depression is linked to low self-esteem and began to theorize that depressed people have a distorted perception of the world. They began studying the cognitive strategies of depressed people to see how those distortions arose.[140,141,142,143,144,145] For example, do depressed people ignore their own successes and good traits, while exaggerating their faults and failures? Some researchers began to conduct careful studies on how depressed people perceived and interpreted events.

These studies eventually produced a very surprising result. Depressed people don't seem to distort things very much; rather, normal (nondepressed) people are the ones who distort.[146] Depressed people seem to be pretty equal in taking the blame for failure and the credit for success, whereas normal people reject blame for failure while claiming plenty of credit for success. Depressed people are pretty accurate about estimating how much control they have over events, whereas normal people overestimate control.[147] Depressed people are pretty accurate at guessing who likes them and who doesn't, whereas normal people overestimate how favorably other people regard them.[148] Instead of trying to understand how depressed people have learned to distort their thinking in a bad way, it seemed imperative to learn how normal people distort their thinking in a positive way. Somehow depressed people—unlike happy, healthy people—simply fail to put a positive spin on the events in their lives.

In 1988, social psychologists Shelley Taylor and Jonathon Brown provided an influential summary of the ways in which well-adjusted, mentally healthy people distort their perception of events. They listed three "positive illusions" that characterize the thought processes of these normal people.[149]

- People overestimate their good qualities (and underestimate their faults). Normal people think they are smarter, more attractive, more likable, more virtuous, easier to get along with, and in other ways better than they actually are. This explains the "above average effect" already noted, by which most people claim to be better than the average person.

- People overestimate their perceived control over events. Normal people tend to think they are largely in control of events in their lives and that what happens to them is generally the result of their own actions. They believe they have the power to make their lives better and to prevent many misfortunes and problems from occurring.

- People are unrealistically optimistic. They think their own personal chances of getting a good job, having a gifted child, acquiring a great deal of money, and experiencing other positive events are better than the chances of the average person like themselves. Conversely, they think their chances of being unemployed, getting a divorce, having a child with a disability, losing a lot of money, being severely injured in an accident, and experiencing other misfortunes are lower than the average person's chances. Each person tends to see his or her own future as somewhat brighter than other people's.

Don't people get into trouble because of these illusions? You might think that these illusions would create a broad overconfidence that could cause people to make poor decisions, such as overcommitting themselves, taking foolish chances, or investing money unwisely. They may sometimes have that effect, but apparently people have a remarkable capacity to set their illusions aside and be realistic when they have to make a decision. People have a special mind-set that goes with making choices.[150,151] Once the decision is made, people then go right back to their optimistic and confident outlook.

Positive illusions flourish partly because of wishful thinking, also called self-deception. The next section will consider some ways people manage this.

How People Fool Themselves

How do people sustain these positive illusions? Don't everyday experiences burst their bubble and force them to face reality? Someone who believes falsely that he is a genius at math might sign up for an advanced math class, for example, and getting a D would seemingly dispel any such illusions of mathematical brilliance. The fact that people seem able to keep these positive illusions intact for long periods of time has prompted social psychologists to examine **self-deception strategies** the mental tricks people use to help them believe things that are false. Normally, of course, these are false beliefs that the person wants to be true.

If people's self-concepts were more affected by their failures than by their successes, then most people would probably consider themselves below average! But we have seen that the opposite is true. Self-deception is a pattern of cognitive tricks and strategies that people use to dismiss or diminish the impact of failures and other kinds of bad feedback. The power of bad feedback can be offset by these mental tricks as long as people use them in a biased fashion, so that successes and good feedback are accepted while failures and criticism are questioned, discredited, and forgotten.

One self-deception strategy is called the **self-serving bias**.[152,153,154] This is a common method of interpreting events (and hence an important part of attribution theory—a broad attempt to explain how people interpret all sorts of social events and outcomes—to be discussed in Chapter 5). Essentially, the person claims credit for success but denies blame for failure. Getting a good grade on a test, for example, is taken as a sign that "I'm really smart and good at this." Getting a bad grade is more likely to be chalked up to external factors, such as not having had a good night's sleep, not having studied the right things, or bad luck. (Also recall the *Tradeoffs* section on self-handicapping, which is a strategy to ensure that the self gets credit for success but no blame for failure.)

A related strategy is to be more skeptical and critical of bad feedback than good feedback. In several studies, researchers had students take a test and then told them at random that they had done either very well or very poorly on the test. Even though they had taken exactly the same test, the people who were told they had done well rated the test as fair and effective, but the people who were told they had done badly thought the test was unfair and poorly designed.[155,156,157] Such tactics enable people to avoid having to revise their self-concepts in light of failure, enabling them to keep their positive illusions intact.

The basic mental processes of attention and memory can also help by being selective. Many people end up remembering good things better than bad things, partly because they spend more time thinking about them and mentally replaying them.[158,159,160,161] Although occasionally failures or criticism stick in one's mind, people usually try not to dwell on them, whereas they enjoy reliving their triumphs and great moments. Selectively focusing on good things can help counteract the power of bad things.

Another strategy makes use of the fact that good and bad are usually relative, as our earlier discussion of social comparison showed. Being able to run a mile in 7 minutes, for example, is neither good nor bad in itself; the evaluation depends on whom you are comparing yourself against. Compared to the speed of expert runners, a 7-minute mile is pathetically slow, but compared to flatfooted couch-potato accountants it is probably terrific. People can turn this to their advantage by choosing their comparison group carefully. People give the most attention to those who are just slightly worse than themselves, because those comparisons make them feel good.[162,163,164] The Japanese have an expression: "Others' misfortunes taste like honey."

Ollvy/Shutterstock.com

If nobody else can do this, I must be pretty special.

self-deception strategies mental tricks people use to help them believe things that are false

self-serving bias a pattern in which people claim credit for success but deny blame for failure

In a similar vein, people skew their impressions of other people so as to convince themselves that their good traits are unusual whereas their faults are commonly found in many other people.[165,166,167] For example, if you are musically talented but have trouble meeting deadlines, you may find yourself thinking that musical talent is rare but procrastination (putting things off, being late, missing deadlines) is common. That makes your fault seem minimal, whereas your good quality makes you special. People are especially inclined to engage in such distortions regarding traits that are central to their self-concepts, and people with high self-esteem are more prone to these distortions than people with low self-esteem. (Probably their high self-esteem is partly sustained by these tricks.)

Yet another strategy relies on the fact that many definitions of good traits are slippery, so people can choose a definition that makes them look good.[168,169,170,171] Most people want to be a good romantic partner, for example, but what exactly defines a good romantic partner? One person can think she is a good romantic partner because she is thoughtful, another can think the same because he is a good listener, and others might think they qualify because they are funny, or easy to get along with, or good in bed, or trustworthy, or able to control their temper. Such shifting criteria may help explain how everyone can regard himself or herself as above average.

Benefits of Self-Esteem

In recent decades, American society has devoted plenty of effort to boosting self-esteem, especially among schoolchildren and other groups considered to need a boost. This was based on the hope that many benefits would flow from high self-esteem. Would high self-esteem cause people to do better in school? Do you have to love yourself before you can love someone else? Will high self-esteem prevent prejudice, violence, drug addiction, and other ills?

Many results have been disappointing. People with high self-esteem do report that they are smarter, are more successful, have more friends, enjoy better relationships, and are better-looking than other people, but objective measures say they aren't. Often high self-esteem amounts to nothing more than a false belief that one is a terrific, superior person. For example, several studies have shown that people with high self-esteem claim to be especially intelligent, but on an actual IQ test they are no smarter than people with low self-esteem.[172] Likewise, they say they are better-looking than other people, but when researchers get people to judge how good-looking people are from photos, the people with high self-esteem get no higher ratings than anyone else.[173,174,175,176] They think they are better-looking, but no one else can tell the difference.

Students with high self-esteem do have slightly higher grades than people with low self-esteem, but high self-esteem does not lead to good grades.[177,178,179,180,181,182,183,184,185,186] If anything, it is the other way around: Getting good grades and doing well in school lead to high self-esteem. As we saw in Chapter 1, the fact that there is a correlation makes it hard to tell what causes what. Self-esteem and good grades are correlated (though weakly), but studies that track people across time have indicated that self-esteem is the result rather than the cause of the good grades. Also, other factors, such as coming from a good family, contribute to both the high self-esteem and the good grades.

In terms of getting along with others, people with high self-esteem believe that they make a great impression on others and are well liked, but in fact there is no difference in how other people evaluate them.[187,188,189,190,191,192,193,194,195] If anything, sometimes people with high self-esteem are obnoxious and turn people off by thinking they are superior.[196,197]

Sexual activity is another important interpersonal process. To learn how it is related to self-esteem, read *The Social Side of Sex*.

High self-esteem has two main benefits.[198] The first is initiative. High self-esteem fosters confidence that you can do the right thing and should act on your best judgment. People with high self-esteem are more willing than other people to speak up in groups or committees. They are more willing to approach people and strike up new friendships. They are more willing to go against other people's advice and do what they think is best. They resist influence better. They are also more adventurous when it comes to experimenting with sex, drugs, and other activities. This is sadly contrary to the goals of researchers and therapists who hoped that high self-esteem would enable young persons to resist such temptations.

Self-Esteem and Saying No to Sex

Is there a link between self-esteem and sexual activity? Researchers have multiple reasons for suggesting that there might be. For one thing, people with low self-esteem have been found to be more vulnerable to social influence than people with high self-esteem, a pattern that social psychologists began to uncover in the 1950s.[199,200,201] This led many experts to hope that increasing self-esteem among young people would enable them to resist peer pressures to participate in sex at a young age. In particular, they thought that girls with low self-esteem might be talked into sex before they were ready.

However, the evidence does not show that high self-esteem helps youngsters resist having sex. In one large and well-designed study, self-esteem was measured among more than 1,000 children at age 11; 10 years later, they were asked whether they had engaged in sexual intercourse by the age of 15. Among the boys, there was no relationship between self-esteem and early sex. Among the girls, there was a relationship—but in the opposite direction from what had been predicted. Girls with higher self-esteem at age 11 were more likely (rather than less likely) than others to have had sex by the age of 15.[202] Other studies have failed to find any relationship at all, however.[203,204]

Most people in our society consider children age 15 or younger to be too young to be having sex, and research suggests that most people begin having sex in their late teen years. People who remain virgins until around the age of 20 are therefore of interest. Is there any link between self-esteem and virginity? The answer is yes, but the link differs by gender.

For many women, apparently, virginity is a positive status, and they may take pride in it. Among men, however, virginity has less of a positive aspect, and many male virgins feel ashamed of their virginity. They may feel that they have failed to appeal to women. This is especially true if the men reach an age where they believe most of their peers are having sex and have regular girlfriends. Hence, there is some link between virginity and low self-esteem in men but not in women.[205,206]

For both genders, but especially for women, decisions about whether to have sex are complicated by the potential for pregnancy. Fear of getting pregnant has historically been an important factor holding women back from sexual activity. In this regard, however, high self-esteem seems to be a risk factor because women with high self-esteem tend to downplay or ignore risks. High self-esteem is often marked by a sense of being special or better than others, and it contributes to a feeling that "bad things will not happen to me." In one study, women wrote down a list of their sexual activities, including whether they took precautions against pregnancy. Then they rated their chances of having an unwanted pregnancy. Women with high self-esteem had essentially the same sex lives and took the same chances as women with low self-esteem, but those with high self-esteem regarded themselves as safer.[207] The researchers concluded that high self-esteem causes women to underestimate the dangers of sex.

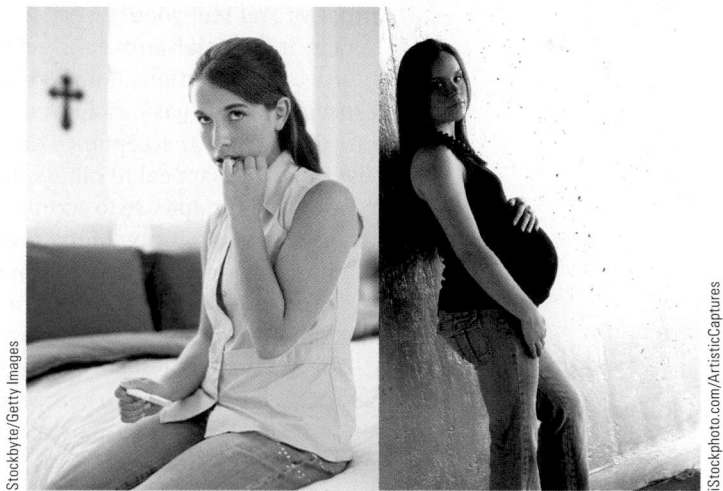

Stockbyte/Getty Images

iStockphoto.com/ArtisticCaptures

High self-esteem is thought to solve many social ills, but it frequently does not. For example, boosting self-esteem does not prevent unplanned pregnancy.

The second advantage of high self-esteem is that it feels good. High self-esteem operates like a stock of good feelings that the person can draw on. When life dumps misfortune on your head, such as when you experience failure or trauma, you can bounce back better if you have high self-esteem, because this is a resource that helps you overcome the bad feelings. People with low self-esteem lack this resource, and therefore misfortune hits them harder. If they don't succeed on the first attempt, people with high self-esteem are willing to try again harder, whereas people with low self-esteem are more likely to give up. Most broadly, people with high self-esteem are happier than people with low self-esteem.[208]

© Cengage Learning

FIGURE 3.7

A gas gauge doesn't make the car go, but it tells you how much fuel you have. When gas gauges indicate that fuel is low, people fill up their gas tanks. According to sociometer theory, self-esteem is like a gauge that tells you how much social approval you have. When self-esteem is low, people try to "fill up" using self-esteem boosts.

A recent study that tracked nearly 2,000 people over a decade confirmed this view of the limited advantages of high self-esteem.[209] Self-esteem produced emotional benefits: People with higher self-esteem at the start of the study later had more positive emotions, were less likely to become depressed, and were more satisfied with their jobs and relationships than other people. But it had no effect at all on objective outcomes, especially career success.

Initiative and good feelings are certainly positive benefits, though they are far less than many self-esteem researchers had hoped. Self-esteem is not the solution to a broad range of psychological and social problems, but it does at least help in those regards.

Why Do We Care?

People are often quite motivated to protect and increase their self-esteem. Indeed, we shall see that many patterns of thinking and acting that social psychologists have demonstrated are based on the desire to maintain one's self-esteem. But why? The preceding section indicated that high self-esteem does not really confer a great many advantages in an objective sense. Why do people care so much about self-esteem if all it does is boost initiative and feel good?

One influential answer is relevant to this book's theme that inner processes serve interpersonal relations. Maybe thinking well of yourself doesn't really matter very much (especially by the basic biological outcome criteria of improving survival or reproduction), but gaining social acceptance does. In this view, self-esteem is essentially a measure of how much you appeal to others. It is noteworthy that self-esteem is mainly based on the reasons that groups use to accept or reject possible members: attractiveness, competence, likability, and morality. Many groups and people avoid and reject people who are unattractive, incompetent, disliked, or dishonest or otherwise immoral. Research has shown that increases in self-esteem come from increases in social acceptance, whereas rejection can sometimes threaten or lower your self-esteem.[210,211]

This view of self-esteem as linked to social acceptance has been called sociometer theory. A **sociometer** (made from the words *social* and *meter*) is a measure of how desirable one would be to other people as a relationship partner, team member, employee, colleague, or in some other way. In this sense, self-esteem is a sociometer because it measures the traits you have according to how much they qualify you for social acceptance. Sociometer theory can explain why people are so concerned with self-esteem: It helps people navigate the long road to social acceptance. Mark Leary, the author of sociometer theory, compares self-esteem to the gas gauge on a car. A gas gauge may seem trivial because it doesn't make the car go forward. But the gas gauge tells you about something that is important—namely, whether there is enough fuel in the car. Just as drivers act out of concern to keep their gas gauge above zero (see **FIGURE 3.7**), so people seem constantly to act so as to preserve their self-esteem.

Sociometer theory is not the only possible explanation for why people might care about self-esteem. Another, simpler theory is that self-esteem feels good (as noted in the previous section), and because people want to feel good, they want to maintain their self-esteem. A more complex variation on that theory invokes the theory of terror management, which holds that fear of death is at the root of all human striving. Terror management theorists assert that having high self-esteem helps shield people from fear of death, so people seek out self-esteem as a way of avoiding a recognition that they are going to die.[212] Another common view is that self-esteem is based mainly on feeling competent rather than on social acceptance. However, recent evidence suggests that feeling accepted has a bigger impact on self-esteem than does feeling competent (though both matter).[213]

sociometer a measure of how desirable one would be to other people

Is High Self-Esteem Always Good?

Focusing mainly on the benefits of high self-esteem might create the impression that high self-esteem is always a good thing. Alas, the benefits of high self-esteem may be balanced by drawbacks, as is the case with many tradeoffs.

The negative aspects of high self-esteem may be especially apparent in the form of narcissism, a trait that is linked to high self-esteem but that captures its worst aspects. The trait of narcissism is based on the Greek myth of Narcissus, a young man who fell in love with his own reflection in the water and did nothing but stare at it until he died. In psychology, **narcissism** refers to excessive self-love and a selfish orientation. Narcissists think very well of themselves and, as a result, are willing to take advantage of others. Among American college students, levels of narcissism have been increasing over time,[214] though some experts dispute the numbers.[215] This self-centered generation has been dubbed "Generation Me."[216]

A clever test of the idea that self-concepts are changing used lyrics from popular songs. The team of researchers[217] took the most popular American songs from the Billboard Hot 100 year-end list for every year from 1980 to 2007. They ran the lyrics for all these songs (totaling almost 90,000 words!) through a computer program that sorted and counted. As the years went by, the songs contained more and more first-person singular pronouns (e.g., *I, me, my*) and fewer and fewer first-person plural words (*we, our*). Words relating to social interactions (like *talking* and *share*) decreased, as did words expressing positive emotions. In contrast, angry and antisocial words, including swear words, increased over these decades. Altogether, these results suggest that what made songs popular in recent decades has been an increase in focus on the self and on angry, antisocial attitudes, while positive emotion and interpersonal connection have lost their appeal in popular music. These results fit well with the evidence that narcissism has increased.

Narcissism is not the same as high self-esteem, but the two are related. Probably the simplest way to understand the link is to think of narcissism as a subset of high self-esteem. That is, nearly all narcissists have high self-esteem, but many people have high self-esteem without being narcissists. To be sure, there has been some controversy about the self-esteem of narcissists. They often act superior to other people and seem to think they deserve to be treated better than others, but clinical psychologists used to think (and some still think) that this egotistical behavior is a disguise that conceals secret feelings of insecurity and low self-esteem. However, research has not been very successful at finding that narcissists really have low self-esteem; indeed, narcissists seem to be confident if not downright conceited through and through. The only area in which they do not seem to rate themselves especially high concerns getting other people to like them, which narcissists are relatively indifferent about. Admiration is more important to them than liking, and they want and expect others to admire them.[218]

Narcissists tend to be more aggressive and violent than other people, especially when they suffer a blow to their egos.[219,220,221] The self-esteem movement had hoped that raising self-esteem would reduce aggression, but there is no sign that that works.

The trait of narcissism is based on the Greek myth of Narcissus, a young man who fell in love with his own reflection in the water. As illustrated in the painting, narcissists are in love with themselves.

narcissism excessive self-love and a selfish orientation

High self-esteem (and not just narcissism) is also associated with higher prejudice.[222,223] People who think well of themselves also tend to think their group is better than other groups, and they discriminate more heavily than other people in favor of their own group.

Narcissists make poor relationship partners in many respects.[224,225,226,227,228] Narcissists typically approach relationships with the attitude "What's in it for me?" and hence do not really try to build a lasting intimacy with another person. They try to associate with glamorous people because they think these others will make them seem glamorous too. They adopt a "game-playing" approach to relationships that helps them maintain power and autonomy without giving much of themselves to the other person. They are also prone to infidelity; if a seemingly more desirable partner comes along, the narcissist will not have many qualms about dumping his or her current partner and hooking up with the new one. More broadly, narcissists are not as loyal to their partners as other people. They are prone to take advantage of their partners when they get the chance. Narcissists often think they deserve someone better, so even if they have a good relationship they may still keep an eye out in case a more attractive or desirable partner comes along. Loving someone who loves himself (or herself) is no picnic because he will readily dump you in favor of someone else.[229]

As we can see, most of the drawbacks of high self-esteem pertain to the person's relations with others. In tradeoff terms, high self-esteem has both costs and benefits, but they are not distributed fairly. The benefits of someone's high self-esteem mostly go to the person himself or herself, whereas the costs of someone's high self-esteem mostly fall on other people.

The previous section noted that people with high self-esteem have more initiative than those with low self-esteem. In general, initiative may be a good thing, but it certainly can contribute to antisocial actions as well. Research on bullies, for example, began with the old idea that bullies secretly suffer from low self-esteem, but this proved false. The most careful studies have found that bullies have high self-esteem, as do the people who help bullies by joining in to torment their victims, but people who stand up to bullies and resist them, including coming to the aid of victims, also have high self-esteem.[230,231] This pattern captures both sides of initiative. People who think well of themselves have more initiative and use it either for bad purposes (bullying others) or for good ones (resisting bullies and protecting victims). Low self-esteem was found mainly among the victims; in fact, the victim role is often a passive one, defined by the absence of initiative.

Persistence in the face of failure also takes initiative (and possibly some resource of good feelings to help overcome discouragement—remember that good feelings were the other benefit of high self-esteem). Many studies have found that people with high self-esteem are more likely than those with low self-esteem to keep trying despite an initial failure.[232,233] In general, we assume that this is a good thing because the chances of eventual success are greater if you keep trying than if you give up. Then again, some endeavors are truly hopeless, lost causes, and continuing to try simply means greater failure. Think of a football coach who keeps calling for a play that never works because the other team knows how to defend against it, or an investor who keeps putting money into a stock that keeps losing, or a scientist who keeps trying to prove a theory that is truly wrong. People with high self-esteem are prone to make that kind of error too. Their persistence in the face of failure can be either a good or a bad thing.[234,235,236,237] In general, though, people with high self-esteem do seem to manage these situations better and make better use of information about when to persist as opposed to when to move on and try something else.[238,239]

Pursuing Self-Esteem

Many people actively pursue self-esteem. Typically they choose some sphere or dimension (such as schoolwork, popularity, or sports) as important to them, invest themselves in it, and try to succeed at it.

Although most people in our culture pursue self-esteem, they go about it in different ways. People who already have high self-esteem pursue it by seeking to dominate others and to increase their competence at valued abilities. People with low self-esteem pursue it by seeking acceptance and validation from others, and especially by trying to avoid failures.[240]

There is increasing evidence that pursuing self-esteem as an end in itself can have harmful consequences.[241] Pursuing self-esteem can compromise the pursuit of competence, as when people choose easy tasks so they can be sure of succeeding. It impairs autonomy because seekers of self-esteem often do whatever others will approve rather than what they themselves might want to do. The pursuit of self-esteem creates feelings of pressure to live up to others' expectations, and therefore it weakens people's intrinsic motivation (their interest in doing something for its own sake). It impairs learning because when self-esteem is on the line people react to setbacks or criticism as threatening events rather than as helpful feedback. It can damage relationships because self-esteem seekers compete against their relationship partners and thereby sometimes undermine intimacy and mutuality. They may also withdraw from partners who are too successful because they feel that they are losing in comparison.[242] Last, the pursuit of self-esteem can be harmful to health, both because it increases stress and because it can lead to unhealthy coping behaviors, such as drinking and smoking, to deal with bad feelings associated with having one's self-esteem on the line.

When people stake their self-esteem on succeeding in some domain, then failure in that domain produces strong negative reactions, including increased anxiety and other negative emotions, as well as drops in self-esteem. If anything, the drops that go with such failures are bigger than the increases that come from success.[243]

1. A person's overall self-evaluation or sense of self-worth constitutes his or her _____ .

   (a)   (b)   (c)   (d)

possible self   self-awareness   self-efficacy   self-esteem

2. Depressed people _____ how favorably other people regard them, whereas normal people _____ how favorably other people regard them.

   (a)   (b)   (c)   (d)

estimate accurately; overestimate   estimate accurately; underestimate   underestimate; estimate accurately   underestimate; overestimate

3. Which of the following is a positive illusion that people hold?

   (a)   (b)   (c)   (d)

People overestimate their strengths and underestimate their faults.   People overestimate their perceived control over events.   People are unrealistically optimistic.   All of the above.

4. When Frank does well on a test, he claims responsibility for the success, but when he does poorly on a test, he denies responsibility and blames his professor for writing a difficult test with ambiguous items. This is an example of _____ .

   (a)   (b)   (c)   (d)

a positive illusion   the overjustification effect   the self-reference effect   the self-serving bias

QUIZ YOURSELF

Self-Esteem, Self-Deception, and Positive Illusions

answers: see pg 111

Self-Presentation

Self-esteem, or egotism, is a common explanation for behavior. Supposedly people do many things—work hard, get in a fight, compete, show off, enjoy compliments, and more—to bolster or protect their self-esteem. Yet why would people care so much about self-esteem? Why would the human psyche be designed to try to prove itself better than other people? Cultural animals do need to care, and care very much, about what *other* people think of them. Could it be that much of what is commonly regarded as egotism, as trying to think well of oneself, is at heart a concern with how others think of you?

The comedian Billy Crystal said, "It is more important to look good than to feel good!" This statement captures the essence of self-presentation.

Undeniably, people do want to think well of themselves. The self-deception strategies we listed earlier generally work so as to enable people to hold favorable views of themselves. (Actually, though, the line between fooling others and fooling yourself turns out to be much fuzzier than one might think. A recent theory proposed that self-deception mainly evolved to enable people to deceive others—because you can be more convincing in arguing your case if you believe it than if you do not.)[244] Although people do want to preserve their self-esteem, on closer inspection it often turns out that they are most concerned with having *other people* view them favorably.[245,246,247] It's fine to like yourself, but what matters more is whether other people like you. In fact, if nobody else likes you, it is difficult to like yourself!

Many research studies do not make much of a distinction between private self-esteem and public esteem, but those who do distinguish them often find that the concern with public esteem is greater. As the comedian Billy Crystal used to say, "It is more important to look good than to feel good!"

This chapter opened with the story of Count Zrínyi, who wanted very much to make a good impression on whoever was going to kill him. Clearly feeling good wasn't his goal because he would be dead. Looking good still mattered.

Probably the concern with looking good to others arises from the basic facts of human nature. Human beings achieve their biological goals of survival and reproduction by means of belonging to social and cultural groups. Getting other people to like you or respect you is very helpful for getting into these groups and staying there. We have said that one theme of human life is the long road to social acceptance. A big part of this road is making good impressions on other people and keeping a good reputation. That is what self-presentation is all about.

Self-presentation is defined as any behavior that seeks to convey some image of self or some information about the self to other people. Any behavior that is intended (even unconsciously) to make an impression on others is included. Self-presentation thus encompasses a wide range of actions, from explicit statements about the self (e.g., "I forgive but I don't forget"), to how you dress or what car you drive, to making excuses or threats, to trying to hide your fear or anger so that other people will think you are cool.

In recent years, social networking Internet sites such as Facebook have emerged as a new medium for self-presentation. People create a site for themselves that presents them as they wish to be seen. A recent study of Facebook and other such networking sites found that most college students participate, but some do not. The nonusers are often disdainful of the time and energy that others invest, and some objected to what they considered phony self-presentations. One woman scornfully told the researchers that someone she knew had listed favorite bands and movies that were chosen simply to make him look cool, as opposed to genuine liking. (She said she had known him for 10 years and he had never mentioned these ostensible favorites!) Users and nonusers of Facebook were similar in many respects, including how much they used the Internet for practical purposes (e.g., buying things, getting information) but differed in how much they used it for expressing themselves (e.g., blogging, creating web pages). The urge to express oneself is thus one reason people use Facebook.[248]

The urge to express oneself is genuine. For example, advice to people on how to act on romantic dates often emphasizes getting the other person to talk about himself or herself. Recent studies have confirmed this wisdom: People like to talk about themselves and feel good when they do.[249] Brain regions associated with pleasure and reward become more active when someone talks about himself or herself, as opposed to talking about other people. Indeed, participants chose to answer questions about themselves even when they could have earned slightly higher amounts of money answering different (i.e., non-self) questions.

Who's Looking?

A great many behavior patterns studied by social psychologists turn out to depend on self-presentation. Researchers have demonstrated this by comparing how people behave in public conditions, when others are present and one's behavior is identified, with private

self-presentation any behavior that seeks to convey some image of self or some information about the self to other people

behavior, when one's actions will remain secret and confidential. If you mainly care about self-esteem, your behavior will be the same regardless of whether someone else is watching. But if you are concerned about what others think (i.e., you are concerned with or motivated by self-presentation), then you will act differently when you are alone than when others are there.

For example, in Chapter 7 you will see that people often change their attitudes to be consistent with their behavior, especially if they have done something out of the ordinary or contrary to their usual beliefs. This pattern occurs mainly when other people are watching; it is much weaker if the behavior is done privately.[250,251] Likewise, when people receive evaluations of their personality or their work, these evaluations have much more impact if they are public (i.e., if other people know about them) than if they are private. Criticism received privately can easily be ignored or forgotten, whereas criticism that is heard by multiple other people must be dealt with. Even if you think the criticism is completely wrong, you cannot just dismiss it or ignore it if other people know about it. That criticism might cause other people to change their impression of you or treat you differently.[252,253,254]

Self-presentation creeps into many behaviors that might not at first seem to have an interpersonal aspect. For example, washing one's hands after using the restroom may seem like a simple matter of personal hygiene. But researchers who have secretly observed how people behave in public restrooms found that washing one's hands is affected by whether other people are watching. Women who used the toilet would usually wash their hands afterward if someone else was in the restroom, but if they believed themselves to be alone, they were more likely to skip washing.[255]

Ed Rode/Getty Images

In his song "Online," Brad Paisley sings about how much cooler he is online. For example, in the real world he works at a pizza joint, drives an old Hyundai, lives with his parents, and is short. Online, however, he is rich, drives a new Maserati, has a black belt in karate, and is tall, thin, and good-looking.

Dieting is also guided by self-presentation. Despite all the talk of how healthy it is to be slim and fit, the strongest motive to lose weight is to make oneself attractive to others. As one expert researcher commented, "No one would diet on a deserted island!"[256]

Even people with severe mental illnesses such as schizophrenia are well attuned to the importance of self-presentation. In a famous study,[257] inmates at a mental hospital were told to report to the head psychiatrist for an interview. On the way, by random assignment, they were told one of two purposes for the interview. Some were told that the purpose of the interview was to evaluate them for possible release from the hospital. You might think that mental patients would be anxious to be released into the outside world, but in fact many have anxieties and fears about that and prefer their safe, structured life in the mental hospital. When the interview began, these patients presented themselves as having serious problems and difficulties, presumably so that the psychiatrist would abandon any plan to release them into the world.

Other patients were told that the purpose of the interview was to decide whether to move them to a locked ward, where more dangerous patients were kept, and where consequently there were fewer comforts and freedoms. These patients presented themselves in the interview as being relatively sane and normal, so as to discourage any thoughts of moving them to the locked ward. Thus, the level of psychopathology (craziness, to put it crudely) displayed by mental patients is at least partly self-presentation. It goes up and down in order to make the desired impression.

When social psychologists first began to recognize the importance of self-presentation, they regarded it as a form of hypocrisy—acting or pretending to be something other than what one is, possibly for bad reasons such as to manipulate others or to feed one's egotism. However, the field gradually recognized that making a good impression and keeping a good reputation constitute a basic and important aspect of human social life. It is not limited to a few phony or hypocritical individuals who seek to convey false impressions. Rather, nearly everyone strives for a good self-presentation as a way of obtaining social acceptance.[258,259] Through self-presentation, people can increase their chances of being accepted by others and can claim a valued identity within the social system, thereby enabling them to maintain their place in the group.

Making an Impression

What makes for a good self-presentation? In many ways, the answers are obvious: One has to show oneself to have good traits and not bad ones. Presenting oneself as competent, friendly, honest, kind, loyal, strong, warm, helpful, and so on, makes for a good self-presentation.[260] The main problem with defining what makes a good self-presentation arises when the values of the self-presenter and the audience diverge. Then the self-presenter faces a tradeoff between being true to his or her own values and making a good impression on the interaction partner (also called the audience). What the person does depends on a variety of factors, including the importance of one's relationship to the audience and the importance of the issue to the self.

It is perhaps not surprising that people often present themselves along the lines favored by their audience. After all, people want to be liked, and conforming to others' values and expectations is a common strategy for achieving that. What is more surprising is that sometimes people deliberately present themselves in ways that they know their audience will not approve. This isn't the same as being more concerned with private reality than public appearance. For example, if Jason really didn't care what others thought, he wouldn't bother telling them he disagreed with them. But sometimes people deliberately make others see them in ways that the others don't approve.

If people are playing to the audience but not giving the audience what it wants, they must have some other motive for how they present themselves. This clues us in to a second important function of self-presentation: claiming identity.

A dramatic single instance of refusing to present oneself in a way the audience would approve occurred in the library at Columbine High School on the terrible day that two students brought guns and began shooting their fellow students. Cassie Bernall was in the library during the shootings, on her knees praying out loud. One of the gunmen asked if anyone there believed in God. Witnesses said that Cassie Bernall told him, "Yes, I believe in God." He shot her to death.[261] Although some details of the story are disputed, it does seem that there was pressure on her to deny her religious faith, which she resisted at the cost of her life. Throughout history, many individuals have been pressured to renounce or reject their faith, and many have died for refusing to give the answers that others wanted to hear. Notice, again, that if she really didn't care about how other people saw her, she could easily have lied and denied her faith. She insisted on making a public statement of what she believed in, and that got her killed.

During the Columbine High School massacre in Colorado, Cassie Bernall was asked by one of the shooters whether she believed in God. She said "yes," and he shot her. She presented herself in a way that the killers didn't like, and she paid with her life.

What kinds of impression are these people trying to make, using their clothing?

Claiming Identity

People aspire to many identities. A person may wish to be recognized as an artist, a talented athlete, an honest businessperson, a defender of certain values. In general, it is not enough simply to persuade yourself that you hold such an identity. Rather, the claims require social validation: Other people must come to perceive you as holding that identity. In an important sense, you cannot be a great artist, or a sports star, or a brilliant student if you are the only one who believes that you are. It becomes necessary to persuade others to see you in that light. Obtaining social validation for your identity claims is the grander task of self-presentation.

People do use self-presentation to advance their claims to identity. In some studies, participants were made to feel either secure or insecure about their claims. For example, among participants who aspired to become expert guitarists, some were told that their personality profiles differed markedly from those of expert guitarists, which conveyed the message that the participant was not on his or her way to becoming one of those experts.[262] Others were told that they fit the profile precisely, which made them feel as if they were doing well on their project of becoming an expert guitarist. They were then asked whether they would like to give guitar lessons to beginners, and if so how many. The people who had been made to feel insecure about their claims to becoming expert guitarists wanted to teach many more lessons than the people who were told they were already looking like expert guitarists. The insecure ones wanted to bolster their claims to being a guitarist by teaching guitar to others because these others would view them as good guitarists.[263]

People will change their behavior to claim identity. A recent study surveyed citizens shortly before an election. Some were asked about the importance of voting. Others were asked about the importance of "being a voter." This subtle difference in phrasing produced a big difference. The ones who thought about the idea in identity terms ("being a voter") went on to vote at higher rates than those who just thought about voting.[264]

Sometimes, the goal of claiming an identity can motivate a person to engage in self-presentation in a way the audience will not like. This is why people sometimes end up arguing about politics, rather than simply agreeing with what the other person says. They identify with their own political views strongly enough that they would rather stand up for what they believe in than make a good, congenial impression on someone who holds different values. The story about Cassie Bernall and religious faith is another example of this.

Of course, what counts as a good impression changes with the times. In recent years, being environmentally conscious has come to be valued by many people. Recent studies show that people favor "green" products, which may be more expensive and lower quality than other goods, when they want to make a good impression.[265] They buy such things when they are thinking about their status in other people's eyes, and especially when they are shopping in public—but not when they are shopping privately (e.g., on the Internet).

Tradeoff: Favorability Versus Plausibility

By and large, people seek to make good impressions, and so they present themselves favorably. A favorable or self-enhancing way of describing oneself prevails in most social psychology studies.[266] Naturally, people do not go to extremes of claiming to be superstars or geniuses, but they tend to present themselves in the best possible light, within the range of what is plausible. One authority on self-presentation has described this as a tradeoff between favorability and plausibility. In plain terms, people present themselves as favorably as they think they can get away with! They may claim to be smart and attractive, but if they think other people will find out that their claims are exaggerated, then they tone down those claims.[267,268] This tendency toward favorable self-presentations dovetails well with the "automatic egotism" described earlier in this chapter: People automatically tend to furnish a very positive image of themselves, unless circumstances dictate otherwise.[269]

What About Modesty?

The tendency toward favorable self-presentation seems well designed to help people make a good first impression on other people. Not surprisingly, it is less needed and hence less common within established relationships. When people are among friends, they often stop boasting or presenting themselves in the best possible light. If anything, modesty seems more natural and common among friends, and it may even be the default or automatic response.[270] One reason for this is that your friends are probably familiar with your faults and failures. If you claim to be better than you are, they may be quick to point out that you are twisting the facts.

Possibly a deeper reason for the prevalence of modesty within long-term relationships and friendships is that it helps people get along better. Most religions have embraced humility as a virtue and regarded pride as either a sin or an obstacle to salvation. One purported secular goal of religion is to promote group harmony, and people probably can get along with humble, modest individuals better than they get along with puffed-up, conceited narcissists. Groups often must divide up resources that vary in quality, such as who gets the best piece of meat or who gets the better place to sleep. Humility and modesty make such divisions easier: "No, you choose." People who think highly of themselves are more likely to think that they deserve the best, and if a group has several such people, the argument can turn nasty.

Some researchers have found that self-enhancement is especially strong in individualistic cultures that place a high emphasis on individual achievement and merit. In contrast, collectivistic cultures that emphasize group harmony above individual rights are less oriented toward self-enhancement.[271] One team of experts has argued, for example, that the Japanese do not go around trying to prove their individual superiority over others; rather, they seek to improve themselves so as to become better members of their social group. If self-enhancement is found in such cultures, it often takes the form of trying to present oneself as a worthy member of the group or as belonging to a highly valued group.[272] Thus, though Japanese may not strive to prove themselves superior to other Japanese individually, many of them do believe that Japanese culture and people together are good and in many ways superior to others.

Self-Presentation and Risky Behavior

Self-presentation is so important to people that they will sometimes risk illness, injury, or even death in order to make a good impression.[273] Many people try to get a suntan because they believe it makes them look attractive and sexy, but sunbathing exposes the skin to dangerous radiation that can (and often does) cause skin cancer. Many young people smoke cigarettes in an effort to look cool, adult, and

Alan Oddie/PhotoEdit

Jessie Jean/Getty Images

Bill Bachmann/PhotoEdit

sophisticated in front of others. Likewise, adolescent drinking is often driven by the belief that drinkers are perceived as tougher, more adult-like, and more rebellious than nondrinkers. Some people fear that others will think badly of them if they purchase condoms or if they suggest using condoms, so they engage in unprotected sex, thereby risking sexually transmitted infections (including AIDS and unexpected pregnancy). Some people drive fast or refuse to wear seat belts in order to project an image of bravery. Others resist wearing helmets when riding bicycles or playing sports. One of your authors (Bushman) bought a bicycle in Amsterdam. The first thing the bike shop did was remove the safety reflectors from the spokes of the tires, and then threw them in the trash. When Bushman asked why, the bike salesperson said, "You don't want to be seen with these on your bike. That's not cool." (Bushman secretly removed the reflectors from the trash, and then put them back on the bike after he left the store. He thought his children needed their father's survival more than he needed to look cool!)

The fact that people will take such risks with their health in order to make a good impression on others indicates that, at some level, gaining social acceptance is felt as an even stronger and more urgent motive than the motivation to stay alive and healthy. Self-presentation can be stronger than self-preservation (as suggested by Billy Crystal's remark, quoted earlier, about looking good versus feeling good!). This is yet another sign that the human psyche is designed to gain and keep a place in a social group.

1. The comedian Billy Crystal used to say, "It is more important to look good than to feel good!" This concern with looking good to others is called _____ .
   - (a) self-awareness
   - (b) self-concept
   - (c) self-handicapping
   - (d) self-presentation

2. John is a young gang member who wants to look tough to his fellow gang members. This concern about looking tough is called _____ .
   - (a) self-awareness
   - (b) self-consciousness
   - (c) self-esteem
   - (d) self-presentation

3. Self-presentation concerns often influence people to engage in _____ actions than they would otherwise engage in.
   - (a) less conservative
   - (b) less risky
   - (c) more conservative
   - (d) more risky

4. People tend to furnish a very positive image of themselves, unless circumstances dictate otherwise. This tendency is called _____ .
   - (a) automatic egotism
   - (b) private self-awareness
   - (c) public self-presentation
   - (d) self-handicapping

answers: see pg 111

What Makes Us *Human*

Putting the Cultural Animal in Perspective

No other animal has a self that can begin to approach the human self in complexity and sophistication. Many of the features that make human beings special can be found in the self.

What is special about the human self begins with self-awareness and self-concept. Self-awareness is quite limited or absent in most other species; indeed, very few animals can even recognize themselves in a mirror. In contrast, people have a remarkable ability to be aware of themselves, to think about themselves, to imagine how others regard them, and to change themselves. Self-awareness has at least two crucial dimensions, public and private, and these are useful for different things. Private self-awareness is useful for evaluating oneself, especially toward goals of self-improvement and self-regulation. Public self-awareness is vital for the task of gaining social acceptance because it enables people to anticipate how others will perceive them.

In humans, self-awareness is more than the name implies (i.e., it is more than just paying attention to self). Self-awareness enables people to compare themselves to standards in a way that other animals cannot. They can evaluate whether they are conforming to cultural standards (such as morals and laws), personal standards (such as goals and ambitions), and many others. This ability makes it possible for people to strive to improve and to behave morally. It also produces some distinctively human problems, such as eating disorders and suicide. Regardless, standards are important. They reveal one theme

of this book: that human behavior is deeply shaped and guided by ideas. Many people deliberately try to become better people according to moral or cultural ideas. Nothing like it has been identified in any other species.

Self-awareness makes self-knowledge possible. Using language, people can express and remember many things about themselves. This process enables self-knowledge to become efficient, useful, and far-reaching. People develop elaborate theories about themselves. Turn on the television and watch any talk show: Even the most boring and shallow people seem to find endless things to say about themselves.

Know thyself! The quest for self-knowledge is another unique part of being human. Most people are eager to learn about themselves. The various motives for self-knowledge (self-enhancement, consistency, and appraisal) are centrally important among human beings but essentially unknown in other animals. Along with these motives go the concern with self-esteem and the cultivation of positive illusions. Self-deception may also be uniquely human. Some animals occasionally deceive each other, but as far as we can tell, only humans lie to themselves.

Another remarkable and distinctive feature of the human self is its ability to take and leave roles. Almost like a professional actor, the human self can take up a role, perform it well, and then stop and move into a different role that requires acting differently. The self can switch roles during the day as it moves from one situation to another (e.g., from office to home or to a bar with friends). The self can also make more lasting changes, such as when a person gets a promotion or a new job. This ability of the human self to change with changing roles, along the way changing how it thinks and behaves, is vital for cultural beings. Successful cultures are large social systems with many different roles. The human self probably evolved to be able to play different roles.

Intrinsic motivation is found in most animal species, but extrinsic motivation is more specific to humans. One common form of extrinsic motivation involves doing something for money, and of course only humans have money. Extrinsic motivation is important for culture because people will do things for the sake of cultural rewards (including money, prestige, status, and fame). These rewards are often vital for inducing people to do things that enable the culture to function properly. Few people have an intrinsic desire to collect garbage, pay taxes, or go to court, but many people do these things because of extrinsic motivation, and the culture operates more effectively when they do. Extrinsic rewards are the start of economic (money) relations because they motivate people to produce more than they need themselves so they can trade some to others and thus get other things they want.

Humans know the difference between inner states and outward appearances (though not all cultures may be as sensitive to this difference as modern, Western ones). People engage in self-presentation, sometimes to make the optimal impression on the audience and sometimes to cement their claims to a particular social identity, gaining validation from having other people accept them in that role. Sometimes people engage in deceptive self-presentation, trying to present themselves as better than they really are. In general, the desire to communicate information about oneself to others is an important aspect of human life.

In short, the self is something that humans know about and care about in ways that would be impossible for most other animals. Humans strive to learn about themselves, to change themselves to fit cultural and other standards, and to get others to regard them favorably. The self is a vital tool for gaining social acceptance and for participating in culture, in ways that only human beings do.

CHAPTER 3 SUMMARY

What Is the Self?

- The three main parts of the self are:
  - Self-knowledge or self-concept.
  - The interpersonal self or public self.
  - The agent or executive function.
- The main purposes of the self include gaining social acceptance and playing social roles.
- People from individualistic cultures understand the self as interdependent (connected to others in a web of social relations), whereas people from collectivist cultures lean toward an independent self-construal (seeing the self as a separate, special or unique, self-contained unit).
- Self-awareness is attention directed at the self, and usually involves evaluating the self.
- Private self-awareness refers to attending to one's inner states; public self-awareness means attending to how one is perceived by others.
- Self-awareness is often unpleasant because people often compare themselves to high standards.
- Being self-aware can make people behave better.
- Human self-awareness is far more extensive and complex than what is found in any other species.
- Self-awareness is vital for self-regulation and adopting others' perspectives.

Where Self-Knowledge Comes From

- The looking-glass self refers to the idea that we learn about ourselves from how others judge us.
- People often do not realize how their minds work.
- The overjustification effect is the tendency for intrinsic motivation to diminish for activities that have become associated with external rewards.
- The phenomenal self or the working self-concept is the part of self-knowledge that is currently active in the person's thoughts.
- Three motivations for wanting self-knowledge are the appraisal motive, the self-enhancement motive, and the consistency motive.
- Self-handicapping involves putting obstacles in the way of one's own performance, so that if one fails, the failure can be blamed on the obstacle, and if one succeeds, one looks especially competent.

Self and Information Processing

- The self-reference effect refers to the finding that information bearing on the self is processed more thoroughly and more deeply, and hence remembered better, than other information.

- Self-concept is likely to change to be consistent with the public self, and with what people want to believe about themselves.

Self-Esteem, Self-Deception, and Positive Illusions

- In many important respects, nondepressed people see the world in a distorted, biased fashion, whereas depressed people can see reality more accurately.
- The self-serving bias leads people to claim credit for success but deny blame for failure.
- People with high self-esteem think they are great, but most people with low self-esteem think they are only mediocre (rather than awful).
- People with low self-esteem do not want to fail, are uncertain about their self-knowledge, focus on self-protection rather than self-enhancement, and are prone to emotional highs and lows.
- Basking in reflected glory refers to people's tendency to want to associate with winners.
- High self-esteem feels good and fosters initiative but does not confer many advantages in an objective sense.
- The sociometer theory suggests that self-esteem is a measure of how socially acceptable you think you are.
- High self-esteem and narcissism are associated with some negative qualities that pertain to relations with others, such as prejudice and aggression.

- Pursuing self-esteem as an end in itself can have harmful consequences.

Self-Presentation

- Most people are more concerned with looking good to others than with private self-esteem.
- Self-presentation is any behavior that seeks to convey some image of self or some information about the self to other people, or that seeks to make an impression on others.
- Nearly everyone strives for a good self-presentation as a way of obtaining social acceptance.
- Self-presentation is so important to people that they sometimes engage in risky or dangerous behavior in order to make a good impression.

What Makes Us Human? Putting the Cultural Animal in Perspective

- What is special about the human self begins with self-awareness and self-concept.
- The self is a vital and distinctively human tool for gaining social acceptance and for participating in culture.

key terms

quiz yourself ANSWERS

1. What Is the Self? **p. 77**
   answers: 1.b   2.b   3.a   4.b

2. Where Self-Knowledge Comes From **p. 88**
   answers: 1.d   2.d   3.d   4.a

3. Self and Information Processing **p. 92**
   answers: 1.d   2.b   3.b   4.c

4. Self-Esteem, Self-Deception, and Positive Illusions **p. 101**
   answers: 1.d   2.a   3.d   4.d

5. Self-Presentation **p. 108**
   answers: 1.d   2.d   3.d   4.a

CHOICES AND ACTIONS
The Self in Control

4

LEARNING OBJECTIVES

1 Distinguish four patterns that influence the choices people make.

2 Analyze how a belief in free will affect behavior.

3 Summarize how a hierarchy of goals affects planning and reaching goals.

4 Explain the TOTE (Test-Operate-Test-Exit) loop.

5 Identify the two main pathways to self-destructive behavior.

Jakub Cejpek/Shutterstock.com

MONEY MATTERS
How Money Can Trick You Into Making Bad Decisions
117

THE SOCIAL SIDE OF SEX
Gender, Sex, and Decisions
119

FOOD FOR THOUGHT
Dieting as Self-Regulation
135

TRADEOFFS
Now Versus Tomorrow: Delay of Gratification
140

WHAT MAKES US HUMAN?
Putting the Cultural Animal in Perspective
143

Terrorists have long chosen airplanes as targets for their violent acts. One of the most dramatic was the destruction of Korean Airlines Flight 858 in 1987. Unlike many such events, this act of terror has been recounted in detail by the perpetrator, a young woman named Kim Hyun Hee, in her book *The Tears of My Soul*.[1]

Kim Hyun Hee grew up in North Korea, a totalitarian communist state where all information is tightly controlled by the government. She learned in school that her country (though in fact a starving nation and an international outcast) was the greatest country in the world and blessed with a godlike leader, Kim Il-Sung. By virtue of her hard work and her father's connections, she was able to attend the country's only major university, and her good record there earned her an invitation to become a special agent for the Korean foreign intelligence service.

One great day she was summoned to meet the director, who told her that she had been assigned to carry out a mission ordered by the Great Leader himself, the most important mission ever attempted by their organization and one that would decide North Korea's national destiny. He explained that she and a comrade would blow up a South Korean commercial airplane. This allegedly would cause the upcoming 1988 Olympics (scheduled for Seoul, South Korea) to be canceled, which in turn would lead to the unification of Korea under the communist government. She said she never understood how destroying a plane and killing some tourists would bring about the country's unification, but she did not question this, and she accepted it on faith. Being assigned such a historic mission was a great honor to her. The director explained that if she succeeded, she would become a national hero, and she and her family would benefit greatly.

At the time, she never thought about the moral issue of killing so many people. "The act of sabotage was a purely technical operation," she recalled later; her attention was focused on the concrete details, rather than guilt or compassion for her victims or even idealistic reflections on her nation's destiny. Airport security was much more casual back then. Her contacts met her at the airport and gave her the parts to the bomb, which she assembled while sitting on the toilet in the women's restroom. She boarded the plane and stowed the bomb (hidden in a briefcase) in the overhead compartment. At a stopover she got off the plane, leaving the bomb there. Later that day, she heard on the news that the plane had exploded, and she mainly felt relief that she had succeeded, plus some pride at having done her part for her country.

She was supposed to make her way home, but she was captured by police. She began to suffer some distress over what she had done. She thought about the happy tourists on the plane, flying home and then abruptly killed. She began to have nightmares, such as that her family members were on the plane and she was shouting at them to get off but they would not listen. For the first time, she was tormented day and night by overwhelming feelings of guilt. She confessed, was sentenced to death, and then was pardoned by the South Korean authorities.

This extraordinary story reveals several important themes about human action:

- Hee's behavior was guided by the values and systems of her culture: Blowing up an airplane was not her idea, but she accepted it and carried it out on faith that it would benefit her nation.

- She trusted that her leaders were good people and knew what they were doing, and she obeyed them without question. She did not notice the moral dilemma in advance and thought only of doing her duty.

- The plans were overly optimistic.

- By herself, she could have achieved very little, but she worked as part of a team.

- Her action followed carefully made plans, though she herself had to make minor adjustments during the mission.

- During the mission, she focused herself on the steps and details, never really questioning whether the project was a good idea in the first place. She focused on how, not why.

- Her nightmares focused on the panicky feeling of being unable to help her family escape.

- During the mission, she thought neither of moral issues nor of national destiny, instead focusing narrowly on the details; only afterward did she start to be troubled with guilt.

- Her behavior was directed toward several goals at different levels; whether you label it a success or a failure depends on which goal you invoke. The mission was a success on its own terms, insofar as the

Kim Hyun Hee, former terrorist and author of *The Tears of My Soul*.

airplane was destroyed and the passengers killed; Hee's capture was the only part that didn't go according to plan. Yet in the broader context, it was a total failure. The 1988 Olympics were held in South Korea as scheduled, and of course the grand goal of uniting the two Koreas under communist rule was not achieved. From the perspective of fulfilling the national destiny, she killed all those people for nothing.

The episode was largely self-defeating her, insofar as she ended up in prison and (temporarily) sentenced to death. But she did not intend to bring herself to that negative outcome. Instead, she was pursuing highly favorable goals both for herself and her country. Her quest for good backfired.

This chapter focuses on making choices and acting on them. The human self—who and what you are—is defined by the choices you make, but the self is also there precisely to help make choices. Indeed, probably the brain itself evolved to help animals make the choices they faced, and the human brain is so large partly to enable humans to cope with all the complex and difficult choices people have. In this chapter we look at how people make choices and why they sometimes make stupid or destructive ones. ●

What You Do, and What It Means

It is possible to talk about animal behavior without asking what the acts or circumstances "mean" to the animal. Skinnerian behaviorism (an approach that emphasized learning from reward and punishment as the main cause of behavior and that dominated psychology in the 1950s and 1960s) did precisely that, with considerable success. Skinnerian behaviorism, however, failed to provide a satisfactory account of human behavior, precisely because of its failure to deal with meaning. As we saw in Chapter 2, human behavior is often guided by ideas, which is to say that it depends on meanings. A bear may go up the hill or not, but the bear's decision is not based on concepts or ideas such as laws, plans, religious duties, flexible schedules, or promises. In contrast, much of human behavior makes no sense if we fail to appreciate what it *means*.

Culture is a network of meaning, and human beings who live in culture act based on meaning; this is what makes them different from other animals. That doesn't imply the psychologists who studied animals were wasting their time. Many of the principles that apply to animal behavior also apply to human behavior. Humans are animals too. But to explain human behavior, one needs more, and one especially needs meaning.

The importance of ideas—what you do depends partly on what it means—reflects the broad theme that inner processes serve interpersonal functions. Meaning depends on language and is therefore learned only through culture. For example, some religions condemn eating beef, others condemn eating pork, others condemn eating all meat; these rules are all learned from the culture, and only humans (with our inner capacity for understanding meaning) can alter their eating habits based on such rules. To go hungry instead of eating forbidden food reflects another theme, of letting social conscience override selfish impulses.

Thinking enables people to make use of meaning. Many psychologists study thinking for its own sake. Thinking probably evolved to help creatures make better choices for guiding their behavior (though this cannot be proven at present). William James, the father of American psychology, once wrote that "thinking is for doing,"[2] and modern social psychologists have shared that view.[3] The only serious alternative is that conscious thinking is for communicating (e.g., talking)[4]—but much communicating ultimately contributes to doing also. One of the most basic uses of thought is to perform actions mentally before doing them physically. You can imagine yourself running a race, or asking someone for a date, or giving a talk in front of an audience, and these imaginary exercises seem to pave the way for really doing them.

How well does it work? As people imagine something, it becomes more plausible and likely to them.[5,6,7,8,9,10] Salespeople make use of this process: Imagine yourself owning this car, they say, and the more you imagine it, the more likely you are to buy it.

B. F. Skinner and his box. But what does it mean to you?

Nina Leen/Time Life Pictures/Getty Images

In one carefully controlled study, some students were told to imagine themselves studying hard for an upcoming exam and doing well on it. These people got significantly higher grades than any other group—an average of 10 points better than the control group. (The control group just kept track of how much they studied without imagining any part of the future.) The ones who imagined themselves studying hard in fact did study longer and harder, which no doubt helped them achieve those high grades. In a different condition, students imagined having done well on the exam, including a vivid scene of looking at the posted grades, following the line across from their number to see a high score, and walking away with a big smile. These people did only slightly (2 points) better than the control group.[11] Apparently just imagining a good outcome isn't as effective as imagining yourself doing all the hard work to produce the success. But all in all, imagination has the power to help make things come true.

Making Choices

Human life is filled with choices. A trip to the grocery store would be a mind-numbing experience if you really confronted all the possible choices, and every year there seem to be more choices to make. One researcher noted that the average American supermarket in 1976 carried 9,000 different products, whereas 15 years later that figure had risen to 30,000![12] Similar patterns can be found everywhere: more television channels, more hairstyles, more churches and religious denominations, more ways to invest your money, more kinds of blue jeans. The progress of culture seems to offer people more and more choices, which must be desirable because people seem to want more choices. But how do they make them?

Two Steps of Choosing

Social psychologists have uncovered several key features of the process of choosing. It helps to recognize that most people handle choosing in two steps.[13] The first step involves whittling the full range of choices down to a limited few. Out of the many dozens of possible cars you might buy (or of the millions of people you might marry!), you discard most of them and zero in on a few options. This step can be done rather quickly. It entails some risk that a potentially good choice will be rejected without careful consideration, but it is the only way that the human mind can deal with a large set of possible choices.

The second step involves more careful comparison of the highlighted options. Once the list of possible cars is down to four or five, you can test-drive them all and look at relevant information about each one. Most research focuses on this second step of decision making because typically researchers study how someone chooses among a few major options, instead of focusing on how someone reduces a large set of choices down to a few. The prevailing assumption is that people perform some sort of mental cost–benefit analysis for each option, looking at the potential good and bad sides, and then add these up and pick the option that comes out best. Although this would seem to be the most rational thing to do, people are often less than fully rational, and their decisions are subject to biases, errors, and other influences. See *Money Matters* to learn about one reason that people make bad decisions.

Influences on Choice

Some of the major patterns that guide people's choices follow:

1. **Risk aversion.** People are more affected by possible losses than by possible gains. In a simple demonstration, participants were asked whether they would take a perfectly fair bet on a coin flip, such that they would win or lose $10. Most people didn't want to bet, presumably because the prospect of losing $10 outweighs the prospect of winning the same amount, even though the odds are exactly equal.[17,18]

   Another study looked at rational versus irrational (foolish) bets. Rational bets conform to what expert statistical risk appraisal would dictate. (For example, a 50% chance to win $20 is better than a 1% chance of winning $100. You evaluate the bet by multiplying the probability times the outcome: $1/2 \times \$20 = \$10$, whereas $1/100 \times \$100 = \$1$.) Researchers found that people were often rational, but when they were not, their irrational behavior was geared toward avoiding losses more often than

risk aversion in decision making, the greater weight given to possible losses than possible gains

MONEY *Matters*

How Money Can Trick You Into Making Bad Decisions

Suppose you have two job offers. One pays $50,000 per year and seems like it would be reasonably relaxed. The other will be stressful but pays better, at $63,000. Which do you choose?

Or suppose that after you get your job you are choosing between two apartments. They are about the same size and quality. One costs more but would enable you to walk to work. The cheaper one would require you to drive about half an hour each way. Which do you choose?

Many people would make these choices based on money—but this would make them less happy in the long run.[14] This is *not* because money is irrelevant to happiness. Having more money is better! But there is a particular illusion that is created by the numerical value of money.

Look again at the differences between the options in these examples. The money difference is quantitative: a matter of degree. The other difference is qualitative: Some feature (e.g., walking to work) is present or absent. People tend to overestimate the impact of quantitative differences on happiness, relative to qualitative differences.

The reason for this is rooted in the difference between how one thinks while deciding versus how one experiences life. When you are deciding, you compare the two options (such as the two apartments). You think about them both at the same time. But once you live in one of them, you cease to think about the other one, by and large. The fact that you saved a certain amount of money by renting the cheaper apartment will vanish from your daily awareness. But whether you can walk to work or must drive half an hour in rush-hour traffic will affect you nearly every day. Even though you stop comparing it to what your life would have been like in the other option, that feature remains to intrude on your daily experience.

The difference between comparing multiple options and experiencing a single one was shown in a different way in another study. Participants considered two different ways of resolving a dispute with a neighbor. In one solution, the participant received $600 and the neighbor received $800. In the other solution, the participant and the neighbor each got $500. When participants had both options to compare, they preferred the first one, because it gave them more money ($600 vs. $500). When participants predicted their reaction to only one of the options (i.e., some participants considered only the first solution, and others considered only the second solution), the first solution received fewer favorable ratings than the second because they got less than the neighbor ($600 vs. $800).[15]

In another study, participants imagined shopping for a music dictionary in a used bookstore and were supposed to say how much they would be willing to pay, from $10 to $50. Some saw descriptions of two dictionaries, whereas others only saw a description of one dictionary. One dictionary had 10,000 entries and was in perfect condition. The other had 20,000 entries and was in perfect condition except for a torn cover. When comparing the two, people were willing to pay more for the one with the torn cover (because it had so much more information). Among participants who saw only one option, however, the torn cover reduced what people were willing to pay because they were not able to appreciate the difference in amount of information between 10,000 versus 20,000 entries.[16]

Thus, when choosing between options, people tend to focus on quantitative differences. But after you have made your choice, you live with what you chose, and the option you did not choose is probably gone from your life. Remember to focus on what you will live with, not just what scores higher on paper when you compare.

Here's the job offer, you'll make $10,000 a month, and work in a relaxed environment with friendly people.

LATER... *Here's the offer: $10,000.50 a month in a stressed environment filled with miserable people and mountains of paperwork.*

Holy cow! That's like, 50 cents more than the previous job offer! I'll take it!

SURRENDER HOPE

The winner of the largest lottery prize in Illinois history, chose to get one "lump sum"—$178 million—rather than $265 million over an extended period of time.

pursuing gains.[19] That is, people seemed more worried about losing than they were attracted by the possibility of winning.

2. **Temporal discounting.** A second influence is that what happens right now weighs more heavily than what might happen in the future. Would you rather have $1,000 today, or $1,200 two weeks from today? The logical choice would be the delayed one because there is very little chance that you could invest the money wisely enough to turn $1,000 into $1,200 in two weeks, so if you take the delayed reward, you will end up with more money. Most people, however, choose the immediate reward. For example, people who buy lottery tickets often choose the single check (immediate) payment option, which means they get all the money at once if they win (sometimes called a "lump sum")—even though they might get more total money if they accept the winnings in more and smaller check amounts.

The discounting of the future can be seen in many contexts beyond money. For one such example that mixes sex and money, see *The Social Side of Sex*.

3. **The certainty effect.** Some features of a decision involve possibilities and odds, whereas others are certain. In buying a car, the likelihood that it will need repairs at a certain cost or frequency or that it will safeguard you in a collision are examples of things that might or might not happen, whereas you can be sure of the color and style you are getting. People tend to place undue weight on things that are certain. This is not to say that they completely ignore safety or repair records and just buy cars based on color, but they do end up relying on color a little more than they mean to do. This tendency to place too much emphasis on definite outcomes is called the **certainty effect.**[20]

For example, suppose you are playing Russian roulette. (A gun has some bullets in it while some of the chambers are empty, and when you play the game you point it at your head and pull the trigger once.) How much would you pay to remove one bullet, assuming either that (a) there are four bullets in the six chambers and two empties, or (b) there is only one bullet and five empties? Reducing the number of bullets from four to three is exactly the same improvement in your chances of surviving the game as is reducing it from one to zero, but most people say they would pay substantially more to eliminate the only bullet. This shows the certainty effect: They want to know they are completely safe. Such processes complicate many decisions about environmental and safety regulations because complete and perfect safety is quite difficult to achieve, yet people might prefer to focus laws and expenditures on trying to reduce risks from 1% to 0% rather than other interventions that might reduce risk from, say, 8% to 4%. Reducing risk from 8% to 4% will save many more people (four times as many) than reducing risk from 1% to 0%.

4. **Keeping options open.** Some people prefer to postpone hard decisions and keep their options open as long as possible. In one study of online shoppers, some were offered a selection of bargains that were only available right away, whereas others had the additional option of coming back later to choose among the same options and bargains. Those who had to buy right away often did so. Those who could put off the decision generally decided to wait, indicating a preference for keeping one's options available

temporal discounting in decision making, the greater weight given to the present over the future

certainty effect in decision making, the greater weight given to definite outcomes than to probabilities

Gender, Sex, and Decisions

Someone of your preferred gender smiles at you and seems to be flirting a bit. There might be a chance to have sex later today. Then again, perhaps the person is just being friendly, and by making romantic or sexual advances you might end up embarrassing yourself and damaging the relationship. Do you make the advances?

The data suggest that the answer may depend on your gender. Men seem much more likely than women to chase after every potential (or even sometimes illusory) chance for sex. The reason for this difference may lie in the fact that evolution has prepared men and women to use different guidelines for making sexual decisions.

One general explanation, called **error management theory**,[21] is that both men and women make decisions so as to minimize the most costly type of error, but men's worst error is not the same as women's. The difference is rooted in a long evolutionary history, during which most males failed to reproduce at all, whereas most females did reproduce. Hence for females the goal is to get the best possible mate, and having sex too readily can defeat that goal. For a woman, to be on the safe side is to say no to sex a little longer, if only to make sure that her partner provides further proof that he is a good man and is devoted to her (and perhaps to make sure no one better is available). In contrast, many male animals will have few or no opportunities to reproduce at all, and so in order to pass along their genes they should take advantage of every chance. It would be folly to pass up a chance for sex today if that opportunity might not be available tomorrow.

These differences are increased by the differences in what the body does to make a baby. If a woman gets pregnant by one man today, and a better partner comes along next week, her body is already committed to the (less attractive) pregnancy, so again it behooves her to wait until she is certain she has the best mate. In contrast, if a man makes one woman pregnant today and then a better partner comes along tomorrow, he is physically capable of impregnating her as well.

A recent study of temporal discounting showed how these sexual impulses can influence even decisions that do not, on the surface, have anything to do with sex. Heterosexual participants in this study had to make choices between sooner smaller rewards (e.g., $5 tomorrow) and larger later ones (e.g., $10 a month from now). After they had made one round of choices, they were exposed to one of four types of stimuli. Some saw 12 pictures of attractive members of the opposite sex. Others saw 12 photos of relatively unattractive members of the opposite sex. Others saw 12 beautiful cars, and a final group saw 12 relatively ugly cars. Then they chose again between sooner smaller and larger later rewards. Only one group showed a substantial shift toward the sooner smaller rewards: men who had looked at the beautiful women. The men in the other three conditions, and the women in all conditions, were relatively unaffected.[22]

Why? Again, evolution has selected men to leap at every mating chance. Apparently the sight of a pretty woman puts men into a mind-set that emphasizes the present and discounts or ignores the future. A pretty woman can induce a man to spend much of his money right away, even at considerable cost to his future financial circumstances. She doesn't even have to try very hard. This study suggests that simply seeing her is enough to cause the man to forget about long-term financial prudence and focus on the here and now.

For Charlie, there was no mistaking the signs... she TOTALLY wanted to have sex with him!

Paula Wright 2012

© Paula Wright 2012

until later. Unfortunately for the sellers, the customers who decided to postpone the decision hardly ever returned to make a purchase. It is hardly surprising that many salespeople make offers that expire immediately.

For some students, keeping a double major is a way of postponing a decision about their future. A double major requires students to divide their time and efforts, so they cannot be as successful at either subject as a single-major student would be, but some people pay this price in order to preserve their options.[23]

Why People Don't Choose

Postponing decisions may be part of a broader pattern called decision avoidance. A review article titled "The Psychology of Doing Nothing"[24] considered different forms this avoidance can take. One, called the **status quo bias** is a simple preference to keep

error management theory the idea that both men and women seek to minimize the most costly type of error, but that men's and women's goals, and hence worst errors, differ

status quo bias the preference to keep things the way they are rather than change

Noel Hendrickson/Blend Images/Corbis

What type of yogurt should I get? There are too many to choose from. I guess I won't get any.

things the way they are instead of changing. Would you want to exchange your home, your romantic partner, your course schedule, for another? The new one is unknown and might have unforeseen problems. People often stick with what they have, even when the alternatives might be better.

Another pattern that leads to doing nothing, called the **omission bias** is taking whatever course of action does not require you to do anything (also called the default option). For example, when you complete a free registration to gain access to a website, often you must mark a particular box if you do not want to receive junk mail and advertisements. Why don't they leave it blank and let you just check it if you want to receive those mailings and ads? Because they want as many people as possible on their mailing list, and they know that many people will not do anything. In principle, it is just as easy for them to make "don't send mail" the default option as to make it "send mail." The omission bias means that many people will do nothing—they will do whatever is the default option—so retailers will get more people on their mailing list by making the default option "send mail" rather than "don't send."

One general theme behind decision avoidance is anticipated regret.[25] People avoid making choices and taking actions that they fear they will regret later on. Apparently people anticipate less regret over doing nothing than over doing something. They also know the status quo better than the alternatives, so there is a greater risk of regret if you decide to change than if you stand pat.

Another theme is that some decisions become too difficult. An influential study showed that people who visited a table with a display of jams were less likely to buy any of them if the table had 24 different varieties than if it had just 6.[26] Some theorists have proposed that modern life offers too many choices.[27]

Subsequent work has not found that people always recoil from too many choices. People like to have many options. Across many different circumstances, there is no general pattern that having more options leads to more avoidance of decisions.[28] Sometimes having too few choices makes people reluctant to choose; for example, many people refuse to buy when they only see one option, even if it seems OK.[29] Hence, it is necessary to dig a bit deeper to see when this does or does not happen.

Basically, we fail to make a selection from a group of options, whether it is a matter of picking a spouse or a toothbrush or a car, for one of two reasons.[30] One is that none of the options seems good enough. The other is that it is hard to tell which one is the best. These two reasons have opposite relationships to the assortment of options. As the number of options increases, it is less and less plausible that none is good enough—but it gets harder and harder to be sure you've chosen the best one. You might test-drive two cars and decide that neither is good enough, but after you've tried two dozen cars, you should have found at least some satisfactory ones. But of course it's harder to pick the best of 24 than the better of 2.

Reactance

The interest in preserving options is the core of an important psychological theory that has held up well over several decades. Called **reactance theory**, it was first proposed by social psychologist Jack Brehm[31,32,33,34,35] and has much in common with the folk notion of "reverse psychology." The central point of reactance theory is that people desire to have freedom of choice and therefore have a negative, aversive reaction to having some of their choices or options taken away by other people or by external forces. The term *reactance* refers specifically to the negative feelings people have when their freedom is reduced. For example, if someone tells you that you cannot see a concert that you have been looking forward to, you will experience reactance, which is an angry, disappointed feeling.

Reactance produces three main consequences.[36] First, it makes you want the forbidden option more and/or makes it seem more attractive. (If you weren't sure you wanted to see

omission bias the tendency to take whatever course of action does not require you to do anything (also called the default option)

reactance theory the idea that people are distressed by loss of freedom or options and seek to reclaim or reassert them

the concert, being told that you can't see it may increase your desire to see it and make you think it is likely to be a really good one.) Second, reactance may make you take steps to try to reclaim the lost option, often described as "reasserting your freedom." (You may try to sneak into the concert after all.) Third, you may feel or act aggressively toward the person who has restricted your freedom.

Many studies have supported reactance theory.[37] Two-year-olds who are told not to play with a particular toy suddenly find that toy more appealing and are more likely to sneak over to it when they think no one is watching. Students who are told they can have their choice of five posters, but then are told that one of them (chosen at random, or even the one that was initially their third choice) is not available, suddenly like that one more and want it more. Labels designed to warn consumers about potentially objectionable material in TV programs, films, video games, and music often have the opposite effect of making people more interested in the "forbidden" media.[38] Most ominously, men who have formed unrealistic expectations of having sex with a particular woman may become angry and even coercive if the woman rejects their advances,[39] especially narcissistic men.[40]

The findings on reactance bring up the broader issues of free will and freedom of action. Regardless of whether someone believes in free will as a genuine phenomenon, one cannot dispute the fact that people are sensitive to how much freedom of choice they have. Reactance theory emphasizes that people are motivated to gain and preserve choices. Having some of their choices taken away by someone else or some external event produces a very negative reaction in most people.

Freedom to Change

Making choices is a major part of life. Animals make simple choices in simple ways, but human beings have a far more complex inner capacity for making choices—which is good because humans face very complex choices. Human choice is also much more momentous than what most animals do. Think of all the choices you make: What courses to take, whom to date and marry, whom to vote for, how to handle your money, what to do on a Sunday afternoon. Understanding choice and decision making is a vital part of any effort to understand human life.

The essence of the idea of freedom is that you can do more than one thing (hence the need to choose among them). This is relevant even to very basic questions such as whether you can choose to change yourself. Some people think their traits are constant and stable, so see little point in trying to change. Others think they can change. For example, some observers have noted that professional (baseball) athletes tend to have different attitudes in the United States and Japan.[41] In general, the American athletes think in terms of innate talent, and hence simply performing up to their ability, whereas the Japanese athletes think of sport in terms of continual improvement through hard work.

That difference in thinking is not confined to athletes. Researcher Carol Dweck[42] has shown that ordinary people and even children can be found exhibiting either style. She uses the term **entity theorists** to refer to people who regard traits as fixed, stable things (entities), as opposed to **incremental theorists** who believe that traits are subject to change and improvement. Entity theorists prefer to do things at which they are good, in order that success can gain them credit and admiration. They dislike criticism or bad feedback intensely (partly because they tend to think that bad traits are permanent). In contrast, incremental theorists are more likely to enjoy learning and challenges; they don't mind criticism or initial failure as much because they expect to improve. Entity theorists often choose the easiest task because they want guaranteed success, whereas incremental theorists prefer harder, more challenging tasks where they can learn.[43]

When students move to a new, more challenging environment, such as from elementary school to middle school, or from high school to college, the entity theorists are often discouraged and overwhelmed, and their performance goes down, whereas the incremental theorists keep striving to improve and often show gains in performance.[44] Likewise, in

Hideo Nomo played for the Kintetsu Buffaloes, a Japanese professional baseball team, from 1990 to 1994. He signed with the Los Angeles Dodgers in 1995 as the first Japanese player in Major League baseball and won the Rookie of the Year award the same year.

entity theorists those who believe that traits are fixed, stable things (entities) and thus people should not be expected to change

incremental theorists those who believe that traits are subject to change and improvement

learned helplessness belief that one's actions will not bring about desired outcomes, leading one to give up and quit trying

lab studies, failure tends to be devastating to entity theorists and even to produce a kind of **learned helplessness** (they quit trying and give up) because they think the failure is proof that they are incompetent losers. In contrast, when incremental theorists fail, they simply try harder to improve.[45]

Ultimately, the difference is between thinking that people are the way they are, period, versus thinking that people are constantly subject to change. People apply these different outlooks both to themselves and to others. Thus, entity theorists tend to interpret other people's behavior as reflecting their traits, whereas incremental theorists interpret them as caused by temporary states and external factors.[46] (See Chapter 5 for a detailed discussion of the difference between internal and external attributions.)

QUIZ YOURSELF
What You Do, and What It Means

1. **Suppose you show up for a paid experiment and receive $10. The researcher says you can double your earnings if the outcome of a coin toss is a head, or lose your earnings if the outcome of a coin toss is a tail. What does research show that most people would do?**

   (a) They would flip the coin and try to get $20.

   (b) They would not flip the coin and keep their $10.

   (c) There is a 50/50 chance that people will flip the coin because the potential gain equals the potential loss.

   (d) The research evidence is mixed.

2. **Mohammed is 4 years old. His mother, a social psychologist, asks whether he would rather have one cookie today or three cookies tomorrow. Mohammed chooses the one cookie today. This illustrates _____ .**

   (a) certainty effect

   (b) planning fallacy

   (c) risk aversion

   (d) temporal discounting

3. **Joni wants to see an R-rated (17+) movie with some friends. However, Joni is only 14, and her parents forbid her to go. Which of the following responses could be predicted from Brehm's psychological reactance theory?**

   (a) Joni would behave aggressively toward her parents.

   (b) Joni would want to see the movie more.

   (c) Joni would sneak into the movie anyway.

   (d) All of the above.

4. **Entity theorists are to incremental theorists as _____ are to _____ .**

   (a) global traits; specific traits

   (b) specific traits; global traits

   (c) stable traits; unstable traits

   (d) unstable traits; stable traits

answers: see pg 145

Freedom of Action

The question of whether people have free will has been debated for centuries, and its importance has been recognized in such fields as theology (religious doctrines), morality, and philosophy.[47] Psychologists are divided on the issue. Many believe that psychology must explain all behavior in terms of causes, and if a behavior is caused, then it is not truly or fully free. Others emphasize the fact that people make choices and could have chosen differently under other circumstances, and in that sense they believe people do have freedom.

Whether to believe in free will is more than just a philosophical debate. In fact, research suggests that belief in free will is valuable for society. When experimental manipulations induced people to reject their belief in free will, they became more willing to cheat on a test and steal money.[48] Similar manipulations showed that disbelieving in free will causes people to become more aggressive and less helpful toward others.[49] These findings say nothing about whether free will really exists—but the belief in it helps cultural animals act in more prosocial ways, thereby helping the social system function better.

More or Less Free

Whatever the ultimate decision is about free will, one cannot dispute that people perceive that they make some choices and that some of these are freer than others. In particular, people have the subjective experience that sometimes they are constrained by external factors, whereas other times they can freely choose what they think is best. In other words, although absolute freedom is debatable, relative freedom is an important feature of social behavior. Among humans, greater freedom is marked by greater behavioral flexibility, controlled processes (as opposed to automatic ones), and self-regulation (deliberately changing one's own states or responses).

In order to live within a culture and human society, humans need a fairly complex and flexible decision-making apparatus. Most animals face choices to some degree, but these are limited in scope and meaning. An animal may have to choose which direction to walk in seeking food, or where to sleep, or whether to fight over some territory or resource. These are important decisions, but they are not nearly as complicated as the choices faced by human beings in our society, such as what college major or occupation to pursue, whether to lie about past sexual experiences, how much effort and time to spend trying to fix one's car before giving up and getting a new one, how much money to offer for a painting or a house, and whether to yield to family pressures about religious matters. Remember, inner processes serve interpersonal events—so the complex demands of living in human society call for an elaborate inner system for making decisions. This elaborate inner system for making decisions is the basis for the common notion of free will.[50] Whether it truly qualifies as free will depends in large part on which of the competing definitions of free will one uses.

As cultural animals, humans rely on meaning to make their choices, and meaning generally offers multiple ways of understanding and deciding. Unlike most other animals, human beings can decide based on abstract rules, moral and ethical principles, laws, plans, contracts, agreements, and the like. This capacity for thinking about a decision or situation in multiple ways requires a flexible capacity for making those decisions.

Free Action Comes from Inside

Self-determination theory is an important perspective on freedom of action. It builds on the research on intrinsic versus extrinsic motivation discussed in Chapter 3. Not all motivations are equal. As the authors of this theory, Ed Deci and Richard Ryan,[51,52,53] point out, people may be motivated to perform well out of a deep passion for excellence or because of a bribe; they may be motivated to behave honestly out of an inner moral sense or because they fear others are watching them; they may be motivated to work hard because they love what they are doing or because they feel pressure to meet a looming deadline. As those three pairs of motivations indicate, people may be motivated by something originating inside them or by some external pressure or force. Doing things to satisfy external pressures is felt to be less free than acting from one's inner promptings. A central point of self-determination theory is that people have an innate need for autonomy, which means that at least some of their activities must be motivated by their inner drives and choices, rather than by external factors.

Believing you are acting autonomously and from intrinsic motivation has many benefits. People who act on that belief derive more satisfaction, are more interested in and excited about what they are doing, have greater confidence, and often perform better, persist longer, and show greater creativity. Their autonomous actions also contribute to vitality, self-esteem, and general well-being (akin to happiness).[54,55,56,57,58,59] They are less prone to

self-determination theory the theory that people need to feel at least some degree of autonomy and internal motivation

fall victim to passivity, alienation, and mental illness. For example, some teachers encourage their students to develop their own interests, make decisions, and in other respects exercise autonomy, whereas other teachers try to control their students. The students of the autonomy-supporting teachers end up more interested in their work, more curious to learn, and more eager for challenges, and they end up learning more.[60,61,62,63,64,65,66,67]

All these studies suggest that different levels of freedom of action have important implications for how people fare. Perhaps most important, when people reach the goals associated with their own autonomous or intrinsic desires, they feel happier and healthier, whereas reaching goals linked to extrinsic motivations is much less able to produce such benefits.[68,69]

Having an Out Versus No Escape

One of the most profound illustrations that perceived freedom produces benefits is the **panic button effect**: Believing that one has an escape option can reduce stress, even if one never makes use of this option. In an early demonstration of this effect, participants were exposed to highly aversive noise stress—blasts of loud noise, delivered at random, unpredictable intervals for irregular lengths of time—while they were trying to solve puzzles. This noise stress made it hard for people to perform their tasks; even afterward, when they sat in a quiet room, people who had been through the noise stress performed worse at a variety of tasks, indicating less concentration, less persistence, and lower frustration tolerance. In this experiment,[70] all participants were exposed to the same noise stress, and all of them had a button on the table in front of them. In reality, the button was not connected to anything, and pressing it would have had no effect.

To some participants, however, the experimenter said that the button would turn off the noise. He said the participant could eliminate the noise if it became too stressful or hard to bear, though he said it would spoil the experiment if the participant pressed it, and he asked the participant not to use the button if possible. No one ever pressed the button. Yet the participants who had this "panic button" available to them did not show all the problems and impairments that the stress had caused. Even though they did not make use of the button to escape the stress, they derived considerable comfort just from knowing it was there.

Thus, even the false belief that one can exert control over events makes them more bearable. Does your neighbor's loud music keep you awake late at night? It may bother you less if you think that you could ask the neighbor to turn it down than if you think you have no choice but to listen to it. Do you suffer when you spend a Friday night alone once in a while? You may feel less lonely if you think you could find some friends or companions than if you think you have no such options.

panic button effect a reduction in stress or suffering due to a belief that one has the option of escaping or controlling the situation, even if one doesn't exercise it

Goals, Plans, Intentions

Ideas and meanings are centrally important to human action, as discussed earlier in the chapter. Meaning connects things; thus, an action has meaning when it is connected to other things or events. One important type of meaning links an action to a goal. Your current action, such as looking at this page, derives meaning from various future events that are presumably your goals, including learning something about social psychology, doing well in the course, getting an education, earning a degree, and preparing for a career. Without those or similar goals, you might still look at this page, but to do so would be relatively pointless and meaningless.

A **goal** is an idea of some desired future state.[72] Goals, in turn, are the (meaningful) link between values and action.[73,74] That is, most people hold certain values, such as family, friends, religion, honesty, success, and health, but these broad and general preferences must be translated into something much more specific in order to serve as guides for behavior. A goal tells you how to pursue and uphold your values.

Goals can also be called personal projects[75] or personal strivings.[76] Most people have more than one goal or project in their life toward which they work and strive at any given time. In fact, when young adults are asked to list their goals and similar personal projects, the average list contains 15 items.[77] Thus, the typical human life nowadays is characterized by a variety of different goals, some of which may be completely unrelated to others, and some of which may even be in conflict (e.g., if they make competing demands on a limited stock of time or money).

Experts disagree as to how goal-oriented other animals are; hence, they disagree about how unique the goal pursuit of human beings is. The experts who believe that animals do pursue goals, in the sense of having mental ideas about future states and trying to make them come true, generally still concede that human beings do this far better and more extensively than other creatures. Animal goals mostly involve the immediate situation and an outcome that is already almost visible, such as climbing a tree or chasing a smaller animal.[78,79] In contrast, human beings pursue goals that may be weeks, years, even decades away, such as in studying and working to become a successful lawyer.

Pursuing distant goals is not as easy as pursuing immediate ones. People may have to interrupt and resume their activities. (While studying to become a lawyer, for example, one must do many things that aren't part of that goal, such as eating, sleeping, and doing laundry!) Self-control is needed to maintain focus and organize one's efforts. Motivation is also likely to fluctuate. During a short-term goal, such as when one is being chased by a bear and wants to get away, motivation stays high throughout, but one's desire to become a lawyer is likely to be stronger on some days than others, and indeed many people change their minds and drop out. Classical motivation theory held that motivation increases as one gets closer to the goal. A modern refinement suggests that the low point for motivation tends to be in the middle of the project. People may start off with high motivation, and it is usually high again as they approach the goal, but during the long slog in the middle, it is likely to wane. Even during tasks done in the same hour, motivation is lower in the middle. For example, when student participants worked on a series of word-making puzzles, they exerted less effort on the middle ones than the early or late ones.[80]

Setting and Pursuing Goals

Where do goals come from? Almost certainly a person's goals reflect the influence of both inner processes and cultural factors. Perhaps the best way to think of this is that the culture sets out a variety of possible goals, and people choose among them depending on their personal wants and needs and also on their immediate circumstances. For example, throughout much of history the goals available to men and women were often quite different; women were barred from many professions, and men were not permitted to be homemakers. Modern Western society has in theory opened up a much wider range of

> "A goal without a plan is just a wish."
>
> — Antoine de Saint-Exupery (1900–1944), French writer and aviator, author of *The Little Prince*[71]

goal an idea of some desired future state

options to both men and women, though both social and personal factors still steer men and women into some different goals and jobs. For example, pressure to earn enough to support a family causes many more men than women to take jobs that may be stressful, unpleasant, or physically dangerous as long as they offer high pay. In such cases, the man's goal of making enough money to attract a mate and support a family causes him to select some goals over other possible goals, such as having a pleasant job and reducing his risk of dying on the job.[81] Women, in contrast, tend to be less guided by materialistic and financial motives in choosing their careers. They give more emphasis to goals of fulfillment, safety, and flexibility.[82] Again, these differences almost certainly reflect the influence of both individual preferences and cultural realities.

Pursuing goals involves at least two major steps, which involve different mental states. The first step includes setting goals (which may involve choosing among competing goals—you can't do everything at once), evaluating how difficult or feasible a goal is, and deciding how much you want to pursue it. The second step is pursuing the goal, which may include planning what to do and carrying out those behaviors.[83,84,85] Let us consider these two mental states in turn (see **TABLE 4.1**).

Setting goals is a time for being realistic. You may be choosing among different possible goals to pursue, or you may simply be deciding whether to commit yourself to a particular goal or not. People in this state are thoughtful and generally seek all sorts of information (both good and bad) about the goals they are contemplating. In this state, the "positive illusions" that characterize a great deal of normal thinking (see Chapter 3) are typically set aside, and people instead tend to be quite accurate about their own capabilities and their chances of successfully achieving the goal.[86,87]

A very different mind-set accompanies pursuing goals. The time for realism is past; instead, optimism and positive illusions help build confidence and foster better performance. The person zeroes in on the one goal and loses interest in information about other goals. Questions of whether and why to pursue the goal are set aside, in favor of questions of how. The goal dominates information processing, such as by drawing attention to opportunities and obstacles, driving the person to develop workable and detailed plans, and stimulating the person to persist and keep trying even in the face of setbacks or interruptions.

Another benefit of goals is that they can bring the person back to resume an activity after an interruption.[88] To get a good grade in a course, for example, you have to perform many activities that are spaced out in time, such as attending class, studying, and reviewing notes, over a period of several months. The goal (the mental idea of doing well in the class) can be important in helping you turn your efforts to pursuing the relevant activities. Even when you are enjoying a television show or practicing your athletic skills, you may stop those activities to attend class or study. Hardly any other animal is capable of making such decisions to stop one activity in order to resume pursuit of a previously pursued goal. Moreover, people who are most successful in life are those who are good at resuming activities after interruptions because most major successes in life require the person to work on them on many different days, interspersed with other activities such as eating and sleeping.

TABLE 4.1 **Mind-Sets and Goals**

	Mind-Set	
	Goal Setting	**Goal Pursuit/Striving**
Function	Deciding what to do	Deciding how to do it, and doing it
Attitude	Open-minded	Closed-minded
Mental focus	Feasibility and desirability	Means and obstacles
Core question	Why should I do it?	How do I do it?
Style of thought	Realistic thinking	Optimistic thinking

Both the deliberate and automatic systems help in the pursuit of goals. The deliberate system does much of the goal setting, especially if the decision about whether to pursue a goal is complicated. The automatic system may also help provide the initiative to resume goals that have been interrupted. Also, crucially, if one step toward a goal is blocked, the deliberate system may be helpful in devising an alternate strategy or route to reach the ultimate goal. The automatic system also contributes in an interesting way. Most people experience the so-called **Zeigarnik effect**, which is a tendency to experience automatic, intrusive thoughts about a goal that one has pursued but whose pursuit has been interrupted. (This is the duplex mind at work: The automatic system signals the conscious mind and deliberate system, which may have moved on to other pursuits, that a previous goal was left uncompleted.) That is, if you start working toward a goal and fail to get there, thoughts about the goal will keep popping into your mind while you are doing other things, as if to remind you to get back on track to finish reaching that goal. Because most human activities naturally form themselves into units so that completing them is a goal, any sort of interruption can produce a Zeigarnik effect. One commonplace experience is turning the radio off in the middle of a song that you like (or even one you don't like), and possibly having that song running through your mind for the rest of the day.

Recent work has even suggested that the Zeigarnik effect can show how conscious and unconscious mind (or automatic and deliberate systems) work together. Unfinished goals normally keep popping into your mind, but if you make a plan for how to reach the goal, these intrusive thoughts stop.[89] In a sense, then, the Zeigarnik effect is a matter of the unconscious mind nagging the conscious mind to make a plan, like a child tugging at the sleeve of an adult to know when and where they will have lunch. The automatic system is great at executing plans but not so good at making them. The deliberate system is inefficient for carrying out plans but excels at making them.

People perform better if they have goals, but some goals are more helpful than others. In general, it is most helpful to have specific goals and goals that are difficult but reachable—goals you have to stretch to reach.[90,91] A broad goal such as "getting an education" does not necessarily improve performance very much; specific goals such as "getting a good grade on my next test" are more helpful. People who shoot for high goals generally do better than those who set easy goals for themselves, unless the goals are so high as to be unrealistic—and therefore discouraging.

Hierarchy of Goals

Goals are not necessarily independent; in fact, most people have interlinked sets of goals. People usually have a hierarchy of goals, with short-term or proximal goals that operate as stepping-stones toward long-term or distal goals. For example, a high school student might decide she wants to be the Chief Executive Officer (CEO) of a major corporation, which would be a distal goal, but if she had only that goal she would be unlikely to get very far. To become a CEO, you need to take many steps, such as getting an education, getting an entry-level job at a corporation, gaining experience, and working your way up through the ranks by way of a series of promotions **(FIGURE 4.1)**. It would be silly to drop out of high school and just look through the want ads in the newspaper for job openings as CEO of a major corporation, but if you only had the big, distal goal of becoming a CEO, without the proximal goals that lead up to it, you might not know any better.[92] The person who has a hierarchy of goals, with many steps leading up to the ultimate distal goal, is far more likely to be successful.

The duplex mind is relevant to goal hierarchies. The automatic system can keep track of the goals and initiate behavior to pursue each step along the way. The deliberate system may be useful, however, when an intermediate goal is blocked. Consciousness (associated with the deliberate system) is flexible at processing information, and it can find a substitute goal when the overarching or ultimate goal is blocked. In the previous example, if you had a plan for becoming CEO but discovered that your corporation never hired a CEO from among its own vice presidents, then you might use your deliberate information-processing system to figure out that once you became vice president you would need to look elsewhere (i.e., other corporations) for openings as a CEO, or else you would have to move laterally as vice president in order to have a chance to come back as CEO. The

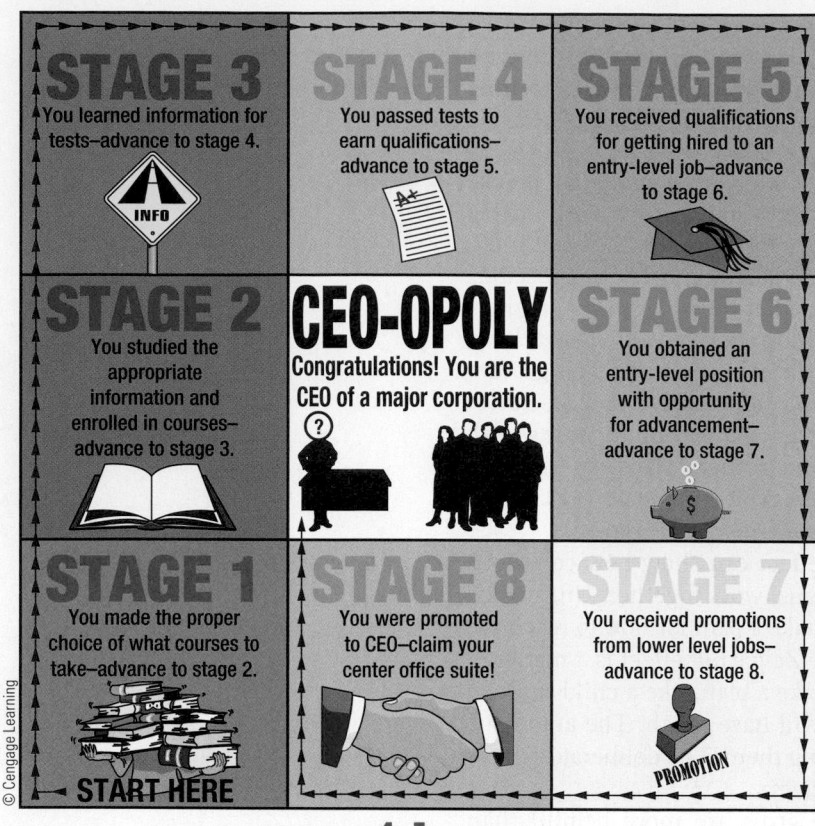

STAGE 3
You learned information for tests–advance to stage 4.

STAGE 4
You passed tests to earn qualifications–advance to stage 5.

STAGE 5
You received qualifications for getting hired to an entry-level job–advance to stage 6.

STAGE 2
You studied the appropriate information and enrolled in courses–advance to stage 3.

CEO-OPOLY
Congratulations! You are the CEO of a major corporation.

STAGE 6
You obtained an entry-level position with opportunity for advancement–advance to stage 7.

STAGE 1
You made the proper choice of what courses to take–advance to stage 2.

START HERE

STAGE 8
You were promoted to CEO–claim your center office suite!

STAGE 7
You received promotions from lower level jobs–advance to stage 8.

PROMOTION

© Cengage Learning

FIGURE 4.1
A hierarchy of goals.

automatic system is much less effective at such flexible thinking; if its plan were blocked, it might be at a loss to find an alternative pathway to the ultimate goal.

We have noted the problems that might arise if you have only distal, ultimate goals without forming a hierarchy of proximal goals. Conversely, people who have only proximal (short-term) goals without the distal (long-term) ones also encounter problems.[93] These people essentially go through life dealing with one issue or problem at a time but without a sense of where they should be going in the long run. They may be good at paying the bills, doing their assigned tasks, and responding to immediate needs or problems in their relationships, but where they end up in life is likely to be the result of a series of accidents and may not necessarily be to their liking. Having only proximal goals is not much better than having only distal goals. To live your life effectively within human society and culture, it is important to have both distal and proximal goals (preferably interlinked). In other words, the most effective approach is to have an idea of where you would like to be in five or ten years (even if you change this goal, it is still important to have one) as well as some ideas of what you need to do this week, this month, and this year in order to get there.

Multiple Goals and Goal Shielding

Nearly everyone has many different goals. That presents a problem, however: How do you decide which to work on? Indeed, how do you prevent worries about unmet goals to distract you when you are working toward another goal? For example, just because you are working on a term paper or problem set, your other goals of finding a romantic partner, getting physically fit, and saving money do not magically disappear—but if you think about them, you won't get your paper finished.

In a sense, the different goals compete inside your mind. Each tries to get you to think about it and work toward it. Not only does the mind have to have a way to set priorities and pursue the top goals, it also needs to keep the others from interfering and distracting you from what you are doing. This process of **goal shielding** sometimes has to keep more important goals at bay. For example, you may regard finding someone to marry as more important than doing your math homework, but if you spend all your time and energy on your love life, you won't get your homework done.

Goal shielding seems to occur naturally, even automatically.[94] When a person starts working toward one goal, the mind automatically shuts other goals away from consciousness. The more committed a person is to the current goal, the more effectively the mind shields this goal by blocking thoughts of other goals.

Different goals are also associated with different people in one's life. Hence being around certain people, or even thinking of them, can shift priorities among goals. As studies have shown, answering questions about a friend made people more helpful than answering questions about a coworker, presumably because the goal of helping is associated with friends more than with coworkers.[95] Thinking of one's mother primed goals of wanting to do well in school; as a result, thoughts of mother motivated people to try harder and perform better, even on laboratory tasks. And the closer people felt emotionally to their mother, the more strongly the thought of her made them want to do well.[96]

Actually, mother may not always be the most effective person to stimulate goal pursuit because people may associate multiple goals with their mothers. Researchers have identified variations on the basic pattern that thinking of a person activates goals that you associate with that person.[97] The more different goals associated with that person, the less

goal shielding occurs when the activation of a focal goal the person is working on inhibits the accessibility of alternative goals

any one of them is activated. And if the other person does not care about the goal, then thinking of him or her does not really get you working toward it. If your mother doesn't happen to care about your schoolwork, then thinking of her won't make you study harder.

One of your textbook authors (Bushman) has a photo of Cael Sanderson in his office. As a college student, Sanderson wrestled at Iowa State University, where he never lost a match (his record was 159–0). *Sports Illustrated* named his college career as the number two most outstanding achievement in college history. He was the first wrestler to appear on a *Wheaties* cereal box. He went on to win a gold medal in wrestling at the 2004 Olympics in Athens. Sanderson was the head wrestling coach at Iowa State University and is currently the head wrestling coach at Penn State University, where he has led his team to several national championships. Bushman remembers Sanderson as a student in his social psychology class. Now his photo inspires Bushman to work harder and strive for excellence.

Successful people actually seem to manage their social lives partly on the basis of these mental connections.[98] When they have a goal, they automatically think more about people who will help them reach that goal or who at least support them in pursuing it. They draw closer to those helpful people and spend more time with them. It may seem unromantic to choose among your friends based on who is most helpful for reaching your goals, but probably that strategy contributes to success.

Reaching Goals: What's the Plan?

Once you have a goal, you can start to plan. Planning is beneficial because it focuses attention on how to reach the goal and typically offers specific guidelines for what to do. People who make specific plans are more likely to take steps toward their goals than people who fail to make plans; in fact, laboratory studies have indicated that making plans motivates people to get started working toward their goals.[99] In one study, students agreed to furnish reports within 48 hours on how they spent their Christmas holidays. Some were asked to make specific plans as to when and where they would write the report; for others, it was left up to them to decide later on. The first group were more than twice as likely as the latter to complete the reports on time.[100] Thus, those who made specific plans were more likely to reach their goals than those who did not.

Plans have two main drawbacks. One is that if they are too detailed and rigid, they can be discouraging. Students taking part in a study of planning were encouraged to make either detailed daily plans for their studying, monthly plans, or no plans. The researchers expected the students with the daily plans to succeed the best, but they did not; those who planned by the month did best.[101,102] (Actually, among the very best students, daily plans were very effective and sometimes surpassed the monthly plans. For everyone else, though, monthly plans worked best.)

Why? Trying to plan every day had several disadvantages. For one thing, making such detailed plans is tiresome and time-consuming, so many participants in the study soon stopped making plans altogether. Another, more important reason was that daily plans are too rigid, which can create feelings of stress and frustration as soon as anything deviates from the plan. Detailed daily plans leave no scope for making changes and choices day by day, even if one figures out better ways to do things or encounters unexpected delays. People enjoy making some choices along the way, as opposed to having everything laid out precisely in advance. When things go wrong, a monthly plan can still be followed with some revisions, but the day-by-day plans are defeated, and the daily planners felt discouraged and frustrated as soon as they were behind schedule. Thus, plans and even specific plans are good, but too much detail and a lack of flexibility can undermine them.[103]

The second drawback of plans is that they tend to be overly optimistic. When was the last time you heard a story on the news saying, "Construction of the new building has been completed eight months ahead of schedule,

© Brad Bushman

Few people achieve perfection in sports or any other domain. Cael Sanderson did it in college wrestling, winning all 159 of his matches. He also won a gold medal in wrestling at the 2004 Olympic Games in Greece. Sanderson was head coach of the wrestling team at Iowa State University, where he wrestled as a student. He is currently the head coach of the wrestling team at Penn State, where he has won two national championships.

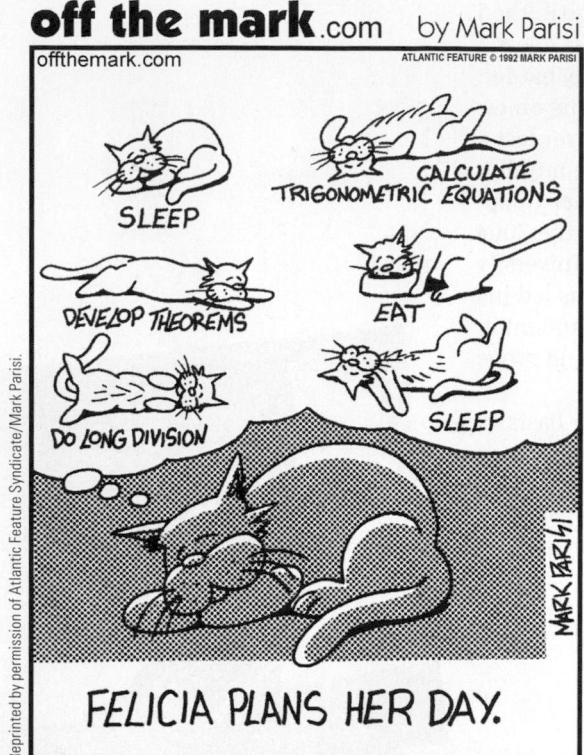

Making daily plans usually is a bad idea (unless you're a cat).

and the total cost was $12 million less than had been projected"? Instead, most projects come in late and over budget. As one famous example, the opera house in Sydney, Australia, now recognized as one of the world's most beautiful and impressive buildings, was started in 1957. The plans said it would cost $7 million and be completed early in 1963. By 1963 it was nowhere near finished and already over budget. The plans were cut back to save time and money, but even so it was not finished until 1973 (10 years late), and the cost had run to more than $100 million![104]

Common Mistakes in Planning

The tendency for plans to underestimate the time and cost probably reflects the optimistic mind-set that people adopt once they have chosen a goal. It is not limited to giant buildings, either. In a very revealing study, students were asked to estimate how long it would take them to finish their thesis, and to furnish both an optimistic estimate and a pessimistic one ("assuming everything went as poorly as it possibly could"). Fewer than a third finished by their best estimate, and fewer than half finished even by their most pessimistic estimate.[105] That is, even when they tried to foresee every possible problem and worst-case scenario, they were still too optimistic. This optimistic bias is related to the **planning fallacy**,[106] defined as the "belief that one's own project will proceed as planned, even while knowing that the vast majority of similar projects have run late."[107]

Another sign that this tendency to make overly optimistic plans comes from people's positive illusions about themselves is that people are pretty accurate at predicting how other people will do. When research participants had to predict how long their roommates or friends would take to complete their projects, the predictions were remarkably accurate. Problems lie not with predicting in general but with the distortions that arise when we think about ourselves. If you want a reliable estimate about how long it will take you to finish some project, don't trust your own judgment—ask someone else who knows you well!

B Lawrence/Alamy

planning fallacy the tendency for plans to be overly optimistic because the planner fails to allow for unexpected problems

The Sydney Opera House: Spectacular architectural achievement or catastrophe of planning … or both?

Optimism seems to run wild when the perspective includes a long future; in the short run, people are fairly realistic. People make their short-run decisions based on what seems feasible, whereas long-range decisions are made with less concern for practical issues and more attention to how desirable something is. For example, would you rather do a difficult but interesting assignment or an easier but more boring one? If the assignment is due this week, students tend to choose the easy/boring one, whereas if the assignment is not due for a month or two, they pick the difficult/interesting one. In another study, the decision about whether to buy tickets for a show depended mainly on the quality of the show if the show was in the distant future, but if the show was soon, people's decisions depended more on the price of the ticket[108,109] (see **FIGURE 4.2**). As crunch time gets closer, people shift their decision criteria from broad, abstract values toward practical concerns. Thus, one of the biggest differences between long-term planning and dealing with present concerns is the greater pressure of practical constraints on the latter.

In general, people naturally feel more strongly about the present than about the distant future, so the here and now takes precedence over future considerations. But to be successful in life, it is usually necessary to consider the future. Overriding one's immediate wishes and feelings may thus be vital for long-term success. Such overriding requires a powerful ability, called self-regulation, which is far more developed in humans than in other species. Self-regulation, which is important for success in pursuing many goals, is examined in the next section.

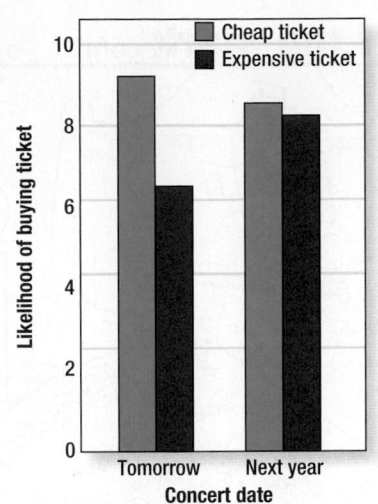

FIGURE 4.2

The high cost of tickets discouraged people from buying them for an imminent concert, but cost seemed irrelevant if the concert was a year away.[109]

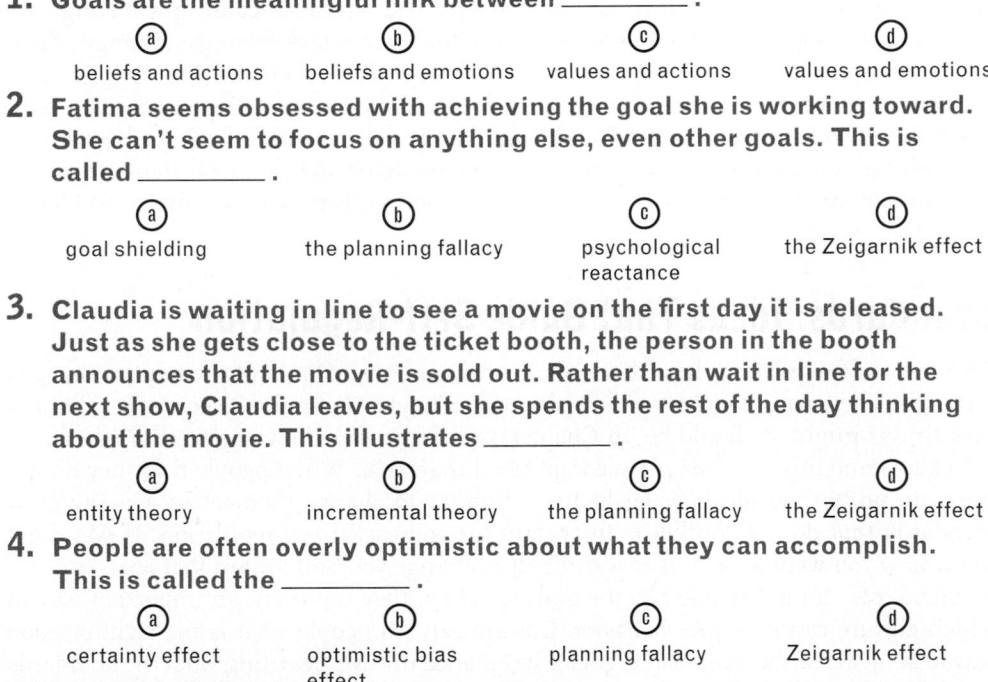

1. **Goals are the meaningful link between _____ .**
    (a) beliefs and actions
    (b) beliefs and emotions
    (c) values and actions
    (d) values and emotions

2. **Fatima seems obsessed with achieving the goal she is working toward. She can't seem to focus on anything else, even other goals. This is called _____ .**
    (a) goal shielding
    (b) the planning fallacy
    (c) psychological reactance
    (d) the Zeigarnik effect

3. **Claudia is waiting in line to see a movie on the first day it is released. Just as she gets close to the ticket booth, the person in the booth announces that the movie is sold out. Rather than wait in line for the next show, Claudia leaves, but she spends the rest of the day thinking about the movie. This illustrates _____ .**
    (a) entity theory
    (b) incremental theory
    (c) the planning fallacy
    (d) the Zeigarnik effect

4. **People are often overly optimistic about what they can accomplish. This is called the _____ .**
    (a) certainty effect
    (b) optimistic bias effect
    (c) planning fallacy
    (d) Zeigarnik effect

QUIZ YOURSELF

Goals, Plans, Intentions

answers: see pg 145

Self-Regulation and Habits

Control and Willpower

Self-regulation refers to the self's capacity to alter its own responses. It is quite similar to the everyday term "self-control." People regulate their thoughts, their emotions, their impulses and desires, and their task performance. Human beings have a much greater

self-regulation the self's capacity to alter its own responses; self-control

off the mark .com   by Mark Parisi
offthemark.com

ATLANTIC FEATURE © 1996 MARK PARISI

capacity for self-regulation than most other creatures, and this is probably a crucial contributor to the human capacity to live in the complex social and cultural worlds we construct. Self-regulation enables people to be flexible, to adapt themselves to many different circumstances, rules, and demands. Self-regulation enables one's social conscience to prevail over selfish impulses, so that people can do what is right and good rather than just indulging their selfish inclinations. In this way, self-regulation enables people to live together and get along much better. This fits the general theme that inner processes serve interpersonal functions. Self-regulation enables people to keep their promises, obey rules, respect others, control their temper, and do other things that make for better interpersonal relations.

Self-regulation predicts success or failure in many different spheres. Most of the problems that afflict people in our society today have some component of inadequate self-regulation: drug and alcohol abuse, addiction, eating disorders, obesity, anxiety and anger control problems, unwanted pregnancy, unsafe sex and sexually transmitted diseases, gambling, overuse of credit cards, debt and bankruptcy, underachievement in school, poor physical fitness, violence and crime, and many more. People who are poor at self-control often end up rejected by their relationship partners, fired by their employers, or even imprisoned for breaking society's laws. People who are good at self-control or self-regulation are more likely to be successful in work, school, relationships, and other important spheres of behavior.[110,111,112,113]

In recent years, various experts have advocated that people make their decisions based on gut feelings, rather than thinking things through. To self-regulation researchers, this sounds like very bad advice, because gut feelings are often swept along by impulsive desires and other momentary feelings. A longitudinal study surveyed adolescents in the 1990s as to whether they rely mainly on their gut feelings when making decisions. The researchers checked the group again 15 years later, when the participants had reached adulthood. The people who said they relied mainly on gut feelings generally earned less money, were more likely to be on food stamps or other government support, and had higher rates of gambling (especially gambling problems) than other people.[114]

Standards: Ideas That Guide Self-Regulation

Effective self-regulation has three main components: standards, monitoring, and strength. The term *standards* was introduced in Chapter 3; it refers to concepts (ideas) of how things might or should be. In Chapter 3 we focused on how people compare themselves to standards, but it is more complicated than that. When people find they do not measure up to their ideals or goals, they often try to change themselves. Having clear standards that do not conflict is important for successful self-regulation. If you don't know how you want to be, it is very difficult to change yourself toward that goal.

Standards can be supplied by the culture. Thus, they represent an important way in which culture can influence behavior. Culture can tell people what is the right or good way to act. Part of the long road to social acceptance involves learning what the standards are—what is fashionable, acceptable, cool, or morally proper. Many youngsters find the early teen years (middle or junior high school) to be especially difficult and unhappy, because social life is changing and it is hard to learn the new standards amid a changing peer group.

Many standards, especially the ones learned from culture, involve what not to do: Don't lie, cheat, steal, spit on the floor, say forbidden words, cut in line, betray a friend, talk back to your teacher, drive when drunk, and so forth. Eight of the Ten Commandments in Judeo-Christian religion specifically say what not to do, and even the other two (honoring parents and keeping the Sabbath day holy) implicitly refer to things that should not be done. As we have repeatedly seen, nature says go and culture says stop. The culture's "stop" rules are standards, and self-regulation is required to implement them.

Monitoring: Watching What You're Doing

The second component of self-control is **monitoring**—keeping track of the behaviors or responses you want to regulate. Indeed, some experts believe that the central purpose of self-awareness (focusing attention on the self) is to promote self-regulation, because as you watch yourself you can monitor how well you are changing to reach your goals or other standards.[115,116] Without self-awareness, self-regulation would be difficult, if not impossible.

The way people monitor themselves is typically summarized as a feedback loop (see **FIGURE 4.3**). An easy-to-remember acronym is **TOTE**, which stands for **T**est, **O**perate, **T**est, and **E**xit.[117,118] The first test is a comparison of self against the standard. For example, if you have resolved to be nicer to your romantic partner, you may occasionally stop to consider how nice you have been toward that person today. If the test reveals a discrepancy—that is, you are not being as nice as you would like—then you move along to the "operate" phase, in which you exert conscious control to change yourself to become nicer. You might remind yourself to say nice things, or perhaps purchase a small gift to express your appreciation to your partner. At some point in the "operate" phase, you may test the self again. Am I being nice enough now? If the answer is no, then more operations (more changes to the self) are required. Eventually, perhaps, the answer is "yes," indicating that you have met the standard, and at this point you can complete the loop by exiting it.

The concept of feedback loops is borrowed from cybernetic theory, developed during and after World War II to help guide missiles toward their targets despite winds and other difficulties.[119] Its most familiar illustration is the thermostat that helps regulate the temperature in a room: The test involves evaluating whether the current temperature is close to the level at which the thermostat has been set, and the "operate" phase involves turning on the heater or air conditioning unit; when another test reveals that the temperature has reached the desired level, the heater or air conditioner is shut off and the loop is exited.

Monitoring is a key ingredient in self-regulation and often presents the best opportunity for immediate improvement in self-regulation. If you want to keep to an exercise program, write on the calendar each day whether you had a workout. If you want to save money, make a list of what you spend your money on each day, and keep closer track of how much you earn and how much you save.

Dieting furnishes a good example of the importance of monitoring. If you are not dieting, you likely pay little or no attention to how much you eat—you may simply eat your fill. Dieters, in contrast, soon begin to keep a close watch on how much they eat and how fattening these foods are (hence the familiar expression "counting calories"). When dieters eat in settings that undermine monitoring, they eat more. In particular, eating while watching television has long been known to increase calorie intake, mainly because people focus their attention on the television program and not on monitoring how much they consume.[120] Likewise, people overeat at parties, where their attention is focused on the other people and activities rather than on how much they eat.[121]

An important study linked eating binges to failures in monitoring.[122] For this purpose, some dieters were induced to break their diet for the day of the experiment, whereas other dieters kept on their diets. Then both groups, plus a sample of nondieters, ate a snack of as many tiny sandwiches as they wanted. Afterward, the researchers asked everyone to

Culture often tells us those things we cannot do, as displayed in this German sign.

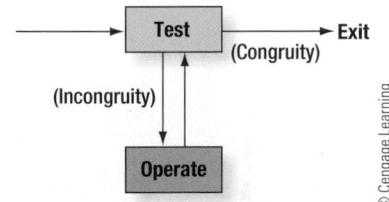

Image courtesy of André Melzer

FIGURE 4.3

TOTE (Test, Operate, Test, Exit) model. The first test is a comparison of self against the standard. In the "operate" phase, match behavior to the standard. Then test again to see if the match is close enough to reduce anxiety. If it is not close enough, keep trying. If it is close enough, stop changing behavior (exit).[115,116]

© Cengage Learning

monitoring keeping track of behaviors or responses to be regulated

TOTE the self-regulation feedback loop of Test, Operate, Test, Exit

estimate how much she or he had eaten. The nondieters were pretty accurate, as were the dieters whose diets had remained intact. But the dieters who had broken their diets made wildly inaccurate estimates of how many tiny sandwiches they had consumed. Apparently once their diet was broken, they stopped keeping track, which then enabled them to eat a great deal without realizing it.

Many factors interfere with monitoring and thereby undermine self-regulation, including emotional distress and being distracted, but probably the most widely recognized and important factor is alcohol intoxication. One effect of alcohol, even in mild doses, is to reduce attention to self,[123] and as we have seen, without monitoring (attending to) yourself, it is very difficult to self-regulate effectively. Hence, people who have consumed alcohol tend to be worse at self-regulating in almost every sphere of behavior that has been studied. Intoxicated people eat more than sober people, perform more violent and aggressive acts, spend more money, smoke more cigarettes, and engage in more inappropriate sexual behavior—and, yes, drinking alcohol even leads to drinking more alcohol when drinkers stop keeping track of how much they drink.[124,125,126,127,128]

Willpower for Change

The third ingredient of self-regulation is the **capacity for change**. This refers to what goes on in the "operate" phase, during which people actually carry out the changes to their states or responses so as to bring them into line with the standards. This capacity corresponds to the popular notion of "willpower," and in fact it does seem to operate like a strength or energy.

Willpower can become depleted when people use it. In an influential early demonstration of this principle,[129] participants arrived having skipped a meal, so most were hungry. The researchers baked fresh chocolate chip cookies in the laboratory, which filled the room with a delicious and tempting aroma. Each participant was seated at a table in front of a stack of these cookies and delectable chocolates, as well as a bowl of radishes. In the important condition, the experimenter told each participant, "You have been assigned to the radish condition," which meant they were supposed to eat only radishes. The experimenter then left the participant alone for five minutes to eat. This task required considerable willpower to resist the tempting chocolates and cookies and eat only the radishes as instructed. In other conditions, participants were permitted to eat cookies and chocolate instead of radishes, or no food was present at all. After this, the participants were set to work on some difficult (actually unsolvable) problems, and the researchers measured how long people kept trying before they gave up, because willpower is also needed to keep trying when you feel discouraged and want to quit. Consistent with the theory that willpower gets used up, the participants in the radish condition quit sooner than participants in the other two conditions. Thus, resisting temptation (in the form of chocolates and cookies) used up some willpower, so those participants had less left over to help them keep working on the frustrating puzzles. The results are depicted in **FIGURE 4.4**.

capacity for change the active phase of self-regulation; willpower

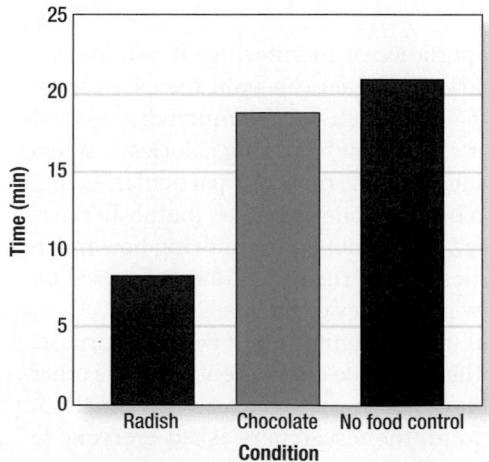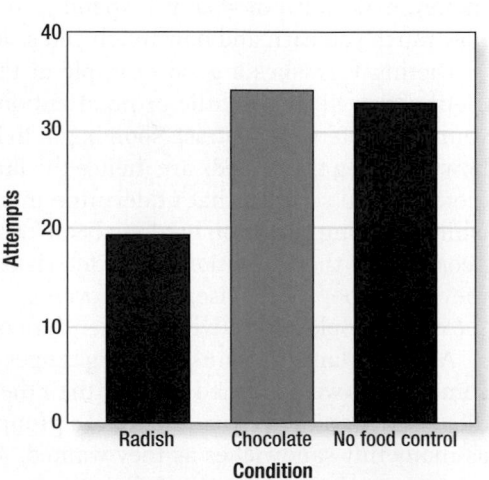

FIGURE **4.4**

People who exercised self-control by eating radishes instead of chocolate gave up more easily on difficult tasks.[129]

© Cengage Learning

A more appealing interpretation of these results would be that eating chocolate made people stronger and more effective. Unfortunately for that view, the participants who ate chocolate were no different from the control participants who ate nothing at all. It was resisting temptation, rather than indulging in chocolate, that was responsible for the experimental results.[130] Thus, willpower can be important for regulating one's eating; in fact, dieting is one of the most common behaviors that depends on self-regulation. To learn more about self-regulation in dieting, see *Food for Thought*.

FOOD FOR *Thought*

Dieting as Self-Regulation

Many people seek to control and restrain their eating and will therefore refrain from eating some tempting food even when it is readily available to them. (Hardly any nonhuman animals do this!) Partly this reflects the progress of culture at providing food. Like most other animals, humans evolved under conditions of periodic scarcities of food, so nature designed human bodies to keep and store food as much as possible. Now that much of the world lives amid ample available food, the body's natural tendency to store fat has turned from a life-saving asset to a life-endangering liability. In 2003, experts calculated that for the first time, more humans worldwide suffer from obesity than are in danger of starving. The problem is too much food, not too little.

Dieting—restricting one's food intake—is the standard response, but it requires self-regulation in order to override the natural desire to eat. To understand dieting as self-regulation, we suggest you imagine yourself going on a diet. What can self-regulation theory tell you about how to succeed? Consider the three main ingredients of self-regulation.

The first is a commitment to standards. A standard would be your goal in terms of weight (or perhaps body measurements such as waist size, or even percentage of body fat). It is helpful to have a realistic idea of what you should weigh. This is a high-level goal that may preside over the whole dieting process (which may take months). It is helpful to set lower-level goals, such as losing a pound or two each week. Many dieters also find it helpful to set standards for food intake, such as not eating more than 1,500 calories per day.

The second ingredient is monitoring. This means keeping track of what you eat, how many calories you consume, and perhaps how much you weigh. External monitoring helps: Rather than relying on memory, keep a journal or diary that records what you eat each day. Also avoid eating in front of the television and other distractions, so you can be aware of how much you eat. If you don't keep track, you are not likely to succeed. Research shows that when dieters break their diets, they often stop keeping track and hence lose any sense of how much they are eating. This can produce an eating binge: You know you are eating too much, but you don't really know how much. The importance of monitoring means that it is important to eat under circumstances in which keeping track of food is possible.

Monitoring weight is another key aspect of dieting. Here the conventional wisdom suggested an exception to the rule to monitor closely. Folk wisdom said that weighing yourself every day can be discouraging because weight fluctuates, so weighing yourself once a week was supposed to be best. Several well-controlled studies have now shown that self-regulation theory is correct after all: People who weigh themselves every day are most successful at losing weight and at keeping it off.[137]

The third ingredient is willpower, or the capacity for change. The self's strength is used for many different activities, and it can be depleted if there are many other demands. An ideal time for dieting is a period of low stress or pressure, stable relationships, and few demands for major decisions. When your willpower is depleted from coping with stress or deadlines, making hard decisions, resisting temptation, or making other efforts to change the self, you will have less strength available for effective dieting. Experiments have shown that dieters eat more when their willpower is depleted.[138]

Sometimes, low level thoughts take precedence... ...no matter how high minded we try to be.

Paula Wright 2012

off the mark .com by Mark Parisi

TODAY'S SPECIAL IS *THE "RESOLUTION BUSTER"*...A FATTY STEAK SMOTHERED IN FRENCH FRIES, MARINATED IN HARD LIQUOR, STUFFED WITH CHOCOLATE CAKE AND TOPPED WITH A CIGARETTE...

offthemark.com 1-3

How does one acquire or increase willpower? Some evidence indicates that willpower resembles a muscle.[131,132] Regular exercise makes you stronger, even though the muscle is temporarily "tired" after a workout. When people perform regular self-control exercises, they show gradual improvements in their capacity for self-control, even on novel tasks. Such exercises may include trying to improve your posture, keep track of what you eat, speak in complete sentences, and use your nondominant hand (your left hand if you're right-handed) to brush your teeth or open doors. Over the long run, these exercises will strengthen your capacity for self-regulation. Just don't perform them right before you are going to need your willpower because that would be like lifting weights just before you have to carry furniture.

Willpower and Decision Fatigue

Many people have an intuitive sense that their willpower fluctuates and so their self-control may get stronger or weaker at different points in the day. But did you know that making decisions also takes willpower? Exerting self-control and making hard choices thus depend on the same supply of energy, and either can affect the other.

One sign that making decisions depletes willpower is that people have poorer self-control after making choices. A series of studies showed that people who made a series of choices later performed worse at self-control.[133] For example, choosing what consumer products they might want caused people to give up faster on a test that required holding one's hand in ice water—a classic lab test of self-control. In a similar vein, students who made choices about what courses to take in the future, or choices about their current course (such as what topics to cover and what educational films to show) did worse thereafter on various lab tests of self-control, such as persevering in solving anagrams.

Such information may have practical consequences. People who have to make many decisions during the day may deplete their willpower, leaving them prone to do things they will regret in the evening, such as eating or drinking too much, or even engaging in sexual or aggressive misbehavior.

Depleted willpower can impair decision making too.[134] When energy is low, decision making changes in various ways, mostly designed to avoid effort. People may prefer to postpone decisions, in effect "deciding not to decide." Their choices are more subject to bias, because they don't think carefully enough to rule out irrelevant factors that could distort the decision. Depleted decision makers also show less tendency to compromise, instead adopting simpler, rigid criteria.

When you have many decisions to make, it is useful to conserve your willpower so as to be able to make the later ones effectively. For example, when you buy a new car, you often must make a long series of decisions. Research has shown that people become increasingly likely to take the standard or default option as they go along, regardless of what the order of decisions is.[135] That is, on the early choices they think hard and choose just what they want, but on the later decisions they tend to take whatever the manufacturer recommends—which can end up increasing the cost of the car significantly. They seemed to suffer from a kind of **decision fatigue**: Having used up their energy on early choices, they took the easy way out on the later ones.

Indeed, a recent study of just this sort of decision fatigue among parole judges raised some disturbing questions about fairness in the legal system. A long-running joke among lawyers asks, "What is justice?" and answers, "Whatever the judge had for breakfast!" Researchers went through the records of parole judges in Israel. These are decisions about whether a particular convict should be released into the community (presumably because he has atoned and reformed) or sent back to prison. The easy and safe decision is simply to send him back to prison, because the judge's reputation is at risk if he approves parole and the released convict commits another crime. Nonetheless, some prisoners have earned the right to be paroled, and the judge must decide.

The researchers found a remarkable pattern.[136] As the day wore on, the judge's decisions became increasingly simple and harsh. The prisoners who came before the judge early in the day, when the judge's willpower was high thanks to a good night's sleep and breakfast, had pretty good odds of being granted parole. Those who came before him

decision fatigue a state of depleted willpower caused by making decisions, which can affect subsequent decisions by causing people to fail to think and choose carefully

(all judges and prisoners were men in this study) late in the day were generally sent back to prison. The only exceptions came right after the judge was able to replenish his energy: after a mid-morning snack break and especially after lunch.

Habits

The previous section focused on self-control, which consists of using deliberate effort to control your actions. **Habits** are in some ways the opposite. Habits occur with relatively little control by the deliberate system. The human mind appears to be set up to use the deliberate system to acquire new behaviors, but as these become performed over and over, they are gradually transferred to the automatic system. To say someone acted out of habit is to say that the person did not necessarily consider the action or alternatives, did not try to perform or resist that action, and may even have been scarcely aware of what he or she was doing.

Using a bad habit to satisfy a goal is a bad idea. For example, some students pull an "all-nighter" to prepare for an exam.

How common are habits? Some studies have sought to find out by having people wear beepers and stop and record what they are doing whenever the beeper goes off (at random intervals throughout the day). By assembling these reports, researchers can develop a broad picture of what people do, and how often. One conclusion from these studies is that almost half the actions people do are things they do pretty much every day in the same place.[139] This suggests that most people have plenty of habits and use them often.

Habits may seem like trouble, such as when people apologize that they did something inappropriate because of "force of habit." Someone may set out to drive to a store and instead follow the habitual route to work or home. Yet habits are not generally opposed to one's goals. According to an influential theory,[140] habits are vestiges of past efforts at pursuing goals. In the driving example, the mistake of driving to work instead of the store may occur because usually your goal is to drive to work.

If anything, current goals are often simply missing from the habitual behavior and irrelevant to it. As one performs the same actions in the same situation over and over, that action becomes associated with that situation or with other relevant cues. Being in that situation sets off automatic processes to enact the behavior just like on other occasions. The deliberate system, one's current goals, and other factors may be completely out of the process.

Eating popcorn while watching a movie is a habit for some people and not others. Researchers gave people free popcorn at the start of one movie. Half the people got delicious, fresh popcorn, but the rest got stale popcorn that had been made a week ago. When people were asked to rate the popcorn, not surprisingly, the fresh popcorn was rated as more pleasant than the stale one, regardless of habit. When it came to how much people ate, however, habits made a big difference. The people who had the habit of eating popcorn at the movies ate just as much popcorn, regardless of whether it was fresh or stale. Meanwhile, people who did not have a popcorn habit ate plenty when it was tasty but ate considerably less of the stale stuff.[141]

But goals are not completely irrelevant to habits. For one thing, they promote the learning of habits. People get the habit of driving a particular way because it took them to their usual goal (e.g., home). Actions that repeatedly help you reach your goals are more likely than others to become habits and indeed strong habits.[142]

Even more important, habits can help sustain pursuit of goals when willpower is low. Success in college, for example, depends on lots of studying. Most students want to succeed, but at various times their motivation (their desire to succeed) may feel weaker than others, and their self-control may also be at a low point. Good study habits can help sustain the effort even when one doesn't feel like it. Recent evidence has shown that during stressful periods, such as exam weeks (when energy is low because of external demands), students act more habitually.[143] For example, those who had a habit of eating a healthy breakfast were more likely to do so. Meanwhile those who had a habit of eating unhealthy breakfasts ate more unhealthy foods. In fact, those who had a habit of reading the newspaper became

habit an acquired behavior that, if followed regularly, will become almost automatic

all the more likely to read it during exams week—even though during exams they should in theory be studying for exams, not reading the paper!

Thus, goals can also conflict with habits. What exactly is bad about bad habits? Eating candy at the movies can be a bad habit, because it conflicts with goals to be healthy, fit, and slim. True, the candy probably served another goal, of enjoying oneself and tasting something good. But this merely shows that people sometimes have conflicting goals. One helpful approach is to remove oneself from the situations that trigger the habit. For example, when people want to quit smoking, they may find that it is easier to do on vacation or after moving to a new home because they are not constantly confronted with the cues and situations that usually triggered the impulse to smoke.

Clearly self-control is often needed to break habits. When self-control resources are depleted, people tend to fall back into bad habits. In a field experiment, participants first identified bad habits they were seeking to break, such as drinking alcohol on weeknights, or good habits they wanted to acquire, such as being punctual to class meetings. On some days, they were randomly assigned tasks to deplete their self-control, such as using their left hand for things they normally did with the right hand. Those days were marked by low success at regulating habits: They were more likely to drink alcohol despite its being a weeknight, or more likely to be late to class.[144]

Without habits, life would be exhausting because every action would require deliberate control. As made clear in Chapter 2, the deliberate system takes effort and energy, whereas the automatic system works much more easily and efficiently. The human mind naturally acquires habits to conserve its energy. Sometimes these habits create problems and require considerable mental exertion to break. But that is the price of getting the benefits of being able to do plenty of daily activities without a struggle. Life would be considerably more difficult without habits.

QUIZ YOURSELF

Self-Regulation and Habits

answers: see pg 145

1. **Self-regulation is most similar to which of the following concepts?**
   - (a) Self-awareness
   - (b) Self-consciousness
   - (c) Self-control
   - (d) Self-esteem

2. **Which of the following refers to a concept or idea of how things could be?**
   - (a) Capacity for change
   - (b) Self-consciousness
   - (c) Self-monitoring
   - (d) Standards

3. **Which common household device best illustrates a feedback loop?**
   - (a) Dishwasher
   - (b) Thermostat
   - (c) Toilet
   - (d) Vacuum

4. **What body part does willpower most resemble?**
   - (a) Bone
   - (b) Eye
   - (c) Muscle
   - (d) Stomach

Irrationality and Self-Destruction

Self-regulation, discussed in the previous section, can help people do what is rational, in the sense of what will produce the best results for them in the long run. We turn now from rational behavior and enlightened self-interest to their opposite: irrational and self-destructive behavior.

Self-Defeating Acts: Being Your Own Worst Enemy

"She has self-destructive tendencies." "The other team didn't beat us, we beat ourselves." "I think he has some kind of death wish." How often have you heard such expressions?

They refer to the common belief that people sometimes do things to bring failure, suffering, or misfortune upon themselves. The psychological term for such actions is **self-defeating behavior**. In everyday language, when people say what someone did was "stupid," they usually mean that it was self-defeating. The "stupid" actions are those that bring about some result contrary to what the person sought, especially if the person might or should have known better.

Self-defeating behavior is paradoxical. Why would self-destructive behavior ever occur? If rational behavior means doing what serves one's enlightened self-interest, how could rational beings do things that are harmful or detrimental to the self? Self-defeating behavior seems to be irrational in the extreme.

Yet without a doubt people do plenty of self-defeating things. Many smoke cigarettes, thereby exposing themselves to lung cancer and other diseases. They eat unhealthy foods, thereby shortening their lives. They engage in risky sex, thereby increasing their chances of getting diseases or creating an unwanted pregnancy. They waste their money or gamble it away. They fail to take their medicine or follow physicians' orders, thereby preventing themselves from regaining health. The list goes on and on.

Most theories assume that psychological processes are designed to increase safety, security, and happiness, and ultimately to increase survival and reproduction. Self-defeating behavior is the opposite. It challenges psychological theory to explain how self-defeating behavior can be reconciled with the general assumption that people behave in adaptive, rational, self-benefiting ways. Many theories have been proposed, including Sigmund Freud's famous conclusion that people have an innate "death drive" that impels them to pursue their own downfall and death.[145] A more recent version of this theory holds that many people, especially women, suffer from a "fear of success." The fear-of-success theory was proposed by Matina Horner,[146] herself the president of one of the most prestigious women's colleges (Radcliffe), who said that many young women believed that if they became too successful in their work they would end up lonely, rejected, and unable to find romantic partners. Because of this fear of success, she theorized, many women sabotage, or at least curtail, their careers.

After many decades of research, social psychologists have begun to establish the main facts about self-defeating behavior. A first conclusion is that people almost never directly seek failure, suffering, or misfortune. Freud's theory of a death drive is apparently wrong. People may perform self-destructive acts, but they do not generally do them out of self-destructive intentions. Likewise, carefully controlled studies have discredited the "fear of success" theory.[147] We have no proof that either men or women ever intentionally sabotage their careers or their work because they consciously (or unconsciously) fear what success will mean for them.

self-defeating behavior any action by which people bring failure, suffering, or misfortune on themselves

Instead, there appear to be two main reasons for self-defeating behavior. One of these involves tradeoffs: Sometimes good and bad outcomes are linked, and in order to get the desired, good outcome, people accept the bad one too. The example of cigarette smoking illustrates this pattern. Yes, smoking causes cancer and other diseases, but hardly anyone decides to smoke in order to get cancer. People smoke for the pleasures and rewards of smoking, including the immediate and pleasant sensations caused by nicotine, and possibly the benefits of impressing others that one is sexy, cool, or mature. They accept some increased risk of lung cancer in order to reap the benefits.

A vivid self-defeating tradeoff was covered in Chapter 3 in *Tradeoffs: Self-Handicapping*. In self-handicapping, you will recall, people create obstacles to their own performance so as to furnish themselves with an excuse for possible failure. The self-handicapper thus sacrifices real chances at success in exchange for protection from the implications of failure.[148] If you are drunk when taking a test, you will likely perform worse than if you were

Many self-defeating behaviors trade off long-term costs for short-term pleasures or benefits.

sober—but you are safe from being proven incompetent because even if you perform badly on the test, people will attribute the failure to the alcohol rather than to low ability. (They may question your judgment for getting drunk before the test, but if you are like many people, you'd rather be seen as undisciplined and fun-loving than as stupid and incompetent.)

Self-defeating tradeoffs are especially likely when the reward is immediate and the cost is delayed. We noted in Chapter 2 that this was one common kind of tradeoff

TRADEOffs

Now Versus Tomorrow: Delay of Gratification

Some people spend their money on fun today rather than save for a rainy day. Some people skimp on medical or dental care in favor of things they would rather do. Some people pursue sexual pleasure without worrying about future consequences. In these and other ways, people come to grief. What these self-defeating behaviors have in common is emphasizing the present over the future. However, human beings thrive and prosper best when they can sacrifice some short-term rewards for the sake of a better future. The ability to make those immediate sacrifices for later rewards is called the **capacity to delay gratification**.

During the 1960s, Walter Mischel and his colleagues developed a clever laboratory method for testing children's capacity to delay gratification.[149,150] Each child would be shown some treat, such as a cookie or a marshmallow. The experimenter would explain to each child that the experimenter was going to leave the room but the child could summon him or her back by ringing a bell on the table. As soon as the child did this, the child would receive the treat. However, if the child could refrain from ringing the bell and just wait until the adult returned, the child would get a bigger reward (e.g., two cookies instead of one). Some children were able to wait and get the larger reward; others succumbed to temptation and rang the bell.

Mischel's task is a classic tradeoff dilemma: whether to take the sooner smaller reward or wait for the larger later one. As we have seen elsewhere in this book, many tradeoffs involve time, especially pitting something right now versus something in the

future. Research using this "delay of gratification" measure has provided the foundations for what we now know about self-regulation, as well as shedding valuable light on self-defeating behavior.

Seeing either the large or the small reward undermined the capacity to hold out. Apparently, seeing what you want stimulates a greater desire for it. Temptation is best resisted by avoiding the sight or thought of it. Many of the children sitting in the room with the bell and the marshmallows came up with this strategy themselves: They would cover their eyes so as not to see the rewards (and be tempted by them), sing, turn around, make up little games, or even take a nap during the waiting period.

Even going to college is an exercise in delay of gratification. Most college students could earn more money, live in a nicer apartment, eat better food, and get a better car and clothes if they dropped out and got a job. College often requires living near the poverty line for several years, but its long-term payoffs are immense: As we saw in Chapter 2, a person with an advanced degree is likely to earn nearly $2 million more than a high school dropout over the course of a 30-year career.

The benefits of being able to delay gratification also emerged in Mischel's subsequent research. He followed up with many of the children years after they had participated in his experiments. Very few psychological traits seem to remain stable from early childhood into adulthood, and fewer yet have been shown to predict success or failure in life. The children who were good at delaying gratification when they were just 4 years old, however, grew into adults who were more popular with friends and family and more successful in universities and jobs

than those who had not been able to resist taking the quick marshmallow in his lab.[151,152] Thus, as they moved through life, being able to resist the impulse to take the immediate payoff really did seem to bring them greater rewards in the long run!

Scholars wonder about whether poor self-control contributes to poverty and inequality. One theory is that people end up poor because they lack self-control and pursue immediate rewards. (Indeed, criminals often have poor self-control, which is a central factor in their criminality.[153]) If poor children lack self-control, perhaps they learned or inherited those traits from their poor parents. A different theory holds that it is rational not to pursue delayed gratification in an unstable, unreliable environment—and poor children are more likely than rich ones to grow up in such an environment. If your parent promises you a treat next week, can you count on it being delivered? If not, then perhaps the sensible thing to do is take what you can get right away. Lab studies have shown that when children get the impression that the adults in the environment are not reliable and trustworthy, they take the immediate reward rather than waiting for delay.[154] Which theory is correct? Further work will tell whether either, neither, or both links poor self-control to low social status.

Radius Images/Getty Images

The ability to delay gratification as a child is a good predictor of later success in life.

(now versus the future). Cigarettes offer immediate pleasure, whereas the cancer and death they may bring lie in the distant future. Many self-defeating acts have this characteristic of sacrificing the future for the sake of the present. Regarding the capacity to give up immediate pleasures for the sake of long-term or delayed benefits, see *Tradeoffs*.

The second pathway to self-defeating behavior involves faulty knowledge and a reliance on strategies that don't work. As with tradeoffs, the person is usually pursuing something positive and good, but the self-defeater chooses a strategy that backfires. Often people do not adequately understand what is effective in the world, either because they do not understand the world or they do not understand themselves correctly. For example, some people procrastinate because they believe that "I do my best work under pressure"[155]—that work left till the last minute will actually end up being better. This is generally false: Leaving things until the last minute typically makes it harder to do an adequate job. Thus, they think that putting things off will help them do better work, but actually it makes them do poorer work. Students who procrastinate get lower grades than other students.[156] When people are tested under identical laboratory conditions, chronic procrastinators perform worse than others, not better.[157] In short, the claim that "I do my best work under pressure" is a false rationalization for almost everyone, and it is particularly false for procrastinators.

Suicide

Suicide has fascinated psychologists and other social scientists for more than a century. At first blush, suicide is the extreme of irrational, self-destructive behavior because it brings a permanent end to the person's chances for happiness or success. People who believe that humans are created by a divine power generally regard suicide as a major sin because it thwarts their god's wishes. People who believe in evolution cannot understand how natural selection would produce an impulse to end one's own life because it goes against the most basic urges toward survival and reproduction. (At most, they might think that sacrificing oneself for one's children might make biological sense, but that would only explain a tiny minority of suicides.) Suicide is essentially unknown among nonhuman animals. Basically, humans are the only creatures who deliberately kill themselves, and many millions have done so.[158] How can this be explained?

Suicide often involves a tradeoff, which as we have seen is one major pathway to self-destructive behavior. Indeed, it often fits the now-versus-future pattern that we have seen as a common tradeoff in human decision making. Suicidal people are often in life circumstances that are acutely unpleasant to them, and their overriding wish is to escape from their emotional distress and feelings of personal worthlessness. They feel miserable and want those feelings to stop. To them, death may seem appealing, not as punishment or violence or suffering (as some theories have proposed) but simply as oblivion. They believe that death will bring peace and an end to their distress and suffering, which looks like an improvement to them. They are willing to trade away their future and all its potential joys in order to gain this immediate relief.

Suicide starts with some discrepancy between expectations (or other standards) and reality. Ironically, suicide rates are often highest in favorable circumstances, such as in rich countries, in places with good climates, or during the fine months of late spring and summer. To be miserable when all around your life seems great for everyone else can be deeply disturbing. Often the suicidal process is set in motion by a significant change for the worse, so that the present seems to fall short of what one has come to expect. For example, rich and poor people commit suicide at about the same rates, but changing from rich to poor produces a big increase in suicide rates. (Going from poor to rich is no problem!) Put another way, suicide does not result from being poor all your life but rather from becoming poor when you are accustomed to being rich. Suicidal college students actually have higher grade point averages than other students—except in their most recent semester, when their grades dipped below average, which probably made them feel that they were falling below what they had come to expect of themselves. Suicidal college students often have parents who expect them to perform well, and the students sometimes feel they cannot meet their parents' expectations.[159,160,161,162,163,164]

capacity to delay gratification the ability to make immediate sacrifices for later rewards

Self-awareness is high among suicidal people; indeed, the human capacity for self-awareness may help explain why nonhuman animals hardly ever kill themselves. In the section on self-awareness in Chapter 3, we saw that people sometimes seek to escape from self-awareness when self-awareness is unpleasant. Suicidal people have often reached this point where self-awareness is acutely painful, and the attempt at suicide may be a desperate, extreme effort to stop ruminating about themselves.[165] In the weeks leading up to a suicide attempt, the person is typically full of thoughts of being a failure, a worthless individual, or an immoral person. Some feel cut off from others, and this too is profoundly upsetting.

You might think that suicidal people would be full of emotional distress, such as anxiety, regret, and guilt, but most studies have found the opposite: Suicidal people tend to be emotionally numb. Apparently, their problems are so upsetting that they respond by shutting down emotionally. They try to avoid thinking about the future or the past and avoid all sorts of abstract, meaningful, or emotional material, focusing instead on the concrete here and now. In the movies, suicide notes are often philosophical: "I've had a good run, but I don't find my life worth living any further; please teach my son to be a good man." In reality, suicide notes tend to be mundane and concrete, such as "I paid the electric bill; tell Fred he can have my video games."[166,167,168,169]

The human mind cannot easily stop thinking meaningfully, and these unfortunate people find that they cannot really keep their thoughts and feelings at bay. Suicide starts to look appealing because it is a way to put an end to the distressing thoughts about how bad the self is. Although suicide trades away one's future for the sake of relief in the here and now, the suicidal person often does not reflect on that because he or she is narrowly focused on the present and not thinking about the future. It is not so much a rejection of one's entire life as an attempt to escape from this week's numbing misery. If you are ever confronted with a friend or relative who is suicidal, besides getting professional help, one emphasis should be to help that person refocus on long-term goals and the pleasures and fulfillments that can still be found in the distant future, regardless of how miserable the foreseeable future may seem.

Another factor that pushes people toward suicide is burdensomeness.[170] Many suicidal individuals are acutely aware of being a burden to others, and they hate that feeling. For example, imagine a man who has long supported his family and after losing his job finds that he has to rely on others to support him. He may start to believe that the people he loves would be better off without him. Therefore, he commits suicide as an act of kindness toward them, relieving them of the burden. Such feelings of guilt may be linked to human nature as cultural animals. People depend on each other and feel bad when they cannot provide for others or reciprocate what others do for them.

No single theory can account for all suicides. The desire to escape from misery may be the most common, but there are other pathways to suicide. This chapter opened with the story of a female terrorist who was prepared to give her own life, and nearly had to do so, in order to destroy a plane full of South Korean tourists. She believed, falsely as it turned out, that killing those people would prevent South Korea from holding the Olympics and would lead to the reunification of her country.

Suicide bombers have been in the news in recent years. The most dramatic were the Arabs who hijacked several airline flights and crashed them into the World Trade Center and the Pentagon in September 2001. Since then, numerous suicide bombers have given their lives to kill other people in various countries in the Middle East and occasionally elsewhere. These people sacrifice themselves to advance a cause such as religion or country, not to escape from a personal hell. (Indeed, some thought they would go directly to heaven for successfully performing their "mission.") Such self-sacrifice represents a commitment to cultural meanings that can override the basic biological drives toward survival and reproduction. Even if one regards them as misguided, futile, or evil, they show how cultural meanings can override biological impulses and cause people to put cultural goals above their own self-interest. Only cultural animals become suicide bombers.

1. In everyday terms, self-defeating behavior is defined as _____ behavior.

(a) experimental
(b) intelligent
(c) stupid
(d) taboo

2. The two main reasons for self-defeating behavior are _____ .

(a) death drive; fear of failure
(b) faulty knowledge; tradeoffs
(c) fear of failure; tradeoffs
(d) faulty knowledge; fear of failure

3. What creatures intentionally kill themselves (i.e., commit suicide)?

(a) Chimps
(b) Gorillas
(c) Humans
(d) All of the above

4. Suicidal people are _____ .

(a) low in self-awareness
(b) high in self-awareness
(c) high in self-handicapping
(d) focused on future consequences

answers: see pg 145

What Makes Us *Human*

Putting the Cultural Animal in Perspective

Behavior occurs among all animals, all the time. What sets humans apart (among other things that will be discussed in other chapters) is an elaborate inner system for controlling behavior. The use of meaning enables human beings to make choices in novel ways and to link their here-and-now actions to far distant realities. Other animals, in contrast, just follow their instincts and respond to the here and now.

Only humans vote in elections, pay taxes, hold wedding ceremonies, make blueprints for the buildings they construct, resort to judges and lawsuits to resolve disputes, create and attend schools and colleges, pray, plan their battles, or celebrate events that occurred before they were born. Animals have sex, but only humans distinguish between meaningless and meaningful sexual relationships. Animals play, but only humans keep score, have referees, and distinguish between meaningful and meaningless games (as in whether the game has playoff implications).

Animals may have a limited understanding of what is happening now, but only humans seem to enrich their understanding of the present by thoughtful links to events in the distant past and future. Indeed, human goals often link what one does now to possible outcomes that lie years away. Thus, human action is not just a here-and-now response but is often designed to help bring about something far off, such as graduation or marriage or retirement. it can also be linked to things that have happened elsewhere or long ago, such as when people celebrate Independence Day or a religious holiday. Moreover, people often follow abstract rules made in distant places by people they will never meet. Most Americans pay income tax, for example, though few have any direct contact with the people who make the tax laws.

Consciousness enables people to use complex reasoning processes to make their decisions via the deliberate system.

They can think about multiple options and do cost–benefit analyses to decide the best course of action.

Self-regulation is not uniquely human, but it seems far better developed among humans than among other species. Our capacity for self-control makes many aspects of human culture possible because it enables us to change ourselves. We can adjust to new norms and opportunities, to changing fads and fashions, to religious doctrines, to new roles and rules. Self-regulation is the key to morality and virtuous behavior, for without the ability to alter one's actions based on general rules, there would be no point in having moral rules. Humans also use self-regulation in ways that other animals don't, ranging from how football players abruptly stop trying to knock their opponents down when the ball goes out of bounds, to instances of people passing up delicious and available food just because they are on a diet.

The capacity for self-directed action has its dark side—namely, irrationality. Just as people are capable of altering their behavior on the basis of rational, enlightened plans, they are also capable of altering it to follow foolish and even self-destructive plans. The brilliance of human innovation is one of the wonders of the world, but humans have also done stupid and costly things on a scale that no other creatures can match. Humans are also alone in the animal kingdom in the occasional willingness of individuals to commit suicide.

Despite these occasional problems and misfortunes, however, human behavior is remarkably special. Perhaps the single greatest advance is freedom: By using meaningful thought, reasoning, and self-regulation, people have been able to free their actions from simply responding to their immediate surroundings. People have choices and make choices, and although choosing is sometimes stressful, people generally benefit from this freedom. When people rise up in revolutions or demonstrations, it is almost always to demand greater freedom, not less freedom. The spread of democracy and liberty thus continues in culture what nature and evolution began—namely, progress toward giving individuals greater freedom.

CHAPTER 4 SUMMARY

What You Do, and What It Means

- Human behavior depends on meaning.
- Inner processes such as thoughts, feelings, and motivations serve interpersonal functions.
- Imagining something makes it more likely to happen.
- Making a choice is typically a two-step process, involving whittling many choices down to a few and then doing a careful comparison of those few.
- Risk aversion refers to the finding that people are more affected by possible losses than by possible gains.
- Temporal discounting refers to the finding that the present is more important than the future in decision making. The further in the future something lies, the less influence it has on the decision.
- In an evolutionary perspective, the most costly type of sexual error for a woman was to reproduce with a nonoptimal male, while the most costly sexual error for a man was to miss an opportunity to have sex and thus possibly to reproduce.
- The certainty effect refers to the tendency to place more emphasis on definite outcomes than on odds and probabilities.
- People may prefer to postpone hard decisions and keep their options open as long as possible.
- The status quo bias is a preference to keep things the way they are rather than change.
- The omission bias (sometimes called the default option) denotes taking whatever course of action that does not require you to do anything.
- People often avoid making decisions because they fear they will later regret their choice.
- Reactance occurs when a freedom or a choice is removed, making the person want the lost option more and perhaps take steps to reclaim it.
- People can think of their traits as fixed and stable (entity theorists) or as subject to change and improvement (incremental theorists).
- Learned helplessness occurs when people think they will fail so they quit trying to succeed.

Freedom of Action

- Belief in free will leads people to act in more prosocial ways.
- Although other animals may have free will, among humans free will has greater behavioral flexibility and can be regulated more easily.
- Humans rely on meaning to make their choices.
- Self-determination theory emphasizes that people need to feel that some of their behavior is caused by their own free will.
- The panic button effect refers to the finding that believing there is an escape option can reduce stress, even if the option is never used.

Goals, Plans, Intentions

- Goals are ideas of some desired future state; they are the meaningful link between values and action.
- Goals tell you what to do in order to pursue and uphold your values, and setting and pursuing goals is a vital job of the self.
- Setting goals includes choosing among possible goals and evaluating their feasibility and desirability.
- Pursuing goals includes planning and carrying out the behaviors to reach goals.
- Both conscious and automatic systems help in the pursuit of goals.
- The Zeigarnik effect states that people remember uncompleted or interrupted tasks better than completed ones.
- People have goal hierarchies; some goals are long term and some are short term.
- Goal shielding is the process of keeping others from interfering with your goals.
- People's plans tend to be overly optimistic, especially over a long time span.

Self-Regulation and Habits

- Self-regulation, or self-control, refers to the self's capacity to alter its own responses; it is essential for cultural animals to adapt to many different demands.
- The three components of self-regulation are standards (concepts of how things should be), monitoring (keeping track of behaviors), and willpower/capacity for change (bringing behavior into line with standards).
- The TOTE model refers to the self-regulation feedback loop of Test, Operate, Test, Exit.
- Willpower is like a muscle, getting depleted after it is used, but getting stronger with exercise.
- A habit is an acquired behavior that, if followed regularly, will become almost automatic.

Irrationality and Self-Destruction

- Self-defeating behavior is defined as any action by which people bring failure, suffering, or misfortune on themselves.
- People engage in self-defeating behavior because they are making tradeoffs or because they are using ineffective strategies, but not usually because they are directly seeking failure.

- The capacity to delay gratification is the ability to make short-term sacrifices in order to get long-term rewards.
- Suicidal people focus on the immediate present at a time when present circumstances may be changing for the worse.

What Makes Us Human? Putting the Cultural Animal in Perspective
- Cultural animals differ from other animals in their elaborate inner systems for controlling behavior.

key terms

capacity for change 134	goal shielding 128	panic button effect 124	self-regulation 131
capacity to delay gratification 140	habit 137	planning fallacy 130	status quo bias 119
certainty effect 118	incremental theorists 121	reactance theory 120	temporal discounting 118
entity theorists 121	learned helplessness 122	risk aversion 116	TOTE 133
error management theory 119	monitoring 133	self-defeating behavior 139	Zeigarnik effect 127
goal 125	omission bias 120	self-determination theory 123	

quiz yourself ANSWERS

1. What You Do, and What It Means **p. 122**
   answers: 1.b   2.d   3.d   4.c

2. Freedom of Action **p. 124**
   answers: 1.b   2.c   3.d   4.b

3. Goals, Plans, Intentions **p. 131**
   answers: 1.c   2.a   3.d   4.c

4. Self-Regulation and Habits **p. 138**
   answers: 1.c   2.d   3.b   4.c

5. Irrationality and Self-Destruction **p. 143**
   answers: 1.c   2.b   3.c   4.b

SOCIAL COGNITION

Arena Creative/Shutterstock.com

5

LEARNING OBJECTIVES

1 Summarize the unique perspective of social cognition.

2 Describe the five elements that distinguish automatic from deliberate processes.

3 Explain how attributes affect our thinking and our behavior.

4 Describe how the four main heuristics affect the way we think.

5 Identify the biases and fallacies that cause errors in thinking.

6 Explain why the shortcuts and styles of thinking are called biases and errors.

Diseases that were once largely eradicated in the United States a generation ago (e.g., whooping cough, measles, mumps) are returning, primarily because parents are deciding not to vaccinate their children for these diseases. For example, consider measles vaccinations. Before routine measles vaccinations were given, there were about 500,000 cases of measles in the United States and a high rate of complications from those cases, including 500 deaths.[1] By 2000, it was declared that the endemic spread of measles in the United States had ended. However, in 2014 measles cases reached a 20-year high,[2] with hundreds of cases being reported. Measles outbreaks have also occurred in many other developed countries (e.g., Australia, Belgium, Canada, the Czech Republic, Germany, Italy, Japan, the Netherlands, New Zealand, Romania, Singapore, the United Kingdom).[3] What has happened?

Typically children received a two-dose vaccine for measles, mumps, and rubella (called the MMR vaccine), with the first dose at age 12–15 months, and the second dose at age 4–6 years.[4] In 1998, a group of 13 researchers led by Andrew Wakefield published an article in the prestigious British medical journal *The Lancet* that reported an examination of 12 children with chronic intestinal disorders who had a history of normal development, followed by severe mental problems.[5] The researchers speculated that the MMR vaccine caused an intestinal infection that damaged the children's brains. Wakefield later coined the term "autistic enterocolitis" for this intestinal disorder. In a press conference, Wakefield recommended that the MMR vaccine be divided into three separate shots given over a longer period of time.

Parents of 8 of the 12 children in the study blamed the MMR vaccine for autistic symptoms in their children. After that, thousands of other parents also claimed that the MMR caused autism in their children. For example, American model Jenny McCarthy blamed vaccinations for her son Evan's autism (even though doctors think Evan has Landau–Kleffner syndrome rather than autism[6]). The U.S. Court of Federal Claims created the National Vaccine Injury Compensation Program to handle all of these claims. However, in three separate rulings the court concluded that the MMR vaccine did not cause autism, and rejected compensation claims from parents of children with autism

The 1998 article by Wakefield and his colleagues set off a wave of large epidemiological studies, but none of these could replicate the link between vaccination and autism. Reviews of the evidence by numerous organizations (e.g., Centers for Disease Control and Prevention, American Academy of Pediatrics, Institute of Medicine, U.S. National Academy of Sciences, U.K. National Health Service, Cochrane Library) concluded that there is no link between the MMR vaccine and autism. For example, the 2012 Cochrane Library review examined data from nearly 15 million children.[7] It too found no link between the vaccine and autism. (And remember, the original study had had only 12 children!)

More recent studies have come to the same conclusion. For example, one 2015 study involving 95,727 participants found no link between the vaccine and autism. The researchers also examined whether each child had a family history of autism, but even for children in this high-risk group there was no link between the vaccine and autism.[8]

Undaunted by the contrary evidence, some critics proposed theories to explain why the MMR vaccine might cause autism. One theory was that the mercury-based preservative thiomersal damaged children's brains. In 1999 the Centers for Disease Control and Prevention and the American Academy of Pediatrics asked vaccine makers to remove thiomersal from vaccines, as a precautionary measure. However, removing thiomersal did not affect autism rates. This theory has since been debunked by all scientific and medical organizations.[9]

After the 1998 article by Wakefield and his colleagues was published, vaccination rates plummeted and the number of measles and mumps cases skyrocketed. Thousands of people have been hospitalized, even though these diseases had been previously controlled.

Since the 1998 study by Wakefield and his colleagues was published, 10 of the 13 authors have retracted the findings.[10] On January 28, 2010, the General Medical Council concluded that the research conducted by Wakefield and his colleagues was unethical, and that the authors had multiple undeclared conflicts of interest (e.g., Wakefield received £55,000—about $94,000—from a group seeking evidence to use against vaccine manufacturers).[11] On February 2, 2010, *The Lancet* "fully retract[ed] this paper from the published record," calling it "an elaborate fraud."[12] In 2011, a series of articles reported that Wakefield and his colleagues had also fabricated some of the data. The presumed disorder "autistic enterocolitis" does not exist—it is bogus. Yet, Wakefield predicted he could make more than $43 million per year by selling diagnostic kits for the new disorder.[13]

The vaccine–autism connection has been described as "the most damaging medical hoax of the last 100 years."[14] The

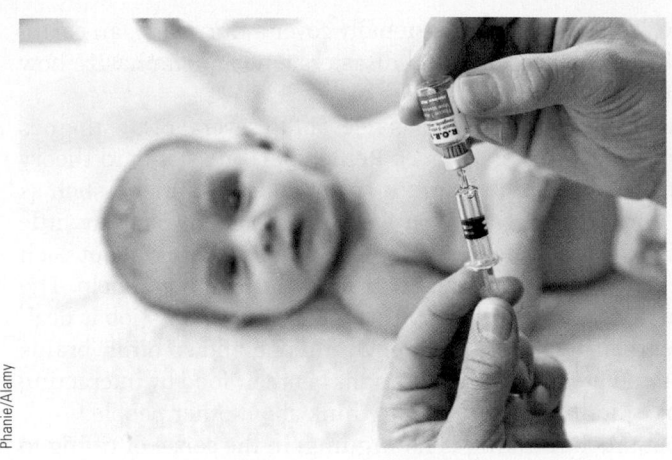

Phanie/Alamy

well-known pediatrician Rahul Parikh stated: "Refusing to vaccinate a child is dangerous not just for that child but for entire communities," and "parents who refuse to vaccinate their kids should pay substantially higher health insurance premiums."[15]

It is therefore shocking that some parents still refuse to vaccinate their children. Instead of believing reviews based on nearly 15 million children, they believe case reports from single individuals like Jenny McCarthy. Indeed, it appears that the anti-vaccine movement has turned into an anti-shot movement. All newborns in the United States are given a routine vitamin K shot because it helps prevent excessive bleeding in those with a deficiency. But some parents are refusing the shot, even though it could mean the difference between life and death for their child.[16]

This chapter sheds light on why things like this occurs. One reason is that misinformation is "sticky"—people can't seem to let go of it.[17] Rejecting information requires cognitive effort. Simply accepting a message as true and the source as credible is easier than weighing the plausibility of the message and its source. Misinformation is especially "sticky" if the topic isn't very important to you or if you have other things on your mind. ●

What Is Social Cognition?

The rise of social cognition in the 1970s marked a fundamental and sweeping change in how social psychologists studied people. Before the 1970s, social psychology was dominated by the doctrine of behaviorism, which held that in order to be scientific, psychologists should only study visible behavior and not make inferences about what was happening inside the person, such as thoughts and feelings. Social psychologists began to realize, however, that it is impossible to understand people without examining how they think and feel. In the 1970s, social psychologists began to focus their studies on people's thoughts and feelings.

Researchers developed methods and techniques to directly and indirectly observe mental processes so that these processes could be studied scientifically. Among the first mental processes that social psychologists studied were attitudes and the motivation to be consistent in one's attitudes (see Chapter 7). The development of attribution theory in the 1960s and 1970s was one of the most important steps in the scientific study of thinking in social psychology. Attribution theory focuses on how people interpret the causes of events, such as external pressures or internal traits. The term **social cognition** became widely used in the 1980s; it encompassed a broad movement to study any sort of thinking by people about people and about social relationships.[18]

Thinking About People: A Special Case?

Social psychologists study how people think about people. Why this topic in particular? Why not study how people think about frogs, or household appliances, or money, or the weather? Cognitive psychologists might study these other topics, but social psychologists focus on people. Is thinking about people special in some way?

In short, yes. People think about other people more than any other topic, and probably more than about all other topics combined.[19] As a brief test, turn on the television and scan the channels. True, some shows are devoted to the physical world, such as those on *Animal Planet* or *The Discovery Channel*. But most shows are about people and their

social cognition a movement in social psychology that began in the 1970s that focused on thoughts about people and about social relationships

relationships with other people. The news may occasionally cover a hurricane, an earthquake, or a tornado, but even footage of these natural disasters tends to emphasize how they affect people. Most news is about people's activities.

The fact that people think a lot about other people is relevant to several of the themes in this textbook, such as "people first" (see Chapter 2). Remember, one standard theory is that the human brain evolved to solve problems in the physical environment, such as making tools, finding shelter, and obtaining food. In fact, people spend relatively little time thinking about these things. Rather, people use their brains to think about each other, implying that humans evolved to rely on each other for information and help. The human mind is designed to participate in society, and this means its primary job is dealing with other people. Birds get their food from their environment, and so birds' brains are focused on trees and worms and predators. Most humans get their food by interacting with other people, and so people's brains are designed to think about other people.

Recent research suggests that much thinking is for arguing, in the sense of trying to convince others.[20] In this view, the purpose of the human brain is not even so much for quietly analyzing other people—rather, it is for communicating with others and influencing them. After all, most people spend relatively little time having their own private thoughts but much more time talking and communicating with other people.[21]

The idea that thinking evolved for arguing may seem implausible, especially if you are the sort of person who hates to argue (though if we say "convince" instead of "argue," it will be hard to say you never do this). But as this chapter examines the ways people reason and the sorts of distortions and slip-ups that afflict human logic, we shall see that these suggest a pattern of arguing for a particular side rather than trying to reason out whatever the truth may be. An added advantage of this view is that it starts from a basic fact of social life, which is that people will often have different opinions as to what would be best to do, and so they need to get others to go along with them. Being able to explain why one's own ideas, wishes, plans, or preferences should prevail is a broadly useful skill, and brains may well have evolved to help that along. It is likely that people who were able to get their way (by arguing) would have survived and reproduced better than people who were less persuasive.

The emphasis on thinking about people—and perhaps arguing with them—shows that inner processes serve interpersonal functions (yet another theme from Chapter 2). Nature (evolution) gave us a powerful brain that can think elaborate thoughts, and this brain is used mainly for helping us relate to others—and not only for garnering social acceptance. You need to understand your enemies and rivals almost as well as you know your friends and lovers. And from time to time you need to convince any and all of them that you are right.

FIGURE 5.1

A plot of brain mass versus body mass for a variety of animals. The open blue circles represent reptiles (including some fish and dinosaurs), the filled purple circles represent mammals (including many birds), and the orange x's represent primates (including humans and their immediate ancestors).[174]

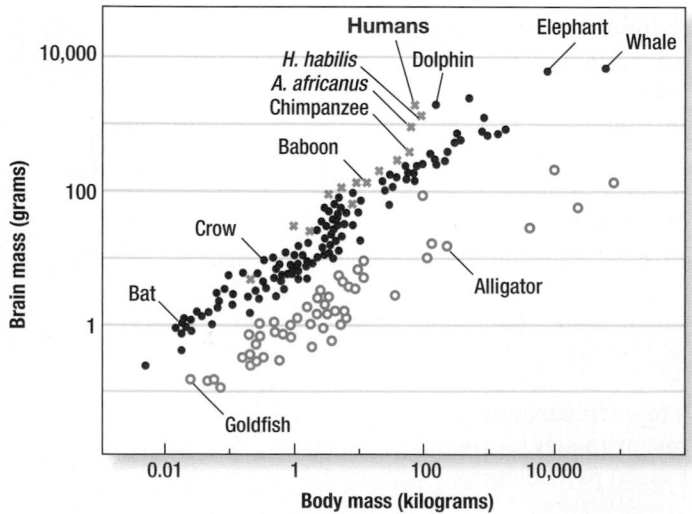

Why People Think, and Why They Don't

Humans can do more and better thinking than any other animal on earth.[22,23,24] Human beings have a brain about the size of a large grapefruit—it weighs about 3 pounds. Although some other animals have larger brains for their body size (e.g., small birds), much of their brain mass is devoted to motor functions (e.g., flying) (see **FIGURE 5.1**). If one compares the size of the cortex (the part of the brain involved in higher-order functions such as thinking) to the rest of the body, humans are at the top of the list.

You might expect that because humans are well equipped to think, they would love to think and would spend all their free time doing it. This is certainly not the case. Researchers have found that often people seem lazy or careless about their thinking. In fact, when experimenters tell people to sit quietly and think, people are unhappy about this, and some would rather receive a mildly painful electric shock.[25] Social psychologists use the term **cognitive miser** to describe people's reluctance to do

cognitive miser a term used to describe people's reluctance to do much extra thinking

much extra thinking.[26] Just as a miser tries to avoid spending money, the cognitive miser tries to avoid thinking too hard or too much. Of course, this isn't entirely a matter of laziness. Thinking takes effort. Although people's capacity to think is greater than other animals, it is limited, so people must conserve their thinking. We have ample evidence that when people's capacity for thinking is already preoccupied, they take even more shortcuts to reduce further the need for thought.[27] They will think hard when engaged in a dispute with someone else, though.

Some people seem to be such numskulls that you wonder whether they had a brain. For example, one young man went into a liquor store, pointed a gun at the clerk, and demanded all the cash in the register. When the bag was full, he demanded a bottle of whisky too. The clerk refused to give up the whisky, saying that he thought the robber was underage. After a brief argument, the robber showed the clerk his driver's license, thereby finally persuading the clerk to hand over the whisky. Of course, the robber was arrested only 2 hours later, after the clerk called the police and gave them the robber's name and address!

Then again, people do think at great length about things that are interesting to them. The legendary genius Albert Einstein published an astonishing 258 articles during his lifetime, dealing with the most complicated issues in physics, and his thinking changed the way that scientists understand the world. Some people spend a great deal of effort thinking about their relationship partners (or how to get one). Some people think about particular events, such as the death of a loved one, for many years afterward. Some people think about soccer (football) all the time and have a seemingly bottomless appetite for the latest game news, anecdotes, and statistics.

Not all thinking is equally difficult. As the theory of the duplex mind indicates, deliberate thinking requires a lot more effort than automatic thinking. People generally prefer to conserve effort by relying on automatic modes of thought when they can. Unfortunately, the automatic system is not very good at some kinds of thinking, such as logical reasoning and mathematics. Therefore, the automatic mind develops various shortcuts, which give rough estimates or pretty good answers. Sometimes, though, people do find it necessary to employ the full power of deliberate thought and analysis.

Automatic and Deliberate Thinking

Humans have a duplex mind, as this book has emphasized (see Chapter 2). Some thinking proceeds by automatic means, whereas other thinking relies on conscious control. To illustrate this point, try the **Stroop test**. In **FIGURE 5.2** you see several rectangles containing different colors. Say the name of the color in each rectangle out loud as quickly as you can. Go one row at a time, from left to right. If you have a timer on your watch

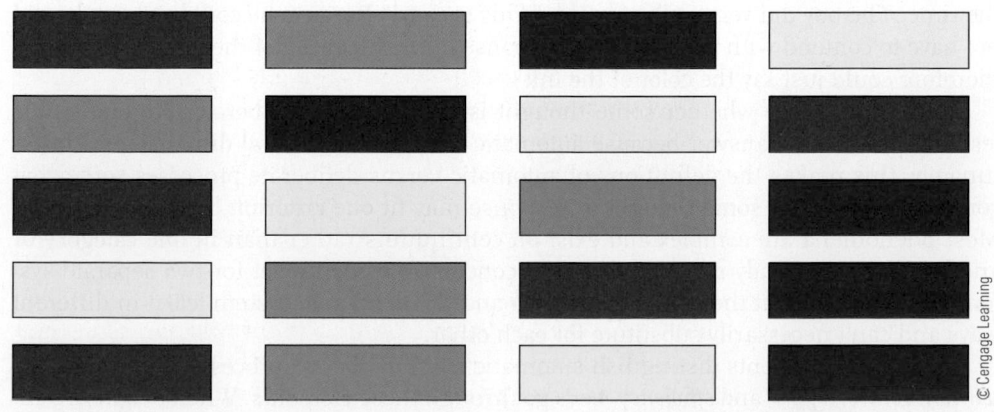

© Cengage Learning

FIGURE **5.2**

Stroop Test 1: Name the color of each rectangle out loud as quickly as you can.

Stroop test a standard measure of effortful control over responses, requiring participants to identify the color of a word (which may name a different color)

FIGURE 5.3
Stroop Test 2: Name the color of each word as quickly as you can, ignoring what the word says.

BLUE	GREEN	BLACK	RED
RED	BLACK	GREEN	BLUE
RED	BLUE	BLACK	GREEN
BLUE	RED	GREEN	BLACK
BLACK	BLUE	GREEN	RED

© Cengage Learning

FIGURE 5.4
Stroop Test 3: As in Test 2, name the color of each word as quickly as you can, ignoring what the word says.

RED	BLUE	GREEN	BLACK
BLACK	BLUE	RED	GREEN
BLUE	BLACK	GREEN	RED
GREEN	BLUE	BLACK	RED
BLUE	BLACK	RED	GREEN

© Cengage Learning

or cell phone, time how long it takes you to do the test. In **FIGURE 5.3** you see several words written in different ink colors. Say the name of the ink color for each word as quickly as you can, ignoring what the word says. Go one row at a time, from left to right. In **FIGURE 5.4** do the same thing—say the ink color, ignoring what the word says. For example, if the word **RED** is printed in blue ink, you should say "blue."

James Ridley Stroop first described the **Stroop effect** in 1935.[28] If you are like most people, it took you longer if the word and ink color didn't match (incongruent) than if they did match (congruent). In the incongruent test (when the word and ink color don't match), the automatic response is to say the word rather than the ink color. It takes conscious effort to override the automatic response and say the ink color instead. One of your textbook authors (Bushman) tried the Stroop test on his son, who was 3 years old at the time. The boy did very well and said, "This is easy!" Because he couldn't read, he did not have to contend with the automatic response of the meaning of the printed word and therefore could just say the color of the ink.

How do we know whether some thought is automatic or deliberate? No one single test can provide the answer because automatic thought has several dimensions. Unfortunately, this makes the definitions of automatic versus deliberate processes somewhat complicated because some thought or response may fit one criterion but not the others. Most phenomena are complex and exist on continuums rather than in one category or another. A recent study reported the most conclusive evidence yet for two separate systems.[29] It showed that the automatic system and the deliberate system learn in different ways and can't necessarily substitute for each other.

At least five elements distinguish automatic from deliberate processes: *awareness, intention, control, effort,* and *efficiency.* Let's go through these elements. When people are engaging in automatic thinking, they may not even be aware that they are thinking. A good example is driving. People who have extensive driving experience don't have to think about how to do it; they just drive. If road conditions become bad, however, deliberate

Stroop effect in the Stroop test, the finding that people have difficulty overriding the automatic tendency to read the word rather than name the ink color

thinking overrides automatic thinking. If it starts to rain or snow, people turn on their windshield wipers, think about whether the roads are slippery, pay more attention to other drivers, and so on. New drivers, in contrast, have to think carefully about what they are doing at all times. Second, automatic thinking is not guided by intention. It may just happen whether you intend it or not. (Indeed, as the Stroop effect shows, automatic thoughts can intrude on your thinking even when you intend to think something else.) Third, automatic thoughts are not subject to deliberate control, so it can be difficult or even impossible to avoid having certain thoughts that have been cued. Fourth, automatic thoughts do not involve effort, whereas deliberate thoughts often involve mental exertion and can feel taxing and tiring. Last, automatic thoughts are highly efficient, unlike deliberate thoughts (which are often slow and cumbersome). To illustrate the difference, suppose we ask you to multiply 3 times 6. The answer comes automatically because you probably memorized it long ago. In contrast, suppose we ask you to multiply 46 times 37, which requires deliberate thought. The differences in intention, control, effort, and efficiency between those two calculations show the relevant differences.

Automatic thinking involves little effort because it relies on knowledge structures. **Knowledge structures** are organized packets of information that are stored in memory. These knowledge structures form when a set of related concepts is frequently brought to mind, or activated. When people think about a concept, it becomes active in memory. Related concepts also become activated (that is, they pop into mind). Over time, as related concepts are frequently activated together, the set of related concepts becomes so strongly linked that activation of one part of the set automatically activates the whole set. For example, the thought of having a cheeseburger might also activate the idea of French fries. Once activated, these knowledge structures simply run their course, like an airplane set on autopilot. The result is automatic thinking.

Different people rely differently on one or the other type of thought. As we have said, both types have advantages. Recent work shows, however, that the deliberative thinkers are better at knowing what they know.[30] For example, a quick intuitive solution might be close but not quite correct, whereas laboriously thinking through the problem furnishes a different answer. The people who use the deliberate style of thinking thus know there are different possible answers, both the intuitive one and the one reached by thinking things through. In contrast, the intuitive people only know the answer that intuition gives, so they are less likely to know whether they got it right. In other words, intuition is often correct and certainly easier—but intuitive people tend to be overconfident rather than knowing what they know.

Schemas

Schemas are knowledge structures that represent substantial information about a concept, its attributes, and its relationships to other concepts. The concept, for example, could be the self, another person, a social category (e.g., politicians), or an object. A schema for dancing, for example, would include movement, rhythm, repetition, and coordination, as well as connections to music, shoes, romance, fashion, art, and perhaps embarrassment. A schema for bears might include fur, claws, danger, climbing trees, hibernating, and growling, as well as relationships to honey, zoos, various football teams (e.g., Chicago Bears), stuffed toys (teddy bears), and drops in stock prices (a "bear market").

Schemas make the complex world much easier to understand. They help organize information by connecting beliefs that are related to each other. They help the mind form expectancies. Hence, if someone asks you to go dancing, you know that person is probably not just telling you to go outside and move around, but perhaps initiating a romantic date, and you should wear nice shoes and be prepared for music.

One type of event that sparks deliberate thinking is a violation of expectancies. In general, people seem to go through their daily lives with a solid idea of what is supposed to happen. When life conforms to what they expect, they don't generally find it necessary to think much about it. When events depart sharply from what people have learned to expect, they may stop and analyze what happened. This is a very useful pattern. People develop an understanding of their social world, and their expectancies and schemas are part of this understanding. You develop schemas through your experiences, and they guide the way you process information. Getting through daily life is much easier if you

knowledge structures organized packets of information that are stored in memory

schemas knowledge structures that represent substantial information about a concept, its attributes, and its relationships to other concepts

1. Hostess greets person

2. Hostess seats person

3. Person pays for food

4. Person orders food from waiter

5. A person enters a restaurant

6. Person looks at menu

7. Person leaves restaurant

8. Person eats food

© Michael Newmann/PhotoEdit

One example of a script is a restaurant script. Try putting the frames above in the correct order. The answer is printed below the frames. The fact that you can do this illustrates that scripts exist.

have schemas and know what to expect. Events that violate your expectancies show that something might be wrong with how you understand the world, so it is worth pausing to analyze the situation. In a club, you ask someone to dance, and the person sometimes nods and accompanies you to the dance floor, or sometimes politely rejects you; all is as expected, with no need to analyze. But if your invitation to dance is met with a big laugh or a hurried departure, you might stop to wonder what went wrong: Are you not allowed to ask people to dance? Is something wrong with the way you look? Do you smell bad?

Scripts

Scripts are knowledge structures that contain information about how people (or other objects) behave under varying circumstances. In a sense, scripts are schemas about certain kinds of events. In films and plays, scripts tell actors what to say and do. In memory, scripts define situations and guide behavior: The person first selects a script to represent the situation, assumes a role in the script, and behaves accordingly. Scripts can be learned by direct experience or by observing others (e.g., parents, siblings, peers, mass media characters).

People learn schemas and scripts that influence how they perceive, interpret, judge, and respond to events in their lives. These various knowledge structures develop over time, beginning in early childhood. The pervasiveness, interconnectedness, and accessibility of any learned knowledge structure is largely determined by the frequency with which it is encountered, imagined, and used. With great frequency, even complex knowledge structures can become automatized—so overlearned that we apply them automatically with little effort or awareness.

scripts knowledge structures that define situations and guide behavior

Priming

You are probably already familiar with the concept of priming. When someone primes an engine (e.g., on a lawn mower), the person pumps gas into the cylinder so that the spark plug will fire more easily, which makes the engine start more easily. The term "prime the pump" refers to government action taken to stimulate the economy (e.g., cutting taxes, reducing interest rates). Memory is filled with concepts. Related concepts are linked together in memory (e.g., the concepts *cradle* and *baby*), as depicted in **FIGURE 5.5**. When one concept becomes primed in memory by thinking about it, related concepts in memory become more accessible. For example, priming the concept "doctor" also makes the concepts "nurse," "hospital," "dentist," and "fever" more accessible in memory (see Figure 5.5). Thus, **priming** is the process by which a given stimulus activates mental pathways, thereby enhancing their accessibility. William James, philosopher and psychologist, described priming as the "wakening of associations." Once a concept has been primed, it can influence the way we interpret new information. For example, numerous studies have shown that people are faster at classifying a target word (e.g., *nurse*) when it is preceded by a related word (e.g., *doctor*) than when it is preceded by an unrelated word (e.g., *butter*).[31,32] The prime doesn't have to be conscious either. Some primes are subliminal, or below the level of conscious awareness. For example, a casino in Windsor, Ontario, Canada, was fined because their electronic slot machines flashed the subliminal message "win" to customers. The idea was that priming the concept "win" would make customers more optimistic so that they would shovel more coins into slot machines. (Apparently the government thought this was unethical; what do you think?)

The power of priming to activate concepts, which then hang around in the mind and can influence subsequent thinking, was demonstrated in an early study.[33] Participants were asked to identify colors while reading words. The words did not seem at all important to the study, but they were actually very important because they were primes. By random assignment, some participants read the words *reckless, conceited, aloof,* and *stubborn,* whereas others read the words *adventurous, self-confident, independent,* and *persistent.* Then all participants were told that the experiment was finished, but they were asked to do a brief task for another, separate experiment. In that supposedly different experiment, they read a paragraph about a man named Donald who was a skydiver, a powerboat racer, and a demolition derby driver, and they were asked to describe the impression they had of Donald. It turned out that the words participants had read earlier influenced their opinions of him. Those who had read the words *reckless, conceited, aloof,* and *stubborn* were more likely to view Donald as having those traits than were participants who had read the other words. That is, the first task had "primed" participants with the ideas of recklessness, stubbornness, and so forth, and once these ideas were activated, they influenced subsequent thinking.

Research has often used priming as a technique to trigger automatic processes. For example, participants in one study first unscrambled sentences by choosing four out of five words to make a grammatically correct sentence.[34] They were told to do this as quickly as possible. In the rude priming version, one of the five words was rude (e.g., *they/her/bother/see/usually*). In the polite priming version, one of the five words was polite (e.g., *they/her/respect/see/usually*). In the neutral priming version, the polite or rude word was replaced by a neutral word (e.g., *they/her/send/see/usually*). Participants were told that after they completed the task, they should come out into the hallway and find the experimenter. The experimenter waited for the participant, while pretending to explain the sentence task to a confederate. The confederate pretended to have a difficult time understanding the task. The experimenter refused to acknowledge the participant, who was waiting patiently for instructions on what to do next. The dependent variable in the study was whether participants interrupted the experimenter within a 10-minute period. Of course, it is rude to interrupt somebody who is speaking to another person. As can be seen in **FIGURE 5.6** participants primed with rude words were much more likely to interrupt the experimenter than were participants primed with polite words. Thus, priming activated the idea of being

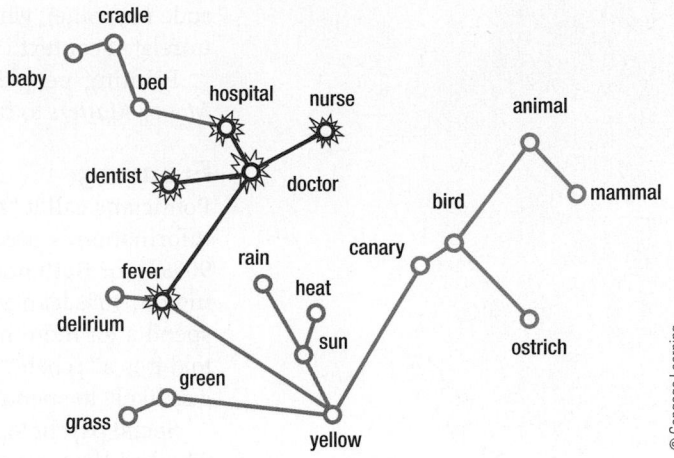

FIGURE 5.5

Human memory can be represented as a network. The nodes represent the concepts. Related concepts are linked in memory.

© Cengage Learning

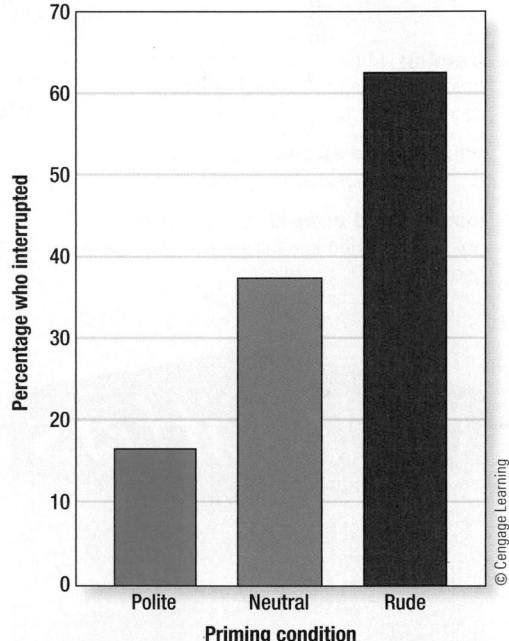

© Cengage Learning

FIGURE 5.6

In one study, participants primed with rude words were much more likely to interrupt the experimenter than were participants in the polite condition.[34]

priming activating an idea in someone's mind so that related ideas are more accessible

rude (or polite), which then lingered in the mind and influenced behavior in a seemingly unrelated context.

Priming people with money changes the way they think about many things. See *Money Matters* to find out how.

Framing

Politicians call it "spin," but social psychologists call it "framing." **Framing** refers to how information is presented to others. Would you rather eat a hamburger that is 10% fat or 90% lean? Both numbers convey the same fact about the same hamburger, but emphasizing the 90% lean aspect sounds much more appetizing. Research has shown that people spend a lot more money when they are told the money is a "bonus" than when they are told it is a "rebate."[36,37] A rebate is the return of a loss of one's own money, so people are less likely to spend it.

Social psychologists have become very interested in the framing of health messages— whether they are more effective if they are framed in terms of gains or losses. **gain-framed appeal** focuses on how doing something will make you healthier (e.g., "Flossing your teeth daily removes particles of food in the mouth, avoiding bacteria, thereby promoting fresh breath."); a **loss-framed appeal** focuses on the downside, such as the potential for greater illness (e.g., "If you do not floss your teeth daily, particles of food remain in the mouth, collecting bacteria, thereby causing bad breath."). Research has shown that gain-framed appeals are more effective when targeting behaviors that prevent the onset of disease, whereas loss-framed appeals are more effective when targeting behaviors that detect diseases that people may already have but not be aware of.[38]

The media can also frame stories in different ways. For example, in 2014 Arizona's governor vetoed a bill that would have allowed business owners who cited their religious beliefs to justify refusing to serve gay customers. The headline for a *Washington Post* article read "Arizona governor vetoes controversial anti-gay bill," whereas the headline for a *Wall Street Journal* article read "Arizona governor vetoes religious-freedom bill."

Framing things sometimes makes unpleasant tasks more palatable. Researchers have even found that framing physical activity as fun rather than exercise reduces overeating later.[39] For example, people who were led to label a hike as an "exercise walk" later ate more dessert at mealtime and consumed more snacks, as compared to people who were led to label the hike as a "scenic walk." Physical activity consumes calories either way, but

framing whether messages stress potential gains (positively framed) or potential losses (negatively framed)

gain-framed appeal focuses on how doing something will add to your health

loss-framed appeal focuses on how not doing something will subtract from your health

MONEY *Matters*

Does Money Make a Difference?

Right now, would you describe what you are doing as "moving my eyes along lines of print," "reading," "doing today's assignment," "gaining knowledge about social psychology," or even "advancing my education"? Those descriptions may all be accurate, but their levels of abstraction differ. Moving one's eyes and reading are fairly concrete, whereas pursuing educational goals is more abstract.

Money seems to shift people toward more abstract styles of thinking, as recent studies showed.[35] Participants had to choose among various groups of descriptions of the same action (like the group in the first sentence of this box). Some previously had the idea of money briefly planted in their minds. These people favored the more abstract descriptions, as compared to others who had not been led to think of money. In another study, people who thought of money sorted objects into fewer, broader categories, as opposites to narrow, specific ones (e.g., birds vs. seagulls, robins, eagles, hawks, and so forth). Those who had not thought of money sorted into the narrower, more specific categories. Using the larger, more all-encompassing categories indicates more abstract thinking.

Not all primes of money led to abstract thinking. Large amounts of money did, but when people had been led to think of small amounts of money, they did not shift to high levels of abstraction. Also, thinking about prices (a specific application of money) made people think in fairly concrete terms. Thinking about a price is often linked to concrete, specific actions (such as whether to buy something).

Money is itself a rather abstract concept. Money is a symbolic store of value. A dollar may be useful for buying a banana at some point, but the dollar bill itself is not edible, nor good for much else. Perhaps it is no accident that humans engage in far more abstract thought than any other animals—and also are the only ones to invent and use money!

framing that as exercise apparently makes people feel they should have some delicious treats as reward. Engaging in fun does not produce that same reaction.

Thought Suppression and Ironic Processes

Most people have had thoughts they would like to erase from their minds. When people want to suppress a thought, their mind sets up two processes. One process keeps a lookout for anything that might remind the person of the unwanted thought. It is an automatic process that checks all incoming information for danger. The other is a deliberate process that redirects attention away from the unpleasant thought. For example, if you are upset that you did not do well on a chemistry test and want to avoid worrying about it, your mind may automatically watch for anything that might remind you of tests or chemistry, and when some cue arises (e.g., seeing the person who sits in front of you in chemistry class), your conscious mind quickly turns attention elsewhere (e.g., you don't say hello to that person). The problem with the deliberate system is that whenever conscious control is relaxed, the automatic system is still watching for cues and may therefore flood the mind with them.[40] This chapter's *Tradeoffs* box describes the pros and cons of unconscious and conscious thought.

As a child, the Russian writer Leo Tolstoy (1828–1910) was once challenged by his older brother Nikolenka to remain standing in a corner until he could stop thinking of a white bear.[41] Poor Leo could think of nothing else. He quickly learned how difficult it is to control thoughts. Researchers have replicated the informal experiment conducted by young Leo Tolstoy in more formal laboratory settings.[42,43,44] Regardless of the setting, the results are the same: People who are told not to think of a white bear cannot rid their minds of the white, furry creatures. People who are trying to overcome vices are better off not suppressing unwanted thoughts of the things they crave. For example, trying not to think about cigarettes only makes it more difficult for smokers to quit.[45] The paradoxical effects of thought suppression have been linked to a variety of psychological disorders, especially anxiety disorders (e.g., phobias, obsessive-compulsive disorders, panic disorder, posttraumatic stress disorder).[46] Even in dreams, suppressed thoughts are more likely to come to mind.[47,48] One review of all previous studies on the topic concluded that suppressing unwanted thoughts often backfires.[49]

If suppressing thoughts does not work, what does work? Research has shown that distraction and even rumination (or contemplation) are more effective than suppression.[50] Mental control is a form of self-regulation, discussed in detail in Chapter 4. *Food for Thought* describes how difficult it is for dieters to control their thoughts and consequently their eating habits.

1. Organized beliefs we have about stimuli in our social world are known as _____.

    ⓐ automatic processes   ⓑ deliberate processes   ⓒ schemas   ⓓ self-concepts

2. What topic do people spend the greatest amount of time thinking about?

    ⓐ Food   ⓑ Money   ⓒ People   ⓓ Weather

3. Which of the following is *not* one of the elements that distinguishes automatic from deliberate processes?

    ⓐ awareness   ⓑ efficiency   ⓒ effort   ⓓ relevance

4. During their first year of medical school, many medical students begin to think that they and other people they know are suffering from serious illness. This phenomenon, known as the medical student syndrome, is probably due to _____.

    ⓐ counterfactual thinking   ⓑ false consensus   ⓒ false uniqueness   ⓓ priming

QUIZ YOURSELF

What Is Social Cognition?

answers: see pg 183

Conscious and Unconscious Thought

Suppose you had a tough choice to make, such as choosing the best apartment to rent. What is the best procedure? Conventional wisdom says to make a list of the pros and cons and then use logic to figure out the best option for you. A different approach—to absorb all the information first and then put it out of your mind for a while—is considered a better option by some. Eventually the right answer pops into your mind.

The second approach has gained scientific respectability in the last few years. Two Dutch psychologists have published influential research making the case for what they call "unconscious thought."[51] As they put it, the brain is a giant organ with many neurons and much activity, and only a tiny portion of it goes on in consciousness. The unconscious can therefore be smarter than consciousness. So letting your unconscious mind help make a decision may be a great way to proceed.

To back up their claim, they reported a series of studies with remarkable findings, often showing that unconscious thought outperforms conscious thought. For example, they used a variation on the apartment choice problem that opened this box. Participants were confronted with a huge amount of information: a dozen different features on each of four apartments. The researchers had rigged the information so that one apartment had mostly good features and another had a more negative overall outlook. They wanted to see whether participants managed to choose what the researchers regarded as the best option.

Some participants had to make their selection immediately after reading all the information. Others had 3 minutes to think consciously about the apartments. A third group, in the unconscious thought condition, had to perform a different mental task that preoccupied their conscious mind for 3 minutes and then choose which apartment. These participants in the unconscious thought condition were more likely to make the optimal choice.[52] Unconscious thinking produced seemingly better results than conscious thinking.

These and similar findings led many experts to start recommending that people rely on unconscious thinking for important decisions. Advice to "sleep on it," "go with your gut feeling," and "don't overthink it" became common. The Dutch researchers won a huge prize for their main article on unconscious thought. But before long there was a backlash from other researchers, who questioned whether unconscious thought was really superior to conscious thought.

One source of objections was based on follow-up experiments. The superiority of unconscious thought over conscious thought has not been replicated consistently.[53] It may depend on fairly artificial constraints, such as requiring the conscious thought to start and end at precise intervals (e.g., 3 minutes).

Other work has shown that conscious thought is genuinely superior to unconscious thought at some things. In particular, the unconscious is not very good at logical reasoning.[54] It doesn't do arithmetic. (When you hear "7 times 4" you automatically think "28," but that doesn't mean the unconscious is actually calculating the answer. More likely, it memorized the answer during elementary school and now just automatically spits out the answer without really understanding the math.)

If consciousness is needed for logic, how could the unconscious even keep up with it (let alone surpass it) in the apartment-choosing problem? Problems like that do not require reasoning or indeed combining information in any complex manner. The "right" answer was simply the apartment that had the most positive and fewest negative features. The unconscious is pretty good at tallying up that one option has more good things than another. It is much less effective at finding new meanings that emerge from combination. For example, *green* is a nice color, and *bread* is good to eat, so to the unconscious *green bread* is simply a double good thing. Likewise, *dead* and *enemy* both connote something bad, so *dead enemy* is doubly bad. It takes conscious thought to notice that the meaning changes when they are combined.[55]

At present, the relative powers and influence of unconscious versus conscious thought comprise an exciting and controversial area, so conclusions are tentative. The best bet seems to be that both conscious and unconscious thought processes have important and valuable—but different—functions. Unconscious thought can really help people sort through information and come to good decisions. But conscious thought is also vital, especially when logical reasoning is helpful.

So when you face a tough decision, a period of unconscious thought might well be useful. But perhaps that should augment and help rather than replace thinking the matter over consciously!

TRADE *Offs*

Ra3rn/Shutterstock.com

Unconscious mind: "you like green and bread—eat it!"

It's the Thought That Counts (or Doesn't Count!) the Calories

How much will someone eat? It depends partly on how hungry the person is. Someone who has not eaten anything for hours will eat more than someone who has just eaten a big meal. At least, that would make sense.

Not everyone follows that pattern, and some people even do the opposite. In one research paradigm, participants come to the lab after not having had anything to eat for several hours.[56] By random assignment, participants are initially given nothing to eat, or a moderate milkshake, or a giant double milkshake. Afterward, participants are given three large containers of ice cream (chocolate, strawberry, and vanilla) to taste and rate. In reality, the researchers simply want to find out how much ice cream people will eat, as a function of whether they are already full (milkshake conditions) or hungry (no-milkshake condition).

Dieters react differently from nondieters in this situation. Nondieters do what you probably expect. Those who just consumed the milkshake eat less ice cream, just enough to enable them to answer the questions on the rating sheet, whereas those who did not get any milkshake tend to chow down on the ice cream.

Dieters, however, show the opposite pattern (**FIGURE 5.7**). That is, dieters who had not been given any milkshake were very restrained in tasting the ice cream. But dieters who had been assigned to drink a milkshake actually ate significantly more ice cream than the others. Researchers dubbed this tendency **counterregulation**—or, more informally, the "what the heck" effect—because the dieters seem to be thinking, "My diet is already blown for the day by drinking that milkshake, so what the heck, I might as well enjoy some ice cream too!"[57]

The fact that the "what the heck" effect is driven by peculiar cognitions, rather than any bodily need for food, was demonstrated in a remarkable series of studies.[58] Apparently whether the dieters think their diet is blown for the day depends more on how they think about certain foods than on the actual number of calories consumed. In one study, some dieters were given a snack of cottage cheese with fruit cocktail, which sounds like diet food but actually contained 580 calories. Others ate a small portion of ice cream that amounted to only 290 calories. Contrary to the actual caloric content, the ones who ate ice cream acted as if their diets were blown and ate more. Those who ate the cottage cheese and fruit cocktail acted as if their diets were still intact, even though their snack had contained twice as many calories as the ice cream.

In another study, dieters had either a high-calorie or a low-calorie salad, or a high-calorie or low-calorie ice cream treat. Regardless of calories, those who ate the ice cream showed the "what the heck" effect, whereas those who had eaten the salads did not. The researchers tried another study in which they told participants precisely how many calories were in the assigned food, and even told them that they would eat this later on. Even under these conditions, dieters who expected to eat ice cream reacted as if their diets were already blown, whereas those who expected to eat salad acted as if their diet were intact, regardless of the caloric content.

None of this makes rational sense. Even if you violate your diet for the day, you should avoid eating more fattening foods. Not only do dieters act as if one lapse ruins their diet for the day so it doesn't matter how much they eat thereafter, they also seem to make those decisions based on rigid ways of thinking about foods, regardless of how many calories the foods contain. Even when the salad contains twice as many calories as the ice cream treat, they act as if salad is good for diets.

If thinking misleads dieters, does it help to avoid thinking? Not really. Trying to suppress thoughts of desired food does not help people restrain their eating.[59,60] Thought suppression only makes people think more about the food they are trying not to think about—a rebound effect.

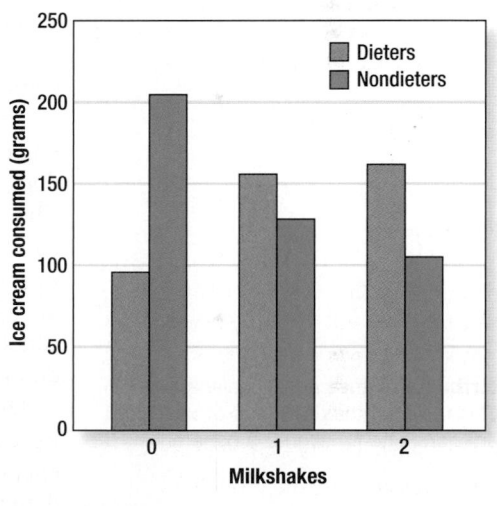

FIGURE 5.7

Nondieters who had had a milkshake ate less ice cream; dieters who had had milkshakes ate more ice cream![56]

Attributions and Explanations: Why Did That Happen?

Why did he do that? Why did she say that? Is she angry? Is he a fool? Is this job too hard for me? Does this good news mean that I am smarter than other people, or just lucky? People ask and answer these questions in their own minds all the time. Making the

counterregulation the "what the heck" effect that occurs when people indulge in a behavior they are trying to regulate after an initial regulation failure

If Calvin falls he wants to make an external attribution for the failure, whereas his teacher wants Calvin to make an internal attribution.

correct inferences is important, but not easy. There is no perfect way to go from what we actually see (e.g., someone's actions) to drawing firm conclusions about what that person is like inside (e.g., stable personality traits).

Attributions are the inferences people make about events in their lives. Indeed, the study of attributions was a revolutionary step in the history of social psychology because it led social psychologists to abandon once and for all the behaviorist tradition that said psychology should only study observable, objective behavior and not talk about thoughts or other inner processes. Attributions opened the way for the study of thoughts and other cognitive processes.

Attributions are a crucial form of information processing that helps determine behavior. Two people may get identical bad grades on a test, but one of them works harder and does better the next time around, whereas the other gives up and drops out of the course. The attributions they make may help explain the difference. One student looked at the bad grade and thought, "I didn't study hard enough," so that person studied harder and improved. The other student looked at the same grade but thought, "I'm no good at this," or "This is too hard for me," or "This class sucks!" or "This teacher fails everyone." Such conclusions do not spur people to try harder because they imply that all such effort is doomed to failure. Instead, they give up.[61]

Differentiating between seeing behavior caused by internal factors and seeing behavior caused by external factors, first proposed by attribution theorist Fritz Heider, has shaped a generation of social psychologists. Research shows, for example, that when students perform poorly in the classroom, teachers make internal attributions (e.g., the student failed because he or she didn't study hard enough), whereas students tend to make external attributions (e.g., the test was too difficult).[62]

It's Not My Fault: Explaining Success and Failure

One early thrust of attribution theory was to map out how people interpret success and failure. The distinction between internal and external causes is certainly important. Success may be due to internal factors of the person such as effort, or could be due to external factors such as luck. Bernard Weiner, another important attribution theorist, proposed a two-dimensional theory of attributions for success and failure.[63] The first dimension was internal versus external; the second dimension was stable versus unstable.

This two-dimensional map of attributions is illustrated in **FIGURE 5.8**. The four possible combinations of internal–external and stable–unstable yield the four main types of attributions that people make when they see themselves or someone else perform. Let us briefly consider each.

Internal, stable attributions involve ability. People may think their success reflects intelligence or talent. Conversely, they may decide that they failed at something because they lack the relevant ability. Ability attributions are very important because they invoke

attributions the causal explanations people give for their own and others' behaviors, and for events in general

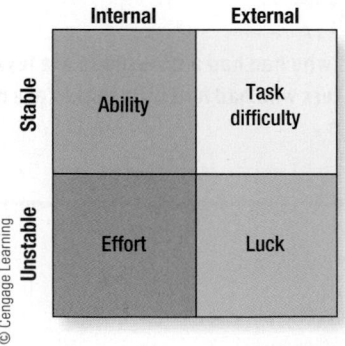

FIGURE **5.8**

Two-dimensional attribution theory illustrating the four possible combinations of internal–external and stable–unstable types.

relatively permanent aspects of the self. People generally like to think that they have high ability, so their attributions may be biased.[64,65]

Internal, unstable attributions involve effort. Effort is unstable because it can change. If you think someone succeeded because she worked very hard, you have little guarantee that she will do well again (because she might not work as hard the next time). Then again, attributing failure to low effort can be very motivating because people may think that they might succeed if they try harder. There are cultural differences on this dimension. People from collectivist cultures emphasize effort, whereas people from individualistic cultures emphasize ability.[66,67]

External, stable attributions point to the difficulty of the task. Success simply indicates the task was easy, whereas failure indicates it was hard. Most other people are likely to get the same result because the crucial cause lies in the task, not in the person doing it.

Last, external and unstable attributions involve luck. If you attribute someone's success or failure to luck, there is very little credit or blame due to the person, nor is there any reason to expect the same result the next time. Attributions are not made in a vacuum. Among other factors, people want to take credit for success but deny blame for failure. This tendency is called the **self-serving bias**. Many studies of attribution have confirmed the widespread operation of the self-serving bias.[68] That is, across many different contexts and settings, people prefer to attribute their successes to ability and effort but tend to attribute their failures to bad luck or task difficulty.[69]

The self-serving bias occurs for several reasons. One reason is simply that interpreting events in that way helps people believe they have high ability and makes people feel good. They can maintain their high opinion of themselves by discounting their failures and maximizing the glory of their successes. However, evidence suggests that the self-serving bias is especially strong when people are explaining their successes and failures to others.[70,71] This would imply that they care more about what others think of them than about how they think of themselves. In other words, the self-serving bias is an important feature of self-presentation, described in Chapter 3 as people's efforts to control the impressions they make on others. (In a sense, self-presentation is about trying to influence the attributions that other people make about you. Thus, this point fits the theme that much thinking is really about how to convince other people.)

The self-presentational nature of the self-serving bias reflects another theme of this book, which is that inner processes serve interpersonal ends. People learn to think in ways that will help them get along better with others. If others see you as an incompetent loser, your chances of being accepted by others (e.g., hired for a good job) are low. Hence, people want to maximize their credit for success while avoiding having their failures reflect badly on themselves.

Related to the self-serving bias is the tendency for individuals to overestimate how much they contributed to a group project. If you ask individuals in a group what percentage they contributed to the project, and add up the percentages, the sum is almost always greater than 100 percent—often much greater![72] Part of the explanation for this effect is that individuals tend to view the other group members as a collective rather than as individuals. When individuals "unpack" the collaborations of the other group members, this bias is reduced.[73,74] Still, mostly people will fail to make that sort of correction, and so they will tend to overestimate how much they contributed. This can complicate the process of sharing credit. After all, it's hard to divide up the pay or credit in a fair manner if both people think they did more than half the work!

You Know I'm Right: The Actor/ Observer Bias

Suppose you go to a store and see a man shouting at the salesclerk. You might be tempted to conclude that the shouting person is a grumpy, obnoxious fellow. After all, obnoxious people certainly are more likely to shout at people in stores than are agreeable, easygoing, nice people.

Then again, the shouting man might see things very differently. If you asked him, "Why are you shouting?"

self-serving bias the tendency to take credit for success but deny blame for failure; or internal attributions for success, external attributions for failure.

In many fights and brawls, each side claims that the other side started it.

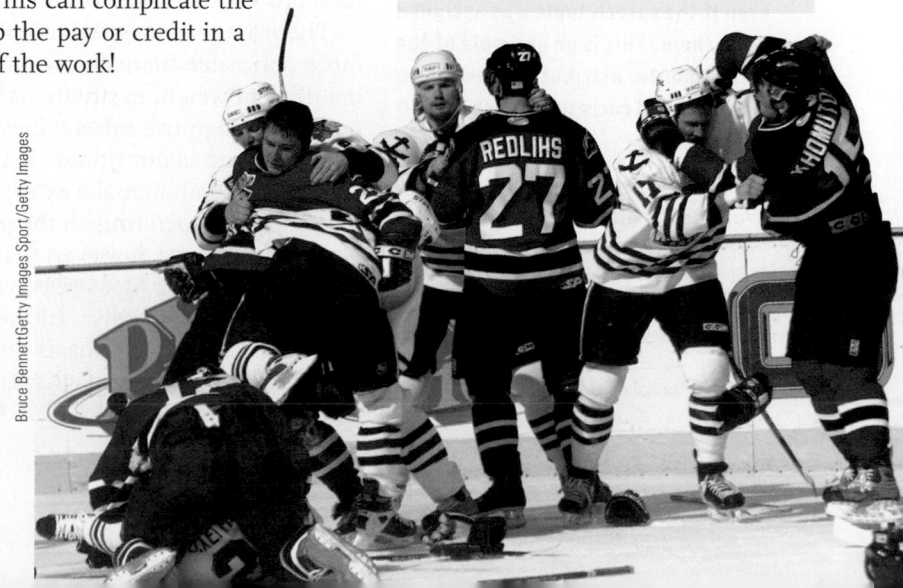

Bruce Bennett/Getty Images Sport/Getty Images

he would be unlikely to give the answer "Because I am an obnoxious person!" More likely, he would say that the store clerk has treated him badly, and perhaps he has experienced a series of frustrations all day long.

In this example, we saw how you can reach very different conclusions (attributions) about the same behavior. The difference has been called the **actor/observer bias**.[75] It is relevant to any situation in which one person (the observer) is watching someone else's (the actor's) behavior. The actor/observer bias can be defined this way: Actors tend to attribute their own behavior to the situation (external), whereas observers tend to attribute actors' behavior to the actors (internal). Put more simply, actors tend to make external attributions, whereas observers make internal attributions.

The actor/observer bias can produce many misunderstandings and disagreements. Indeed, in an argument, it may be common for both sides to see themselves as responding to what the other does. "He started it!" is a common complaint, often heard on both sides, because each side attributes its own behavior to the situation but the others' behavior to their traits and other dispositions. It seems natural to infer that *they* are fighting because they are mean, whereas *we* are fighting because they attacked us. Or, in the simpler words of pro hockey player Barry Beck on a brawl that broke out in one game, "We have only one person to blame, and that's each other!"

Some psychologists have focused on the observer side of the actor/observer bias, labeling it the **fundamental attribution error** (also sometimes called **correspondence bias**). People have a bias to attribute another person's behavior to internal or dispositional causes (e.g., personality traits, attitudes) to a much greater extent than they should. People fail to take full notice and consideration of the external factors (e.g., the situation, constraints of the social environment) that are operating on the person.

For example, is the person who commits an act of aggression a beast? Is the person who donates money to charity an altruist? To answer this kind of question, people make inferences on the basis of factors such as choice and intention. Intentional behavior that is freely chosen is more informative about a person than is behavior that is coerced. Participants in a classic study[76] read a speech, ostensibly written by a college student, that either favored or opposed Fidel Castro, who was then the communist leader of Cuba and an outspoken enemy of America. The participants were instructed to try to figure out the true attitude of the essay writer. Half of the participants were told that the student who wrote the essay had freely chosen to take this position. The other participants were told that the student was assigned the position by a professor. The study results are depicted in **FIGURE 5.9**. When asked to estimate the student's true attitude, participants were more likely to assume that there was a correspondence between his or her essay (behavior) and attitude (disposition) when the student had a choice than when the student had no choice.

However, crucially, the participants in that study were willing to make internal attributions even when they were told the essay writer had had no choice. Logically, you cannot infer anything about someone's true opinion if the person's behavior was forced by the situation. This is the fundamental attribution error in action: People discounted the situational pressures to write a pro-Castro essay and concluded that the writer must have pro-Castro opinions.

There are several explanations for the fundamental attribution error. First, behavior is more noticeable than situational factors, which are often hidden. Second, people assign insufficient weight to situational causes even when they are made aware of them. Third, people are cognitive misers; they often take quick and easy answers rather than thinking long and hard about things. It takes considerably less cognitive effort to make internal attributions than to make external attributions by thinking about all the external factors that might be operating on the person.

We should note, however, that the fundamental attribution error might not be so fundamental after all. Most research shows that the fundamental attribution error is more common in individualist cultures than in collectivist cultures.[77,78,79] Collectivist cultures tend to place more emphasis on situational explanations of behavior than individualist cultures do.[80] Western civilization pioneered the idea that each person is an individual who can think and act as a unit. Hence people who live in Western civilization (like North

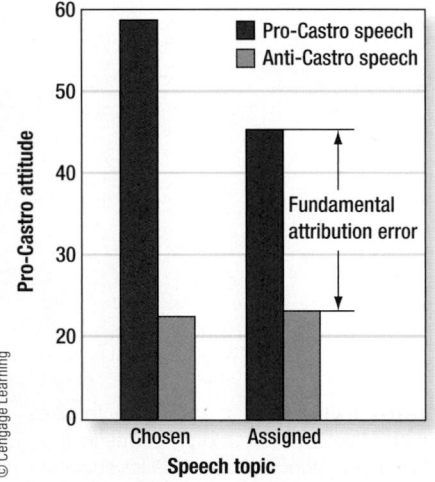

FIGURE 5.9

Participants in a classic study thought that students who wrote a pro-Castro speech had pro-Castro attitudes, even if the speech topic was assigned to them. This is an example of the fundamental attribution error (also called correspondence bias).[76]

actor/observer bias the tendency for actors to make external attributions and observers to make internal attributions

fundamental attribution error (correspondence bias) the tendency for observers to attribute other people's behavior to internal or dispositional causes and to downplay situational causes

America and Europe) may be especially prone to attribute actions to causes inside the person. Recent experiments in China and the United States suggest that the Western style of thinking is designed to improve control over the world, whereas collectivistic thought styles are more about acceptance and harmony. When Asians desire control, they shift and think more like Westerners.[81]

Challenging Attribution Theory

Recent work has begun to question the very existence of the actor/observer bias, however, especially when one sorts it out from the self-serving bias. Combining results from many different studies, Bertram Malle has concluded that there was no consistent tendency for observers to make more dispositional attributions than actors.[82]

Indeed, he has concluded that the influential theory of the actor/observer bias is wrong. Still, genuine differences exist between how actors and observers explain actions.[83] Actors are more likely than observers to state reasons for how they acted ("I bought a motorcycle to save gas" vs. "He bought a motorcycle because he can't afford high gas prices"). Actors are also more likely to explain their acts by citing their beliefs ("I come here for lunch *because they make* the best hamburgers"), whereas observers point to the actors' desires ("He comes here for lunch *because he likes* the hamburgers").

Thus, the difference between drawing conclusions about self and drawing conclusions about others remains important. People judge others by their actions but judge themselves by their (generally good) intentions.[84] They can discount their own bad actions by saying, "I didn't mean to do that," thus giving themselves a break that they do not give to others.

Taking this a step further, research has shown that people regard others as conformists but do not regard themselves as conformists to the same degree, again because they rely on introspection.[85] That is, if they see another person purchasing the same kind of car or shirt or grill that neighbors have already bought, they assume that the other person is conforming. When they themselves purchase the same item under the same circumstances, they do not perceive themselves as conforming. Rather, they look inside and perceive that they thought it was a good buy or something that seemed useful to them for personal reasons. For example, in one study,[86] students read about campus issues and were given (false and random) information about what a panel of students had decided. The students generally went along with the panel's recommendations, but they denied doing so out of conformity. However, they thought that other students would go along because of conformity. People do not see in themselves any desire to conform to others, so they do not chalk up their own behavior to conformity. The catch is that conformity pressures and processes may be mostly outside of consciousness, so people do not realize that they are conforming. They can see conformity in others but not in themselves. As the authors put it, the result is that the individual thinks he or she is "alone in a crowd of sheep."[87] Though we are all doing the same thing, everyone else is conforming, but I am not.

Explaining Actions: A Different Approach

The work by Malle and his colleagues has forced a new look at how people actually explain events.[88] Malle examined people's explanations—rather than relying on rating scales— and concluded that people distinguish between intentional and unintentional action. (Fritz Heider emphasized this in his original book, but even the social psychologists who were most inspired by Heider's work neglected that idea in favor of the internal–external dimension.)[89]

Intentional behavior is typically interpreted and explained on the basis of reasons. If you meant to do it, people assume you have a reason, and that is the explanation. In contrast, unintentional behavior is explained more by causes, which are often outside the person. If the causes are inside the person, they may be something the person is not aware of (e.g., such as if the behavior was a side effect of some medication).

1. **You and I work on a joint project, and it succeeds. In describing our relative contributions to the project, you assume that your contribution is greater than mine, but I assume that my contribution is greater than yours. This illustrates the _____.**
   - (a) actor/observer bias
   - (b) false consensus effect
   - (c) fundamental attribution error
   - (d) self-serving bias

2. **Jose reads Sarina's essay that strongly supports capital punishment. Jose knows that Sarina had been assigned the task of writing the essay favoring capital punishment by her debate teacher. Jose is likely to _____.**
   - (a) believe that Sarina opposes capital punishment
   - (b) believe that Sarina does, at least to some extent, favor capital punishment
   - (c) believe that Sarina's position on capital punishment is neutral
   - (d) reach no conclusion about Sarina's real position on capital punishment

3. **Which of the following is *not* an explanation given for the fundamental attribution error?**
   - (a) Behavior is more noticeable than situational factors.
   - (b) People assign insufficient weight to situational causes even when they are made aware of them.
   - (c) People are cognitive misers.
   - (d) People are high in need for cognition.

4. **According to Bertram Malle, what is the most important dimension people use when making attributions about the behavior of others?**
   - (a) Global–specific
   - (b) Intentional–accidental
   - (c) Internal–external
   - (d) Stable–unstable

answers: see pg 183

Heuristics: Mental Shortcuts

> **"Everything should be made as simple as possible, but not simpler."[90]**
> ~ Albert Einstein

People have to make judgments and inferences about uncertain outcomes all the time, and they do it using limited information. What is the likelihood I will get a speeding ticket if I drive at 50 miles per hour when the speed limit is 40? What is the likelihood of my professor giving an unannounced quiz today in class? What is the likelihood that I will get a high-paying job if I major in psychology? What is the likelihood that this person will say yes if I ask him or her out on a date? What is the likelihood of divorce if I marry this person? What is the likelihood of getting pregnant or catching a sexually transmitted disease if I have unprotected sex with my partner?

As we have seen, deliberate conscious thinking is difficult and requires effort, so most people prefer to rely on automatic processing when they can. Usually the automatic system works very well. The automatic system, however, is not smart enough to perform all the complex operations of reasoning; instead, it relies on shortcuts. These mental shortcuts, called **heuristics** provide quick estimates (though sometimes inaccurate ones) for decisions about uncertain events. Heuristics greatly simplify our lives. Although people use several heuristics, we will feature four common ones: (a) representativeness, (b) availability, (c) simulation, and (d) anchoring and adjustment.[91] Other shortcuts will be discussed later. For example, stereotypes, sometimes considered to be heuristics, will be covered in Chapter 13 on prejudice and intergroup relations.

heuristics mental shortcuts that provide quick estimates about the likelihood of uncertain events

representativeness heuristic the tendency to judge the frequency or likelihood of an event by the extent to which it resembles the typical case

Representativeness Heuristic

The **representativeness heuristic** is the tendency to judge the frequency or likelihood of an event by the extent to which it resembles the typical case. For example, in a series of 10 coin tosses, where H is heads and T is tails, most people judge the series HHTTHTHTTH to be more likely than the series HHHHHHHHHH even though both series are equally likely. The reason is that the first series looks more random than the second series. It "represents" our idea of what a random series should look like.

Heavy reliance on the representativeness heuristic leads people to ignore other factors that help shape events, such as rules of chance, independence, and base rate information. Consider the following example:

> Tom is a 41-year-old who reads nonfiction books, listens to National Public Radio, and plays tennis in his spare time. Which is more likely?
>
> **a.** Tom is an Ivy League professor.
> **b.** Tom is a truck driver.

Most people answer (a) because Tom seems like a typical Ivy League professor. People fail to consider, however, that there are a lot more truck drivers than there are Ivy League professors. Thus, in making that judgment, people rely on one kind of information (representativeness, which means how well Tom resembles the category of professors) instead of another (how many people are in the category). The representativeness heuristic is related to the base rate fallacy described later in this chapter.

Availability Heuristic

The **availability heuristic** is the tendency to judge the frequency or likelihood of an event by the ease with which relevant instances come to mind. The ease with which relevant instances come to mind is influenced not only by the actual frequency but also by factors such as how salient or noticeable the event is, how recent the event is, and whether attention was paid to the event.

For example, people overestimate the frequency of dramatic deaths and underestimate the frequency of less dramatic deaths.[92] Airplane crash deaths are much more dramatic than deaths caused by tobacco use, and they get a lot more attention from the mass media, which makes them stand out in memory (high availability). As a result, people think they are common. In fact, three jumbo jets full of passengers crashing every day for a year would not equal the number of deaths per year caused by tobacco use. Tobacco kills about 6 million people a year.[93] It also takes tobacco a long time to kill a person, so deaths due to tobacco aren't as salient as deaths due to airplane crashes.

The availability heuristic might also help explain extrasensory perception (ESP) beliefs. Have you had a dream and later found that the dream came true? This has happened to most people. It might be because this event is more salient than the other possible events, as is shown in **FIGURE 5.10.**

It takes a skilled observer to notice when an expected event does *not* occur. For example, consider an incident in the story "Silver Blaze" from Sir Arthur Conan Doyle's *The Memoirs of Sherlock Holmes*.[94] Colonel Ross owned a horse named Silver Blaze, the favorite for the Wessex Cup. Silver Blaze had mysteriously disappeared, and the horse's trainer, John Staker, had been murdered. Inspector Gregory asked Sherlock Holmes to help investigate the case. During the investigation, Colonel Ross asked Sherlock Holmes, "Is there anything else to which you wish to draw my attention?" Holmes replied, "Yes, to the curious incident of the dog in the nighttime." Ross answered, "But the dog did nothing in the nighttime!" Holmes responded, "That is the curious incident." The dog was kept in the same stable as Silver Blaze. Three boys were also in the stable; two slept in the loft while the third kept watch. The stable boy who kept watch had been drugged with opium. Holmes explained, "Though someone had been in and had fetched out a horse, he had not barked enough to arouse the two lads in the loft. Obviously the midnight visitor was someone whom the dog knew well." From this, the famous detective was able to figure out that it was the trainer who had taken the horse that night.

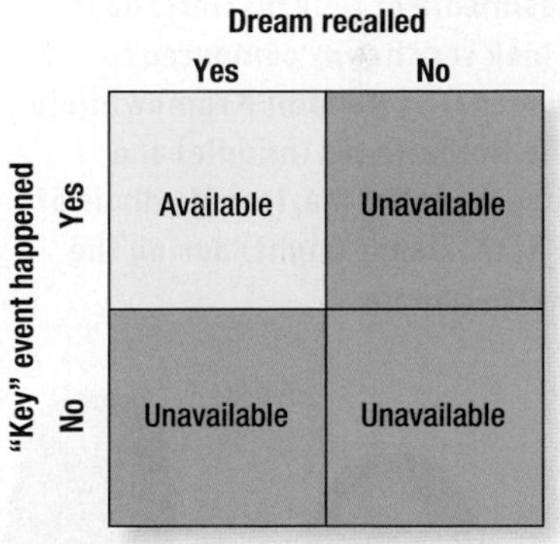

Dream recalled

		Yes	No
"Key" event happened	**Yes**	Available	Unavailable
	No	Unavailable	Unavailable

© Cengage Learning

FIGURE **5.10**

The availability heuristic provides one explanation of ESP beliefs. People remember salient events, but forget nonsalient events.

availability heuristic the tendency to judge the frequency or likelihood of an event by the ease with which relevant instances come to mind

Simulation Heuristic

The **simulation heuristic** is the tendency to judge the frequency or likelihood of an event by the ease with which you can imagine (or mentally simulate) it. More easily imagined events are judged to be more likely than other events. When people imagine what might have been, emotional reactions to events are intensified.

Consider the following hypothetical example:[95]

> Mr. Crane and Mr. Tees were scheduled to leave the airport on different flights, at the same time. They traveled from town in the same limousine, were caught in a traffic jam, and arrived at the airport 30 minutes after the scheduled departure time of their flights. Mr. Crane is told that his flight left on time. Mr. Tees is told that his flight was delayed and just left 5 minutes ago. Who is more upset, Mr. Crane or Mr. Tees?

Most people think Mr. Tees would be more upset than Mr. Crane. The reason is that it is easier for people to imagine how Mr. Tees could have made his flight (e.g., if only the plane had waited a little longer, if only the traffic jam had cleared a few minutes earlier). In contrast, Mr. Crane had no chance of making his flight even if one of those things had been different.

In another study,[96] researchers videotaped television coverage of the Olympic Games. They showed participants the immediate reactions of bronze and silver medalists at the end of the competition, and on the podium when they received their awards. Participants rated the bronze medalists to be happier than the silver medalists! Why? Although the silver medalists received a higher award than the bronze medalists, it was easier for them to imagine winning the gold medal. For the bronze medal winners, it was a close call to be on the podium with a medal at all. If a few small things had been different, they might have finished in fourth place and received no medal. Satisfaction depends on thoughts about what might have been.

The simulation heuristic addresses these "if only" thoughts, also called counterfactual thoughts. We discuss counterfactual thinking in more detail later in this chapter.

Anchoring and Adjustment Heuristic

In estimating how frequent or likely an event is, people use a starting point (called an anchor) and then make adjustments up and down from this starting point. This mental shortcut or heuristic is called **anchoring and adjustment**. For example, if one party in a negotiation starts by suggesting a price or condition, then the other party is likely to base its counteroffer on this anchor. People use anchors even if they know they are just random numbers. Crucially, most research finds that people remain close, typically too close, to the anchor.[97] The anchor has far more impact than it deserves.

Some research participants were asked to estimate what percentage of the United Nations was made up of African countries.[98] Before they made their estimate, they were given an anchor that was ostensibly random and had no meaningful link to the correct answer. The researcher spun a *Wheel of Fortune* type wheel that contained the numbers 0–100. The wheel was rigged so that it stopped on 10 for half the participants and on 65 for the other half. These numbers were the anchors. Participants were asked if the percentage of African countries was higher or lower than the number on the wheel. The estimating task was the same for both groups, so in theory they should have made similar estimates, but both groups stuck close to their anchor. The average estimate of participants who had been given the random number 10 was 25%, whereas the average estimate of those given the random number 65 was 45%. This study illustrates that people are

---

simulation heuristic the tendency to judge the frequency or likelihood of an event by the ease with which you can imagine (or mentally simulate) it

anchoring and adjustment the tendency to judge the frequency or likelihood of an event by using a starting point (called an anchor) and then making adjustments up or down.

Silver medalist Aliaksandra Herasimenia of Belarus (left) does not look very happy compared to gold medalist Ranomi Kromowidjojo of the Netherlands (middle) and bronze medalist Marleen Veldhuis of The Netherlands (right) during the medal ceremony.

Clive Rose/Getty Images Sport/Getty Images

influenced by an initial anchor value even though it may be unreliable (indeed, it was seemingly chosen at random).

TABLE 5.1 summarizes the definitions and examples of the four heuristics we have discussed. The next section discusses the most common cognitive errors people make.

TABLE 5.1 The Most Common Mental Shortcuts (or Heuristics) That People Use

Heuristic	Definition	Example
Representativeness	The tendency to judge the frequency or likelihood of an event by the extent to which it "resembles" the typical case	In a series of 10 coin tosses, most people judge the series HHTTHTHTTH to be more likely than the series HHHHHHHHHH (where H is heads and T is tails), even though both are equally likely.
Availability	The tendency to judge the frequency or likelihood of an event by the ease with which relevant instances come to mind	People overestimate the frequency of dramatic deaths (e.g., dying in an airplane crash) and underestimate the frequency of less dramatic deaths (e.g., dying from lung cancer).
Simulation	The tendency to judge the frequency or likelihood of an event by the ease with which you can imagine (or mentally simulate) an event	In the Olympics, bronze medalists appear to be happier than silver medalists because it is easier for a silver medalist to imagine being a gold medalist.
Anchoring and adjustment	The tendency to judge the frequency or likelihood of an event by using a starting point (called an anchor) and then making adjustments up and down from this starting point	If one party in a negotiation starts by suggesting a price or condition, then the other party is likely to base its counteroffer on this anchor.

1. **The strategy of judging the likelihood of things by how well they match particular prototypes constitutes the _____ heuristic.**
   - (a) availability
   - (b) matching
   - (c) representativeness
   - (d) vividness

2. **People's greater fear of flying than of driving can probably best be explained by the _____ heuristic.**
   - (a) anchoring and adjustment
   - (b) availability
   - (c) representativeness
   - (d) simulation

3. **"If only I hadn't driven home from work using a different route," thinks Minh, "then my car would not have been hit in the rear by that other driver!" Minh's statement most clearly reflects _____.**
   - (a) the availability heuristic
   - (b) a self-serving bias
   - (c) counterfactual thinking
   - (d) the self-fulfilling prophecy

4. **Masako asked two friends to estimate the number of people living in Tokyo. The correct answer, according to the 2000 census, was just over 12 million. She asked the first friend whether it was more or less than 8 million. She asked the second friend whether it was more or less than 16 million. The first friend guessed 9 million people, whereas the second friend guessed 15 million people. The difference in estimates can best be explained using the _____ heuristic.**
   - (a) anchoring and adjustment
   - (b) availability
   - (c) representativeness
   - (d) simulation

answers: see pg 183

Flawed or Clever Thinking?

Social psychologists have long taken a particular approach to understand human thinking—but objections have led to the consideration of a new, different approach. We have already seen this with attribution theory. The long-standing assumption was that people first decide whether person versus situation factors cause behavior, but now a different view says people start by distinguishing intended versus unintended actions (though both views are based on Heider's 1958 book).[99]

A similar dispute questions whether people's thinking is full of errors and biases, or is instead very effective and well tailored for its purposes. The standard view that people's thinking is full of errors and biases among other flaws has dominated the field for decades (including previous editions of this textbook!). The gist is that the world is full of information that is extensive and complicated, and the human mind is lazy, so people acquire all sorts of mental shortcuts. People favor these shortcuts because they often get the right answer, or at least a good enough answer, while saving plenty of time and effort, but they do open the door for errors and biases. The best approach would be to do the careful, hard thinking of analyzing all the information, using logic, mathematical calculations, and statistical reasoning, but because those are hard, people take the easy way out. The heuristics we covered in the previous section are easy to understand in that way, as is the roster of errors and biases we cover in the next section.

Thus, the standard view is that people think in order to find the truth, but their thinking suffers from mistakes and shortcomings stemming largely from laziness and from various motivated biases (e.g., wishful thinking). The alternative view gives people more credit than that. This alternative has two prongs. One was mentioned at the start of the chapter. It says that people evolved to think in order to argue with others and convince them of their side, rather than to figure out the truth alone. (We'll see examples in the next section.) The other prong suggests that the shortcuts and heuristics actually work quite well. It says that it is wrong and foolish to claim that the proper way to think is to perform extensive calculations, using logic and math. Math is good when one has complete and perfect information to work with, but that is rarely true. It says that often people do better with simple rules and guides.

As a vivid illustration,[100] consider the news story in which an airplane flew into a flock of birds upon takeoff. Several of the birds went into the jet engines and shut them down, leaving the plane coasting through the air with no power. The pilot had to make a quick decision as to whether he could glide back to the airport and land there safely. Such a calculation can be made quite precisely, provided that one knows the plane's current speed and weight, its altitude, the relevant distances, and a few other things (e.g., effects of wind). But of course the pilot did not have all that information handy, and even if he did, computing them in his head would be risky because a single mistake could mean death for everyone on the plane.

Instead, the pilot relied on one simple heuristic. When you look out the front window of a gliding plane at a point in the horizon, if that point starts to rise in your windshield, you won't make it that far. The pilot looked at the airport in the distance, and when that seemed to rise, that meant the plane was dropping too fast to get there. He abandoned the plan to fly to the airport and instead steered the plane to land in the river, where it stayed afloat long enough for everyone to be rescued. Thus, in this case, he did better by following the simple heuristic than by trying to do the full calculation.

With that in mind, let's take a look at some of social psychology's classic findings about how people think.

"It was easier when you went to school, Dad. That was before the information age."

1. The current view of attributions assumes that people try to explain the behavior of others start by focusing on _____ actions.

   (a) external versus internal   (b) global versus specific   (c) intended versus unintended   (d) stable versus unstable

2. Which of the following standard views of heuristic thinking may be incorrect based on the current evidence?

   (a) automatic   (b) effortless   (c) flawed   (d) quick

3. According to the standard view, people think in order to find _____.

   (a) the truth   (b) a good approximate answer   (c) an answer that agrees with what they already believe   (d) an answer that will be persuasive to others

4. According to the current view, people think in order to find _____.

   (a) the truth   (b) a good approximate answer   (c) an answer that agrees with what they already believe   (d) an answer that will be persuasive to others

answers: see pg 183

(So-Called) Errors and Biases

One theme of this book is the duplex mind. The human mind has two main systems: the automatic system and the deliberate system. The automatic system helps people deal with information overload. The job of the automatic system is to make quick, fairly accurate judgments and decisions, whereas the deliberate system works more slowly and thoroughly to make more precise judgments and decisions. Because most people are cognitive misers and do not like to expend mental effort, they rely heavily on the automatic system. The automatic system takes shortcuts, such as by using heuristics. Even though the automatic system is very good at helping people make fast decisions (it can do it in milliseconds!), it is not very good at making precise calculations, such as probabilities. Thus, the automatic system is prone to make several kinds of cognitive errors. Even on such important personal questions as to how many sex partners one has had, people's thinking is subject to biases. For example, many studies have found dramatic but logically implausible differences in how men and women answer the question of how many sex partners they have had. Read *The Social Side of Sex* to find out more.

People generally have access to two types of information: (a) statistical information from a large number of people, and (b) case history information from a small number of people (even a single case). Although people would make much better decisions if they paid the most attention to statistical information, they generally pay the most attention to case history information.[119] For example, when buying a new car, people are more influenced by what a few friends tell them about a car (case history information) than they are by what hundreds of people say about the car in *Consumer Reports* (statistical information). Even if the car has an outstanding repair record and is rated very highly by consumers, they won't buy it if their friend owned a similar car once and said it was a "lemon."

Or at least, that is how social psychologists have thought about such patterns for decades: as irrational mistakes. But the new approach suggests a more positive view. Maybe people do pretty well by trusting a friend's direct experience than relying on statistics in some magazine. And maybe the issue is for arguing. Suppose your friend complained about a certain car being a lemon, and then you went out and bought the same kind of

The Social Side of Sex

Counting Sex Partners

At some point in the development of most intimate relationships, the two individuals ask each other how many people they have previously had sex with. A simple question with a simple answer, right? Hardly! In fact, even when people give supposedly honest answers to physicians or researchers, the answers are subject to distortion from a variety of sources.[101,102] One sign of distortion is that in all surveys, men report many more sex partners than women. For example, ABC News conducted a national poll and reported on the show *PrimeTime Live* that the average American man has had sex with 20 partners but the average American woman has had only 6 partners.[103] Similarly unequal results, though usually with lower numbers, have been reported in all other studies.[104,105] These inequalities are logically impossible. If we count only heterosexual behavior, and if there are roughly the same number of men as women, then the average numbers of sex partners must be equal. Every time a man has sex with a new woman, the woman also has sex with a new man. How can the numbers be so different? And same-sex behavior is not enough to explain the gap. If the ABC News numbers were correct, then the average American man would have had sex with 6 women and 14 men! Most evidence indicates that same-gender sex is much rarer than that.[106]

Most experts suspect that tallies of sex partners are affected by motivation. Men want to claim to have had many sex partners because that indicates that they are handsome, charming, and virile.

Women, however, want to claim relatively few partners because women value being choosy and look down on others who have had many partners.[107,108,109] Still, how do these motivations translate into different tallies of sex partners?

One possible answer is that people lie. Men might invent more partners than they have had, and women might deny or conveniently forget some of their past partners. This is not a full explanation. The gender difference in sex partners is found even on anonymous surveys, in which people would have little to gain by lying and would supposedly not be embarrassed by the truth. Still, there are some signs of it. When researchers hooked people up to lie detectors, they changed their answers to the question about how many sex partners they had. Women, in particular, reported more partners when they were connected to lie detectors than when they could just write a number on a questionnaire.[110]

Another possible answer is that differences are due to sex with prostitutes or homosexual activity. Few surveys include prostitutes, so these women (some of whom have had sex with thousands of men) could skew the data. These sex acts would be counted by the men but not by the women in the research sample (because prostitutes were not included in the female sample). These do contribute something to the finding that men have more sex partners than women. However, some researchers have calculated that there is not nearly enough prostitution to account for the large gender difference in tallies of partners.[111,112] The same goes for homosexual activity. True, gay males typically have more partners than gay females, but gay males are a relatively small segment of the population. Even when

data are restricted to heterosexual and non-prostitute sex, men report more partners than women.[113]

Research on social cognition has identified two processes that help produce the difference. One is a difference in how people count. People who have had more than six partners do not always keep an exact count. When asked how many partners they have had, they can either try to make a mental list, or they can estimate. Apparently, women usually answer by making a mental list, but this procedure is prone to underestimating (because it is easy to forget something that may have happened once or twice some years ago). In contrast, men tend to estimate, and estimating tends to produce inflated numbers (because men round up: a true figure of 22 might produce an estimated answer of "about 25"). Accordingly, when men and women try to give honest answers, they may still furnish systematically distorted numbers.[114,115,116]

The other process involves shifting criteria. What exactly counts as sex? Research has shown that men are more likely than women to include borderline cases such as oral sex.[117] There is no truly correct answer, and so, as social cognition researchers have found in many spheres, people use criteria that suit them and make them feel good.[118] Women want to report relatively few sex partners, so if they only had oral sex with someone they feel justified in saying they did not have sex. Men want to have higher tallies, so they think it is reasonable to include oral sex. No doubt some people do lie about their sexual histories. But even when they try to tell the truth, they may furnish heavily biased answers. Moreover, these answers are distorted in the directions that give people the answers they prefer.

---

car, and it too turned out to be a lemon—you'd have a hard time justifying your behavior to your friend. "I told you so!" the friend would say, and your lame response, "But the magazine said its statistics were good" wouldn't help much.

Let's be clear and not overstate. Most experts agree that doing the full calculations is the best way when thorough and clear information is available. But usually it's not. The question is whether to do hard calculations with the available but inadequate data, or to rely on heuristics and rules of thumb. It's also about whether thinking is an often-fallible procedure for reaching the truth or a pretty effective way of arguing one side. Both sides of that debate host lively arguments. (Notice, however, that even scientists often reach the truth by arguing both sides and seeing which one can produce the most convincing evidence!)

Sometimes the consequences are much more important than what car to buy. To return to the story that opened this chapter, parents must decide whether to vaccinate their children. If they ignore the overwhelming statistical evidence and rely instead on personal anecdotes, they might decide not to vaccinate their children, which could prove fatal.

Confirmation Bias

Jonathan Cainer was born in the United Kingdom in 1958.[120] He dropped out of school when he was 15 years old, pumped gas at a service station, and played in a band called *Strange Cloud*. In the early 1980s, he moved to the United States and became a manager at a nightclub in Los Angeles. There he met a psychic poet named Charles John Quatro, who told him he would someday write an astrology column read by millions. Cainer returned to the United Kingdom and enrolled at the Faculty of Astrological Studies in London. Today he does indeed write an astrology newspaper column that is read by millions of people all over the world.

Are you impressed by the accuracy of Quatro's prediction regarding Cainer's future as an astrology columnist? We can predict your answer to this question, even though we have never met you (and we are not psychics). If you believe in astrology, we predict that you will be impressed. If you don't believe in astrology, we predict that you will not be impressed. Were we correct? Told you so!

This example illustrates the **confirmation bias** defined as the tendency to notice information that confirms one's beliefs, and to ignore information that disconfirms one's beliefs.[121] Philosopher Francis Bacon said, "It is the peculiar and perpetual error of the human understanding to be more moved and excited by affirmatives than by negatives."[122] Beliefs in paranormal phenomena such as telepathy can be explained by the confirmation bias.[123] The confirmation bias isn't limited to paranormal beliefs, however. This bias extends to a wide variety of beliefs.[124]

To learn the truth, it would be best to give equal consideration to confirming and disconfirming evidence. The tendency to pay more attention to confirming than disconfirming evidence has long been regarded as typical of how human thought is sabotaged by bias leading to error. But look at it again from the perspective that human reasoning is designed for arguing, not for figuring out the truth. If you are trying to argue your case, you want evidence that helps you, not evidence that goes against your side. It turns out that people are pretty good at finding disconfirming evidence when they have to argue against something.[125] To return to the example of Quatro's prediction about Cainer, people who disbelieve in astrology can probably generate several reasons not to be impressed by that story. Thus, the confirmation bias may not be a flaw in human thinking—it's just a standard pattern that helps people do what thinking is primarily for, namely argue and convince.

Illusory Correlations

An **illusory correlation** occurs when people overestimate the link between variables that are related only slightly or not at all.[126] For example, people overestimate the frequency of undesirable behavior by minority group members. One explanation for this tendency is that minority group status and undesirable behaviors are both relatively rare. Because people are sensitive to rare events, the occurrence of two rare events together is especially noticeable.

Consider some experiments on illusory correlation.[127] Participants read a series of sentences describing a desirable or an undesirable behavior from a person belonging to group A or B (e.g., "John, a member of Group A, visited a sick friend in the hospital." "Allen, a member of Group B, dented the fender of a parked car and didn't leave his name."). Overall, two-thirds of the behaviors were desirable for both groups, and

confirmation bias the tendency to notice and search for information that confirms one's beliefs and to ignore information that disconfirms one's beliefs

illusory correlation the tendency to overestimate the link between variables that are related only slightly or not at all

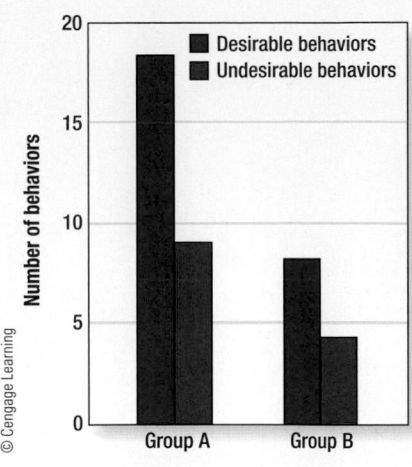

FIGURE 5.11

Actual correlation study. Two-thirds of the behaviors were performed by Group A members (the majority), and two-thirds of the behaviors were desirable for both.[127]

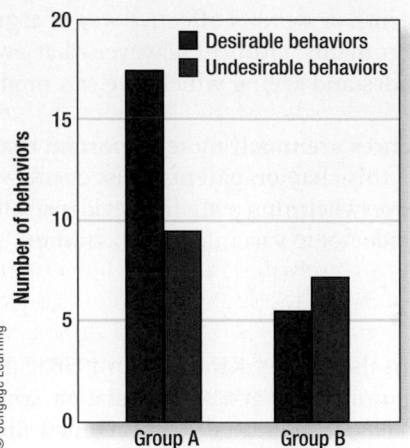

FIGURE 5.12

Illusory correlation study. Even though two-thirds of the behaviors committed by Group B members were desirable, participants "recalled" Group B members committing more undesirable behaviors than desirable behaviors.[127]

two-thirds involved a member of Group A—the majority (see **FIGURE 5.11**). Participants then estimated the number of desirable and undesirable behaviors performed by members of each group. The ratio of desirable to undesirable behaviors was the same for the two groups, so the estimates should have been the same for the two groups, but they were not. Participants overestimated the number of undesirable behaviors performed by Group B (minority) members; in fact, they estimated more undesirable behaviors than desirable behaviors from Group B members (see **FIGURE 5.12**). Illusory correlations can even occur after exposure to only one unusual behavior performed by only one member of an unfamiliar group (e.g., Ben, a Jehovah's Witness, owns a pet sloth) called **one-shot illusory correlations**.[128]

The mass media contribute to these illusory correlations. For example, if a mentally ill person shoots a famous person (e.g., Mark Chapman shoots Beatles guitarist John Lennon; John Hinckley Jr. shoots former U.S. President Ronald Reagan), the media draw attention to the mental status of the assassin. Assassinations and mental hospitalizations are both relatively rare, making the combination especially noticeable. Such media reporting adds to the illusion of a correlation between mental illness and violent behavior. The rate of violence among those with severe mental illness is not particularly high, and is not higher than those without mental illness.[129]

Again, the idea that thinking is for arguing offers a fresh perspective. Illusory correlations are errors if the purpose of thinking is to find the truth. But saying two things go together can be a very convincing argument, and if your opponent is reduced to saying something feeble like, "Well, they don't *always* go together," you have the upper hand in the dispute.

Base Rate Fallacy

The **base rate fallacy** is the tendency to ignore or underuse base rate information (information about most people) and instead to be influenced by the distinctive features of the case being judged. Many cognitive errors are the result of people not paying attention to base rates. Consider the following example:[130]

> A town has two hospitals. In the larger hospital, about 45 babies are born every day; in the smaller hospital, about 15 babies are born every day. In one year, each hospital recorded the number of days on which more than 60% of the babies born were boys. Which hospital recorded more such days?
>
> **a.** EXTlarge hospital
>
> **b.** The small hospital
>
> **c.** About the same number of days (within 5% of each other)

one-shot illusory correlation an illusory correlation that occurs after exposure to only one unusual behavior performed by only one member of an unfamiliar group

base rate fallacy the tendency to ignore or underuse base rate information and instead to be influenced by the distinctive features of the case being judged

Most people answer (c). People don't consider the fact that variability decreases as sample size increases. Think about flipping a coin 10 times and getting 6 heads versus flipping a coin 1,000 times and getting 600 heads. You are much more likely to get 6 heads in 10 flips than to get 600 heads in 1,000 flips. Tournaments that eliminate teams after a single loss (e.g., World Cup soccer, National Football League playoffs, college basketball tournament) allow underdogs a better chance to win, as compared to tournaments in which each round is a series of games (e.g., National Basketball Association playoffs, World Series in baseball). In a single game, the weaker team might get lucky and win. Across many games, the better team will tend to win more often.

Soccer is especially vulnerable to the effects of small samples, because soccer games tend to have low scores such as 1–0. Sometimes only one goal is scored in the entire championship game, and that goal decides the winner. Thus, one moment of luck can crown the underdog as champion. In contrast, a seven-game World Series of baseball may easily contain 40–50 points scored, and a seven-game basketball series will typically have over more than 1,000 points, which makes it quite difficult for a relatively inferior team to beat the odds and win just by luck.

The base rate fallacy may simply reflect a broader pattern by which people are not naturally skilled at statistical reasoning. On this point, the newer view of heuristics as adaptive or as designed for arguing is not that helpful, and the base rate fallacy may really be an error. After all, even if you can do the base rate calculations yourself, the person you are arguing against may not understand the argument, and so it won't help you convince that person.

Gambler's Fallacy and the Hot Hand

Suppose you flip a coin 10 times. You flip 9 heads in a row. What is your next flip more likely to be?

a. Heads

b. Tails

c. Heads and tails are equally likely.

Hot hand players answer (a) because they think they have a "hot" hand and their luck will continue. **Gambler's fallacy** players answer (b) because they think their luck will change and that a tails is "due." These biases may both stem from the same source—the representativeness heuristic. The correct answer is (c). If people think about it, they would agree that heads and tails are equally likely on any given flip. They might also agree that the outcome of any flip does not depend on the outcome of the previous flip.

These are both errors if one accepts the assumption that each flip is truly random and independent of the others. But perhaps that is rare in the real world. When dealing with strangers, trust is a big issue. If you saw someone flip "heads" 9 times in a row, would you really want to bet on tails the next time, at even money, as the statisticians say you should? More likely, the person has a trick coin or has mastered some skill at making the flip come out heads. Certainly if your friends said not to bet on tails, and you did so anyhow and lost, they would say "we told you not to bet!" and you'd have a difficult time arguing that what you did was sensible.

To test these biases in the real world, researchers conducted a study in a casino in Nevada.[131] Participants were videotaped while playing roulette. Because a roulette wheel consists of 38 numbers, 1/38, or 2.6%, of the bets should fall on each number. The researchers could look at how each person bet over time. Most players exhibited both biases. Gambler's fallacy players were also more likely to be hot hand players. Statisticians like to say that state lotteries are a tax on people who are bad at math. The tax is especially high for gambler's fallacy and hot hand players. Again, though, the point may simply be that the mind is not designed to deal with truly random events and the statistics that go with them. Predicting future behavior from past behavior is often a sensible strategy and an effective argument.

hot hand the tendency for gamblers who get lucky to think they have a "hot" hand and their luck will continue

gambler's fallacy the tendency to believe that a particular chance event is affected by previous events and that chance events will "even out" in the short run

False Consensus Effect

People tend to overestimate the number of people who share their opinions, attitudes, values, and beliefs. This tendency is called the **false consensus effect**.[132,133] An early demonstration[134] asked students whether they would walk around campus carrying a sign that said "Eat at Joe's." Later they were asked how many other people they thought would be willing to carry such a sign. Those who agreed to carry the sign said that 62% of other people would also agree to carry the sign. Those who refused to carry the sign said that only 33% of other people would carry the sign. Obviously both can't be right, and one or both groups tended to overestimate the proportion of people who would respond the same way they themselves had.

The availability heuristic provides one possible explanation of the false consensus effect. When asked to predict what other people are like, people use the information that is most readily available—information about themselves and their friends. Because people tend to associate with similar others, this available information might lead people to overestimate the percentage of the population that is similar to themselves. Another explanation is that people want to believe their views and actions are the correct ones, so they assume others would concur. Yet another explanation is that people use their own reaction as an "anchor" (remember the anchoring and adjustment heuristic?) and adjust it when having to furnish a broad prediction about people in general; as usual, they tend to remain too close to the anchor.

A study of over a thousand people on Facebook found that friends routinely overestimated how much they had similar opinions.[135] They failed to realize how much they disagreed, even when they claimed to discuss the issues. People seem to surmise their friends' opinions by projecting their own views and by relying on stereotypes about their friends.

False Uniqueness Effect

People tend to underestimate the number of people who share their most prized characteristics and abilities. This tendency is called the **false uniqueness effect**.[136] For example, religious people believe that other people are more likely to believe in paranormal phenomena but are less likely to hold religious beliefs than they are.[137,138] Similarly, people who engage in desirable health-protective behaviors (e.g., exercising regularly, getting regular checkups, eating healthy foods), underestimate the number of other people who engage in similar behaviors.[139] It appears that people overestimate consensus when it comes to their undesirable characteristics (false consensus) but underestimate consensus when it comes to their desirable characteristics (false uniqueness). As noted in the previous section, they also overestimate consensus for their opinions and preferences.

This mixture of overestimating and underestimating can be remembered easily by noting that all distortions are in the direction most helpful for self-esteem. That is, you can feel good about yourself if your opinions are correct, and one sign of correctness is that most people agree with you (so you overestimate consensus for opinions). You can feel good about yourself if your faults are ones that many people have (so overestimate consensus regarding faults). And you can feel especially good about yourself if your talents and virtues are rare and exceptional ones that few people can match (so underestimate consensus regarding good characteristics). Probably this pattern is no accident. As we saw in Chapter 3, people like to think well of themselves, and many patterns of bias and distortion help them achieve and maintain their favorable self-views.

Perseverance of Theories

Generating explanations of social facts is one common mental activity. When research participants read a newspaper article claiming that risk-takers made the best firefighters, they were able to come up with multiple explanations why that would be so. The experimenters, however, had created the newspaper article. Other participants read a different (bogus) article making the opposite claim, that risk-avoiders made the best

false consensus effect the tendency to overestimate the number of other people who share one's opinions, attitudes, values, and beliefs

false uniqueness effect the tendency to underestimate the number of other people who share one's most prized characteristics and abilities

firefighters. Those participants were just as good at coming up with explanations. As we said in Chapter 1, common sense can explain most things in hindsight!

But then the experiment took a curious turn. The experimenter told the participants that the news story on which they had based their thinking was a pure fiction created by the researchers for this study. Surprisingly, however, when participants rated their opinions on what sorts of people made the best firefighters, they stuck with what they had been thinking—even though the evidence for it had been completely demolished.[140] These findings were the first demonstration of what came to be known as **theory perseverance** effects. Once the mind draws a conclusion, it tends to stick with that conclusion unless there is overwhelming evidence to change it. Merely losing the evidence on which the conclusion is based does not seem to shake people's belief.

One interpretation of the theory perseverance effect is that the mind is quite impressed with its own activity. Once people had thought about why risk-seekers made the best firefighters, their minds clung to that conclusion. Thus people may get stuck with false beliefs. Then again, if thinking is designed for arguing, theory perseverance is not surprising. Losing some of the evidence for the side you are arguing does not make you want to switch sides. Indeed, when people argue, if some of the evidence they cite is discredited, they quickly move along to use other arguments.

The cognitive miser may also be relevant. Rejecting information takes more cognitive effort than accepting it.[141]

Statistical Regression

In the 19th century, Sir Francis Galton introduced the concept of **statistical regression** (also called **regression to the mean**), which refers to the statistical tendency for extreme scores or extreme behavior to return toward the average. In his study of men's heights, Galton found that the tallest men usually had sons shorter than themselves, whereas the shortest men usually had sons taller than themselves. In both cases, the height of the children was less extreme than the height of the fathers.

To make it onto the cover of a major sports magazine, such as *Sports Illustrated,* an athlete or team must perform exceptionally well in addition to being lucky. However, appearing on the cover of *Sports Illustrated* got the reputation of being a jinx because athletes consistently performed worse afterward. The belief in the *Sports Illustrated* jinx is so strong that some athletes have even refused to appear on the cover.[142]

Many people attribute the subsequent poor performance to internal factors rather than to chance (e.g., after appearing on the cover of *Sports Illustrated,* athletes feel so much pressure that they choke). But the "*Sports Illustrated* jinx" can also be explained by the concept of regression to the mean.[143] The magazine puts a team or athlete on the cover after an exceptionally good performance, and regression to the mean dictates that in most cases the next performance won't be as great, just as really short men don't usually have sons who are even shorter. If the magazine instead used cover photos featuring teams that had performed unbelievably badly that week, the magazine would get a reputation as a miracle worker for improving a team's luck and performance! But that too would be just a misunderstanding of regression to the mean.

In summary, the key to regression to the mean is that when one selects an instance (or a group) for extreme performance, it is almost always true that one will have selected a more extreme instance than is warranted. When events deviate from the average, people are more likely to think about the bad exceptions than about the good exceptions.

Illusion of Control

During a summer drought, retired farmer Elmer Carlson arranged a rain dance by 16 Hopis in Audubon, Iowa. The next day an inch of rain fell. "The miracles are still here, we just need to ask for them," explained Carlson.

The belief that people can control totally chance situations is called the **illusion of control**.[144,145] For example, gamblers in casinos who are playing craps often roll the dice harder for high numbers and softer for low numbers. People like to be in control of their

theory perseverance proposes that once the mind draws a conclusion, it tends to stick with that conclusion unless there is overwhelming evidence to change it

statistical regression (regression to the mean) the statistical tendency for extreme scores or extreme behavior to be followed by others that are less extreme and closer to average

illusion of control the false belief that one can influence certain events, especially random or chance ones

own fate. The illusion of control has been shown to influence people to take more risks. Research on traders working in investment banks found that traders who had an illusion of control took more risks and lost more money than other traders.[146]

Counterfactual Thinking

Counterfactual means "contrary to the facts." **Counterfactual thinking** involves imagining alternatives to past or present factual events or circumstances.[147] Counterfactual thinking is familiar to everyone, even if they have not heard the term before. We have all thought about "what might have been," if people had only behaved differently. What if you had studied harder in high school? What if your parents had never met? What if the other candidate had won the election? Douglas Hofstadter,[148] cognitive science professor at Indiana University and author of the Pulitzer Prize–winning *Gödel, Escher, Bach: An Eternal Golden Braid,* wrote, "Think how immeasurably poorer our mental lives would be if we didn't have this creative capacity for slipping out of the midst of reality into soft 'what ifs'!" Recent work has confirmed this richness: Counterfactual thinking makes life more meaningful. When people reflect on important life events, like winning a scholarship or meeting a romantic partner, these feel all the more meaningful when people consider how they might never have happened.[149]

Counterfactual thinking influences how students take tests.[150] When taking multiple-choice tests, many students choose what they initially think is the correct answer. After thinking about it more, however, they begin to doubt their so-called first instinct and think that another answer is even better. Are students better off staying with their first choice, or should they switch their answer? About 75% of students think it is better to stick with their initial answer. Most college professors also believe that students should stick with their initial answer. Some test preparation guides also give the same advice: "Exercise great caution if you decide to change your answer. Experience indicates that many students who change answers change to the wrong answer."[151] However, virtually all studies show that students are better off switching answers.[152] This tendency has been dubbed the **first instinct fallacy**. It is defined as the false belief that it is better not to change one's first answer even if one starts to think that a different answer is correct.

So why do many students, professors, and test guide writers succumb to this fallacy? Research on counterfactual thinking can shed light on this issue. Assume that you got the answer wrong in the end and therefore engaged in counterfactual thinking about what you might have done to get it right. You'd probably feel the most regret if you had first written down the correct answer and then changed it to a wrong one. You'd feel less regret if you had first written the wrong answer and then refused to change it, because in that scenario you had never put down the right answer. Having first written the correct answer and then erased it makes you feel that you were so close to getting it correct that changing was a terrible mistake.

Counterfactual thinking can envision outcomes that were either better or worse than what actually happened. **Upward counterfactuals** involve alternatives that are better than actuality, whereas **downward counterfactuals** are alternatives that are worse than actuality.[153,154] For example, when Dwyane looks back on her honeymoon, she can think it could have gone better (e.g., "We should have gone to a more exotic place!") or that it could have been worse (e.g., "Good thing we didn't get robbed!"). People make far more upward than downward counterfactuals, which is probably a good thing because it causes people to consider how to make things better in the future.[155] For example, if Eduardo looks back on his exam and regrets not studying harder so he could have earned a higher grade, he will probably study harder next time. In contrast, if Eduardo looks back on his exam with relief that he did not fail it, he probably will not study harder next time.

Downward counterfactuals have their uses, of course. In particular, they help people feel better in the aftermath of misfortune.[156] When something bad happens, people say, "It could have been worse," and contemplating those even more terrible counterfactuals is comforting.

counterfactual thinking imagining alternatives to past or present events or circumstances

first instinct fallacy the false belief that it is better not to change one's first answer on a test even if one starts to think that a different answer is correct

upward counterfactuals imagining alternatives that are better than actuality

downward counterfactuals imagining alternatives that are worse than actuality

Ultimately, counterfactual thinking is probably one of the crucial traits that help people create and sustain the marvels of human society and culture. Most animals can barely perceive and understand their immediate surroundings, but people can dream of how it can be different. Democracy, women's liberation, and wireless technology did not exist in nature, but human beings were able to look at life as it was and imagine how it could be different, and these imaginings helped them change the world for the better.

The concepts of counterfactual thinking and regret are sometimes used interchangeably. Although the two concepts are related, they are not the same thing.[157] One important difference is that regrets are feelings, whereas counterfactuals are thoughts. **Regret** involves feeling sorry for misfortunes, limitations, losses, transgressions, shortcomings, or mistakes.[158]

The various cognitive biases and (so-called) errors discussed in this section are summarized in **TABLE 5.2.**

regret involves feeling sorry for one's misfortunes, limitations, losses, transgressions, shortcomings, or mistakes

TABLE 5.2 **Common Cognitive Errors**

Error or Bias	Definition	Example
Confirmation bias	The tendency to notice information that confirms one's beliefs and to ignore information that disconfirms one's beliefs	Looking for evidence that your horoscope is true if you believe in astrology, and ignoring evidence that is inconsistent with your horoscope
Illusory correlation	The tendency to overestimate the link between variables that are related only slightly or not at all	Believing that mentally ill individuals are violent and dangerous
Base rate fallacy	The tendency to ignore or underuse base rate information and instead to be influenced by the distinctive features of the case being judged	Thinking that it is equally likely to have 60% of births be male in a small or a large hospital
Gambler's fallacy	The tendency to believe that a particular chance event is affected by previous events, and that chance events will "even out" in the short run	Believing that one is more likely to get a *heads* on a coin toss after the sequence TTTTTTTTT than after the sequence THHTTHTHT
Hot hand	The tendency for gamblers who get lucky to think they have a "hot" hand and their luck will continue	Believing that one is more likely to get a *tails* on a coin toss after the sequence TTTTTTTTT than after the sequence THHTTHTHT
False consensus effect	The tendency for people to overestimate the number of other people who share their opinions, attitudes, values, and beliefs	Believing that most people have the same religious beliefs as you do
False uniqueness effect	The tendency for people to underestimate the number of other people who share their most prized characteristics and abilities	If a person exercises regularly, underestimating the number of other people who also exercise regularly
Theory perseverance	The tendency to stick with a conclusion unless there is overwhelming evidence to change it	Continuing to dislike someone because you heard she was mean to your friend, even though you later find out she was not mean to your friend
Statistical regression	The statistical tendency for extreme scores or extreme behavior to return toward the average	The "*Sports Illustrated* jinx," in which athletic performance usually declines after appearing on the cover of *Sports Illustrated*
Illusion of control	The belief that one can control totally chance situations	For gamblers, throwing dice softly for low numbers and hard for high numbers
Counterfactual thinking	Imagining alternatives to past or present factual events or circumstances	After getting in a car wreck, thinking "what if" I had gone home using a different route

QUIZ YOURSELF

[So-Called] Errors and Biases

answers: see pg 183

1. **Gamblers who throw dice softly to get low numbers and who throw harder to get high numbers are demonstrating _____.**
   - (a) the base rate fallacy
   - (b) the gambler's fallacy
   - (c) the illusion of control
   - (d) regression to the mean

2. **Which sequence of six coin flips is least likely to occur?**
   - (a) TTTTTT
   - (b) TTTTTH
   - (c) THHTTH
   - (d) All of the above are equally likely to occur.

3. **If you scored 99 out of 100 on your first social psychology exam, you are likely to score lower on the second exam, even if you are equally knowledgeable about the material on both exams. This is an example of _____.**
   - (a) base rate fallacy
   - (b) confirmation bias
   - (c) false uniqueness effect
   - (d) regression to the mean

4. **Gustov gets in an accident in which his new car is totaled, but he received only minor injuries. Gustov thinks to himself, "At least I'm still alive. I could have died." This type of thinking illustrates which of the following concepts?**
   - (a) Downward counterfactual
   - (b) Regression to the mean
   - (c) Regret
   - (d) Upward counterfactual

Are Most People Really Just Kind of Stupid?

Sometimes social cognition researchers are accused of perpetuating the idea that people are basically stupid. This is because these researchers show that people make so many cognitive errors. Would nature have selected stupid people to reproduce and pass on their genes to subsequent generations? We doubt it. The kinds of errors people make are not random—they are quite predictable. Many may not even be errors at all, as we have said: They might just reflect a style of thinking geared toward arguing one's case and convincing others, rather than trying to reason out the truth, whatever it may be.

More often than not, heuristics provide the correct answers, or at least answers that are good enough. The automatic system is also incredibly fast, capable of making decisions in milliseconds. People can even process information outside of conscious awareness.

It is possible that some errors may only occur in the social psychological laboratory—not in the real world. Other errors are corrected socially, such as when people give us feedback on what we did wrong. Still other errors can cancel each other out, if they occur in random combinations.

Evolutionary psychologists have argued that when it comes to the really important decisions, those involving survival and reproduction, people make relatively few stupid decisions.[159,160,161] Perhaps this is because they use the deliberate system rather than the automatic system when it comes to making important decisions. The quick and approximate answers provided by the automatic system are not good enough, and people expend the mental energy required to make these important decisions.

Reducing Cognitive Errors

Even if the errors aren't all that serious, who wants to make errors? Several factors can reduce cognitive errors. People can be taught to use relevant statistical probabilities rather than ignore them.[162] Even crash courses on statistical reasoning are helpful in reducing cognitive errors.[163,164] Making the information easier to process can also improve decision-making ability and reduce cognitive errors.

One of the most effective ways of **debiasing** people from the tendency to make cognitive errors is to get them to use deliberate processing (such as conscious reasoning) rather than automatic processing. Some examples include encouraging people to consider multiple alternatives,[165,166,167] to rely less on memory,[168,169] to use explicit decision rules[170,171] to search for disconfirmatory information,[172] and to use meta-cognition.[173] **Meta-cognition** literally means "thinking about thinking." It is a reflective approach to problem solving that involves stepping back from the immediate problem to examine and reflect on the thinking process. Examples include quizzing oneself to evaluate one's understanding of what one has read in a textbook, planning how to approach a math exam, and evaluating progress toward achieving a learning goal (e.g., memorizing the periodic table of the elements for your chemistry class).

debiasing reducing errors and biases by getting people to use deliberate processing rather than automatic processing

meta-cognition reflecting on one's own thought processes

1. **What system is mainly responsible for the cognitive errors that people make?**

   (a) Automatic system (b) Deliberate system (c) Primary system (d) Secondary system

2. **People make fewer cognitive errors when they are making decisions about _____.**

   (a) trivial matters (e.g., what brand of toothpaste to buy)
   (b) important matters (e.g., what major to select in college)
   (c) very serious matters (e.g., survival and reproduction)
   (d) None of the above; cognitive errors are the same for the three types of matters.

3. **Which type of graduate training that teaches statistical reasoning is most effective in reducing cognitive errors?**

   (a) Business (b) Chemistry (c) Law (d) Psychology

4. **The analysis of cognitions is called _____.**

   (a) counterfactual thinking
   (b) explicit decision rules
   (c) meta-cognition
   (d) statistical reasoning

QUIZ YOURSELF

Are Most People Really Just Kind of Stupid?

answers: see pg 183

What Makes Us *Human*

Putting the Cultural Animal in Perspective

The special or unique features of human psychology are readily visible in this chapter. Experts debate the question "Do animals think?" (i.e., nonhuman animals), but the debate usually focuses on whether the very simple cognitive activities of animals, such as forming an expectancy and perceiving that it is violated, qualify as thinking. Only a few overly sentimental pet owners believe that animals can formulate complex thoughts or understand long sentences—let alone begin to match the higher flights of human thought, such as in philosophical or religious contemplation, theories of physics and chemistry, poetry, epic narratives, or even arguments about why a football game or blind date turned out as it did. Only humans think in those ways.

The remarkable power of human thought is seen not just in the use of symbolism, but in the combining of symbols. People use language to do most of their thinking, and human thought typically combines many small concepts into complex ideas, stories, or theories. A dog can learn several dozen one-word commands, but only humans can string together a long set of words to make sentences, paragraphs, long stories, speeches, or a book like this.

The capacity to use language opens up new worlds of thought, as it lets people explore the linkages of meaning. People can do mathematical and financial calculations, conduct cost–benefit analyses, and reason logically. Without language, other animals can engage in only the very simplest, most trivial versions of those forms of thought, or none at all.

The duplex mind is another distinctive feature of human thinking. Automatic processing is probably something both humans and animals have, but the powers of the conscious mind are more uniquely human. Only humans can perform the rule-based, systematic, precise thinking that the deliberate system does, such as mathematical calculations, logical reasoning, and detailed cost–benefit comparisons of multiple options when facing a decision.

The simple fact is that most complex patterns of thought are uniquely human. Humans can analyze a complex situation and make attributions about why something happened (and they can also debate with each other about those attributions, to reach a consensual explanation). Only humans use heuristics. False consensus and false uniqueness biases are limited to humans.

Only humans engage in counterfactual thinking, which can be extremely helpful in enabling people to change their behavior in the future. Only humans suffer agonies of rumination and regret about what might have been, but that same power of counterfactual thinking has been a crucial aid to human progress. Over the centuries, people have looked around them at the state of the world and imagined how it could be better. Nature did not give us schools, written language, dental care, recorded music, airplane travel, or the justice system, but counterfactual thinking has enabled people to dream of such improvements—and then to help them become reality.

We saw in Chapter 3 that humans have a much more complex conception of self than other animals. This complex knowledge structure influences thought in many ways. Only humans will show self-serving biases or actor/observer differences, and only humans can learn to correct for these biases.

The remarkable power of human thought creates both unique errors and unique capabilities to understand the truth. In other words, the special properties of the human mind lead to both right and wrong answers that other animals wouldn't get. Only humans can succumb to the base rate fallacy because only humans can use base rates at all, so only humans can learn to use them correctly. Only humans fall prey to the regression fallacy, but only humans can develop an accurate understanding of regression to the mean and can therefore learn to avoid the mistake.

In short, most of the material in this chapter would be absent in a book on the psychology of other animals because human cognition is generally unlike what is found in other species. This sweeping difference is quite unlike what we will see in the next chapter on emotion. That is because advanced cognitive processes are relatively new in evolution and specific to human beings, whereas emotion goes far back in evolutionary time. Thus, many animals have emotional reactions and expressions that resemble human ones in crucial respects. Even so, the fact that we can think about our emotions (and their causes) is likely to change them, as we shall see. For humans and human social life, thinking changes almost everything.

CHAPTER 5 SUMMARY

What Is Social Cognition?

- Social cognition is the study of any sort of thinking by people about people and about social relationships.

- People think about other people more than any other topic, and probably more than about all other topics combined.

- The human mind is designed to participate in society, and this means its primary job is dealing with other people.

- People think about other people in order to be accepted by them, or to compete with or avoid them.

- The term *cognitive miser* refers to people's reluctance to do much extra thinking.

- People generally prefer to conserve effort by relying on automatic modes of thought when they can.

- Knowledge structures are organized packets of information that are stored in memory.

- Schemas are knowledge structures that represent substantial information about a concept, its attributes, and its relationships to other concepts.

- A violation of expectancies sparks deliberate thinking.
- Scripts are knowledge structures that contain information about how people (or other objects) behave under varying circumstances; scripts define situations and guide behavior.
- At least three main types of goals guide how people think:
  - Find the right answer to some problem or question.
  - Reach a particular, preferred conclusion.
  - Reach a pretty good answer or decision quickly.
- In the Stroop effect, the automatic response is to say the word rather than the ink color.
- The four elements that distinguish automatic from deliberate processes are intention, effort, control, and efficiency.
- Priming is the tendency for frequently or recently activated concepts to become more accessible in memory.
- Framing is how something is presented.
- Trying to suppress a thought can have the paradoxical effect of increasing the thought.
- In the counter-regulation or "what the heck" effect, dieters eat more if they believe they have broken their diets than if they are hungry.

Attributions and Explanations: Why Did That Happen?

- Attributions are the inferences people make about events in their lives.
- Internal, stable attributions involve ability; internal, unstable attributions involve effort; external, stable attributions point to the difficulty of the task; and external, unstable attributions involve luck.
- The self-serving bias suggests that people want to take credit for success but deny blame for failure.
- The actor/observer bias states that actors tend to make external attributions, whereas observers make internal attributions.
- The fundamental attribution error (also sometimes called correspondence bias) refers to the finding that people have a bias to attribute another person's behavior to internal or dispositional causes.
- A major attribution dimension is whether one believes another person's behavior was intentional versus accidental.

Heuristics: Mental Shortcuts

- Heuristics are mental shortcuts or rules of thumb.
- The representativeness heuristic is the tendency to judge the frequency or likelihood of an event by the extent to which it resembles the typical case.
- The availability heuristic is the tendency to judge the frequency or likelihood of an event by the ease with which relevant instances come to mind.
- The simulation heuristic is the tendency to judge the frequency or likelihood of an event by the ease with which you can imagine (or mentally simulate) an event.

- The anchoring and adjustment heuristic suggests that when people estimate how frequent or likely an event is, they use a starting point (called an anchor) and then make adjustments up and down from this starting point.

Flawed or Clever Thinking?

- According to the standard view, the purpose of thinking was to discover the truth. Heuristic and automatic thinking was viewed as flawed and biased.
- According to the current view, thinking is for arguing and persuading others. Heuristic is not viewed as flawed and biased; indeed it often provides an excellent answer.

(So-Called) Errors and Biases

- People may make cognitive errors because they are more concerned about arguing their point of view than about finding the truth.
- Information overload is the state of having too much information to make a decision or remain informed about a topic.
- Estimation and shifting criteria can result in biased counts of sexual partners.
- People generally have access to two types of information:
  - Statistical information from a large number of people.
  - Case history information from a small number of people.
- People generally pay the most attention to case history information.
- Confirmation bias is the tendency to notice information that confirms one's beliefs and to ignore information that disconfirms one's beliefs.
- An illusory correlation occurs when people overestimate the link between variables that are related only slightly or not at all. It can occur even after one exposure called one-shot illusory correlations.
- The mass media contribute to illusory correlations by focusing on rare events.
- The base rate fallacy is the tendency to ignore or underuse base rate information and instead to be influenced by the distinctive features of the case being judged.
- The hot hand is the tendency for gamblers who get lucky to think they have a "hot" hand and their luck will continue.
- The gambler's fallacy is the tendency to believe that a particular chance event is affected by previous events and that chance events will "even out" in the short run.
- The false consensus effect is the tendency to overestimate the number of people who share one's opinions, attitudes, values, or beliefs.
- The false uniqueness effect describes the finding that people tend to underestimate the number of people who share their most prized characteristics and abilities.
- The theory perseverance proposes that once the mind draws a conclusion, it tends to stick with that conclusion unless there is overwhelming evidence to change it.
- Statistical regression (also called regression to the mean) refers to the statistical tendency for extreme scores or extreme behavior to return toward the average.

- One major evolutionary purpose of thinking is to decide how to respond when one's goals are blocked.
- The belief that people can control totally chance situations is called the illusion of control.
- Counterfactual thinking involves imagining alternatives to past or present factual events or circumstances.
- Upward counterfactuals posit alternatives that are better than actuality, whereas downward counterfactuals posit alternatives that are worse than actuality.
- Regret involves feeling sorry for misfortunes, limitations, losses, transgressions, shortcomings, or mistakes.
- Regrets are feelings, whereas counterfactuals are thoughts.

Are Most People Really Just Kind of Stupid?
- More often than not, heuristics provide the correct answers, or at least answers that are good enough.
- Relying less on memory, considering multiple alternatives, using meta-cognition, searching for disconfirmatory information, and using explicit decision rules are all techniques that can reduce cognitive errors.

What Makes Us Human? Putting the Cultural Animal in Perspective
- The remarkable power of human thought creates both unique errors and unique capabilities to find the truth.

key terms

quiz yourself ANSWERS

1. What Is Social Cognition? **p.157**
   answers: 1.c 2.c 3.d 4.d

2. Attributions and Explanations: Why Did That Happen? **p.164**
   answers: 1.d 2.b 3.d 4.b

3. Heuristics: Mental Shortcuts **p.167**
   answers: 1.c 2.b 3.c 4.a

4. Flawed or Clever Thinking? **p.169**
   answers: 1.c 2.c 3.a 4.d

5. (So-Called) Errors and Biases **p.178**
   answers: 1.c 2.d 3.d 4.a

6. Are Most People Really Just Kind of Stupid? **p.179**
   answers: 1.a 2.c 3.d 4.c

EMOTION AND AFFECT

6

LEARNING OBJECTIVES

1 Explain the duplex mind's contribution to our emotional experience, and contrast conscious emotion and automatic affect.

2 Compare the three theories of emotion, and identify the role of physiological arousal.

3 Explain how specific emotions—like happiness, anger, guilt, shame, and disgust—serve interpersonal functions.

4 Describe the role of emotion in feelings of belongingness and relationships, in behavior, in thinking and learning, and in decision making.

5 Describe the research on whether emotions differ across gender and culture.

6 Summarize physiological changes associated with different emotions and explain how they can contribute to our conscious experience of emotions.

7 Define emotional intelligence and explain how it relates to emotional regulation.

Spam or junk e-mail messages are the plague of the digital age. Filters don't always work either. Most people get plenty of spam each day, and they waste a lot of time just deleting these junk e-mail messages.

The flood of spam is enough to make anyone fuming mad! Or is it? People respond to spam very differently. Consider two real people who appeared in the news for how they responded to spam. The first story is about Charles Booher, a Silicon Valley computer programmer.[1] Booher was arrested for threatening to torture and kill employees of the company who bombarded his computer with spam ads promising to enlarge his penis. According to prosecutors, Booher threatened to mail a "package full of Anthrax spores" to the company, to "disable" an employee with a bullet and torture him with a power drill and ice pick, and to hunt down and castrate the employees unless they removed him from their e-mail list. Booher used intimidating return e-mail addresses, such as Satan@hell.org. He admitted that he had behaved badly but said that he did so because the company had rendered his computer almost unusable for about two months by a barrage of pop-up advertising and e-mail messages. Booher was arrested for the threats he made, facing a possible 5-year prison sentence and a $250,000 fine, but was released on $75,000 bond. He later committed suicide.

The second story is about a musician from Ottawa, Canada, named Brad Turcotte.[2] Like the rest of us, Turcotte is bombarded with spam e-mail. He said, "I was just staring at my inbox one day and looking at all these ridiculous subject lines"—such as Feel Better Now, Look and Feel Years Younger, and Do You Measure Up, to name but a few—"and I started thinking that some of these were pretty surreal and bizarre. And at the same time, I had been having trouble coming up with titles for some of my songs, so I started thinking that maybe there was something here." As a one-man band called *Brad Sucks,* Brad Turcotte wrote and recorded a song called "Look and Feel Years Younger." He recruited other musicians through the Internet to write additional songs, and assembled a CD of 14 songs titled *Outside the Inbox.* He sells the CDs on the Internet, and so far he has sold hundreds of CDs and hundreds of thousands of downloads. "I was surprised that so many people caught on to it," he said. "I thought it might just be a fun, goofy thing to do. It only occurred to me afterwards, oh, right, everyone gets this. Everyone in the world. How could I forget?"

Both men had the same problem and the same negative emotional reaction, but they coped with it very differently. Neither could get rid of the anger or irritation by simply deciding to feel better, so they both ended up doing something. In one case the anger led to violent, possibly dangerous responses, but in the other it led to positive, creative responses. Emotional states are often so compelling that we struggle to feel good—these struggles range from the creative to the criminal.

Emotions make life rich and colorful, and they influence how people act, though not always in a good way (e.g., crimes of passion!). They still pose something of a mystery. Why do people have emotions? Why is the emotion system set up the way it is? We will try to answer these important questions in this chapter.

One clue is that emotions are mostly outside our conscious control, even though we may feel them consciously. (That's why neither Booher nor Turcotte could just shrug off their anger and feel good.) Emotions provide a feedback system.

Courtesy of Brad Turcotte

Courtesy of Brad Turcotte

After being bombarded with lots of spam e-mail, Brad Turcotte organized a compilation CD called *Outside the Inbox*, in which he and other musicians wrote songs based on the subject lines of spam e-mail, such as "Look and Feel Years Younger."

off the mark .com   by Mark Parisi

ATLANTIC FEATURE © 2002 MARK PARISI

@☼❋#!! SPAM...

✉ ANTLER ENLARGEMENT
✉ WANT BIGGER ANTLERS?
✉ ENLARGE YOUR ANTLERS
✉ ANTLER SIZE MATTERS
IMPROVE YOUR MATING SEASO

DELETE

MARK PARISI/ offthemark.com

Reprinted by permission of Atlantic Feature Syndicate/Mark Parisi.

They bring us information about the world and about our activities in it. They reward and punish us, so we learn to set up our lives in ways that avoid bad emotions and maximize good emotions. Consider guilt as an example. Guilt helps us know we did something wrong. To avoid guilt, people may change their behavior in advance: They may try to keep their promises, obey the rules, treat other people kindly, and so on. If people could escape guilt just by deciding not to feel guilty, there would be less need to behave well in order to avoid guilt. If you could control your emotions, then anytime you started to feel guilty, you could just turn those feelings off and everything would be fine (at least as far as how you feel is concerned). Guilt can give us feedback and guide our behavior, but only if it and similar emotions are outside of our conscious control. ●

What Is Emotion?

It turns out to be fiendishly difficult to provide a definition of emotion, or even to provide several definitions of distinct concepts related to emotion. Some psychologists use the terms *emotion, affect,* and *mood* interchangeably, whereas others treat the terms as distinct concepts. The most common definitions emphasize **emotion** as a full-blown, conscious state that is clearly linked to some event. Emotion is thus a reaction to something, and the person who has the emotion knows it. You may feel angry because someone insulted you, or happy because you got an "A" on your social psychology test, or sad because your grandmother died. In contrast, **mood** is sometimes defined as a feeling state that is not clearly linked to some event. You may not know why you are in a good or bad mood, but you do know that you feel happy or sad. The third concept, **affect** (pronounced 'AF-ekt; note that this word is a noun, not the verb, which is pronounced ∂-'fekt) is sometimes defined as a result of mapping all emotions onto a single good–bad dimension. Positive affect encompasses all good emotions, such as joy, bliss, happiness, love, and contentment. Negative affect encompasses all bad emotions, such as anger, anxiety, fear, jealousy, and grief. Most researchers argue that positive and negative affect are separate dimensions, not opposite ends of the same dimension.[4,5,6,7] Affective reactions can occur without consciousness. You can have a quick positive or negative feeling about something as simple as a word without being fully conscious of it.

Emotions are very important to humans, and the ability to recognize emotions starts very young. Babies as young as 3 months old can "hear" emotions. Researchers scanned the brains of 21 babies and found that their brains responded to tapes playing "emotional sounds," such as laughing and crying.[8] The limbic brain region, which regulates emotions, responded strongly to negative or sad sounds, but it did not differentiate between neutral and happy sounds. These findings are consistent with the general principle that bad is stronger than good.[9]

> "Everyone knows what an emotion is, until asked to give a definition."
> — Beverly Fehr and James Russell[3]

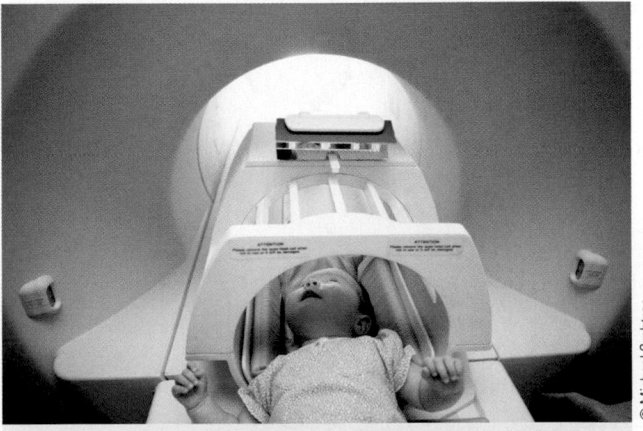

© Michael Crabtree

Using brain scan technology, researchers recently found that babies three months old could "hear" different emotions. The limbic brain region of their brains, which regulate emotions, responded strongly to negative or sad sounds, but did not differentiate between neutral and happy sounds.

emotion a conscious evaluative reaction that is clearly linked to some event

mood a feeling state that is not clearly linked to some event

affect the automatic response that something is good (positive affect) or bad (negative affect)

conscious emotion a powerful and clearly unified feeling state, such as anger or joy

automatic affect a quick response of liking or disliking toward something

Conscious Emotion versus Automatic Affect

Regardless of how people use the terms *emotion, mood,* and *affect,* two quite different phenomena need to be distinguished. These correspond roughly to the two dimensions of the duplex mind. One is **conscious emotion** which is felt as a powerful, single (unified) feeling state. The other is **automatic affect** which is felt as liking or disliking, or as good and bad feelings toward something, and may occur outside of consciousness.

We will use the term *emotion* to refer to the conscious reaction, often including a bodily response, to something. In contrast, we use the term *affect* to refer to the automatic response that something is good or bad (liking versus disliking). Affective reactions to things that are "good" and "bad" are automatic and very fast, occurring in the first microseconds of thought. As soon as you know what something is, you start to know whether you like or dislike it.[10] This initial evaluation even occurs for things people have never encountered before, such as nonsense words like "juvalamu."[11] In contrast, full-blown emotion takes time.

There is no point in trying to decide whether automatic affect or conscious emotion is more important. Both are important, and it would be a mistake to assume that everything we learn about one of them applies to the other as well.

Emotions have both mental and physical aspects. In the next section we explore the physical aspects of emotional arousal.

1. Conscious is to unconscious as _____ is to _____.

   (a) affect; emotion
   (b) emotion; affect
   (c) affect; mood
   (d) mood; affect

2. Affect is generally mapped onto _____ dimensions.

   (a) good and bad
   (b) masculine and feminine
   (c) specific and universal
   (d) strong and weak

3. Affective reactions to things that are "good" and "bad" generally occur in the first _____ of thought.

   (a) microseconds
   (b) seconds
   (c) minutes
   (d) Hours

4. Fatima feels deep sadness because her dog died. What term most accurately describes what Fatima is feeling?

   (a) Affect
   (b) Emotion
   (c) Mood
   (d) All of the above

Emotional Arousal

One reason that people are fascinated by emotions is that they bridge the mind and the body. Emotions have both mental aspects (such as subjective feelings and interpretations) and physical aspects (such as a racing heartbeat or tears). The challenge is to say how the mental and physical aspects of emotion are linked together. One important area of connection involves the bodily response of arousal, which is linked to most conscious emotions, though not necessarily to automatic affect. **Arousal** is a physiological response that occurs within the body, including a faster heartbeat and faster or heavier breathing. It should not be confused with sexual arousal, as it is a general bodily state. We will say more about it as we cover the competing theories of emotion.

arousal a physiological reaction, including faster heartbeat and faster or heavier breathing, linked to most conscious emotions

James–Lange theory of emotion the proposition that the bodily processes of emotion come first and the mind's perception o these bodily reactions then creates the subjective feeling of emotion

James–Lange Theory of Emotion

In 1884, American psychologist William James and Danish psychologist Carl Lange both independently proposed a theory linking the mental and physical aspects of emotion, which is now called the **James–Lange theory of emotion**.[12] James[13] described the theory as follows:

> My theory . . . is that *the bodily changes follow directly the perception of the exciting fact, and that our feeling of the same changes as they occur is the emotion.* Common

sense says: we lose our fortune, are sorry and weep; we meet a bear, are frightened and run; we are insulted by a rival, are angry and strike. The hypothesis here to be defended says that this order of sequence is incorrect, . . . we feel sorry because we cry, angry because we strike, afraid because we tremble, and not that we cry, strike, or tremble, because we are sorry, angry, or fearful, as the case may be. [italics in original]

The James–Lange theory of emotion suggests that the bodily processes of emotion come first and the mind's perception of these bodily reactions then creates the subjective feeling of emotion (see **FIGURE 6.1**). When something happens, your body and brain supposedly perceive it and respond to it, and these physiological events form the basis for the emotion you feel.

Researchers tried for many years to prove the James–Lange theory, but they were largely unsuccessful. One important aspect of the theory is that different emotions must arise from different bodily responses. Data from many studies suggested, however, that the body's response seemed to be very similar for different emotions. Whatever emotion the person felt, the body just showed a standard arousal pattern. Even tears, for example, are not limited to sadness, because people sometimes cry when they are happy or angry or afraid, and many others do not cry when they are sad. Tears, therefore, are not just a sign of sadness, but more likely a sign of intense feeling.

The James–Lange theory did, however, lead to an important contemporary hypothesis—the **facial feedback hypothesis**.[14,15,16] According to the facial feedback hypothesis, facial expressions can evoke or magnify emotions because the brain reacts to what the facial muscles are doing. Several studies have found support for this hypothesis. One of the cleverest manipulations of facial feedback consisted of having participants hold a pen either between their lips or their teeth while rating cartoons.[17] This sounds like a trivial difference, but try it: When you hold the pen between your teeth, your face resembles a smile, whereas when you hold it between your lips, your face resembles a frown. The facial feedback hypothesis holds that if you are smiling, you will enjoy things more than if you are frowning, and this is what researchers found. Participants who held the pen in their teeth thought the cartoons were funnier than did participants who held the pen in their lips. Thus, if you put on a happy face, you will be happier and enjoy external events more.

| Emotional Stimulus | → | Physiological Arousal | → | Experienced Emotion |

FIGURE **6.1**

James–Lange theory of emotion: The emotional stimulus (e.g., hearing footsteps behind you in a dark alley) produces physiological arousal (e.g., increased heart rate), which then produces an experienced emotion (e.g., fear).

facial feedback hypothesis the idea that feedback from the face muscles evokes or magnifies emotions

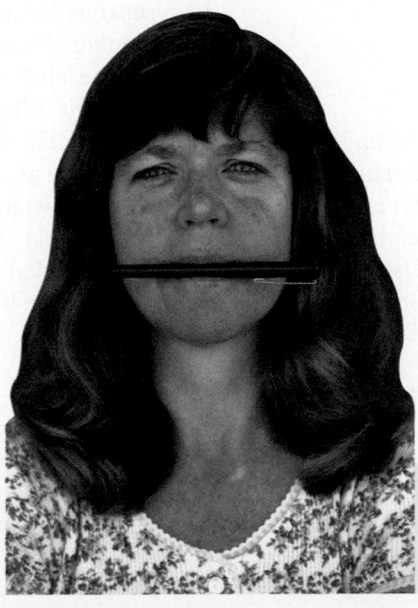

In research studies, people who held a pen with their teeth smiled and felt happier, whereas people who held the pen with their lips frowned and felt sad.

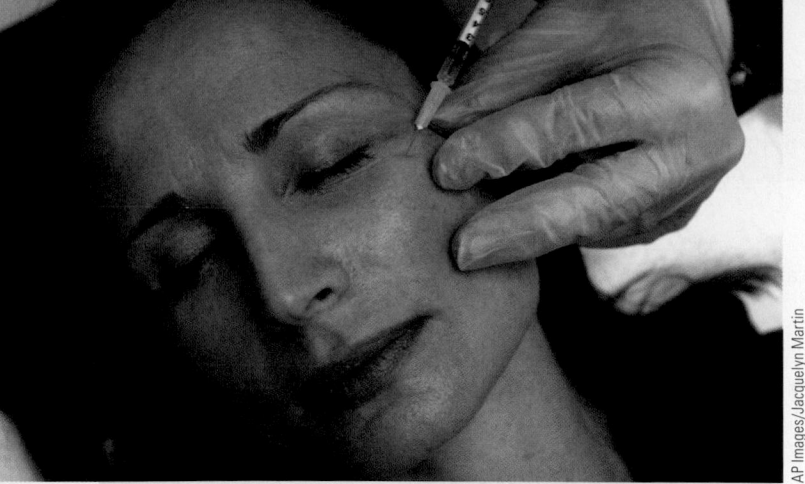

AP Images/Jacquelyn Martin

Although Botox cosmetic injections may make people look younger, they can impair the ability to recognize emotional expressions in others.

Facial feedback may also help us recognize emotional expressions in others. A study[18] found that Botox cosmetic injections, which are used to reduce wrinkles and other signs of aging, can have an unintended negative side effect—they reduce muscular feedback from the face, so the brain doesn't get all the usual input that helps it use emotional information. Female patients in cosmetic clinics who received Botox injections were less accurate in recognizing emotional expressions in others than were participants who received dermal filler injections that do not reduce facial feedback. Seeing people smile normally makes you start to smile a little, and that helps your brain understand their emotions. If you've had Botox, your face doesn't react to the other person's smile (or frown or whatever emotional expression), and this impairs your ability to understand other people's emotions.

Schachter–Singer Theory of Emotion

Modern social psychology has been greatly influenced by a theory put forward by Stanley Schachter and Jerome Singer in the early 1960s.[19,20] They developed it partly in response to the failure of the James–Lange theory. Instead of claiming that the feeling of emotion is a direct result of the bodily reaction, Schachter and Singer said that emotion has two separate components—physiological arousal and cognitive label—each of which is crucial (see **FIGURE 6.2**). Physiological arousal is similar in all emotions. (Remember, this was the problem scientists found when testing the James–Lange theory.) The cognitive label is different for each emotion. The arousal is the mix of feelings you get when your sympathetic nervous system is activated: The heart beats faster, more blood flows to the muscles and brain, the bronchioles in the lungs dilate so that more oxygen goes into the blood, and so on. The feeling of nervousness, such as when you are ready for a big test or a major public performance, is what it is like to have arousal by itself. (Again, this is not to be confused with sexual arousal, which we later discuss in a separate box.) Nervousness is thus a kind of generic emotional state: the arousal part of the emotion, without the label.

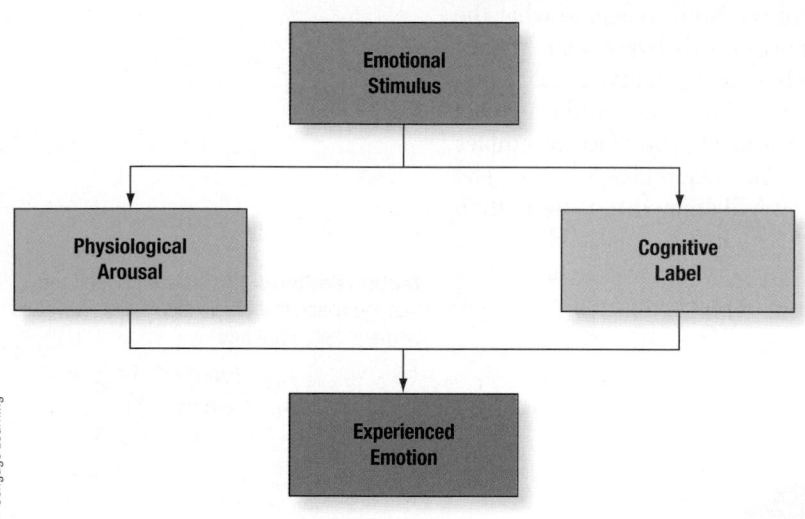

© Cengage Learning

FIGURE **6.2**

Schachter–Singer theory of emotion. The emotional stimulus (e.g., hearing footsteps behind you in a dark alley) produces physiological arousal (e.g., increased heart rate) and a cognitive label, which produces an experienced emotion (e.g., fear).

In the **Schachter–Singer theory of emotion**, emotion is something like a television program. The arousal is the on/off switch and volume control: It determines that there is going to be an emotion, and how strong it will be. The cognitive label is like the channel switch: It dictates what emotion will be felt.

Sometimes the mind might not realize that the body is aroused, or why. *The Social Side of Sex* discusses this problem in connection with a particularly interesting form of physical excitement—sexual arousal. Read the box to find out more about how sexual arousal is related to emotions!

Misattribution of Arousal

One intriguing aspect of the Schachter–Singer theory is that it allows for arousal states to be mislabeled or relabeled. That is, arousal may arise for one reason but get another label, thereby producing a different reaction. For example, someone may not realize that what he or she is drinking has caffeine (e.g., mistaking regular coffee for decaffeinated coffee), which may create an arousal state. The mind then searches for a label to make sense of the emotional state. If something frustrating happens, someone who has this

Schachter–Singer theory of emotion the idea that emotion has two components: a bodily state of arousal and a cognitive label that specifies the emotion

extra, unexplained arousal may get much angrier than he or she would otherwise. This process is called **excitation transfer**.[21] The arousal from the first event (drinking caffeinated tea) transfers to the second event (frustration).

There have been several important experimental demonstrations of mislabeling or relabeling arousal. In Schachter and Singer's original studies,[22] participants were told that the researchers were studying the "effects of vitamin injections on visual skills." By the flip of a coin, participants received an injection of either adrenaline (epinephrine) or a placebo (saline solution, which has no effects; it was included just to control for any effects of having someone stick a needle into your arm). Adrenaline is a stimulant that causes your heart rate, blood pressure, and breathing rate to increase. Participants who received the adrenaline shot were either informed or not informed about the "side effects" of the drug (e.g., it causes heart pounding, trembling hands, etc.). Everyone was told that the injection contained the vitamins, but of course there were no actual vitamins.

Next, participants were exposed to a confederate who acted either happy and joyous (by playing with paper, rubber bands, pencils, folders, and hula hoops) or angry and resentful (provoked by a questionnaire that asked many nosy, offensive questions, such as "Which member of your immediate family does not bathe or wash regularly?"). The researchers secretly observed to see whether the participant would join in and show similar emotion. The strongest emotional reactions were found among the people who had both received the stimulant, rather than the placebo, and been told that the injection would not have any side effects. The ones who received the stimulant and were told that it was a stimulant attributed their arousal state to the injection rather than to the situation, so they did not label it as an emotional state.

excitation transfer the idea that arousal from one event can transfer to a later event

sex guilt feeling guilty about sexual thoughts, acts, or fantasies.

The Social Side of *Sex*

Can People be Wrong about Whether They Are Sexually Aroused?

Sexual arousal is one form of arousal. You might think it is simpler and clearer than emotional arousal because emotional arousal can be associated with such a wide spectrum of emotions, whereas sexual arousal is specific and focused. Yet sexual arousal has its ambiguities, too.

One source of ambiguity is that the brain and the genitals are not always on the same page. Sexual stimulation may affect the brain, or the genitals, or neither, or both. Research suggests that the disconnect between the brain and the genitals is greater among women than men. That is, the link between self-reported arousal (i.e., whether people consciously believe they are sexually turned on) and physiological measures of sexual arousal in the genitals are correlated about 0.60 in men but only about 0.25 in women.[23] Remember, correlations range in size from +/−1 (a perfect, exact match) to 0 (completely unrelated, no connection at all). By conventional values, a "small" correlation is 0.1, a "moderate" correlation is 0.3, and a "large" correlation is 0.5.[24] Thus, the correlation is quite large for men, but less than moderate for women.

There is plenty of room for divergence in both genders, especially if the person's attitudes prescribe certain reactions that differ from what the body finds exciting. In one classic study,[25] men's feelings about homosexuality were surveyed, and researchers chose heterosexual men who were the most tolerant of gay sex and others who were most strongly opposed to it. Then all the participants watched some films of gay men having sex with each other. The researchers measured both the feelings the men had while watching these films and their physiological response. The latter test used a device (called the penile plethysmograph) that wraps a rubber band around the penis to measure how erect it becomes.

The two measures yielded opposite findings. The men who had said they were most strongly opposed to homosexuality reported that they did not like the gay films at all and that they were not turned on. The physiological data, however, showed that those men were the ones most aroused by the films.

A comparable finding emerged from research on **sex guilt** (i.e., feeling guilty about sexual thoughts, acts, or fantasies) in women.[26] In this work, women watched sexually explicit film clips. Women with high levels of sex guilt reported on questionnaires that they did not enjoy the films, and they rated their sexual arousal to the films as lower than any other women in the study. However, physiological measures of arousal—which assess the degree of lubrication in the vagina (measured using a device called a vaginal photoplethysmograph)—indicated that these women were actually more aroused than the other women in the study. Thus, some women who claim to be turned off by erotic films are actually turned on by them.

Sex guilt involves moral objections to erotic activities (possibly including thoughts and fantasies) and reproaching oneself for erotic desires or actions.

Perhaps the best-known demonstration of mislabeling arousal was a study done in Vancouver, Canada, where people can cross a scenic but scary bridge hanging by cords over a deep gorge.[27] According to the authors, the bridge has many features that might be arousing, such as "(a) a tendency to tilt, sway, and wobble, creating the impression that one is about to fall over the side; (b) very low handrails of wire cable which contribute to this impression; and (c) a 230-foot (70.1-meter) drop to rocks and shallow rapids below the bridge." The "control condition" bridge located further upriver was made of heavy cedar wood, did not tilt or sway, had sturdy handrails, and was only a few feet (less than a meter) above a small stream. The researchers stationed an attractive woman on both bridges, and she approached men who were crossing the bridge to ask them to complete a short questionnaire. After participants completed the questionnaire, the attractive female offered to explain the study in more detail when she had more time. She tore off a corner of a sheet of paper, wrote down her name and phone number, and invited each participant to call her if he wanted to talk further. Each researcher kept track of whether the men actually called her.

The reasoning was that crossing the bridge would create an arousal state of fear, and then a conversation with a beautiful woman would lead them to label their fear-based arousal as attraction to her. Sure enough, the men who had crossed the suspension bridge were more likely to call the female researcher than were men who had crossed the stable bridge (even though it was the same woman). The researchers proposed that fear can be converted into love.

Perhaps you can use excitation transfer theory to improve your love life! Take your lover on an exciting date, such as to an amusement park or an action-packed movie, and then kiss him or her. According to excitation transfer theory, the arousal from the amusement ride or movie will transfer to raise your date's attraction to you.

Is the bodily arousal state really the same in all emotions? Subsequent research suggested that there is not just one single state underlying all emotions. More plausibly, there are at least two basic arousal states that feel quite different. One of these is pleasant and the other unpleasant. Many research studies have been done with neutral states, such as someone receiving caffeine or another stimulant (e.g., exercising, watching a sexually explicit movie), and it does seem that these states can be converted into almost any emotion, good or bad. However, emotional arousal that comes from actual events, generated by the body in response to experience rather than chemically induced, is usually either good or bad. "Good" arousal cannot be converted into "bad" arousal, nor can "bad" arousal be converted into "good" arousal.[28,29] Some studies have explicitly shown

Capilano Canyon Suspension Bridge in North Vancouver, British Columbia, Canada. The bridge is 450 feet long (137.2 meters), 5 feet wide (1.5 meters), and hangs 230 feet (70.1 meters) above a rocky gorge. Men who had crossed this bridge were more likely to call a female research assistant than were men who had crossed a low, stable bridge. [27]

that when people experience pleasant arousal, they will not misattribute that state as an unpleasant emotion, or vice versa.[30]

Indeed, the only study that seems to suggest a successful conversion of a bad emotion into a good one is the Vancouver suspension bridge study described earlier,[31] and even this study is ambiguous. Remember, the key measure of attraction was whether the men called the woman, and this did not occur until much later. There is no way of knowing when they decided they liked the woman enough to call her—on the bridge, just after the bridge, or even the next day when remembering the experience. The notion that fear converted into love may be a misinterpretation of that study—maybe it was the relief or elation or bravado they felt after crossing the bridge that was converted into love. If so, then the results indicated converting one positive emotion into another, which would be more in line with subsequent findings.

If there are two types of naturally occurring arousal states—one good and one bad—the explanation of why real, everyday emotions can't be converted may lie with automatic affect. Remember, conscious emotion takes time to build, but automatic affect arises quickly. If an arousal starts to build to form the basis for a conscious emotional reaction, it will be shaped by the automatic reaction, so it too will feel good or bad. Hence, it will be hard to re-label a bad emotion as a good one, or vice versa. Converting one positive emotion into a different positive one, such as turning joy into pride, will be much easier. A warning to the wise: Always watch out for emotional overreactions fueled by caffeine!

QUIZ YOURSELF

Emotional Arousal

answers: see pg 226

1. **Which theory of emotion predicts that we are angry because we hit someone?**

   (a) Cannon–Bard   (b) James–Lange   (c) Schachter–Singer   (d) None of the above

2. **Which theory of emotion predicts that arousal from an event can be mislabeled?**

   (a) Cannon–Bard   (b) James–Lange   (c) Schachter–Singer   (d) None of the above

3. **Tyrone had a stressful day at the office, so he stopped at the gym on the way home to work out. Even after he gets home, Tyrone still feels wound up. When his wife remarks in passing that he forgot to take out the trash, Tyrone responds by yelling and cursing at his wife. Tyrone's overreaction to his wife's comment illustrates _____.**

   (a) catharsis   (b) disinhibition   (c) desensitization   (d) excitation transfer

4. **How many basic arousal states are there?**

   (a) One   (b) Two   (c) Three   (d) Four

Some Important Emotions

In this section we describe five important emotions: happiness, anger, guilt, shame, and disgust. In reading about each of these emotions, it is helpful to think back to one of this textbook's most important themes—namely, that inner processes serve interpersonal functions. To be sure, some emotions may serve more basic biological needs, especially survival and reproduction. But even there, people mainly achieve survival and reproduction by forming and maintaining good relationships with other people. Hence, for example, we may miss the point if we merely ask, "How could feeling guilty ever benefit the person who feels that way?" Instead, it will be more enlightening to ask, "How does feeling guilty help a person maintain good relationships with others?"

Happiness

One of the most compelling works of fiction to emerge from the Cold War is *One Day in the Life of Ivan Denisovich* by Alexander Solzhenitsyn. The main character has been sent to a prison labor camp in Siberia, Russia for 10 years, and he knows there is no guarantee that he will actually be released when his time is up. The situation is bleak. No family or loved ones ever visit him, and he is only allowed two letters per year. He has to work hard outdoors in freezing temperatures, with worn-out clothes that leave his fingers and toes constantly numb. He has no entertainment, not even something to read, and sleeps on a rock-hard bed in a room full of other prisoners. He never catches a glimpse of a woman. He has little chance of escape, and anyone who did manage to escape would probably just freeze to death in the vast empty land. Yet on the last page of the book, the hero looks back on his day (remember, the whole book covers just one ordinary day in the middle of his 10-year prison sentence) and reflects that he was pretty lucky—it was "almost a happy day." He falls into a contented sleep.

How could someone have an "almost happy day" in a Siberian prison camp? The writer's goal was to draw attention to the millions of Russians who suffered terribly in the prison camp system. This is what made the story brilliant: Instead of describing a day that was totally awful, the author presented a relatively "good day" in such a miserable setting. The story shows the power of comparisons and expectations. If you expect the worst—and as a Siberian prisoner you would soon come to expect that—then anything slightly better than the very worst can seem quite good by contrast. The good events that surpassed his expectations seem pathetic to most of us. His dinner was two bowls of bad oatmeal, instead of one; he had avoided the worst work assignments; he had managed to get a little tobacco (the camp's only luxury); and he had found a small piece of metal, not useful for anything he could readily imagine, but maybe someday it might come in handy in some unknown way.

Defining Happiness

What is happiness, and how can it be reached? The term *happiness* is used in different ways to refer to slightly different phenomena. Human beings and many animals share one form of happiness, and it refers simply to feeling good right now. When you get something to eat or you warm up in the sun after being cold, you feel good, and you react with happy feelings.

Other forms of happiness are unique to human beings, in part because they involve a broader time span and the meaningful integration of multiple experiences. Thus, someone might be a happy person because he enjoys many positive emotional experiences, or because she hardly ever feels bad emotions. Indeed, one measure of happiness is **affect balance**. the frequency of positive emotions minus the frequency of negative emotions.

The most complex form of happiness is sometimes called **life satisfaction**. It involves not only evaluating how your life is generally, but also how it compares to some standard. Probably most animals can feel good or bad, but only humans have life satisfaction because only humans can think meaningfully about their life as a whole and decide whether it measures up to their hopes and goals. Life satisfaction has a much broader time span than current emotion and affect balance.

Objective Roots of Happiness

What would make you happy? Most people answer this question by referring to objective circumstances. They think they would be happy if they had something along these lines: plenty of money, a good job, a happy marriage or at least a good romantic relationship, perhaps children, some friends, good health, and a nice place to live. With one exception, they are correct because people who do have those things are happier than people who do not have them. Note that most of those objective predictors involve succeeding by

affect balance the frequency of positive emotions minus the frequency of negative emotions

life satisfaction an evaluation of how one's life is generally and how it compares to some standard

biological and cultural standards. Thus, if people strive to feel good, they will do things that the culture values (such as marrying and succeeding at a good job), and if everyone were to do those things, the culture would thrive and flourish.

The one odd exception is having children. Couples who have children are less happy than couples who have no children.[32] The drop in happiness has been shown repeatedly, with many different research samples and methods. It goes against intuitive beliefs, and in fact most parents expect that having children will increase their happiness. What's more, they continue to believe that having children has made them happier, even though the research clearly shows otherwise. Possibly this is because parenthood is riddled with self-deception and illusion. Parents do not want to believe that they made a big mistake by having children, and they also want to rationalize the efforts and sacrifices they have made. Having children is, however, a powerful source of meaning in life, so that even if becoming a parent reduces happiness, it does make life richer and more meaningful.[33]

Honey, are you happy we had kids?

Culture plays a big role in all this. Nearly all cultures encourage people to have children (by birth or adoption), and toward that end they help promote the idea (even when false) that having children will make you happy. If enough people expect to become happy by having babies, the culture will increase in population, which cultures have generally found to be advantageous. Cultures that do not produce new generations will not survive, so nearly all successful cultures encourage reproduction. Moreover, cultures compete against others, and at some very basic level, those that have more people will triumph over those with fewer. It is not surprising that most cultures glorify parenthood and bestow social approval on those who reproduce most. For a while, the former Soviet Union even gave medals to women who had the most children. This may seem odd, but it is merely a more explicit form of the approval that is found all over the world. Most likely it was motivated by urgent pragmatic forces: The Soviet Union suffered more deaths than any other country during World War II, so replenishing the population was more urgently needed there than in other countries.

The fact that having children reduces happiness may actually be a fairly recent, modern phenomenon.[34] Throughout most of history, most people were farmers, and they lived in societies that offered no social security systems, pensions, or other means of support. When you grew too old to work the farm, you would starve, unless you had children to take over the farm and support you. Childlessness was a disaster for a married couple, in terms of their practical and economic prospects. Only when the family changed from an economic unit to a haven of intimate relationships did the emotional impact of parenthood shift to become more negative.

Many readers are worried when they learn that having children is likely to reduce their happiness. Don't be! Most people want to have children, and do, and end up glad they did, even though along the way they are less happy than they would otherwise have been. The human mind is very good at forgetting bad things and emphasizing good ones. Also, if you want to reduce the negative effect on happiness, you can take several steps. The first is to have a stable relationship to avoid the added stresses of being a single parent. The second is to prolong the "newlywed" phase of life between marriage and birth of first child, rather than rushing into parenthood. That phase may allow the relationship to become stronger, enabling it to withstand the stresses of parenthood better. (Also, many studies have confirmed that the interval between the wedding day and the birth of the first child is one of life's happiest times, especially for women.)[35] Third, save up some money, which can be used to cover new expenses and thereby reduce some of the financial stresses that parenthood puts on the couple. After all, children can be expensive! The average cost of raising a child until age 18 is about $250,000.[36] Having a savings cushion can help avoid much unhappiness.

After World War II in the former Soviet Union, women who had lots of children were given medals.

The surprising thing about the objective predictors of happiness, however, is that the effects are weak. Yes, people with plenty of money are happier than people who don't have much money, but the difference is quite small. Apparently money can buy happiness, but not very much of it. There is only one objective circumstance that has been shown to make a big difference in happiness, and that involves social connections. People who are alone in the world are much less happy than people who have strong, rich social networks. (This strong link shows once again that inner processes, in this case happiness, are linked to interpersonal relationships, in this case forming and maintaining good connections to other people. The human emotional system is set up so that it is very hard for a person to be happy while alone in life.)

For all other circumstances, even including health, injury, money, and career, the differences are small. If you think that reaching your goals will make you happy, you are likely to be disappointed, even though technically you are right. Generally, people who meet their goals are briefly happy, but then they go back to where they were before. People who reach their career goal may experience some temporary happiness, but they do not live happily ever after. Most things wear off pretty soon.

The Hedonic Treadmill

The tendency for objective changes to wear off led some social psychologists to speak of the **hedonic treadmill**.[37,38,39,40,41,42] Like a person on a treadmill, you may take big steps forward but end up in the same place. A big success at work or in romance will bring joy for a while, but then the person goes back to being as happy or unhappy as before. That doesn't mean that everyone goes back to the same level. Happy people go back to being happy, and unhappy ones go back to their former level of unhappiness.[43]

In one of the most dramatic illustrations of the hedonic treadmill, researchers studied people who had won the state lottery (thereby gaining hundreds of thousands of dollars) and other people who had been severely paralyzed in an accident.[44] Such events are among the most extremely good or bad things that can happen to someone. At first, of course, the lottery winners were very happy, whereas the accident victims were very unhappy. A year afterward, however, the effects had largely worn off. Winning the lottery was wonderful, but the winners seemed to have lost their ability to appreciate everyday pleasures such as a friendly conversation or a sunset. Additionally, sudden wealth brought a number of problems: Annoying, needy relatives came out of the woodwork, tax problems brought new headaches, and the like. In general, a year after the big event the differences in happiness were not very noticeable.

It appeared that people got over big good events faster than they got over big bad events. People did not recover emotionally from being paralyzed as fast or as thoroughly as they got over the joy of winning the state lottery. Two large studies that tracked people across many years found that the hedonic treadmill does not work very well when life gets worse.[45] That is, people who suffered a disabling injury became less happy than they had been and, though they adjusted somewhat, they tended not to get back to being as happy as they had been before the accident.

Subjective Roots of Happiness

If objective circumstances do not cause happiness, then what does? Happiness appears to lie more in our outlook and personality than in our circumstances. In a sense, some people are "born happy," whereas others remain grumpy and miserable no matter what happens. Longitudinal research has looked at a long list of objective predictors of happiness and, as usual, found very weak relationships to happiness.[46,47,48] This pattern held true for people who were tracked for a decade. Much can change in 10 years, including most of one's objective circumstances. Ten years from now you will probably have a different job, a different home, different friends, different hobbies, a different amount of money, possibly some different family members. Yet, the strongest predictor of each person's happiness turned out to be how happy the person had been 10 years before.[49] It is not perfect, of course. Some people do change for the better or worse over long periods of time, but they are the exception. In general, people who are happy now will be happy in the future, whereas those who are grumpy or depressed or irritable now will continue to

hedonic treadmill a theory proposing that people stay at about the same level of happiness regardless of what happens to them be so. Major events bring joy or sorrow, but these feelings wear off, and people go back to their own baseline. If you want to be married to a happy person in 10 years, find someone who is happy today (and preferably someone who was happy before meeting you!). Statistically, that person is your best bet for someone who will be happy in the future.

One reason happiness often remains the same across time is that happiness is rooted in one's outlook and approach to life. The importance of one's outlook is evident in the difference between subjective and objective predictors of happiness. In general, subjective predictors are much stronger. *Subjective* refers to how you feel about something, whereas *objective* refers to the something. Thus, how much money you make (objectively) has only a weak relationship to happiness, but how you feel about your income (subjectively) is a strong predictor of happiness. How healthy you are (objectively), measured by how often you got sick this year, has only a weak relationship to your happiness, but how satisfied you are with your health (subjectively) is stronger. Being married has only a weak impact on happiness, but being happily married is a strong factor.

Increasing Happiness

The "positive psychology" movement has begun to look for actions or exercises that can increase happiness. Some findings are promising. Several psychological patterns have been shown to increase happiness, such as forgiving others, expressing gratitude, counting up good things that have happened recently, practicing religious beliefs, and being optimistic.[50,51,52,53,54,55,56] These all share the idea of focusing one's attention on positive things. For example, one exercise you might try if you want to raise your happiness is to sit down once or twice a week and make a list of the good things that have happened to you. Research studies have confirmed that people who do this end up happier than control participants who do not.[57]

Regardless of what causes happiness, happy people are healthy people. For example, consider the results from a fascinating study of Catholic nuns.[58] On September 22, 1930, the Mother Superior of the North American sisters sent a letter requesting that each Catholic nun "write a short sketch of [her] life. This account should not contain more than two to three hundred words and should be written on a single sheet of paper . . . include place of birth, parentage, interesting and edifying events of childhood, schools attended, influences that led to the convent, religious life, and outstanding events." More than 60 years later, these 180 sketches were scored for positive emotions. The researchers found that nuns who expressed high positive emotions lived about 10 years longer than the nuns who expressed low positive emotion! Positive emotions are apparently good for your health, though the results are correlational, so we cannot be sure whether the positive emotion is a cause of good health or merely a sign of it.

In another fascinating study,[59] researchers examined the 1952 Baseball Register photos of 230 Major League Baseball players. Researchers coded whether each player had "no smile" (i.e., stared blankly at the camera), a "partial smile" (i.e., the muscles around his mouth were only slightly raised), or a "full smile" (i.e., a wide grin, with both cheeks raised—also known as a Duchenne smile). Of the 230 players, 46 were still alive. Players who had not smiled in the photos died at age 72.9 years (on average), players with partial smiles died at age 75.0, and players with full smiles died at age 79.9 years. The results remained significant even after controlling for other variables related to mortality (e.g., marital status, BMI). Again, we do not know whether frequent smiling was a cause or just a sign of a long life. But smiling a bit more certainly can't hurt your chances! Remember the facial feedback hypothesis.

Research shows that baseball players with big smiles (top right) in their official photo lived 5 years longer than those with slight smiles and 7 years longer than those with no smiles. Smile—you just might live longer!

Q32/Alamy

Q27/Alamy

Q27/Alamy

Positive emotions may have direct effects on the body that improve health, such as boosting the immune system. It may also be that happiness is linked to good social relations, as we have seen, and perhaps good social relations promote health, whereas being alone in the world weakens bodily health. The link between health and belongingness could also go in either direction or both. Maybe people are drawn to associate with happy people while avoiding sad or grumpy types (thus happiness affects belongingness). Or maybe having good social relations makes people happy whereas being alone reduces happiness (thus belongingness affects happiness). Maybe both are correct. There is even another possibility, which is that some underlying trait predisposes people to get along with others and to be happy.

Where you live also makes a difference. A recent 5-year study[60] measured the happiness of employees who relocated from the city to greener areas, compared with happiness of employees who relocated in the reverse direction. Results found that relocating to greener areas was associated with more happiness. Other research shows that even imagining yourself outdoors in nature increases happiness.[61]

Happy All the Time?

Scholars have even begun to debate whether happiness is always good.[62] There is certainly a case to be made that happiness is simply all good. For one thing, it feels pleasant, and preferring pleasure over pain and good feelings over bad ones is natural. For another, there are benefits to happiness. Indeed, recent research using large national samples from three different countries showed that people who are happier (in the sense of higher life satisfaction) later had better outcomes than less happy people.[63] Happy people were more likely to get married and less likely to get divorced or separated. They were less likely to lose their jobs or change jobs, and less likely to move to a new home. They were more likely to conceive a child, which as we saw is a somewhat mixed blessing in terms of happiness—but of course reproduction is central to natural selection. Evolution might favor happy people, if they are more likely than unhappy ones to have children.

On the other hand, various findings suggest that some people who seem extremely happy are actually less healthy, more rigid, and prone to overlook genuine dangers and threats. To use an extreme example, people who suffer from mania exhibit high levels of happiness but are prone to taking dangerous risks and often suffer problems in work and social life. Feeling very happy may also be counterproductive in some situations, such as funerals. Happy feelings can blunt negative emotions, leaving people without important signals and other benefits of negative emotion. (As one example, expressing anger is often helpful in a negotiation, and so an overly happy negotiator might not get a good result.)

Negative emotions presumably serve useful functions, and so sometimes it is appropriate and helpful to feel bad.[64] Sadness and other bad moods can improve memory as well as the accuracy of some judgments. Interpersonally, bad moods enable people to detect when others are lying and to resist social influence, and it also reduces bias due to stereotypes and prejudice. Unpleasant emotions cause people to focus away from the self, attending more to the environment and analyzing things carefully, whereas pleasant emotions signal that the external world is fine and so the person can turn inward and take it easy.

Is pursuing happiness good? People want to become happy, but perhaps they succeed best at that by trying to do good work and earn the trust and affection of other people, rather than trying directly to be happy. Indeed, some lab studies have found that trying to be happy sometimes backfires, leaving people less happy than participants in a control condition who simply experienced things without pushing themselves to feel good.[65] It is perhaps better to let happiness be a reward for good deeds than to make it an end in itself.

Nobody thinks being constantly miserable is best. But perhaps someone can be too happy, or happy at the wrong times. Perhaps the healthiest pattern is to experience a broad variety of emotions, as suggested by some recent work. People who are happy all the time are only using part of their emotional repertoire and may be missing out on some valuable parts of the human experience. The term "**emodiversity**" refers to how much a person experiences the variety and abundance of different human emotions.

emodiversity degree to which a person experiences the variety and relative abundance of human emotions

High emodiversity is linked to better mental and physical health,[66] though it is hard to say what causes what.

Emodiversity does not necessarily mean extremity of emotion. A person can have plenty of emodiversity even though all emotions are relatively mild. The extremity of emotional reactions is a separate topic that has interested researchers. Some people often experience intense emotions, both positive and negative, whereas others rarely feel intense emotions of any sort. *Tradeoffs* describes the tradeoff of feeling versus not feeling intense emotions.

Anger

Anger is an emotional response to a real or imagined threat or provocation. Anger can range in intensity from mild irritation to extreme rage. Many events make people angry. These events can be interpersonal such as a provocation, or they can be stressors such as frustration, physical pain, exposure to violent media, or discomfort caused by heat, crowding, noise, or foul odors.[71] Chemicals inside the body, such as the hormone testosterone, also contribute to getting angry.[72]

Much of life can be understood as deriving from approach and avoidance tendencies. Approach and avoidance are rooted in simple processes of animal learning (e.g., does the animal move forward to check out the new stimulus, or does it run away?). Emotions, including anger, are often helpful signals for what to approach and avoid. Generally, positive emotions signal to approach something, typically because it is good. Negative emotions are

anger an emotional response to a real or imagined threat or provocation

Affect Intensity: Emotional Roller Coaster or Even Keel?

TRADE Offs

Nearly everyone wants to be happy, and the emotional formula for happiness seems simple: plenty of good feelings and as few bad ones as possible. Unfortunately, life doesn't always cooperate. Over the last couple of decades, researchers have begun to recognize that some people have many intense experiences, both good and bad, whereas others have relatively few.

One of the most systematic treatments of this difference is based on the Affect Intensity Measure (AIM).[67] Some sample items from the scale are: "When I'm happy, I feel like I'm bursting with joy" and "When I am nervous, I get shaky all over." People who score low on the scale have relatively few emotional reactions, and these tend to be rather subdued. In contrast, people who score high have strong emotions to all sorts of events. Consistent with traditional stereotypes, one study found that advanced

art college students had higher scores on the AIM than did advanced science college students.[68] That is, future artists generally live with plenty of extreme emotions, whereas future scientists generally have more subdued emotional lives.

Which is better? Affect intensity appears to be a genuine tradeoff. People who score low on the AIM can go through life on a fairly even keel. They don't become too bothered about problems and stresses, but then again they don't feel swept away with passionate joy very often either. In contrast, life is an emotional rollercoaster for people with high affect intensity. Thus, you get both the good and the bad, or neither.

The quality of your life circumstances may dictate which is preferable. If your life is in a positive groove, well under control, so that most experiences are good, then you may well get more meaningful enjoyment if you have high affective intensity. In contrast, if your life is filled with unpredictable, uncontrollable events, some of which are very bad, you may well prefer to have low affect intensity. You don't want to take the good with the bad if there is too much bad.

This tradeoff can affect the most intense and personal of relationships. People who have been hurt in love may become reluctant to let themselves fall in love again. Historians have even suggested that in past centuries people were reluctant to love their children because the high rate of child mortality would lead to heartbreak.[69,70] In Europe, for example, if a woman from a good family had a baby, she would often send it out to the country to be nursed, even though objectively its chances of survival were slightly lower there (because the country was poorer) than if the child stayed with her. Preventing the woman from nursing her own baby kept maternal feelings of love to a minimum, so the mother was less hurt if the baby died. Older children were often sent out to live in other people's households starting when they were 6 or 7, so parents might not develop the lasting emotional bond to their children that comes from living together year after year. Once public health improved, however, and most children could be expected to survive into adulthood, parents could afford the risk of loving their children more, and they began to keep their children with them until they were nearly grown up.

mostly avoidance signals, because they tell you something is bad. Fear, sadness, jealousy, anxiety, depressed feelings, and others tend to motivate people to avoid and withdraw.

Anger is a rare example of an emotion that feels bad but nonetheless signals approach.[73] Being angry often makes people want to approach or confront the problem, such as by fixing it or at least arguing with the person whoever made them angry. Anger can be a powerful force in helping people stand up for what they believe is right. The American Revolution, the civil rights movement, the feminist movement, and other causes probably used anger to motivate people to take action against unfair practices. Anger is often linked to aggression (as will be explored in Chapter 10). The association between anger and approach motivation may thus be due to the increase in aggressive motivation that typically accompanies anger.

Anger is widely recognized as a problem. It is one of the most heavily regulated emotions, in the sense that cultures have many different norms about anger. Some of these norms conflict with each other. For example, norms say that sometimes it is justifiable to be angry, other times anger is wholly inappropriate, and yet other times there is an obligation to be angry.[74] In another sense, however, anger is one of the least regulated emotions. When people are surveyed about how they control their emotions, they typically report that they have fewer and less effective techniques for controlling anger than for controlling other emotions.[75]

Is Anger Maladaptive?

Anger seems maladaptive today—useless, counterproductive, harmful, divisive, and problematic. When people become angry, they do things they will regret later. They are impulsive, aggressive, and worse. Why would anger exist if it is harmful and maladaptive? It is reasonable to assume that it is (or was) adaptive, or else natural selection would likely have favored people who did not feel anger, and anger would gradually have disappeared from the human repertoire of emotions. In other words, despite all its faults and drawbacks, anger must have some positive value that helps the organism survive—or at least it must have had some positive value in the evolutionary past. Whether anger is suited to today's cultures and social circumstances is another question, however.

One line of explanation is that anger is adaptive because it motivates the person to act aggressively and assertively. The broader context is that emotions exist in order to motivate actions, and each emotion points toward a certain kind of act. Anger helps get people ready to defend themselves, assert their rights, pursue goals that might be blocked, and perform other useful acts.

A second line of explanation begins by objecting to the first: Why not go directly to the aggression? Why become angry first? Anger tips off your foes that you might attack them, allowing them to prepare themselves or even attack you preemptively. The second explanation is that anger helps reduce aggression. This may seem paradoxical because studies show that people are more aggressive when they are angry than when they are not.[76] But that evidence could be misleading, because both anger and aggression occur in situations in which there is conflict, frustration, or provocation. If human beings had evolved to skip feeling anger and go directly to aggression, there would still be plenty of aggression. Hence, in this second view, anger helps warn friends and family that something is wrong and aggression may be coming. This gives people time to resolve the conflict before it reaches the point of violence. Anger may therefore actually reduce aggression, compared to what the world would be like if people went directly into aggressive action as soon as they experienced conflict or frustration. For example, some powerful people manage to get their way with just a brief frown of displeasure or a slight raising of the voice: A hint of anger is enough to make other people scurry to do their bidding, and the powerful person hardly ever has to express a full-blown angry outburst, let alone engage in aggressive action.

Thus, anger may be social in an important sense, and in fact it may help enable people to live together. If anger is a warning sign of impending aggression, anger may help defuse conflict and prevent aggression. Yet as a sign of conflict and problem, anger may be antisocial. Moreover, the action-motivating function of anger may conflict with the social conflict-defusing aspect. Angry people may say or do things that make the problem worse.

If one person wants to go out and the other wants to stay in, conflict is already there—but angry, insulting remarks will aggravate it and make it harder to reach a compromise. Research on negotiation has shown some social benefits of anger. When two people are negotiating and one shows anger, the other takes this as a sign to give in. It is a sign that the angry person will not compromise or make concessions, so one had best go along.[77,78,79] Anger is thus useful for a negotiator. To be sure, people dislike angry negotiators, so anger can backfire, especially if the non-angry negotiator has other options. But if they have to settle a negotiation, they concede more to the angry than to the non-angry person.

People seem aware that anger can be useful. Some people actually try to increase their angry feelings when they anticipate a social interaction in which anger might be useful, such as a difficult confrontation with a rival or enemy. Moreover, they are right: Sometimes anger does improve performance in such difficult situations.[80]

A final perspective on the causes of anger is the potential mismatch between people's natural reactions and the complexity of modern social life. Many emotional reactions developed during a time of simpler life circumstances. Anger might help you have the arousal to fight off a predatory animal, but it may be useless and even counterproductive to have the same feelings toward your computer when the hard drive crashes.

Dealing with Anger

Because it is unpleasant, many people want to get rid of their anger when they experience it. There are three possible ways of dealing with anger. One standard approach that has been endorsed by many societies is never to show anger. (Nature supplies the impulse to be angry, but culture tells people to try to stop it.) It can end up prompting people to stuff their anger deep inside and repress it. There is some evidence that this is a costly strategy. Long-term concealed anger can be quite destructive to the person, increasing the risk of such illnesses as heart disease.[81] On the other hand, as we have seen, inner states follow outward expressions (as in the facial feedback hypothesis, discussed earlier), so if people generally act as if to show they are not angry, some anger may be diminished.

A second approach is to vent one's anger. This view treats anger as a kind of inner pressure or corrosive substance that builds up over time and does harm unless it is released. The **catharsis theory** falls in this category because it holds that expressing anger (including verbal expression or even aggressive, violent action) produces a healthy release of emotion and is therefore good for the psyche. Catharsis theory, which can be traced back through Sigmund Freud to Aristotle, is elegant and appealing. Unfortunately, the facts and findings do not show that venting one's anger has positive value. On the contrary, it tends to make people more aggressive afterward and to exacerbate interpersonal conflicts.[82] Venting anger is also linked to higher risk of heart disease.[83,84,85] Even among people who believe in the value of venting and catharsis, and even when people enjoy their venting and feel some satisfaction from it, venting anger increases subsequent aggression, even against innocent bystanders.[86]

One variation of venting is intense physical exercise. When angry, some people go running or try some other form of physical workout. Although exercise is good for your heart, it is not good for reducing anger.[87] The reason exercise doesn't work is that it increases rather than decreases arousal levels (recall the earlier section on arousal in emotion). When people become angry, their physiological arousal increases. The goal is to decrease arousal rather than increase it. Also, if someone provokes you after exercising, excitation transfer might occur.[88] That is, the arousal from the exercise might transfer to the response to the provocation, producing an exaggerated and possibly more violent response.

In a nutshell, venting anger may be like using gasoline to put out a fire: It just feeds the flame. Venting keeps arousal levels high and keeps aggressive thoughts and angry feelings alive.

The third approach is to try to get rid of one's anger. This solution is important because the problems of both the other approaches (i.e., stuffing and venting) arise because the person stays angry. The important thing is to stop feeling angry. All emotions, including anger, consist of bodily states (such as arousal) and mental meanings. To get rid of anger, you can change either of those. Anger can be reduced by getting rid of the arousal state, such as by relaxing or by counting to 10 before responding. Anger can also be addressed

catharsis theory the proposition that expressing negative emotions produces a healthy release of those emotions and is therefore good for the psyche

Bettmann/Corbis

Ted Bundy in court. Bundy was a serial killer who murdered dozens of women. He was electrocuted in a Florida prison on January 24, 1989.

guilt an unpleasant moral emotion associated with a specific instance in which one has acted badly or wrongly

shame a moral emotion that, like guilt, involves feeling bad but, unlike guilt, spreads to the whole person

by mental tactics, such as by reframing the problem or conflict, or by distracting oneself and turning one's attention to other, more pleasant topics. Certain behaviors can also help get rid of anger. For example, doing something such as petting a puppy, watching a comedy, making love, or performing a good deed can help because those acts are incompatible with anger and the angry state becomes impossible to sustain.[89]

Guilt and Shame

What do you think of the view of guilt expressed in this quotation? Many people agree with it. Guilt does have a bad reputation in our culture. If you visit the "pop psychology" section in a bookstore, you are likely to find several books telling you how to get rid of guilt. The underlying idea is that guilt is a useless (or even harmful) form of self-inflicted suffering. Most people seek to avoid guilt like the plague.

Then again, perhaps guilt deserves more credit than it gets. This quotation was actually from Ted Bundy, a notorious mass murderer who killed at least 30 women in seven different states. Bundy described himself as "the most cold-hearted son of a bitch you'll ever meet."[91] Bundy was executed in an electric chair in Florida in 1989. Perhaps if he had felt a little more guilt himself, Bundy might have refrained from his criminal acts and some of those women (and Bundy himself) would be alive today.

Research by social psychologists has gradually painted a picture of guilt that differs starkly from the negative view held by our culture (and by Ted Bundy). Guilt is actually quite good for society and for close relationships. You would not want to have a boss, a lover, a roommate, or a business partner who had no sense of guilt. Such people exist (they are called psychopaths), but they are often a disaster to those around them.[92] They exploit and harm others, help themselves at the expense of others, and feel no remorse about those they hurt.

Guilt versus Shame

What is guilt? **Guilt** is a negative emotional feeling, and it is usually associated with some implicit reproach that one has acted badly or wrongly. By and large, everyone occasionally does something wrong; the difference between people lies in whether they feel bad about it or not. Recent research suggests that guilt triggers specific behaviors intended to right the wrong, rather than simply doing anything that might help guilty people feel good about themselves.[93] Guilt is especially associated with acts that could damage a relationship about which one cares.

Guilt must be distinguished from **shame**.[94] The difference lies in how widely the bad feeling is generalized. Guilt focuses narrowly on the action, whereas shame spreads to the whole person. Guilt says, "I did a bad thing." Shame says, "I am a bad person."

Research based on that distinction has repeatedly shown that shame is usually destructive, whereas guilt is usually constructive. This may be worth keeping in mind when you deal with your assistants and workers, or your family members, or even your romantic partners. How do you criticize them when they do something wrong? Calling their attention to what they did wrong may seem necessary, but phrasing your criticism in terms of being a bad person (e.g., "you rotten creep") is not nearly as constructive as allowing them to be a good person who did a bad thing (e.g., "you did a bad thing"). Thus, one should avoid making internal negative stable attributions about others (see Chapter 5). There is, after all, no remedy for being a bad person, so shame makes people want to withdraw and hide, or to lash out in anger. In contrast, guilt signifies a good person who did a bad thing, and there are plenty of ways that a good person can remedy an isolated bad act: apologize, make amends, reaffirm one's commitment to the relationship, promise not to repeat the misdeed, and so forth.

Effects of Guilt

Guilt motivates people to do good acts, such as apologizing. Apologies can help repair damage to relationships because they (a) convey the implicit agreement that the act was wrong, (b) suggest that the person will try not to do it again, and (c) counteract any implication that the bad action meant that the person does not care about the relationship.

For example, if your partner cooks you a lovely dinner but you arrive an hour late and the food is spoiled, your partner may not care very much about the food itself, but the implication that you do not care about the relationship can be very upsetting. A sincere apology cannot revive the spoiled food, but it may prevent your partner from feeling that you do not care about the relationship.[95,96,97]

Guilt also motivates people to make amends. When people feel guilty about something they have done, they try harder to perform positive or good actions. They are more likely to learn a lesson and try to behave better in the future. This too can help salvage a relationship from the damage done by some misbehavior.

For example, half the participants in one study[98] were induced to tell a lie. A previous participant (actually a confederate) told them all about the study and what the correct answers to a test were before the experimenter arrived. Soon thereafter, the experimenter came and asked participants if they had heard anything at all about the study. All participants said no. Thus, half of the participants lied (because in fact they had all heard about the study). After the study was over, the experimenter said that participants were free to go, but added that if they had extra time they could help him fill in bubble sheets for another study (an incredibly boring task). Participants who had not been induced to lie volunteered to help fill in bubble sheets for 2 minutes on average, whereas participants who had been induced to lie volunteered to help fill in bubble sheets for 63 minutes! The lying participants were apparently attempting to wash away their guilt by being more helpful. Guilt made them more willing to do something nice.

off the mark.com   by Mark Parisi

YUP, THAT'S MY JOB... PRETTY DISGUSTING, HUH? I CAN'T THINK OF ANYTHING MORE HUMILIATING. I'M SO ASHAMED. BY THE WAY, WHAT DO YOU DO?

©1997 MARK PARISI   offthemark.com

Reprinted by permission of Atlantic Feature Syndicate/Mark Parisi

Many social psychology studies have found that guilt makes people behave in more socially desirable ways.[99,100,101] These research findings suggest that guilt is good for relationships, even though feeling guilty will be unpleasant. Sometimes, in order to make a relationship more successful, people must sacrifice their own selfish interests and do what is best for the other person. (Indeed, one theme of this book has been the need to rely on conscience and self-regulation to overcome selfish impulses in order for civilized society and strong human relationships to survive.) Guilt is one force that pushes people toward making those relationship-enhancing sacrifices.

Thus, guilt can help make you a better person. Does it make your own life better? Guilt has a positive effect on relationships. Even beyond this, there may be benefits of guilt. In a provocative series of studies, researchers showed that guilt can increase pleasure, mainly because people have learned to associate guilt with pleasures such as eating, drinking, and having fun when they should be working. Participants who were primed with the notion of guilt reported higher subsequent enjoyment of various activities, including looking at profiles on a dating website, buying or eating a candy bar, and watching an entertaining film.[102] Thus, ironically, a bit of guilt can increase one's happiness!

Guilt and Relationships

Some forms of guilt do not revolve around doing anything wrong. Sometimes people feel guilty simply because others have suffered more than they have. The term **survivor guilt** emerged after World War II based on observations of victims who had not suffered as much as others. Some people who survived the mass murder campaigns in concentration camps felt guilty for having survived when so many others died. Likewise, people who survive other natural or human-caused disasters feel guilty for having lived when so many others died. These people had not done anything wrong, but the phenomenon of survivor guilt shows that people are deeply sensitive to a sense of fairness and have some unease when life is "unfair" in their favor. (It is easy to be upset about unfairness when you are the one who got less than others; even some animals react to such unfairness, but animals do not seem to mind getting more than their share.) A more modern version of survivor guilt has been observed during economic recessions, when large firms must lay off many workers as in the current financial crisis. Those who remain often have some feelings of guilt for keeping their jobs when other deserving individuals have lost theirs.[103]

survivor guilt an unpleasant emotion associated with living through an experience during which other people died.

All of this depicts guilt as a very interpersonal emotion, and it is. The stereotype of guilt depicts it as a solitary emotion, but even if someone feels guilty while alone, most likely the guilt is about something interpersonal. People mainly feel guilty about things they have done to others—hurting them, ignoring them, letting them down, or failing to meet their expectations. Moreover, they mainly feel guilty toward people they care about. Guilt is more linked to close relationships than other emotions. For example, people may often be afraid of total strangers, or annoyed by casual acquaintances, or frustrated by someone in a store or restaurant, but guilt is mainly felt toward family, good friends, and other loved ones.[104]

Guilt over hurting someone else depends partly on how useful that other person is, according to recent experiments.[105] For example, participants felt somewhat guilty when their choices resulted in assigning another person to do an unpleasant task instead of a fun one. They felt much guiltier when they learned that the other person would later decide how to divide the money reward among the group than when the other person had no such power. The transgression and the other person's suffering were the same, so in moral principle the guilt should have been the same. But guilt focuses on relationships that are beneficial to us. That is presumably why people feel more guilt toward their mother and romantic partner than toward strangers.

Guilt is one emotion that people actively try to make others feel. Some people become quite skilled at knowing what to say to make someone else feel guilty. As always, though, the guilt depends on the relationship, and a stranger may have a hard time making you feel guilty. The essence of most guilt-inducing strategies is "See how you are hurting me." If you do not care about that person, you may not feel guilty for hurting him or her. In contrast, if the person is someone you love and care about, you will usually change your behavior to avoid hurting the person.

Guilt is thus an emotion well suited to cultural animals such as human beings. It depends on one's connections to others, and it makes people maintain better relationships with others. It also benefits a large system of interrelationships, which is what a culture is. And it encourages people to live up to cultural standards and rules.[106]

Washing Away the Guilt

The classic literature offers examples of people who try to wash away their guilt by washing their hands. A story in the Bible relates that Pontius Pilate, the Roman governor of Jerusalem, washed his hands and declared himself blameless after decreeing that Jesus would be crucified.[107] Likewise, in Shakespeare's play *Macbeth,* Lady Macbeth attempted to wash away her guilt of plotting King Duncan's murder by compulsively washing her hands. Purity is a central notion of morality[108] and cleansing makes one feel pure and clean.[109] In baptisms and other religious rituals, water is often used to wash away sin and make the person clean and virtuous. Research by modern social psychologists has confirmed that the average person actually does feel less guilty after washing his or her hands.[110] Because guilt often makes people do good deeds such as helping, washing one's hands can make one less helpful.[111]

Disgust

Disgust may not seem like an emotion, but it is considered to be one—and one that psychologists have begun to recognize as important. **Disgust** can be defined as a strong negative feeling of repugnance and revulsion. It is captured by statements such as "grossed out" or "yuck!" It is different from anger, in that anger motivates people to approach rather than avoid things, whereas disgust is a strong cue to avoid something.[112] Disgust is "the voice in our heads . . . the voice of our ancestors telling us to avoid infectious disease and social parasites."[113] The prototype of disgust is the feeling of wanting to vomit after eating something that is intolerable and that the body naturally wishes to expel as fast as possible (hence the urge to vomit). It is not confined to humans and may be widespread in the animal kingdom because it helps motivate animals not to eat things that could make them sick or even kill them. Disgust thus helps keep people healthy.[114]

Disgust may be especially important among humans because our constitution is delicate compared to most other animals, and there are many things we should not eat; yet

Research shows that washing one's hands can actually reduce feelings of guilt, as when Pilate washed his hands after sanctioning the crucifixion of Jesus Christ.

disgust a strong negative feeling of repugnance and revulsion

human children naturally try to learn about things by putting them in their mouths. Paul Rozin led research into disgust by having adult and child research participants watch him put a sterilized dead cockroach into a glass of apple juice and then removing it and offering them a drink from the glass. Most adults said no, and indeed many refused even a fresh drink of apple juice in a different cup, but some of the children had no objection to drinking from the glass with the cockroach.

Women seem to have stronger disgust reactions than men.[115] Men high in masculinity are less willing to show disgust. There are various theories to explain this, including males being socialized to do dirty jobs, but the gender difference may reflect the importance of health for reproduction. Pregnant women typically are highly sensitive to disgust, which nature may have arranged because an infection would endanger the fetus.

Although disgust is unpleasant, it does have its benefits. It can motivate a broad range of healthy behaviors, beyond avoidance of things that will make you sick. Most health workers now appreciate that many people do not wash their hands often enough, including after going to the toilet. Cultivating a sense of disgust helps motivate

Kyodo/Newscom

Some governments (such as Australia's) require cigarette companies to put disgusting pictures on cigarette packs to motivate people to quit smoking.

people to wash more often. Another use of disgust to motivate healthy behavior is in the policies by which some governments (such as Australia's) require cigarette companies to put disgusting pictures on cigarette packs to motivate people to quit smoking.

Disgust can be considered part of a "behavioral immune system" that supports health.[116] The body's inner immune system for fighting off infections requires considerable energy and is not always successful, so it is safer to avoid things that could bring infection. This system does more than stop people from eating spoiled food. It may discourage people from being friendly toward strangers when there are concerns about disease. It may motivate people to avoid having sex or even being friends with people whose faces have ugly marks on them because in the past some diseases left marks on the face. Indeed, sex brings two people into such close contact that many germs can be exchanged, so it carries a disease risk, especially with someone who has slept with many partners. Sexual disgust may therefore motivate people to avoid risky partners, and finding prostitutes or other highly promiscuous people "disgusting" may protect one's health.

Indeed, in our ancestral past, people living together were likely to have had and survived the same diseases, so interacting more with them was relatively safe (because by this point you are probably immune to those illnesses). Strangers, on the other hand, could have diseases you have not yet had, so they posed a greater risk of bringing you new infections. Some thinkers have concluded that prejudice against outgroups may be partly derived from the greater risk of infection that came from socializing with them.[117] The more people feel disgust toward particular groups of other people, the more prejudice they show against those groups,[118] such as obese people,[119] and even some religious groups, such as Muslims[120] and atheists.[121] Groups regarded as disgusting are even viewed as not quite human.[122]

People also regard some forms of immoral behavior as disgusting, and they elicit similar facial responses and attitudes as do unpalatable foods, filthy restrooms, and bloody wounds.[123] In particular, behaviors associated with purity, such as cleanliness and physical health (also sexual propriety) are particularly linked to disgust. The more strongly research participants find an activity disgusting (like reading about a brother and sister kissing passionately), the more strongly they condemn it. Even being disgusted by a film caused people to make harsher moral judgments about some activity unrelated to the film, when the behavior violated the moral virtue of purity. For example, feeling disgusted caused people to make especially strong moral condemnation of a person they read about who bought a chicken at a supermarket, had sex with it, then cooked and ate it. Disgust had less relevance to moral judgments about unfairness or interpersonal harm.[124] In other research, participants made harsher judgments of immoral behavior if they were in a room that stank (something the researchers achieved by dousing the room with "fart spray" before the session) than in a non-stinky room.[125] The disgusting smell affected moral judgments on everything from sex between first cousins to laziness.

Andy Butterton/PA Photos/Landov

How immoral is sex before dinner?

1. **One measure of happiness, affect balance, is equal to _____.**

(a) the frequency of the positive emotions

(b) the frequency of positive emotions divided by the frequency of negative emotions

(c) the frequency of positive emotions minus the frequency of negative emotions

(d) the frequency of positive emotions plus the frequency of negative emotions

2. **Mimi just won the lottery in the state where she lives. What is her emotional response likely to be over time?**

(a) Mimi will be very happy at first and will remain very happy.

(b) Mimi will be very happy at first, but she will later return to her level of happiness before she won the lottery.

(c) Mimi will be very happy at first, but she will later become very depressed after the good feeling wears off.

(d) Mimi's initial and subsequent level of happiness will not change from what it was before she won the lottery.

3. **Bill thinks that if he's irritated with his children, he'll feel better and be less inclined to hit them if he just yells and screams. Bill believes in the notion of _____.**

(a) catharsis

(b) displacement

(c) excitation transfer

(d) negative reinforcement

4. **Which statement best describes the research about guilt and shame?**

(a) Guilt and shame are both good for the individual and society.

(b) Guilt and shame are both bad for the individual and society.

(c) Guilt is bad and shame is good for the individual and society.

(d) Guilt is good and shame is bad for the individual and society.

answers: see pg 226

Why Do We Have Emotions?

If emotions were confusing and destructive reactions that generally made people do stupid things, then natural selection would probably have phased them out long ago because people who had fewer and weaker emotions would fare better than people with plenty of strong emotions. Although some science fiction characters (like the alien Mr. Spock on *Star Trek*) may do fine without emotions, humans who lack emotions seem to have great difficulties in life.[126] It is true that sometimes emotions are confusing and cause people to do stupid, irrational, even self-destructive things. But all that tells us is that the benefits of emotion must be that much greater, because the benefits have to offset those costs.

One thing seems clear: Emotions make up an important and powerful feedback system. Emotions tell us whether something is good or bad. You don't have much emotion over things you don't care about! Caring (motivation) is therefore one ingredient necessary for making emotion. As we go through life and things happen to us, emotions follow along afterward and help stamp in the strong sense that each event was good or bad. This is true for both automatic affect and conscious emotion. Whatever else emotions may do, they help formulate our reactions to whatever has just happened.

Emotions Promote Belongingness

Emotions help people get along better. This may seem surprising at first because we are quick to notice when someone else's emotions make that person hard to get along with. Mostly, however, people's emotions promote their ties to others. (Imagine trying to be friends with someone who never showed or felt any emotion.)

The best way to appreciate this is to look at the emotions people have when they either form or break a social bond with someone else. Forming social bonds is linked to positive emotions.[127,128,129,130,131,132,133,134,135,136,137,138] People are happy at weddings (even if they cry!). They are usually delighted when they join a fraternity or sorority (even if they have to go through a hazing process first!). They are excited or at least relieved when they get a job. Having children is revealing: People are usually all full of joyful smiles when they have children, even though in the long run being a parent leads to lower happiness in life, probably because of the stresses and demands of parenting.

Conversely, a host of bad emotions is linked to events that end, damage, or threaten relationships. Having an enemy leads to fear or hate. Divorce and other forms of social rejection foster sadness, depression, and anger. Being treated badly or rejected unfairly causes anger. Doing something that hurts a loved one causes guilt. The threat that your partner might leave you for someone else causes jealousy. The prospect of being abandoned and alone causes anxiety. Losing a loved one causes grief.

Happy feelings often reflect healthy relationships,[139] whereas hurt feelings often reflect damaged relationships.[140] If you want to feel good and avoid emotional distress, form and maintain good social relationships with other people! Social contact, especially with loved ones, can help people deal with stressful emotions. Female research participants who were anticipating painful electric shocks showed big reductions in stress if they were permitted to hold their husband's hand during the waiting period.[141] The biggest stress-reduction gains were found among the women whose marriages were happiest (indicating they may have felt the strongest positive social connections). There was some benefit, though less, from holding a stranger's hand or holding hands with a husband in a not-so-happy marriage. Thus, a moment of physical contact with another person can reduce bad emotions caused by stress, and the greatest emotional boost comes from holding hands with someone you love. The results from this study are depicted in **FIGURE 6.3**. Recent research suggests that human touch can also help people with low self-esteem cope with anxiety about dying.[142]

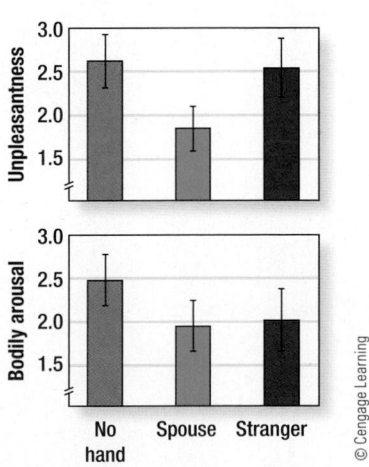

© Cengage Learning

FIGURE 6.3

Holding someone's hand reduces how unpleasant stressful events are judged to be and even reduces bodily arousal, especially if the person is your spouse.[141]

The fact that emotions promote belongingness is yet another important instance of our general theme that what happens inside people serves what happens between people. Emotions (inner processes) help promote good interpersonal relations. People want to feel good and avoid bad emotions, and this desire impels them to try to form and maintain good relationships.

Emotions Communicate Social Information

Emotions fit the general pattern that nature says go, culture says stop. Children do not need to be taught to have emotions. Rather, they learn to conceal their feelings when appropriate. Apparently, the natural state of an emotion includes visible display, so that others can tell what you are feeling.

Emotions are thus not purely for the inside. No one can tell your thoughts unless you choose to speak them, but people can read your emotions. Evolution must have benefited people whose emotions were read by others. Possibly this starts with babies, who cannot take care of themselves and therefore have to let their caregivers know when they feel bad (such as by crying). We have also suggested that anger could help prevent harm by signaling that one is unhappy, so that there is time to discuss the problem rather than having a fistfight.

In Chapter 9, we will see that much prosocial behavior (e.g., helping others) is motivated by empathy, which involves being able to feel what someone else is feeling. Here again, it is beneficial to show emotions that can be easily read by others. They are more likely to help you if they feel your pain or share your distress.

Indeed, there is a variety of evidence that emotions can be contagious,[143] presumably because there is value (probably for strengthening social bonds) to having people be in a similar emotional state. Recently, some researchers have begun to use social media to examine how emotions spread. One experiment used the News Feed feature of Facebook. It manipulated the emotional content of news about friends, either suppressing more positive or more negative emotional content.[144] People's own posts tended to conform to the emotional content of what they had seen on their News Feed. For example, if positive information was omitted from their News Feed, users tended to post more emotionally negative information themselves. The researchers even found a general effect for emotionality: People whose News Feed contained less emotional information (good or bad) were less likely to post anything emotional themselves the next day.

Another recent study looked at the impact of rainy days on millions of Facebook users.[145] To examine how emotions spread, they looked at how Facebook updates changed when it rained. They found that negative updates increased by 1.16% and positive updates decreased by 1.19% when it rained. Then they looked at the friends of the people who posted the updates to see if moods are contagious. They found that every negative update generated an additional 1.29 negative updates, whereas every positive update generated an additional 1.75 positive updates.

Emotions Cause Behavior—Sort Of

Traditionally it has been assumed that emotions guide behavior. This view is consistent with what we know about physiological arousal. Arousal gets the body ready for action.[146,147] Some theorists have proposed that emotion does not exist without a readiness for action.[148] Other theorists have proposed that implicit muscle movements are part of emotion.[149] That is, an emotion naturally and normally starts your body moving.

Then again, maybe emotions do not guide behavior. People have plenty of emotions without doing anything. Additionally, we do not associate most emotions with any single action. Maybe fear prompts you to run away, but it is slow; if you depended on having full-blown fear, you would not escape fast enough. Maybe anger inspires you to fight, but most angry people don't fight. What is the single behavior that is supposed to follow from guilt? From love? From joy?

The objection that emotion is too slow to guide behavior applies mainly to conscious emotion, of course. Automatic affect—the feeling of liking or disliking something—arises in a fraction of a second and therefore can be very helpful. When walking through a crowded room, you may meet someone unexpectedly, and you might have to decide whether to smile at that person or go the other way. The fast automatic reaction that tells you whether you like or dislike that person can be a big help. If you had to wait around for arousal to build and a full-fledged conscious emotion to occur, it would be too late to help you make that decision.

Food for Thought talks about whether moods guide eating behavior.

When emotion causes behavior, it is often because the person wants to change or escape the emotional state. For example, researchers have long known that sad, depressed moods make people more helpful.[158,159,160,161] This could be true for multiple reasons—for example, that sadness makes people have more empathy for another person's suffering and need, or that sadness makes people less concerned about their own welfare. Then again, perhaps sadness makes people more concerned about themselves, in that they want to feel better. One team of researchers hit on an ingenious way to test this theory.[162] They put people in either a happy, sad, or neutral mood. They also gave everyone a pill. Some were told the pill had no side effects, but others were told that the pill would freeze or fix their emotional state for about an hour, which meant that whatever mood or emotion they currently had would continue for another hour. The point of this mood-freezing manipulation was that it made people think it was useless to try to feel better. The group of sad participants whose pills supposedly had no side effects were more helpful than others, consistent with previous findings that sadness increases helping. The mood-freeze participants, however, did not increase in helpfulness. The researchers concluded that sad moods only lead to greater helping if people believe that helping will make them feel better. The emotion (sadness) does not directly cause behavior; rather, it makes people look for ways to escape the bad feeling.

FOOD FOR *Thought*

Mood and Food

Positive moods lead to preferences for healthy food, whereas negative moods lead to preferences for unhealthy food.[150] People who feel bad often eat badly. For example, people who are depressed or lonely will eat foods that are typically high in sugar, fat, and carbohydrates. Such foods are called "comfort foods" because they are often associated with childhood and home cooking (and thus the comfort of having a parent take care of you). They also provide a sense of well-being—at least until you start feeling guilty for eating them!

Many studies have linked food and mood, as shown in a study of 60 obese women with binge-eating disorders.[151] Binge eaters consume a large amount of food at one time. Sometimes they also feel out of control when eating. By the flip of a coin, half these women were assigned to fast for 14 hours, so they would be very hungry, whereas the rest did not fast. All the women were then induced to have either a negative or a neutral mood, and then they were served a buffet meal (so they could eat as much as they wanted). How much the women ate depended on their mood but not on whether they had fasted. In other words, being in a bad mood had a bigger effect on how much these women ate than how food deprived they were! The bad mood led to more eating, and eating seemed to help cheer the women up.

Other studies have reported similar results: Being in a bad mood leads to binge eating and a feeling of being out of control when eating.[152,153] A comparison of binge-eating-disordered adults, nonclinical binge eaters, and adults who did not binge eat found that all three groups overate in response to negative emotions.[154] The effect of mood on food intake is not limited to people with eating disorders—it applies to all adults. In contrast, inducing a positive mood was shown to reduce the number of cookies people ate.[155]

This doesn't mean that bad moods automatically or directly cause people to eat. Rather, eating seems to be a strategy for making yourself feel better. In one study,[156] half the participants were told that eating would not change their mood. Then all were put into a sad, depressed mood by having them imagine they were the driver in a car accident that killed a child. Those who had been told that eating wouldn't make them feel good did not eat any more than those in a neutral-mood control condition. Only those who thought eating might make them feel better indulged in heavy eating in response to the bad mood. Thus, it is wrong to say simply that emotion "causes" behavior. Emotional distress drives people to want to feel better, and they choose actions that they think will cheer them up. These findings are consistent with mood maintenance theory, which argues that people who are in a good mood try to maintain that good mood as long as they can.[157]

There is another reason to suspect that the purpose of emotion is not directly causing behavior. When emotion does cause behavior, as in the so-called heat of passion, it often produces behaviors that are not wise or beneficial to the individual. For example, angry people often say and do things that they later regret, such as calling their boss an idiot.[163] Evolution favors traits that bring benefits and advantages. If emotions mainly caused foolish actions, then natural selection would have gradually phased emotion out of the human psyche. The irrationality of emotional actions is therefore a reason to suspect that the natural purpose of emotion lies elsewhere.

One seeming exception to the view that emotions do not cause behavior is communication. It seems that emotions are meant to be communicated, and, in this sense, emotions do cause behavior. It may be natural to show one's feelings and artificial to hide them. Young children, for example, typically express their emotions freely and without reserve. As they grow up, they slowly learn to hide them sometimes, which is another sign that the influence of socialization is to restrain and conceal feelings rather than to instill them. Once again, nature says go and culture says stop!

Emotions Guide Thinking and Learning

As the previous section showed, emotion may or may not guide behavior directly. The link between emotion and behavior is far from clear, but emotion does influence thinking and learning. As we said earlier, emotions make up a feedback system that helps people process information about the world and their own actions in it. Emotions change the way people think and sometimes help them learn better.

A long-standing stereotype held that emotions undermine rational thinking and make people do foolish, crazy things. However, psychological studies have shown that people who lack emotions (often because of brain injuries or other problems) are not really better off. They have great difficulty adjusting to life and making decisions. For example, a researcher described asking one such patient which of two dates would be better for his next appointment. The man spent most of an hour thinking of all the potential reasons to choose one or the other date, thus showing that he could analyze and think very logically, but he could not manage to choose between them. Finally the researcher just picked one date, and the man immediately said, "Fine!"[164]

Research with such patients has also shown that emotions help people learn from their mistakes. Without emotions, people don't learn. Participants in one study had to draw from various decks of cards.[165] In some decks, the cards generally signaled that the participant would win a small amount of money. In other decks, the amounts of money were larger, but one could lose as well as win. Normal people with normal emotional responses would play the game by sampling each deck, and when they drew a card that cost them a large sum they would then avoid that deck for a while. The negative emotional reaction helped them learn to regard those decks as bad. The patients without emotion (due to damage to a particular brain area) failed to learn. Even after they lost a big sum they would go right back to the same deck, often losing much more money in the process.

Thus, emotions help people learn. The mere fact of having an emotion alters memory: It makes people remember important things better while impairing memory for low-priority information. In lab studies, for example, when people saw an emotionally arousing picture, they remembered the preceding (irrelevant) picture even better than normal—provided it was important to them.[166] If not important, they remembered that previous picture worse than otherwise (i.e., without the later emotional surge). Thus, both positive and negative arousal seem to operate like a filter that puts priorities on what gets into memory and what gets ignored and forgotten.

Emotions also help learning from experience. Bad emotions may help people think about their mistakes and learn how to avoid repeating them. Sometimes this process is aided by counterfactual thinking, which is the process of thinking about what might have been (see Chapter 5). Emotions make people engage in more counterfactual thinking, as in "I wish I hadn't said that" or "If I hadn't wasted time arguing on the phone, I would have gotten there on time" or "I should have asked that attractive person for his/her phone number."[167]

Emotion can constitute valuable information that people learn about the world. According to the **affect-as-information hypothesis**,[168] people judge something as good or bad by asking themselves, "How do I feel about it?" If they feel good, they conclude that the thing is good. If they feel bad, then whatever they are dealing with must be bad. Research has shown that mood effects are eliminated when people misattribute their mood to an irrelevant source, such as the weather. Researchers in one study sampled phone numbers from the student directory, assigned them to sunny versus rainy conditions by the flip of a coin, and waited for suitable days.[169] The sunny days were the first two sunny spring days after a long period of gray overcast. For the first time in months, students went outside to play Frisbee. The rainy days were several days into a period of low-hanging clouds and rain. The interviewer pretended to call from out of town and asked a few questions about life satisfaction. The crucial manipulation was whether the interviewer first asked as an aside, "By the way, how's the weather down there?" This question was asked to draw students' attention to a plausible source of their present mood. Because the researchers weren't sure that this would work, they also included a condition in which the interviewer told students that the study was about "how the weather affects people's mood." The results showed that students were more satisfied with their lives on sunny days than on rainy days, but only when their attention was not drawn to the weather. Asking "How's the weather down there?" eliminated the effect of weather on people's life satisfaction.

When people are in an emotional state, they seem to see the world in a more emotional way, and this changes the way they process information. People put things in categories based more on their emotional tone than on their meaning. For example, does the word *joke* go more with *speech* or with *sunbeam*? People who are not having an emotion at the moment tend to group *joke* with *speech* because both involve talking (a logical grouping). In contrast, people who are happy or sad tend to group *joke* with *sunbeam* because both words have positive emotional meanings. Emotion thus attunes you to emotional connections out in the world.[170]

(Anticipated) Emotion Guides Decisions and Choices

We said earlier that emotions are a feedback system in the sense that they give us dramatic and powerful evaluations of whatever has just happened. In a sense, therefore, emotions focus on the recent past. Is that any help toward the future? One way they could help would be with learning, as noted previously. Another, however, is that people can learn to anticipate how they will feel if something happens. As a result, they can begin to guide their behavior based on how they expect to feel. If emotion rewards and punishes behavior, then perhaps people decide how to act based on how they expect to feel afterward. They avoid acts that they expect will make them feel sad, angry, guilty, or embarrassed, and they favor acts that they think will make them feel happy, satisfied, or relieved.

Thus, *anticipated* emotion is important. Indeed, a recent review found that anticipated emotion has a much stronger effect on human thought and behavior than does actual emotion.[171] Guilt is a good example: Guilt can really organize someone's life even if one hardly ever feels guilty. If guilt does its job, the person will anticipate and avoid acts that might lead to guilt. The person will end up behaving in a morally and socially desirable manner, and hence will almost never actually have to feel guilty.

Humans are the only animals that can travel mentally through time, preview a variety of different futures, and choose the one they think will bring them the greatest pleasure (or the least pain). **Affective forecasting** is the ability to predict one's emotional reactions to future events.[172] How do you think you would feel, and how long would this emotional state last, if (a) you won first prize in some athletic tournament, (b) you found out your romantic partner was having an affair with another person, (c) you got a great job offer with a high starting salary, or (d) you were wrongly accused of cheating and had to withdraw from the university? Most people are fairly accurate at predicting which emotions they would feel, but they substantially overestimate how long they would feel that way. People also overestimate the intensity of their emotional

affect-as-information hypothesis the idea that people judge something as good or bad by asking themselves "How do I feel about it?"

affective forecasting the ability to predict one's emotional reactions to future events

reactions.[173] The odds are that if any of these things did happen to you, you would get over it and return to your normal emotional state faster than you think. People are rarely happy or unhappy for as long as they expect to be. This error may occur because people focus too much attention on the event in question and not enough attention on other future events.[174]

Is it a problem that our predictive powers are seriously flawed? It may be a blessing rather than a curse, according to social psychologist Dan Gilbert:

> Imagine a world in which some people realize that external events have much less impact than others believe they do. Those who make that realization might not be particularly motivated to change the external events. But one of the reasons we protect our children, for example, is that we believe we would be devastated if they were harmed or killed. So these predictions may be very effective in motivating us to do the things we as a society need to do, even though they might be inaccurate on an individual level. Anyone who wanted to cure affective forecasters of their inferential ills would be wise to measure both the costs and benefits of forecasting errors.[175]

Still, predicting wrongly could carry some costs. Revenge, for example, is something people often pursue on the basis of affective forecasting errors.[176] People believe that punishing someone who did something bad will bring them satisfaction and a feeling of closure. In reality, when people get revenge by punishing someone else, they continue to ruminate about the event and end up feeling worse than people who did not have the opportunity to take revenge. (The latter tend to move on and gradually forget about the issue.) Even when it comes to something as simple as deciding whether to go for a walk indoors (on a treadmill) or outdoors, people lose out because they fail to predict these emotions.[177] The outdoors walk produces a better mood than the indoors walk, but people fail to predict this, and so they miss a chance to feel good. (And note that both these examples involve predicting too little emotion rather than too much—consistent with Gilbert's comment, quoted above, saying that predicting too much emotion may be more helpful than predicting too little!)

Anticipated emotion can be a powerful guide to behavior, though psychologists have just begun to study the ways in which this happens. Thus far, one of the most studied effects of anticipated emotion is anticipated regret. Some researchers have argued that people make decisions more on the basis of how they expect to feel than on the basis of a fully logical, rational analysis of what will yield the greatest reward.[178] Decision making shows a "status quo bias," which means that people tend to stick with what they have and be overly reluctant to make changes, even if changing would logically put them in a better position. These researchers explain the status quo bias on the basis of anticipated regret: If you made the wrong decision, you would probably regret it more if you had made a change (thus relinquished the good situation you had in favor of a worse one) than if you had stuck with what you had.

Imagine this in the context of a romantic relationship: You have a reasonably good relationship, but someone else comes along who seems potentially an even better partner for you, though it is hard to be certain. According to the anticipated emotion theory, your decision will be based on considering how much you will regret either decision if it is wrong. If you stay with your pretty good partner even though the other partner could have been better, you may feel some regret. But you would feel even more regret if you dumped your pretty good partner and went off with the other one, and that turned out to have been a mistake. Anticipating the greater possible regret of making the second kind of mistake (dumping your current partner in favor of the new one) will bias the decision-making process toward staying with the status quo.

Emotions Help and Hurt Decision Making

We have already seen that without emotions, people have trouble making up their minds. They can think through the good and bad features of different choices, but they have trouble settling on which one is best. Decisions are also guided by anticipated emotion, usually for the better. On the other hand, the traditional awareness that people make bad decisions under the influence of emotion suggests that emotion can harm decisions as well as helping them. Only recently has decision research started to take seriously the role of emotions in the choices and decisions people make.[179]

Evolution seems to have prepared humans and other primates to experience fear and anxiety in response to certain objects (e.g., snakes, spiders). Anxiety has been called "the shadow of intelligence" because it motivates people to plan ahead and avoid taking unnecessary risks.[180] According to the **risk-as-feelings hypothesis**,[181] people react to risky situations based on how severe the worst outcome is and how likely it is to occur. They do this at a gut level. If their gut tells them the situation is too risky, they avoid it. (In terms of the duplex mind, gut reactions usually refer to the automatic system—in this case, automatic affective reactions.)

Strong conscious emotions can also influence people to engage in risky behavior and ignore future consequences. Sexual arousal often interferes with decision-making ability. For example, male research participants who saw sexually appealing photographs thought they were less likely to contract a sexually transmitted disease from a high-risk partner than did men who saw nonsexual photographs.[182]

Thus, their feeling of sexual arousal prevented them from appraising the danger accurately. Negative emotional responses to sex such as anxiety, guilt, and fear interfere with sexual behavior and also interfere with learning and retaining sexually relevant material, such as contraceptive information.[186] Other negative emotions, such as depression, are associated with maladaptive decision making.[187] To see how negative emotions affect how much money we spend, see the *Money Matters* box.

In summary, emotions call attention to good and bad outcomes but seem to make people disregard probabilities and odds. Anticipated emotions generally seem to help and

risk-as-feelings hypothesis the idea that people rely on emotional processes to evaluate risk, with the result that their judgments may be biased by emotional factors

Emotions and Prices

Money experts generally advise you to avoid making financial decisions on the basis of emotion. But emotion is an important and common feature of everyday life, and it is unrealistic to expect people to be able to wait until all their emotions have subsided whenever they want to buy or sell anything. Hence, it is useful to know how emotion can affect financial decisions—even emotion that is left over from other events.

The effects of two leftover emotions on buying and selling decisions was investigated in an important study— disgust and sadness.[183] Participants first watched a film clip designed to induce an emotional state. Some saw a sad scene from a film in which a boy witnesses his father's death. Others saw a disgusting scene in which a man plunges into an unflushed, filthy public toilet in the hope of finding a dose of heroin. Participants in the neutral control condition saw a brief nature video.

Some participants had received a highlighter pen set as a gift, and they were later asked how much they would sell it for. For the other participants, the price they would pay for the pen set was assessed. (To avoid the problem that some participants might not have much money with them, the researchers asked them to choose between the highlighter set and various amounts of money they could receive instead.) Note that the buying and selling had nothing to do with the emotional states from the film clips, and in fact participants thought they were doing two separate experiments.

Disgust is naturally caused by eating something bad, so it predisposes the body to want to get rid of what is inside it and avoid taking in anything new.[184,185] In naming prices, people acted as if the highlighter set were the cause of their disgust. They lowered their selling price, which is a good way to get rid of something. They also lowered the price they were willing to pay for it, which reduces the chances of acquiring it.

Sadness reflects a general judgment about something as bad, so the message of sadness is "Let's change something!" As with disgust, sadness induced people to lower their selling price, which increases the odds of selling the item and hence making a change. Unlike disgust, however, sadness caused people to increase what they were willing to pay for the highlighter set, which increased the odds of another kind of change, namely acquiring something.

From B.L. Fredrickson. The value of positive emotions. *American Scientist, 91*, 330–335. Reprinted by permission.

Intellectual resources	Physical resources
• Develop problem-solving skills • Learn new information	• Develop coordination • Develop strength and cardiovascular health

Social resources	Psychological resources
• Solidify bonds • Make new bonds	• Develop resilience and optimism • Develop sense of identity and goal orientation

FIGURE 6.4

Positive emotions broaden and expand an individual's attention and mind-set. These broadened mind-sets, in turn, build an individual's intellectual, physical, social, and psychological resources.[191]

inform decision making, but current emotional states can bias the process and lead to risky or foolish choices.

Positive Emotions Counteract Negative Emotions

Positive emotions are studied far less than negative emotions.[188] Compared to negative emotions, there are fewer positive emotions, and they are relatively undifferentiated. For example, it is difficult to distinguish joy, amusement, happiness, and contentment. In contrast, it is easier to distinguish anger, fear, sadness, and disgust.

What adaptive function do positive emotions serve? How did they help our ancestors survive? One possible answer is that positive emotions appear to solve problems of personal growth and development. According to the **broaden-and-build theory** of positive emotions, positive emotions prepare an individual for later hard times.[189,190,191] Positive emotions broaden and expand an individual's attention and mind-set. For example, joy broadens by creating urges to play, push the limits, and become creative.[192,193] These broadened mind-sets, in turn, build an individual's physical, intellectual, and social resources (see **FIGURE 6.4**).

Some research has shown that positive events are strongly related to positive emotions but not negative emotions, whereas negative events are strongly related to negative emotions but not positive emotions.[194] However, in some studies, bad events affected both good and bad emotions, whereas good events mainly affected good emotions.[195,196] In any case, this line of thought suggests that the value of positive emotions is found mainly in connection with positive events. Against that view, however, research suggests that much of the value of positive emotions may lie in their power to overcome or prevent bad emotions.

Other Benefits of Positive Emotions

Being in a good mood helps flexibility, creativity, and problem-solving ability. For example, researchers put some physicians in a good mood by giving them some candy.[197] Physicians in the control group received no candy. Both groups of physicians were given a case of a patient with liver disease, and researchers timed how long it took them to diagnose the case. Physicians who received the candy were 19% faster and showed fewer distortions and more flexible thinking in comparison to physicians who received no candy. (The results could not be due to a "sugar high" because the physicians were told to eat the candy after the study was over, and all of them waited.)

Being in a bad mood does not help flexibility and creativity. For example, research participants who thought about the French documentary *Night and Fog*, which is about the World War II concentration camps, did not perform better than individuals in a neutral mood.[198] Thus, the effects are probably not due to mere arousal because both positive and negative moods can increase arousal.

Work can benefit from positive emotions. People in a positive mood also perform better, are more persistent, try harder, and are more motivated than people in a neutral or negative mood.[199,200] People are more motivated to perform tasks they enjoy doing, and being in a good mood makes tasks more enjoyable.

Being in a good mood can also serve a protective function. People in a good mood tend to avoid risks, such as in gambling.[201] People in a good mood want to remain in a good mood, and they would feel bad if they gambled away their earnings.

Having a positive mood does, however, have a darker side. People in a positive mood are less logical,[202] have poorer short-term memory,[203] and are more easily distracted by irrelevant information.[204] These effects might be due to the fact that positive moods promote heuristic thinking that relies on mental short cuts.

broaden-and-build theory the proposition that positive emotions expand an individual's attention and mind-set and promote increasing one's resources

1. _____ emotions are generally associated with forming social bonds, whereas _____ emotions are generally associated with breaking social bonds.

(a) Unpleasant; pleasant

(b) Pleasant; unpleasant

(c) High arousal; low arousal

(d) Low arousal; high arousal

2. According to the affect-as-information hypothesis, people judge something as good or bad by asking themselves which of the following questions?

(a) How do I feel about it?"

(b) "What do I think about it?"

(c) "When does it affect me most?"

(d) All of the above

3. People generally _____ how long they will feel a particular emotion.

(a) underestimate

(b) accurately estimate

(c) overestimate

(d) All of the above, depending on whether the emotion is pleasant or unpleasant.

4. Which of the following emotions motivates people to plan ahead and avoid taking unnecessary risks?

(a) Anger

(b) Anxiety

(c) Happiness

(d) Sadness

answers: see pg 226

Group Differences in Emotion

Are Emotions Different Across Cultures?

Do people in different cultures have different emotional lives? For many years experts assumed that the answer was "yes." They thought that cultural differences would lead to huge differences in inner lives so that you could not begin to understand how someone from another culture might feel. This view has lost ground, however, and some experts now agree that most emotions may be quite similar across cultural boundaries.

Paul Ekman and his colleagues have identified six basic emotions that can be reliably inferred from facial expressions (see photographs): anger, surprise, disgust, happiness (or joy), fear, and sadness.[205] Their research group showed these photos to people all over the world, and regardless of cultural differences, people interpreted the same facial expression as indicating the same inner emotion. A meta-analysis showed that people living in 37 countries on five continents inferred the same basic emotions from photos of facial expressions.[206] These findings suggest that, based on facial cues, people have similar emotions everywhere and can recognize and understand one another despite their very different cultural backgrounds.

Are Women More Emotional Than Men?

A long-standing stereotype depicts women as more emotional than men. Women are supposed to be more readily overcome with feelings and to be more guided by them, in contrast to men, who make decisions based on cool, rational deliberation. Is this stereotype accurate?

A large-scale study had adult married men and women carry beepers around.[207] Whenever they heard a beep, they were supposed to stop what they were doing and fill out a quick rating of their current mood and emotional state. The researchers obtained thousands of emotion reports of what men and women felt as they went about their daily activities. Many statistical analyses comparing men and women yielded a general result: no gender differences. Men and women were remarkably alike in the degree to which they reported feelings at any point on the emotional continuum—strong bad emotions, strong good ones, mild bad, mild good, neutral.

Other research with similar methods has obtained similar findings: Daily emotional experience is essentially the same regardless of gender.[208] Adolescent boys do report extreme positive feelings a little less often than girls, although both girls and boys experienced extreme negative emotions such as anger.[209] In laboratory studies, women sometimes report stronger emotional reactions,[210] although this outcome could be affected by social norms that put pressure on men to underreport emotional reactions. Lab studies that use physiological measures do not find women to show stronger reactions. If anything, those measures suggest that men sometimes have stronger emotional reactions than women.[211]

One way to get around social norms (such as exhorting men to restrain emotion) is to look at small children. These studies fail to find greater female emotionality—if anything, the opposite. As far back as 1931, research showed that little boys have more frequent angry outbursts and temper tantrums than girls.[212] Studies of infants either find no difference in emotionality or find that baby boys are more emotionally intense than baby girls.[213,214,215] Observations of boys' play indicate that they seek out exciting, arousing themes but try to learn to manage fear and other emotions.[216] In games, boys put an emphasis on keeping their emotions under control so that feelings do not disrupt the game. Disputes are settled by appealing to abstract rules or, if necessary, replaying the disputed event, whereas girls' games are likely to end when emotion erupts. Partly for this reason, boys' games last longer than girls' games. Boys may find it more difficult than girls to calm themselves down when upset, so they work harder to avoid emotion in the first place. This pattern continues into adulthood and marriage: When married couples argue, husbands show stronger and longer-lasting physiological arousal than wives. As a result, husbands tend to avoid marital conflicts, whereas wives are more willing to argue and confront their spouse with problems.[217]

All these findings begin to suggest a very different conclusion: Men may be slightly *more* emotional than women, whereas women feel more willing to report their emotions and claim to have stronger feelings. Social norms may put pressure on men to stifle their emotions and not admit to having strong feelings, but the greater emotionality of women may be an illusion. Similar patterns are found in empathy research: On self-report measures, women claim to have more empathy than men, but when research uses objective measures of understanding the emotional states of others, no gender difference is found.[218]

What about love? Here too there is scant support for the female emotionality. Men confess "I love you" before women do, and men feel happier than women when someone expresses love to them.[219] Men fall in love faster than women, and women fall out of love faster than men.[220,221,222] Men have more experiences of loving someone who does not love them back, whereas women have more experiences of receiving love but not reciprocating it.[223] When a love relationship breaks up in a heterosexual relationship, men suffer more intense emotional distress than women.[224]

In short, the traditional stereotype of female emotionality is wrong, at least in Western society where most of the research has been conducted. Based on the research findings, one could even speculate that men are more emotional than women. The findings of greater male emotionality in love and work, plus during infancy, fit this pattern. Possibly male emotion has presented problems for society, as when male emotion leads to violence, risk taking, intoxication, and other potential problems. Holding up an ideal of men as cool, rational, and unemotional may be a way for society to keep the dangers of male emotion under control.

1. **How many "basic" facial emotions have been observed across dozens of different cultures?**

   ⓐ Two ⓑ Four ⓒ Six ⓓ Eight

2. **Which of the following lists contains only "basic" facial emotions (i.e., biologically determined, culturally universal in expression)?**

   ⓐ Anger, disappointment, disgust   ⓑ Fear, hope, surprise   ⓒ Happiness, indifference, sadness   ⓓ Happiness, sadness, surprise

3. **Which of the following statements is true?**

   ⓐ Young boys are more emotional than young girls   ⓑ Men are more emotional than women   ⓒ None of the above   ⓓ All of the above

4. **Which of the following is the conclusion of research evidence regarding emotional expression in males and females?**

   ⓐ Females are more emotional than males.   ⓑ Males are more emotional than females.   ⓒ Males and females don't differ much in how emotional they are.   ⓓ None of the above

answers: see pg 226

Arousal, Attention, and Performance

We noted earlier that emotion contains arousal, in the sense of being physically excited. Many people believe that emotional arousal is harmful—that it is better to calm down, especially when one is trying to make a logical decision or perform effectively in a crisis. Yet the arousal that goes with emotion seems designed by nature to make a person perform better, not worse. For example, when the person is aroused, more oxygen is sent to the brain and muscles than otherwise. So, is emotional arousal good or bad?

One answer is that the relationship between arousal and performance is an upside-down U-shaped curve. That is, increasing arousal first makes for better performance, then for worse. Put another way, some arousal is better than none, but too much arousal can hurt performance. In 1908 Robert Yerkes and John Dodson proposed this view based on their studies with rats.[225] **FIGURE 6.5** illustrates this **Yerkes–Dodson law**. (Psychologists are reluctant to call something a "law," but this finding is so reliable and has been replicated so many times that it is considered a law.) The curve is lower for complex tasks than for simple tasks because performance is generally lower for complex tasks. In both cases, though, the link between arousal and performance resembles an inverted (upside-down) U, going up and then back down.

Arousal also seems good for narrowing and focusing attention. This is probably why people drink coffee or tea when they work: They want to be alert and focused, and consuming a drink that arouses them will produce that state. A famous theory by psychologist J. A. Easterbrook proposed that one major effect of arousal is to narrow attention, and this can explain both slopes of the inverted U-shaped curve that Yerkes and Dodson proposed.[226] Easterbrook's main idea was that arousal makes the mind eliminate information and

Yerkes-Dodson law the proposition that some arousal is better than none, but too much can hurt performance

FIGURE 6.5

According to the Yerkes-Dodson law, some arousal is better than none, but too much can hurt performance.

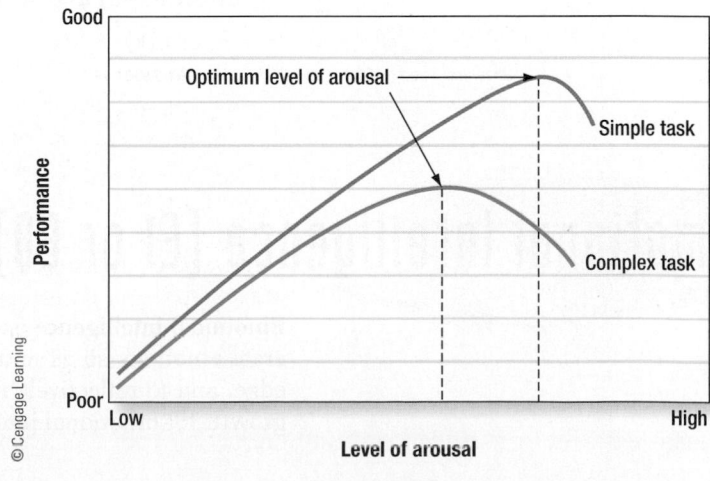

© Cengage Learning

focus more narrowly. When people have very low arousal, they do not perform very well because the mind is deluged with all sorts of information (including much that is unhelpful or irrelevant, such as noise outside when you are studying), so it has a difficult time focusing on the task at hand. As arousal increases, the mind begins to screen out irrelevant information, which helps it focus better on the task at hand, and performance improves. At some point, corresponding to the peak on the curve and the best possible performance, the mind is processing all the information relevant to the task and nothing else. That's when you do your best work.

However, as arousal increases beyond that point, the mind continues to focus ever more narrowly—and this further narrowing requires that it throw out helpful, task-relevant information (because all the irrelevant information has already been screened out, so only the good stuff is left). Hence, highly aroused people will be intensely, narrowly focused on what they are doing, but they may miss crucial information that is relevant or helpful. As a result, they end up performing worse than people with a moderate level of arousal.

The effects of stress on thinking appear to go along with Easterbrook's theory.[227] Under stress, people focus more narrowly on the task at hand, so up to a point, stress makes people perform better—but beyond that point, stress makes people ignore relevant information. Research using multiple-choice tests has shown how this can happen. Under stress, people just scan the multiple answers until they find one that seems correct, and they pick that one, sometimes without considering all the options. Thus, if answer B sounds good, they might choose it without even considering answer D. This gets them done faster, but they may make more mistakes, especially if D was really a better answer than B.[228,229]

QUIZ YOURSELF

Arousal, Attention, and Performance

answers: see pg 226

1. According to the Yerkes–Dodson law, there is a(n) _____ curve between arousal and performance.

   (a) bell-shaped   (b) inverted U-shaped   (c) J-shaped   (d) U-shaped

2. The curve between arousal and performance is _____ for complex tasks than for simple tasks.

   (a) broader   (b) higher   (c) lower   (d) narrower

3. According to Easterbrook, arousal influences performance by _____ attention.

   (a) broadening   (b) decreasing   (c) increasing   (d) narrowing

4. Under high levels of arousal, what answer on a four-item multiple-choice test are students least likely to consider?

   (a) Answer A   (b) Answer B   (c) Answer C   (d) Answer D

Emotional Intelligence (EI or EQ)

Emotional intelligence is defined as "the ability to perceive emotions, to access and generate emotions so as to assist thought, to understand emotions and emotional knowledge, and to reflectively regulate emotions so as to promote emotional and intellectual growth."[231] Emotional intelligence is denoted by EI or EQ rather than IQ.

Emotional intelligence has four parts. The first is Perceiving Emotions, defined as the ability to recognize how you and those around you are feeling. It also involves perceiving emotions in objects, art, stories, music, and other stimuli. The second is Facilitating Thought, defined as the ability to generate an emotion and then reason with this emotion. The third is Understanding Emotions, defined as the ability to understand complex emotions and how emotions can transition from one stage to another. The fourth is Managing Emotions, defined as the ability to be open to feelings, and to modulate them in oneself and others so as to promote personal understanding and growth.

People high on emotional intelligence are better than others at affective forecasting (predicting future emotional states) and less susceptible to common errors. That is, they predict their future emotions more accurately than other people. Scoring high on Managing Emotions was particularly conducive to being able to predict future emotions correctly.[232,233]

Emotional intelligence seems especially important in the business world. For example, employees of a Fortune 400 insurance company who had previously scored high on emotional intelligence scores received greater merit increases, held higher company rank, and received higher ratings from peers and supervisors than did employees with low scores.[234] Emotional intelligence is positive related to job performance in both Western[235] and Eastern[236] cultures, to leadership skills,[237] and to mental and physical health.[238] People with high emotional intelligence have fewer alcohol-related problems than other people,[239] possibly because they know how to manage their emotions without getting drunk. Recent meta-analyses report that emotional intelligence is also positively related to romantic relationship satisfaction,[240] academic success,[241] and constructive conflict management in leaders.[242]

Recent research suggests that there is a dark side to emotional intelligence. There is a **dark triad of personality** consisting of narcissism, psychopathy, and Machiavellianism.[243] Recall from Chapter 3 that narcissists are selfish individuals with inflated egos. Psychopaths show a pervasive disregard for, and violation of, the rights of others. They are callous and unemotional individuals. "Machiavellianism" comes from the Italian philosopher and writer Niccolò Machiavelli. Machiavelli advocated using any means necessary to gain raw political power, including aggression and violence. People with these dark personality traits tend to be high in emotional intelligence, but they use their emotional intelligence to manipulate others.[244,245] This dark triad of personality is also related to aggression (see Chapter 10).

> "Many people with IQs of 160 work for people with IQs of 100, if the former have poor interpersonal intelligence and the latter have a high one."
> — Howard Gardner[230]

emotional intelligence the ability to perceive, access and generate, understand, and reflectively regulate emotions

dark triad of personality consists of narcissism, psychopathy, and Machiavellianism.

QUIZ YOURSELF

Emotional Intelligence (EI or EQ)

answers: see pg 226

1. **Which branch of emotional intelligence involves the most basic psychological processes?**
   - (a) Facilitating thought
   - (b) Perceiving emotions
   - (c) Managing emotions
   - (d) Understanding emotions

2. **Which branch of emotional intelligence involves the most psychologically integrated processes?**
   - (a) Facilitating thought
   - (b) Perceiving emotions
   - (c) Managing emotions
   - (d) Understanding emotions

3. **Emotional intelligence is negatively related to _____.**
   - (a) alcohol-related problems
   - (b) leadership skills
   - (c) work performance
   - (d) mental and physical health

4. **What dimention of the "dark triad of personality" is related to emotional intelligence?**
   - (a) Machiavellianism
   - (b) Narcissism
   - (c) Psychopathy
   - (d) All of the above

Affect Regulation

One reason that emotional intelligence is beneficial is that it can help people control and regulate their feelings. When emotions run out of control, they can wreak havoc on inner and interpersonal processes. Indeed, so-called mental illness is often marked by severe emotional problems, and some experts have concluded that people who are poor at controlling their own emotional reactions are more likely to fall victim to such mental illnesses.[246,247,248]

Chapter 4 presented research on self-regulation, and we saw that the ability to self-regulate is important and valuable in many spheres of life. People do regularly seek to control their thoughts, desires, and actions. They often try to control emotions too but encounter an added difficulty: For the most part, emotions cannot be directly controlled. That is, if you are feeling bad, you cannot just decide to be happy and succeed by a simple act of will, in the same sense that you can drag yourself out of bed when you don't feel like getting up. Emotion control is a special case of self-regulation, and generally people have to rely on indirect strategies.

How to Cheer Up

One research group ambitiously attempted to map out people's affect regulation strategies.[249] They used a series of questionnaire studies to find out what strategies people use to cope with a bad mood and make themselves feel better. Their list of strategies points to the different ways that emotion and mood can be altered.

One strategy is simply to do things that produce good feelings. People may cheer themselves up by eating something tasty, having sex, listening to music, or shopping (especially buying oneself a gift).[250,251] A strategy that overlaps with this one involves simply doing something to take one's mind off the problem, such as watching television, changing one's location, avoiding the source of the problem, or taking a shower. Note that neither of these strategies addresses the original problem or source of bad feelings; instead, people seek to create a positive, pleasant state to replace the unpleasant one.

Earlier in this chapter we saw that physical arousal is an important part of emotion. Hence for many people, raising or lowering their arousal is a promising strategy for affect regulation.[252] Arousal control strategies include exercising, drinking coffee or other caffeine product to increase arousal, or drinking alcohol, taking a nap, and using relaxation techniques to decrease arousal. Exercise may be an especially interesting strategy because it first increases arousal but later, as one gets tired, decreases it.

Seeking social support is another common strategy for controlling emotion. People may call their friends when they feel bad. Others go out and actively seek others' company. This fits our theme of putting people first: Even to deal with their own problem emotions, people turn to other people. When you are upset about almost anything, you can go spend time with people who like you, and the odds are good that you will end up feeling better. Note that this does not solve the original problem that made you feel bad, but it does help you stop feeling bad.

A very different set of affect regulation strategies is based on trying to deal directly with the problem (the one that gave rise to the bad feelings) in some way. Many people report trying to reframe the problem, such as by putting it into perspective or trying to see a conflict from the other person's side. Some try to use humor to make light of the problem and cheer themselves up. Others seek to vent their feelings, as by pounding a pillow, screaming, or crying (venting might feel good, but it usually just makes things worse). Religious activities such as praying help some people cope with their troubles; indeed, some studies have found religious activities were rated as among the most effective strategies for regulating affect.[253] For example, prayer is an effective way to reduce angry feelings and aggressive behaviors.[254] Imagining the situation from a more distant, third-person perspective, like a fly on a wall, can also reduce angry feelings and aggressive behaviors[255]

To be sure, many of the strategies may work by more than one means. Exercise might bring both distraction and arousal control. Making jokes may be a way of spending time with others and reframing the problem as less serious than it seemed at first. Having sex may generate good feelings, distract one from the problem, and create a state of tiredness. If you're upset about having lost $100 because of a stupid purchasing decision, then making jokes or having sex or playing tennis does not change the original problem in the least, but it could make you feel better.

Not all strategies are equally effective. The data are very complex, but if people had to choose one strategy as most effective, it might be exercise.[256] If you're feeling sad or depressed, exercise can energize you and lift your mood. However, exercising to get rid of anger might backfire because it keeps arousal levels high rather than reducing them.[257] Listening to music was also rated very highly as effective for changing a bad mood, as was seeking out social support. At the other extreme, watching television and trying to be alone were rated among the least successful ways of coping with a bad mood.

Affect Regulation Goals

In principle, affect regulation can have at least six different goals: One can seek to get into, get out of, or prolong a good mood, and the same three options apply to a bad mood.[258] At first you might wonder why anyone would ever want to get out of a good mood or into a bad one, but in some situations it is inappropriate or even counterproductive to seem (or feel) overly happy. A physician may be in a terrifically happy mood one day, for example, but if she has to tell a patient that his illness is incurable and that he will die soon, a beaming smile may seem out of place. Likewise, an activist who has to present a case of injustice may find that an angry mood will be more effective than a cheerful, happy-go-lucky one.

In particular, people often seek to cultivate neutral moods prior to social interactions. In a series of laboratory studies, researchers first induced good or bad moods by exposing participants to music and then allowed them to select either cheerful or depressing reading material.[259] Some participants expected to meet and talk with someone new; these participants chose reading material *opposite* to their current mood—happy people chose sad readings, and sad people chose happy readings—presumably as a way to bring them out of their current feeling and bring them into a cool, neutral mood. (In contrast, people who did not anticipate an interaction chose mood-congruent readings—happy people chose happy readings, and sad people chose sad ones.) The implication is that people get ready for social interaction with a new partner by trying to get out of either a good or bad mood and into a neutral state.

Further work has shown that how people regulate their emotional states prior to social interaction is often very specific to the context.[260] People who expect to interact with a depressed person often seek out positive stimuli that will make them even happier— possibly because they expect (rightly) that it will be depressing to talk to a depressed person and they want to fortify themselves with an extra good mood to help them resist being brought down. People who are going to interact with a close relationship partner do not seem to change their moods, possibly because they intend to share their good or bad feelings with the partner. In any case, it is clearly wrong to assume that all affect regulation is aimed at trying to feel better right away.

Sometimes people even seek to cultivate anger. People in one study preferred to listen to angry music rather than other types of music when they expected a social interaction that would require confrontation and assertion (see **FIGURE 6.6A**).[261] (In

FIGURE **6.6**

(a) Preferences for anger-inducing, neutral, and exciting activities (i.e., listening to music and recalling events) when anticipating performing confrontational and nonconfrontational tasks.[80]

(b) Residual performance in the confrontational and nonconfrontational computer games, as a function of music condition.[80]

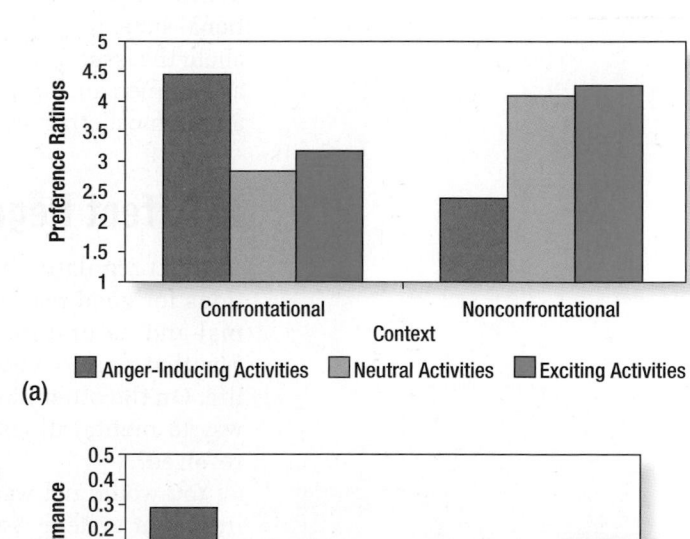

(a)

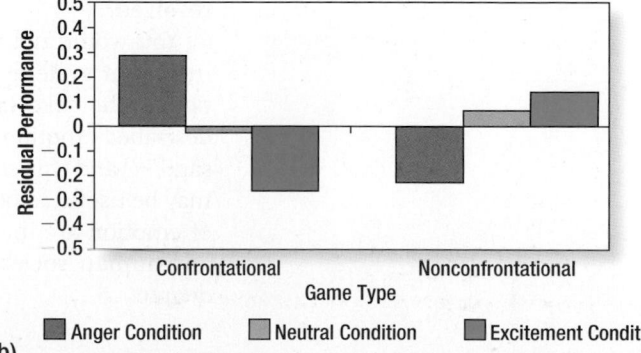

(b)

contrast, participants anticipating a cooperative or constructive social interaction chose other types of music.) Thus, people seemed to anticipate that anger might be a useful emotion in the upcoming interaction, so they chose stimuli to help them get and stay mad. What's more, it worked! The angrier participants performed better in the confrontational situation. The results are depicted in **FIGURE 6.6B**.

Thus, people seem to seek out emotions partly on the basis of what will be useful and helpful in their social interactions. This desire to be effective competes with the desire to feel good, of course. Many strategies of emotion regulation are simply aimed at the goal of getting out of a bad mood or into a good one.[262,263]

Gender Differences in Emotion Control Strategies

Men and women may cope with bad moods in some different ways, although in general research shows that men and women are more similar than different.[264] One general theory is that when feeling depressed, women frequently respond with rumination, as in thinking about the problem, whereas men more commonly try to distract themselves with other thoughts or activities.[265] This may contribute to the higher rate of depression among women because ruminating about why you are depressed is more likely to prolong the bad feelings than shifting your attention onto something more cheerful, such as a sports event or hobby. Men often seek to keep themselves busy doing some task or chore, which not only may take their mind off their troubles but may also furnish some good feelings of success and efficacy if they can achieve something useful.

Another difference can be found in what people consume. Women are more likely than men to turn to food when they feel bad.[266,267] In contrast, men turn to alcohol and drugs to cope with the same feelings.[268,269,270,271] In a nutshell, women eat and men drink to regulate their moods. (Both strategies have obvious drawbacks!)

Other gender differences exist in mood regulation strategies.[272] When seeking to feel better, men are more likely than women to use humor to make light of the problem (a tendency that some women may find annoying if they do not think the problem is funny!). Men are also more prone to report that sexual activity is a good way to improve their emotional state. In contrast, women are more likely to go shopping or to call someone to talk about the issue. Still, overall, as we saw in the earlier section on gender and emotion, men and women are far more similar than different in their overall experiences with emotion and in most other areas as well.

Is Affect Regulation Safe?

Is affect regulation a good idea? This chapter has emphasized that people have emotions for good reasons; if you prevent your emotions from functioning in their normal and natural manner, you may deprive yourself of their valuable guidance. We saw that people who lack emotions often have difficulty finding their way through life. On the other hand, we have seen that poor emotion regulation can also point the way to mental illness and other problems. How can this seeming contradiction be resolved?

You would not want to live without emotions entirely. Then again, emotions are an imperfect system. Sometimes, undoubtedly, emotions overreact to a situation; in particular, they may last past the point at which they have served their function. One expert described emotion regulation as "the ability to hang up the phone after getting the message,"[273] and this seems a very apt characterization. Once emotions have done their job, it may be useful to be able to control them. In any case, culture teaches people that displays of emotion are inappropriate on many occasions. To be a successful member of almost any human society requires the ability to regulate one's emotional reactions to some degree.

1. There is a(n) _____ relationship between emotional control and mental health.
   - (a) upside-down U
   - (b) negative
   - (c) null
   - (d) positive

2. What is the most effective strategy for improving a bad mood?
   - (a) Exercise
   - (b) Trying to be alone
   - (c) Watching television
   - (d) All of the above are equally effective for improving a bad mood.

3. Before interacting with someone who is depressed, what type of stimuli do people seek out?
   - (a) Angry
   - (b) Frightening
   - (c) Happy
   - (d) Sad

4. To regulate their moods, women tend to _____, whereas men tend to _____.
   - (a) eat; drink
   - (b) ruminate; distract themselves
   - (c) not use humor; use humor
   - (d) all of the above

answers: see pg 226

What Makes Us *Human*

Putting the Cultural Animal in Perspective

Humans are hardly the only species to have feelings. Fear, rage, joy, and even something close to love can be found in other animals. But human emotion is special in certain ways. Probably the most important is that human emotion is tied to meaning. People can respond emotionally to ideas, concepts, and the like. They cry at weddings, not because the spectacle of marriage is inherently sad, but because the idea of pledging to love the same person for the rest of one's life is deeply meaningful. Likewise, some ideas, such as freedom, justice, and nationality, have so much emotional power that they can make people willing to sacrifice their lives for them.

The importance of meaning, and thus of ideas, in human emotion is also reflected in Schachter and Singer's theory,[274] which emphasizes that a bodily reaction needs a cognitive label (an idea) in order to become a full-fledged emotion. Ideas are also central to human happiness. An animal is happy or unhappy depending mainly on what has happened in the last few minutes, but people can reflect on their lives as a whole and be satisfied or discontented. The power of ideas also enables people to suffer (or benefit) from misattribution of arousal because the use of cognitive labels for inner states creates the possibility of switching labels or attaching a mistaken label. One emotion can be converted into another, as in the study in which fear and relief (from the suspension bridge) were converted into romantic attraction. Ideas can transform emotions, even after the bodily response is already in full gear.

Ideas also give human beings a larger range of subtle emotional differences than is found in most other species. As we said, many animals show fear, rage, and joy, but human beings have hundreds of different words for emotional states. Humans probably have so many different words for emotion because there are so many subtle differences in their emotional states. Being able to process so many subtly different ideas enables human emotion to be fine-tuned into many more subtly different grades of feeling.

Emotions are a vital help to people in navigating the long road to social acceptance. People who lack emotions do not fare well in human society. The distinctive complexity of human emotion is probably tied to some of the other tools we have seen that humans use to cultivate social acceptance. The human self, for example, is more elaborate and complex than what other animals have, and the complex self brings with it self-conscious emotions that inform and aid its activities. As an important example, the distinction between guilt and shame (doing a bad thing versus being a bad person) is probably beyond what most animals could understand; humans may be the only creatures who make use of that distinction.

Emotion is also linked to cognition (another tool used by humans on the road to social acceptance) in many and complex ways. We have already suggested that the human capacity for meaningful thought produces many more shades of emotional experience than would otherwise be possible, including many subtle distinctions between similar emotions (again, think of guilt versus shame). Humans are able to rely on anticipated emotion in their decision making, and even if their affective forecasting is sometimes off base, it can still inform and help human decision making in ways that would be impossible for almost any other creature.

The cognitive capabilities of human beings enable them to learn about their emotions too. Emotional intelligence is a concept that may be largely useless in discussing most other animals, but many people develop an emotional intelligence that can sometimes be more useful than other forms of intelligence. Emotional intelligence—using the ideas associated with emotions—enables people to function and succeed better amid the complexities of human society and culture. Although people high in narcissism, psychopathy, and Machiavellianism also tend to be high in emotional intelligence, they use it to manipulate others.

Emotional intelligence includes the power to regulate one's emotions (as in trying to control one's emotional state), and humans have cultivated that power much more than other animals. People learn how to conceal their emotions, which may be an important manifestation of the general principle that nature says go (i.e., the same kinds of events produce the same emotions in all cultures) but culture says stop (i.e., people learn to hide or express their emotions differently depending on cultural norms and rules). Emotion regulation itself—such as in trying to stop feeling angry or to cheer up—shows how people deliberately exert control over their inner states. The very pursuit of happiness is also something that makes us human because it depends on several unique human abilities—such as the ability to think about a different emotional state from what one is currently feeling—to form a goal of moving from one state to another, to integrate inner states across time (remember, only humans can understand happiness in terms of broad satisfaction with one's life in general), and to save up information about how to move from one state into a happier one.

Ultimately, emotions make human life more meaningful and satisfying. A human life without emotion would be handicapped because a person without emotions would be without an important tool, but there is more to it than that: A life without emotion would be empty and dull. Human beings care about their emotional lives in ways that other animals almost certainly don't.

CHAPTER 6 SUMMARY

What Is Emotion?

- Emotions are mostly outside our conscious control, even though we may feel them consciously.

- An emotion is a conscious reaction to something; a mood is a feeling state that is not clearly linked to some event; affect is the automatic response that something is good or bad (liking versus disliking).

- Positive affect encompasses all good emotions, such as joy, bliss, love, and contentment; negative affect encompasses; all bad emotions, such as anger, anxiety, fear, jealousy, and grief.

Emotional Arousal

- Emotions have both mental aspects (such as subjective feelings and interpretations) and physical ones (such as a racing heartbeat or tears).

- James and Lange proposed that the bodily processes of emotion come first, and then the mind's perception of these bodily reactions creates the subjective feeling of emotion. Proponents of the James–Lange theory of emotion failed to find specific arousal patterns for different emotions.

- According to the facial feedback hypothesis, feedback from the face muscles evokes or magnifies emotions.

- Schachter and Singer proposed that emotion has two components. One, the bodily state of arousal, is the same in all emotions. The other, the cognitive label, is different for each emotion.

- Sexual stimulation may affect the brain, the genitals, neither, or both.

- In excitation transfer, the arousal from one event transfers to a subsequent event.

Some Important Emotions

- Affect balance is the frequency of positive emotions minus the frequency of negative emotions.
- Couples who have children are less happy than couples who do not have children.
- People who are alone in the world are much less happy than people who have strong, rich social networks.
- The hedonic treadmill describes the tendency to revert to one's usual level of happiness soon after an emotional event.
- Happiness is rooted in one's outlook and approach to life, as well as in one's genes.
- Forgiving others, being grateful for blessings, practicing religious beliefs, sharing good feelings, and being optimistic can all increase happiness.
- Happiness is linked to a variety of good outcomes, including health and success in life.
- Anger is an emotional response to a real or imagined threat or provocation.
- The catharsis theory holds that expressing anger produces a healthy release of emotion and is therefore good for the psyche, but research demonstrates that catharsis increases anger and aggression and has negative health consequences.
- Shame is usually destructive, whereas guilt is usually constructive.
- Guilt motivates people to do good acts and make amends to repair damage to relationships.
- Disgust is a strong negative feeling of repugnance and revulsion. It motivates healthy behavior.

Why Do We Have Emotions?

- At least two basic arousal patterns—pleasant and unpleasant—underlie emotions.
- Emotions comprise an important and powerful feedback system, telling us whether something is good or bad.
- Positive emotions are linked to forming social bonds, whereas bad emotions are linked to various events that end, damage, or threaten relationships.
- Emotion rarely causes behavior directly.
- People who lack emotions have great difficulty adjusting to life and making decisions.
- Emotions help people learn from their mistakes. Without emotions, people don't learn.
- According to the affect-as-information hypothesis, people judge something as good or bad by asking themselves how they feel about it.
- Affective forecasting is the ability to predict one's emotional reactions to future events.
- According to the risk-as-feelings hypothesis, people react to risky situations based on how severe the situation is and how likely it is to occur.

- Strong conscious emotions can also influence people to engage in risky behavior and ignore future consequences. Emotions call attention to good and bad outcomes but seem to make people disregard probabilities and odds.
- The broaden-and-build theory of positive emotions suggests that positive emotions expand an individual's attention and mind-set, which, in turn, builds an individual's resources.
- Positive moods can increase flexibility, creativity, and problem-solving ability. People in a good mood perform better, are more persistent, try harder, and are more motivated than people in a neutral mood.
- Good moods can serve a protective function because individuals in a good mood tend to avoid taking risks.

Group Differences in Emotion

- Six basic emotions have been observed in numerous cultures: anger, surprise, disgust, happiness, fear, and sadness. People of different cultures can reliably recognize posed facial expressions of these emotions.
- Men and women have similar emotional lives. Men may be slightly more emotional than women, but women may feel more willing to report their emotions and claim to have stronger feelings.
- Men fall in love faster than women, and women fall out of love faster than men.

Arousal, Attention, and Performance

- Arousal serves to narrow and focus attention. Some arousal is better than none, but too much arousal can hurt performance.

Emotional Intelligence (EI or EQ)

- Emotional intelligence is the ability to perceive emotions, to access and generate emotions so as to assist thought, to understand emotions and emotional knowledge, and to reflectively regulate emotions so as to promote emotional and intellectual growth.
- People high in narcissism, psychopathy, and Machiavellianism (called the "dark triad" of personality) tend to be high in emotional intelligence, but they use it to manipulate others.

Affect Regulation

- People attempt to regulate their emotions by doing things that feel good, distracting themselves from negative emotions, controlling their arousal, seeking social support, or dealing with the emotion-causing issue directly.

What Makes Us Human? Putting the Cultural Animal in Perspective

- In humans, emotion is tied to meaning.

key terms

quiz yourself ANSWERS

1. What Is Emotion? **p.188**
   answers: 1.b   2.a   3.a   4.b

2. Emotional Arousal **p.193**
   answers: 1.b   2.c   3.d   4.b

3. Some Important Emotions **p.206**
   answers: 1.c   2.b   3.a   4.d

4. Why Do We Have Emotions? **p.215**
   answers: 1.b   2.a   3.c   4.b

5. Group Differences in Emotion **p.217**
   answers: 1.c   2.d   3.c   4.c

6. Arousal, Attention, and Performance **p.218**
   answers: 1.b   2.c   3.d   4.d

7. Emotional Intelligence (EI or EQ) **p.219**
   answers: 1.b   2.c   3.b   4.a

8. Affect Regulation **p.223**
   answers: 1.d   2.a   3.c   4.d

ATTITUDES, BELIEFS, AND CONSISTENCY

7

LEARNING OBJECTIVES

1 Define attitudes and why people have them.

2 Describe how attitudes are formed.

3 Summarize how the major consistency theories and the duplex mind relate to attitudes.

4 Explain the relationship between attitudes and behavior.

5 Debate the role of attitudes in coping with trauma.

When he was a sophomore at Harvard University in 2003, Mark Zuckerberg developed a website called *Facemash,* in which users rated which of two female Harvard students they thought was "hottest."[1] Zuckerberg got the photos by hacking into Harvard's computer network. In just four hours, the Facemash site attracted 450 visitors and 22,000 photo-views.[2] Although Harvard charged Zuckerberg with breach of security, violating copyrights, and violating individual privacy, these charges were dropped.[3] Zuckerberg had his friends with skills in programming, graphic arts, and business help him develop and promote the website. Within one month over half of the undergraduate students at Harvard registered to use the site. It was later made available to other elite universities in America (e.g., Princeton, Yale, Stanford).

In 2004, the name of the website was changed to *The Facebook,* and the word *The* was dropped in 2005. The term *Facebook* comes from the informal name of a book that some universities give to new students so they can get to know each other better. To use Facebook, individuals must register and be at least 13 years old, although proof of age is not required. Facebook surpassed

over a billion active users in 2012—about a third of all the people in the world who have Internet access.[4] What made this phenomenon so wildly popular?

Once registered, Facebook users can develop a personal profile that includes a profile photo as well as information about themselves, such as their gender, birthday, relationship status, family members, where they are from, where they live now, where they went to school, what job they have, religious views, political views, what languages they speak, etc. Users can also express their attitudes about a wide variety of topics, by indicating their "likes," such as music (genre and artists), books, movies, television programs, favorite athletes, favorite sports teams, interests (e.g., hiking, traveling, skiing), and people who inspire them. Users can post almost anything on their Facebook page, such as comments, photos, videos, and links to favorite web pages. In short, Facebook lets people communicate information about themselves to the world at large.

Attitudes (this chapter's topic!) are an important part of Facebook. Registered friends can indicate their attitudes by

pressing the "Like" button, which has a "thumb's up" icon, by writing their own comment, or both. At present, Facebook's "Like" button gets about 2.7 billion clicks every day. Apparently, many people "like" to express positive opinions! As of 2014, Shakira might have the most popular Facebook page, with over 87.7 million "likes." Facebook users can even vote on the policies for governing the site, by indicating which policy they "like" the most.

While positive attitudes ("likes") are eagerly sought and communicated, negative ones are discouraged. Users have a choice between no response and liking, but there is no simple option for expressing dislike or disapproval. However, Facebook is adding a "dislike" button.

On Facebook, 2.7 million users showed their support for legalizing same-sex marriage by changing their profile picture to the Human Rights Campaign's equality sign on a red square background.[5] According to a Human Rights Campaign spokesperson, "Red is a symbol for love, and that's what marriage is all about. We wanted to give people an opportunity to show their support for marriage equality in a public and visible way."[6] Thus,

AP Images/Paul Sakuma

Mark Zuckerberg and his friends developed Facebook while they were undergraduate students at Harvard University.

Like-a-hug

SIPA USA/Melissakitchow.com via Sipa USA/Newscom

Like-A-Hug Vest inflates each time you get a "like" on Facebook.

Facebook allows people to express their attitudes about important and trivial topics, and to see what attitudes other people have.

A U.S. Department of State bureau spent $630,000 over two years on Facebook advertising campaigns, which increased the number of "likes" from about 100,000 to over 2.5 million.[7] Thus, a government agency was able to use Facebook to increase the government's popularity among users, by getting them to express favorable attitudes.

Scientists at the Massachusetts Institute of Technology (MIT) have designed a vest called "Like-A-Hug Vest" that inflates and "hugs" you each time a Facebook friend "likes" one of your posts.[8] The designer said the vest helps the wearer "feel the warmth, encouragement, support or love that we feel when we receive hugs."

The designers of Facebook have incorporated many digital substitutes for normal social interaction. Facebook users can "poke" their "friends" to get their attention, and they can "chat" with their "friends" in real time online. Facebook users can update their "status," which informs their "friends" where they are and what they are doing. People can also play games with their "friends" on Facebook.

One can also get applications (apps) for Facebook, such as EnemyGraph, which contains an "Enemy" button that enables users to indicate what they dislike.[9] The developers wanted to use the term "dislike" rather than "enemy," but the word "dislike" is banned by the service (even though the word "enemy" seems far more negative). Again, it is revealing that the original Facebook developers shunned the expression of negative attitudes, and so users need a different application in order to express disliking.

Research has shown that Facebook users tend to be more extraverted and narcissistic, but less conscientious and socially lonely, in comparison to nonusers.[10] Shy people tend to spend more time than other people on Facebook,[11,12] perhaps because it is less intimidating than face-to-face interaction.[13]

Sometimes, however, students place information on their Facebook page that employers might find inappropriate.[14] Almost half of prospective employers use social networks sites to check out job applicants, and they use Facebook more than LinkedIn.[15] About 35% of applicants are rejected because of information employers find posted on their Facebook page. You might think that attitudes would be irrelevant, but some kinds of Facebook attitude posts contribute to turn off potential employers. These include bad-mouthing a previous employee, colleague, or client (which conveys the impression that you might be difficult to work with), and expressing prejudicial, discriminatory attitudes.

Recent research suggests that "likes" on Facebook can spread like a contagious disease.[16] If you "like" an article on Facebook, someone else who reads it is also more likely to also "like" it—32% more likely. Perhaps attitudes, like emotions covered in Chapter 6, are socially contagious. At present it is not clear whether what spreads is the actual positive attitude or merely the inclination to express it, but either sheds important light on the interpersonal spread of attitudes.

Using epidemiological models, researchers have predicted that Facebook will lose 80% of its users by 2017 and will die out like a contagious disease by 2020.[17] The basic idea behind epidemiological models is that user adoption is analogous to "infection" and user abandonment is analogous to "recovery."

Of course, people can also express their attitudes using other social media (e.g., Twitter, YouTube). In the digital age, people can express their attitudes easier and more often than ever before, and to much larger audiences. Sometimes videos go viral (i.e., spread like a virus) and attract very large audiences. For example, the video PSY - GANGNAM STYLE (강남스타일) M/V has over 2 billion views.

In this chapter, we discuss what attitudes are, how they are formed, what purpose they serve, and how they differ from beliefs. In the next chapter, we discuss attitude change, or persuasion. ●

What Are Attitudes and Why Do People Have Them?

Why are attitudes so important? And why specifically are they so important to social psychology? Some attitudes seem trivial, but others are clearly important. Attitudes can be important insofar as they predict behaviors. For example, does a person's attitude toward the environment predict whether he or she will recycle, take public transportation, ride a bike, car pool, use energy-efficient light bulbs, and so on?

Attitudes versus Beliefs

Attitudes differ from beliefs. **Beliefs** are pieces of information (facts or opinions) about something. **Attitudes** are global evaluations toward some object or issue (e.g., you like or dislike something, you are in favor of or opposed to some position).[19] If you think that a certain person is president or that it is cloudy outside, that's a belief. An attitude is whether you like this person as president, or the clouds. Logically, attitudes are for choosing, whereas beliefs are for explaining. Beliefs and attitudes both serve interpersonal functions. People need to influence how others choose, and people also need to explain things to others.

Dual Attitudes

"She says she likes jazz, but somehow she never seems to listen to it, and in fact when it comes on the radio she usually changes the station!" **Dual attitudes** are defined as different evaluations of the same attitude object: an automatic attitude and a deliberate attitude.[20] This dual model of attitudes fits the duplex-mind theme of this book. **Automatic attitudes** are very fast evaluative, "gut-level" responses that people don't think a great deal about. In contrast, **deliberate attitudes** are more reflective responses that people think more carefully about. Although this distinction between automatic and deliberate attitudes is very popular with current researchers, it has been around for a very long time.[21] Sometimes automatic and deliberate attitudes are inconsistent. In the United States, for example, few people from any ethnic group admit to holding racial prejudices, and most sincerely espouse the ideals of racial equality, yet many people show negative automatic responses toward other races.[22]

Automatic attitudes are more difficult to measure than deliberate attitudes. Most measures of automatic attitudes involve measuring reaction times to stimuli. The faster the reaction time, the more accessible the attitude is assumed to be.

Some researchers have questioned the distinction between automatic and deliberate attitudes altogether.[23,24] They argue that it is inappropriate and unjustified to conclude that there are two different types of attitudes solely on the basis of automatic and deliberate measures leading to differing assessments of individuals' attitudes. They argue that the automatic/deliberate distinction applies to the level of measurement, not to the actual attitudes. For another question about dual attitudes, read the *Tradeoffs* box.

Why People Have Attitudes

Most animals don't need very many attitudes. They know what they like to eat (what tastes good), what fellow animals they like or dislike, and where they like to sleep. Their world is not very complex (compared to that of humans), and a few simple attitudes can serve them well.

In contrast, human life is now highly complex, and people need to have a broad assortment of attitudes. People are asked to vote on many issues and candidates in elections. When shopping, they are presented with literally thousands of different choices within one supermarket or department store. Even if they know they want a particular product,

beliefs pieces of information about something; facts or opinions

attitudes global evaluations toward some object or issue

dual attitudes different evaluations of the same attitude object held by the same person (perhaps one deliberate, the other automatic)

automatic attitudes very fast evaluative, "gut-level" responses that people don't think a great deal about

deliberate attitudes reflective responses that people think more carefully about

What Is the Real Attitude?

TRADE Offs

Dual attitudes present a dilemma for judging people. How do you judge someone whose dual attitudes conflict, which means that a person holds two different attitudes that are incompatible with one another? Should we judge a person based on the deliberate attitude—or based on the automatic one?

Suppose a person was brought up to endorse certain attitudes strongly, such as religious or political views. Then during adulthood the person thinks deeply about these issues and decides to change. The person's actions may reflect the new attitude, including voting and donating money—but the views learned from childhood are still strongly entrenched in the unconscious. Should we judge the person based on the automatic attitudes leftover from childhood, or the ones deliberately chosen by the adult?

Prejudice involves a particularly sensitive version of this dilemma. Hardly any Americans outwardly express racist attitudes any more, although they do seem to express more automatic racist attitudes. Do we judge a person based on explicit statements of being tolerant and egalitarian, or based on the reaction-time evidence suggesting an automatic racist bias?

Addiction presents another sensitive and complex case of dual attitudes. Many addicts desire their drugs (or whatever it is that they are addicted to) but also desire to recover from addiction and stop using. Do we judge them positively because of their earnest desire to be cured? Or do we judge them based on their automatic craving for destructive substances?

Further complicating the judgment question is the possibility of deception. People can lie about their true feelings, so in a sense explicit expressions of deliberate attitudes are less reliable than indicators of automatic attitudes (which are hard to fake). For example, a bigot might know that expressing prejudice is socially unacceptable and therefore might claim to be tolerant. Such possibilities make people more inclined to treat the automatic attitude as the "real" one. But in those cases, what was misleading was not the true, deliberate attitude, but only what the person expressed.

---

such as a pair of gloves, they face a vast array of potential choices, and having some attitudes can help (e.g., mittens are better than gloves because they are warmer, or gloves are better than mittens because the fingers are more usable; leather is fashionable, but harder to maintain, plus some animal had to die; brown gloves might clash with my blue coat). Attitudes are necessary and adaptive for humans. They help us adjust to new situations, seeking out those things in our environment that reward us and avoiding those things that punish us. Attitudes can even be a matter of life or death, influencing whether people take risks.

Attitudes are mainly used to sort things into "good" and "bad" categories. The world is full of information (see Chapter 5), but just figuring things out and understanding them isn't enough. You can only make your way through a complicated world if you can sort things into good and bad. Sure enough, good and bad are among the most basic categories of thought. Although these categories are abstract, children understand them very early in life, especially the category "bad." In one study of children 2 to 6 years old, bad pictures were more readily identified than good pictures at all ages beyond 2 years, 5 months.[25] This probably reflects one of the most basic psychological principles: Bad is stronger than good.[26,27]

As soon as you know what something is, you start to know whether you like or dislike it.[28] This initial evaluation is immediate and unconscious, occurring in the first microsecond of thought. This initial evaluation even occurs for things people have never encountered before, such as nonsense words. For example, the nonsense word *juvalamu* is very pleasing, the nonsense word *bargulum* is moderately pleasing, and the nonsense word *chakaka* is very displeasing.[29] Although people can easily override the initial, automatic evaluation with further thought, the initial evaluation stands if no further thought is given. According to John Bargh, who led this team of researchers (and no doubt inspired the word *bargulum!*), "We have yet to find something the mind regards with complete impartiality, without at least a mild judgment of liking or disliking."[30] Put another way, people have attitudes about everything.

Attitudes are tremendously helpful in making choices. Perhaps it doesn't matter which person you think ought to be eliminated next on TV shows such as *American Idol*,

Survivor, The Bachelor, or *The Bachelorette.* When you have to choose what courses to take next semester, however, you will find that attitudes come in very handy. Without attitudes, you face a bewildering array of options, all respectable intellectual endeavors, all taught by presumably competent faculty, all offering useful knowledge or at least something interesting. How can you choose, unless you have attitudes that say this course will be more interesting, or that one will be more useful to your chosen career, or that one will lead to a higher paying job, and that other one is likely to be dreadfully boring?

Previous research has shown that possessing an attitude increases the ease, speed, and quality of decision making.[31] Thus, attitudes appear to have great functional value. Evidence for this came in a study in which first-year college students completed measures of negative life events and health at two points in time.[32] Students who entered college knowing their likes and dislikes on academically relevant issues experienced better physical and mental health in the new college setting than did other students. Thus, having plenty of attitudes is even good for your health!

QUIZ YOURSELF

What are Attitudes and Why do People Have Them?

answers: see pg 255

1. **Which concept can be defined as pieces of information (facts or opinions) about something?**

   (a) Attitudes   (b) Beliefs   (c) Intentions   (d) Values

2. **Which concept can be defined as a global evaluation?**

   (a) Attitude   (b) Belief   (c) Intention   (d) Value

3. **Fast evaluation is to slow evaluation as _____ is to _____.**

   (a) automatic attitude; deliberate attitude   (b) deliberate attitude; automatic attitude   (c) primacy effect; recency effect   (d) recency effect; primacy effect

4. **Dual attitudes refer to _____ and _____ attitudes.**

   (a) automatic; deliberate   (b) new; old   (c) private; public   (d) rewarded; unrewarded

How Attitudes Are Formed

Formation of Attitudes

Several explanations have been offered for how attitudes are formed. We shall look at relatively simple explanations (mere exposure, classical conditioning, body movements) and also at more complicated explanations (operant conditioning, social learning).

Mere Exposure Effect

Most people have heard the aphorism "familiarity breeds contempt." It is false. (Winston Churchill is said to have once rebutted the assertion that familiarity breeds contempt by pointing out that without a certain amount of familiarity, it is impossible to breed anything!) Hundreds of studies have shown that "familiarity breeds liking."[33] The **mere exposure effect** is the tendency for novel stimuli to be liked more after the individual has been repeatedly exposed to them. In 1968, social psychologist Robert Zajonc proposed that "mere repeated exposure of the individual to a stimulus is a sufficient condition for the enhancement of his attitude toward it."[34] In plainer terms, just seeing something

mere exposure effect the tendency for people to come to like things simply because they see or encounter them repeatedly

over and over is enough to make you like it. To test his mere exposure hypothesis, Zajonc conducted a series of studies in which participants were exposed to novel stimuli (e.g., Turkish words, Chinese-like characters, and yearbook photos of strangers).[35] The more frequently participants saw each stimulus, the more they liked it (see **FIGURE 7.1**). Subsequent research has shown that mere exposure to more meaningful stimuli, such as faces of people from different races, can increase liking for similar faces that have never been seen.[36]

The mere exposure effect can also influence attitudes toward oneself. Female college students brought a close female friend with them to do an experiment.[37] The researchers took a photograph of each student and made two prints from it—a true print and a mirror (reversed) print. Participants liked the mirror print better than the true print, whereas their friends liked the true print better than the mirror print. A follow-up study found the same result when female participants brought their boyfriends. Why? Both groups liked what they had been exposed to most frequently. People most commonly see themselves in a reversed image, as when they look in the mirror. In contrast, your friends mostly see your true image because they look directly at you rather than seeing you in a mirror.

The mere exposure effect appears to be quite robust. It even occurs for animals other than humans, such as crickets[38] and chickens.[39] Why does it occur? It seems that when people are exposed to novel stimuli over and over again, they feel more positively about them.[40]

This general rule has a couple of exceptions. If you initially dislike something, being exposed to it repeatedly will not make you like it more. In fact, it will make you like it less.[41,42] For example, if you hear a song on the radio that you hate, the more you hear it, the more you will hate it. The same is true for threatening stimuli (e.g., angry faces)—the more people are exposed to them, the less they like them.[43,44]

This chapter started with the story of Facebook. The mere exposure effect seems like a great boon to Facebook users. As they use it more, they like it more. They also see more of their friends on it, which will cause them to like those friends more.

Embodied Attitudes

The famous biologist Charles Darwin thought attitudes were evident in bodily states, such as leaning toward or away from something. In an early classic demonstration,[45] college students were told that the researchers were conducting a marketing study for a headphone company "determined to create the ultimate headphones in terms of sound and comfort." After trying on six different headphones, participants listened to a simulated radio broadcast of an editorial commentator discussing tuition at their university. By the flip of a coin, half the participants heard the commentator argue that tuition should be increased, whereas the other half heard the commentator argue that tuition should be decreased. The experimenter said that it was important that headphones would function well despite movement, so some participants were instructed to move their heads while listening. Some were told to move their heads up and down (like nodding agreement): These ended up agreeing with the message even if it meant their tuition would be increased. Others were told to move their heads from side to side (like shaking their head no). These ended up disagreeing with the message. Thus, the randomly assigned bodily movements shaped people's attitudes toward what they heard.

Classical Conditioning

Research has shown that attitudes can be formed through **classical conditioning**.[46] Ivan Pavlov, a Nobel Prize–winning Russian scientist, developed the theory of classical conditioning and demonstrated it in his experiments with dogs. Meat powder (**unconditioned stimulus**) makes the dog's mouth water (**unconditioned response**). The first time a researcher rings a bell (**neutral stimulus**), the dog's mouth does not water. However, if the

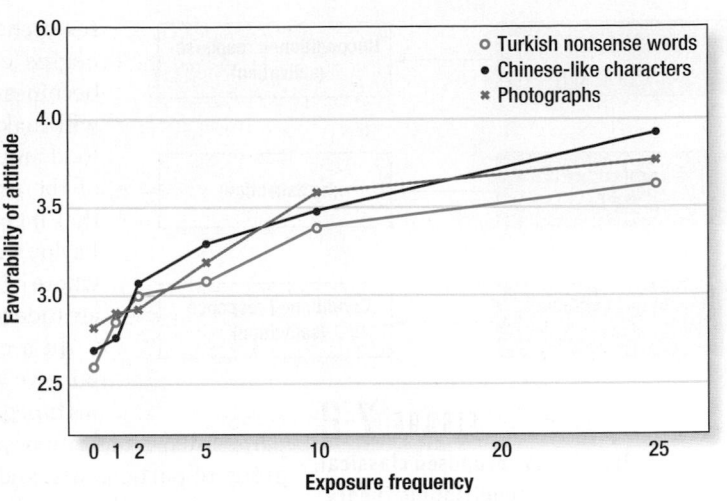

FIGURE **7.1**

Relation between frequency of mere exposure to Turkish words, Chinese-like characters, and yearbook photos of strangers and attitudes toward these stimuli.[35]

classical conditioning a type of learning in which, through repeated pairings, a neutral stimulus comes to evoke a conditioned response

unconditioned stimulus a stimulus (e.g., meat powder) that naturally evokes a particular response (salivation)

unconditioned response a naturally occurring response (e.g., salivation)

neutral stimulus a stimulus (e.g., Pavlov's bell) that initially evokes no response

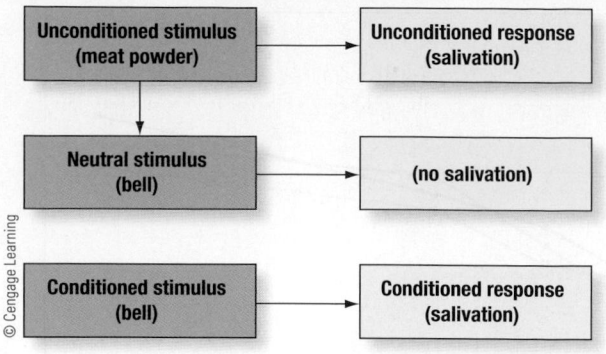

FIGURE 7.2

Ivan Pavlov proposed classical conditioning theory.

researcher rings the bell every time the dog gets meat powder, the dog begins to expect that every time it hears the bell it will be fed, and the bell becomes a **conditioned stimulus**. Eventually, the sound of the bell alone will make the dog's mouth water (**conditioned response**), even with no food around (see **FIGURE 7.2**). This principle is one of the foundations of the psychology of learning, and social psychologists have proposed that it could explain the formation of attitudes in humans. In a sense, Pavlov's dog developed a positive attitude toward the sound of the bell, where it had not had any attitude before, simply because the dog's positive attitude toward meat gradually became linked to the sound of the bell.

In a classic study,[47] the word *Dutch* was systematically paired with positive words (e.g., *vacation, gift*), whereas the word *Swedish* was paired with negative words (e.g., *bitter, failure*). When tested afterward, participants rated Dutch more positively than Swedish. The pairing was reversed for a second group of participants, and they rated Swedish more positively than Dutch. Classical conditioning may help explain the development of prejudice against social groups that are frequently associated with negative information in the media,[48] such as Muslims being associated with terrorism in the popular press.[49]

Advertisers use classical conditioning to their advantage by linking their products with famous or attractive people. For example, famous athletes such as LeBron James, Christano Renaldo, Neymar Jr, Serena Williams, and Tiger Woods have endorsed Nike shoes, which should make attitudes toward Nike shoes more positive. That's also why advertisers may cancel their contracts with famous people who behave badly or illegally, so customers will not develop negative attitudes toward their products. For example, Nike and other sponsors dropped former bicyclist Lance Armstrong following his drug scandal,[50] former National Football League (NFL) player Ray Rice after videos emerged showing him beating his fiancé unconscious in an elevator,[51] and former NFL player Adrian Peterson after he was arrested for beating his 4-year-old son.[52]

Other pairings seem questionable. For example, on the TV show *American Idol,* the "American Idol" logo is used to cover someone's mouth every time that person swears or makes an obscene gesture (e.g., sticking up their middle finger, mooning the camera). What might Dr. Pavlov have to say about associating the show's logo with vulgar, obscene swear words?

Operant Conditioning

Attitudes can also be formed through **operant conditioning** (also called **instrumental conditioning**). In this type of conditioning, developed by behaviorists such as Edward Thorndike and B. F. Skinner, participants are more likely to repeat behaviors that have been rewarded and less likely to repeat behaviors that have been punished. For example, if parents or teachers praise a child for doing well on math problems, then the child may develop a more positive attitude toward math. Students in one study received either an "A" or a "D" (the grade was actually decided by the flip of a coin) on the essays each wrote.[53] Even though the grades were randomly determined, students who received an "A" reported more favorable attitudes toward the topic than did students who received a "D." (Don't worry; your social psychology instructor won't be assigning grades in your class randomly!) Parents, teachers, and other adults often use operant conditioning by praising children for expressing what they consider to be socially desirable attitudes.

Facebook seems likely to gain from both classical and operant conditioning. One goes online and sees one's friends, whom one likes, and so Facebook (like Pavlov's bell) will get associated with positive things. And when people use Facebook, they may feel rewarded by positive connections with others, which will also improve their positive attitude toward Facebook. In contrast, the "Enemy" button should have the opposite effect.

Social Learning

By the early 1960s it became clear that conditioning by itself could not explain complex social behaviors. Psychologist Albert Bandura theorized that the most powerful learning processes in understanding social behavior involved **social learning** (also called **observational learning imitation,** or **vicarious learning**).[54,55,56] According to social learning theory, people

conditioned stimulus a neutral stimulus that, through repeated pairings with an unconditioned stimulus, comes to evoke a conditioned response

conditioned response a response that, through repeated pairings, is evoked by a formerly neutral stimulus

operant conditioning (instrumental conditioning) a type of learning in which people are more likely to repeat behaviors that have been rewarded and less likely to repeat behaviors that have been punished

social learning (observational learning, imitation, vicarious learning) a type of learning in which people are more likely to imitate behaviors if they have seen others rewarded for performing them, and less likely to imitate behaviors if they have seen others punished for performing them

Many viewers' attitudes about musical performances have been shaped by watching the judges on the TV program *American Idol*.

learn how to behave by observing and imitating others. In several classic experiments, Bandura showed that young children imitated specific aggressive acts they observed in aggressive models, for example, hitting a "Bobo" doll (a large inflatable toy) that they had seen an actor hit. Furthermore, he developed the concept of vicarious learning of aggression by showing that children were especially likely to imitate other people who had been rewarded for behaving aggressively.[57,58] Bandura argued that this imitation was the key to social learning. The idea is that people do not just imitate the specific social behaviors they see, but they make cognitive inferences based on their observations, and these inferences lead to generalizations in behavior. What is important is how the child interprets social events, and how competent the child feels in responding in different ways.[59] These cognitions provide a basis for stability of behavior tendencies across a variety of situations. Watching Mommy hit Daddy (or vice versa) may not only increase a child's likelihood of hitting. It may also increase the child's belief that hitting is okay when someone provokes you. Once again, the capacity to learn from others is important for enabling humans to be cultural beings.

Of course, social learning theory can also explain how attitudes are developed. For example, many teens learn what attitudes are acceptable by watching whether other teens are rewarded or punished for endorsing certain music, clothing styles, hairstyles, and convictions.[60] Social media such as Facebook, Twitter, and YouTube makes this process more efficient because one can learn about the attitudes of many other people. Indeed, the recording and tallying of "likes" has become a widely influential measure of popular attitudes, now reverberating through the business world too. Facebook's prohibition of the word "dislike" may hamper the spread of negative attitudes. Is that a good or a bad thing? (In other words, what's your attitude toward that policy?)

Polarization

Sometimes our attitudes about something can become stronger or weaker simply by thinking more about it. When we think about something, we may generate new ideas or insights that we did not consider when we formed our initial attitudes. Research suggests that as people reflect on their attitudes they become more extreme, an effect known as attitude polarization.[61,62,63,64] Even just thinking about an issue can move a person toward holding a more extreme attitude.

Furthermore, people who hold strong attitudes on certain issues are likely to evaluate relevant evidence in a biased manner. They tend to accept at face value evidence that confirms what they already believe, whereas they tend to be more critical of evidence that goes against their beliefs. Thus, even if people see an equal amount of confirming and disconfirming evidence (so that logically their attitude should not change), they become even more convinced of their initial attitudes and adopt them more strongly. The attitude polarization effect is especially likely to occur in people who have strong initial attitudes.[65] In a famous study,[66] proponents and opponents of the death penalty read studies about the death penalty. The results showed that both groups were biased in favor of studies that matched their initial opinion on the death penalty. As a result, their attitudes became more polarized—the proponents became more in favor of the death penalty, whereas the opponents became more opposed to it—even though all had read the same information! Attitude polarization also occurs sometimes because people are reluctant to admit they are wrong. As they think more about an issue, they tend to convince themselves that they were right all along.

Other studies show that people are more accepting of evidence presented by ingroup members (members of one's own group) than by outgroup members (members of a different group).[67] People are especially skeptical of evidence presented by outgroup members who are different from themselves. (Thus, even though Facebook promotes contact between many different people, users may mainly interact with friends and other ingroup members, so that they mainly share information with like-minded people.) All of this reflects another theme we have seen repeatedly in this book: putting people first. People rely on others for information, and they especially rely on people who are similar to themselves. If people are biased to accept information from ingroup members, then most groups will tend to hold fairly similar opinions on many issues. This may make it easier for the group to work together. Alternatively, it may foster poor decision making. These issues are discussed in more detail in Chapter 14.

attitude polarization the finding that people's attitudes become more extreme as they reflect on them

QUIZ YOURSELF
How Attitudes Are Formed

1. Alissa heard a new song on the radio that she likes. A company used the same song in its advertising jingle, and the song was played over and over, so she was repeatedly exposed to the song. Alissa's attitude toward the song is likely to _____ .

   (a) become ambivalent   (b) become more negative   (c) become more positive   (d) remain the same

2. If the word *pink* is followed by negative words and frowns from his mother, the toddler learns to respond negatively to the word *pink*. This is an example of _____ .

   (a) classical conditioning   (b) operant conditioning   (c) social learning   (d) verbal learning

3. Juan wasn't sure whether he was in favor of capital punishment or not. However, after receiving an "A" on a speech paper denouncing capital punishment, he decides that capital punishment is ineffective and inhumane. This is an example of _____.

   (a) classical conditioning   (b) operant conditioning   (c) social learning   (d) verbal learning

4. After 3-year-old Davis sees his dad shaving, he covers his own face with shaving cream. This is an example of _____ .

   (a) classical conditioning   (b) operant conditioning   (c) social learning   (d) verbal learning

answers: see pg 255

Consistency

Inconsistency does not much trouble dogs or bugs, but people feel some inner pressure to resolve it. To reduce their feelings of inconsistency, people may have to seek out new information or reinterpret old information, realign or even abandon cherished beliefs, or change patterns of behavior. People don't like it when their beliefs, attitudes, and behaviors are inconsistent. (Nor do they approve of inconsistency in others!) This drive for consistency is a central component of several theories in social psychology.

Most consistency theories have three things in common. First, they specify the conditions that are required for consistency and inconsistency of cognitions. Second, they assume that inconsistency is unpleasant and therefore motivates people to restore consistency. Third, they specify the conditions that are needed to restore consistency. In general, people choose the path of least resistance to restore consistency. Because attitudes are easier to change than behaviors, people often change their attitudes. Next, we review the most influential consistency theory—cognitive dissonance theory. We then show how the duplex mind copes with inconsistency.

Cognitive Dissonance and Attitude Change

One of the most important applications of consistency to social phenomena is called **cognitive dissonance theory**. According to this theory, conflicting thoughts cause psychological discomfort (cognitive dissonance). It is a theory about how people rationalize their behavior so as to bring their attitudes into line with their actions.

The origins of cognitive dissonance theory lay in some confusing findings that emerged from persuasion research during its first flowering in the 1950s. At that time, psychology was dominated by operant conditioning theory (see "Formation of Attitudes" section earlier in this chapter), which was based on the simple idea that when people are rewarded, they will do more of whatever led to the reward. Applied to persuasion, operant conditioning theory held that the best way to get people to change their attitudes was to get them to act in the desired manner and then reward them for doing so. If you want people to like Brussels sprouts, get them to say they like sprouts and then pay them big bucks for saying so. It sounded reasonable, but it never seemed to work very well. If anything, the people who said it for less money seemed to end up believing it more— opposite to operant conditioning theory.

Along came social psychologist Leon Festinger, who proposed that inconsistencies produce an unpleasant mental state called **cognitive dissonance**. He said that people want to maintain consistency, so when they catch themselves being inconsistent they feel bad. The reason that paying somebody big bucks to claim to like Brussels sprouts didn't produce any actual liking was that the money resolved the inconsistency: "I don't really like them, but if you pay me a lot to say I like them, I'll say so." The more interesting case, thought Festinger, was when the pay was minimal: "I didn't think I liked Brussels sprouts, but I said I like them, and I was willing to say so without getting much money. I'm not a liar. I must really like them after all." *Money Matters* describes how one classic experiment provided evidence for cognitive dissonance theory.

Justifying Effort

A second memorable study of cognitive dissonance, published the same year, introduced the idea of **effort justification**.[68] According to cognitive dissonance theory, people want to convince themselves that all their hard work and effort are worthwhile. This particular study was stimulated by controversies on college campuses surrounding "hazing" initiations at fraternities and sororities. People who wanted to join those organizations often had to go through embarrassing or painful initiation rituals, such as being spanked

cognitive dissonance the uncomfortable feeling people experience when they have two thoughts or cognitions conflict with one another

cognitive dissonance theory the theory that inconsistencies produce psychological discomfort, leading people to rationalize their behavior or change their attitudes

effort justification the finding that when people suffer or work hard or make sacrifices, they will try to convince themselves that it is worthwhile

Would You Sell Your Soul for $1?

In 1959, Leon Festinger and his colleague J. Merrill Carlsmith published a classic experiment to demonstrate how dissonance worked.[133] It involved getting people to say they liked something they really didn't like by paying them. The core question was how much pay would produce the most attitude change. Traditional reinforcement theory assumed that the more pay they received (the bigger the reward), the more people would come to believe what they said. Dissonance theory predicted the opposite: Small pay would produce the most attitude change.

Each participant came for a study called "Measures of Performance." The experimenter said it had to do with performing routine tasks, such as those found in factories. The experiment itself was excruciatingly boring. The participant spent the first half hour taking 12 little wooden spools off a tray one at a time, then putting them back on the tray, then off again, over and over and over. The second half hour was no better: The participant had to turn 48 square pegs a quarter turn clockwise, then again, and again, and again. Finally, when the participant was probably about bored to tears, the experimenter said that the study was over but then explained that there were some hidden wrinkles to the experiment—it was really about trying to motivate people to perform these routine, repetitious tasks. To do that, he employed a confederate who pretended to be a previous participant in the study and who would tell real participants that the task was fun, exciting, interesting, fascinating, and great. The experimenter said the study's purpose was to see whether people who heard these glowing tributes performed better than others.

Then came the crucial part. The experimenter said that another participant was scheduled to arrive in a few minutes, and the confederate who was supposed to be there had called to cancel. The experimenter asked the participant to "fill in" and perform the confederate's job, which just entailed telling the next participant that the experiment was really interesting. Obviously this was false—the participant knew how deadly boring the task was—but the participant didn't want to refuse the request and so agreed to do what the experimenter asked. The experimenter paid the participant either $1 or $20 for performing this service. (Participants in the control group skipped this part of the experiment; they were not asked to lie and were paid nothing.) The next participant (who was actually a confederate) came in, the participant told this person that the task was really interesting, the confederate expressed some skepticism, the participant insisted, and the confederate finally agreed.

Later, in a different room, another researcher asked the participant to rate how much he or she had enjoyed the experiment. The results are shown in **FIGURE 7.3**. Participants had essentially lied for either $1 or $20, and they had a chance to undo the lie by convincing themselves that they did find the experiment enjoyable. Those who had been paid $20 did not say the task was enjoyable; their ratings were no different from those of participants who had not been asked to lie. They had experienced no dissonance: They were willing to tell a lie for $20 (especially in the name of science; and $20 in 1959 would be equivalent to over $160 today). But those who had been paid only $1 still had some dissonance, and they changed their attitudes. They said the task really had been interesting. It was a way of rationalizing their behavior so as to resolve the inconsistency: They could reassure themselves that they had not actually lied.

Thus, people are willing to do questionable things for large sums of money. But when they perform the same actions for a small amount of money, people feel a need to rationalize and justify those actions, so they change their attitudes.

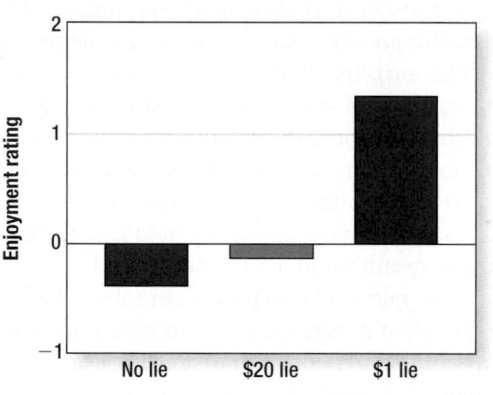

© Cengage Learning

FIGURE **7.3**

Participants who had been paid $1 to lie about how enjoyable the experiment was rated it as more enjoyable than did those in the other two groups, which were not significantly different from each other.[133]

or performing demeaning tasks for the older members of the organization. College administrators often sought to clamp down on these practices, but fraternity and sorority members said that these experiences helped forge strong ties to the group. Dissonance researchers thought that perhaps the students were right.

The experiment was disguised as a group discussion on sex, which back in the 1950s was pretty racy stuff. The participants were all college women who had signed up to join one of these groups. When the participant arrived, the experimenter (a man) said that the group had met several times already, and one problem had surfaced, which was that some people were too embarrassed to talk about sex. Did the participant think she could talk freely? All the women said yes. In the control condition, the experimenter said okay, she could join the group. But in the other conditions, he said that she would have to pass an embarrassment test. Some participants were given a mild test, in which they merely had to say a few words such as *virgin* and *prostitute* out loud to the male experimenter. Others, however, were given a more severe initiation in which they had to recite obscene words and read sexually explicit passages from paperback novels out loud to the male experimenter. For most participants, this was an embarrassing and unpleasant experience.

At the end of the test, the experimenter told each participant that she had passed and could join the interesting group—indeed could listen in on the discussion taking place right then. The supposedly interesting group turned out to consist of several biology graduate students droning on pointlessly about dull things like mating patterns among cockroaches. The measure was how well the participant liked what she heard and how much she liked the group. The women who had had no test or only a mild test recognized how boring and useless it all was and said they didn't like the discussion or the group. But the women who had gone through the stressful, unpleasant initiation (the highly embarrassing test) rated the discussion and group much more favorably. As the fraternity members were saying, people who suffered more to get into a group ended up liking the group more. That was the only way to convince themselves that their suffering had been worthwhile. The mind's own drive for consistency is behind the process.

A rare and remarkable recent study confirmed the benefits of painful rituals for group identification. In connection with a religious festival in Mauritius, young adult men were randomly assigned to one of three roles. One group took part in ritual consisting of singing and praying. Another performed the Kavadi, a painful ritual requiring piercing the skin with needles, dragging a cart attached by hooks to the skin, and climbing a mountain barefoot. A third group observed the Kavadi. The men who performed or watched the painful Kavadi later donated more to the temple and identified more with Mauritius than the men who did the easy ritual.[69] Thus, taking part in the painful ritual made the men identify more with the large social group and act in a more prosocial manner.

Thus, dissonance makes people seek to justify and rationalize any suffering or effort they have made. Perhaps surprisingly, dissonance reduction processes can make people accept their suffering and even choose to continue it. *Food for Thought* describes how people will sometimes choose to suffer as a consequence of expecting to suffer, even if the choice is as unappealing as eating a worm!

Justifying Choices

The next big advance in cognitive dissonance theory was centered around having a choice, which is very important to people (see Chapter 4). (We also noted earlier in this chapter that attitudes are most helpful for choosing, so it would be useful and adaptive to review and revise attitudes when making choices.) If you perform an action but do not have any choice, you

To reduce dissonance, people like to justify the effort they put into a task.

"There are so many choices of socks to choose from. If they all were the same, they would always match!"

Would You Eat a Bug or a Worm?

Would you eat a worm? Television reality shows like *Survivor* typically include an episode in which people are asked to eat a variety of bugs, worms, and other foods that may be regarded as delicacies in some parts of the world but that strike most Americans as gross and unappealing, if not downright disgusting.

Yet social psychologists have found in multiple studies that if they set up the situational factors correctly, people—even modern American college students—will eat worms or bugs. This isn't because students think eating worms is about the same as eating dorm food! On the contrary, most start off with substantially negative attitudes toward eating such foods, but their attitudes can change.

One of the most thorough and revealing studies of worm eating looked at the underlying attitudes and beliefs that had to change.[70] On the first day of the study, participants filled out questionnaires. On the second day, each participant was ushered into a laboratory room and told the task would be performed there. In one condition, participants were told the task would involve weight discrimination—judging which of two items was heavier than the other. Other participants were told their assigned task would be to eat a worm. The lab was set up with a plate containing a (dead) worm, as well as a fork, a napkin, and a glass of water for the worm-eating task, and a scale, some weights, and some paper to record responses for the weights task. The participant was left alone for a while, to allow time to think about the impending task. Then came an attitude questionnaire, so the researchers could track people's attitudes about the task.

After a time the experimenter returned and said he had made a mistake. Instead of being assigned the one task, the participant was supposed to be allowed to choose whether to do the worm-eating task or the weight discrimination task. Among the participants who had been told they were assigned to the weight discrimination task and then were given the chance to eat a worm instead, all (100%) said something to the effect of "no, thanks!" All these participants stuck with the emotionally neutral weight discrimination task.

Among those who had expected to eat the worm and then were given the chance to do the weight discrimination task, however, most (80%) stuck with the worm or at least said they did not have a preference. This may seem surprising, but the questionnaire data revealed that changed attitudes helped mediate the choice. Most of these people had changed their views by increasing their belief that (a) I am brave, (b) I deserve to suffer, or (c) eating a worm isn't so bad. The people who failed to change any of these beliefs made up the 20% who jumped at the chance to do the weight discrimination task instead.

Thus, this study shows that sometimes people will choose to suffer as a consequence of expecting to suffer—but only if they have coped by changing some of their relevant beliefs and attitudes.

Anders Ryman/Encyclopedia/Corbis

Would you eat a worm?

don't have to rationalize or justify it. In these studies,[71] students were encouraged to write an essay saying that various controversial speakers should be banned from college campuses, which was contrary to what most students believed (they supported free speech and their own freedom to listen). Some were told that this was their assigned task in the experiment. Others were told, "We would really appreciate it if you would do this, but it's entirely up to you to decide." Most people willingly agreed to the experimenter's request. Only the people in the latter (high-choice) condition experienced dissonance and changed their attitudes toward greater agreement with their essays.

People also experience dissonance when they make difficult choices. For example, should you major in A or B? Should you attend college A or B? Should you accept the job offer from company A or B? Should you get married or remain single? Every decision involves tradeoffs (see Chapter 2), but people like to reduce their dissonance by justifying their choices. This type of dissonance is called **post-decision dissonance**. In particular, if the decision was a close call, you can reduce dissonance afterward by deciding that what you chose was far better than what you rejected.

post-decision dissonance cognitive dissonance experienced after making a difficult choice, typically reduced by increasing the attractiveness of the chosen alternative and decreasing the attractiveness of rejected alternatives

Advances in Dissonance Theory

Another step forward came when researchers began to ask themselves what dissonance felt like. Was it an arousal state—that is, a bodily reaction in which the heart beats faster and in other respects the person seems more tense and nervous? In other words, does dissonance resemble an emotional reaction? A series of studies indicated that the answer is yes. When people performed actions contrary to their attitudes, they often felt acutely uncomfortable. If this feeling was blocked, they did not change their attitude. If they had this feeling but thought it was due to something else (specifically, a pill they had been given, along with instructions that the pill would make them feel tense and aroused), they did not change their attitudes.[72,73] Only people who felt discomfort *and* attributed it to their inconsistent behavior were driven to rationalize what they had done. They alone changed their attitudes to match their actions. Dissonance is marked not only by arousal, but also by an unpleasant arousal. It feels bad.

Another advance in dissonance theory linked the reaction to the interpersonal sphere. People may have some desire to be consistent in the privacy of their minds, but they have a much stronger desire to be seen by other people as consistent. We live in a social world in which people expect each other to be consistent. People who say one thing one day and something else another day are criticized as liars, hypocrites, gullible weaklings, untrustworthy or unreliable chameleons, and worse. It is important to act consistently when in the presence of others. This interpersonal dimension invokes the importance of self-presentation, discussed in Chapter 3: What is inside is often driven by what happens between people. Consistency may be yet another case in which inner processes serve interpersonal relations. On the long road to social acceptance, people learn that others expect them to be consistent and may reject them if they are inconsistent.

Many studies have shown the importance of self-presentation (that is, the effort to make a good impression or keep a good reputation) in cognitive dissonance. For example, when people act in ways that are contrary to their attitudes, the effects depend on who is looking. Writing an essay that violates your beliefs has little effect if it is done privately and anonymously, whereas if you have to put your name on it, you are more likely to feel dissonance and to change your attitude to match what you wrote. Telling someone that a task was interesting doesn't seem to have an effect if that person doesn't listen or doesn't believe you, but if you actually convince someone, then you feel a much greater need to convince yourself, too.

Dissonance Theory and the Media

To avoid the dissonance that comes from hearing conflicting attitudes, people often purposely seek out media that confirm what they already believe—called **selective exposure**.[74] For example, conservative Americans might follow the media Twitter feeds of *Weekly Standard*, Michelle Malkin, Andrew Breitbart, Sean Hannity, and *Daily Caller*, whereas liberal Americans might follow Ezra Klein, *The Nation*, *Mother Jones*, *Salon*, and *Daily Kos*.[75] Indeed, some Internet sites (e.g., Google, Facebook) intentionally use algorithms to expose you to material that is consistent with your attitudes—called a **filter bubble**.[76] The use of filter bubbles could be considered forced selective exposure.

Is the Drive for Consistency Rooted in Nature or Nurture?

Social psychologists have debated for decades the question of whether consistency is rooted in nature or nurture. Cultural variation would be one indication that it is learned. Some evidence indicates that the same basic drive for consistency can be found in very different cultures,[77] but making choices does not seem to cause dissonance processes among East Asians the way it does for North Americans.[78,79,80] On the other hand, the influence of social pressures toward consistency probably strengthens the drive. Either way, the root probably lies in the fact that groups of people can get along better if the people understand each other, and understanding each other is easier if people are consistent. People expect and pressure each other to be consistent, and people respond to these pressures and

selective exposure refers to the tendency of individuals to select information that supports their preexisting views and avoid information that contradicts their preexisting views

filter bubbles are algorithms used on the Internet to selectively guess what information a user would like to see based on information available about that use (e.g., previous web pages viewed, click behavior) expectations by seeking to be consistent. Quite possibly the drive for consistency is both rooted in our biological nature and strengthened by learning and socialization.

Indeed, the drive toward consistency may also embody a principle we saw in Chapter 5 (on social cognition): Human thinking and reasoning processes seem designed primarily for arguing. It is not that there is some peculiar feature of brain cells that renders them averse to contradiction. Rather, if you contradict yourself while arguing with someone, you are likely to lose the argument. So evolution may have shaped the brain for arguing and thereby instilled a sensitivity toward inconsistency. Still, how people argue may be influenced by local, cultural conditions, so the consistency drive may vary somewhat from one culture to another.

Most likely the drive toward consistency involves both parts of the duplex mind. The automatic system can learn to detect inconsistencies and send out alarm signals (distress, arousal). The deliberate system then steps in and finds some resolution to the inconsistency by thinking about how to rationalize or rethink things. It is also possible that some modes of dissonance reduction are automatic.

1. **Don says he values the environment. Someone reminds Don that he litters, wastes water, eats a lot of meat, drives a gas-guzzling car alone, and never uses public transportation. Don feels a certain amount of mental discomfort, which is most likely _____ .**

   (a) attitude polarization
   (b) cognitive dissonance
   (c) effort justification
   (d) negative attitude change

2. **Cognitive dissonance theory predicts that when there is little external justification for having performed an act, dissonance will be _____ and attitude change will _____ .**

   (a) high; occur
   (b) high; not occur
   (c) low; occur
   (d) low; not occur

3. **Which statement summarizes the basic idea underlying effort justification?**

   (a) Less leads to more.
   (b) More leads to less.
   (c) Suffering leads to liking.
   (d) Liking leads to suffering.

4. **The specific process of avoiding information that is different from what one already believes is called _____ .**

   (a) cognitive dissonance
   (b) predictive selection
   (c) rationality
   (d) selective exposure

Do Attitudes Really Predict Behaviors?

Psychology calls itself a behavioral science, which means that it seeks to predict and explain behavior. Attitudes are supposedly worth studying because they guide behavior. People act on the basis of what they like and dislike. Or do they? This is an important question, because if attitudes can't predict behavior, there would be little point in studying them.

Researchers have been examining the link between attitudes and behaviors for decades. An early sign that this link might be weak came before World War II. In the 1930s, many Americans did not like the Chinese for a variety of reasons, including a common perception that Chinese immigrants were taking American jobs. In 1934, a social psychologist and a young Chinese couple drove 10,000 miles across the country.[81] They stopped at 184 restaurants and 66 hotels, auto camps, and tourist homes. They received service at all establishments, except for one dilapidated auto camp where the owner refused to lodge them and called them "Japs." Six months later, the social psychologist sent a questionnaire to the same establishments, asking whether they would accommodate Chinese guests. About 92% said they would *not* accommodate Chinese guests. This raised an early warning signal about attitudes: These business owners, at least, expressed attitudes that differed sharply from their actual behavior.

Attacking Attitudes

Most social psychologists had accepted Gordon Allport's assertion that the attitude is the most important concept in psychology. Accordingly, they were surprised when Alan Wicker wrote an article in 1969 arguing that attitudes were a trivial, peripheral phenomenon.[82] After reviewing the results from 47 studies, Wicker concluded that attitudes did not cause behavior or even predict it very well. He even went so far as to suggest that social psychology abandon the concept of attitude, and that researchers should study more important things instead! He wrote, "Taken as a whole, these studies suggest that it is considerably more likely that attitudes will be unrelated or only slightly related to overt behaviors than that attitudes will be closely related to actions."

Once you set aside the assumption that people are generally consistent, it is not hard to find evidence that attitudes can differ from behavior. For example, a leader of an anti-pornography campaign was arrested with a prostitute. He had paid her for sex and was carrying a bottle of Viagra (a sex aid). To read about some interesting studies on attitude–behavior (A–B) consistency in sexual behavior, see *The Social Side of Sex*.

A–B problem the problem of inconsistency between attitudes (A) and behaviors (B)

The Social Side of *Sex*

A–B Inconsistency and Erotic Plasticity

As we have seen, attitude researchers have struggled with what they call the **A–B problem** the inconsistency between attitudes (A) and behaviors (B). Sex provides ample room for contradictions between people's attitudes and their actual behaviors. One general prediction derives from the view that female sexuality is more open than male sexuality to influence from social, cultural, and situational factors.[83] If that is correct, then women should show lower attitude–behavior consistency than men because women's sexual responses depend much more on the immediate situation and various other social influences. What a man wants may be the same regardless of context, but if the woman's sexual response depends on what it means, then her general attitude won't predict specific behaviors as accurately as his.

Same-gender sexual activity is one place where attitudes and behaviors diverge. A major survey asked people both about their attitudes toward homosexual activity ("Do you like the idea of having sex with someone of your own gender?") and about their actual behavior ("Have you had sex with someone of your own gender during the past year?") For men, the two questions overlapped heavily: A large majority (85%) of the men who favored homosexual activity had engaged in it during the past year. In contrast, attitudes and behaviors were much less consistent for women: Less than half the women who liked the idea had actually done it recently.[84]

The gender gap in consistency can be found in heterosexual behavior, too. Multiple studies have looked at whether people engage in sexual activity of which they do not approve, and all have found that women do this far more than men.[85,86,87]

Most people believe they should use condoms, especially when having sex with new or unfamiliar partners, but many people fail to do so. The gap between pro-condom attitudes and non-condom-using behaviors is larger among women than men (which is ironic, given that a condom detracts from male enjoyment more than female enjoyment).[88] Likewise, most people strongly favor being faithful to their partners if they have a committed relationship, but many people do occasionally indulge in kissing or sexual intercourse, or anything in between, with other partners. Again, women's behavior is more inconsistent than men's. In one study, men's attitudes regarding infidelity explained about 33% of their behavior, whereas women's attitudes explained only 11%.[89]

One solution to the A–B problem is for social psychologists to measure very specific attitudes. This doesn't resolve the gender problem, though. Several studies have measured whether people had sex on an occasion when they did not feel desire for sex. Both men and women do this (e.g., usually to please a partner who is feeling amorous), but more women than men do it.[90,91]

Apart from the special case of opportunity constraints, men's attitudes predict their sexual behavior much better than women's. The reason is not that women are generally inconsistent (indeed, no such general pattern exists outside of sexual activity). Rather, women's sexual responses are specific to the person, the situation, and what it all means, so their general attitudes are not highly relevant. In contrast, men tend to like and dislike the same things day in and day out, regardless of specific situations, so their general attitudes predict their behavior much better.

Defending Attitudes

Wicker's 1969 critique provoked a crisis in the field. Many social psychologists had spent their careers studying attitudes, and they were very disturbed to hear that attitudes were just little ideas flitting around inside people's minds that had no connection to what the people actually did. Attitude researchers circled the wagons to defend themselves, seeking ways to show how attitudes actually might have a closer link to behavior.

General Attitudes and Specific Behaviors

A first response in defense of attitudes was that the gap between general attitudes and specific behaviors was too big.[92] Researchers might ask what someone's attitude was toward helping people and then measure whether the person was willing to donate blood. The problem is that someone might be in favor of helping people generally, but might be afraid of needles. In contrast, if researchers measured attitudes toward giving blood, these attitudes were much better predictors of whether the person would actually give blood. The solution, though it did help indicate that attitudes could predict behavior, sacrificed broad general attitudes and put a burden on researchers to measure a vast number of very specific attitudes rather than a few general ones.

Behavior Aggregation

Another solution to the problem of attitude–behavior inconsistency comes from aggregating behavior, which means combining across many different behaviors on different occasions.[93] A person's attitude toward helping others might fare better if we didn't measure behavior by a single test, such as giving blood. Instead, we could add up whether the person gives blood, plus whether the person donates money to charity, plus whether the person volunteers to work with the homeless, plus whether the person stops to help a handicapped person cross the street, and so on. A person with a more positive attitude toward helping others will perform more of these behaviors, and this could add up to a substantial difference, even though the general attitude's link to any single behavior may be weak or unreliable.

Broad Attitude in Context

A third solution is that general attitudes can help cause behavior, but only if they are prominent in the person's conscious mind and influence how the person thinks about the choices he or she faces.[94] When asked to give blood, the person might say "no" despite having a favorable attitude toward helping others, because the person might not think of the question in terms of helping others. (The person might think of it in terms of being scared of needles, or of needing all his or her blood for a tennis match or hot date later that day!) If you first caused the person to reflect on his or her attitude toward helping others, then when the request for a blood donation came along, the person would see it as an opportunity to help, and hence the person's willingness to give blood would be shaped by that broad attitude. The broad attitude can influence specific behavior, but only if it has a chance to shape how the person interprets and construes the specifics of the here-and-now situation.

accessibility how easily something comes to mind

Attitude Accessibility

Accessibility refers to how easily the attitude comes to mind. Highly accessible attitudes can be quite influential because they come to mind very easily.[95,96] Obviously, an attitude that does not easily come to mind will have little opportunity to exert influence on thought, emotion, and behavior. One meta-analysis of 88 studies found that attitudes that are certain, stable, consistent, accessible, and based on direct experience are especially effective in predicting behavior.[97]

Behavioral Intentions

Another approach was to consider the role of behavioral intentions on the link between attitudes and behaviors. Behavioral intentions are a key component of the theory of planned behavior, which is depicted in **FIGURE 7.4**.[98] As the title of this theory

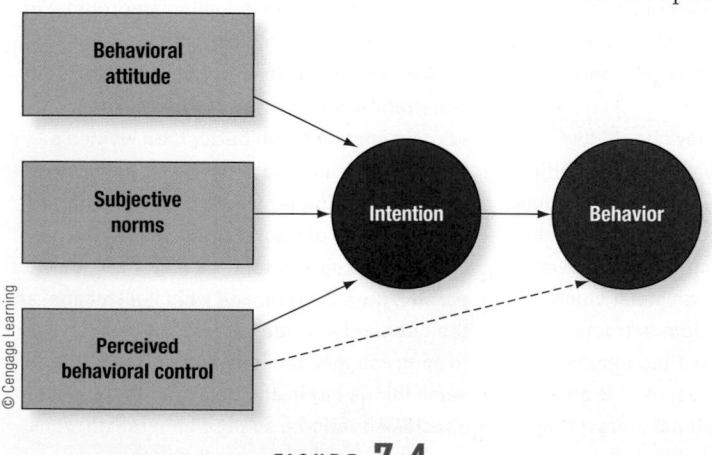

© Cengage Learning

FIGURE 7.4
The theory of planned behavior.

suggests, **behavioral intentions** refer to whether the person plans to perform the behavior in question. If a person intends to do a behavior, then it is likely that he or she will actually do it.

As can be seen in **FIGURE 7.4**, behavioral intentions are not only determined by the person's attitude but also by subjective norms and perceived behavioral control.

Subjective norms are the person's perceptions about whether significant others think he or she should perform the behavior in question or not. **Perceived behavioral control** refers to the person's beliefs about whether he or she can actually perform the behavior. A meta-analytic review of 185 studies found that the theory of planned behavior explained 27% of the variance in behavior—an impressive amount considering how difficult it is to predict human behavior.[99]

1. In 1934, a social psychologist and a Chinese couple drove 10,000 miles across the country, stopping at numerous hotels and restaurants. The Chinese couple received service at all of the establishments except one. Six months later, LaPiere sent a questionnaire to the same establishments, asking whether they would accommodate Chinese guests. How many said they would accommodate Chinese guests?

   (a) More than 90%   (b) About 75% of them   (c) About 25% of them   (d) Less than 10%

2. After reviewing the results from 47 studies, what did Wicker conclude in his 1969 article about the relationship between attitudes and behaviors?

   (a) It is almost perfect.   (b) It is strong.   (c) It is moderate in size.   (d) It is so weak that the concept of attitudes should be abandoned.

3. According to Gordon Allport, what is the most important concept in psychology?

   (a) Aggression   (b) Attitudes   (c) Discrimination   (d) Social influence

4. The best way to predict whether people will go see *Harry Potter and the Deathly Hallows: Part 2* is to assess their attitudes toward _____.

   (a) boxing   (b) films   (c) the seven previous Harry Potter films   (d) sports

answers: see pg 255

Beliefs and Believing

Consistency is an important issue for beliefs just as much as for attitudes. You want your beliefs about the world to be consistent with the world.

Believing versus Doubting

"I understand what you're saying, but I don't believe it!" Clearly, the gap between understanding and believing appears to be big. Or is it? Recent research has suggested that doubting/disbelieving is separate from understanding—but believing immediately, *automatically* accompanies understanding. Consider the title of one article on this pattern: "You Can't Not Believe Everything You Read"![100] As soon as you understand it, you

behavioral intentions an individual's plans to perform the behavior in question

subjective norms an individual's perceptions about whether significant others think he or she should (or should not) perform the behavior in question

perceived behavioral control an individual's beliefs about whether he or she can actually perform the behavior in question

believe it; only then, and only maybe, do you take a second step of changing your mind. If someone tells you the moon is made of green cheese, you believe it for a brief moment, even though you probably quickly change your mind.

The difference is important. Believing and disbelieving are not on an equal par. If for some reason the mind is prevented from taking the second step of changing your mind, you might just go on believing that the moon is made of green cheese. It is very hard to take in information while withholding all judgment about whether it is correct. The first impulse is to believe what you hear (or read).

The duplex mind may be implicated here. The automatic system automatically believes the information it is given. The deliberate system can override this belief by deciding that it is false. If you only use automatic processing, you will believe lots of things that aren't true.[101,102]

Children, for example, are notoriously gullible. If believing and disbelieving were equal acts that occurred at the same step, then children would first learn to understand without either believing or disbelieving anything, and then gradually learn to judge information as true or false. This is not what happens, though. Children first believe everything they are told, and only later learn to doubt and question.[103] Likewise, in lab studies, people who are supplied with information while they are distracted (such as when the experimenter tells them to remember a phone number for later) end up believing things they are told more than people who are not distracted. The distraction prevents them from taking the second step of thinking something like, "Wait a minute, this can't be right!"

Out in the world, religious and political cults are sometimes accused of "brainwashing" their members into believing strange things. To strengthen belief in their ideas, they often make sure their converts are tired or distracted (even by physical pain, hunger from fasting, or discomfort) when the doctrines are presented. If you wanted people to understand your cult's ideas best, you would want them rested and alert when you presented your teachings, but if you want someone to believe everything, then you should present your ideas when the person is not at full mental power. Tired or distracted people do not make it to the second step (of doubt); they stop at the first step, which combines understanding and believing.[104,105]

In short, when you understand something, believing it is automatic, whereas to doubt and question it may require controlled, conscious thought. The automatic system is fairly uncritical and accepts as true whatever it is told. The deliberate mind can override this and change from belief to disbelief. But as we know, deliberate activity requires time and effort, which people do not always have.

Belief Perseverance

Once beliefs form, they are resistant to change. This is true even of false beliefs that have been discredited. This effect is called **belief perseverance**. In an influential study,[106] participants were given 25 real and fictitious suicide notes and were told to identify the real ones. By the flip of a coin, participants were told either that they had correctly identified 24 of the 25 (success feedback) or that they had correctly identified only 10 of the 25 (worse than random chance, the failure feedback). Both groups were told that the average was 16 correct. At the end of the study, all participants were told that the feedback they had received was bogus. Nevertheless, participants who had received success feedback thought they were more accurate on the current test and that they would be more accurate on a future test than did participants who had received failure feedback. Participants thus continued to believe the feedback even though the researcher had discredited it.

A classic study about belief perseverance was mentioned in Chapter 5.[107] Half the participants read cases suggesting that risk-taking people make better firefighters than cautious people, whereas the other half read cases suggesting that cautious people make better firefighters than risk-taking people. Both groups of participants were told to come up with theories explaining the cases they had read. Then participants were told that the study was over and that the cases they had read were bogus. However, participants did

belief perseverance the finding that once beliefs form, they are resistant to change, even if the information on which they are based is discredited

not abandon their theories, even though the researcher had discredited the evidence on which they were based.

The good news is that there is a remedy for belief perseverance. Explaining the opposite theory (e.g., why a cautious person might make a better firefighter than a risk-taking person) reduces or eliminates belief perseverance.[108,109] If you want to understand things correctly, it is good to cultivate the habit of trying out the opposite theory to whatever theory you initially believe. Note that this trick makes use of the social cognition principle that reasoning is for arguing. To get a balanced, unbiased view in your mind, it helps to try to argue both sides. Put another way, try to play the "devil's advocate," is the popular phrase referring to deliberately arguing the opposite side. The term comes from group processes: The Catholic Church worried that someone with a checkered past might become pope, partly because none of the cardinals would dare criticize their possible future boss. Therefore, when choosing a new pope, they would appoint someone to be the "devil's advocate" whose sacred obligation was to argue that the candidate was unfit to be pope. That way all the objections would be heard.

Belief and Coping

Beliefs help people understand the world around them. This is especially apparent when people experience serious problems, such as misfortunes or disasters. The general term for how people attempt to deal with traumas and go back to functioning effectively in life is **coping**. The study of coping is an important opportunity for social psychologists to understand beliefs.

Something that puzzled psychologists for decades was that the psychological harm can be far more lasting, or even permanent, compared to the physical or pragmatic harm. People are sometimes quite upset over having their apartment robbed, even though they may not have lost much of value and most of the loss is repaid by an insurance company. Some rape victims may be traumatized for years even though they suffer no lasting or permanent physical harm. How can these processes be understood? Bodily injury and monetary loss may be two components of trauma, but clearly there is something else.

One important answer is that a crime affects a victim's beliefs about the world. These beliefs are called **assumptive worlds**, a term that expresses the view that people live in social worlds based on their assumptions about how things operate.[110] These include three main types of assumptions, all of which help people live healthy and happy lives, but any of which can be shattered when one is a victim of a crime:

1. **The world is benevolent.** Basically, people are nice, life is safe, and one can count on good things happening most of the time.

2. **The world is fair and just.** The world is fair, so people generally get what they deserve and deserve what they get. If you follow the rules and treat others with fairness and kindness, you can expect to be treated that way yourself.

3. **I am a good person.** I am someone of value and therefore deserve good things to happen to me.

If someone steals your wallet, or vandalizes your car, or assaults you during a stroll in the park, this creates a problem because it violates those beliefs. As you try to explain to yourself how such a thing can happen, you may feel that you cannot continue to maintain those three beliefs as well as you did before. Ultimately, effective coping may involve figuring out how to explain the crime while still permitting yourself to continue believing that, by and large, the world is benevolent and fair and that you are a good person who deserves good things.

This view of coping helps explain a surprising finding that emerged from a study that showed blaming oneself is often a good way to cope.[111] That study interviewed

off the mark .com   by Mark Parisi

I CAN DEAL WITH IT... I'VE BEEN EATEN BY A SNAKE, BUT I'LL JUST GO ON WITH MY LIFE... I'M OKAY!

LEWIS TESTS THE LIMITS OF POSITIVE THINKING.

Coping is easier for some people than others.

coping how people attempt to deal with stressful traumas and go back to functioning effectively in life

assumptive worlds the view that people live in social worlds based on certain beliefs (assumptions) about reality

individuals who had been paralyzed in serious accidents. All the victims had asked the question "why me?" and nearly all had come up with an answer. To the researchers' surprise, it did not seem to matter what explanation they came up with—fate, God's will, their own mistakes, the actions of others, or other factors. The big difference was whether they did or did not have an explanation. Those who had found an explanation coped better than those who had not, as rated by hospital staff and others. This finding was surprising because most psychologists at the time assumed that blaming oneself for misfortune or trauma would be bad for the person. Therapists who heard a patient blame himself or herself would often rush in to insist that such an explanation was wrong, and the person should avoid self-blame. Yet self-blame seemed to work just fine in helping people cope. The researchers' explanation was that blaming oneself can actually help people achieve a sense of control. The paralyzed victims would say things like, "It was my fault; I was driving too fast" or "I wanted to impress my friends, so I jumped off the roof onto the trampoline, even though I knew it was risky." If people believe that their own foolish actions caused their misfortunes, it helps them feel that they can avoid future misfortunes by not repeating those mistakes. In contrast, people who cannot explain their misfortunes to themselves are more likely to think that something bad could happen to them again, regardless of what they do. They feel much more vulnerable and have a hard time getting over what happened.

Not all self-blame is good, of course. There is an important distinction between blaming oneself for one's actions and blaming oneself for being a bad person. Someone who reacts to being robbed or injured by thinking, "I am a worthless person and I deserve to have bad things happen to me" is not going to bounce back very effectively. This type of thinking is likely to lead to feelings of shame, which are destructive. It is much more helpful to think, "I am basically a good and competent person, and I foolishly took a risk that brought this harm to me—so if I act more wisely in the future, I can avoid further problems." This type of thinking is likely to lead to feelings of guilt and even confidence, which are constructive. (See Chapter 6 for a discussion on the difference between shame and guilt.)

The upshot is that mental processes play a central role in helping people cope with and recover from misfortunes. A broad theory of **cognitive coping** was put forward by Shelley Taylor, who outlined several kinds of beliefs that need to be bolstered or restored in the wake of trauma.[112] Her original work focused on women who had breast cancer, but the ideas have been applied in many other contexts since then.

One important type of cognitive coping is based on the belief that whatever happened could have been worse, so at least the person was somewhat lucky. The technical term for this is **downward comparison**.[113] People compare themselves and their situations to other people who are worse off, and this makes people feel better about themselves. For example, women whose breast cancer resulted in surgery to remove a lump from the breast compared themselves to others who had lost an entire breast or both breasts. The reverse comparison, called an **upward comparison**, was rare or absent: No woman who lost an entire breast compared herself with women who had only had the lumpectomy. In everyday life, many people seem to understand this principle because "it could have been a lot worse" is a standard phrase that people say to someone to whom something bad has just happened.

Other beliefs in cognitive coping pertain to self-esteem and control. Victims of trauma and misfortune often need to find some way to restore their belief that they are good people and that they can exert control over what happens to them. Taylor observed that many women cultivated beliefs that they could control their cancer and prevent it from coming back, even though these beliefs often had little or no medical validity. The women thought that by eating certain foods or acting in a certain way (even by getting a divorce), they could keep themselves safe. These beliefs, although wrong according to medical knowledge (and many were later proven wrong because the cancer did eventually come back), were a great source of comfort that improved their well-being.

cognitive coping the idea that beliefs play a central role in helping people cope with and recover from misfortunes

downward comparison the act of comparing oneself to people who are worse off

upward comparison the act of comparing oneself to people who are better off

Still another type of helpful belief is that all things have some useful or higher purpose. The majority of women in Taylor's research sample reported positive changes in their lives that had come from having breast cancer. Many said they had learned to appreciate what was truly important in life, such as love and family, and had learned not to get upset over minor things. Religious beliefs are also helpful to people under these circumstances because people can accept on faith that God has some purpose for letting these misfortunes occur to them, or even that their suffering made them stronger or helped test and cement their faith. Others look to their own good deeds. A woman named Maureen Fischer suffered badly when her 3-year-old daughter died from a brain tumor, but she turned this tragedy into something good by raising money for and founding a hospitality lodge where families with very sick children could come for free vacations. In this way, her daughter's death helped her find a way to bring joy and comfort to many other suffering families.

When people encounter disasters or suffering, their beliefs must help them get by, and sometimes these beliefs must change. Even so, consistency is important in dictating whether beliefs will be helpful or not. Some traumas seem to contradict beliefs—such as assumptions about the world being a safe, benevolent, and fair place—that people need in order to go on living. Coping requires finding a way to make the trauma seem compatible or even consistent with those beliefs. Other beliefs help frame the problem in a way that makes it more tolerable, such as believing that the misfortune could have been much worse, or believing that the bad event led to some good purpose.

Religious Belief

Religion involves a very important category of beliefs. Science cannot generally say anything about whether religious beliefs are true or false. Regardless of objective truth, however, psychology can shed light on why some people accept religious beliefs, whereas other people reject those same beliefs. It can also explore the benefits that people get from believing in religion, again regardless of whether those beliefs cannot be proven to be true.

The appeal of religion throughout history has been partly its ability to explain the world, especially those things that cannot be explained by science. Religion can explain both large and small things. It can explain grand issues, such as where the sun, earth, and moon came from, where the person (or soul) existed before birth, and what happens after death; but religion can also explain smaller things, such as why your child got sick. (Again, we are not saying the religious explanations are true or false—but remember, coping depends on having an explanation, regardless of whether it is true or false.)

Religious beliefs can help people cope with stress.[114,115] For example, people recover more quickly from being sexually assaulted if they use religion to cope with the traumatic event.[116] People who rely on religion to help them cope are also less likely to fall back on ineffective coping strategies, such as drinking alcohol.[117]

Research has shown that appealing to a superordinate (high, all-encompassing) principle or power is an effective way to reduce dissonance.[118] For example, between 1831 and 1844, a preacher named William Miller launched the Great Second Advent Awakening, also known as the Millerite Movement.[119] Based on his study of the biblical verse in Daniel 8:14, Miller calculated that Jesus Christ would return to earth sometime between March 21, 1843, and March 21, 1844. After those dates passed with no evidence that Jesus was back, Samuel Snow, a follower of Miller, used the biblical verse in Habakkuk 2:3 to extend the date to October 22, 1844. (Note how changing these details allowed people to maintain consistency in the overriding belief.) When that prophecy also failed, thousands of believers left the movement, calling the prophecy the "Great Disappointment." Some of the followers, however, concluded that the prophecy predicted not that Jesus Christ would return to earth on October 22, 1844, but that a special ministry in heaven would be formed on that date. They continued to believe in Miller's teachings.

When Harold Camping predicted the end of the world to be May 21, 2011, some of his followers (called "ambassadors") left their homes, spouses, children, pets, and everything they owned, to travel around in a caravan to tell others about the upcoming end of the world.

Michelle V. Agins/The New York Times/Redux

More recently, radio evangelist Harold Camping predicted the rapture would occur on May 21, 1988. The rapture is the event described in the Bible, where the righteous people on the earth will be "caught up" to meet Jesus Christ in the clouds at the time of his second coming.[120] When that date came and went with no rapture, Camping revised the prediction to September 6, 1994, and then May 21, 2011. After these predictions also proved to be inaccurate, Camping once again changed the date to October 21, 2011. Some followers of Camping (called "ambassadors") left their homes, spouses, children, pets, and everything they owned, to travel around in a caravan to tell others about the upcoming end of the world.[121] When October 21, 2011 passed without incident, the *International Business Times* called Camping a "false prophet,"[122] and *Time* magazine listed Camping's predictions in their "Top 10 Failed Predictions."[123]

Despite the benefits of religious beliefs, the road to religious belief sometimes contains stumbling blocks.[124,125] At a cognitive level, people may have trouble dealing with inconsistent doctrines or resolving existential questions. At a more emotional level, some religious doctrines and practices can elicit feelings of fear and guilt. People may also experience feelings of anger or resentment toward God when tragedies occur in their lives.[126] Religion offers great benefits to many believers, but maintaining faith is not always easy.

Irrational Belief

People believe lots of seemingly crazy things, even though they have no rational basis for these beliefs.[127] These include paranormal beliefs (about Bigfoot, UFOs, etc.), as well as beliefs that are logically and statistically flawed (e.g., the belief that you can influence the outcome of a sports event that you are watching on television, or the belief that random events even out in the short run). We explored some of these irrational beliefs in Chapter 5. When it comes to irrational beliefs, the minuses probably outweigh the pluses. People who hold irrational beliefs are more anxious,[128] cope less well with terminal illnesses,[129] are more likely to become depressed over time,[130] and have lower levels of self-esteem.[131] People who think they are lucky are more likely to gamble and may therefore squander their money trying to beat long odds or to recoup large amounts of money they have already lost.

How do gamblers sustain their optimism as their losses mount? After all, if you lose more than you win (as most gamblers do), you should logically conclude either that you aren't lucky or that gambling is a foolish thing to do with your money, so you should stop. An intriguing series of studies suggests that gamblers maintain their positive (irrational) beliefs by using a series of tricks. In particular, they convince themselves that many losses were "near wins," so they don't count those against themselves. Thus, if they bet on sports, they feel lucky and smart if they win the bet, and they feel unlucky or dumb if their team loses by a wide margin. But if they lose by a small margin, they tell themselves that they should have won. This permits them to remain confident that they will win in the future.[132]

1. **Which is faster, believing or disbelieving?**
   - (a) Believing
   - (b) Disbelieving
   - (c) They are equally fast.
   - (d) It depends on how old the person is.

2. **Sometimes even social psychologists are reluctant to give up their pet theories, even when the data contradict those theories. This tendency is called _____ .**
   - (a) assumptive world beliefs
   - (b) belief perseverance
   - (c) mere exposure effect
   - (d) the A–B problem

3. **Which of the following incidents would violate an assumptive world belief?**
   - (a) Getting a flat tire.
   - (b) Slipping and falling on the highway on the ice.
   - (c) Getting beaten up by a bully at school.
   - (d) All of the above

4. **Trent was in a serious car crash. He totaled his car and broke his collarbone. Trent considered himself very unlucky. While in the hospital, he saw a story on the local news about another car accident in which the driver totaled his car and suffered serious brain damage. After hearing the news report, Trent now considers himself lucky rather than unlucky. What type of social comparison did Trent make?**
   - (a) Downward
   - (b) Lateral
   - (c) Upward
   - (d) None of the above

answers: see pg 255

What Makes Us Human

Putting the Cultural Animal in Perspective

Humans are not unique in having attitudes. Animals have attitudes, at least in the sense that they like and dislike certain things. But humans have far more attitudes than other animals, and the mental processes associated with them are far more complex. The way attitudes and beliefs operate is much more complicated among humans. For one thing, consistency pressures seem much more central in human than in animal functioning. It is doubtful that animals can really understand inconsistency beyond very simple events (e.g., expecting something and suddenly not finding it). We have little reason to think that animals engage in rationalization, whereas humans are quick to rationalize, especially when they experience cognitive dissonance.

One reason for the greater human concern with consistency is that we use language in dealing with each other. Humans explain their actions to each other and argue with each other. Inconsistency weakens arguments and explanations, and listeners are often quick to point out any inconsistencies. So people strive to be consistent as they prepare what to say.

The way people think creates other special processes involving attitudes and beliefs. People can hold dual attitudes, in which their deliberate attitude differs from their automatic response; animals that lack higher-level cognitions don't have that kind of inner conflict. We saw that simply thinking about an issue causes people's opinions to become polarized, but most animals would not be capable of that much thinking and hence wouldn't have to cope with its polarizing consequence. We also saw that doubting and questioning, and ultimately rejecting a belief as untrue, is often a second step in human thinking that may require conscious thought. Nonprimates probably lack the capacity to make true/false judgments. In practice, that probably means they believe everything that is presented to them and don't make judgments about whether something is true or false. Much of the great progress in human culture, from science to philosophy, involves carefully considering multiple views and rejecting those that are found to be false. Without the capacity to judge something as false, animals have been unable to develop science or philosophy.

Humans also use attitudes and beliefs much more extensively than other animals in how they relate to the world around them. We develop elaborate sets of beliefs to help us understand the world. (Again, only humans have developed science, religion, and philosophy.) Beliefs have another benefit, in that they can help people cope with misfortune. To an animal, a bad event (such as an injury) is just a practical matter, but for humans bad events affect their beliefs about the world, and people can use or modify those beliefs to help themselves bounce back.

CHAPTER 7 SUMMARY

What Are Attitudes and Why Do People Have Them?

- Beliefs are pieces of information, facts, or opinions; attitudes are broad evaluations (liking or disliking) toward some object or issue.
- Automatic attitudes are automatic, nonconscious, evaluative responses; deliberate attitudes are controlled, conscious, evaluative responses.
- Dual attitudes refer to having different, competing attitudes, one deliberate and the other automatic.
- People may not be aware of all their own attitudes.
- Attitudes help deal with the complex social world. People need far more attitudes than most animals.
- As soon as you know what something is, you start to know whether you like or dislike it (in the first microsecond of thought).
- To be impartial—as a judge or referee is supposed to—may require overcoming one's attitudes.
- Attitudes are tremendously helpful in making choices. Possessing an attitude increases the ease, speed, and quality of decision making.

How Attitudes Are Formed

- The mere exposure effect is the tendency for novel stimuli to be liked more after the individual has been repeatedly exposed to them. Familiarity breeds liking!
- Classical conditioning (also called Pavlovian conditioning) is the repeated pairing of an unconditioned stimulus with a conditioned stimulus, until the conditioned stimulus elicits a response similar to that elicited by the unconditioned stimulus.
- Classical conditioning may help explain the development of prejudiced attitudes against social groups that are frequently associated with negative information in the media.
- Advertisers use classical conditioning to direct attitudes by linking their products with famous or attractive people or with feeling good.
- Operant conditioning (also called instrumental conditioning) is a type of learning. People are more likely to repeat behaviors that have been rewarded and are less likely to repeat behaviors that have been punished.
- Social learning (also called observational learning, imitation, or vicarious learning) is the type of learning in which people are more likely to imitate behaviors if they have seen others rewarded for performing those behaviors, and are less likely to imitate behaviors if they have seen others punished for performing them.
- Attitudes can be formed or changed through operant conditioning, classical conditioning, or observational learning.
- Attitude polarization is the tendency for attitudes to become more extreme as people think about or reflect on their attitudes, especially if they held strong attitudes to begin with.
- If people see an equal amount of confirming and disconfirming evidence, they become even more convinced of their initial attitudes and adopt them more strongly.

- People are more accepting of evidence presented by ingroup members and more skeptical of evidence presented by outgroup members.

Consistency

- To reduce their feelings of inconsistency, people may have to seek out new or reinterpret old information, realign or abandon cherished beliefs, or change patterns of behavior. People will generally choose the easiest of these (the path of least resistance), which often means changing their attitudes.
  - Consistency theories have three parts:
  - They specify the conditions that are required for consistency and inconsistency of cognitions.
  - They assume that inconsistency is unpleasant and therefore motivates people to restore consistency.
  - They specify the conditions that are needed to restore consistency.
- According to cognitive dissonance theory, discrepancies between attitudes and behaviors produce psychological discomfort (cognitive dissonance), which causes people to rationalize their behavior so as to bring their attitudes into line with their actions.
- People who were paid a small amount to lie came to change their attitudes to believe their own lie; people who were paid a large amount to lie did not.
- Effort justification is the idea that people who expend a great deal of effort will want to convince themselves that their effort was worthwhile.
- People will sometimes choose to suffer as a consequence of expecting to suffer, if they have coped with their expectation by changing some of their relevant beliefs and attitudes.
- People who suffer more to get into a group end up liking the group more.
- Choice is necessary for dissonance and attitude change.
- Dissonance is marked by unpleasant arousal.
- People may have some desire to be consistent in the privacy of their minds, but they have a much stronger desire to be seen by other people as consistent.
- People selectively expose themselves to information that supports their preexisting views and avoid information that contradicts their preexisting views.
- Some Internet sites use filter bubbles to expose users to information that they think the user will like
- The drive for consistency may be rooted in our biological nature and strengthened by learning and socialization, and it may involve both parts of the duplex mind.

Do Attitudes Really Predict Behaviors?

- The A–B problem is the problem of inconsistency between attitudes (A) and behaviors (B). The link between attitudes and behaviors is often weak.
- Men's general attitudes predict their sexual behavior much better than women's.

- Attitudes predict behavior best if any or all of the following conditions are met:
  - Attitude measures are very specific.
  - Behaviors are aggregated across time and different situations.
  - Attitudes are consciously prominent and influence how the person thinks about the choices he or she faces.
  - Attitudes are highly accessible (i.e., they come to mind easily).

Beliefs and Believing

- The automatic system just believes; the deliberate system can override this belief by deciding that it is false.
- Belief perseverance is the idea that once beliefs form, they are resistant to change.
- Explaining the opposite theory reduces or eliminates belief perseverance.
- *Coping* is the general term for how people attempt to deal with traumas and go back to functioning effectively in life.
- *Assumptive worlds* is a term for the view that people form a complex understanding of their world and live according to that. Their assumptions typically include the following, any of which can be violated by misfortune or trauma:
  - The world is benevolent.
  - The world is fair.
  - I am a good person.
- Blaming oneself can be a good way to cope, if one blames oneself for having made a mistake, as opposed to blaming oneself for being a bad person.

- Cognitive coping identifies several kinds of beliefs that need to be bolstered or restored in the wake of trauma, including the following:
  - Reevaluate the trauma using downward comparison, in which people compare themselves and their situations to other people who are worse off.
  - Restore self-esteem.
  - Restore belief in control.
  - Find positive changes resulting from the trauma.
- Irrational beliefs are often maintained despite contradictory evidence.

What Makes Us Human? Putting the Cultural Animal in Perspective

- Although animals have some attitudes (e.g., they have likes and dislikes), humans have many more attitudes.
- Humans also have far more complex attitudes than other animals do.
- Only humans rationalize their behaviors by changing their attitudes.
- Because humans have conscious thought, they can question, doubt, and reject a belief as untrue. Other animals lack this ability.
- Only humans develop elaborate sets of beliefs to help them understand the world.

key terms

A–B problem 245	classical conditioning 235	dual attitudes 232	post-decision dissonance 242
accessibility 246	cognitive coping 250	effort justification 239	selective exposure 243
assumptive worlds 249	cognitive dissonance 239	filter bubbles 243	social learning (observational learning, imitation, vicarious learning) 236
attitude polarization 238	cognitive dissonance theory 239	mere exposure effect 234	
attitudes 232	conditioned response 236	neutral stimulus 235	
automatic attitudes 232	conditioned stimulus 236	operant conditioning (instrumental conditioning) 236	subjective norms 247
behavioral intentions 247	coping 249		unconditioned response 235
belief perseverance 248	deliberate attitudes 232		unconditioned stimulus 235
beliefs 232	downward comparison 250	perceived behavioral control 247	upward comparison 250

quiz yourself ANSWERS

1. What Are Attitudes and Why Do People Have Them? **p.234**
   answers: 1.b 2.a 3.a 4.a

2. How Attitudes Are Formed **p.238**
   answers: 1.c 2.a 3.b 4.c

3. Consistency **p.244**
   answers: 1.b 2.a 3.c 4.d

4. Do Attitudes Really Predict Behaviors? **p.247**
   answers: 1.d 2.d 3.b 4.c

5. Beliefs and Believing **p.253**
   answers: 1.a 2.b 3.d 4.a

SOCIAL INFLUENCE AND PERSUASION

LEARNING OBJECTIVES

1 Distinguish normative and informational influence.

2 Categorize the techniques of social influence in terms of the four basic principles and describe ways of resisting these techniques.

3 Explain how a persuasion attempt can be described by "who says what to whom," and identify which factors of each element are most likely to elicit successful persuasion.

4 Summarize the two routes to persuasion, applying the concept of the duplex mind to describe the two routes.

5 Describe some of the steps you can take to increase your resistance to persuasive attempts to change your attitudes.

iStockphoto.com/OJO_Images

James Warren Jones was born in Crete, Indiana, during the height of the Great Depression, on May 13, 1931.[1] His father was not an important part of his life and was thought to be a member of the Ku Klux Klan. His mother essentially raised him alone. As a child, a Pentecostal woman who lived in his neighborhood also influenced Jones. As a teen, Jones became a devout member of the Church of the Nazarene. He earned degrees from Indiana University and Butler University.

In September 1954, Jones was invited to preach at an Assemblies of God Pentecostal church. Although the church liked Jones and wanted to hire him, they would not approve his request for an interracial congregation. Jones decided to form his own interracial church on April 4, 1955, which he called the Wings of Deliverance. The church's name was later changed to the Peoples Temple. In 1960, the Peoples Temple was officially made a member of the Christian Church (Disciples of Christ) denomination in Indianapolis, and Jones was ordained as a minister, even though he had no formal theological training.

In 1965, Jones moved his congregation to northern California, where he said racial equality could grow unhindered. Jones also thought California would be a safer place than Indiana if a nuclear war broke out.[2] Seventy families, half black and half white, followed Jones to California.[3] In California, the members of the Peoples Temple lived a communal life. All items of value (income, real estate, insurance policies) were given to Jones, who liquidated and redistributed them equally among the members. Jones believed in catharsis (see Chapters 6 and 10), which involved public punishment for transgressions.[4] Guilt or innocence was determined by a vote of the congregation. Guilty children were often brutally spanked by Jones. Guilty adults were placed in a ring and forced to "box" with bigger and stronger congregation members. In California, the church grew to 20,000 members, and Jones amassed a fortune estimated at more than $15 million (worth over $112 million today).

In 1977, paranoia and unfavorable press reports led Jones to move his congregation again, this time to 4,000 acres of dense jungle in Guyana, on the northern coast of South America. At first only 50 people lived in this new community called Jonestown, but it grew to more than 900 residents. Conditions in the jungle were harsh. People worked long hours, lived in dormitories, and mainly ate beans and rice (meat and vegetables were reserved for meals with visitors). Meanwhile, Jones worked far fewer hours and lived in his own private house with a well-stocked refrigerator. Jones claimed that he needed the refrigerator because he had a blood sugar problem.

Much of the religion that Jones practiced was borrowed from the Pentecostal movement. Jones claimed to have the power to "discern spirits," the power of healing, and the prophetic ability to see into the future.[5] Jones also proclaimed himself to be the Second Coming of Christ.

Jones installed loudspeakers in Jonestown, and used them to indoctrinate his followers. He "read" the news to his followers, and frequently "portrayed the United States as beset by racial and economic problems."[6] Jones developed a belief called Translation, in which he and his followers would all die together and would move to another planet for an afterlife of bliss and harmony. He used the loudspeakers to practice what he called White Nights. In the middle of the night, sirens blared over the loudspeakers, and the residents would gather in the central pavilion. At the gathering, Jones told them that attacks by mercenaries were imminent, that the end was near, and that they would need to make the ultimate sacrifice for "the Cause." They lined up and drank a liquid described as poison, expecting to die. When they did not die, Jones told them that they had passed the "loyalty test."[7] However, he told them that if ever the colony was actually threatened by mercenaries, "revolutionary suicide" would be real, and it would demonstrate their devotion to "the Cause." Jones hired armed guards to fend off a possible mercenary invasion. The guards were also told to prevent residents from leaving Jonestown.

A few people did manage to leave Jonestown. Some of them formed a group called Concerned Relatives, which alleged that Jones had brainwashed his followers and was holding them in Guyana against their will.[8] The group found a voice in Congress through California Congressman Leo Ryan. On November 14, 1978, Ryan, a small group of media representatives, and several members of the Concerned Relatives group departed for Jonestown.[9] Ryan and his party interviewed several Jonestown residents, some of whom expressed a desire to leave. Jones told Ryan that the residents of Jonestown could come and go as they pleased. However, when Ryan attempted to take a group of 16 Jonestown residents back to the United States, armed guards opened fire on them, killing Ryan, three media representatives, and one Jonestown resident.[10]

Fearing retribution, Jones summoned his followers to the central pavilion. He said the end was near and the time had come for them to commit "revolutionary suicide." One woman dissented, but her opinion was quickly suppressed.[11] Jones ordered the residents to drink purple Kool-Aid (a flavored, sugary drink) laced with cyanide and a variety of sedatives and tranquilizers. The residents were organized into lines. First to drink were

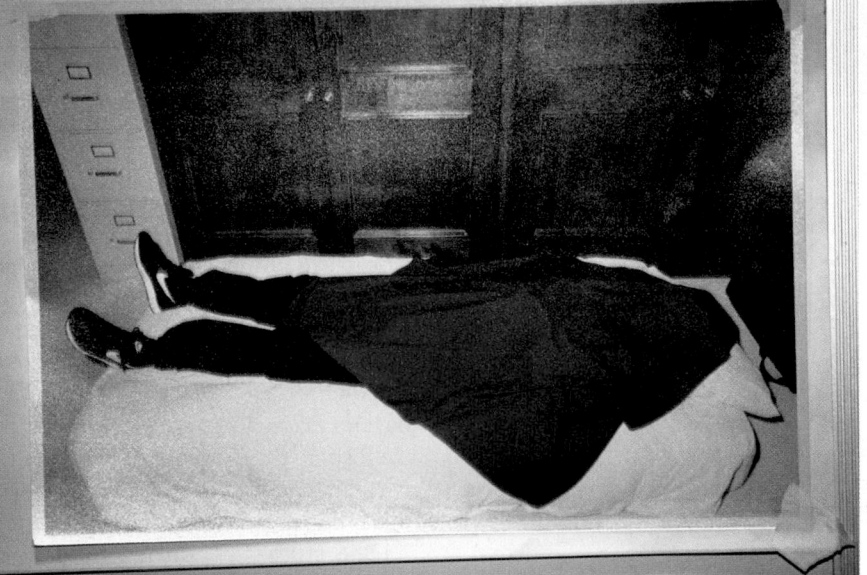

Jim Jones (left). At Jonestown, 914 people committed suicide (right). Only a few fled into the jungle to escape. Marshall Applewhite convinced 38 members of the Heaven's Gate cult to commit suicide.

the infants and children; many mothers poured the poison down their children's throats.[12] In the end, the body count was 914 people, including 276 children. Jones himself died by shooting himself in the head rather than drinking the poisoned Kool-Aid. A few residents fled into the jungle and survived.

This chapter is about social influence. The Peoples Temple story illustrates the extremes to which people can be influenced: hundreds of people voluntarily took their own lives. The Peoples Temple is perhaps the largest mass suicide in recent history, but others have occurred since then. Between 1994 and 1997, about 74 members of the Order of the Solar Temple committed suicide (usually on the dates of equinoxes and solstices).[13] They left letters stating they believed that their deaths provided an escape from the "hypocrisies and oppression of this world," and that they were "moving on to Sirius" (the brightest star in the night sky). In 1997, Marshall Applewhite and 38 other members of his Heaven's Gate cult committed mass suicide to "evacuate this Earth" which they believed was about to be "recycled."[14,15] To reach the Next Level of existence, they supposedly would board an alien spaceship that followed the

Hale-Bopp Comet. They lived together in a 9,200-square-foot (855-square-meter) Rancho Santa Fé, California, mansion they rented called "the Monastery" and "the Craft." They believed "to be eligible for membership in the Next Level, humans would have to shed every attachment to the planet." This means that members gave up family, friends, sex, jobs, money, all earthly possessions, and even their individuality (they were only referred to by first names). Indeed, eight male members (including Applewhite) had been castrated.[16] They believed that their bodies were only "vehicles"—decaying "containers" for their souls. Authorities found the dead lying in bunk beds, with their faces and torsos covered by a square, purple cloth. They were all dressed identically in black shirts and sweat pants, with new black-and-white Nike shoes, and armband patches reading "Heaven's Gate Away Team." Each member carried a five-dollar bill and three quarters in their pockets, for an "interplanetary toll." The group spent $10,000 on "alien abduction insurance," which covered up to 50 members.[17] Each body also had a travel bag next to it on the floor. Autopsies revealed that they had consumed a mixture of barbiturates and alcohol to induce

unconsciousness, followed by suffocation by a plastic bag placed over the head and secured at the neck with rubber bands.

Suicide bombers are another example of individuals who have been persuaded to voluntarily give up their own lives for the ostensible benefit of religious or political goals.

How could the leaders of the Peoples Temple and Heaven's Gate have had so much influence over their followers as to induce more than 900 of them to commit suicide? The use of force is one simple way to influence others. Aggression can be regarded as a form of social influence (see Chapter 10). Although aggression works in the short run, it backfires in the long run. Aggression has many unintended consequences and side effects that limit its usefulness. In addition, cultures generally frown on aggression and seek to restrain it. Accordingly, people have developed other, nonaggressive ways to influence each other.

As social animals, people are exceptionally responsive to each other. As cultural animals, people rely on each other for information about the world and for guidance about how to act in uncertain situations. This dependency on others creates opportunities for social influence. ●

Two Types of Social Influence

Social psychologists distinguish between two major categories of social influence: normative and informational.[18] Let us consider each of these in turn.

Being Liked and Accepted: Normative Influence

Normative influence involves going along with the crowd in order to be liked and accepted. As other chapters have emphasized, humans have a fundamental need to belong to social groups. Being accepted and included improves one's chances for survival (and improves life in many other ways). However, there is a long road to acceptance within the group. To live together, people usually need to agree on a set of common beliefs, values, attitudes, and behaviors that reduce ingroup threats and act for the common good. Therefore, people learn to conform to their group's rules. The more we see others behaving in a certain way or making particular decisions, the more we feel inclined to follow suit. This happens even when we are in a group of complete strangers: we will go along with the others to avoid looking like a fool.

The studies conducted by Solomon Asch illustrate the power of normative influence (also see Chapters 1 and 9).[19] Asch asked participants to judge which of three lines matched a comparison line. In some studies, the participant was asked last in a group of confederates, all of whom had been instructed to give the same wrong answer. Asch found that many participants went along with the confederates and gave the wrong answer, even though they could plainly see it was wrong, rather than deviate from the group. In some studies, Asch varied the discrepancy between the standard line and the comparison lines to discover the point at which the error made by the confederates was so glaring that no participants would conform. These manipulations did not eliminate the effect: Participants went along with the group

normative influence going along with the crowd in order to be liked and accepted

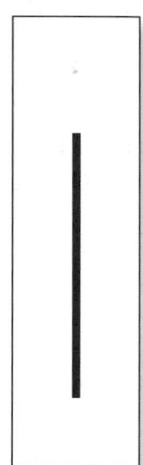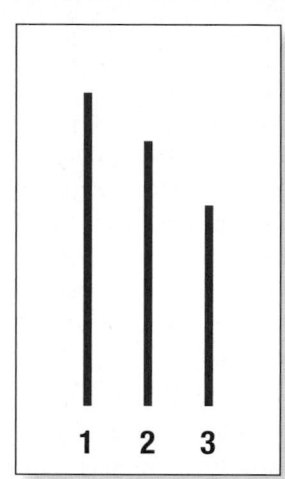

1 2 3

© Cengage Learning

© Archives of the History of American Psychology/U of Akron

Archives of the History of American Psychology/University of Akron

In the studies conducted by Asch, participants chose line 1, 2, or 3 as matching the comparison line (line in the box to the left of lines 1, 2, and 3). During the experiment, six of the seven people were confederates who gave the wrong answer (top right image). Most participants went along with the group even though the group gave an obviously wrong answer.

even when the group made flagrant errors. To be accepted by the group was more important to participants than to be correct.

Several factors influence whether people will conform to group norms. Asch varied the number of unanimous confederates from 1 to 15.[20] He found that conformity increases as group size increases up to a point, then it levels off (see **FIGURE 8.1**).

In another study, one of the confederates was a "dissenter" who always gave the correct answer.[21] A single dissenter reduced conformity by about one-fourth. In addition, participants who gave the correct answer reported feelings of warmth and closeness toward the dissenter. Asch wondered whether the dissenter reduced conformity because he was accurate or because he deviated from the other confederates. So Asch conducted another study in which the dissenter disagreed with the other confederates but chose another incorrect answer. Half the time the dissenter made a moderate error, choosing a line that was incorrect but not too far off; the other half of the time the dissenter made an extreme error. The results showed that when the dissenter made a moderate error, conformity decreased by about one-third; when the participants did make errors, most were moderate rather than extreme. When the dissenter made an extreme error, conformity decreased by almost three-fourths! Furthermore, when participants did make errors—and this occurred on only 9% of the trials—all of the errors were moderate, none extreme. Thus, the extreme dissenter had a remarkably freeing effect on participants. The implication is that people feel considerable pressure to conform to a group if everyone agrees, but if group members disagree about even the smallest point, then people become willing to stand up for what they believe.

When people deviate from group norms, they may pay a heavy price, including social rejection (see Chapter 11 for more on the psychology of rejection). Social rejection can be painful. Asch found that people would agree with the group, even when they knew the group was wrong, rather than suffer social rejection. Other research has shown that people who deviate from the group do indeed run a heightened risk of being rejected. For example, in an early study,[22] groups of eight individuals discussed the case of a juvenile delinquent named Johnny Rocco. Each group consisted of five real participants and three confederates. One confederate, the "deviant," adopted the extreme position of punishing Rocco severely and did not deviate from this position during group discussion. A second confederate, the "slider," first adopted the extreme position of punishing Rocco but then "slid" toward the position adopted by most group members. A third confederate, the "mode," adopted the position of most group members. At the end of the group discussion, the experimenter told everyone that a smaller group was needed for the next group discussion, so that the group needed to vote one member out. Most groups voted out the deviant. A review of similar studies showed that groups are quick to reject deviants or nonconformists.[23] Rejection is more likely when there are only one or two nonconformists than when there are many nonconformists.[24]

Being Correct: Informational Influence

If you look at a pinpoint of light in a dark room, the light appears to move even though it does not actually move at all. This illusion of movement, caused by very slight movements of the eye, is called the **autokinetic effect**.

Muzafer Sherif used the autokinetic effect to study the formation of group norms.[25] **Group norms** are the beliefs or behaviors that a group of people accepts as normal. Sherif asked individual participants in a dark room to estimate how far the light moved. Their individual estimates ranged from about 1 inch to about 8 inches (2.54 to 20.32 centimeters). They repeated this process on subsequent days, but in the presence of two other participants. As participants heard the estimates provided by others, their individual answers converged and became more similar (see **FIGURE 8.2**).

These social norms are not temporary, either; they can last at least one year.[26] These social norms can also be transmitted from one person to another. In another study that used the autokinetic effect,[27] researchers had a confederate give an inflated estimate of how far the light moved in the presence of a real participant. The confederate was then replaced

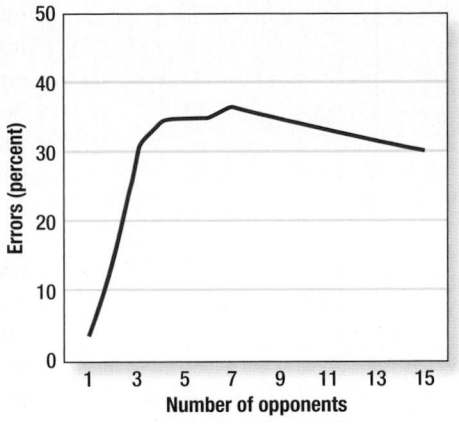

Size of the majority that opposed them had an effect on the participants. With a single opponent, the participant erred only 3.6% of the time; with two opponents, he erred 13.6%; three, 31.8%; four, 35.1%; six, 35.2%; seven, 37.1%; nine, 35.1%; fifteen, 31.2%.

© Cengage Learning

FIGURE **8.1**

Effect of group size on conformity in the Asch experiment: As the number of confederates increased from one to four, conformity increased dramatically; as more confederates were added, conformity leveled off.[19]

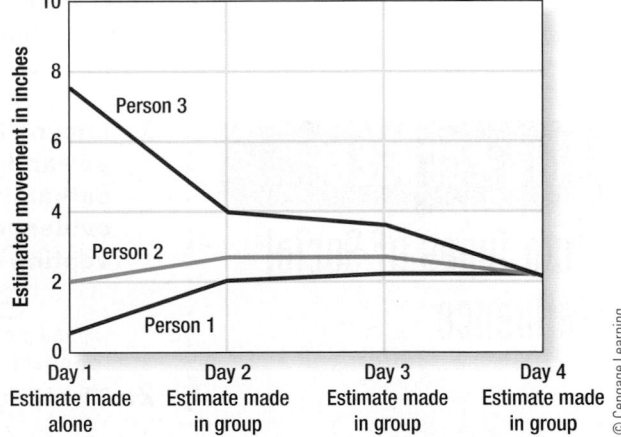

© Cengage Learning

FIGURE **8.2**

Sherif used the autokinetic effect to study the development of group norms.[25]

autokinetic effect illusion, caused by very slight movements of the eye, that a stationary point of light in a dark room is moving

group norms the beliefs or behaviors that a group of people accepts as normal

by a real participant, who was in turn replaced by another real participant, and so on. The inflated estimate persisted over five generations of research participants. Thus, people ended up conforming to the (false) norms set by someone who was by this point long gone.

The studies conducted by Sherif indicate a second type of social influence called informational influence. **Informational influence** involves going along with the crowd because you think the crowd knows more than you do (rather than because you want to be liked, as with normative social influence). It fits the "people first" theme we have seen throughout this book: People get valuable information from others, and sometimes they give more weight to what others think than to what their own eyes and ears tell them.

Two types of situations increase susceptibility to informational influence: (a) ambiguous situations, in which people do not know how to behave, and (b) crisis situations, in which people don't have time to think for themselves. In these situations, people conform to what others do because they assume that those other people must know what they are doing. Sometimes this assumption is wrong—others really do not know more than we do. In fact, others may assume that we know more than they do! In some cases, nobody knows anything, which is called a state of **pluralistic ignorance** (also see Chapter 9).

In short, there are two different kinds of social influence: normative and informational. A key difference is whether the conforming person comes to believe that others are right (informational) or believes they are wrong but conforms simply to avoid rejection, ridicule, hostility, or other kinds of punishment (normative). Informational social influence helps produce **private acceptance**—a genuine inner belief that others are right. Normative social influence may elicit mere **public compliance**—outwardly going along with the group but maintaining a private, inner belief that the group is wrong, or at least entertaining serious doubts about the group's decision.

The Jonestown example contained both types of influence. Some people probably believed that Jones was a great religious leader with correct views because others who expressed those beliefs surrounded him. Others went along under pressure of punishment and threat of death. As a less extreme example, some people become vegetarian because they believe it is a healthier lifestyle and better for the planet (private acceptance), whereas others might become vegetarian because all their friends think it is trendy and cool, even though inwardly they still love to eat meat (public compliance).

informational influence going along with the crowd because you think the crowd knows more than you do

pluralistic ignorance looking to others for cues about how to behave, while they are looking to you; collective misinterpretation

private acceptance a genuine inner belief that others are right

public compliance outwardly going along with the group but maintaining a private, inner belief that the group is probably wrong

QUIZ YOURSELF
Two Types of Social Influence

1. **Lucyna initially believes that when she becomes angry it is helpful to yell and scream to vent her anger. This emotional cleansing is called catharsis. After listening to her professor's lecture on the research evidence contradicting catharsis, Lucyna no longer believes that venting works. This change in belief illustrates _____.**

   (a) the autokinetic effect
   (b) informational influence
   (c) normative influence
   (d) public compliance

2. **The autokinetic effect is a(n) _____.**

   (a) false group consensus
   (b) group norm
   (c) illusion of perceived movement
   (d) influential bias in social influence

3. **The type of conformity based on a fear of social rejection is called _____.**

   (a) ingratiation
   (b) modeling
   (c) private acceptance
   (d) public compliance

4. **Tyrone plans to vote for candidate Duck in the local elections. Before he votes, his friends explain why they're going to vote for candidate Goose. In the voting booth, Tyrone votes for candidate Goose. This is an example of _____.**

   (a) private acceptance
   (b) psychological reactance
   (c) public compliance
   (d) reciprocity

answers: see pg 289

Techniques of Social Influence

The previous section discussed influence as a matter of people feeling pressure to conform. In those cases, the influencer only offers information or dangles the possibility of social acceptance. In this section, we look at how influencers take a more active approach to altering another person's behavior, in ways that go far beyond conformity.

As Chapter 5 suggested, a primary purpose of human reasoning is to influence others, such as by arguing.[28] Social influence techniques can be organized according to four basic principles: (1) commitment and consistency, (2) reciprocation, (3) scarcity, and (4) capturing and disrupting attention. Not all the techniques in the following sections were discovered by social psychologists. As you will see, salespersons have been experimenting with ways of influencing people for a very long time.

Techniques Based on Commitment and Consistency

Several techniques of influence are based on the principle of commitment and consistency.[29] Once people make a commitment, they feel pressure (both from inside themselves and from others) to behave consistently with that commitment. Inconsistent behavior causes a form of psychological discomfort called cognitive dissonance (see Chapter 7). The influence techniques in this section exploit that principle: Get the person to commit to what you want, and the person is likely to do it. Seemingly trivial commitments can lead to substantial compliance on more important things.

Foot-in-the-Door Technique

Cult recruiters don't just ask a complete stranger on the street, "Hey, you! Do you want to give us all your belongings and join our cult today?" Getting someone to join a cult and stay with it up through mass suicide takes powerful influence. How Jim Jones recruited followers is very revealing.[30] Members of the Peoples Temple would ask a passerby to help for just five minutes by stuffing and mailing a few envelopes. Jim Jones explained, "They came back for more. You know, once I get somebody, I can get them to do anything." When the person became a member of the Peoples Temple, monetary contributions were voluntary at first. Then, Jones asked for a 10% contribution, or tithe. After that, he required a 25% contribution. Finally, he required members to give him everything they had—a 100% contribution. Another example: Jones asked his followers to move from Indiana to California before he asked them to move to Jonestown in the jungles of Guyana.

The technique in the examples above is called the **foot-in-the-door technique**. It is based on the principle of starting with a small request in order to get eventual compliance with a much larger request. The term refers to the efforts of old-fashioned door-to-door salespeople to get "one foot in the door" as a prerequisite to getting their whole body into the house. (The assumption was that the customer won't slam the door in your face as long as your foot is in the way.) Complying with small requests seems like no big deal, but it increases the likelihood of complying with larger requests later on. It is easier to comply the second time than the first time. If requests get bigger slowly and gradually, the person may be more willing to comply with each one than if the other had started with a large request.

In a classic study conducted in the 1960s,[31] researchers telephoned housewives in California and asked if they would answer a few questions about the household products they used. Three days later, the researcher called again. This time, the housewives were asked if a survey team of five or six men could come into their homes for two hours to catalog all their household products. The investigators found that the women who agreed to the small request were more than twice as likely to agree to the two-hour request than a group of housewives who were asked only the larger request (53% versus 22%).

foot-in-the-door technique influence technique based on commitment, in which one starts with a small request in order to gain eventual compliance with a larger request

"Would you like to super-size that?"

Car salespeople sometimes use the low-ball technique.

Low-Ball Technique

A second approach that shifts from a smaller request to a larger request is the **low-ball technique**. In this technique, the requester first gets a person to comply with a seemingly low-cost request and only later reveals hidden additional costs. Car salespeople sometimes try this technique on potential customers. You come into a car dealership and test drive a car you really want to buy. The salesperson quotes you an excellent price, you agree to the deal, and you sign an offer. The salesperson goes to talk to the sales manager and then returns with some "bad news" (e.g., you will only get $400 on your trade-in, rather than the $2,000 you had been promised; the wireless audio system with 18 speakers costs extra, even though the salesperson had told you it came with the car; or perhaps the sales price you were offered was an error and must be raised $500). The original price is really a "low ball" that the salesperson threw at you.

In one test of the low-ball influence technique, college students were recruited to participate in a study on "thinking processes" that was to be conducted at 7:00 in the morning.[32] Half of the students were thrown a low ball: The researcher asked if they would be interested in participating in a study on thinking processes *before* telling them they would have to be at the lab at 7 a.m. After they agreed to participate, the researcher told them the bad news about the early scheduling. Even though the researcher gave them a chance to change their minds, 56% agreed to participate. In contrast, among students who were told of the starting time before they made a commitment, only 24% agreed to participate. The low-balled participants were also more likely than the others to actually show up for the study. Thus, the low-ball technique increased both promises to comply and actual compliance.

Although the low-ball technique is considered unscrupulous, it often works. Why? As with the foot-in-the-door technique, it is based on the principle of commitment and consistency. Commitments have a tendency to "grow their own legs";[33] that is, people often add new reasons and justifications to support their initial commitment. One lesson we learned from cognitive dissonance theory is that people like to justify their decisions (see Chapter 7). Your initial decision to buy the car was based on a single "leg"—the great initial offer the salesperson quoted you. But then other legs start growing. You like the color. It's fast. It smells good inside. The wireless sound system that connects to your new iPhone sounds great. And so on. The salesperson then throws a low ball that knocks over the leg that initially held up your decision to buy the car (the great initial offer), but the decision doesn't fall through because now all the new legs are holding it up. You fulfill your commitment and buy the car.

Bait-and-Switch Technique

Car salespeople also use a technique called **bait-and-switch**. The car dealership places an ad for a car at a great price, but when you get to the showroom the car is "sold out." The dealership placed the ad simply to get you into the showroom. Once you are there, they can try to sell you another car. You are baited with one car (usually a stripped-down model with no options, sold at an unbelievably low price), and then you are switched to another car (usually a fully loaded model that goes for a much higher price). The American Bar Association warns consumers that this technique is illegal and fraudulent.

The bait-and-switch technique is used by businesses other than car sales. For example, you may go to a store because they advertised a product you want, but when you get to the store you discover that the product is sold out. Since you are already at the store, you decide to go shopping anyway. The ad served its purpose—it got you into the store.

The bait-and-switch technique, like the low-ball and foot-in-the-door techniques, is based on the principle of commitment and consistency.[34] It gets people to make a psychological commitment, and then relies on consistency pressures to keep them loyal to this commitment even when the influencer changes the terms.

low-ball technique influence technique based on commitment, in which one first gets a person to comply with a seemingly low-cost request and only later reveals hidden additional costs

bait-and-switch technique influence technique based on commitment, in which one draws people in with an attractive offer that is unavailable and then switches them to a less attractive offer that is available

Labeling Technique

The **labeling technique** is another way to induce compliance. It involves assigning a label to an individual and then requesting a favor that is consistent with the label. Former Egyptian President Anwar Sadat used the labeling technique to persuade those he negotiated with.[35] Before negotiations began, Sadat would tell his opponents that they and the citizens of their country were widely known for being cooperative and fair. In doing so, Sadat gave his opponents a label to live up to. According to former Secretary of State Henry Kissinger, Sadat was a successful negotiator because he understood how to get others to act on his behalf by giving them a reputation to uphold. The labeling technique is related to the self-fulfilling prophecy (see Chapter 13). People tend to live up to the positive labels others give them.

Research has shown that the labeling technique can persuade both children and adults. Elementary school children who are told by an adult "You look to me like the kind of girl (or boy) who understands how important it is to write correctly" were more likely to choose a penmanship task several days later than were children who were not labeled.[36] Similarly, adults who were previously told that they were "above average citizens" were more likely to vote several days later than were adults previously told that they were "average citizens."[37]

The labeling technique is also based on the commitment and consistency principle. Whether positive labels are assigned by oneself or by others, people like to live up to them. Labeling also uses the importance of self-concepts (see Chapter 3). How people think about themselves can influence their behavior. Thus, if you want to influence that person's behavior, an effective technique is to get the person to think of himself or herself in a manner that will produce the desired result. A person who thinks of herself as helpful will often be more helpful than a person who doesn't.

People also do not want to be labeled as cheap. Hence, they may find it hard to refuse a very small request. To see how this can lead to persuasion, read the *Money Matters* box.

Defenses Against Techniques Based on Commitment and Consistency

Several influence techniques are based on the principle of commitment and consistency, including the foot-in-the-door technique, the low-ball technique, the bait-and-switch technique, the labeling technique, and the legitimization-of-paltry-favors technique. The commitment and consistency principle is a great time saver. If people had to weigh the pros and cons of each decision, they would soon feel overwhelmed, and they would not

labeling technique influence technique based on consistency, in which one assigns a label to an individual and then requests a favor that is consistent with the label

---

MONEY *Matters*

Even a Penny Will Help

Asking for donations is hard work, and one gets used to refusals. Researchers developed a clever technique to make it harder for people to say no. In their study,[38] some confederates simply asked for a donation to the American Cancer Society, while others added the phrase "Even a penny (cent) will help." Adding the latter phrase nearly doubled the rate at which people said yes and gave a donation.

Of course, getting donations of only a penny would not really be of much help to the American Cancer Society! But the researchers found that the average size of the donations did not change, even while more people donated. Thus, the even-a-penny method produced many more donations of the same approximate size, resulting in a big increase in total amount.

Why? Most reasons people give for refusing resemble, "I do not have enough money to donate," but such reasons do not work with the even-a-penny method. Everyone can afford to give a penny! To refuse a request when even a penny would be acceptable might make the refuser feel cheap and petty. Apparently, though, once people decide to go ahead and donate, they donate the amount they would normally give (rather than just giving a penny).

© Shebeko/Shutterstock.com

be able to function. It is much easier to make a commitment once and then behave consistently with that commitment.

The power of the commitment and consistency principle comes from the sense of obligation it creates. When people freely make commitments, they feel obligated to behave consistently with those commitments. Behaving inconsistently has personal and interpersonal costs. Personally, inconsistency between one's attitudes and actions can result in cognitive dissonance, which is an unpleasant emotional response (see Chapter 7). Interpersonally, if your inconsistent behaviors affect others, you may suffer social rejection and ostracism, which don't feel good either. However, you should *not* feel obligated to behave consistently with a commitment that you were tricked into making. If it is not clear whether you were tricked into making a commitment, ask yourself this question: "Knowing what I know now, if I could go back in time, would I make the same commitment?"[39] If the answer is "yes," behave consistently with the commitment. If the answer is "no," don't do it!

Another way to resist influence is to make a public commitment to your position.[40] Commitments are much more binding when they are made in public than when they are made in private. Standing up for your convictions in public makes you less susceptible to what others have to say.

Techniques Based on Reciprocation

Reciprocity—if you take care of me, I will take care of you—is one of the foundations of culture. All cultures understand reciprocity and expect people to obey its norms. The appreciation of reciprocity is deeply rooted in human nature; one sign of this is that people feel guilty if someone does them a favor and they cannot repay it in some way. This sentiment is the foundation for some of the best moral behavior and good treatment of others. Unfortunately, it is also something that sneaky people can exploit to influence others. Two influence techniques are based on reciprocation: door-in-the-face and that's-not-all.[41]

Door-in-the-Face Technique

An effective way to get people to comply with a request is to start by making an inflated request (that will most likely be rejected) and then retreat to a smaller request. The smaller request, the one that was desired all along, is likely to be accepted because it appears to be a concession. This is called the **door-in-the-face technique** because the first refusal is like slamming a door in the face of the person making the request. It is opposite of the foot-in-the door technique, which starts with a small request in order to get compliance to a larger request. In negotiations between labor and management, both sides often use this tactic. They initially make extreme demands that they do not expect to get. Later they retreat to more reasonable demands. Although the expression "door in the face" vividly describes the procedure, the key to compliance is not the initial refusal but rather reciprocity. After the first offer is refused, the salesperson or negotiator makes a more reasonable offer, and people feel obliged to reciprocate this seemingly kind and generous offer by becoming more agreeable themselves.

To demonstrate the door-in-the-face method, researchers asked people if they would volunteer two hours per week for at least two years in a community mental health agency.[42] They all said "No." Next, they were asked if they would volunteer for two hours on a single occasion. About 76% of participants volunteered. In contrast, only 29% volunteered if they were just asked to work two hours on a single occasion (without the prior request for two years). Moreover, the door-in-the-face people were not simply agreeing without meaning to follow through. Among all those who volunteered, 85% of participants in the door-in-the-face group showed up, whereas only 50% of participants in the control group showed up, which coincides with the commitment and consistency principle described earlier.

The door-in-the-face technique does not work, however, if the first request is so extreme that it is seen as unreasonable.[43] The door-in-the-face technique also does not work if different people make the first and second requests.[44] This probably reflects the importance of reciprocation. The key to getting someone to agree is to pretend you are

door-in-the-face technique influence technique based on reciprocity, in which one starts with an inflated request and then retreats to a smaller request that appears to be a concession

The door-in-the-face technique is often effective.

doing the person a favor by reducing your request to a much more reasonable level, so the person will feel an obligation to agree to it. If the second offer or request comes from someone different, no sense of reciprocal obligation is created.

That's-Not-All Technique

The **that's-not-all technique** like the door-in-the-face technique, begins with an inflated request. However, before the person can respond, the requester "sweetens" the deal by offering a discount or bonus. Perhaps you've seen this technique on television. First, the "regular" price is reduced, and then several additional bonuses are added, such as getting two items for the price of one.

At a cupcake booth on a college campus, researchers conducted a field experiment to test the that's-not-all technique.[45] Customers were randomly assigned to one of three conditions. In the that's-not-all group, one researcher told the customer that the cupcakes cost $1.25. At this point, a second researcher tapped the first researcher on the shoulder. Before the customer could say anything, the first researcher raised his hand and said, "Wait a second." After a brief conversation with the

"How much would you pay for all the secrets of the universe? Wait, don't answer yet. You also get this six-quart covered combination spaghetti pot and clam steamer. Now how much would you pay?"

The that's-not-all technique is effective, too.

second researcher, the first researcher told the customer that he would lower the price to $1.00 because they were planning to close the booth soon. In the bargain group, the participant was told, "These are only $1.00 now. We were selling them for $1.25 earlier." In the control group, customers were simply told that the cupcakes cost $1.00. The results showed that more customers in the "that's-not-all" group bought cupcakes (55%) than in the bargain (25%) or control (20%) groups. Customers in the "that's-not-all" group most likely complied more because they felt as if the researcher were doing them a personal favor, whereas in the bargain group, the researcher did the same favor for everyone. People felt most obligated to reciprocate when they believed the seller was making an exception for them personally.

The that's-not-all technique, like the door-in-the-face technique, is based on reciprocal concessions and a sense of personal obligation. When a stranger or interaction partner does something kind for you, you feel an obligation to do something nice or kind in return. A discount or bonus can increase compliance by sweetening the deal. Reciprocity is one of the most basic traits of human beings because it goes to the essence of what a cultural

that's-not-all technique influence technique based on reciprocity, in which one first makes an inflated request but, before the person can respond, sweetens the deal by offering a discount or bonus

animal is. It is in our genes to pay back what others do for us and to recognize when other people do—or do not—reciprocate. Thus, people can be readily exploited by unscrupulous salespeople who take advantage of their basic human tendency to reciprocate.

Defenses Against Techniques Based on Reciprocation

Ralph Waldo Emerson said, "Pay every debt, as if God wrote the bill." He was advocating the value of the principle of reciprocation: People should feel obligated to repay favors and concessions. If people don't reciprocate, they feel guilty. Guilt often induces prosocial behavior (see Chapter 6).

Generally, the principle of reciprocation is beneficial to society. It allows us to give, knowing that if people cast their bread upon the water it will come back to them, as the Judeo-Christian Bible advises.[46] The problem is that some people (those who want to persuade us) cast a crumb on the water and expect a loaf of bread in return. For example, a charitable organization may give us inexpensive address labels and expect a large donation in return.

This chapter discussed two influence techniques based on reciprocal concessions: the door-in-the-face technique and the that's-not-all technique. How do we defend ourselves against people who use these techniques to manipulate us? Robert Cialdini, a social psychologist famous for his studies on influence, recommends that we accept initial favors or concessions in good faith, but be ready to define them as tricks if they prove to be tricks.[47] Once they are defined as tricks, we will no longer feel obligated to reciprocate them with a favor or concession. The reciprocation rule says that favors are to be repaid with favors. Tricks do not have to be repaid with favors!

Techniques Based on Scarcity

According to the scarcity principle, rare opportunities are more valuable than plentiful opportunities. Even everyday items can become valuable when they are scarce. For example, the starting bid for a one-of-a-kind rock that looks like barbecued pork was $1,255,000 on an eBay auction. People quickly get caught up in competitive situations for valuable items.

Scarcity is sometimes used as a heuristic cue in decision making—what is rare is good. The scarcity heuristic is illustrated by the results of a consumer preferences study.[48] Participants were each given a cookie to taste and rate. Some participants received the cookie from a jar containing 10 cookies, whereas others received the cookie from a jar containing only 2 cookies. Even though the cookies were identical, the people who took the cookie from the jar containing only 2 cookies rated it higher than did the people who took the cookie from the jar containing 10 cookies.

One reason why the scarcity principle works is because it takes more effort to obtain rare items than plentiful items. Often we have to compete with others for scarce opportunities. Perhaps that is why potential lovers and potential employees "play hard to get." They want others to think that they are a hot commodity with lots of options. If you don't agree to the person's request, you could lose a valuable partner or employee.

Another reason why the scarcity principle works is that people, especially those from individualistic cultures, highly value their freedom. As opportunities become scarce, we lose our freedom to obtain them. When our personal freedom is threatened, we experience an unpleasant emotional response called psychological reactance (see Chapter 4). This unpleasant emotion motivates us to obtain the scarce opportunity.

Various influence techniques are based on scarcity. One is the **limited-number technique** saying that only a limited number of these products will be available. Another is the **fast-approaching-deadline technique** saying that an item or a price is only available for a limited time (e.g., last day of sale). The point of both is that your chances to buy the product are limited, either by how few there are or by the deadline.

Defenses Against Techniques Based on Scarcity

The principle of scarcity generally serves people well. Scarce items usually are more valuable than plentiful items. In the influence business, however, people often use the

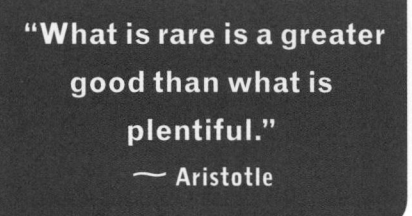

> "What is rare is a greater good than what is plentiful."
> — Aristotle

limited-number technique influence technique based on scarcity, in which one tells people that an item is in short supply

fast-approaching-deadline technique influence technique based on scarcity, in which one tells people an item or a price is only available for a limited time

scarcity principle to convince us that their products are scarce and that we should get them now, while we can, even when plenty may be in stock.

We discussed two techniques based on scarcity: the limited-number technique and the fast-approaching-deadline technique. How do we defend ourselves against people who use these techniques to influence us? It is easier said than done! Our natural response to scarcity is to panic. We want to seize the opportunity before it slips away. When our freedom is threatened, we experience psychological reactance (see Chapter 4). Unfortunately, this emotional response to scarcity interferes with our ability to think clearly. Robert Cialdini recommends a two-stage process of resistance.[49] First, we should use the tide of emotional arousal we feel in response to scarce items as a cue to stop short. We need to calm ourselves so we can think clearly and rationally. Second, we should ask why we want the item. Is it because it is scarce, or is it because of its own merits? "Because it is the last day of a sale" or "because it is the last one" is not a good reason for purchasing an item. We should buy something only if we really want it, not because it is scarce.

Techniques Based on Capturing and Disrupting Attention

Other influence techniques try to capture the attention of the target of influence, or try to distract the target of influence. When influencers have strong arguments, they want to attract the attention of targets because they want people to think about the convincing arguments. When influencers have weak arguments, they want to disrupt the attention of targets so they won't think too deeply about the unconvincing arguments (also see discussion of the elaboration likelihood model in a later section of this chapter).

Pique Technique

Often when panhandlers approach us, they ask, "Can you spare a quarter?" or "Can you spare any change?" People who live in large cities have heard these requests so many times that they often just ignore the panhandler and move on. Pedestrians have a refusal script in mind the instant they see a panhandler, such as "Sorry, I don't have any change." To be effective, the panhandler must disrupt this refusal script and capture the pedestrian's attention. The **pique technique** captures the pedestrian's attention by making the request novel. In a field study,[50] confederates disguised as panhandlers asked pedestrians whether they had any change, or they asked them whether they had 17 cents. Thirty-seven percent of pedestrians complied with the request for 17 cents, whereas only 23% complied with the spare change request. It helps to grab people's attention before they tune out.

The pique technique has also been used to influence drivers to slow down in residential areas. Aspen, Colorado, has a new speed limit in its residential area—14 miles per hour (mph) (or 22.53 kph). "It gets people's attention," said Aspen's mayor. "I don't think many people even notice regular speed limit signs anymore."[51] Based on this research, the mayor is probably right.

Disrupt-Then-Reframe

In the **disrupt-then-reframe technique** a non sequitur or unexpected element is introduced to provide a momentary disruption. The disruption absorbs critical thinking functions and prevents individuals from processing the persuasive message. The requester then reframes the message in a positive light.

For example, researchers managed to disrupt attention by stating the price of Christmas cards in pennies (rather than dollars) before stating, "It's a bargain!"[52] When homeowners were told that a package of eight cards cost $3, about 40% of the homeowners bought the cards. When homeowners were told the cards cost 300 pennies (the disruption), "which is a bargain" (the reframing), about 80% of the homeowners bought the cards. To work, this technique requires both the disruption and the reframing, in that order. Distraction prevents people from processing persuasive messages at a deep level.

As you may have noticed, many influence and persuasion techniques are based on the duplex mind. In many cases, persuaders want to influence someone to do something

pique technique influence technique in which one captures people's attention, as by making a novel request.

disrupt-then-reframe technique influence technique in which one disrupts critical thinking by introducing an unexpected element, then reframes the message in a positive light

that he or she would not sensibly do. The deliberate mind is therefore the enemy, and the persuaders seek to neutralize and bypass it by working with the automatic mind. For example, your willingness to buy something ought to be the same regardless of whether its price is 3 dollars or 300 cents. But it takes deliberate processing to recognize that those are the same and that one's willingness to buy should be the same. The automatic system is more susceptible to such tricks and biases, so persuaders prefer to work with it—and to keep the deliberate mind from getting involved.

Defenses Against Techniques Based on Capturing and Disrupting Attention

The pique technique is based on capturing attention. It catches people off guard, so they comply without thinking. Thus, the antidote is to stop and think before acting. Whether someone asks you for a quarter or for 17 cents should not determine whether you comply.

The disrupt-then-reframe technique is based on disrupting attention. Distraction increases persuasion for weak messages and decreases persuasion for strong messages. The key, therefore, is to eliminate the distraction so you can process the message at a deep level.

QUIZ YOURSELF

Techniques of Social Influence

answers: see pg 289

1. The technique in which an influencer prefaces the real request by first getting the person to agree to a smaller request is called the _____ technique.

   (a) door-in-the-face   (b) foot-in-the-door   (c) low-ball   (d) pique

2. The class first asks their professor to cancel the next exam. The professor says, "No way!" The class then asks the professor to postpone the exam one week. The professor says, "Okay." This is an example of what technique?

   (a) Disrupt-then-reframe   (b) Door-in-the-face   (c) Foot-in-the-door   (d) Low-ball

3. Mohamed accepts a job to shingle the roof of a house. He later learns that he also is expected to shingle the detached garage as part of the original agreement. This is an example of what technique?

   (a) Door-in-the-face   (b) Legitimization of paltry favors   (c) Low-ball   (d) That's-not-all

4. Which of the following is an explanation of the fast-approaching-deadline technique?

   (a) Capturing and disrupting attention   (b) Commitment and consistency   (c) Reciprocity   (d) Scarcity

Persuasion

One important form of social influence is persuasion. A primary purpose of the human brain is to influence others and argue with them in an attempt to persuade them.[53] **Persuasion** is an attempt to change a person's attitude. (See Chapter 7 for a discussion on attitudes.) The scientific study of persuasion can be traced back to Carl Hovland, a social psychologist at Yale University. Hovland received a contract from the U.S. Army to study the morale of soldiers. President Franklin D. Roosevelt was worried that American

persuasion an attempt to change a person's attitude

soldiers would lose their will to fight Japan after defeating the German Nazis. White House adviser Lowell Mellett was told that the newly drafted soldiers "haven't the slightest enthusiasm for this war or this cause. They are not grouchy, they are not mutinous, they just don't give a tinker's dam."[54] The Army Morale Branch tried to improve soldier morale, but failed due to the "deadly effects of prepared lectures indifferently read to bored troops." The War Department hired Frank Capra, of Fox and Disney studios, to produce a series of films called *Why We Fight*. From 1942 to 1945 Hovland worked in Washington, D.C., to study the effects of these films on soldier morale.[55] Hovland conducted more than 50 experiments on persuasion and found that although the films were successful in helping soldiers understand the factual basis of the war, they were unsuccessful at motivating soldiers to fight the war. Soldiers were no more eager to die for America after watching films than before.

After the war, Hovland returned to Yale University. The Rockefeller Foundation gave him a grant to continue his studies on persuasion and communication. Hovland and his colleagues conducted a systematic program of research that analyzed the process and effectiveness of persuasion in terms of "who says what to whom."[56] The "who" component is the source of the message, such as a person who is making a speech. The "says what" component is the actual message, such as the content of the speech. The "to whom" component is the audience, the people who hear the speech. Whether persuasion succeeds or fails can be shaped by any and all of those factors.

Aristotle had proposed these same three components of persuasion more than 2,000 years before Hovland was born. In *Rhetoric*, Aristotle specified three components of the persuasive process: the speaker, the subject of the speech, and the hearer to whom the speech is addressed.[57] Aristotle also identified three elements necessary to persuade an audience: (a) emotional appeal (pathos), (b) intellectual appeal (logos), and (c) charisma (ethos). As we have seen, when social psychologists take up an idea, they often find they are not the first to have thought of it. But they can test and evaluate ideas using the experimental method and thereby make an important, original contribution to understanding. Aristotle was brilliant, but he conducted no experiments. Many seemingly brilliant ideas turn out to be wrong, and only careful testing can determine which ones are correct.

Who: The Source

Perhaps the most important characteristics of the source of a message are credibility and likability. Let's look at both of these important characteristics.

Source Credibility

The **source** is the individual who delivers the message. A source can be credible or not credible. According to the Merriam-Webster dictionary, credibility is "the quality or power of inspiring belief." However, a source may inspire belief in some situations but not others. For example, an actor like Brad Pitt is a credible source for acting, but he is not a credible source on China or Tibet. Sometimes people are downright uncredible sources. For example, a university professor from Rome invited Francesco Schettino, the former skipper of the Costa Concordia cruise ship, to give a two-hour lecture on the topic of "best emergency practices." Italy's education minister was upset by this choice because at the time Schettino was on trial for manslaughter and abandoning ship when the luxury cruise ship he captained hit a reef and sank. The ship contained 4,229 people, and 32 of them died. Schettino is probably the worst possible choice for a lecture on best emergency practices since he violated many of them.

Speaker credibility was the topic of a famous early series of studies by Hovland and Weiss.[58] For example, participants read one speech advocating the development of atomic submarines. By random assignment, the speaker was said to be either a well-known physicist (Robert J. Oppenheimer, called the "father of the atomic bomb") or a writer for *Pravda* (the newspaper of the Communist Party in the former Soviet Union). Participants reported their opinions about the topics in the speeches before, immediately after, and a month after reading the speeches. The results showed that immediately after reading the speech, highly credible sources produced more opinion change than did less credible sources.

> "You shouldn't speak until you know what you're talking about. Reporters ask me what I feel China should do about Tibet. Who cares what I think China should do? I'm an actor! They hand me a script. I act. I'm here for entertainment. Basically, when you whittle everything away, I'm a grown man who puts on makeup."
> — Brad Pitt, American actor

source the individual who delivers the message

A month later, however, opinion for the less credible source increased and that for the highly credible source decreased. Therefore, in the long run, the overall amount of opinion change was about the same for the two sources. Hovland and Weiss called this the **sleeper effect**. Over time, people separated the message from the messenger. If they remembered the speech, they forgot who gave it. Subsequent research has shown that the sleeper effect is a very reliable effect.[61]

What makes a source credible? Hovland identified two characteristics: **expertise** which is how much the source knows, and **trustworthiness** which is whether the source will honestly tell you what he or she knows. Experts can influence us because we assume they know what they are talking about. But experts cannot be persuasive unless we trust them. A Gallup poll of American adults showed that the general public perceived lobbyists, car salespeople, members of Congress, and advertisers as the least trustworthy people.[62] After the U.S. government shutdown in 2013, people liked Congress *less* than hemorrhoids, dog poop, zombies, witches, cockroaches, toenail fungus, jury duty, potholes, and the IRS (Internal Revenue Service that collects taxes), to name a few.[63] Those considered most trustworthy were nurses, military officers, pharmacists, and grade school teachers. The main difference between the two groups of people is that the first group has something to sell, and therefore something to gain—your money! Corroborating the results of this poll, research shows that a physician from a drug company claiming that its company's

sleeper effect the finding that, over time, people separate the message from the messenger

expertise how much a source knows

trustworthiness whether a source will honestly tell you what he or she knows

convert communicators people perceived as credible sources because they are arguing against their own previously held attitudes and behaviors

FOOD FOR *Thought*

Convert Communicators and Health Messages

Usually experts must be trustworthy to be credible. However, people can make up for their deficits in trustworthiness by arguing against their past transgressions. Such people are called **convert communicators** and they can be quite persuasive.[59] This tactic is especially effective when used by low-status communicators that audiences might otherwise ignore. Because of the commitment and consistency principle, we take notice when people argue against their previously held attitudes and behaviors. Drug addicts, alcoholics, and chain-smokers may lack status and prestige, but they can still be very credible sources when they tell us how they overcame their undesirable behaviors.

For example, for many years Subway ads featured Jared Fogle, a man who lost an amazing 235 pounds by eating low-calorie, low-fat Subway sandwiches instead of high-calorie, high-fat foods. In less than a year, he went from 425 pounds to 190 pounds. Obese people may listen to Jared because he was probably heavier than they are now and they may be impressed by how much weight

he lost. Jared Fogle was a good convert communicator until he become involved in child pornography and started paying minors for sex.

Convert communicators are likable because they are similar to audience members. They also show a sense of mastery because they were able to overcome their undesirable behavior, which enhances their credibility. For example, research has shown that a reformed alcoholic is a much more persuasive source than a lifelong teetotaler on the subject of the importance of abstaining from alcohol.

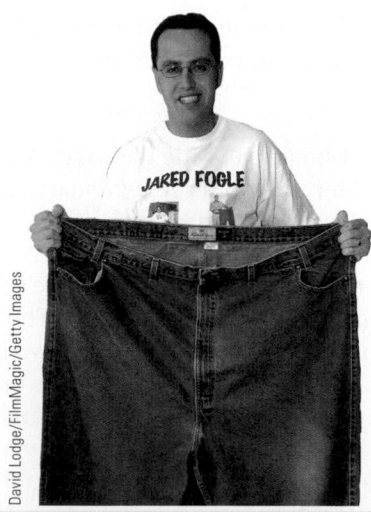

David Lodge/FilmMagic/Getty Images

Convert communicators who describe how they overcame obstacles can be very persuasive. For example, Jared Fogle lost 235 pounds in less than a year by eating low-calorie, low-fat Subway sandwiches instead of high-calorie, high-fat foods. The company took advantage of his credibility by featuring him in their advertisements.

Italy's education minister was outraged after discovering that the captain of the sunken Italian cruise ship, the Costa Concordia, had been invited to deliver a lecture to La Sapienza university students on "best emergency practices."

drug was safe was less persuasive than the Food and Drug Administration (FDA) making the same claim.[64] *Food for Thought* explains yet another way that communicators can be persuasive by being especially trustworthy.

Powerful speakers are assumed to be credible sources.[65,66] Powerless speech, such as speech containing disclaimers (e.g., "I'm not an expert, but ..."), detracts from the speaker's credibility and therefore is less successful at exerting influence.

Although he didn't conduct any research on the topic, Aristotle recognized the importance of source credibility in persuasion. According to Aristotle, "Persuasion is accomplished by a character whenever the speech is held in such a way as to render the speaker worthy of credence." According to Aristotle, credible speakers display "(i) practical intelligence (*phronêsis*), (ii) a virtuous character, and (iii) good will."[67] Aristotle's list of characteristics resembles those proposed by Hovland's group. Practical intelligence is similar to expertise—expert sources are intelligent and know what they are talking about. "Virtuous character" and goodwill are similar to trustworthiness—trustworthy sources appear to be honest, virtuous, and good-willed. Aristotle argued that if the speaker displayed practical intelligence without virtuosity and goodwill, the audience would doubt the speaker's aims, but that if the speaker displayed all three characteristics, "it cannot rationally be doubted that his suggestions are credible." It is not necessary that the speaker actually possess any of these characteristics—only that the audience believes that the speaker has these characteristics.

In addition to the perceived character of a speaker, other factors make a speaker more or less credible. One such factor is how fast the speaker talks. Does talking fast make a speaker more credible? To find out, see *Tradeoffs*.

Source Likability

We are also persuaded by sources we like. Two important factors that influence whether we like someone are similarity and physical attractiveness. In a study that examined source similarity, students at the University of California, Santa Barbara, read a speech advocating the use of standardized test scores in college admissions.[71] The arguments for using the scores were either strong or weak. Strong arguments were persuasive when the delegate who wrote the speech was a fellow student at the University of California, Santa Barbara, but not when the delegate was a student at the University of New Hampshire. (Weak arguments were not persuasive regardless of who wrote the speech.) Thus, overall, the similar source was more persuasive than the dissimilar source.

Should Speakers Talk Fast or Slow?

People who are trying to persuade others, such as car salespeople and auctioneers, talk really fast. Is talking fast a good strategy or a bad one? Two early field experiments found that fast speakers were more persuasive than slow speakers.[68] In the first study, participants were adults in public locations such as parks and shopping malls. A researcher posing as a radio announcer stopped people and asked them to evaluate the radio program for that day, which was on "The Danger of Drinking Coffee." The message argued that coffee was bad because it contains caffeine, a poisonous drug that causes heart damage, migraine headaches, stomach ulcers, and a host of other problems. The speaker who delivered the message was either a "locksmith" (low credibility source) or a biochemist (high credibility source). People either heard a slow speaker or one who spoke almost twice as many words per minute (195 vs. 102). Overall, the high-speed message was more persuasive than the low-speed message, and the high credible source was more persuasive than the low credible source.

In the second study, the researchers used an unfamiliar topic instead: "The Dangers of Hydroponically Grown Vegetables." Again, the faster the speech, the more persuasive the message was judged to be. Fast speakers were also judged to be more intelligent, knowledgeable, and objective. The authors concluded, "Beware of the fast talker."

According to these results, speaking fast makes people think you are more credible.

This is good if thinking is shallow. But if thinking would have been deep, then fast talking distracts people from processing the arguments. This could reduce persuasion if the arguments supporting the message are strong, but it can increase persuasion if the arguments supporting the message are weak. The listener does not have time to figure out that the fast talker's arguments are flawed.

Fast talking can backfire.[69] Researchers approached undergraduate students and had them listen to a message about a recently passed law that raised the legal age for purchasing and consuming alcoholic beverages from 19 to 21 years. (Before conducting the study, the researchers found out that almost all students were opposed to the new law; they wanted to be able to drink legally at age 19 rather than 21.) By the flip of a coin, students heard a speech in favor of the new law (counterattitudinal group) or a speech that opposed the new law (the proattitudinal group). The speech was delivered at a slow (144 words per minute), moderate (182 words per minute), or fast (214 words per minute) rate. As with earlier studies,[70] this study found that as speech rate increased, the perceived credibility of speakers also increased. The more

important question is whether the speech influenced the students' attitudes. As can be seen in **FIGURE 8.3** as speech rate increased, students showed more agreement with the counterattitudinal message but less agreement with the proattitudinal message. Thus, persuaders should talk fast if their arguments are weak so listeners won't have time to think about the arguments. If their arguments are strong, persuaders should talk more slowly, so listeners can think about and appreciate the arguments. Perhaps this is why auctioneers talk really fast. They don't want the bidders to think too deeply about the money they are spending!

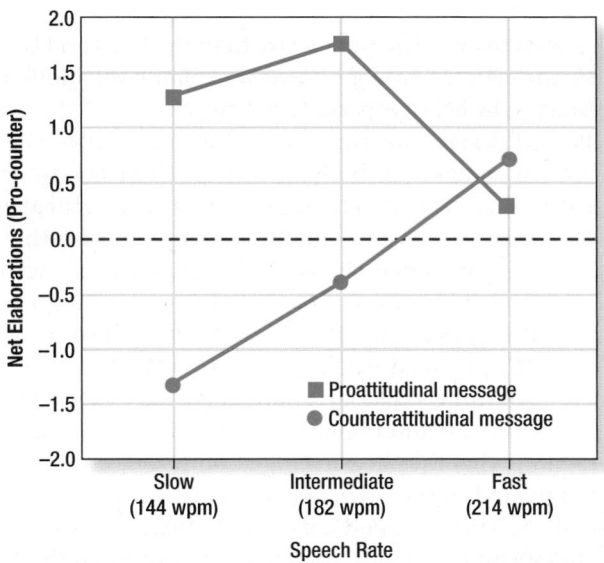

FIGURE 8.3

Speaking fast is good if the audience thinks your arguments are weak (because they won't have time to think about them), but it is bad if the audience thinks your arguments are strong.[69]

Physical attractiveness produces a positive reaction from others (see Chapter 11). We assume that attractive people also possess many other desirable traits—including traits that can influence how persuasive a person is, such as intelligence. This is called the **halo effect**. For example, attractive political candidates are more effective at persuading people to vote for them than are unattractive candidates, even though many voters deny the impact of attractiveness on electability.[72,73]

Says What: The Message

Messages can vary on several dimensions. In this section, we examine some of the most important ones.

Reason Versus Emotion

There are two approaches in presenting a persuasive message. One can present the cold, hard facts, or one can appeal to emotions. Which approach works best? Well-educated and analytical people are more responsive to arguments based on logic and reason.[74]

Emotional responses can also be very effective. In *Rhetoric,* Aristotle wrote that the success of a persuasive message depends on the emotional state of the audience; "for we do not judge in the same way when we grieve and rejoice or when we are friendly and hostile."[75] Research has shown that people who are in a good mood are more receptive to persuasive messages than other people. One study found that persuasion was increased when college students ate peanuts and drank soft drinks while reading the messages.[76]

Using humor is one way to put an audience in a good mood. About 40% of all ads employ humor.[77] Research shows that people pay more attention to humorous messages than to serious messages.[78] Humor can also make the source more likable.[79] On the downside, people may remember that a message was funny but forget what the message was about.[80]

Humor isn't the only emotional approach that speakers can use—fear is another option. Do scare tactics work to persuade people? If so, how much should you scare them? Should you just unnerve them a little, or scare the daylights out of them? Carl Hovland based his persuasion research on learning theory, which focuses on the link between the stimulus and the response. Hovland predicted that a frightening message (the stimulus) would increase arousal, attention, and comprehension of the message, which would result in attitude change (the response). Attitude change, in turn, should function as a reinforcement because it reduces the fear. Fear appeal and attitude change may have an **inverted (upside-down) U-shaped relationship**, according to Irving Janis.[81] Attitude change is lowest for no fear and extremely high fear appeals, with the most attitude change occurring for moderate fear appeals. Subsequent research has shown that fear appeals are persuasive if they do not paralyze the audience with fear, if the audience is susceptible to the danger, and if the audience is told how to avoid the danger.[82] A meta-analysis of 105 studies involving about 18,000 participants found that fear appeals are especially effective if people feel vulnerable to the threat.[83] The research on fear appeals is affecting public policy. For example, the Canadian government now requires that half the surface on a cigarette pack be devoted to graphic images of the hazards of smoking. Research indicates that written warnings accompanied by pictures are 60 times more likely to inspire smokers to quit than are written warnings alone.[84] In this case, the target audience knows exactly how to avoid the danger—quit smoking. Even advertisers want to frighten us into buying their products. Who wants to get caught with bad breath, dandruff, and stinky armpits? Fear appeals can be persuasive, as long as people don't become too afraid. For an illustration of fear's effect on attitudes, see *Social Side of Sex.*

One-Sided Versus Two-Sided Messages

Another factor in persuasion is how a message is conveyed. That is, does the presenter offer only one side of the argument, or are both sides given? One interesting example of one-sided versus two-sided messages can be found in political campaigns. One-sided messages are more effective when audience members are less educated or have already made up their minds on the issue.

When you're only No. 2, you try harder. Or else.

Little fish have to keep moving all of the time. The big ones never stop picking on them.

Avis knows all about the problems of little fish.

We're only No. 2 in rent a cars. We'd be swallowed up if we didn't try harder.

Avis can't afford to relax.

There's no rest for us.

We're always emptying ashtrays. Making sure gas tanks are full before we rent our cars. Seeing that the batteries are full of life. Checking our windshield wipers.

And the cars we rent out can't be anything less than spanking new Plymouths.

And since we're not the big fish, you won't feel like a sardine when you come to our counter.

We're not jammed with customers.

Advertisers can sometimes enhance sales by seeming to argue against their own self-interests. Consumers think the advertisers are more honest and are therefore more persuaded by the ad.

inverted (upside-down) U-shaped relationship a relationship that looks like an upside-down U when plotted

Scared into Safe Sex?

The so-called sexual revolution of the 1960s produced a widespread increase in sexual activity in the 1970s. People began having sex at younger ages, more premarital and extramarital sex, and more sex partners. However, in the 1980s the AIDS epidemic burst into public consciousness. An incurable and fatal disease, AIDS made the free and easy sexual behavior of the 1970s seem dangerous and irresponsible.

Although some people did become more careful about their sex partners, it did not seem likely that entire nations would go back to the degree of sexual abstinence that had been the norm in the 1950s. (To be sure, attitudes about sex change more rapidly than realities, and many historians believe that both the sexual abstinence of the 1950s and the sexual freedom of the 1970s have been overstated.) Accordingly, there was a movement to influence people, perhaps especially young people, about the dangers of AIDS. But what sort of influence would be most effective?

One approach used messages that would generate the maximum amount of fear, by emphasizing that one careless sex act can lead to a painful, grisly death. Many organizations thought this was the best way to go. However, they had not turned to social psychologists to learn whether inspiring fear is a good way to change attitudes and behaviors. Social psychologists had repeatedly found that strong fear-inspiring messages often backfire, failing to yield the desired changes in behavior.[85,86] People just "turn off" if you scare them too much.

In a series of studies on the specific effect of fear-inspiring anti-AIDS films, researchers reasoned that some people would find depictions of AIDS victims personally threatening and, as a result, would deny their fear and ignore the message.[87] Researchers showed emotionally powerful films about AIDS to sexually active college students. These films depicted young people discussing how they had gotten AIDS and how their lives had changed. The films were explicitly made to instill a sense of fear and vulnerability in young people so as to influence their sexual behavior toward more caution and restraint.

The films backfired. The sexually active young people who saw the films rejected the fear-inducing message. They rated their own risk of getting AIDS in the next five years as significantly lower than did a control sample of participants who had not seen any film. (Control participants in one study read pamphlets about AIDS prevention; in the other study they did not have any AIDS messages at all.) Thus, the film designed to make people worry more about their risk actually made them worry less.

Ironically, the films did succeed in increasing perceived risk among one group of people: Virgins (participants who had never had sex) who watched the same films rated their risk of AIDS as higher than virgins in the control conditions.

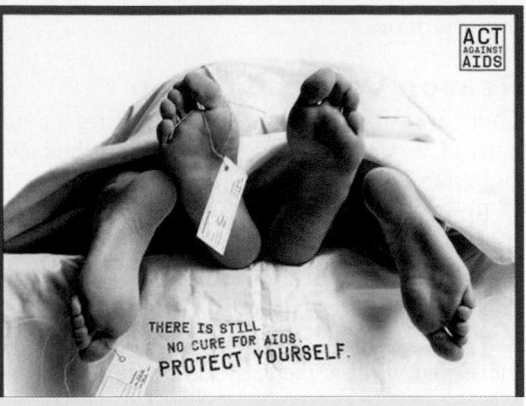

THERE IS STILL NO CURE FOR AIDS. PROTECT YOURSELF.

© Courtesy of The Centers for Disease Control and Prevention

Strong fear appeals can often backfire.

At the end of the experimental session, the researchers offered all participants some informational pamphlets about AIDS to take home. These results confirmed the conclusion that some people were denying the reality of risk. Sexually active people who had watched the films took fewer pamphlets than control participants. Virgins who watched the film took more pamphlets than virgins in the control condition.

With sex, as with other behaviors, instilling fear is an unreliable mode of influence. People resist feeling bad, and they may resist the influence attempt that uses fear. Sexually active people do live with some risk of AIDS; in order to avoid facing that risk, they rejected the message and lowered their perception of danger. Only virgins, for whom AIDS is not a current danger, were able to attend to the fear-inducing message and respond with a plausibly increased awareness of risk.

Should a political candidate talk only about his or her own strengths, or also about the opponent's weaknesses? In politics, negative campaigning is defined as trying to depict one's opponent as bad. Instead of focusing on what is good about one's own candidate, a negative advertisement talks mainly about the other side and tries to turn voters against him or her. Polls indicate that many voters disapprove of negative campaigning, and many candidates say they will refrain from criticizing their opponents. Nonetheless, one has only to watch television in the later stages of almost any major campaign to see negative advertisements.

Why are negative political ads so common? Do they really work? The results of social psychology research on negative campaigning have been mixed. In many cases, negative

Sean Gardner/Getty Images

Marc Serota/Getty Images

campaigning involves tradeoffs. One cost is that negative campaigning tends to produce lower evaluations of both candidates. In several laboratory studies, participants read campaign ads that were either positive or negative. When both sides used negative ads, the participants perceived both candidates more negatively.[88] Negative ads also made participants less likely to say they would vote, at least if voting was difficult (e.g., because of bad weather).[89] Negative campaigning may be most effective as a desperation measure by a candidate who is far behind in the polls and is willing to try anything to make the election closer. Even if a race is pretty close, candidates may turn negative in an attempt to get ahead.

Negative campaigning does not win very many votes, but perhaps that is not its goal—instead, the goal is to reduce the other side's votes. If voters for the other side stay home while one's own supporters are fanatical enough to vote despite an ugly, negative campaign, it might still work. Further research is needed before we can know whether the tradeoff yields more benefits than costs.

Repetition

Persuasive messages, such as advertisements, are often shown repeatedly. Does this help or hurt the message? Recall that the mere exposure effect is the tendency for novel stimuli to be liked more after the individual has been exposed to them repeatedly (see Chapter 7). Accumulated research confirms that repeated exposure to ads does influence memory for ads.[90] The initial attitude toward the product makes a difference.[91] If the person has a neutral or positive response to the message initially, then repeated exposure can make the message more persuasive; if the person hates the message right off the bat, hearing it again and again will only make things worse.

Even if audience members initially like the message, they don't want to hear it too many times, or advertisement wear-out might occur. **Advertisement wear-out** is defined as a "condition of inattention and possible irritation that occurs after an audience or target market has encountered a specific advertisement too many times."[92] A good example is Flo, the perky car insurance cashier (played by Stephanie Courtney), who debuted in 2008.[93] In 2009 the *Boston Herald* called her "the commercial break's new sweetheart" and said she was "attaining TV ad icon status."[94] Initially the ads were appealing and people even dressed up as Flo for Halloween. After appearing in over 50 ads, however, Flo was losing her initial appeal. Of course, it is possible that the advertising industry overstates the danger of wear-out, because the greater the perceived danger of wear-out, the faster companies buy new ad campaigns, and the more money advertisers make. Advertisers have to influence their clients as well as the people who watch their ads! One good way to prevent advertisement wear-out is to use **repetition with variation**—repeat the same information, but in a varied format.[95,96]

advertisement wear-out inattention and irritation that occurs after an audience has encountered the same advertisement too many times

repetition with variation repeating the same information, but in a varied format

To Whom: The Audience

In studying persuasion, one cannot ignore the characteristics of audience members, such as how intelligent they are. Some people are easier to persuade than others, and certain persuasion techniques work better on some people than on others.

Intelligence

The studies conducted by Hovland and his colleagues showed that more intelligent soldiers learned more from the films, analyzed the ideas more thoroughly, and were more persuaded by two-sided arguments than by one-sided arguments.[97,98] Building on this research, Hovland's colleague William McGuire developed a model for persuasion that emphasized processes such as reception and yielding.[99] **Receptivity** refers to whether you "get" the message (Did you pay attention to it? Do you understand it?). **Yielding** refers to whether you "accept" the message (Did you believe it? Were you persuaded by it?). McGuire found that audience members with high self-esteem were receptive to persuasive messages because they had confidence in their initial positions. However, they did not yield to the message because they were satisfied with their existing attitudes. He also found that audience members with high intelligence were receptive to persuasive messages because they had longer attention spans and were better able to comprehend arguments. They too did not yield because they had confidence in their existing attitudes. Later work has largely confirmed McGuire's model.[100] Moderately intelligent people and people with moderate self-esteem levels are easiest to persuade. Thus, there is an inverted-U relationship between intelligence and persuasion and between self-esteem and persuasion.

AP Images/David Adame

Flo, the perky car insurance cashier, may be starting to lose her initial appeal after being featured in over 50 advertisements.

Need for Cognition

Most people are mentally lazy; they are cognitive misers (see Chapter 5). In contrast, people high in need for cognition like to think, analyze situations, and solve mental problems. **Need for cognition** is "the tendency for an individual to engage in and enjoy effortful thinking."[101] For example, people high in need for cognition may be more likely than others to watch the debates in a presidential election because they like to think about the issues and candidates.[102] Some sample items from the Need for Cognition scale are "I like to have the responsibility of handling a situation that requires a lot of thinking" and "I prefer my life to be filled with puzzles that I must solve." Research has shown that people high in need for cognition are more persuaded by strong arguments and are less persuaded by weak arguments than are people low in need for cognition.[103]

Concern About Public Image

Some people, such as those high on the traits of self-monitoring (see Chapter 11) and public self-consciousness (see Chapter 3), are very concerned about their public image (recall the discussion of self-presentation in Chapter 3). Persuasive messages that focus on name brands and stylish products appeal to such people. In one study,[104] people high in self-monitoring gave ads that focused on image (e.g., "Barclay ... You can see the difference") higher ratings than ads that focused on quality (e.g., "Barclay ... You can taste the difference"). Another study showed that people high in public self-consciousness were even concerned about the brand of peanut butter they ate.[105] Even though the jars contained the same peanut butter, individuals high in public self-consciousness gave the jar with the generic label very negative ratings and gave the jar with the name brand label very positive ratings. If publicly self-conscious people are concerned about the brand of peanut butter they buy, they are probably even more concerned about the clothes and shoes they wear and the cars they drive.

Cultural Differences

People from individualist cultures tend to place more emphasis on the individual, whereas people from collectivist cultures tend to place more emphasis on the group. One cross-cultural study tested what types of advertisements appealed to members of these two

receptivity whether you "get" (pay attention to, understand) the message

yielding whether you "accept" (believe, and especially whether you change your attitude to agree with) the message

need for cognition a tendency to engage in and enjoy effortful thinking, analysis, and mental problem solving

cultures.[106] One set of ads focused on the person (e.g., "Treat yourself to a breath-freshening experience"); the other set of advertisements focused on the group (e.g., "Share this breath-freshening experience"). Americans (from an individualistic culture) were more persuaded by the individualistic ads, whereas South Koreans (collectivistic) were more persuaded by the collectivist ads. Another study showed that Americans had more favorable attitudes toward products that offered "separateness," whereas Chinese had more favorable attitudes toward products that offered "togetherness."[107] The implication is that people are more persuaded by messages that match their culture's general attitudes.

Overheard Messages

Other research has shown that if people think they are overhearing a message, they are more persuaded than if they see it as a sales pitch aimed directly at them.[108] People are more persuaded by messages that do not seem to be designed to influence them. Advertisers sometimes use this "overheard communicator trick" to persuade consumers.

Research has shown that advertisements with omitted conclusions are more persuasive than advertisements with conclusions.[109] Consumers appear to be more strongly influenced by the advertised message if they draw the conclusion on their own.

When ads appear on television, most people leave the room, surf channels, or fast forward through them if they have a DVR. That is why advertisers sometimes use product placement in television shows or movies. For example, Lark cigarettes paid $350,000 to have James Bond smoke their cigarettes in *License to Kill*. One reason product placements work so well is that people don't realize that advertisers are trying to influence them, so they let down their guard. Advertising executive David Ogilvy said, "A good advertisement is one which sells the product without drawing attention to itself."[110] Product placement occurs in most forms of media, including video games. For example, product placement is very prominent in racing video games. Players recall the products placed immediately after the game and also months later.[111] "Overheard" messages can be quite persuasive.

Distraction

We saw earlier that distraction is sometimes helpful to influence because it gets the conscious mind out of the way (leaving the more gullible automatic system to deal with the message). Persuasion researchers have shown that distraction can help persuasion by preventing the conscious mind from thinking of counterarguments.[112] College students read a persuasive message that argued against the Greek system on campus. Because these students belonged to (Greek) fraternities, they were not very receptive to the message. By the flip of a coin, half of the students were distracted by a cartoon while they read the message. The cartoon distracted participants from mentally arguing against the message.

Distraction isn't always helpful. If you have a really good argument but the person listening is distracted, he or she won't understand how good your case is. **TABLE 8.1**.

TABLE 8.1 Major Findings of the Line of Persuasion Research Conducted by Hovland and His Colleagues		
What Types of Sources Are Most Persuasive?	**What Types of Messages Are Most Persuasive?**	**Who Is Receptive to Persuasive Messages?**
Highly credible sources	Logical messages—mainly with educated, analytical people	People who are in a good mood
Likable sources	Moderately fear-inducing messages	People of average intelligence and self-esteem
Convert communicators	Two-sided messages	People concerned about their public image (high self-monitoring, high public self-consciousness)
Sources who argue against their own self-interest	Moderately discrepant messages	Very young or very old people
	Messages that are repeated (but may backfire)	

summarizes the major results of persuasion studies conducted by Hovland, his colleagues, and other researchers.

Two Routes to Persuasion

One theme of this book has been the duplex mind: The mind has two systems, one deliberate and the other automatic. Influence attempts can operate using either system. That is, some forms of influence rely on appealing to conscious, rational, deliberate processing, whereas other forms rely on activating automatic responses. One appeals to enlightened self-interest; the other appeals to motivations or responses that may not be fully understood. Illicit or "tricky" forms of persuasion rely more on the latter. Both types of influence can be successful.

Social psychologists have avidly studied persuasion at least since the 1940s and have reported many findings, some of them seemingly contradictory or incompatible. For example, distraction sometimes increases and sometimes decreases persuasion. To resolve these problems, the **elaboration likelihood model** or **ELM** for short,[113] and the **heuristic/systematic model**[114] suggest two routes to persuasion. (The two theories are quite similar, and experts use either set of terms.) One route involves deliberate processing, whereas the other route involves automatic processing. These routes correspond with the duplex mind. We describe the ELM and refer to the heuristic/systematic model when the two models differ.

The route to persuasion that involves deliberate processing is called the **central route** (or **systematic processing** in the heuristic/systematic model); it is depicted on the top path in **FIGURE 8.4**. Persuasion that occurs along the central route involves careful and thoughtful consideration of the content of the message. The route that involves automatic processing is called the **peripheral route** (or **heuristic processing** in the heuristic/systematic model); it is depicted on the bottom path in Figure 8.4. Persuasion that occurs along the peripheral route involves the influence of some simple cue, such as how attractive the source is. We will start at the left of the figure and work our way to the right side.

First, the person encounters a persuasive message (e.g., "Vote for Emily"). The first question is whether the person is motivated to process the message. This is influenced by two factors: personal relevance and need for cognition. **Personal relevance** refers to whether people expect the issue "to have significant consequences for their own lives."[115] The more personally relevant the issue, the more motivated people are to think about the persuasive message at a deep level. Some issues have personal relevance throughout our lives (e.g., the tax structure of the country we live in, the quality of water and air where we live); other issues have personal relevance for a certain period of time (e.g., raising college tuition, the price of textbooks); still others have personal relevance only under very transient conditions (e.g., dishwasher ads are personally relevant only when a person is shopping for a dishwasher). The other factor that influences motivation to process the persuasive message is need for cognition. As mentioned previously, people high in

elaboration likelihood model (ELM) theory that posits two routes to persuasion, via either conscious or automatic processing

heuristic/systematic model theory that posits two routes to persuasion, via either conscious or automatic processing

central route (systematic processing) the route to persuasion that involves careful and thoughtful consideration of the content of the message (conscious processing)

peripheral route (heuristic processing) the route to persuasion that involves some simple cue, such as attractiveness of the source (automatic processing)

personal relevance degree to which people expect an issue to have significant consequences for their own lives

FIGURE **8.4**
Elaboration likelihood model (ELM) of persuasion.

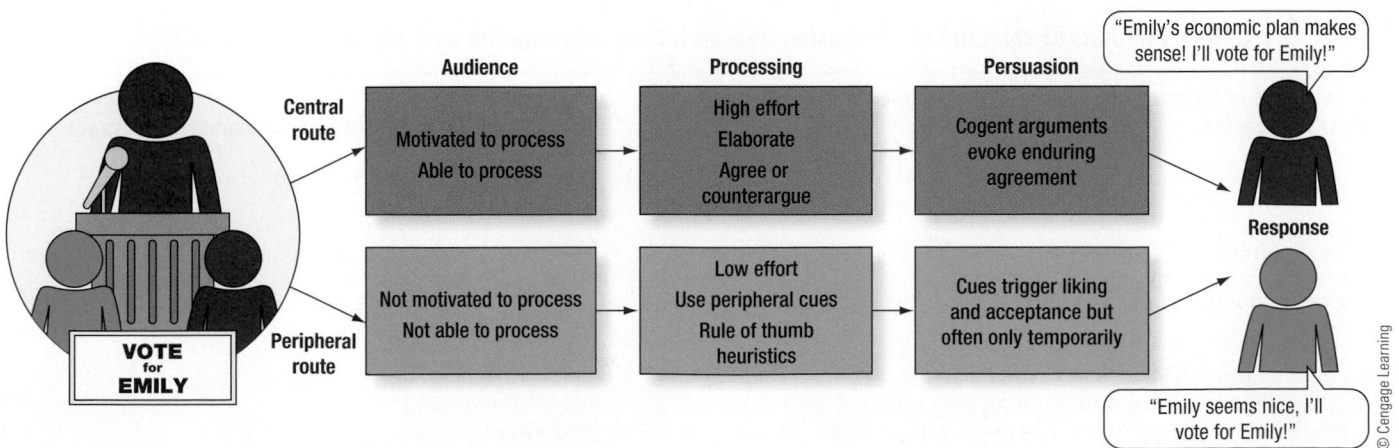

need for cognition like to think and are therefore more likely than people low in need for cognition to think about the message at a deep level. Thus, both situational and personal factors (i.e., need for cognition) influence personal relevance. Recent research shows that messages processed at a deep level are especially resistant to change.[116]

Just because people are motivated to process a message does not mean they will be able to process it. Two factors influence one's ability to process the message: distractions and knowledge. As we saw, distraction disrupts the ability to think about a persuasive message. Participants in one study were exposed to ads for a variety of consumer products.[117] Half the participants were distracted by having them count the number of random clicks on a tape recording. Weak arguments were more effective with distracted participants, probably because they were unable to think carefully about the message and discover its weaknesses. In contrast, strong arguments worked best on the central route—that is, when people were not distracted and could think consciously about the message.

Deliberate (central route) processing also depends on having sufficient knowledge to appreciate a message and possibly to understand what is wrong with it. This factor may help explain why females are more easily persuaded than males in some domains, whereas males are more easily persuaded than females in other domains. College students in one study were shown 36 photos.[118] Half the photos depicted football tackles (high male knowledge), and half depicted current fashions (high female knowledge). On the back of the picture were written comments from a "previous participant" (actually a confederate) that contained factual information (e.g., the dress is blue, the runner's feet are off the ground) or an evaluation (e.g., that's a great tackle) that was either accurate or inaccurate. When comments were completely factual or were accurate, men and women were equally persuaded. The effects of inaccurate evaluations, however, depended on the participant's knowledge about the topic. Men were less persuaded than women by inaccurate evaluations of football tackles, whereas women were less persuaded than men by inaccurate evaluations of fashion. Thus, both situational (i.e., distraction) and personal (i.e., knowledge) factors influence motivation.

If a person is motivated and able to process the message, the outcome of the processing that occurs depends on the quality of the arguments and the initial attitude. A persuasive message can be either strong or weak. When arguments are strong, thinking about them leads people to recognize their validity and to come up with further thoughts that support the message. In contrast, thinking about a message with weak arguments leads people to recognize its flaws and to come up with thoughts that argue against the message. Strong messages lead to strong positive attitude change, whereas weak messages can lead to attitude change in the opposite direction.

Of course, the person's initial attitude sets some limits on how much the attitude can change. If the person has a very strong initial attitude, even a very strong opposing message may fail to change it. Additionally, people process information in a biased way: They are much more critical of messages that go against their views than of messages that agree with their initial attitude.[119] If people are not motivated or able to process a message, they may be persuaded by cues peripheral to the message. Some examples of peripheral cues are

- Experts know best.
- The more arguments, the better.
- Expensive products are good.
- Rare products are good.
- What is beautiful is good.

College freshmen read a message about senior comprehensive exams as part of an experiment.[120] Those in the high relevance group were told that the exams would be instituted at their university within two years (Yikes! I have to take the test to graduate!). Students in the low relevance group were told that the exams would be instituted within 10 years (Who cares? I'll be gone by then!). The source of the message was either an expert (a university dean) or a nonexpert (a high school student). The source of the message had little or no impact on highly involved students. They had to take the exam regardless of the source of the message. Participants who were not highly involved, however, were more persuaded by the dean than by the high school student.

In summary, attitude change can take two routes. People who think about the message travel down the central route, whereas people who don't think about the message take the peripheral route. Attitude change that occurs via the peripheral route tends to be weak. It is temporary, is vulnerable to change, and does not predict future behavior very well. Persuasion by the central route produces much more durable and powerful attitude change, and it predicts behavior very well. But of course the central route is often the more difficult one to use because you actually have to have strong, effective arguments.

QUIZ YOURSELF
Persuasion

1. **Pauline reads an article citing several reasons for having life insurance. When she notices that the article is really an insurance company advertisement, she decides that life insurance is a waste of money. When the topic of insurance comes up a few weeks later, Pauline thinks that life insurance is a good use of money. This change in attitude over time represents the _____ effect.**

   (a) primacy   (b) reactance   (c) recency   (d) sleeper

2. **Maureen is very intelligent, Audrey is moderately intelligent, and Denise is not very intelligent. A two-sided persuasive message will probably be most effective on _____.**

   (a) Audrey   (b) Denise   (c) Maureen   (d) The three women should be equally affected

3. **While listening half-heartedly to a lecture, Jamaal hears his professor cite several reasons why playing violent video games increases aggression. Jamaal accepts these reasons solely because his professor has been correct before. In this example, Jamaal is using _____ processing.**

   (a) alpha   (b) central route   (c) omega   (d) peripheral route

4. **Research shows that a person who is distracted from a message is more likely to be persuaded by that message. The elaboration likelihood model explains this by suggesting that _____.**

   (a) distractions take up most of the person's peripheral processing ability   (b) distractions serve as cues for rewards and punishments concerning being persuaded   (c) a distracting attitude makes the source more likable   (d) distractions prevent people from engaging in central route processing of information

answers: see pg 289

Resisting Social Influence Techniques

The Borg ("Cyborg") are among the most evil villains in space encountered by the *Star Trek* crew. They are a species that looks half human, half machine. When the Borg encounter a new species, they say, "This is the Borg Collective. Prepare to be assimilated. We will add your biological and technological distinctiveness to our own. You will adapt to service us. Resistance is futile." Sometimes the people who want to influence us seem like the Borg trying to assimilate us—resistance seems futile. In the case of persuasion, however, resistance need not be futile. You can take steps to increase your resistance to persuasive attempts to change your attitudes.

Attitude Inoculation

People brought up in a germ-free environment are highly vulnerable to diseases because their bodies have not built up antibodies to attack them. Medicine has helped to solve this problem by inoculating people: Exposing people to weakened doses of viruses (as in a flu shot) helps make their immune systems stronger. William McGuire and his colleagues transferred the concept of inoculation to the study of attitudes.[121,122,123,124] They argued that cultural truisms (e.g., "Smoking is bad for your health") should be especially vulnerable to counterarguments because they exist in a kind of "germ-free" environment where their validity is never challenged. They argued that in order to immunize people against persuasion, it is good to expose them to some of the counter-arguments against these cultural truisms and let them build up defenses against the counterarguments. Of course, being exposed to too many counterarguments, like too heavy a dose of the live virus, could have the opposite effect, reducing resistance rather than strengthening it.

Research has shown that inoculation works in the real world. For example, middle and high school students can be inoculated against peer pressure to smoke.[125,126,127] Researchers taught high school students to say "She is not really liberated if she is hooked on tobacco" in response to a cigarette ad that implied modern, liberated women smoke. They also role-play situations in which peers try to persuade them to smoke. After being called "chicken" for not taking a cigarette, they answer with statements like "I'd be a real chicken if I smoked just to impress you." In these studies, inoculated children are about half as likely as un-inoculated children to begin smoking.

Credit card debt is a growing problem worldwide, and college students aren't immune to it. Credit card companies often target college students because they

The Borg on *Star Trek* are a species that attempt to assimilate all other species (left). They live as a collective in a cube (right). When the Borg encounter a new species, they try to assimilate them. Sometimes the people who want to gain influence over us seem like the Borg. The good news is that you have defenses at your disposal to shield you against those who wield weapons of influence.

College students are bombarded by ads from credit card companies. Fortunately, they can be inoculated against these ads.

are quick to use credit cards and slow to pay them back (because students don't have much money). A degree isn't the only thing students leave college with. Many also leave with a mountain of credit card debt. One student said, "My credit card problems were a major added worry to everything else and . . . made my freshman year horrible."[128] Fortunately, college students can be inoculated against persuasive attempts to acquire and use credit cards.[129] Students who were taught by researchers how to critically evaluate persuasive messages in credit card advertisements were able to resist these ads.

One theory of persuasion is based on the statement, "What doesn't kill me makes me stronger."[130] According to this theory, when people resist persuasion, they become more confident in their initial attitudes. When people think they have successfully resisted persuasion, they decide that their initial attitude is correct and therefore feel more certain about it. Such a pattern helps explain why inoculating people by exposing them to weak arguments can protect them against stronger arguments.

Forewarned Is Forearmed

Sneak attacks on attitudes can be devastating. If people know an attack is coming, however, they can prepare to defend themselves. High school students in a study were forewarned either 2 or 10 minutes in advance that they would hear a speech on "Why Teenagers Should Not Be Allowed to Drive" (not a very popular message, as you might guess).[131] The remaining students heard the same talk, but received no forewarning. The results showed that students who received no forewarning were persuaded the most, followed by those who received 2 minutes' warning, followed by those who received 10 minutes' warning. When people believe that someone is trying to persuade them (and take away their freedom of choice), they experience an unpleasant emotional response called psychological reactance, which motivates them to resist the persuasive attempt (see Chapter 4). Often people will do exactly the opposite of what they are being persuaded to do; this is called **negative attitude change** or a **boomerang effect**. The parents of Romeo and Juliet in Shakespeare's play found this out when their efforts to end the romance only drove the young lovebirds closer together.

Stockpile Resources

To deal with persuasion attempts, we should use all the resources at our disposal: physical, cognitive, and social. In the Iraq War, American soldiers used sleep deprivation and music to break Iraqi prisoners' resistance.[132] The music included songs from the heavy metal group Metallica and from children's television programs (*Sesame Street, Barney*) because Iraqi prisoners hated both types of music. As discussed in the section on the mere exposure effect in Chapter 7, repeated exposure to a disliked stimulus (such as unpleasant music) makes people dislike the stimulus even more. As discussed in Chapter 6, unpleasant events put people in a bad mood. People don't like being in a bad mood, but it takes a lot of effort to repair a bad mood. If people use their cognitive resources to repair a bad mood, they have fewer resources available to fight off persuasive attempts.

Although using irritating music may be a new tactic, sleep deprivation is a very common tactic used on POWs (prisoners of war) during times of war. We all function

negative attitude change (boomerang effect) doing exactly the opposite of what one is being persuaded to do

In the Iraq war, U.S. soldiers tortured Iraqi soldiers by forcing them to listen to music from the heavy metal group Metallica (left) and from the public television show *Barney* (right).

much better after a good night's sleep. People may be more susceptible to persuasion tactics when they are tired.[133] When we hear someone make a statement, we immediately accept the statement as being true, regardless of whether it is actually true. It is only with mental effort that we recognize the statement to be false and reject it. All of this happens in a fraction of a second. People usually have enough cognitive energy and motivation to mentally reject statements that sound false, but when people are tired, their mental energy levels drop, and they become more susceptible to false statements.

QUIZ YOURSELF
Resisting Social Influence Techniques

1. **When I am driving my car and someone tailgates me to make me go faster, I slow down. This is an example of _____.**

   (a) cognitive dissonance   (b) door-in-the-face   (c) low-balling   (d) psychological reactance

2. **Knowing in advance that we are a target of a persuasive message is called _____.**

   (a) cognitive dissonance   (b) elaboration   (c) forewarning   (d) psychological reactance

3. **The theory that exposure to weak versions of a persuasive message increases later resistance to that message is called _____.**

   (a) attitude inoculation   (b) negative attitude change   (c) psychological reactance   (d) the sleeper effect

4. **Cialdini says that we should accept initial favors or concessions in good faith, but be ready to define them as tricks if they prove to be tricks. This defense is most effective for techniques based on the _____ principle.**

   (a) capturing and disrupting attention   (b) commitment and consistency   (c) reciprocation   (d) scarcity

answers: see pg 289

What Makes Us *Human*

All social animals rely on others for some of what they want and need, so they face the same basic problems of needing to influence others, at least sometimes. The need to exert social influence is not limited to human beings. But the need may be more extensive in humans than in other animals, given how much human activity depends on working together with others and participating in flexible social systems. Moreover, some methods of influence, and of resisting influence, are distinctly human.

The duplex mind is rather distinctively human, so only humans have two routes to persuasion. In particular, human beings have a special capacity for cognitive reasoning and thinking, so the central, or systematic, route to persuasion works better with humans than with any other animal. Likewise, logical reasoning and humor are only useful influence techniques with humans because only humans have logic and humor.

The extent to which people think about what others tell them, thereby elaborating on and embellishing a simple persuasive message, also reflects the extensive makeup of the human self. As we saw, getting people to label themselves as being a certain kind of person is an effective way to change their behavior. People have elaborate self-concepts that can be swayed in this way. With most other animals, the scope for influence by labeling the self-concept would be much smaller.

As cultural beings, humans are characterized by a social life filled with elaborate norms and implicit rules. Many persuasion techniques make use of these norms and rules. Humans everywhere recognize the norm of reciprocity, based on an abstract concept of fairness, and they accept obligations to reciprocate what is done for them. As we have seen, several influence techniques capitalize on norms of fairness and reciprocity. Although all human groups seem to have reciprocity norms, there may be important cultural differences in what needs to be reciprocated and what counts as reciprocation.

Another special dimension of the complexity of human social life is our ability to anticipate and care about how others perceive us, and to alter our behavior to make an impression. The distinction between private acceptance and public compliance is crucial to understanding human influence, but it is mostly irrelevant to understanding influence among other animals. Humans have a much more elaborate inner self and a more advanced understanding of the difference between inner sentiments and overt, expressive acts than other creatures. In plainer terms, only humans respond to social pressure by saying things they don't mean, or by going along with the crowd while keeping doubts to themselves.

The moral rules that are common to human cultures also capitalize on the human capacity for feeling guilty over violations of interpersonal norms, and persuaders can play on people's guilt to influence them. The door-in-the-face and foot-in-the-door techniques, for example, may well operate by making the person start to feel guilty.

Although we have focused on special opportunities to influence people, there is another side: People are uniquely able to resist influence and persuasion. Most of the means of resisting influence involve use of conscious control over responses (wait until your emotional reaction has subsided before making a decision), shifting among perspectives (consider an alternative view), and conscious reasoning (evaluate the message logically). These capacities are pretty much absent outside of our species. People, therefore, have special powers and weapons that enable them to avoid being swayed.

CHAPTER 8 SUMMARY

Two Types of Social Influence

- Normative influence involves going along with the crowd in order to be liked and accepted.
- People from collectivist countries are more likely to be influenced by group norms than are people from individualist countries.
- Conformity increases as group size increases (up to a point, then it levels off).
- People will conform to a group in which everyone agrees, but if group members disagree about even the smallest point, then people become willing to stand up for what they believe and go against the majority.
- People who deviate from a group are often rejected by the group.
- Group norms are the beliefs or behaviors a group of people accepts as normal.
- Informational influence involves going along with the crowd because you think the crowd knows more than you do, such as when
  - The situation is ambiguous, so people do not know how to behave.
  - There is a crisis and people don't have time to think for themselves.

Techniques of Social Influence

- The foot-in-the-door technique gets someone to comply with a large request by first making a small request.
- The low-ball technique involves shifting from a smaller request to a larger request after the person has committed to the small request.

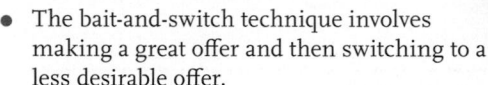

- The bait-and-switch technique involves making a great offer and then switching to a less desirable offer.
- The labeling technique involves assigning a label to an individual and then requesting a favor that is consistent with that label.
- The legitimization-of-paltry-favors technique involves asking for a very small contribution in order to get a larger contribution.
- The door-in-the-face technique involves making an inflated request (that will most likely be rejected) and then retreating to a smaller request. (It only works if the first request is not too extreme and if the same person makes both requests.)
- The that's-not-all technique begins with an inflated request that is quickly followed by a discount or bonus.
- According to the scarcity principle, rare opportunities are more valuable than plentiful opportunities.

- With the limited-number technique, the customer is told that items exist in a limited supply.
- With the fast-approaching-deadline technique, the customer is told that items can only be obtained for a limited time.
- When our personal freedom is threatened, we experience an unpleasant emotional response called psychological reactance, which motivates us to do what is forbidden.
- The pique technique captures the target's attention by making the request novel to increase the chances of compliance with the persuasive request.
- In the disrupt-then-reframe technique, a non sequitur or unexpected element is introduced to provide a momentary disruption that interrupts critical thinking and increases the chances of compliance with the persuasive request.

Persuasion

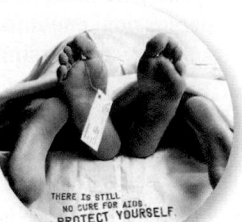

- Persuasion is an attempt to change a person's attitude.
- According to the sleeper effect, over time people separate the message from the messenger.
- Two characteristics can influence source credibility:
  - Expertise—how much the source knows.
  - Trustworthiness—how honest the source is.
- Fast talkers are assumed to be more credible and intelligent than slow talkers (as long as the speech is not too fast to be comprehended).
- Powerful speakers are believed to be credible.
- Powerless speech includes compound requests and disclaimers.
- Convert communicators make up for their deficits in trustworthiness by arguing against their past transgressions.
  - They can be very persuasive.
  - They are likable because they are similar to audience members.
  - They show a sense of mastery because they were able to overcome their undesirable behavior.
- Similarity and physical attractiveness increase liking and therefore increase persuasion.
- People who are in a good mood are more receptive to persuasive messages.
- Instilling fear is an unreliable mode of influence; moderate fear appeals are more persuasive than high or low fear appeals.
- One-sided persuasive messages work best when the audience is not able to process the message thoroughly; two-sided messages work best when the audience can process the message thoroughly.

- Message discrepancy is the difference between the initial attitude of the audience and the content of the speaker's message.

- Repetition polarizes initial responses to the persuasive message, although advertising wear-out can occur when an ad is repeated too many times.

- Audience members with moderate levels of self-esteem and intelligence are most affected by persuasive messages.

- Need for cognition is the tendency for an individual to engage in and enjoy effortful thinking.

- People high in need for cognition are more persuaded by strong arguments and are less persuaded by weak arguments than are people low in need for cognition.

- Overheard messages are more persuasive than direct attempts to change attitudes.

- If the message is weak, distraction makes the message more effective, but if the message is strong, then distraction makes the message less effective.

- The elaboration likelihood model (ELM) and the heuristic/systematic model are similar. They describe two routes to persuasion: one involving conscious processing and one involving automatic processing.

- The route that involves conscious processing is called the central route or systematic processing. The route that involves automatic processing is called the peripheral route or heuristic processing.

- Personal relevance is the degree to which people expect an issue to have significant consequences for their own lives.

- Two factors influence our ability to process a message: whether we are free from distractions and whether we have sufficient knowledge.

- Peripheral cues such as source expertise have no effect on people who are motivated to process a persuasive message, but they can have an effect on people who are not motivated to process the message.

Resisting Social Influence Techniques

- In order to immunize people against persuasion, it is good to expose them to some of the counterarguments and let them build up defenses against the counterarguments.

- When people resist persuasion, they become more confident in their initial attitudes.

- If people are forewarned that a persuasive message is coming, they are less persuaded by it.

- The boomerang effect (negative attitude change) results from psychological reactance to the persuasive attempt; the result is an attitude opposite to the persuasive message.

What Makes Us Human? Putting the Cultural Animal in Perspective

- The duplex mind is only found in humans, so only humans have two routes to persuasion.

- Inner traits and processes play a much bigger role in human influence than in influence in nonhuman animals.

- Many persuasion techniques rely on norms and implicit rules. Humans have far more elaborate norms and implicit rules than nonhuman animals.

- Probably only humans feel guilty if they break norms and rules.

- The distinction between private acceptance and public compliance plays a much bigger role in human influence than in influence in nonhuman animals.

- Humor can be a factor in persuasion, but nonhuman animals probably do not have a sense of humor.

- Only humans appear able to resist influence and persuasion.

key terms

quiz yourself ANSWERS

1. Two Types of Social Influence **p.262**
   answers: 1.b   2.c   3.d   4.a

2. Techniques of Social Influence **p.270**
   answers: 1.b   2.b   3.c   4.d

3. Persuasion **p.282**
   answers: 1.d   2.c   3.d   4.d

4. Resisting Social Influence Techniques **p.285**
   answers: 1.d   2.c   3.a   4.c

PROSOCIAL BEHAVIOR

Doing What's Best for Others

9

LEARNING OBJECTIVES

1 Explain how reciprocity, social responsibility, equity, and equality create different motivations to help others.

2 Compare and contrast the different kinds of prosocial behaviors, such as cooperation, forgiveness, obedience, conformity and trust.

3 Analyze the different explanations and motives for helping.

4 Describe who is most likely to help and who is most likely to receive help.

5 Elucidate the five steps of bystander intervention.

6 Discuss the ways to increase helping.

Alloy Photography/Veer

by Catherine Ryan Hyde (and 2000 film) *Pay It Forward*, a 12-year-old boy does favors for three individuals and, when asked how they can repay him, tells them to "pay it forward" by doing favors for three others, who then are to be instructed to pay it forward to three more recipients. The book has been translated into at least 23 different languages. Many people have been inspired by the novel and movie.

For example, a 26-year-old named Dean Young from California decided to start giving a homeless man leftover homemade chocolate chip cookies from the restaurant he worked at, rather than throwing them away. Dean learned that when the man came back from serving overseas in the military, he discovered that his wife had sold everything he owned, emptied their joint bank account, and moved to Mexico with another man. He had no family either. After giving the man cookies for about a month, Dean took the man to a motel, gave him a small bag of toiletries (e.g., razor, toothbrush, scissors), and told him to get cleaned up and get a good sleep because they were going to look for jobs together the next day. When Dean dropped the man off at the motel he had "long scraggly beard and mane of mangy hair and so much dirt crusted on his skin it made him look 80!" When he returned the next day, Dean was shocked to see how good the 25-year-old man looked. Dean bought the man a new suit and found him a good job working with computers, a skill the man possessed. The only problem was the job

was in downtown Los Angeles. Dean said, "I'll pay your motel, meals, and get you passes for the Green Line to get to and from work until you can support yourself again." When he offered to pay the money back, Dean replied, "Tell you what, when you get to the point where you're back on your feet and financially secure enough to pay me back for what I've done for you, turn and go the opposite direction away from where I am. Keep going until you come across someone that can benefit from your kindness, your charity, your friendship and help them the way I helped you or anyway they need you to help them." A few years later, Dean saw the man at the restaurant where he worked. The man vigorously shook Dean's hand, and told him how he "paid it forward." The former homeless man met an inner city boy from a broken home. He became a big brother father figure for the boy. The boy loved baseball. The man helped the boy and his friends form a baseball team, bought them uniforms and equipment, and even became their coach. He also took them to several Dodger games. Someday that inner city boy might also "pay it forward" by helping someone else in need.

As another example, one person saw that tires on a truck were badly worn and bought new tires for the person, asking that the person also do something nice for a complete stranger one day.

Social scientists call this "pay it forward" concept "upstream reciprocity,"

defined as passing benefits on to third parties instead of returning benefits to one's benefactors.[1] Many cities, states, provinces, and territories have issued *Pay it Forward* proclamations. The "pay it forward" concept has become a worldwide movement to send "ripples of kindness" around the world. In 2014, people from 70 countries participated in *Pay it Forward* Day. The response was so overwhelming that there will be an international *Pay It Forward* Day each year from now on. Even on Facebook there is a *Pay it Forward* post going around that says: "I'm participating in a *Pay it Forward* initiative. The first five people who comment on this status with "I'm in" will receive a surprise from me at some point during this calendar year— anything from a book, a ticket, something home-grown, purchased, homemade, a postcard, absolutely any surprise! There will be no warning and it will happen when the mood comes over me or if I see something that I believe would suit you and make you happy. These five people must make the same offer on their Facebook status. Once my first five have commented "I'm in" I will forward you this message to put as your status (don't share it) so we can form a web connection of kindness. Let's do more nice and loving things this year, without any reason other than to make each other smile and to show that we think of each other. Here's to a more enjoyable, friendly, and love filled year! Thank you!" ●

You do not know me but I saw that you needed some tires for your truck and I wanted to do something nice for a stranger because one day a stranger did the same for me. The receipt is in the envelope and all you have to do is go by Warehouse Tire on 3rd Street and ask for Steven Hodges and they will be put them on for free. All I ask is that one day you do something nice for a complete stranger.

The concept of *Pay it Forward*—doing a favor for someone and asking that person to do the same in the future—can promote prosocial behavior. For example, one person saw that tires on a truck were badly worn and bought new tires for the person, and left a note asking that the person do something nice for someone else.

Is Helping Contagious?

Sometimes social psychologists seem to focus on the negative things people do. The famous American historian Howard Zinn said:

> To be hopeful in bad times is not just foolishly romantic. It is based on the fact that human history is a history not only of cruelty, but also of compassion, sacrifice, courage, and kindness. What we choose to emphasize in this complex history will determine our lives. If we see only the worst, it destroys our capacity to do something. If we remember those times and places—and there are so many—where people have behaved magnificently, this gives us the energy to act, and at least the possibility of sending this spinning top of a world in a different direction. And if we do act, in however small a way, we don't have to wait for some grand utopian future. The future is an infinite succession of presents, and to live now as we think human beings should live, in defiance of all that is bad around us, is itself a marvelous victory.

As Zinn noted, people can and do behave magnificently. For example, recently a man was boarding a train in Perth, Australia, when he slipped and trapped his leg in the gap between the train and the platform. If the train left, the man might lose his leg or his life. Hundreds of fellow passengers pushed on the train and literally lifted it up so the man could get his leg out.[2]

The dying wish of Aaron Collins—a young man from Kentucky—was to leave an "awesome" tip of at least $500 to a waiter or waitress. Aaron's brother Seth and their mother Tina gave a $500 tip to a waitress at a pizza joint. They posted a video of it on a blog called "Aaron's Wish." Many strangers were moved by the video, and began donating money to a foundation set up in Aaron's name (aaroncollins.org). So far, over 100 waiters or waitresses have received $500 tips in many states throughout the United States. Recent research has even shown that cooperative behavior can be contagious, passing from person to person to person.[3]

Mercury Press and Media Limited

Mercury Press and Media Limited

Fellow passengers saved a man by collectively lifting a train so he could get his leg out of the gap between the train and the platform.

What Is Prosocial Behavior?

Prosocial behavior is defined as doing something that is good for other people or for society as a whole. Prosocial behavior includes behavior that respects others or allows society to operate. Culture is a whole that is more than the sum of its parts, but only if people cooperate and follow the rules will culture be able to yield its benefits. In a nutshell, prosocial behavior builds relationships. It is the opposite of antisocial behavior, which means doing something bad for others or for society. Antisocial behavior usually destroys relationships (see Chapter 10).

Social psychologists have had a peculiar relationship with prosocial behavior. Most social psychology textbooks feature helping as the main prosocial behavior, while ignoring most other prosocial behaviors. When they discuss conformity, obedience, and other forms of following the rules, textbooks have often been sharply critical, suggesting that these are bad things. It is true that obedience and conformity can be bad—mindless obedience to a demented leader such as Hitler can produce all sorts of terrible consequences. For the most part, however, obedience and conformity are good things. Society would collapse if people didn't follow most of the rules most of the time. For example, consider what would happen if people decided to ignore traffic rules, such as "Stop," "Wrong Way," "Yield," and "Speed Limit" signs. Traffic accidents and fatalities would increase sharply! Likewise, imagine what would happen if most people just took things from stores without paying, or ignored the tax laws, or if restaurant employees did not wash their hands after using the bathroom, or if grocery stores disobeyed health regulations and sold rotten food.

Obeying the rules, conforming to socially accepted standards of proper behavior, and cooperating with others are important forms of prosocial behavior. Helping—which most social psychology textbooks treat as the quintessential form of prosocial behavior—is actually something of an "extra" or a luxury. We admire the spirit of "paying it forward," but society could function just fine if nobody did that. More broadly, society and culture can still bring immense benefits if people do not perform altruistic, self-sacrificing acts of helping. If no one obeys the rules, however, society will fall apart and chaos will reign. Following rules is essential. Helping is less essential, though certainly helping makes the world a much nicer place, and some forms of helping (such as what parents do for their small children) are probably vital for the survival of the species.

We rely on other people to follow their own self-interest while obeying the rules. They sell us their food in exchange for our money, which is good for them and for us. No helping or self-sacrifice on their part is necessary, but it is vital that they obey the rules by not selling us spoiled meat or committing other fraudulent acts.

Imagine two societies, one in which people are happy and healthy, and another in which people are fearful, poor, and desperate. What might account for the difference? The happy society is likely full of people who cooperate with each other, respect each other, follow the rules, and contribute to the general welfare. The unhappy society is likely full of people who break the rules; its social life is marked by crime, corruption, distrust, betrayal, and wide-ranging general insecurity.

A society in which people respect and follow the rules is said to have an effective **rule of law**. If there are no laws, or if laws exist but are widely ignored and disobeyed, the rule of law is said to be lacking. The rule of law may occasionally annoy us, such as when you get a speeding ticket, but in reality the rule of law is usually a huge boost to the quality of life. If you lived in a society where the rule of law had broken down, or had not yet appeared, you would find life hard and dangerous. Indeed, researchers have found a positive correlation between happiness and rule of law, across many societies.[4]

Fairness and justice are also important factors in predicting prosocial behavior. If employees perceive the company they work for to be fair and just, they are more likely to be good "company citizens."[5] For example, they are more likely to voluntarily help others in the workplace and more likely to promote the excellence of their employer, without

prosocial behavior doing something that is good for other people or for society as a whole

rule of law when members of a society (including its most powerful leaders) respect and follow its rules

Christopher Futcher/Getty Images

Others will see how much you contribute.

any promise of reward for these behaviors. The crucial point is that people behave better when they think the rules are fair.

The presence of others can stimulate prosocial behavior, such as when someone acts more properly because other people are watching. Dogs will stay off the furniture and out of the trash when their owners are present, but they blithely break those rules when alone. Humans may have more of a conscience, but they also still respond to the presence or absence of others. Public circumstances generally promote prosocial behavior, as shown by an interesting experiment. Participants[6] sat alone in a room and followed tape-recorded instructions. Half believed that they were being observed via a one-way mirror (public condition), whereas others believed that no one was watching (private condition). At the end of the experiment, the tape-recorded instructions invited the participant to make a donation by leaving some change in the jar on the table. The results showed that donations were seven times higher in the public condition than in the private condition. Apparently, one important reason for generous helping is to make (or sustain) a good impression on those who are watching.

One purpose of prosocial behavior, especially at cost to self, is to get oneself accepted into the group, so doing prosocial things without recognition is less beneficial. Self-interest dictates acting prosocially if it helps one belong to the group. That is probably why prosocial behavior increases when others are watching. Other studies have shown that favors increase compliance in both private and public settings, but compliance is greater in public settings.[7]

It may seem cynical to say that people's prosocial actions are motivated by wanting to make a good impression, but one can also see this pattern in a positive light. One theme of this book has been that people travel a long road to social acceptance. People do many things to get others to like them, and prosocial behavior is no exception.

Born to Reciprocate

Reciprocity is defined as the obligation to return in kind what another has done for us. Folk wisdom recognizes reciprocity with such sayings as "You scratch my back, and I'll

reciprocity the obligation to return in kind what another has done for us

off the mark.com   by Mark Parisi

I'M A LOUSY TIPPER AND I'D LIKE YOUR RUDEST WAITRESS SO I WON'T FEEL GUILTY ABOUT IT...

offthemark.com

Reprinted by permission of Atlantic Feature Syndicate/Mark Parisi.

scratch yours." Reciprocity norms are found in all cultures in the world.[8] If I do something for you, and you don't do anything back for me, I'm likely to be upset or offended, and next time around I may not do something for you. If you do something for me, and I don't reciprocate, I'm likely to feel guilty about it.

The reciprocity norm is so powerful that it even applies to situations in which you do not ask for the favor. Phil Kunz, a sociology professor at Brigham Young University in Provo, Utah, sent 578 Christmas cards to a sample of complete strangers living in Chicago, Illinois.[9] When somebody sends you a card, you feel obligated to send one back. Does this apply even to complete strangers? Apparently so, because Dr. Kunz received a total of 117 cards from people who had no idea who he was. He also received several unexpected long-distance telephone calls from people who had received one of his Christmas cards. Although most of the cards just contained signatures, a significant number of them contained handwritten notes, long letters, and pictures of family and pets. Only 6 of the 117 people who sent Kunz cards said they couldn't remember him.

Most often people consider reciprocity to be direct—you help someone who may help you later. However, scientists have argued that some reciprocity may be indirect—help someone and receive help from someone else, even strangers who know you only through reputation.[10] Helping someone or refusing to help has an impact on one's reputation within the group. We all know people who are consistently helpful, and others who are not.

Does reciprocity apply to seeking help as well as giving help? Often you might need or want help, but you might not always accept help and certainly might not always seek it out. People's willingness to request or accept help often depends on whether they think they will be able to pay it back (i.e., reciprocity). If they don't think they can pay the helper back, they are less willing to let someone help them.[11] This is especially a problem among the elderly because their declining health and income are barriers to reciprocating.[12] As a result, elderly people may refuse to ask for help even when they need it, simply because they believe they will not be able to pay it back.

When someone helps you, you probably feel grateful for the assistance. **Gratitude** is defined as a positive emotion that results from the perception that one has benefited from the costly, intentional, voluntary action of another person.[13]

People often have an acute sense of fairness when they are on the receiving end of someone else's generosity or benevolence, and they prefer to accept help when they think they can pay the person back. We discuss this sense of fairness in the next section.

Born to Be Fair

The central theme of this book is that human beings are cultural animals, that the impulse to belong to culture is in our genes. Fairness is a cultural norm. **Norms** are standards established by society to tell its members what types of behavior are typical or expected. Norms that promote fairness can have an important influence on whether people contribute to the common good.[14] Two such norms are equity and equality. **Equity** means that each person receives benefits in proportion to what he or she has contributed (e.g., the person who does the most work gets the highest pay). **Equality** means that everyone gets the same amount. Both kinds of fairness are used and understood much more widely by humans than by any other animal.

According to some evolutionary theories, an individual's ability to reproduce depends largely on his or her position within the social group.[15] In order to maintain fitness-enhancing relationships, the individual must continually invest time, energy, and resources in building good relationships with others in the social group. To take without giving something back runs the risk that others might resent you and might ultimately reject or exclude you from the group. After all, few groups can afford to have lots of members (other than babies, perhaps) who take and take without contributing anything. It will

gratitude a positive emotion that results from the perception that one has benefited from the costly, intentional, voluntary action of another person

norms standards established by society to tell its members what types of behavior are typical or expected

equity the idea that each person receives benefits in proportion to what he or she contributes

equality the idea that everyone gets the same amount, regardless of what he or she contributes

be hard to pass on your genes to the next generation when the people you want to mate with shun you.

People are designed by nature (so to speak) to belong to a system based on fairness and social exchange. As one sign of the importance of fairness to human nature, the feeling that one has no value to others—that you are a taker rather than a giver—is a major cause of depression.[16] To be sure, there are plenty of obnoxious people who take more than they give, but most of them don't see themselves that way. People who do see themselves as taking more than they give may become depressed. To avoid depression, people may seek to contribute their fair share.

Some suicides may reflect the same concern with being fair and reciprocal. We saw in Chapter 4 that human beings differ from most other animals in that they commit suicide. One reason some people commit suicide is that they think they are a burden on other people—that others do things for them that they cannot reciprocate, so the others would be better off if they were dead.[17,18] Of course, people are not better off when someone commits suicide. Suicide has numerous negative effects on those left behind. Not only do the survivors miss the dead person, they may even blame themselves for the suicide.

The concern with fairness makes people feel bad when they don't contribute their fair share, but it can also affect people who think that their good performance makes others feel bad. When we outperform others, we may have mixed emotions. On the one hand, we may feel a sense of pride and pleasure because we have surpassed the competition. On the other hand, we may feel fear and anxiety because those we have outperformed might reject us or retaliate. Interpersonal concern about the consequences of outperforming others has been called **sensitivity about being the target of a threatening upward comparison**.[19] Outperformers often become distressed when they believe that others are envious that they did not perform as well. In reality, however, losers have more to worry about than winners. Research shows that participants are more aggressive against someone they beat (i.e., losers) than against someone who beat them (i.e., winners).[20]

Is reciprocity unique to humans? More simply, do animals understand the concept "fairness"? A study of monkeys provides a fascinating answer.[21] The researchers trained monkeys to fetch rocks. Each monkey was rewarded with a slice of cucumber for each rock it fetched. The monkeys could see each other getting these rewards, and they soon learned to keep fetching rocks to get cucumber slices. Then, however, the researchers randomly gave some monkeys a grape instead of a cucumber slice for their rocks. To a monkey, a grape is a much better treat than a slice of cucumber. The monkeys who got the grapes were very happy about this. The other monkeys were mad, however. They acted as if it were unfair that they only got the cucumber slice for the same act that earned other monkeys a grape. The ones who didn't get the grapes protested, such as by refusing to fetch more rocks ("going on strike") or by angrily flinging the cucumber slice away. This study attracted international media attention, with the implication being that monkeys understand fairness and object to unfairness.

But do they really? Perhaps the study was overinterpreted. Yes, a monkey is smart enough to protest when it is treated unfairly. If, however, unfairness per se is the problem, then the monkeys who received the grapes should have protested too. But they didn't. Researchers who study fairness distinguish between two kinds of unfairness, namely being **underbenefited** (getting less than you deserve) and being **overbenefited** (getting more than you deserve). Monkeys and several other animals seem to have an acute sense of when they are underbenefited. However, only humans seem to worry about being overbenefited. A full-blown sense of fairness, one that encompasses both aspects, is found only among humans. For people to be truly fair, they must object to being overbenefited as well as to being underbenefited (even if the latter is stronger).

People (unlike other animals) do feel guilty when they are overbenefited. In lab studies, people feel guilty if they receive a larger reward than others for performing the same

> "...it's better in fact to be guilty of manslaughter than of fraud about what is fair and just."
> — Plato, *The Republic and Other Works*

sensitivity about being the target of a threatening upward comparison interpersonal concern about the consequences of outperforming others

underbenefited getting less than you deserve

overbenefited getting more than you deserve

amount or same quality of work.[22] Getting less than your fair share provokes anger and resentment, but getting more than your fair share produces guilt.[23] (See Chapter 6 for a discussions of anger and guilt.)

People who harm others (perhaps without meaning to do so) prefer to do something nice for the person they harm, and they prefer the nice act to exactly match the harm they did, so that fairness and equity are restored.[24] They act as if the harm they did creates a debt to that person, and they desire to "pay it back" so as to get the relationship back on an even, fair footing.

QUIZ YOURSELF

What Is Prosocial Behavior?

answers: see pg 329

1. **Henrietta helped Maurille when her first child was born. When Henrietta has her first child, Maurille thinks she ought to help Henrietta. This type of helping illustrates the norm of _____ .**

   ⓐ equity ⓑ reciprocity ⓒ social justice ⓓ social responsibility

2. **Albert thinks that because he has more job experience than others on his shift, he should make more money than they do. This illustrates the norm of _____ .**

   ⓐ equality ⓑ equity ⓒ reciprocity ⓓ social responsibility

3. **At the local soup kitchen, volunteers give everyone one bowl of soup regardless of how much money they have or how hungry they are. This type of helping illustrates the norm of _____ .**

   ⓐ equality ⓑ equity ⓒ reciprocity ⓓ social responsibility

4. **Feeling guilty about receiving more than one's fair share is found in _____ .**

   ⓐ animals other than humans ⓑ only humans ⓒ both (a) and (b) ⓓ neither (a) nor (b)

Morality

This chapter is about prosocial behavior. One way to think of behavior is that it encompasses actions that are morally good. Thus, understanding morality is one key to understanding prosocial behavior. We have said that people seem to be born to reciprocate and to be fair. That suggests that they are born with a readiness to learn moral rules and act on them.

All known human societies have morals, which are a set of rules about what actions are right versus wrong. Moral rules tell people what they should do. In general, moral rules encourage people to do what is best for the social group, which often requires restraining selfish and other antisocial impulses. This sheds light on a key theme of this chapter, which is that in the long run everyone is better off when people cooperate—but people are often tempted to be selfish instead, and so it is necessary to encourage people to cooperate, such as by having and enforcing rules.

Moral issues arise frequently in everyday life. When researchers contacted people at randomly chosen moments during the day, one out of every three or four responses indicated that the person had experienced a moral or immoral action (by self or others, including just witnessing) within the past hour.[25] Having people do immoral things to you reduces your happiness significantly—and, conversely, happiness goes up when people do morally good things to you. Performing morally good actions is thus a way that people make each other feel better. It also increases one's sense of purpose.

One might assume that performing immoral actions would be a strong cause of unhappiness, not least because people would feel guilty and regretful. While it is true that performing immoral actions does tend to reduce levels of happiness, the effect is not strong or consistent. Inconsistency arises in part from the surprising fact that many people seem to get pleasure from doing immoral things—a "cheater's high," as described by one set of researchers.[26] They showed that people expect that dishonest and immoral behavior will make them feel bad, but contrary to their expectations, many of them feel a surge of positive emotion. This seems often to be based on a feeling of self-satisfaction, even perhaps a thrill, based on having cheated and gotten away with it.

Time of day seems to matter. Evidence for a "morning morality effect" shows that people seem to be at their virtuous best in the morning, and the likelihood of immoral actions increases later in the day.[27] One likely reason concerns self-control, which was covered in Chapter 4. It takes self-control to do what is morally right rather than acting on impulse or selfish motives. Self-control depends on an energy resource, which tends to be in good shape after a night's sleep but gets depleted during the day.

Morals often contribute to inner conflict—particularly when you are tempted to do something that will benefit yourself but you know it would be morally wrong. For example, someone might be tempted to steal some money but holds back because stealing is immoral. A recent article with the simple title "Moral Actor, Selfish Agent" concluded that what many people do is try to appear to be moral (like an actor playing a role) while quietly being selfish.[28] The moral version of this self is thus an act that one puts on for others, because it is highly desirable to be perceived as a morally good person. People regard their moral actor self as idealistic, while they see their selfish agent self as realistic.

Many people associate morality with reasoning from principles. An early and influential line of research sought to classify people by the quality of their **moral reasoning**. This was done by presenting them with a dilemma and asking them to explain their judgment. A frequently used dilemma involved a man whose wife was deathly ill, and he could not afford the expensive medicine to save her life—but he had an opportunity to steal it. Should he steal? What mattered was not the specific answer of yes or no, but the quality of reasoning the person displayed while thinking about it.

But then psychologists began to notice that when people were confronted with moral dilemmas in their own lives, they often did not stop to engage in reasoning from principles. Instead, they seemed to be guided by a sense of what "feels right." Researchers began to study **moral intuitions** instead of moral reasoning.

Research began to show that people's moral intuitions have more influence than reasoning.[29] New dilemmas were devised, such as a case in which a brother and sister decided to have sex one time, used protection (and so had no consequences of pregnancy or disease), enjoyed it, never did it again, and ultimately felt their relationship had been strengthened by this one adventure. Most research participants condemned this as wrong. The reasons they gave were contradicted. For example, some pointed out that incest increases the odds of producing birth defects; but the example specified that the act did not cause pregnancy. Others said that incest might become habit-forming or damage the sibling relationship, but again the story ruled those out. Yet despite the failure of their reasons, most participants continued to condemn the incest as morally wrong. Some said things like, "I can't explain why, I just know it's wrong." Such sentiments capture the crucial point: The moral judgment was based on intuitive feelings, not reasoning from principles.

Are moral principles irrelevant? No. Often people must explain and justify their actions to others, and invoking shared moral principles is an effective way to do this.[30] People who perform immoral acts risk being excluded from important social groups: divorced, fired, even imprisoned.

Soon, researchers began to explore other irrational patterns of moral judgment. In one, people imagine a runaway trolley that is headed toward killing five people, and they are asked whether they would throw a switch to shift the trolley onto another track, where it will kill one person.[31] Many people say they would throw the switch, thereby killing an innocent person, in order to save the five.[32] However, if it were necessary to have physical

moral reasoning using logical deductions to make moral judgments based on abstract principles of right and wrong

moral intuitions judgments (about whether an action is right or wrong) that occur automatically and rely on emotional feelings

contact with the victim (pushing him off a bridge in front of the trolley to stop it from killing the others ahead), they generally say they would not. The moral principle is the same: sacrificing one innocent person to save five other lives. But apparently moral intuitions respect a big difference between the two ways of killing someone (throwing a switch vs. pushing a human body off a bridge).

Another dilemma concerns the head of a large corporation who is told about a possible new venture that would increase profits and would either help or harm the environment. He responds that he cares only about the environment, not about profits, and he approves the plan, which then does have the predicted effect on the environment.[33] If the outcome is harm, then research participants generally condemn him for having intentionally harmed the environment. But if the outcome is help, they do not give him credit for intentionally helping.[34] Again, the moral principle should seemingly predict no difference, because in both cases he explicitly said he did not care about the environment.

Political behavior is often guided by strong moral values. Recent work has proposed that moral differences may contribute to some of the disagreements between political liberals and conservatives. The broader idea is that moral judgments in general can be traced to five different foundations, which are like basic values. Liberals prize and use two of the five, whereas conservatives prize all five of them.[35]

One broad moral foundation is disapproval of people hurting each other. Another is the importance of fairness, which includes the assumption that people should generally reciprocate good treatment by others. These are the two that both liberals and conservatives uphold. The other three, which appeal mainly to conservatives, are respect for legitimate authority, loyalty to one's group (this includes patriotism), and purity/sanctity. Purity includes the value of cleanliness, in both the literal physical sense (e.g., wash hands before touching the flag or a holy book), and symbolic (e.g., ritual purification, sexual innocence). Subtle cues that evoke these values can affect people's political opinions. For example, when people encountered a dispenser of hand sanitizer, they expressed more conservative political views than when not thus reminded of purity.[36]

Thus, morality is more than an abstract topic for debate by philosophers. It reaches into many corners of social life, including emotion, judgment, impression formation, and politics. Morality is what enables people to agree that prosocial actions are indeed prosocial. More broadly, moral rules create the shared understandings of how to act—which are one of the foundations of human culture and society.

QUIZ YOURSELF
Morality

1. **What human societies have morals?**
   - (a) Developed countries
   - (b) Religious countries
   - (c) Third-world countries
   - (d) All of the above

2. **What time of day are people most moral?**
   - (a) Morning
   - (b) Afternoon
   - (c) Evening
   - (d) Morality does not depend on the time of day

3. **People expect to feel _____ when they engage in immoral behavior, and they actually feel _____ after engaging in immoral behavior.**
   - (a) bad; bad
   - (b) bad; good
   - (c) good; bad
   - (d) good; good

4. **Moral judgments in general can be traced to five different foundations: (1) disapproval of people hurting each other, (2) fairness, (3) respect for legitimate authority, (4) loyalty to one's group, and (5) purity/sanctity. Conservatives tend to value all five, whereas liberals tend to value which two?**
   - (a) disapproval of hurting others; fairness
   - (b) disapproval of hurting others; loyalty to one's group
   - (c) fairness; loyalty to one's group
   - (d) fairness; purity/sanctity

answers: see pg 329

Cooperation, Forgiveness, Obedience, Conformity, and Trust

Cooperation

Cooperation is a vital and relatively simple form of prosocial behavior. **Cooperation** is based on reciprocity: You do your part, and someone else does his or her part, and together you work toward common goals. Cooperating is vital for social groups to succeed, especially if they are to flourish in the sense of the whole being more than the sum of its parts.

Psychologists have studied cooperation by using the **prisoner's dilemma**, which forces people to choose between a cooperative act and another act that combines being competitive, exploitative, and defensive. The prisoner's dilemma, a widely studied tradeoff, is discussed in detail in the *Tradeoffs* box.

Political scientist Robert Axelrod once held a computer tournament designed to investigate the prisoner's dilemma situation using the payoff matrix shown in **TABLE 9.1**. Contestants in the tournament submitted computer programs that would compete in a prisoner's dilemma game for 200 rounds. These followed many different strategies, such as being antagonistic every round, cooperating every round, or deciding each move at random.

The strategy that gained the most points for the player was tit-for-tat:[37] Just do whatever the other player did last time. If the other player cooperated, then you should cooperate too. If the other player made the competitive move, then you should too. Obviously tit-for-tat is closely based on reciprocation, and it is no accident that reciprocation works so well: It promotes cooperation when the other person is cooperative, but it also protects you from being taken advantage of when the other person is exploitative.

Undoubtedly some people are more cooperative than others. One difference lies in how people interpret the situation. Cooperators see the prisoner's dilemma and related situations as an issue of good versus bad behavior (with cooperation being good). Competitors see it as weak versus strong, with cooperation being weak.[38,39] It is hardly surprising that people are more prone to cooperate if they think of cooperation as a sign of moral goodness than as a sign of weakness.

What happens when people with different approaches are matched in the prisoner's dilemma game? Sadly, the results show that exploitation trumps cooperation.[40,41,42] When both players favor cooperation, not surprisingly, they both tend to cooperate (and do pretty well). When both lean toward competition, then the game soon degenerates into everyone choosing the competitive response on every trial, and no one ends up doing well. When there is one of each, the game likewise degenerates into mutual exploitation and defensiveness. Thus, two virtuous people can do well by each other, but if either one plays selfishly, trust and cooperation are soon destroyed. This is an important and profound insight into how people relate to each other. If both people want to cooperate, they can succeed in doing so, for mutual benefit. If either one is not cooperative, then cooperation is typically doomed. Cooperation is a fragile tendency, easily destroyed. This probably reflects the facts of evolution: Across most species, competition is the norm and cooperation is rare. For example, research has shown that pigeons usually defect during a tit-for-tat condition of a prisoner's

TABLE 9.1 Prisoner's Dilemma: Computer Tournament

	Player 1 (Antagonistic)	Player 2 (Cooperative)
Player 2 (Antagonistic)	Both get 1 point	Player 1 gets 0 points
		Player 2 gets 5 points
Player 2 (Cooperative)	Player 2 gets 0 points	Both get 3 points
	Player 1 gets 5 points	

cooperation working together with someone for mutual or reciprocal benefit

prisoner's dilemma a game that forces people to choose between cooperation and competition

dilemma game even though it means earning only one-third of the food that they could have earned if they had cooperated.[43] Humans are much better at cooperating than most other animals, but this should be regarded as small progress in overcoming the naturally competitive tendencies that are still alive and well (and strong) in humans too.

Cooperation: The Big Picture

The prisoner's dilemma game offers a choice between cooperation and competition, as if those were on the same level. We noted that competition seems to be stronger, in the sense that if one person cooperates and the other competes, pretty soon both are competing. There may be important reasons for this.

In evolution, competition is much older and more deeply rooted than cooperation. Plenty of research with great apes (humankind's closest biological relatives) has shown that they compete very readily and cunningly, but the idea of cooperating with non-kin seems never even to occur to them.[44] Their few activities that sometimes look like cooperation (e.g., hunting in groups) are not truly cooperative, because each animal is really just out for itself.

Cooperation is a vital foundation of culture. The fact that animals do not cooperate probably contributes to the fact that they do not get very far at creating culture. The willingness to trust strangers and cooperate with them enabled humans to create civilization, with all its benefits. Indeed, although social psychologists have long emphasized research on helping, and stories about helpful people (including the "pay it forward" story with which this chapter opened) inspire admiration, helping is much less important than cooperation for the success of the human species.

The human tendency is not to trust and cooperate with everybody, indiscriminately. Rather, people tend to cooperate with members of their group. Often this is motivated by competition and threats from other groups. After all, if there were a battle between two groups, one of whom cooperated with each other and the other did not, the cooperators would likely win. Recent evidence shows that threats of violence make people more agreeable, trusting, and cooperative—but mainly with members of their own group.[45] In lab studies, threat made participants more willing to work with their own group and less willing to work with other groups. Even at the national level, countries that spent more money on their military forces showed more trust toward ingroup members and less toward outgroup members.

Cooperation requires each person to make sacrifices so that all can benefit. People who break these rules undermine the system and ruin it for everyone. For example, if lots of people started making and using counterfeit money, people would have to stop trusting the money they got, and society would lose the benefits of being able to use money. Social norms, moral principles, and laws help people know when it is appropriate to cooperate.

Unlike other animals, humans will punish someone who breaks rules, even if they were not personally victimized. A dog might try to bite another dog who takes its food, but no one has ever seen a third dog intervene to make the second dog respect the property of the first. Humans will not only do this. Some fascinating research using an economic game (similar to the prisoner's dilemma) has shown that many people will even accept costs, as in a reduction of their own pay, in order to punish someone else who breaks the rules.[46] This pattern is called "altruistic punishment," because the punisher is individually worse off as a result of punishing the rule-breaker, but the punisher helps the collective good by encouraging everyone to follow the rules. People engage in more altruistic punishment when they are thinking about how members of a group are similar to each other,[47] like a functioning social network.

Another way people help enforce rules is through gossip. Gossip has a bad reputation, but it is often used to communicate accurate information about others. People who break the rules develop bad reputations, and so others know not to trust them. When research participants saw another person betray someone's trust and refuse to cooperate, they passed this information along to others who might have to decide whether to trust and cooperate with that same person.[48] Indeed, it made people feel better to pass along this gossip. Moreover, when people know that gossip is likely to occur, they become more cooperative and less selfish. All these findings indicate how much human social behavior is attuned to the importance of cooperation and trust.

The Prisoner's Dilemma

The prisoner's dilemma is a classic tradeoff that many psychologists have adapted for use in research. The dilemma arises in a story about two criminals, whom we will call Bart and Mack (see **TABLE 9.2**). They are arrested on suspicion of having committed armed robbery, and sure enough they are found to be carrying concealed weapons, but the police do not have enough evidence to link them to the robbery. Accordingly, the police question them separately. Both men are invited to confess to the crime and hence betray the other. What happens to either of them depends on how both of them react.

One possibility is that neither man confesses to the crime. This is the prosocial option (well, prosocial when crime isn't involved!): They cooperate with each other and reject the police's deals. If this happens, they can only be convicted of the minor charge of carrying concealed weapons. Both men will get a light jail sentence.

Another possibility is that one man will confess and the other will not. If Bart confesses and Mack holds out, then the police will let Bart turn state's evidence. In reward for his testimony against Mack, Bart can go free (the best possible outcome for Bart); the police will be able to get Mack convicted of the robbery, and he will get a long prison sentence (the worst possible outcome for Mack). Of course, the outcomes are reversed if Bart holds out and Mack confesses.

The last possibility is that both confess. The police then do not have to give anyone a free pass because both men have incriminated themselves. Both will go to prison for moderately long sentences, though perhaps not as long as the sentence that one gets if the other betrays him.

From the player's perspective, the dilemma is thus whether to confess and betray your partner or to hold out and cooperate with him. In a broader sense, your choice between a cooperative response and an antagonistic response. Confessing betrays your partner for your own benefit, and it also protects you in case your partner seeks to betray you. Cooperating (refusing to confess) involves taking a risk that could bring a good outcome for both people, but leaves you vulnerable to the longest sentence if your partner chooses to confess. Put another way, you will both be better off if both cooperate and refuse to confess because you both get light sentences. However, you can get the best outcome for yourself by confessing while your partner holds out, so many people will be tempted to try that route.

Yet another way of understanding the tradeoff is that it is between what is best for you versus what is best for everyone. What is best for you is to confess because you either get off totally free (if your partner holds out) or get a medium rather than a long sentence (if you both betray each other). But the best outcome for both partners is achieved if you both refuse to confess. This is the dilemma of human cultural life in a nutshell: whether to selfishly pursue your own impulses, regardless of the rules and other people's welfare, or instead to do what is best for all.

Researchers recently tested the prisoner's dilemma game with actual prisoners.[49] They compared female prisoners to female college students in Germany. Surprisingly, they found that prisoners were far more cooperative than expected, even more cooperative than the college students.

TABLE 9.2 Prisoner's Dilemma: Original Story Version: What Would You Choose?

Although it is commonly believed that women are more cooperative than men, a meta-analysis of 50 years of research involving 31,642 participants in 18 different countries concluded that overall men are just as cooperative as women.[51] There are some interesting gender differences in cooperation. Male–male interactions are more cooperative than female–female interactions. In mixed-sex interactions, however, women were more cooperative than men. These findings make sense from an evolutionary perspective.[52] Ancestral men needed to cooperate to acquire resources, such as food and property. For example, if men did not cooperate during hunting and warfare, nobody would get any food, and wars would be lost. Ancestral women usually migrated between groups, and they would have been interacting mostly with women who tended not to be relatives. Such social interactions were likely rife with sexual competition, which could explain lower cooperation in female–female interactions.

According to the recent book *Warriors and Worriers: The Survival of the Sexes*,[53] men evolved to fight wars and battles together, whereas women evolved to bear and care for their children, which they cannot do alone. Men therefore form lasting bonds with other men, with whom they will work together and fight enemies together. Women seek someone to help provide for them and their children, and that usually means a man rather than another woman (who will have her own children who need support). Women therefore do not tend to form lasting, productive bonds with other women their age. Rather, they seek to form attachments to men. This could account for the pattern of cooperation shown in prisoner's dilemma games (and much else). Still, there are many opinions and theories about gender differences, and not all of them would embrace this analysis.

Successful cooperation also seems to depend on communication. If communication is difficult, there is less cooperation.[56] Communication allows for the emergence of cooperation.[57] Cooperation drops sharply when partners avoid discussion during a prisoner's dilemma game.[58] Can money reduce cooperation and helping? To find out, see *Money Matters*.

Forgiveness

Forgiveness is an important category of prosocial behavior.[59] **Forgiveness** refers to ceasing to feel angry toward and ceasing to seek retribution against someone who has wronged you. According to theories of fairness, reciprocity, and equity, if someone does something bad to you, that person owes you a kind of debt—an obligation to do something positive for you to offset the bad deed. Forgiveness in that context involves releasing the person from this obligation, just as one might cancel a monetary debt. This does not mean that you condone what the person did. It just means that you won't hold it against him or her.

As we have seen, human beings have longer-lasting relationships than most other animals, and forgiveness is an important contributor to this. When people hurt, disappoint, or betray each other, the bad feelings can damage the relationship and drive the people to leave it. Forgiveness can help heal the relationship and enable people to go on living or working together.[60] The more strongly someone is committed to a particular relationship, the more likely he or she is to forgive an offense by the other partner.[61]

Forgiveness is an important part of a successful romantic or marital relationship, as is increasingly recognized by both researchers and spouses themselves.[62,63] Couples that

non-zero-sum game an interaction in which both participants can win (or lose)

zero-sum game a situation in which one person's gain is another's loss

forgiveness ceasing to feel angry toward or seek retribution against someone who has wronged you

forgive each other have higher levels of relationship satisfaction.[64,65] But what causes what—the tendency to forgive or relationship satisfaction? Researchers have recently begun tracking couples over time, to see which comes first.[66] Partners who forgave each other for doing something wrong were happier than other couples six months later. In contrast, earlier satisfaction with the relationship did not predict later forgiveness. This pattern of findings indicates that forgiveness leads to better relationships, not vice versa.

The benefits of forgiveness have been well documented in research. It is fairly obvious that being forgiven is beneficial to the person who did something wrong because that person no longer needs to feel guilty or owes a debt to the one who has been hurt. Perhaps more surprisingly, forgiveness also has great benefits for the forgivers. They report better physical and mental health than victims who hold grudges.[67,68,69]

The downside of forgiveness may be that it invites people to offend again. So far, research has yielded mixed results. Some findings indicate that offenders are glad to be forgiven and often feel grateful, which may motivate them to perform more good deeds. For example, participants in one study[70] were led to believe they had accidentally broken some laboratory equipment. They received a message of forgiveness, or retribution, or both, or neither. Later, the experimenter asked for a favor. Those who had been forgiven were most willing to do the favor. Thus, instead of inviting repeat offenses, forgiveness led to more prosocial behavior. On the other hand, a recent study of married couples found that *refusing* to forgive a partner led to long-term declines in aggression. Spouses who were readily forgiven continued to engage in hurtful actions toward their partners.[71]

Mostly, though, forgiveness leads to more satisfying relationships. One pathway is that when someone refuses to forgive a loved one for doing something wrong, this tends to come up again in future conflicts, making them harder to resolve.[72] "It's just like when

"FORGIVE YOU?... SURE I'LL FORGIVE YOU... THE MOMENT I SEE SOMETHING I REALLY WANT ON THE SHOPPING CHANNEL."

© Edgar Argo/CartoonStock

you forgot my birthday last year!" When each new conflict prompts the couple to bring up unforgiven old grudges, minor arguments quickly become major fights, and this sets the couple on the downward spiral that is typical of unhappy, problem-filled relationships (see Chapter 12). Forgiveness can help prevent this destructive pattern from starting.

Forgiveness is linked to seeing the other person's perspective and hence avoiding some cognitive biases that can drive people apart. When any two people have a conflict, especially if one does something to hurt the other, people tend to perceive and understand it in biased ways. The victim tends to emphasize all the bad consequences ("That really hurt my feelings"), whereas the perpetrator may focus on external factors that reduce his or her blame ("I couldn't help it"). Hence, they don't understand or sympathize with each other. People in highly satisfying dating relationships don't show those biases.[73] Instead, they see the other person's point of view better ("I know you couldn't help it"). Couples who think that way are more willing to forgive each other and hence better able to recover from a misdeed. Forgiveness helps couples get past even such relationship-threatening events as sexual infidelity, enabling the relationship to survive and recover.[74]

Why don't people forgive? Research has identified several major barriers that reduce willingness to forgive. One fairly obvious factor is the severity of the offense: The worse the person treated you, the harder it is to forgive.[75] Another is a low level of commitment to the relationship.[76] In a sense, forgiving is making a generous offer to renounce anger and claims for retribution as a way of helping to repair and strengthen the relationship, and people are more willing to do this for relationships that are more important to them. Apologies also help elicit forgiveness. When someone has wronged you but is sincerely remorseful and expresses an apology, you are much more willing to forgive than when no such apology or remorse is expressed.[77,78]

Inner processes also can lead toward or away from forgiveness. In particular, how the person thinks about the transgression can be decisive. If you think that you might easily have performed a similar offense, you become more willing to forgive.[79] In contrast, ruminating about what someone did to you can increase anger, which in turn makes forgiveness less likely.[80]

Some persons are also more forgiving than others. Religious people forgive more readily than nonreligious people,[81] in part because religions generally promote and encourage values that help people live together, and in fact some religions prominently extol forgiving as an important virtue. For example, the most famous and widely repeated prayer in the Christian religion couples a request for forgiveness with a promise to forgive others: "And forgive us our debts, as we forgive our debtors."[82]

Forgiving others requires inhibiting impulses to lash out aggressively at those who have harmed us. Cognitive executive functions are the mental abilities that help us attend to, organize, plan, and achieve goals. They also help us inhibit inappropriate behaviors. It is therefore not surprising that people with more advanced cognitive executive functions are more forgiving of others.[83] In a similar vein, people high in trait self-control are also more forgiving of others.[84]

In contrast, narcissistic individuals are less likely than others to forgive when they have been offended.[85,86] These conceited and self-centered individuals have a broad belief that they deserve special, preferential treatment, and they are outraged when someone offends them. They are easily offended and generally think they deserve some major compensation before they will consider forgiving.

Obedience

Obedience to orders can be prosocial, and in many respects it is highly desirable that people carry out the orders of their superiors. Groups such as military units, corporations, surgical teams, and sports teams cannot function effectively without some degree of obedience. If people refuse to follow the leader's directions, the group degenerates into an ineffective collection of individuals.

Social psychologists have generally taken a dim view of obedience. This attitude can be traced to a classic series of studies conducted by Stanley Milgram in the 1960s.[87] His research interest, like that of many psychologists at the time, was shaped by the

obedience following orders from an authority figure

disturbing events of World War II, including large-scale massacres of civilians by Nazi German troops. After the war, the international outcry against these atrocities presented an ongoing challenge to social science to account for how seemingly ordinary, decent, well-intentioned individuals could do such things. Many of the killers defended themselves by saying "I was only following orders." The odds are that if someone asked you whether you might have helped kill Jews, homosexuals, Roma (gypsies), communists, and other defenseless civilians if you had lived in Nazi Germany, you would say "no way!" Yet these refusals stand in contrast to how so many German citizens actually behaved.

Milgram set up a study to see whether Americans would in fact follow orders that might injure or possibly kill someone. Participants were recruited for a study on learning, and when they arrived they were told that they would play the role of a teacher who would deliver electric shocks as punishment for mistakes made by a learner. They met the learner: a mild-mannered, middle-aged man who was actually a confederate. The man mentioned that he had a heart condition.

The experimenter showed the participant an impressive-looking shock delivery apparatus, which had a row of switches with labels running from "Mild shock" up to "Danger: Severe shock" and then to "XXX." The experimenter said that each time the learner made a mistake, the participant should flick a switch, starting from the mildest shock (15 volts) and working upward toward the most severe shock (450 volts), in 15-volt increments. The experimenter said that although the shocks were painful, they would not be dangerous.

They started the exercise, and the learner kept making mistakes. The participant sat by the experimenter, who instructed him or her to deliver shocks. Although the learner was in another room, the participant could still hear him. (Subsequent studies showed that people were less willing to deliver severe shocks if the learner was in the same room with them, as opposed to being out of sight.) If the participant hesitated, the experimenter had a standard series of prods that commanded the participant to continue. To make it harder to continue, the learner followed a script that included groaning, screaming in pain, banging on the wall, and shouting that he had a heart

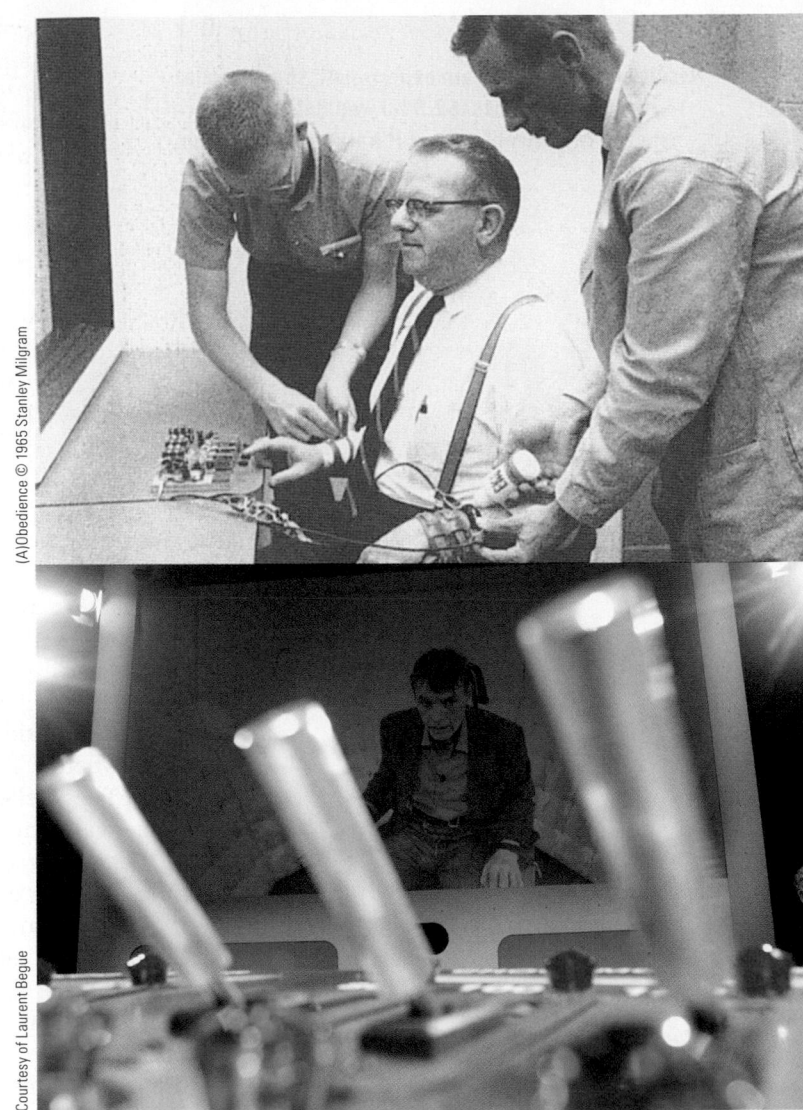

Conducting the Milgram study, the experimenter attaches shock electrodes to the wrists of the "learner" (actually a confederate) while the "teacher" (the real participant) helps out.

condition, that his heart was starting to bother him, and that he did not want to continue the study. Eventually the learner stopped responding at all, so for all the participant knew, the learner had passed out or died. The experimenter, however, said to treat no response as a mistake and therefore to continue delivering higher shocks.

Before he ran the study, Milgram surveyed a group of psychiatrists for predictions as to what would happen. How many participants would go all the way and deliver the most severe shock of 450 volts? The psychiatrists had faith that the participants would resist authority, and they predicted that only 1 in 1,000 (0.10%) would be willing to deliver the most severe shocks. In the actual study, the majority of participants (62.5%) went all the way up to the maximum shock (see **FIGURE 9.1**)! To be sure, this wasn't easy for them: Many showed acute signs of distress, such as sweating, making sounds, and sometimes having fits of nervous laughter that seemed out of control, but they still did what they were told.

In 2009, social psychologist Jerry Burger replicated Milgram's findings and found nearly identical results, although he had to stop at 150 volts for ethical reasons.[88] Even after hearing cries of pain, 70% of participants kept shocking (Milgram found that 80% of participants kept shocking after 150 volts).

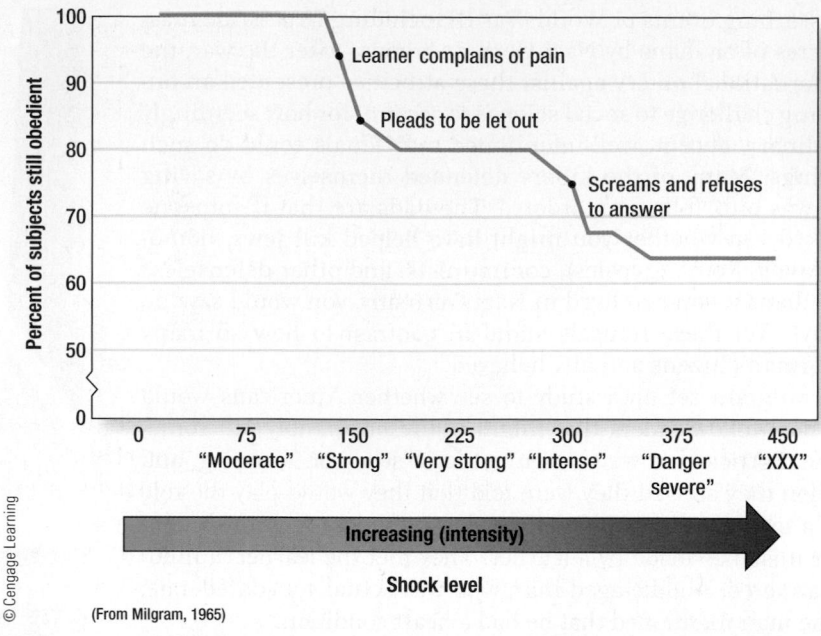

FIGURE 9.1

Results from the Milgram experiment, showing that most participants (62.5%) would deliver severe shocks to someone even if it harmed that person.

(From Milgram, 1965)

© Cengage Learning

Much has been said and written about Milgram's studies (including some serious debates as to whether it is ethical for researchers to put their participants through such experiences). The intellectual community was deeply shocked (no pun intended) to learn how far American citizens would obey orders to hurt another person, despite the moral lessons of Nazi Germany. Many people use Milgram's studies to emphasize the point that human behavior is more strongly influenced by the situation than by the person. However, recent research suggests that there are important individual differences in obedience. For example, agreeable people are more obedient than others, whereas people who lean to the "left" (liberal) politically are less obedient than others.[89]

Milgram's research has given obedience a bad name. His study was published in the early 1960s, and the rest of that decade saw a broad countercultural movement in which many young and some older people became hostile to authority and asserted that disobedience was a positive good, a right, and even an obligation. Bumper stickers such as "Question Authority!" abounded.

Yet, again, obedience can usually be a good thing. As we have already noted, very few organizations can function properly without obedience. Even families would fall apart if children refused to obey their parents' rules. Milgram's study focused on a peculiar situation in which obedience has morally bad outcomes, but this is exceptional. In most situations, obedience produces good outcomes. For example, how could a football team win a game if the pass receivers refused to obey the quarterback's play calling, or indeed if they disobeyed the orders of the referees? What would happen if people refused to obey traffic signals?

The fact that people obeyed Milgram's instructions may reveal an important fact about human nature, and one that depicts it as less morally bankrupt than is often said. People are naturally inclined to belong to groups, to seek social acceptance, and to put other people first. When a seemingly legitimate authority figure gives them commands, they tend to obey. This tendency does contain some danger, such as when a misguided, power-hungry, or irresponsible leader gives immoral commands. But the willingness to obey authority figures is probably an important and positive aspect of human psychology that enables people to live effectively in large groups (and hence in culture). Obedience is ultimately prosocial behavior because it supports group life and helps cultures to succeed. Milgram's studies provide cautionary evidence that obedience can be abused and can, under extraordinary circumstances, lead to immoral actions. But those circumstances are rare exceptions, and they should not blind us to the (mostly) prosocial benefits of obedience.

In a sense, participants who refused to obey the authority figure in a Milgram study were still obeying some rules—typically moral rules. Human cultural life sometimes contains conflicting rules, and sometimes people obey the wrong ones. If your professor tells you that obedience is bad, then try this: During the next exam, discuss the questions in a loud voice with the students seated near you, and if the professor objects, bring up the Milgram study's ostensible lesson that obedience to authority is bad. You're likely to see the professor suddenly change her or his tune about the value of obeying rules! (Don't actually try this. You might get expelled from your university!)

Homogeneous Originality by CIAgent

Conformity

Conformity is going along with the crowd (see Chapter 8). Like obedience, conformity has had a bad reputation among social psychologists, and this stems in part from influential early studies that depicted people doing foolish, irrational, or bad things in order to conform. The broader point, however, may be that conformity is prosocial, insofar as the studies show how people put other people first and exhibit a strong desire to get along with others. If people put themselves first, by being selfish, prosocial behavior decreases.[90]

People conform to the behavior of others more, and in general conform to social norms more, when others are watching than when unobserved.[91] For example, do people wash their hands after using the toilet in a public restroom? One study found that most women (77%) did—but only if they thought someone else was in the restroom too.[92] Among the women who thought they were alone, only a minority (39%) washed their hands. Presumably men would act about the same. (So if your date goes to the bathroom alone, you might think twice about holding hands!) The motivation behind socially desirable behavior (such as washing hands after using the toilet) can be to gain acceptance and approval from others.

Research shows that the presence of conformists dramatically increases the group size for which cooperation can be sustained.[93] In other words, a tendency toward conformity helps people to function well in large groups. Large groups are good for culture because there are more people (than in small groups) with which to share information, cooperate, exchange goods and services, and so forth.

Cultures vary in the degree to which they value conformity. A recent study[94] compared conformity in several dozen countries and concluded that pressures to conform were strictest in places where the risk of disease was highest. Because many diseases are contagious, people can interact safely only if they trust that others are following safe practices to restrict disease (such as being clean). In places where there are few germs around, cultures tend to let people do whatever they want, but that sort of tolerant individualism risks allowing unsafe practices and spreading disease when there are many germs.

To learn more about conformity as it relates to restaurants, see *Food for Thought*. It includes information that might change the way you order your food for years to come.

Trust

Trust is a strong belief in the reliability and validity of someone or something. Trust is another vital part of prosocial behavior among humans. Trust enables strangers and other nonrelatives to cooperate. Economists say that every economic transaction involves some degree of trust. (After all, when you buy something online, you are giving money to strangers you have not even seen, and you trust that they will send you the goods you paid for.) Yet economists also argue that rational people should not trust strangers, because they might get burned. However, recent research shows that people actually show an "excess" of trust to strangers.[95] That is, they trust strangers more than they probably should, including when they are not confident that the other stranger will do the right thing. The implication is that people (at least in many modern societies) respect a social norm that prohibits treating a stranger as untrustworthy, until and unless there is some reason to do so. People think they have an obligation to trust strangers, and they often feel guilty if they do not trust them. (To be sure, the trust is likely to be quickly withdrawn if the other person behaves

conformity going along with the crowd, that is, saying or doing whatever other people are doing

trust a confidence that others will provide benefits and/or not harm you, even if they may be tempted to do otherwise

badly. But to start off interacting with someone new, the norm in our culture is to show a willingness to trust.) Remember from Chapter 6 that guilt often motivates prosocial behavior. Trust links past, present, and future, and in that sense is particularly important for the kinds of cooperation that comprise human culture and social life.

Social psychologists have recently begun to study trust.[96] As the Dutch saying goes, "Trust comes by foot and leaves by horse!"—trust is slow to build up and then quick to unravel. The prisoner's dilemma game, for example, relies on trust: You make a cooperative play in the expectation that the other person will do likewise instead of betraying you for a bigger reward (see *Tradeoffs* box for a description of the prisoner's dilemma game). When people play the game over many rounds, trust is built up slowly as both continue to cooperate. A betrayal of trust early in the game usually spells the end of trust. If the same happens later in the game, after some trust has been established, it can recover.[97]

Recent research has found that people trust strangers with easier to pronounce names (e.g., "Andrian Babeshko" versus "Czeslaw Ratynska"), even when those strangers are from the same foreign country.[98] Comedian Stephen Colbert calls this effect "truthiness," defined as "truth that comes from the gut, not books." The effect might be due to the duplex mind. As lead researcher said, "information that's difficult to process signals danger," so weird names evoke an automatic distrust.

FOOD FOR *Thought*

Restaurants, Rules, and the Bad Taste of Nonconformity

Earlier in this chapter we suggested that conforming to rules is an important form of prosocial behavior, without which society would disintegrate into chaos. The Outback Steakhouse restaurant has for years advertised "No Rules" as its slogan. Do they really mean no rules apply? If you and six friends ate an ample meal there and then refused to pay, citing "no rules" as your justification, would the restaurant managers approve? Or how about if you grabbed food off the plates of other diners, or decided to run naked through their kitchen (violating Food and Drug Administration rules, which are in force regardless of the restaurant's advertising slogans or policies). If you were to try any or all of these behaviors at the nearest Outback Steakhouse, you'll quickly discover that they have plenty of rules after all.

Not all restaurant behavior involves conforming. In fact, psychologists have recently documented a curious pattern of deliberate nonconformity among restaurant diners. The surprising thing, though, is that

it often leaves people less satisfied with their meal than they might otherwise have been.

"I'll have the chicken."

"Hey, I was going to order the chicken! But that's OK, I'll order something else."

Have you ever heard such an exchange? When people eat together in a restaurant, they often act as if there were only one of each item on the menu and feel some obligation not to order the same food that someone else in the party has already ordered. Of course, there is no need to order different things. The restaurant almost certainly has enough chicken for everyone who wants it. Nonetheless, people seem to feel they should order different things.

A careful research project confirmed that people do in fact order different foods.[99] In their first study, they tracked the orders of hundreds of diners at a restaurant, to see how often people ordered the same versus different entrees. They then used a computer simulation to form other groups at random, for comparison purposes. This comparison showed that people who eat together order different foods more often than they would by chance.

In a second experiment, they let people order from a menu of different beers. By random assignment, some of the groups had to order in secret, whereas the others ordered aloud in the usual manner. When diners didn't know what the others were

having, they often ordered the same beer, but when they heard someone else order a particular beer, they switched to order something different.

This impulse to order something different makes people less satisfied with their food or drink. The researchers found that when diners ordered in secret (and therefore often ordered the same thing), they were pretty happy with what they had. When they ordered aloud, the person who ordered first (and therefore got what he or she wanted) was also pretty happy. But things weren't so good for the people who ordered later and often made a point of not ordering the same item that the first person had ordered. Those individuals were less satisfied with what they got.

It's not entirely clear why people feel the urge to order something different. Perhaps they just think that conformity is bad, so they try to avoid conforming to what someone else has done. But conformity is not really so bad. The people who order the same item, when it is their first choice, end up enjoying it more than the ones who switch to a second choice just to be different.

Apparently, the best practice is just to order your first choice, even if somebody else has already ordered it. Your second choice really won't taste as good, on average. Instead of trying to be different and nonconforming, just order what you would like best!

In general, people tend to be trusting, perhaps a bit more than is entirely safe. The "trust game," developed by behavioral economists, involves giving participants some money and telling them they can keep it or send any part of it off to someone else. Whatever they send will be tripled by the experimenter, and then the recipient can decide whether to keep it all or send part of it back. Obviously sending it off increases the money, and if the other person can be trusted to share the benefits, both people are better off. But there is no guarantee that you will get anything back, so trust is risky. In general, people send off a substantial amount of money, and others (strangers) generally reward their trust by splitting what they get.[100]

Although this work is in its early stages, some interesting facts have emerged. People trust others with good self-control, presumably because they can be expected to behave properly and resist selfish impulses.[101] People tend to distrust atheists, possibly because people think the fear of God is an important source of virtue.[102] Trust is an important factor in building commitment in close relationships.[103,104] Lonely people are much less trusting than other people.[105]

1. Psychiatrists predicted that _____ participants would go all the way in Milgram's experiment, giving the maximum shock level (450 volts) to the confederate.

(a) 1 in 10 (b) 1 in 50 (c) 1 in 100 (d) 1 in 1,000

2. A hockey coach orders a player to injure an opposing team's star player. Although the player is personally opposed to intentionally injuring other players, he follows the coach's order. This illustrates _____.

(a) conformity (b) compliance (c) cooperation (d) obedience

3. The results from Milgram's experiments are generally taken to show that _____.

(a) males are more physically aggressive than females (b) people can be sadistic (c) people often are resistant to situational pressures (d) situational pressures can overwhelm individual differences

4. The tendency for people to go along with the crowd is called _____.

(a) compliance (b) conformity (c) cooperation (d) obedience

answers: see pg 329

Why Do People Help Others?

People might have several different motives for helping. In this section we explore some of the possible reasons why people help others.

Evolutionary Benefits

It is clear that receiving help increases the likelihood of passing one's genes on to the next generation, but what about giving help? In the animal world, the costs of helping are easy to spot. A hungry animal that gives its food to another has less left for itself. Selfish animals that don't share are less likely to starve. Hence evolution should generally favor selfish, unhelpful creatures. Indeed, Richard Dawkins (1976/1989) wrote a book titled *The Selfish Gene*.[106] According to Dawkins, genes are selfish in that they build "survival machines" (like human beings!) to increase the number of copies of themselves. In an interview, Dawkins said: "Genes try to maximize their chance of survival. The successful ones crawl down through the generations. The losers, and their hosts, die off. A gene for helping the group could not persist if it endangered the survival of the individual."[107]

One way that evolution might support some helping is between parents and children. Parents who helped their children more would be more successful at passing on their genes. Although evolution favors helping one's children, children have less at stake in the survival of their parents' genes. Thus, parents should be more devoted to their children, and more willing to make sacrifices to benefit them, than children should be to their parents. In general, we should help people who have our genes, a theory known as **kin selection**.[108,109] For example, you should be more likely to help a sibling (who shares one-half of your genes) than a nephew (who shares one-fourth of your genes) or a cousin (who shares one-eighth of your genes). Plenty of research evidence suggests that people do help their family members and close relatives more than they help other people. In both life-or-death and everyday situations, we are more likely to help others who share our genes.[110] However, life-or-death helping is affected more strongly by genetic relatedness than is everyday helping (see **FIGURE 9.2**).

Research has also shown that genetically identical twins (who share 100% of their genes) help each other significantly more than fraternal twins (who share 50% of their genes).[111] Likewise, survivors of a fire at a vacation complex said that when they realized the complex was on fire, they were much more likely to search for family members than for friends.[112]

Thus, the natural patterns of helping (that favor family and other kin) are still there in human nature. However, people do help strangers and non-kin much more than other animals do. People are not just like other animals, but they are not completely different either. Humans are cultural animals, selected by nature to participate with nonrelatives in a larger society. Our natural inclinations to help kin have been amplified via emotional responses to translate into more far-reaching actions, such as empathy.

Empathy is an emotional response that corresponds to the feelings of the other person. When people see a person in distress, they usually feel that person's distress; when they see a person who is sad, they feel that person's sadness. The sharing of feelings makes people want to help the sufferer to feel better. Empathy is an especially important emotion when it comes to understanding why people help. Dramatic evidence for this was provided in a study of 18-month-old toddlers.[113] When the adult researcher dropped something, the human toddlers immediately tried to help, such as by crawling over to where it was, picking it up, and giving it to him. (The babies also seemed to understand and empathize with the adult's mental state. If the researcher simply threw something on the floor, the babies didn't help retrieve it. They only helped if the adult seemed to want help.) The researchers then repeated this experiment with chimpanzees. The chimps were much less helpful, even though the human researcher was a familiar friend. This work suggests that humans are hardwired to cooperate and help each other from early in life, and that this is something that sets humans apart from even their closest animal relatives.

Unfortunately, some evidence suggests empathy levels are decreasing in college students.[114] Empathy scores have dropped 40% over the past 30 years or so. Compared with college students of the late 1970s, current students are less likely to agree with statements such as "I sometimes try to understand my friends better by imagining how things look from their perspective," and "I often have tender, concerned feelings for people less fortunate than me." The authors speculated, "College students today may be so busy worrying about themselves and their own issues that they don't have time to spend empathizing

FIGURE 9.2

As genetic relatedness increases, helping also increases, in both everyday situations and life-or-death situations.[182]

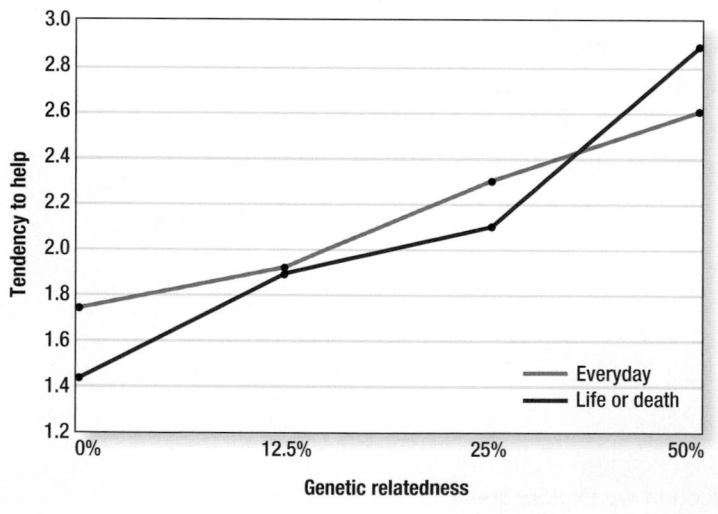

kin selection the evolutionary tendency to help people who have our genes

empathy reacting to another person's emotional state by experiencing the same emotional state

with others."[115] The media might also play a role in reducing empathy. For example, research shows that playing violent video games reduce feelings of empathy and makes people numb to the pain and suffering of others,[116] perhaps because violent games require players to adopt the role of the killer rather than the victim. Playing violent video games also decreases prosocial behavior such as cooperation and helping others.[117,118]

Two Motives for Helping: Altruism and Egoism

The 19th-century philosopher Auguste Comte (1875) described two forms of helping based on very different motives. One form he called **egoistic helping** in which the helper wants something in return for offering help. The helper's goal is to increase his or her own welfare (such as by making a friend, creating an obligation to reciprocate, or just making oneself feel good). The other form he called **altruistic helping** in which the helper expects nothing in return for offering help. The helper's goal in this case is to increase another's welfare. Psychologists, philosophers, and others have debated this distinction ever since.

These two different types of helping are produced by two different types of motives (see **FIGURE 9.3**). Altruistic helping is motivated by empathy. The sharing of feelings makes people want to help the sufferer to feel better.

According to the **empathy–altruism hypothesis**,[119] empathy motivates people to reduce other people's distress, as by helping or comforting them. How can we tell the difference between egoistic and altruistic motives? When empathy is low, people can reduce their own distress either by helping the person in need or by escaping the situation so they don't have to see the person suffer any longer. If empathy is high, however, then simply shutting your eyes or leaving the situation won't work because the other person is still suffering. In that case, the only solution is to help the victim feel better.

Untangling these different motives for helping has been an ongoing challenge for social psychologists. One study[120] was presented to participants as a test of the effects of stress on task performance. Through a rigged lottery, the "other participant" (actually a confederate named Elaine) was assigned to perform 10 trials of a task while receiving random electric shocks (the stressor) on each trial. The real participant watched Elaine over a closed-circuit TV. Before the study began, the participant overheard a conversation in which Elaine told the experimenter that she was afraid of receiving the shocks because as a child she had been thrown from a horse into an electric fence. Ever since that experience, she had been terrified of electricity. The experimenter apologized but said Elaine would have to receive the shocks anyway because she had lost the coin toss.

To increase empathy, the researchers told half of the participants that Elaine's values and interests were very similar to their own (high-empathy condition). The other participants were told that Elaine's values and interests were quite different (low-empathy condition). People feel more empathy toward those they believe are similar to themselves than toward dissimilar people. To test for egoistic motives for helping, the researchers also manipulated how difficult it was to escape. In the easy-escape condition, participants were told that they could leave after watching Elaine get shocked on the first two trials. In the difficult-escape condition, participants were told that they would have to watch all 10 trials. Participants who were only concerned about their own feelings would not have

egoistic helping when a helper seeks to increase his or her own welfare by helping another

altruistic helping when a helper seeks to increase another's welfare and expects nothing in return

empathy–altruism hypothesis the idea that empathy motivates people to reduce other people's distress, as by helping or comforting

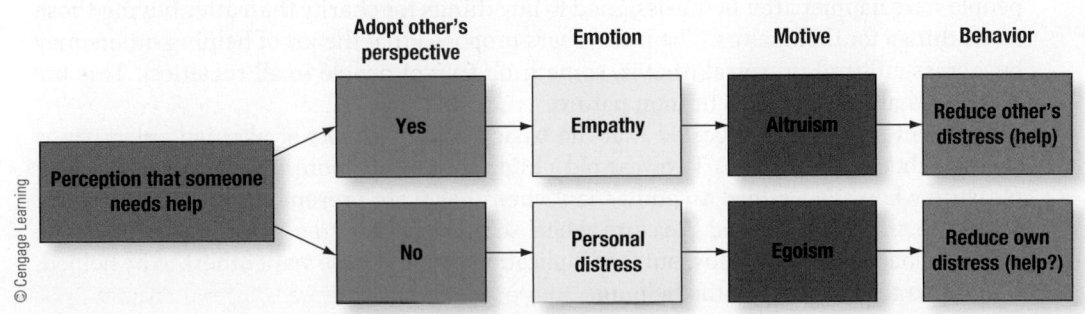

© Cengage Learning

FIGURE 9.3

Two routes to helping: The top route is motivated by altruism, whereas the bottom route is motivated by egoism

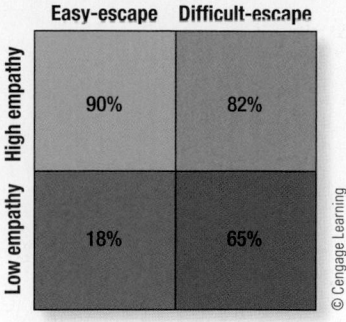

	Easy-escape	Difficult-escape
High empathy	90%	82%
Low empathy	18%	65%

© Cengage Learning

FIGURE 9.4

People in the high-empathy group helped regardless of whether escape was easy or difficulty. In the low-empathy group, people helped mainly when they could not escape.[183]

to help Elaine in the easy-escape condition. Instead they could just walk away and forget about her suffering.

After watching Elaine suffer through two trials, the participant was asked whether she would be willing to trade places with Elaine as a way of helping her avoid further suffering. Consistent with empathy–altruism theory, almost all the participants in the high-empathy group traded places with Elaine, regardless of whether it was easy or difficult to escape (see **FIGURE 9.4**). In the low-empathy group, however participants did not offer to take Elaine's place if it was easy for them to escape the unpleasant task of watching Elaine suffer. If it was difficult to escape, more than half of them traded places with Elaine (rather than watch her suffer longer).

This study provided evidence for both kinds of helping. In the low-empathy condition, people helped only to make themselves feel good. If they could walk away and ignore the victim's suffering, many chose that path. In contrast, people who felt high empathy helped regardless of whether they were allowed to escape. High-empathy helping is centered on the victim's needs, not on one's own prospects for feeling good.

Is Altruism Possible?

As they conducted research on whether helping is driven by empathy and sympathy for victims or by the selfish desire to feel better, social psychologists gradually became involved in a centuries-old debate about whether people are basically good or evil—or, more to the point, basically good or selfish. Many philosophers have asked whether people really perform morally good actions such as altruistic helping if they are motivated by a desire to feel good. In a nutshell, the argument is this: If you donate money to charity or help a needy victim because it makes you feel good to do so, aren't you really just being selfish and self-serving? Ultimately the question becomes: Is genuine altruism even possible?

Social psychologists have split on this debate. Nobody disputes that some helping can be egoistical, in the sense that people sometimes help in order to gain benefits for themselves such as improved mood or a good reputation. They disagree as to whether egoism is the only motive. Some point out that people will help even when they could feel better by other, simpler means, such as by escaping the situation (as in the previous study with Elaine). They also think it is sad to dismiss so much genuine helping as mere selfishness—after all, helping someone for selfish reasons deserves to be recognized as something more positive and socially desirable than not helping or hurting someone for selfish reasons! Others have argued, however, that even empathic helping is a way to make oneself feel better. The debate goes on today.

Our view is that the debate cannot be resolved because it asks the wrong question. It may well be true that people feel better when they help, and that these good feelings promote helping. But instead of supporting a negative conclusion about people—that people are always basically selfish—this should foster a more positive, optimistic view. Isn't it great that natural selection influenced human beings to be able to get pleasure from helping others?

The idea that people are naturally designed to get pleasure from helping others has begun to gain support. A recent investigation compared people across 136 different countries, including lab studies in some quite different cultures (e.g., Canada, India, Uganda). Everywhere, people got pleasure from spending money on other people.[121] In one study, people were happier after being assigned to buy things for charity than after buying those same things for themselves. The researchers proposed that the joy of helping others may be a cross-cultural universal (that is, something true of people in all societies). This fits the view that it is built into human nature.

A recent study has suggested that the basic key to this sort of altruistic pleasure is seeing others receive help. Two-year-old children showed more physiological signs of pleasure when they helped an adult than when they were prevented from helping him. Crucially, they also showed pleasure when someone else came along and helped the adult.[122] That is only one study, but the implication is that people want others to be helped, more than they want to do the helping.

Although people assume that altruistic helping exists, it might not.

The conflict between selfish impulses and social conscience has been one theme of this book. Often people have to be socialized to resist selfish impulses so as to do what is best for society and culture.[123] Children must be taught to share, to take turns, and to respect the property of others, for example. The fact that nature has enabled people to feel empathy for the suffering of others and to feel good when they lend help is one (very welcome and constructive) way to avoid that conflict. The social conscience is there to make people do what is best for others (and best for society at large) even when doing so means overriding selfish impulses. The fact that people can get satisfaction from helping others makes it easier for the social conscience to accomplish this. If no one ever got any satisfaction from doing good deeds, there would probably be far fewer good deeds.

Selfishness may be part of human nature, but so is helpfulness. Human beings help their children and kin, their friends, and sometimes even total strangers. It is unfair to call them selfish just because this helping is often motivated by the fact that helping feels good. The innately prepared pleasure we get from helping is one important element in the basic goodness of human nature.[124,125]

Are some people more likely to help than others? If so, who are they? We discuss this topic in the next section.

QUIZ YOURSELF
Why Do People Help Others?

1. **Jean Luc's house is on fire. His grandparents, wife, children, and cousins are in the house. Based on kin selection theory, whom should he save first?**

   (a) His children   (b) His cousins   (c) His grandparents   (d) His wife

2. **Eliza trips, falls, and begins to cry. When Mariah sees Eliza crying in pain, she starts to cry too. Mariah's response is called _____.**

   (a) altruism   (b) egoism   (c) empathy   (d) reactance

3. **After seeing a victim of misfortune, empathy motivates us to _____.**

   (a) gain the approval of bystanders   (b) gain the approval of the victim   (c) reduce our own discomfort   (d) reduce the discomfort of the victim

4. **After seeing a victim of misfortune, personal distress motivates us to _____.**

   (a) gain the approval of bystanders   (b) gain the approval of the victim   (c) reduce our own discomfort   (d) reduce the discomfort of the victim

answers: see pg 329

Who Helps Whom?

Before we look at specific factors that differentiate who helps whom, let us consider the big picture. One thing that is special and remarkable about humans is their willingness to help others, even unrelated others. Imagine that you were offered a chance to get a nice reward for yourself, maybe money or good food. You could either get it just for yourself, or you could get a duplicate of your reward delivered to someone you had known for 15 years (and still get your own full reward). Which would you choose? Most people would eagerly choose to benefit a friend or acquaintance, especially if they could do so without cost to themselves.

Yet when this exact experiment was tried on chimps, the results were quite different. Chimps are biologically similar to human beings,[126] but they did not show any interest in helping their longtime (15-year) acquaintances. They took the reward for themselves, but they did not do the kind favor for others.[127] Thus, the basic motive to bring help and benefits to others who aren't blood relatives appears to be something that sets human beings apart from our closest animal relatives.

Helpful Personality

Eva Fogelman studied the family backgrounds of rescuers of Jews in Nazi-occupied Europe, where Jews were being rounded up and sent to death camps, and found some common denominators: "a nurturing, loving home: an altruistic parent or beloved caretaker who served as a role model for altruistic behavior; a tolerance for people who were different."[128] Other researchers studied 231 Gentiles who rescued Jews and 126 nonrescuers of the same age, gender, education, and geographic location during the war.[129] Rescuers had higher ethical values, had stronger beliefs in equity, had greater empathy, and were more likely to see all people as equal.

Some people are clearly more altruistic than others. In a typical questionnaire measure of altruistic personality,[130] respondents are asked to indicate the frequency with which they have engaged in specific prosocial behaviors within the past year, such as helping others (e.g., "I have donated blood") and giving to charity (e.g., "I have given money, goods, or clothes to a charity"). This scale, called the Self Report Altruism Scale, has been shown to correlate with peer ratings of altruism, completion of an organ donor card, and paper-and-pencil measures of prosocial orientation.[131] The altruistic personality also appears to have a genetic component.[132]

Similarity

Research has shown that people are more likely to help similar others than dissimilar others. (Even in the study reported above, with Elaine the confederate, people who thought she was similar to them were more willing to help her than people who thought she was different.) The similarity bias especially works for outward symbols that are readily identifiable, such as similar apparel.[133] For example, recent research shows that international students are more likely to help other international students from similar countries than other international students from different countries.[134]

Gender

Research indicates that males are more helpful than females in the broader public sphere, toward strangers, and in emergency settings.[135] For example, since 1904 the Carnegie Hero Fund Commission has given awards to "heroes," defined as "a civilian who voluntarily risks his or her own life, knowingly, to an extraordinary degree while saving or attempting to save the life of another person."[136] More than 90% of the individuals who have received Carnegie medals have been men. Women are more helpful in the family sphere, in close relationships, and in situations that require repeated contact over a long period of time such as in volunteering.[137] Compared to males, females tend to feel more sympathy and empathy for people who need help.[138,139]

When it comes to receiving help, females are more likely to receive help than are males, regardless of whether the helper is male or female. If a car has a flat tire, for example, people are more likely to stop and help if the owner is female than if the owner is male.[140,141]

Males and females also differ in the types of help they offer their friends and relatives in sexual relationships. Read *The Social Side of Sex* to find out how.

Beautiful Victims

One of the most robust findings in the helping literature is that people are more likely to help attractive individuals than unattractive individuals. This holds true for male and female helpers and for males and females in need of help. This finding has been shown in both laboratory and field settings.[142] It has been shown in emergency situations and in nonemergency situations. In one study,[143] for example, people using phone booths at airports found a completed application form in the booth, a photograph of the applicant, and an addressed, stamped envelope. Half of the photos depicted an attractive applicant; the

The Social Side of *Sex*

Helping, Sex, and Friends

A sexual relationship may seem like a private matter between two people, but in fact people depend on help from their friends and relatives in multiple ways. Just meeting sex partners is often a matter of relying on one's network. One landmark study of sexual practices found that less than half the people met their sex partners or marriage partners by introducing themselves, such as by approaching someone at a bar.[144] (Also, self-introductions were more likely to lead to short-term affairs rather than long-term relationships.) In contrast, many people were introduced to their lovers by friends, coworkers, or relatives. Family members were responsible for bringing together relatively few sex partners, but the likelihood of those relationships lasting was especially high, probably because your family knows you and will only introduce you to someone who is likely to be a good match. If your mother or brother introduces you to someone, it is probably not for the sake of casual sex but rather someone with whom you might have a stable and happy long-term relationship.

Online dating services, however, have reduced the need to rely on family members and friends to find partners. People even use online dating services to find sex partners.[145] A 2002 article from *Wired* magazine stated: "Twenty years from now, the idea that someone looking for love without looking for it online will be silly, akin to skipping the card catalog to instead wander the stacks because 'the right books are found only by accident.' Serendipity is the hallmark of inefficient markets, and the marketplace of love, like it or not, is becoming more efficient."[146] This prediction is accurate and seems to have come true before the 2022 target date.

Helping is also apparent in how people act on spring break, which for many college students is a brief, exciting time of intense partying and sexual opportunity. A team of researchers followed a sample of Canadian students who traveled to Florida for one spring break.[147] They found that most traveled in same-sex groups. On the way down, many of these groups made pacts or other agreements to help each other during the week. These agreements differed for men and women. The men generally promised to help each other find a partner to have sex with. They would agree that they all wanted to have sex and that they would support each other's efforts. If they were sharing a room, they would make plans as to how to keep it discreetly available in case one of them wanted to bring a woman there

for sex. (For example, the others might agree to stay out late or even sleep on the beach if someone was there having sex.) The women, in contrast, made agreements to help each other avoid having sex. They usually agreed that their goal was to refrain from sex, unless one happened to find true love. They promised each other, for example, that if one of them got drunk and was being "hit on" (that is, targeted with romantic or sexual advances) by a particular man, the others would swoop in and bring her safely away. If they were sharing a room, they might promise not to leave one of them alone in it with a man. Thus, heterosexual men and women differ dramatically in how they help their friends in sexual situations.

Why? The most likely explanation is rooted in the social exchange theory of sex (see Chapter 12).[148] In that view, society treats heterosexual sex as something that men want from women, so men give women other resources (love, commitment, respect, attention, money) in exchange. Spring break sex is typically "free" sex that is not accompanied by commitment or other resources. From the exchange perspective, free sex signifies a good deal for men and a bad one for women. That is why men will try to support and help each other to engage in free sex, whereas women will try to support and help each other to avoid that sort of sex.

Maxi Spreewald/Getty Images

Women, especially beautiful women, are most likely to receive help.

other half depicted an unattractive applicant. Callers were much more likely to mail applications for attractive applicants than for unattractive applicants.

In another study,[149] male college students walking by the student health center were approached by a woman who said she desperately needed money for a tetanus shot. Male students were more likely to give the woman money if she was attractive than if she was unattractive.

Belief in a Just World

When the British marched a group of German civilians around the Belsen concentration camp at the end of World War II to show them what their soldiers had done, one civilian said, "What terrible criminals these prisoners must have been to receive such treatment."[150] This statement was not made by a guard who was trying to justify his behavior to reduce cognitive dissonance; it was made by an innocent civilian. Why was this person blaming the victim? One possible explanation is that the person believed that the world is a just place where people get what they deserve and deserve what they get, a phenomenon referred to as **belief in a just world**.[151,152,153]

One unfortunate consequence of belief in a just world is that it leads people to blame the victim. They assume that those who suffer a bad fate had it coming to them. For example, people assume that rape victims must have behaved or dressed provocatively, that poor people are lazy, and that sick people are responsible for their illness. On the other hand, "blaming the victim" has become such a taboo and condemned response in the social sciences that many people today will refuse to blame a victim even when the victim does bear some of the blame. Research on violence and aggression has frequently shown, for example, that many violent acts stem from incidents in which both people provoked or attacked each other. Two patrons in a bar may start by exchanging insults, move along to shoving and hitting, and end up in a violent fight in which one is injured or killed. The killer is certainly to blame, but the so-called victim also deserves some blame under those circumstances. Victims generally deserve sympathy, and some are indeed entirely free from blame, but other victims do share responsibility for what happened to them.

People who believe the world is just (fair) will help others, but only if they think those people deserve the help.[154] People who believe in a just world are not helpful toward victims who are perceived to be responsible for their own predicament.[155] People who believe most strongly in a just world express more negative attitudes toward helping the elderly because they believe that the elderly are responsible for meeting their own social, economic, and health needs.[156]

Belief in a just world can sometimes promote helping because the helper desires to deserve good outcomes. Again, the essence of believing in a just world is that people deserve what they get and get what they deserve. By extension, if you help others, you are a good and deserving person, so you can expect good things to happen to you. This can take on an almost superstitious aspect, as when people perform good or helpful acts in the expectation that they will be rewarded later.

Students sometimes show this sort of superstitious helping. Students at one college were asked to volunteer to do a good deed, such as serving as a reader for blind students or doing extra psychology experiments.[157] During the routine parts of the semester, helping was fairly low, and it made no difference whether the students had high or low belief in a just world. However, when the request came just before exam time, the students who believed in a just world were significantly more willing to help. Presumably they thought at some level that their good deeds would be rewarded by better luck and a better grade on the exam: If good things happen to good people, then it may help to do good deeds so as to become a good person.

Emotion and Mood

belief in a just world the assumption that life is essentially fair, that people generally get what they deserve and deserve what they get

In general, positive feelings increase helping. Research has shown that helping is increased by all kinds of pleasant situations, such as sunny weather,[158] eating a cookie,[159]

imagining a Hawaiian vacation,[160] and playing a relaxing video game.[161] One possible explanation for this phenomenon is that people want to maintain a good mood, and acting helpfully toward another person may allow them to sustain their good feelings (see Chapter 6).

On the other hand, bad emotions can sometimes increase helping. One way to resolve these findings is to suggest that some negative emotions may promote helping more than others. (Thus, perhaps guilt motivates helping, whereas shame or anger makes people unhelpful.) Another possibility is that the same emotion can have different effects. Focusing on yourself versus the victim can make a big difference, for example, even when the emotion is the same.

Bystander Helping in Emergencies

On March 13, 1964, a young woman named Kitty Genovese was attacked by a knife-wielding rapist outside her apartment in Queens, New York. News reports said her screams for help aroused 38 of her neighbors. Many watched from their windows while, for 35 minutes, she tried to escape. None called the police or sought to help in any other manner. In fact, her attacker left her twice and then returned each time; if someone had come to help her into the building during those intervals, she would have lived. Some of the witnesses didn't help because they thought it was a lover's quarrel. The *New York Times* article that described the event was titled "Thirty-Eight Who Saw Murder Didn't Call the Police."

The incident made the national news and ignited a storm of controversy. How could people just sit by and let a woman be murdered? Talking heads weighed in with their theories about urban decay, alienation, and other roots of the seemingly heartless indifference of the onlookers. Although some facts of this case have been disputed,[162] it led to a long line of social psychology studies on why bystanders might fail to help a victim in an emergency.

Most of the intellectuals who appeared on the news to discuss the Genovese murder assumed that the reasons for failing to help lay within the person. In a sense, they made what Chapter 5 described as the "fundamental attribution error": They underestimated

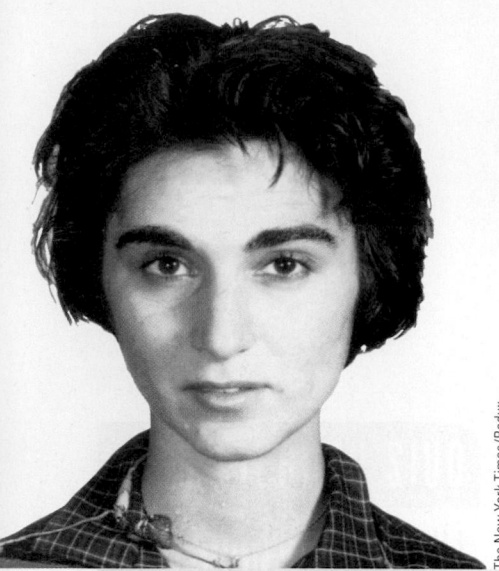

On March 13, 1964, Kitty Genovese was attacked by a knife-wielding rapist outside her apartment in Queens, New York, while several of her neighbors watched from their windows.

The New York Times/Redux

bystander effect the finding that people are less likely to offer help when they are in a group than when they are alone

the importance of situational factors and assumed behavior reflected the values and traits of the unresponsive bystanders. Even so, no news reporters could induce any of the bystanders to say, "I really didn't care whether that young woman lived or died." It fell to social psychologists to show that the special power of such emergency situations could explain what came to be known as the **bystander effect**. People are less likely to offer help when they are in the presence of others than when they are alone. Recent research shows the bystander effect even occurs in young children.[163]

Five Steps to Helping

Two social psychologists, John Darley and Bibb Latané, whose offices were a few minutes from the site of the Genovese murder, took the lead in studying the bystander effect. Gradually they came to recognize an absurd aspect of the controversy: the assumption that helping would be the normal, natural response. Instead, they proposed that there are at least five steps to helping in an emergency situation (see **FIGURE 9.5**). These amounted to five possible reasons that people would not help. A victim would only get help if the bystander resolved all five of these steps in the optimal way. Crucially, the presence of a crowd can interfere with helping at each of the five steps.

Step 1: Notice That Something Is Happening

The first step is to notice that something is happening. One obstacle to noticing the incident is being distracted: People who are busy or preoccupied are less likely to notice what is happening around them. Of course, people are more distracted when others are around than when alone. In a clever experiment,[164] male college students completed a questionnaire in a room, either alone or with two strangers. While they were working, smoke started coming into the room through a wall vent. Students who were alone noticed the

FIGURE 9.5
Five steps to helping and the obstacles encountered at each step.[184]

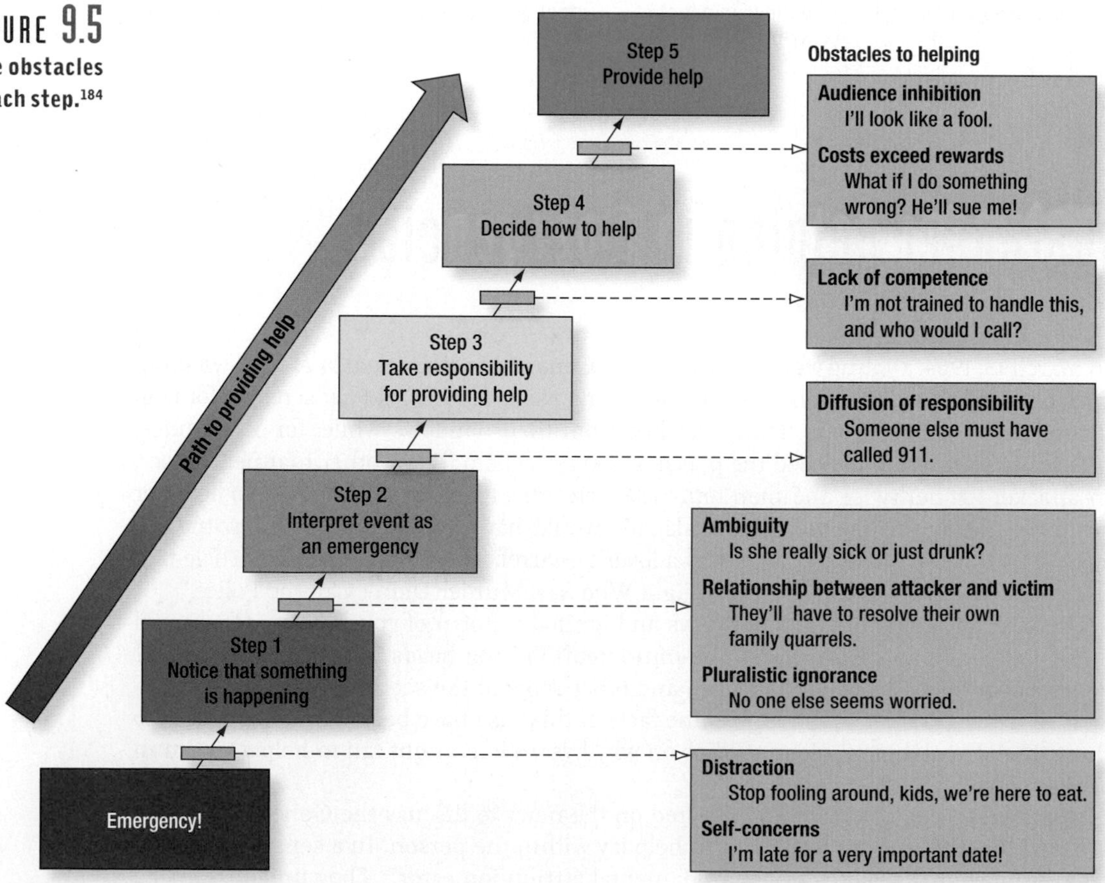

Path to providing help

Step 5
Provide help

Step 4
Decide how to help

Step 3
Take responsibility for providing help

Step 2
Interpret event as an emergency

Step 1
Notice that something is happening

Emergency!

Obstacles to helping

Audience inhibition
I'll look like a fool.

Costs exceed rewards
What if I do something wrong? He'll sue me!

Lack of competence
I'm not trained to handle this, and who would I call?

Diffusion of responsibility
Someone else must have called 911.

Ambiguity
Is she really sick or just drunk?

Relationship between attacker and victim
They'll have to resolve their own family quarrels.

Pluralistic ignorance
No one else seems worried.

Distraction
Stop fooling around, kids, we're here to eat.

Self-concerns
I'm late for a very important date!

smoke right away. In contrast, those in groups took about four times as long to notice the smoke (even though there were more people there to notice it!). The difference may be crucial in some emergency situations, such as a fire.

Step 2: Interpret Meaning of Event

Once you have noticed something is happening, the second step is to interpret the meaning of the event. Is it an emergency or not? Few people encounter emergencies on a regular basis, and emergencies do not usually come with obvious labels. How someone interprets these ambiguous situations can be decisive. For example, you notice a man stagger down the street and then slump onto the ground. Is he having a heart attack, so that your timely intervention might be needed to save his life? Or is he merely drunk, so that if you rush over to him your reward might be nothing more than having him puke on your shoes?

Sometimes it is hard to tell whether an event is an emergency. When it is easy to tell, people are more likely to intervene. To show the power of interpretations, researchers staged a physical fight between a man and a woman.[165] Bystanders offered help 65% of the time when she shouted, "Get away from me; I don't know you." Bystanders offered help only 19% of the time when she shouted, "Get away from me; I don't know why I ever married you." Perhaps they interpreted the event as a marital spat rather than as an emergency. Similarly, some of the bystanders who witnessed the Kitty Genovese murder thought it was only a lover's quarrel.

What are the obstacles to helping at this step? People often look to others for clues about how to behave. We think that others might know something that we don't know. If others do not react to an event, we conclude that it is not an emergency because otherwise they would be reacting. This phenomenon of collective misinterpretation is called **pluralistic ignorance**. We forget that others, in turn, might be looking to us for clues about how to behave. They assume that we know more than they do. Nobody reacts, because everybody assumes that others know more than they do, when in reality nobody knows anything. Everybody is certain that nothing is wrong, when actually the event is an emergency! In simpler terms, "I'm not really sure what is going on, so I'll just mimic everyone else."

Pluralistic ignorance is not restricted to emergency situations. Have you ever sat through a class feeling completely lost and confused about the material being presented? You want to ask a question, but you're too embarrassed to ask it. No one else is saying anything, so you assume that everybody else understands the material. In fact, the other students are probably just as confused as you are. Pluralistic ignorance in the classroom can prevent learning, and in an emergency situation it can prevent helping. Others often don't know as much as we give them credit for.

Step 3: Take Responsibility for Providing Help

The third step is taking responsibility for providing help. You might notice that something is happening, and decide that it is an emergency, but that is not enough. You must

pluralistic ignorance looking to others for cues about how to behave, while they are looking to you; collective misinterpretation

Pluralistic ignorance in the classroom can interfere with learning.

be willing to take responsibility for helping. The obstacle to this step of helping is called **diffusion of responsibility**. With several potential helpers around, the personal responsibility of each bystander is reduced. If you are the only person present, 100% of the responsibility for providing help rests on your shoulders; if two people are present, each has 50% responsibility; if three people are present, each has about 33% responsibility; if four people are present, each has 25% responsibility; and so on. In crowds, people think, "Perhaps someone else will help; perhaps someone else has already called for help." With everyone thinking that someone else will help or has helped, nobody helps.

The importance of diffusion of responsibility was demonstrated in lab experiments conducted by researchers at New York University, not far from where Kitty Genovese was killed.[166] Participants believed they were taking part in a group discussion over an intercom system. During the session, another participant (actually a prerecorded voice) apparently started having a seizure and called for help. Participants who thought they were part of a six-person group generally did not help because they thought someone else would do so. In contrast, if the participant thought he or she was the only one who knew about the victim's seizure, the participant helped almost every time.

Step 4: Know How to Help

The fourth step is deciding how to help. Having assumed the responsibility to help, the person must now figure out what to do. An obstacle to offering direct help is the feeling of lack of competence—people don't feel qualified to help, or they think that somebody else is more qualified to help than they are. Researchers have shown that there is no bystander effect for those who feel competent to intervene directly. In one study,[167] female participants were either registered nurses or general education students. On their way to the lab, participants passed by a workman (actually a confederate) who was standing on a ladder, fixing a light fixture. In the lab, participants worked on a task either alone or with a confederate who was pretending to be another participant and whose instructions were to sit still and do nothing during the upcoming accident. In the hall, participants heard the ladder fall over, they heard a thud, and then they heard the workman groaning in pain. The vast majority of nurses helped, regardless of whether they were working alone or with a passive bystander. For them, lack of competence was no obstacle to helping. General education students were much more likely to help if they were working alone than if they were working with a passive bystander.

People who don't feel competent to offer direct help can still offer indirect help, which involves calling someone else to help. In the age of cell phones, offering indirect help is quite easy, and it may often be the wisest and safest course of action. Physical injuries are best handled by people with proper training, such as ambulance workers. Dangerous

diffusion of responsibility the reduction in feeling responsible that occurs when others are present

situations are best handled by people with proper training, such as police officers. Stalled motorist problems are best handled by people with proper training, such as the highway patrol. Calling others for help is still being helpful.

Step 5: Provide Help

The fifth and final step is to take action by offering help (see **TABLE 9.3**). There are obstacles to helping at this step also. One obstacle is called **audience inhibition**—people don't want to feel foolish in front of others if they offer help and the person does not want help. People also might not help if the costs outweigh the benefits.[168] For example, people might not want to get their hands or clothes dirty, or they might not have enough time. We discuss the issue of lack of time being an obstacle to helping in the next section.

Too Busy to Help?

One of the more moving and memorable stories from the New Testament in the Bible has come to be known as the parable of the Good Samaritan. It goes like this:

> A certain man went down from Jerusalem to Jericho, and fell among thieves, which stripped him of his raiment, and wounded him, and departed, leaving him half dead. And by chance there came down a certain priest that way: and when he saw him, he passed by on the other side. And likewise a Levite, when he was at the place, came and looked on him, and passed by on the other side. But a certain Samaritan, as he journeyed, came where he was: and when he saw him, he had compassion on him. And went to him, and bound up his wounds, pouring in oil and wine, and set him on his own beast, and brought him to an inn, and took care of him. And on the morrow when he departed, he took out two pence, and gave them to the host, and said unto him, Take care of him; and whatsoever thou spendest more, when I come again, I will repay thee. (Luke 10:30–35, King James Version)

Would the parable of the Good Samaritan actually prompt bystanders to help in an emergency? To find out, researchers recruited students at the Princeton Theological Seminary who were studying to be ministers.[169] Half of them came to the psychology building expecting to give a talk about the Good Samaritan parable, so that the issue of helping needy victims should have been prominent in their minds. The remaining students were told to give a talk on job opportunities for seminary students.

Does being in a hurry make bystanders less likely to help in an emergency? To find out, students were also divided into low, moderate, and high "hurry" conditions. When they arrived at the lab for their appointment, they were told that their talk would be given

audience inhibition failure to help in front of others for fear of feeling like a fool if one's offer of help is rejected

TABLE 9.3	Some Costs and Benefits of Helping	
	Helping	**Not Helping**
Costs	Lose time	Guilt
	Injury	Social disapproval
	Legal liability	Legal liability
	Worsen situation	
Benefits	Self praise	Avoid risk of injury
	Reward	Avoid risks of helping
	Social approval	

in an auditorium in another building and were sent on their way. Those in the low-hurry condition were told that they were ahead of schedule and had plenty of time. Those in the moderate-hurry condition were told that they were right on schedule. Those in the high-hurry condition were told that they were late and that their audience was waiting for them. On the way to give their speech, all participants passed a man (actually a confederate) who was slumped in a doorway, coughing and groaning. The measure of helping was whether students stopped to help the man.

The topic of the upcoming speech—and thus whether participants were thinking about career prospects or about the New Testament's most famous story of bystander helping—had no effect on helping. Several seminary students going to give a talk on the parable of the Good Samaritan literally stepped over the victim as they hurried on their way! Time pressures, however, had a significant effect on helping. Participants in the low-hurry condition were more than six times more likely to help than were participants in the high-hurry condition. The more time people had, the more likely they were to help.

1. **As the number of witnesses present at an emergency situation increases, the probability of any given individual helping _____ .**

   (a) decreases
   (b) increases
   (c) increases then levels off
   (d) remains the same

2. **The fire alarm goes off. Nina doesn't move because she's uncertain about what's going on. She assumes that other people don't move because they know it's just a fire drill. Nina's thoughts illustrate _____ .**

   (a) diffusion of responsibility
   (b) the discounting principle
   (c) normative social influence
   (d) pluralistic ignorance

3. **When Dick sees a neighbor's house on fire with a crowd of people standing around it, he doesn't call the fire department. He assumes that other neighbors who also saw the fire have already called the fire department. Dick's thoughts illustrate _____ .**

   (a) diffusion of responsibility
   (b) the discounting principle
   (c) normative social influence
   (d) pluralistic ignorance

4. **In the Good Samaritan study,[170] participants varied in the amount of help that they offered to an (apparently) unconscious man as a function of their _____ .**

   (a) free time
   (b) gender
   (c) major
   (d) religiosity

How Can We Increase Helping?

Getting Help in a Public Setting

People aren't cold and uncaring when it comes to helping others; they are just uncertain about what to do. If you need help in an emergency setting, your best bet is to reduce the uncertainties of those around you concerning your condition and their responsibilities.[171] If you need emergency help when in a crowd of people, pick a face out of the crowd. Stare, speak, and point directly at that person. Say, "You, sir, in the red T-shirt, I need help. Call an ambulance now."

With that one statement you have reduced all the obstacles that might prevent or delay help.

- He notices you (reduces distraction).
- He understands that help is needed (reduces pluralistic ignorance).
- He understands that he, not someone else, is responsible for providing help (reduces diffusion of responsibility).
- He understands exactly how to provide help (reduces concerns about lack of competence).
- He should not be inhibited by an audience (reduces audience inhibition).

Decades of research have shown that if you follow this advice, you will maximize the likelihood of receiving help in a public setting.

Once people understand the situational factors that interfere with helping in emergency situations, they should be more likely to help. In one study,[172] students heard a lecture on why bystanders often don't help. Other students heard a different lecture or no lecture at all. As part of a different study in a different location, students found themselves walking with an unresponsive confederate past someone sprawled beneath a bicycle. The group that heard the lecture was much more likely to help (67% vs. 27%). The researchers replicated the study by separating the lecture and the opportunity to help by two weeks. Two weeks later, when encountering a person slumped over, the group that had heard the lecture was still much more likely to help (43% vs. 25%). (See, taking a social psychology course can help you become a better person!)

Provide Helpful Models

If unresponsive models interfere with helping, as often occurs in public when bystanders fail to offer help, can helpful models increase helping? The answer is a resounding yes. In one study,[173] fourth- and fifth-graders played a bowling game in which gift certificates could be earned. The gift certificates could be traded for candy and toys. Near the bowling game was a box labeled "Trenton Orphans Fund." The box also contained pictures of orphans in ragged clothing. Half the students were exposed to a helpful adult model, and half were not. Each time the adult model won gift certificates, he put half of them in the orphan box and said, "If you would like to give some of your gift certificates to them you can, but you do not have to." Students who were not exposed to the model were told the same thing. The students were then left alone to play the game. The results showed that 48% of students who were exposed to the adult model helped the orphans, whereas 0% of students who were not exposed to the adult model helped the orphans. If the researchers had included a child model condition, donations might have been even higher than for the adult model condition because people are more influenced by similar others.

The models don't need to be live either. Filmed models also work. Research has shown that prosocial television programs such as *Lassie, Mr. Rogers' Neighborhood, Barney,* and *Sesame Street* increase helpful behavior in children.[174] Prosocial video games[175] and music with prosocial lyrics[176] can also increase prosocial behavior. Another way to model helpful behavior is to be a **volunteer**. Over 1 in 4 Americans volunteer through or for an organization at least once a year.[177] The median amount of time spent on volunteering activities is 50 hours. Some possible activities included collecting, preparing, distributing, or serving food, fundraising, and tutoring or teaching others.

Teach Moral Inclusion

Often people sort others into "us" (people who belong to the same group or category as we do, called ingroup members) and "them" (people who belong to a different group or category than we do, called outgroup members). (Chapter 13 describes the distinction between ingroups and outgroups in more detail.) One way to increase helping is to make

> "Example is not the main thing in influencing others. It is the only thing."
> — Albert Schweitzer, humanitarian, theologian, missionary, organist, and medical doctor

> "The more a soul is held captive by love, the more [that person] is identified with all humanity."
> — Mother Teresa

volunteering a planned, long-term, nonimpulsive decision to help others

everybody on this planet a member of your "ingroup." People, regardless of how they differ from us (e.g., ethnic background, gender, sexual orientation, religion), are still part of the human family and are worthy of our help. This is called **moral inclusion**.

There is a new scale to measure this tendency, called the Identification With All Humanity Scale.[178] It contains nine items; some sample items are:

1. How much do you identify with (that is, feel a part of, feel love toward, have concern for) each of the following?

    a. people in my community

    b. Americans

    c. All humans everywhere

2. When they are in need, how much do you want to help:

    a. people in my community

    b. Americans

    c. People all over the world

Research shows that fewer than 15% of American respondents identify as much with all humanity as with Americans and people in their community.[179] But those who do tend to be more empathic and less prejudiced, ethnocentric, authoritarian, and dominant than others. They also tend to be more concerned about global issues (e.g., climate change), humanitarian needs, and support for universal rights. They put their money where their mouth is too, by financially supporting such causes. They value the lives of outgroup members (Afghanis) as much as ingroup members (Americans). Researchers also found that members of a major humanitarian charity and of a major human rights organization had significantly higher scores on this scale than a general adult sample. In summary, the tendency to identify with all humanity is positively related to many prosocial behaviors.

moral inclusion involves treating all people as ingroup members

QUIZ YOURSELF

How Can We Increase Helping?

1. **At which stage do potential helpers weigh the costs of helping versus not helping before making their decisions?**

   (a) Assuming responsibility to help
   (b) Providing help
   (c) Interpreting the situation as an emergency
   (d) Noticing the emergency

2. **TV programs such as *Barney*, *Lassie*, and *Mr. Rogers' Neighborhood* have been shown to _____ helpful behavior in children.**

   (a) decrease
   (b) increase
   (c) have no effect on
   (d) Not enough research has been conducted to answer this question.

3. **Volunteerism is to other forms of helping as _____ is to _____ .**

   (a) altruistic; egoistic
   (b) egoistic; altruistic
   (c) impulsive; nonimpulsive
   (d) nonimpulsive; impulsive

4. **Treating everyone as a member of your ingroup is known as _____ .**

   (a) diffusion of responsibility
   (b) moral inclusion
   (c) kin selection
   (d) pluralistic ignorance

answers: see pg 329

What Makes Us *Human*

This chapter has given you a look at the brighter side of human nature (but get ready for the darker side in the next chapter!). Prosocial behavior shows people doing things that bring benefits to others and help their culture and society to operate successfully. Traditionally, social psychologists have emphasized helping, but there are many other important forms of prosocial behavior. We may be inspired by the heroic acts, but society's successful functioning depends less on that sort of occasional, spectacular heroism than on everyday prosocial behavior like following rules, cooperating, reciprocating, forgiving, taking turns, and obeying legitimate authority. If most people do those things most of the time, the cultural system can succeed in making everyone better off. Recent centuries of human history have gradually seen power shift from individuals (such as kings who could command or decree whatever they wanted) to the rule of law, and in the process life has gotten safer and happier for most people. Even today, happiness levels are higher in countries with a strong rule of law than in those that lack the rule of law.[180]

Perhaps the most sweeping and important difference in prosocial behavior between humans and other animals is that humans will do prosocial things for others who are not family members. As with most animals, human helping gives first priority to family members and loved ones, but human beings will also do nice things for total strangers. Sharing your food with your mother or your son does not indicate anything special about your humanity—many other animals would do the same. But donating money or blood to benefit people you will never meet is distinctively, and remarkably, human. In fact, we saw that 18-month-old human toddlers will even help non-kin voluntarily, and that they are more helpful than older chimps in similar situations. Nature seems to have prepared people to understand and care about each other and to offer help when possible.

Some animals can learn to follow rules, but usually these are very specific rules, made and enforced by another (typically bigger) animal whose presence is often essential for enforcing the rules. Rule following took a big leap with human evolution. People can follow laws, moral principles, and other rules even when they are alone, and they can apply them to novel situations, making following rules a vital form of prosocial behavior.

Obedience is related to following rules. Again, many animals can learn to obey specific commands. Only humans expect each other to tell the difference between legitimate and wrongful authority and to obey only the former. Even the military has come around (after atrocities such as the My Lai massacre during the Vietnam War and the Abu Ghraib prison abuses during the Iraq War) to advocating that soldiers have a duty to disobey orders that are improper. Studies such as Milgram's[181] have shown that it is hard for people to disobey direct orders from seemingly legitimate authority figures, but it can be done. The human being is (sometimes, at least) an autonomous, thinking, moral agent, even when receiving orders.

Conformity is simpler and cruder than following rules because all it requires is the ability to see what others are doing and the desire to do the same. Many animals exhibit a herd instinct sort of conformity, in which they unthinkingly copy the behavior of others. Unlike other animals, people exchange information with each other and rely on what others tell them to learn about the world.

Likewise, the beginnings of reciprocity can be seen among animals, but typically this involves sharing with kin. Humans can reciprocate with strangers. Cooperation, too, is more advanced in humans than in many other species. Some animals seem to cooperate, in that they do complementary things, but mostly these are fixed action patterns. Humans can decide to cooperate or not, and often they decide to cooperate.

Reciprocity and cooperation indicate some understanding of fairness. (If you don't pay it back, you're not being fair.) Some other animals have a crude understanding of fairness, but mostly they are upset when they are underbenefited. Humans often feel guilty or uncomfortable when they are overbenefited too.

Last, empathy may be more centrally important to human helping than to the prosocial behavior of other animals. People are much better than most other creatures at understanding what someone else is feeling, and this capacity to appreciate someone else's pain and suffering is an important factor in promoting helping behavior.

CHAPTER 9 SUMMARY

Is Helping Contagious?

- Helping and cooperative behavior can be contagious, passing from person to person to person.

What Is Prosocial Behavior?

- Prosocial behavior involves doing good for others or society; it builds relationships and allows society to function.
- Obeying rules, conforming to norms, cooperating, and helping are all forms of prosocial behavior.
- Public circumstances generally promote prosocial behavior. That is, people behave better when others are watching and know who they are.
- Reciprocity is the obligation to return in kind what another has done for us.
- Equity means that each person receives benefits in proportion to what he or she did. Equality means that everyone gets the same amount, regardless of performance.
- A full sense of fairness, recognizing both underbenefits and overbenefits, is important in humans but probably absent in other animals.

Cooperation, Forgiveness, Obedience, Conformity, and Trust

- Prisoner's dilemma is a game that consists of tradeoffs between cooperation and competition.
- Zero-sum games are those in which the winnings and losings add up to zero, so that one's gain is another's loss. Non-zero-sum games are those in which both participants can win (or lose).
- If one member of a pair is not cooperative, then cooperation is typically doomed.
- Communication improves the chances of cooperation.
- Forgiveness helps repair relationships and provides health benefits to both the forgiver and the forgiven person.
- Forgiveness is more likely when the offense or hurt was minor and when the offending person apologizes. People who are religious, are committed to the relationship, and are not self-centered or narcissistic are more willing to forgive than other people.
- A majority of participants in Milgram's experiments delivered extreme shocks to a screaming victim in obedience to an authority figure.
- Although mindless obedience can be bad, in most cases society is better off if people obey society's rules.
- Conformity means going along with the crowd. It can be good or bad.
- Conformity and obedience can be prosocial behaviors, in that they make it easier to get along with others and for society to function.

Why Do People Help Others?

- The evolutionary theory of kin selection suggests that we prefer to help others who are related to us.
- Altruistic helping is motivated by empathy, an emotional response that corresponds to the feelings of the other person because it motivates people to reduce others' distress.

Who Helps Whom?

- Many people get pleasure from helping others.
- People are more likely to help similar others than dissimilar others.
- Males are more helpful than females in the broader public sphere, toward strangers, and in emergencies, whereas females are more helpful in the family sphere, in close relationships, and in volunteering.
- Females are more likely to receive help than are males, regardless of whether the helper is male or female.
- People are more likely to help attractive individuals than unattractive individuals.
- Belief in a just world refers to the finding that people believe that the world is mostly fair and that people usually get what they deserve.
- People who believe the world is just will help others, but only if they think those people deserve the help.
- Positive moods generally increase helping, but some bad moods, such as guilt, can also promote helping.

Bystander Helping in Emergencies

- The bystander effect is the finding that people are less likely to offer help when they are in a group than when they are alone.
- The five steps to helping during an emergency are
  - Notice that something is happening.
  - Interpret the event as an emergency.
  - Take responsibility for providing help.
  - Know what to do.
  - Take action and provide help.
- Pluralistic ignorance involves thinking others know something that we don't know, even if others don't know it either.
- Diffusion of responsibility refers to the reduction in helping that occurs when multiple bystanders all assume that others will take the responsibility of helping.
- People who are in a hurry help less than those who aren't, even if those in a hurry are thinking about the Good Samaritan.

How Can We Increase Helping?

- Helping can be increased by
  - Reducing uncertainties
  - Educating others about bystander indifference
  - Providing helpful models
  - Teaching moral inclusion (making others a part of the ingroup)

What Makes Us Human? Putting the Cultural Animal in Perspective

- Humans, unlike other animals, frequently act in a prosocial manner toward others who are not family members.
- Rule following, obedience, and conformity are often depicted as negative acts, but for the most part are prosocial acts.

key terms

altruistic helping 313
audience inhibition 323
belief in a just world 318
bystander effect 320
conformity 309
cooperation 301
diffusion of responsibility 322
egoistic helping 313

empathy 312
empathy–altruism hypothesis 313
equality 296
equity 296
forgiveness 304
gratitude 296
kin selection 312
moral inclusion 326

non-zero-sum game 304
norms 296
obedience 306
overbenefited 297
pluralistic ignorance 321
prisoner's dilemma 301
prosocial behavior 294
reciprocity 295

rule of law 294
sensitivity about being the target of a threatening upward comparison 297
trust 309
underbenefited 297
volunteering 325
zero-sum game 304

quiz yourself ANSWERS

1. What Is Prosocial Behavior? **p.298**
   answers: 1.b 2.b 3.a 4.d

2. Morality **p.300**
   answers: 1.d 2.a 3.b 4.a

3. Cooperation, Forgiveness, Obedience, Conformity, and Trust **p.311**
   answers: 1.d 2.d 3.d 4.b

4. Why Do People Help Others? **p.315**
   answers: 1.a 2.c 3.d 4.c

5. Who Helps Whom? **p.319**
   answers: 1.a 2.a 3.d 4.b

6. Bystander Helping in Emergencies **p.324**
   answers: 1.a 2.d 3.a 4.a

7. How Can We Increase Helping? **p.326**
   answers: 1.b 2.b 3.d 4.b

AGGRESSION & ANTISOCIAL BEHAVIOR

10

LEARNING OBJECTIVES

1 Define the different types of aggression.

2 Debate the role of nature versus nurture in human aggression, and analyze the effects of culture on aggressive impulses.

3 Identify the inner causes of aggression.

4 Describe the interpersonal causes of aggression.

5 Compare the external causes of aggression to the internal and interpersonal causes.

6 Discuss the role of culture and self-views in producing violence and aggression.

7 Identify other, nonaggressive forms of antisocial behavior.

Rwanda, a country

located in east-central Africa, was originally home to the Hutus.[1,2] About 600 years ago, the Tutsis, a tall warrior people that lived in Ethiopia, invaded and conquered the area and installed a king with extensive powers. Although the Hutus greatly outnumbered the Tutsis, they agreed to raise crops for the Tutsis in exchange for protection from hostile intruders. In 1890, Rwanda became part of German East Africa. In 1916, during World War I, Belgium invaded the German territories, and after the war Rwanda came under Belgian rule.

Traditionally, the differences between Hutus and Tutsis were occupational rather than ethnic. The Hutus had the low-status farming jobs, whereas the Tutsis had the high-status cattle-herding jobs. In terms of appearance, the Hutus tended to be short and square, whereas the Tutsis were tall and thin. That may have been true 600 years ago, but today it is not possible to tell them apart. The two groups not only look the same, they also speak the same language, inhabit the same parts of the country, follow the same traditions, and intermarry.

The Belgians considered the Tutsis as superior to the Hutus and even gave out identity cards classifying individuals as Hutu or Tutsi. Tutsis (not surprisingly) agreed with the Belgians and enjoyed better jobs, educational opportunities, and living conditions for decades. Resentment among the Hutus gradually

built up, culminating in 1959 in a series of riots that overthrew the ruling Tutsi king. During these riots, more than 20,000 Tutsis were killed, and many more fled to nearby countries. When Belgium relinquished power and granted Rwanda independence in 1962, the Hutus took control of the country; many Tutsis left Rwanda and went to live in neighboring Burundi.

With the Hutus in power, the Tutsis were used as the scapegoats for every problem the country faced. Hate media fueled the fire. For example, a 1992 leaflet picturing a machete asked the question: "What shall we do to complete the social revolution of 1959?" In 1993, Burundi President Melchior Ndadaye, a Hutu, was assassinated by hardline Tutsi soldiers. The media used the assassination to incite anger against Tutsis. The media falsely reported that the president had been tortured and castrated. (This harked back to cultural practices: In precolonial times, some Tutsi kings castrated defeated enemy rulers.)

On April 6, 1994, Rwandan President Juvenal Habyarimana, a Hutu, was killed when his plane was shot down above the airport. Nobody was sure who shot down the plane, but the Tutsis were blamed. Soon genocidal murders began, encouraged by media propaganda. Radio broadcasts called for a "final war" to "exterminate the (Tutsi) cockroaches." The United Nations (U.N.) commander in charge of peacekeeping operations at the time, General Romeo Dallaire, said: "Simply jamming [the] broadcasts and replacing them with messages of peace and reconciliation would have had a significant impact on the course of events."[3] As this chapter will discuss, the power of mass media to promote or restrain

violence has been a lively topic of scientific research.

Not all broadcasters participated in the hate campaign. Thomas Kamilindi, a Hutu, resigned from a state-run radio station because he refused to broadcast hate messages. Kamilindi was called a "dog" and was almost killed for "sympathizing" with the Tutsis. A commander who happened to pass by just as a soldier pointed a gun at Kamilindi's head saved him. Kamilindi later discovered that his 5-year-old daughter had been murdered while she was visiting her Tutsi maternal grandparents, and his father had been murdered too. (One of your textbook authors—Brad Bushman—was a mentor to Kamilindi for a year while he was a Knight-Wallace Journalism Fellow at the University of Michigan.)

In just 100 days, about 800,000 Tutsis and their sympathizers were killed with guns, machetes, sticks, and stones. Hutus were given incentives for killing

Some of the victims of the 1994 massacre in Rwanda.

AP Photo/Brennan Linsley

Today some Tutsis are forgiving the Hutus that murdered family members.

Melanie Stetson Freeman/The Christian Science Monitor via Getty Images

Tutsis, such as money, food, and even the dead Tutsis' houses and property. Imagine the people in your hometown taking up their kitchen carving knives and carpentry tools to slaughter their neighbors.

Hate media were also used to incite rape and sexual assault against Tutsi women. For example, leaflets contained statements such as "You Tutsi women think that you are too good for us" and "Let us see what a Tutsi woman tastes like." A 1996 U.N. report stated that "rape was the rule and its absence the exception." The report also stated that "rape was systematic and was used as a 'weapon' by the perpetrators of the massacres." The report estimated that between 250,000 and 500,000 Tutsi women and girls had been raped, many by men who were HIV positive and knew it.[4]

The international community largely stood aside during the genocide. Initial reports were sporadic and difficult to believe, and international law generally discourages countries from interfering in the internal affairs of others. (Mass killings inside one country are thus more difficult to stop than an invasion of one country by another.) U.N. troops withdrew after the murder of 10 of their soldiers. The

U.S. government was reluctant to involve itself in the "local conflict" in Rwanda and refused to label the killings as "genocide," a decision that former President Bill Clinton later came to regret. In a TV interview Clinton stated that he believes if he had sent 5,000 U.S. peacekeepers, more than 500,000 lives could have been saved.[5]

There was an ironic twist at the end, when the international community finally did send in troops to stop the bloodshed. A Tutsi army led by Paul Kagame (Rwanda's president today) conquered the country. This stopped violence against Tutsis but sent the Hutus into a panic, for fear the Tutsis would extract brutal revenge. The U.N. troops had been told to stop all killings, and they found themselves in the peculiar position of having to protect mainly Hutus, including many who had taken part in the genocide.

Unfortunately, violent and aggressive behavior often has unintended consequences. Violence often begets more violence. The 1994 genocide that occurred in Rwanda was the precipitating factor in starting the first Congo war, which resulted in 3.8 million deaths— the bloodiest war since World War II.[6] Beginning in April 1994, more than 2 million Rwandans fled to neighboring

countries. Most went to Zaire (now called the Democratic Republic of Congo). Many of the refugees were Hutu militia forces (*Interahamwe*) who wanted to escape the Tutsi-led government that took control of Rwanda following the genocide. In October 1996, the Rwandan troops tried to forcibly oust President Mobutu Sese Seko, a dictator who had ruled Zaire for decades, which started the conflict.

As horrific as the Rwanda genocide was, there were and continue to be isolated incidences of good, inspiring acts that came from it. During the genocide, hotel manager Paul Rusesabagina sheltered 1,268 Tutsis (and their sympathizers) while mobs outside his hotel shouted for their blood.[7] Among those saved were Kamilindi, his wife, and their surviving daughter. This true story formed the basis for the 2004 movie *Hotel Rwanda*. Another bright spot is that some Rwandans today are forgiving and reconciling with those who murdered their children, friends, siblings, and parents during the 1994 genocide.[8]

The genocide in Rwanda illustrates several important points about aggression and violence. The mass media can promote aggression. Frustrated people can sometimes lash out at the source of their frustration in violent ways. Aggressors often dehumanize their victims, such as by calling them "cockroaches" or "dogs." Not just combatants but innocent people can be victims, in huge numbers. Violent actions can have unintended consequences, such as stimulating further violent actions. On the other hand, it also illustrates that people can resist situational forces that increase aggression. Thomas Kamilindi quit his job and refused to broadcast hate messages. Paul Rusesabagina refused to let the Hutu soldiers kill the Tutsis taking refuge in the hotel he was managing. Some Rwandans today are reconciling with those who participated in the genocide. Forgiveness is possible, even for the most extreme actions.

Early psychological theories (such as Freud's) depicted aggression as the outburst of powerful inner forces.

More recent theories have considered aggression as a kind of strategic behavior that people use to influence others, get what they want, and defend certain ideas that they see as under attack.[9,10] Understanding aggression is important not only to social psychologists but also to society at large. One can adopt either a pessimistic or an optimistic view of aggression in human life. On the pessimistic side, there is a great deal of aggression, and it is sad to think how much avoidable suffering it causes all over the world. On the optimistic side, many situations could lead to aggression, but aggression arises in only a few of them, so somehow most people manage to inhibit their aggressive tendencies most of the time. And as we shall see, there is evidence that aggression and violence decrease as culture progresses. ●

Defining Aggression, Violence, and Antisocial Behavior

What is aggression? In everyday conversation, some people may describe a salesperson who tries really hard to sell merchandise as "aggressive." The salesperson does not, however, want to harm potential customers. Most social psychologists define human **aggression** as any behavior intended to harm another person who does not want to be harmed.[11] This definition includes three important features. First, aggression is a behavior—you can see it. Aggression is not an emotion, such as anger (see Chapter 6 for a discussion of emotion). Aggression is not a thought, such as mentally rehearsing a murder (see Chapter 5 for a discussion of cognition). Second, aggression is intentional (not accidental), and the intent is to harm. For example, a dentist might intentionally give a patient a shot of anesthetic (which hurts!), but the goal is to help rather than hurt the patient. Third, the definition stipulates that the victim wants to avoid the harm. Thus, again, the dental patient is excluded because she or he is not seeking to avoid the harm (in fact, the patient probably booked the appointment weeks in advance and paid to have the dental work done). Suicide and sadomasochistic sex play are also not included because again the victim actively seeks to be harmed. Note that behaviors that are intended to harm others are still acts of aggression even if they don't actually harm them. For example, if a person shoots a gun at you but misses, it is still an act of aggression.

It is useful to distinguish among various forms and functions of aggression. By "forms" we mean how the aggressive act is expressed, such as *physically* (e.g., hitting, kicking, stabbing, shooting) or *verbally* (e.g., yelling, screaming, swearing, name calling). In **displaced aggression**, a substitute aggression target is used.[12] For example, a man is berated by his boss at work but does not retaliate. When he gets home, he kicks his dog or yells at a family member instead.

Different forms of aggression can be expressed directly or indirectly. In **direct aggression**, the victim is physically present; in **indirect aggression**, the victim is absent. For example, physical aggression can be direct (e.g., hitting a person in the face) or indirect (e.g., burning his house down while he is away). Likewise, verbal aggression can be direct (e.g., screaming in a person's face) or indirect (e.g., spreading rumors behind her back). Males are more likely than females to use direct aggression, whereas females are more likely than males to use indirect aggression.[13]

Aggressive acts may also differ in their function or motivation. Consider two examples. In the first, a husband finds his wife and her lover together in bed. He grabs his rifle from the closet and shoots and kills them both. In the second, a "hit man" uses a rifle to kill another person for money. The form of aggression is the same (shooting and killing victims with a rifle); however, the motives appear quite different. In the first example, the husband is probably motivated by anger. He is enraged when he finds his wife making love to another man, so he shoots them both. In the second example, the "hit man" is motivated by money. The "hit man" probably does not hate his victim. He might not even know his victim, but he kills the person anyway for the money.

aggression any behavior intended to harm another person who is motivated to avoid the harm

displaced aggression any behavior that intentionally harms a substitute target rather than the provocateur

direct aggression any behavior that intentionally harms another person who is physically present

indirect aggression any behavior that intentionally harms another person who is physically absent

To capture different functions or motives for aggression, psychologists make a distinction between **reactive aggression** (also called hostile, affective, angry, impulsive, or retaliatory aggression) and **proactive aggression** (also called **instrumental aggression**).[14,15,16] Reactive aggression is "hot," impulsive, angry behavior that is motivated by a desire to harm someone. Proactive aggression is "cold," premeditated, calculated behavior that is motivated by some other goal (obtaining money, restoring one's image, restoring justice). Some social psychologists have argued that it is difficult (if not impossible) to distinguish between reactive and proactive aggression because they are highly correlated and because motives are often mixed.[17]

Bullying refers to persistent aggression by a perpetrator against a victim for the purpose of establishing a power relationship over the victim.[18] The key feature of bullying over other acts of aggression is its persistent nature—the bully repeatedly picks on the victim. **Cyberbullying** refers to the use of the Internet (e.g., e-mail, social network sites, blogs, instant messages, tweets, sending personal photos or videos) to bully others. In cyberbullying the perpetrator can be anonymous, especially when using instant messaging. Although bullies at school tend to be bigger and stronger than their victims, cyberbullies can harm others regardless of how big and strong they are.

Researchers also use the term *violent* in a more precise way than the general public. A meteorologist might call a storm "violent" if it has intense winds, rain, thunder, lightning, or hail. Most social psychologists define **violence** as aggression that has as its goal extreme physical harm, such as injury or death. For example, one child pushing another off a tricycle is an act of aggression but is not an act of violence. One person intentionally hitting, kicking, shooting, or stabbing another person is an act of violence. Thus, all violent acts are aggressive acts, but not all aggressive acts are violent—only the ones designed to cause extreme physical harm are violent. The U.S. Federal Bureau of Investigation (FBI) classifies four crimes as "violent"—homicide, aggravated assault, forcible rape, and robbery.

Antisocial behavior is a term that research psychologists have used in casual and somewhat inconsistent ways (though clinicians have a more precise definition). In general, it seems to refer to behavior that either damages interpersonal relationships or is culturally undesirable. Aggression is often equated with antisocial behavior.[19,20] Others have pointed out, however, that aggression is often a social as well as an antisocial strategy, in that it is a way that people seek to manage their social lives, such as by influencing the behavior of others to get what they want.[21] Littering, cheating, lying, and stealing, on the other hand, are behaviors that qualify as antisocial but may or may not be aggressive.

Is the World More or Less Violent Now Than in the Past?

Although the world seems more violent today than ever before, Daniel Webster was right—the world is less violent now than in the past. Quantitative studies of body counts, such as the proportion of prehistoric skeletons with axe and arrowhead wounds, suggest that prehistoric societies were far more violent than our own.[22] Although one can kill a lot more people with a bomb than with an axe, the death rates per battle were much higher in the past. Estimates show that if the wars of the 20th century had killed the same proportion of the population as ancient tribal wars, then the death toll would have been 20 times higher—2 billion rather than 100 million.[23]

More recent data also show that violence has declined over time. European murder rates have decreased dramatically since the Middle Ages.[24,25] For example, estimated murders in England dropped from 24 per 100,000 in the 14th century to 0.6 per 100,000 by the early 1960s. The major decline in violence seems to have occurred in the 17th century during the Age of Reason, beginning in the Netherlands and England and then spreading to other European countries.[26]

> **"Let us thank God that we live in an age when something has influence besides the bayonet."**
> — Daniel Webster

reactive aggression (also called **hostile aggression**) "hot," impulsive, angry behavior motivated by a desire to harm someone

proactive aggression (also called **instrumental aggression**) "cold," premeditated, calculated harmful behavior that is a means to some practical or material end

bullying persistent aggression by a perpetrator against a victim for the purpose of establishing a power relationship over the victim

cyberbullying the use of the Internet (e.g., e-mail, social network sites, blogs) to bully others

violence aggression that has as its goal extreme physical harm, such as injury or death

antisocial behavior behavior that either damages interpersonal relationships or is culturally undesirable

Stapelton Collection/Fine Art/Corbis

AP Photo/U.S. Signal Corps

Although modern weapons such as the bomb the Americans dropped on Hiroshima can kill a lot more people than ancient weapons, the world is actually a more peaceful place today than in the past.

Global violence has been falling steadily since the middle of the 20th century (despite horrific episodes like the Rwanda massacres).[27] For example, the number of battle deaths in wars between countries has declined from more than 65,000 per year in the 1950s to fewer than 2,000 per year in the 2000s. Globally, the number of armed conflicts and combat deaths, the number of military coups, and the number of deadly violence campaigns waged against civilians have declined. As can be seen in **FIGURE 10.1**, violence levels have decreased worldwide in the 20th century.

A number of other observations are consistent with the idea that human society is becoming less violent over time. Steven Pinker, author of a popular book covering much of the research on the long-term decline in violence, notes: "Cruelty as entertainment, human sacrifice to indulge superstition, slavery as a labor-saving device, conquest as the mission statement of government, genocide as a means of acquiring real estate, torture and mutilation as routine punishment, ...—all were common features of life for most of human history. But, today, they are rare to nonexistent in the West, far less common elsewhere than they used to be, concealed when they do occur, and widely condemned when they are brought to light" (p. 18).[28]

In today's digital age we certainly are more informed about wars and other acts of violence than in past ages. "If it bleeds, it leads" seems to be the rule used to determine what news stories to focus on. Citizen journalists around the world also make use of social media such as Facebook, Twitter, and YouTube to "show and tell" the world about unjustified acts of violence. Because violent images are more available to us now than ever before, we might assume that violence levels are also higher. However, that perception might be due to the availability heuristic (see Chapter 5); when we can readily recall violent acts, we assume that violent acts are common. In reality, over time this planet is actually becoming a more peaceful place to live. (At least for humans; animals have not changed their behavior much, and species continue to go extinct at tragic rates, mostly due to loss of habitat caused by humans.)

The fact that aggression and violence are decreasing over time is consistent with one of this book's key themes: Nature says yes and culture says no. One of the main goals of

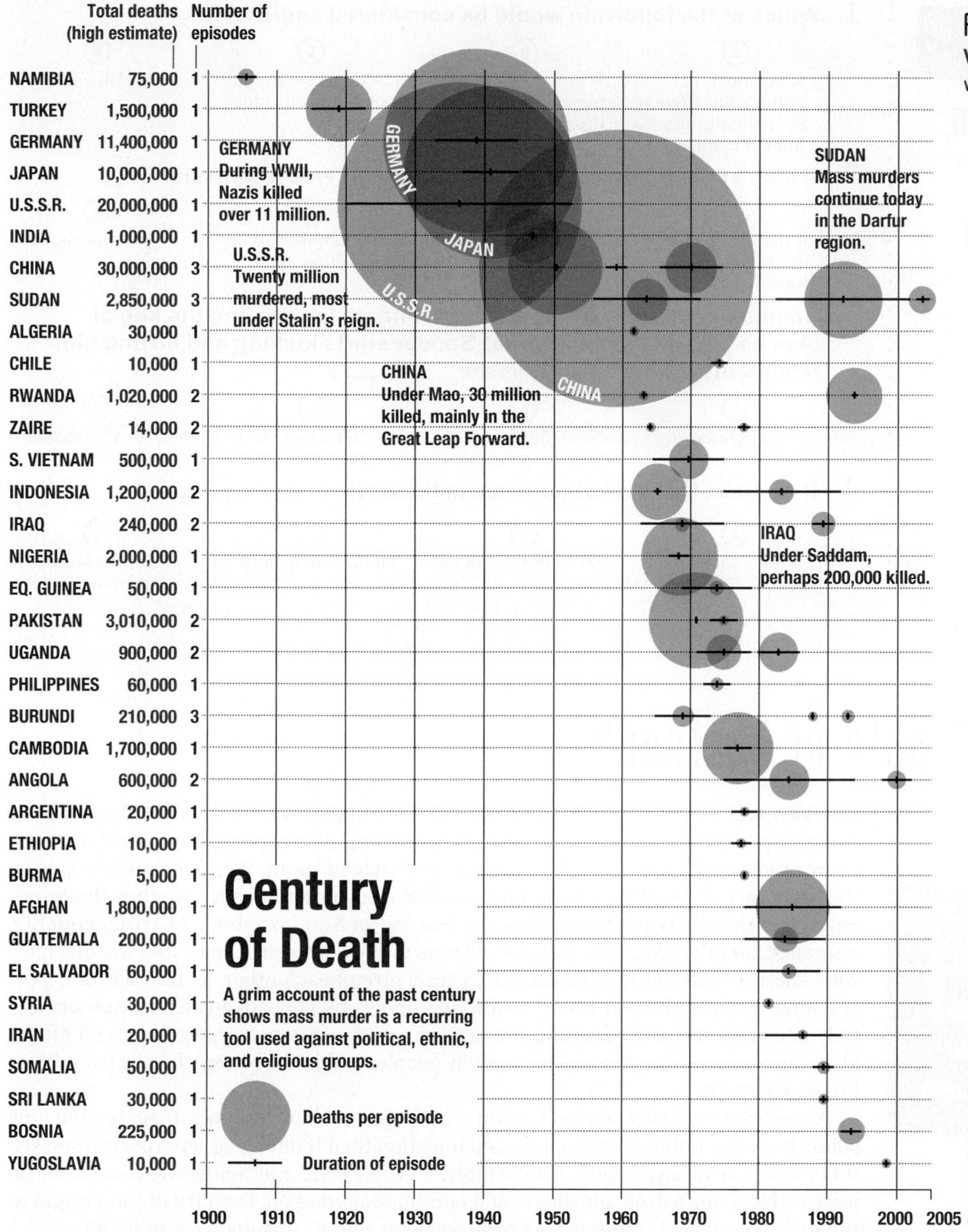

FIGURE 10.1
Violence levels have decreased
worldwide in the 20th century.

Total deaths (high estimate)	Number of episodes
NAMIBIA 75,000	1
TURKEY 1,500,000	1
GERMANY 11,400,000	1
JAPAN 10,000,000	1
U.S.S.R. 20,000,000	1
INDIA 1,000,000	1
CHINA 30,000,000	3
SUDAN 2,850,000	3
ALGERIA 30,000	1
CHILE 10,000	1
RWANDA 1,020,000	2
ZAIRE 14,000	2
S. VIETNAM 500,000	1
INDONESIA 1,200,000	2
IRAQ 240,000	2
NIGERIA 2,000,000	1
EQ. GUINEA 50,000	1
PAKISTAN 3,010,000	2
UGANDA 900,000	2
PHILIPPINES 60,000	1
BURUNDI 210,000	3
CAMBODIA 1,700,000	1
ANGOLA 600,000	2
ARGENTINA 20,000	1
ETHIOPIA 10,000	1
BURMA 5,000	1
AFGHAN 1,800,000	1
GUATEMALA 200,000	1
EL SALVADOR 60,000	1
SYRIA 30,000	1
IRAN 20,000	1
SOMALIA 50,000	1
SRI LANKA 30,000	1
BOSNIA 225,000	1
YUGOSLAVIA 10,000	1

GERMANY During WWII, Nazis killed over 11 million.

U.S.S.R. Twenty million murdered, most under Stalin's reign.

CHINA Under Mao, 30 million killed, mainly in the Great Leap Forward.

SUDAN Mass murders continue today in the Darfur region.

IRAQ Under Saddam, perhaps 200,000 killed.

Century of Death

A grim account of the past century shows mass murder is a recurring tool used against political, ethnic, and religious groups.

Deaths per episode

Duration of episode

1900 1910 1920 1930 1940 1950 1960 1970 1980 1990 2000 2005

Courtesy of Professor Barbara Harff

culture is to reduce aggression. When two social animals want the same thing, aggression is the main way of settling who gets it. Culture offers other, better ways of settling conflict: negotiation, property rights, money, courts of law, compromise, religious and moral rules, and the like. The main exception has been rivalries between cultures, which sometimes are settled with aggression. Even so, culture has sought to reduce these conflicts, such as with the Geneva Convention and other rules of war that constrain violence. World organizations such as the United Nations also try to reduce aggression between countries.

QUIZ YOURSELF

Defining Aggression, Violence, and Antisocial Behavior

answers: see pg 368

1. Which of the following would be considered aggression?

(a) A baseball batter's line drive accidentally hits the pitcher in the knee.

(b) A girl attempts to punch her little brother, but misses.

(c) A depressed man commits suicide.

(d) All of the above

2. Which of the following would not be considered aggression?

(a) A dentist giving a patient a shot of Novocain

(b) A depressed man committing suicide

(c) A sadomasochistic interaction

(d) All of the above

3. Sander becomes so angry at his roommate for stealing the keg of beer he bought for a party that Sander starts kicking and hitting him repeatedly. Sander's actions are _____ .

(a) aggressive

(b) violent

(c) aggressive and violent

(d) neither aggressive nor violent

4. Over time, the level of violence in the world has _____ .

(a) decreased

(b) remained the same

(c) increased linearly

(d) increased exponentially

Is Aggression Innate or Learned?

> "The tendency of aggression ... constitutes the most powerful obstacle to culture."
>
> — Sigmund Freud (1856–1939)

The 19th and 20th centuries saw many attempts to improve society. The hope was to design a perfect society so that people could live together in peace, love, and harmony. Communism was based on these ideals, and indeed many Western intellectuals in the early part of the 20th century supported the Soviet Union because they thought it embodied the Christian ideals they had learned in Sunday school: sharing, equality, tolerance, and the like.[29] Some went so far as to say that Jesus Christ and his disciples were the first communists because they took care of each other, shared all their possessions freely with each other, and made decisions collectively. Communism was only one of the plans for making the perfect society. Democracy, fascism, and others also aimed at creating a society in which people could all live together in friendly or loving harmony.

Aggression gradually emerged as the crux of the problem, however. If aggression only stems from frustration, exploitation, and injustice, then if one designed a perfect society, there would be no aggression. For example, if people were only aggressive because of injustice, then eliminating injustice would eliminate aggression. Even frustration might in theory be eliminated, and much aggression along with it. (But don't count on it!)

On the other hand, if people are naturally, innately aggressive, then no amount of social engineering will be able to get rid of it. No matter how well a society is designed, people will still be aggressive. Perfect social harmony will prove elusive. If people are inherently aggressive, then aggression will always be with us, and society or culture needs to find ways of living with it, such as by passing laws to punish wrongful aggression.

Instinct Theories

The instinct theory of aggression, first given scientific prominence by Charles Darwin,[30] views aggressive behavior as an evolutionary adaptation that had enabled creatures to survive better. This instinct presumably developed during the course of evolution because it promoted survival of individuals. Because fighting is closely linked to mating, the aggressive instinct helped ensure that only the strongest individuals would pass on their genes to future generations.

Sigmund Freud[31] argued that human motivational forces, such as sex and aggression, are based on instincts. An **instinct** is an innate (inborn, biologically programmed) tendency to seek a particular goal, such as food, water, or sex. In his early writings, Freud proposed the drive for sensory and sexual gratification as the primary human instinct. He called this constructive, life-giving instinct **eros**. After witnessing the horrific carnage of World War I, however, Freud concluded that a single, positive life force could not be responsible for so much violence. He proposed, therefore, that humans also have a destructive, death instinct, which he called **thanatos**.

Freud's views undoubtedly influenced Konrad Lorenz,[32] whose instinct theory of aggression posited a buildup of aggressive urges (like hydraulic pressure inside a closed environment) that, if not released through some other activity, would inevitably lead to aggression. Although little empirical evidence has ever been found to support this "hydraulic" model of aggression, the theory that aggression results from the buildup of an internal drive or tension that must be released still has a profound influence on clinical psychology. It motivates popular venting and cathartic therapies even though numerous studies have found no evidence supporting the hydraulic model.[33,34,35]

Empirical evidence supporting the existence of innate, relatively automatic aggressive responses has been demonstrated for many species.[36] For example, in the male Stickleback fish, a red object triggers attack 100% of the time.[37] However, no such innate aggressive response has been demonstrated in humans.[38]

Learning Theories

According to social learning theory,[39,40,41] aggression is not an innate drive like hunger in search of gratification. People learn aggressive behaviors the same way they learn other social behaviors—by direct experience and by observing others. In social learning theory, the shift is from internal causes to external ones. According to this theory, people observe and copy the behavior of others—called **modeling**. Modeling can weaken or strengthen aggressive responding. If the model is rewarded for behaving aggressively, further aggression (both by the model and by the observer) becomes more likely. If the model is punished for behaving aggressively, further aggression becomes less likely.

To demonstrate the social learning of aggression, Albert Bandura and his colleagues[42] allowed preschool children to watch an aggressive adult role model, a non-aggressive model, or no model. The aggressive model abused a large, inflated clown called a Bobo doll. The model laid the Bobo doll on its side, sat on it, punched it repeatedly in the nose, and said, "Sock him in the nose." The model then beat the doll on the head with a mallet and said, "Hit him down." The model tossed the doll up in the air and said, "Throw him in the air." The model kicked the doll about the room, saying, "Kick him" and "Pow." In contrast, the nonaggressive model played with nonviolent toys the entire time, so children in that condition saw no aggressive activity. After 10 minutes, the experimenter entered the room, informed the child that he or she would now go to another game room, and said good-bye to the model. The other room contained both aggressive toys (a Bobo doll, a mallet and pegboard, dart guns, and a tetherball with a face painted on it), and some nonaggressive toys (a tea set, crayons and paper, a ball, dolls, teddy bears, cars and trucks, and plastic farm animals). The children who had watched the aggressive model showed the highest levels of aggression (see **FIGURE 10.2**). Even watching the aggression on television was enough to make children more aggressive; Bandura and his colleagues replicated their findings using filmed models.[43]

instinct an innate (inborn, biologically programmed) tendency to seek a particular goal, such as food, water, or sex

eros in Freudian theory, the constructive, life-giving instinct

thanatos in Freudian theory, the destructive, death instinct

modeling observing and copying or imitating the behavior of others

Bandura's studies showed that children readily imitated filmed aggressive adult models.

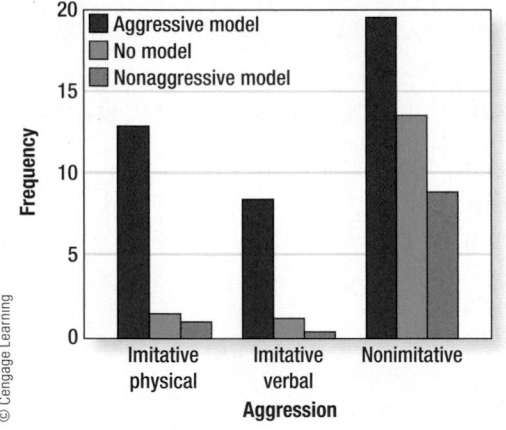

FIGURE 10.2

Results from a Bobo doll study conducted by Bandura and his colleagues. Children exposed to aggressive models behaved more aggressively than did children exposed to nonaggressive models or no models.[282]

To be sure, these studies do not meet our definition of human aggression because the aggressive act is targeted at a Bobo doll rather than a real person. However, many other studies have shown that aggressive models can influence people of all ages to behave more aggressively toward human targets. In one study,[44] children could help or hurt another child's chance of winning a prize by pressing either a green "HELP" button or a red "HURT" button. Participants were told that when they pressed the "HURT" button, a handle that the other child was turning would get really hot and burn him. (In reality, of course, there was no child in the other room, and no one got burned.) Children who had watched a violent film pressed the "HURT" button down longer than did children who had watched a nonviolent film.

These experiments don't exactly show that aggression is learned. They do, however, show that inhibitions against aggression can be overcome if a model acts out aggressively. Although all creatures are innately disposed to learn some things better and faster than others, learning is still important. The impulse to lash out against someone who hurts or threatens or humiliates you may be natural and universal (nature says go), but the rules governing action or restraint depend heavily on culture (culture says stop). Some anthropologists and others believe that without cultural encouragement, there would be no aggression,[45] but the majority of social scientists disagree, partly because aggression has been found everywhere. The nonviolent human being, not the violent one, is the product of culture.

Nature *and* Nurture

Many experts on aggression (and your textbook authors) favor a middle ground in this nature-versus-nurture dispute. Both learning and instinct are relevant.

As already noted, learning clearly plays a role. People can learn how to behave aggressively. Even more important and more commonly, they learn how to restrain aggression. People learn and mostly obey complicated rules about aggression. Some remarkable evidence of this can be seen in American football games. Urged on by coaches and fans to "beat" and "destroy" their opponents, the defensive players charge at the quarterback as ferociously as they can, eager to slam into him and knock him to the ground. But they have to be able to stop this attempted aggression at a split-second's notice when the quarterback steps out of bounds, or he throws the ball, or the referee blows the whistle, to avoid being penalized for "roughing the passer."

As for nature, it is hard to dispute that aggression is found all over the world, and indeed some of its patterns are universal. For example, in all known societies, young adult men mainly perpetrate violence.[46] In no society do the majority of violent criminals turn out to be elderly women, for example.

Most likely, the Freudian theory of innate aggression needs a major overhaul. Freud and others thought aggression was like hunger: The need bubbles up from inside and has to be satisfied in some way. In that view, the aggressive drive is independent of circumstances. In contrast, perhaps natural selection has led to aggressive impulses as a way to respond to certain (social) events, such as someone else's getting something you want. To appreciate the difference, imagine what life would be like if you always got everything you wanted. According to the Freudian view, you would still have aggressive impulses, because the aggressive drive would still arise repeatedly and make you want to hit people or smash things. In contrast, if aggression is merely an innate response to not getting what you want, you might in principle never have an aggressive impulse if you always got what you wanted.

Humans don't have to learn to behave aggressively—rather, aggression seems to come naturally. They learn how to control their aggressive impulses. Thus, it may be natural to feel aggressive impulses in response to certain provocations. But cultural beings learn to bring those natural impulses under control so as to follow the rules. This fits the theme that nature says go, whereas culture says stop. All known human societies have rules against aggression, though they may consider some aggression acceptable. For human beings who live in culture, aggression is subject to rules and limits. And as we have seen, the gradual progress of human culture has led to a gradual but large reduction in rates of aggression and violence. Culture's "stop" message is slowly succeeding.

© Mauritius/SuperStock

Aggressive instincts can be modified so that even cats and rats can live together peacefully.

QUIZ YOURSELF
Is Aggression Innate or Learned?

1. **In Freud's theory, life-giving instinct is to death instinct as _____ is to _____ .**

   - (a) eros; thanatos
   - (b) thanatos; eros
   - (c) id; superego
   - (d) superego; id

2. **Learning is to instinct as _____ is to _____ .**

   - (a) external forces; internal forces
   - (b) internal forces; external forces
   - (c) Sigmund Freud; Konrad Lorenz
   - (d) Konrad Lorenz; Sigmund Freud

3. **Abdul believes that children are aggressive because they imitate what they see family members and media characters do. Abdul's beliefs are consistent with _____ theory.**

   - (a) Freudian
   - (b) frustration
   - (c) instinct
   - (d) social learning

4. **The wide variation in homicide rates across different countries illustrates the effect of _____ on violence and aggression.**

   - (a) aggressive cues
   - (b) frustration
   - (c) nature
   - (d) nurture

answers: see pg 368

Inner Causes of Aggression

Frustration

In 1939 a group of psychologists from Yale University published a book titled *Frustration and Aggression*.[47] In this book, they proposed the **frustration–aggression hypothesis**, which they summarized on the first page of their book with these two bold statements: (a) "the occurrence of aggressive behavior always presupposes the existence of frustration," and (b) "the existence of frustration always leads to some form of aggression." (Note the strong use of "always" in both sentences; social psychologists today hardly ever dare say "always" or "never"!) They defined **frustration** as blocking or interfering with a goal. The Yale group formulated the frustration-aggression hypothesis based on the early writings of Sigmund Freud.[48] Freud believed that people are primarily motivated to seek pleasure and avoid pain. People were presumed to be frustrated when their pleasure-seeking or pain-avoiding behavior was blocked. Freud regarded aggression as the "primordial reaction" to frustration. (As we saw earlier, Freud eventually revised his theory to include an aggressive instinct, but the Yale group favored his earlier theory.)

Neal Miller, one of the original authors of *Frustration and Aggression*, was quick to tone down the second statement of the frustration-aggression hypothesis.[49] He changed that statement to: "Frustration produces instigations to a number of different types of response, one of which is an instigation to some form of aggression" (p. 338). Miller continued to hold that the first statement of the hypothesis (aggression is *always* preceded by frustration) was true.

Most experts today think Miller and his colleagues went too far by using the word "always" in their theory. Aggression can exist without frustration, and frustration without aggression. Still, there is no denying the basic truth that frustration often increases aggression.

The Rwanda genocide was triggered in part by frustration on the part of Hutus that the Tutsis were so much better off than they were, even though they were the minority group. The frustration of the majority Hutus dated back to having to submit to a Tutsi king. Of course, frustration does not justify the Hutus' slaughtering the Tutsis, but it may partly explain their actions.

Being in a Bad Mood

Angry, frustrated, distraught, upset people have long been regarded as being prone to aggressive behavior. As the previous section showed, psychologists have long believed that frustration causes aggression, and the data have confirmed that—but it is not the whole story because some aggression is not caused by frustration. More recently, Leonard Berkowitz (sometimes considered the grandfather of the social psychology of aggression, and the academic grandfather of Bushman) proposed that all states of negative affect—not just frustration—deserve to be recognized as causes of aggression.[50] To be sure, not all varieties of negative affect have been tested for aggression-enhancing effects, but it is clear that some of them are quite capable of increasing aggression. When researchers want to elicit high levels of aggression in the laboratory, they typically start by inducing some aversive emotional state, such as anger or indignation. But perhaps it is too much to state that all negative emotions promote aggression. Indeed, guilt, which is a negative emotion, increases prosocial behavior[51] and decreases aggressive behavior.[52]

Why do unpleasant moods increase aggression? One possible explanation is that angry people aggress in the hope that doing so will enable them to feel better. Research has consistently shown that people who feel bad often try to remedy or repair their moods.[53] Because many people believe that venting is a healthy way to reduce anger and aggression (see Chapter 6), they might vent by lashing out at others to improve their mood. Experimental research supports this hypothesis about trying to feel better.[54] These

frustration–aggression hypothesis proposal that "the occurrence of aggressive behavior always presupposes the existence of frustration," and "the existence of frustration always leads to some form of aggression"

frustration blockage of or interference with a personal goal

studies replicated the standard finding that anger increases aggression—but also found a revealing exception. When participants believed that their angry mood would not change for the next hour no matter what they did (ostensibly because of side effects of a pill they had taken, which temporarily "froze" their mood), anger did not lead to aggression. The implication is that anger does not *directly* or *inevitably* cause aggression. Rather, angry people attack others because they believe that lashing out will help get rid of their anger and enable them to feel better.

As we saw in Chapter 6, many emotions are characterized by a bodily state called arousal, which is a feeling of excitement or tenseness. (This does not refer to specifically sexual arousal, which is an unusual and special case.) Moreover, we saw that arousal caused by one event can sometimes be transferred to something else, thereby increasing one's reaction to it. Aggression can be increased by "excitation transfer." That is, arousal deriving from nonaggressive sources (such as physical exercise or an erotic nonviolent movie) can be mistaken for anger and can therefore increase aggression. Studies have randomly assigned participants to exercise by riding a stationary bike, or to skip the workout.[55] Afterwards, participants were provoked or not provoked by a confederate. Participants were then given an opportunity to punish the confederate by shocking him. The highest levels of aggression were found among participants who had both ridden the bike and been provoked (see **FIGURE 10.3**). The provocation produced the anger, which was then fueled by excitation transfer from the workout.

The fact that aversive emotional states lead to aggression has been asserted for decades and supported by many research findings. However, it is important to point out that being in a bad mood is neither a necessary nor a sufficient condition (nor a justification) for aggression. There is negative affect without aggression, and vice versa.

Hostile Cognitive Biases

As we noted in Chapter 5, the attributions people make for another person's behavior can have a strong influence on their own behavior. Perceptions can be more important than reality when it comes to understanding human thought and behavior. People are more likely to behave aggressively when they perceive ambiguous behaviors from others as stemming from hostile intentions than when they perceive the same behaviors as coming from benign intentions. When an ambiguous event occurs, do we give others the benefit of the doubt, or do we assume they are out to get us? This is a question of attributions. Some people assume that others are out to attack them, even if they are not. That is, they automatically (and sometimes mistakenly) attribute hostile intent to other people.

The **hostile attribution bias** is the tendency to perceive ambiguous actions by others as indicating aggressive intent. For example, if a person bumps into you, a hostile attribution would be that the person did it on purpose to harm or annoy you. A meta-analysis of 41 studies involving more than 6,000 participants showed a strong relationship between hostile attribution of intent and aggressive behavior in children.[56] This relationship holds for adults, too.[57]

Two other related biases have been proposed: the hostile perception bias and the hostile expectation bias. The **hostile perception bias** is the tendency to perceive social interactions in general as being aggressive. The hostile *attribution* bias pertains specifically to whether someone is attacking you, but the hostile *perception* bias pertains to whether other people are attacking each other, such as seeing two other people having a conversation and inferring that they are arguing or getting ready to fight. Research has shown that this bias is more prevalent in aggressive individuals than in nonaggressive individuals.[58] Even something as subtle as an advertisement for alcohol can increase hostile perceptions, perhaps because most people strongly associate alcohol with aggression.[59]

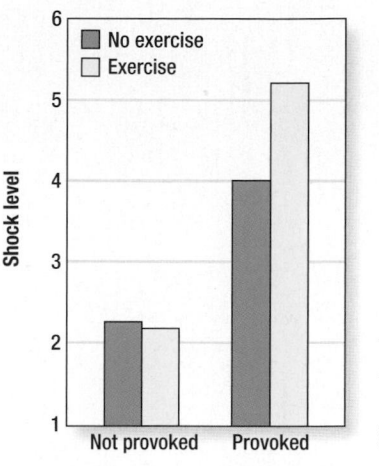

FIGURE 10.3

Arousal from physical exercise can transfer to a provocation and therefore increase aggression. As shown in this figure, the most aggressive participants in this study were those who first exercised and were later provoked.[283]

off the mark .com — by Mark Parisi
offthemark.com

SO... MAKIN' FUN OF ME?

© 2004 MARK PARISI DIST. BY UFS., INC.

Some people have a hostile attribution bias—they interpret the ambiguous actions of others as hostile actions.

hostile attribution bias the tendency to perceive ambiguous actions by others as aggressive

hostile perception bias the tendency to perceive social interactions in general as being aggressive

Aggressive people see the world as a hostile place. The **hostile expectation bias** is the tendency to expect others to react to potential conflicts with aggression. Individuals who are characteristically aggressive are more likely than nonaggressive individuals to expect others to behave in an aggressive manner.[60] For example, if you bump into another person, a hostile expectation would be that the person will assume that you did it on purpose and will attack you in return. Of course, people are more likely to behave aggressively themselves if they expect others to behave aggressively. Playing a violent video game can increase the hostile expectation bias,[61,62] which, in turn, can increase aggression levels after the game has been turned off.[63] In contrast, playing a prosocial video game can decrease the hostile expectation bias.[64]

In summary, aggressive people have inner biases that make them (a) expect others to react aggressively, (b) view ambiguous acts as aggressive, and (c) assume that when someone does something to hurt or offend them, it was deliberately and intentionally designed to have that hurtful effect even if it was accidental or benign. Such biases are an impediment to peace and harmony in our social world. If more people could give each other the benefit of the doubt more often, the world would be a less violent place.

Recent research suggests that hostile biases can be changed![65] Participants were teens in a youth program that were considered high risk for committing a crime. Indeed, 70% already had an official record of criminal convictions. Participants saw 15 faces on a continuum that ranged from clearly happy to clearly angry, with several ambiguous faces in between. First, teens indicated the point in the continuum when the faces changed from happy to angry. Next, teens were randomly assigned to treatment or control groups. The treatment consisted of telling the teens that two of the faces they thought were angry were in fact happy. They were told this each day for four days, just to make sure they got it. To measure the effect of the treatment, staff members recorded incidents of aggressive behavior the week prior to the experiment, and two weeks after the experiment. The results showed that teens in the treatment group were significantly less aggressive than those in the control group.

hostile expectation bias the tendency to assume that people will react to potential conflicts with aggression

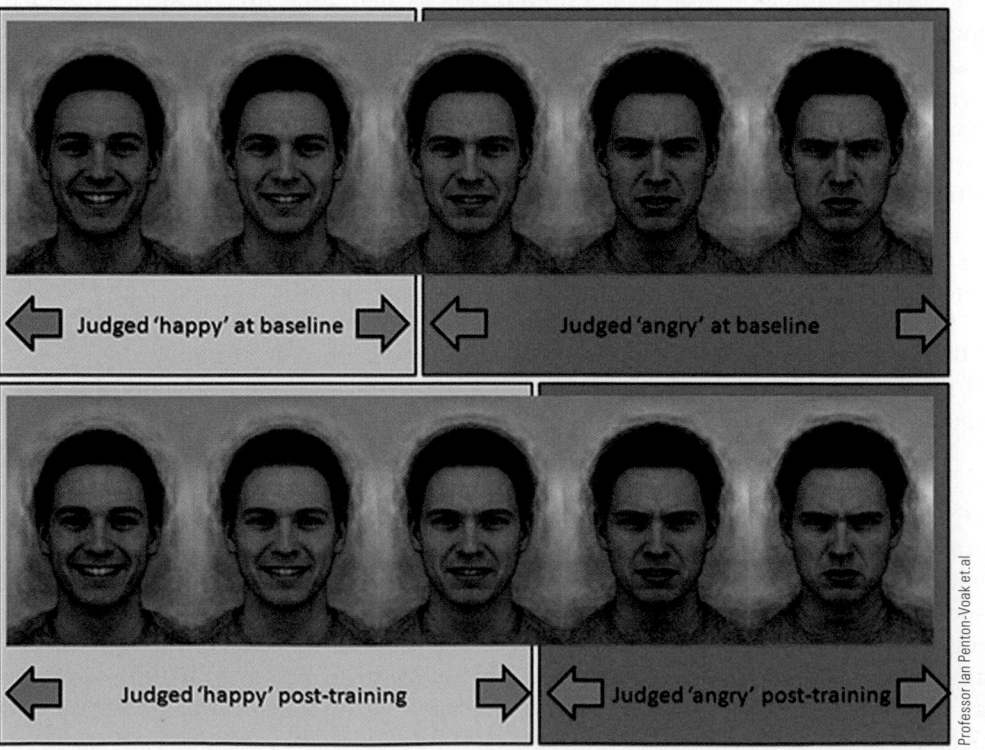

Professor Ian Penton-Voak et.al

Age and Aggression

Children do not commit many violent crimes, especially as compared to young adult men. Yet Richard Tremblay has provided evidence that very young children are in fact the most aggressive human beings on earth.[66] His research team observed toddlers in day-care settings and recorded that about 25% of interactions involve some kind of physical aggression (e.g., a child pushes another child out of the way and takes her toy). No adult group, not even violent youth gangs or hardened criminals, resorts to physical aggression 25% of the time. (Remember our definitions, though: Most toddler aggression isn't severe enough to qualify as violence, and it is sometimes difficult to determine intent in toddlers.) It is fortunate for all of us that toddlers are small, weak, and unlikely to be carrying guns!

Few dared to enter the territory of the dreaded "Cribs Gang."

The high level of aggression among toddlers again fits the theme that nature says go and culture says stop. Human children naturally rely on physical aggression to resolve their disputes, including influencing other toddlers to get what they want. Toddlers may resort to aggression 25% of the time, but as they grow up, they learn to inhibit aggression.

Although most people become less aggressive over time, a small subset of people become *more* aggressive over time. The most dangerous years for this small subset of individuals (and for society) are late adolescence and early adulthood. This is because aggressive acts become more extreme (e.g., weapons are used more frequently). Official records show that violent criminal offending is highest for individuals (especially men) between 15 and 30 years old, and declines significantly after that.[67]

Gender Differences in Aggression and Violence

Two males bump into each other:

> *First Male:* Hey, watch it!
> *Second Male:* No, YOU watch it!
> *First Male:* Oh, yeah?
> (They deliberately bump into each other again.)

Two females in an identical situation:

> *First Female:* I'm sorry!
> *Second Female:* No, it's my fault!
> *First Female:* Say, those are cute shoes!
> (They go shopping.)[68]

Of course the above interaction is just hypothetical (and stereotypical), but it does illustrate a fundamental difference in how males and females differ in response to stressful situations. This difference also occurs among animals other than humans. For example, research shows that when male rats are under stress, they respond by either fighting or running away, called the **fight or flight syndrome**.[69] In contrast, female rats respond to stress by nurturing others and making friends, called the **tend and befriend syndrome**.[70]

Gender differences in aggression are very noticeable by the preschool years, with boys showing higher levels of physical aggression than girls.[71] In later elementary grades and in adolescence, gender differences increase. Indirect aggression becomes much greater for girls than boys, physical aggression becomes much greater for boys than girls, and verbal aggression is about the same for girls and boys.[72,73] These gender differences culminate in dramatic differences in physically violent behavior in young adulthood, reflected in huge gender differences in murder rates. There is no known

Aggressiveness peaks at age 2. Fortunately it is curtailed by nap times, curfews, limited strength, and general incompetence.

SOURCE: Tremblay (2000).

fight or flight syndrome a response to stress that involves aggressing against others or running away

tend and befriend syndrome a response to stress that involves nurturing others and making friends

"It's a guy thing."

Donald Reilly/The New Yorker Collection/The Cartoon Bank

relational aggression (also called **social aggression**) behavior that involves intentionally harming another person's social relationships, feelings of acceptance, or inclusion within a group

society in which women commit most of the violent crimes;[74] the gender difference in violence is universal.

Why? When something is universal, the common assumption is that it is at least partly innate. One answer would therefore be that males are innately more aggressive than females. A related answer is that during evolution, whether a male was able to reproduce depended on his status and rank among the males in his group—and those in turn depended on aggression. To get access to females and thereby have a chance to make babies, a male had to fight and dominate other males. Vestiges of this pattern have been shown in modern college students. After thinking about an intense sexual experience, college men (but not women) became more aggressive—and only toward other men, not toward women.[75] Thus, the thought of sex stimulates the male's concern with needing to dominate other males physically.

Nevertheless, it would be wrong to think that females are never physically aggressive. Females do display physical aggression in social interactions, particularly when other females provoke them.[76] Laboratory studies with college students often yield higher aggression by men, but provocation apparently has a greater effect on aggression than does biological sex. Gender differences in lab aggression shrink under high provocation.[77] When it comes to heterosexual domestic partners, women are slightly *more* likely than men to use physical aggression against their partners![78,79] However, men are more likely than women to inflict serious injuries and death on their partners (i.e., violence), probably because men tend to be taller, heavier, and stronger than women on average.

Females are much more likely than males to engage in **relational aggression** (also called **social aggression**), defined as intentionally harming another person's social relationships, feelings of acceptance, or inclusion within a group.[80] Some examples of relational aggression include saying bad things about people behind their backs, withdrawing affection to get what you want, excluding others from your circle of friends, and giving someone the "silent treatment." Early research focused mainly on the negative effect of relational aggression, especially on the unfortunate targets. However, recent research has shown that relational aggression may also have a positive effect—it can strengthen friendships through the sharing of sensitive and intimate information.[81] Whether it is a good thing for two women to deepen their friendship by harming another woman is, of course, debatable.

Interpersonal Causes of Aggression

Selfishness and Influence

One broad theory argues that aggression should be understood as a form of social influence.[82] Instead of a learned response, or a reaction to frustration, or an eruption of innate drives, aggression is mainly viewed as a means for people to get what they want. This theory highlights the social rather than the antisocial nature of aggression, because it depicts aggression as a way in which people relate to others.

Creatures that don't take care of themselves tend not to survive and reproduce, so evolution has made most animals (including humans) selfish.[83] Humans can rise above their selfishness, but the selfish core is still there. Social life inevitably breeds some degree of conflict between selfish beings, such as when two people want the same food or the same mate, when both want to occupy a nice spot, or even when both want to watch different programs on the same television set! Aggression is one means that social animals use to resolve some of these disputes.

When do people resort to aggression to get what they want? Several factors play a role.[84] The more they want the reward (think of saving the life of someone you love), the more willing people are to use violence to get it. People are more likely to resort to aggression when they believe it will bring success, such as if the other person seems unlikely to retaliate. (If the other person is bigger and stronger than you, then aggression does not seem a promising way to get what you want.) Some people regard physical violence as immoral and will not engage in it under almost any circumstances, whereas others are far less inhibited.

Blaming someone for unfair actions can lead to aggressive retaliation. The most commonly cited unfair things that people do include disloyalty, disregarding the feelings of others, hostility, breaking promises and other agreements, selfishness, rudeness, lateness, and vicious gossip.[85,86] People use many means to strike back or punish someone who has wronged them, ranging from directly hitting the person, to spreading nasty rumors, to committing property crimes such as burglary or vandalism. In fact, one study of arson (setting fires) in Houston concluded that three out of five arsons were done as a way of getting revenge for some perceived unjust mistreatment.[87] For example, people set fires to punish a bar or restaurant that had thrown them out, or to get back at an ex-lover.

In short, aggression is a strategy that many social animals (including humans) use to help them get what they want. To learn about one particular case—namely, sexual aggression—see *The Social Side of Sex*. Human culture may invoke laws and moral principles to try to get people to resolve their disputes using peaceful means, and most people probably agree that nonviolent means are better, but every day, all over the world, many people find themselves resorting to aggression or violence to get something or just to get even.

Domestic Violence: Hurting Those We Love

Domestic violence (also called **family violence** or **intimate-partner violence**) is violence that occurs within the home, between people who have a close relationship with each other. Examples of domestic violence include a husband beating his wife, a mother hurting her child, a parent sexually molesting a child, brothers and sisters hitting each other, a child witnessing parents fighting, and an adult striking an elderly parent. If anything, aggression is highest between siblings.[88] The U.S. Surgeon General declared domestic violence to be the number one health risk in the United States. Women in noncommitted relationships are especially at risk. The risk of being the victim of domestic violence for women who are separated, divorced, cohabiting with a partner, or never married is three times higher than the risk for married women.[89] It can occur in heterosexual, homosexual, or bisexual relationships. It is mainly women who report incidents of domestic violence to the police.[90]

domestic violence (also called **family violence** or **intimate-partner violence**) physically harmful actions that occur within the home or family, between people who have a close relationship with each other

We have seen that many people use aggression to get what they want from others, and one thing that people sometimes want—and use force to get—is sex. Most cultures recognize the problem that some men force women to have sex against their will. The opposite problem, of women forcing men to have sex, has generally been ignored, though surveys suggest it also occurs.[91] Still, when women force men to have sex, the traumatic consequences appear to be much less than what female rape victims suffer.[92] Sometimes, too, men force other men to have sex, and women force other women. Male coercion of females is generally considered to be the most serious social problem, however. Of course, sexual coercion occurs within homosexual relationships as well as heterosexual relationships.

Defining rape or sexual coercion is a difficult issue that has compounded the problem of understanding, because sexual coercion consists of multiple phenomena that almost certainly have different causes. Some researchers have favored broad, loose definitions of sexual coercion, using one big category that includes everything from being attacked, beaten, and forced to have intercourse by a stranger to the case of a young man who kisses a woman against her will. Efforts to understand the causes of sexual coercion depend heavily on such definitions. Because there are far more cases resembling the stolen kiss than the forcible stranger rape, the stolen kiss data can crowd out the violent stranger rapes. The National Health and Social Life Survey[93] found that between 15% and 22% of women had been forced into some sexual activity against their will, but only 1% were forced by strangers. The majority of victims, in fact, said the person who forced them was someone they were in love with at the time.

Even if a woman is in love with the man who forced her, or has consented to kissing or petting with him, or even if she has previously (or subsequently) consented to sex with that man, that does not make any kind of forced sexual activity any less of a crime. A woman (or a man, for that matter) always has the right to refuse sexual advances from any person at any time, and it is both highly immoral and illegal to continue to demand sex when one's partner has indicated an unwillingness to go any further. It is upsetting and even traumatic to be subjected to unwanted sexual advances, whether one knows the attacker or not. However, researchers who use broad definitions of sexual coercion and then combine all acts when evaluating the harm done to victims may seriously underestimate the negative effects of some of the most atrocious acts of sexual violence.

How the victims fare depends on which definition of rape is used. Victims of violent rape, especially by strangers, often suffer lasting problems, including fear and anxiety, depression, and sexual problems.[94,95] Many blame themselves. Some withdraw from other people and become socially isolated. In contrast, when looser definitions of sexual coercion were used in other studies, the results suggested much less lasting trauma. Often the man apologized and the woman simply forgave him and went on to consider him a friend.[96] Three out of five rape victims said they had had consensual sex with the rapist on a previous occasion, and two out of five had some consensual activity (such as making out or oral sex) on the same day as the rape.[97] Two out of five rape victims said they would consent to having sex with the rapist on a later occasion.[98] Almost certainly these data are not based on violent stranger rapes—they refer instead to acquaintance and date rape patterns, which are different in some ways (though still immoral).

The old stereotype of the rapist was either a woman hater or a man who lacked social skills and could not get sex via romance and persuasion and therefore resorted to violence. Research, including studies on date rapists, has painted a very different picture.[99,100] Sexually coercive men generally have other sex partners and indeed may have more sex than noncoercive men. A sexually coercive man generally does not hate women, but he may devalue them, may have little empathy for their concerns or suffering, and is likely to feel that women have hurt or betrayed him in the past. His peer group places high emphasis on sexual conquests, and he wants to have some to boast about. He is therefore motivated to downplay his use of force or coercion and claim instead that he had consensual sex (because it bolsters his ego and reputation). In fact, he probably prefers not to use force, but he is willing to use any means he can, including trickery, false promises, untrue declarations of love, and force, to get sex. He has high sexual motivation and enjoys impersonal, uncommitted sex. If his crime was date rape, it was often preceded by some consensual activity such as oral sex; when the woman wanted to stop, he forced her to continue. He thinks very highly of himself and may well have narcissistic personality patterns, including the sense that he deserves special rewards such as sexual favors.[101] He may think the woman owes him sex and that he is only using a bit of force to claim what he deserves. Therefore, he may not even admit to himself that what he is doing is immoral and illegal.

Men are also victims of domestic violence, although it is often underreported. As was noted earlier, women actually attack their relationship partners slightly more often than men do, although women don't cause as much physical harm. The average husband is taller, stronger, and heavier than his wife, so if they get into a physical fight, she is much more likely to be injured or killed than he is. Domestic violence also occurs in relationships involving homosexual men and women.[102] Physically weaker family members, such as children or elderly parents, are especially at risk of becoming domestic violence victims because they cannot fight back. Domestic violence not only immediately harms victims, but it can also produce long-term harmful consequences (e.g., depression, anxiety, insomnia, loneliness, social dysfunction, somatic symptoms).[103,104]

The same factors that influence aggression against strangers also appear to influence aggression against loved ones. The "perfect storm" combination of causes for domestic violence appears to be a combination of strong instigating factors (e.g., provocation, rejection), strong impelling factors (e.g., trait aggressiveness, hostile attribution bias), and weak inhibitor factors (e.g., low self-control, alcohol intoxication).[105]

Research shows that husbands who want to control their wives are more likely to assault them.[106] Abusive spouses also tend to be abusive parents.[107] Parents who were abused as children are significantly more likely than others to abuse their own children.[108,109] However, one should not overstate this relationship, as is often done. By far, most victims of abuse do not become abusers themselves.

Domestic violence is not a recent phenomenon; it has a long history. Gradually, culture is intervening to prohibit and punish it. This indicates the slow process of culture entering more and more previously private spheres to say "stop" by exerting control over aggression. The American Puritan tradition regarded the nuclear family as sacrosanct and held that no one should intervene in how parents raise their children, but modern American culture is increasingly rejecting that view to insist that parents refrain from aggressive and violent treatment. Corporal punishment of children (including spanking) at home is legal in all 50 states in the United States, but it is illegal at school in 31 of the 50 states and in 37 different countries, starting with Sweden in 1979.[110]

JJ Grandville "Les cent proverbs" 1845

Qui aime bien châtie bien.

An illustration from French caricaturist Jean Ignace Isidore Gérard's (pseudonym J. J. Grandville) *Les cent proverbs* captioned "Qui aime bien châtie bien" (*Who loves well, punishes well*), showing a man spanking a child in the foreground, and a husband beating his wife in the background. JJ Grandville "*Les cent proverbs*" 1845

QUIZ YOURSELF

Interpersonal Causes of Aggression

1. What theory of aggression posits that people use aggression to restore justice?

(a) Frustration–aggression theory

(b) Instinct theory

(c) Social influence theory

(d) Social learning theory

2. Which group of people is especially at risk for domestic violence?

(a) Men in committed relationships

(b) Men in noncommitted relationships

(c) Women in committed relationships

(d) Women in noncommitted relationships

3. Which of the following statements is false?

(a) Women attack their relationship partners more often than men do.

(b) In an attack, men cause more damage than women do.

(c) The average husband is taller, stronger, and heavier than his wife.

(d) All of the above are true.

4. Domestic violence is especially likely to occur when instigating factors are _____, impelling factors are _____, and inhibiting factors are _____ .

(a) strong; strong; strong

(b) strong; strong; weak

(c) strong; weak; weak

(d) weak; weak; weak

answers: see pg 368

External Causes of Aggression

Weapons Effect

> "Guns not only permit violence, they can stimulate it as well. The finger pulls the trigger, but the trigger may also be pulling the finger."
>
> — Leonard Berkowitz, Emeritus Professor of Psychology, University of Wisconsin

Obviously, using a weapon can increase aggression and violence, but can just seeing a weapon increase aggression? In 1967, Leonard Berkowitz and Anthony LePage conducted a study to find out.[111] Angry participants were seated at a table that had a shotgun and a revolver on it—or, in the control condition, badminton racquets and shuttlecocks. The items on the table were described as part of another experiment that the researcher had supposedly forgotten to put away. The participant was supposed to decide what level of electric shock to deliver to a confederate, and the electric shocks were used to measure aggression. The experimenter told participants to ignore the items, but apparently they could not. Participants who saw the guns were more aggressive than were participants who saw the sports items.

Several other studies have replicated this effect, which has been dubbed the **weapons effect**. This effect has been replicated many times.[112] Indeed, you don't even need to be consciously aware of the fact that you have seen a weapon for it to affect you. In a recent study, participants who were exposed to words describing weapons (e.g., "gun") for only 17/100ths of a second were more aggressive afterward in comparison to participants exposed to nonaggressive words.[113]

Some studies have tested the weapons effect outside of the lab. In one field experiment,[114] for example, a confederate driving a pickup truck purposely remained stalled at a traffic light to see whether the motorists trapped behind him would honk their horns (the measure of aggression). The truck contained either a military rifle in a gun rack, or no rifle. More motorists honked at the pickup truck with a rifle than at the pickup truck with no rifle. What is amazing about this study is that you would have to be pretty foolish to honk your horn at a driver with a military rifle in his truck! These findings again bring up the duplex mind. Horn honking was probably not a product of logical, conscious thought. Most likely, it was mediated by the automatic system. The guns activated aggressive tendencies via a nonconscious, automatic response, making people react more aggressively than they would have otherwise.[115]

The horn-honking study raises another question: Are drivers with guns in their cars more likely to drive aggressively? Research shows they are.[116] A representative sample of over 2,000 U.S. drivers found that those who had a gun in the car were significantly more likely to make obscene gestures at other motorists (23% vs. 16%), aggressively follow another vehicle too closely (14% vs. 8%), or both (6.3% vs. 2.8%), even after controlling for potential confounding factors such as gender, age, urbanization, census region, and driving frequency.

The presence of weapons can also increase hostile biases. For example, recent research shows that holding a gun makes people believe that others are also holding guns (as opposed to neutral objects such as a cell phone).[117]

Recent research shows that acts of gun violence in Hollywood movies rated PG-13 (for ages 13+) have tripled since the rating was introduced in 1985.[118] Indeed, since 2012 PG-13 films contain more gun violence than movies rated R (for ages 17+). The changing levels of gun violence over time can be seen clearly by comparing movies with their sequels. For example, the 1990 movie "Die Hard 2" was rated R, but it contains less gun violence than the 2007 movie "Live Free or Die Hard" that was rated PG-13. Similarly, the 2003 movie "Terminator 3: Rise of the Machines" was rated R, but it contained less gun violence than the 2009 movie "Terminator Salvation" that was rated PG-13. These findings contradict the Motion Picture Association of America (MPAA) webpage, which says: "A PG-13 motion picture may go beyond the PG rating in theme, violence, nudity, sensuality, language, adult activities or other elements, but does not reach the restricted R category."

In American society, weapons are often visible to bystanders. For example, following the 2014 police shooting of Michael Brown—an unarmed black teen from Ferguson, Missouri—there was some discussion about the militarization of police forces.[119] It is possible that

weapons effect the increase in aggression that occurs as a result of the mere presence of a weapon

AP Images/Jeff Roberson

seeing police officers dressed in full combat gear could produce a weapons effect, thereby increasing (rather than decreasing) aggression, violence, and other antisocial behaviors.

Human beings are very good at quickly identifying potentially dangerous, threatening stimuli such as spiders and snakes. Such stimuli also automatically elicit fear. These responses are adaptive from an evolutionary perspective because some spiders and snakes are poisonous, and our ancient ancestors who could identify them quickly and were frightened by them were more likely to avoid them and live to pass their genes on to the next generation. Recent research shows that people can identify guns as quickly as they can identify spiders and snakes.[120,121,122] These findings are very interesting because guns are modern threats and cannot be explained using evolutionary principles. Yet guns are a far bigger threat to more people today than spiders or snakes. Of the over 40,000 known species of spiders, only about 200 species (0.5%) have dangerous or potentially lethal bites.[123] Poisonous spiders such as black widows and brown recluses kill about six Americans each year.[124] Poisonous snakes such as rattlesnakes kill about five.[125] In comparison, guns kill over 30,000 Americans each year.[126]

Mass Media

As we saw in the opening story about the genocide in Rwanda, the mass media can increase aggression. Social scientists have extensively studied the effects on aggression of exposure to violent media.

Public debate on the link between violent media and youth violence can become especially contentious in the wake of a shooting rampage.[127] In many rampage shootings, the perpetrator puts on a uniform (e.g., hockey mask, trench coat, movie costume, military uniform), as if following a media script. The perpetrator then collects several guns and ammunition, goes to a place where many people are gathered, kills as many people as possible, and then often kills himself (or is killed by the police). It is tempting for some to conclude that violent media caused the shooting rampage. However, it is impossible to make causal inferences about the link between exposure to violent media and violent criminal behavior because it is unethical to conduct experimental studies in which research participants can commit violent crimes such as rampage shootings (see Chapter 1). Violent behavior is complex and is caused by multiple factors, often acting together. The more extreme the violent behavior (e.g., from hitting, to shooting, to rampage shooting), the more complex the causality may be.

One can, however, draw causal inferences about the link between exposure to media violence and aggressive behavior in milder forms than violence. Hundreds of experiments

FIGURE 10.4

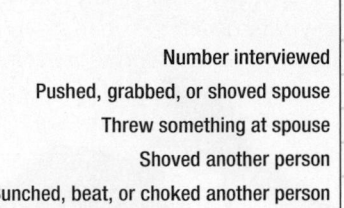

Women as well as men who were heavy childhood viewers of violent TV shows were much more likely to have abused their spouses and assaulted another adult at least once in the last year, according to self-reports, other-reports, and police records.[284]

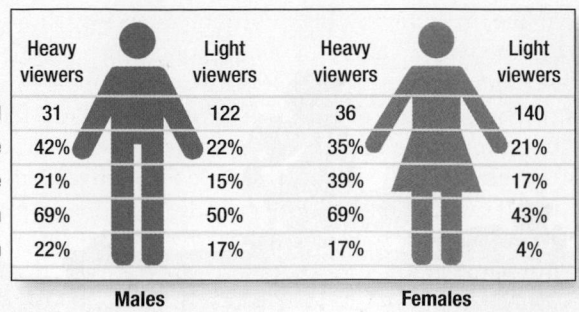

	Males		Females	
	Heavy viewers	Light viewers	Heavy viewers	Light viewers
Number interviewed	31	122	36	140
Pushed, grabbed, or shoved spouse	42%	22%	35%	21%
Threw something at spouse	21%	15%	39%	17%
Shoved another person	69%	50%	69%	43%
Bunched, beat, or choked another person	22%	17%	17%	4%

have shown that exposure to media violence causes an increase in aggressive behavior.[128,129,130] Studies also have shown that parents who set limits on the amount and content of children's media use provide a powerful protective factor against aggression.[131]

Longitudinal studies have shown that violent media effects persist over time. In a 15-year longitudinal study involving 329 participants,[132] for example, heavy viewers of violent TV shows in first and third grade were three times more likely to be convicted of criminal behavior by the time they were in their 20s. They were also more likely to abuse their spouses and assault other people (see **FIGURE 10.4**).

In 2011 the U.S. Supreme Court struck down a California law that restricted the sale and rental of violent video games to minors.[133] That decision, however, was based on First Amendment (i.e., freedom of speech) grounds, not on public safety or scientific grounds.[134] The scientific evidence on this issue is clear. One meta-analysis[135] of 381 effects from research reports involving over 130,000 participants "nails the coffin shut on doubts that violent video games stimulate aggression."[136] This meta-analysis showed that violent games increase aggressive thoughts, angry feelings, physiological arousal (e.g., heart rate, blood pressure), and aggressive behaviors and decrease empathic feelings and prosocial behaviors. Similar effects were obtained for males and females of all ages, regardless of their age, and regardless of what country they lived in. More recent meta-analyses have found similar effects.[137] Recent research also shows that people are especially aggressive after playing a violent video game as a character that is stereotypically violent. In one study, both male and female participants were more aggressive after playing a violent game as male character than as a female character, but the effect was larger for male participants (probably because male participants identified with the male character more than female participants did).[138] In another study, white participants were more aggressive after playing a violent game as a black character than as a white character.[139]

Some people think there is a "debate" about violent media effects. Although there is never complete consensus on any scientific topic, including violent media effects, the overwhelming majority of pediatricians (about 90%) and media researchers (about 67%) *strongly agree* or *agree* that violent screen media (i.e., television programs, movies, Internet sites, video games) increase aggression in children.[140] The rest are about even divided between *disagree* or *strongly disagree* and *neither agree nor disagree*.

One other type of media deserves special mention: violent media that contain sex, such as rape depictions. As we saw in the opening story, hate media may have contributed to the rape and sexual assault of women and girls during the 1994 genocide in Rwanda. Several social psychological experiments have found that violent sexual media increase aggression against women.[141] There are also long-term effects of viewing violent sexual media, such as desensitization to the pain and suffering experienced by women who have been the victims of sexual assault. Research has shown that even several days after watching violent sex scenes in "slasher" films, men still displayed an increased tolerance for aggression directed toward women.[142,143]

Unpleasant Environments

One common belief shared by writers, philosophers, and laypersons alike is that hot temperatures increase aggression and violence. This belief has even crept into the English

> "I pray thee, good Mercutio, let's retire; The day is hot, the Capulets abroad, And, if we meet, we shall not 'scape a brawl, For now, these hot days, is the mad blood stirring."
>
> — William Shakespeare, *Romeo and Juliet*, Act 3, Sc 1

language, as indicated by common phrases such as "hot-headed," "hot-tempered," "hot under the collar," and "my blood is boiling." Research evidence is consistent with this belief. The evidence from laboratory experiments, field experiments, correlational studies, and archival studies of violent crimes indicates that hotter temperatures are associated with higher levels of aggression and violence.[144] Studies that compare the violence rates of regions that differ in climate have found that hotter regions have higher violent crime rates.[145] Time period studies generally have found higher violence rates in hot years, hot seasons, hot months, and hot days than cold ones.[146,147]

Temperatures can even influence judgments about criminals and their crimes. Recent research[148] found that participants in a room with a low temperature (67.8 °F; 19.9 °C) judged a criminal to be more "cold-blooded" and the crime he committed to be more premeditated, whereas participants in a room with a high temperature (79.2 °F; 26.2 °C) judged the same criminal to be more "hot-headed" and his crime to be more impulsive. The temperature of the control group room was moderate (74.8 °F; 23.8° C).

When people think of the consequences of global warming (the observation that the weather all over the world is getting a little hotter year by year), they focus mainly on the impact of rising temperatures on droughts, agricultural crops, flooding, and extreme weather. However, there is also an impact of global warming on aggression and violence.[149] A comprehensive review of the 60 most rigorous studies conducted to date found strong causal evidence linking climate change to human conflict.[150]

Other unpleasant environmental events can also increase aggression. Numerous studies have shown that loud noises can increase aggression, including traffic noise,[151] especially when it is uncontrollable.[152,153] Foul odors,[154] secondhand smoke,[155] and air pollution[156] can also increase aggression. For example, one woman was arrested for throwing a knife at her boyfriend after he deliberately passed gas in her face while they were watching TV.[157]

Social stress may be even more unpleasant than nonsocial stress. **Density** (the number of people in a given area) and **crowding** (the subjective and unpleasant feeling that there are too many people in a given area) are not the same thing. Crowding is a better predictor of aggression than density per se. In fact, high population density can produce positive emotions and behaviors in desirable environments, such as in football stadiums or concert halls. Crowding, on the other hand, can increase aggression in undesirable environments, such as in psychiatric wards[158] and prisons.[159]

Chemical Influences

Hormones and Neurotransmitters

Like all behaviors, aggression is mediated by changes in chemical reactions and interactions within the brain. Two naturally occurring chemicals in the brain, testosterone and serotonin, have been closely linked with aggression. **Testosterone** is the male sex hormone. Although both males and females have testosterone, males have much more of it. Levels peak during puberty and begin to decline around age 23. Testosterone has repeatedly been linked to aggression in both sexes. In his book *The Trouble with Testosterone,* Robert Sapolsky provides a concise description of the seemingly direct association between testosterone and aggression: "Remove the source of testosterone in species after species and levels of aggression typically plummet. Reinstate normal testosterone levels afterward with injections of synthetic testosterone, and aggression returns."[160] For example, rats that received testosterone injections for 12 weeks responded with more aggression when their tails were pinched than did rats that received placebo injections.[161]

One problem with establishing a link between testosterone and aggression is that behavioral outcomes closely related to aggression also affect circulating testosterone levels.[162] For example, laboratory studies of competitions have shown that males who win games usually experience an increase in testosterone, and some female winners do, too.[163,164,165] This research strongly suggests a reciprocal influence between testosterone and aggression in humans. Higher levels of plasma testosterone probably increase aggression slightly, but the outcome of winning and dominating affects testosterone levels just as much. To be sure, if high testosterone makes someone pick a fight that he or she loses, his or her testosterone may drop afterward.

> "So, if anatomy is destiny then testosterone is doom."
> — Al Goldstein, pornographer

density the number of people divided by the area of the space they share

crowding the subjective and unpleasant feeling that there are too many people in a given area

testosterone the male sex hormone, high levels of which have been linked to aggression and violence in both animals and humans

In human brains, information is communicated between neurons (nerve cells) by the movement of chemicals across a small gap called the synapse. The chemical messengers are called neurotransmitters. **Serotonin** is one of these neurotransmitters; it has been called the "feel good" neurotransmitter. Not enough of it makes people feel bad and may therefore increase aggression. In correlational studies, levels of serotonin in the brain have been negatively related to aggression and violence in both humans[166,167] and nonhuman primates.[168,169]

Perhaps the best evidence of the influence of serotonin on aggression comes from laboratory experiments that use the drug tryptophan to increase serotonin. Experimental studies have shown that decreasing tryptophan increases aggression, whereas increasing tryptophan decreases aggression.[170,171,172] The question of just *how* serotonin influences aggression has been the subject of considerable debate. Most researchers agree that serotonin has an indirect rather than a direct effect on aggression, such as by increasing impulsive tendencies and reducing aggressive inhibitions.[173]

Alcohol and Other Drugs of Abuse

Alcohol is by far the chemical that has received the most attention from aggression researchers. Alcohol has long been associated with violent and aggressive behavior. In fact, sometimes alcohol is deliberately used to promote aggression. The military historian John Keegan noted that it has been standard practice for many centuries to issue soldiers some alcohol before they went into battle, both to reduce fear and to increase aggression.[174] There is ample evidence of a correlation between alcohol and aggression. A meta-analytic review of 130 studies found that alcohol was correlated with both criminal and domestic violence.[175] As was stated in Chapter 1, correlation does not necessarily imply causation. However, meta-analytic reviews of experimental studies come to the same conclusion—alcohol increases aggression.[176,177,178]

In one recent study, religious participants were significantly less aggressive than nonreligious people after consuming a placebo beverage, but were significantly more aggressive than nonreligious participants after consuming an alcoholic beverage.[179] This is relevant to the theme that nature says go and culture says stop. Religion, after all, is an important societal institution that often says to stop violence. Apparently this works with sober people—but not with intoxicated ones.

There are several possible explanations for why alcohol increases aggressive tendencies. One explanation is that alcohol reduces inhibitions.[180] Normally people have strong inhibitions against behaving aggressively, and alcohol reduces these inhibitions. To use a car analogy, alcohol increases aggression by cutting the brake line rather than by stepping on the gas. Alcohol might increase aggression by decreasing glucose levels, which provide the brain with the fuel it needs to exercise self-control (see Chapter 4).[181] Alcohol might also reduce inhibitions by decreasing serotonin levels.[182]

Another explanation is that alcohol has a "myopic" (nearsighted) or narrowing effect on attention.[183] This causes people to focus attention only on the most salient features of a situation (e.g., provocation) and not pay attention to more subtle features. A third explanation is that alcohol increases aggression by decreasing self-awareness.[184] As was noted in Chapter 3, people become more aware of their internal standards when attention is focused on the self. Most people have internal standards against behaving aggressively, but alcohol reduces people's ability to focus on these internal standards. A fourth explanation is that alcohol disrupts executive functions,[185] the cognitive abilities that help us plan, organize, reason, and control our emotions. A fifth explanation is that alcohol increases aggression because people expect it to. In many cultures, drinking occasions are culturally agreed-on "time-out" periods when people are not held responsible for their actions. People who behave aggressively while intoxicated can therefore "blame the bottle" for their actions.

Does all of this mean that aggression is somehow contained in alcohol? No. Alcohol increases rather than causes violent or aggressive tendencies. Factors that normally increase aggression (e.g., provocation, frustration, aggressive cues, violent media) have a stronger effect on intoxicated people than on sober people.[186] Put another way, alcohol

serotonin the "feel good" neurotransmitter, low levels of which have been linked to aggression and violence in both animals and humans

mainly seems to increase aggression in combination with other factors. If someone insults or attacks you, your response will be more violent if you are drunk than sober. When there is no provocation, however, the effect of alcohol on aggression may be negligible. Plenty of people enjoy an occasional drink without turning violent.

If what you drink can affect aggression, what about what you eat? *Food for Thought* summarizes some intriguing findings about this link.

FOOD FOR *Thought*

Is There a Link Between Diet and Violence?

In his memoirs about his life as a violent youth gang member in Los Angeles, "Monster" Kody Scott reflected that whenever he started to spend a serious amount of time with his gang, he often began to feel grumpy and irritable after a few days.[187] He thought this might have something to do with what he ate at those times. Most gang members do not go home for dinner to eat a balanced meal with plenty of vegetables, fruit, vitamins, protein, fiber, and other nutritious foods. Instead, they eat erratically, often late at night, and almost exclusively from fast-food outlets that serve fatty, sweet, and fried foods. "Monster" thought that subsisting on junk food for weeks at a time might contribute to the readiness of gang members to react violently when provoked.

Is this plausible? Is there a link between diet and violence rates? During the early 1980s, a criminologist named Stephen Schoenthaler instituted dietary changes in a dozen juvenile correctional institutions. He simply removed two types of foods from their diets: fried foods (e.g., hamburgers, sausages, French fries) and sugary foods (e.g., cookies, milkshakes, soft drinks). His data, which involved 8,076 juvenile delinquents, showed that removing these unhealthy foods led to a 47% reduction in antisocial behavior, including assaults, insubordination, suicide attempts, and rule violations. Schoenthaler notes that "the more violent the bad behavior [before dietary interventions began], the more the improvement."[188]

Vitamin supplements also reduce antisocial behavior in juvenile delinquents. In a typical study, Schoenthaler gave a vitamin supplement to 71 inmates of a state juvenile detention facility. He compared antisocial behavior when prisoners were getting the supplement versus when they were getting a placebo. The result was a startling improvement in behavior with the supplement. Total violence fell by two-thirds. Escape attempts and going AWOL (absent without official leave) plummeted from 79 incidents to 13. Property crimes dropped by half.

The vitamin supplement results obtained for juvenile delinquents have also been obtained for adult prisoners. Researchers in the United Kingdom gave 231 young adult prisoners either a placebo or a vitamin supplement.[189] Prisoners receiving vitamin supplements for a minimum of two weeks were involved in 35% fewer violent and antisocial infractions than those who received a placebo. The lead author on the study, Dr. Bernard Gesch, a physiologist at Oxford University, said, "Since the 1950s there has been a ten-fold increase in offences. How else can we explain that but by diet? ... The main change over that period has been in nutrients." An over-the-counter vitamin supplement seems like an inexpensive way to reduce antisocial behavior.

So perhaps "Monster" was right: Junk food can help make someone into a violent "monster." Much more research is needed, but at present the link between diet and violence appears to be real and significant.[190] Obviously, no one is suggesting that gang violence would disappear if only we could get a few young men to eat more fruits and vegetables. But it is very plausible that some diets make people more irritable than others, and that rates of violence can be affected by diet.

QUIZ YOURSELF

External Causes of Aggression

1. **Research suggests that the mere sight of a weapon can _____ .**
   (a) elicit frustration
   (b) increase aggression
   (c) prevent violence
   (d) produce catharsis

2. **There is _____ relationship between alcohol and aggression.**
   (a) a negative
   (b) no
   (c) a positive
   (d) None of the above

3. **There is _____ relationship between hot temperatures and aggression.**
   (a) a negative
   (b) no
   (c) a positive
   (d) None of the above

4. **Low levels of _____ are associated with high levels of aggression.**
   (a) adrenaline
   (b) alcohol
   (c) serotonin
   (d) testosterone

answers: see pg 368

In this section we discuss the role of culture and self-views in aggression and violence.

Norms and Values

Amok is one of the few Malay words used in the English language. The term, which dates back to 1665, means "a murderous or violently uncontrollable frenzy that occurs chiefly among Malays."[191] **Running amok**, roughly translated, means going berserk. Historically, the typical pattern was that a young Malay man who had suffered some loss of face or other setback would run amok, heedlessly performing violent acts (and sometimes not-so-coincidentally damaging the property of the people who had done him wrong). The Malays believed that these responses were normal and natural and that it was impossible for young men to restrain their wild, aggressive actions under those circumstances. However, when the British colonial administration disapproved of the practice and began to hold the young men responsible for their actions and to punish them for the harm they did, most Malays stopped running amok.[192]

The history of "running amok" thus reveals some important points about aggression. First, it shows the influence of culture: The violence was accepted by one culture and prohibited by another; when the local culture changed, the practice died out. Second, it shows that cultures can promote violence without placing a positive value on it. There is no sign that the Malays approved of running amok or thought it was a good, socially desirable form of action, but positive value wasn't necessary. All that was needed was for the culture to believe that it was normal for people to lose control under some circumstances and act violently as a result. Third, it shows that when people believe their aggression is beyond control, they are often mistaken: The supposedly "uncontrollable" pattern of running amok died out when the British cracked down on it. The influence of culture was thus mediated through self-control.

Some cultures or subcultures place positive value on fighting and aggression, at least in the sense of giving more respect to men who fight well. But researchers have not been successful at showing that people value fighting and violence. Even in youth gangs, most members say they don't like or approve of the violence. Violence is nowhere regarded as a positive good or end in itself. More often, violence may receive grudging acceptance as a necessary evil.

The link between culture and violence brings us back to the theme that nature says go and culture says stop. Some cultures condone losing control and engaging in violence under some circumstances, but they don't positively encourage it. For example, if a man catches his wife having sex with another man, many cultures forgive him for violence, up to and including killing one or both of them. Still, this is not the same as regarding killing them as a good thing. Nowhere are men given medals or prizes for killing their unfaithful wives and their lovers. When nature supplies the impulse to behave violently, culture sometimes tells people to stop; when culture falls silent, tolerating or condoning violence, then aggression will rise. Cultures can become more violent without positively encouraging violence; all that is necessary is to stop saying no.

Self-Control

In 1990, two criminologists published a book called *A General Theory of Crime*.[193] Such a brazen title was bound to stir controversy. After all, there are many crimes and many causes, so the idea of putting forward a single theory was pretty bold. What would their theory feature? Poverty? Frustration? Genetics? Violent media? Bad parenting? As it turned out, their main theory boiled down to poor self-control. Research has shown that poor self-control is one of the "strongest known correlates of crime" (p. 952).[194] And poor self-control is a better predictor of violent crimes than of nonviolent crimes.[195] Self-control is covered in detail in Chapter 4; we discuss it only briefly here. The concept of self-control is related to other factors in aggression that we have already discussed. For example,

running amok according to Malaysian culture, refers to behavior of a young man who becomes "uncontrollably" violent after receiving a blow to his ego

intoxicated people have less control over their aggressive behavior than do sober people, perhaps because alcohol interferes with executive functions. Children 1 to 3 years old have difficulty controlling their behavior and are also quite aggressive.

The emphasis on poor self-control as a cause of crime is consistent with some themes of this book. We have seen that the conflict between selfish impulses and social conscience crops up over and over. Most crime is selfish because it seeks to benefit the individual at others' expense. Society mostly tries to socialize people to restrain aggressive and criminal impulses; indeed, by definition, culture and society try to get people to obey the norms and rules of good, law-abiding behavior. (Even criminal parents do not usually teach or encourage their children to commit crimes, contrary to one stereotype.)

Gottfredson and Hirschi provided plenty of data to back up their theory. For one thing, criminals seem to be impulsive individuals who don't show much respect for rules in general. In the movies, criminals often specialize in one specific kind of crime, almost like any other job. But in reality, most criminals are arrested multiple times—for different crimes. If self-control is a general capacity for bringing one's behavior into line with rules and standards, most criminals lack it.

Another sign is that the lives of criminals show low self-control even in behaviors that are not against the law. They are more likely than law-abiding citizens to smoke cigarettes, to be involved in traffic accidents, to be involved in unplanned pregnancies, to fail to show up for work or school regularly, and the like.

Social psychology has found many causes of violence, including frustration, anger or insult, alcohol intoxication, violence in the media, and hot temperatures. This raises the question of why there isn't more violence than there is. After all, who hasn't experienced frustration, anger, insult, alcohol, media violence, or hot weather in the past year? Yet most people do not hurt or kill anyone. These factors may give rise to violent impulses, but mostly people restrain themselves. Violence starts when self-control stops.

Wounded Pride

For years, most social psychologists accepted the view that most aggression derived from low self-esteem. From murderers to playground bullies, violent individuals were assumed to have low opinions of themselves. Research, however, has contradicted that view.[196] If anything, violent individuals typically think they are better than others and have grandiose or inflated opinions of their own worth. Think of the most aggressive, violent person

Heinrich Hoffmann/Getty Images

Hitler probably did not have low self-esteem. In fact, the eminent psychoanalyst Erich Fromm said that Hitler had narcissistic personality disorder. Most of the men seen here adoring their Führer will be dead in a few years because of his violent decisions. Tens of millions of others, too.

you know, from history or personal experience. That person probably did not have low self-esteem. For example, Adolf Hitler probably did not have low self-esteem.

Aggression often starts when someone comes along and questions or challenges those favorable self-views. Wounded pride seems to be the most apt descriptor of how self-views are linked to aggression.

This is not to say that high self-esteem causes aggression. Indeed, most people with high self-esteem are not aggressive. But violent individuals typically have the trait of narcissism, which includes thinking oneself superior or special, feeling entitled to preferential treatment, being willing to exploit others, having low empathy with "lesser" human beings, and entertaining grandiose fantasies or other ideas about oneself as a great person.[197] The term *narcissism* comes from the Greek myth about a handsome man who falls in love with his own reflection in the water.

The Narcissistic Personality Inventory is a 40-item self-report scale that measures narcissism.[198] Several studies have shown that people who score high on the Narcissistic Personality Inventory respond with high levels of aggression when they receive a blow to their egos.[199] Violent prisoners also have much higher narcissism scores than nonviolent people.[200] Recent research involving a large nationally representative sample of Americans shows that people high in narcissism and low in self-control are especially prone to violence.[201]

The wounded pride factor has found its way into so much aggression research that it is often scarcely noticed. Most laboratory studies on aggression include some kind of provocation in the form of an insult delivered to the participant by the person toward whom the participant will later be able to aggress. Without such an insult, most studies find hardly any aggression. Essentially, most studies of aggression simply show that other factors can increase or decrease the effect of wounded pride. Without an insult, alcohol and violent movies typically do not produce a significant increase in aggression. Even the contribution of narcissism depends on the insult. When narcissists receive praise, they are no more aggressive than anybody else.[202]

Both nature and culture may contribute to the importance of wounded pride in causing violence. In nature, many (mainly male) animals compete for status, and some fighting is required to reach and keep a high rank. Fighting is often a response to a challenge to one's favorable position. In humans, this translates into thinking you have to defend your good name or good opinion of yourself by lashing at anyone who tries to attack it. As for culture, the concept of "honor" has often required violent action to maintain it, as the next section explains.

Culture of Honor

Sam Houston needed his mother's permission to join the army in the War of 1812 because he was not yet 21 years old. His mother, Elizabeth Houston, agreed to let him join, and gave him two gifts before he left.[203] One was a gold ring with the word *honor* inscribed inside; Houston wore this ring until his death. The other gift was a musket (i.e., muzzle-loaded rifle used by infantry), which his mother gave him with the following admonition:

> "My son, take this musket and never disgrace it; for remember, I had rather all my sons should fill one honorable grave, than that one of them should turn his back to save his life. Go, and remember, too, that while the door of my cottage is open to brave men, it is eternally shut against cowards."

Houston was from the southern United States. He was born in Virginia in 1793 and moved to Tennessee after his father died in 1807. In 1832 he moved to Texas, and went on to become one of the heroes of that state. In fact, he was in command of the Texas soldiers who won their independence by defeating the Mexican army, shouting, "Remember the Alamo!" Texas later became the southern tip of the United States, and its largest city was named after Sam Houston.

Sam Houston at San Jacinto.

The southern United States has long been associated with higher levels of violent attitudes and behaviors than the northern United States. In comparison to northern states, southern states have more homicides per capita, have fewer restrictions on gun ownership, allow people to shoot assailants and burglars without retreating first, are more accepting of corporal punishment of children at home and in schools, and are more supportive of any wars involving U.S. troops.[204] People from southern states are also more tolerant of domestic violence.[205]

Social psychologists Dov Cohen and Richard Nisbett hypothesized that these regional differences are caused by a **culture of honor**, which calls for a violent response to threats to one's honor.[206] This culture apparently dates back to the Europeans who first came to the United States. The northern United States was settled by English and Dutch farmers, whereas the South was settled by Scottish and Irish herders. Sam Houston was of Scottish-Irish descent. A thief could become rich quickly by stealing another person's herd. The same was not true of agricultural crops in the North; it is difficult to quickly steal 50 acres of corn plants. Men had to be ready to protect their herds with a violent response. A person who did not respond in this way would be branded as an easy mark.

A similar culture of violence exists in the western United States, the so-called Wild West, where one could also lose one's wealth quickly by not protecting one's herd. (Cowboys herded cows, hence the name.) Even the names of places and businesses are more violent in the South and West than elsewhere.[207] An analysis of place names (e.g., lakes, summits, parks, cities, towns) in the United States found that 80% of the places with violent names were located in the South and West. Some examples are Gun Point, Florida; War, West Virginia; and Rifle, Colorado. Similarly, 68% of the businesses in the United States with violent names (e.g., "War Taxi" and "Rifle Realty," even "Shotgun Willy's Daycare Center" and "Shotgun Willie's Strip Club"!) were located in the South and West. (Would you really want to leave your child with Shotgun Willy?)

However, this violent culture isn't confined to the southern and western United States. Cultural anthropologists have observed that herding cultures throughout the world tend to be more violent than farming ones.[208,209,210]

Other examples of honor cultures include Latin American and Middle Eastern countries. The victims of cultures of honor are not always men. In some societies, women are killed if they bring "dishonor" to their family, such as by refusing to accept an arranged marriage, seeking a divorce (even from an abusive husband), committing adultery, or having sex before marriage (even if the man forced her). This practice, called **honor killing**, supposedly restores the family's honor from the disgrace caused by the woman. Thousands of women are killed each year in this way, mainly in Western Asia, North Africa, and parts of South Asia.[211]

Humiliation appears to be the primary cause of violence and aggression in cultures of honor.[212] **Humiliation** is a state of disgrace or loss of self-respect (or of respect from others). It is related to the concept of shame that was discussed in Chapter 6, but the two states are not the same.[213] If someone insults you, and you judge the insult to be justified, then you feel shame (if you think you are a bad person, or you feel guilt if you do not think you are a bad person). If you judge the insult to be unjustified, then you feel humiliation. In honor cultures, there is nothing worse than being humiliated, and the culturally approved response to humiliation is swift and intense retaliation.

Humiliation may also be an important cause of terrorism.[214] To many people in the Middle East, having the United States and its allies occupy their countries is humiliating. This occupation may encourage suicide bombings and other acts of terrorism. Interviews with terrorists led Jessica Stern, who serves on the Hoover Institution Task Force on National Security and Law, to conclude that the primary motivation for terrorism is "overwhelming feelings of humiliation."[215] For example, the founder of the Muslim Jambaz Force said, "Muslims have been overpowered by the West. Our ego hurts. We are not able to live up to our own standards for ourselves." Osama bin Laden's deputy, Ayman Zawahiri, told Islam youth to carry arms and defend their religion with pride and dignity rather than submit to the humiliation of Western globalization. According to Stern, "Holy wars take off when there is a large supply of young men who feel humiliated and

culture of honor a society that places high value on individual respect, strength, and virtue, and accepts and justifies violent action in response to threats to one's honor

honor killing killing another individual who has brought "dishonor" to the family (e.g., a woman who has committed adultery)

humiliation a state of disgrace or loss of self-respect (or of respect from others)

deprived; when leaders emerge who know how to capitalize on those feelings; and when a segment of society is willing to fund them."

In fact, the Holocaust, genocide, ethnic cleansing, terrorism, and suicide bombings may all have their roots in humiliation.[216] For example, World War II was triggered, at least in part, by the humiliation that the Versailles Treaty inflicted on Germany after World War I. Hitler attacked his neighbors in part to retaliate for past humiliations inflicted on Germany. Hitler may have perpetrated the Holocaust to avert future humiliation that he feared from "World Jewry." After World War II, the Marshall Plan was designed to bring dignity and respect rather than humiliation to Germany. Instead of starting World War III, Germany has become a cooperative and peaceful member of the European family.

Other Antisocial Behavior

Aggression and violence aren't the only forms of antisocial behaviors, although they are the forms social psychologists have studied the most. In this section we examine four other common forms of antisocial behavior: (1) lying, (2) cheating, (3) stealing, and (4) littering.

Lying

Lying is not telling the truth. Most people lie at least once per day.[217] However, about half of all lies are told by 5% of the population—so-called "habitual liars."[218]

Sometimes the stakes for lying are low, such as being embarrassed if one is caught. At other times the stakes are very high, such as lying to a spouse about infidelity or lying to a country about the reasons for going to war. When it comes to getting a job, people often lie about their qualifications and skills to increase the chance that they will be hired.[219] People also lie on social network sites such as Facebook to promote themselves.[220]

The cliché "all's fair in love and war" suggests that it is okay to lie to gain advantages in these high-stakes situations. Social psychologists have done a lot more research on lying for love than on lying for war, and they have found that people are quick to tell lies if it will

> "I was not lying. I said things that later on seemed to be untrue."
>
> ~ Richard Nixon, discussing Watergate

lying deliberately making a false statement, usually to mislead someone.

improve their love (or sex) lives. Both men and women are willing to lie to increase their chances of going out with an attractive partner.[221] The less attractive people are (as determined by independent judges), the more likely they are to lie about their height, weight, and age to online dating partners.[222] Lying is less common for very high-stakes issues in sexual relationships, such as whether the person has AIDS.[223] Lying in romantic relationships tends to be reciprocal—if one partner lies, the other also lies.[224] As expected, lying is associated with less commitment to the relationship.

Lying takes more cognitive resources than telling the truth.[225] Lying generally requires coordination between both parts of the duplex mind (Chapter 2): The automatic system knows what the truth is, and the deliberate system says something else while also concealing any telltale signs that what the person is saying is false.

Recent research shows that telling fewer lies is linked to better health and relationships. In this study, participants were randomly assigned to two groups. One group was told to stop telling lies during the duration of the study (10 weeks). The other (control) group received no instructions about lying. The group that refrained from telling lies got sick less often over the course of 10 weeks, were less depressed, and said their social interactions with others were smoother.

Detecting Liars

Is it possible to reliably detect lying? "Liar, liar, pants on fire!" is a phrase that children like to use when they think another child is lying. It would be much easier to identify liars if their pants were on fire. Because pants don't spontaneously combust when people lie, more subtle cues must be used. Sometimes outside information is available, such as when facts or witnesses directly contradict the lie. When outside information is unavailable, people often rely on verbal and nonverbal cues. In one study, over 500 research participants were shown videotapes of college women who either lied or did not lie.[226] The participants included law enforcement personnel, including members of the U.S. Secret Service, Central Intelligence Agency (CIA), Federal Bureau of Investigation (FBI), National Security Agency, Drug Enforcement Agency, and California police and judges, as well as psychiatrists, college students, and working adults. Note that many of these deal with liars as part of their jobs. The women in the videotapes had been told to describe the enjoyment of a film. Half the women saw a nature film and were therefore telling the truth. The other women saw a very gruesome and upsetting film and were therefore lying. Could the observers spot the difference? Only the Secret Service personnel detected lying at better than chance levels. In general, people are not very good at detecting liars.[227] Even when children tell lies, adults have difficulty distinguishing them, and experts are no better than novices.[228]

Textual analysis programs generally do better than people at detecting lying, even better than experts. They can detect lying at better than chance levels, correctly detecting liars at least 60% of the time (still far from perfect!).[229] When liars tell stories, the stories are not complex, they contain fewer self and other references, and they contain more negative emotion words. Of course, textual analysis programs cannot detect nonverbal cues.

Sometimes a mechanical device known as a polygraph (popularly called a lie detector) is used to "detect" lies. A polygraph measures physiological responses such as blood pressure, pulse, respiration, and skin conductivity while the subject is asked and answers a series of questions, on the theory that false answers will produce distinctive measurements. The problem with lie detector tests is that they can make it look as though someone is lying, even if the person is telling the truth. In 1998 the U.S. Supreme Court concluded: "There is simply no consensus that polygraph evidence is reliable."

Cheating

Cheating is widely recognized as an antisocial, undesirable behavior, yet it is widespread. People even cheat on video games that are meant to be fun, as indicated by the popularity of cheat codes and websites.[230] Cheating occurs among some athletes, who take performance-enhancing drugs to increase their competitiveness.[231] It occurs among many students, who cheat out of a "desire to get ahead" in school.[232] Although most

> "A thing worth having is a thing worth cheating for."
> — W. C. Fields (1880–1946)

students acknowledge that cheating is wrong, more than 75% admit to having cheated in high school or college.[233] Some students even cheat on free online courses that don't count toward anything.[234] Even some teachers cheat by raising test scores for students to create the illusion of massive educational gains.[235]

It is much easier for students to cheat in the digital age, too. The Internet makes term paper access remarkably easy, allowing many students to plagiarize part or all of their written school assignments.[236] To **plagiarize** means "to steal and pass off (the ideas or words of another) as one's own without crediting the source."[237] Some schools are cracking down on cheaters. At the University of California at Davis, for example, students receive No. 2 pencils with their exams that read, "Fill in your own bubble or be in trouble."[238] Other professors use plagiarism-checking websites to screen student papers.

Students aren't the only ones who plagiarize. Politicians do it too. For example, three pages of U.S. Senator Rand Paul's (Republican–Kentucky) 2013 book *Government Bullies* was cut and pasted verbatim from a 2003 case study by the Heritage Foundation.[239]

Although getting ahead is probably the primary reason why people cheat, there might also be other reasons. For example, recent research suggests that cheating can even trigger positive affect—called the "cheater's high."[240] For example, Frank Abagnale described the experience of cheating as "the most delightful sensation I'd ever experienced." Abagnale passed himself off as a pilot, a lawyer, and a physician, all before he turned 21. In 5 years, he had used 8 identities and passed bad checks worth over $2.5 million in 26 countries. To be sure, he benefited financially (at least until he was caught) by all that cheating—but he did also enjoy it. Experiments have shown that people can get pleasure by cheating even though they expected to feel guilty rather than self-satisfied, and even apart from the benefit of acquiring money.[241] Some of the enjoyment seems to come from getting away with something illicit and sneaky.

Research has begun to explore some causes of cheating. Cheating violates the rules that enable society to function, and so it goes against one's social conscience. Refraining from cheating is part of being a morally responsible member of society. When feelings of moral responsibility are undermined, such when people come to disbelieve that they have free will, cheating becomes more likely.[242] In a similar vein, when people's capacity for self-control has been weakened (by ego depletion; see Chapter 4), their tendency to lie and cheat increases.[243]

plagiarize to claim the ideas or words of another person as one's own without crediting that person

Creativity and Cheating

TRADE Offs

Cheating involves breaking rules. As we have said, rules enable culture to function, so cheating is antisocial in a fundamental way, because it ruins the basis for civilization. Yet breaking rules can have positive benefits in some ways. Creativity often involves violating rules (though usually creativity does not harm innocent victims, like cheating does). Is there a link? Some fascinating recent experiments showed that people become more creative after cheating.[244] This is not just a matter of the type of person who breaks rules being both more creative and more willing to cheat. Ordinary people who were randomly assigned to engage in cheating (as opposed to being honest) went on to perform more creatively as a result. These results are no justification for the immoral act of cheating, but they do indicate a psychological link. Cheating makes people feel that rules do not matter, and this can boost their ability to think creatively.

Thus, cheating causes creativity. It works the other way, too: Creativity leads to cheating. The rule-breaking mind-set helps. Another factor is that a creative mentality finds it easier to come up with justifications for morally dubious behavior, as compared to an uncreative mind-set.[245] So creative people are able to rationalize their unethical actions.

Cheating does lead to more cheating, though. When people do dishonest things, their minds tend to shut down their knowledge of moral rules. Experimental participants who were induced to cheat after having read an honor code were less able than other participants to remember the honor code afterward—even when offered a chance to earn money for correctly remembering the moral rules.[246]

Cheating is sometimes done for money, as is stealing (which the next section will cover. To learn more about links between money and antisocial behavior, read the *Money Matters* box.

No one will be surprised that people sometimes do dishonest things to get money. Indeed, many people have heard or read the Bible verse that "the love of money is the root of all kinds of evil."[247] But it seems that even the mere idea of money can be enough to elicit antisocial behavior. Merely thinking of the idea of money has been shown to increase cheating behavior.[248]

Then again, people do have moral scruples about money also. One study allowed students to solve problems and score their own answer sheets. Each correct solution earned them 50 cents. Some students were paid directly in cash. They cheated to some degree. Others were paid in tokens, which in a couple minutes they exchanged for cash. They cheated considerably more.[249] Thus, simply creating a mental separation between the cheating and the money (by using the tokens) increased cheating. Probably people have fewer scruples about taking extra tokens than extra money.

Some recent work has suggested that people have two sets of associations to the idea of money—with opposite moral effects. Chinese researchers tested this by having some people briefly handle old, dirty, crumpled money that had been buried in mud for several days. Other participants counted fresh, crisp, new banknotes. Compared to controls who handled only paper rather than money, those who handled the dirty money went on to behave in immoral, antisocial ways. But those who had handled clean, new money behaved in exceptionally moral, prosocial ways.[250] The explanation is that the use of money in society depends on fairness, trust, and honesty, and so money can evoke these positive values, even though ordinary, dirty money also evokes notions of selfish greed and unethical dirty tricks.

Desire for money has certainly been the root of much evil, but it also has motivated many positive things in society. The antisocial aspect of money seems to be the more prominent association for most people, but alongside it there is often a more positive view.

Stealing

Most companies lose about 5% of their annual revenue to employee theft.[251] The U.S. Chamber of Commerce[252] estimates that 75% of all employees steal at least once, and that 50% of those employees steal repeatedly. They may steal the company's product (e.g., waiters helping themselves to food) or just office supplies or money. Employees are especially likely to steal from employers when they feel they are being treated unfairly.[253] Employees can also steal time, such as by arriving to work late, leaving work early, taking longer lunches or breaks than company policy allows, and "surfing" the web or playing video games on company time. Research shows that employees who think such behavior is normal are more likely to engage in it.[254]

Not only do employees steal from employers, but customers steal too. Shoplifting (also known as a "five-finger discount") involves the theft of goods from a retail establishment. Shoplifting is found among males and females and all different races, ethnicities, and social classes, though patterns and incidence may vary.[255] (Males tend to use backpacks, whereas females tend to use strollers.) Retail theft is over $16 billion per year in the United States alone.[256] The average shoplifter who gets caught is found to have about $200 worth of stolen merchandise in his or her possession.[257]

As we saw with cheating, shoplifting is motivated by more than the desire to acquire material possessions. Many people do it for the excitement and thrill of getting away with something. The items they steal are often soon forgotten, left unused in a drawer or thrown away—which shows that the motivation to steal was not to acquire something important but rather for the temporary excitement of doing the deed.[258]

People can even steal your identity! **Identity theft** is defined as stealing someone else's personal information (e.g., Social Security number, bank account, credit card number) and using it without their permission, usually to obtain money or goods.[259] According to the Federal Trade Commission, "It is a serious crime that can wreak havoc with your finances, credit history, and reputation."[260] In one extreme case of identity theft,[261] a convicted criminal racked up over $100,000 of credit card debt, obtained a federal home loan, and bought homes, motorcycles, and handguns in the victim's name, before filing for bankruptcy (also in the victim's name). It took the victim more than four years and

> "But he that filches from me my good name
> Robs me of that which not enriches him
> And makes me poor indeed."
> — Shakespeare, Othello, Act iii. Sc. 3.

identity theft consists of stealing someone's personal information (e.g., Social Security number, bank account, credit card number) and using it without their permission, usually to obtain money or goods.

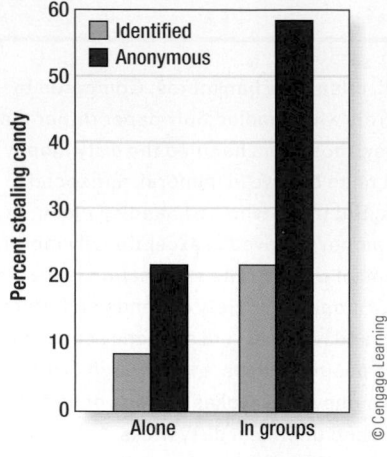

FIGURE 10.5

Children were most likely to steal candy when they were not identifiable and when they were in a group.[285]

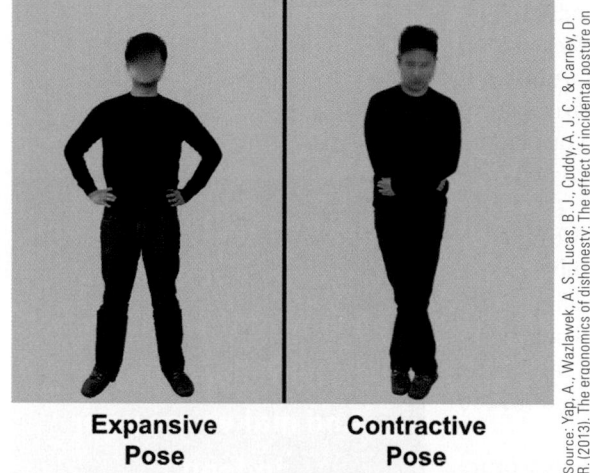

Expansive Pose | **Contractive Pose**

Researchers have found that people are more likely to engage in antisocial behavior when they adopt expansive body postures (compared to contractive body postures).

Source: Yap, A., Wazlawek, A. S., Lucas, B. J., Cuddy, A. J. C., & Carney, D. R. (2013). The ergonomics of dishonesty: The effect of incidental posture on stealing, cheating, and traffic violations. *Psychological Science, 24*(11), 2281-2289. DOI: 10.1177/0956797613492425

deindividuation a sense of anonymity and loss of individuality, as in a large group, making people especially likely to engage in antisocial behaviors such as theft

more than $15,000 of his own money to restore his credit and reputation. Cases like this prompted the U.S. Congress to make identity theft a federal offense in 1998. Identity theft costs corporations over $20 billion per year and costs victims over $2 billion and 100 million hours of their personal time.[262]

Social psychologists have studied stealing and other antisocial behaviors and the factors that contribute to them. One such factor is the presence of others. The presence of others increases arousal (see Chapter 14 on groups). When people are in large groups, they become anonymous and lose their sense of individuality, a state called **deindividuation**. People in a deindividuated state are especially likely to engage in antisocial behaviors, such as theft. In a clever study,[263] children who were trick-or-treating on Halloween were greeted by an experimenter who said, "You may take one of the candies. I have to go back to my work in another room." Some children go trick-or-treating alone, and some go in groups. By the flip of a coin, half of the children were assigned to an identifiable group, and half were assigned to an anonymous group. The experimenter asked each child in the identifiable group what his or her name was and where he or she lived. The experimenter then carefully repeated each child's name and address to let the child know that he or she could be identified. The experimenter did not identify the children in the anonymous group. A hidden observer recorded whether each child took more than one piece of candy from a large bowl. Children were most likely to steal candy when they were in a group and when the experimenter could not identify them (see **FIGURE 10.5**). Research shows that theft can also be reduced when people believe that others are watching them, such as on closed-circuit television.[264]

In a series of studies,[265] researchers found antisocial behavior—cheating on a test, stealing money, and breaking traffic laws—as well as feelings of power increased when expansive body postures (compared to contractive body postures) were induced. In both animals and humans, power and dominance are expressed through expansive, open-bodied postures that take up more space. Researchers also found that cars with more expansive driver's seats were more likely to be illegally parked on New York City streets than cars with more contractive driver's seats.

The video game *Grand Theft Auto* glorifies stealing cars. In one recent study,[266] Italian high school students were randomly assigned to play a violent video game (one of the *Grand Theft Auto* video games), or a nonviolent video game. After playing the game, participants completed a logical test, and were told they could get a raffle ticket for each item they got correctly. The raffle tickets could be used to win attractive prizes, such as new iPads. The researcher gave them a large envelope of raffle tickets, and told them to take the number of tickets they earned, and then left the room. Violent game players stole eight times more tickets than nonviolent game players did. Consistent with many other studies, violent game players were also significantly more aggressive than nonviolent game players (i.e., they gave an ostensible partner longer and louder unpleasant noise blasts through headphones).

Littering

Litter is a big problem in many places. When everybody else seems to be littering, individuals are more likely to litter, too.[267,268] Cigarette butts are the most common form of litter in many states.[269] For example, each year 140 million cigarette butts are tossed onto Texas highways. Although convicts pick up some of the litter, hired crews (paid with taxpayer dollars) pick up 90% of it. To fight the problem, which was costing the state $20 million a year to clean up, the Texas Department of Transportation hired Mike Blair and Tim McClure, from an advertising company, to come up with a catchy anti-littering slogan.[270] The target audience was 18- to 24-year-old males who thought it was their "God-given right" to toss beer cans and other trash out the windows of their trucks. McClure came up with the slogan in an "aha" moment when he saw some garbage and remembered how his mother would always tell him his room was a mess, and came up with the slogan "Don't

Mess With Texas." The word litter is associated with animals like cats. "Mess seemed like it would resonate better," he said. This slogan plays on the pride of Texans in their home state—they love their state so much that they should not ruin it with litter. (The slogan was also designed to seem aggressive and macho, so as to appeal to the young men who were perceived as the source of much littering and who might not respond as well to a seemingly effeminate slogan such as "Please Be Clean." "Don't Mess With Texas" is well suited to a culture of honor state!)

Litter is not only unattractive, but it can also cause health problems to humans and animals. One recent study found that about 80% of smokers littered their cigarette butts, and that 74% of smokers did not extinguish their butts, sometimes before tossing them into a trashcan, which was a fire risk.[271] Litter such as broken bottles can also cause injuries and flat tires.[272] How can litter be reduced? One way is through anti-littering norms.[273,274,275] **Norms** are social standards that prescribe what people ought to do. Litter can be reduced by anti-littering norms, especially **injunctive norms** that specify what most others approve or disapprove of. In contrast, **descriptive norms**, which specify what most people do, seem not effective at reducing littering. Messages that explicitly command people not to litter are less effective than messages that appeal to social norms.[276] This may be due to **psychological reactance**—the unpleasant emotional response people experience when someone is trying to restrict their freedom to engage in a behavior. Such threats frequently backfire (see Chapter 4 for a more detailed description of psychological reactance).

One reason norms might work is because people feel guilty if they don't follow them. As we learned in Chapter 6 on emotions, guilt can have a positive impact on people's behavior, including reducing litter. After a littering campaign, people said they would feel guilty if they littered.[277]

Other factors can help, too. Research has shown that recycling can substantially reduce litter.[278] Paying a deposit on cans and bottles reduces that type of litter, although it has little impact on other types of litter.[279] An adequate supply of trash cans also helps reduce litter.[280,281] In summary, making it convenient or rewarding for people to get rid of trash is effective.

Don't Mess With Texas $10-1000 FINE FOR LITTERING

Annette Udvardi/PhotoEdit

The Texas Department of Transportation launched a campaign with the motto "Don't Mess With Texas" to combat the litter problem.

norms social standards that prescribe what people ought to do

injunctive norms norms that specify what most others approve or disapprove of

descriptive norms norms that specify what most people do

psychological reactance the unpleasant emotional response people experience when someone is trying to restrict their freedom to engage in a desired behavior

answers: see pg 368

QUIZ YOURSELF
Other Antisocial Behavior

1. **What is the impact of the Internet on school cheating?**
   - (a) The Internet has decreased school cheating.
   - (b) The Internet has not affected school cheating.
   - (c) The Internet has increased school cheating.
   - (d) More research is needed to determine the impact of the Internet on school cheating.

2. **Which of the following can increase self-awareness?**
   - (a) Alcohol
   - (b) Audience
   - (c) Darkness
   - (d) All of the above

3. **Tamika attends a football game, and her team wins. The fans rush the field and tear down a goal post. Tamika happily joins them, and tears down a goal post with her fellow students. Tamika is probably experiencing _____ .**
   - (a) cognitive dissonance
   - (b) deindividuation
   - (c) psychological reactance
   - (d) self-awareness

4. **What type of norm is most effective at reducing litter?**
   - (a) Injunctive
   - (b) Descriptive
   - (c) Both (a) and (b)
   - (d) Neither (a) nor (b)

Aggression provides a curious perspective on what makes us human. In some ways, humans are far more aggressive than our biological relatives. Most fighting between animals of the same species stops far short of serious injury or death, whereas humans kill each other. Only humans have invented tools to increase aggression, and these (from spears and guns to nuclear weapons) have greatly escalated the harm people can do to each other. Only humans have been able to accumulate knowledge across generations (a hallmark of culture) so as to create weapons of mass destruction that are capable of destroying entire nations and possibly even wiping out the entire human population of the planet.

Only humans kill for ideas, such as religion or honor or political ideals. Only humans commit genocide, defined as the attempt to kill everyone in a particular racial or ethnic category. Only humans declare war on other groups, maintain military establishments to prepare for war in time of peace, and bestow honors on the individuals who kill their enemies most brilliantly or effectively. Only humans deliberately create chemical substances (such as alcohol) that make them more violent.

Still, human culture is unique in its devices for restraining aggression. Only humans commit crimes, in part because only humans can enact laws that define socially undesirable acts as crimes. The long history of culture is in part a story of placing ever more careful and thorough restraints on aggression, ranging from ancient moral laws ("Thou shalt not kill") to laws that forbid teachers from using corporal punishment on students or prohibit people from sending hostile e-mail messages (i.e., cyberbullying). Only humans have police forces that deter and punish criminals—though, again, the police must often use violence to stop violence. This is the paradox of culture: Step by step, it has created the technology to do more harm while also creating laws and other devices to reduce and prevent harm, another example of a tradeoff (involving very high stakes). Yet the level of violence and aggression in the world has decreased over time, and continues to do so.

The elaborate mental apparatus that people have has transformed aggression, too. Factors such as the hostile attributional bias are probably unique to humans, because only humans make inferences about someone else's intentions. A hostile attributional bias is a way of interpreting the behavior of others—"I think you intended to hurt me!"—that increases the likelihood of an aggressive response. Animals know whether they were hurt or not, but they probably do not have much capacity to choose an aggressive or a nonaggressive reaction based on whether they think the hurt was inflicted intentionally or accidentally.

Aggression is not the only kind of antisocial behavior. The same paradox can be seen in other behaviors. Culture creates new opportunities for antisocial behavior, such as insurance fraud, insider trading, overcharging, and all sorts of scams. At the same time, culture seeks to promote and reward behavior that follows the rules. Insider trading was unknown in biblical times, but so were the laws against it.

The impulses to commit aggression and other antisocial acts are deeply rooted in the social nature of human beings. Social animals are generally selfish, and because they get what they want from other animals, they are often tempted to exploit or hurt others. The human capacity for self-control is probably much more extensive than what other animals have, and it is responsible for the fact that people mostly refrain from acting on their violent and antisocial impulses.

CHAPTER 10 SUMMARY

Defining Aggression, Violence, and Antisocial Behavior

- Aggression is any behavior that intentionally harms another person who is motivated to avoid the harm. Violence is aggression that has extreme harm as its goal.

- Antisocial behavior refers to behavior that either damages interpersonal relations or is culturally undesirable.

- Aggressive acts frequently fail to produce the intended, desired consequences and often bring about serious unintended consequences, mostly antisocial ones.

- Aggression is universal, but cultural rules restrict and govern aggression in different ways.

- Aggression evolved to help social animals deal with their social lives, but culture, as a better way of being social, offers new, nonviolent ways of resolving conflicts and problems.

Is Aggression Innate or Learned?

- Freud (and others) proposed that people have an innate instinct that causes them to behave aggressively.

- According to social learning theory, aggression is not an innate drive but rather a learned behavior.

- When people observe and copy the behavior of others, this is called modeling.

- Inhibitions against aggression can be overcome if a model acts out aggressively.
- Learning and cultural socialization can subdue or encourage innate aggressive impulses and aggressive action.
- Aggression is a product of both nature and learning.

Inner Causes of Aggression

- The original frustration-aggression hypothesis states that the occurrence of aggressive behavior always presupposes the existence of frustration and the existence of frustration always leads to some form of aggression.
- There can be aggression without frustration, and frustration without aggression, but aggression is increased by frustration.
- Unpleasant moods increase aggression, but being in a bad mood is neither a necessary nor a sufficient condition for aggression.
- Anger does not directly or inevitably cause aggression, but the belief that aggression will help get rid of anger does increase aggression.
- The hostile attribution bias is the tendency to perceive ambiguous actions by others as intentionally hostile.
- The hostile perception bias is the tendency to perceive social interactions in general as being aggressive.
- The hostile expectation bias is the tendency to expect others to react to potential conflicts with aggression.
- About 25% of toddler interactions in day-care settings involve some kind of physical aggression.
- In all known societies, young men just past the age of puberty commit most of the violent crimes and acts.

Interpersonal Causes of Aggression

- Domestic violence (also called family violence or intimate-partner violence) is violence that occurs within the home, between people who have a close relationship with each other (such as parents and children, spouses, and siblings).
- The sibling relationship is the most violent relationship in the world.
- In 1984, the U.S. Surgeon General declared domestic violence to be the number one health risk in the United States.
- Women attack their relationship partners slightly more often than men do, but women don't cause as much harm.

External Causes of Aggression

- People behave more aggressively in the mere presence of a weapon.
- Exposure to violent media increases aggression.
- Hotter temperatures are associated with higher levels of aggression and violence.
- Unpleasant environmental events, such as noise, crowding, foul odors, air pollution, and secondhand smoke, can increase aggression.
- Increases in testosterone, junk food, and alcohol lead to increased aggression. Decreases in serotonin and increases in vitamins reduce aggression.

Self and Culture

- Running amok, roughly translated, means going berserk. Cultural changes in running amok show that when people believe their aggression is beyond control, they are often mistaken.
- Poor self-control is an important cause of crime.
- Violent individuals, rather than having low self-esteem, typically think themselves better than other people and have grandiose or inflated opinions of their own worth.
- The term *narcissism* describes the condition of thinking oneself superior or special, feeling entitled to preferential treatment, being willing to exploit others, having low empathy with "lesser" human beings, and entertaining grandiose fantasies or other ideas about oneself as a great person.
- Much aggression involves wounded pride, so narcissists are especially likely to become aggressive.
- The southern United States has a culture of honor, which accepts and even calls for violent responses to threats to one's honor.
- Humiliation (a state of disgrace or loss of respect) appears to be a primary cause of violence and aggression in cultures of honor.

Other Antisocial Behavior

- Lying, swearing, cheating, stealing, and littering are forms of antisocial behavior.
- Deindividuated people are more likely to steal than people who can be readily identified.
- Norms are social standards that prescribe what people ought to do.
- Injunctive norms specify what most others approve or disapprove.

What Makes Us Human? Putting the Cultural Animal in Perspective

- Human cultures mostly attempt to restrain violence and aggression.

key terms

quiz yourself ANSWERS

1. Defining Aggression and Antisocial Behavior **p.338**
   answers: 1.b 2.d 3.c 4.a

2. Is Aggression Innate or Learned? **p.341**
   answers: 1.a 2.a 3.d 4.d

3. Inner Causes of Aggression **p.346**
   answers: 1.d 2.a 3.a 4.b

4. Interpersonal Causes of Aggression **p.349**
   answers: 1.c 2.d 3.d 4.b

5. External Causes of Aggression **p.355**
   answers: 1.b 2.c 3.c 4.c

6. Self and Culture **p.360**
   answers: 1.c 2.d 3.a 4.c

7. Other Antisocial Behavior **p.365**
   answers: 1.c 2.b 3.b 4.a

INTERPERSONAL ATTRACTION AND REJECTION

11

LEARNING OBJECTIVES

1 Differentiate the two ingredients for belongingness, and debate why the need to belong is a basic need for a cultural animal.

2 Contrast the variables that predict who will like whom.

3 Identify two strategies for getting someone to like you that confirm the importance of interpersonal rewards, and explain how reciprocity has a powerful effect on liking.

4 Compare the inner reactions to the behavioral effects of rejection.

5 Analyze what makes people feel lonely and describe the conditions that lead to social rejection.

Mangostock/Veer

In 2003, an attractive young woman named Melana Scantlin signed up to be on one of those reality shows in which the female central character meets around 20 different guys, who compete for her affections. She was to eliminate them steadily and ideally end up marrying the winner.

She told the producers of the show that she wanted to meet and marry a man with good inner qualities. She said she cared little about physical attractiveness and was much more concerned with personality and other inner traits. Perhaps she sincerely thought that good looks and other superficial traits were not her concern, but when the show's bus opened and a series of very ordinary looking men came up to meet her, she struggled to hide her dismay, and hidden cameras later captured her complaining about the men's lack of physical charms. Some of the men were obese, others were bald, and few were genuinely handsome.

The men had been told that the woman was looking for personality rather than good looks, but they were soon disappointed. As one disgruntled suitor pointed out, by the second day of eliminations, she had sent home every man weighing over 200 pounds. Meanwhile, one man clearly regarded himself as better looking than everyone else, and this narcissistic fellow engaged in a variety of bullying maneuvers and putdowns that made most characters regard him as a jerk, but Melana went out of her way to convince herself that he was not a jerk. During the round in which she sent all the tubby and balding men home, she was seen lying on the floor with the narcissistic fellow with their arms around each other, kissing passionately.

Late in the game, after Melana had whittled the set of eligible men down to a handful of candidates, the producers surprised everyone by adding several new male suitors—this time all young and handsome, if rather shallow in some ways. This was the test to see how good looks would fare against the inner qualities she had presumably found among the average ones. After that point, whenever Melana had to choose someone for a date, she invariably chose one of the handsome young fellows. (She did say she already knew the original men and needed dates with the new guys to give them a fair chance.) More men were sent home, until she was down to the final two. One was the last of the original "average Joes"; the other was a handsome newcomer. On final dates, she discovered that Adam, the last of the average Joes, was not so average: He was in fact a millionaire who owned several luxury homes, had part-ownership in a bar, and had a successful career as an investor. He noticed that she suddenly warmed up to him, becoming more flirtatious and affectionate toward him when he revealed his assets. Perhaps it was too late, however. She chose the other finalist: Jason, a handsome but shallow waiter who at age 26 was still living with his parents. The relationship did not last, despite his looks.

Melana would not be the first person to choose physical attractiveness over other traits. What made her story so dramatic was that she had initially insisted that she was not interested in surface appearance and instead wanted inner qualities in a man.

Like most reality shows, *Average Joe* was about acceptance and rejection. The show revolved around a large group of people who were rejected one by one, or sometimes in groups, until at last the "winner" was the person who staved off rejection

the longest (think *American Idol, Survivor, Big Brother, The Bachelor, The Bachelorette, The Apprentice,* and others). The woman in *Average Joe* could only accept one man, presumably as a husband or long-term relationship partner, and along the way she had to reject everyone else.

Like reality television (though perhaps the resemblance ends there!), this chapter is about attraction, social acceptance, and rejection. **Attraction** refers to anything that draws two or more people together, making them want to be together and possibly to form a lasting relationship. In social psychology it is especially used to refer to what makes people like (or start to love) each other. **Social acceptance** means that other people have come to like you, respect you, approve of you, and in general regard you in ways that will lead them to include you in their groups and relationships. **Rejection**, also known as **social exclusion**, is the opposite of acceptance: It means that others exclude you, so that you are not able to form or keep a social bond with them.

The quest for social acceptance is not limited to human beings. All social animals need to be accepted. Likewise, social rejection is a problem and a source of distress for many social animals as

Melana and Jason.

© NBC/Courtesy: Everett Collection. Frederick M. Brown/Getty Images

J Kottmann/AGE Fotostock

Rejected by females, male fruit flies turn to alcohol.

well as for human beings. Indeed, social rejection is even a problem for insects. Recent research found that male fruit flies that were spurned by female fruit flies drank more alcohol afterward![1] The basic patterns in this chapter—attraction based on similarity or good looks, rejection of those who are different—are more linked to the social than the cultural aspect of human nature.

It is not surprising that people have developed many ways to make themselves attractive to others. One cautionary note, which we suspect Melana Scantlin may someday recognize, is that the traits that make someone most attractive upon first meeting are not always the same traits that make for a successful relationship. Testosterone levels provide one example of this sort of tradeoff, as *Tradeoffs* explains. ●

The Need to Belong

Why is social attraction important? Forming bonds is a big part of human life. Social animals (including plenty of nonhuman ones) survive and reproduce mainly by way of their relationships with others. In order to survive, it is vital to form and maintain some relationships. Forming relationships involves securing acceptance, which often depends on getting others to feel and think positively about you. That (along with the flip side, rejection) is the focus of this chapter. Sustaining long-term close relationships will be the focus of the next chapter.

Belongingness as a Basic Need

People survive and reproduce better if they have relationships, but that doesn't mean they only want relationships for those reasons. Most likely, the "need to belong" is a powerful drive within the human psyche, and it affects people who are neither worried about survival nor urgently interested in reproduction. In our evolutionary past, the people who had a stronger need to belong probably fared better than other people, so that today's humans are mainly descended from ancestors who had a strong need to belong.[2,3,4] This book's theme of "putting people first" is probably linked to the need to belong. Human beings relate to their physical environment by relating to other people first. We get even our basic food and shelter from other people, rather than directly from nature. People who didn't care about being with other people probably didn't live as well or as long as those who formed strong social networks, and the need to belong helps make people want to form those networks. To enjoy the benefits of culture, people have to have an inner drive to connect with other people.

The universality of the need to belong was once aptly summarized by social psychologist Warren Jones in his research on loneliness: "In two decades of studying loneliness, I have met many people who say they have no friends. I have never met anyone who didn't want to have any friends."[5] Converging evidence from other sources casts doubt on the stereotype that some people are by nature loners or are indifferent to human social contact. True, some people may want many friends, whereas others are content with just a few, but everybody needs somebody. Even religious hermits, who supposedly live alone in nature, typically rely heavily on one or two people who visit them regularly (e.g., in their cave) and supply much-needed human contact. Full deprivation of interpersonal contact is extremely stressful for everyone. That is why solitary confinement is considered an extreme form of punishment in prisons. It is said that prisoners at San Quentin who were sentenced to solitary confinement and had no communication with each other resorted to desperate measures just to achieve some

attraction anything that draws two or more people together, making them want to be together and possibly to form a lasting relationship

social acceptance a situation in which other people have come to like you, respect you, approve of you, and include you in their groups and relationships

rejection (social exclusion) being prevented by others from forming or keeping a social bond with them; the opposite of acceptance

Testosterone—A Blessing and a Curse

Testosterone is a hormone associated with masculinity. Both men and women have it, though men have 9 or 10 times as much as women. (Women are somewhat more sensitive to it, though men are still more affected by testosterone overall, because they have so much more.) Most people, both men and women, tend to admire manly traits (especially in men), and they look upon testosterone as a good thing.

The researcher Jim Dabbs, one of psychology's leading experts on testosterone, reported that as he became known for this research, he received many inquiries from individuals about whether it was possible to increase their testosterone level. No one ever asked him about how to reduce it! Such one-sided interest suggests that people think very favorably of testosterone and will do almost anything for more of it. People don't seem to appreciate the tradeoffs, which come through much more clearly in Dabbs's book[6] on the hormone. In reality,

TRADE Offs

testosterone is a very mixed blessing, both for the individual who has it and for others connected with that person. High-testosterone men are more exciting but less reliable. They are restless in many ways, shown by their frequent interest in exploring new places and meeting new people, but this also makes them less prone to stay at home and take care of their families (see **FIGURE 11.1**).

Nature seems to have recognized that testosterone is better suited for finding mates than for maintaining stable families, and it has made some remarkable adjustments.[7] First, testosterone reaches its peak in young men around the age of 20 and declines steadily after that, so that it is highest during the years of single male competition but lower over the more family-centered years that typically follow.

The right circumstances help turn it on: One study showed that males who simply came into contact with a female confederate while waiting in line for an experiment had higher testosterone levels than men who came in contact with a male

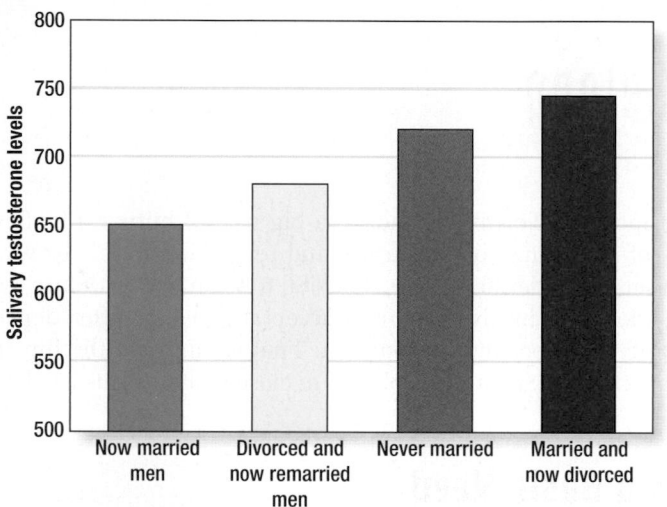

FIGURE 11.1
These data link low testosterone to a stable marriage; higher levels go with single status and divorce.

© Cengage Learning

Josh Mitchell/Getty Images

Prisoners in San Quentin who were sentenced to solitary confinement and had no communication with each other resorted to desperate measures just to achieve some connection with other humans, such as speaking to other prisoners through toilet pipes.

connection with other humans: Many of the men learned to speak down into their toilets, so the sound could pass through the pipes into other cells. They generally did not know who they were talking with, probably could not communicate very effectively, and might not have much to talk about—and the prospect of talking with your head stuck inside your toilet would be off-putting to many—but it was worth it to them just to hear another voice and know that theirs was heard. If the only road to social acceptance requires putting your head into a toilet, many people will do it.

Talking into toilets may seem bizarre to you, or outside your realm of experience. More commonly, you probably know people who rely on the Internet for much of their social life and social contact. The Internet allows people to interact with strangers and feel as though they can form social connections without much risk or anxiety.[14,15,16] Some people manage to satisfy the need to belong by spending time in Internet chat rooms, where they may have intimate conversations with other people. Some who suffer from social anxiety or have feelings that society rejects and stigmatizes—so that opening up face to face with people

baloocartoons.com

"Give Mr. Fogarty his testosterone injection, Nurse, and then run like the dickens!"

BZ Tons by Brian Zaikowski

People will do almost anything for more testosterone.

confederate.[8] Second, when a young man becomes a father, his testosterone level typically drops. In fact, in one experiment, men who were soon to become fathers held a baby doll wrapped in a blanket that had previously been around a real baby (and therefore still had some baby smell), and after just a half hour these men experienced a significant decrease in their testosterone levels.[9]

Testosterone makes one more willing to take risks.[10] The tradeoffs there are obvious.

High-testosterone men are more likely to perform heroic acts—and criminal ones, both of which involve risk taking. Competition also involves risk, and high-testosterone individuals are much more eager than others to compete in all sorts of spheres. If you don't compete, you can't win, but you can't lose either. The low-testosterone man may prefer to sit safely and comfortably on the sidelines, but the one with high testosterone wants to jump into the fray and test his mettle.

Testosterone seems to help promote high sex drive, in both men and women. Transsexuals who get testosterone shots (which help turn a woman into a man) report that they have more feelings of sexual desire and sexual interest.[11] Those who get testosterone blockers, which reduce the effect of testosterone, report a drop in sex drive. Among typical heterosexual individuals, higher levels of testosterone in both men and women are linked to higher sex drives in many studies, though some studies find no differences.[12] Whenever a relation is found, however, it links high testosterone to more desire.

As we saw in Chapter 10, high-testosterone men are also more violent than others. The aggressive and sexual

United Artists/Handout/Getty Images

Bold adventures, passionate romances, but early graves.

passions that come with high testosterone are accompanied by a corresponding lesser interest in simpler, gentler pleasures. Men with low testosterone are kinder, more trustworthy, and more affectionate.

High testosterone may lead to an exciting life, but a difficult one. The fascination with sex and violence can produce risky activities and problems. Probably such individuals have more active sex lives, but they also have shorter lives.[13] So all those people clamoring to raise their testosterone levels should be careful what they wish for!

they know is threatening, even dangerous—find they can communicate about their inner selves with complete strangers under the safe protection of anonymity that the Internet offers.

Talking into toilets is just one extreme and vivid instance of how hard people will work to connect with others. The long road to social acceptance has been a repeated theme of this book, and this chapter will show the variety of ways in which people strive to gain acceptance—and the variety of ways they suffer when they fail to connect with others. Nobody wants to end up all alone in the world; in fact, most human beings could hardly survive by themselves. As this chapter will show, people work long and hard to secure acceptance by others and to avoid rejection.

Social animals probably developed a kind of "herd instinct" long ago, but the human need to belong goes beyond that. A herd is a large collection of animals that all do pretty much the same thing. In contrast, humans often play distinct roles and have all sorts of specific, individual relationships with other members of the group. We have some evidence that the animal species most closely related to human beings have more complex social lives than other kinds of animals, in part because they can understand relations among others. One monkey can recognize that two other monkeys have an alliance, or that they might form one, or that they are enemies who may be prone to fight against each other, and the monkey might adjust its own behavior toward these others accordingly. Humans do the same. In fact, one thought-provoking theory has proposed that the driving force behind the evolution of intelligence and the brain was social: Animals developed larger, smarter brains in order to keep track of more relationships and more complicated social networks.[17]

FOR THE LAST TIME, NO!

The need to belong is an important need!

The **need to belong** is defined as the desire to form and maintain close, lasting relationships with some other individuals.[18,19,20,21,22,23] Without this motive, people might just live alone; they would certainly be willing to abandon a partner as soon as he or she became annoying. The need to belong drives people to affiliate, commit, and remain together, and it makes them reluctant to live alone. People usually form relationships easily and readily, such as with neighbors and work colleagues. They are reluctant to let relationships end, even if they do not see any clear purpose in continuing the relationship. For example, when workers at a corporation go through a training group exercise in which they meet regularly for a set period of time, the group typically resists its impending breakup, such as by promising to remain in touch with each other and even planning reunions.[24,25,26] The group's purpose will be over, and in fact most of these planned reunions never take place, but nobody wants to admit that the interpersonal connections are coming to an end. By the same token, when people break off a romantic relationship, they usually say they want to preserve some parts of their intimate connection despite terminating the romantic connection. "Let's just be friends" is the common breakup line, though in reality most ex-lovers do not sustain close friendships with each other.[27] Promising to remain friends is usually just a way to avoid the fact that a social bond is being broken.

Indeed, people are often reluctant to put an end even to bad relationships. People remain in relationships even with violent, abusive partners. This has been an enduring puzzle to psychologists and a source of vexation to therapists. A breathtaking variety of theories have been put forward to explain why women stay with men who humiliate or beat them, though it has been hard to prove any one of these theories correct, and many views (such as that some women have a masochistic desire to be beaten and abused) have been discredited. The broadest and simplest explanation is that breaking off relationships goes against the basic tendencies of human nature. We are designed to connect, not to separate, and even if the relationship is bad, we have a deeply rooted impulse not to terminate it. (Chapter 12 will cover more material about why people stay in bad relationships, especially in the section on the investment model.)

Two Ingredients to Belongingness

What exactly do people want? The need to belong has two parts.[28] First, people want some kind of regular social contacts. Of course, not all interactions are equally satisfying. Aversive social contacts, such as fighting and arguing, do not satisfy the need to belong. Positive social contacts are better, though neutral ones, such as watching television together or simply having breakfast together, are also satisfying. Second, people want the stable framework of some ongoing relationship in which the people share a mutual concern for each other.

Having either of these without the other produces partial satisfaction. For example, people who have many encounters with other people but without the relationship framework are better off than people who are fully isolated, but they are not fully satisfied either. Imagine being a tollbooth collector who interacts with people all day long but never sees anyone for more than a minute or two and mostly just says the same few words over and over. The same goes for telemarketers, who may speak to many people on the phone but without any real connection. Prostitutes have rather intimate interactions with many individuals, but again without the context of an ongoing relationship these are not satisfying.[29,30,31]

Conversely, people who have the stable context without the frequent interactions also suffer from the lack of face-to-face contact, even though they may treasure the relationship. Long-distance relationships or so-called commuter marriages reveal this pattern: The partners place great value on the bond they have with their far-off lover, but they yearn to spend more time together.[32,33,34,35,36,37]

People may want to belong, but most do not seek to make new friends endlessly. Some people want more friends than others, but most people seem to think that having about four to six close relationships is enough.[38,39] That is, if you have about five people who care

need to belong the desire to form and maintain close, lasting relationships with other individuals about you, whose company you enjoy, and with whom you can spend time on a regular basis, you probably feel fairly satisfied with your social life. (Most adults want at least one of those relationships to be a romantic pairing.) If you have fewer than that, you may be on the lookout for more. Few people seem eager to have more. In one survey, the majority of college students rated "having a few close friends" as extremely important, whereas "having lots of casual friends" was relatively unimportant.[40]

Another sign is how people act in people-rich settings such as universities. Because universities draw so many people, in principle, you could interact with someone new every day. As you may notice, that's not how people actually conduct their social lives. Most students form a social circle of about half a dozen other people and devote their time and energy to interacting with the members of this circle rather than to constantly seeking new friends.[41]

Not Belonging Is Bad for You

The need to belong is called a need, rather than merely a want, because when it is thwarted, people suffer more than just being unhappy. (A want is something that we can live without; a need is something that we have to have in order to be healthy.) Failure to satisfy the need to belong leads to significant health problems, including a higher risk of death. Death rates from all kinds of diseases are higher among people without social connections than among those with social connections.[42] People who are alone in the world have more physical and mental health problems than people who belong to a good social network.[43,44,45,46,47,48,49,50,51,52] Loneliness is hard on the body, impairing its natural powers including the immune system and its ability to recover from sickness or injury.[53]

There are plenty of other benefits to belonging (as if health and happiness were not enough!). Recent work has even linked belongingness to the meaning of life. Feeling connected to a strong network of relationships makes people see life as more meaningful.[54] Conversely, a lack of social connection can make life seem relatively meaningless.

Best Friends, Lovers, and Groups

Are close friends and romantic relationships the main or only way to satisfy the need to belong? In principle, cultural animals like human beings have another option: They can "belong" to a group or organization. Some people may find those social connections satisfying even if they do not form close friendships there.[55] As we shall see later in this chapter, some people can satisfy their wish for belongingness and keep loneliness at bay by feeling connected to a group or organization (even a university, or a professional sports team of which they are only fans). This seems to work better for men than for women.[56]

QUIZ YOURSELF

The Need to Belong

answers: see pg 401

1. In the reality TV show *Average Joe,* Melana based her choice of partners on _____ .

   (a) personality
   (b) physical attractiveness
   (c) wealth
   (d) All of the above

2. What hormone has been linked with masculine traits such as aggressiveness and dominance?

   (a) Cortisol
   (b) Estrogen
   (c) Progesterone
   (d) Testosterone

3. The need to belong has two parts, _____ and _____ .

   (a) business contacts; pleasure contacts
   (b) female contacts; male contacts
   (c) regular social contacts; an ongoing relationship
   (d) All of the above

4. Most people seem to think that having about _____ close relationships is enough.

   (a) 1 to 3
   (b) 4 to 6
   (c) 7 to 9
   (d) 10 to 12

Attraction: Who Likes Whom?

Social psychologists have labored long and hard to study the start of possible friendships and other forms of liking. Two people who are just meeting may come to like each other, or they may not. Which way they go depends on a variety of factors. Social psychology's task has been to identify those factors.

Some social psychologists, such as the influential researcher Edward E. Jones,[57] approached the question of attraction by studying what people actively do to try to make someone like them. (The term **ingratiation** is used for this, although ingratiation also has the connotation of being something a bit sneaky or manipulative.) This is a useful complement to the simple studies of who likes whom. Imagine you met someone and wanted to get that person to like you, either as a friend or as a romantic partner. What would you do? Jones found that people seem to have an intuitive knowledge of what fosters attraction, and they use that knowledge to get other people to like them. We will see several examples in the coming sections.

Not much will prove surprising in these research findings. People like good-looking, friendly people who are similar to themselves in important ways, and they like people who are nice to them. Still, let us review the main conclusions.

Similarity, Complementarity, Oppositeness

Two old clichés make opposite predictions about who likes whom. "Birds of a feather flock together" suggests that people mainly like others who resemble themselves, whereas "opposites attract" points to the contrary conclusion—that people are drawn to people dissimilar to themselves. Note that in such circumstances, whatever result social psychologists produce will look in retrospect like common sense. (This is why you shouldn't rely only on common sense when taking your social psychology exams! See Chapter 1 for a discussion on the weaknesses of common sense.)

In any case, decades of research by social psychologists have produced a clear and definitive winner in this battle of the clichés. Opposites do not attract very often. The birds of a feather are the ones who end up flocking together and staying together. In social psychology's terms, similarity is a common and potent cause of attraction.[58]

Most likely, you can see this yourself. Classify yourself on several major dimensions along which people differ. Choose ones that matter to you—perhaps age, race, level of education, liberal/conservative, religious or not, athletic or not, rich or poor. Then classify your several closest friends. The odds are that you and your close friends will fall in similar categories far more often than in different ones. People who want to influence us are well aware of this principle; sometimes they try to get us to like them by claiming that they are similar to us.

The appeal of similarity was illustrated in an amusing way by a news story. A man and a woman made contact via the Internet and began to exchange e-mails. They discovered they had a great deal in common, and they became attracted to each other. They "dated" for about six months via e-mail messages, though they did not reveal their names. The woman was also older than she had led the man to believe, so when he asked for her picture, she sent him a photo from a magazine. As their emotions grew stronger, the man pressured the woman to meet him for a romantic rendezvous. She finally relented and agreed to meet him on a dark beach. He went there, heart pounding, and saw a woman waiting for him as promised, wearing white shorts and a pink tank top. He spoke to her and she turned around, and they both got a shock: She was his mother! Obviously, nobody wants to date his own mother (especially because she was still married to his father, who became a laughing-stock when the story hit the news and who took a very dim view of the whole episode).[59] But family members generally are quite similar to each other, so it is not surprising that when their identities were concealed they had many similarities that produced the attraction.

Similarity can promote liking in many spheres. Having friends who like to do the same things you like to do can be important. After all, if none of your friends

ingratiation what people actively do to try to make someone like them

likes to play tennis, how are you going to find someone to play with? Some people compartmentalize their social lives more than others. People who are high in **self-monitoring**[60,61,62,63] seek to maximize each social situation, whereas those low in that trait pay more attention to permanent connections and feelings rather than fluctuating ones. Hence, the high self-monitor tennis player would prefer to play tennis with the best (or most evenly matched) tennis player in his or her circle of friends, whereas the low self-monitor would prefer to play tennis with his or her best friend, regardless of tennis ability.

Some of the most striking effects of similarity are found in marriage, even though marriage, which usually binds together two people of opposite genders, is often assumed to be one of the spheres where opposite or at least complementary (thus different) traits promote attraction. In fact, most spouses are similar in many basic respects. For example, husband and wife tend to have similar levels of intelligence.[64] (When you get married, don't call your spouse an idiot, because your spouse's IQ probably is close to your own!) Married partners are also similar on other dimensions, including physical attractiveness, education, and socioeconomic status.[65] Similarity contributes not only to the initial attraction but to the development of close bonds. Couples who are more similar to each other in attractiveness are more likely to progress toward more loving and committed relationships[66] (see **FIGURE 11.2**).

The **matching hypothesis** states that people tend to pair up with others who are equally attractive.[67,68,69] This is especially true among lovers, but it also is true among friends. It occurs in same-sex and in opposite-sex relationships.

Why does similarity promote attraction? The pattern seems widespread and probably very deeply rooted in the psyche, so explanations should probably invoke simple, basic tendencies. If human beings were naturally selected "for" culture, and we evolved under conditions of competing cultures, people who attached themselves strongly to similar others would have an advantage. People who were drawn more to the different, the exotic, the foreign, might detach from their group and join another, but this would be risky. Newcomers aren't trusted as much as long-familiar mates.[70] Hence, people who preferred to form bonds with people very different from themselves might tend to leave behind fewer offspring than people who attached themselves to others like themselves. Another contributing factor is that most people start off life surrounded by family members, so we learn to love by loving people who are quite similar to us.

Some evidence indicates that matching is driven more by rejecting dissimilar others than by liking similar others.[71] In fact, as people get to know each other and find out about dissimilarities, liking goes down. Most people believe that the more they know about someone, the more they like that person—but in reality, they tend to like someone less as they learn more. They start off assuming the other person will be similar. But once they find some dissimilarities, these seem to multiply, so that new evidence confirms dissimilarity and reduces liking. In an online dating study, researchers found, sure enough, that after the date was over people knew more about the dating partner but liked him or her less than previously.[72]

The attraction to similar others is probably social rather than cultural (see Chapter 2 for a discussion of the distinction between social and cultural animals). That is, the pattern that similarity promotes liking is not something that originates with human beings living in culture but rather something that originated among animals that formed into groups to help each other live better. Groups composed of similar animals would probably help each other live better. If anything, culture has raised the value of diversity and complementarity because cultural systems can take advantage of different roles and different talents.

Thus, as culture progresses and forms large, complex, interacting groups, there may be more need for complementarity. The movement toward diversity in organizations and the workplace may reflect an attempt to capitalize on the value of being different (see Chapter 14). But when people pick their friends and lovers, they still tend to look for those who are similar to themselves.

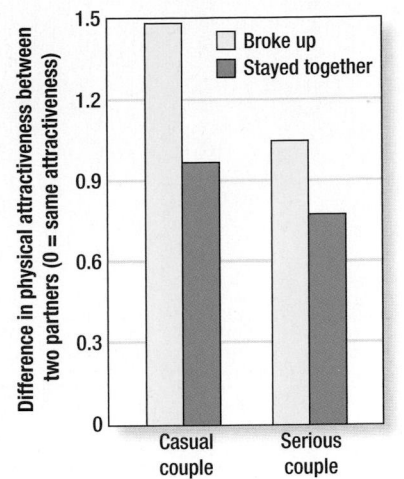

FIGURE 11.2

Dissimilarity in physical attractiveness increases the risk of breaking up.[199]

self-monitoring the ability to change one's behavior for different situations

matching hypothesis the proposition that people tend to pair up with others who are equally attractive

Social Rewards: You Make Me Feel Good

For several decades, psychological theory was dominated by **reinforcement theory**, which held that people and animals will perform behaviors that have been rewarded more than other behaviors. Applied to the issue of interpersonal attraction, this theory predicted that people would mainly like others who are rewarding to them—those who benefit them or make them feel good.

Two themes of ingratiation research confirm the importance of interpersonal rewards.[73] A first broad strategy for getting someone to like you is to do favors for that person. By definition, favors bring benefits to the recipient, and so favors make the person feel positively toward the person who did the favor. A man who wants a woman to like him will often do a broad variety of favors for her, such as sending her flowers, buying her dinner, and giving her gifts. Now and then people will recognize a favor as manipulative and resent it,[74] but in general favors are a good way to promote liking.

The second broad strategy involves praise. Most people feel good when they receive a compliment, so if you want someone to like you, you will probably be tempted to give that person plenty of compliments. Telling people what you like about them and what you see as their best traits is by and large a good way to go through life because it both reinforces the traits you approve of and makes people like you. The only limitation is that if people see the praise as manipulative or insincere, they may discount it. Otherwise, however, praising people is a reliable way to get them to like you.[75]

Consider Joe Girard, for example. Joe made a living selling cars in Detroit, Michigan. He was so successful at his job that he was listed in the *Guinness Book of World Records* as the "Greatest Car Salesman." Every day he worked, Joe sold an average of five cars and trucks. Joe was once asked the secret of his success. His response was: "Finding the salesman you like, plus the price. Put them together, and you get a deal." In other words, getting people to like him was as important as money. He probably helped his business with repeat customers, too. Each month Joe would send a postcard to thousands of his former customers. The postcard contained only five words: "I like you! Joe Girard."[76] Praise can even help you sell cars.

Why do rewards promote liking? This is no big mystery. Rewards mean getting what you want. Any organism should learn to like people, places, animals, or things that provide it with what it wants and needs. This may be as simple as classical conditioning: You learn to associate feeling good with being with someone, so naturally you like that person more.

Tit for Tat: Reciprocity and Liking

Chapter 9 emphasized that reciprocity is important for culture and therefore for human beings. Culture depends on reciprocity: If I do something for you, you should do something for me in return. Reciprocity is also important in liking. Having someone like you is powerful at a deep, gut level: It is hard to resist liking that person in return.

If there is a single trait that stands out as most valued in social relationships, it is trustworthiness.[77] Why should trustworthiness be the single most important trait for social appeal? When you form a bond with someone, you expect to do positive things for that person. Trustworthiness means that you can expect the other person to reciprocate. That is an important and effective foundation for a good relationship.

Multiple studies have confirmed the simple principle that liking begets (reciprocal) liking, and it is so obvious and intuitively correct that few studies now bother to focus on it. Still, whenever participants receive feedback that someone else likes them, they almost invariably feel a surge of affection for that person. The power of reciprocal liking seems to be universal. Thus, even research that finds differences between cultures in how people think about friendships and how they attract new friends still finds the common principle: If someone likes you, it is hard to resist liking that person in return.[78]

Reciprocation can take other forms and in that respect can imply similarity. In nonverbal behavior, reciprocity can take the form of mimicking. In one well-known study,[79] participants interacted with a confederate whom they wanted to like them. Sometimes

Each month Joe Girard sends each of his former customers (over 13,000 of them!) a postcard that says: "I like you! Joe Girard." This may be one reason why Joe Girard is listed in the *Guinness Book of World Records* as the "Greatest Car Salesman."

reinforcement theory the proposition that people and animals will perform behaviors that have been rewarded more than they will perform other behaviors

the confederate touched his or her face during the conversation, and other times the confederate wiggled his or her foot. Without realizing what they were doing, participants mimicked these behaviors themselves. A follow-up study showed that mimicry is often successful as a means of increasing liking. Participants talked to a confederate who had been trained to mimic the participant's nonverbal behavior (or not). When the confederate performed the same nonverbal behaviors as the participant—for example, wiggling her foot in response to seeing the participant wiggle her foot—the participant ended up liking the confederate more.[80] That may help explain why human babies quickly learn to mimic the people they see: Babies need people to like them!

We started this chapter by describing the *Average Joe* television reality show that featured Melana Scantlin. The sequel, *Average Joe: Hawaii*, had another beautiful woman courted by a bevy of ordinary-looking men. In this series, one of the nerdy-looking men adopted an

I'm starting to like you more and more.

unusual strategy, which was to declare himself wildly in love with the woman early in the game. It is a risky strategy, at least assuming that the declarations of love were truthful, because to fall in love with someone far more attractive than yourself (not to mention someone who was being courted by a couple of dozen other men!) makes you highly vulnerable to heartbreak. In this case, however, it had a powerful impact. The gorgeous young woman responded to the nerdy man's love for her, and she repeatedly selected him to continue in the game, even after the producers introduced a row of handsome young alternative suitors. The thoroughly smitten young man made it into the final round of two men, although she, like Melana Scantlin in the first game, ultimately chose the shallow but handsome fellow over the passionately devoted but average-looking guy. (Then the handsome guy dumped her.) Still, he had gone much further than he otherwise could have, simply by loving the woman unreservedly. It was hard for her to resist the fact that he loved her so much.

Reciprocation of liking may have a hugely powerful effect in everyday friendships. Its impact is more of a problem in romance, however. The difference may lie in the simple truth that you can have many friends but usually only one love relationship, in most cultures.

Research on one-sided, unrequited love has confirmed that people are positively attracted when they learn that someone else likes them—but if they do not want to reciprocate those feelings, they soon start to find the other person's attraction to them to be a burden or problem. If you were to find out that someone has a crush on you, your first reaction would almost certainly be positive because it is good to be loved. But if you did not really want that person as your partner, soon you would feel uncomfortable around him or her. Initially it is flattering to learn that someone likes you, but if you do not want to marry that person, your later reaction is a struggle with guilt and a search for ways to let the person down easily.[81]

Reciprocity brings us back to the broad theme of humans as cultural animals. If people liked those who liked them, this reciprocity would make people better suited to culture. Creatures who mainly liked those who disliked them would have a difficult time forming the network of relationships that makes culture possible. You are safer and better off among people who like you than among people who don't care about you one way or the other.

It's hard to say no to someone who really loves you.

Putting people first, to mention another theme of this book, seems to work best when it involves people who like us and are similar to us.

You Seem Trustworthy: Moral Traits

Many people can have fun with someone who is not particularly scrupulous about moral behavior, and they may even enjoy someone who breaks the rules now and then. But if you want to form a long-term relationship with someone, you will generally be happier if that person is a moral person.

Nobody disputes that people like people who are warm and friendly. But is that the main criterion? Recent evidence suggests that global impressions depend more on moral character than on warmth. Honest, trustworthiness, fairness, and courage have a big impact on the impressions people form—much more than warmth, sense of humor, sociability, and agreeableness.[82]

After all, liking is not the only thing that matters. Relationships need trust also, and trust depends on moral traits. People earn trust by having good self-control, which is a vital basis for moral behavior (see Chapter 4).[83] In fact, even people with low self-control choose partners with high self-control, contrary to the usual pattern of being attracted to similar others (which would predict that people with low self-control would be attracted to others who also have low self-control).[84] Again, this indicates judging people by moral traits, not friendliness.

Indeed, the importance of a person's moral character in interpersonal attraction and relationship formation is not just changing the latter. It is also changing how psychologists think about morality. For decades, the focus has been on how people judge actions. Recent work has suggested, however, that morality may be more about judging people.[85] After all, an action is in the past, but the future may require a person to decide whether someone will make a good partner or not. Moral judgment, including blame and praise, may be a vital basis for making future choices about relationships.

You Again: Mere Exposure

What we have seen so far is hardly surprising. People like those who are similar to them, who like them back, and who make them feel good. But another pattern is less intuitively obvious. Apparently people sometimes like others based on nothing more than familiarity. That is, they grow to like people whom they encounter on a regular basis. This **propinquity** (nearness) effect is robust and reliable. A classic study tracked friendship formation in a dormitory, and it found that people made friends (as well as enemies) most frequently among the people who lived close to them.[86]

Chapter 7 on attitudes described the mere exposure effect: People come to hold more positive attitudes toward familiar stimuli than toward novel, unfamiliar ones. Merely seeing or encountering something or someone on a regular basis increases liking (unless you dislike the person initially, then it leads to more disliking).

An extension of the mere exposure effect involves shared experiences. For example, many years from now in some far-off place you may meet a stranger and discover during the conversation that the two of you attended the same college or came from the same home town or had the same kind of pet. Logically, there is little reason that this should promote liking, but the odds are that you and this other person will begin to have friendly feelings toward each other based on this shared experience.

People seem to develop positive feelings toward someone even if the shared experiences were bad. Laboratory participants who are strangers and have no common bond except that they experience electric shock together end up liking each other more![87] A similar conclusion emerges from research on combat veterans. Going through combat is mostly a highly stressful, dangerous, sad, and terrifying experience, marked by loud noise, confusion, death and injury to friends, and uncertainty about one's own survival. Yet military groups who experience combat seem to bond to each other from the experience. One sign is that military reunions are better attended by groups who went through combat than by groups who did not.[88]

propinquity being near someone on a regular basis

Why do familiarity and shared experiences promote liking? The effect of familiarity and shared experiences goes beyond simple explanations in terms of conditioning (positive associations). Most likely it is very deeply rooted in the psyche, which means its roots are far back in our evolutionary history. One should perhaps ask why even very simple animals would prefer familiar stimuli or familiar other animals. A tendency to grow fond of the familiar would help stamp in the preference for a stable environment (so animals might learn to like their homes). It would certainly promote stable social bonds. Imagine, for example, that nature programmed animals in the opposite way, so that familiarity led to contempt or some other form of disliking. How would families stay together? How would friendships, alliances, or other partnerships survive? If you always preferred a stranger to someone you knew, social life would be in constant turmoil and turnover. In contrast, if you automatically grew to like the people you saw regularly, you would soon prefer them over strangers, and groups would form and stabilize easily. Given the advantages of stable groups (e.g., people know each other, know how to work together, know how to make decisions together, know how to adjust to each other), it is not surprising that nature favored animals that grew to like (rather than dislike) each other on the basis of familiarity.

As with all these patterns, it is important not to overstate them. Of course, we do not grow to love everyone we see on a regular basis. Some people are a pain in the neck, and seeing them every day will not make them seem like adorable sweethearts. There is even an interesting pattern of research suggesting that a partner's annoying habits grow more annoying with repeated exposure (see **FIGURE 11.3**). This is called the **social allergy effect** based on the analogy to ordinary allergies, which grow worse over time. If you have a slight allergy to cats and you move in with a romantic partner who has a cat, your cat allergy is likely to grow more severe as you are exposed to the cat more frequently. In the same way, early in a relationship you may be only slightly bothered by how your partner chews with her mouth open, or picks his toenails while watching television, or keeps repeating some stupid phrase such as "like, wow"—but this slight irritation will most likely grow more bothersome over time.[89,90,91,92] In short, familiarity and repeated exposure can sometimes make bad things worse. But the most common consequence is that people grow to like people (and places and things) that become familiar to them.

This increase in liking caused by familiarity, like nearly every social psychology effect, involves a shift in the odds rather than a black-and-white absolute difference. In this case, seeing someone regularly and becoming familiar with that person leads to a slight increase in the odds that you will end up liking that person. The mere exposure effect is probably an important part of the propinquity effect, noted earlier. We like those who live near us because we see them frequently.

Looking Good

In the Melana Scantlin story that started the chapter, a beautiful and desirable woman chose a physically attractive man over one with substance and success. Such a choice is not uncommon. When all else is equal, most people show a substantial preference for attractive over unattractive others. Even when all else is not equal, physical good looks count for a lot and can trump other good points.

Some of the advantages of good looks fall into the stereotype that has been called the **what is beautiful is good effect**. That is, people assume that physically attractive people will be superior to others on many other traits. These traits include happiness, sexual warmth, popularity, and even intelligence and success.[93,94,95] To be sure, not all good traits are assumed to be linked to attractiveness. Beautiful women and handsome men are not assumed to be more honest than others, for example. Researchers have also found some evidence of cultural variation. South Koreans, for example, place more value than North Americans on honesty and compassionate concern for others, and South Koreans also are more likely to think that attractive people will rank higher than average on those traits.[96]

Good looks can outweigh other factors in attraction. (To see how one group of researchers tried to put a dollar value on physical attributes, read *Money Matters*.) Indeed, this fact produced one of the most famous disappointments in social psychology's research on

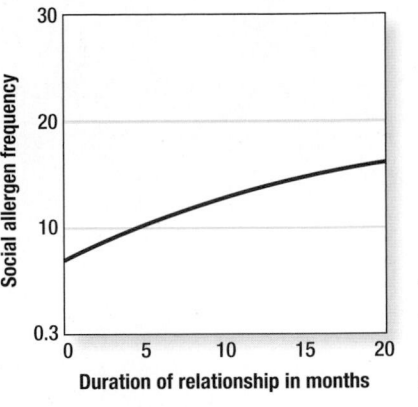

FIGURE 11.3

The longer the relationship continues, the more people are bothered by their partner's minor annoying habits, and the more negative emotion they have in response to them.

social allergy effect the idea that a partner's annoying habits become more annoying over time

what is beautiful is good effect the assumption that physically attractive people will be superior to others on many other traits

attraction. A group of researchers set up a campus dating service to test their various theories about interpersonal liking.[97] They collected all sorts of information about the students in their pool; then they matched them at random and sent them out on dates. The researchers favored theories emphasizing similarity and reciprocity: They thought people who were most similar to each other on various attributes would enjoy their dates the most. This was not what happened. Instead, the main conclusion was that the dating partner's attractiveness was the strongest predictor of how much people enjoyed the date: The more attractive your partner was, the better you liked him or her. The fancy theories about matching and similarity and reciprocity couldn't shine through the overwhelming preference for the best-looking partners.

It is perhaps understandable that people want their dating partners and romantic partners to be physically attractive (see *The Social Side of Sex*). But good looks are valued in many other, nonromantic settings as well. Attractive children are more popular among other children than their less attractive peers, and teachers like them more, too.[98,99,100] Research even shows that 3-month-old babies prefer to look at more attractive faces.[101] Good-looking people do better in job interviews, including for jobs that are not based on looks.[102,103] We saw in the chapter on prosocial behavior that attractive people sometimes get more help in emergency situations.[104]

For men, modern clothing is linked more to displaying wealth and status than showing off the body as a sex object. Women in one study were asked to rate how attractive they found men as potential husbands, dates, or lovers, based on seeing photographs of them.[109] The researchers had actually taken two photos of each man. In one photo, the man wore classy and expensive clothes, including a navy blue blazer, nice tie, and Rolex watch. For the other photo, each man put on a Burger King server outfit, complete with hat. Women expressed very little desire to meet, date, sleep with, or marry the men they

MONEY *Matters*

Is Manhood Measured in Dollars or Inches?

What is the measure of a man? Women have long known that physical dimensions are a key component of their own attractiveness, and women's concern with losing weight and being thin is at least partly rooted in the competition to be desirable to men. One relevant measure is the ratio of waist size to hip size. Researchers have found that men are more attracted to women with a ratio of about 0.7, and they have clear preferences when they judge a woman only by her silhouette.[105] A low ratio like 0.7 is compatible with the so-called hourglass figure that men find desirable. If the ratio is higher, as it is for women with bigger bellies, attraction is less.

In an effort to see whether women would judge men by equally simple (some might

say shallow!) criteria, researchers prepared silhouette drawings of men with varying waist-to-hip ratios and asked women to rate them for attractiveness.[106] Sure enough, women did have a slight preference for a certain body shape in men, with a waist-to-hip ratio of around 0.9 and normal overall weight. Of course, this doesn't necessarily mean very much because that was all the information the women had on which to judge the men, and the effect was small.

In a final study, therefore, researchers added a second variable: how much money the man earned. Waist-to-hip ratio still mattered, a little, but the amount of money the man made was much more important, especially when women were judging him as a partner for a long-term relationship or marriage. Women much preferred the men with high incomes over the low-paid ones. Dollars mattered more than inches, though for maximum appeal, both the right body and a high income were needed.

Of course, waistline is not the only part of a man that can be measured in inches. Being tall matters, and there is in fact some tradeoff between money and height, according to research done with an online dating service.[107] Women's choices depended on both men's height and their salaries. Taller was better, but money could compensate. Thus, a man who was 5 feet 8 inches (1.73 meters) tall could get as many dates as a man who was 6 feet (1.78 meters) tall, provided that the shorter man made more money— precisely, $146,000 per year more! For a 5-foot 2-inch (1.57 meters) man to do as well as a 6-footer, he would need to earn an extra $277,000.

The news for short men is not all bad, however. Women may express some preference for dating tall men, but when they meet them, they do not find them any more attractive. Moreover, short men report having had just as many dates as tall men, so obviously they find ways of overcoming any prejudice against them.[108]

saw wearing Burger King outfits, probably because those outfits are associated with low status and not much money. The very same men attracted much more interest when dressed up in classy, expensive clothes.

Body shape is another component of attractiveness and sex appeal. A so-called hourglass figure composed of a narrow waist with wider hips and shoulders is most appealing in both men and women, though naturally the widest shoulders are seen as more attractive in a man than a woman. The ideal figure varies from culture to culture. For example, plump women are regarded as more attractive by some cultures than by others, though being very obese is not regarded as lovely by almost any culture. Even within a culture, standards of beauty change. For example, the weight of *Playboy* centerfolds and Miss America Pageant contestants and winners has decreased substantially since 1960.[110]

The sources of cultural variation in ideal body weight are not fully known, although one factor may be whether food is scarce. That is, in a culture where there is often not enough to eat, a plump woman is probably rich and healthy, whereas a skinny woman is more in danger of starving or might have a disease. Men in such cultures might prefer slightly larger women because their bodies will be better able to support a baby. Of course, the men don't necessarily think about whether the woman can nurse a baby. It is just that the men who for whatever reason were attracted to the plumper women were more successful at passing on their genes, whereas the men who liked the skinniest women produced fewer surviving babies.

The ideal beauty standard for American women has become thinner over time.

Attraction in the 21st Century: Online Dating

Dogs, birds, and giraffes meet their mates today much the same way they always have, but human mating customs have changed repeatedly over the centuries. In the 1800s, much romance was conducted on the front porch, where the gentleman caller talked to the young lady with her mother present and sometimes with his romantic rivals also earnestly trying to dominate the conversation. The 20th century invented "dates" (the term originally referred to an encounter with a prostitute), especially as motorcars enabled young couples to seek livelier environments than Mom's front porch. Trips to the movies were a staple of mid-century dates. Dances have long been popular ways of getting to know romantic partners, though the settings and dances changed over the decades. Elsewhere in the world, the variety is even greater, including marriages arranged by parents so that the young couple first meet each other at their wedding, as well as people going to priests or professional matchmakers to get help finding a partner.

In the 21st century, many people seek romantic partners via new, online dating services, such as eHarmony and Match.com. Not long ago, computers were owned by big corporations and operated mainly by professional nerds and their lackeys, but now young men and women use computers as instruments of romance. They can sign up to a service that lets them peruse information about large numbers of potential partners and contact ones they find appealing.

How has online dating changed romance? The Association for Psychological Science appointed a blue-ribbon panel of experts to review the latest research and draw some conclusions. Their 60-page report was published in 2012.[117]

To start with the obvious, the researchers documented several key differences between online dating and the more conventional (offline) sort. First, online dating greatly expands the range of potential partners and the ease of meeting them. College students can meet single people in classes and around campus, but once a person leaves college, the prospects for encountering eligible partners shrink markedly: One meets a few people at work, or is "set up" on a blind date by a third party, or chats up strangers in bars. In contrast, the online supply can seem almost limitless, at least in a large city.

Most people can agree fairly well on who is beautiful and who isn't, but it is much harder to say why someone is beautiful. Also, people agree more about women than about men, possibly because physical attractiveness counts more for women than for men.[111] In lab studies, both men and women automatically looked more at beautiful women (more than handsome men) in a group of faces.[112] Probably the reasons differed. The men see beautiful women as potential mates. The women see them as potential rivals and want to check out the competition. (Did it ever strike you as odd that not only are men's magazines filled with pictures of beautiful women—but so are women's magazines?)

Evolutionary psychologists generally think that female beauty is linked to signs of being a good mate and potential partner, which especially means being young and healthy. If cultural variation in beauty were random, you might expect that gray hair and wrinkled skin would be regarded as beautiful in some cultures, but no known culture treats old-looking women as more beautiful than younger-looking ones. A clear complexion is nearly always prized, possibly because it was a sign of health: Many infectious diseases such as pox left permanent marks on the skin, so clear skin would be one sign of a healthy mate. Today's men and women are descended from male ancestors who chose young and healthy-looking women.

Symmetry is a surprisingly powerful source of beauty. That is, people whose faces and bodies are exactly the same on both sides are regarded as more attractive than people whose right side is different from the left side. Symmetry is a sign of two important things: being healthy and having good genes. Faults or defects in someone's genes produce discrepancies between the left and right sides. The most symmetrical person presumably has the fewest genetic defects.

One of the most remarkable demonstrations of the power of symmetry began by measuring a series of body parts (such as earlobes and little fingers) of young adult men, to see how closely they matched. Then the researchers asked each man to sleep in a T-shirt some night when he did not use deodorant or cologne. Each man brought the T-shirt to the lab and left it there. A sample of young women then sniffed each T-shirt and rated how good it smelled (of course without knowing which men had worn them). They also informed the researchers of when they had had their last menstrual period. The most symmetrical men's T-shirts were rated as smelling the best, and this effect was mainly found among the women who were at the point in the menstrual cycle at which they would be most fertile. Thus, when women are most prone to get pregnant, they are most drawn to the bodily smell of men who were most symmetrical and hence would probably have the best genes.[113]

Researchers also demonstrated the importance of symmetry by doubling images. That is, researchers took facial photos of people, then cut each photo down the middle, threw out one side at random, and filled in the blank with the mirror image of the other side. For example, they might create a photo of you by taking the left side of your face, making a mirror image of it, and attaching the mirror image (as the right side) to the real left side. The result was faces that looked much like the original people but were more exactly symmetrical. Participants consistently rated these reworked images as more attractive than the original faces. Thus, increasing the symmetry of a face made it seem more attractive.

Another source of beauty is typicality. That is, people who look different from others are generally regarded as less attractive. This theory was proposed two centuries ago by the German philosopher Immanuel Kant,[114] who thought that the mind reviews all the faces it has ever seen, forms a sort of average or composite, and regards that as the most attractive. Recent advances in computer technology finally made it possible to test his theory by morphing faces together to make up an average. In a landmark study, researchers started with 16 different faces that varied in attractiveness. Then they combined pairs of faces using computer imaging software, so that they made 8 new faces, each of which was an "average" of two of the original faces. They then merged these again by pairs, and again, ultimately creating a single image that was the average of all 16. Participants consistently rated the original, actual faces as less attractive than the 2-face composites; the 4-face composites got even higher ratings; and the images that had been made by averaging all 16 faces were rated as the most beautiful.[115]

Further work has shown that the ultimate, most attractive faces are not really averages of everyone, but rather averages of the faces that are high on the other indices of beauty, such as youth and health. That is, a face that averages across the entire life span, including a baby, a little girl, an adolescent, a young adult, a middle-aged woman, and an old woman, is not as attractive as a face that is made by averaging a group of young adult women.

The preference for slender versus fuller figures seems to change fairly easily. In fact, men can change their preferences even within the same day! One study stopped Princeton students going to dinner or coming back from it to furnish ratings of attractiveness of women from photos. The hungry men (before dinner) preferred plumper women than the men who were full from dinner.[116]

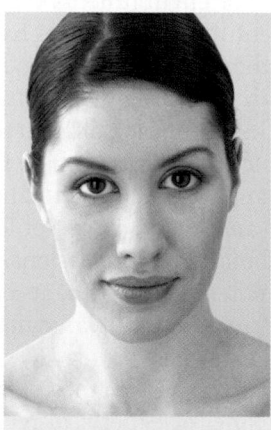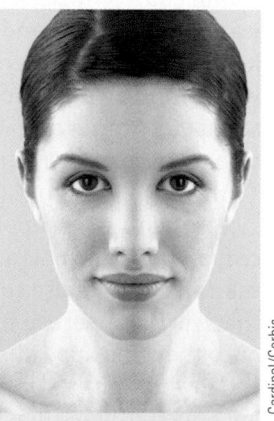

Cardinal/Corbis

Which photo is more attractive? The one on the left shows the actual face; the one on the right was made by duplicating the left side on the right, so that the face is perfectly symmetrical. Most people find the one on the right to be more attractive than the true picture.

Second, online dating enables people to communicate via computer before they meet in person, and in some cases these contacts can be extensive. You can send messages back and forth with a potential partner for days, weeks, even months before meeting face to face. This enables you to get to know much about the partner, make preliminary evaluations (perhaps finding out reasons not to meet, which are less awkwardly handled by e-mail than in the middle of a romantic dinner), and build some degree of relationship before you are ever in the same room together.

Third, several online services offer to help you search out the best partners from your database. They use formulas and algorithms that select the people who will match up with you best.

There are drawbacks, to be sure. People do not always tell the truth in their online profiles. One study checked online claims against actual measurements and found that 81% of the dating profiles contained lies about height, weight, or age.[118] Men tend to overstate their height, and women understate their weight.

On the harder question of whether online dating really improves outcomes, the panel's report had mixed answers. Yes, online dating vastly increases the number of potential partners, but one encounters them in the form of online profiles that can fail to include crucial information, and having thousands of potential partners may reduce the effort to work at getting to know any particular one. Communicating by computer can be helpful, but it is not a substitute for face-to-face interaction. As for the claims to find your soul mate by combing through the files with mathematical formulas—well, these are simply not plausible, as the panel concluded. Thus, online dating seems here to stay, and it does have its advantages, but it is not a magic recipe for finding love, and it may create its own set of problems and difficulties.

So far we have focused on what makes people attractive and attracted to each other. In the next section we turn to the other side of the coin: social rejection and exclusion.

Finding love has changed over time.

1. Based on attraction research, which of these proverbs is most accurate?

   (a) "The early bird gets the worm."   (b) "Birds of a feather flock together."   (c) "Opposites attract."   (d) "Out of sight, out of mind."

2. If you live next to someone, what outcome is most likely?

   (a) You will become friends with that person.   (b) You will become enemies with that person.   (c) Both (a) and (b)   (d) Neither (a) nor (b)

3. If people are seated according to their last names using a seating chart, those with last names that start with the same letter often end up becoming good friends. This finding can be explained by _____.

   (a) ingratiation   (b) propinquity   (c) need for belonging   (d) similarity

4. According to the what is beautiful is good effect, attractive people have a number of other desirable traits. Which of the following is not one of these traits, at least in Western cultures?

   (a) Happiness   (b) Honesty   (c) Intelligence   (d) Popularity

Rejection

One day a young man named Kip Williams was walking through a park, and unexpectedly he saw a Frisbee spinning toward him. He caught it and looked about for its source. Two other guys waved to him, and he threw it back to them. Everyone smiled, and the three of them threw the Frisbee around for a few minutes. Then, oddly, the other two stopped throwing him the Frisbee and ignored him. He stood there for a few minutes, his smile gradually fading, until he realized that they weren't going to include him anymore. Feeling surprisingly sick and sad, he turned and slunk away.

In most cases that would have been the end of the story, but Williams went on to become a social psychologist. He remembered the experience and his emotional reaction. After all, why should he have expected the others to keep him in their game forever, and why should he even care? He hadn't gone to the park expecting to play Frisbee; he didn't know the guys, so they didn't owe him anything; and he didn't lose anything of importance or value. Yet somehow at a gut level he had been quite upset by the way the two fellows had excluded him. He turned his attention to the study of what happens when someone is rejected, excluded, or ignored. Kip Williams has even designed a virtual game called *Cyberball* that can be used to reproduce the situation of the excluded Frisbee player, for research purposes (see **FIGURE 11.4**).

Ostracism refers to being excluded, rejected, and ignored by others. The term comes from ancient Greece. One custom in Athens was that if a person behaved offensively or too aggressively, someone would write that person's name on a piece of broken pottery and put it in one of the large containers allocated in public places. These pieces of pottery, called *ostraka* (from which the word *ostracism* is derived) were collected and tallied, and if one person was named on 6,000 *ostraka,* the entire community agreed to give that person the silent treatment for 10 years: no one would speak to or interact with that person.

Nowadays the term *ostracism* is used for smaller-scale practices of ignoring, as when a person refuses to speak to his or her spouse for a period of time. The close-knit Amish community will sometimes ostracize someone who is regarded as having violated the community's rules, such as by cheating someone, breaking religious rules, or misbehaving sexually. The silence is sometimes also used in military groups, such as if someone

ostracism being excluded, rejected, and ignored by others

Including the third player — Excluding the third player

© Cengage Learning

FIGURE 11.4

Psychologists have many ways to make participants feel socially excluded for short periods so they can evaluate the effects social exclusion has on everything from brain activity to sharing cookies. Many experiments use this *Cyberball* game, developed by Kip Williams of Purdue University. The participant, represented by the little hand in the foreground, is initially included in the game of catch with the other two players, who are really just part of a computer program. Midway through the game, the other players throw the ball between themselves, excluding the participant, whose little hand is left with nothing to do.

is believed to have cheated or broken the military code of honor. In such cases, no one speaks to the person or even acknowledges his existence. No one looks at you or responds to anything you say. Lt. Henry Flipper, the first black man to go to West Point, had to endure that treatment for his entire four years of college because the other cadets believed that it was inappropriate for an African American to study there to become an officer in the army.[119]

We opened this section with the brief story about Kip Williams being ostracized by strangers for a few minutes. Such experiences may be unpleasant, but when one is ostracized by significant others, or over a long period of time, the impact is almost certainly considerably worse.[120] The fact that some people (like Williams himself in the Frisbee story) feel bad after even a few minutes of ostracism attests to the power and importance that the human psyche attaches to being socially accepted. To be ostracized for months at a time by a spouse or parent can be devastating.

Much ostracism is informal, and some targets do not even know why they are being ostracized. One woman reported in an interview that her father had ostracized her off and on since she was 12, and she was now 40. Despairing of ever having a warm connection to her family again, she moved halfway around the world. Eventually her siblings contacted her and told her that her father was expected to die soon. This was one last chance to make up, so she made the long flight home, booked into a hotel, and finally went to the hospital. Even then she was torn between the desire to connect and the fear of being rejected again. She stood outside her father's hospital room struggling within herself as to what to say and whether to go in. Summoning all her courage, she finally walked in and looked at the now frail but still recognizable man lying on the bed. He was surprised to see her. "Oh Daddy, please don't leave me," she said. The old man's eyes filled with tears, but then he turned his face to the wall and never said a word to her. That was the last time she ever saw him. (As the researcher, Williams found these stories so hard to bear that he had to hire research assistants to take over the rest of the interviews.)

Kean Collection/Archive Photos/Getty Images

Lt. Henry Flipper was the first African American to graduate from West Point in 1877. He was ostracized the entire time he was a student at West Point.

It is easy and appropriate to feel sorry for the victims of ostracism. Still, it is important to appreciate both perspectives. When someone is rude or offensive or behaves very badly, it may be appropriate to challenge their behavior in some way. However, simply refusing to interact with the offensive person may be easier than confronting him or her. Experiments have found that it depletes energy to confront someone who behaves badly, and some people may turn to ostracizing the bad person as a strategy that subtly expresses disapproval but also conserves energy.[121]

Effects of Rejection: Inner Reactions

Nobody thinks it's fun to be rejected, to be thrown out of a group, or to have your heart broken. The inner states that arise in response to rejection are almost uniformly negative. People who are repeatedly or continually ostracized by others over a long period of time report a broad variety of problems: pain, illness, depression, suicidal thoughts, eating disorders, helplessness, promiscuity.[122,123] Their self-esteem suffers, and they feel worthless. Some of them say life seems meaningless and pointless.[124,125] All of these findings underscore the central point that people are designed by nature to want to be accepted into social groups and relationships.

Being rejected repeatedly can cause people to develop expectations that other people will reject them too. This forms the basis of a personality trait called **rejection sensitivity**. Sometimes these expectations make people so hypersensitive to possible rejection that they become reluctant to open up or get close to others for fear of being hurt. This can set up a vicious circle in which rejection sensitivity causes people to push others away (so as to reduce the risk of getting hurt), which then damages relationships, causing more rejection and increasing the sensitivity.[126,127]

The common experience "you hurt my feelings" is usually tied to an implicit message that "you don't care about our relationship."[128] Anything a person does or says that suggests the person doesn't care about you as much as you care about him or her, or doesn't care about the relationship as much as you do, can hurt your feelings. Obviously, rejection almost always involves the sense that the rejecter doesn't care about the relationship—so hurt feelings are common. Perhaps surprisingly, it doesn't seem to matter much whether people actively try to reject you or do it more casually or thoughtlessly. Your feelings may be deeply hurt even if the other person never intended to hurt you and never thought about you at all, such as if your romantic partner forgot your birthday. Instead, the amount of hurt feelings depends on how much you care about the relationship and how clear a sign you received that the other person doesn't care as much.[129]

Not all rejection produces an immediate wave of emotional distress, however. In fact, the initial reaction to rejection is often closer to numbness, "feeling nothing," than anxiety or sadness.[130] This is possibly rooted in biology: The body reacts to the pain of social rejection with the same response it uses to physical pain, and severe pain often deadens the body to all feeling.[131,132,133,134,135,136] People who suffer terrible physical injuries, such as a broken bone or severe wound, may become numb, and sometimes athletes who are injured during a game don't fully feel the pain until the game is over. This could help explain why rejected people sometimes do antisocial things that might alienate other people further: They have become numb to the pain of social exclusion and hence don't realize that what they are doing might drive people away.

Indeed, social rejection affects the body in ways similar to physical injury. When people who have recently broken up with a romantic partner look at a photo or other reminder of that person, their brains respond with activity in the same places that respond to physical pain.[137] Social psychologist Nathan DeWall was struck by the parallels between social and physical pain, and he began to wonder whether taking a painkiller like aspirin or Tylenol (acetaminophen) would reduce suffering from social rejection just as it seems to reduce physical pain. He recruited samples of students to take a couple pills every day, by random assignment either Tylenol or a placebo. After a few days, those taking Tylenol reported fewer "hurt feelings" and other signs of being bothered by rejection. Their social self-esteem increased, even though other aspects of self-esteem (e.g., about their schoolwork) were unaffected. The placebo group showed no change. A lab study with

rejection sensitivity a tendency to expect rejection from others and to become hypersensitive to possible rejection

brain scans showed the same benefit: Painkillers reduced responses to being rejected and ostracized.[138] Thus, distress over social events is really processed in the body in ways that resemble the response to physical injuries. Of course, one should not become addicted to painkillers just to numb social pain.

The numb or stunned feeling that comes from a strong (and especially an unexpected) rejection can interfere with normal psychological functioning. Rejection interferes with cognitive processing: In simple terms, rejection makes people temporarily stupid. They are less effective at processing complex information such as reasoning.[139] Rejection also undermines self-regulation: In the aftermath of rejection, people become more impulsive, more inclined to do something they will regret later (but that may seem appealing now).[140] Rejected people may, for example, blow their diets by eating a giant cake or a large serving of ice cream, or they may waste a large amount of money. See *Food for Thought* for some experimental findings on rejection and eating.

Other bodily effects of rejection have begun to be studied. At some unconscious level, people link temperature with social processes. Being surrounded by loving friends is warm; being rejected is cold. Lonely people seem to feel physically cold, to the extent that they take more hot baths to warm up![141] Conversely, being physically cold can make people feel lonelier.

FOOD FOR *Thought*

Social Rejection and the Jar of Cookies

The love of your life, or at least the person you thought was the love of your life, storms out the door, saying, "I don't ever want to see you again!" and calling you a variety of names like loser, creep, and hopelessly inept lover. According to one stereotype, you might go home and eat an entire cheesecake, or a whole gallon of ice cream.

What does research say? The stereotype is actually fairly accurate. Social anxiety and fears of rejection are linked to eating binges and eating disorders.[142,143,144,145] In lab studies, rejected people are more prone to eat fattening or junk food.[146] This fits the more general pattern that rejection impairs self-regulation. People may want to eat cake, ice cream, or French fries much of the time, but usually they restrain these impulses because they know such foods are bad for them. After experiencing a rejection, however, the restraints are undermined. In one study, rejected people ate nearly twice as many cookies as people who had been accepted by a group (see **FIGURE 11.5**).[147] They also rated the cookies as tasting better,

though the increased eating was statistically independent of the taste ratings, and some people ate more cookies even though they didn't find the taste particularly appealing. ("I didn't like the cookies, but I couldn't stop eating them!" said one participant who had been rejected by the group.)

The results seem to reflect a breakdown in control rather than an increase in hunger. If the food doesn't taste good but is good for you, rejection produces the opposite pattern (of reduced consumption). In one study, researchers exhorted participants (both verbally and with a cash incentive) to consume a healthy but very bad-tasting beverage consisting of unsweetened Kool-Aid mixed with both water and vinegar. The brew resembled some medicines and health drinks that taste bad but are worth consuming for their health benefits. (Vinegar is actually good for you.) Participants who had just experienced social acceptance or had received neutral feedback made themselves consume about 8 ounces of the gross-tasting drink, but rejected people averaged only about 2 ounces[148] (see **FIGURE 11.5**).

What these results have in common with the cookie-eating study is self-regulation. People need self-regulation to prevent themselves from eating junk foods, just as

they need it to make themselves consume things they don't like but are good for them. On both counts, rejected people fared worse.

The bottom line is that rejected people do not self-regulate their eating as well as other people. They eat more junk food, and they consume less of what is good for them.

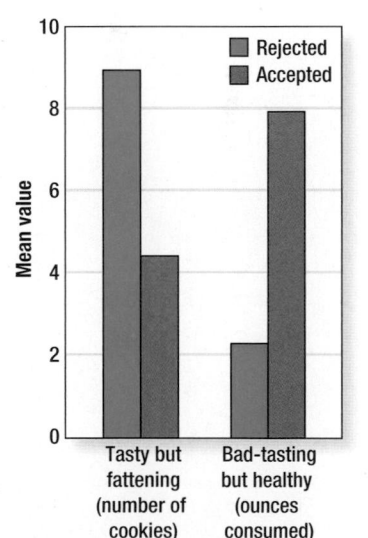

FIGURE 11.5

Rejection weakens self-control: Rejected persons ate more cookies but drank less.[140]

The conflict between social conscience and selfish impulse is an important theme of social psychology. Apparently, most people resolve this in favor of doing the sort of proper, generous, unselfish actions that society approves—but mainly if they enjoy and anticipate social acceptance. Rejection appears to change how people approach that conflict, making them more prone to favor the selfish impulse. Acting in a socially conscientious manner (such as waiting in line, paying taxes, or refraining from littering) often requires some degree of effort and sacrifice, and those sacrifices are compensated by the rewards of social acceptance. Accordingly, if people reject you, you may feel less inclined to make those efforts and sacrifices.

One more constructive response to rejection is to become more attuned to social cues and information about other people. Rejection makes people start to look about, cautiously, for new potential friends.[149] Participants in one experiment were rejected (or not) and then were permitted to read other people's diaries. The rejected people showed an increase in attention to the interpersonal events in the diaries, such as whether the diary writer had a date or played tennis with someone else.[150] When rejected people think they might have a chance to form a bond with someone or even to get back together with the person who rejected them, they focus their attention on this possibility and think at length about their possible relationship partners. Indeed, being able to think about people who do love you may shelter you from the pain of being rejected by someone else. Participants in another study who brought along a photograph of someone who loved them fared better and felt better after being rejected in the lab than did people who had no photos, and also better than someone who had brought photos of a favorite celebrity.[151]

What about outsiders who find their own way and thus create or discover things that people in the mainstream might miss? A provocative recent investigation showed that being rejected can actually increase creativity, though only for some people.[152] Participants who were rejected by a group scored higher on tests of creativity than others who were accepted. The increase in creativity was mainly found among people who desired to be different and unique, and those who thought of themselves as independent from others, so it is not safe to recommend rejecting people as a way of making everyone more creative! And measuring creativity is a tricky business, so the findings in these studies might not generalize to other measures. Still, it is encouraging to think that some people can respond to rejection in a positive manner, seeing the world in fresh, creative ways.

Behavioral Effects of Rejection

How should rejected people act? Conroy's novel *The Prince of Tides* tells the story of a young man from a rural area who went to a major state university in a big city. At the end of fraternity rush, he was stunned to learn that not a single fraternity offered him a bid. By chance he met a young woman who was in a similar predicament; the two formed a bond, eventually falling in love and marrying. They decided that if they were not to spend all their time at parties and other Greek life functions, they would devote themselves to their studies, and they achieved top grades (in fact the woman graduated first in her class). They also resolved to help others: The man became a teacher and the woman a physician. This story shows an ideal, exemplary response to rejection, marked by forming new social bonds, improving intellectual work, and engaging in prosocial behavior.

Social psychology studies have painted a very different picture of how people react to rejection, however. As we saw earlier in this chapter, rejected participants show decreases rather than increases in intelligent thought, and indeed IQ test performance often drops substantially among people who have just been rejected. Instead of seeking to form new social bonds, rejected people often treat new interaction partners with skepticism, aloofness, avoidance, or even outright hostility.[153] Instead of devoting themselves to others, rejected people are typically less generous, less cooperative, and less helpful than others, and they are more willing to cheat or break rules of good behavior.[154] They act in shortsighted, impulsive, even self-destructive ways.[155]

Repeated experiences of rejection or social exclusion (being left out of social groups) can create aggressive tendencies. One study surveyed high school students about various groups in their school, such as "jocks," "potheads," and popular kids. Students reported that they frequently imagined attacking, beating, shooting, and otherwise harming people in groups that had rejected or humiliated them.[156]

School violence grabbed America's attention in the 1990s. The media publicized a series of incidents in which students took guns or other weapons to school and killed other students. Sometimes these were precisely targeted, such as when one killed his ex-girlfriend's new boyfriend. Other shootings seemed more random, such as when a student opened fire in a cafeteria where 400 students were dining, and the widely spraying bullets killed several students and wounded quite a few more.

What drove these students to lethal violence? One common theme was feeling socially excluded. It was never the most popular, well-loved students who brought guns to school and opened fire; rather, it was those who felt picked on, excluded, and rejected by others. A careful investigation of 15 of these incidents concluded that at least 13 of them involved young men who were going through long and painful experiences of being rejected by others.[157]

Aggression and rejection are linked in multiple ways. Aggression can lead to rejection. For example, young children in particular tend to exclude and avoid other children who start fights or engage in bullying (though as the students reach adolescence, this pattern of rejection diminishes, and aggressive adolescents are sometimes accepted by others).[158] In lab studies, students who receive an experience of being rejected by others tend to show high levels of aggression toward someone who offends or provokes them—and, ominously, they are also more aggressive than average toward neutral people who haven't done anything bad to them.[159]

There are a few glimmers of hope. In particular, if the rejected person has some prospect of being accepted or included, either back into the group that excluded him or her or into a new group, then the rejected person's behavior is more positive and prosocial. If someone comes along and is kind to the rejected person, such as by praising the person or being nice in other ways, the rejected person may respond favorably, as by refraining from aggression, by cooperating, or by conforming.[160,161] Rejected people who have a chance to form a new friendship may engage in positive nonverbal behaviors, such as mimicking the nonverbal behavior of the new person;[162] as we have seen, nonverbal mimicry is a positive behavior that helps people come to like each other.

School shooters are typically rejected teens who feel like social outcasts.

AP Images/Mark Duncan

Loneliness

Loneliness is the painful feeling of wanting more human contact or connection than you have. The stereotype of the lonely person is a socially inept loser who doesn't know how to get along with others, who perhaps has little to offer other people, who has few or no friends, and who spends much of the time alone, perhaps envying other people who have friends and lovers. But recent research has begun to paint a very different picture. Lonely people are not that different from non-lonely people. They do not differ in intelligence or attractiveness. They spend about the same amount of time interacting with other people.[163] Thus, lonely does not mean alone: Loneliness is essentially independent of the quantity of relationships or social interaction.[164]

Not all lonely people are the same, either. Researchers have recognized variations in loneliness. It may be quite common for people to feel a temporary loneliness when they move to a new place and are separated from their friends and family. In many cases, those feelings go away as soon as the person starts making friends at the new home. Other people, however, suffer from chronic loneliness that may last for months or years. In general, when researchers speak of lonely people, they are referring to people who suffer chronic loneliness that has lasted for a substantial period of time and is not showing signs of letting up.

By and large, the lonely do not lack social skills, though they somehow fail to use them as much as others (they can get along well with others, but they don't).[165] The main deficiency that has been established is that lonely people are poorer at figuring out other people's emotional states.[166] This lack of emotional sensitivity could be either a cause of loneliness (because it makes it harder to attract and keep friends), or possibly a result, or perhaps both.

These findings indicate that loneliness is much more complex than simply a failure to find other people to be with. You can be lonely living in a densely populated city like New York. You can even be lonely when married, though married people are on average a bit less likely to be lonely than single people.[167,168] Being far from home is one strong predictor of loneliness,[169] which is probably one reason that in many cultures people live their entire lives close to their place of birth and are reluctant to relocate, even for a seemingly great career opportunity.

The long road to social acceptance is a theme to which we have returned repeatedly, and apparently some people find the road too long and difficult—but they pay a price for not making the full effort. Staying close to family is one strategy that seems to shorten the road, in the sense that if your family lives nearby, you have easier and readier access to some forms of social acceptance than if you live far away.

Loneliness originates in a gap between the amount or quality of social relationships that you have and the amount or quality that you want. In principle this can be because you want a normal amount but have less than that—or because you have a normal amount but want a great deal more.[170]

In theory, loneliness can also be an issue of either the quality or the quantity of relationships. You might be lonely because you don't have enough contact with others, or because the time you spend with others does not satisfy your needs. In practice, the data suggest that most loneliness stems from a lack of close, satisfying relationships. Lonely people may spend plenty of time with other people, but just talking to many different people is not good enough, and people may suffer if they do not feel that enough people care about them and want to maintain a long-term, close relationship. Put another way, loneliness is typically rooted in the quality rather than the quantity of social interaction:[171] Lonely people spend plenty of time with others, but they do not come away from these interactions feeling satisfied. To be sure, most research on loneliness has focused on people who live in large cities or universities, and people who are lonely when there are many others around are probably suffering from a lack of quality rather than quantity. Living far from others, such as if you

You can be lonely even when surrounded by people.

loneliness the painful feeling of wanting more human contact or connection than you have

worked as a forest ranger in the Arctic, might produce loneliness for lack of quantity of interaction. Still, in the modern world, most loneliness is linked to quality rather than quantity of interaction.

Relationships to large groups or organizations are relevant for men, though apparently not for women. That is, a man who has few or no close friends but feels strongly connected to his corporation or university or sports team will probably not suffer from loneliness, but a woman in the same circumstance will typically still feel lonely because women tend to care less about large organizations than men do.[172]

Some people can even stave off loneliness by forming attachments to celebrities or people they see on television. Women who watch many situation comedies feel less lonely than other women who have the same number of friends and lovers but do not watch as many shows.[173] Apparently the televised characters come to feel like friends and family to them, especially if they watch the same shows regularly and develop feelings about the characters. Women tend to care more about close relationships with family and friends than men do.

Other people fight off loneliness by forming quasi-relationships with nonhuman entities. For example, they might bond with a dog or cat, or treat a potted plant like a person. Some people even name their cars and treat them like family members.[174] A vivid depiction of such a strategy was provided in the movie *Castaway,* in which Tom Hanks played a Federal Express worker who was stranded on a desert island for many months with no human contact at all. To keep himself sane and stave off loneliness, he painted a face on a volleyball that washed up on the island with him, named the ball "Wilson," and talked to it as if it were a close human friend. In fact, he risked his life to "rescue" Wilson when the ball floated away from his raft.

Loneliness takes its toll on the body. Lonely people sleep as much as non-lonely people, but the sleep is not as good or as refreshing, and they may end up feeling chronically tired. They spend the same amount of time in bed as others, but the lonely person is more prone to lie there awake or to wake up during the night.[175,176] Loneliness also seems to be bad for one's physical health. Lonely people take longer than others to recover from stress, illness, or injury.[177] The poor health stems from several factors, including sleep problems. As lonely people get older, they drink more alcohol and overeat more, and they fail to take care of themselves in many ways. They feel more stress and cope with it more poorly.[178]

What Leads to Social Rejection?

We have seen that being rejected or socially excluded is generally painful and harmful. Why do people inflict such rejection on each other? Several lines of research are starting to furnish answers.

Children are rejected by their peers for three main reasons.[179] First, aggressive children are rejected, possibly because children do not like violence and will avoid bullies and others whom they regard as dangerous. Second, some children withdraw from contact with others, and they in turn are rejected by others. The avoidance of withdrawn, isolated children escalates into adolescence, thereby creating a particular problem for people who move toward adulthood becoming more and more disconnected from social groups.

Third, and related to the other two, deviance leads to rejection. Children who are different in any obvious fashion are more likely to be rejected. Children reject others who look different, act differently, or otherwise seem different. Being handicapped, belonging to a racial minority, speaking differently, not knowing the locally favored style of music or clothing, not watching the same television shows or listening to the same music,

© Blend Images/SuperStock

A relationship with your pet can stave off loneliness.

having an unusual family arrangement (e.g., living with a grandmother rather than parents, or having two daddies or two mommies), or speaking with an accent—any of these can cause a child to be rejected by others. Even being clearly less intelligent or more intelligent than most of the other kids in the class can elicit rejection. This does not mean that the children make a deliberate or conscious decision that they do not approve of someone's personality or lifestyle. In terms of the duplex mind, the reaction against those who are different is probably automatic, and the reaction that leads children to reject others is probably rooted in automatic processes. Remember what you read in the section on attraction: People tend to like others who are similar to them and especially to dislike people who are different. The cruel, rejecting behavior of children may simply be an early form of this general pattern.

Among adults, the simplest and most general explanation for rejection is deviance.[180] Groups reject others who are different in important or meaningful ways from the rest of the group. Indeed, groups seem to find deviants threatening, and they are more bothered by a nonconformist or poor performer who is in the group than by one who is outside the group.[181] This is important evidence of the importance of group solidarity. Someone who is different from your group, but is not part of your group, doesn't threaten the unity of your group. In contrast, someone who is different to the same degree but still belongs to your group undermines group unity. Groups reject insiders more than outsiders for the same degree of deviance.[182]

Bad performance by a member of your own group is rated more negatively than an identically bad performance by someone who is not in the ingroup.[183,184] Conversely, good performance by an ingroup member of the ingroup is rated more positively than identically good performance by an outgroup member. Apparently, groups want their members to be successful, and they will reject members who are prone to failure.

Much deviance involves breaking the rules. Deviants don't do what they are expected or supposed to do. As we saw in the chapter on prosocial behavior, groups can only operate successfully if most people follow most of the rules most of the time, so each act of deviance presents some problem or threat to the success of the group. Deviants therefore undermine the quality of life for the rest of the group. If no one ever steals, for example, you don't need to worry about being robbed, so you don't need to lock your doors, buy security systems, pay for insurance, and take other precautions. The Qur'an (the holy book of Islam) prescribes that societies should cut off the hands of thieves, even someone who just steals a piece of fruit. This strikes many people in other cultures as unfair and excessive, but most likely the underlying sentiment is that the thief isn't just taking someone's piece of fruit—the thief is undermining the trust and security that everyone else would otherwise enjoy. A severe punishment might be justified if it would actually prevent people from doing things that spoil group life for everyone else. In other words, we miss the point if we view Islamic law as cruel or overly punitive for cutting off someone's hand as punishment for stealing a piece of fruit: The hand is cut off because stealing in general undermines trust and degrades the whole fabric of social relationships.

A further reason that groups may reject deviants lies in the so-called **bad apple effect**.[185] This effect is named after the cliché that one bad apple can spoil the whole barrel because the rot that infects one apple can spread to other apples. Applied to social behavior, the implication is that one person who breaks the rules can inspire other people to follow his or her example. As the example of stealing illustrated, the issue from the point of view of society as a whole is that if some people get away with stealing, then others may be tempted to steal also, and chaos can result. Sadly, bad apples seem to inspire more copycats than good apples: People are more easily swayed to follow the example of deviant misbehavior than of virtuous, exemplary, or heroic action.[186] Thus, if you break the group's rules, the group may believe it is best to reject or expel you, lest others follow your bad example.

The threat of being expelled or rejected does seem to be an important force in producing good behavior. When participants were expelled from a group after they had followed the example of a bad apple—and then were reinstated in the group, ostensibly due to an accident or technical problem—they subsequently behaved much better and more prosocially than others, generally following the example of the good rather than the bad

bad apple effect the idea that one person who breaks the rules can inspire other people to break the rules also

apples.[187] Even the threat of being expelled is sometimes enough to discourage people from following bad apples.[188] This is probably an important explanation for why rejection is so powerful and important in life. Human groups need people to follow rules and conform to shared values, and the threat of rejection is a strong force encouraging them to do so.

The link between rejection and deviance has been confirmed in research on families. A large survey[189] asked people what were the worst things that family members do to each other, and how these behaviors related to being rejected by the family. The most commonly cited bad behaviors were seen as justifying expelling someone from the family. Most of these behaviors involved violating the basic rules or expectations that govern how family members are supposed to treat each other. These included rejection, abandonment, disloyalty, sexual abuse, and betrayal, in addition to watching your loved one become (or marry) a loser or criminal.

This research was not meant to pass moral judgment on whether such behaviors justify expulsion from the family. The point is simply that the threat of expulsion discourages people from doing those things to their loved ones. The net result is that family members treat each other better, and the family bonds remain stronger. The (very real) pain of rejection serves the function of holding families and other groups together.

Romantic Rejection and Unrequited Love

Most people experience romantic rejection at some point. They wanted someone for a romantic partner, but that person failed to match those feelings and declined any offers of a relationship. These failed romances can occasionally develop into serious problems, ranging from suicidal despair to violent stalking.

One impressive early paper on romantic rejection used attribution theory to understand the reasons women gave for refusing an offer of a date.[190] As we saw in Chapter 5, many attributions can be sorted along two dimensions: internal/external and stable/unstable. The reasons the women privately held for refusing dates tended to be internal to the man and stable: There was something seriously wrong with him, as she saw it (internal). Also, his deficit was viewed as relatively permanent (stable). But the reasons women gave the men for refusing the date were external and unstable. Thus, when a man she didn't fancy asked her for a date on Friday, she might say that she couldn't go out with him that night because her parents were coming to visit. This reason is external (it has nothing to do with him) and unstable (it pertains only to that particular night, or perhaps that weekend). People are often surprised when the romance-seekers they reject come around again and keep trying, but trying again would seem natural under those circumstances. She can't go out with him this Friday because her parents are coming to visit—so why not ask her out for next Friday? In contrast, if she said, "I can't go out with you because you're not very good-looking, you don't have enough money, you're not smart enough for me, and you smell bad," he would probably be much less likely to respond with "OK, then how about next Friday?" All those reasons for her refusing the offer for this Friday would also apply to next Friday.

Unrequited love is defined as a situation in which one person loves another but the other does not return that love. It is a common experience among adolescents and young adults, and most single people have at least one experience a year in which they have a crush on someone who does not have similar feelings toward them, or (conversely) in which they do not reciprocate someone else's feelings of romantic attraction toward them. The two roles are quite different and go with very different types of feelings. Most men and women have experience in both roles, though men have more experiences of being the rejected lovers, and women are more often in the rejecting role.[191,192]

The rejected lovers experience a kind of emotional roller coaster, in which they alternate between hopeful, exciting, passionate feelings, and insecure despair. They suffer intensely, but they are also drawn to the good parts, and they tend to look back on a failed love with some bittersweet affection. In contrast, the rejecters tend to think there was nothing good about the episode, and they are more likely to wish the whole thing had never happened.[193,194]

© Jonathan Tennant/Alamy

Even adults are often threatened by people who look "different."

unrequited love a situation in which one person loves another but the other does not return that love

off the mark.com   by Mark Parisi

THIS JUDGE IS KNOWN FOR HIS STRICT RESTRAINING ORDERS...

offthemark.com   ©2008 MARK PARISI DIST. BY UFS INC.

Restraining orders for stalkers can sometimes be strict. Don't stalk!

Rejection is felt as a blow to one's self-esteem. Broken-hearted lovers often wonder if something is wrong with them, or if they somehow have some inner flaw that prevented the other from becoming romantically attracted to them. They try to find some way to bolster their self-esteem, and nothing seems to work quite so well as finding a new lover.

Broken-hearted lovers may engage in stalking behaviors toward the rejecter. **Stalking** refers to persisting in romantic or courtship behavior (e.g., repeated phone calls) or other behaviors that frighten and harass the rejecter in the relationship.[195,196,197] Although unrequited love is something that both genders experience, women are disproportionately the victims of stalkers (possibly because they are more likely than men to be the rejecters). Data from the National Violence Against Women Survey showed that women report being stalked in the context of current or former romantic partners (marriage, cohabitation, or dating), whereas men rarely reported being stalked in the context of a current or former romantic relationship.[198] Male and female victims of stalking reported feeling that their safety was being threatened and some even carried weapons to protect themselves far more than nonvictims (45% vs. 29%) Thus, the sting of unrequited love may lead rejected people to stalk their rejecters, and this tendency is particularly strong among rejected men.

For the rejecters, the problem is not low self-esteem but guilt. As the concept of a need to belong implies, people are designed to form and maintain relationships, not to reject them, and most people find that refusing someone's offer of love is difficult. They feel guilty for hurting the other person, and to minimize feelings of guilt they strive to convince themselves that they never led the other person on, so that the other person's love and resultant suffering were not their fault. Guilt is a central part of the difficulty of rejecting someone, and this difficulty is probably linked to a basic fact about human nature: Humans are programmed to form and maintain social bonds, and breaking bonds goes against the grain. Even if you don't want someone's love, it is difficult and sometimes painful to refuse it.

The message of rejection is difficult for both persons. The rejecter feels guilty and wants to avoid hurting the other person's feelings. The person who is about to be rejected is often eager to grasp at straws and seize on any sign of possible encouragement. It is therefore no wonder that the message often does not get communicated very well: The one doesn't want to say it, and the other doesn't want to hear it.

As we have seen, the road to social acceptance is often long. Rarely does it seem longer or harder than in unrequited love. Loving someone who does not return your feelings can be extremely discouraging and painful. And even rejecting someone's love is not usually easy.

stalking persisting in romantic, courtship, or other behaviors that frighten and harass the rejecter in a relationship

QUIZ YOURSELF

Rejection

answers: see pg 401

1. **Being excluded, rejected, and ignored by others is what social psychologists call _____ .**

   (a) propinquity   (b) loneliness   (c) ostracism   (d) bad apple effect

2. **What personality trait is formed as a result of repeated rejection?**

   (a) Extraversion   (b) Introversion   (c) Rejection sensitivity   (d) Self-monitoring

3. **What is the main difference between lonely and non-lonely people?**

   (a) Lonely people are less attractive.   (b) Lonely people are less emotionally sensitive.   (c) Lonely people are less intelligent.   (d) Lonely people are less socially skilled.

4. **Loneliness is primarily determined by the _____ of relationships.**

   (a) quality   (b) quantity   (c) both (a) and (b)   (d) neither (a) nor (b)

What Makes Us *Human*

Much of what we have seen in this chapter is not unique to human beings. Many social animals seek social acceptance and try to avoid being rejected. Good-looking, rewarding, similar others are attractive. Deviants are vulnerable to rejection. Most social animals (and that category includes nearly all the close biological relatives of humankind) want to be allowed to belong to a group and want to avoid being rejected or excluded.

The human quest for belongingness has, however, some special features, or at least twists. The basic need to belong may be the same in humans as in other animals, but some of the processes are different. People use language to form and maintain relationships, and this enables them to disclose much more information about themselves. People can be similar or dissimilar on many dimensions that other animals cannot process: religion, favorite sports team, zodiac sign, political opinions, and many more. More broadly, humans traverse a long road to social acceptance, which means they have to spend a large and ongoing amount of time and energy to secure and maintain their place in the social group. A bird or frog can gain access to the group simply by being there and joining in, but humans who seek social acceptance need money, skills, the right clothes, an understanding of complex social norms, and much else.

Human social systems are more complex than those of other creatures, so there is more emphasis on being special or unique. We have seen that being similar is important for attraction, in humans as in other animals, but culture also places value on diversity. A culture is a system, and a system made up of all identical parts is not much of a system. Whether you are finding a niche in your career or persuading a loved one to choose you instead of a romantic rival, you may often feel some pressure to establish yourself as different or special. Put very simply, if you can do something useful that no one else in your small group can do (find a particular food, make fire, install plumbing, fix computers, prepare income tax returns, kick long field goals), you are safe: They cannot afford to exclude you. The strategy of promoting social acceptance via unique abilities is largely unknown outside of human beings, but it is very important in our human social life. Put more simply, most social animals seek acceptance via similarity, and humans do too, but only humans cultivate social acceptance by trying to be special or different.

Another striking difference is that human relationships are not just between the two people involved: They often require some validation or recognition by the culture. Animals have families, but these do not have legal status. If the father becomes separated from his offspring, he is not required—except among humans—to pay child support year after year. Both humans and animals experience romantic attraction and sexual mating, but only humans formalize the bond with a wedding license and a ceremony, so that every member of the large social group recognizes the bond and knows what it means. Animals can break up just by wandering off, whereas married humans require a divorce court. In the same vein, many animals neglect or even abuse their young, but only humans have formal systems to stop this, such as police or legal intervention. Animals may sometimes work together to build something, but only humans sign contracts or incorporate their partnerships or sue each other when the project fails.

Divorce courts, police interventions, and lawsuits may seem like an unpleasant aspect of human relationships. What have we done to ourselves? Yet these institutions represent something very positive: Human society has sought to protect people from betrayal and abuse by their relationship partners. Culture recognizes, validates, and encourages relationships, and ultimately it reduces some of the risk and suffering that go with the process of connecting with someone. If two animals work together to get some food and then the bigger one takes it all, the smaller one is simply out of luck. The more vulnerable human being, however, may go to court or try some other cultural recourse, and because the system is there, the stronger one is less likely to cheat or betray in the first place. In such ways, culture makes relationships stronger and better.

CHAPTER 11 SUMMARY

The Need to Belong

- Social acceptance means getting others to like you, respect you, approve of you, and in general want to have some kind of relationship with you.

- Rejection, also known as social exclusion, means that others exclude you, so that you are not able to form or keep a social bond with them.

- Testosterone, a hormone associated with masculinity, is a mixed blessing, both for the individual who has it and for others connected with that person; it is better suited to finding mates than to maintaining stable families.

- The need to belong, defined as the desire to form and maintain close, lasting relationships, is a powerful drive within the human psyche.

- According to social brain theory, the driving force behind the evolution of intelligence and the brain was the need to understand others so as to form and maintain social relationships.
- People usually form relationships easily and readily but are reluctant to let relationships end.
- The need to belong has two parts:
  - Regular social contact with others.
  - Close, stable, mutually intimate contact.
- Failure to satisfy the need to belong leads to significant health problems, up to and including a higher risk of death.

Attraction: Who Likes Whom?

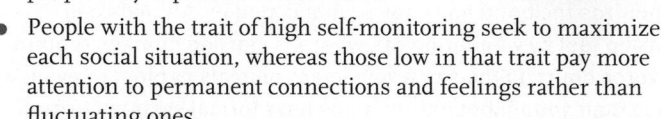

- Ingratiation is actively to try to make someone like you.
- Similarity is a common and significant cause of attraction.
- People prepare for social interaction by shifting to become more similar to the people they expect to interact with.
- People with the trait of high self-monitoring seek to maximize each social situation, whereas those low in that trait pay more attention to permanent connections and feelings rather than fluctuating ones.
- The matching hypothesis states that people tend to pair up with others who are equally attractive.
- As culture progresses and forms large, complex, interacting groups, there may be more need for complementarity, but when people pick their friends and lovers, they still tend to look for those who are similar to themselves.
- In general, favors are a good way to promote liking.
- Praising people is a reliable way to get them to like you.
- Liking begets (reciprocal) liking.
- Mimicry is often successful as a means of increasing liking.
- Propinquity (being near someone on a regular basis) causes attraction, but it also can to lead to conflict and friction.
- Familiarity breeds liking.
- The social allergy effect refers to the finding that a partner's annoying habits grow more annoying with repeated exposure.
- When all else is equal, most people show a substantial preference for attractive over unattractive others.
- The what is beautiful is good effect suggests that people assume that physically attractive people will be superior to others on many other traits.
- Attractive children are more popular with other children than their less attractive peers, and teachers like them more, too.
- Evolutionary psychologists generally think that beauty is linked to signs of being a good mate and potential partner, which especially means being young and healthy.
- Symmetry is a powerful source of beauty.
- Average faces are more attractive than individual faces.
- Women are more attracted to men who look rich and successful.

- Many people find romantic partners online, which has both advantages (e.g., more potential partners to choose from) and disadvantages (e.g., easier for potential partners to mislead others or even lie to them).

Rejection

- Ostracism refers to being excluded, rejected, and ignored by others.
- Being rejected repeatedly can cause people to develop expectations that others will reject them, resulting in a personality trait called rejection sensitivity.
- "You hurt my feelings" is usually tied to an implicit message that "you don't care about our relationship."
- The initial reaction to rejection is often closer to numbness than to anxiety or sadness. It can interfere with normal psychological and cognitive functioning.
- Pain killers such as Tylenol can reduce social pain as well as physical pain.
- Rejection undermines self-regulation and often makes people behave selfishly rather than acting in a socially conscientious manner.
- Repeated experiences of rejection or social exclusion can create aggressive tendencies.
- Aggression can lead to rejection.
- Loneliness is the painful feeling of wanting more human contact or connection (either more quantity or quality of relationships) than you have.
- There are very few differences between lonely and non-lonely people, with the major exception that lonely people are poorer at figuring out other people's emotional states.
- Loneliness is bad for physical health.
- Children are rejected by their peers for three main reasons:
  - Because they are aggressive or violent.
  - Because they are withdrawn or socially isolated.
  - Because they are different from other children in some way.
- Among adults, the simplest and most general explanation for rejection is deviance.
- Groups reject insiders more than outsiders for the same degree of deviance.
- The bad apple effect suggests that one person who breaks the rules can inspire other people to follow his or her example.
- Humans are programmed to form and maintain social bonds; breaking them goes against the grain and makes the rejecter feel guilty.

What Makes Us Human? Putting the Cultural Animal in Perspective

- Human social systems are more complex than those of other creatures, so there is more emphasis on each individual being special or unique.
- Human relationships often require some validation or recognition by the culture.

key terms

attraction 373
bad apple effect 396
ingratiation 378
loneliness 394
matching hypothesis 379

need to belong 376
ostracism 388
propinquity 382
reinforcement theory 380
rejection (social exclusion) 373

rejection sensitivity 390
self-monitoring 379
social acceptance 373
social allergy effect 383
stalking 398

unrequited love 397
what is beautiful is good
    effect 383

quiz yourself ANSWERS

1. The Need to Belong **p.377**
   answers: 1.b 2.d 3.c 4.b

2. Attraction: Who Likes Whom? **p.388**
   answers: 1.b 2.c 3.b 4.b

3. Rejection **p.398**
   answers: 1.c 2.c 3.b 4.a

CLOSE RELATIONSHIPS
Passion, Intimacy, and Sexuality

LEARNING OBJECTIVES

1 Describe the different types of love.

2 Differentiate exchange and communal relationships.

3 Describe the four styles of attachment.

4 Identify the factors that are important to maintaining relationships over time.

5 Use the theories of sexuality to explain sexual attitudes and behavior.

6 Summarize the work on sexual jealousy.

Fancy Photography/Veer

The Spencer family gave birth to their third daughter in July of 1961. Her parents could hardly have suspected that their daughter would become a royal princess and the heartthrob of millions. Their own marriage crumbled, and years later Diana said she never forgot the sound of her mother's footsteps crunching on the gravel driveway as she left their home on the day of their divorce in 1969. In 1975 her father became the Earl of Spencer, which automatically elevated his family (including Diana) into the aristocracy. At school, Diana was a mediocre student but a good athlete. She did not go on to college. Instead, she worked at a series of dull jobs.

In 1977 Diana and her older sister Sarah were invited to a party, where they met Charles, the Prince of Wales. Sarah was originally regarded as the more promising girlfriend for him, and he dated her for a while, but soon Charles found himself attracted to the blossoming young beauty Diana. The attraction was mutual.

The match seemed improbable, which lent the entire episode the aura of a fairy tale. On their wedding day in 1981, he was 32 years old, whereas she was just 19. He was in line to become king of England, whereas she was working as a kindergarten assistant. The public continued to see him as a somewhat odd-looking and awkward fellow, whereas Diana was soon accepted as one of the world's great beauties, and her wardrobe became a source of fascination and imitation throughout the world. Their first public appearances were marked by an easygoing rapport between them and by a seemingly obvious pleasure in each other's company. When their engagement was announced, reporters asked them whether they were in love, and both said "Yes!" though Charles added "whatever love means" (a line that certainly won him no points as a dashing, romantic suitor!).

Their wedding, shortly before Diana's 20th birthday, was an international event. An estimated 600,000 people lined the streets to watch the wedding party go from Buckingham Palace to St. Paul's Cathedral. Millions of people around the world watched it on television. Diana later said that on that day she was "so in love with my husband that I couldn't take my eyes off him" and that she felt herself the luckiest woman in the world. And even if the prince did look a bit odd, the lavishly spectacular wedding seemed a perfect ending for a fairy tale in which an ordinary schoolgirl grew up, fell in love with a (sort of) handsome prince, married him in the so-called wedding of the century, thence to settle down and wait until they would someday become king and queen. In reality, the fairy tale was not over but would take a non-fairy-tale turn in the coming months.

Diana quickly became pregnant and produced a son who also would become heir to the throne, and two years later the couple had another son. The public took "Princess Di" into its heart, and she responded by trying to be perfect in her role. She supported charity causes, visited hospitals, and did other good deeds, all the while trying to raise their royal sons properly. Everything seemed perfect.

But things were not perfect, and indeed the marriage went downhill, first secretly, then more publicly. Her husband, Charles, did not come to love her as she wanted. Indeed, when they first got engaged, he privately told a friend he did not love her yet (though he expected that he would soon). More problematically, he retained strong ties to his mistress, Camilla Parker Bowles, even inviting her to the wedding, and continued his sexual affair with her after the wedding. Camilla Parker Bowles was also married at the time and had two children of her own. Diana later said in a BBC interview, "There were three of us in the marriage. It was a bit crowded." Her assessment won her widespread sympathy, though some subsequent reports have claimed that her comment was not entirely honest because at that time there was a fourth person in the marriage too—namely, Diana's lover.

Apparently, once the princess concluded that she was not getting the love she wanted from her husband, she sought it elsewhere. She had an affair with a handsome riding instructor on the palace staff. He fell hard for her. After five years, she broke it off. (The head of palace security took the riding instructor aside and told him how to deal with the breakup: "Well, look, you know, if it's over, consider yourself to have been in a very privileged position. Really, that's the end of it. Live with that memory.") She was hurt when he wrote a book about his affair with her.

Prince Charles and Diana, Princess of Wales, on their wedding day, July 29, 1981.

Keystone/Hulton Archive/Getty Images

AP Images/John Stillwell/Pool

Prince Charles and his lover Camilla Parker Bowles who later became his second wife.

Another affair, this time with an art dealer, also ended badly when the man broke up with her and went back to his wife. The man started receiving nuisance hang-up calls, and after several hundred of these he went to the police, who traced the calls to the princess. (In some contexts, such behavior can be considered stalking, though no one is likely to prosecute a royal princess for it.) Another affair with a professional athlete also led to a highly publicized blowup.

These were hard times for Diana. She developed psychological symptoms, including eating disorders and self-mutilation (cutting herself). She worried that the royal family was plotting to ruin her image and even to kill her. She was intensely lonely and depressed. She heard her separation from Charles announced on the radio and thought "the fairy tale [has] come to an end." Four years later, in 1996, they were officially divorced.

In 1997, she thought she had finally found a new love to satisfy her. She told a friend, "I'm no longer lonely. I know what love is now." There were several men in her life, and there is some dispute as to which relationship she meant. We may never know, because on the last day of August she was killed in a car crash in the Pont de l'Alma road tunnel in Paris. Her death provoked an international outpouring of grief, including huge demonstrations of affection in London and elsewhere. The authorities were shocked by how many people came to express their grief and how many people's lives she had seemingly touched in some way. It is estimated that 6 million people crowded the streets of London for her funeral procession. A giant crowd listened via loudspeakers outside the funeral ceremony, and their applause

was so loud that the people indoors were disturbed to hear it.

The public reaction to her death was so strong that the authorities planned a ceremony a year later to commemorate its anniversary. Turnout was much lower than expected. Apparently the public had gotten over its grief. The love of the public is short-lived, resembling passion more than intimacy or commitment. There was, however, a revival of affection for Diana in 2005, when Charles announced his intention to marry his longtime mistress Camilla. Diana's fans protested the marriage. A second revival occurred in 2011, when Prince William, the elder son of Prince Charles and Diana, married Catherine Middleton, whose parents were once flight attendants. ●

Chris Ison/PA Photos/Landov

Prince William, elder son of Prince Charles and Diana, Princess of Wales, kissing Miss Catherine Middleton on their wedding day.

What Is Love?

"I'm a 17-year-old girl and I think I'm in love, but my parents say I don't know what real love is. What is love and how can I tell if I'm really in love?"[1] Thus wrote a young woman to the Kinsey Institute, asking an earnest and personal question—and one that most people have struggled with at some point.

No simple answer can be given. Part of the problem is that there is more than one kind of love, so more than one phenomenon needs to be explained. The same person might feel different kinds of love toward several different people, even at the same point in his or her life. Most American adults say "I love you" into the telephone to their mothers on Mother's Day, for example, but what they mean by those three words is probably quite

different from what they mean when saying "I love you" while kissing and hugging the person to whom they are engaged to be married.

Although the next section will distinguish two main types of love, recent work addressing the question of "What is love?" has produced one common feature that most people endorse. It is investment in the well-being of the other for his or her own sake. In other words, if James truly loves Angela, then he wants her to be happy, healthy, successful, and otherwise well off, regardless of any benefit to himself. In recent studies, participants rated this investment in the other's well-being as an end in itself as a common and essential feature of very different kinds of love relationship, including romantic love, parental love, nonsexual love between two adult female friends, and the caring love someone who takes care of a chronically ill man.[2] Caring for the other person regardless of one's personal gain may thus be a defining aspect of love in general.

Passionate and Companionate Love

An important distinction between two main kinds of love has emerged from many years of research.[3] The experts called the two kinds of love "passionate" and "companionate." By **passionate love** they mean having strong feelings of longing, desire, and excitement toward a special person. Passionate love (also called **romantic love**) makes people want to spend as much time as possible together, to touch each other and engage in other physical intimacies (often including sex), to think about each other and feel joy merely upon seeing each other, and to exhibit other patterns that suggest strong emotions.

In contrast, **companionate love** (sometimes called **affectionate love**) is less strongly emotional; it tends to be calmer and more serene. Companionate love means perceiving the other person as your soul mate or special partner. It signifies a high level of mutual understanding and caring and in many cases a commitment to make the relationship succeed. As the term implies, companionate love is what makes people want to remain each other's good companions. Someone high in companionate love is likely to say things like "My wife is my best friend." That kind of love is not the same as what usually motivates people to start a new sexual relationship, but it may be essential to a successful long-term marriage.

There is probably a physiological, even biochemical, difference between the two kinds of love. People who feel passionately in love have high levels of phenylethylamine (PEA), a neurotransmitter that enables information to travel from one brain cell to another.[4,5] This chemical produces strong emotional feelings, including those "tingling" sensations of excitement and euphoria that you get when the person you love walks into the room or holds your hand. It also helps produce high intensity and frequency of sexual desire. The emotional churning and the sense of being in an altered state (sometimes compared to being high on drugs) is very likely linked to some chemical in the body, and PEA is a leading candidate, although further research is needed, and passionate love may affect more than one chemical. In any case, companionate love does not seem to be characterized by these elevated levels of PEA.

Love and Culture

Love changes over the years.

The PEA response suggests that passionate love involves something more basic than cultural learning, although undoubtedly culture can work with or against the biochemical responses to love objects. The question of whether romantic love is universal or is simply a product of Western culture has been fiercely debated. Some authorities[6] have argued that romantic love is a cultural construction, possibly introduced into Western culture by the Crusaders or troubadours, who brought it from the Middle East and elaborated it into its mythological status at the royal courts of Europe (where most marriages were arranged for political reasons, so passionate love flourished in extramarital affairs), and then embraced as one of the culture's main goals and values during the so-called Romantic Period (roughly 1775–1850). From the social constructionist view, cultural values and meanings have shaped personal feelings and changed the way people run their lives, and the cultural construction of love is an important case in point.

passionate love (romantic love) strong feelings of longing, desire, and excitement toward a special person

companionate love (affectionate love) mutual understanding and caring to make the relationship succeed

More recent cross-cultural work, however, has begun to suggest that passionate love is not merely a product of Western culture. In 1995, anthropologist William Jankowiak published a painstaking, influential book titled *Romantic Passion: A Universal Experience?*[7] His answer was yes. Careful anthropological investigations led him to the conclusion that romantic love is indeed found everywhere (that is, in the vast majority of cultures he surveyed around the world, though not in every single one). This is not to suggest that culture plays no role. The forms and expressions of romantic passion vary significantly, as does the culture's attitude toward passionate love. Modern Western culture (whose influence is certainly spreading through many parts of the world) has come to regard passionate love as an important part of life, so that if you never experience it, you will have missed out on a major form of fulfillment. Possibly, people in other cultures feel love as we do but do not place the same value on it and do not feel that a life without passionate love is by definition a lesser life.

Romantic love is not just an invention of Western culture.

© Peter Coombs/Alamy

In fact, passionate love may seem like a form of temporary insanity. Thus, although most cultures have recognized the existence of passionate love, different cultures and even different eras in Western culture have held very different attitudes toward it. One historian concluded that in bygone centuries in Europe, people regarded passionate love as a form of mental imbalance that made people feel and act in strange, even crazy ways. They did not think that passionate love was a good reason to marry someone; indeed, proposing marriage while in love would strike them as similar to making any major life decision while drunk or on drugs! And they certainly didn't think that passionate love made a good basis for marriage.[8] Companionate love seemed a much better bet.

Passionate love may therefore be found among humans everywhere, but how they experience it and how they regard it may depend on their culture. People are hooked into their cultural system, and the system can influence how they love.

Love Across Time

Companionate love may be harder to create than passionate love, which often arises spontaneously and without people trying to fall in love. Companionate love is what makes a good marriage or a stable, trustworthy, lasting relationship, but it takes sustained work and effort to build trust, intimacy, and other foundations of companionate love. Passionate love may be the most effective emotion for starting a relationship; companionate love may be the most effective emotion for making it succeed and survive in the long run.

One reason for skepticism about passionate love as the basis for marriage is that it tends to be temporary.[9] This is hard for most people to appreciate, especially young people who may not yet have spent many years in the same romantic relationship and who think that their passionate feelings are sure to be permanent. But most people experience passionate love for a relatively brief period in a relationship—a year, perhaps, or two or three at most, if one is very lucky. A few lucky couples report still feeling passionate love even after many years together, but these are rare exceptions to the general pattern of declining passion.[10,11] If the relationship continues, it tends to rely more on companionate love. A successful long-term relationship thus depends on making an effective transition from one kind of love to the other.

A behavioral sign of the decrease in passion can be found in data about frequency of sexual intercourse. Many studies have found that as time goes by, the average married couple has sex less and less often.[12,13,14,15,16,17] Newlyweds generally live up to the stereotype

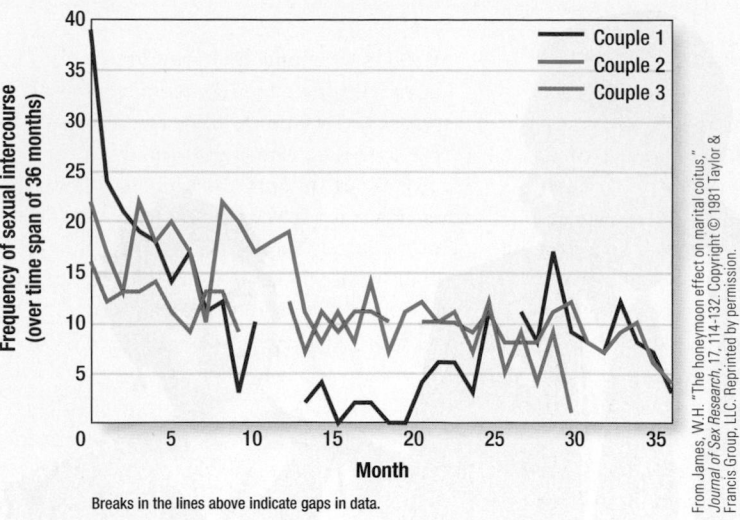

Frequency of sexual intercourse (over time span of 36 months)

Couple 1
Couple 2
Couple 3

Month

Breaks in the lines above indicate gaps in data.

From James, W.H. "The honeymoon effect on marital coitus." *Journal of Sex Research*, 17, 114-132. Copyright © 1981 Taylor & Francis Group, LLC. Reprinted by permission.

FIGURE 12.1

For most couples, sex is most frequent during the first month and first year after their wedding and declines after that. [237]

of passionate young lovers who have relatively frequent sex. But this does not last. Research shows that the frequency of sexual intercourse declines by about half after the first year of marriage, from about 18 times per month during the first year to about 9 times per month in the second year.[18] It continues to decrease more slowly after that (see **FIGURE 12.1**). Likewise, studies that follow married couples over many years find that they start off having sex relatively often, but that this frequent rate decreases sharply at first and then continues to go down as the couple grows old together.[19] The decline in frequency of sex is not entirely due to aging. If a couple has a long marriage, their frequency of sex goes down, but if they then divorce and remarry, they typically show a big increase in sexual frequency with their new partners.[20] To learn more about the relationship between marriage and sex, see *Tradeoffs*.

The biochemical rush associated with high levels of PEA (if that is indeed the chemical component of love) is thus not destined to be permanent. It is probably a feature linked to new love and the forming of a new relationship bond. Unfortunately, many people probably mistake its normal and natural decline for a sign that they are no longer in love. They stop feeling swept away, and in particular their feelings of sexual desire for each other may dwindle to the individuals' normal, baseline levels, but the two people may mistake this process to mean that they have lost interest in each other or, even more ominously, that the other person has ceased to love them.

The story of Prince Charles and Diana, at the beginning of this chapter, illustrates the difference between passionate and companionate love. The start of their romance captured the world's imagination because it seemingly embodied the vital features of passionate love: a beautiful woman, a royal prince, blossoming attraction culminating in a spectacular wedding and then the birth of two handsome sons. Apparently, though, Charles and Diana failed to make the transition to companionate love, and their years together were not marked by intimacy, mutual devotion, and becoming each other's best friend. When passionate love fails to convert into companionate love (regardless of whether that is actually what transpired between Charles and Diana), the story line is likely to be one of a wonderful, romantic beginning followed by a downward spiral of stress, disappointment, estrangement, and ultimate failure. Fortunately, many people avoid that fate and do sustain a happy marriage for a long time or even a lifetime.

Sternberg's Triangle

Robert Sternberg has proposed a more elaborate theory of the nature of love.[22] Instead of speaking of two different kinds of love, Sternberg proposed that love is composed of three different ingredients (see **FIGURE 12.2**). The first of these is **passion**, which he explained in terms of feelings of romantic attraction, physical attraction to the other person, and sexual interest. Passion is largely an emotional state and is characterized by high bodily arousal: When you feel passion, your heart beats more rapidly than usual, you become excited and alert, and you may also feel sexual arousal. Passion makes people want to be together and in many cases makes them want to kiss, hold hands, and perhaps have sex.

passion an emotional state characterized by high bodily arousal, such as increased heart rate and blood pressure

FIGURE 12.2

The triangle on the left represents a relationship that is high in intimacy and passion, but low in commitment. The triangle on the right represents a relationship that is high in intimacy and commitment but low in passion.

© Cengage Learning

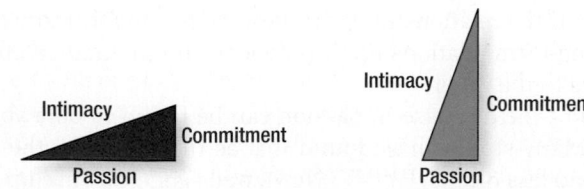

Intimacy — Commitment — Passion

Intimacy — Commitment — Passion

Sex In and Out of Marriage

It often seems as if married and single people envy each other. Single people think it must be wonderful to have a loving, devoted sex partner who sleeps with you every night, and they anticipate that getting married finally brings on a lifetime of great sex. Married people imagine that single life is full of sexual adventure and novelty, trying new acts and new partners anytime one wants instead of going to bed with the same old person according to the same old routine.

Of course, people have many reasons to marry (or not to marry), but we focus here on the links between marriage and sex, as indicated by the National Health and Social Life Survey.[21] The data suggest, first, that neither of the stereotypes invoked in the preceding paragraph is entirely correct. Frequent passionate sex, as seen in movies and novels, appears to be fairly unusual, and only a tiny fraction (8%) of married or single people have sex more than three times per week. Married people do have more sex than single people, or at least more than single people who are not cohabiting with a romantic partner. Living together without marriage is marked by the highest rates of sexual activity, though living together may not be the cause; unmarried cohabitation is mainly found among young people early in a relationship, and such individuals may have more sexual desire than older, long-married couples. Cohabitors also do not have many of the distractions of married life, such as small children, who can interfere with time and energy (and even privacy!) needed for sex. If you compare married people and single cohabitors of the same age, the frequency of sex is pretty similar, although the married people still have sex somewhat less often.

Thus, married people have more sex, in terms of quantity—but what about quality? Quality of sex is harder to measure, but one index might be how long people spend on a given sex act. By this measure, it looks as though single people have better sex. Married sex is more likely than unmarried sex to be finished in less than 15 minutes. Single persons are more likely than married ones to spend more than an hour on a single sexual event. Single people are also more likely than married ones to say that their most recent sex act included some activity beyond basic genital intercourse, which is another sign that they put effort and imagination into sex.

Not all signs of quality favor the single. When asked whether their most recent sex partner brought them physical or emotional satisfaction, married people are more likely than single ones to say yes. (Orgasm rates were nearly identical, however.) This may be partly because the marriage relationship contains love (and hence emotional satisfaction), and partly because a married spouse knows how to please you better than someone who is unfamiliar with your body. Single people are more likely than married ones to report consuming alcohol before sex, and alcohol does interfere with sexual responsiveness. Then again, at least the single people who drink before sex share the enjoyment of drinking; married people are prone to drink alone before sex, if at all.

One last and probably unsurprising difference is that single people have more sex partners than married ones. Though not all married people are faithful, most are, so marriage really does seem to entail settling down with one regular sex partner. Single people are more likely than married ones to have had several sex partners in the past year—then again, they are also more likely to have had none at all.

The relationship between marriage and sex thus appears to be a tradeoff. Married people have more frequent sex. Single people have more partners. Married people benefit from a partner who knows their responses and who loves them. Single people spend more time and energy on each sex act and try more things. For many single people, life alternates between periods of exciting sex with a new partner and periods of no sex with any partner. For many married people, sex conforms to a stable and regular pattern of familiar activities, once or twice a week.

The second ingredient in Sternberg's scheme is **intimacy**. Intimacy, in his view, is the common core of all love relationships. It refers to feeling close to the other person. Empathy is important in intimacy; indeed, intimacy includes a sense of understanding the partner and being understood by him or her. Intimacy also entails a mutual concern for each other's welfare and happiness. When two people have a high degree of intimacy, they have a basic feeling of caring and concern about one another, they want each other to be happy and healthy, and they may often seek to do things that will benefit each other. Intimate partners try to take care of each other, and they emphasize communication about their lives, feelings, and problems.

The third ingredient is decision and **commitment**. Sternberg observed that when many people speak of love, they refer more to a conscious decision than to a feeling state. Emotions come and go, but commitments based on decisions remain constant unless they are deliberately revoked. For example, if you ask someone whether she loves her husband or her children, she may say, "Of course!" without having to think about it. If love referred only to passion, she would have to stop and examine her emotions at

intimacy a feeling of closeness, mutual understanding, and mutual concern for each other's welfare and happiness

commitment a conscious decision that remains constant

off the mark.com by Mark Parisi

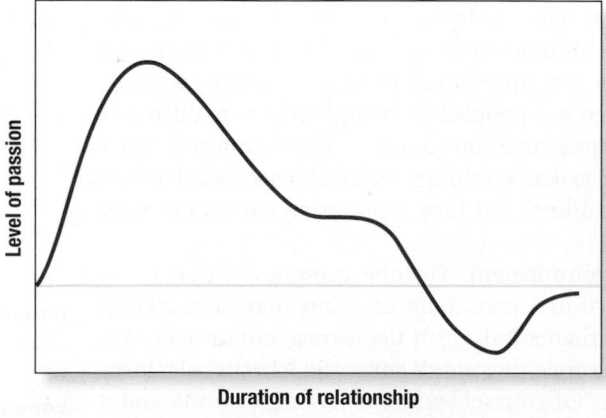

HOW ABOUT IF I JUST WRITE YOUR NAME IN SUNSCREEN AND GET A BAD SUNBURN INSTEAD?

TATTOOS
LYNN
OPEN

MARK PARISI 8-20

This man does not seem committed to his partner.

that moment to see whether she actually felt passionate attraction toward the other person. But if love means commitment, and she has made that commitment, then she can say, "Of course!" without requiring a survey of her current inner feelings.

Passion, intimacy, and commitment are not three different "kinds" of love. Instead, Sternberg proposed that any given love relationship can mix those three ingredients in any combination. Some love relationships might have high intimacy, high commitment, but low passion. Others might have plenty of passion and commitment but little intimacy. Can you think of examples of those types? The first (high intimacy and commitment but low passion) might describe a marriage that is still strong after many decades. The second might describe a "whirlwind romance" in which two people fall madly in love and marry quickly, before they have gotten to know each other very well.

An ideal love might contain substantial measures of all three ingredients. If none of the three is present, Sternberg would say, there is no love. In his research, he concluded that intimacy is the most common ingredient; relatively few relationships utterly lack intimacy. Still, the feeling called "love at first sight" usually involves low intimacy; you hardly know the person yet, and passion is the main ingredient.

The three ingredients typically have different time courses. Passion can arise quickly—but as already noted, passion also tends to diminish after a while. Intimacy, in contrast, arises more slowly but can continue increasing for a long time, and it often remains high after it stops rising.[23,24] One theme of this book is the long road to social acceptance, and nowhere is the length of this road more obvious than in the slow, long-term development of an intimate relationship. The bond of intimacy continues to solidify for years. Last, decisions and commitments are typically made at particular points in time (such as agreeing to stop dating other people, or proposing marriage).

The shift from passionate to companionate love is explained by Sternberg's theory in terms of a change in the mixture of love's three ingredients (see **FIGURE 12.3**). Companionate love emphasizes intimacy and commitment, whereas passionate love consists mainly of passion (obviously). Commitment may help solidify the trust and mutual concern that contribute to companionate love. Thus, a typical long-term sexual relationship might start out consisting mainly of passion, but over time the intimacy grows stronger as passion grows weaker, and at some point a decision is made to solidify a long-range commitment. Commitment can help keep the couple together during periods of conflict or dissatisfaction, which many couples experience sooner or later. If the commitment is not made, or if intimacy does not grow, then the relationship is likely to break up after the early stage. The couple may still experience a great deal of passion, but once the

FIGURE 12.3

Passion and intimacy have different time courses over a relationship. Passion increases dramatically and then tends to decline steadily over time, whereas intimacy starts low and tends to increase over time.

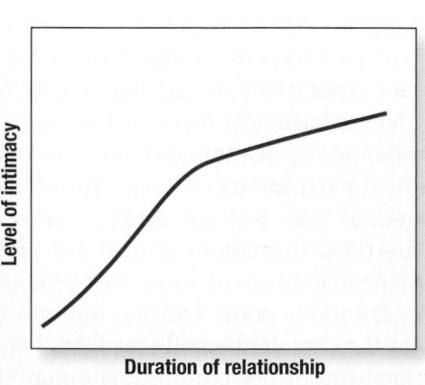

Level of passion

Duration of relationship

Level of intimacy

Duration of relationship

passion dies down, there may be little to replace it, and they will run out of reasons to stay together.

Benefits of Commitment

Of the three components in Sternberg's theory of love, passion and intimacy are familiar to everyone, but commitment may seem like a surprise as a third. Social psychologists have begun to explore relationship commitment more recently than the other two. What makes people make the leap and tie the knot?

An appealing relationship, with lots of passion and rising intimacy, is one factor that makes people ready to commit. But another may be fear of being single.[25] Many people have a deep fear of ending up alone in life. These fears motivate people to "settle for less": They lower their standards for relationship partners. They are more willing to pair up and stay with lower-quality partners, as compared to people with less fear of being single. If dissatisfied with a relationship, they are less likely to initiate a breakup, because they are afraid of being alone.

When a commitment is made, however, it changes the relationship, typically by making it stronger. Commitment may not matter much as long as both partners are deliriously happy together, but it helps when there are problems and conflicts. A commitment such as marriage may motivate a couple to work out their differences rather than splitting up. Even the problems may be contained better: Recent studies showed that romantic couples respond less aggressively to each other's provocations and misdeeds (such as criticizing the partner, flirting with someone else, or neglecting each other's needs and desires) to the extent that they were committed.[26] That is, commitment to the relationship reduced aggression within it.

That doesn't mean that commitment prevents problems. It can make them worse, in a way. After all, the more you care about the relationship, the more its problems will disturb you. The benefits of commitment are more visible over time than at once. A well-designed recent study found that higher levels of relationship commitment made people more sensitive and vulnerable to relationship problems in the short run—but also made them more resilient to these problems in the long run.[27] The two may go together. Being bothered by conflicts right away may motivate people to address them and solve them, which they can do better with a stronger commitment basis.

Weddings are themselves important devices for commitment, because the young couple makes formal statements of commitment to each other. Weddings are of course something that only cultural animals do. Other animals may mate for long periods, even for life, but they do not cement the bond with a meaningful public ceremony. Some recent work has examined effects of wedding characteristics on commitment.[28] Perhaps surprisingly, spending a large amount of money on the ring or the wedding ceremony failed to reduce the likelihood of divorce and in fact may have increased it. That is, couples who spent more on the wedding and the ring had higher rates of divorce. What did reduce the likelihood of divorce was having a lot of people at the wedding. Thus, the beneficial effects of the wedding are more about the impact on one's social world than about spending a lot of money.

The role of physical attractiveness and sexual desire in marriage has been much disputed. New data suggest that women whose male partners valued them for their bodies had higher satisfaction with the relationship than other women—provided that the man also valued her other traits and was committed.[29] Being valued for her body by a man whose commitment was low or who failed to appreciate other (non-body) qualities did lower the women's satisfaction. The implication for men who want happy wives and girlfriends is to show commitment and appreciate the woman's other qualities, but then also to express plenty of desire and appreciation for her physical charms too. Similar results are found for being valued for sex, as in being a good sex partner and engaging in frequent sex:[30] In a committed relationship, that increases the woman's satisfaction with the relationship, even though it decreases her satisfaction when commitment is weak.

QUIZ YOURSELF

What Is Love?

answers: see pg 445

1. Passionate love is an aspect of _____ .

(a) Eastern culture

(b) Western culture

(c) both Eastern and Western cultures

(d) neither Eastern nor Western cultures

2. Passionate love is to companionate love as _____ love is to _____ love.

(a) affectionate; romantic

(b) committed; intimate

(c) married; single

(d) romantic; affectionate

3. People who feel passionately in love have high levels of _____ .

(a) acetylcholine

(b) dopamine

(c) epinephrine

(d) phenylethylamine

4. In the triangle theory of love, what does companionate love stem from?

(a) Commitment

(b) Intimacy

(c) Passion

(d) Both (a) and (b)

Different Types of Relationships

Not all people are the same, nor are all relationships the same. Let us consider some of the basic differences in how people relate to each other.

Exchange Versus Communal

There are at least two different basic types of relationship. These can be called exchange and communal relationships.[31,32] **Exchange relationships** are based on reciprocity and fairness; each person does something for the other mainly in the expectation of getting some direct benefit in return. **Communal relationships**, in contrast, are based on mutual love and concern; in this type of relationship, people do things for each other without expecting to be repaid. The relationship between a family dentist and a regular customer would be one example of a long-term exchange relationship: The dentist and client may be friendly to each other and even enjoy seeing each other, but the basis of their interaction is still the exchange of dental care for money. In contrast, a long-term communal relationship might exist between two sisters, who help each other out during difficult times by giving emotional support and even money without expecting that the other will pay it back.

One difference between communal and exchange relationships is whether the people keep track. Thus, some couples that live together keep track of who pays which bills, who buys the groceries, and so forth, to make sure that everything is equal. Other couples live together in a more communal fashion, putting all their money into a joint bank account and letting either one spend it without having to check with the other. Even in terms of chores and doing favors for each other, some couples keep careful track, while others don't. In the lab, researchers have measured communal versus exchange orientation by having participants work on puzzles one after the other and noting whether they choose to use different colored pens (so each person's contribution is readily visible in a distinctive color) or the same colored pen (so that it becomes impossible to tell who did what). People who want or have communal relationships are more likely to use the same colored pen.[33,34] By doing that, they do not keep track of their respective contributions.

In general, social psychologists assume that communal relationships are more mature and desirable than exchange relationships. If you found out that a couple had been married for 10 years but still kept separate bank accounts and kept careful track of who paid

exchange relationships relationships based on reciprocity and fairness, in which people expect something in return

communal relationships relationships based on mutual love and concern, without expectation of repayment

for what, you would probably think something was wrong with the relationship, and you might question their commitment to each other. In fact, couples who pool their money in a communal fashion while living together are more likely to remain together and to get married than cohabiting couples who keep their relationship on an exchange basis by maintaining separate accounts.[35]

This bias in favor of communal relationships, however, is specific to close or intimate relationships. Across the broader society, exchange relationships seem much more powerful for driving progress and increasing wealth.[36] The communal societies in which possessions are shared freely by all tend to be simple, even relatively primitive cultures. The rich and flourishing cultures have all apparently become that way by taking advantage of social and economic exchange because the rewards for success encourage achievement, innovation, and risk taking. Thus, ultimately, there may be a tradeoff between the two types of relationship. Exchange relationships promote achievement, increase wealth, and ultimately drive progress, whereas communal relationships make people feel safe and secure and provide a haven where others care for you regardless of how much you achieve. This tradeoff may explain why most people in modern societies ultimately try to have some of both. They spend their working lives in a network of exchange relationships, where their salary and other rewards are directly proportional to what they accomplish, and where they do things for others specifically in order to get money or other rewards in return. Meanwhile, they try to set up their families on a communal basis, where people care for each other without keeping track of who contributed what and everyone shares with everyone else.

In any case, communal interactions are healthier and more mature in close relationships. People in communal close relationships help each other more than do people in exchange close relationships.[37] They feel better about helping each other[38] and are more responsive to each other's emotional states.[39] They keep track of each other's needs rather than what the other does for them, and this attention to the other's needs reflects an ongoing concern to take care of each other.[40,41] Communal relationships also promote a greater sense of unity and shared identity, so the relationship feels more solid.

The underlying reality may be that communal and exchange relationships are based on different rules. Exchange relationships are based on reciprocity. In exchange relationships, you should only allow someone to do something for you if you are ready to repay that favor. Fairness and even exchange are uppermost concerns. In contrast, communal relationships are based on the norm of mutual concern. You can let the other person do things for you without any immediate idea of how to repay it, just as you would be willing to do a great deal for your partner without expecting anything in return. Instead of equality and repayment, the underlying rules involve caring for the other person and being available and ready to provide support, help, and other resources whenever the person needs you.

Attachment

During the dark days of World War II, London, England, endured daily bombings by the German air force. London was the nation's capital, and it was necessary for many people to remain at work there, but many parents decided to send their children to live out in the country, where the danger from bombs was much less. Although this practice promoted safety, it required many small children to be separated from their parents for significant periods of time. A British psychologist, John Bowlby, observed how the children dealt with these separations, and on this basis he began to formulate a theory about different styles of attachment.[42] This theory was revived by relationships researchers in the 1980s and has become an influential, powerful way of understanding all close relationships (especially romantic ones).

Like many psychologists of his era, Bowlby was influenced by both Freudian and learning psychology, and these views treated adult behavior as shaped by early childhood experiences. Bowlby thought that how adults relate to others—romantic partners, work colleagues and bosses, even organizations—would essentially copy or repeat the style of interaction they had learned in childhood. He saw some children deal with separation from parents by

Relationship questionnaire

_____ A. I am somewhat uncomfortable being close to others; I find it difficult to trust them completely, difficult to allow myself to depend on them. I am nervous when anyone gets too close, and often, others want me to be more intimate than I feel comfortable being.

_____ B. I find it relatively easy to get close to others and am comfortable depending on them and having them depend on me. I don't worry about being abandoned or about someone getting too close to me.

_____ C. I find that others are reluctant to get as close as I would like. I often worry that my partner doesn't really love me or won't want to stay with me. I want to get very close to my partner, and this sometimes scares people away.

FIGURE 12.4

Three attachment styles: anxious/ ambivalent (A), secure (B), and avoidant (C) from a one-item measure.
SOURCE: Hazan and Shaver (1987).

attachment theory a theory that classifies people into four attachment styles (secure, preoccupied, dismissing avoidant, and fearful avoidant) based on two dimensions (anxiety and avoidance)

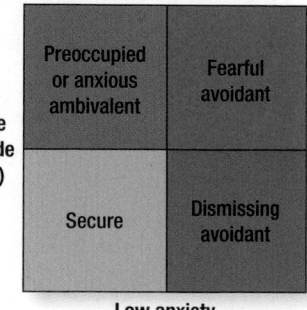

High anxiety
(Negative attitude toward self)

| Preoccupied or anxious ambivalent | Fearful avoidant |
| Secure | Dismissing avoidant |

Low avoidance
(Positive attitude toward others)

High avoidance
(Negative attitude toward others)

Low anxiety
(Positive attitude toward self)

FIGURE 12.5

Two dimensions of attachment: anxiety and avoidance.

clinging and crying and refusing to let go; others pretended they didn't like their parents and didn't care whether they were there or not; still others seemed to deal with the separation in a sad but accepting manner. He thought that these early experiences would shape how the children would later carry on their adult relationships. Bowlby's descriptions of the styles of interaction have influenced subsequent work, but today the weight of opinion does not favor the view that adult styles of interaction are strongly shaped by early childhood experiences. Many people change and develop new styles of relating long after early childhood. (Also, when research findings do indicate that a person has remained the same from childhood into adulthood, researchers today note that this could reflect some underlying genetic trait rather than the causal influence of childhood experiences.)

Types of Attachment

The original theory identified three types of attachment. John Bowlby's observations were extended by Phillip Shaver and his colleagues[43,44,45] to describe adult relationships, including love and romantic relationships. Shaver's group found that people could classify themselves reliably. It wasn't even necessary to use a long, fancy questionnaire; a single item (see **FIGURE 12.4**) was enough to sort people into categories. The categories range along a continuum from pulling close to pushing away. At one extreme lie the clinging types who want to be as close as possible, who ideally would like to experience a complete merger with someone else, and whose problems stem from the fact that others don't want to be as close as they do. This style of attachment is called anxious/ambivalent. At the other extreme one finds the *avoidant* individuals, who are uncomfortable when others want to get too close and who try to maintain some distance between themselves and relationship partners.

In the middle, between the anxious and avoidant styles, are the secure individuals. *Secure attachment* is characterized by a comfortable balance: The secure person is happy to become close and intimate with others and does not worry inordinately about being abandoned or hurt. Earlier, we noted that the difference between communal and exchange relationships is a kind of tradeoff, in that both have advantages in appropriate contexts. In that sense, neither communal nor exchange is inherently better than the other. All attachment styles are not equal, however. In almost all published studies, the secure attachment style produces the best outcomes.

The best that can be said for the other attachment styles is that they provide some limited kind of defense mechanisms or ways of coping with painful relationships. In fact, the avoidant attachment style is thought to start when parents (especially mothers) reject or neglect their babies, fail to express affection and other emotions, avoid physical contact, and fail to provide comfort when the babies are upset.[46] An upset baby whose mother fails to provide comfort may learn to turn off the desire to be close to the mother as a way of preventing itself from feeling worse.[47]

Two Dimensions of Attachment?

As the study of attachment styles evolved, researchers gradually moved from the single dimension (running from anxious/ambivalent to secure to avoidant) in favor of a two-dimensional **attachment theory**.[48,49,50,51,52] The two dimensions are now called *anxiety* and *avoidance*. A simple way to remember them is that one dimension (anxiety) refers to attitudes toward the self and the other dimension (avoidance) refers to attitudes toward the other person. Though both of these dimensions should be understood as a continuum, we can use a simple high-versus-low split on each dimension to create vivid images of four different attachment styles (see **FIGURE 12.5**). Thus, the new theory offers four styles, instead of the three in the earlier version, mainly by splitting the "avoidant" category into two.

The first of the four styles is, again, **secure attachment**. Securely attached people are low on anxiety and low on avoidance (or, to put it another way, they have favorable attitudes toward both self and others). They are good at close relationships. They trust their partners, share their feelings, provide support and comfort (and happily receive these as well), and enjoy their relationships. Their relationships tend to be stronger, more durable, more satisfying, and more intimate than those of people in the other categories.[53,54]

The second category is called **preoccupied attachment**, though some researchers still prefer the original term **anxious/ambivalent**. People in this category are low on avoidance, reflecting the fact that they want and enjoy closeness to the other person, but they tend to have high anxiety and a more negative attitude toward themselves. These individuals want to merge and cling but worry that their relationship partners will abandon them, possibly because they think their partners will discover their faults and flaws.[55,56,57,58,59] Preoccupied individuals tend to see partners as inconsistent, unreliable, and reluctant to commit. They seek more and more closeness, and their frequent efforts to force others to remain close to them can cause their partners to perceive them as overly controlling (or even "suffocating"). Preoccupied individuals may provide large amounts of comfort, support, and care to others, but sometimes they provide too much, partly because they provide care more to satisfy their own need to connect than out of any genuine sensitivity to their partner's needs.[60,61,62]

In the third type, **dismissing avoidant attachment**, people see themselves as worthy, adequate individuals (thus low anxiety) but seek to prevent relationships from becoming too close.[63,64] They view partners as unreliable, unavailable, and uncaring. They seek to rely on themselves rather than on others. Their relationships are marked by more distance, lower commitment, and lower enjoyment than those of secure or preoccupied individuals. Their partners sometimes see them as withdrawn or aloof and as reluctant to open up (that is, they are slow to disclose personal feelings and experiences). They provide less care and support to their loved ones than do secure or preoccupied people.

Fourth, **fearful avoidant attachment** is characterized by both high anxiety and high avoidance. These people have low opinions of themselves and keep others from becoming close. They view potential relationship partners as untrustworthy, uncaring, and otherwise unavailable. They worry that they are unlovable. Given their issues with both self and others, this worry may not be entirely unfounded!

How firm are these styles? Although each person may have a habitual attachment style, anyone can occasionally have a relationship with a different style, partly because of the partner's influence.[65] You might normally be secure, for example, but you might find yourself preoccupied in a particular relationship, especially if the partner treats you in an erratic or anxiety-producing manner.

In many ways, the avoidant individuals (both dismissing and fearful) present the biggest theoretical puzzle.[66,67] We have said that the need to belong and the desire for close relationships is common to all human beings, yet at least on the surface avoidant people seem to push others away rather than keep them close. Do avoidant people thus lack the need to belong? Avoidant individuals do desire and seek out connections with others. But, they worry that if they give in to these wishes and become close to others, they will be hurt. Thus, the fear of closeness lies alongside the need to belong, and the two urges can come into conflict. Quite possibly their fear of closeness originates in previous experiences, whether very early in life such as having had a distant or rejecting mother, or as a result of early romantic experiences that ended in pain and suffering. Put another way, avoidant individuals have the same basic need to belong as other people, but they seem to learn to turn it off or disconnect it to avoid being hurt. Outwardly they may act as if they are indifferent to closeness with others, but secretly they often suffer a great deal during separations.[68,69]

Avoidant individuals thus perform a delicate balancing act. They want contact and relatedness with other people, but they seek to avoid becoming too close. In a sense, they want human connection and companionship but without allowing too much intimacy. Some

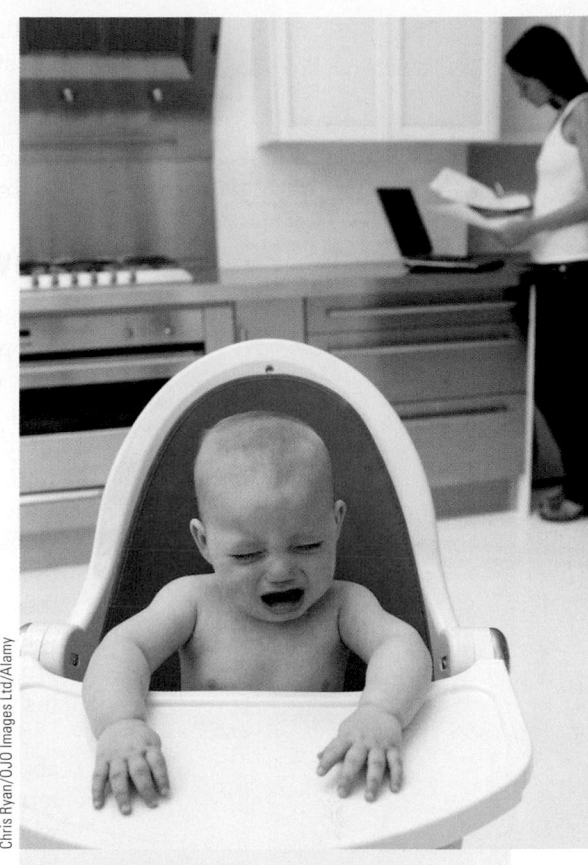

Chris Ryan/OJO Images Ltd/Alamy

Avoidance problems later in life may in part be due to being ignored as a child.

secure attachment style of attachment in which people are low on anxiety and low on avoidance; they trust their partners, share their feelings, provide and receive support and comfort, and enjoy their relationships

preoccupied (anxious/ambivalent) attachment style of attachment in which people are low on avoidance but high on anxiety; they want and enjoy closeness but worry that their relationship partners will abandon them

dismissing avoidant attachment style of attachment in which people are low on anxiety but high on avoidance; they tend to view partners as unreliable, unavailable, and uncaring

fearful avoidant attachment style of attachment in which people have both high anxiety and high avoidance; they have low opinions of themselves and keep others from getting close

deal with this by keeping multiple relationships going at the same time, so that if one partner starts to get too close, they can shift emphasis to another. Others manage the problem by frequently introducing conflict into a relationship, such as by getting into fights and arguments over seemingly minor things. That way they can stay connected to someone but prevent the relationship from becoming too close. Others simply set up their social lives so that they keep interactions relatively short, thus preventing intimacy from developing.[70]

Loving People Who Love Themselves

"First you must love yourself, and only then are you ready to love someone else"—this is a popular belief in our culture. It is variously attributed to the psychological thinkers Erik Erikson, Carl Rogers, and Abraham Maslow, but it is probably a misreading of their works. Erikson said that people must resolve their identity crisis and know who they are before they are ready to start working on intimacy.[71] He didn't say you had to love yourself—merely know yourself (and it is even questionable whether knowing yourself is a prerequisite for having a good relationship). Rogers focused on self-actualization (the global process of cultivating your talents and becoming a better person all around) rather than self-love. He also thought that people needed to receive unconditional love before they were ready to reach self-actualization.[72] This is in a sense the opposite of the idea that self-love comes first; instead, being loved comes first, self-esteem later. Maslow likewise proposed that belongingness and love needs were more basic than self-esteem needs;[73] his views, too, run contrary to the theory that self-esteem comes first, love later.

Still, those theories are no more than theories. What do the facts and findings say about loving yourself and loving others? The evidence is at best weak and inconsistent in terms of showing that loving yourself contributes to loving others. In some cases, people who love themselves lavishly are less likely to love anyone else.

Let us begin with self-esteem. People with low self-esteem engage in a variety of behaviors that can undermine a relationship.[74,75] They are skeptical or distrustful when their partners express love or support, and sometimes they act as if they expect their partners to dump them. Still, these problematic behaviors do not seem to translate into breaking up faster. One possible reason is that people with high self-esteem do other, different things that are bad for relationships. When problems or conflicts occur in a relationship, people with high self-esteem are quicker to decide "I don't have to put up with this!" and to contemplate ending the relationship.[76,77] Probably the different levels of self-esteem contribute to those different reactions. People with low self-esteem doubt that they are lovable, so they expect others to leave them. People with high self-esteem think they are lovable, so they think they can find a new partner relatively easily. The net result may be that people who have either high or low self-esteem break up at about the same rate, but for different reasons. The other side of the coin is that people of all levels of self-esteem can have lasting, successful relationships.

The damage that self-love can do to relationship harmony is magnified if one looks at narcissism (see also Chapters 3 and 10), which is a personality type based on very high self-love. Narcissists have high self-esteem and a strong though somewhat unstable self-love, but these qualities do not make for good relationships; indeed, their selfishness and other qualities may harm relationships. They approach relationships in a game-playing spirit of having fun or as a pragmatic way of getting what they want (including sex).[78] They seek out successful, beautiful, admired people to date because they think they are similar to them, and they believe that the glamour or prestige of their partners makes them look good.[79]

Getting along with a narcissist is no picnic! Narcissists tend to hog the credit when things go well but blame their partners when things go badly,[80,81,82,83,84] which can certainly put a strain on a relationship. In an observational study in which couples discussed problems that threatened their self-esteem, narcissists had fewer positive interactions with their spouses than other people did.[85]

off the mark.com   by Mark Parisi

ARG! HOW CAN WE HAVE A DECENT CONVERSATION WHEN YOU'RE SO FULL OF YOURSELF?!

offthemark.com   ATLANTIC FEATURE © 1995 MARK PARISI

Reprinted by permission of Atlantic Feature Syndicate/Mark Parisi

Being in a relationship with a narcissist is no picnic. Because they are so full of themselves, they don't think about others.

Ultimately, narcissists tend to be less committed to love relationships than other people are.[86] Narcissists tend to keep one eye on the relationship but another eye out to see whether a better partner might come along. Narcissists think they are superior beings and overestimate how attractive they are; as a result, they think they can and should have the most desirable romantic partners. A narcissist may love you for the time being, but he or she will dump you as soon as a better prospect comes along.

If self-love leads to loving others, narcissists should be the world's best lovers because they love themselves the most. The evidence suggests the opposite, however: In narcissists, at least, loving yourself detracts from loving others. Narcissists are interested in others mainly as a way of boosting their own inflated views of themselves. Hence, their relationships tend to be prone to breakup. This may help explain why marriages among celebrities often end in divorce: Being a celebrity tends to push people to become more narcissistic (partly because they are widely admired and highly paid), and this often leads to relationship problems, especially when new partners are constantly and readily available.

Although narcissism is one problematic extreme, some less extreme versions of self-love and self-esteem may be helpful for relationships. A more minimal form of self-love is **self-acceptance**, which means simply regarding yourself as being a reasonably good person as you are. The same study that found narcissism to be linked to fewer positive interactions with the spouse found that self-acceptance was linked to more positive interactions.[87] These findings suggest that having a very negative, critical attitude toward yourself can interfere with the capacity to love. The best summary of current knowledge on this issue is to say that either extreme of self-love or self-hate is likely to be detrimental to intimacy. Conversely, someone with a simple and secure appreciation of self, without being conceited or overblown, may be the best romantic partner.

QUIZ YOURSELF

Different Types of Relationships

answers: see pg 445

1. **Exchange relationship is to communal relationship as _____ is to _____ .**

   (a) concern; reciprocity   (b) passion; concern   (c) reciprocity; concern   (d) reciprocity; passion

2. **What attachment style is associated with high levels of anxiety and high levels of avoidance?**

   (a) Dismissing avoidant   (b) Fearful avoidant   (c) Preoccupied   (d) Secure

3. **Individuals who see themselves as worthy and adequate but seek to prevent relationships from becoming too close have what type of attachment style?**

   (a) Dismissing avoidant   (b) Fearful avoidant   (c) Preoccupied   (d) Secure

4. **What personality trait is associated with a grandiose, inflated view of the self?**

   (a) Narcissism   (b) Self-acceptance   (c) Self-efficacy   (d) Self-esteem

Maintaining Relationships

Information is available everywhere about how people form new relationships. Countless books, movies, and studies look at how people become attracted to each other and reach the point of making a commitment to carry on an intimate relationship. Most people have some idea about how to do this. In contrast, how people manage to keep a relationship

self-acceptance regarding yourself as being a reasonably good person as you are

going, sometimes for 40 years or more, seems a mystery. Social psychology is only gradually beginning to provide answers to the question of how people keep their relationships alive and well.

What goes on between partners in a long-term relationship? How do they keep it going? What causes some relationships to succeed while others fail? These processes have fascinated social psychologists in recent decades.

Whether relationships continue depends partly on how people deal with temptation, especially the temptation to seek other possible partners. One social psychologist had people in dating relationships look at photos of attractive members of the opposite sex and recorded how long they looked at them. He contacted the participants months later to see whether they were still together with the same relationship partner. The longer they had looked at the photos, the more likely they were to break up. Apparently, exposing yourself to temptation (even just by looking at photos of attractive members of the opposite sex) is one sign that the person may be drifting toward breaking up.[88]

There is some evidence that men and women respond to relationship threats and temptations in different ways. In a series of studies, people who were in committed relationships were introduced to an attractive single person (or, in other studies, imagined this experience). Women reacted to meeting a desirable man by increasing their commitment to their current partner, such as by tolerating his faults more, thinking more positively about him, or increasing their commitment to him. Men, on the other hand, reacted to meeting an attractive single woman by reducing their commitment to their current partner and becoming more critical of her.[89] The implication is that meeting a tempting new partner makes men entertain the possibility of a new relationship instead of the one they have, whereas women try to defend their current relationship.

We saw in the previous chapter that physical good looks matter a great deal for initial attraction. Stereotypes suggest that beauty matters more to men than women, especially in the beginning, because other things take precedence in a long-term relationship. A classic rock song by Jimmy Soul that hit #1 on the Billboard and R&B charts in 1963 even advised men that "If you wanna be happy for the rest of your life, never make a pretty woman your wife!" and went on to advise men to "Get an ugly girl to marry you."

As usual, with the accumulation of data, the picture becomes more complicated. For marital satisfaction, the woman's looks matter more than the man's.[90] That is, men with attractive wives were happier about the marriage and stayed higher in relationship satisfaction than men with less attractive wives. The man's looks had little impact on the woman's satisfaction. Further work suggests, however, that the part of indifference to male beauty can be chalked up to birth control pills. These pills alter women's hormones and change their patterns of sexual response. When women stop taking birth-control pills, their relationship satisfaction changes, depending on their partner's looks.[91] Women with good-looking husbands became more satisfied when they stopped taking the pill, but those with less handsome husbands experienced a decrease in satisfaction.

I Love You More Each Day(?)

Many people in happy marriages say that their relationships continue to grow and improve over the years. People striving to have good and lasting relationships want to know what secrets or actions enable this to happen. If you form a relationship when you are falling in love, everything seems wonderful and perfect. How can things continue to get even better than that?

The data suggest a very different picture. People may say and even believe their relationships are getting better, but usually they are mistaken. Evidence came from a study that had people report on their relationship quality year after year, and also report on changes. People in happy relationships consistently said their relationship was better each year. But if you compared how they rated it this year with how they rated it last year, there was no change. The ever-improving relationship is largely a myth. Good relationships essentially stay the same over long periods of time.[92]

Those were the happy relationships. Many longitudinal studies that track couples over years find essentially two outcomes: Some stay the same, and others get worse.[93,94,95]

Relationships start off good, and either they stay good or they go downhill. The problem of how to have a good long-term relationship is therefore not finding a way to make it better and better—rather, the crucial thing is to avoid the downward spiral. Moreover, once relationships begin to deteriorate, it is apparently quite difficult and unusual to stop this process. The most important challenge is therefore to prevent the downward spiral from starting.

Which type will your relationship be? Intriguing new findings suggest that it is possible to predict decline from early in the relationship. A longitudinal study tracked newlywed couples for four years. At the start of the study, they were all asked to rate their partners. They also did a complex task designed to assess unconscious, automatic attitudes. The simple, conscious ratings had no predictive power, but the relationships marked by positive unconscious attitudes toward each other held up better than the relationships with less positive automatic responses.[96] In a sense, then, the seeds of your divorce may be present at your wedding—but you won't be consciously aware of them. Put another way, most newlyweds have a conscious belief that they are happy together and the relationship is great, but these happy thoughts are there in roughly equal measure in the doomed relationships and in the ones that will thrive and last. The unconscious, however, already has begun to have the feelings that will predict which way the relationship will go.

In reality, most relationships do not improve steadily.

Many things can contribute to the downward spiral. These are especially likely when taking care of oneself and one's own needs is detrimental to the relationship. Making your partner feel guilty is one such process.[97,98] People who are insecure about the relationship are especially worried when the partner criticizes them or misbehaves in other ways. (Insecurity can be linked to anxious attachment styles; see above.) They respond to such conflicts and problems by expressing a high level of hurt feelings and other distress, which makes the partner feel guilty. Seeing the partner express remorse and guilt is reassuring to them, because it indicates that the partner is committed and cares about them. Unfortunately, exaggerating your distress to make your partner feel guilty has a negative effect in the long run, because it reduces the partner's satisfaction with the relationship.[99] Thus, before you make yourself feel better by inducing guilt in your partner, think twice about the damage that might do in the long run!

Investing in Relationships That Last

The question "Why do people stay with their long-term relationship partners?" was the focus of years of research by relationships expert Caryl Rusbult.[100] She began by noting the simpleminded answer: People stay with relationships when they are happy and satisfied. This is not wrong, but it is not a full explanation. People who were satisfied with their relationships were more likely than unsatisfied partners to stay together, but the statistical link was surprisingly weak—which meant that some other factors must be at work.

Eventually Rusbult and her colleagues developed a theory called the **investment model**, with three factors. The first factor, sure enough, is satisfaction. Do you like your partner? Are you glad you have this particular relationship? Do you enjoy spending time together? Does your partner please and satisfy you? If your answers are yes, the relationship is more likely to survive. This is hardly surprising.

The second factor is the quality of available alternatives. Maybe your relationship is not really satisfying, but you don't see anyone better available. In that case, you might remain in an unsatisfying relationship. Conversely, your relationship may be pretty good and satisfying, but if someone clearly better than your partner comes along and makes you an offer, you may be tempted to leave. Here, Rusbult's theory makes the important point that a decision on whether to stay or leave a particular relationship doesn't depend only on how you evaluate that relationship. The decision also depends on whether you could be happier with someone else.

investment model theory that uses three factors—satisfaction, alternatives, and investments—to explain why people stay with their long-term relationship partners

© Jose Luis Pelaez, Inc. /Corbis

Commitment to one's relationship is weaker when many high-quality alternative partners are available.

The third factor is how much the individual has invested in the relationship. Rusbult notes that many investments are "sunk costs," which means that the person has put time, effort, emotion, and other resources into a relationship and cannot get them back out. If you have struggled for two years to get your partner to understand your feelings or respect your needs, and you then break up and start over with someone else, all that struggle is lost. You may have to repeat it all with your new partner. A couple that has spent 20 years together, amassing savings, coordinating careers, raising children, and the like, may be resistant to change simply because they have invested so much in the relationship and do not want to lose it. Even if another attractive partner comes along, they may cling to the relationship that they have worked hard to build. When an old married person dies, friends sometimes tell the widow or widower, "You don't get over it; you get used to it." The implication is that the lost partner is not replaceable. Even if you remarry, you cannot rebuild what you may have shared with someone for many decades of your adult life.

Each of these three factors alone has a weak (though significant) ability to predict whether couples stay together or break apart. Putting the three together provides a very (statistically) strong basis for prediction. If you are satisfied with the relationship, don't see appealing alternatives, and have invested a great deal in the relationship, you will almost certainly remain committed to it. Charles and Diana, whose relationship story opened this chapter, were clearly not satisfied and had plenty of alternatives, and these facts probably helped cause their relationship to break up even though they had invested a fair amount (public statements, time, money, love, plus the raising of children) in it.

The investment theory can even explain some of the phenomena that have puzzled psychologists for decades, including why people (especially women) remain in relationships with physically violent, abusive partners.[101] Logically, one would think that if your partner hits, hurts, or abuses you, you should immediately get out of that relationship and find someone else. Satisfaction is generally not very high in abusive relationships. But many abuse victims do not believe they have alternatives. Some believe they are not attractive enough to find someone else (a belief that the abusive spouse sometimes encourages). At the same time, many abuse victims invest a great deal in making the relationship work, often over long-term cycles in which brief episodes of violent abuse are followed by repentance, making up, sharing feelings, and promising to do better in the future. The victim may be reluctant to toss aside all that has been achieved and take a chance on a new partner who may be no better.

Are Married People Happier?

Love and other close, intimate relationships make up a major part of life. Most people in North America today, and probably most people in most other modern cultures, believe that to miss out on love and intimacy would be to live a poorer, emptier life, compared to people who experience those things. In Chapter 11 we saw that having social bonds is linked to better mental and physical health on all sorts of measures. Many of those advantages have been specifically linked to marriage: People who marry live longer and healthier lives than people who never marry, and people who stay married live longer and better than those who divorce.[102,103,104]

Some qualifications are needed before you start thinking, "I'd better marry somebody, anybody, as soon as possible!" Unhappy marriages produce considerable stress and other bad effects that can nullify the advantages of marriage and in some cases leave people worse off married than alone.[105,106,107,108] Thus, not just marriage but happy marriage may be the most important thing. There may also be a gender difference, though more data are needed. To men, the big difference is being married versus not married, but for women, the quality of the relationship (happy versus unhappy) seems more powerful.[109]

Chapter 1 discussed how the conclusions from research depend on the methods. The data on the advantages of marriage have some built-in ambiguities because of the research methods. We saw in Chapter 1 that research cannot easily establish causality unless it uses random assignment to conditions, and of course no researchers can randomly assign people to be married versus single. It is possible that people who are healthier and saner to start with are more likely to marry, so their better health might not be a result of the marriage. Research has shown that some inborn, genetic factors steer people toward marriage, whereas other genetic factors guide other people toward remaining single.[110] That is, married people are genetically different from lifelong single people, on average, and some of those differences could contribute to the differences in health and longevity. For example, a person born with a genetic problem that caused many health problems over the years might find it harder than a healthy person to marry (because people prefer to marry healthy, attractive partners) and also might be more likely to die at a young age (because of the health problems).

Then again, some of the differences in outcomes are probably caused by the benefits of marriage. For example, Catholic priests do not live as long or as healthy lives as do Protestant ministers.[111] It does not seem likely that genetic traits steer men into Catholic versus Protestant faith—so the difference in how long they live is more likely due to the fact that only the Protestant clergy marry.

Thinking Styles of Couples

Certainly people do some things that help their relationships succeed. High on the list are ways in which the couple deals with problems and conflicts. If you live with someone for many years, there is a high likelihood that sooner or later the person will be unpleasant or difficult, at least occasionally. It is also likely that conflicts will arise when the two of you want different things, such as spending a vacation at the beach or visiting one person's parents, or when you disagree about money.

Some research has compared happy couples with unhappy couples. Seeing how those two types of couples differ, especially in how they deal with problems and conflicts, can shed light on what makes some couples happier than others.

Some of the crucial differences between happy and unhappy couples are based on the attributions they make. (As we saw in Chapter 5, attributions are inferences about the causes of events.) In strong, happy relationships, partners seem willing to give the partner the benefit of the doubt most of the time. For example, researchers asked people how they would respond when the partner did something unpleasant, as opposed to doing something pleasant.[112] The happy couples said they would probably attribute the partner's unpleasant behavior to some external factor, such as thinking that the person must be under stress at work. In contrast, when the partner does something pleasant, the member of a happy couple was likely to view this as further proof of what a good person the partner is. In short, good acts were attributed to the partner's inner qualities, whereas bad acts were dismissed as due to external factors. The researchers called this pattern (internal attributions for good behavior, external for bad) the **relationship-enhancing style of attribution** (see **FIGURE 12.6**). It strengthens the relationship by making the partners see each other in a positive light.

The unhappy couples interpreted events along the opposite lines. If the partner did something good, they tended to think it was due to external factors. For example, if the husband brought the wife flowers, she might think, "He must have just gotten those on sale" or even "He did something wrong and is trying to cover it up." If the partner did something bad, the person would think, "Well, that's just typical!" and see it as a reflection of the kind of person the partner was. Thus, bad acts were attributed to the partner's inner qualities, whereas good acts were dismissed as due to external factors. The researchers called this pattern the **distress-maintaining style of attribution** (see **FIGURE 12.6**).

These styles of thinking explain why it is often so difficult to save a relationship that is in trouble, even with the aid of professional marriage therapists. Getting people to change their actions and treat each other better is certainly an important first step, but

relationship-enhancing style of attribution tendency of happy couples to attribute their partner's good acts to internal factors and bad acts to external factors

distress-maintaining style of attribution tendency of unhappy couples to attribute their partner's good acts to external factors and bad acts to internal factors

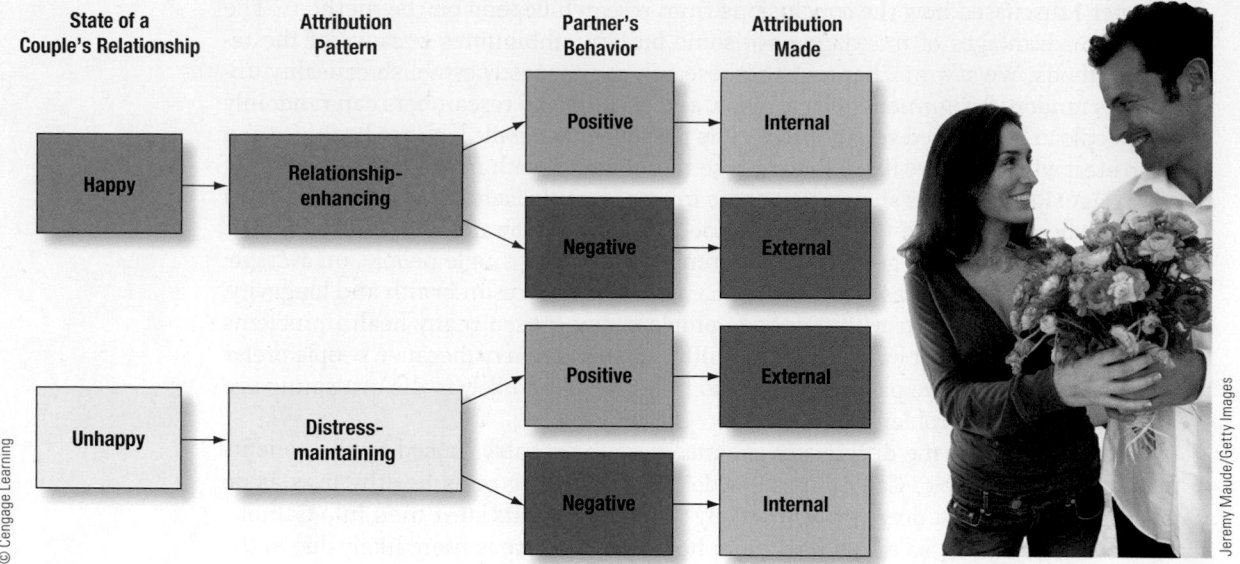

State of a Couple's Relationship	Attribution Pattern	Partner's Behavior	Attribution Made
Happy	Relationship-enhancing	Positive	Internal
		Negative	External
Unhappy	Distress-maintaining	Positive	External
		Negative	Internal

© Cengage Learning

Jeremy Maude/Getty Images

FIGURE 12.6

What attribution does she make for his gift? "He must love me very much." "He must have done something wrong and wants to pacify me." "He must have gotten those on sale." "He's such a sweetheart." "He probably wants something from me."

once the distress-maintaining attributional pattern is in place, good actions tend to be discounted. You may decide to try to be nicer to your partner in order to try to strengthen the relationship, but your partner is likely to dismiss your positive acts. ("You're only being nice because the therapist told you to!") Meanwhile, even if you are trying to be good, you may occasionally slip up and say or do something unkind—in which case your distress-maintaining partner is likely to see this as the "real" you emerging again. You can't win, at least as long as your partner follows the distress-maintaining style of thinking.

Trust is an important factor that guides how people think about relationships and partners. People who trust their partners more can take more responsibility for conflicts (such as by accepting blame), because they are confident that the partner will act in their best interests in general. Lacking trust, one has to look out more for oneself. Several recent studies tracked couples over time and had them report on their conflicts and partner misdeeds both when they happened and then quite a bit later (from memory).[113] In high trust relationships, people's memories showed something much like the relationship-enhancing style of attribution: They remembered the partner's misdeeds less often and rated them as less severe than they had initially. In low-trust relationships, no such bias was apparent, and memories of partner misdeeds remain sharp and painful.

Other important thought processes include how people look at the relationship itself. Happy couples tend to exaggerate how wonderful the relationship is. When problems arise, they may see them as isolated incidents. In this way, they sustain a view that the relationship is great. People's ratings of their dating relationships tend to be more positive and optimistic than the ratings of those same relationships by the young lovers' parents and roommates.[114] (The roommates' predictions about whether the relationship would last were the most accurate!)

When couples start to move toward breaking up, the partners often reassess the relationship, wherein they go back and reinterpret past events as far less wonderful and positive than they seemed at the time.[115] For example, many happy couples maintain a highly romanticized story of how they first met, suggesting that they discovered that they were truly meant for each other and that they really turned each other on because they had a terrific rapport. When the same couple is preparing for breakup or divorce, they create a new version of the story of how they first met, suggesting that it was just an accident, that they happened to be lonely or sexually desperate and were willing to strike up a romance with anybody who happened to be there, or that the attraction was based on false impressions.

Another important process is devaluing alternatives. One study had people who were in relationships rate the attractiveness of several potential dating partners.[116] The people in the most committed relationships gave these potential partners low ratings, especially when the other person was attractive and would actually have been available as a possible dating partner. These circumstances were considered to be the most threatening, and so the devaluing of alternatives was probably a defensive response against the danger of becoming interested in someone else. Sure enough, in another study, those same researchers found that people who failed to devalue alternatives were more likely to break up than people who did. In other words, people in lasting relationships did not find other people appealing, whereas people in doomed relationships (the ones that later broke up) found other people appealing and even increased their attraction to them over time. Remember the study that let people look at attractive photos of opposite-sex individuals for as long as they wanted, the duration of looking predicted whether they broke up with their current partner: Those who looked longest were most likely to break up.[117]

In another study, young heterosexual participants who were in relationships rated photos of young opposite-sex persons as less attractive than did people who were not in relationships.[118] The two groups did not differ in how they rated young same-sex individuals or older opposite-sex individuals—neither of which constituted a potential threat to their current dating relationship. Thus, only the potential alternative partners were devalued. The implication is that closing your mind to other potential partners is one way to help keep your relationship safe.

Being Yourself: Is Honesty the Best Policy?

Listen to the discussions on television about what is best for long-term relationship success, and one common theme is honesty. The prevailing wisdom is that honesty is crucial, even essential, for relationship success. You have to be able to be yourself and show yourself as you really are, and your partner has to honestly accept this.

Then again, when you are shopping with your romantic partner and she or he asks, "Does this garment make me look fat?" should you honestly say, "Yes, but no more than most of your other clothes"? Honesty may be overrated. After all, people who are wildly, passionately in love often idealize and overestimate their partners—is that necessarily a bad thing? Why does love make us see each other as better than we are, if seeing each other accurately is best for relationship success?

There are in fact two very different views about honesty's role in successful relationships. One holds that honesty is the best policy: It is best if two people understand each other fully and correctly, communicate all their feelings, and accept each other for who they are. The other is that the people should idealize each other and see each other in a positively biased fashion.

During passionate love, two people generally take a very positive, even distorted view of each other. Friends will say, "What does he see in her?" or "I can't believe she thinks he's so brilliant." Moreover, the lovers tend to encourage and help each other to see each other in this idealized fashion. On dates, they wear their best clothes and are on their best behavior: thoughtful, charming, considerate, and proper. A woman might be careful that her new boyfriend only sees her when her hair is combed and she is wearing makeup. A man may clean up his language and monitor the opinions he expresses so as to make a good impression.

Because of these practices, people fall in love with an idealized version of each other. Such illusions may be difficult to sustain over the long run. Still, does that mean people should rush into honesty? Perhaps. You probably do want to be known and loved for who you really are. You might feel insecure if your partner has never seen the "real" you and instead has only known you on your best behavior. You may feel that if the other person ever found out what you are really like, he or she would reject and abandon you. The love between Charles and Diana may have started off with both people idealizing

off the mark .com   by Mark Parisi

GEORGE...DO I LOOK FAT?

WASHINGTON ABOUT TO BREAK HIS "CANNOT TELL A LIE" COMMITMENT.

Honesty sometimes is not the best policy, even if you are George Washington and "cannot tell a lie."

Time 1 — Time 2

Idealize each other → Still in love

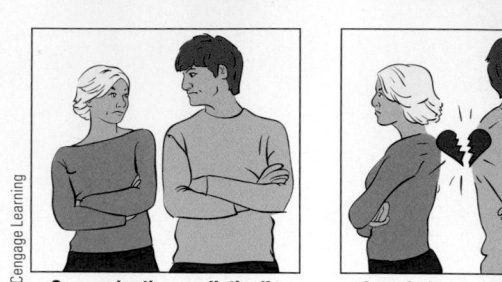

See each other realistically → Less in love, or broken up

© Cengage Learning

FIGURE 12.7
Idealize each other and you will stay together longer.

each other, but when the fairy tale ended and reality set in, the problems began.

The question then becomes, should you try to preserve your partner's idealized version of you for as long as possible? Or should you reveal your true self, with all your flaws and failings, and seek to be accepted that way?

Research has provided conflicting answers. Work by William Swann and his colleagues[119,120] (see also Chapter 3) sought to show that people desire others to see them as they see themselves. (Admittedly, most people see themselves in a positively distorted fashion, so this is not the same as all-out honesty.) These researchers found that different rules apply in dating as opposed to marriage. When dating, people were most intimate with partners who viewed them most favorably. Within marriage, however, people were most intimate with partners who saw them as they saw themselves. In fact, people with low self-esteem were more intimate with partners who viewed them relatively less favorably than with partners who thought highly of them.[121]

In contrast, studies by Sandra Murray and John Holmes support the idealization view.[122,123,124,125] In their studies, couples were assessed on how much they idealized each other, as well as on relationship satisfaction. The researchers then followed up with the couples after many months to see whether they were still dating and, if so, how they were doing. They found that people who saw each other in the most positive fashion had the happiest relationships—and the most durable ones (that is, least likely to break up). Moreover, the idealization seemed to be the crucial cause. Having a very positive view of the other person at Time 1 led to a happier relationship at (later) Time 2, but a happy relationship at Time 1 did not predict a positive opinion of the partner at Time 2 (see **FIGURE 12.7**). This finding is consistent with the relationship-enhancing style of thought discussed in the previous section: People who downplay their partners' bad points and emphasize their partners' good points have the happiest relationships.

One resolution of these seemingly discrepant findings has to do with what aspects of self are being measured.[126] Swann's studies measured very specific features of the self, whereas Murray and Holmes measured global, overall appreciation. It is therefore plausible that both findings are correct. People may want their partner to see them accurately in the little things but to hold a broadly positive view of them in the vague, general sense. It is better for your partner to know accurately whether you are good at fixing the car, balancing the checkbook, being on time for a date, or acting in a charming and respectful manner in front of your partner's parents. If your partner vastly overestimates you on any of those, you may be headed for trouble! But at the same time, you probably want your partner to think that you are a wonderful person in general. If your partner has a somewhat inflated view of what a nice person you are, how intelligent you are, or how physically attractive you are, this may help the relationship to survive.

Another, perhaps deeper way to reconcile these findings is that people want selective confirmation of how they think of themselves—neither total honesty nor total illusion. They want their partners to see them at their best, which is a real and valid part of who they are, as opposed to seeing either the full nasty truth or a fictional version that is unrealistically perfect. The most attractive, brilliant, and charming, but still genuine, version of yourself is the one you'd like your partner to believe is the real you. The relationship-enhancing style of thought focuses on your partner's best traits and ignores the bad ones, but it does not fabricate nonexistent good traits.

It is therefore probably a good idea to stay on your best behavior for a relatively long period of time. Relationships do benefit when the people can sustain highly favorable views of each other. You want to allow your partner to see you at your best and to keep up a somewhat idealized view of the kind of person you are.

The marriages among the middle class during the Victorian period (late 19th century, before World War I) are often mocked these days as phony and pretentious. In those marriages, husband and wife would dress up for dinner together. They sometimes addressed each other in relatively formal terms. They did not necessarily pour out all their inner feelings to each other but kept some distance. They tried to keep up good, proper behavior even when alone together. In a sense, they remained on their best behavior, so that 5 or 25 years into a marriage they still acted almost as if they were still courting. To the modern sensibility, these practices seem like a silly way to go about having a close relationship with someone. The modern mind thinks that people should share everything about themselves.

But perhaps the Victorian practices deserve to be reconsidered. In fact, the middle-class Victorians had the longest lasting marriages in Western history, on average.[127,128,129] How can you make a relationship tolerable for 40 years? Perhaps the Victorians had a valid solution: Be on your best behavior. Research lends support to this view. Rather than requiring your partner to see you at your worst, such as sitting on the couch in dirty underwear and scratching yourself, or pouring forth all sorts of neurotically insecure thoughts, you want to help your partner continue to idealize you. On a first date, most people dress and act carefully so as to make the best impression they can. Perhaps if they continued to do this through many years of committed relationship and marriage, they would get better results.

Sexuality

Are love and sex the same thing? Undoubtedly they overlap in many cases and are often intertwined. But a recent social theory proposes that they have two separate biological bases, which can sometimes result in confusion.

This theory was put forward by Lisa Diamond[130,131] based on her studies of female sexuality through time. Diamond's basic point is that humans form relationships based on two separate systems, which can reinforce each other or be in conflict. One of these is the attachment system (see the earlier section on attachment theory). This is an urge to connect and form close social bonds with a few individuals. The other system is the sex drive, based on the principles of mating. Diamond says that evolution probably shaped the sex drive to focus on the opposite gender (because only heterosexual sex can create children). The attachment drive, in contrast, is probably gender neutral. Most children (boys and girls) form their first attachment to their mother, and later develop close friendships or attachments to other people, often primarily of their own gender.

If attachment and sexuality remained completely separate, there might be no problem, but most human beings mix intimacy with sex. The natural sex drive might dictate an initial preference for opposite-gender sex partners, but the attachment drive can promote intimacy between people of the same gender, and sometimes this can result in sexual attraction, too.

A curious pattern that Diamond observed in her data led her to conclude that attachment and sex were somewhat separate, independent systems that can produce these surprising effects. She found that many women identified themselves as heterosexual but then found themselves having a homosexual (lesbian) relationship. At that point, these women might identify themselves as lesbians. Crucially, however, the lesbian orientation often did not outlast the relationship: If the woman broke up with her girlfriend, she would not go looking for another woman, but instead would often find a man as her next romantic partner. Her affair with another woman was thus not a sign of a deep, fixed, unchangeably lesbian orientation. Instead, it was a result of her love and intimacy with a particular human being who happened to be a woman. She might have lesbian love with her, but when the relationship ended, she would revert to a heterosexual preference, and her next partner would be a man.

Diamond[132] concluded that if there is a "gay gene," love is not on it. Love comes from the attachment drive, and that drive is independent of gender. You can love both your mother and your father, both your son and your daughter, both your best male and best female friend. A gay gene (if it exists) would stipulate sexual orientation, so it might dictate which gender you would want to have sex with, but it would not limit your ability to experience love and intimacy with either gender. Attachment can lead to sexual desire, and sexual intimacy can promote attachment, so the two are not entirely independent—which is why sometimes people find themselves attracted to someone of the "wrong" gender, however they have defined it.

Theories of Sexuality

Researchers have identified several basic theoretical approaches to sex. Especially popular and influential during the 1970s were **social constructionist theories**, which asserted that cultural forces and socialization shape how people assign meaning to their lives, with the result that sexual attitudes and behaviors vary widely based on culture.[133,134] It is no accident that this view was most influential during the peak years of the "sexual revolution" (1960s to 1970s). The sexual revolution had changed sexual attitudes and behaviors so rapidly in such a short time that it seemed as though almost any further changes would be possible. The rapid and extensive changes attested to the power of culture to shape the sex drive, contrary to views of sexual desire as innately programmed.

The social constructionist approach to sex acknowledges that there may be some biological foundations to sex, but most forms of sexual desire are seen as the result of cultural conditioning. Who wants to do what to whom (sexually) is seen as a result of social and political influences, including upbringing and media influence. Gender differences in sexuality are seen as highly changeable roles that are created by society to serve political or other goals. Feminist theory, which also reached a peak at this time, allied itself closely with the social constructionist approach to sex. In that view, women's sexuality was shaped by how men had long sought to control and oppress women; again, cultural influences (in this case, the influence of male-dominated culture on women) were seen as decisive.[135]

Evolutionary theory emerged in the 1970s and 1980s to provide a radically different view of sex. **Evolutionary theory** asserts that the sex drive has been shaped by natural selection and that its forms therefore tend to be innate.[136,137] Those patterns of sexual desire that led prehistoric men and women to have the most children would win in the evolutionary competition, with the result that people today are mainly descended from people who had those patterns of desire. For example, many prehistoric men might have been attracted to old women instead of young women, but old women usually do not have

social constructionist theories theories asserting that attitudes and behaviors, including sexual desire and sexual behavior, are strongly shaped by culture and socialization

evolutionary theory theory of sexuality asserting that the sex drive has been shaped by natural selection and that its forms thus tend to be innate

Piotr Malecki/Getty Images

Constructionist theories emphasize that sexual attitudes and behaviors are shaped by cultural influences.

babies. The men who mated with old women would therefore not pass on their genes. As a result, today's men would all be descended from men who preferred younger women.[138]

The evolutionary approach sees gender differences as rooted in biology and hence as less flexible and less influenced by politics and culture than is suggested by the social constructionist view. One basis for gender differences lies in different reproductive strategies. People today are descended from those ancestors who raised the most children, but what succeeded best for one gender may not be the same as what worked best for the other. A woman can have only a few babies in her lifetime; each one occupies her body for about nine months and typically makes demands on her time and energy for years. Hence, a woman would by nature be cautious about sex and mating because each pregnancy is a huge investment for her. A man, on the other hand, can make a baby with only a few minutes of pleasure. Biologically, he could walk away and never expend any more time, effort, or other resources on that baby, yet still have passed along his genes. Hence, brief, casual, one-time sexual encounters will be more appealing to men than to women.[139]

Men can also be much less choosy than women about their partners, for the same reason. After all, the quality of your offspring depends on both your genes and those of your partner. If a woman gets pregnant by a low-quality man and then a better man comes along, she cannot make another baby for many months (by which time the better mate may be long gone). Hence, the most effective strategy for women would involve being cautious and choosy before consenting to sex. In contrast, if a man gets a low-quality woman pregnant and then a better partner comes along, he can make a baby with the new woman almost immediately. Having sex with low-quality partners is thus more costly for women than for men.[140,141] As one sign of this, when researchers ask people what is the minimum IQ you would want to have in a sex partner, women give much higher numbers than men.[142]

The same logic would predict differences in the desired number of sex partners. A woman can get pregnant only about once a year regardless of how many men she has sex with, whereas a man can make many different babies if he has sex with many different women. Moreover, for a woman, getting pregnant is not the only or main issue; she also wants a man to help provide for her and her children. (For example, if she has two small children and is pregnant with a third, she may find it hard to get food for her family by herself, especially if getting food requires chasing animals

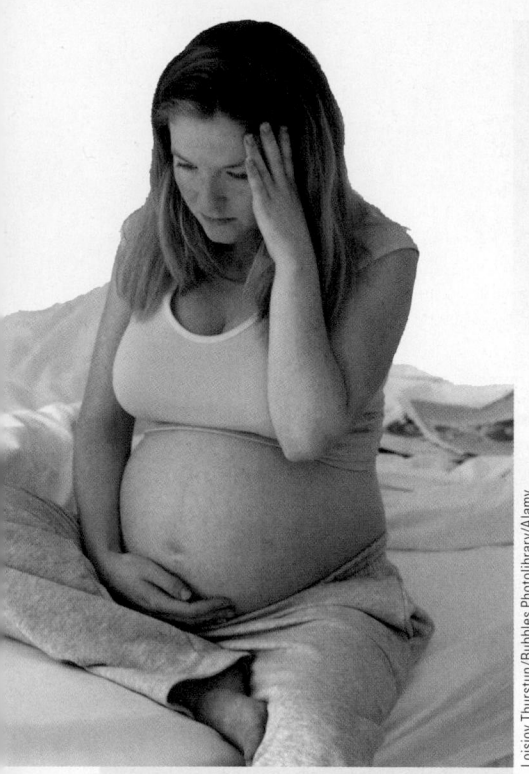

A woman pays a higher biological price than a man for making a poor choice of sex partners, and so it behooves women to be more cautious than men about sex.

Loisjoy Thurstun/Bubbles Photolibrary/Alamy

or climbing trees.) Hence, she may want to form a close relationship with a man whom she can trust to stick around and provide for her and her children. A woman with one intimate partner is more likely to receive male care over a long term than a woman who changes partners frequently. Nature may therefore have shaped women to desire sex mainly in the context of committed, lasting relationships. Men, in contrast, can be successful at passing on their genes by having sex with many different partners.

A third theoretical perspective on sexuality is based on **social exchange theory**, which seeks to understand social behavior by analyzing the costs and benefits of interacting with each other.[143,144,145,146] In this view, sex is a resource that women have and men want. Men therefore have to give women other resources in exchange for sex.[147,148] These resources may include money, attention, respect, love, and commitment. Male sexuality is not seen as having much value for social exchange, whereas most cultures place a high value on female sexuality. Most cultures do not place as much value on virginity or marital fidelity in men as in women. (Indeed, some commentators think that the marriage of Charles and Diana was partly shaped by pressure on Charles to marry a virgin, on the assumption that a future king should not marry someone who has already had other sex partners. It is doubtful that a female heir to the throne would be under similar pressure to marry a male virgin.) Likewise, in the extreme, women can sell sex for money— prostitution has been found all over the world in many different cultures—whereas that option is not widely available to men (except for a small number who, like women, cater to male customers).

Social exchange theory provides an economic perspective on sex. In essence, women's sexuality is the supply, and men's sexuality creates the demand. Moreover, people are hooked into the system, in the sense that their sexual decisions are affected by what other people in their peer group or community are doing. The "price" of sex, which is to say how much the man must invest before the woman consents to sex, may vary according to the standard laws of supply and demand. You may have noticed the difference if you have attended a school or college where one gender far outnumbers the other: The minority gender has much more influence. When men outnumber women (so that the supply of sex is lower than demand), the price is high: People have relatively little premarital or extramarital sex, and men must usually make a serious commitment before they can have sex. If a man doesn't want to make the commitment, he has few alternatives available and will probably just not have much sex. In contrast, when women outnumber men (such as after a major war or in some low-income groups where many men have been lost to violence, prison, suicide, or outmigration), the price of sex drops, and women cannot usually demand much from the man in exchange for sex. If she refuses sex, he can just move on and get it from someone else. A recent major study of modern American campuses has shown that sexual norms have in fact shifted toward more readily available, low-commitment sex as the proportion of female students has increased.[149]

Sex and Gender

Stereotypes about gender and sexuality include the following: (a) Men want sex more than women. (b) Men separate love and sex more than women. (c) Women's sexuality is more natural, whereas men's sexuality reflects more cultural influence. (d) Women serve as "gatekeepers" who restrict the total amount of sex and decide whether and when sex will happen. Two of these are correct, and two are incorrect; can you pick which ones are which?

The first stereotype asserts that there is a gender difference in strength of sex drive. During the 1970s, sex was seen as an unmitigated good; to say that men had a stronger sex drive implied that they were somehow better than women. However, the notion that more sex is always better was soon discredited as AIDS, unwanted pregnancies, and other problems surfaced. So it is perhaps possible now to take a fresh look at whether there is a gender difference in sex drive without worrying that some possible conclusions will be politically incorrect.

social exchange theory theory that seeks to understand social behavior by analyzing the costs and benefits of interacting with each other; it assumes that sex is a resource that women have and men want

Nearly all the evidence supports the view that men have a stronger sex drive than women (see **FIGURE 12.8**). What behaviors do you think would reveal the strength of sex drive? Almost any form of overtly sexual behavior you might suggest is something men do more than women. Men think about sex more often, are aroused more often, desire sex more often, desire more sex partners, and desire more different kinds of sex acts than women. Men initiate sex more and refuse sex less than women. Men take more risks and expend more resources to get sex. Men want sex earlier in the relationship, want it more often during the relationship, and even want it more in old age. Men have more positive attitudes about their own genitals than do women, and they also have more positive attitudes about their partner's genitals than do women. Men find it harder to live without sex. (For example, some religious callings require people to give up sex, but all evidence suggests that men fail at this far more often than women.) And men rate their sex drives as stronger than women rate theirs. Essentially, every measure and every study point to greater sexual motivation among men.[150] Some experts still disagree,[151] though their work has come under fire for its methods.[152]

One of the largest and most consistent gender differences is in the desire for casual, uncommitted sex,[153] which is probably based in a simple desire to have sex with different partners. The term **Coolidge effect** was coined to refer to the sexually arousing power of a new partner. Specifically, a male animal would have sex and researchers would measure how long it took until he could become aroused again, as a function of having either the same partner or a new partner willing to copulate with him.[154] Males typically were more rapidly and more aroused by the new partner than by the familiar one.[155]

The term *Coolidge effect* is based on an amusing story about former U.S. President Calvin Coolidge, who was known for being a man of very few words. Once he and the First Lady toured a farm and were shown around separately. The First Lady noticed that the chicken area had many females but only one male. She inquired about this seeming imbalance, and the farmer assured her that the cock was in fact able to perform sexually dozens of times every night. "Please point that out to Mr. Coolidge," she told the farmer. A short time later, when the president came to this area, the farmer dutifully said that the First Lady had specifically asked him to tell the president that the rooster was able to have sex over and over each night. "Same hen every time?" asked the president, and the farmer answered that no, these prodigious sexual feats involved copulating with many different hens. "Point that out to Mrs. Coolidge," said the laconic president.

None of this should be taken to mean that women do not enjoy sex, or should not enjoy it. Enjoyment and desire are different. Also, at times (such as when newly falling in love) when women do desire sex almost as much as men, and certainly some women regularly desire more than some men. Many couples find that their sexual desires seem to match almost perfectly when they are falling in love, and they get married expecting a lifelong rich sexual relationship—but when the passionate phase wears off, they revert to their different baselines, and the husband usually wants sex more than the wife.

An Australian researcher persuaded a sample of married couples to keep daily reports of their sexual activities, for a book called *The Sex Diaries*.[156] She was hoping for steamy stories, and she got a few, but to her surprise the far more common report was that the wife had lost most of her interest in sex within a couple years after the wedding, while the husband continued to want to have sex. The researcher commented that many married women talk to each other about their clever little strategies for avoiding sex (e.g., starting an argument just before bedtime), without realizing how much anguish and disappointment their refusals caused the husbands. One husband had become so frustrated by his wife's rejection of his advances that he said he would wait until she initiated sex—with the result that they had had no sex for nine years! In such cases, one can feel sympathy for both persons. It is difficult for a wife to be subjected to frequent pressure to

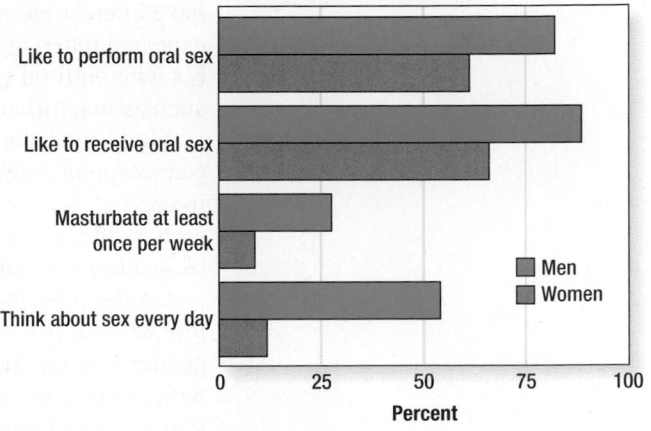

© Cengage Learning

FIGURE 12.8

More men than women report high sexual desire on almost every measure, but some differences are bigger than others.

Popperfoto/Getty Images

President Calvin Coolidge and First Lady Grace Coolidge.

Coolidge effect the sexually arousing power of a new partner (greater than the appeal of a familiar partner)

have intercourse when she does not want to. It is also difficult for a husband who never expected marriage to require him to give up most or all his sexual pleasure, especially if his wife both refuses most of his advances and disapproves of him finding other outlets such as masturbation or pornography.

The second stereotype was that men can separate sex and love more than women. This stereotype probably arose from a valid observation, which was that men are much more interested than women in having sex without love. (The evolutionary theory, described earlier, offers a strong explanation for why this should be true.) Men do surpass women in seeking and enjoying sex without love.

On the other hand, love and sex can be separated in the opposite manner—enjoying love without sex—and it appears that women find this more acceptable. Thus, as to which gender can separate love from sex better, we have a seeming standoff: Men accept sex without love, whereas women accept love without sex. (Both genders, however, probably find love combined with sex to be the best.) To resolve this standoff, one national survey asked people whether they agreed with the statement "Love and sex are two different things."[157] More women than men agreed with this statement. In that sense, women separate sex and love more than men. Hence, the stereotype that men separate love from sex more easily than women is wrong.

The third stereotype has depicted women as closer to nature and men as closer to culture. This is relevant to the clash of theories we noted earlier: Is the sex drive mainly determined by culture, politics, and socialization, or by genes, hormones, and innate biological motivations? The answer does differ by gender—but in the way opposite to the stereotype.

To be sure, both nature and culture have an influence on every human being's sexuality. The balance between nature and culture can be expressed in terms of **erotic plasticity**, defined as the degree to which the sex drive can be shaped and altered by social, cultural, and situational forces. High plasticity indicates that culture can shape the person's sex drive to a great extent, whereas a more "natural" and inflexible sex drive would have low plasticity.

Considerable evidence shows that women have higher erotic plasticity than men.[158,159] (It is not necessarily better or worse to have high plasticity.) Adult women often go through many changes in their sexual feelings and desires, whereas men remain much more constant through life.[160] Even switching back and forth between heterosexual and homosexual forms of sexuality is more common among women than men.[161,162] A man's sexual desires at age 20 are probably the same ones he will have at age 60, except for the natural diminishment due to aging. In contrast, a woman may have changed her desires and feelings several times along the way.[163,164] Another sign is that many social and cultural factors have a stronger influence on female than male sexuality. For example, highly educated women have quite different sex lives than uneducated women, and highly religious women have very different sex lives than nonreligious women—but for men, the corresponding differences are much smaller.[165,166] Thus, two powerful cultural forces (religion and education) affect female sexuality more strongly than male sexuality.

The difference in plasticity suggests a fairly basic difference in how the sex drive operates. We have seen that culture influences what things mean. Women's sexual responses typically depend on what sex means: who the partner is, what sex might signify about the relationship, what other couples are doing at similar stages, how she feels about the sexual partner, and what her sexual activity might signify about her as a person. Male sexuality seems much more to be a bodily, physical response. For example, a man who likes oral sex might well enjoy it whenever and wherever (and with whomever) the opportunity arises, but a woman who likes oral sex will only want it under certain circumstances and in contexts that carry the right meanings.

In short, the third stereotype is wrong, even specifically backward. Male sexuality is closer to nature and less affected by culture; women's sexuality is less biological and more closely tied to social and cultural meanings.

erotic plasticity the degree to which the sex drive can be shaped and altered by social, cultural, and situational forces

The fourth stereotype depicted women as the gatekeepers who restrict sex and decide whether and when it will happen. This is correct. Because men are not very choosy or cautious about sex, they are usually willing to have it under a wide variety of circumstances. Women are much more selective and hence become the ones who make the decision. Many findings confirm that women are the sexual gatekeepers. For example, a study of couples in various relationship stages[167] considered the category of "reluctant virgins"— people who had a dating partner and wanted to be having sex but were not having it because their partner did not consent. This category was filled almost entirely with men. The implication is that men were ready for sex fairly early, but whether sex happened depended on the woman's choice.

One revealing study surveyed dating couples at Pennsylvania State University. Researchers asked how many dates participants thought there should be before sex. They also asked each participant to estimate how many dates other people thought there should be before sex. The results were surprising: Nearly everyone thought that other people were leaping into bed faster than they themselves were. (For example, women thought that they would have sex after an average of 18 dates, but women typically estimated that other women would have sex after about 13 dates). Crucially, the researchers compared when the individual wanted to start having sex and when the couple actually did start having sex. The correlation between what men wanted and what happened was not significantly different from zero. In other words, the man's wishes were essentially irrelevant to whether or when the couple actually did have sex. In contrast, there was a very high correlation between the woman's preferences and the couple's activities.[168] Thus, a heterosexual couple starts having sex when the woman thinks it is appropriate; usually the man has been ready and waiting for some time.

Many dates involve eating together, and it is fair to assume that eating together usually precedes having sex together. To learn more about the effects of dieting on sex, read *Food for Thought*.

Homosexuality

All these findings apply mainly to heterosexual relationships. In many respects, homosexual romance, sex, and love are quite similar to what happens between heterosexuals

Eating in Front of a Cute Guy

In the movie (and novel) *Gone With the Wind*, the heroine, Scarlett O'Hara, prepares for a dinner party by eating a meal at home. Asked about the seeming absurdity of eating just before dinner, she explains her behavior in self-presentational terms: A lady is expected to eat very little, so even though she is going to a dinner party, she will make the best impression if she hardly eats anything there. And because she is a hungry human being, the best way for her to refrain from eating the delicious food at the party is to be satiated before she goes!

Research has confirmed that people, perhaps especially women, eat sparingly in the presence of an attractive member of the opposite sex. In a laboratory study, college students ate a meal in the presence of an attractive male or female confederate. Both men and women ate less in the presence of an opposite-gender than a same-sex confederate.[169] Moreover, the reduced eating was correlated with the motive to gain social approval by doing what is socially

desirable, for both men and women. For women, additionally, the restraint on eating was linked to the wish to seem feminine. Thus, female eating in particular is tied to the pressures to please others and live up to cultural ideals of femininity.

The importance of making a good impression on a potential dating partner was confirmed in other work where participants had the opportunity to eat snack foods (peanuts and M&M candies) while engaged in a get-acquainted conversation with a confederate. The confederate was either male or female. Half the time the confederate was presented as a desirable and interesting person, but half the time the confederate came across as something of a narrow-minded loser who had no hobbies or interests other than watching television, who had no career goals other than making money, and who claimed to already be in a romantic relationship. Female participants ate by far the least when in the presence of the attractive, desirable, and available man; they ate more in the presence of a woman or an unattractive man.[170] Thus, they seemed to restrain their eating for self-presentational reasons, mainly to make a good impression on a potential dating partner. The results were less clear-cut for male participants.

They ate less in the presence of a woman than in the presence of a man, but the woman's availability and desirability did not seem to affect their eating. Men's restraint may be a matter of politeness and general norms that are activated by any woman, rather than a particular effort to make a good impression.

Thus, restraining one's food intake may be more important to women seeking to make a good impression on a potential dating partner than it is to men. This was confirmed in another study, in which female participants were given feedback suggesting that they had scored as either masculine or feminine in terms of their interests and personality. When women received private feedback that they were feminine, they ate less, consistent with the view that femininity operates as a cue to refrain from eating. But in another condition, the women were told that their male partners had seen their masculine/feminine scores. The women who thought their partner knew they had scored as "masculine" ate the lowest amount of any group in the experiment. Presumably they sought to reestablish their feminine image by eating lightly, thereby conforming to the cultural ideal of femininity.

(for example, the desire for multiple partners is more common among male than female homosexuals),[171] but there are some unique aspects. For one, without clearly defined gender roles, homosexuals may feel freer to negotiate their roles in romance and sex without conforming to how society has trained people to act. Of course, this can also make things a bit more awkward, precisely because one does not have a culturally determined script. For example, if you are a heterosexual, you probably know how to act on a date with someone of the opposite sex, but if you were on a date with a member of your own sex, you would be constrained by fewer standard rules to say who should pay the bill, who should hold the door for whom, and so forth.

The basic fact that homosexuality exists all over the world and survives generation after generation poses a fundamental challenge to some of the major theories discussed so far. If sexuality is a product of cultural conditioning, how can homosexuality continue to exist? Most cultures have condemned homosexuality to varying degrees, and dominant cultures have often taken a fairly extreme position that homosexuality is sinful, illegal, and socially undesirable. If cultural socialization shapes sexuality, why is anyone a homosexual? On the other hand, if the sex drive is shaped by evolution based on natural selection and success at reproduction, then again homosexuality should have vanished long ago because homosexual sex does not produce children. How would a "gay gene" be passed along to future generations, if gay sex does not produce children?

At present we have no satisfactory answers. One intriguing theory, put forward by social psychologist Daryl Bem is known as EBE, for "exotic becomes erotic."[172,173] It is based on Schachter's theory of emotion,[174] discussed in Chapter 6, which holds that emotions arise when people have a bodily response of arousal and then put a label on it. Bem proposed that a specific gene for homosexuality does not exist but proposed that genes do contribute to temperament. Heterosexual development proceeds because boys and girls are temperamentally different and therefore play mainly with their own gender during childhood. To boys, therefore, other boys are familiar, whereas girls are different and "exotic." In adolescence, the boy may start to spend time around girls and will find himself nervous and otherwise aroused because they are different. He then learns to label this as sexual arousal. For heterosexual girls, the reverse applies: Boys seem different and exotic, so being around them is more arousing, and this arousal becomes labeled as romantic and sexual attraction.

Homosexuals, in Bem's theory, follow a similar process, except that during childhood they typically play with the other gender rather than their own. Some boys are temperamentally suited to prefer quiet play with girls rather than rough-and-tumble play with boys. When these boys reach adolescence, girls seem familiar, whereas other boys seem exotic. The nervousness arising from boys then gets labeled as sexual arousal. The reverse applies to girls, though as Bem noted, girls are more likely than boys to grow up having regular contact with and playmates of both genders.[175] (Bem suggested that women may be more bisexual than men precisely because they grow up around both boys and girls.)

At least one crucial step in Bem's theory—the labeling of nervousness as sexual arousal, leading to homosexual self-identification—has not yet been supported (or contradicted, for that matter) by data, probably because it is unethical to do properly controlled experiments that might transform someone into a homosexual. Bem's theory fits well with the research findings available at the time he developed it (the 1990s), but at present it still rests partly on speculation. If Bem's theory does not turn out to be correct, then researchers must keep on looking for the mysterious combination of nature (genes, hormones) and social experiences that leads to homosexuality. Almost certainly there will be a combination of nature and nurture. For example, if one identical twin is gay, then the odds are about 50% that the other twin is gay.[176] This is far above chance, which indicates that genes have something to do with it. But it is far short of a full explanation: If identical twins share 100% of their genes, then they should share 100% of genetic traits (such as eye color), whereas homosexuality is only shared at 50%. Social influences and personal experiences must explain the 50% of cases in which one twin is gay and the other is not.

Another reason to be cautious about Bem's theory is that it says that attraction is based on being different. We saw in Chapter 11 that friendship and other forms of attraction are more commonly based on similarity than difference (that is, "opposites attract" is not usually correct, whereas "birds of a feather flock together" is usually correct). It is possible that sexual desire is different, and indeed sexual attraction to the opposite gender is more common than attraction to one's own gender. Sexual desire may therefore be a special case. Still, more research is needed before psychology can claim to have a solid understanding of these matters.

Extradyadic Sex

In the course of long relationships, many couples have some conflicts about sex. One person may want to try some sex act that the other doesn't, or one may simply want sex more often than the other. In theory, the logical solution might be to find another partner. After all, if your husband doesn't want to play tennis with you, you just find another tennis partner and tell your husband about it later. Alas, that approach doesn't seem to work so well with sex.

In most long-term romantic relationships, the two partners expect each other to refrain from having sex with anyone else. When one person violates that expectation, the other is likely to be upset, and the relationship may be damaged or may even break up. This chapter began with the story of Charles and Diana, and though their marriage may have had multiple problems, it seems likely that the frequent infidelities by both of them contributed to their difficulties and eventual divorce. Even the term *infidelity* conveys a value judgment of disapproval (which is why many researchers prefer more neutral terms such as extramarital sex or even the broader term **extradyadic sex**, which is not limited to cases involving marriage).

Some couples have an "open" relationship, by which they mean that they are permitted to have sex with other people. During the sexual revolution of the 1970s, during which many people aspired to have such relationships and even to participate openly in sex with other people, extramarital sex was not regarded as being unfaithful.

Rare or Common?

Different surveys have reported different rates of extramarital sex. Some conclude that nearly half of married people eventually stray;[177] other studies conclude that extramarital sex is quite rare. There are several reasons for the different numbers, but two of them are important. First, the rate of extramarital sex has probably changed. It may have been more common and more tolerated in the 1970s than afterward, especially when the herpes and AIDS epidemics became widely known. Second, different studies use different sampling methods, and people who volunteer to answer a survey about sex are more likely to report extensive sexual experience than people who do not volunteer.[178,179,180]

The most reliable numbers suggest that there is far less extramarital sex (indeed far less sex altogether) than you might think from movies, novels, TV shows, and celebrity news. According to the National Health and Social Life Survey, more than 75% of husbands and 90% of wives claim to have been completely faithful over the entire period of their marriage.[181] Using another well-constructed national sample, researchers concluded that 23% of men and 12% of women have ever engaged in extramarital sex (including in a previous marriage).[182] Even if these numbers are precisely accurate, the actual rates of infidelity may end up being a little higher because some people who have not yet had an affair will eventually do so. Still, that is not likely to make a huge difference, so one must assume that monogamy and fidelity are the norm. Estimates that half of married men have affairs[183] are probably not accurate. The truth is closer to 1 out of 3 or 4 husbands, and 1 out of 9 or 10 wives, has sex with someone other than the spouse while married. Moreover, many of these are one-time occurrences in the course of a long marriage. In any given year, more than 90% of husbands and wives remain sexually faithful to their spouses.

To be sure, all these data are based on self-reports (what people are willing to tell an interviewer or report on a questionnaire), and it is hard to rule out the possibility that people claim to be more faithful than they are. In recent years, DNA tests have begun to confirm that many children (between 5% and 15%, according to most experts on paternity testing) are not biologically related to the man they believe is their father, presumably because the mother conceived the child through extramarital sex.[184] If that many women actually have children as a result of secret affairs, then the total amount of extramarital sex by women is probably much higher than we have assumed, and higher than many women are admitting.

Evolutionary psychologists[185] have pointed out that having such affairs and duping the husband into raising the children as if they were his own is a strategy that makes good sense from the (admittedly amoral) standpoint of passing on one's genes. Highly successful and attractive men may have the best genes, and so a woman can make the best offspring by conceiving a child with such a man, even if he is not willing to marry her. To receive long-term financial support and care, she may need to marry a different man who might not have such good genes, but if he believes her children are his, he will take good care of them and provide for them. It does appear to be true that millions of men in North America and Western Europe have been fooled into raising children who are not their own.[186] Some experts have proposed that for a woman to dupe a man into raising children who were secretly conceived via extramarital sex is more immoral than rape.[187]

Extradyadic Sex and Breakups

Extramarital sex is a risk factor for breaking up. That is, people who remain faithful are more likely to stay together than people who have sex with other partners.[188] This is true

extradyadic sex having sex with someone other than one's regular relationship partner

AP Images/Chicago Sun-Times, Robert A. Davis

even for couples who have an "open marriage" or other understanding that permits extramarital sex.[189] In a national survey, 38% of men who had had extramarital sex had also gotten a divorce, whereas only 15% of the fully faithful husbands had divorced. Among women, the corresponding numbers were 20% and 8%.[190] Thus, having extramarital sex was associated with more than double the divorce rate, as compared to fidelity.

One cannot leap to the conclusion, however, that extramarital sex causes divorce. After all, researchers cannot randomly assign people to have or not have extramarital sex, which is the sort of research design needed for firm conclusions about causality (see Chapter 1). Some people may be deeply unhappy about their marriage and have an affair as a result of their dissatisfaction. The affair could therefore be a symptom rather than a cause of the marital unhappiness, and perhaps those people would have gotten a divorce even if they had not had an affair.

People often view their own infidelities (if they have committed them) as a result rather than a cause of the problems in their relationships.[191] Their partner's infidelities, however, are seen as an important cause leading directly to the relationship problems and even to the breakup. This finding probably reflects a self-serving bias (discussed in Chapter 5): People see their own misbehavior as being caused by external factors and not producing bad consequences but see their partner's actions in a less favorable light; in short, they would prefer to blame the divorce on their partner's actions rather than on their own. Still, these data do suggest that the causal arrow can point in either direction: Marital problems can lead to infidelity, or vice versa. In a famous television interview, Diana attributed her marital problems to Charles's infidelities, but she neglected to mention her own. If she was like most people, she was quick to say that her partner's sexual activities with others had damaged the marriage, whereas her own outside sexual activities were merely a result of the problems in the marriage—in effect, blaming him but not herself for similar actions.

We also should not overstate the link. Affairs do not lead inevitably to breaking up. In fact, only a small minority of extramarital affairs lead to divorce.[192] Infidelity is a risk factor, but the risk remains fairly small. Still, the affair is often a bigger risk than people anticipate. One researcher found that many people in her sample began their extramarital affairs with the firm belief that they could control the new sexual involvement and that their marriage would not be affected.[193] Often they were wrong. In particular, many people find themselves falling in love with their extramarital sex partners, especially when they have sex repeatedly or on a regular basis over a period of months. The strong emotional involvement often develops into a threat to the marriage, indeed more than the sex itself. Even if the marriage survives, it may be damaged or shaken by one person's love for someone else.

These patterns fit several themes. We saw earlier in this chapter that looking at tempting alternative partners can lead to breaking up one's current relationship, and now we see that having sex or romance with other partners likewise puts the relationship at risk. Avoiding those temptations is thus one constructive strategy to help preserve a relationship. One theme of this book is that nature says go and culture says stop. It is apparently natural to feel tempted from time to time to admire or even pursue alternative partners, but people can learn to resist and overcome these temptations (as culture prescribes). Another theme is the importance of self-regulation for overriding antisocial impulses. Being happily married or attached does not mean that the automatic system is indifferent to other possible partners. Self-regulation (here, in the form of stopping oneself from pursuing other partners) is a big part of the work that goes into making a relationship succeed.

Extradyadic Activity in Dating Relationships

Infidelity has also been studied in dating relationships. In dating relationships "extradyadic relations" is defined as erotic kissing, petting, or intercourse with someone other than your steady dating partner, and studies have found that 71% of men and 57% of women had experienced this (either by doing it or having their partner do it).[194] Despite the high frequency of experiences, most people expressed low tolerance and a negative attitude toward such activity. Many people disapproved of such activities but occasionally engaged in them anyway. The self-serving bias was apparent there too. In this research, people rated their own extradyadic relations as less bad than their partner's. When asked how much the extradyadic relations had caused pain and suffering, only 9% of men and 14% of women said their own infidelity had hurt their partner a great deal. In contrast, 45% of men and 30% of women said their partner's infidelity had hurt them a great deal. As usual, people seem more willing to make excuses for their own misbehavior than for their partner's!

Jealousy and Possessiveness

In medieval Europe, there were relatively few police and courts, and the system of law enforcement was not equal to the task of maintaining order. If people misbehaved or committed crimes, it often fell to the community itself to take action. One common form of punishment for less serious crimes and offenses was called the *charivari* (French word) or *shivaree* (English word). The whole village would gather together at some crucial place,

Romeo Ranoco/Reuters/Landov

In medieval Europe, charivari involved banging pots and pans, as depicted here, to punish the husband of an adulterous woman, as well as less serious crimes. It is still practiced in some parts of the world today.

such as outside the house of the offender. They would bring pots and other items and bang them together to make a loud noise. They would also shout or chant insulting remarks and might make embarrassing sounds. The point was to humiliate the offender.[195] The charivari was used to punish adultery. If a wife had sex with a man other than her husband, and enough people found out, the village would stage a charivari. Ironically, though, the charivari was not generally used to punish the adulterous woman or her lover. Instead, the village would punish the husband. The implication was that he had not satisfied his wife sexually or exerted sufficient control over her behavior, so he needed to be punished. Apparently, if a man's wife had sex with another man, it was the husband's fault.[196]

The husband's humiliation, whether implicitly felt in the mere shame of his wife's infidelity, or explicitly recognized through the charivari, suggests an important link between jealousy and pride or self-esteem. When two people decide to have an extramarital affair, they often think mainly of themselves, and they may not intend any harm to their spouses. But if the affair comes to light, the spouses will have a variety of negative reactions, and these are often linked to a feeling of humiliation. Finding out that your spouse or romantic partner has been unfaithful is often a serious blow to your pride. Sure enough, people married to unfaithful partners have lower self-esteem than people married to faithful partners.[197]

Jealousy is a common response to partner infidelity, and many people feel jealous over even fairly minor signs that the partner might be interested in someone else, such as a flirtatious conversation at a party. Researchers distinguish jealousy from envy on the basis that jealousy is a fear of losing something that you have, whereas envy is a desire for something you do not have.[198]

Cultural Perspective

Some experts believe that jealousy is a product of social roles and expectations. In particular, some argue that Western societies have made men believe that women are their property, so men are jealous and sexually possessive of women. If only the culture taught people differently, the emotion of jealousy might disappear, according to this view.

Support for the cultural theory of jealousy came most famously from the anthropologist Margaret Mead's work *Coming of Age in Samoa,* though subsequent researchers have questioned her methods and conclusions and have even suggested that the handful of Samoans she interviewed were joking. Mead claimed that the Samoans did not have sexual jealousy or possessiveness. They allow their partners to share intimate interactions with others.[199] Similar observations have been made about Native American (Eskimo) cultures, in which male houseguests sometimes have sex with the hostess, with her husband's permission.

More recent work, however, has questioned those seemingly idyllic, nonpossessive attitudes. Sexual jealousy is found in all cultures and societies, although its forms, rules, and expressions may vary from one to another.[200,201] Eskimos do in fact have considerable sexual jealousy. The occasional sharing of a wife's sexual favors occurs only under certain circumstances, including consent by everyone involved and usually a desire to form a closer relationship between the two families. A cross-cultural study of 92 different societies and cultures found sexual jealousy in all of them, although again how they dealt with it varied.[202] In some, for example, a husband was permitted to beat or even kill his wife if he caught her having sex with another man, whereas other cultures prohibited such violent responses. Another survey found that different countries focused jealousy on different acts—for example, kissing someone other than your spouse elicits jealousy in some but is permitted in others—but again jealousy was found everywhere, and the various cultures were more similar than different.[203]

These findings suggest that society can modify and channel jealousy but cannot effectively eliminate it. Apparently, some degree of sexual possessiveness is deeply rooted in human nature. It is normal and natural to feel jealous if you find your partner has had sexual relations with someone else.

Evolutionary Perspective

The apparent universality of jealousy suggests that we should look to biological and evolutionary patterns to help explain it. Jealousy has a strong evolutionary defense, but these reasons differ somewhat for men as opposed to women.[204] These differences can be traced to the differences in male versus female reproductive systems. Both men and women supposedly want to pass on their genes, but the possibilities and dangers differ.

Men know that their wives can only have a few children, and normally just one at a time. Hence, a major threat to the man's reproductive goal is the possibility that another man might make his wife pregnant. Throughout most of history, it was impossible for men to know whether the children borne by their female partners were in fact the men's own offspring, so they faced a constant danger of raising the children of other men. The only solution was to keep strict control over the wife's sexual behavior. In various cultures, some men have kept their wives locked up and guarded, such as in a harem. Other men insisted that their wives wear iron chastity belts, which were originally designed as protection against rape but soon were adapted to help men retain confidence in their wives' fidelity. Such practices are largely absent in the modern Western world, though some men (and a few women) use threatened or actual physical violence to pressure

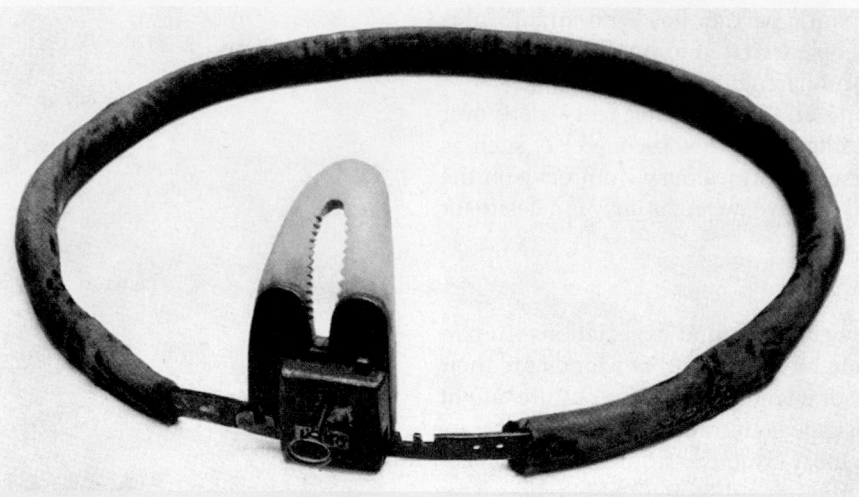

In the past men required women to use chastity belts to make sure they didn't have sex with other men.

their partners into remaining faithful. Because suspicions of jealousy can be unfounded, this violence sometimes hurts innocent victims. Even if the partner has been unfaithful (and, as noted above, DNA tests suggest that paternity fraud is still an important issue),[205] perpetrating or threatening physical violence against a romantic partner is immoral and illegal.

For women, the threat is different. If a woman's husband has sex with another woman, he has only expended a small quantity of sperm, and there is plenty more where that came from! The sperm itself is thus no great loss, and a single sex act does not therefore constitute much of a threat. On the other hand, the woman may depend on the man to provide her with food and other resources, as well as provide for her children. If he becomes involved with another woman, he may bestow some of his resources on her, which would leave the wife and her children in a poorer position. Men are well aware that women seek men who have resources, and this influences their behavior (see *Money Matters*). Hence, the greatest threat to the woman is the possibility that the man will become emotionally involved with someone else and therefore withhold these crucial resources.

This evolutionary theory about gender differences in sexual possessiveness was put to experimental tests in which students were asked a difficult question: Would it be worse for the person you love to have a one-time sexual encounter with another person without any emotional involvement, or for the person you love to have a lasting, emotionally intimate relationship with a member of your gender—but one that did not include sexual intercourse?

To be sure, neither men nor women were very happy with either possible scenario. But when forced to choose, they could do so—and their choices differed by gender. The majority of men (60%) objected more strongly to the sexual infidelity. In contrast, the women objected more to the emotional infidelity (only 17% objected more to the sexual infidelity).[206] These findings fit the evolutionary view: Male possessiveness focuses heavily on the sex act and is less concerned with intimate conversations, whereas female possessiveness emphasizes the emotional relationship and is less concerned with the sex act itself.

As is often the case, subsequent work has made the picture more complicated. In particular, men are often upset over both sexual and emotional relationships that link their wives or girlfriends with another man.[207,208,209] Also, some people assume that one form of infidelity will lead to the other, so the difference between sexual and emotional infidelity may not be as simple as the hypothetical dilemma posed by the experimenters makes it seem.[210] Nonetheless, researchers have reason to think that men and women do experience jealousy somewhat differently on average and may worry about different aspects of what their partners do with other lovers.

Causes of Jealousy

Jealousy thus seems to be a product of both the person and the situation. This impression is confirmed if we ask about the accuracy of people's jealous suspicions. To be sure, there are some cases of false jealousy; in particular, abusive individuals who have jealous rages and become physically violent toward their partners often are acting on suspicions that are completely unfounded.[215,216] Many jealous suspicions are, however, accurate.

In one large-scale investigation, researchers interviewed both husband and wife separately and then compared notes. Thus, they could ask the husband whether he believed his wife had ever been unfaithful and then check his response against his wife's actual (confidential) answer as to whether she had in fact strayed. They found that most

Women are attracted to men partly on the basis of thinking men will be generous providers. At some level, men seem to know this. Thoughts of women, sexuality, and mating change the way that men handle money.

One classic tradeoff involves now versus later. With money, people sometimes must choose between taking some money now versus getting a larger amount later. In research, as in life, the choice is often such that waiting for the larger amount will bring the best outcome in the long run, but when people feel money pressure in the heat of the moment, they will accept less in order to have it immediately. After men looked at sexy pictures or handled brassieres, they were more inclined to take the money now rather than waiting for more money later.[211]

The importance of sexual attraction was shown in a study where participants choose between receiving a modest amount of money (e.g., $15) right away and receiving a larger sum (e.g., $50) several weeks later. Most people in most conditions were willing to wait for the larger reward, but men who had looked at pictures of attractive women shifted toward taking the money right away.[212] No such shift was found if the men looked at pictures of unattractive women, or pictures of attractive or unattractive cars. Women looking at pictures of men likewise were unaffected. Thus, the urgency to have money now stems from male desire for attractive females.

The so-called ultimatum game (a popular research method) involves having one person decide how to divide payment between self and another person. The other person can then either accept the deal or refuse it, and if he or she refuses, neither person gets anything. The second person, "the responder," is thus sometimes faced with a choice between money and pride. For example, if both persons worked on the task, and the divider offers to split a $10 payment by keeping $8 and giving the responder only $2, the responder faces an unpleasant choice. The $2 is unfair and a bit humiliating, but then again it is arguably better to take $2 than nothing. In general, men tend to refuse such unfair offers in order to preserve their pride. But if the previous part of the experiment had involved having the men look at pictures of women in bikinis and lingerie, the men tend to swallow their pride and take the money.[213]

The underlying principle appears to be that when men are thinking about wooing women, they realize that money is important to have because women choose men on that basis. An early investigation showed that after men had looked at pictures of attractive women, they placed higher value on money and expressed greater ambition to become financially successful in life, as compared to men who looked at photos of older, relatively unattractive women.[214] Similar effects were found just by having men fill out the questionnaires in the presence of attractive women, as opposed to being in the presence of only other men. Thus, attraction to women makes men want money.

---

suspicions of infidelity were justified. Only about 10% of wives' suspicions and 13% of husbands' suspicions were mistaken.[217] Thus, paranoid (false) jealousy is fairly unusual, although it certainly does exist. In marriage, at least, people who suspect their spouses of being unfaithful are usually correct. (The rates of unfounded suspicion were higher among couples who were living together without being married. For both men and women, slightly more than 20% of the people who suspected their cohabiting partners had been unfaithful were wrong.)

This is not to say that the partner always knows. In many cases, the partner falsely believed that the spouse had been faithful. Across various categories, these amounted to between 20% and 30% of unfaithful partners.[218] A study of college dating couples found that a large number were unaware of their partners' genuine infidelities.[219] Thus, a sizable minority of people manage to keep their affairs secret from their partners. But among spouses who suspected infidelity, most were correct. In any case, the evidence suggests that most but not all jealous suspicions have some valid basis.

Jealousy and Type of Interloper

The identity of the interloper (that is, the third person who has sex with one member of a romantic couple) also has an impact on how jealous people get. A common reaction to learning of a partner's infidelity is to disparage the interloper: "If you had to have an affair, did you have to choose such a loser?"[220] But such reactions tend to be irrational. After all, would you prefer your partner to have sex with someone who is not a suitable partner (and hence no competition to you)—or with somebody who is terrific? Remember, jealousy is essentially a response to a threat to your romantic attachment, so the less of a threat the interloper is, the less jealous you should feel. A loser won't steal your partner away, but a desirable, eligible person might.

This reasoning led some social psychologists to predict that people's jealousy would depend on how their own traits stacked up against those of the interloper. Their results fit very well with the view of jealousy as responding to threat. Even if the other person was reasonably talented, people were less jealous as long as those talents did not resemble their own. The worst jealousy occurred when the partner became involved with someone whose abilities exceeded their own, in the same area.[221,222] Thus, if you are a student in medical school, and your partner sleeps with an athlete, you may be unhappy about it, but your jealousy may remain at only a moderate level. Your jealousy would be much worse if your partner slept with someone who (like you) is also a medical student, and it will be worst of all if that other person has better grades than you or already has a medical degree. Similarly, if you are an athlete, then you'll be more jealous about your partner having sex with another athlete than with a medical student, and if the interloper's athletic skills surpass your own you will be extremely jealous.

Even the gender of the other person is important. Researchers found that men are less jealous and upset if their girlfriend has sex with a woman than with a man.[223] Probably this is because they believe that another man might steal the girlfriend away, whereas a woman would not be able to do so. Ironically, however, the same researchers found that women were less upset if their boyfriend had sex with another woman than with a man. In other words, both men and woman seem to object more strongly to a male interloper than to a female interloper. Women are regarded as less threatening. This fits the economic (exchange) theory of sexuality discussed earlier: In sex, women give something of value, whereas men take.

Social Reality

Thus far, however, we have not mentioned what may be the biggest factor of all in determining jealousy: the number of other people who know about the extradyadic sex.[224] If you learn that your partner has had a highly discreet, secret affair, you may well be upset, but your jealousy will not reach the highest levels. The worst situation is apparently to realize that you are the last person in your social network to learn about your partner's affair. By the time you find out, most of your friends already know about it, as do various other people. In simple terms, the more other people know about your partner's affair, the more upset and jealous you are likely to be.

Why does it matter so much what other people think? Probably this brings us back self-presentation and reputation. Your partner's affair makes you look bad. It makes you look like an incompetent lover who is unable to control your partner or keep him or her satisfied. This is why other people's knowledge becomes so important. The more other people know about the affair, the more they know something that reflects badly on you. The textbook theme of "putting people first" entails that people care about what others think, and that applies very strongly to sex.

Researchers sometimes use the term **social reality** to refer to public awareness of some event.[225] If something happens but nobody knows about it, it does not have much social reality (although it has objective reality). It is therefore possible to go on with life afterward and more or less pretend that the whole episode never happened. In contrast, if other people know about it, it is harder to ignore it or put it behind you.

Social reality is thus an important determinant of jealousy. If many other people know about your partner's infidelity, you may find it difficult to continue with the relationship. You have to face them, after all, and you may wonder when you go out with your partner whether other people are looking at the two of you and thinking about your partner's infidelity.

Culture, Female Sexuality, and the Double Standard

All known cultures seek to regulate sex in some ways. The reason is not hard to guess. Unregulated sexual behavior produces all sorts of social turmoil and disruption: jealous partners committing acts of violence, collapsing marriages, unwanted babies, epidemics

social reality beliefs held in common by several or many people; public awareness

of sexually transmitted diseases. Some relevant evidence emerged from an anthropological study of one African society that was very permissive with regard to sex, so that both premarital and extramarital sex were common.[226] Although many individuals derived excitement and enjoyment from these activities, the social costs were huge. In particular, sexually transmitted diseases rendered around 40% of the woman unable to bear children—which was both a lasting source of heartbreak to these unfortunate individuals (and their husbands) and a significant disruption in how society would pass along resources from one generation to the next.

In sex, nature certainly says "go" whereas culture often pleads "stop!" These pleas have generally been directed more at women than at men, resulting in a widespread pattern called the cultural suppression of female sexuality. Why women? Different explanations have been put forward. One follows from what was said earlier about female erotic plasticity: Women's sexuality responds to cultural influences better than men's, so if a culture wants to control sexuality, it will be more successful focusing on women.

Another, more common explanation is that the cultural suppression of female sexuality is rooted in men's wish to control women. A related explanation has to do with **paternity uncertainty**—the fact that a man cannot be sure that the children born to his female partner are his. Aristotle once said, "Mothers are fonder than fathers of their children because they are more certain they are their own." To be sure, recent advances in DNA testing have finally made it possible for a man to be certain. Research with these techniques has consistently found that a great many women trick their husbands into supporting children fathered by an illicit lover, a fact that some feminists have regarded with pride,[227] though it has also spawned a men's rights movement that seeks to release divorced men from paying child support for children who are not genetically related to them. According to the paternity uncertainty view, men try to stifle female sexuality in order to make their wives less interested in having sex with other partners. This interpretation does not have much direct evidence, however.

Much discussion of the cultural suppression of female sexuality has focused on the so-called double standard of sexual morality. The **double standard** is defined as a pattern of moral judgment that says specific sexual behaviors (especially premarital sex) are acceptable for men but immoral for women. By the conventional view, this double standard is a mechanism by which men seek to control women's sexuality.

The view of the double standard as reflecting male control of women received a severe blow in one of the most comprehensive and influential reviews of published research on sexuality.[228] In every study that had found evidence of a double standard, women supported it more than men. Apparently, women are the ones who condemn other women while permitting men to do similar things. For example, a large national survey in 1965 (before the sexual revolution had gotten far) asked whether a woman who engaged in premarital sex was immoral.[229] "Yes" answers were received from 42% of men but from 91% of women (we will discuss this difference further in a few paragraphs). Thus, women condemned other women much more harshly than men condemned them. Subsequent work confirmed this in another way. Female college students were asked whether they themselves believed in the double standard (nearly all said no) and whether they thought others believed it (most said yes)—and if so, who these others were. Far more said the condemnation of women came from other women than from men.[230] (The rest said it came from both genders equally.)

In retrospect, evidence for the double standard has always been much weaker than is often assumed. A series of careful studies tried multiple ways of measuring it and found either no double standard or even a **reverse double standard**—that people condemned men more than women for the same sexual behavior.[231]

A methodological error in past work had created a false impression of widespread belief in a double standard. The error was rooted in the fact that women are generally less permissive than men about sexual morality in general. For example, national surveys from the 1930s to the 1950s asked people whether premarital sex was acceptable for everyone, acceptable for no one, or acceptable for men but not for women.[232] Only the last option indicates a true double standard, and only a tiny fraction of respondents endorsed it. But there was a gender difference: Women tended to say premarital sex was acceptable

paternity uncertainty the fact that a man cannot be sure that the children born to his female partner are his

double standard condemning women more than men for the same sexual behavior (e.g., premarital sex)

reverse double standard condemning men more than women for the same sexual behavior (e.g., premarital sex)

for no one, whereas men tended to say it was acceptable for everyone. Careless researchers were misled into thinking support for a double standard was widespread. They confused "being rated acceptable *by* men" as meaning "being rated acceptable *for* men." In reality, most men and most women made judgments that showed no double standard.

Thus, the double standard is weaker than assumed and, more surprisingly, is supported by women more than men. Moreover, the importance of women and the female community in restraining sex is not limited to these few moral judgments. In fact, the cultural control of female sexuality comes primarily from women, and the pressures on women to restrain their sexual activities come from other women. Thus, it is women who punish the sexually active woman or girl with gossip and a bad reputation, who promote religious or moral injunctions to refrain from sex, who tell girls about the dangers of sex and pregnancy, and who in some cultures support and carry out surgical procedures that impair the woman's physical capacity to enjoy sex.[233]

Why would women seek to restrain each other's sexuality? The answer is probably based neither on pathology nor on self-destructive motives, but rather may lie in a simple and rational response to women's situation. The social exchange theory of sex (described previously) offers a clear explanation. For most of history, women have lacked opportunities to acquire wealth, education, power, and other resources to provide themselves with a good life. A woman's sexuality has often been the main resource she had with which to bargain (by making a favorable marriage) for access to the good life. It was therefore important for each woman to maintain as high an exchange value as possible for her sexuality. As with any resource, the price depends on supply and demand; restricting the supply raises the price. To the extent that the community of women could restrain each other's sexuality, they all stood to benefit from the higher value.

When men can get sex without offering much in return, women derive relatively little benefit from their sexual favors. In contrast, when sex is not readily available, men may offer women a great deal in return for sex, including love and commitment, long-term financial support, and other resources. Such offerings have been crucial to women's well-being in cultures and historical periods in which women were unable to provide for themselves in other ways. Rather than being passive dupes or victims of culture, women appear to have responded in rational ways so as to make the best of their circumstances. Putting pressure on each other to restrain sexual behavior has sometimes been in women's best interests.

QUIZ YOURSELF

Sexuality

1. **Which theory proposes that sexual attitudes and behaviors are the result of cultural forces and socialization?**
   - (a) Attachment theory
   - (b) Evolutionary theory
   - (c) Social construction theory
   - (d) Social exchange theory

2. **When men outnumber women, the price of sex _____ .**
   - (a) decreases
   - (b) increases
   - (c) increases then decreases
   - (d) stays the same

3. **Bjorn loves his wife, but he discovers that she has been unfaithful to him. To make matters worse, everyone knows she has been unfaithful to him. The common knowledge that Bjorn's wife has been unfaithful to him is called _____ .**
   - (a) double standard
   - (b) reverse double standard
   - (c) social construction
   - (d) social reality

4. **Waldo believes that premarital sex is acceptable for men but unacceptable for women. This belief illustrates _____ .**
   - (a) double standard
   - (b) erotic plasticity
   - (c) reverse double standard
   - (d) social construction

answers: see pg 445

What Makes Us *Human*

Sexual attraction and mating are found throughout nature, but they take on new and added dimensions among human beings. For one thing, long-term monogamous mating is much more common among human beings than among other species, especially apes and other primates. The ability to stay sexually faithful to one partner for decades appears to be quite specific to humans.[234,235]

Culture helps. The view that humans are "naturally" monogamous is contradicted by data indicating that polygamy has been common in many societies and cultures. Only after some historical struggles did most modern cultures ban polygamy and insist that you can only marry one spouse at a time. Were people not thus influenced by culture, monogamy would be less common.

The effect of human culture on love and mating can perhaps be most plainly seen in divorce. If two animals have a sexual relationship that fails to satisfy them, especially if they frequently annoy and aggravate each other, they can dissolve their relationship just by walking away. Human beings require the culture's permission, which often entails hiring lawyers and negotiating for months over what will happen to their jointly owned property and their children.

The cultural control of close relationships extends far beyond divorce, of course. Many laws regulate what goes on in the family, affecting everything from hitting family members to bequeathing them money. Culture also shapes relationships via informal influence, such as how relationships and sex are depicted in the mass media, which in turn helps shape how people treat each other. No other species has ever changed or reinvented its gender roles to the extent that human beings have done. In general, these changes have been positive: Unlike some animals, for example, humans are culturally discouraged from eating or beating their offspring.

Sex itself has been profoundly affected by culture. Formal laws have prohibited various sex acts (for example, oral and anal sex have been illegal in many cultures) and various kinds of sex partners (same-gender partners, relatives, or underage children). The mixture of economic, moral, and religious factors that created the cultural control of female sexuality is almost impossible to imagine in any other species. Patterns of sexual activity changed in many ways during the 20th century, with its so-called sexual revolution(s), including vast increases in premarital sex and oral sex. Among the many factors contributing to these changes were the improvements in birth control technology. Only cultural (human) animals have been able to invent new ways of controlling pregnancy and to change their sexual norms on that basis.

Perhaps the biggest difference is in human intimacy. Having mastered language, people have been able to create complex, intricate selves. Forming a close relationship often begins with a great deal of talking, by which people reveal and disclose their inner selves to each other. Indeed, one theory of language has proposed that the reason humans evolved to use language was to promote close relationships[236] because talking enabled people to get to know each other and stay connected much more efficiently than the methods used by other primates. It is almost impossible to imagine a human marriage or other close relationship without language and conversation. The slow building of intimacy by talking to each other for years is an important aspect of the long road that people follow to form bonds with each other.

The seemingly endless human fascination with love and sex has also produced a steady stream of cultural activities to depict and celebrate them. The basic inclinations toward sex and mating may be rooted in biology and shared across many species, but in human art they are transformed into something grander and more meaningful. Most of the music you hear consists of songs about love. Most books and movies have some coverage of love, not even counting the pornography industry that finds a ready market for simple depictions of sex. In fact, if you took away love (including sex) and violence (including crime), it is hard to imagine the American film industry surviving at all! Poetry too has long favored themes of love and romance, whereas no baboons or turtles write love sonnets to their sweethearts. Attractive nude young women (and men) have been favorite subjects for painters and sculptors. In short, much of human culture is about close relationships, love, and sexuality.

One of the most interesting and curious facts about human sex is that most people use a face-to-face position for intercourse. Most other mammals, including the great apes who are believed to be humans' closest biological relatives, rely on having the male enter the female from behind. Why are humans different? Possibly the more upright human posture for walking contributed by changing the direction of the internal organs. A more social explanation, however, points to something special and wonderful about human nature. The face-to-face position enables lovers to look into each other's eyes, kiss each other on the lips, and say sweet things to each other during sex. In that way, it is more compatible with promoting intimacy and sharing deep feelings of love. Quite possibly the earliest humans who began to make love in this position found that they were able to transform sex into a more meaningful act and one that would, by increasing love and intimacy, help build stronger families—and so perhaps their offspring fared better than people who still favored the older, animal positions for sex. If so, then the combination of love, intimacy, and sex is a crucial part of what makes us human.

CHAPTER 12 SUMMARY

- Good relationships are good for you. Married people (especially happily married people) live longer, healthier lives than single or divorced people.

What Is Love?

- Passionate love (also called romantic love) refers to having strong feelings of longing, desire, and excitement toward a special person.

- Companionate love (sometimes called affectionate love) refers to a high level of mutual understanding, caring, and commitment to make the relationship succeed.

- Passionate love is found all over the world, but the forms and expressions of romantic passion vary significantly from one culture to another.

- Companionate love is important for a long, happy marriage or a stable, trustworthy, lasting relationship.

- Married people have sex more often and more satisfyingly, but single people spend more time at each sexual episode and have more different partners.

- Sternberg proposed that love is composed of passion, intimacy, and commitment, and that these three ingredients can vary in strength in different relationships.

Different Types of Relationships

- Exchange relationships are based on reciprocity and fairness.

- Communal relationships are based on love and concern for each other, without expectation of direct, equal repayment.

- Communal relationships are more desirable in intimate relationships, but exchange relationships are more powerful for driving progress and increasing wealth in larger groups.

- The four kinds or styles of attachment are
  - Secure attachment, characterized by comfort with intimacy and no excessive fears of abandonment.
  - Dismissing avoidant attachment, characterized by avoidance of intimacy and discomfort with close relationships while viewing partners as unreliable, unavailable, and uncaring.
  - Fearful avoidant attachment, characterized by avoidance of intimacy and discomfort with close relationships while viewing the self as unlovable.
  - Preoccupied (or anxious/ambivalent) attachment, characterized by excessive desire for closeness to the point of desiring to merge with the partner, and worry about abandonment.

- Self-love and narcissism may not be beneficial to good relationships, but self-acceptance may help one get along with others.

Maintaining Relationships

- People in good relationships often think their relationships are getting better and better, but research suggests they actually stay at the same (good) level.

- The three factors of the investment model are
  - Satisfaction with the partner.
  - Quality of alternative partners.
  - Investment (sunk costs) in the relationship.

- The relationship-enhancing style of attribution involves attributing good acts to the partner's inner qualities and attributing bad acts to external factors. The distress-maintaining style of attribution is just the opposite.

- People in love generally hold idealized versions of each other.

- Relationships can thrive when couples remain on their best behavior with each other.

Sexuality

- Diamond's work suggests that attachment/love and sex are two separate psychological systems in humans, so love and sex don't always match.

- Social constructionist theories of sex assert that sexual attitudes and behaviors vary widely based on culture and learning. These theories seek to understand how personal experiences and cultural influences shape sexual desire and behavior.

- Evolutionary theory emphasizes that the sex drive was shaped by natural selection. Evolutionary psychologists seek to understand innate patterns of sexual desire and behavior.

- The social exchange theory views sex as a resource that women have and that men want and are willing to exchange other resources for.

- On average, men have a stronger sex drive than women.

- The stereotype that men separate love from sex more easily than women is wrong.

- Women show more erotic plasticity than men, meaning that women's sex drive can be shaped and altered by social, cultural, and situational forces, whereas men are more driven by innate, biological needs.

- Women act as the gatekeepers who restrict sex and decide whether and when it will happen.

- Sexual jealousy is found in all cultures and societies, although its forms, rules, and expressions may vary from one to another, suggesting that some degree of sexual possessiveness is deeply rooted in human nature.

- Jealousy can focus on either a sexual or an emotional connection to an outsider. Men may focus more strongly on the sexual aspect than women.

- The more other people know about your partner's infidelity, the more upset and jealous you are likely to be.

- All known cultures seek to regulate sex in some ways.

- Paternity uncertainty refers to the fact that a man cannot be sure that the children born to his female partner are his (at least until recent advances in DNA testing).

- The sexual double standard is defined as a pattern of moral judgment that says specific sexual behaviors are acceptable for men but immoral for women. It is supported more by women than by men.

- Across different cultures, it has sometimes been in women's best interests to put pressure on each other to restrain sexual behavior.

What Makes Us Human? Putting the Cultural Animal in Perspective

- Long-term monogamous mating is much more common among human beings than among other species.

key terms

attachment theory 414
commitment 409
communal relationships 412
companionate love (affectionate love) 406
Coolidge effect 429
dismissing avoidant attachment 415
distress-maintaining style of attribution 421

double standard 441
erotic plasticity 430
evolutionary theory 426
exchange relationships 412
extradyadic sex 434
fearful avoidant attachment 415
intimacy 409
investment model 419
passion 408

passionate love (romantic love) 406
paternity uncertainty 441
preoccupied (anxious/ ambivalent) attachment 415
relationship-enhancing style of attribution 421
reverse double standard 441
secure attachment 415
self-acceptance 417

social constructionist theories 426
social exchange theory 428
social reality 440

quiz yourself ANSWERS

1. **What Is Love?** p.412
   answers: 1.c 2.d 3.d 4.d

2. **Different Types of Relationships** p.417
   answers: 1.c 2.b 3.a 4.a

3. **Maintaining Relationships** p.425
   answers: 1.b 2.b 3.b 4.c

4. **Sexuality** p.442
   answers: 1.c 2.b 3.d 4.a

PREJUDICE AND INTERGROUP RELATIONS

13

Ariel Skelley/Getty Images

LEARNING OBJECTIVES

1 Identify the differences between prejudice, discrimination, and stereotyping.

2 Evaluate how and why stereotypes and discrimination impact targets.

3 Debate the innate versus cultural causes of prejudice and stereotyping.

4 Summarize research on the accuracy of stereotypes.

5 Discuss how inner processes can affect prejudice.

6 Explain how stereotypes actually operate and how they can be overcome.

7 Describe the impact of prejudice on targets.

Most **people are familiar** with zoos in which animals are confined in pens and cages. People might be less familiar with the long history of human zoos in which Africans and conquered indigenous peoples were also kept in pens and cages as if they were animals.[1] The euphemistic term for these human zoos is "ethnological expositions." The crude term for them is "freak shows."

Regardless of what they were called, real people were "on display" for others to see. Human zoos have a very long history. "In 1492 Columbus sailed the ocean blue" (as the old rhyme goes), and in 1493 he kidnapped indigenous Americans and brought them to the Spanish court. In the 16th century, the Aztec ruler Montezuma displayed humans such as dwarves, albinos, and hunchbacks, along with animals in his zoo in Tenochtitlán (now central Mexico City).[2] Also in the 16th century, the Italian Cardinal Hippolytus Medici had a collection of "Barbarians" speaking over 20 languages, along with exotic animals.[3] In the mid-1800s, P. T. Barnum (co-founder of Barnum & Bailey Circus) had public displays of "human freaks." In the 1870s, human zoos could be found in many major cities of the Western World, such as New York, USA, London, UK, Hamburg, Germany, Antwerp, Belgium, Barcelona, Spain, Milan, Italy, and Warsaw, Poland.[4] In 1889, the World's Fair was held in Paris, France. Although the main symbol of the fair was the Eiffel Tower, the main attraction was the "Negro village" (*village nègre*) where 400 Africans were displayed for over 6.3 million visitors to see.[5] In 1896, the Cincinnati Zoo invited 100 Native Americans from the Sioux tribe to establish a village at the zoo, where they lived for three months.[6] In 1904, the main exhibit of the World's Fair in St. Louis was a display of "primitive" peoples from the Philippines, as well as the Apache Chief Geronimo.[7] In 1906, the Bronx Zoo in New York displayed the Congolese pygmy Ota Benga in a cage labeled "The Missing Link" (in the evolutionary chain) along with chimpanzees and an orangutan.[8] In 1958, the World's Fair in Brussels, Belgium, had a Congolese village.[9] In 1994 an Ivory Coast village was included as part of an African safari in Port-Saint-Père, France.[10] As late as 2005, an African village was included in the Augsburg zoo in Germany, despite widespread criticism that the village was racist.[11] ●

Library of Congress Prints and Photographs Division [LC-DIG-ggbain-22741]

Ota Benga, a Congolese pygmy, at the Bronx Zoo in New York in 1906.

Bain News Service, publisher

Human Zoo at Luna Park, a Coney Island Amusement Park in New York, 1905. It featured Filipino natives.

ABCs of Intergroup Relationships: Prejudice, Discrimination, and Stereotypes

Prejudice is derived from the Latin term for prejudging. It refers to evaluating a person or multiple persons based on membership in a group or category of people. Thus, prejudice involves attitudes toward categories of people, which can be used to judge individuals without being based on the individual's actions or personal traits.

Perhaps the best-known form of prejudice is **racism**, which is defined as having negative views toward people based on race (which is often, though not always, considered a biological category). Racism can take the form of overt, blanket statements of disliking and disparaging groups. In some settings, people are uncomfortable about their prejudices. This creates a pattern that some social psychologists have dubbed **aversive racism**.[12] Aversive racists simultaneously hold egalitarian values and negative (aversive or unpleasant) feelings toward people of other races. They believe in racial equality and equal opportunity, but they also feel uncomfortable around minorities and try to avoid them when possible. For example, when white Americans are talking to black Americans, they may sit farther away, maintain less eye contact, talk in a less friendly manner, and end discussions sooner than they do when talking to other whites.[13] Such a pattern may indicate that the white people were nervous and uncomfortable, but it could also mean that they felt inner conflict about having negative views toward the African Americans based on race.

Prejudiced feelings sometimes lead people to discriminate against others. **Discrimination** refers to unequal treatment of different people based on the groups or categories to which they belong. An example of discrimination against Native Americans would be the practice of keeping them on reservations instead of letting them live wherever they want. Prejudice can exist without discrimination, if people hold negative views but don't act unfairly. Sometimes discrimination can occur without prejudiced feelings. For example, suppose that a state police force sets a requirement that its officers must all be at least 6 feet (1.83 meters) tall, because it believes that "height equals might" and that criminals won't take short officers seriously. This height requirement would discriminate against women, Hispanics, and Asians because they are generally shorter than 6 feet tall. To read about discrimination in paying athletes of different races, see the *Money Matters* box.

Stereotypes are beliefs that associate groups of people with certain traits. Stereotypes refer to what we believe or think about various groups. They can be good or bad. For example, one might stereotype older people as wise (good) or as slow (bad). Stereotypes are sometimes difficult to change. One reason is that people tend to throw exceptions to the stereotype's general rule into a separate category, called a **subtype**.[15] For example, if a man meets a woman who doesn't fit the stereotype of the warm and nurturing type, he can either discard or modify his stereotype of women, or he can put her into a subtype, such as "career woman" or an "athlete."[16]

Prejudice, discrimination, and stereotypes are the ABCs of intergroup relationships. The **A**ffective component is prejudice, the **B**ehavioral component is discrimination, and the **C**ognitive component is stereotyping.

The human mind seems naturally inclined to sort objects into groups rather than thinking about each object separately. This process of **categorization** makes it much easier to make sense of a complicated world. The process of sorting people into groups on the basis of characteristics they have in common (such as race, ethnicity, gender, age, religion, or sexual orientation) is called **social categorization**. As we saw in Chapter 5, people tend to be "cognitive misers," which means they generally think in easy, simple ways that

prejudice a negative feeling toward an individual based solely on his or her membership in a particular group

racism prejudiced attitudes toward a particular race

aversive racism simultaneously holding egalitarian values and negative feelings toward people of other races

discrimination unequal treatment of different people based on the groups or categories to which they belong

stereotypes beliefs that associate groups of people with certain traits

subtypes categories that people use for individuals who do not fit a general stereotype

categorization the natural tendency of humans to sort objects into groups

social categorization the process of sorting people into groups on the basis of characteristics they have in common (e.g., race, gender, age, religion, sexual orientation)

MONEY*Matters*

Racial Discrimination in Sports: Paying More to Win

Many people argue that racial integration and diversity produce value for organizations. The evidence behind this claim has been mixed at best. But recent analyses of the economics of sport have begun to show that racial discrimination is in fact costly for some teams.

One of the best studies on the cost of discrimination in sports involved English football (soccer) teams.[14] These teams provided a useful test because teams were relatively free to hire athletes as they saw fit, which included the option of discriminating by race. There were also no salary caps, revenue sharing, and other financial regulations that distort the economic marketplace. In the 1970s, black players began to enter the major league, and some teams hired them eagerly, whereas others chose not to do so. Given the relatively free market for talent, the result was that black players got lower salaries than white players, regardless of ability. (This was the case because a player could get a higher salary when more teams wanted to bid for his services.)

Another way of putting this is that black players cost less than white players, at any level of ability. It did not matter whether white or black players were better overall. All that mattered was that, whatever the player's talent level, his salary would be lower if he was black, so the team that hired him instead of a white player in effect got a bargain: a better player for the same money.

In general, teams with higher payrolls get better players and therefore win more games. But when the researcher analyzed teams for the number of black players they had, he found that using more black players allowed teams to win more games for the same amount of money. A team that had no black players would have to pay 5% more overall in player salaries to achieve the same win–loss record as a team that did have black players.

Thus, organizations do pay a price for racial discrimination. Hiring the best talent available regardless of race is the most effective strategy. To refuse to hire based on race means paying more or winning less, or both.

minimize mental effort. Categorizing people is an easy and efficient way of simplifying the world and reducing mental effort. When people form an impression of a person, they typically use what personal information they have about the individual, but invoking stereotypes is a relatively easy way to fill in gaps in this knowledge.

Modern objections to stereotyping and prejudice go far beyond the chance of an inaccurate prediction, of course. Today, people object to stereotyping and prejudice even if the stereotypes are reasonably accurate.

Women are stereotypically warm and nurturing. When a man sees a woman who does not meet this stereotype, such as these female Islamic State (IS) fighters, he can either discard or modify his stereotype of women, or he can put them into a subtype.

Javad Moghimi/ParsPix/ABACAUSA.COM/Newscom

The view that prejudice and stereotyping are morally wrong is a product of modern Western culture. Several centuries ago, Western culture shifted to the view that each person had a right to be judged as an individual, regardless of his or her category. Prior to that, there was greater acceptance of judging people based on categories and groups. Even legal judgment followed such principles. For example, if a man rebelled against the local ruler, the ruler might have the man's entire extended family imprisoned or executed.[17] Nowadays, punishing the whole family for one individual's crime would seem unjust and unfair.

Biased judgments based on stereotypes and prejudices are not only unfair and immoral; in some cases, they can have lethal consequences. For example, in 2014 a white police officer shot an unarmed black teenager named Michael Brown in Ferguson, Missouri, which sparked conflict and unrest between the police and citizens for several days.[18]

If a police officer possessed the stereotypic expectation that black people are more likely to be violent and aggressive than white people, it could influence split-second decisions whether to shoot black suspects, with tragic consequences. Indeed, research using computer simulations (similar to video games) has found that people, whether police officers or college students, are more likely to mistakenly shoot at unarmed black suspects than unarmed white suspects.[19,20,21,22,23] That is, when a research participant sees an ambiguous scene with a possibly dangerous man who may or may not be armed, the participant is more likely to shoot at the man if he is black than if he is white (even if he is not actually armed). Although it is tempting to treat this as an instance of anti-black prejudice among white people, the bias is not confined to white

Alex Wong/Getty Images

Does Hillary Clinton fit the stereotype of the warm and nurturing woman? If not, people may throw her into a subtype such as "career woman."

© Michael Newman/PhotoEdit

© Michael Newman/PhotoEdit

When viewing an ambiguous scene with a possibly dangerous man who may or may not be armed, participants are more likely to shoot at the man if he is black than if he is white.

A makeshift memorial for Michael Brown, the black, unarmed teenager who was shot by a white police officer in Ferguson, Missouri.

research participants: African Americans are also more likely to shoot at the possibly threatening man if he is black than if he is white.

One big difference between sorting people and sorting things is the level of emotional involvement. For example, when sorting people into heterosexual, bisexual, or homosexual categories, the sorter belongs to one of the categories and feels emotionally attached to it. In contrast, someone who sorts fruits into apples and oranges is probably not emotionally attached to these categories. **Outgroup members** ("them") are people who belong to a different group or category than we do. **Ingroup members** ("us") are people who belong to the same group or category as we do.

Most people assume that outgroup members are more similar to each other than ingroup members are to each other. This false assumption, known as the **outgroup homogeneity bias** is reflected in statements such as "They're all alike" and "If you've seen one, you've seen them all!" In fact, one of the earliest studies of outgroup homogeneity used campus fraternities at a university. The researchers found that students believed that the members of their own fraternity had many different traits, values, and activities, but that members of other fraternities were much more similar to each other.[24]

In fact, people see outgroup members as even looking similar to one another. Have you ever felt embarrassed because of confusing two people of a different racial group than your own? If so, you're not alone. Research has shown that eyewitnesses are more accurate at identifying people of their own racial group than at identifying people of a different racial group.[25,26] However, when outgroup members are angry, the opposite is true.[27] Angry outgroup members are easier to identify than are angry ingroup members. This finding reflects the importance of keeping track of dangerous people. Angry members of another group may pose a major threat, so the human mind automatically pays close attention to them and makes a strong mental note of who those people are.

Outgroup homogeneity bias has a simple explanation: We don't have as much exposure to outgroup members as we do to ingroup members. Thus, we don't have much chance to learn about how outgroup members differ from one another. This lack of exposure can have several negative consequences such as prejudice.

outgroup members people who belong to a different group or category than we do

ingroup members people who belong to the same group or category as we do

outgroup homogeneity bias the assumption that outgroup members are more similar to one another than ingroup members are to one another

1. Prejudice is to discrimination as _____ is to _____ .

   (a) affect; behavior
   (b) affect; cognition
   (c) cognition; affect
   (d) cognition; behavior

2. Which of the following refers to the tendency that some people have to simultaneously (1) hold egalitarian values, and (2) experience negative feelings when interacting with minority groups?

   (a) aversive racism
   (b) contact hypothesis
   (c) discontinuity effect
   (d) social dominance orientation

3. One reason why people hold on to their stereotypes—even in the face of refuting evidence—is that they tend to view pieces of refuting evidence as "exceptions," which constitute their own (new) categories. That is, they tend to create _____ .

   (a) biases
   (b) prototypes
   (c) subtypes
   (d) typologies

4. Becca is a store clerk. While she is shopping at another store on her day off, she runs into a very rude store clerk and a very rude manager. Becca will probably conclude _____ .

   (a) most store clerks and managers tend to be rude
   (b) most store clerks but not necessarily managers tend to be rude
   (c) most managers but not necessarily store clerks tend to be rude
   (d) neither most store clerks nor most managers tend to be rude

answers: see pg 489

Common Prejudices and Targets

Prejudice is based on perceived differences among groups of people. Some prejudices build on external characteristics that are readily visible, such as race, gender, weight, or clothing (e.g., turbans worn by some Sikh and Muslim men; burqu and head scarves worn by some Muslim women; small hats called yarmulkes or kippas worn by some Jewish men). Probably the most widely discussed prejudice in modern North America is racial prejudice (racism), followed by gender prejudice (sexism). Racial prejudice has been an important social problem, particularly prejudices held by European Americans about African Americans.

Most people claim not to be prejudiced, but then again perhaps they just think that is the right thing to say. Sometimes behavior differs from expressed attitudes. One study of online dating found that 50% of the white women and 80% of the white men said that race didn't matter to them—hence they would be willing to date anyone from any race.[28] But if you look at how those people responded to dating ads, race did seem to matter. The white women who said race did not matter to them sent 97% of their responses to white men. Likewise, the white men who were supposedly open to any race sent 90% of their responses to white women. Thus, these people claimed not to care about race, but when actually contacting someone to date, they showed a strong preference for their own race.

Society has sought for decades to reduce or erase racial and gender prejudices. While people may at least strive to conceal if not overcome their racial and gender prejudices, other prejudices are often held with much less inner conflict or debate, such as against Muslims, atheists, obese individuals, and homosexuals.

> "If we were to wake up some morning and find that everyone was the same race, creed and color, we would find some other cause for prejudice by noon."
>
> — George Aiken, former Governor and U.S. Senator from Vermont

Muslims

Fill in the blank: Islamic ___. For many people living in the Western world, the words that come to mind are negative, violent ones such as "extremist," "fundamentalist," "insurgent," "militant," "jihadist," "mujahideen," or "terrorist." People rarely associate other religions with these negative, violent words. Adherents of the religion of Islam are called Muslims. The word Muslim means "one who submits to Allah (God)." There are about 1.6 billion Muslims, or 23% of the world's population, making Islam the second-largest religion after Christianity.[29] Islam began on the Arabian Peninsula in the 7th century. Although most Arabs are Muslims, a majority of the world's Muslims are not Arabs. Indonesia contains the largest percentage of the world Muslim population—about 209 million (13%).

Prejudice and discrimination against Arabs and Muslims living in the United States has increased dramatically since Islamic terrorists hijacked American airplanes and crashed them into New York City and Washington, D.C., on September 11, 2001.[30] For example, they have been removed from airplanes without probable cause, out of fear they might be terrorists. Women in head scarves have been jeered and insulted. Mosques (Islamic places of worship) have been sprayed with graffiti and bullets. Highly visible forms of discrimination (e.g., vandalism, assault) are relatively rare; pleas from the government, civil liberties groups, and others imply that such acts are socially and legally unacceptable. Less visible forms of discrimination, however, persist. For example, in the year following the September 11, 2001, attacks, the Equal Opportunity Employment Commission received 706 complaints of workplace discrimination against Arab Americans, 383 more than in the year before the September 11, 2001, attacks.[31] Despite a November 2001 joint initiative undertaken by the Equal Employment Opportunity Commission, the Justice Department, and the Labor Department to decrease such discrimination, workplace discrimination against Arabs and Muslims has continued to increase.[32] In workplace discrimination cases, it is often unclear whether the disputed action (e.g., job termination) is motivated by prejudice or other causes (e.g., poor job performance).

One study focused on less visible forms of discrimination against Arabs.[33] The researchers used a modern variation of Stanley Milgram's "lost letter" technique[34] to examine prejudice toward socially undesirable groups.[35] Milgram dropped self-addressed, stamped envelopes around a college campus and counted the number of lost letters that

Since September 11, 2001, discrimination against Arabs has increased in the United States.

AP Images/Ryan Remiorz

were mailed. People mailed more letters addressed to socially desirable groups (e.g., a medical research group) than to socially undesirable groups (e.g., a communist organization). In one study, white American college students received a "lost e-mail" message addressed to a person with an Arab surname (e.g., Mohammed or Fatima Hameed) or a European American surname (e.g., Peter or Julianne Brice). The e-mail stated that the intended recipient either had or had not won a prestigious four-year college scholarship. The e-mail requested a reply within 48 hours. Thus, if the participant did not forward the e-mail, the student would not be able to benefit from a scholarship worth tens of thousands of dollars. Participants had all completed a measure of prejudiced attitudes toward Arabs a few weeks before they received the e-mail message. The scale had items such as "I can hardly imagine myself voting for an Arab-American who is running for an important political office." As can be seen in **FIGURE 13.1**, prejudiced participants tended to pass along bad news but not pass along good news to the Arab target.

Other research has found similar results.[36] In a Swedish university, researchers dropped 100 unsealed envelopes around campus. Half the letters were addressed to a person with a common Swedish surname (A. Andersson), whereas the other half were addressed to a person with a common Muslim surname (A. Abdullah). Only initials were used for the first name to eliminate possible gender effects. The envelopes contained money (three SEK20 bills—about $9). The Swedish students returned 58% of the letters with a Swedish surname but only 36% of the letters with a Muslim surname.

The news media can play a key role in fueling prejudice against Muslims. By linking Islam with terror, the media can increase prejudice against all Muslims.[37]

Sometimes the media even misreport that Muslims committed a terrorist act when they did not. On July 22, 2011, for example, Anders Behring Breivik, a conservative, right-wing Christian with strong anti-Muslim and anti-immigration beliefs, bombed government buildings in Oslo, Norway, that resulted in 8 deaths, and then shot 69 people at a youth camp. Initially, some media outlets claimed that a Muslim terrorist committed these acts.[38]

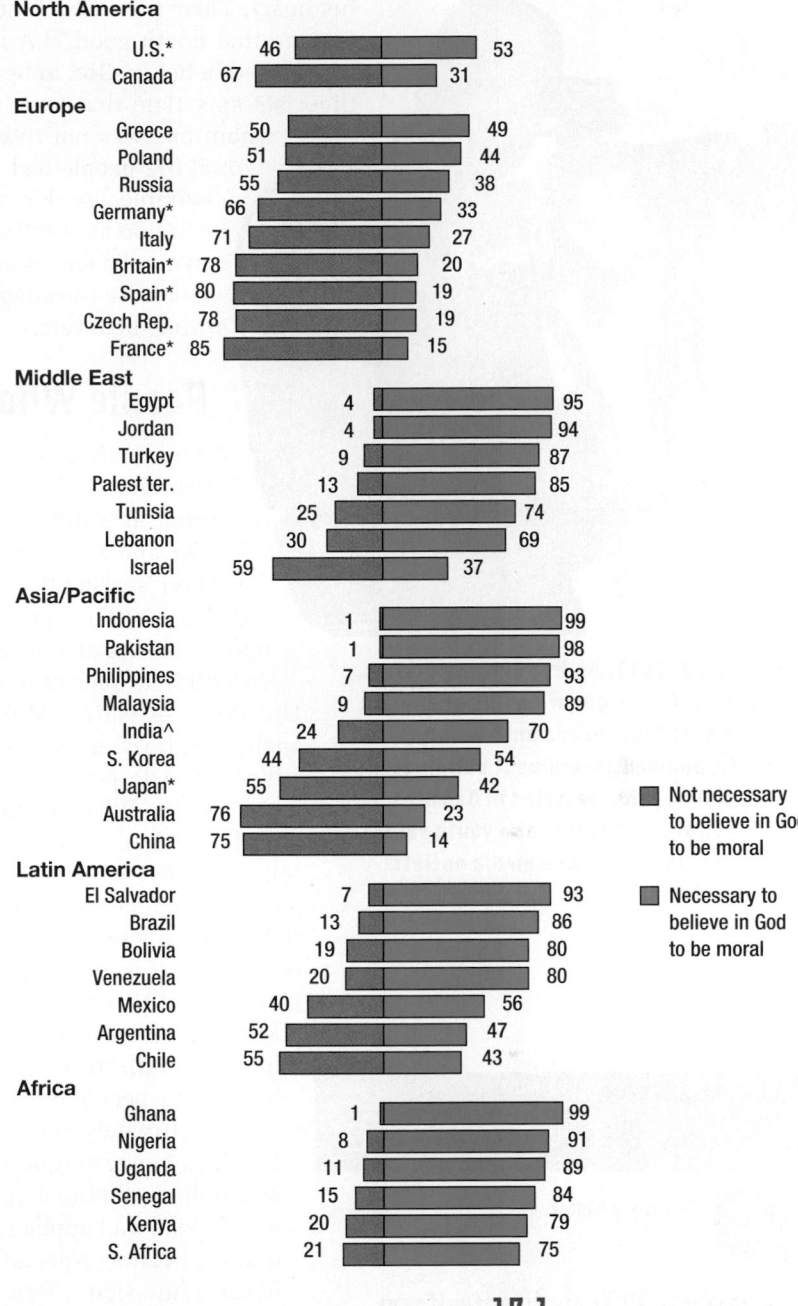

FIGURE 13.1
Belief in God Essential to Morality?[44]

Atheists

Atheists are also disliked around the world in communities in which the majority of individuals are religious.[39] Kalei Wilson, age 15, and her brother Ben, age 17, tried to organize an atheist club in her high school in Canton, North Carolina, but they gave up after their family received numerous threats and verbal attacks.[40] The U.S. Air Force told a sergeant that he will have to leave the military unless he agrees to take an oath containing the phrase "so help me God."[41]

Prejudice toward atheists seems to be rooted in distrust.[42] Religious people often consider belief in God a precondition for moral behavior. Scriptures such as this one from the Old Testament in the Bible reinforce such beliefs: "The fool hath said in

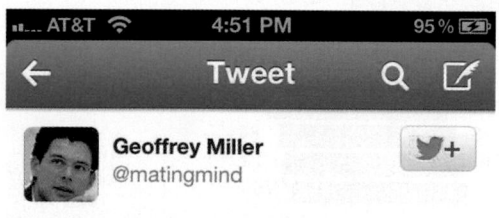

AFP/Getty Images

his heart, *There is* no God. They are corrupt, they have done abominable works, *there is* none that doeth good."[43] A recent poll found that 22 of the 40 countries surveyed considered belief in God to be necessary for morality and good values.[44] Evolutionary theorists speculate that trusting kin comes more naturally than trusting people to whom one was not related, and religious communities may appeal to this by making people feel like they are related to each other. Many religions, for example, speak of their god as a father and address other members of the religion as "brother and sister." Atheists are seen as someone who has no symbolic family and therefore cannot be trusted. Undoubtedly this dovetails with the suggestion that atheists have no fear of divine punishment, unlike believers.

People Who Are Overweight

Another highly visible characteristic of individuals subject to prejudicial attitudes is obesity. Although some clothes may be "revealing" or "slimming," it is difficult to hide one's weight. Abercrombie and Fitch refuses to sell XL and XXL women sizes because the company does not want overweight women wearing their brand (although they do sell XL and XXL men's sizes).[45] Unlike racist and sexist attitudes, many people will openly admit and even act upon their negative attitudes toward obese people (see *Food for Thought*).

In 2013, a professor of evolutionary psychology from New Mexico State University—Geoffrey Miller—tweeted the following comment: "Dear obese PhD applicants: if you didn't have the willpower to stop eating carbs, you won't have the willpower to do a dissertation #truth."[67] Later the same day, he deleted the tweet but it was too late. What he thought was a private tweet, was actually public. People had already captured the tweet with screen shots and sent it through cyberspace. Then Miller tweeted "sincere apologies," noting first that the "idiotic, impulsive, and badly judged tweet does not reflect my true views, values, or standards" and then adding: "Obviously my previous tweet does not represent the selection policies of any university, or my own selection criteria." The university also issued a statement: "The University of New Mexico administration and faculty were surprised by Dr. Geoffrey Miller's tweet. We are deeply concerned about the impact of the statement, which in no way reflects the policies or admission standards of UNM. We are investigating every aspect of this incident and will take appropriate action."[68]

Unfortunately, recent research confirms that there is indeed a bias against admitting overweight and obese students to college. In one recent study,[69] researchers obtained the height, weight, and recommendation letters for 97 people who had applied to a psychology graduate program. Researchers found that applicants (especially females) with a higher body weight had significantly fewer admission offers, even though body weight was unrelated to the overall quality of their recommendation letters. In another recent study,[70] male and female participants were asked to determine which female candidates they would be most and least likely to admit to a university on the basis of a variety of factors, including body size. Results showed only 6% of the overweight and obese women were selected for admission compared to 60% of the underweight women.

On July 22, 2011, Anders Behring Breivik, a conservative, right-wing Christian with strong anti-Muslim and anti-immigration beliefs, bombed government buildings in Oslo, Norway that resulted in 8 deaths, and then shot 69 people at a youth camp. Initially, however, some media outlets claimed the killer was Muslim.

www.insidehighered.com

Homosexuals

Although a person's sexual orientation is not as readily visible as his or her race, gender, or weight, anti-gay prejudices are often quite strong, even from family members. Consider, for example, the experience of Nathan Hoskins.[71] Nathan grew up in rural Kentucky. He knew from an early age that he was gay. "When I was in sixth grade, I had met a good friend and he wasn't interested in girls," he said. The friend mailed him a Valentine's Day card, but his mother got it before

Prejudice Against the Obese

In the United States, diet and activity level are the leading causes of death behind tobacco, and the gap is shrinking over time. Diet and activity are associated with almost every health risk known. However, obesity has other negative effects besides health risks, the biggest of which is the stigma associated with being fat. Anti-fat attitudes are strong, and they begin as early as preschool.[46] Five-year-old children say they would rather lose an arm than be fat.[47] Anti-fat attitudes are even stronger for adolescents than for children, especially among females.[48] The stigma is strong despite the fact that so many people are fat. In the United States, about two out of every three adults are considered either overweight or obese.[49]

Research has shown that compared to normal weight people, overweight people are considered to be less intelligent, less hardworking, less attractive, less popular, less successful, less strong-willed, and less trustworthy.[50,51,52,53,54] Obese people are also assumed to be less conscientious, less agreeable, less emotionally stable, and less extraverted than "normal weight" individuals, even though these stereotypes are false.[55] College students said they would rather marry a cocaine user, shoplifter, embezzler, or blind person than an obese person.[56]

The stigma associated with obesity is also contagious, as research has shown. Participants[57] indicated whether they thought male job applicants should be hired. Half the participants saw a photo of the applicant sitting next to a normal-sized woman, whereas the other half saw the same applicant sitting next to an obese woman. The woman was actually the same person, but in the obese condition she wore an obese prosthesis (a "fat suit") to make her look fat. The results showed that the applicants were rated more negatively if they were shown sitting next to an obese woman. This effect is called **stigma by association**.

Being fat can even cost you money, especially if you are a woman.[58] Obese women earn about 6% less than other women, and obese men about 3% less than other men. The cumulative effect can be significant. An obese worker who is paid $1.25 less an hour over a 40-year career will end up earning $100,000 less.

In a nationally representative sample of Swedish adults, obese individuals were more likely to experience workplace and health care discrimination than normal weight individuals.[59] Even the nurses and doctors who treat them have strong negative attitudes and reactions toward obese patients.[60] Recent research found that medical students are also prejudiced against obese people.[61] "If doctors assume obese patients are lazy or lack willpower, they will be less likely to spend time counseling patients about lifestyle changes they could make," the lead author on the research said. "Doctors also may be less likely to recommend formal weight loss programs if they assume their patient is unlikely to follow through."[62]

Unlike many unfortunate fates that may befall a person, obesity is considered by many people to be self-inflicted.[63,64,65] Thus, people are likely to blame fat people for their plight.[66] Obesity has many costs indeed!

---

he could hide it from her. When he got off the bus, she was standing on the front porch holding the card. "She took me into the house and pulled her shotgun out of the closet. She loaded it in front of me and put it in my hands and told me to hold on to that. She led me outside, and she put me in the back of the car. And she drove out into the country," he said. Once they arrived at a remote place, Hoskins explained what happened next: "She stood me up against a tree. She took the shotgun out of my hands, and she put it to my head. She said, 'this is the tree that I'd take my son to and blow his head off if he ever decided to be a faggot.'" He says at that moment he realized he had to do whatever it took not to be gay. "And I tried very hard. And I was a great liar for many years." He was married for nine years before he divorced and came out. A couple of years later he asked his mom about that incident. She laughed. He said, "Mom, I just want to hear one time that what you did was wrong," but she couldn't say it.

People are especially likely to feel prejudice toward gays and lesbians if they believe that homosexuality is a lifestyle choice rather than a biological predisposition.[72] However, the American Psychological Association pamphlet on the topic states, "most people experience little or no sense of choice about their sexual orientation."[73] After all, who would choose to be gay if it means being persecuted and rejected by society, peers, and possibly even family members? It also begs the question, "When did heterosexual people choose to be straight?"[74]

> "Is fat really the worst thing a human being can be? Is fat worse than vindictive, jealous, shallow, boring, evil, or cruel? Not to me."
> — J. K. Rowling

stigma by association rejection of those who associate with stigmatized others

Like other targets of prejudice, research has shown that lesbian, gay, bisexual, and transgender (LGBT) individuals are not treated equally in the workplace, in the military, and even on the street. In one study of workplace discrimination against gay men,[75] pairs of fictitious résumés were sent in response to 1,769 job postings in seven states. One résumé in each pair was randomly assigned experience in either a gay campus organization or another liberal campus organization—Progressive and Socialist Alliance. Overall, gay applicants had a lower chance of being invited for an interview (7.2% versus 11.5%). The chance of a gay applicant being invited for an interview were much lower in the Southern and Midwestern states (Florida, Texas, Ohio) than in the Western and Northeastern states (California, Nevada, Pennsylvania, New York)—4.9% versus 9.0%, probably because the Western and Northeastern states are more supportive of gay rights (e.g., they allow same-sex marriage and civil unions and have stricter hate crime and antidiscrimination laws). This finding is consistent with other research showing that gay bashing is higher when people think homosexuals' rights and benefits are illegitimate than when they think they are legitimate.[76]

Similarly, employers subject to antidiscrimination laws were more likely to invite a gay applicant for an interview than were employers not subject to antidiscrimination laws—6% versus 3%. Employers who mentioned masculine characteristics in the job ads (e.g., "makes decisions independently," "aggressive self-starter") were less likely to invite gay applicants for interviews than employers who did not mention masculine characteristics—4.8% versus 8.1°%, perhaps because they thought gay men lacked these characteristics.

Some businesses even turn away gay customers. Arizona lawmakers passed a bill to allow businesses to refuse service to customers for religious reasons, such as when the customers are gay.[77] However, the governor of Arizona vetoed the bill.[78]

From 1993 until 2011, the U.S. military prohibited discriminating against "closet" homosexuals serving in the military, although it barred "open" homosexuals. In 2011, the U.S. military repealed the "Don't Ask Don't Tell" policy, allowing "open" homosexuals to serve in the military. However, transgendered individuals (who self-identify as a male, female, both, or neither) are still barred from serving in all branches of the military.[79]

J. C. Penney's decision to hire Ellen DeGeneres—a gay celebrity—as its spokesperson drew widespread support from some and threats of protest from others.

Of course, prejudice toward LGBT isn't confined to formal organizations. In one study,[80] male and female confederates who wore either a black T-shirt without words or a black T-shirt with containing the words "Gay pride" in big, bright red letters asked pedestrians for change for a parking meter. Pedestrians were much less likely to help the confederate if he or she wore a "Gay pride" T-shirt.

Many people who would never admit to holding a negative stereotype about another race will freely and openly say that they think homosexuals are bad.[81] Researchers have begun to study homophobia. Phobias are excessive fears, so **homophobia** is an excessive fear of homosexuals or homosexual behavior. Research shows that participants with homophobic attitudes (e.g., "Gay people make me nervous" and "I would hit a homosexual for coming on to me") are more aggressive against gay men.[82,83] Other research shows that homophobic participants were more likely to believe negative stereotypes about homosexuals (e.g., "Gays and lesbians are more promiscuous than straight people") and were less likely to believe positive stereotypes (e.g., "Gays and lesbians are more artistic than straight people").[84] (For information on the roots of anti-gay prejudice, see *The Social Side of Sex*.)

Opposition to gay rights is most pronounced among people with conservative political and religious beliefs,[94] and among people who are disgusted by homosexuality.[95] Indeed, if people are induced to feel disgusted, they are more prejudiced against homosexuals.[96] There are also cultural differences in tolerance toward homosexuality. For example, Dutch children living with lesbian parents are more open about growing up in a lesbian family, are less homophobic, and have fewer emotional and behavioral problems than American children in similar families.[97]

One sign of increasing tolerance concerns same-sex marriage. Support for same-sex marriage has increased dramatically over time, especially among younger Americans. Since 2011, the percent of Americans who favor same-sex marriage has been greater than the percent who oppose it.[98]

Of course there are other potential targets of prejudice besides the common targets we have discussed, such as people with stigmas. **Stigmas** include characteristics of individuals that are considered socially unacceptable. Besides overweight, other stigmas include mental illness, sickness, poverty, and physical blemishes.

off the mark.com — by Mark Parisi

WE DON'T KNOW WHAT TO MAKE OF THIS, MR. STEIER, BUT WE FIND OURSELVES WISHING YOU'D PUT A SHIRT ON...

MarkParisi@aol.com · offthemark.com · ©2004 MARK PARISI DIST. BY UFS, INC.

Reprinted by permission of Atlantic Feature Syndicate/Mark Parisi.

Individuals with stigmas are often the targets of prejudice and discrimination.

homophobia is an excessive fear of homosexuals or homosexual behavior.

stigmas characteristics of individuals that are considered socially unacceptable (e.g., being overweight, mentally ill, sick, poor, or physically scarred)

QUIZ YOURSELF
Common Prejudices and Targets

1. **The second leading cause of preventable death in the United States is _____ .**
   - (a) alcohol
   - (b) diet and activity level
   - (c) tobacco
   - (d) toxic agents

2. **Research shows that atheists are considered to be _____ than religious people.**
   - (a) less intelligent
   - (b) less trustworthy
   - (c) more noncommittal
   - (d) more cruel

3. **Research shows that compared to non-obese people, obese people are less _____ .**
   - (a) agreeable
   - (b) conscientious
   - (c) emotionally stable
   - (d) None of the above

4. **Which of the following is not thought to be a major motivator of anti-gay prejudice?**
   - (a) Feelings of disgust
   - (b) Desire to have more possible relationship partners
   - (c) Fear of having to refuse homosexual advances
   - (d) Fear that one might enjoy homosexuality

answers: see pg 489

Roots of Anti-Gay Prejudice

Why are people prejudiced against homosexuals? As noted in the text, the prejudice is strong, and many consider it normal and natural to abhor sexual deviance. Some people invoke religious or biblical statements condemning homosexuality, but most likely those statements are a result rather than an original cause of anti-gay bias. Other people think it is simple to say that homosexuality is unnatural, but in fact homosexual activity is found in many other species besides humans (e.g., beetles, birds, dolphins, fruit bats, orangutans, sheep).[85] Homosexuality is also found all over the world among humans. Nature, at least, does not regard homosexuality as unnatural. At most, homosexual activity does not produce offspring, so people who think the only purpose of sex is to make babies might find fault with gay sex.

There are some curious facts about anti-gay prejudice. It is stronger among men than women,[86] even though men are more likely than women to take part in homosexual activity and to be homosexuals.[87] Then again, the apparently greater tolerance among women could be due to the fact that when people answer questions about homosexuality, they think mainly of male homosexuality. To correct for this methodological problem, researchers have asked participants separate questions about attitudes toward male versus female homosexuality, and found that both men and women were more intolerant of homosexuality in their own gender.[88,89]

Simple logic might dictate the opposite. After all, if you were the only heterosexual man in your town (because all the others were gay), you would be in a great position to choose the most desirable women for yourself. Put another way, every man who turns out to be gay reduces the competition for the number of available women for heterosexual men. Conversely, when people of the opposite sex turn out to be gay, a heterosexual's odds of finding an ideal mate are reduced. Heterosexuals ought logically to be delighted to learn that members of their own gender are gay and ought to be more opposed to homosexuality in the opposite gender. But that's not what the data say.

At present, the most likely explanation is that people's attitudes are mainly rooted in fear that they themselves will be the target of romantic or sexual advances from homosexuals. Heterosexuals do not want to be in the position of having to reject homosexual overtures.[90] That may be why they are more strongly opposed to homosexuality in their own gender.

A second explanation may be that they fear that they might have a positive response to homosexual advances. We saw in Chapter 6 that the men who expressed the strongest anti-gay views were also the most sexually aroused by watching gay pornography, though the men were reluctant to admit it, and their arousal was only verified by measuring their erectile responses.[91] The fear of one's own possible reactions might explain why people often treat homosexuals with such strong reactions of disgust and hatred, as if the homosexuals represented a dangerous threat.

A third (related) explanation may be fear of what others might think. Recent research shows that heterosexual men, but not heterosexual women, may exhibit prejudice against gays in order to distance themselves from gays and prove to others "I'm not gay ... I'm a real man!"[92] In fact, even people who do not express anti-gay prejudice may avoid spending time with openly gay people, such as by declining to work together on a class project.[93] This is because people fear that others will regard them gay if they are seen with gay friends. Heterosexual people do not want to be mistaken for homosexuals.

Some female Japanese macaques, like these two in Kyoto, prefer to be with females, even when males are present in their group.

Tom Brakefield/Photodisc/Getty Images

Many people believe homosexuality is unnatural, but in fact homosexual activity has been found all over the world in humans and in nonhuman species.

AP Images/Dan Peled

Why Prejudice Exists

Why does prejudice exist? One view holds that prejudice is a product of a wicked culture. By this view, children start off innocent, trusting, and accepting of all others, but they are taught through socializing agents (including parents and the mass media) to dislike and reject certain groups.

There is certainly something correct in the view that stereotypes and prejudices are learned through socialization. Stereotypes often contain specific information about specific groups, and this information must be learned (as opposed to being innate knowledge). On the other hand, the tendency to hold stereotypes and prejudices may be innate. Children do not turn out on close inspection to be sweet, accepting, and tolerant. Even children as young as 6 months judge others based on race.[99] As we saw in Chapter 11, children everywhere seem instantly ready to reject anyone who is different in any way. There is even evidence that many primates naturally treat members of other groups as enemies.[100] Although the predisposition to categorize by stereotypes may be innate, the content of stereotypes is certainly learned through socialization.

At present, your authors have reluctantly come to the conclusion that prejudice is natural. As we shall see in the later section on overcoming prejudice, it seems that people automatically and normally know stereotypes and think of them, whereas they have to exert themselves to override them. More important perhaps, prejudices are found all over the world; we know of no culture in which gender stereotypes are unknown, or where members of rival groups view each other with only respect and admiration. That doesn't make prejudice right or acceptable, but as social scientists we should not be surprised to find it.

The conclusion is that the tendency to align with similar others and square off against different others, including forming negative stereotypes of them and discriminating against them, is deeply rooted in the human psyche. Some social psychologists noted early on that if two groups were involved in a laboratory study, and the experimenter allowed one person to decide how much to pay each participant, the person would usually give more money to members of his or her own group than to members of the other group, even if the groups were chosen completely at random.[101,102,103,104,105] Various theories were proposed to explain this finding. Was it because people felt similar to members of their own group? Was it because they had grown to like them? Was it because they had had conflict with the outgroup? Was it because they expected members of their own group to repay the good treatment later on?

A European research team led by Henri Tajfel decided to conduct a program of studies that would determine what caused these patterns of **ingroup favoritism** (preferential treatment of, or more favorable attitudes toward, people in one's own group, as compared to people in other groups). They formed an experimental plan: They would start out with groups that were so meaningless that people would not show any in group favoritism; then they would gradually add in other variables (such as the presumption that the group members were similar to each other, or had to depend on each other, or had common goals) and see at what point the ingroup favoritism started.

But the plan failed—for a very revealing reason. It failed because the research team could never get to the starting point. They were unable to make a group that seemed so arbitrary or trivial that no ingroup favoritism was found. If the experimenters did nothing more than flip a coin to assign participants to a "red team" and a "blue team," the red team members soon began to think that the blue team members were stupid or obnoxious or immoral, and they would favor other red team members if they could.[106] This automatic preference for members of one's own group even in the absence of pragmatic benefit or personal relationship is called the **minimal group effect**.

These findings suggest that people are normally and naturally ready to go along with dividing the world up into "us" and "them" and to adopt a negative stance toward "them."

ingroup favoritism preferential treatment of, or more favorable attitudes toward, people in one's own group

minimal group effect the finding that people show favoritism toward ingroup members even when group membership is randomly determined

Prejudice and discrimination follow naturally from this tendency. As we said, the content of stereotypes may be learned, but the readiness to hold stereotypes is deeply rooted and not easily overcome.

Prejudice may be yet another sphere in which nature says go, whereas culture sometimes says stop. Nature has prepared human beings to divide the world into "us" and "them" and to hold prejudices against "them." This mind-set may have been very helpful in early human evolution, during which people survived by belonging to groups that cooperated—and during which people in other groups were often dangerous.

Culture sometimes strives to teach people to overcome their prejudices. Modern diverse cultures in particular struggle to get people to set aside their prejudices and treat each other with fairness and tolerance, but the struggle is not an easy one, and total success has proven elusive. There has been some progress, such as in attitudes toward same-sex marriage becoming more accepting over time in the United States.[107] In addition, more and more countries are legalizing same-sex marriage around the world. The Netherlands was the first country to legalize same-sex marriage in 2000, but since then several other countries have followed suit: Belgium in 2003; Canada and Spain in 2005; South Africa in 2006; Norway and Sweden in 2009; Argentina, Iceland, and Portugal in 2010; Denmark in 2012; Brazil, England, Wales, France, New Zealand, and Uruguay in 2013; and Luxembourg and Scotland in 2014; and the United States in 2015.[108] Since 2009, same-sex marriage has been legal in some jurisdictions in Mexico.

Of course, culture does not always say stop. As we noted earlier, the content of stereotypes is almost always learned, and people learn from their culture what members of other groups are supposedly like. That goes for stereotypes that are fairly accurate and ones that are wildly distorted.

Us Versus Them: Groups in Competition

In the 1950s, Muzafer Sherif conducted a study at Robber's Cave State Park in Oklahoma.[109] The park, named after a cave that was once supposedly inhabited by robbers, was located in a remote area far from external influences. Participants were 22 white, middle-class, 11-year-old boys who thought they were going on a summer camp experience. Little did they know that the camp was being run by a social psychologist! Sherif divided the boys into two groups of 11 that were approximately equal in athletic ability and camping experience. He then transported the two groups to the park in separate buses and assigned them to cabins located in different areas of the park. The study was conducted in three stages, with each stage lasting about one week.

During the first stage, the two groups of boys had no contact with each other. The boys in each group cooperated in activities such as swimming, pitching tents, preparing meals, and hiking. During this stage, the boys in each group became good friends. One group called itself the Rattlers; the other group called itself the Eagles. Both groups made flags and stenciled the group names on their T-shirts.

During the second stage, the two groups met each other and competed in contests such as baseball and tug-of-war. The stakes were high because the winners took home valuable prizes including trophies, medals, cash, and pocketknives. The two groups began eating together in a common mess hall, where the prizes were on display for all to see. The contests produced strong feelings of prejudice toward the other group. These showed up first in name-calling, such as calling the other boys "pigs," "sissies," "cheaters," and "stinkers." Before long, the boys started committing physical acts of aggression. Following their first loss at a baseball game, the Eagles burned the Rattlers' flag, and the Eagles' leader proclaimed "You can tell those guys I did it ... I'll fight 'em." The next day, the Rattlers burned the Eagles' flag in retaliation. When the Eagles won a tug-of-war by sitting down and digging in their heels, the Rattlers accused them of cheating and that night invaded their cabin, overturning beds, tearing out mosquito netting, and causing extensive damage. The next morning, the Eagles took revenge on the Rattlers' cabin, and then began to store rocks to throw at the Rattlers if they retaliated.

The Eagles eventually won the tournament and took home the valuable prizes. No consolation prizes were given to the losers. The defeated Rattlers immediately raided the

Eagles' cabin and stole the prizes, which provoked further fighting. Things became so bad that the camp counselors were forced to intervene. At the end of the second stage, it was fair to say that the opposing groups of boys hated each other. It had taken only a week and a few competitions to transform groups of 11-year-old campers into violent haters.

The third stage was designed to reduce the hostility between groups. The researchers soon found out that creating hostility between groups was much easier than reducing it (another sign that people are predisposed to develop negative feelings toward outgroups)! First, the researchers tried telling each group good things about the boys in the other group. This attempt failed miserably. Neither group believed the propaganda. Next, the psychologists tried noncompetitive contact, such as having the boys watch movies together, eat meals together, and shoot off fireworks together on the Fourth of July. This didn't work either. It just gave the boys another chance to express their hostile prejudices. For example, when the boys ate together, they ended up having food fights.

Finally the researchers tried to induce cooperation by having the boys work together toward shared goals, called **superordinate goals**. The researchers rigged some urgent problems that the boys could solve only by working together. First, the camp's water supply failed. The camp staff blamed the problem on "vandals." The Eagles and Rattlers inspected the water lines separately but found no problems. They came together at the source of water, a large tank that was practically full, where they discovered a sack stuffed inside the water faucet. The boys worked together on the faucet for more than 45 minutes. Finally they fixed it, and the two groups rejoiced together. The second superordinate goal involved showing a feature-length movie. The staff called the boys together and said they could get one of two films, *Treasure Island* or *Kidnapped*. Both groups yelled approval of these films. After some discussion, one Rattler said, "Everyone who wants *Treasure Island* raise their hands." Most of the boys voted for this film. The staff said that the film would cost $15 (a serious amount of money in those days), and the camp could not afford to pay the whole amount. After some more discussion, the boys arrived at a solution— each group would pay $3.50 and the camp would pay the remaining $8.00. The boys even decided to eat dinner together.

By the end of the third stage, negative stereotypes of outgroup members had decreased dramatically (see **FIGURE 13.2**). At breakfast and lunch on the last day of camp, many boys sat next to boys in the other group. The boys agreed that they wanted to return to Oklahoma City all together on one bus, instead of going home in separate buses. When the staff agreed to the request, some of the boys actually cheered. The Rattlers even agreed to use the $5 they had won in a contest to buy malts for all the boys at a rest stop.

Several theories have been proposed to explain prejudice, such as the prejudice that existed between the Eagles and Rattlers. **Realistic conflict theory** provides one explanation of prejudice.[110] According to this theory, competition over scarce resources leads to intergroup hostility and conflict. A common example is a situation in which jobs are scarce and an established group blames immigrants for "taking the food out of our children's mouths." By **competition** we mean that some people attain their goals only if other people do not.[111] By **cooperation** we mean that people work together with others to help all of them achieve their goals.[112] In the Robber's Cave study, competition over valued prizes such as cash and pocketknives led to an all-out feud between two groups of ordinary 11-year-old boys. The two groups of boys quickly came to loathe each other even though they didn't differ on any visible dimension, such as racial or ethnic background. In everyday life, where it is easier to distinguish "us" from "them" on the basis of obvious physical traits, prejudice and hostility may arise even more swiftly.

According to realistic conflict theory, groups should have the most negative attitudes toward their rivals, and these attitudes should be strongest, when resources are scarce and groups must compete for them. (Everyone needs food, water, and air to live, but

Sometimes people have to work together to achieve superordinate goals that no single person could achieve alone (such as getting the box of cookies off the top of the fridge).

© Danny Vincenz 2012

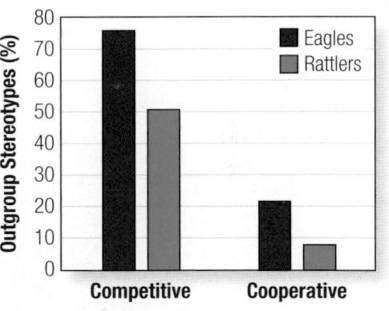

© Cengage Learning

FIGURE 13.2

Percent of outgroup members classified negatively after competition and after cooperation.[109]

superordinate goals goals that can be achieved only by cooperating and working with others

realistic conflict theory the idea that competition over scarce resources leads to intergroup hostility and conflict

competition situation in which people can attain their goals only if others do not

cooperation situation in which people must work together with others to help all achieve their goals

few groups fight over air because there is plenty for everyone. In contrast, fighting over food has a long history, and some predictions are that as the world's supply of freshwater begins to run short over the course of this century, conflicts over water will increase.) Competition is not a part of every society. *Tradeoffs* describes 25 peaceful, cooperative, noncompetitive societies.

One could argue that realistic conflict theory is just frustration–aggression theory (see Chapter 10) applied to group conflict. Competition is a zero-sum game in which one side's gain is the other side's frustration. Hence people form negative attitudes toward competing outgroups because they frustrate your own group's efforts to get what you want.

Evolution may have had a hand in instilling the human readiness to form groups and hold prejudices against rival groups. Hunter-gatherer groups lived under conditions of fairly scarce resources, which is why they roamed over large areas. If two groups tried to spend the summer in the same area, there might not be enough food for both groups, so one group would have to leave. The groups would therefore be natural enemies. If one group contained people who readily formed prejudices against the others and acted quickly to drive the others out, whereas the other group failed to develop such attitudes, the more prejudiced group would very likely win the competition for scarce resources.

Most discussions of prejudice and stereotyping today focus on unfavorable treatment of the outgroup, but that is simply the other side of the coin of preferential or favorable treatment of the ingroup. For example, if a wealthy African American businessman gives a large sum of money to make scholarships available for African American students, is he discriminating against non-blacks (who are not eligible for his money) or helping members of his own group? Both are correct. When we understand prejudice as doing positive, favorable deeds for members of one's own group, it is easier to see how this could be favored in evolution and become part of human nature. Imagine human beings who didn't do anything special or nice for members of their own families or for the people with whom they lived and worked. Such people might well have lost out in natural selection, if pitted against groups in which most members helped and supported one another.

The idea of ingroup selection brings up the broader issue of whether prejudice is really based on love or hate. Hating the enemy may be the flip side of the coin of loving one's own group. Ironically, prejudice affects even judgments about whether people are motivated by love or hate. Participants in a series of studies rated their own group as motivated mainly by love, whereas they saw outgroups as motivated by hate.[122] Republicans and Democrats both saw each other as driven mainly by hate—and saw their own party members as motivated by love. Similar patterns emerged with Israelis and Palestinians, two groups with different religious and ethnic backgrounds that have clashed endlessly in the Middle East.

The challenges of living in a diverse society have sensitized modern individuals to the problems created by prejudices. People from different groups seem ready to distrust each other and develop negative views of each other. It is important to remember that humans evolved under conditions in which they interacted mainly with members of their own group, not other groups. (In other words, diverse societies are a fairly modern invention.) Groups whose members wanted to help and support one another probably flourished better than groups that didn't. But in modern life people have to live in harmony with people who belong to very different groups. This is not what we evolved for, but it is the reality of modern life.

Numerous studies have shown that groups are more prone to hostile competition than individuals are, a finding that has been dubbed the **discontinuity effect**.[123] The discontinuity effect appears to be motivated by fear and greed.[124,125] People don't trust the members of other groups, so they grab as many resources as they can. If the outgroup is cooperative, they will take advantage of it. However, intergroup competitiveness is not inevitable. For example, we can reduce it by having people think about the long-term effects of their actions.[126] Making group members identifiable will also reduce intergroup competitiveness.[127] Recall from Chapter 10 that when people become deindividuated (identities are concealed), they are more likely to perform antisocial actions.

discontinuity effect the finding that groups are more extreme, and often more hostile, than individuals

Competition Versus Cooperation

Many people in the United States and other Western societies perceive the world as a dog-eat-dog place in which people compete to survive and prosper. Not all societies adopt this view of competition. In an analysis of 25 cooperative, peaceful societies, researchers found that competition did not exist in 23 of the 25 societies.[113] In these 23 societies, even the games children play lack competition. For example, the !Kung children of Namibia and Botswana in southern Africa love to play a game called *zeni.* The children use a stick to throw into the air a weight that is attached by a thong to a feather. Then they use the stick to try to catch the object. Although the children exhibit widely different skill levels, they do not compete against each other. They just play the game for fun.[114]

TRADE *Offs*

The !Kung children of Namibia and Botswana in southern Africa love to play a noncompetitive game called *zeni* where they use a stick to throw into the air a weight that is attached by a thong to a feather and then to try to catch the object.

The Piaroa of Venezuela are intensely opposed to competition and even put it in the same category as cannibalism.[115] The Chewong of the Malay Peninsula are so opposed to competition that they don't even have a word for it in their language.[116] The Tristan Islanders had virtually no knowledge of competition until 1961, when they were forced to relocate to Great Britain for two years after a volcano erupted on their island. The Tristan Islanders did not fit in well with the highly competitive English society.[117] The Ifaluk, who live on a small Pacific atoll in the Federated States of Micronesia, value most highly a person who is *maluwelu* (calm, quiet, respectful, obedient, kind, gentle). The word *maluwelu* is also used to describe a lagoon when the wind is calm. They strongly devalue traits such as showing off, being disrespectful, and displaying personal possessions.[118] The Birhor, a tribal society of central India, do not compete for scarce resources and rarely accumulate possessions.[119]

Competition was found in 2 of the 25 peaceful societies, but it was limited to competition in business dealings. More than 100 years ago, the Fipa of western Tanzania transformed their society from one based on violence and war to one based on nonviolence and peace. The Fipa are very competitive in their business dealings, but the competition is constructive and peaceful.[120] The other competitive peaceful society is the Jains of India. The Jains believe in *ahimas* (nonviolence), and they take vows to avoid any socially harmful acts, including stealing and lying. Yet they are quite competitive in the business world. An analysis of these studies does not prove that competition leads to violence, but it does show that cultures have the power to say "stop" even though our natural tendency is to compete for limited resources.

However, there might be a tradeoff to embracing cooperation and shunning competition. These 25 cooperative, peaceful societies are not very successful or powerful, in either economic or political terms. Competition may produce prejudice, hostility, and aggression, but it also produces progress and advancement. Communism sought to eliminate competition (at least based on greed) by eliminating private ownership and private property, but without incentives it was an economic failure. The effect can be summed up in one of the stock phrases that Soviet-bloc workers used to say before the collapse of European communism: "They pretend to pay us, and we pretend to work." Many small European countries competed for centuries for local power, at great cost in warfare and suffering, but as a result European military skills and technology so far surpassed those of the rest of the world that Europeans were able to conquer and colonize most other peoples they encountered. Indeed, according to some analyses, the competition among many small, neighboring countries was a central fact that enabled Europe to surpass and overpower other cultures that had once been clearly more powerful.[121] Competition has costs, but it also offers gains.

Dancers from Ifaluk, one of the 25 peaceful, cooperative societies studied by Bruce Bonta found in the world (1997).

Anthony Bannister/Gallo Images/Documentary Value/Corbis

© Eric Metzgar/Triton Films

The crucial implication of the discontinuity effect is that groups won't usually get along as well as individuals. To illustrate, imagine two people from different races who have a dispute; they sit down, one-to-one, and try to resolve the issue. What are the odds that they can work it out? Now imagine that the dispute is between groups—six people of one race and six of the other. What are the odds that these groups can reach an acceptable compromise? The discontinuity effect holds that the two groups will be less likely to find a mutually agreeable compromise than the two individuals. One Asian and one African can perhaps find a mutually satisfactory compromise; six Asians talking to six Africans might not. This is not a reflection on the particular races but rather on universal human nature.

Ignorance? The Contact Hypothesis

Another view is that prejudice stems from ignorance. According to this view, people who have very little contact with other groups have no information about them, so they try to fill the gap by forming stereotypes. If people could resolve ignorance by having more interactions and getting more firsthand information about outgroups, prejudice would diminish or even disappear.

More than 50 years ago, Gordon Allport proposed the **contact hypothesis** which states that regular interaction between members of different groups reduces prejudice, providing that it occurs under favorable conditions.[128] According to this hypothesis, negative prejudices arise and survive because the two groups don't have much contact with each other. Bringing conflicting groups together supposedly reduces prejudicial feelings as members of different groups come to know and understand one another. For example, integrating children of different racial backgrounds should reduce prejudice as these students interact with one another and learn more about each other.

Research has shown some support for the contact hypothesis, provided that the contact is pleasant and positive and other conditions are met.[129,130] When the contact is not mutually satisfying, the result can be an increase in hostility and prejudice.[131] In line with the "bad is stronger than good" principle,[132] negative contact seems to outweigh positive contact.[133] (Remember what happened in the "Robbers Cave" study, described earlier, when the two antagonistic groups of boys were brought together for more contact—the

contact hypothesis the idea that regular interaction between members of different groups reduces prejudice, providing that it occurs under favorable conditions

Over time, roommates of different races become less prejudiced.

time spent together led to more fighting.) When contact occurs under positive conditions, people feel good inside. This good feeling, in turn, leads to less prejudice.[134,135] These positive feelings, in turn, predicted less prejudiced behavior a year later. A longitudinal study of 1,655 secondary school students from Belgium, England, and Germany showed a reciprocal relationship between contact and prejudice.[136] Not only did contact reduce prejudice, but prejudiced people also avoid contact with minority group members. Contact can even work for common targets of prejudice, such as Muslims[137] and gays and lesbians.[138]

In fact, the positive contact need not be direct to work. Vicarious indirect contact through the media can work to reduce prejudice in direct contact situations.[139] Even imagining positive interactions with outgroup members can reduce prejudice toward them.[140] Some researchers have argued that it is time to rename the "contact hypothesis" the "contact theory" because the scientific evidence has grown to a point that it is quite convincing.[141]

Rationalizations for Oppression

Some social psychologists have sought to explain prejudice and stereotyping on the basis of the political goals of the powerful group.[142] They propose, for example, that white Americans constructed stereotypes of African Americans as inferior beings to justify keeping them in an inferior position in society. Likewise, some feminists have suggested that men invented stereotypes of women simply to rationalize men's continued oppression of women. For example, the view that women were unsuited for higher education (even to the extent of bizarre medical theories proposing that if a woman studied too much, her uterus would come loose and wander aimlessly around inside her body) might have been invented so that men could justify refusing to admit women to universities. Traditional female stereotypes can be used to justify the oppression of women.[143]

The fact that stereotypes can justify social inequality does not mean that stereotypes were deliberately invented as part of a conspiracy to oppress certain people. Rather, it suggests that people in positions of relative power and wealth find stereotypes to be an appealing way of explaining their superiority.

Stereotypes as Heuristics

The previous section presented stereotypes as a kind of conspiracy, claiming that people deliberately invented stereotypes for devious, manipulative ends. A simpler and less insidious view is that people often rely on stereotypes as mental shortcuts, just as they simplify the world in countless other ways. In Chapter 5, we saw that people use a variety of heuristics to help them understand the world in clear, simple ways. Stereotypes may be heuristics, too. Gordon Allport described stereotyping as "the law of least effort."[144] It is difficult and tiring to get to know each individual on his or her own merits, starting with a completely open mind, and to form a valid, carefully tested impression of each person. It is much easier to go through life prejudging people and assuming they will fit general stereotypes based on quickly recognizable categories. Such generalizations appeal to the lazy mind or cognitive miser.

Research has shown that stereotypes are energy-saving devices.[145] Participants performed two tasks at the same time. In one task they were to form an impression of another person using a list of traits. Half of the participants saw only the name of the person they were to form an impression of (e.g., John), whereas the other half also saw a stereotypic label (e.g., John—skinhead). Underneath the name was a list of 10 traits, of which half were consistent with the stereotype (e.g., for skinheads: rebellious, aggressive, dishonest, untrustworthy, dangerous) and half were not (e.g., lucky, observant, modest, optimistic, curious). The other task involved listening to a prose passage (that had nothing to do with the stereotypes) and trying to remember what they heard. Participants' performance on both tasks was tested. Participants who saw a stereotype label recalled twice as many stereotypical traits as did participants who did not see the label. They also remembered more information about the prose passage. Thus, when people were encouraged to use stereotypes, they actually had better memory for other, unrelated information—because

Stereotypes on the savannah...

Paula Wright 2012

© Paula Wright 2012

they were able to save mental energy by stereotyping the skinheads. Similar effects were obtained in a follow-up study even when the stereotype labels were presented subliminally. Using stereotypes enabled people to process more information, consistent with the view that stereotypes are useful tools that enable people to understand others more easily (and, in these cases, more accurately, too). In simple terms, people use stereotypes to simplify the process of thinking about other people.

People use stereotypes when their ability to judge is diminished. One clever study sorted participants into "morning people," who like to wake up early but get sleepy early in the evening, versus "night people," who have energy long after dark but find it hard to drag themselves out of bed in the morning.[146] Each group was tested for how much it used stereotype thinking in the morning versus at night. Morning people are more prone to use stereotypes at night (when they are tired) than in the morning (when they are alert). Night people do the opposite: They rely on stereotypes more in the morning than at night. These findings fit the broader point that people use stereotypes to conserve effort and energy.

People learn the content of stereotypes mainly from other people in their group. That is because people spend much more time with ingroup members than with outgroup members. This fits one of the themes of this book—"putting people first." People rely on other people for information about the world, rather than learn about the world through direct experience. If you have a stereotype about Russians, you probably learned it from your non-Russian friends rather than from direct observation of Russians.

Prejudice and Self-Esteem

We have seen that most stereotypes are negative and that most prejudices depict outgroups as inferior or as having bad traits. Several reasons for this have been suggested. One simple motivational explanation for the negative tone of most stereotypes is that people use them to boost self-esteem. The basic idea is that most people want to have high self-esteem, which is one of the most common assumptions underlying a great deal of research in social psychology. High self-esteem feels good. Applied to prejudice, the idea is that by regarding members of other groups as inferior, people enhance their self-esteem by virtue of belonging to their own group. Put another way, if all the other groups are inferior, then your own group must be superior—so you must be pretty good to belong to it. In this way, prejudice can be self-affirming. By using stereotypes to justify and act on prejudices, people can claim for themselves a feeling of mastery and self-worth.[147] For a summary of why prejudice exists, see **TABLE 13.1**.

TABLE 13.1	Explanations for Why Prejudice Exists		
Explanation	**Definition**	**Example**	
Competition	According to realistic conflict theory, competition over scarce resources leads to intergroup hostility and conflict.	Competition over good housing, schools, and jobs can lead to hostility toward outgroup members.	
Ignorance	People who have very little contact with other groups have no information about them, and so they attempt to fill the gap by forming stereotypes.	People who have little contact with Muslims may assume that they all support the jihad against the West.	
Rationalizations for oppression	To retain their status, powerful groups justify and rationalize prejudice against less powerful groups.	Some feminists have suggested that men invented stereotypes of women simply to rationalize continued oppression of women.	
Stereotypes as heuristics	To simplify their world, people often rely on stereotypes as mental shortcuts or heuristics.	Rather than collect information about each African American individually, it requires less mental effort to stereotype them all as good at music and sports.	
Prejudice boosts self-esteem	People can feel better about themselves if they consider their own group superior and all other groups inferior.	People might feel better about themselves if they think their own religion is the only true one and all others are false.	

1. **If some participants are randomly assigned to a "red group" and others are assigned to a "gray group," the "red group" members will think they are superior to the "gray group" members, whereas the "gray group" members will think they are superior to the "red group" members. What is this phenomenon called?**

   (a) Discontinuity effect (b) Minimal group effect (c) Outgroup favoritism (d) Outgroup homogeneity bias

2. **The Robber's Cave study provides _____ .**

   (a) evidence that stereotypes once formed can almost never be changed (b) evidence that competition is necessary to the creation of intergroup conflict (c) evidence that mere contact will greatly reduce intergroup hostility (d) None of the above

3. **According to the discontinuity effect, _____ .**

   (a) both groups and individuals are influenced by competition (b) groups are more influenced by competition than individuals are (c) individuals are more influenced by competition than groups are (d) neither groups nor individuals are influenced by competition

4. **What does the research indicate about the contact hypothesis?**

   (a) Contact with outgroup members decreases prejudice, regardless of the context in which it occurs. (b) Contact with outgroup members decreases prejudice in negative contexts. (c) Contact with outgroup members decreases prejudice in positive contexts. (d) Contact with outgroup members increases prejudice regardless of the context in which it occurs.

answers: see pg 489

QUIZ YOURSELF
Why Prejudice Exists

Content of Prejudice and Stereotypes

In this section we examine the content of prejudice and stereotypes. One might say that people today have a stereotype about stereotypes, which is that stereotypes are typically both wrong and negative. Is that stereotype accurate?

Are Stereotypes Always Wrong, Mostly Wrong, or Mostly Right?

In the Stereotypes as Heuristics section, we covered the theory that stereotypes are heuristics. As we saw in Chapter 5, people use heuristics and other shortcuts in their thinking to conserve mental effort and time, and to help them make decisions when they lack full information. Heuristics can lead to errors, but heuristics survive because they often produce the right answer. This has led some researchers to wonder whether some stereotypes have some element of accuracy. For example, you might have the stereotype that men are taller than women, and so when meeting a married couple you would generally expect the husband to be taller than the wife. Sometimes you would be wrong because some women are taller than their husbands. Still, you would be right most of the time.

That, after all, is how heuristics work. They take an approach that is true most of the time and follow it as if it were always true. Researchers have investigated gender stereotypes to see how big the kernel of truth was.[148] The findings were disturbing to some because they suggested that people's stereotypes are accurate in both content and degree. Participants listed the traits men and women differed on, and indicated how large they thought the difference was. When these estimates were compared against published studies on actual gender differences, the results showed that the stereotypes were mostly quite accurate. That is, not only were participants correct about what traits were different between men and women—they were also pretty accurate at estimating the size of the differences.

A thorough review of stereotype accuracy and inaccuracy found remarkable accuracy, with some notable exceptions.[149] Most studies found that people's judgments about racial and ethnic differences averaged within 20% of the objective facts. Hence, severe inaccuracies were not common. Most studies found the same general level of accuracy for gender stereotypes. On the other hand, political stereotypes were consistently inaccurate: Democrats and Republicans do not perceive each other very accurately.[150] Stereotypes about personality traits based on countries were also not very accurate.[151] For example, if we were to ask you what sort of personality is typical among Germans, or French, or Brazilians, you might be able to come up with an answer, but it is not likely very accurate. Moreover, even the evidence of accuracy in general does not translate into everyone being correct. Although the average level of accuracy was high, in every study there were plenty of individuals who expressed wildly inaccurate stereotypes.

Recent research suggests that stereotypes of age differences in personality traits are accurate across 26 nations.[152] Adolescents were consistently seen as impulsive, rebellious, undisciplined, and openness, whereas old people were consistently seen lower on impulsivity, activity, antagonism, and openness. These consensual age group stereotypes correlated strongly with actual personality test scores.

The high level of accuracy in modern stereotypes may also indicate that stereotyping has changed. Most participants in these studies were modern university students, who have been taught to be careful about using stereotypes and avoiding unfair prejudice. Decades ago, German Nazis stereotyped Jews as greedy, ruthless individuals conspiring to destroy their country as a step toward world domination—a mistaken notion that contributed to horrific mass murder.

Even accurate stereotypes may be generalized unfairly and inaccurately. As we noted, a stereotype that women are shorter than men is accurate but may be wrong in many specific cases. A more dangerous version of that kind of mistake was found in connection with hurricanes. Hurricanes named after women kill more people than hurricanes named after men.[153] This may seem surprising, as hurricanes are named in alternating fashion so that the gender is random. Plus, of course, hurricanes do not know their own names. The most likely explanation is that female hurricanes are no worse than male ones—but the names evoke the stereotypes that men are more violent and dangerous than women, so people take fewer precautions when the approaching hurricane has a female rather than a male name.

Another question regarding the accuracy of stereotypes is what happens when people judge a particular other person. Meta-analyses that combine the results of many different studies have generally concluded that there is a genuine effect of stereotypes on judgment of individual persons, but it is a pretty small one.[154] In contrast, people rely quite heavily on information specific to the person when making judgments about that person.[155] In other words, when people meet someone and form an impression of that person, they mostly rely on whatever they learn about that individual, and they may fill in the gaps with stereotypes to a small extent. This fits the view that stereotypes operate like heuristics; they are used to help make judgments when information is lacking or uncertain.

Prejudice has multiple roots. To the extent that prejudices are held as a heuristic way of understanding the social world, people may try to hold fairly accurate stereotypes. In contrast, to the extent that people hold prejudices in order to bolster their own self-esteem at the expense of others, or to rationalize the status quo and justify their oppression of disadvantaged minorities, stereotypes may be exaggerated or even entirely fabricated and hence have little or no factual basis.

Are Stereotypes Always Negative?

Are stereotypes always negative? No, of course not. Many people hold the stereotype that Asian Americans are good at math, or engineering, or schoolwork in general, or that African Americans have superior talents in a variety of culturally valued spheres such as music and sports. A once-popular stereotype that fat people were jolly contributed to how Santa Claus became depicted. If Santa were invented today, he would almost certainly be fashionably slim and debonair! Conversely, if a new character were introduced today as a fat old man with a long beard and a silly red pantsuit, he probably would be a bad guy or troublemaker.

Negative stereotypes generally present more of a cultural problem than positive ones, because they entail prejudging a person as having faults. But positive stereotypes can also be harmful, although the harm may not be as readily apparent. Consider, for example, the difference between hostile sexism and benevolent sexism.[156] Hostile sexism is exemplified by what feminists labeled as "male chauvinist pigs" who view women in a derogatory manner. Benevolent sexism is exemplified by chivalrous men who open doors for women and insist on paying for dinner. Benevolent sexism seems to paint a favorable view of women, but it is also grounded in gender stereotypes. Some researchers have argued that benevolent sexism is worse than hostile sexism for women's cognitive performance.[157] In addition, women who have benevolent sexist attitudes are more likely to perceive safety restrictions (e.g., not driving alone on a long trip) as justified and for their own good.[158] Along the same lines, some researchers complain about benevolent sexism because they make women content with the status quo.[159] Benevolent sexism may be more harmful than hostile sexism because some women may accept it or even enjoy it. In some parts of the world, such as the southern United States, benevolent sexism is even considered to be romantic.

Benevolent sexism may be a tradeoff: It gives women some benefits but reinforces stereotypes. In July 2012, a crazed gunman opened fire in a Colorado movie theater, shooting randomly into the audience, killing a dozen people. Three different young men acted quickly to shield their girlfriends with their bodies, such as by pushing her down onto the floor and lying on top of her. These men died, and their girlfriends lived. Were these men heroes, or sexist oppressors? Or both? There were no reported cases in which women died to save their boyfriends, nor of men sacrificing themselves to save male friends. The critics of "benevolent sexism" could cite those facts as evidence that the young men who died for their dates were acting out of sexist prejudice. (Your textbook authors see them as heroes.)

1. Research has shown that stereotypes about women are _____ .

(a) accurate in content and degree

(b) accurate in content, but inaccurate in degree

(c) inaccurate in content, but accurate in degree

(d) inaccurate in content and degree

2. Joe is the kind of man who likes to hold doors open for women, buy them flowers and chocolates, pay for their meals, and in general put them on a pedestal. Joe is demonstrating _____ .

(a) benevolent sexism

(b) hostile sexism

(c) both benevolent and hostile sexism

(d) neither benevolent nor hostile sexism

3. What type of sexism leads to the greatest reductions on cognitive performance tests in women?

(a) Benevolent sexism leads to the greatest reductions in cognitive performance.

(b) Hostile sexism leads to the greatest reductions in cognitive performance.

(c) Reductions in cognitive performance are similar for benevolent and hostile sexism.

(d) Neither benevolent nor hostile sexism lead to reductions in cognitive performance.

4. Benevolent sexism is considered romantic in what part of the United States?

(a) Eastern

(b) Northern

(c) Southern

(d) Western

Inner Processes

Inner processes (e.g., emotions) can also contribute to prejudice and stereotyping. Stereotypes can form simply on the basis of **salience**—a psychological term roughly meaning "obviousness."[160,161] We described one of these studies in Chapter 5 when we discussed illusory correlations.[162] That is, simply standing out can contribute to stereotyping. If you were, say, the first blond person to arrive on an island, people would pay extra attention to what you did, and if you did something memorable (say, you did something to disgrace a local church), people would remember that "blond people are against religion," and the next blonds to arrive would have to cope with that stereotype.

The research findings based on salience are interesting because they show how stereotypes can form from purely cognitive (mental) processes, without any influence of emotion or motivation. When motivation enters the picture, it can greatly increase the likelihood of prejudice. One classic formulation of motivated prejudice is scapegoat theory. In ancient times, on the Day of Atonement (Yom Kippur), Moses' older brother Aaron symbolically placed all the sins of the children of Israel on the head of a goat, who was then sent into the wilderness to perish.[163] The peoples' sins were supposed to perish along with the unfortunate scapegoat.

Scapegoat theory proposes that people blame their problems and misfortunes on outgroups, which contributes to negative attitudes toward these outgroups. This process is linked to attribution theory, discussed in Chapter 5, which looks at how people infer the causes of events. One theme introduced there was the **self-serving bias**. People like to take credit for success but refuse blame for problems and failures. When times are bad, people prefer to blame others (scapegoats) rather than their own bad judgment or incompetence.

salience being obvious or standing out

scapegoat theory the idea that blaming problems and misfortunes on outgroups contributes to negative attitudes toward these outgroups

self-serving bias the tendency for people to take credit for success but refuse blame for problems and failures

Recent work suggests that scapegoating can derive from two different motivational roots.[164] One is a quest for moral affirmation and superiority. The person's responsibility for bad outcomes is transferred onto the scapegoat, so guilt and other feelings of moral inferiority are reduced. The other motivation is a desire for control. Many negative events have complex causes that are hard to fathom and even harder to control. In contrast, blaming a scapegoat is simple and straightforward, and it restores the person's sense of having control.

Scapegoating creates friction in any diverse society. Throughout Western history, the Jews have suffered repeatedly as a result of being blamed for the problems of Christian societies. Jews were blamed for the death of Jesus, even though it was the Romans who actually performed the execution. Before long, however, Romans were European and Christian (and the pope himself lived in Rome), so the Christian community in Europe preferred to put the blame on the Jewish outgroup rather than on members of their own ingroup.

Even in the 20th century, Jews were scapegoats. Germans were shocked and baffled by their country's abrupt surrender in World War I (which, thanks in part to battlefield standstills and government propaganda, they had thought they were winning all along). When the Nazis accused the Jews of having stabbed the German war effort in the back, many Germans found this theory more believable and appealing than blaming their own leaders and politicians, and the wide acceptance of this theory helped fuel the hostility toward Jews that enabled the murderous Holocaust. Note that this likely served both motives for scapegoating: It enabled non-Jewish Germans to feel no responsibility for their nation's defeat and collapse, and it offered the false promise that Germans could regain control of their fate by treating the Jews as a dastardly enemy.

Social psychologists conducted a famous test of scapegoat theory using race relations in the United States. Researchers correlated the market price of cotton with the frequency of interracial lynching incidents in the southern United States over a period of 49 years, 1882 to 1930.[165] Lynching is execution by a vigilante mob. Typically, a group of people would hang or otherwise kill someone who has been accused of a crime but not legally convicted, and of course such killings are themselves both illegal and immoral. The researchers chose the price of cotton because many white families in the South made their living by growing cotton. Because the amount they could grow in a given year stayed about the same (given how much land they owned), a drop in cotton prices meant a big drop in income and hence financial problems for many. The researchers reasoned that when people were thus poorer than usual, they would want to blame their troubles on an outgroup, and they thought African Americans would make a convenient scapegoat. Hence, they reasoned, illegal violence against African Americans (as measured by lynching) would go up when cotton prices went down. That's what they found. Subsequent work with more elaborate statistical methods reconfirmed this hypothesis.[166]

To be sure, the correlation between cotton prices and interracial lynching is not necessarily a pattern of scapegoating. Recall that correlation does not mean causation. The relationship might be explained on other, related grounds, such as frustration (resulting from low cotton prices and less money) leading to aggression. Still, whatever the inner processes, it does suggest that harsh times cause people to behave more aggressively toward outgroups.

Research indicates that conflict and stress tend to bring out stereotypes. The subtitle of one set of studies is "She's fine if she praised me but incompetent if she criticized me."[167] In these studies, college students evaluated female university instructors as less competent than male instructors after receiving negative evaluations from them but not after receiving positive evaluations from them. Students who were praised by a woman or by students who watched someone else receive praise or criticism from a woman did not use the stereotype that women are less competent than men.

Similar findings have been reported for racial stereotypes. People are more likely to use racial stereotypes when there is a disagreement or conflict than when everyone agrees.[168] For example, white participants in one study read about a court case, gave their verdict, and then observed a videotape of a black or white fellow juror who either agreed or disagreed with the participant's verdict.[169] Later, on a computerized test, participants showed faster reaction times to black stereotypical words when black fellow jurors had disagreed with them. Thus, stereotypes may lie buried and forgotten much of the time, but when a black person disagrees with a white person, the stereotypes start leaping to mind.

Emotional stress can activate stereotypes and lead to distortions in how people see the world. A team of researchers collected facial photos of people of different races, including whites, Arabs, and blacks.[170] The photos were carefully chosen to have no particular expressions, and participants who were themselves in a calm or neutral state rated them all that way. However, in one experimental condition, participants first viewed scenes from a horror movie that induced fearful states. When these participants looked at the same faces, they saw the faces of people from other races as angry and threatening, though they did not show any change in how they perceived the faces of people from their own race. Moreover, these effects occurred mainly among people who held stereotypes of the other races as dangerous and threatening. For example, whites who regarded Arabs as dangerous tended to see the blank Arab faces as angry and threatening (when the white perceivers were already afraid). But whites who did not hold that stereotype of Arabs did not shift in how they perceived the Arab faces.

How does prejudice operate? One simple theory is that people simply prejudge others based on their assumptions. Some stereotypes may operate that way, but social psychology research has suggested that the actual process is often more subtle and complex. Some research shows that people use their stereotypes more as hypotheses to be tested than as rules that can be applied in all cases. In an influential experiment,[171] students were exposed to background information about a schoolgirl named Hannah. Some participants saw a videotape that depicted her as from a rich, privileged family, whereas others saw a videotape that depicted her as from a poor, working-class family. The participants were then asked to guess how well she was doing in school. The typical prejudice and stereotype would predict that the girl from the upper-class background would be doing better in school than the girl from the working-class background, but the researchers found no such difference. Participants were not willing to leap from knowing her background (and holding broad stereotypes) to making predictions or assumptions about her intellectual ability.

Meanwhile, other participants saw a second videotape. It depicted Hannah taking an oral test in school. There was only one version of this videotape, and it depicted Hannah's performance as inconsistent. Sometimes she seemed to perform quite well, but at other points she seemed bored by the test and not able to furnish the proper answers.

You might think that seeing someone take a test of intellectual ability would eliminate the effect of stereotypes, but in fact the Hannah experiment found exactly the opposite. The stereotypes based on family background emerged only among people who saw Hannah taking the test. The mechanism was probably one of **confirmation bias**, which we saw in Chapter 5 is a tendency to focus more on evidence that supports (confirms) one's expectations than on evidence that contradicts them. The participants who believed Hannah came from a rich family paid more attention to the parts of the test on which she was doing well, and so concluded that their expectations (that rich children do better in school) were confirmed. Meanwhile, the participants who believed she came from a poor family focused on the parts of the test on which she did poorly; they too concluded that their expectations (that poor children perform worse) were confirmed.

The participants did not truly prejudge Hannah. Their prejudices did not lead to firm assumptions about how smart she would be; instead, the prejudices functioned more like expectations, which they then sought to test against Hannah's behavior. Unfortunately, perhaps, they ended up viewing her behavior in a biased manner, so their ultimate impression of her was biased.

confirmation bias the tendency to focus more on evidence that supports one's expectations than on evidence that contradicts them

1. The psychological term for obviousness is _____ .

  (a) heterogeneous   (b) homogeneous   (c) nonsalience   (d) salience

2. What theory proposes that people blame their problems and misfortunes on outgroups?

  (a) Catharsis theory   (b) Realistic conflict theory   (c) Relative deprivation theory   (d) Scapegoat theory

3. In a famous 1940 study, researchers found that as cotton prices decreased, the number of lynchings _____ .

  (a) decreased   (b) increased   (c) increased and then decreased   (d) was not affected

4. Lea believes that all Muslims are terrorists. She searches for evidence on the Internet and finds lots of "evidence" to support his belief. Lea is exhibiting _____ .

  (a) the confirmation bias   (b) the false consensus effect   (c) an illusory correlation   (d) the self-serving bias

answers: see pg 489

Overcoming Stereotypes, Reducing Prejudice

How prejudiced are Americans today? One view that can be heard on many talk shows that focus on race relations is that the United States is a deeply prejudiced, racist society. A contrary view is this:

> The sociological truths are that America, while still flawed in its race relations, is now the least racist white-majority society in the world; has a better record of legal protection of minorities than any other society, white or black; offers more opportunities to a greater number of black persons than any other society, including all those of Africa.[173]

This comment may sound as though it came from someone unfamiliar with American problems or unsympathetic to African Americans, but in fact the source was Orlando Patterson, a highly respected black scholar who was chair of the African American Studies program at Harvard University.

Which view is correct? Both could be. It depends on what the standard is. Compared to our American ideals of full tolerance and equality, there is still far too much prejudice, as the first characterization suggests. Compared to most other societies in the history of the world, however, the United States is remarkably tolerant, equal, and supportive, as Patterson's comment expresses.

It is undeniable that prejudice exists in the United States today. Contrary to what some people have claimed, the race problem still exists even though the nation now has twice elected its first non-white president—Barack Obama. Indeed, to eliminate prejudice completely seems an impossible ideal. Still, modern Americans have come far in overcoming many prejudices and stereotypes. Most people now believe that prejudices based on race and gender are unfair and even immoral, and if people do know those stereotypes, they may try not to let them cloud their judgment of individuals. In most societies in world history, a person's race and gender would steer the person toward one

> "The greatest and noblest pleasure which men can have in this world is to discover new truths; and the next is to shake off old prejudices."[172]
> — Frederick the Great, 18th-century King of Prussia

It is true that America elected its first non-white president, Barack Obama, in 2008. It is not true, however, that racism is no longer a problem in America.

sort of life, with one set of opportunities and not others, but modern American society has come remarkably far in removing those obstacles. Though the society was created by white men, and the government still is disproportionately composed of white men, the laws and court rulings issued by those men have changed society so that African Americans, women, and other categories of people can run for president (and win), serve on the Supreme Court, rise to the top of universities and corporations, represent their country in international diplomacy, and in other ways have access to the best positions and rewards the culture has to offer. Indeed, in many cases the white men made rules to give preferential treatment to women and non-white men (e.g., affirmative action policies).

None of this should be taken to imply that prejudice has been conquered or that cruel, immoral, and sometimes vicious acts of prejudice and discrimination have ceased. Prejudice is still a force in the United States; its influence ranges from hate crimes to demeaning ethnic jokes. The point is merely that American society has made considerable progress in fighting against some important kinds of prejudice, especially those based on race and gender.

Conscious Override

If prejudice is natural, and culture sometimes wants to say "stop" to prejudice, those who hold prejudiced views must consciously override the response. The battle against prejudice is fought between the two halves of the duplex mind. The automatic system may often sustain prejudices, for many of the reasons we have already noted: Stereotypes simplify the world and help people make snap judgments; thus, they appeal to the automatic system (which is usually looking for ways to process information quickly). The conscious system can strive to overcome those prejudices and stereotypes so as to support equality and avoid prejudging individuals.

Numerous studies have shown that people harbor prejudiced attitudes toward particular social groups at the implicit or unconscious level, even though they honestly report having no prejudiced attitudes at the explicit or conscious level[174,175,176,177] (also see Chapter 7). Unconscious prejudiced attitude measures have been found to do a good job in predicting behavior, especially spontaneous behaviors.[178] Likewise, unconscious racist attitude measures have been shown to do a better job of predicting workplace discrimination in hiring practices than explicitly stated, conscious attitude measures.[179] Implicit attitude measures about alcohol did a better job of predicting drinking behavior than did explicit attitude measures.[180] Because people are reluctant to admit that they have racist attitudes or drinking problems, what they say in response to explicit questions is not always a good predictor of behavior.

Most implicit attitude measures compare prejudice toward blacks relative to whites. Thus, it is difficult to know whether racism is due to liking whites, disliking blacks, or both. Recent research shows that these measures indicate disliking blacks rather than liking whites.[181] Intriguing evidence about this inner struggle to overcome prejudice was provided in research examining the aftereffects of talking with someone of a different race.[182,183] As we saw in Chapter 4, self-regulation operates like a muscle that gets tired after use. Participants showed just such tiredness: They performed worse than other participants (who had spoken to someone of their own race) on a standard test of self-regulation (the Stroop task, which requires people to override their first impulse in order to give the correct response; see Chapter 5). The effect was strongest for participants who had the strongest prejudices. Thus, when people talk to someone from another race, they have to carefully regulate themselves in order to hide their prejudices and to make sure they do not say anything that could be interpreted as offensive or biased. This extra effort takes its toll, leaving people less able to self-regulate afterward. People do exert themselves consciously to overcome and hide their prejudices, even though the effort may be costly.

Of course, in many cases the conscious mind is quite comfortable hanging onto its prejudices and does not try to override the prejudicial reaction of the automatic system. The difference can perhaps be appreciated by comparing anti-black and anti-obese prejudices in the United States today. Most Americans regard racial prejudice as immoral and will consciously strive to avoid thinking or expressing negative stereotypes of African Americans. In contrast, many people are content to think and express negative stereotypes of obese people; they do not consciously try to override the automatic reaction (possibly unless they are talking to an obese person).

Mental Processes of Nonprejudiced People

The view that overcoming prejudice is based on conflict between conscious and automatic responses emerged from an important series of studies.[184] This research sought to find which mental processes underlay prejudice by seeking to ascertain what was different between prejudiced and nonprejudiced people. A questionnaire was used to classify people as either prejudiced or nonprejudiced, and people who were at both extremes took part. A series of tests were used to see where the difference lies.

The first hypothesis was that the difference lies in knowledge of stereotypes: Maybe nonprejudiced people are not familiar with the stereotypes. Upon testing both groups, however, the researcher found that they had equal knowledge of the content of stereotypes.

The second hypothesis was that the difference lies in whether the stereotype is activated (i.e., whether it springs to mind) when one encounters a member of the group. Nonprejudiced people might know the stereotype of African Americans, for example, but might not think of the stereotype when they encounter a real person. This too proved to be wrong: Both prejudiced and nonprejudiced people do think of the stereotype when they encounter someone from the stereotyped group. This suggested that the automatic system was at work, automatically retrieving the prejudicial information when it recognized a member of the category.

The third hypothesis, therefore, was that the automatic system operates in similar ways in both prejudiced and nonprejudiced people, but nonprejudiced people employ their conscious processing to override the stereotype and replace prejudiced thoughts with thoughts more in line with their values of tolerance, fairness, and equality. This hypothesis proved correct. Nonprejudiced people still know and think of stereotypes, but they override them. This fits our theme that nature says go and culture says stop: It is normal and natural to have some degree of prejudice, but the conscious mind can learn to overcome these reactions and treat people in a fair and tolerant manner. Thus, the duplex mind was crucial. The automatic responses of prejudiced people are similar to those of nonprejudiced people. The difference lies in the conscious system and its override of automatic responses that conflict with conscious values.

Discrimination in Reverse

Research has shown that when people are accused of prejudice, they often exert themselves to prove the opposite. In an early laboratory study,[185] for example, white participants who thought of themselves as relatively unprejudiced were either accused or not accused by the experimenter of being racist. After leaving the study, participants encountered a black or white panhandler (actually a confederate) who asked for money. The black panhandler received more money from participants who had been accused of racism than from other participants (not accused of racism). The white panhandler received an equal amount of money from the two groups of participants. Thus, white people gave more money to the black confederate to prove they were not racists.

In another study,[186] black couples and white couples (actually confederates) visited 40 different Canadian restaurants that had advertised dress code regulations, including jacket and tie for male diners. The male partner in each couple violated the dress code by wearing a turtleneck sweater instead of a dress shirt and tie; thus, according to restaurant policy, the restaurant could refuse service to them. When a black couple entered the restaurant first, they were served 75% of the time; when a white couple entered first, they were served only 30% of the time. The restaurant personnel may have had no conscious prejudices, but they subtly showed a reverse discrimination pattern. They treated the black couple more favorably in order to avoid the appearance of being biased.

There was a revealing twist in the restaurant study's data. About 45 minutes after the first couple arrived, the second couple from the other race arrived, and they too violated the dress code. In general, the second couple was treated the same as the first. However, the decision how to react depended on which couple arrived first, and this initial decision showed the reverse discrimination pattern. If the black couple arrived first, then they were seated despite breaking the rules; if later a white couple also broke the rules, they too were seated. If the white couple arrived first, they were usually turned away, and once the restaurant staff had refused service to the white couple, they felt justified in turning away the black couple on the same basis.

Thus, people overcome prejudice by making conscious efforts to be fair and equal in how they treat others. Many people try extra hard to avoid anything that could be interpreted as showing racism or sexism. People may not try as hard to overcome and override prejudices against gay people, obese people, and others. But the progress in overcoming racism and sexism shows the way toward possibly reducing these other prejudices as well, so that Western society can live up to its ideals of judging each person as an individual rather than prejudging him or her as a member of a group or category.

Motives for Overcoming Prejudice

The previous sections have suggested two different reasons for wanting to overcome prejudice. One is a possibly heartfelt dedication to equality and a corresponding belief that prejudice is morally wrong. The other is an appreciation that expressing prejudice could elicit social disapproval. For example, most white Americans report that they do not want to respond with prejudice toward African Americans, but is this a sincere desire to promote equality or merely a strategic reluctance to say things that might make some people angry?

Both motives are real, but different people may emphasize one or the other (or neither).[187] A measure has been developed that can help classify people's responses according to these two motives. The measure assesses Internal Motivation to Respond Without Prejudice, which is understood as a motivation based on a strong inner belief that prejudice is wrong. It also assesses External Motivation to Respond Without Prejudice, which is essentially a sense that it is socially unwise to express opinions that others will regard as socially undesirable or politically incorrect. **FIGURE 13.3** contains the items for both these scales. The scales can also be modified to assess motives to avoid prejudice against gay people, obese people, Muslims, or any other group. The internal and external motivations to avoid prejudice are not mutually exclusive. Some people have one, some have both, and others have neither.

People's source of motivation to respond without prejudice (i.e., the *reason* why they are motivated) has important implications for behavior. For example, people who are only externally motivated to respond without prejudice report low-prejudice attitudes and beliefs when they have to provide their responses out loud to an experimenter or another person. However, if they are allowed to write their answers on a questionnaire in an anonymous setting, they report attitudes that are more prejudiced. Thus, they shift their answers across settings depending on whether others will be privy to their responses. In contrast, people who are internally motivated to respond without prejudice report low-prejudice attitudes and beliefs regardless of how or to whom they provide their answers. Those neither internally nor externally motivated report moderately prejudiced attitudes regardless of the setting. (Very few present-day Americans consistently express strong racial prejudices.)

Although externally motivated people shift their responses to comply with social pressure to respond without prejudice, this public conformity comes at a price. White people who are primarily externally motivated to respond without prejudice become angry when

FIGURE 13.3

Test yourself: What is your motivation to overcome prejudice?

Copyright © 1998 by the American Psychological Association. Reprinted by permission.[244]

Internal Motivation to Respond Without Prejudice

1. I attempt to act in nonprejudiced ways toward black people because it is personally important to me.
2. According to my personal values, using stereotypes about black people is OK (reverse scored.)
3. I am personally motivated by my beliefs to be nonprejudiced toward black people.
4. Because of my personal values, I believe that using stereotypes about black people is wrong.
5. Being nonprejudiced toward black people is important to my self-concept.

External Motivation to Respond Without Prejudice

1. Because of today's PC (politically correct) standards, I try to appear nonprejudiced toward black people.
2. I try to hide any negative thoughts about black people in order to avoid negative reactions from others.
3. If I acted prejudiced toward black people, I would be concerned that others would be angry with me.
4. I attempt to appear nonprejudiced toward black people in order to avoid disapproval from others.
5. I try to act nonprejudiced toward black people because of pressure from others.

Note: Answer each item on a scale running from 1 = strongly disagree to 9 = strongly agree. For #2 on the Internal Motivation scale, subtract your answer from 10. Then add across items, and divide by the number of items. The average score for college students is about 8 for the Internal Motivation scale and about 5 for the External Motivation scale.[188]

they feel pressured to respond in a politically correct manner. When they are released from such pressure (i.e., when they are no longer under the watchful eye of a nonprejudiced audience), they respond with a backlash and actually express more prejudice than if they had not been pressured to respond without prejudice.[188]

White people who are primarily internally motivated to avoid prejudice have more deeply internalized, well-practiced nonprejudiced reactions than the other groups. This inner commitment to overcome prejudice allows them to override and replace any unwanted biased responses, including even very subtle biases that can occur automatically and with hardly any conscious recognition, resulting in more effective control of prejudice.[189,190]

Contact

As we learned earlier, prejudice can be reduced by contact.[191,192,193] Sometimes even vicarious contact can work, such as knowing that a good friend who is a member of your group has a close relationship with an outgroup member.[194] Although overt expressions of prejudice can be reduced by direct educational and attitude-change techniques (see Chapter 8), more covert expressions of prejudice, such as deliberate avoidance or mild harassment, can be reduced by intergroup contact.[195]

Political correctness is the norm in the United States today.

Superordinate Goals

As Sherif discovered, cooperating to achieve common goals is one powerful antidote to intergroup conflict. When the Eagles and Rattlers worked together to achieve common goals, they stopped hating each other and even grew to like each other. Other studies have found similar results. In one study,[196] researchers found that when children play cooperative games, their aggressive behavior decreases, and their cooperative behavior increases. In contrast, when they play competitive games, their aggressive behavior increases and their cooperative behavior decreases.

One technique used to achieve a common goal is the jigsaw classroom. The **jigsaw classroom** is a cooperative learning technique developed to reduce feelings of prejudice.[197,198,199] Just as each piece of a jigsaw puzzle is necessary to complete the puzzle, some contribution from each student in a jigsaw classroom is necessary to complete an assignment. For example, after each person learns as much as possible about his or her assigned topic, students from different groups who were assigned the same topic meet together to become experts on their topic. Once each individual is up to speed, the jigsaw groups reconvene, and members share with each other what they have learned. Group members must work together as a team to accomplish a common goal.

Several studies have shown positive outcomes for jigsaw classrooms. Research shows that participation in jigsaw classrooms decreases racial prejudice and increases academic performance.[200,201] The jigsaw classroom has been successfully applied in countries other than the United States.[202,203]

jigsaw classroom a cooperative learning technique for reducing feelings of prejudice by having students interact and cooperate to learn material

QUIZ YOURSELF

Overcoming Stereotypes, Reducing Prejudice

1. **In the United States, people are most likely to consciously override prejudicial feelings for what group of individuals?**
   - (a) African Americans
   - (b) Arab Americans
   - (c) Homosexuals
   - (d) Obese individuals

2. **A state police force has set a height requirement of 5 feet 10 inches (1.8 meters) for all officers. This requirement is not related to job effectiveness, but it generally excludes Hispanics, Asians, and women from the police force. The height requirement most clearly reflects _____ .**
   - (a) ingroup bias and outgroup homogeneity bias
   - (b) racism and sexism
   - (c) scapegoating and self-serving bias
   - (d) stereotyping and prejudice

3. **Jett can think of many interesting ideas, but he isn't a very good writer. Kiowa is an excellent writer, but he is not very creative. In order to write a book, the two of them form a team. Writing a book in this example is a _____ goal.**
   - (a) coordinate
   - (b) subordinate
   - (c) superordinate
   - (d) none of the above

4. **What type of classroom has been shown to reduce prejudiced feelings?**
   - (a) Active learning
   - (b) Integrated
   - (c) Jigsaw
   - (d) Segregated

answers: see pg 489

Impact of Prejudice on Targets

No culture seems immune to stereotypes, prejudice, and discrimination. Most cultures have stereotypes, at least of rival external groups. If two countries have recently fought against each other in a war, each will likely have some prejudices and stereotypes about the other, and most likely rather negative ones.

In addition, diverse cultures typically have to contend with the fact that members of different groups or categories have stereotypes about the other groups. As one example, all societies have both men and women, and your textbook authors would be very surprised to find any society in which men and women do not hold some stereotypes about each other. Likewise, most democracies have different political parties, and the members of both parties hold prejudices and stereotypes about the opposing parties.

What effects do prejudices and stereotypes have on their targets? What is it like to grow up in a culture that regards you as unattractive, or incompetent, or dangerous? Or, for that matter, what is it like to live in a culture that expects you to be wise and kind? In his famous "I Have a Dream" speech, Martin Luther King Jr. said: "Being a Negro in America means trying to smile when you want to cry. It means the pain of watching your children grow up with clouds of inferiority in their mental skies. It means having your legs cut off, and then being condemned for being a cripple."

Probably the most common reaction is that people dislike being stereotyped; they want to be known and judged as individuals. Being stereotyped in a negative manner is especially unpleasant. In a series of studies, women who used feminist doctrines to express negative stereotypes of men elicited reactions that sometimes took the form of sexual harassment.[204] The experimenters instructed the men to select stimulus pictures to send to a woman via e-mail. Some of the available pictures were of nature and animals and were thus neutral, but others were sexually explicit and even pornographic images, and in all conditions the women had indicated that they found such pictures offensive. To expose someone to sexual materials against that person's explicit wishes is a form of sexual harassment. Men were most likely to choose such pictures if the woman had stereotyped men in a degrading or insulting manner. Though this finding does not excuse or justify sexual harassment, it does indicate that reactions to being stereotyped can be quite negative and even hostile or aggressive.

Self-Fulfilling Prophecies

Once we accept the expectations of others, we tend to behave in a manner that is consistent with those expectations, and as a result the expectations come true. This is called a **self-fulfilling prophecy**.[205] A self-fulfilling prophecy is an expectation about the future that tends to come true partly *because* it is expected.

A self-fulfilling prophecy involves three stages.[206] First, a person believes that a certain event will happen in the future. Second, this expectation, or prophecy, leads to a new behavior that the person would have not engaged in without the expectation. Third, the expected event takes place (partly as a result of the change in behavior), and the prophecy is fulfilled. A vivid example is the collapse of the Last National Bank, which was a stable and solvent financial institution in the early 1930s during the Great Depression in the United States. First, people began to believe (incorrectly) that the Last National Bank was on the verge of bankruptcy. Second, the people who had accounts at the bank panicked and withdrew all their money. Third, the bank collapsed. The initial belief (that the bank was ready to collapse) was false, but once people withdrew all their money, the bank really did collapse.

Several studies have found results that are consistent with the self-fulfilling prophecy. In one famous research demonstration of this effect, participants were children from 18 classrooms.[207] The researchers gave all participants an IQ test and then randomly chose 20% of the children from each room and told the teachers they were "intellectual bloomers." Teachers were told that these bloomers would show remarkable gains in IQ during the coming year. By the end of the year, these randomly designated "intellectual bloomers" really did bloom. They improved their IQ scores by an average of 12 points, as compared with gains of 8 points among other students. Thus, teachers' expectations, which were initially false and baseless, became a reality, probably because the teachers focused more positive attention on the students whom they expected would bloom.

A comprehensive literature review found that although self-fulfilling prophecies do occur in the classroom, the effects are relatively small.[208] Teacher expectations do predict student performance, but that is because teacher's expectations are often accurate, not because the expectations become self-fulfilling prophecies.

self-fulfilling prophecy a prediction that ensures, by the behavior it generates, that it will come true

The concept of the self-fulfilling prophecy offers one way to predict the effects of stereotypes on their targets. People often live up or down to what is expected of them, especially if others treat them in certain ways based on those expectations. Applied to stereotypes, a self-fulfilling prophecy would mean that people would come to act like the stereotypes others hold of them.[209]

Most social scientists have long assumed that self-fulfilling prophecy effects would be the main, most powerful way that stereotypes affect their targets. They assumed that people could not entirely resist internalizing the stereotypes that society held of them. However, people often can and do resist. One of the most surprising contradictions to the self-fulfilling prophecy effect formed the basis for a new line of theory and research, discussed in the next section.

Stigma and Self-Protection

Throughout much of American history, the culture has held stereotypes of African Americans as inferior to European Americans in various ways. Some of these probably originated during the period of slavery. Black people were stereotyped as lazy, intellectually backward, and childlike. These stereotypes most likely reflected the fundamental attribution error (see Chapter 5), which attributes people's behavior to their inner traits even when it was really caused by external circumstances. All over the world, slaves have generally been lazy as far as their masters are concerned,[210] and why shouldn't they be? People rise above laziness in response to incentives that reward hard work, such as money, power, and status, but these were all denied to slaves. Likewise, American slaves had almost no opportunity for schooling or education, without which intellectual attainments are difficult if not impossible. Many aspects of the slave's role resemble the child's role: few rights, utter dependency on others, inability to make decisions about one's own life, and the inability to express any striving for long-term future goals. Any sensible person would behave that way in that situation, and it is unfortunate but perhaps understandable that observers made the mistake of seeing those behaviors as reflecting slaves' innate traits rather than situational forces.

What survived into the 20th century, long after slavery had been abolished, was a general perception of African Americans as inferior to European Americans. What were the consequences for African Americans born in that new era? Most social scientists assumed that African Americans could not help internalizing those negative views to some degree, just as with any self-fulfilling prophecy. The broadest result of American prejudices would therefore be that African Americans would have low self-esteem. To live in a culture that regards you and treats you as a second-class citizen would, seemingly inevitably, cause you to see yourself that way. The low self-esteem could then perhaps explain many behavioral patterns that might be observed, from lower occupational attainment to crime and violence.

This line of thought was standard, but in the late 1980s it was turned upside down by a surprising finding. Researchers reviewed dozens of studies and established a startling conclusion: African Americans on average do not suffer from low self-esteem.[211] If anything, African Americans have higher self-esteem than white Americans. Subsequent work has verified this finding and shown that African Americans are actually somewhat different from other minority groups in this regard.[212] Most American minority groups do have somewhat lower self-esteem than mainstream European Americans, but African Americans continue to score consistently higher on self-esteem.[213]

How could this be? No one disputed the fact that American society had held prejudices that regarded black people as inferior. How did they manage not only to resist internalizing the message, but to end up with higher self-esteem than other groups? Researchers have offered three answers, each of which is rooted in cognitive strategies and processes similar to those covered in Chapter 5.[214]

The first involved social comparison—specifically, the choice of comparison targets. To an animal living in the forest, success and failure can probably be measured directly in terms of getting something to eat, but to cultural beings, success and failure are relative. Your salary, for example, might be a measure of how well you are doing, but by itself it doesn't mean much. Salary is an index of success only in comparison to what other people are earning. People compare themselves to those within their own group. The self-esteem of a minority group might therefore not suffer from the fact that its members earn less than members of other groups. The earnings of other groups are regarded as irrelevant. They mainly compare themselves against each other.

The second involves the criteria of self-worth. People judge themselves by many criteria. As we saw in Chapter 3 on the self, people often choose criteria on which they do well and avoid criteria that make them look bad. If you're good at basket weaving or meteorology, you may decide that those are important measures of self-worth, but if you are bad at them, you may decide that they are trivial and irrelevant. Groups, too, can reject or discount the standards that make them look bad, focusing instead on the things they do well.

The third process involves attribution theory (again!). We noted earlier in this chapter that the self-serving bias (making internal attributions for successes and external attributions for failures) can help explain the thinking and actions of people who hold stereotypes. It may also help explain reactions to prejudice. Some disadvantaged minority groups might protect their self-esteem by attributing their problems to other people's prejudices against them. Assume, for example, that most people's lives contain some successes and some failures, and that each individual's self-esteem will depend on how he or she adds those up. If you can use the self-serving bias to dismiss your failures as irrelevant to your worth, your self-esteem can be higher than if you blame yourself for your failures. Despite all its costs and harm, prejudice does offer one advantage to the target—an external attribution for failure. Targets of prejudice can blame their failures and problems on prejudice. As a result, they can base their self-esteem mainly on their successes, and their self-esteem will rise.

A subsequent experiment confirmed that attributing failure to prejudice can protect self-esteem.[215] African American college students wrote an essay and received feedback that was critical and negative. This feedback came from a white American confederate pretending to be another participant. Did the criticism cause a drop in self-esteem? It depended on attributions. Half the participants believed that the other participant knew who they were, including their race. These participants showed no drop in self-esteem, because they inferred that the bad evaluation reflected the prejudices of the evaluator. Criticism based on prejudice should not lower one's self-esteem, of course, so the participants who made this attribution (that the bad evaluation was caused by prejudice) shrugged it off. In contrast, the other participants were told that the evaluator knew nothing about them. They could not dismiss the evaluation as a result of racial prejudice because they thought the evaluator did not know their race. Their self-esteem did suffer (temporarily) as a result of the bad evaluation.

Thus, although both groups received exactly the same evaluation, only one group experienced a drop in self-esteem. Of course, those participants had no proof or evidence that the evaluation was motivated by racial prejudice, and in reality the evaluation (exactly the same for everyone) was decided by the experimental procedure. All that differed was that one group was able to conclude that prejudice might be one possible cause of it, and they apparently used this possibility as a basis for dismissing the criticism and maintaining their self-esteem.

If nothing else, these findings show that people are not just passive recipients of social influence. Cultures tell some groups that they are inferior, but many members of those groups successfully reject such messages.

Another form of self-protection against stigmas is to actively conceal them. Researchers have long recognized the important difference between visible and invisible stigmas. A woman who is black and a lesbian, for example, must deal with the fact that everyone can immediately see that she is black, whereas her homosexuality can be concealed. Recent work suggests that people who conceal their stigmatized identities "internalize the closet," which means that they become adept at keeping some parts of their self-concept secret.[216] In Chapter 3 we considered the important distinction between public self (the image one presents to the world) and private self (how one views oneself). Gay persons who keep their homosexuality secret learn to maintain a public (seemingly non-gay) identity, while also keeping a private concept of self that contains plenty that is not shared with the world. Similar patterns were found among people who concealed their strong religious beliefs from nonbelieving peers.

Competitive Victimhood

You might assume that nobody wants to be a victim. After all, being a victim is associated with being passive, with suffering mistreatment by others, and with general unhappiness. Yet in recent years various scholars have argued that in modern society, various people and groups compete to claim victim status.[217,218] Being a victim entitles a person to others' sympathy and emotional support, possibly extending to financial and legal entitlements. The victim's role enjoys a kind of moral privilege. It is considered taboo in many circles to reproach victims for any sort of misbehavior. No doubt this reflects the fact that many victims are innocent and both need and deserve help, and blaming them for their troubles could be seen as supporting the oppressors (who often blame their victims for sometimes completely made-up misdeeds).

Yet other people may claim victim status precisely because of the moral, legal, or financial advantages inherent in the role. Indeed, as this edition of the textbook was being prepared, American society was rocked by several scandals in which college students falsely claimed to have been raped, thereby causing some innocent young men to be stigmatized and punished.[219] The University of Virginia shut down its entire fraternity system after the magazine *Rolling Stone* published an article in which a female college student claimed she was gang-raped as part of a fraternity initiation, and the ban remained even after the magazine retracted the story.

Laboratory research has now shown that people compete for victim status. Both men and women responded to accusations that their gender discriminated against the other by insisting that their own gender was victimized. Similar findings were obtained for race and age, and even for different groups of university members (i.e., students vs. staff). Thus, when people are accused of belonging to a group that oppresses others, they assert that members of their group are victims. Earlier work showed that claiming victim status reduces guilty feelings.[220] For example, Jews who were reminded of how many Jews were killed by Hitler's troops felt less guilty about Jews' harmful treatment of Palestinians. Likewise, Americans felt less guilty about their country's harmful actions in Iraq if the Americans had been reminded of terrorist attacks against America or even just reminded of the Pearl Harbor bombing by the Japanese in 1941. Claiming to be a victim—including based on events in the distant past—serves to reduce one's guilt, even for seemingly irrelevant acts.

Stereotype Threat

We have seen that people do not like being stereotyped and often strive extra hard to show that they do not fit negative stereotypes of their group. Sometimes stereotypes can even create **self-defeating prophecies**. This observation has been elaborated in a profound way by several social psychologists, who noted that when a stereotype might apply, people fear that their behavior will confirm it. This fear is called **stereotype threat**.[221] When people fear that they will be negatively stereotyped, their performance suffers.

Stereotype threat may operate most powerfully when it is difficult to contradict. Thus, if your group is stereotyped as liking greasy food, you can relatively easily show that it does not apply to you, simply by choosing healthier, nongreasy foods when others are watching. In contrast, if your group is stereotyped as being bad at singing, you would have to sing well in order to contradict it, and singing well (especially when you are nervous because of stereotype threat!) may be quite difficult.

Intellectual performance is of particular interest because of its importance in American culture and society. Girls score slightly lower than boys on math tests, even when they are gifted children.[222] The difference seems to be due to mathematical reasoning, because females can do simple arithmetical computations better than males. In a similar vein, African American students score lower on many tests than European American students.[223,224] Social psychologists wondered whether these gender and race differences might be partly due to stereotype threat, and they conducted a series of studies to test this hypothesis.

self-defeating prophecy a prediction that ensures, by the behavior it generates, that it will not come true

stereotype threat the fear that one might confirm the stereotypes that others hold

© JupiterImages/Brand X/Alamy

Jim Zuckerman/Spirit/Corbis

Several studies played on the stereotype that women perform worse than men on mathematical tests.[225] When the math test was described as producing no gender differences, women performed as well as men. However, when the math test was described as producing gender differences, women performed worse than men. Women feared that if they did poorly, it would reinforce people's beliefs about female inferiority at math, and the resulting worry contributed to lowering their performance. Even subtle cues can produce this effect, such as when the experimenter is male rather than female.[226] The effects are especially large if women are concerned that performing poorly will reflect badly on all women rather than on them personally.[227] The same thing happens to white men when the comparison group is Asian men (who are stereotyped to be good at math).[228]

Other studies have taken on the controversial issue of racial differences in intellectual performance. Although IQ tests have been accused of racial bias, defenders of the tests have argued that they are designed to predict performance in school, and the tests (which predict the performance of white students quite accurately) often predict higher grades for black students than the students actually end up achieving. Could that discrepancy be due to stereotype threat? In an important study,[229] researchers told some participants that the test had been shown to have no racial bias and no racial differences. In that condition, African American participants performed as well as their college admission standardized test scores would predict. Other participants received no such instruction, so the stereotype threat ("If I do badly, it will confirm people's stereotype of African Americans as intellectually inferior") remained an important force in the situation. In that situation, African Americans performed worse than others and worse than their college admission standardized test scores would predict. Other research has shown that under stereotype threat, African Americans experience an increase in blood pressure.[230] Eliminating the stereotype threat does not entirely eliminate the test-score gap between blacks and whites,[231,232,233] but it does eliminate the troubling pattern in which many students perform below what their college admission standardized test scores predict.

A meta-analytic review found that stereotype threat does impair test performance for women and minorities.[234] Why does the impairment occur? Anxiety appears to be the culprit. Confirming negative stereotypes makes people anxious, and the more anxious people are, the more their performance suffers.[235,236] When people become anxious, they try to calm down, but this takes a lot of effort and mental resources, which depletes people of the mental resources they need to perform well on the test.[237] Indeed, people who experience a stereotype threat show activity in the part of their brain involved in emotional processing rather than in the part of their brain involved in thinking and reasoning.[238]

Fortunately, there is a silver lining on this dark cloud of stereotype threat. Recent research shows that people can be inoculated against stereotype threat.[239] In one study, older people did better on a math test if they first interacted with their grandchildren than if they did not. Even imagining interacting with younger people improved performance. When older people interact with younger people, they feel less anxious about their test performance.

Nearly everyone is a member of some group that is sometimes the target of stereotyping. Stereotype threat can affect everyone. Minority groups sometimes hold the stereotype of European Americans as prejudiced, so in interracial interactions white people sometimes worry lest anything they say be interpreted as a sign of prejudice.

Indeed, this sort of stereotype threat makes interracial interactions more difficult for all concerned. Research on interactions between black and white people has found that both groups approached these interactions with heightened anxiety, for just these reasons.[240,241] Black people worried that their white interaction partners would be biased against them, so they feared behaving in ways that might justify these prejudices. Meanwhile, the white participants worried that they would be perceived as prejudiced by their black interaction partners, and they too feared that they might do something to confirm those stereotypes.

Stereotype threat should promote sympathy for minority groups, especially in difficult performance contexts. It is hard enough to perform well on your own, but it is that much more difficult to perform well while worrying that others will take failure as confirmation of negative stereotypes. No one likes to fail, and many people will avoid some risks in order to reduce the chances of failure. If failure reflects not only on you but also on an entire category of people to which you belong, the burden of failure is greatly increased, and it is not surprising that some people will withdraw in order to avoid such pressure.

answers: see pg 489

QUIZ YOURSELF
Impact of Prejudice on Targets

1. Once we have adopted a certain expectation, we tend to behave in a manner that is consistent with that expectation, and the expectation comes true. This effect is called the _____ .

    (a) discontinuity effect
    (b) false consensus effect
    (c) minimal group effect
    (d) self-fulfilling prophecy

2. Compared to European Americans, African Americans generally have _____ levels of self-esteem.

    (a) higher
    (b) more unstable
    (c) lower
    (d) similar

3. In a social interaction between blacks and whites, which group tends to become more anxious?

    (a) Blacks
    (b) Whites
    (c) Both blacks and whites
    (d) Neither blacks nor whites

4. Mr. Trig, a high school math teacher, communicates to his class that he thinks boys tend to do better in math than girls. As a result, some of the girls in his class become anxious about doing math problems. The girls are experiencing _____ .

    (a) stereotype threat
    (b) discontinuity effect
    (c) the scapegoating effect
    (d) social identity threat

Are Social Psychologists Biased?

Many social psychologists see their research as part of the battle against prejudice. This serves liberal ideals of fairness, justice, and equal opportunity, not to mention reducing hatred and violence. Simply put, most social psychologists would declare themselves opposed to prejudice.

That fact made the scientific community quite sensitive when some members began to suggest that the field of social psychology is biased—specifically, biased against political conservatives.[242] At the major national meeting of social psychology in 2001, one speaker asked for a show of hands indicating political affiliation. About 800 raised their hands to identify with liberalism, as compared with only 3 who admitted to being conservative. (In fact, only 20 claimed to be moderate or centrist, plus 12 libertarians.) More systematic surveys suggest that psychologists are about 10 to 15 times more likely to identify as liberals than conservatives—while in the general U.S. population, Gallup polls suggest that there are twice as many conservatives as liberals. Probably the 800-to-3 difference in the show of hands was so big because a few conservatives were afraid to express their views in public.

At present, the field of social psychology is debating whether its so-called "liberal bias" is a problem and what should be done about it. Almost certainly, a liberal bias shapes how research questions are asked and how data are interpreted. Editors may prefer to publish research findings that fit liberal rather than conservative views. In fact, liberals may even prevent research from being conducted if they do not approve of the political overtones. Disturbing evidence came from research on ethics boards, which all research-oriented universities have in order to decide whether a given study is safe and suitable to conduct with the student population. Researchers submitted identical research designs to 150 different universities' ethics boards, asking for permission to run the same study, which was concerned with prejudice and discrimination.[243] The applications were the same except for one detail: Half were described as attempting to study discrimination (i.e., against ethnic minorities), whereas the others were described as studying "reverse discrimination (i.e., against white males). There should have been no difference, because the procedures were exactly the same and thus equally safe, as well as equally valid in terms of scientific quality. But the boards rejected more applications that referred to "reverse discrimination," which goes against liberal bias, than when they referred simply to discrimination, which is congenial to liberal bias.

In writing this textbook, we have tried to be fair to both liberal and conservative political views. Still, we are covering the field as it is, and the body of scientific knowledge may itself be altered by liberal bias. This is a concern for anyone who prizes scientific truth above political ideals.

What Makes Us Human

Putting the Cultural Animal in Perspective

Conflict between groups is not unique to humans. As cultural animals, however, humans surround group conflict with meanings, values, and other ideas. Having a hostile feeling toward a rival group may be something that many animals experience, but creating a negative stereotype of the other group is something that requires the powerful mental apparatus of the human mind.

Moreover, the content of stereotypes and prejudices is generally learned, and as we saw, it is not so much learned by direct experience as from other people similar to oneself. Deliberately passing social ideas to the young is something that sets humans apart, and in general it is one of the wonders of human nature—but humans also teach stereotypes and prejudices to their children. This is not to say that children are naturally inclined toward love and tolerance of everyone. Human children seem all too ready to reject anyone who is different, so they quickly and readily acquire negative views of other groups.

Culture increases the scope and importance of prejudices. If a fish were prejudiced toward another group of fish, it might avoid interacting with them, but this would not affect the other fish very much. Humans, in contrast, rely on each other and their social network for their livelihoods. Prejudice can interfere with someone's chances to get a particular job, live in a desirable home, hold political office, and choose a desired mate. Victims of discrimination lose out on many cultural rewards, from prestige and self-esteem to money. People may use prejudices and stereotypes to strengthen the bonds within their group. This shows once again the theme that inner processes serve interpersonal relations: People form and maintain stereotypes because those mental structures help them deal with the social world.

But there is another, more positive side to human nature. Unlike other animals, humans can rise above their prejudices and feelings. People can reinvent and restructure the society in which they live—indeed, the processes of social change seem to go on relentlessly, at least in the modern world. People can also change themselves, by questioning their values and pushing themselves to think, feel, and act differently.

Thus, only humans have been able to rise above their natural antagonisms and create a society in which people from different, even formerly competing, groups can live together in peace, tolerance, and harmony. In the past century, the United States (like many other countries) has seen dramatic improvements in the social respect and opportunities offered to women, and it has moved far toward racial equality and tolerance, too. In many countries of the world, people from different groups that once hated, despised, and fought each other now live side by side and cooperate actively in a respectful, smoothly functioning system. The capacity for progress of this sort is one of the biggest advantages of human culture. The progress toward defeating prejudice and discrimination—though still incomplete and imperfect—is a very positive indication of what makes us human.

CHAPTER 13 SUMMARY

ABCs of Intergroup Relationships: Prejudice, Discrimination, and Stereotypes

- Prejudice is a negative feeling or attitude toward an individual based solely on his or her membership in a particular group.
- Discrimination refers to unequal treatment of different people based on the groups or categories to which they belong.
- Stereotypes are beliefs that associate groups of people with certain traits.
- The view that prejudice and stereotyping are morally wrong is a product of modern, Western culture. Many cultures tolerate stereotyping.
- Most stereotypes are negative, and most prejudices depict outgroups as inferior or as having bad traits.
- Outgroup members ("they") are people who belong to a different group or category than we do.
- Ingroup members ("we") are people who belong to the same group or category as we do.
- The outgroup homogeneity bias assumes that outgroup members are more similar to one another than ingroup members are to one another.
- Stigmas include characteristics of individuals that are considered socially unappealing, such as being overweight, mentally ill, sick, or poor, or having a physical blemish.
- Stigma by association shows that people are discriminated against for merely being associated with a stigmatized person.

Common Prejudices and Targets

- Both men and women are more intolerant of homosexuality in their own gender than in the opposite gender.
- Although stereotypes often contain culturally specific information, the tendency to form stereotypes and prejudices may be innate.

- People automatically and normally know stereotypes and think of them, whereas they have to exert themselves to override them.

Why Prejudice Exists

- Ingroup favoritism is preferential treatment of, or more favorable attitudes toward, people in one's own group, as compared to people in other groups.
- Realistic conflict theory suggests that competition over scarce resources leads to intergroup hostility and conflict; hostilities form when groups compete against each other.
- Some societies have little or no competition. These are typically peaceful, economically undeveloped groups.
- Competition has costs, but it also has benefits.
- Evolution may have had a hand in instilling the human readiness to form groups and hold prejudices against rival groups.
- The discontinuity effect suggests that groups are more prone to hostile competitiveness than individuals are.
- The contact hypothesis proposes that regular interaction between members of different groups reduces prejudice, providing that it occurs under favorable conditions.
- People often rely on stereotypes as heuristics (mental shortcuts).
- By using stereotypes to justify and act on prejudices, people can increase their feelings of self-worth.

Content of Prejudice and Stereotypes

- Some stereotypes are accurate, others are wrong, and others are partly true but overgeneralized.
- Stereotypes can form from purely cognitive processes, without any influence of emotion or motivation. Still, emotion or motivation can greatly increase the likelihood of prejudice.

Inner Processes

- Scapegoat theory proposes that people blame their problems and misfortunes on outgroups.

- Conflict and stress tend to bring out stereotypes and prejudice.
- People use their stereotypes more as hypotheses to be tested than as rules that can be applied in all cases.
- American society has made considerable progress in fighting against some important kinds of prejudice, especially those based on race and gender.
- The automatic system may often sustain prejudices, whereas the conscious system may strive to overcome those prejudices and stereotypes.
- When people are accused of prejudice, they often exert themselves to prove the opposite.

Overcoming Stereotypes, Reducing Prejudice

- People overcome prejudice by making conscious efforts to be fair and equal.
- The internal (belief that prejudice is morally wrong) and external (desire to avoid social disapproval) motivations for avoiding prejudice are not mutually exclusive.
- The jigsaw classroom, developed to reduce prejudice, is a cooperative learning technique in which group members must work together as a team and share unique information to accomplish a common goal.

Impact of Prejudice on Targets

- The self-fulfilling prophecy effect proposes that people will come to act in accordance with the stereotypes that others hold of them.

- Stereotypes can also create a self-defeating prophecy, which ensures, by the behavior it generates, that it will not come true.
- Cultures may tell some groups that they are inferior, but many members of those groups successfully reject such messages.
- Compared to European Americans, African Americans generally have higher levels of self-esteem.
- Stereotype threat is the fear that a stereotype might apply and that one's behavior might confirm it.
- Stereotype threat makes interracial interactions anxiety provoking for both races because both worry about confirming stereotypes about themselves.
- Unlike other animals, only humans have been able to rise above their natural antagonisms and create a society in which people from different, even formerly competing, groups can live together in peace, tolerance, and harmony.

What Makes Us Human?

- Although conflict between groups is not unique to humans, humans surround group conflict with meanings, values, and other ideas.
- Humans are the only animals that deliberately pass social ideas on to their young.
- People may use prejudices and stereotypes to strengthen the bonds within their group.
- Unlike other animals, humans can rise above their prejudices and feelings.

key terms

aversive racism 449	homophobia 459	racism 449	stereotype threat 484
categorization 449	ingroup favoritism 461	realistic conflict theory 463	stereotypes 449
competition 463	ingroup members 452	salience 472	stigma by association 457
confirmation bias 474	jigsaw classroom 480	scapegoat theory 472	stigmas 459
contact hypothesis 466	minimal group effect 461	self-defeating prophecy 484	subtypes 449
cooperation 463	outgroup homogeneity bias 452	self-fulfilling prophecy 481	superordinate goals 463
discontinuity effect 464	outgroup members 452	self-serving bias 472	
discrimination 449	prejudice 449	social categorization 449	

quiz yourself ANSWERS

1. ABCs of Intergroup Relationships: Prejudice, Discrimination, and Stereotypes **p.453**
   answers: 1.a 2.a 3.c 4.c

2. Common Prejudices and Targets **p.459**
   answers: 1.b 2.b 3.b 4.d

3. Why Prejudice Exists **p.469**
   answers: 1.b 2.b 3.b 4.c

4. Content of Prejudice and Stereotypes **p.472**
   answers: 1.a 2.a 3.a 4.c

5. Inner Processes **p.475**
   answers: 1.d 2.d 3.b 4.a

6. Overcoming Stereotypes, Reducing Prejudice **p.480**
   answers: 1.a 2.b 3.c 4.c

7. Impact of Prejudice on Targets **p.486**
   answers: 1.d 2.a 3.c 4.a

GROUPS

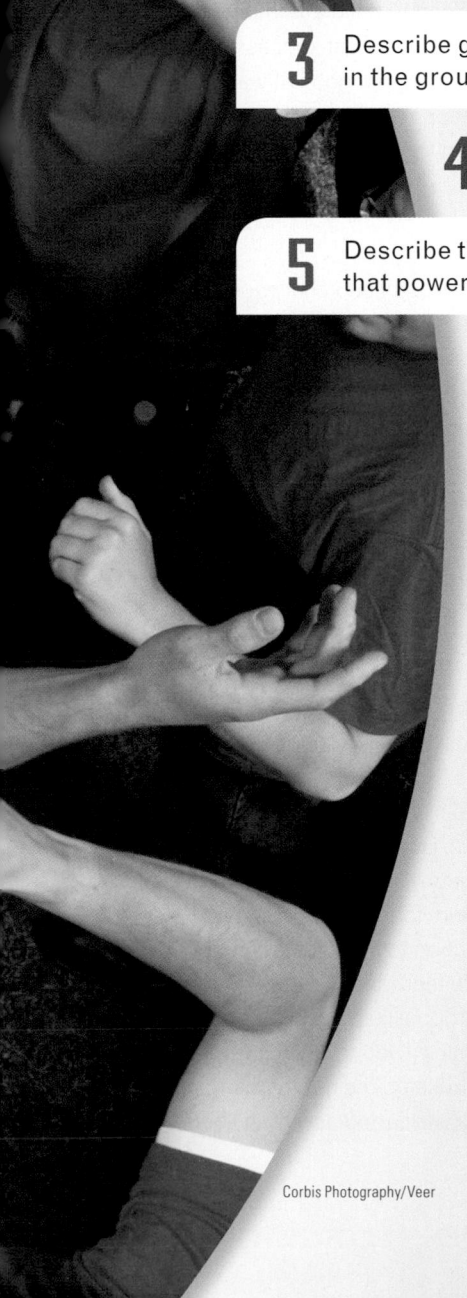

Corbis Photography/Veer

14

LEARNING OBJECTIVES

1 Explain how humans, as cultural animals, form groups that differ from the groups of other social animals, emphasizing how selves and roles alter the nature of human groups.

2 Discuss how roles and the inner processes of the self affect group behavior.

3 Describe group outcomes that result from being individually identified in the group versus feeling submerged in the group.

4 Describe how individuals within a group share information, including brainstorming and groupthink.

5 Describe the traits of successful leadership and the five crucial effects that power has on people.

In **1863 a well-to-do** Michigan farming family gave birth to a son. As a boy, Henry never took to farming, instead showing an abiding interest in mechanical things. He became popular in his neighborhood for fixing people's watches. At age 16 he took a job as an apprentice machinist. Eventually he joined the Edison Engineering Company and at the age of 30 was their chief engineer.

Local travel at the time depended on horses, but clever inventors around the country were experimenting with ways to make self-propelled ("automobile") vehicles. Henry began to tinker with internal combustion engines and began to work on a car (calling it the "Quadricycle," to link it with the popular bicycle). His neighbors had taken to calling him "Crazy Henry" because he spent his evenings and weekends shut up in his garage with his contraption. But they were impressed when late one night he got the car moving. According to legend, it smashed a hole in the side of the garage and drove around the neighborhood with Henry at the wheel.

The car market didn't seem very large. In the year 1900, barely 1 in 10,000 Americans owned an automobile. Nobody expected cars would someday swarm everywhere. Cars were in the news, though. A Vermont man, accompanied by a mechanic and a dog named Bud (all three wearing goggles) made the first coast-to-coast car trip in 65 days, after which they were hailed as national heroes.

Henry went to work for the fledgling Detroit Automobile Company. In two years, it didn't even manage to sell six cars. The company went bankrupt, and Henry was fired. Unemployed, he entered some automobile races and won them. This attention attracted some new financial backers. In 1903 Henry and some other men started the Ford Motor Company, with himself as vice president and chief engineer. A quiet banker named Gray was the first president, but Ford's racing fame dictated that they name the firm after him. The manufacturing system involved having two or three men work together to make a car. Obviously these men had to have enormous skill and knowledge, which made their work relatively expensive. The company was initially only able to make three cars per day, using parts made by other companies. Henry looked for ways to make the production more efficient. In 1907 Henry said that his goal was to create "a motor car for the great multitude."

The first coast-to-coast car trip included two men and a dog.

Up until this point, cars were rare and expensive machines, usually custom-made toys for the rich. More than 240 companies had been formed to build automobiles, so the prospects for great success by any one company were not good. It wasn't even clear that gasoline-powered engines would become the norm. In 1906, a steam-powered car (the Stanley Steamer) set the car speed record by going 127 miles per hour.

A big opportunity and challenge arose when the Ford company developed the Model T. This was the first practical car that ordinary people could afford. Henry threw out the tradition of custom-built cars and made them all exactly the same, even offering only one color. (Henry's remark, "The customer can have any color he wants so long as it's black," became famous.) The design of the Model T did not change from the first one built in 1908 until the final, 15-millionth one in 1927.

Four years after the first Model T was made, three out of every four cars in America were Model Ts. Even in 1918, half of all cars sold in the United States would be Model T Fords. But this escalating demand called for a much more efficient (and cheaper) system for making these cars.

Ford's solution to this problem is the reason we are featuring this story in the chapter on groups. Ford wrote, "Nothing is particularly hard if you divide it into small jobs."[1] Ford broke up the manufacture of the car into 84 steps and assigned each

Henry Ford (1888) and his Quadricycle (1896).

An Assembly Line
of the
Ford Motor Company

Rykoff Collection/ Encyclopedia/Corbis

In 1913 Henry Ford introduced the assembly line into his factory, which greatly improved productivity rates.

one to a different worker. Thus, instead of two or three master craftsmen making each car, a great many men worked on each car. Each man, rather than knowing how to build an entire car, could specialize in just one small job. At first, Ford tried a system in which the cars being built were set up on a row of sawhorses. Each worker would do his part on the first vehicle and then move on to the next one. Runners brought parts for each job and left them next to each car. This cut production time down to about 17 hours per car, and Ford workers were soon producing 26,000 cars a month. But there were constant problems. The parts didn't all arrive at the same pace, so many workers had to stand around and wait before they could do their next task. In addition, a fair amount of time was lost as the workers moved around.

The biggest breakthrough came in 1913, with what became known as the assembly line. (Earlier versions had been tried, dating back to 1901.) Instead of having workers move from one car to another, with parts being delivered to constantly changing locations, Ford decided that each worker could stay in one place with a pile of ready parts. The cars would move along a conveyer belt. The initial experiment was done using ropes and pulleys to pull the cars along the belt, but the success of this plan quickly led

to using a continuous chain pulled by a motor. Once this plan was adopted and a few bugs worked out, the time to make a new car dropped to 93 minutes. At the height of production, a new car rolled off the assembly line every 24 seconds. The car's price dropped as low as $99.

By dividing the task into many parts, Ford found that he could hire workers without expecting them to master a great deal of information about manufacturing cars. It takes a long time for a person to learn how to build an entire car; learning to do one small task might take only a few days. The assembly line was a tremendous success, and Ford became the largest car manufacturer in the world.

There was a problem, however: Many workers disliked the repetitious, boring, low-paid work. Many quit, and Ford was constantly hiring and training new workers. Henry came up with another stroke of genius to solve this problem. He would resist the temptation to pay the workers the minimum amount. He announced a new minimum wage of $5 per day, more than double the average at the time. This made him a hero to the working class, a role he accepted. "A business that makes nothing but money is a poor kind of business," he said in a later interview. Other capitalists called Ford "a traitor to his class," complaining that he

was raising expectations and the cost of labor everywhere, but he ignored their complaints. Ordinary people flocked to work for him—and, with their higher wages, began buying Model T cars themselves. Business boomed. Ford reaped other benefits, including improved loyalty of his employees, and he saved money on training. Later he boasted that paying $5 a day was one of the smartest cost-cutting moves he had ever made.[2]

Can groups outperform individuals? Of course a group of 10 people can probably accomplish more than one person, but can a 10-person group outperform 10 people working alone? Culture enables human beings to form groups that can do things that no groups of other animals can, like build and operate a fishing boat, or publish a newspaper, or install artificial heat in everyone's home. To be sure, sometimes a group is less than the sum of its parts. But culture makes it possible (not guaranteed, but possible) for the group to become more than the sum of its parts, as illustrated in this story about Henry Ford.

What does this story exemplify about the social psychology of groups? A strong and persevering leader, experimenting with new ideas and methods, and good organization can breed success, of course. And by sharing rewards with his followers, Ford increased their loyalty, which also helped the group.

But most of all, the assembly line took division of labor to a new level. When ants or wolves hunt, they do so in a kind of swarm in which most individuals perform the same act. The individual acts are interchangeable. On the Ford moving assembly line, in contrast, each person performed a different job requiring some limited but specific knowledge or skill. Using this method, a group of people, each having minimal knowledge and skill, could produce something magnificent. The group was far more than the sum of its members. This is one important key to how human beings can use the power of culture to make groups that can achieve far more than collections of individuals operating alone. Interactive, complementary roles can make up a powerful system. ●

What Groups Are and Do

A **group** is a collection of people with something in common. Usually the group consists of people who have common interests and characteristics and periodically do something together. Still, some researchers use "group" to mean a category of people who do not all interact or even encounter each other, such as Hispanic Americans or athletes. Although most people think of a group as at least half a dozen members, many psychologists insist that, technically, two people (a "dyad") can be a group.

Indeed, the question of precisely what criteria need to be met in order for several people to qualify as a "group" is itself the target of research. That is because some groups seem more like groups than others, and so instead of a simple yes-or-no rule about what makes a group, it is more useful and accurate to think of group-ness as on a continuum. One could say that Canadians are a group, but that is a very large and diverse group, and most of the members don't know each other. Forty strangers on a bus don't make much of a group. Forty people waiting in line for football tickets may be a bit more like a group, given their common goal and perhaps their shared loyalty to their team. Forty people working together on an assembly line or football team make a much more coherent group. Yes, a dyad can be a group, but it is perhaps a special kind of group, and the processes and dynamics of a dyad (e.g., two people in a romantic relationship) are probably different from what goes on in a larger group. For one thing, two people can really relate as equals and make their decisions jointly so that each is satisfied, but a group of 100 probably cannot make decisions in that way; they will need either a leader who makes decisions or a democratic voting system that lets the preferences of the majority determine the decision.

What makes a group feel united? As we said, a football team is more like a group than 40 strangers on a bus, for several reasons.[3,4] They have a common identity, exemplified by the team name, whereas the strangers on the bus do not. The team members interact frequently with one another, unlike the strangers on the bus who often sit silently and don't talk to each other. The team members depend on one another, whereas the bus passengers do not. The team members work together toward common goals, again unlike the bus riders. The team members have common beliefs values, and practices, such as about the importance of football, and they are similar in other respects such as athleticism and gender, whereas the bus riders share only their faith that the bus will take them closer to their different destinations. The team members share emotionally powerful experiences, such as in winning or losing big games, whereas the bus riders do not.

group a collection of at least two people who are doing or being something together

In fact, if something emotionally powerful were to happen to the bus, such as being hijacked or having an accident, the riders might start to act and feel more like a group. One famous example was the United Airlines flight 93 that was hijacked by terrorists on that fateful September day in 2001. Several passengers and crew made telephone calls aboard the flight, learned about the terrorist attacks on the World Trade Center and the Pentagon, and made a joint effort to regain control of the plane. The plane crashed in a field near Shanksville, Pennsylvania, about 150 miles (240 km) northwest of Washington, D.C., killing all on board including 40 passengers and crew and 4 hijackers. An analysis of the flight recorders revealed that passengers and crew prevented the aircraft from reaching the hijackers' intended target, thought to be either the White House or U.S. Capitol.

Thus, one factor is whether the members of a group feel similar to each other. For this reason, more diverse groups

Conflict between groups helps solidify feelings of belonging to a group.

Sara Wolfram/Getty Images Sport/Getty Images

Is a Marriage a Group?

The questions about what constitute a group have gone beyond technical debates among social science researchers. All known societies have some form of marriage, but they disagree about what kind of group can marry. In the modern world, most marriages are dyads: two people, a man and a woman. But other groups can be married too, such as same-sex dyads. Gay marriage has been legal in many countries for years, beginning with the Netherlands in 2001. In the United States, many states have also legalized gay marriage or civil unions. In the past, most societies have included polygamy, a form of marriage in which one husband would have several wives. Today many Islamic countries, such as Saudi Arabia, permit a man to have up to four wives. Marriage systems in which one wife has multiple husbands is rare but not entirely unknown (especially in societies with shortages of women).

Should marriage be a dyad? Monogamy is often described as a benefit to women, and most women say they prefer it rather than polygamy, but it is not clear that this is rational. All else being equal, polygamy would seem to favor heterosexual women by offering more choices. It creates a surplus of single men, because a few men take up many wives, leaving far more single men than women. Even a woman who wants a monogamous marriage may be better off in a polygamous society, because polygamy creates a large selection of available men. Plus, of course, women have more options under polygamy: Some women would prefer to be the second or third wife of a rich, handsome man, rather than the sole wife of a homely, dull, poor one. In contrast, monogamy clearly favors the majority of men, especially the less powerful ones, because it enables every man to have a potential wife. Most likely, monogamy replaced polygamy in step with social reforms that favored greater equality among men.

Marriage fits many aspects of the definition of a group. It has a common identity (often symbolized by taking identical last names). Spouses interact frequently. They depend on each other. They work toward common goals, such as raising a family. They are often quite similar in many respects ranging from political and religious beliefs to intelligence and physical attractiveness. Yet they are also often different in many ways. Division of labor is common in marriage: Traditionally, the wife took care of the home, made and repaired the clothes, tended the sick, and stored and cooked the food, while the man did the heavy farm work (or, later, earned most of the money), provided protection, and built or repaired the dwelling. Today, spousal roles continue to change and adapt, but most married couples still divide up their tasks in some ways. Groups share emotional experiences, and certainly marital love and sex would certainly count as such.

Indeed, it is possible to regard any couple engaging in sex as a dyad, at least a temporary one: Sex partners work together toward a common goal, share an intense experience, are typically similar to each other, often feel an emotional connection, and so forth. To be sure, sex sometimes occurs in larger groups, which raises the question of why most sex is dyadic.

Group sex, whether it is a matter of three people in bed together or a larger group having a wild orgy, often attracts attention but is fairly rare in practice.[5] It seems reasonable to estimate that over 99% of sex acts in the world today involve just two people. Quite possibly this simply reflects the difficulty of getting multiple people to consent; it is often difficult for just two people to reach the point of agreeing that they want to have sex, and so getting seven or eight people to decide to jump in bed together might be much more difficult!

---

may find it harder to come together as a group, compared to groups that start off being similar. Then again, diversity brings other benefits; to appreciate these, see *Trade offs* on diversity.

Most likely another factor is the presence of an outgroup, especially a rival or enemy. Sports teams are often cohesive groups, not simply because they wear uniforms of the same color, but because they frequently have to work together for the common good against a common opponent. A team that merely practiced, without ever playing against an opponent, would probably not feel so unified. It is quite possible that the deeply rooted human impulse to form social groups was partly stimulated by competition among groups.

If a lone person wanted something—the fruit on a particular tree, for example—and a group also wanted it, the group would almost always win. Over evolutionary history, loners would therefore be losers, whereas the people who passed on their genes toward future generations would be the ones who formed groups.[11]

What, then, do groups accomplish? Answers to this can be found at both the social and cultural level. Social animals tend to live in groups, because groups provide several clear benefits. They promote safety, they find and share food, and they can do tasks that no one individual can do alone.

Diversity in Groups

The novelist Jerzy Kosinski filled his novels with vivid, moving stories from his personal life, which included many hardships. Kosinski himself eventually committed suicide. The title of his novel *The Painted Bird* refers to a story in which a character would capture a black bird and then, holding the blindfolded bird in one hand, dab it with different colors of paint until the bird was a collage of all colors of the rainbow. When no black feathers remained visible, he would remove the hood and release the frightened animal. The bird would quickly soar up into the sky, a beautiful spectacle of flying colors. Soon another black bird would come by and strike at it, however, and then another and another, until the painted bird disappeared in a mass of black birds that tore it to pieces.

The story captures a sad truth of nature: Often animals that look different from the others are targeted for rejection and outright violence. Animals do not seem to value diversity in their groups. They are not even content with excluding those who are different, but often actively destroy them.

American society has committed itself to promoting diversity, and there is much talk everywhere about how groups and institutions (work groups, universities, sports teams, and the like) will perform better if they are diverse. But is diversity always better? Is it safe for Americans to assume that they will always be able to outperform other, less diverse societies, such as the Chinese and Japanese? Diversity has both costs and benefits. Homogeneous (that

TRADE Offs

is, not diverse) groups may have some advantages, too, along with their drawbacks. Many advocates of diversity oppose women's colleges or African American schools (because they exclude male or nonblack students), but such institutions have provided good educations for many students, and a cautious scientist would not insist that more diverse school populations always produce better results. (Of course, some people might oppose same-sex colleges on moral grounds even if they do provide a first-rate education.)

Research by social psychologists suggests that diversity involves tradeoffs.[6] On the plus side, diverse groups can be more flexible and creative than groups marked by greater similarity among the members. Greater diversity can bring together more perspectives and possibly more information. Groups can be smarter than the smartest individuals, but only if different people contribute different information to the mix.[7] Diverse groups, by definition, have a better chance of bringing together different information than similar groups.

Recent research has confirmed that a group's collective wisdom can exceed the sum of its individual members, but only if the individual members have diverse and different views.[8] In fact, a group of diverse individuals can make better decisions than a group of similar individuals that are much smarter. The reason is that the errors of diverse people tend to cancel each other out, so when you average them you get the best answer. In contrast, similar individuals tend to make the same types of errors, so

when you average them you really don't gain much.

On the minus side, diversity can make it harder for people to cooperate and work together. The different backgrounds can result in poor communication and misunderstandings. Often diverse groups perform less well than other groups. The difficulty in getting very different people to work together can result in frustration, resentment, low morale, and even feelings of alienation from (or reduced commitment to) the group.[9]

One way to resolve the conflict is to take into account different kinds of diversity. The benefits of diversity come from having people with different knowledge and skills, so they can complement each other. In contrast, groups benefit much less from other kinds of diversity, such as getting people with different ethnicities, nationalities, backgrounds, and the like.[10] The misunderstandings, distrust, and other communicative problems arise more readily given that sort of diversity.

This tradeoff helps explain one seeming paradox that will be seen throughout this chapter. Groups perform best if people are individually identified and perform their separate, distinct roles. Yet groups have all sorts of pressures that push everyone to be and become the same. Why are such widespread conformity pressures observed in so many groups, if diversity is superior? The tentative answer for now is that diversity can produce benefits, but it has costs as well. Indeed, the advantages of diversity in groups may be limited to cultural animals because they involve sharing information and role differentiation.

Human groups are not just social but also cultural, and culture greatly increases what groups can do.[12] Cultural groups preserve information in the group and pass it along to future generations, greatly increasing the benefit of being able to absorb and communicate information. Cultural groups also benefit from role differentiation. Everyone specializes at something, in effect becoming an expert at his or her role, and the result is that all of the jobs are performed by experts.

Ford's assembly line exemplifies these advantages of groups. Knowledge about how to make cars was accumulated and preserved by the group, enabling it to be gradually improved. The first assembly line had the workers, rather than the cars, move along the line. The second, improved version had the cars move down the line, pulled along by ropes. The third version had a motorized conveyor belt move the cars along. Furthermore, the company used information and reasoning to reorganize itself to make the assembly system better. And the essence of the assembly line is division of labor. Instead of having two or three men make the entire car, the new system used many workers, each of whom specialized in a few simple tasks. The result was impressive improvements in the ability to make more cars better, faster, and cheaper.

QUIZ YOURSELF
What Groups Are and Do

1. **Which of the following is a group?**

   (a) Three children; playing hide-and-go-seek

   (b) Three neighbors; having a barbecue

   (c) Three strangers; quietly waiting for a bus

   (d) Three students; working together on a class project

2. **In one high school class, the teacher lets students select their own groups to work on an important class project. As expected, similar students group themselves together. In another class, the teacher randomly divides students into groups, so dissimilar students are often grouped together. Which is likely to be the main advantage of the dissimilar groups over the homogeneous (similar) ones?**

   (a) The dissimilar (heterogeneous) groups will be more cooperative.

   (b) The dissimilar groups will be more efficient.

   (c) The dissimilar groups will generate a greater variety of information.

   (d) The dissimilar groups will have higher morale.

3. **Which of the following greatly increased the production of automobiles in Henry Ford's plants?**

   (a) The added health benefits workers received

   (b) The assembly line

   (c) The higher pay workers received

   (d) The longer work week

4. **Which of the following is an advantage of a group?**

   (a) Groups can provide safety in numbers.

   (b) Groups can help each other find food.

   (c) Groups can make difficult tasks easier to perform.

   (d) All of the above

answers: see pg 525

Groups, Roles, and Selves

A vital and distinctive feature of human groups is that many of them are made up of distinct, well-defined, individual roles. Each person has a different job to do, and each person can specialize and become an expert at that job. The different jobs complement each other, so the joint effort improves total performance. The assembly line thus reveals a crucial advantage that cultural groups have over merely social groups, such as wolves or bees. Complementary roles produce better results than simply having everyone chip in and do the same thing.

The advantages of specialized roles were recognized long before Henry Ford invented the assembly line. In medieval farming villages, for example, it was probably good to have a blacksmith. But if everyone tried to be a blacksmith, the village would starve. The same goes for musicians, artists, and priests. When human groups advanced to the point that they did not need every person to be producing as much food as possible all the time, they became able to support musicians, artists, and priests. But if everyone in a tribe or village wanted to be a musician, the group would be unable to survive. Today, the same goes for teachers, police officers, physicians, plumbers, fortune-tellers, prostitutes, computer repair technicians, comedians, airline flight attendants, and barbers. Human roles only work in the context of a large system when most other people do something else.

Identifying individual people with their unique roles within the group is an important key to the success of human groups. In this chapter, we will see repeatedly that groups do better when people are individually identified and perform their unique roles. In contrast, when people blend together into a group and lose their unique place, such as by submerging their identities into the group, the groups perform less well and sometimes produce downright ugly results.

Social psychologists coined the term **deindividuation** to refer to loss of self-awareness and of individual accountability in a group. The term, from the same root as "individual," implies a loss of individuality. Deindividuated participants in lab studies often behaved badly, such as stealing, aggressing, or doing other antisocial things.[13,14] We shall see repeatedly in this chapter that group processes can produce costly and destructive results when people submerge their individual identities in the group. As Stanislaus Lezczynski, King of Poland, observed: "No snowflake in an avalanche ever feels responsible."

Although this conclusion has emerged in a halting way from laboratory findings, it was also spectacularly confirmed by some of the major historical movements of the 20th century. For example, the essence of fascist movements was that the individual should be submerged in the group, and the individual's self-interest should be subordinated to the best interests of the group. The most successful fascists (at least for a while) were the German Nazis, who did achieve some impressive successes in rebuilding a shattered, starving nation and fighting a war against the combined great powers of the world, but whose inner dynamics degenerated into a level of shocking cruelty and evil that went beyond what had been seen in other places—and that ultimately resulted in the sweeping destruction of their own country. Germany's experiment with deindividuation was thus a disaster for all concerned.

deindividuation the loss of self-awareness and of individual accountability in a group

Before closing this section, it is important to appreciate a few other important points about role differentiation. First, in a culture, the roles are defined by the system; they exist independently of the individual. The United States has one president, 100 senators,

Keystone/Hulton Archive/Getty Images

Hulton-Deutsch Collection/Historical/Corbis

Movements such as National Socialism (Nazism) submerge individual identity into the group. The results have often been destructive, for themselves and others.

and nine Supreme Court justices. A select few individuals occupy those roles today, but after all those men and women are dead and gone, those roles will still exist and be occupied by other individuals. The system creates the role, and different human beings occupy it, each one coming and going. When you get a job, it will most likely be a position that someone else had before you and someone else will have after you.

The split between people and roles means that people must have selves that are flexible enough to adopt (and occasionally drop) roles. Ants, for example, benefit from a social system that has several different roles, but each ant is programmed by nature for only one role, and ants do not change jobs very often. In human society, new roles become available all the time. Individual humans often have careers that involve a series of different jobs and different roles.

Belonging to a human cultural group thus involves two separate demands. One is to find common values and other sources of similarity that can cement one's allegiance to the group. The other is to find some special or even unique role within the group.

Todd Maisel/AFP/Getty Images

Most individuals have multiple roles.

QUIZ YOURSELF

Groups, Roles, and Selves

1. **When normally shy Devan is at a hockey game, he often gets swept away in the excitement. He is no longer self-conscious and, as a result, often does and says things that he later regrets. Hockey games seem to create in Devan a state of _____ .**
   - (a) catharsis
   - (b) deindividuation
   - (c) excitation transfer
   - (d) pluralistic ignorance

2. **Circumstances that increase _____ will decrease _____ .**
   - (a) anonymity; empathy
   - (b) anonymity; diffusion of responsibility
   - (c) self-awareness; deindividuation
   - (d) self-awareness; empathy

3. **What type of movement suggests that self-interest should be subordinated to the best interests of the group?**
   - (a) Fascism
   - (b) Anarchy
   - (c) Capitalism
   - (d) Democracy

4. **What is the most distinctive feature of human groups over nonhuman groups?**
   - (a) Distinct well-defined, individual roles
   - (b) Collective roles that many individuals fill
   - (c) The existence of group leaders
   - (d) The existence of subordinates within the group

answers: see pg 525

Group Action

Many people do many things in groups. The effect of working in a group (as compared to working alone) is variable: Sometimes the group produces improvement; other times, disaster. Social psychologists have spent years mapping out these effects.

One theme we have already suggested is that the effects of groups are often negative when people are submerged in the group. In contrast, when people retain their individual identities and feel personally accountable for their actions, many of the bad effects of groups are prevented or reduced, and the positive effects of groups are more common. Identifying people and holding them accountable for their actions produces better outcomes. To be sure, accountability is not a cure-all for the broad range of lapses, mistakes, and mental biases people show in groups. But when people believe they may have to justify their actions and decisions to other people, they tend to be more careful and thorough in their thinking, including using all the information available to them and thinking about how they would respond to possible criticisms.[15] People cooperate more with others when they are individually identified, whereas the anonymity of groups produces more greed, fear, and other dangerous reactions.[16]

Social Facilitation

Many experts regard Norman Triplett's (1897–1898) work as the first social psychology experiments (see Chapter 1). While watching bicycle races, he noticed that cyclists who raced alone against the clock generally were slower than those who raced against competitors. In an early experiment, he instructed children to wind fishing reels as fast as they could. Those who did this task alone were slower than those who did it when someone else was competing against them. Triplett thought that the presence of others stimulated a competitive instinct, causing people to work harder.

But further work showed that competition was not necessary. Some people performed better merely because observers, as opposed to competitors, were present.[17,18] This finding led to the tentative conclusion that **evaluation apprehension** (concern about how others are evaluating you) is the driving factor. People increase effort when others are present because they want the others to evaluate them favorably.

A bigger problem for the theory is that the presence of others doesn't always make people perform better. Have you ever given a speech or performance in front of a large audience? Many people find that unnerving and make mistakes.[19,20,21,22,23] If an audience always made you do better, people would never "choke under pressure."

These diverse, seemingly conflicting sets of observations were integrated into an exciting theory proposed by social psychologist Robert Zajonc. His theory was rooted in observations of animal learning.[24] Zajonc proposed that being in the presence of other people (or, for animals, other members of the same species) is arousing: It makes one breathe faster, makes the heart beat faster, sends adrenaline through the system, and so forth. One well-known effect of arousal (note this is not sexual arousal, but any sort of physical excitement) is to increase the **dominant response**, which is defined as the most common response in that situation. Thus, whatever you normally tend to do, you will do it even more when in the presence of others. The essence of Zajonc's **social facilitation theory** (see **FIGURE 14.1**) is that the presence of others increases the dominant response tendency.[25] For example, if you usually (though not always) choose hamburgers over hot dogs, then choosing hamburgers is your dominant response in that situation. When others are present, you will be especially likely to choose a hamburger.

The dominant response theory can explain both the good and the bad effects of the presence of others—both the faster cycling times in the presence of competition and the mistakes the amateur pianist makes when playing for an audience. For familiar, easy, and well-learned behaviors, the dominant response is to perform well, and performance increases when others are watching. For difficult, unfamiliar tasks, the dominant response is to perform less well, so mistakes become more common when others are watching.

The social facilitation theory has been confirmed by many studies.[26] In fact, one investigation even found it among cockroaches

evaluation apprehension concern about how others are judging you and/or your performance

dominant response the most common reaction to a given situation

social facilitation theory proposition that the presence of others increases the dominant response tendency

FIGURE 14.1

Robert Zajonc's theory of social facilitation: The presence of others increases arousal. Arousal increases whatever response is dominant. If the dominant response is correct, performance increases. If the dominant response is incorrect, performance decreases.

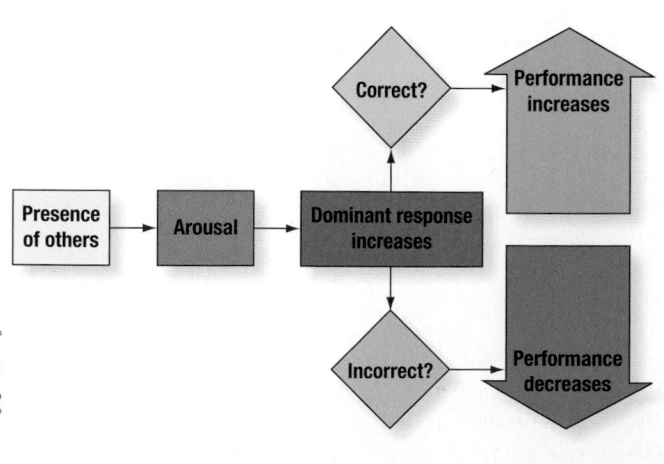

(see **FIGURE 14.2**).[27] Cockroaches probably do not suffer evaluation apprehension or other complex human motives, so this finding was best explained in the simple, basic terms of arousal increasing the dominant response.

Social facilitation theory has many applications to the real world. For example, many modern offices have more public shared space (such as large rooms where everyone is present) than private offices. Is this a good design decision? It depends. If the employees are working on simple or well-learned tasks, then this design works well because the presence of others should increase their performance. On the other hand, if the employees are working on complex or creative tasks, the design is bad because the presence of others is likely to decrease their performance. The Ford assembly line worked well in part because the tasks were simple, so the dominant response was to perform them correctly.

More recent work has concluded that social facilitation effects depend on three processes.[28] Bodily arousal confers more energy and increases the dominant response. Evaluation apprehension makes people strive to make a good impression (but also creates worries). And some degree of distraction occurs, insofar as people start paying attention to each other rather than the task. Evaluation apprehension and distraction both fit the "putting people first" orientation we have seen over and over in this textbook, because people care about what other people think of them.

The presence of others can also influence food consumption, as described in *Food for Thought*.

To be sure, evaluation apprehension does affect performance among humans, and it may intensify the effects of others' presence. A judgmental observer has a stronger effect than a blindfolded bystander.[29] The possibility of evaluation seems to inspire certain kinds of people to do their best. In particular, **narcissists** are individuals who regard themselves as better than others and are constantly trying to win the admiration of others. These glory hounds perform best when others are watching or when important rewards are riding on the outcome of their performance, whereas they tend to slack off when there is no opportunity to bring credit to themselves.[30] This pattern, however, can elicit resentment from other group members, who recognize that the narcissist is not a team player but rather is looking for individual honors.

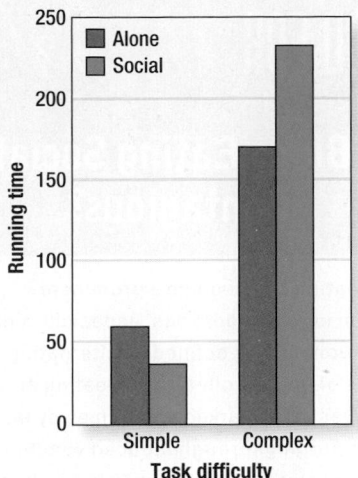

FIGURE 14.2

In a study, cockroaches completed simple mazes more quickly when they ran in the presence of four other cockroaches than when they ran alone. In contrast, cockroaches completed complex mazes more quickly when they ran alone than when they ran in the presence of four other cockroaches.[27]

Social Loafing

The preceding section showed that the presence of others can make people perform better, especially on easy and familiar tasks. But wait: Around the same time that Triplett was noticing that cyclists rode faster when other cyclists were present, a French engineer named Max Ringelmann was coming to a very different conclusion (see Chapter 1). Ringelmann observed farm workers and noticed that as new men were added, the total output didn't seem to increase as much as it should. He conducted experiments in which men pulled carts either alone or together. In theory, two men should pull twice as hard (200%) as one (and if social facilitation theory is at work here, two men should pull more than twice as hard!)—but in fact two men pulled only 186% as hard. When four men worked together, the drop in total effort was even bigger. In eight-man teams, each man was not even pulling half as hard as the lone men. Here was a clear example of a human group being less than the sum of its parts: Somehow the men didn't seem to work as hard in a team as they did when alone.[31] What went wrong?

Several factors reduce an individual's productivity when working in a group, such as difficulty coordinating efforts with others. But subsequent research confirmed a pattern that came to be known as **social loafing**. People reduce effort when working in a group, compared to when working alone.[32] In lab studies, for example, participants were assigned to make as much noise as possible by clapping and shouting. Recordings verified that they were louder (indicating greater effort) when working alone than in a group. Three people, each cheering alone, made about as much total noise as six people cheering together.

The pattern of social loafing has also been called the **free rider problem**.[33] This term is probably derived from trams, subways, and buses in Europe, which rely on the honor system for payment: People are supposed to buy a ticket and punch it or scan a debit card when they climb on board. The money from these tickets pays for the transportation

narcissists individuals who regard themselves as better than others and are constantly trying to win the admiration of others

social loafing (free rider problem) the finding that people reduce effort when working in a group, compared to when working alone

Binge eating has become a prominent problem in recent decades, especially among young women. It is defined by alternating periods of uncontrolled, lavish eating and of severe restraint marked sometimes by fasting or even purging through induced vomiting or taking laxatives. It is associated with the clinical diagnosis of bulimia (based on Latin for "ox hunger"). These patterns were rarely noted or observed prior to the 1960s, but they have quickly become a serious problem. Recent estimates suggest that between 1 out of 20 and 1 out of 5 female college students engages in this behavior.

How could a pattern of problem behavior change so quickly from relatively unknown to widespread? Part of the answer lies in group processes. Research on college sororities found that binge-eating patterns seemed to be contagious, in the sense that they spread through the group.[34] Binge eating was most commonly noted when groups of young women, all about the same age, interacted regularly. Young women who joined sororities would adopt the behavior patterns of the group—sometimes including binge eating.

In fact, binge eating was associated with popularity in the sororities. There were two different patterns. In one, the more a young woman engaged in binge eating, the more popular she was. This suggests that women perceived binge eating as a pathway to social success. It also indicates that binge eating carried no social penalty. On the contrary, apparently the group rewarded binge eating, as the women who engaged in it most frequently were most highly regarded by the other group members.

The other pattern was only slightly less worrisome. One sorority apparently had norms for the optimal amount of binge eating. The most popular women were those who were closest to these norms. Thus, there was apparently at least some disapproval directed toward the most extreme binge eaters. Still, women who failed to engage in binge eating also paid a price in terms of lower popularity.

The second pattern, indicating social norms for binge eating, is consistent with the idea that women picked up the habit from their friends. Sure enough, the research on sororities found that a woman's tendency toward binge eating had typically become quite similar to that of her friends by the end of the academic year.[35] In other words, members of the group became more like their friends over time. Because the members of the sorority typically engaged in binge eating, new members adopted this pattern as they made friends.

Image Source/Getty Images

Evaluation apprehension is bad for the appetite.

system. But some people simply get on and ride without paying. They thus take free rides, letting others provide the money that keeps the system going.

Free riders presumably know they are cheating the system and taking advantage of others. In lab studies, most social loafers say they are working as hard as they can, even though the experimental results prove that they aren't. Apparently, many people are not aware that they are socially loafing, or at least they are reluctant to admit it.[36]

Why does social loafing occur? One important factor is the feeling of being submerged in the group, and therefore not being individually accountable. When the contributions of individual group members are identified, so that everyone (or at least the leader) knows who did what, social loafing is greatly reduced.[37,38] People are less likely to steal free rides on the subway if they will be identified than if they think they can do it anonymously. Likewise, people work harder for their team or group if they believe that others will know if they slack off.[39] Ford's assembly line may have benefited from the fact that each person performed a different job, so it would be possible to identify a lazy employee who did poor work.

The importance of individual identification exemplifies the theme we have already noted: Groups produce more negative effects when individual identities are submerged in the group. During the 1980s and 1990s, "accountability" became a major buzzword in American businesses. Accountability meant that each person was held individually responsible for his or her decisions and job performance. The drive for accountability was fueled in part by the growing recognition that a lack of individual accountability contributes to social loafing.

The difference between feeling individually accountable versus submerged in the group probably holds the key to the apparent contradiction between Ringelmann and Triplett. Remember, Triplett found that people performed better when others were present, but Ringelmann found the opposite. In Triplett's studies, performers were individually identified; in fact, they were often competing against one another. In Ringelmann's observations, the men were yoked together pulling carts, and no one could know how hard any individual man pulled. Competition and accountability lead to greater effort, but submersion in the group leads to social loafing.

A related cause of social loafing is the desire not to be a sucker.[40] Once members of a group begin to suspect that others are loafing, they loaf too, because they do not want to do all the work on behalf of others. If you and a friend had to paint the garage, and your friend spent most of the time texting and taking calls on her cell phone while you did most of the painting, you might well feel that you had been foolish to do more than your fair share of the work, especially if credit (and pay) was shared equally between the two of you. This pattern has also been called the **bad apple effect**,[41,42,43] based on the folk observation that one bad apple can spoil all the other apples. One loafer can thus cause other workers to loaf as well.

Although it looks like these people are pulling the rope as hard as they can, research shows that they would pull harder if they were pulling alone.

Again, individual identification helps overcome the tendency to loaf. People are less prone to copy a social loafer if they believe they will get credit or blame for their own work. When people believe their own contribution to the group is unique, especially if it is also important and meaningful, they are less likely to loaf.[44]

How is social loafing to be reconciled with social facilitation? The pattern of social facilitation is deeply rooted in nature and indeed is found in other species. Nature, apparently, has prepared people to become excited when others are around, and this can make for better performance. Social loafing and especially the bad apple effect appear to be much more distinctively human, insofar as people must often force themselves to do work that they dislike. Only humans worry about being a sucker, and perhaps only humans can reason through to the conclusion that they might as well enjoy the same benefit as others for half the effort, if they can get away with it.

Punishing Cheaters and Free Riders

Social psychologists have been using game-based methods to study people's motives for several decades, and recently economists have begun to adopt similar research methods. One influential finding is that when participants recognize that other players are showing signs of social loafing or free riding, they will punish them—even if it costs the participant money to punish the free rider.[45]

This finding was shocking to many economists. Certainly free riders can gradually undermine the system for everyone, but economists generally assume that rational human beings will maximize their own payoffs. Why would they give up some of their own money to punish a free rider, rather than just doing the best they can for themselves and leaving the free rider problem to others? Economists even came up with a name for this—**altruistic punishment**.[46] It is altruistic in the sense that the individual sacrifices his or her own gain for the betterment of all, by punishing people who cheat the system. This might be compared to a bystander who risks injury in order to stop a crime, such as by attacking the criminal.

The irrationality of altruistic punishment suggests that it may involve something very deeply rooted in the psyche, which fits the theme of this book that natural selection has favored humans who are able to participate in a cultural society. One trait that would fit that description very well would be a deeply rooted impulse to punish people who cheat or

bad apple effect the idea that one social loafer can cause other people to loaf as well

altruistic punishment the finding that people will sometimes sacrifice their own gain for the betterment of all, by punishing people who cheat the system

May I please see some ID?

beat the system. Culture depends on a system, and those who cheat the system can ruin it for everyone. Altruistic punishers may suffer in the short run, but in the long run they are likely to benefit. A group of people who are all willing to punish cheaters and free riders will have a safer, fairer system—and hence may survive and reproduce better—than a group of people who don't guard their culture against cheating and free riding.

Deindividuation and Mob Violence

Earlier in this chapter, we introduced another form of being submerged in the group: deindividuation. The term signifies a loss of individuality, and research now defines it as a loss of individual accountability and reduction of self-awareness, mainly due to the presence of others.[47,48,49] Social psychologists quickly reached the (preliminary) conclusion that deindividuation makes people more willing to act on their own impulses, which can increase antisocial behavior (see Chapter 10). We have seen that in many situations nature says go, whereas culture says stop. Apparently, one way that culture says "stop" is by holding people individually accountable for their actions, and when people become anonymous and not identifiable, they are less likely to heed the culture's pleas to stop. It is in a sense ironic that merging into the group can make people behave less in accordance with cultural values, because cultural values are group values. Thus, as people merge into the group, they sometimes feel freer to go against the group's values. Loss of individual accountability enables people to take advantage of the group for personal gain.

One review of all the published studies on deindividuation found that the effects of deindividuation are somewhat erratic, which calls into question any general conclusion such as "deindividuated people are more violent."[50] The review found that whether or not members of the group were anonymous to one another didn't seem to matter much, but being anonymous to outsiders did make people more willing to violate norms, such as by stealing and cheating. Likewise, what mattered in terms of self-awareness was whether people were attuned to how other people regarded them, not whether they were privately thinking about themselves. Thus, deindividuation makes people more willing to behave badly insofar as they cease worrying about what others think of them. Meanwhile, accountability emerged as the single biggest factor in predicting aggression. As we have said, people behave most in line with general social norms when they feel individually accountable for their acts. When not accountable, they will go along with what others are doing at the moment, even when these situational norms go against what is generally considered morally good. This is probably how looting happens during a riot: Most people believe stealing is wrong, but when one is submerged in the group and other members of the group are stealing, the individual goes along with the here-and-now group and steals, too.

Shared Resources and the Commons Dilemma

Land, food, money, tools, jewels, and other resources can be held in two ways. One is private property, in which a single person owns the resource. The other is to have resources shared by the group, so that people take what they need and leave the rest to others. The march of human history has seen a dramatic shift in ownership patterns. The earliest humans seem to have had relatively few possessions, and much of what they had was shared communally by the family, tribe, or other group. Modern Western civilizations, in contrast, have adopted private ownership of most goods, though communal ownership is still sometimes seen within families (e.g., any member of the family is permitted to take and eat food from the family refrigerator).

Private ownership has severe social costs. One is inequality. About 1% of the world population is estimated to hold 40% of world wealth.[51] This income disparity was a large factor for the "Occupy" movements that began on Wall Street in New York City, but quickly spread to all states. The 99% of Americans were sick and tired of 1% controlling the lion's share of resources. Another possible inequality can occur when ambitious and greedy private owners take advantage of others to increase their share. Religious orders in many parts of the world have insisted that clergy and other people who devote their lives to spiritual striving renounce worldly possessions, sometimes taking a vow of poverty. In a very different manner, some social movements such as socialism and communism have advocated reducing or abolishing private property so that people will share ownership of valuable resources and not seek to exploit one another.

The Occupy movement was a protest against the wealthiest 1% (e.g., banks) by the other 99%.

Yet joint, communal ownership has costs, too (thus indicating another tradeoff!). Resources that are not owned by anyone do not receive the preserving care that they get from individual owners. Communism became notorious for pollution and waste because individuals had no incentive to take care of the publicly owned resources. On a smaller scale, you might notice that your friends who live in dorm rooms or rental properties do not take care of these dwellings as carefully as they do their rooms at home or as carefully as people who own their own home.

Social psychologists became interested in the problems of communal resources under the name of the **commons dilemma**—the tendency for shared or jointly owned resources to be squandered and not used in an optimal or advantageous fashion. The term comes from the "tragedy of the commons," a pattern in which common grazing areas would get overused and become useless.[52] A more contemporary version is the worldwide dwindling of fish stocks. Because the fish in the sea belong to no one until they are caught, fishing boats just catch as many as they can, and eventually too few fish are left to reproduce and replenish the fish population.

Two kinds of conflict occur in the commons dilemma, both of which have been seen repeatedly in this book. The first is social conscience versus selfish impulse: People take things for themselves even when it hurts the group as a whole. The second involves time (again, the tradeoff of "now versus later"). To manage a resource for the long run, it is best to restrain oneself in the present. People could actually benefit their own selfish goals best if they would all simply go slowly, allowing the resource to replenish itself fully. But that is not what people do. They take most of the resource now, leaving little for later.

Communication helps. When people can communicate and urge each other to show restraint, they do not use up the resource as fast.[53] Unfortunately, they still tend to take too much, so the resource is still badly managed and ends up being depleted prematurely.

Another factor is the behavior of others. When people observe that others are greedily taking more for themselves rather than showing restraint in order to benefit everyone over the long term, they tend to copy this behavior. Earlier in this chapter we saw that the tendency to follow bad behavior is called the bad apple effect. When people observe others behaving well, they also tend to behave more favorably, but people copy bad behavior more quickly and readily than they copy good behavior.

commons dilemma the tendency for shared or jointly owned resources to be squandered and not used in an optimal or advantageous fashion

1. **The presence of others helps individual performance on _____ tasks and hurts individual performance on _____ tasks.**

   (a) boring; interesting   (b) interesting; boring   (c) easy; difficult   (d) difficult; easy

2. **Professor Walleye Bass finds that having other faculty members observe his class improves his lectures. This improvement is the result of _____ .**

   (a) evaluation apprehension   (b) mere presence   (c) social loafing   (d) None of the above

3. **Easy identification of the contributions of group members _____ .**

   (a) decreases group efficiency   (b) decreases evaluation apprehension   (c) decreases social facilitation   (d) decreases social loafing

4. **Snap, Crackle, and Pop have a group project in their nutrition class. They write a paper on breakfast nutrition. Snap and Crackle do all the work, whereas Pop does little or no work. Because grades are assigned to groups of students, Snap, Crackle, and Pop all get "A"s. Pop's "A" grade illustrates _____ .**

   (a) a free ride   (b) downward social comparison   (c) the bad apple effect   (d) upward social comparison

answers: see pg 525

How Groups Think

Groups should seemingly be smarter than individuals. Folk wisdom says that two heads are better than one, so 10 heads ought to be better yet. The general principle is that groups are smarter than individuals. But are they? The following sections will reveal a mixture of answers.

Before we are too critical of groups, however, it is important to remember the theme that humans evolved to belong to cultural groups—groups that share and preserve information. It is normal and natural for people to share information and to look to others for information. Moreover, if information is to be shared through a group, members of human groups will have the natural tendency to think alike. Social psychologists have been good at finding absurd or destructive excesses of this tendency, such as when everyone in a group clings to a false belief. But these excesses are probably linked to basic tendencies that are neither absurd nor destructive. Groups do far more good than harm.

Brainstorming, and the Wisdom of Groups

Although fields such as advertising often borrow ideas from psychology, sometimes the advertising people get there first. Brainstorming is an idea that was developed by advertising executives in the 1950s to increase the creativity of their groups, and only after it had made its mark in ad groups did psychologists begin to conduct research on it. **Brainstorming** is a form of creative thinking in groups, using a procedure in which all group members are encouraged to generate as many ideas as possible without holding back or worrying about being wrong. They are also encouraged to build on each other's ideas. The core assumption is that creative people can feed off each other's thinking processes and creative energy, thereby coming up with more and better ideas than could the same number of people working alone.

brainstorming a form of creative thinking in groups, using a procedure in which all group members are encouraged to generate as many ideas as possible while interacting and stimulating each other

The benefits of brainstorming have been gradually confirmed by careful research. Compared against the same number of people working alone, people working together in a brainstorming group session enjoy the process of generating ideas more than people who toil alone. When they finish the work, they evaluate it more favorably, rating it as more creative and successful. People who work alone but hear about brainstorming groups also immediately recognize the advantages of brainstorming and express the belief that they would do better if they were in a brainstorming group.[54,55]

But that's all. If you read the preceding paragraph carefully, you probably noticed that it didn't say that the brainstorming groups actually performed better—only that they thought they were better, and they had more fun. When researchers actually check the quality and quantity of ideas, the performance of brainstorming groups is quite disappointing. A meta-analysis that combined the results of 18 separate studies concluded that the output of brainstorming groups is substantially lower than that of people working separately.[56] Eight people working individually produce more ideas than eight people brainstorming. Nor does brainstorming increase quality by sacrificing quantity; the quality of work coming out of the brainstorming groups is lower, too. In short, brainstorming doesn't improve creative output—it reduces it.

The brainstorming research was disappointing but not surprising. There is a long tradition of groups being regarded as having negative traits: immoral, dangerous, stupid, impulsive, violent, and even beastly.[57] The French writer Gustave le Bon[58] wrote in 1895 that when people come together in a group, they lose their ability to think as reasonable human beings and instead become dominated by the "group mind," which effectively moves them to a lower, more animalistic level of evolution.

Francis Galton (1822–1911), the pioneering scientist who stimulated much research in psychology, thought that most people were not very intelligent, and groups of people even less so. One day he attended a fair where there was a contest to guess the weight of a steer. The very large animal was there to be viewed, but the contest was made more difficult by the rule that the guess had to be how much the creature would weigh after being slaughtered and prepared for sale. People paid a small amount for a ticket, on which they would write their guesses, and the most accurate guess would win a prize. Some contestants were cattle farmers or butchers who might have had some knowledge of meat weights, but most others knew little about it and couldn't offer much more than a guess based on whim or a lucky number. After the contest, Galton obtained the 800 tickets and did some statistics on the guesses, hoping to provide more data on the foolishness and stupidity of the herd of common people.[59]

The correct answer was 1,198 pounds (543.4 kg). When Galton compiled the 800 guesses, thinking they would be way off, he found their average to be 1,197. He was stunned. How could all those unintelligent, uninformed people produce an almost perfect answer?

This anecdote was used by James Surowiecki to open his book *The Wisdom of Crowds*.[60] Surowiecki's work is an important counterweight to the long tradition of research indicating that groups produce stupid judgments. He has compiled an impressive list of patterns in which the collective wisdom turns out to be smarter than even the experts. For example, no expert on sports is consistently able to predict the outcome of sports events better than the final betting line, which is directly based on the bets of many individuals, even though those bets are distorted by wishful thinking, whims, guesses, and favorite colors. Likewise, almost no stockbroker can consistently pick winning stocks better than the market as a whole.

One of the most dramatic, if less scientific, illustrations of the power of collective wisdom comes from the television show *Who Wants to Be a Millionaire?* In this game show, contestants could win large sums of money by giving only correct answers to a series of multiple-choice question, each with four possible

"O.K., we've set up the manufacturing facitlities, organized the distribution network, hired the marketing expertise, and allocated the advertising budget. Any ideas for a product?"

People enjoy brainstorming and think it works, but it does not.

In the television game show *Who Wants to Be a Millionaire?* people who are stumped get more questions correct when they poll the studio audience (91%) than when they ask an expert (65%). Surely they aren't smarter than a favorite expert!

answers. When stumped, the contestant could either call an expert (selected in advance, usually the smartest or most knowledgeable person the contestant knows) or poll the studio audience. Surowiecki went through the statistics on how these "lifelines" worked out. Calling an expert was pretty good, producing the correct answer about two-thirds (65%) of the time. But polling the studio audience yielded the right answer 91% of the time! Thus, a crowd of random people sitting in a television studio was more likely to get the right answer than a carefully chosen expert.

It is remarkable to think that large groups of people are smarter than the smartest individuals, but under the right circumstances they are. "It's as if we've been programmed to be collectively smart," said Surowiecki[61]—a conclusion that resonates with our view of humans as cultural animals who learn about the world by sharing information. People assume that getting lots of independent opinions from average people simply multiplies mediocrity. But in fact it makes for collective wisdom. You'd need a super-expert, or possibly a very advanced technical problem (rocket scientists really do know a few crucial things!), before an expert would perform better than a crowd.

But the conditions that enable crowds to achieve this high level of intelligent functioning are often violated, as we will see below in connection with groupthink and other group processes. These conditions include diversity of opinion and independence. That is, each person must be able to think for himself or herself, and each person must be able to get some information from his or her own perspective. If everyone is forced or pressured to think the same thing, or if their main information is seeing what everyone else does, watch out—group wisdom may degenerate into group stupidity. On the other hand, the wisdom of crowds works well when individuals disagree, hold diverse opinions, and even have plenty of (various) biases.[62]

Recent findings have shown how fragile the "wisdom of crowds" effect is. If people are merely aware of what others are thinking, they start to conform, and the group as a whole becomes less accurate. Ironically, people become more confident as their answers converge with those of others, so the group as a whole is more sure of being accurate but is actually less accurate![63]

Many people working independently, all getting their own bits of information, often produce a surprisingly accurate average. If someone can pull together that information, the group can be wise. But when groups fall into the trap of following each other or conforming to dominant views, their power is lost. These conclusions fit this book's theme of regarding humans as cultural animals. In order to perform effectively, people must operate as separate, independent members of a group, pooling and sharing their diverse information. Only then do people become "collectively smart," in Surowiecki's words.

You may notice a seeming contradiction. Groups can be smarter than individuals, yet brainstorming groups don't perform as well as independent individuals. But brainstorming groups don't meet Surowiecki's criteria for success. Group members don't work independently and contribute their separate ideas—rather, they interact, which raises the likelihood that some will feel left out, will defer to the opinions of others, will be too shy to criticize the group, or in other ways will be held back from contributing what they can.

Why Do People Love Teams?

We have seen that groups often do not perform as well as a number of individuals working alone (though groups do usually outperform a single person). Why do people love the idea of working in groups? Why do American companies want everyone to be a "team player"? Why do they form teams?

The section on brainstorming suggested a partial answer. It noted that people believe teams will outperform the same number of people working individually (even though that belief often turns out to be wrong). Maybe people are just stuck in a mistaken view of reality and make their decisions based on that mistake.

A more complex and reasonable answer was furnished by research.[64] A large body of research finds a consistent pattern. Many people, including business managers, believe that teams are highly effective for improving performance, but in reality the majority of teams don't live up to their reputation (either in the lab or in real business organizations). If performance were the only measure, then most corporations and other organizations should forget about teamwork and cultivate individual excellence. But performance is not the only measure, and working in teams has many side benefits. People enjoy working with others rather than alone. Working in teams satisfies their need to belong. It enables them to feel confident, effective, and superior (if only because many members of teams think they are the star, or at least a crucial team member who deserves a large share of the credit for any success the team has). The enjoyment and other psychological benefits of teams may explain why people are so eager to form and join them, even if they really do not improve performance most of the time.

Transactive Memory: Here, You Remember This

As we have seen, groups are most likely to be "collectively smart" if members' minds work independently. The best strategy may be for members to specialize as to who remembers what. In a world of information overload, there is simply too much for any one person to remember. Hence, the solution: Different people should focus on different things. Remember Ford's assembly line: Instead of hiring mechanics who know how to build an entire car, he could hire people with little knowledge and just train them on a specific skill.

The idea that information is dispersed through the group runs directly contrary to the old "group mind" theories, according to which thinking in groups is mainly a matter of having everyone think the same thing. Noting this contradiction, some psychologists coined the term **transactive memory** to refer to a process by which members of a small group remember different kinds of information.[65,66] For example, when the electricity goes out and you need a candle, it helps if you can remember where the candles are. But it is almost as good if you know that your roommate remembers where they are. You don't have to remember everything yourself.

What makes a group most effective is if group members know about what they know and can shift responsibility for remembering to the best-suited individuals.[67] For example, a romantic couple moving in together might start off by having the woman do the cooking because that fits traditional roles and assumptions, but as they get to know each other, they might realize that the man is more interested in food and has a better memory for recipes, so they could reallocate the role to him. In lab studies, intimate couples who worked face to face performed the best on group memory tasks.[68] They did better than pairs of strangers and better than couples who were not face to face. The crucial difference was that by looking at each other, they could tell which of them knew the answer best.

Transactive memory begins at the learning stage, not just at the remembering stage. Groups perform better when they are trained together, in part because they can help slot people into particular roles for learning different things. That is, the group can speed its learning by figuring out who is good at what parts of the task. As a result, each person can concentrate on learning his or her specialty, rather than everyone trying to learn everything.[69,70]

Groupthink

The term **groupthink** was borrowed from novelist George Orwell, who used it in his novel about totalitarianism called *1984*. The term refers to the tendency of group members to think alike.[71,72] Social psychologists use it specifically to mean a style of thought in which

transactive memory a process by which members of a small group remember different kinds of information

groupthink the tendency of group members to think alike, especially when doing so leads to bad decisions

the group clings to a shared but flawed or mistaken view of the world rather than being open to learning the truth. In decision making, groupthink means that the group sticks to its preferred course of action, refusing to consider alternatives fairly and refusing to recognize the dangers or flaws in its plan.

The roots of groupthink probably lie in the desire to get along. Members of a group do not want to spend all their time arguing, nor do they want the other members to dislike them. They most enjoy being together and working together when they all agree. In principle, a group will have the most information if people bring diverse viewpoints and air conflicting opinions (as noted in the preceding section), but such discussions can be difficult and unpleasant. Hence, people become reluctant to criticize the group, attack its basic beliefs, or question each other. This creates the illusion that everyone is in agreement.

Several aspects of a situation make groupthink more likely. First, the group tends to be fairly similar and cohesive to start with (and then becomes more so as a result of groupthink). That is, the members of the group share many views and ideas in common, and they tend to get along well with each other. Second, a strong, directive leader makes groupthink more likely. Third, the group may be isolated in some sense from others, so that it is not exposed to disturbing facts or contrary views. Fourth, the group may have high self-esteem, regarding itself as a superior, elite collection of people who do not need to worry about what outsiders think or want.

Social psychologists have identified several important signs that indicate when groupthink is occurring. First, there is pressure toward conformity. Groupthink originates in people's desire to get along and, toward that end, to hold the same views and opinions.

A second sign is an appearance of unanimous agreement. Because dissent is suppressed, people get the impression that everyone in the group agrees with the group's plans or views. In group meetings, members mainly express support and agreement. The illusion of consensus is sometimes furthered by **self-censorship** which means that individuals decide not to express their doubts or bring up information that goes against the group's plans and views. Thus, many individual members of the group may have doubts or know things that spell trouble for the group, but everyone thinks that no one else does, so each person decides not to rock the boat. This creates a vicious circle: Because no one is willing to express any doubts, the impression that no one (else) has any doubts becomes very strong.

An illusion of invulnerability is a third sign. When the experts all agree, it is easy to think that nothing can go wrong. Information about risks, costs, and dangers is suppressed, everyone expresses faith and optimism, and this creates the sense that the group can accomplish almost anything. Many of the worst disasters in history have arisen because this sort of illusion of invulnerability caused groups to make decisions without fully appreciating the flaws and dangers in their plan.

A sense of moral superiority is a fourth sign. Such groups regard themselves as good and virtuous. They hold high ideals and believe that they live up to them better than other people. This belief reinforces the patterns of self-censorship and pressure to conform that we have already noted.

A fifth sign is a tendency to underestimate opponents. Groupthink helps groups regard themselves as superior. The other side of the coin is that their opponents and enemies are regarded with disrespect, disdain, and contempt. Groups who are engaging in groupthink may refuse to negotiate with their enemies because they think they are evil. They do not fear their enemies because they regard them as weak. This can prove costly, because if you underestimate your enemies, your chances for success are much less than you think, and your plans will not go smoothly.

Foolish Committees

Most organizations rely on committees to study issues and make decisions. This approach is based on an eminently sensible principle: It may be hard for a single person to know all sides of an issue and all aspects of a problem. By bringing together a group of people with different knowledge and different viewpoints, the outcome

self-censorship choosing not to express doubts or other information that goes against a group's plans and views

can be improved. Ideally, each person contributes something different, the group members respect each other's opinions, and the committee can achieve a broad level of wisdom and understanding that is above and beyond what anyone working alone could accomplish.

But ask anyone with extensive experience whether committees generally achieve high levels of wisdom and understanding. Most likely, the answer will be a laugh or a roll of the eyes. What goes wrong?

Careful laboratory studies of group decisions have begun to reveal the problems that cause committees to fail to live up to their promise. One important factor is that members of a committee want to get along with each other, so they focus more on what they have in common than on their different perspectives. These pressures toward group harmony end up stifling the free exchange of information.

In one set of studies, the experimenter told a group of participants to decide which of two job candidates should be hired. Each member of the group was given some information about the two candidates. There were seven reasons to hire Anderson and only four reasons to hire Baker, and the group had all of the reasons—so, logically, the committee should have chosen Anderson. Yet most groups ended up choosing Baker, who was objectively the poorer candidate.[73,74]

The roots of the wrong decision lay in how the information was distributed. The researchers gave each member of the group the same four reasons for choosing Baker, but they gave each person only one of the reasons for choosing Anderson. Each person got a different reason for choosing Anderson, so if the committee members managed to pool their knowledge, they would realize that there were more reasons to hire Anderson. After all, that is how committees are supposed to work, by bringing together all the different information that the various members have.

But they didn't manage to pool their information. Instead of talking about all seven different reasons for hiring Anderson, they mainly talked about the four reasons for hiring Baker. That is, their group discussion focused on what they all knew in common, rather than on the unique information each person had.

Thus, a committee can end up being less than the sum of its parts, even in purely informational terms. Instead of bringing together different views and information, committees often narrow their focus to what they have in common. Information is lost rather than gained.

Group Polarization and the "Risky Shift"

As we saw in the last section, committees are often formed on the principle that many people working together can be smarter and make better decisions than individuals working alone. Yet often the decisions of committees seem foolish. This has prompted research into how groups make decisions.

Early on, social psychologists stumbled onto a peculiar pattern in group decision making, which they dubbed the risky shift.[75,76] The **risky shift** was defined as a tendency for groups to take greater risks than the same individuals (on average) would have decided to take individually. Somehow the process of talking about the dilemma moved the group toward a more extreme, risky view. (If you read the earlier section on groupthink, this result will not surprise you!)

Rather soon after the risky shift was discovered, exceptions began to appear. Sometimes the group would shift toward more cautious decisions, which was the opposite of a risky shift. (Some social psychologists began to speak of a "stingy shift" or a "conservative shift.") For a time, the whole line of research was mired in arguments and confusion, but the correct principle began to emerge in later studies. The effect of groups is not invariably either a risky or a stingy shift. Rather, the primary effect is to drive the group toward a greater extreme in whatever direction it was already headed.[77] If the group leans initially toward risk, then group discussion will yield greater risk. If the group leans toward caution, discussion will make it all the more cautious.

The movement toward either extreme became known as the **group polarization effect**. (Polarization means moving away from the middle, toward either extreme.) It can

risky shift a tendency for groups to take greater risks than the same individuals (on average) would have decided to take individually

group polarization effect a shift toward a more extreme position resulting from group discussion

FIGURE 14.3

Group polarization occurs when group discussion leads people to become more extreme in the direction of their initial opinions.

Copyright © 2008 The McGraw-Hill Companies, Inc. Reprinted by permission.[125]

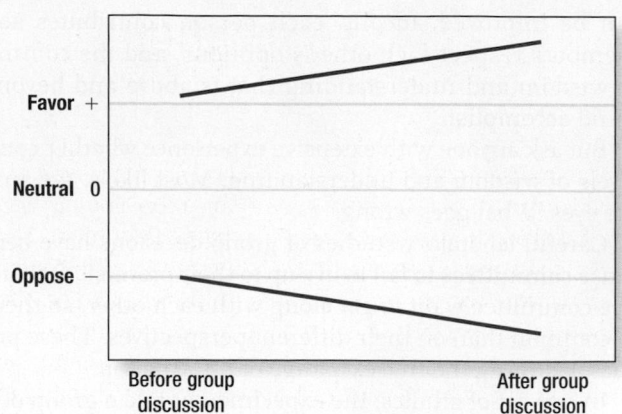

be defined as a shift toward a more extreme position resulting from group discussion (illustrated in **FIGURE 14.3**).

Group polarization depends on the fact that people in the group are fairly similar, so that they all initially lean in the same direction (e.g., they are all somewhat inclined to take a risk). This resembles what tends to happen in everyday life. Even when a large and diverse set of people are all thrown together, such as first-year students arriving at college, they soon sort themselves into groups of like-minded individuals. (As we saw in the chapter on attraction, similarity is a common and strong basis for forming friendships.) As a result, most people spend most of their time interacting with people who think and feel rather similarly. Hence, when they discuss issues, they accentuate each other's beliefs and feelings, thereby contributing to group polarization.

QUIZ YOURSELF
How Groups Think

1. **Which of the following is not an effect of brainstorming in groups?**

   (a) People have more fun working in groups than alone.

   (b) People think that the quality and quantity of answers are better when they work in groups than when they work alone.

   (c) The quality and quantity of answers are better when people work in groups than when they work alone.

   (d) All of the above are effects of brainstorming in groups.

2. **Samantha is considering a new product line to compete with the leading manufacturer in her business. Although her staff wonders privately if the new product is a good idea, they support her decision rather than undermine her authority. This is an example of _____ .**

   (a) deindividuation

   (b) group polarization

   (c) groupthink

   (d) risky shift

3. **Which of the following is *not* a symptom of groupthink?**

   (a) Conformity pressure

   (b) Overestimating opponents

   (c) Illusion of unanimity

   (d) Sense of moral superiority

4. **The Department of Psychology is in the process of hiring a new faculty member. Although the individual members of the search committee tend to favor hiring Dr. Slight Favorite, most are still somewhat uncertain as to how they will finally vote. Friday afternoon they will discuss the candidate. What will be the most likely outcome of their deliberations?**

   (a) They will decide to hire Dr. Slight Favorite.

   (b) They will decide not to hire Dr. Slight Favorite.

   (c) They will be deadlocked.

   (d) They will form another committee.

answers: see pg 525

Power and Leadership

Many groups strive for equality. In modern marriage, in particular, the ideal is that husband and wife own everything in common and make decisions equally, with respect and consideration for each other. In parallel, democracy is spreading through the world, with its similar emphasis on equality and joint decision making. In a democracy, each person's vote counts the same, and millions of votes may be counted in order to decide something important.

In practice, however, equality is not very efficient for making decisions, and it may have other drawbacks. Instead of full equality, most groups have leaders. Large groups don't just have leaders, they typically have a hierarchy of power, ranging from a leader at the top, down through several ranks of others who have some authority but must respect what the top leader says, down to the lowest levels of people who take orders and directives but cannot give them. Try to imagine, for example, an army that did away with all ranks and ascribed equal authority to every soldier, so that the army would never take action unless everyone (or at least a majority) voted in favor. No armies actually operate like this—and probably for very good reasons! Such an army would probably never manage to decide to fight a battle. And if it did, it would probably be hopeless at deciding what tactics to use amid the chaos, noise, trauma, and confusion of battle. Bad commanders have caused many battles to be lost, but an army without commanders would be even worse off, and it would probably lose every time.

> "Being powerful is like being a lady. If you have to tell people you are, you aren't."
> — Margaret Thatcher

Leadership

Leadership is vitally important but poorly understood. Bad leaders can ruin countries, organizations, or military units. One team of researchers sought to determine how big an impact the Chief Executive Officer (CEO, the highest ranking person in the organization) has on the performance of a company, as reflected in its profits. They concluded that the answer was about 14%, or one-seventh.[78] That is a huge impact for one person to have. Another study concluded that high-performing executives added an average of $25 million to the value of their company, as compared with average performers.[79]

The importance of leadership emerged from an expansive study of corporate success called Good to Great.[80] The research group scanned the Fortune 1000 to identify companies that had 15 years of below-average performance followed by 15 years of above-average performance. They found 11 companies that had undergone this sort of sustained improvement, and then the research team tried to identify what these improving companies had in common. To the surprise of the researchers, the biggest common factor was leadership: All the companies had been transformed by a new CEO who took over the organization and improved its performance.

Moreover, two traits characterized the 11 CEOs who led their companies to lasting success. One was being modest and humble. This conclusion came as a shock at the time because the business world had been much enamored of celebrity CEOs with flamboyant, self-promoting styles and probably streaks of narcissism. The other important trait was extreme persistence, also known as "fierce resolve."[81] These leaders made decisions and stuck with them, even if the early results were disappointing. Recall the story about Henry Ford that opened this chapter: His first two car companies were failures, and his first attempt at a low-cost Ford, the Model N, was not very successful, but he stayed the course and achieved legendary success with the Model T.

Additional evidence suggests that most good leaders are perceived as having several basic traits.[82,83,84] Good leaders are decisive; they make a decision and stick with it. They are competent at the group's tasks. (Among hunter/gatherer tribes, which were the norm for most human beings in prehistoric times, the headman was usually one of the best hunters in the group.) Good leaders are seen as having integrity; they are honest and have good moral character (or at least they are perceived that way). Last, they have vision—

some concept of what the group can become or achieve—and they use this vision to motivate other people to set aside self-interest in order to work toward the group's goals.

Recall, from the emotion chapter (Chapter 6), how guilt motivates concern for others and socially constructive behavior, whereas shame is generally antisocial? Being prone to guilt (and not shame) makes a better leader.[85] Guilt-prone people are seen as more desirable leaders, and they actually take charge more. Indeed, a study of performance in business organizations found that workers with higher guilt-proneness were rated as more effective leaders, as well as being more responsible for others, by their co-workers, supervisors, and subordinates. The guilt finding stands out in particular because much other research has found that people prefer leaders with plenty of positive emotions. But guilt's special link to responsible concern for others may be particularly helpful for leaders.

Another useful way of thinking about leadership divides the leader role into two components: task orientation and relationship orientation.[86] Task orientation means getting the job done well, and it is no accident that the best workers are often promoted into leader roles. Task-oriented leaders focus on planning, motivating, coordinating inputs from group members, setting goals, and providing feedback. Relationship orientation refers to maintaining good relationships among the group. Boosting morale, resolving conflicts, taking care of group members, and promoting group spirit are important parts of this component. Many leaders are good at one or the other of these two components of leadership, but a high-quality leader must be good at both.

Narcissists may not necessarily make great leaders, but that does not mean that narcissism and leadership are not linked. Narcissists may be more likely than others to become group leaders, for better or worse. In lab studies, groups of four strangers were assembled with no leader and assigned to discuss a problem and make a recommendation. The researchers tracked who emerged as a leader in each group. In every study, people scoring high on the trait of narcissism were most likely to emerge as leaders.[87] This appeared to be less a matter of seeking attention than of simply wanting to be in control and having the confidence to speak up frequently. Their confidence caused other group members to defer to them.

Speaking up and being assertive in other ways may help a person move into a leadership role, but it is not necessarily a recipe for successful leadership. Studies of MBA (master of business administration degree) students and actual business managers have found that as assertiveness increases, leadership quality first increases—and then decreases.[88] Assertiveness was defined as the tendency to speak up for, defend, and promote one's values and goals. Leaders who were low in assertiveness were seen as unable to motivate people and unable to get things done, so they were ineffective. At the other extreme, highly assertive leaders were viewed negatively in interpersonal terms (even if effective in some ways): unfriendly, bossy, manipulative, and generally not likable.

The mixed effects of assertiveness mesh well with the idea of the two components of leadership. Assertiveness may be helpful for the task dimension but harmful for the interpersonal dimension. The best leaders seem to strike the right balance of being somewhat but not too assertive.

Toxic Leaders

Bad leaders can be disastrous. History has many examples of leaders who have brought ruin, misery, and death to their followers (recall the example of Jim Jones in Chapter 8). One leader who has gone from an international hero to a despised pariah is Robert Mugabe, and his story is sobering.

Mugabe was a leader of the black uprising in Rhodesia, a relatively rich country in southern Africa. When his revolution succeeded, he became the first president of his country, newly renamed Zimbabwe. Representatives from 96 countries attended the independence ceremony in 1980, in which Mugabe promised peace and reconciliation, even assuring the 200,000 white citizens that he would be their friend and ally. The country had been impoverished by the war, but it had tremendous natural resources, including rich farmland and diamond mines, as well as a strong industrial base. Zimbabwe was seen as the potential breadbasket of southern Africa, able to grow enough food to feed much of the rest of the continent.

Robert Mugabe, President of Zimbabwe.

AP Images/Tsvangirayi Mukwazhi

Over time, Mugabe narrowed his goals and focused ever more on increasing and cementing his own power. In the process he turned the once prosperous country from a breadbasket to a basket case. His talk of making the country rich through capitalism was abandoned in favor of Marxist politics, which brought poverty. Racial reconciliation was abandoned when the black majority grew impatient with Mugabe's policies, and in a transparent bid for popular support he announced that the government would confiscate farms owned by white people and give them to poor black peasants. This drove most of the white people out of the country, taking some knowledge and skills with them. Then, instead of giving the confiscated farms to poor and hungry black citizens, he gave the best to his cronies and loyalists, many of whom were already rich and few of whom knew anything about farming. Food production fell dramatically, and soon many Zimbabweans were starving. Instead of exporting food to other countries, as it had once done, Zimbabwe became dependent on donations of food from the outside world. Mugabe pressed ahead: "If I see anyone with cold feet," he said, "I'll put hot irons under them."

Zimbabwe could not even buy food because the economy was in a catastrophic state. Inflation reached such high levels that the money became virtually worthless. The majority of the workforce was unemployed. Meanwhile the corrupt government continued to pay lavish salaries to its leaders, along with other perks such as frequent brand-new Mercedes cars. Although the government was clearly going broke, Mugabe sent his army into a seemingly pointless civil war in the Congo, on the other side of Africa, at the cost of a million U.S. dollars a day. He sought to cheer up his impoverished citizens with publicity stunts, like conducting a lottery for a huge cash prize, selected from every citizen with a bank account. (By suspicious coincidence, the lottery officials found that Mugabe himself won the huge prize—a bit ironically, as he was one of the few Zimbabweans who did not need the money!)

In 2002, Mugabe came up for reelection, and by now he faced a serious chance that the disillusioned masses would vote him out. He rigged the election shamelessly, including sponsoring systematic violence against members of the opposition party (and throwing the opposing presidential candidate into prison on trumped-up charges of treason). Colin Powell, America's first black Secretary of State, observed that Mugabe had blatantly stolen his victory. At the next election, in 2007, Mugabe came in second in the first round and looked certain to lose the runoff, whereupon his supporters became so violent against the opposition party that Mugabe's election opponent withdrew from the race.

The starving masses waited in line for food handouts from foreign donors, but Mugabe's men refused to give food to anyone who could not produce a membership card in their party. Many of the world's governments protested against how Mugabe had stolen the election, but he dismissed their accusations as nothing more than racism and continued to cement his hold on power while driving his country into ever greater ruin. When the Archbishop Desmond Tutu, a highly respected black leader who had won the Nobel Peace Prize, dared to call Mugabe a tyrant, Mugabe denounced him as an "angry, evil, and embittered little bishop." Most outsiders thought the archbishop was right.

Bosses can also make bad leaders. American business is home to plenty of bad bosses. Many surveys have found that between two-thirds and three-quarters of workers say the worst aspect of their job is their immediate boss.[89] Perhaps such surveys bring out a tendency to complain, but other, more objective methods of assessing managerial performance yield an average estimate that about half the bosses in the United States are inept.[90]

What makes some leaders so disastrous for their followers? Research has begun to fill in the picture of what makes a bad boss. After surveying many findings, one research study identified four patterns.[91] One was simply that the person was promoted above his or her abilities and never managed to adjust to the demands and responsibilities of the new job. A second pattern was failure to build a team, by making poor hiring choices. This may sound obvious, but it is often difficult to choose the right people for the team, especially because almost everyone knows that during a job interview you should try to project an image as a cooperative, reliable, talented, and motivated worker. Bad bosses may give top jobs to their friends and choose team members based on loyalty to the boss rather than competence (like Mugabe), or they may simply be unable to judge people effectively.

The third pattern of bad bosses involved poor interpersonal skills that created conflicts between the leader and subordinates. For example, some leaders may be arrogant and thus offend their group by demanding outward shows of respect and deference. ("Because I said so, that's why!") Others are simply insensitive—they don't know or don't care about the people who work for them. And the fourth pattern involved interpersonal actions that undermined the group's ability to work together, such as betraying someone's trust, failing to keep promises, taking advantage of subordinates, or frequently changing his or her mind.

One admirable attempt to distinguish dangerous leaders from others began by noting that politicians do not differ in mental health from the rest of the population, so a certain number of mentally ill people (even clinically insane) will come to power here and there. The successful ones may be able to think effectively, but the madness will be found in their emotional lives.[92]

In particular, the dangerous leaders suffer from "emotional disregard and disconnection from others."[93] This disconnection is not necessarily harmful in anyone, and even a leader with that characteristic will not necessarily turn to violence or evil, becoming instead a legalistic or technocratic ruler. However, when the emotional disconnection is combined with a proneness to violence, there is disaster in the making. Such a leader will be willing to undertake destructive projects, pursuing dreams of glory and grandeur (or even just vindictive grudges and hatreds) without worrying much about how his or her followers may be put at risk of intense suffering. Napoleon and Hitler are good examples. Although most histories focus on their conflicts with other nations and on the struggles and sufferings of their enemies and victims, it is instructive to recall what happened to their own followers. France was bled white by Napoleon's wars, and a generation had to cope with a lack of men who could serve as heirs, husbands, and fathers. Germany suffered even worse from Hitler's wars. Napoleon once responded to the news of the battlefield deaths of his own troops by saying that "soldiers are meant to be killed," a chilling comment that revealed how little emotional connection he felt with the agony and sacrifice of the young men who followed him.

Three characteristics seem typical of dangerous leaders.[94] First was the indifference toward the suffering of people, along with devaluation of other people in general. This allows the leader to manipulate, exploit, and even kill without regret. Second, the dangerous leader is intolerant of criticism, and he or she will often take steps to suppress dissent. Stifling the free press and imprisoning dissidents are often early signs of a dangerous leader. (Mugabe, for example, has repeatedly arrested journalists who criticize his regime, and his opponent in the 2002 election was arrested for treason and could have

Myself, your glorious leader.

All in a day's work?

been condemned to death.) Third, a dangerous leader has a grandiose sense of national entitlement. This corresponds to the egotism that we have already seen in Chapter 10 on aggression as characterizing violent and dangerous individuals.

What Is Power?

Power is an important aspect of leadership, insofar as leaders make decisions that affect the group. **Power** means one person's control over another person.

Power can seem addictive. People who get a taste of power often show patterns of seeking more power. The careers of many powerful individuals, from Napoleon to John D. Rockefeller, suggest a steady rise in their grasping for ever greater power, even though the amount of power they already have seems enough to satisfy any normal person's needs and indeed far exceeds what normal folks can even dream of attaining. Napoleon, for example, was already emperor of France and held power over conquered territories all around Europe, including Germany, Austria, and Poland. Why did he need to attack Russia, too?

Although power is normally understood as an aspect of control, a famous essay by political scientist Hans Morgenthau proposed that it is linked to belongingness as well.[95] Morgenthau compared power to love, although at first blush the two may seem totally different. Yet both power and love effectively merge separate individuals. The difference is that love entails a more or less equal and mutual union, whereas power effects a one-sided union in which the will of the powerful person is imposed on the subordinate. Morgenthau went on to point out that this unequal merging (unlike love) ultimately fails to save the powerful person from loneliness because the self of the subordinate effectively disappears; even at the moment of peak domination, the powerful person finds himself or herself alone again after all. Morgenthau suggests that this dissatisfaction explains why powerful people seek even more power, thinking that this will help them escape from loneliness. It also explains why powerful people often insist on displays of love from their underlings ("our beloved leader"). Yet it continues to be lonely at the top.

People are often afraid to question the leader.

Effects of Power on Leaders

The imbalance in power causes a variety of effects, many of which appear harmful. A British nobleman, Lord Acton, is credited with saying: "Power tends to corrupt, and absolute power corrupts absolutely." Is this a reason why it is good to keep changing one's leaders?

The corrupting effects of power have been studied by assigning participants to be managers over groups of workers. By random assignment, some of the managers had considerable power, such as the ability to give pay raises and bonuses, to deduct pay, to reassign workers, and even to fire them. The other, low-power managers had no such powers and simply had the title of manager. Both were supposed to get their workers to perform well.[96,97]

The managers without objective powers urged the workers to do better, praised them, proposed goals and targets, and gave advice. These tactics are quite reasonable ways to influence people, but the powerful managers spurned them. Instead they issued commands, made threats, and also made promises or offers of money (using the powers they held). The ones who were given power began to use it more and more over time. What they said was part of throwing their power around.

How do powerful people perceive their underlings? These studies also measured how the managers in his research rated their workers. The actual performance of the workers was carefully controlled by the experimenter so that it was identical in the two conditions (powerful versus not-so-powerful managers). Yet the managers perceived these objectively identical workers in quite different ways. The managers with more power evaluated the performance of their workers much more poorly than did the managers who lacked

power one person's control over another person, including what happens to that person

objective power.[98] Powerful bosses gave their workers little credit for the work they did, preferring to see the workers as simply carrying out the commands of the manager. In this way, the powerful managers took credit for what was accomplished without forming a favorable view of the employees. In contrast, the managers with less power believed that the workers' own motivation and efforts were mainly responsible for what was achieved, and they rated the workers more favorably overall. Having power makes you look down on others and underestimate their worth.

Some of the detrimental effects of power on leaders are linked to how followers treat them. A study of American business CEOs (topmost leaders) found that their subordinates frequently flattered them and expressed agreement with their opinions even when the subordinates privately felt differently. This ingratiating flattery boosted the narcissistic egotism of the bosses. This in turn made the CEOs think they were doing great, to the extent that they downplayed problems in the company and failed to take action to solve them. In the long run, these egotistical mistakes increased the chance that the CEO be fired.[99] So if you find yourself in position of powerful leadership, don't listen too carefully to the flattery and agreement from your underlings!

Followers forgive and tolerate misbehavior by leaders much more readily than similar misbehavior by other group members. In several studies, for example, people read about a soccer player who broke the game's rules by yelling and cursing at the referee and the opposing team, also refusing to shake hands at the end of the game.[100] Participants rated that player more favorably if he was the leader than merely a member of the team. In another study, a team of participants played a lab game for money, and one of the players cheated to help the team. Again, that player was rated better if a leader than simply another member. It may be natural for group members to support their leader, but turning a blind eye to leader misdeeds is a potentially dangerous form of such support.

How do powerful people treat their followers? The prisoner's dilemma game (discussed in Chapter 9 on prosocial behavior) forces people to make a choice between two moves. One is cooperative; the other is exploitative, self-serving, and defensive. Researchers have used the game to see how powerful versus less powerful people treated each other. The highly powerful individuals favored self-serving responses rather than cooperative ones. Even when low-power people showed a consistent pattern of being willing to cooperate, high-power people would often continue to take advantage of them and pursue their individual goals.[101] Highly powerful people seem to disregard and even prey on the weak. These patterns certainly support Lord Acton's comment that power tends to corrupt.

Recent works suggest that the corrupting effect comes from the power, not the high status that often accompanies power. Status means that others respect and admire you. Experimental participants accorded high status were exceptionally fair and generous toward others. In contrast, power is control over others, and participants who were assigned high power were relatively unfair and unjust toward others.[102] The nastiest folks were the ones who got high power but low status. They treated others very badly. High status helped offset the negative effects of power.

Then again, not all power corrupts, and some people wield it in positive ways. Social psychologists have searched for a more balanced theory about power that can recognize its benefits as well as its costs. One general theory of power proposed that power has five crucial effects.[103]

Emotion

Power feels good. People with power are more likely to feel positive, pleasant emotions and to express these good feelings. For example, people who report feeling more dominant and powerful in life, such as those in leadership roles, generally report more positive and happy emotions.[104] People who lack power are more prone to feel and express negative emotions such as guilt and depression.

Rewards Versus Punishments

Power makes people attend more to rewards than to punishments, whereas lack of power has the opposite effect. Essentially, power focuses its possessors on the possibility of getting what they want. It makes them more likely to pursue whatever rewards appeal to them, including money, sex, attention, food, possessions, and success. Put another way, they look for opportunities.

They also ignore constraints. Lab studies show that people in power positions tend to overlook or forget information that might prevent them from reaching their goals.[105] Hence they may go ahead and pursue unrealistic or risky strategies, because they are not attuned to potential problems and obstacles. Power undermines caution.

Adaptability

Powerful people seem to think in terms of how they can use circumstances, benefit from them, or work with them. Powerful people change their behavior more across different situations than do powerless people.[106] You might think that low-power people bend to situations while high-power people remain true to their inner feelings, but the reverse seems to be true. Changing to fit the situation enables the powerful person to get the most out of it. For example, powerful people plan more leisure on weekends and more work during the week, compared to less powerful people. A low-power person might plan to spend a weekend reading a novel, for example, regardless of the season, but a powerful person will take more heed of the special opportunities of winter as opposed to summer (e.g., skiing, going to the beach).

Adapting one's plans and actions to get the most out of situational opportunities is not the same as being at the mercy of the situation. Even though powerful people may change how they act, they are not pushed around by the situation. As the title of a recent article states, "Power reduces the press [as in pressure] of the situation."[107] High- versus low-power participants in their studies responded in different ways to seemingly identical situations. High-power people perceived more choices, conformed less to the opinions expressed by others, and generated creative ideas that were further apart from what other people had already put forward, as compared to people low in power. In contrast, people who lack power shift their attention more to threats and dangers. Instead of thinking about how to get what they want, they focus more on how to avoid losing what they have, and they are more prone to see ambiguous situations as dangerous or threatening.

The phrase "thinking outside the box" has become something of a cliché in recent years; nonetheless, it is relevant here. If we think of the situation as the "box," then power enables people to think outside the box, but that includes finding ways to use the box to their own best advantage. People low in power remain inside the box in their thinking, and hence they may never fully appreciate what the box could do for them.

The Duplex Mind

As we have seen in this book's repeated references to the duplex mind, mental processes can be sorted into deliberate, controlled ones and relatively automatic ones. Power seems to make people rely more on automatic processing, whereas people who lack power engage in more deliberate thinking.[108] The reason is probably that the greater vulnerability of people low in power makes them feel the need to think carefully before acting. People who are held accountable for their actions—which is typical of people with low power—think in more complex ways, such as considering both sides of an issue rather than simply emphasizing the side they favor.[109,110] Powerful people are rarely told by others that they are wrong, so they become lazy in their thinking, and easy or lazy thinking is the specialty of the automatic system.

Approach Versus Inhibition

Last, power removes inhibitions against acting, whereas a lack of power makes people more inhibited. In a sense, this theme underlies all the others because it inclines powerful people to act assertively to pursue the rewards they want (including using others to help them get what they want), which brings the positive feeling of pursuing and getting these rewards.

The approach or action orientation makes powerful people more likely than others to engage in socially inappropriate behavior. Powerful people sometimes get into trouble when they act on their impulses without thinking about possible consequences. Many politicians (across the political spectrum!) have had their careers damaged because of minor sexual misdeeds. There is also some evidence that sexual harassment occurs because powerful men automatically think of sex in connection with power.[111] This automatic thinking, along with the tendency to act impulsively to pursue what one wants (and, perhaps crucially, the willingness to regard others as means toward one's own satisfaction), increases the likelihood of trying to pressure subordinates into granting sexual favors.

As we have seen, Henry Ford used his power to create a better system that enriched himself, his family, his workers, and his stockholders, and that also enriched society by providing a convenient and appealing mode of travel. Other leaders have brought disaster to their followers. Is power ultimately good or bad? Perhaps neither, according to some recent social psychology studies. These studies suggest that power increases the tendency to take action, and this can be for good or ill.

A series of studies suggested that power leads to action even if the power is logically irrelevant to the action.[112] That is, power seems to create a state of mind that favors action. Lacking power, in contrast, brings a wait-and-see mental state marked by inhibition and inaction. In one of these studies, participants played the card game blackjack after being assigned the role of either manager or worker (builder) on a separate task. Although being manager had nothing to do with the blackjack game, the managers were more likely to follow the active strategy of taking an additional card, whereas the low-power participants tended to stick with the cards they had been dealt and not ask for a new one. In another study, mental states were manipulated by having people remember and write about prior experiences in which they had either held power over someone or been subjected to another person's power. They performed this task while seated in a room in which an annoying fan was blowing directly on them. People in the high-power condition (those who were writing about having power over someone else) were more likely than those in the low-power condition to get up and move the fan or turn it off.

One of these studies is particularly relevant to the question of whether power is used for good or bad ends.[113] States of mind were manipulated again by having participants write about personal experiences of having power or being at the mercy of someone else's power. Half the participants played a commons dilemma game, in which people could passively allow the common resource to remain large (and grow) or could actively and selfishly take money for themselves. The other participants played a different kind of game in which the active response was to donate money for a public good, whereas the passive response was to keep one's own money and rely on others to be generous. In both games, the high-power participants took the active response, whereas the low-power participants tended to be more passive. Thus, power increased the tendency to take action both for selfish gain and for the benefit of others. Power doesn't always corrupt— sometimes it ennobles, too.

The idea that power can cut both ways was also supported in research that compared leaders who felt a communal bond with their followers and other leaders who were out for themselves without caring so much about others. The leaders who had a communal bond with their followers typically wanted to use their power to improve the lot of their underlings; in fact, many of them felt an obligation to do so. As

Feeling powerful makes you more likely to ask for another card. (But it doesn't make you more likely to win!)

a result, these leaders used their power to take care of their followers. In contrast, leaders who were out for themselves used their power for their own good, often to the harm or detriment of their followers.[114] Thus, again, power can be used to harm or to benefit those who are at the mercy of the powerful.

Preserving Power

Power can perhaps be addictive: People who get it gradually become increasingly concerned with preserving their power. The more they perceive a threat of losing power, the more they may concentrate on trying to conserve it. We saw in the example of Mugabe a case in which a ruler started out trying to do the best for all his citizens and over time became focused on advancing his cronies and consolidating his power, even to the detriment of the citizens. He may be exceptionally bad, but he is far from unique in this. If you follow world news, you will read many stories about various leaders who seek to change their country's constitution to allow them to remain in power longer and longer, or who perform other damaging actions so as to preserve their position.

Lab studies have shed light on the power-clinging mentality. Leaders of experimental groups were faced with choices between doing what was best for the group and what was best for them, including maintaining their power position. Mostly, leaders did what was best for the group (though keep in mind that these were mainly student research participants who had just been assigned to be leaders, as opposed to people who had had years to become addicted to power). But when there was a threat to their power, many leaders changed their priorities to favor preserving their position.[115] For example, they might exclude a highly talented group member who could really help the group perform (but might threaten the leader's authority). They blocked talented subordinates from having influence over the group's decisions. Also, following the ancient Chinese writer Sun-Tzu's advice to "keep your friends close, but your enemies closer," they took careful note of what other group members might threaten their situation (such as by performing really well) and tried to stay close to that person, presumably to keep a close eye on what that person did.[116]

There was one situation in which even the threatened leaders tended to do what is best, such as picking the best people even though these might outshine the leader. That was when they were competing against another group. Even leaders who put their own interests first will sometimes switch so as to take care of the group when it has to win a competition against an outgroup.

Effects of Power on Followers

Let us turn attention now from those with power to their subordinates. Being in a subordinate position, according to our definition of power, means that another person can decide what happens to you and that you may be forced to do things you do not want to do. Not surprisingly, subordinates pay extra attention to the powerful person and try to understand him or her. Careful laboratory studies have shown that when people are dependent on someone else, they spend extra time thinking about that person, analyzing that person's behavior, and trying to figure out that person's traits and personality.[117]

When there is conflict, the person with less power is at an obvious disadvantage. Hence, people with less power will be especially prone to foster peace and harmony. When subordinates ask for peace and cooperation, the powerful person may simply take this as a given and not be very responsive, whereas when the powerful person asks for peace and harmony, low-power people should be highly receptive. Some evidence for this was provided by laboratory studies with experimental games: Lab participants low in power responded very positively when the high-power person suggested cooperation and an end to conflict.[118]

Another fascinating study showed that people low in power adapt to the expectations of high-power people, even without realizing it.[119] Participants in this study were given randomly assigned, bogus information about the ostensible personality traits of their interaction partners. Power was manipulated in terms of which person was permitted to make decisions about the next phase of the study. The two participants then had a 10-minute conversation, which was tape-recorded in such a way that each person was recorded on a separate channel. Judges who did not know the experimental manipulation then listened to what each person said and rated whether the person showed those traits that the partner had been anticipating. Low-power individuals ended up acting the way their high-power partners expected, more than the reverse. Many were unaware that they changed their behavior, and some of the changes were to the individual's own disadvantage. Thus, when power is unequal, the lower-ranking person may unwittingly make a variety of changes in behavior as influenced by the unstated expectations of the person high in power, even if the low-power person might not want to make those changes.

Sometimes power takes the form of controlling how much money people get. Lack of money is no laughing matter, yet people without money seem to laugh more (see *Money Matters*).

Legitimate Leadership

The maintenance of power often depends on legitimizing myths.[120] **Legitimizing myths** purport to explain and justify why people in power deserve to be in power. In an ostensible meritocracy, those in power have to contend that they have superior merit, such as by being smarter, more talented, or harder working than those who rank below them. After all, some degree of inequality is inevitable, and nearly all societies have power structures, so the crucial question is whether the inequality of power is fair and legitimate. The individuals or groups in power must typically find some reason that everyone will accept as establishing that their power is indeed fair and legitimate.

Indeed, the desire for legitimacy may be a common concern of powerful people, not least because it makes their job easier: Underlings will follow commands and cooperate better with leaders who are seen as legitimate than with others. When most nations were ruled by kings, many kings claimed "divine right," which is to say that they sought legitimacy by insisting that the supreme god had intended for them to rule. Indeed, the long and turbulent history of the relation between religion and politics has much to do with what the two systems offer each other: Religions offer legitimacy but lack power,

legitimizing myths explanations used to justify why people in power deserve to be in power

---

MONEY*Matters*

Money, Power, and Laughter

Who laughs more, rich and powerful people, or poor and dependent ones? Existing theories offer bases for predicting both answers. Rich and powerful people can do what they want, so perhaps they feel free to let go and laugh, whereas those low in power wait to see whether others laugh first. Alternatively, people low in power might laugh at the powerful person's jokes, as a way of ingratiating themselves.

To test these hypotheses, researchers assigned participants to high- or low-

power roles and then measured how much they laughed at someone's jokes. Power was manipulated by control over money: Participants were told that a cash prize would be given to someone and either they or someone else would have the final decision. Then they interacted with someone who managed to tell several jokes, including both funny and unfunny ones. The researchers secretly recorded how much the participant laughed.

Low power led to more laughing. Apparently, having someone else control your money makes you more prone to laugh—regardless of whether the jokes are funny or not. Indeed, the researchers had difficulty coding the laughter according to whether the jokes were funny or not because low-power people seemed to laugh

even at odd times when nothing funny had been said.[121]

Was this laughter a ploy to ingratiate themselves with the powerful person? Not necessarily. In one of the studies, participants merely watched a video of someone talking, so that nobody would seemingly know whether they laughed or not. They still laughed more. They also laughed more when they were interacting with a co-worker who had no more money or power than they did.

Laughter may well be a strategy for making friends, because people like people who laugh.[122,123] Apparently, people who lack money and power are eager to make friends with anyone (not just those who are powerful). They become more prone to laugh at anybody's jokes—even if the jokes aren't funny!

while rulers have power but want legitimacy, so they make natural allies. In democratic systems, rulers claim legitimacy by virtue of being elected by a majority vote. But incompetent, immoral, or illegal actions can quickly rob an elected leader of this legitimacy.

In short, the quest to bolster legitimacy is typically an ongoing problem for those in power. Even as they hold and exercise power, they must remain on the lookout for ideas or values that can be used to justify their position of power and their influence over others.

QUIZ YOURSELF
Power and Leadership

1. **What two traits are possessed by CEOs who lead their companies to lasting success?**

   (a) Good looks and intelligence (b) Humility and persistence (c) Persistence and intelligence (d) Narcissism and persistence

2. **Powerful is to powerlessness as _____ is to _____ .**

   (a) affect; cognition (b) cognition; affect (c) approach; inhibition (d) inhibition; approach

3. **Research has shown that in the prisoner's dilemma game, more powerful people choose to _____ and less powerful people choose to _____ .**

   (a) cooperate; cooperate (b) cooperate; defect (c) defect; cooperate (d) defect; defect

4. **Research shows that power leads to _____ .**

   (a) action (b) competition (c) cooperation (d) inaction

answers: see pg 525

Putting the Cultural Animal in Perspective

What Makes Us Human

In this chapter we have glimpsed some of the best and the worst of human nature. Sometimes, as in violent lynch mobs and mass murder campaigns, groups bring out the worst in people and enable them to do things much more terrible than they would likely do alone. Other times, as on the assembly line, groups manage to achieve things that would be far beyond the powers of all the same group members acting individually.

One pattern we have seen is that submerging the individual in the group often leads to bad outcomes such as violence, groupthink, and the waste of resources in the commons dilemma, whereas keeping people individually identified and accountable helps to promote positive results. Humans are perhaps much better equipped than other animals to maintain separate, accountable identities, so humans can benefit from groups in ways that most other animals cannot.

Role differentiation and the division of labor help make human groups especially effective. People can take on and adapt to different roles, and they can design and function in a group that is a network of individually defined roles. Culture is especially powerful for creating such systems of interlocking, complementary roles. It is possible that human beings first created culture in order to enjoy some of these benefits of group systems. Groups of animals may have a couple of roles, such as male and female, or leader and follower, but human groups such as corporations and universities can consist of hundreds of different roles with separate jobs and distinct functions.

The distinctively human traits make some effects stronger than those found in animals. We saw that social facilitation occurs in animals (even cockroaches!), but among humans the impact of others is intensified by evaluation apprehension. People are better than animals at anticipating how others will evaluate them and at adjusting their behavior accordingly.

Communication is important to the success of many groups. As language users, people can communicate much more effectively than other animals. To be sure, this does not always lead to good results because (as in groupthink) people can use their words to put pressure on others to conform to a faulty idea. By and large, though, good communication is central to the great success of human groups.

Power and leadership are found in the animal world, but they too take on new dimensions in human society. For one thing, the power of communication enables humans to preside over much larger groups. (Millions of U.S. citizens follow the laws made by their government, for example, even though they might never meet the president or any member of Congress face to face.)

More impressively, perhaps, humans have gradually developed means of transferring power without violence. Among most animals, power is held by the strongest male, who has his way with food and females until another male comes along and physically defeats him. Through most of human history, many rulers retained power until their death. A remarkable achievement of the modern era has been the democratic transfer of power, whereby the person or party that loses an election will peacefully turn over power to a new set of rulers. In some parts of the world, this has still never happened, but the tide of history seems to spread peaceful democratic transition to more and more places.

Restricting power has been one of the great achievements of human culture. As we saw, in groups of animals, the leader can do almost anything he (or less often she) wants. Humans have gradually learned to hold their leaders accountable. The progress of culture has included imposing more and more restrictions on power, so that even the topmost leaders can be arrested, put on trial, and removed from office against their will. Even in the family, the husband or father no longer holds the extreme power over his wife and children that was common in many earlier societies, a power that at times has extended to life and death. Humans use laws—which are among the most powerful elements of culture—to restrict and restrain the uses of power. In this way, abuses of power can be reduced, and life can become better for the vast majority of people.

CHAPTER 14 SUMMARY

What Groups Are and Do

- Humans can use the power of culture to form groups that can achieve far more than collections of individuals operating alone.
- In human evolution, a tendency to form groups may have been beneficial because
  - Group members can find safety in numbers.
  - Group members can help each other find food.
  - Groups can accomplish tasks that would be too difficult for lone individuals.
- Cultural groups preserve information and pass it along to future generations.
- Cultural groups can use information, as well as reason from experience, to organize themselves.
- Cultural groups benefit from role differentiation and division of labor.

Groups, Roles, and Selves

- Complementary roles (as in the role differentiation of cultural groups) produce better results than simply having everyone do the same thing.
- Human roles work in the context of a large system in which most other people do something else.
- In fascist movements, the individual's self-interest is subordinated to the best interests of the group.
- Putting the best interests of the collective (that is, society as a whole) above those of the individual makes tyranny more likely.

- Culture creates roles that are independent of the individuals who occupy those roles.
- Human selves are flexible enough to take on (and occasionally drop) roles.
- Identifying people in groups and holding them accountable for their actions produces better outcomes.

Group Action

- Zajonc's theory of social facilitation states that the presence of others increases arousal, which increases the dominant response tendency (the most common response in that situation).
- Social facilitation theory states that the presence of others can make people perform better, especially on easy and familiar tasks.
- The presence of others can change people's eating patterns.
- Narcissists are individuals who regard themselves as better than others and are constantly trying to win the admiration of others.
- Evaluation apprehension may intensify the effects of others' presence.
- Social loafing (also called the free rider problem) refers to the finding that people reduce effort when working in a group, compared to when working alone, especially if their work is not individually identifiable.
- The bad apple effect refers to the finding that one loafer can cause other workers to loaf as well.
- Deindividuation refers to a loss of self-awareness and of individual accountability in a group, which can lead to antisocial behavior.

- The commons dilemma is the tendency for shared or jointly owned resources to be squandered and not used in an optimal or advantageous fashion (the "tragedy of the commons").
- Communication, personality, mood, and the behavior of others all affect the tendency to overuse a common resource (the commons dilemma).

How Groups Think

- Brainstorming involves encouraging group members to share and generate as many ideas as possible without holding back or worrying about being wrong; it produces less creative output but is liked better than working separately.
- Large groups of people can make better predictions than the smartest members of the group if people operate as separate, independent members and then pool and share their diverse information.
- Transactive memory refers to a process by which the members of a small group remember different kinds of information.
- Groupthink refers to the tendency of group members to think alike. It is especially likely if the group
  - Is similar and cohesive.
  - Has a strong, directive leader.
  - Is isolated from other ideas.
  - Has high self-esteem.
- Groupthink is marked by these symptoms:
  - Pressure toward conformity.
  - An appearance of unanimous agreement.
  - An illusion of invulnerability.
  - A sense of moral superiority.
  - Underestimation of opponents.
- Groups tend to focus more on information held in common by all members than on unique information each person has.

- The risky shift is the tendency for groups to take greater risks than the same individuals (on average) would have decided to take individually.
- The group polarization effect is defined as a shift toward a more extreme position resulting from group discussion.

Power and Leadership

- Large groups typically have a hierarchy of power.
- Successful leaders are humble and extremely persistent.
- People who are perceived as good leaders have integrity, decisiveness, competence, and vision.
- Power refers to one person's control over another person's outcomes and behavior.
- Power has five crucial effects on the powerful: it feels good, it alters attention to rewards and punishments, it changes the relationships between people, it makes people rely more on automatic processing, and it removes inhibitions against taking action.
- People with less power are especially prone to fostering peace and harmony. They adapt to the expectations of high-power people, even without realizing it.
- Legitimizing myths purport to explain why those in power deserve to be in power.

What Makes Us Human? Putting the Cultural Animal in Perspective

- Submerging the individual in the group often leads to bad outcomes.
- Humans have gradually developed means of transferring power without violence.
- Restricting power has been one of the great achievements of human culture.

key terms

altruistic punishment 503
bad apple effect 503
brainstorming 506
commons dilemma 505
deindividuation 498

dominant response 500
evaluation apprehension 500
group 494
group polarization effect 511
groupthink 509

legitimizing myths 522
narcissists 501
power 517
risky shift 511
self-censorship 510

social facilitation theory 500
social loafing (free rider problem) 501
transactive memory 509

quiz yourself ANSWERS

1. What Groups Are and Do p.497
   answers: 1.c 2.c 3.b 4.d
2. Groups, Roles, and Selves p.499
   answers: 1.b 2.c 3.a 4.a
3. Group Action p.506
   answers: 1.c 2.a 3.d 4.a

4. How Groups Think p.512
   answers: 1.c 2.c 3.b 4.a
5. Power and Leadership p.523
   answers: 1.b 2.c 3.c 4.a

A–B problem the problem of inconsistency between attitudes (A) and behaviors (B)

ABC triad Affect (how people feel inside), Behavior (what people do), Cognition (what people think about)

accessibility how easily something comes to mind

actor/observer bias the tendency for actors to make external attributions and observers to make internal attributions

advertisement wear-out inattention and irritation that occurs after an audience has encountered the same advertisement too many times

affect the automatic response that something is good (positive affect) or bad (negative affect)

affect-as-information hypothesis the idea that people judge something as good or bad by asking themselves "How do I feel about it?"

affect balance the frequency of positive emotions minus the frequency of negative emotions

affective commitment an employee's emotional attachment to the organization that makes the employee want to stay in the organization

affective forecasting the ability to predict one's emotional reactions to future events

agent self (executive function) the part of the self involved in control, including both control over other people and self-control

aggression any behavior intended to harm another person who is motivated to avoid the harm

altruistic helping when a helper seeks to increase another's welfare and expects nothing in return

altruistic punishment the finding that people will sometimes sacrifice their own gain for the betterment of all, by punishing people who cheat the system

ambient environment sensory surroundings, including temperature, odor, and sound

anchoring and adjustment the tendency to judge the frequency or likelihood of an event by using a starting point (called an anchor) and then making adjustments up or down.

anger an emotional response to a real or imagined threat or provocation

anthropology the study of human culture—the shared values, beliefs, and practices of a group of people

antisocial behavior behavior that either damages interpersonal relationships or is culturally undesirable

applied research research that focuses on solving particular practical problems

appraisal motive the simple desire to learn the truth about oneself, whatever it is

appraisals how we think about a situation or event

arousal a physiological reaction, including faster heartbeat and faster or heavier breathing, linked to most conscious emotions

assumptive worlds the view that people live in social worlds based on certain beliefs (assumptions) about reality

attachment theory a theory that classifies people into four attachment styles (secure, preoccupied, dismissing avoidant, and fearful avoidant) based on two dimensions (anxiety and avoidance)

attitude polarization the finding that people's attitudes become more extreme as they reflect on them

attitudes global evaluations toward some object or issue

attitudes at work satisfaction with the work itself, pay and benefits, supervision, co-workers, promotion opportunities, working conditions, and job security

attraction anything that draws two or more people together, making them want to be together and possibly to form a lasting relationship

attribution cognitive process of assigning meaning to a symptom or behavior

attributions the causal explanations people give for their own and others' behaviors, and for events in general

audience inhibition failure to help in front of others for fear of feeling like a fool if one's offer of help is rejected

authoritarian personality a pattern of cross-situational attitudes and behaviors that reflects conventional values, respect for authority figures, and a desire to punish others who defy authority

autokinetic effect illusion, caused by very slight movements of the eye, that a stationary point of light in a dark room is moving

automatic affect a quick response of liking or disliking toward something

automatic attitudes very fast evaluative, "gut-level" responses that people don't think a great deal about

automatic egotism response by the automatic system that "everything good is me, and everything bad is not me"

automatic system the part of the mind outside of consciousness that performs simple operations

availability heuristic the tendency to judge the frequency or likelihood of an event by the ease with which relevant instances come to mind

aversive racism simultaneously holding egalitarian values and negative feelings toward people of other races

bad apple effect the idea that one person who breaks the rules can inspire other people to break the rules also

bait-and-switch influence technique based on commitment, in which one draws people in with an attractive offer that is unavailable and then switches them to a less attractive offer that is available

base rate fallacy the tendency to ignore or underuse base rate information and instead to be influenced by the distinctive features of the case being judged

basic research research that focuses on a general understanding of basic principles that can be applied to many different problems

behavioral intentions an individual's plans to perform the behavior in question

behaviorism theoretical approach that seeks to explain behavior in terms of learning principles, without reference to inner states, thoughts, or feelings

belief in a just world the assumption that life is essentially fair, that people generally get what they deserve and deserve what they get

belief perseverance the finding that once beliefs form, they are resistant to change, even if the information on which they are based is discredited

beliefs pieces of information about something; facts or opinions

between-subjects design participants are exposed to only one level of the independent variable

biological psychology (physiological psychology, neuroscience) the study of what happens in the brain, nervous system, and other aspects of the body

biopsychosocial approach acknowledging that our health has biological, psychological, and social determinants

blank lineup a lineup in which all the lineup members are known to be innocent of the crime

brainstorming a form of creative thinking in groups, using a procedure in which all group members are encouraged to generate as many ideas as possible while interacting and stimulating each other

brand loyalty the degree to which a customer holds a positive attitude toward a brand, has a commitment to it, and intends to continue purchasing it

broaden-and-build theory the proposition that positive emotions expand an individual's attention and mind-set and promote increasing one's resources

bullying persistent aggression by a perpetrator against a victim for the purpose of establishing a power relationship over the victim

bystander effect the finding that people are less likely to offer help when they are in a group than when they are alone

can-do factors the maximum performance an employee can exhibit

capacity for change the active phase of self-regulation; willpower

capacity to delay gratification the ability to make immediate sacrifices for later rewards

categorization the natural tendency of humans to sort objects into groups

catharsis theory the proposition that expressing negative emotions produces a healthy release of those emotions and is therefore good for the psyche

central route (systematic processing) the route to persuasion that involves careful and thoughtful consideration of the content of the message (conscious processing)

certainty effect in decision making, the greater weight given to definite outcomes than to probabilities

challenge for cause a request made by an attorney that a potential juror be removed from the jury panel because he or she is clearly biased and will be unable to hear the case fairly

change of venue moving a trial to a new location where there has been less pretrial publicity

classical conditioning a type of learning in which, through repeated pairings, a neutral stimulus comes to evoke a conditioned response

clinical psychology branch of psychology that focuses on behavior disorders and other forms of mental illness, and how to treat them

cognitive appraisal model Lazarus's theory of how thinking plays a strong role in stress

cognitive control the sense people have about the predictability or controllability of their situation

cognitive coping the idea that beliefs play a central role in helping people cope with and recover from misfortunes

cognitive dissonance the uncomfortable feeling people experience when they have two thoughts or cognitions conflict with one another

cognitive dissonance theory the theory that inconsistencies produce psychological discomfort, leading people to rationalize their behavior or change their attitudes

cognitive miser a term used to describe people's reluctance to do much extra thinking

cognitive psychology the study of thought processes, such as how memory works and what people notice

commitment a conscious decision that remains constant

commons dilemma the tendency for shared or jointly owned resources to be squandered and not used in an optimal or advantageous fashion

communal relationships relationships based on mutual love and concern, without expectation of repayment

companionate love (affectionate love) mutual understanding and caring to make the relationship succeed

competition situation in which people can attain their goals only if others do not

conditioned response a response that, through repeated pairings, is evoked by a formerly neutral stimulus

conditioned stimulus a neutral stimulus that, through repeated pairings with an unconditioned stimulus, comes to evoke a conditioned response

confederate a research assistant pretending to be another participant in a study

confirmation bias the tendency to notice and search for information that confirms one's beliefs and to ignore information that disconfirms one's beliefs

confirmation bias the tendency to look for information that supports our views

conformity going along with the crowd, that is, saying or doing whatever other people are doing

confounding occurs when two the effects of variables cannot be separated

conscious emotion a powerful and clearly unified feeling state, such as anger or joy

consent form a document that participants receive before a study begins; the form contains enough information about the study procedures, including any potential harm they (or others) might experience, so participants can decide if they want to participate

consistency motive a desire to get feedback that confirms what the person already believes about himself or herself

conspicuous consumption the purchase and prominent display of luxury goods to provide evidence of a consumer's ability to afford them

construct validity of the cause extent to which the independent variable is a valid representation of the theoretical stimulus

construct validity of the effect extent to which the dependent variable is a valid representation of the theoretical response

contact hypothesis the idea that regular interaction between members of different groups reduces prejudice, providing that it occurs under favorable conditions

continuance commitment commitment that results when an employee remains with a company because of the high cost of losing organizational membership including monetary and social costs

continuance delaying a trial until the level of media attention to the crime has decreased in order to reduce the prejudicial effects of pretrial publicity

convert communicators people perceived as credible sources because they are arguing against their own previously held attitudes and behaviors

Coolidge effect the sexually arousing power of a new partner (greater than the appeal of a familiar partner)

cooperation working together with someone for mutual or reciprocal benefit

coping individual efforts made to manage distressing problems and emotions that affect the physical and psychological outcomes of stress

correct rejection when a witness correctly states that the person who committed the crime is not present in a lineup

correlation the relationship or association between two variables

correlation coefficient (r) the statistical relationship or association between two variables

correlational approach a nonexperimental method in which the researcher merely observes whether variables are associated or related

counterfactual thinking imagining alternatives to past or present events or circumstances

counterproductive behaviors any intentional behavior on the part of an organizational member viewed by the organization as contrary to its legitimate interests

counterregulation the "what the heck" effect that occurs when people indulge in a behavior they are trying to regulate after an initial regulation failure

crowding the subjective and unpleasant feeling that there are too many people in a given area

cultural animal theory the view that evolution shaped the human psyche so as to enable humans to create and take part in culture

culture an information-based system that includes shared ideas and common ways of doing things

culture of honor a society that places high value on individual respect, strength, and virtue, and accepts and justifies violent action in response to threats to one's honor

cyberbullying the use of the Internet (e.g., e-mail, social network sites, blogs) to bully others

dark triad of personality consists of narcissism, psychopathy, and Machiavellianism

death qualification the special jury selection process that occurs in capital cases with the purpose of excluding jurors who would not be able to weigh the evidence fairly because of their death penalty attitudes

debiasing reducing errors and biases by getting people to use deliberate processing rather than automatic processing

debriefing an oral or written statement participants receive at the end of a psychological study; it serves two main purposes: (1) to fully inform participants about the study and answer any questions they have, and (2) to reduce or eliminate any stress or harm the participant experienced by being in the study

deception studies research studies that withhold information from participants or intentionally mislead them about the purpose of the study

decision fatigue a state of depleted willpower caused by making decisions, which can affect subsequent decisions by causing people to fail to think and choose carefully

deindividuation a sense of anonymity and loss of individuality, as in a large group, making people especially likely to engage in antisocial behaviors such as theft

deliberate attitudes reflective responses that people think more carefully about

deliberate system the part of the mind that performs complex operations

demand characteristics features of an experiment that communicate to the participant the experimenter's hypothesis

density the number of people divided by the area of the space they share

dependent variable the variable in a study that represents the result of the events and processes

descriptive norms norms that specify what most people do

developmental psychology the study of how people change across their lives, from conception and birth to old age and death

diffusion of responsibility the reduction in feeling responsible that occurs when others are present

direct aggression any behavior that intentionally harms another person who is physically present

discontinuity effect the finding that groups are more extreme, and often more hostile, than individuals

discrimination unequal treatment of different people based on the groups or categories to which they belong

disgust a strong negative feeling of repugnance and revulsion

dismissing avoidant attachment style of attachment in which people are low on anxiety but high on avoidance; they tend to view partners as unreliable, unavailable, and uncaring

displaced aggression any behavior that intentionally harms a substitute target rather than the provocateur

disrupt-then-reframe technique influence technique in which one disrupts critical thinking by introducing an unexpected element, then reframes the message in a positive light

distress-maintaining style of attribution tendency of unhappy couples to attribute their partner's good acts to external factors and bad acts to internal factors

domestic violence (also called **family violence** or **intimate-partner violence**) physically harmful actions that occur within the home or family, between people who have a close relationship with each other

dominant response a behavior that takes very little effort or thought and is frequently the default or habitual response to a specific situation

door-in-the-face technique influence technique based on reciprocity, in which one starts with an inflated request and then retreats to a smaller request that appears to be a concession

double standard condemning women more than men for the same sexual behavior (e.g., premarital sex)

double-blind testing a lineup administration in which neither the police officer nor the witness knows which lineup member is the suspect

downward comparison the act of comparing oneself to people who are worse off

downward counterfactuals imagining alternatives that are worse than actuality

downward social comparison comparing yourself to people worse off than you

dual attitudes different evaluations of the same attitude object held by the same person (perhaps one deliberate, the other automatic)

duplex mind the idea that the mind has two different processing systems (deliberate and automatic)

economics the study of the production, distribution, and consumption of goods and services, and the study of money

effort justification the finding that when people suffer or work hard or make sacrifices, they will try to convince themselves that it is worthwhile

egoistic helping when a helper seeks to increase his or her own welfare by helping another

elaboration likelihood model (ELM) theory that posits two routes to persuasion, via either conscious or automatic processing

emodiversity degree to which a person experiences the variety and relative abundance of human emotions

emotion a conscious evaluative reaction that is clearly linked to some event

emotional intelligence the ability to perceive, access and generate, understand, and reflectively regulate emotions

empathy reacting to another person's emotional state by experiencing the same emotional state

empathy–altruism hypothesis the idea that empathy motivates people to reduce other people's distress, as by helping or comforting

endowment effect the finding that items gain in value to the person who owns them

entity theorists those who believe that traits are fixed, stable things (entities) and thus people should not be expected to change

equality the idea that everyone gets the same amount, regardless of what he or she contributes

equity the idea that each person receives benefits in proportion to what he or she contributes

eros in Freudian theory, the constructive, life-giving instinct

erotic plasticity the degree to which the sex drive can be shaped and altered by social, cultural, and situational forces

error management theory the idea that both men and women seek to minimize the most costly type of error, but that men's and women's goals, and hence worst errors, differ

estimator variables characteristics of the witness, the crime, and the witness's testimony that are not under the control of the justice system but that may provide information about the likely accuracy of an eyewitness identification

ethnographic a research method that attempts to provide a close understanding of people and cultures

evaluation apprehension concern about how others are judging you and/or your performance

evolutionary theory theory of sexuality asserting that the sex drive has been shaped by natural selection and that its forms thus tend to be innate

exchange relationships relationships based on reciprocity and fairness, in which people expect something in return

excitation transfer the idea that arousal from one event can transfer to a later event

experiment a study in which the researcher manipulates an independent variable and randomly assigns people to groups (levels of the independent variable)

experimental realism the extent to which study participants get so caught up in the procedures that they forget they are in an experiment

expertise how much a source knows

external validity the extent to which the findings from a study can be generalized to other people, other settings, and other time periods

extradyadic sex having sex with someone other than one's regular relationship partner

extrinsic motivation performing an activity because of something that results from it

facial feedback hypothesis the idea that feedback from the face muscles evokes or magnifies emotions

false (mistaken) identification when a witness incorrectly identifies an innocent suspect as the person who committed a crime

false consensus effect the tendency to overestimate the number of other people who share one's opinions, attitudes, values, and beliefs

false uniqueness effect the tendency to underestimate the number of other people who share one's most prized characteristics and abilities

fast-approaching-deadline technique influence technique based on scarcity, in which one tells people an item or a price is only available for a limited time

fearful avoidant attachment style of attachment in which people have both high anxiety and high avoidance; they have low opinions of themselves and keep others from getting close

field experiment an experiment conducted in a real-world setting

fight or flight syndrome a response to stress that involves aggressing against others or running away

fight-or-flight response Cannon's theory of stress explaining physiological responses in our body

fillers lineup members other than the suspect who are known to be innocent of the crime

filter bubbles are algorithms used on the Internet to selectively guess what information a user would like to see based on information available about that use (e.g., previous web pages viewed, click behavior)

first instinct fallacy the false belief that it is better not to change one's first answer on a test even if one starts to think that a different answer is correct

foot-in-the-door technique influence technique based on commitment, in which one starts with a small request in order to gain eventual compliance with a larger request

forgiveness ceasing to feel angry toward or seek retribution against someone who has wronged you

framing whether messages stress potential gains (positively framed) or potential losses (negatively framed)

Freudian psychoanalysis theoretical approach that seeks to explain behavior by looking at the deep unconscious forces inside the person

frustration blockage of or interference with a personal goal

frustration–aggression hypothesis proposal that "the occurrence of aggressive behavior always presupposes the existence of frustration," and "the existence of frustration always leads to some form of aggression"

fundamental attribution error (correspondence bias) the tendency for observers to attribute other people's behavior to internal or dispositional causes and to downplay situational causes

gain-framed appeal focuses on how doing something will add to your health

gambler's fallacy the tendency to believe that a particular chance event is affected by previous events and that chance events will "even out" in the short run

general adaptation syndrome Selye's stage theory of how we respond to all stressors in a similar way

generalized other a combination of other people's views that tells you who and what you are

geo-targeting the strategy of exposing only individuals within a specific geographic region to a particular ad campaign

goal an idea of some desired future state

goal shielding occurs when the activation of a focal goal the person is working on inhibits the accessibility of alternative goals

gratitude a positive emotion that results from the perception that one has benefited from the costly, intentional, voluntary action of another person

group a collection of at least two people who are doing or being something together

group norms the beliefs or behaviors that a group of people accepts as normal

group polarization effect a shift toward a more extreme position resulting from group discussion

groupthink the tendency of group members to think alike, especially when doing so leads to bad decisions

guilt an unpleasant moral emotion associated with a specific instance in which one has acted badly or wrongly

habit an acquired behavior that, if followed regularly, will become almost automatic

halo effect the assumption that because people have one desirable trait (e.g., attractiveness), they also possess many other desirable traits (e.g., intelligence)

health a state of complete physical, mental, and social well-being

health belief model theory that posits that beliefs about the effectiveness, ease, and consequences of doing (or not doing) a certain behavior determine whether we do (or do not do) that behavior

health psychology an interdisciplinary subspecialty of psychology dedicated to promoting and maintaining health and preventing and treating illness

healthy behaviors any specific behaviors that maintain and enhance health

hedonic treadmill a theory proposing that people stay at about the same level of happiness regardless of what happens to them

heuristic/systematic model theory that posits two routes to persuasion, via either conscious or automatic processing

heuristics mental shortcuts that provide quick estimates about the likelihood of uncertain events

history the study of past events

hit (correct identification) when a witness accurately identifies the person who committed a crime from a lineup

homeostasis the ideal level of bodily functions

homophobia is an excessive fear of homosexuals or homosexual behavior.

honor killing killing another individual who has brought "dishonor" to the family (e.g., a woman who has committed adultery)

hostile attribution bias the tendency to perceive ambiguous actions by others as aggressive

hostile expectation bias the tendency to assume that people will react to potential conflicts with aggression

hostile perception bias the tendency to perceive social interactions in general as being aggressive

hostile work environment a form of sexual harassment when an employee experiences workplace harassment such as provocative pictures that make the environment an offensive place to work

hot hand the tendency for gamblers who get lucky to think they have a "hot" hand and their luck will continue

humiliation a state of disgrace or loss of self-respect (or of respect from others)

hypochondriacs people who are constantly worried about their health

hypocrisy induction a technique for effecting behavior change by confronting people with the inconsistency between their attitudes and their behavior

hypothesis an idea about the possible nature of reality; a prediction tested in an experiment

identity theft consists of stealing someone's personal information (e.g., Social Security number, bank account, credit card number) and using it without their permission, usually to obtain money or goods

illusion of control the false belief that one can influence certain events, especially random or chance ones

illusory correlation the tendency to overestimate the link between variables that are related only slightly or not at all

implicit personality theories a set of beliefs, developed through experience, about how demographic characteristics and attitudes are interrelated

incorrect rejection when a witness fails to identify the suspect in a target-present lineup

incremental theorists those who believe that traits are subject to change and improvement

independent self-construal a self-concept that emphasizes what makes the self different and sets it apart from others

independent variable the variable manipulated by the researcher that is assumed to lead to changes in the dependent variable

indirect aggression any behavior that intentionally harms another person who is physically absent

individual good–collective bad trap when a destructive behavior by one person is of little consequence but has disastrous results when repeated by many (e.g., overgrazing)

informational influence going along with the crowd because you think the crowd knows more than you do

ingratiation what people actively do to try to make someone like them

ingroup favoritism preferential treatment of, or more favorable attitudes toward, people in one's own group

ingroup members people who belong to the same group or category as we do

injunctive norms norms that specify what most others approve or disapprove of

instinct an innate (inborn, biologically programmed) tendency to seek a particular goal, such as food, water, or sex

Institutional Review Board (IRB) is a committee that makes sure that a research study conducted in university settings is ethical. The board must contain at least one scientist, one nonscientist, and one person not affiliated with the university

interdependent self-construal a self-concept that emphasizes what connects the self to other people and groups

internal validity the extent to which changes in the independent variable caused changes in the dependent variable

interpersonal self (public self) the image of the self that is conveyed to others

intervention any program or message providing information or structure to change a behavior

intimacy a feeling of closeness, mutual understanding, and mutual concern for each other's welfare and happiness

intrinsic motivation wanting to perform an activity for its own sake

introspection the process by which a person examines the contents of his or her mind and mental states

inverted (upside-down) U-shaped relationship a relationship that looks like an upside-down U when plotted

investment model theory that uses three factors—satisfaction, alternatives, and investments—to explain why people stay with their long-term relationship partners

James–Lange theory of emotion the proposition that the bodily processes of emotion come first and the mind's perception o these bodily reactions then creates the subjective feeling of emotion

jigsaw classroom a cooperative learning technique for reducing feelings of prejudice by having students interact and cooperate to learn material

job analysis the identification of the critical elements of a job; it documents the tasks, working conditions, and human attributes needed to do the job

job withdrawal behaviors employees use to avoid their job

kin selection the evolutionary tendency to help people who have our genes

knowledge structures organized packets of information that are stored in memory

labeling technique influence technique based on consistency, in which one assigns a label to an individual and then requests a favor that is consistent with the label

lateral cycling selling or giving a previously purchased product to someone else to use for its intended purpose

leadership a social influence process in which a person steers members of the group toward a goal

learned helplessness belief that one's actions will not bring about desired outcomes, leading one to give up and quit trying

legitimizing myths explanations used to justify why people in power deserve to be in power

life satisfaction an evaluation of how one's life is generally and how it compares to some standard

limited-number technique influence technique based on scarcity, in which one tells people that an item is in short supply

lineup a police procedure in which a witness to the crime is shown a suspect (or a picture of the suspect) along with several other people (or photos of people) to see if the witness recognizes one of the lineup members as the person who committed the crime

loneliness the painful feeling of wanting more human contact or connection than you have

looking-glass self the idea that people learn about themselves by imagining how they appear to others

loss-framed appeal focuses on how not doing something will subtract from your health

low-ball technique influence technique based on commitment, in which one first gets a person to comply with a seemingly low-cost request and only later reveals hidden additional costs

lying deliberately making a false statement, usually to mislead someone.

margin of error a statistic measure of the amount of random sampling error in a survey's results—for example, a 3% margin of error means that the survey's result could be 3% lower or 3% higher than the average response—the larger the sample is, the smaller the margin of error is

match-to-culprit description choosing lineup fillers who share features of the culprit mentioned in the witness's description of the culprit but who vary on other features

match-to-suspect choosing lineup fillers who have features that are similar to the features of the suspect the police have in custody

matching hypothesis the proposition that people tend to pair up with others who are equally attractive

mentoring training that occurs when a current and often long-term employee (the mentor) is paired with a new employee

mere exposure effect the tendency for people to come to like things simply because they see or encounter them repeatedly

meta-analysis a quantitative literature review that combines the statistical results (e.g., correlation coefficients) from all studies conducted on a topic

meta-cognition reflecting on one's own thought processes

minimal group effect the finding that people show favoritism toward ingroup members even when group membership is randomly determined

missing hero trap when information of actual or potential disaster (e.g., toxic spill) is withheld from those affected by it

modeling observing and copying or imitating the behavior of others

monitoring keeping track of behaviors or responses to be regulated

mood a feeling state that is not clearly linked to some event

moral inclusion involves treating all people as ingroup members

moral intuitions judgments (about whether an action is right or wrong) that occur automatically and rely on emotional feelings

moral reasoning using logical deductions to make moral judgments based on abstract principles of right and wrong

mundane realism refers to whether the setting of an experiment physically resembles the real world

mutation a new gene or combination of genes

narcissism excessive self-love and a selfish orientation

narcissists individuals who regard themselves as better than others and are constantly trying to win the admiration of others

natural selection the process whereby those members of a species that survive and reproduce most effectively are the ones that pass along their genes to future generations

nature the physical world around us, including its laws and processes

need for cognition a tendency to engage in and enjoy effortful thinking, analysis, and mental problem solving

need to belong the desire to form and maintain close, lasting relationships with other individuals

negative attitude change (boomerang effect) doing exactly the opposite of what one is being persuaded to do

netnography ethnographic research applied to internet and social media communications to better understand the group and individual members

sentiment analysis often using computers and analytical techniques on words in postings, this type of analysis provides companies with information about how people feel about their products or services

neutral stimulus a stimulus (e.g., Pavlov's bell) that initially evokes no response

noise annoying, unwanted sound

non-zero-sum game an interaction in which both participants can win (or lose)

normative commitment a commitment to the organization based on feelings of obligation

normative influence going along with the crowd in order to be liked and accepted

norms standards established by society to tell its members what types of behavior are typical or expected

obedience following orders from an authority figure

Occupational Information Network, or O*NET a comprehensive, detailed, and flexible set of job descriptors that can be used to find information to include in a job description; salary and occupational outlook are also provided

omission bias the tendency to take whatever course of action does not require you to do anything (also called the default option)

one-person trap when the consequences of a destructive behavior affect only the individual (e.g., overeating)

one-shot illusory correlation an illusory correlation that occurs after exposure to only one unusual behavior performed by only one member of an unfamiliar group

online virtual memories online versions of cemeteries and other places to remember people

operant conditioning (instrumental conditioning) a type of learning in which people are more likely to repeat behaviors that have been rewarded and less likely to repeat behaviors that have been punished

operational definitions observable operations, procedures, and measurements that are based on the independent and dependent variables

organizational citizenship behaviors (OCBs) behaviors employees engage in that go beyond what is expected by the leaders of the organization.

organizational culture the cognitive component that includes the shared assumptions and beliefs of the organization

organizational justice employees' perceptions of fairness of treatment in the workplace

organizational socialization the process by which organizational members become a part of, or are absorbed into, the culture of the organization

organizational withdrawal type of withdrawal comprised of work and job withdrawal

ostracism being excluded, rejected, and ignored by others

outgroup homogeneity bias the assumption that outgroup members are more similar to one another than ingroup members are to one another

outgroup members people who belong to a different group or category than we do

overbenefited getting more than you deserve

overjustification effect the tendency for intrinsic motivation to diminish for activities that have become associated with rewards

own-race bias the finding that witnesses are more accurate in identifying members of their own race than members of another race

panic button effect a reduction in stress or suffering due to a belief that one has the option of escaping or controlling the situation, even if one doesn't exercise it

passion an emotional state characterized by high bodily arousal, such as increased heart rate and blood pressure

passionate love (romantic love) strong feelings of longing, desire, and excitement toward a special person

paternity uncertainty the fact that a man cannot be sure that the children born to his female partner are his

perceived behavioral control an individual's beliefs about whether he or she can actually perform the behavior in question

peremptory challenge a method of removing a potential juror from a jury panel in which the attorney need not specify the reason

performance reviews evaluations of employees' job performance usually conducted by their direct supervisor on an annual or semi-annual basis

peripheral route (heuristic processing) the route to persuasion that involves some simple cue, such as attractiveness of the source (automatic processing)

personal relevance degree to which people expect an issue to have significant consequences for their own lives

personal space an area with invisible boundaries that surrounds us

personality psychology the branch of psychology that focuses on important differences between individuals

personalization a way of marking our territory with improvements or decorations that are unique reflections of our personal identity

persuasion an attempt to change a person's attitude

phenomenal self (working self-concept) the image of self that is currently active in the person's thoughts

philosophy "love of wisdom"; the pursuit of knowledge about fundamental matters such as life, death, meaning, reality, and truth

pique technique influence technique in which one captures people's attention, as by making a novel request.

plagiarize to claim the ideas or words of another person as one's own without crediting that person

planning fallacy the tendency for plans to be overly optimistic because the planner fails to allow for unexpected problems

pluralistic ignorance looking to others for cues about how to behave, while they are looking to you; collective misinterpretation

political science the study of political organizations and institutions, especially governments

polychronic activity engaging in more than one activity or behavior at a time

population the total number of people under consideration

post-decision dissonance cognitive dissonance experienced after making a difficult choice, typically reduced by increasing the attractiveness of the chosen alternative and decreasing the attractiveness of rejected alternatives

post-traumatic stress disorder post-disaster behavioral symptoms including sleep disorders, social withdrawal, uncontrollable thoughts about the event, and a desire to avoid thoughts of the event

power one person's control over another person, including what happens to that person

praxis practical ways of doing things

prejudice a negative feeling toward an individual based solely on his or her membership in a particular group

preoccupied (anxious/ambivalent) attachment style of attachment in which people are low on avoidance but high on anxiety; they want and enjoy closeness but worry that their relationship partners will abandon them

primary territory area, such as a bedroom, that is highly personalized and considered off limits to those not invited to enter

priming activating an idea in someone's mind so that related ideas are more accessible

prisoner's dilemma a game that forces people to choose between cooperation and competition

private acceptance a genuine inner belief that others are right

private self-awareness looking inward on the private aspects of the self, including emotions, thoughts, desires, and traits

proactive aggression (also called **instrumental aggression**) "cold," premeditated, calculated harmful behavior that is a means to some practical or material end

product misuse using a product for an unintended purpose or without regard to instructions or usage suggestions

prompts cues that convey a message and remind people to do something

propinquity being near someone on a regular basis

prosocial behavior doing something that is good for other people or for society as a whole

psyche a broader term for mind, encompassing emotions, desires, perceptions, and all other psychological processes

psychological reactance the unpleasant emotional response people experience when someone is trying to restrict their freedom to engage in a desired behavior

psychology the study of human behavior

public compliance outwardly going along with the group but maintaining a private, inner belief that the group is probably wrong

public self-awareness looking outward on the public aspects of the self that others can see and evaluate

public self-consciousness thinking about how others perceive you

public territory area that is open to anyone who is not specifically excluded

quasi-experiment a type of study in which the researcher can manipulate an independent variable but cannot random assign participants to conditions

quid pro quo a form of sexual harassment that means "in exchange for this, I'll give you that"

racism prejudiced attitudes toward a particular race

random assignment procedure whereby each study participant has an equal chance of being in each treatment group

random sample a sample wherein each person in the population has an equal chance of being selected

reactance an unpleasant emotional response that people often experience when someone is trying to restrict their freedom

reactance theory the idea that people are distressed by loss of freedom or options and seek to reclaim or reassert them

reactive aggression (also called **hostile aggression**) "hot," impulsive, angry behavior motivated by a desire to harm someone

realistic conflict theory the idea that competition over scarce resources leads to intergroup hostility and conflict

receptivity whether you "get" (pay attention to, understand) the message

reciprocity the obligation to return in kind what another has done for us

recruitment the process organizations use to identify qualified individuals for a job

regret involves feeling sorry for one's misfortunes, limitations, losses, transgressions, shortcomings, or mistakes

reinforcement theory the proposition that people and animals will perform behaviors that have been rewarded more than they will perform other behaviors

rejection (social exclusion) being prevented by others from forming or keeping a social bond with them; the opposite of acceptance

rejection sensitivity a tendency to expect rejection from others and to become hypersensitive to possible rejection

relational aggression (also called **social aggression**) behavior that involves intentionally harming another person's social relationships, feelings of acceptance, or inclusion within a group

relationship-enhancing style of attribution tendency of happy couples to attribute their partner's good acts to internal factors and bad acts to external factors

reliability consistency of measurement

repetition with variation repeating the same information, but in a varied format

replication repeating a study to see if the effect is reliable

representativeness heuristic the tendency to judge the frequency or likelihood of an event by the extent to which it resembles the typical case

reproduction producing babies that survive long enough to also reproduce

reverse double standard condemning men more than women for the same sexual behavior (e.g., premarital sex)

risk-as-feelings hypothesis the idea that people rely on emotional processes to evaluate risk, with the result that their judgments may be biased by emotional factors

risk aversion in decision making, the greater weight given to possible losses than possible gains

risky shift a tendency for groups to take greater risks than the same individuals (on average) would have decided to take individually

rule of law when members of a society (including its most powerful leaders) respect and follow its rules

running amok according to Malaysian culture, refers to behavior of a young man who becomes "uncontrollably" violent after receiving a blow to his ego

salience being obvious or standing out

scapegoat theory the idea that blaming problems and misfortunes on outgroups contributes to negative attitudes toward these outgroups

Schachter–Singer theory of emotion the idea that emotion has two components: a bodily state of arousal and a cognitive label that specifies the emotion

schemas knowledge structures that represent substantial information about a concept, its attributes, and its relationships to other concepts

scripts knowledge structures that define situations and guide behavior

secondary territory area, such as the desk you usually sit at, that you don't really own but nonetheless consider to be "yours"

secure attachment style of attachment in which people are low on anxiety and low on avoidance; they trust their partners, share their feelings, provide and receive support and comfort, and enjoy their relationships

selective exposure refers to the tendency of individuals to select information that supports their preexisting views and avoid information that contradicts their preexisting views

self-acceptance regarding yourself as being a reasonably good person as you are

self-awareness attention directed at the self

self-censorship choosing not to express doubts or other information that goes against a group's plans and views

self-deception strategies mental tricks people use to help them believe things that are false

self-defeating behavior any action by which people bring failure, suffering, or misfortune on themselves

self-defeating prophecy a prediction that ensures, by the behavior it generates, that it will not come true

self-determination theory the theory that people need to feel at least some degree of autonomy and internal motivation

self-enhancement motive the desire to learn favorable or flattering things about the self

self-esteem how favorably someone evaluates himself or herself

self-fulfilling prophecy a prediction that ensures, by the behavior it generates, that it will come true

self-handicapping putting obstacles in the way of one's own performance so that anticipated or possible failure can be blamed on the obstacle instead of on lack of ability

self-knowledge (self-concept) a set of beliefs about oneself

self-monitoring the ability to change one's behavior for different situations

self-perception theory the theory that people observe their own behavior to infer what they are thinking and how they are feeling

self-presentation any behavior that seeks to convey some image of self or some information about the self to other people

self-protection trying to avoid loss of esteem

self-reference effect the finding that information bearing on the self is processed more thoroughly and more deeply, and hence remembered better, than other information

self-regulation the process people use to control and change their thoughts, feelings, and behaviors

self-serving bias the tendency to take credit for success but deny blame for failure; or internal attributions for success, external attributions for failure

sensitivity about being the target of a threatening upward comparison interpersonal concern about the consequences of outperforming others

sensory overload when the amount of information to be processed exceeds the individual's capacity to sort out what is relevant from what is not

sequential lineup a lineup presentation procedure in which a witness views each lineup member in turn, making a yes/no decision about each lineup member before proceeding to the next member

serotonin the "feel good" neurotransmitter, low levels of which have been linked to aggression and violence in both animals and humans

sex guilt feeling guilty about sexual thoughts, acts, or fantasies

shame a moral emotion that, like guilt, involves feeling bad but, unlike guilt, spreads to the whole person

shrinkage the loss of money or Inventory from shoplifting and/or employee theft

simulation heuristic the tendency to judge the frequency or likelihood of an event by the ease with which you can imagine (or mentally simulate) it

simultaneous lineup the traditional lineup presentation procedure in which witnesses view all lineup members at the same time

sleeper effect the finding that, over time, people separate the message from the messenger

social acceptance a situation in which other people have come to like you, respect you, approve of you, and include you in their groups and relationships

social allergy effect the idea that a partner's annoying habits become more annoying over time

social animals animals that seek connections to others and prefer to live, work, and play with other members of their species

social categorization the process of sorting people into groups on the basis of characteristics they have in common (e.g., race, gender, age, religion, sexual orientation)

social cognition a movement in social psychology that began in the 1970s that focused on thoughts about people and about social relationships

social comparison examining the difference between oneself and another person

social constructionist theories theories asserting that attitudes and behaviors, including sexual desire and sexual behavior, are strongly shaped by culture and socialization

social exchange theory theory that seeks to understand social behavior by analyzing the costs and benefits of interacting with each other; it assumes that sex is a resource that women have and men want

social facilitation theory proposition that the presence of others increases the dominant response tendency

social learning (observational learning, imitation, vicarious learning) a type of learning in which people are more likely to imitate behaviors if they have seen others rewarded for performing them, and less likely to imitate behaviors if they have seen others punished for performing them

social loafing (free rider problem) the finding that people reduce effort when working in a group, compared to when working alone

social psychology the scientific study of how people affect and are affected by others

social reality beliefs held in common by several or many people; public awareness

social roles the different roles a person plays, as in a play or a movie

social support emotional, informational, or instrumental assistance from others

sociology the study of human societies and the groups that form those societies

sociometer a measure of how desirable one would be to other people

source the individual who delivers the message

stalking persisting in romantic, courtship, or other behaviors that frighten and harass the rejecter in a relationship

standards ideas (concepts) of how things might possibly be

statistical regression (regression to the mean) the statistical tendency for extreme scores or extreme behavior to be followed by others that are less extreme and closer to average

status quo bias the preference to keep things the way they are rather than change

stereotype threat the fear that one might confirm the stereotypes that others hold

stereotypes beliefs that associate groups of people with certain traits

stigma by association rejection of those who associate with stigmatized others

stigmas characteristics of individuals that are considered socially unacceptable (e.g., being overweight, mentally ill, sick, poor, or physically scarred)

stimulus sampling using more than one exemplar of a stimulus (e.g., more than one violent video game)

stress the upsetting of homeostasis

Stroop effect in the Stroop test, the finding that people have difficulty overriding the automatic tendency to read the word rather than name the ink color

Stroop test a standard measure of effortful control over responses, requiring participants to identify the color of a word (which may name a different color)

structured interview interview conducted by a trained interviewer that has standardized questions based on a job analysis, a specific question order, and a predetermined scoring or answer key

subjective norms an individual's perceptions about whether significant others think he or she should (or should not) perform the behavior in question

subtypes categories that people use for individuals who do not fit a general stereotype

superordinate goals goals that can be achieved only by cooperating and working with others

survival living longer

survivor guilt an unpleasant emotion associated with living through an experience during which other people died

system variables characteristics of a lineup administration that are under the control of the criminal justice system and that influence the accuracy of eyewitness identifications

target-absent lineup a lineup in which the person who committed the crime is not present in the lineup

target-present lineup a lineup in which the person who committed the crime is one of the lineup members

temporal discounting in decision making, the greater weight given to the present over the future

tend and befriend syndrome a response to stress that involves nurturing others and making friends

tend and befriend Taylor and colleagues' theory of how women react to stress differently than men

territoriality the tendency to stake out an area and a willingness to defend that area from intruders

testosterone the male sex hormone, high levels of which have been linked to aggression and violence in both animals and humans

tests the measurement of carefully chosen samples of behavior

thanatos in Freudian theory, the destructive, death instinct

that's-not-all technique influence technique based on reciprocity, in which one first makes an inflated request but, before the person can respond, sweetens the deal by offering a discount or bonus

theories unobservable constructs that are linked together in some logical way

theory of evolution a theory proposed by Charles Darwin to explain how change occurs in nature

theory of planned behavior theory to explain how intentions predict behaviors

theory perseverance proposes that once the mind draws a conclusion, it tends to stick with that conclusion unless there is overwhelming evidence to change it

time poverty a feeling of having less time available than is required to meet the demands of everyday living

Title VII of the Civil Rights Act of 1964 federal legislation that prohibits discrimination based on race, color, religion, sex, and national origin (Big 5)

TOTE the self-regulation feedback loop of Test, Operate, Test, Exit

tradeoff a choice in which taking or maximizing one benefit requires either accepting a cost or sacrificing another benefit

transactive memory a process by which members of a small group remember different kinds of information

transtheoretical model the stages we progress through during behavior change

trust a confidence that others will provide benefits and/or not harm you, even if they may be tempted to do otherwise

trustworthiness whether a source will honestly tell you what he or she knows

unconditioned response a naturally occurring response (e.g., salivation)

unconditioned stimulus a stimulus (e.g., meat powder) that naturally evokes a particular response (salivation)

underbenefited getting less than you deserve

unrequited love a situation in which one person loves another but the other does not return that love

unstructured interview interview conducted by an untrained interviewer that is informal and unplanned, with random questions and no scoring key

upward comparison the act of comparing oneself to people who are better off

upward counterfactuals imagining alternatives that are better than actuality

upward social comparison comparing yourself to people better than you

usage situation the context in which a product is used.

validity the accuracy of a test in measuring what it is intended to measure

venire members of the community who are called to the courthouse to form a jury pool

violence aggression that has as its goal extreme physical harm, such as injury or death

voir dire the legal proceeding in which attorneys and judges attempt to uncover bias among those people who have been called for jury duty

volunteering a planned, long-term, nonimpulsive decision to help others

weapon focus when a witness focuses on the weapon carried by a culprit, causing a decrease in accuracy for memory of the culprit's face

weapons effect the increase in aggression that occurs as a result of the mere presence of a weapon

what is beautiful is good effect the assumption that physically attractive people will be superior to others on many other traits

will-do factors the normal or typical performance by an employee

within-subjects design participants are exposed to all levels of the independent variable

work groups two or more employees who (a) exist to perform organizationally relevant tasks, (b) share one or more common goals, (c) interact socially, (d) exhibit task interdependencies, (e) maintain and manage boundaries, and (f) are embedded in an organizational context that sets boundaries, constrains the team, and influences exchanges with other units in the broader entity

work withdrawal behaviors employees use to avoid their work

workforce planning the process used by managers to determine their needs with regard to human resources including retaining their talented employees, promoting employees, as well as removing poor performers.

Yerkes–Dodson law the proposition that some arousal is better than none, but too much can hurt performance

yielding whether you "accept" (believe, and especially whether you change your attitude to agree with) the message

Zeigarnik effect a tendency to experience automatic, intrusive thoughts about a goal whose pursuit has been interrupted

zero-sum game a situation in which one person's gain is another's loss

CHAPTER 1
The Mission & the Method

1. Kelly, J. (2014). When these stuffed squirrels went on the auction block, bidders went nuts. Washington Post. Retrieved from http://www.washingtonpost.com/local/when-these-stuffed-squirrels-went-on-the-auction-block-bidders-went-nuts/2014/04/08/b792b472-be5e-11e3-b195-dd0c1174052c_story.html
2. Associated Press. (2013, February 25). Homeless man to get more than $100,000 for good deed. Retrieved from http://www.thestar.com/news/world/2013/02/25/homeless_man_to_get_more_than_100000_for_good_deed.html
3. Associated Press (2013, May 7). Airman who led sex assault unit charged in groping. Retrieved from http://bigstory.ap.org/article/airman-who-led-sex-assault-unit-charged-groping
4. Triplett, N. (1897). The dynamogenic factors in peacemaking and competition. *American Journal of Psychology, 9,* 507–533.
5. Ringelmann, M. (1913). Recherches sur les moteurs animés: Travail de l'homme. *Annales de l'Institut National Argonomique,* 2e srie, tom 12, 1–40.
6. McDougall, William (1960. Original work published 1908). *An Introduction to Social Psychology* (23rd ed.). University Paperbacks. Imprint of Methuen & Co (London) and Barnes & Noble (New York), pp. xxi–xxii (Note: Preface to 23rd edition commences p. xxi, with date of this preface [October 1936] on p. xxii.)
7. Ross, Edward A. (1974. Original work published 1908). *Social Psychology.* New York: Arno Press.
8. Allport, F. H. (1924). *Social psychology.* Boston: Houghton Mifflin Company.
9. Allport, G. W. (1954). The historical background of modern social psychology. In G. Lindzey (Ed.), *Handbook of social psychology* (Vol. 1, pp. 3–56). Cambridge, MA: Addison-Wesley.
10. Lewin, K. (1936). *Principles of topological psychology.* New York: McGraw-Hill.
11. Milgram, S. (1974). *Obedience to authority; An experimental view.* New York: Harper and Row.
12. Milgram, S. (1973, December). The perils of obedience. *Harper's,* 62–66.
13. Bargh, J. A., Chen, M., & Burrows, L. (1996). Automaticity of social behavior: Direct effects of trait construct and stereotype activation on action. *Journal of Personality and Social Psychology, 71*(2), 230–244.
14. O'Brien, E. H., Anastasio, P. A., & Bushman, B. J. (2011). Time crawls when you're not having fun: Feeling entitled makes dull tasks drag on. *Personality and Social Psychology Bulletin, 37*(10), 1287–1296.
15. George Santayana (1905) *Reason in Common Sense,* p. 284, volume 1 of *The Life of Reason* (1905–1906) at Project Gutenberg https://en.wikiquote.org/wiki/George_Santayana.
16. Stephan, C. W. & Stephan, W. G. (1985). *Two Social Psychologies: An Integrative Approach.* Homewood, IL: Dorsey.
17. Funder, D. C. (2001). Personality. *Annual Review of Psychology, 52,* 197–221.
18. Lewin, K. (1951). *Field theory in social science: Selected theoretical papers* (D. Cartwright, Ed.). New York: Harper Torchbooks. Quote on p. 169.
19. Hoff Sommers, C. (1994). *Who stole feminism? How women have betrayed women.* New York: Touchstone.
20. Rogow, A. A, Carey, G. L., & Farrell, C. (1957). The significance of aphorisms in American culture. *Sociology and Social Research, 41,* 417–420.
21. Teigen, H. (1986). Old truths or fresh insights? A study of students' evaluations of proverbs. *British Journal of Social Psychology, 25,* 43–50.
22. McLeod, J. M., & Pan, Z. (2005). Concept explication and theory construction. In S. Dunwoody, L. B. Becker, D. M. McLeod, & G. M. Kosicki (Eds.), *The evolution of key mass communication concepts* (pp. 13–76). Creskill, NJ: Hampton Press.
23. Buss, A. H. (1961). *The psychology of aggression.* New York: John Wiley.
24. Dollard, J., Doob, L., Miller, N., Mowrer, O., & Sears, R. (1939). *Frustration and aggression.* New Haven, CT: Yale University Press.
25. Harris, M. B. (1974). Mediators between frustration and aggression in a field experiment. *Journal of Experimental Social Psychology, 10*(6), 561–571.
26. Harris, M. B. (1976). Instigators and inhibitors of aggression in a field experiment. *Journal of Social Psychology, 98*(1), 27–38.
27. Cook, T. D., & Campbell, D. T. (1979). *Quasi-experimentation* (pp. 37–94). Boston: Houghton Mifflin.
28. Middlemist, R. D., Knowles, E. S., & Matter, C. F. (1976). Personal space invasions in the lavatory: Suggestive evidence for arousal. *Journal of Personality and Social Psychology, 33*(5), 541–546.
29. Orne, M. T. (1962). On the social psychology of the psychological experiment: With particular reference to demand characteristics and their implications. *American Psychologist, 17*(11), 776–783.
30. Epley, N., & Huff, C. (1998). Suspicion, affective response, and educational benefit as a result of deception in psychology research. *Personality and Social Psychology bulletin, 24,* 759–768.
31. Cook, T. D., & Campbell, D. T. (1979). *Quasi-experimentation* (pp. 37–94). Boston: Houghton Mifflin.
32. Wells, G. L., & Windschitl, P. D. (1999). Stimulus sampling and social psychological experimentation. *Personality and Social Psychology Bulletin, 25,* 1115–1125.
33. Brehm, J. W. (1966). *A theory of psychological reactance.* New York: Academic Press.
34. Ruback, R. B. & Juieng, D. (1997). Territorial defense in parking lots: Retaliation against waiting drivers. *Journal of Applied Social Psychology, 27,* 821–834.
35. Harris, M. B. (1974). Mediators between frustration and aggression in a field experiment. *Journal of Experimental Social Psychology, 10*(6), 561–571.
36. Aronson, E., & Carlsmith, J. M. (1968). Experimentation in social psychology. In G. Lindzey & E. Aronson (Eds.), *Handbook of Social Psychology* (2nd ed., Vol. 2, pp. 1–79). Reading, MA: Addison-Wesley.
37. Berkowitz, L., & Donnerstein, E. (1982). External validity is more than skin deep. *American Psychologist, 37,* 245–257.
38. Wynder, E. L., & Graham, E. A. (1950). Tobacco smoking as a possible etiological factor in bronchiogenic carcinoma. *Journal of the American Medical Association, 143,* 329–336.
39. Anderson, C. A., & Dill, K. E. (2000). Video games and aggressive thoughts, feelings, and behavior in laboratory and real life. *Journal of Personality and Social Psychology, 78*(4), 772–790.
40. Cohen, J. (1988). *Statistical power analysis for the behavioral sciences* (2nd ed.). New York: Academic Press.
41. The Onion (2014, June 24). Report: Only predictor of happy marriage is if husband ever won wife big stuffed animal at amusement park. Retrieved from: http://www.theonion.com/articles/report-only-predictor-of-happy-marriage-is-if-husb,36353/
42. Election polls—Accuracy record in presidential elections. Retrieved from http://www.gallup.com/poll/9442/election-polls-accuracy-record-presidential-elections.aspx
43. CNN Poll: Support for legal marijuana soaring (2014, January 6). Retrieved from http://politicalticker.blogs.cnn.com/2014/01/06/cnn-poll-support-for-legal-marijuana-soaring/
44. Schuman, H., & Scott, J. (1987). Problems in the use of survey questions to measure public opinion. *Science, 236*(4804), 957–959.
45. Schwarz, N. (1999). Self-reports: How the questions shape the answers. *American Psychologist, 54*(2), 93-105. doi: 10.1037/0003-066X.54.2.93
46. Kim, J., Glaser, P., & Smith, T. W. (2011). The polls—trends: Trends in surveys on surveys. *Public Opinion Quarterly, 75*(1), 165–191.
47. Koole, S. L., & Lakens, D. (2012). Rewarding replications: A sure and simple way to improve psychological science. *Perspectives in Psychological Science, 7*(6), 608–614. doi: 10.1177/1745691612462586
48. Oakes, W. (1972). External validity and the use of real people as subjects. *American Psychologist, 27,* 959–962.
49. Sears, D. O. (1986). College sophomores in the laboratory: Influences of a narrow data base on social psychology's view of human nature. *Journal of Personality and Social Psychology, 51,* 515–530.
50. Anderson, C. A., Shibuya, A., Ihori, N., Swing, E. L., Bushman, B. J., Sakamoto, A., Rothstein, H. R., Saleem, M., & Barlett, C. P. (2010). Violent video game effects on aggression, empathy, and prosocial behavior in Eastern and Western countries: A meta-analytic review. *Psychological Bulletin, 136*(2), 151–173.
51. Bond, R., & Smith, P. B (1996). *Culture and conformity: A meta-analysis of studies using Asch's (1952b 1956) line judgment task.* Psychological Bulletin, 119 (1), 111–137.

CHAPTER 2
Culture and Nature

1. Colapinto, J. (2000). *As nature made him: The boy who was raised as a girl.* New York: HarperCollins.
2. Colapinto, J. (2000). *As nature made him: The boy who was raised as a girl.* New York: HarperCollins.
3. Joiner, T. (2005). *Why people die by suicide.* Cambridge, MA: Harvard University Press.
4. de Waal, F. B. M. (2002). Evolutionary psychology: The wheat and the chaff. *Current Directions in Psychological Science, 11,* 187–191.
5. Buss, D. M. (1994). *The evolution of desire: Strategies of human mating.* New York: Basic Books.
6. Symons, D. (1979). *The evolution of human sexuality.* New York: Oxford University Press.
7. Trivers, R. (1972). Parental investment and sexual selection. In B. Campbell (Ed.), *Sexual selection and the descent of man: 1871–1971* (pp. 136–179). Chicago: Aldine.
8. Schmitt, D. P. (2003). Universal sex differences in the desire for sexual variety: Tests from 52 nations, 6 continents, and 13 islands. *Journal of Personality and Social Psychology, 85,* 85–104.
9. Dunbar, R. I. M. (1993). Coevolution of neocortical size, group size, and language in humans. *Behavioral and Brain Sciences, 16,* 681–694.
10. Dunbar, R. I. M. (1996). *Grooming, gossip, and the evolution of language.* Cambridge, MA: Harvard University Press.
11. Powell, J., Lewis, P.A., Roberts, N., Garcia-Finana, M., & Dunbar, R.I.M. (2012). Orbital prefrontal cortex volume predicts social network size: An imaging study of individual differences in humans. *Proceedings of the Royal Society B, 279,* 2157–2162.
12. Aronson, E. (2007). *The social animal.* New York: Worth.
13. de Waal, F. B. M. (2002). Evolutionary psychology: The wheat and the chaff. *Current Directions in Psychological Science, 11,* 187–191.
14. Boyd, R., & Richerson, P. J. (1985). *Culture and the evolutionary process.* Chicago: University of Chicago Press.
15. Shteynberg, G., Hirsh, J. B., Apfelbaum, E. P., Larsen, J. T., Galinsky, A. D., & Roese, N. J. (2014, August 25). Feeling more together: Group attention intensifies emotion. *Emotion.* Advance online publication. http://dx.doi.org/10.1037/a0037697

16. Shteynberg, G., & Apfelbaum, A. P. (2013). The power of shared experience: Simultaneous observation with similar others facilitates social learning. *Social Psychological and Personality Science, 4*, 738–744.

17. Thomas, K. A., DeScioli, P., Haque, O. S., & Pinker, S. (2014). The psychology of coordination and common knowledge. *Journal of Personality and Social Psychology*, Advance online publication. http://dx.doi.org/10.1037/a0037037

18. Davies, G. (2002). *A history of money from ancient times to the present day.* Cardiff: University of Wales Press.

19. Lea, S. E. G., & Webley, P. (2006). Money as tool, money as drug: The biological psychology of a strong incentive. *Behavioral and Brain Sciences, 29*, 161–209.

20. Lea, S. E. G., & Webley, P. (2006). Money as tool, money as drug: The biological psychology of a strong incentive. *Behavioral and Brain Sciences, 29*, 161–209.

21. Levitt, S. J., & Dubner, S. D. (2005). *Freakonomics: A rogue economist explores the hidden side of everything.* New York: Morrow.

22. Van Boven, L., & Gilovich, T. (2003). To do or to have? That is the question. *Journal of Personality and Social Psychology, 85*, 1193–1202.

23. Caprariello, P. A. & Reis, H. T. (2013). To do, to have, or to share? Valuing experiences over material possessions depends on the involvement of others. *Journal of Personality and Social Psychology, 104*, 199–215.

24. Blackwell, B., & Hutchins, I. (1994). *Delights of the garden.* New York: Doubleday.

25. Frey, R. G. (1983). *Rights, killing, and suffering: Moral vegetarianism and applied ethics.* Oxford: Blackwell.

26. Ritson, J. (1802). *An essay on abstinence from animal food, as a moral duty.* London: Richard Phillips.

27. Tansey, G., & D'Silva, J. (1999). *The meat business: Devouring a hungry planet.* New York: St. Martin's Press.

28. Walters, K. S., & Portmess, L. (Eds.). (1999). *Ethical vegetarianism: From Pythagoras to Peter Singer.* Albany: State University of New York Press.

29. Grondin, S., Deshaies, P., & Nault, L. P. (1984). Trimestres de naissance et participation au hockey et au volleyball. *La Revue Quebecoise de l'Activité Physique, 2*, 97–103.

30. Musch, J., & Grondin, S. (2001). Unequal competition as an impediment to personal development: A review of the relative age effect in sport. *Developmental Review, 21*, 147–167.

31. Pedersen, W. C., Miller, L. C., Putcha-Bhagavatula, A. D., & Yang, Y. (2002). Evolved sex differences in the number of partners desired? The long and short of it. *Psychological Science, 13*, 157–161.

32. Tannahill, R. (1980). *Sex in history.* London: Scarborough House.

33. Frayser, S. G. (1985). *Varieties of sexual experience: An anthropological perspective on human sexuality.* New Haven, CT: HRAF Press.

34. Herdt, G. (1984). Ritualized homosexual behavior in the male cults of Melanesia, 1862–1983: An introduction. In G. Herdt (Ed.), *Ritualized homosexuality in Melanesia* (pp. 1–82). Berkeley: University of California Press.

35. Musch, J., & Grondin, S. (2001). Unequal competition as an impediment to personal development: A review of the relative age effect in sport. *Developmental Review, 21*, 147–167.

36. Dickinson, D. J., & Larsen, J. D. (1963). The effects of chronological age in months on school achievement. *Journal of Educational Research, 56*, 492–493.

37. Hauck, A., & Finch, A. (1993). The effect of relative age on achievement in middle school. *Psychology in the Schools, 30*, 74–79.

38. Maddux, C. D., Stacy, D., & Scott, M. (1981). School entry age in a group of gifted children. *Gifted Child Quarterly, 25*, 180–184.

39. DeMeis, J., & Stearns, E. (1992). Relationship of school entrance age to academic and social performance. *Journal of Educational Research, 86*, 21–27.

40. Vandello, J. A., Bosson, J. K., Cohen, D., Burnaford, R. M., & Weaver, J. R. (2008). Precarious manhood. *Journal of Personality and Social Psychology, 95*, 1325–1339.

41. Vandello, J. A., Bosson, J. K., Cohen, D., Burnaford, R. M., & Weaver, J. R. (2008). Precarious manhood. *Journal of Personality and Social Psychology, 95*, 1325–1339.

42. Harris, M. (1974). *Cows, pigs, wars, and witches: The riddles of culture.* New York: Random House.

43. Harris, M. (1977). *Cannibals and kings: The origins of culture.* New York: Random House.

44. Murray, D. R., Trudeau, R., & Schaller, M. (2011). On the origins of cultural differences in conformity: Four tests of the pathogen prevalence hypothesis. *Personality and Social Psychology Bulletin, 37*, 318–329.

45. Fincher, C. L., Thornhill, R., Murray, D. R., & Schaller, M. (2008). Pathogen prevalence predicts human cross-cultural variability in individualism/collectivism. *Proceedings of the Royal Society B, 275*, 1279–1285.

46. Park, J. H., & Schaller, M. (2009). Parasites, minds and cultures. *The Psychologist, 22*, 942–945.

47. Schaller, M., & Murray, D. R. (2008). Pathogens, personality, and culture: Disease prevalence predicts worldwide variability in sociosexuality, extraversion, and openness to experience. *Journal of Personality and Social Psychology, 95*, 212–221.

48. Schaller, M., & Murray, D. R. (2008). Pathogens, personality, and culture: Disease prevalence predicts worldwide variability in sociosexuality, extraversion, and openness to experience. *Journal of Personality and Social Psychology, 95*, 212–221.

49. Boyd, R., & Richerson, P. J. (1985). *Culture and the evolutionary process.* Chicago: University of Chicago Press.

50. Boyd, R., & Richerson, P. J. (2005). *The origin and evolution of cultures.* New York: Oxford University Press

51. Baumeister, R. F. (2005). *The cultural animal: Human nature, meaning, and social life.* New York: Oxford University Press.

52. Baumeister, R. F. (2005). *The cultural animal: Human nature, meaning, and social life.* New York: Oxford University Press.

53. Boyd, R., & Richerson, P. J. (1985). *Culture and the evolutionary process.* Chicago: University of Chicago Press.

54. Litt, C. J. (1981). Children's attachment to transitional objects: A study of two pediatric populations. *American Journal of Orthopsychiatry, 51*, 131–139.

55. Barry, H., III, & Paxson, L. M. (1971). Infancy and early childhood: Cross-cultural codes II. *Ethnology, 10*, 466–508.

56. Leung, K., & Bond, M. H. (2004). Social axioms: A model for social beliefs in multicultural perspective. In M. Zanna (Ed.), *Advances in experimental social psychology* (Vol. 36, pp. 119–197). New York: Academic Press.

57. Koider, S., Andrillon, T., Barbosa, L. S., Goupil L., & Bekinschtein, T. A. (2014). Inducing task-relevant responses to speech in the sleeping brain. *Current Biology, 24*, 1–7.

58. Oswald, I., Taylor, A. M., & Treisman, M. (1960). Discriminative responses to stimulation during human sleep. *Brain, 83*, 440–453.

59. Strack, F., & Deutsch, R. (2004). Reflective and impulsive determinants of social behavior. *Personality and Social Psychology Review, 8*(3), 220–247.

60. Gazzaniga, M. S. (1998). *The mind's past.* Berkeley: University of California Press.

61. Gazzaniga, M. S. (2003, January). *The when, where, what, and why of conscious experience.* Paper presented at the 25th Annual National Institute on the Teaching of Psychology Convention, St. Petersburg Beach, FL.

62. Wegner, D. M. (2002). *The illusion of conscious will.* Cambridge, MA: MIT Press.

63. Bargh, J. A. (1982). Attention and automaticity in the processing of self-relevant information. *Journal of Personality and Social Psychology, 43*, 425–436.

64. Bargh, J. A. (1994). The four horsemen of automaticity: Awareness, intention, efficiency, and control in social cognition. In R. S. Wyer, Jr., & T. K. Srull (Eds.), *Handbook of social cognition* (pp. 1–40). Hillsdale, NJ: Erlbaum.

65. Bargh, J. A., Chen, M., & Burrows, L. (1996). Automaticity of social behavior: Direct effects of trait construct and stereotype activation on action. *Journal of Personality and Social Psychology, 71*, 230–244.

66. Bargh, J. A., Gollwitzer, P. M., Lee-Chai, A., Barndollar, K., & Trötschel, R. (2001). The automated will: Nonconscious activation and pursuit of behavioral goals. *Journal of Personality and Social Psychology, 81*, 1014–1027.

67. Lieberman, M. D., Gaunt, R., Gilbert, D. T., & Trope, Y. (2002). Reflection and reflexion: A social cognitive neuroscience approach to attributional inference. *Advances in Experimental Social Psychology, 34*, 199–249.

68. Bargh, J. A. (1994). The four horsemen of automaticity: Awareness, intention, efficiency, and control in social cognition. In R. S. Wyer, Jr., & T. K. Srull (Eds.), *Handbook of social cognition* (pp. 1–40). Hillsdale, NJ: Erlbaum.

69. Lieberman, M. D., Gaunt, R., Gilbert, D. T., & Trope, Y. (2002). Reflection and reflexion: A social cognitive neuroscience approach to attributional inference. *Advances in Experimental Social Psychology, 34*, 199–249.

70. Van der Wal, R.C., & van Dillen, L.F. (2013). Leaving a flat taste in your mouth: Task load reduces taste perception. *Psychological Science, 24*, 1277–1284.

71. DeWall, C. N., Baumeister, R. F., & Masicampo, E. J. (2008). Evidence that logical reasoning depends on conscious processing. *Consciousness and Cognition. 17*, 628–645.

72. Kahneman, D., & Frederick, S. (2002). Representativeness revisited: Attribute substitution in intuitive judgment. In T. Gilovich, D. Griffin, & D. Kahneman (Eds.), *Heuristics and biases* (pp. 49–81). New York: Cambridge University Press.

73. Kahneman, D. (2011). *Thinking, fast and slow.* New York: Farrar, Straus, and Giroux.

74. Strack, F., & Deutsch, R. (2004). Reflective and impulsive determinants of social behavior. *Personality and Social Psychology Review, 8*(3), 220–247.

75. Baumeister, R. F., Masicampo, E. J., & Vohs, K. D. (2011). Do conscious thoughts cause behavior? *Annual Review of Psychology, 62*, 331–361.

76. Peters, K., & Kashima, Y. (2007). From social talk to social action: Shaping the social triad with emotion sharing. *Journal of Personality and Social Psychology, 93*, 780–797.

77. Walton, G. M., Cohen, G. L., Cwir, D., & Spencer, S. J. (2012). Mere belonging: The power of social connections. *Journal of Personality and Social Psychology, 102*, 513–532.

78. Cesario, J., Plaks, J. E., & Higgins, E. T. (2006). Automatic social behavior as motivated preparation to interact. *Journal of Personality and Social Psychology, 90*, 893–910.

79. Loersch, C., & Arbuckle, N.L. (2013). Unraveling the mystery of music: Music as an evolved group process. *Journal of Personality and Social Psychology, 105*, 777–798.

80. Freud, S. (1961). *Civilization and its discontents* (standard ed.). London: Norton. (Original work published 1930).

81. Baumeister, R. F., Heatherton, T. F., & Tice, D. M. (1994). *Losing control: How and why people fail at self-regulation.* San Diego: Academic Press.

82. Ridley, M. (1993). *The red queen: Sex and evolution in human nature.* New York: Penguin.

83. Ridley, M. (2004). *Evolution* (3rd ed.). Oxford: Blackwell Science.

84. Baumeister, R. F., Reis, H. T., & Delespaul, P. A. E. G. (1995). Subjective and experiential correlates of guilt in everyday life. *Personality and Social Psychology Bulletin, 21,* 1256–1268.

85. Tangney, J. P., & Dearing, R. L. (2002). *Shame and guilt.* New York: Guilford Press.

86. Rozin, P., Markwith, M., & McCauley, C. (1994). Sensitivity to indirect contacts with other persons: AIDS aversion as a composite of aversion to strangers, infection, moral taint, and misfortune. *Journal of Abnormal Psychology, 103,* 495–505.

87. Pryor, J. B., Reeder, G. D., Yeadon, C., & Hesson-McInnis, M. (2004). A dual-process model of reactions to perceived stigma. *Journal of Personality and Social Psychology, 87,* 436–452.

88. Mischel, W. (1974). Processes in delay of gratification. In L. Berkowitz (Ed.), *Advances in experimental social psychology* (Vol. 7, pp. 249–292). San Diego: Academic Press.

89. Mischel, W. (1996). From good intentions to willpower. In P. Gollwitzer & J. Bargh (Eds.), *The psychology of action* (pp. 197–218). New York: Guilford Press.

90. Dion, J., & Mellor, B. (2004, August). Is sport really good for you? *EnRoute,* pp. 33–34.

91. Roberts, W. A. (2002). Are animals stuck in time? *Psychological Bulletin, 128,* 473–489.

92. Luce, M. F. (1998). Choosing to avoid: Coping with negatively emotion-laden consumer decisions. *Journal of Consumer Research, 24,* 409–433.

93. Luce, M. F., Bettman, J. R., & Payne, J. W. (1997). Choice processing in emotionally difficult decisions. *Journal of Experimental Psychology: Learning, Memory, and Cognition, 23,* 384–405.

94. Luce, M. F., Bettman, J. R., & Payne, J. W. (2001). *Emotional decisions: Tradeoff difficulty and coping in consumer choice.* Chicago: University of Chicago Press.

95. Tetlock, P. E. (1981). Pre- to post-election shifts in presidential rhetoric: Impression management or cognitive adjustment? *Journal of Personality and Social Psychology, 41,* 207–212.

96. Tetlock, P. E. (2000). Coping with trade-offs: Psychological constraints and political implications. In S. Lupia, M. McCubbins, & S. Popkin (Eds.), *Political reasoning and choice.* Berkeley: University of California Press.

97. Van Beest, I., & Williams, K. D. (2006). When inclusion costs and ostracism pays, ostracism still hurts. *Journal of Personality and Social Psychology, 91,* 918–928.

98. Asch, S. E. (1955, November). Opinions and social pressure. *Scientific American,* 31–35.

99. Asch, S. E. (1956). Studies of independence and conformity: I. A minority of one against a unanimous majority. *Psychological Monographs, 70* (No. 416).

100. Bond, R. A., & Smith, P. B. (1996). Culture and conformity: A meta-analysis of studies using Asch's (1952, 1956) line judgment task. *Psychological Bulletin, 119,* 111–137.

101. Hilmert, C. J., Kulik, J. A., & Christenfeld, N. J. (2006). Positive and negative opinion modeling: The influence of another's similarity and dissimilarity. *Journal of Personality and Social Psychology, 90,* 440–452.

CHAPTER 3
The Self

1. Turnbull, S. (2003). *The Ottoman Empire 1326–1699.* New York: Routledge.

2. James, W. (1948). *Psychology.* Cleveland, OH: World Publishing. (Original work published 1892).

3. Sennett, R. (1974). *The fall of public man.* New York: Random House.

4. Stone, L. (1977). *The family, sex and marriage in England: 1500–1800.* London: Perennial.

5. Weintraub, K. J. (1978). *The value of the individual: Self and circumstance in autobiography.* Chicago: University of Chicago Press.

6. Baumeister, R. F. (1987). How the self became a problem: A psychological review of historical research. *Journal of Personality and Social Psychology, 52,* 163–176.

7. Turner, R. H. (1976). The real self: From institution to impulse. *American Journal of Sociology, 81,* 989–1016.

8. Goffman, E. (1959). *The presentation of self in everyday life.* New York: Doubleday Anchor.

9. Markus, H. R., & Kitayama, S. (1991). Culture and the self: Implications for cognition, emotion, and motivation. *Psychological Review, 98,* 224–253. See also Triandis, H. C. (1989). The self and social behavior in differing cultural contexts. *Psychological Review, 96,* 506–520.

10. Clark, D. (1986). *The missing link.* New York: Humansphere.

11. Biddle, B. J., & Thomas, E. J. (1966). *Role theory: Concepts and research.* New York: Wiley.

12. Mead, G. H. (1934). *Mind, self and society.* Chicago: University of Chicago Press.

13. Goffman, E. (1959). *The presentation of self in everyday life.* New York: Doubleday Anchor.

14. Duval, S., & Wicklund, R. (1972). *A theory of objective self-awareness.* New York: Academic Press.

15. Fenigstein, A., Scheier, M. F., & Buss, A. H. (1975). Public and private self-consciousness: Assessment and theory. *Journal of Consulting and Clinical Psychology, 43,* 522–527.

16. Carver, C. S., & Scheier, M. F. (1981). *Attention and self-regulation: A control therapy approach to human behavior.* New York: Springer Press.

17. Kagan, J. (1981). *The second year: The emergence of self-awareness.* Cambridge, MA: Harvard University Press.

18. Becker, A. E., Burwell, R. A., Herzog, D. B., Hamburg, P., & Gilman, S. E. (2002). Eating behaviours and attitudes following prolonged exposure to television among ethnic Fijian adolescent girls. *British Journal of Psychiatry, 180,* 509–514.

19. Botta, R. A. (2000). The mirror of television: A comparison of black and white adolescents' body image. *Journal of Communication, 50,* 144–159.

20. Harrison, K. (2000). The body electric: Thin-ideal media and eating disorders in adolescents. *Journal of Communication, 50,* 119–143.

21. Harrison, K. (2001). Ourselves, our bodies: Thin-ideal media, self-discrepancies, and eating disorder symptomatology in adolescents. *Journal of Social and Clinical Psychology, 20,* 289–323.

22. Harrison, K. (2003). Television viewers' ideal body proportions: The case of the curvaceously thin woman. *Sex Roles, 48,* 255–264.

23. Lavine, H., Sweeney, D., & Wagner, S. H. (1999). Depicting women as sex objects in television advertising: Effects on body dissatisfaction. *Personality and Social Psychology Bulletin, 25,* 1049–1058.

24. Tiggemann, M., & Pickering, A. S. (1996). Role of television in adolescent women's body dissatisfaction and drive for thinness. *International Journal of Eating Disorders, 20,* 199–220.

25. Silvia, P. J., & Duval, T. S. (2001). Objective self-awareness theory: Recent progress and enduring problems. *Personality and Social Psychology Review, 5,* 230–241.

26. Diener, E., & Wallbom, M. (1976). Effects of self-awareness on antinormative behavior. *Journal of Research in Personality, 10,* 107–111.

27. Sentyrz, S. M., & Bushman, B. J. (1998). Mirror, mirror on the wall, who's the thinnest one of all? Effects of self-awareness on consumption of fatty, reduced-fat, and fat-free products. *Journal of Applied Psychology, 83,* 944–949.

28. Heatherton, T. F., Polivy, J., Herman, C. P., & Baumeister, R. F. (1993). Self-awareness, task failure and disinhibition: How attentional focus affects eating. *Journal of Personality, 61,* 49–61.

29. Scheier, M. F., Fenigstein, A., & Buss, A. H. (1974). Self-awareness and physical aggression. *Journal of Experimental Social Psychology, 10,* 264–273.

30. Smith, G. E., Gerrard, M., & Gibbons, F. X. (1997). Self-esteem and the relation between risk behavior and perceptions of vulnerability to unplanned pregnancy in college women. *Health Psychology, 16,* 137–146.

31. Pryor, J. B., Gibbons, F. X., Wicklund, R. A., Fazio, R. H., & Hood, R. (1977). Self-focused attention and self-report validity. *Journal of Personality, 45,* 513–527.

32. Greenberg, J., & Musham, C. (1981). Avoiding and seeking self-focused attention. *Journal of Research in Personality, 15,* 191–200.

33. Hull, J. G. (1981). A self-awareness model of the causes and effects of alcohol consumption. *Journal of Abnormal Psychology, 90,* 586–600.

34. Hull, J. G., Levenson, R. W., Young, R. D., & Scher, K. J. (1983). Self-awareness-reducing effects of alcohol consumption. *Journal of Personality and Social Personality, 44,* 461–473.

35. Baumeister, R. F. (1990). Suicide as escape from self. *Psychological Review, 97,* 90–113.

36. Chatard, A., & Selimbegovic, L. (2011). When self-destructive thoughts flash through the mind: Failure to meet standards affects the accessibility of suicide-related thoughts. *Journal of Personality and Social Psychology, 100,* 587–605.

37. Carver, C. S., & Scheier, M. F. (1981). *Attention and self-regulation: A control therapy approach to human behavior.* New York: Springer Press.

38. Carver, C. S., & Scheier, M. F. (1990). Origins and functions of positive and negative affect: A control-process view. *Psychological Review, 97,* 19–35.

39. Heatherton, T. F., & Baumeister, R. F. (1991). Binge eating as escape from self-awareness. *Psychological Bulletin, 110,* 86–108.

40. Blanchard, F. A., & Frost, R. O. (1983). Two factors of restraint: Concern for dieting and fluctuations. *Behavior Research and Therapy, 21,* 259–267.

41. Heatherton, T. F., Polivy, J., & Herman, C. P. (1989). Restraint and internal responsiveness: Effects of placebo manipulations of hunger state on eating. *Journal of Abnormal Psychology, 98,* 89–92.

42. Cooley, C. H. (1902). *Human nature and the social order.* New York: Charles Scribner's Sons.

43. Mead, G. H. (1934). *Mind, self and society.* Chicago: University of Chicago Press.

44. Shrauger, J. S., & Shoeneman, T. J. (1979). Symbolic interactionist view of self-concept: Through the looking glass darkly. *Psychological Bulletin, 86,* 549–573.

45. Tesser, A., & Rosen, S. (1975). The reluctance to transmit bad news. In L. Berkowitz (Ed.), *Advances in experimental social psychology* (Vol. 8, pp. 193–232). New York: Academic Press.

46. Rosenberg, M. (1979). *Conceiving the self.* New York: Basic Books.

47. Nisbett, R. E., & Wilson, T. D. (1977). Telling more than we can know: Verbal reports on mental processes. *Psychological Review, 84,* 231–259.

48. Nisbett, R. E., & Wilson, T. D. (1977). Telling more than we can know: Verbal reports on mental processes. *Psychological Review, 84,* 231–259.

49. Smith, G. H., & Engel, R. (1968). Influence of a female model on perceived characteristics of an automobile. *Proceedings of the Annual Convention of the American Psychological Association, 3,* 681–682.

50. Nisbett, R. E., & Wilson, T. D. (1977). Telling more than we can know: Verbal reports on mental processes. *Psychological Review, 84,* 231–259.

51. Vazire, S. (2010). Who knows what about a person? The Self-Other Knowledge Asymmetry (SOKA) model. *Journal of Personality and Social Psychology, 98,* 281–300.

52. Festinger, L. (1954). A theory of social comparison processes. *Human Relations, 7,* 117–140.

53. Tesser, A. (1988). Toward a self-evaluation maintenance model of social behavior. In L. Berkowitz (Ed.), *Advances in experimental social psychology* (Vol. 21, pp. 181–227). San Diego: Academic Press.

54. Bem, D. J. (1965). An experimental analysis of self-persuasion. *Journal of Experimental Social*

Psychology, 1, 199–218. Jones. E. E., & Gerard, H. B. (1967). *Foundations of social psychology*. New York: Wiley.

55. Jones, E. E., & Gerard, H. B. (1967). *Foundations of social psychology*. New York: Wiley.

56. Markus, H. R., & Kunda, Z. (1986). Stability and malleability in the self-concept in the perception of others. *Journal of Personality and Social Psychology, 51*, 858–866.

57. Deci, E. L. (1971). The effects of externally mediated rewards on intrinsic motivation. *Journal of Personality and Social Psychology, 18*, 105–115.

58. Deci, E. L., Koestner, R., & Ryan, R. M. (1999). A meta-analytic review of experiments examining the effects of extrinsic rewards on intrinsic motivation. *Psychological Bulletin, 125*, 627–668.

59. Cameron, J., Banko, K. M., & Pierce, W. D. (2001). Pervasive negative effects of rewards on intrinsic motivation: The myth continues. *The Behavior Analyst, 24*, 1–44.

60. Deci, E. L. (1971). The effects of externally mediated rewards on intrinsic motivation. *Journal of Personality and Social Psychology, 18*, 105–115.

61. Lepper, M. P., Greene, D., & Nisbett, R. E. (1973). Undermining children's intrinsic interest with extrinsic reward: A test of the "overjustification" hypothesis. *Journal of Personality and Social Psychology, 28*, 129–137.

62. Deci, E. L., Koestner, R., & Ryan, R. M. (1999). A meta-analytic review of experiments examining the effects of extrinsic rewards on intrinsic motivation. *Psychological Bulletin, 125*, 627–668.

63. Cameron, J., Banko, K. M., & Pierce, W. D. (2001). Pervasive negative effects of rewards on intrinsic motivation: The myth continues. *The Behavior Analyst, 24*, 1–44.

64. Rosenfeld, D. L., Folger, R., & Adelman, H. F. (1980). When rewards reflect competence: A qualification of the overjustification effect. *Journal of Personality and Social Psychology, 39*, 368–376.

65. Cameron, J., Banko, K. M., & Pierce, W. D. (2001). Pervasive negative effects of rewards on intrinsic motivation: The myth continues. *The Behavior Analyst, 24*, 1–44.

66. Deci, E. L., Koestner, R., & Ryan, R. M. (1999). A meta-analytic review of experiments examining the effects of extrinsic rewards on intrinsic motivation. *Psychological Bulletin, 125*, 627–668.

67. Wrzesniewski, A., Schwartz, B., Cong, X., Kane, M., Omar, A., & Kolditz, T. (2014). Multiple types of motives don't multiply the motivation of West Point cadets. *PNAS, 111*, 10990–10995.

68. McGuire, W. J., McGuire, C. V., Child, P., & Fujioka, T. (1978). Salience of ethnicity in the spontaneous self-concept as a function of one's ethnic distinctiveness in the social environment. *Journal of Personality and Social Psychology, 36*, 511–520.

69. McGuire, W. J., McGuire, C. V., Child, P., & Winton, W. (1979). Effects of household gender composition on the salience of one's gender in the spontaneous self-concept. *Journal of Experimental Social Psychology, 15*, 77–90.

70. Lord, C. G., & Saenz, D. S. (1985). Memory deficits and memory surfeits: Differential cognitive consequences of tokenism for tokens and observers. *Journal of Personality and Social Psychology, 49*, 918–926.

71. Wakslak, C. J., Nussbaum, S., Liberman, N., & Trope, Y. (2008). Representations of the self in the near and distant future. *Journal of Personality and Social Psychology, 95*, 751–773.

72. Kirkpatrick, L. A., & Ellis, B. J. (2001). An evolutionary-psychological perspective on self-esteem: Multiple domains and multiple functions. In G. J. O. Fletcher & M. S. Clark (Eds.), *Blackwell handbook of social psychology: Vol. 2. Interpersonal processes* (pp. 411–436). Oxford: Blackwell.

73. Trope, Y. (1983). Self-assessment in achievement behavior. In J. Suls & A. Greenwald (Eds.), *Psychological perspectives on the self* (Vol. 2, pp. 93–121). Hillsdale, NJ: Erlbaum.

74. Trope, Y. (1986). Self-enhancement and self-assessment in achievement behavior. In R. Sorrentino & E. T. Higgins (Eds.), *Handbook of motivation and cognition* (Vol. 2, pp. 350–378). New York: Guilford Press.

75. Sedikides, C. S., & Gregg, A. P. (2008). Self-enhancement: Food for thought. *Perspectives on Psychological Science, 3*, 102–116.

76. Swann, W. B., Jr. (1985). The self as architect of social reality. In B. Schlenker (Ed.), *The self and social life* (pp. 100–125). New York: McGraw-Hill.

77. Swann, W. B., Jr. (1987). Identity negotiation: Where two roads meet. *Journal of Personality and Social Psychology, 53*, 1038–1051.

78. Sedikides, C. (1993). Assessment, enhancement, and verification determinants of the self-evaluation process. *Journal of Personality and Social Psychology, 65*, 317–338.

79. Kim, Y.-H., Chiu, C., & Zou, Z. (2010). Know thyself: Misperceptions of actual performance undermine achievement motivation, future performance, and subjective well-being. *Journal of Personality and Social Psychology, 99*, 395–409.

80. Kim, Y.-H., Chiu, C., & Zou, Z. (2010). Know thyself: Misperceptions of actual performance undermine achievement motivation, future performance, and subjective well-being. *Journal of Personality and Social Psychology, 99*, 395–409.

81. Kwan, V. S., John, O., Robin, R., & Kuang, L. (2008). Conceptualizing and assessing self-enhancement bias: A componential approach. *Journal of Personality and Social Psychology, 94*, 1062–1077.

82. Jussim, L., HsiuJu, Y., & Aiello, J. R. (1995). Self-consistency, self-enhancement, and accuracy in reactions to feedback. *Journal of Experimental Social Psychology, 31*, 322–356.

83. McFarlin, D. B., & Blascovich, J. (1981). Effects of self-esteem and performance on future affective preferences and cognitive expectations. *Journal of Personality and Social Psychology, 40*, 521–531.

84. Shrauger, J. S. (1975). Responses to evaluation as a function of initial self-perceptions. *Psychological Bulletin, 82*, 581–596.

85. Swann, W. B., Jr., Griffin, J. J., Predmore, S., & Gaines, B. (1987). The cognitive-affective crossfire: When self-consistency confronts self-enhancement. *Journal of Personality and Social Psychology, 52*, 881–889.

86. Hirt, E. R., Deppe, R. K., & Gordon, L. J. (1991). Self-reported versus behavioral self-handicapping: Empirical evidence for a theoretical distinction. *Journal of Personality and Social Psychology, 61*, 981–991.

87. Jones, E. E., & Berglas, S. (1978). Control of attributions about the self through self-handicapping strategies: The appeal of alcohol and the role of underachievement. *Personality and Social Psychology Bulletin, 4*, 200–206.

88. Smith, T. W., Snyder C. R., & Perkins S. C. (1983). The self-serving function of hypochondriacal complaints: Physical symptoms as self-handicapping strategies. *Journal of Personality and Social Psychology, 44*, 787–797.

89. Snyder, C. R., & Higgins, R. L. (1990). *Self-handicapping: The paradox that isn't*. Norwell, MA: Kluwer.

90. Kolditz, T., & Arkin, R. M. (1982). An impression management interpretation of the self-handicapping phenomenon. *Journal of Personality and Social Psychology, 43*, 492–502.

91. Tice, D. M. (1991). Esteem protection or enhancement? Self-handicapping motives and attributions differ by trait self-esteem. *Journal of Personality and Social Psychology, 60*, 711–725.

92. Berglas, S., & Jones, E. E. (1978). Drug choice as a self-handicapping strategy in response to non-contingent success. *Journal of Personality and Social Psychology, 36*, 405–417.

93. Berglas, S. C., & Baumeister, R. F. (1993). *Your own worst enemy: Understanding the paradox of self-defeating behavior*. New York: Basic Books.

94. Paulhus, D. L., & Levitt, K. (1987). Desirable responding triggered by affect: Automatic egotism? *Journal of Personality and Social Psychology, 52*, 245–259.

95. Swann, W. B., Jr., Hixon, J. G., Stein-Seroussi, A., & Gilbert, D. T. (1990). The fleeting gleam of praise: Cognitive processes underlying behavioral reactions to self-relevant feedback. *Journal of Personality and Social Psychology, 59*, 17–26.

96. Swann, W. B., Jr., Stein-Seroussi, A., & Giesler, R. B. (1992). Why people self-verify. *Journal of Personality and Social Psychology, 62*, 392–401.

97. Rogers, T. B., Kuiper, N. A., & Kirker, W. S. (1977). Self-reference and the encoding of personal information. *Journal of Personality and Social Psychology, 35*, 677–688.

98. Rogers, T. B., Kuiper, N. A., & Kirker, W. S. (1977). Self-reference and the encoding of personal information. *Journal of Personality and Social Psychology, 35*, 677–688.

99. Greenwald, A. G., & Banaji, M. R. (1989). The self as a memory system: Powerful, but ordinary. *Journal of Personality and Social Psychology, 57*, 41–54.

100. Higgins, E. T., & Bargh, J. A. (1987). Social cognition and social perception. *Annual Review of Psychology, 38*, 369–425.

101. Klein, S. B., & Kihlstrom, J. F. (1986). Elaboration, organization, and the self-reference effect in memory. *Journal of Experimental Psychology: General, 115*, 26–39.

102. Symons, C. S., & Johnson, B. T. (1997). The self-reference effect in memory: A meta-analysis. *Psychological Bulletin, 121*, 371–394.

103. Kahneman, D., Knetsch, J. L., & Thaler, R. H. (1990). Experimental tests of the endowment effect and the Coase theorem. *Journal of Political Economy, 98*(6), 1325–1348.

104. Beggan, J. K. (1992). On the social nature of nonsocial perception: The mere ownership effect. *Journal of Personality and Social Psychology, 62*, 229–237.

105. Langer, E. J. (1975). The illusion of control. *Journal of Personality and Social Psychology, 32*, 311–328.

106. Jones, E. E., Rhodewalt, F., Berglas, S., & Skelton, J. A. (1981). Effects of strategic self-presentation on subsequent self-esteem. *Journal of Personality and Social Psychology, 41*, 407–421.

107. Rhodewalt, F., & Agustdottir, S. (1986). Effects of self-presentation on the phenomenal self. *Journal of Personality and Social Psychology, 50*, 47–55.

108. Jones, E. E., & Nisbett, R. E. (1971). *The actor and the observer: Divergent perceptions of the causes of behavior*. New York: General Learning Press.

109. Backteman, G., & Magnusson, D. (1981). Longitudinal stability of personality characteristics. *Journal of Personality, 49*, 148–160.

110. Caspi, A., & Roberts, B. W. (2001). Personality development across the life course: The argument for change and continuity. *Psychological Inquiry, 12*, 49–66.

111. Epstein, S. (1979). The stability of behavior: I. On predicting most of the people much of the time. *Journal of Personality and Social Psychology, 37*, 1097–1126.

112. Eron, L. D., & Huesmann, L. R. (1990). The stability of aggressive behavior—even into the third generation. In M. Lewis & S. M. Miller (Eds.), *Handbook of developmental psychopathology* (pp. 147–156). New York: Plenum Press.

113. Harter, S. (1993). Causes and consequences of low self-esteem in children and adolescents. In R. F. Baumeister (Ed.), *Self-esteem: The puzzle of low self-regard* (pp. 87–116). New York: Plenum Press.

114. Group for the Advancement of Psychiatry. (1957). *Methods of forceful indoctrination: Observations and interviews*. New York: Author.

115. Heatherton, T. F., & Nichols, P. A. (1994). Personal accounts of successful versus failed attempts at life change. *Personality and Social Psychology Bulletin, 20*, 664–675.

116. Fazio, R. H., Effrein, E. A., & Falender, V. J. (1981). Self-perceptions following social interaction. *Journal of Personality and Social Psychology, 41,* 232–242.

117. Tice, D. M. (1992). Self-presentation and self-concept change: The looking-glass self is also a magnifying glass. *Journal of Personality and Social Psychology, 63,* 435–451.

118. Schlenker, B. R., Dlugolecki, D. W., & Doherty, K. J. (1994). The impact of self-presentations on self-appraisals and behaviors: The power of public commitment. *Personality and Social Psychology Bulletin, 20,* 20–33.

119. Ross, M. (1989). The relation of implicit theories to the construction of personal histories. *Psychological Review, 96,* 341–357.

120. Conway, M., & Ross, M. (1984). Getting what you want by revising what you had. *Journal of Personality and Social Psychology, 47,* 738–748.

121. Ross, M. (1989). The relation of implicit theories to the construction of personal histories. *Psychological Review, 96,* 341–357.

122. McFarlin, D. B., & Blascovich, J. (1981). Effects of self-esteem and performance on future affective preferences and cognitive expectations. *Journal of Personality and Social Psychology, 40,* 521–531.

123. Campbell, J. D. (1990). Self-esteem and clarity of the self-concept. *Journal of Personality and Social Psychology, 59,* 538–549.

124. Baumeister, R. F., Hutton, D. G., & Tice, D. M. (1989). Cognitive processes during deliberate self-presentation: How self-presenters alter and misinterpret the behavior of their interaction partners. *Journal of Experimental Social Psychology, 25,* 59–78.

125. Campbell, J. D., Chew, B., & Scratchley, L. S. (1991). Cognitive and emotional reactions to daily events: The effects of self-esteem and self complexity. *Journal of Personality, 59,* 473–505.

126. Branden, N. (1994). *The six pillars of self-esteem.* New York: Bantam Books.

127. Bushman, B. J., Moeller, S. J., & Crocker, J. (2011). Sweets, sex, or self-esteem? Comparing the value of self-esteem boosts with other pleasant rewards. *Journal of Personality, 79*(5), 993–1012.

128. Bushman, B. J., Moeller, S. J., Konrath, S., & Crocker, J. (2012). Investigating the link between liking versus wanting self-esteem and depression in a nationally representative sample of American adults. *Journal of Personality, 80*(5), 1455-1471. DOI: 10.1111/j.1467-6494.2012.00781.x.

129. Twenge, J. M. (2006). *Generation me.* New York: Free Press.

130. Twenge, J. M., & Campbell, W. K. (2001). Age and birth cohort differences in self-esteem: A cross-temporal meta-analysis. *Personality and Social Psychology Review, 5,* 321–344.

131. Svenson, O. (1981). Are we less risky and more skillful than our fellow drivers? *Acta Psychologica, 47,* 143–51.

132. College Board. (1976–1977). *Student descriptive questionnaire.* Princeton, NJ: Educational Testing Service.

133. Gilovich, T. (1991). *How we know what isn't so.* New York: Free Press.

134. Kling, K. C., Hyde, J. S., Showers, C. J., & Buswell, B. N. (1999). Gender differences in self-esteem: A meta-analysis. *Psychological Bulletin, 125,* 470–500.

135. Crocker, J., & Major, B. (1989). Social stigma and self-esteem: The self-protective properties of stigma. *Psychological Review, 96,* 608–630.

136. Gray-Little, B., & Hafdahl, A. R., (2000). Factors influencing racial comparisons of self-esteem: A quantitative synthesis. *Psychological Bulletin, 126,* 26–54.

137. Twenge, J., & Crocker, J. (2002). Race, ethnicity, and self-esteem: Meta-analyses comparing whites, blacks, Hispanics, Asians, and Native Americans, including a commentary on Gray-Little and Hafdahl (2000). *Psychological Bulletin, 128,* 371–408.

138. Twenge, J., & Crocker, J. (2002). Race, ethnicity, and self-esteem: Meta-analyses comparing whites, blacks, Hispanics, Asians, and Native Americans, including a commentary on Gray-Little and Hafdahl (2000). *Psychological Bulletin, 128,* 371–408.

139. Sedikides, C., Meek, R., Alicke, M. D., & Taylor, S. (2013). Behind bars but above the bar: Prisoners consider themselves more prosocial than non-prisoners. *British Journal of Social Psychology, 53,* 396–403.

140. Beck, A. T. (1976). *Cognitive therapy and the emotional disorders.* New York: Meridian.

141. Beck, A. T. (1988). *Cognitive therapy of depression: A personal reflection.* The Malcolm Millar Lecture in Psychotherapy. Aberdeen: Scottish Cultural Press.

142. Beck, A. T., & Burns, D. (1978). Cognitive therapy of depressed suicidal outpatients. In J. O. Cole, A. F. Schatzberg & S. H. Frazier (Eds.), *Depression: Biology, psychodynamics, and treatment* (pp. 199–211). New York: Plenum Press.

143. Clark, D. A., Beck, A. T., & Brown, G. (1989). Cognitive mediation in general psychiatric outpatients: A test of the content specificity hypothesis. *Journal of Personality and Social Psychology, 56,* 958–964.

144. Ottaviani, R., & Beck, A. T. (1987). Cognitive aspects of panic disorders. *Journal of Anxiety Disorders, 1,* 15–28.

145. Shaw, B. F., & Beck, A. T. (1977). The treatment of depression with cognitive therapy. In A. Ellis & R. Grieger (Eds.), *Handbook of rational emotive therapy* (pp. 309–326). New York: Springer.

146. Moore, M. T., & Fresco, D. M. (2012). Depressive realism: A meta-analytic review. *Clinical Psychology Review, 32,* 496–509.

147. Alloy, L. B., & Abramson, L. Y. (1979). Judgment of contingency in depressed and nondepressed students: Sadder but wiser? *Journal of Experimental Psychology: General, 108*(4), 441–485.

148. Lewinsohn, P. M., Mischel, W., Chaplin, W., & Barton, R. (1980). Social competence and depression: The role of illusory self-perceptions. *Journal of Abnormal Psychology, 89,* 203–212.

149. Taylor, S. E., & Brown, J. D. (1988). Illusion and well-being: A social psychological perspective on mental health. *Psychological Bulletin, 103,* 193–210.

150. Gollwitzer, P. M., & Kinney, R. F. (1989). Effects of deliberative and implemental mind-sets on the illusion of control. *Journal of Personality and Social Psychology, 56,* 531–542.

151. Taylor, S. E., & Gollwitzer, P. M. (1995). Effects of mindset on positive illusions. *Journal of Personality and Social Psychology, 69,* 213–226.

152. Gonzales, M., Pederson, J., Manning, D., & Wetter, D. (1990). Pardon my gaffe: Effects of sex, status, and consequence severity on accounts. *Journal of Personality and Social Psychology, 58,* 610–621.

153. Weary, G. (1980). Examination of affect and egotism as mediators of bias in causal attributions. *Journal of Experimental Social Psychology, 38,* 348–357.

154. Zuckerman, M. (1979). Attribution of success and failure revisited, or: The motivational bias is alive and well in attribution theory. *Journal of Personality, 47,* 245–287.

155. Kunda, Z. (1990). The case for motivated reasoning. *Psychological Bulletin, 108,* 480–498.

156. Pyszczynski, T., Greenberg, J., & Holt, K. (1985). Maintaining consistency between self-serving beliefs and available data: A bias in information processing. *Personality and Social Psychology Bulletin, 11,* 179–190.

157. Wyer, R. S., & Frey, D. (1983). The effects of feedback about self and others on the cognitive processing of feedback-relevant information. *Journal of Experimental Social Psychology, 19,* 540–559.

158. Baumeister, R. F., & Cairns, K. J. (1992). Repression and self-presentation: When audiences interfere with self-deceptive strategies. *Journal of Personality and Social Psychology, 62,* 851–862.

159. Crary, W. G. (1966). Reactions to incongruent self-experiences. *Journal of Consulting Psychology, 30,* 246–252.

160. Kuiper, N. A., & Derry, P. A. (1982). Depressed and nondepressed content self-reference in mild depression. *Journal of Personality, 50,* 67–79.

161. Mischel, W., Ebbesen, E. B., & Zeiss, A. R. (1976). Determinants of selective memory about the self. *Journal of Consulting and Clinical Psychology, 44,* 92–103.

162. Crocker, J., & Major, B. (1989). Social stigma and self-esteem: The self-protective properties of stigma. *Psychological Review, 96,* 608–630.

163. Taylor, S. E. (1983). Adjustment to threatening events: A theory of cognitive adaptation. *American Psychologist, 38,* 1161–1173.

164. Wills, T. A. (1981). Downward comparison principles in social psychology. *Psychological Bulletin, 90,* 245–271.

165. Campbell, J. D. (1986). Similarity and uniqueness: The effects of attribute type, relevance, and individual differences in self-esteem and depression. *Journal of Personality and Social Psychology, 50,* 281–294.

166. Marks, G. (1984). Thinking one's abilities are unique and one's opinions are common. *Personality and Social Psychology Bulletin, 10,* 203–208.

167. Suls, J., & Wan, C. K. (1987). In search of the false uniqueness phenomenon: Fear and estimates of social consensus. *Journal of Personality and Social Psychology, 52,* 211–217.

168. Dunning, D., & McElwee, R. O. (1995). Idiosyncratic trait definitions: Implications for self-description and social judgment. *Journal of Personality and Social Psychology, 68,* 936–946.

169. Dunning, D., Meyerowitz, J. A., & Holzberg, A. D. (1989). Ambiguity and self-evaluation: The role of idiosyncratic trait definitions in self-serving assessments of ability. *Journal of Personality and Social Psychology, 57,* 1082–1090.

170. Dunning, D., Perie, M., & Story, A. L. (1991). Self-serving prototypes of social categories. *Journal of Personality and Social Psychology, 61,* 957–968.

171. Dunning, D., & Perretta, S. (2002). Automaticity and eyewitness accuracy: A 10-to-12 second rule for distinguishing accurate from inaccurate positive identifications. *Journal of Applied Psychology, 87,* 951–962.

172. Gabriel, M. T., Critelli, J. W., & Ee, J. S. (1994). Narcissistic illusions in self-evaluations of intelligence and attractiveness. *Journal of Personality, 62,* 143–155.

173. Bowles, T. (1999). Focusing on time orientation to explain adolescent self concept and academic achievement: Part II. Testing a model. *Journal of Applied Health Behaviour, 1,* 1–8.

174. Diener, E., Wolsic, B., & Fujita, F. (1995). Physical attractiveness and subjective well-being. *Journal of Personality and Social Psychology, 69,* 120–129.

175. Gabriel, M. T., Critelli, J. W., & Ee, J. S. (1994). Narcissistic illusions in self-evaluations of intelligence and attractiveness. *Journal of Personality, 62,* 143–155.

176. Miller, C. T., & Downey, K. T. (1999). A meta-analysis of heavyweight and self-esteem. *Personality and Social Psychology Review, 3,* 68–84.

177. Bachman, J. G., & O'Malley, P. M. (1977). Self-esteem in young men: A longitudinal analysis of the impact of educational and occupational attainment. *Journal of Personality and Social Psychology, 35,* 365–380.

178. Bachman, J. G., & O'Malley, P. M. (1986). Self-concepts, self-esteem, and educational experiences: The frog pond revisited (again). *Journal of Personality and Social Psychology, 50,* 35–46.

179. Baumeister, R. F., Campbell, J. D., Krueger, J. I., & Vohs, K. D. (2003). Does high self-esteem cause better performance, interpersonal success, happiness, or healthier lifestyles? *Psychological Science in the Public Interest, 4,* 1–44.

180. Forsyth, D. R., & Kerr, N. A. (1999, August). *Are adaptive illusions adaptive?* Poster presented at the annual meeting of the American Psychological Association, Boston, MA.

181. Maruyama, G., Rubin, R. A., & Kingsbury, G. G. (1981). Self-esteem and educational achievement: Independent constructs with a common cause? *Journal of Personality and Social Psychology, 40,* 962–975.

182. Pottebaum, S. M., Keith, T. Z., & Ehly, S. W. (1986). Is there a causal relation between self-concept and academic achievement? *Journal of Educational Research, 79,* 140–144.

183. Rosenberg, M., Schooler, C., & Schoenbach, C. (1989). Self-esteem and adolescent problems: Modeling reciprocal effects. *American Sociological Review, 54,* 1004–1018.

184. Scheirer, M. A., & Kraut, R. E. (1979). Increased educational achievement via self-concept change. *Review of Educational Research, 49,* 131–150.

185. Skaalvik, E. M., & Hagtvet, K. A. (1990). Academic achievement and self-concept: An analysis of causal predominance in a developmental perspective. *Journal of Personality and Social Psychology, 58,* 292–307.

186. Wylie, R. C. (1979). *The self-concept: Vol. 2. Theory and research on selected topics.* Lincoln: University of Nebraska Press.

187. Adams, G. R., Ryan, B. A., Ketsetzis, M., & Keating, L. (2000). Rule compliance and peer sociability: A study of family process, parent-child school-focused interactions and children's classroom behavior. *Journal of Family Psychology, 14,* 237–250.

188. Battistich, V., Solomon, D., & Delucchi, K. (1993). Interaction processes and student outcomes in cooperative learning groups. *The Elementary School Journal, 94,* 19–32.

189. Baumeister, R. F., Campbell, J. D., Krueger, J. I., & Vohs, K. D. (2003). Does high self-esteem cause better performance, interpersonal success, happiness, or healthier lifestyles? *Psychological Science in the Public Interest, 4,* 1–44.

190. Bishop, J. A., & Inderbitzen, H. M. (1995). Peer acceptance and friendship: An investigation of their relation to self-esteem. *Journal of Early Adolescence, 15,* 476–489.

191. Brockner, J., & Lloyd, K. (1986). Self-esteem and likability: Separating fact from fantasy. *Journal of Research in Personality, 20,* 496–508.

192. Buhrmester, D., Furman, W., Wittenberg, M. T., & Reis, H. T. (1988). Five domains of interpersonal competence in peer relationships. *Journal of Personality and Social Psychology, 55,* 991–1008.

193. Campbell, J. D., & Fehr, B. A. (1990). Self-esteem and perceptions of conveyed impressions: Is negative affectivity associated with greater realism? *Journal of Personality and Social Psychology, 58,* 122–133.

194. Glendenning, A., & Inglis, D. (1999). Smoking behaviour in youth: The problem of low self-esteem? *Journal of Adolescence, 22,* 673–682.

195. Keefe, K., & Berndt, T. J. (1996). Relations of friendship quality to self-esteem in early adolescence. *Journal of Early Adolescence, 16,* 110–129.

196. Heatherton, T. F., & Vohs, K. D. (2000). Interpersonal evaluations following threats to self: Role of self-esteem. *Journal of Personality and Social Psychology, 78,* 725–736.

197. Colvin, C. R., Block, J., & Funder, D. C. (1995). Overly positive evaluations and personality: Negative implications for mental health. *Journal of Personality and Social Psychology, 68,* 1152–1162.

198. Baumeister, R. F., Campbell, J. D., Krueger, J. I., & Vohs, K. D. (2003). Does high self-esteem cause better performance, interpersonal success, happiness, or healthier lifestyles? *Psychological Science in the Public Interest, 4,* 1–44.

199. Brockner, J. (1983). Low self-esteem and behavioral plasticity: Some implications. In L. Wheeler & P. Shaver (Eds.), *Review of personality and social psychology, Vol. 4* (pp. 237–271). Beverly Hills, CA: Sage.

200. Janis, I. L. (1954). Personality correlates of susceptibility to persuasion. *Journal of Personality, 22,* 504–518.

201. Janis, I. L., & Field, P. (1959). Sex differences and personality factors related to persuasibility. In C. Hovland & I. Janis (Eds.), *Personality and persuasibility* (pp. 55–68, 300–302). New Haven, CT: Yale University Press.

202. Paul, C., Fitzjohn, J., Herbison, P., & Dickson, N. (2000). The determinants of sexual intercourse before age 16. *Journal of Adolescent Health, 27,* 136–147.

203. Langer, L. M., & Tubman, J. G. (1997). Risky sexual behavior among substance-abusing adolescents: Psychosocial and contextual factors. *American Journal of Orthopsychiatry, 67,* 315–322.

204. McGee, R., & Williams, S. (2000). Does low self-esteem predict health compromising behaviours among adolescents? *Journal of Adolescence, 23,* 569–582.

205. Sprecher, S., & Regan, P. C. (1996). College virgins: How men and women perceive their sexual status. *Journal of Sex Research, 33,* 3–15.

206. Walsh, A. (1991). Self-esteem and sexual behavior: Exploring gender differences. *Sex Roles, 25,* 441–450.

207. Smith, G. E., Gerrard, M., & Gibbons, F. X. (1997). Self-esteem and the relation between risk behavior and perceptions of vulnerability to unplanned pregnancy in college women. *Health Psychology, 16,* 137–146.

208. Diener, E., & Diener, M. (1995). Cross-cultural correlates of life satisfaction and self-esteem. *Journal of Personality and Social Psychology, 68,* 653–663.

209. Orth, U., Robins, R. W., & Widaman, K. F. (2012). Life-span development of self-esteem and its effects on important life outcomes. *Journal of Personality and Social Psychology, 102,* 1271–1288.

210. Leary, M. R., Tambor, E. S., Terdal, S. K., & Downs, D. L. (1995). Self-esteem as an interpersonal monitor: The sociometer hypothesis. *Journal of Personality Psychology, 68,* 518–530.

211. Leary, M. R., & Baumeister, R. F. (2000). The nature and function of self-esteem: Sociometer theory. In M. Zanna (Ed.), *Advances in experimental social psychology* (Vol. 32, pp. 1–62). San Diego: Academic Press.

212. Greenberg, J., Solomon, S., & Pyszczynski, T. (1997). Terror management theory of self-esteem and cultural worldviews: Empirical assessments and conceptual refinements. In M. P. Zanna (Ed.), *Advances in experimental social psychology* (Vol. 29, pp. 61–139). San Diego: Academic Press.

213. Koch, E. J., & Shepperd, J. A. (2008). Testing competence and acceptance explanations of self-esteem. *Self and Identity, 7,* 54–74.

214. Twenge, J. M., Konrath, S., Foster, J. D., Campbell, W. K., & Bushman, B. J. (2008). Egos inflating over time: A cross-temporal meta-analysis of the Narcissistic Personality Inventory. *Journal of Personality, 76,* 875–901.

215. Trzesniewski, K. H., Donnellan, M. B., & Robins, R. W. (2008). Is "Generation Me" really more narcissistic than previous generations? *Journal of Personality, 76,* 903–917.

216. Twenge, J. M. (2006). *Generation Me.* New York: Free Press.

217. DeWall, C. N., Pond, R. S., Campbell, W. K., & Twenge, J. M. (2011). Tuning in to psychological change: Linguistic markers of psychological traits and emotions over time in popular U.S. song lyrics. *Psychology of Aesthetics, Creativity, and the Arts, 5,* 200–207.

218. Morf, C. C., & Rhodewalt, F. (2001). Unraveling the paradoxes of narcissism: A dynamic self-regulatory processing model. *Psychological Inquiry, 12,* 177–196.

219. Bushman, B. J., & Baumeister, R. F. (1998). Threatened egotism, narcissism, self-esteem, and direct and displaced aggression: Does self-love or self-hate lead to violence? *Journal of Personality and Social Psychology, 75,* 219–229.

220. Bushman, B. J., & Baumeister, R. F. (2002). Does self-love or self-hate lead to violence. *Journal of Research in Personality, 36,* 543–545.

221. Bushman, B. J., Bonacci, A. M., Van Dijk, M., & Baumeister, R. F. (2003). Narcissism, sexual refusal, and sexual aggression: Testing a narcissistic reactance model of sexual coercion. *Journal of Personality and Social Psychology, 84,* 1027–1040.

222. Aberson, C. L., Healy, M., & Romero, V. (2000). Ingroup bias and self-esteem: A meta-analysis. *Personality and Social Psychology Review, 4,* 157–173.

223. Crocker, J., & Schwartz, I. (1985). Prejudice and ingroup favoritism in a minimal intergroup situation: Effects of self-esteem. *Personality and Social Psychology Bulletin, 11,* 379–386.

224. Buss, D. M., & Shackelford, T. K. (1997). From vigilance to violence: Mate retention tactics in married couples. *Journal of Personality and Social Psychology, 72,* 346–361.

225. Campbell, W. K. (1999). Narcissism and romantic attraction. *Journal of Personality and Social Psychology, 77,* 1254–1270.

226. Campbell, W. K. (2005). *When you love a man who loves himself.* Naperville, IL: Sourcebooks.

227. Campbell, W. K., & Foster, C. A. (2002). Narcissism and commitment in romantic relationships: An Investment Model analysis. *Personality and Social Psychology Bulletin, 28,* 484–495.

228. Campbell, W. K., Foster, C. A., & Finkel, E. J. (2002). Does self-love lead to love for others? A story of narcissistic game playing. *Journal of Personality and Social Psychology, 83,* 340–354.

229. Campbell, W. K. (2005). *When you love a man who loves himself.* Naperville, IL: Sourcebooks.

230. Olweus, D. (1994). Bullying at school: Long-term outcomes for the victims and an effective school-based intervention program. In R. Huesmann (Ed.), *Aggressive behavior: Current perspectives* (pp. 97–130). New York: Plenum Press.

231. Salmivalli, C., Kaukiainen, A., Kaistaniemi, L., & Lagerspetz, K. M. J. (1999). Self-evaluated self-esteem, peer-evaluated self-esteem, and defensive egotism as predictors of adolescents' participation in bullying situations. *Personality and Social Psychology Bulletin, 25,* 1268–1278.

232. Perez, R. C. (1973). The effect of experimentally induced failure, self-esteem and sex on cognitive differentiation. *Journal of Abnormal Psychology, 81,* 74–79.

233. Shrauger, J. S., & Sorman, P. B. (1977). Self-evaluations, initial success and failure, and improvement as determinants of persistence. *Journal of Consulting and Clinical Psychology, 45,* 784–795.

234. Janoff-Bulman, R., & Brickman, P. (1982). Expectations and what people learn from failure. In N. T. Feather (Ed.), *Expectations and actions: Expectancy-value models in psychology* (pp. 207–237). Hillsdale, NJ: Erlbaum.

235. McFarlin, D. B. (1985). Persistence in the face of failure: The impact of self-esteem and contingency information. *Personality and Social Psychology Bulletin, 11,* 153–163.

236. McFarlin, D. B., Baumeister, R. F., & Blascovich, J. (1984). On knowing when to quit: Task failure, self-esteem, advice, and nonproductive persistence. *Journal of Personality, 52,* 138–155.

237. Sandelands, L. E., Brockner, J., & Glynn, M. A. (1988). If at first you don't succeed, try, try again: Effects of persistence-performance contingencies, ego involvement, and self-esteem on task persistence. *Journal of Applied Psychology, 73,* 208–216.

238. Di Paula, A., & Campbell, J. D. (2002). Self-esteem and persistence in the face of failure. *Journal of Personality and Social Psychology, 83,* 711–724.

239. McFarlin, D. B. (1985). Persistence in the face of failure: The impact of self-esteem and contingency information. *Personality and Social Psychology Bulletin, 11,* 153–163.

240. Crocker, J., & Park, L. E. (2004). The costly pursuit of self-esteem. *Psychological Bulletin, 130,* 392–414.

241. Crocker, J., & Park, L. E. (2004). The costly pursuit of self-esteem. *Psychological Bulletin, 130,* 392–414.

242. Tesser, A. (1988). Toward a self-evaluation maintenance model of social behavior. In L. Berkowitz (Ed.), *Advances in experimental social psychology* (Vol. 21, pp. 181–227). San Diego: Academic Press.

243. Crocker, J., Sommers, S. R., & Luhtanen, R. K. (2002). Hopes dashed and dreams fulfilled: Contingencies of self-worth and admissions to graduate school. *Personality and Social Psychology Bulletin, 28,* 1275–1286.

244. Von Hippel, W., & Trivers, R. (2011). The evolution and psychology of self-deception. *Behavioral and Brain Sciences, 34,* 1–56.

245. Baumeister, R. F. (1982). A self-presentational view of social phenomena. *Psychological Bulletin, 91,* 3–26.

246. Goffman, E. (1959). *The presentation of self in everyday life.* New York: Doubleday Anchor.

247. Schlenker, B. R. (1980). *Impression management: The self-concept, social identity, and interpersonal relations.* Monterey, CA: Brooks/Cole.

248. Tufekci, Z. (2008). Grooming, gossip, Facebook, and Myspace: What can we learn about these sites from those who won't assimilate? *Information, Communication & Society, 11,* 544–564.

249. Tamir, D. I., & Mitchell, J. P. (2012). Disclosing information about the self is intrinsically rewarding. *PNAS, 109,* 8038–3043.

250. Baumeister, R. F., & Tice, D. M. (1984). Role of self-presentation and choice in cognitive dissonance under forced compliance: Necessary or sufficient causes? *Journal of Personality and Social Psychology, 46,* 5–13.

251. Tedeschi, J. T., Schlenker, B. R., & Bonoma, T. V. (1971). Cognitive dissonance: Private ratiocination or public spectacle? *American Psychologist, 26,* 685–695.

252. Baumeister, R. F., & Cairns, K. J. (1992). Repression and self-presentation: When audiences interfere with self-deceptive strategies. *Journal of Personality and Social Psychology, 62,* 851–862.

253. Baumeister, R. F., & Jones, E. E. (1978). When self-presentation is constrained by the target's knowledge: Consistency and compensation. *Journal of Personality and Social Psychology, 36,* 608–618.

254. Greenberg, J., & Pyszczynski, J. (1985). Compensatory self-inflation: A response to the threat to self-regard of public failure. *Journal of Personality and Social Psychology, 49,* 273–280.

255. Munger, K., & Harris, S. J. (1989). Effects of an observer on handwashing in a public restroom. *Perceptual and Motor Skills, 69,* 733–734.

256. Heatherton, T. F., personal communication, 1993.

257. Braginski, B. M., Braginski, D. D., & Ring, K. (1969). *Methods of madness: The mental hospital as a last resort.* New York: Holt, Rinehart & Winston.

258. Goffman, E. (1959). *The presentation of self in everyday life.* New York: Doubleday Anchor.

259. Schlenker, B. R. (1980). *Impression management: The self-concept, social identity, and interpersonal relations.* Monterey, CA: Brooks/Cole.

260. Schlenker, B. R. (1980). *Impression management: The self-concept, social identity, and interpersonal relations.* Monterey, CA: Brooks/Cole.

261. Faith, heroics and bedtime snacks hailed at Columbine funerals. (1999, April 26). *CNN.* Retrieved from http://www.cnn.com/US/9904/26/school.shooting.funeral/

262. Wicklund, R. A., & Gollwitzer, P. M. (1982). *Symbolic self-completion.* Hillsdale, NJ: Erlbaum.

263. Wicklund, R. A., & Gollwitzer, P. M. (1982). *Symbolic self-completion.* Hillsdale, NJ: Erlbaum.

264. Bryan, C. J., Walton, G. M., Rogers, T., & Dweck, C. S. (2011). Motivating voter turnout by invoking the self. *PNAS, 108*(31), 12653–12656.

265. Griskevicius, V., Tybur, J. M., & Van den Bergh, B. (2010). Going green to be seen: Status, reputation, and conspicuous conservation. *Journal of Personality and Social Psychology, 98,* 392–404.

266. Schlenker, B. R. (1975). Self-presentation: Managing the impression of consistency when reality interferes with self-enhancement. *Journal of Personality and Social Psychology, 32,* 1030–1037.

267. Schlenker, B. R. (1975). Self-presentation: Managing the impression of consistency when reality interferes with self-enhancement. *Journal of Personality and Social Psychology, 32,* 1030–1037.

268. Schlenker, B. R. (1980). *Impression management: The self-concept, social identity, and interpersonal relations.* Monterey, CA: Brooks/Cole.

269. Paulhus, D. L., & Levitt, K. (1987). Desirable responding triggered by affect: Automatic egotism? *Journal of Personality and Social Psychology, 52,* 245–259.

270. Tice, D. M., Butler, J. L., Muraven, M. B., & Stillwell, A. M. (1995). When modesty prevails: Differential favorability of self-presentation to friends and strangers. *Journal of Personality and Social Psychology, 69,* 1120–1138.

271. Heine, S. J., Lehman, D. R., Markus, H. R., & Kitayama, S. (1999). Is there a universal need for positive self-regard? *Psychological Review, 106,* 766–794.

272. Sedikides, C., Gaertner, L., & Toguchi, Y. (2003). Pancultural self-enhancement. *Journal of Personality and Social Psychology, 84,* 60–70.

273. Leary, M. R., Tchividjian, L. R., & Kraxberger, B. E. (1994). Self-presentation can be hazardous to your health: Impression management and health risk. *Health Psychology, 13,* 461–470.

274. Bushman, B. J., Moeller, S. J., Konrath, S., & Crocker, J. (2012). Investigating the link between liking versus wanting self-esteem and depression in a nationally representative sample of American adults. *Journal of Personality, 80*(5), 1455–1471. DOI: 10.1111/j.1467-6494.2012.00781.x.

275. Bushman, B. J., Moeller, S. J., & Crocker, J. (2011). Sweets, sex, or self-esteem? Comparing the value of self-esteem boosts with other pleasant rewards. *Journal of Personality, 79*(5), 993–1012. DOI: 10.1111/j.1467-6494.2011.00712.x

276. Markus, H. R., & Kitayama, S. (1991). Culture and the self: Implications for cognition, emotion, and motivation. *Psychological Review, 98,* 224–253. Copyright © 1991 by the American Psychological Association. Reprinted by permission.

CHAPTER 4
Choices and Actions: The Self in Control

1. Hee, K. H. (1993). *The tears of my soul.* New York: Morrow.

2. James, W. (1890). *Principles of psychology.* New York: Holt.

3. Fiske, S. T. (1992). Thinking is for doing: Portraits of social cognition from daguerreotype to laserphoto. *Journal of Personality and Social Psychology, 63,* 877–889.

4. Baumeister, R. F., & Masicampo, E. J. (2010). Conscious thought is for facilitating social and cultural interactions: How mental simulations serve the animal-culture interface. *Psychological Review, 117,* 945–971.

5. Anderson, C. A. (1983). Imagination and expectation: The effect of imagining behavioral scripts on personal intentions. *Journal of Personality and Social Psychology, 45,* 293–305.

6. Anderson, C. A., & Sechler, E. S. (1986). Effects of explanation and counterexplanation on the development and use of social theories. *Journal of Personality and Social Psychology, 20,* 24–34.

7. Carroll, J. S. (1978). The effect of imagining an event on expectations for the event: An interpretation in terms of the availability heuristic. *Journal of Experimental Social Psychology, 14,* 88–96.

8. Gregory, L. W., Cialdini, R. B., & Carpenter, K. M. (1982). Self-relevant scenarios as mediator of likelihood estimates and compliance: Does imagining make it so? *Journal of Personality and Social Psychology, 43,* 89–99.

9. Hirt, E. R., & Sherman, S. J. (1985). The role of prior knowledge in explaining hypothetical events. *Journal of Experimental Social Psychology, 21,* 519–543.

10. Sherman, S. T., Zehner, K. S., Johnson, J., & Hirt, E. R. (1983). Social explanation: The role of timing, set, and recall on subjective likelihood estimates. *Journal of Personality and Social Psychology, 44,* 1127–1143.

11. Taylor, S. E., & Pham, L. B. (1996). Mental simulation, motivation, and action. In P. M. Gollwitzer & J. A. Bargh (Eds.), *The psychology of action: Linking cognition and motivation to behavior* (pp. 219–235). New York: Guilford Press.

12. Waldman, S. (1992, January 27). The tyranny of choice: Why the consumer revolution is ruining your life. *New Republic,* 22–25.

13. Kahneman, D., & Tversky, A. (1979). Prospect theory: An analysis of decision under risk. *Econometrica, 47,* 263–291.

14. Hsee, C. K., & Zhang, J. (2004). Distinction bias: Misprediction and mischoice due to joint evaluation. *Journal of Personality and Social Psychology, 86*(5), 680–695.

15. Bazerman, M. H., Loewenstein, G. F., & White, S. B. (1992). Reversals of preference in allocation decisions: Judging an alternative versus choosing among alternatives. *Administrative Science Quarterly, 37*(2), 220–240.

16. Hsee, C. K. (1996). The evaluability hypothesis: An explanation for preference reversals between joint and separate evaluations of alternatives. *Organizational Behavior and Human Decision Processes, 67*(3), 247–257.

17. Kahneman, D., & Tversky, A. (1984). Choices, values, and frames. *American Psychologist, 39,* 341–350.

18. Tversky, A., & Kahneman, D. (1983). Extensional vs. intuitive reasoning: The conjunction fallacy in probability judgment. *Psychological Review, 91,* 293–315.

19. Atthowe, J. M. (1960). Types of conflict and their resolution: A reinterpretation. *Journal of Experimental Psychology, 59,* 1–9.

20. Kahneman, D., & Tversky, A. (1979). Prospect theory: An analysis of decision under risk. *Econometrica, 47,* 263–291.

21. Haselton, M. G., & Buss, D. M. (2000). Error management theory: A new perspective on biases in cross-sex mind reading. *Journal of Personality and Social Psychology, 78,* 81–91.

22. Wilson, M., & Daly M. (2003). Do pretty women inspire men to discount the future? *Biology Letters (Proc. R. Soc. Lond. B; Suppl.* doi: 10.1098/rsbl.2003.0134, online 12/12/2003)

23. Shin, J., & Ariely, D. (2004). Keeping doors open: The effect of unavailability on incentives to keep options open. *Management Science, 50,* 575–586.

24. Anderson, C. J. (2003). The psychology of doing nothing: Forms of decision avoidance result from reason and emotion. *Psychological Bulletin, 129,* 139–167.

25. Anderson, C. J. (2003). The psychology of doing nothing: Forms of decision avoidance result from reason and emotion. *Psychological Bulletin, 129,* 139–167.

26. Iyengar, S. S., & Lepper, M. R. (2000). When choice is demotivating: Can one desire too much of a good thing? *Journal of Personality and Social Psychology, 79,* 995–1006.

27. Schwartz, B. (2004, April). The tyranny of choice. *Scientific American,* 72–75.

28. Scheibehenne, B., Greifeneder, R., & Todd, P. M. (2008, November). *Can there ever be too many options? Re-assessing the effect of choice overload.* Paper presented at the annual meeting of the Society for Judgment and Decision Making, Chicago.

29. Mochon, D. (2008, November). *Single option aversion: When the illusion of choices reduces deferral.* Paper presented at the annual meeting of the Society for Judgment and Decision Making, Chicago.

30. White, C. M., Reisen, N., & Hoffrage, U. (2008, November). *Choice deferral can arise from absolute evaluation or relative comparison.* Paper presented at the annual meeting of the Society for Judgment and Decision Making, Chicago.

31. Brehm, J. W. (1966). *A theory of psychological reactance*. New York: Academic Press.

32. Brehm, J. W. (1972). *Responses to loss of freedom: A theory of psychological reactance*. Morristown, NJ: General Learning Press.

33. Brehm, S. S., & Brehm, J. W. (1981). *Psychological reactance*. New York: Wiley.

34. Wicklund, R. A. (1974). *Freedom and reactance*. Potomac, MD: Erlbaum.

35. Wortman, C. B., & Brehm, J. W. (1975). Responses to uncontrollable outcomes: An integration of reactance theory and the learned helplessness model. In L. Berkowitz (Ed.), *Advances in experimental social psychology* (Vol. 8, pp. 277–336). New York: Academic Press.

36. Brehm, J. W. (1966). *A theory of psychological reactance*. New York: Academic Press.

37. Brehm, S. S., & Brehm, J. W. (1981). *Psychological reactance*. New York: Wiley.

38. Bushman, B. J., & Cantor, J. (2003). Media ratings for violence and sex: Implications for policy makers and parents. *American Psychologist, 58*, 130–141.

39. Baumeister, R. F., Catanese, K. R., & Wallace, H. M. (2002). Conquest by force: A narcissistic reactance theory of rape and sexual coercion. *Review of General Psychology, 6*, 92–135.

40. Bushman, B. J., Bonacci, A. M., Van Dijk, M., & Baumeister, R. F. (2003). Narcissism, sexual refusal, and sexual aggression: Testing a narcissistic reactance model of sexual coercion. *Journal of Personality and Social Psychology, 84*, 1027–1040.

41. Heine, S. J., Lehman, D. R., Markus, H. R., & Kitayama, S. (1999). Is there a universal need for positive self-regard? *Psychological Review, 106*, 766–794.

42. Dweck, C. S. (1996). Implicit theories as organizers of goals and behavior. In P. Gollwitzer & J. Bargh (Eds.), *The psychology of action: Linking cognition and motivation to behavior* (pp. 69–91). New York: Guilford Press.

43. Dweck, C. S., & Leggett, E. L. (1988). A social-cognitive approach to motivation and personality. *Psychological Review, 95*, 256–273.

44. Henderson, V., & Dweck, C. S. (1990). Achievement and motivation in adolescence: A new model and data. In S. Feldman & G. Elliott (Eds.), *At the threshold: The developing adolescent* (pp. 308–329). Cambridge, MA: Harvard University Press.

45. Zhao, W., & Dweck, C. S. (1994). *Implicit theories and vulnerability to depression-like responses*. Unpublished manuscript, Columbia University, New York. Cited in Dweck, C. S. (1996). Implicit theories as organizers of goals and behavior. In P. Gollwitzer & J. Bargh (Eds.), *The psychology of action: Linking cognition and motivation to behavior* (pp. 69–91). New York: Guilford Press.

46. Dweck, C. S. (1996). Implicit theories as organizers of goals and behavior. In P. Gollwitzer & J. Bargh (Eds.), *The psychology of action: Linking cognition and motivation to behavior* (pp. 69–91). New York: Guilford Press.

47. Kant, I. (1967). *Kritik der praktischen Vernunft* [Critique of practical reason]. Hamburg: Felix Meiner Verlag. (Original work published 1797).

48. Vohs, K. D., & Schooler, J. (2008). The value of believing in free will: Encouraging a belief in determinism increases cheating. *Psychological Science, 19*, 49–54.

49. Baumeister, R. F., Masicampo, E. J., & DeWall, C. N. (2009). Prosocial benefits of feeling free: Disbelief in free will increases aggression and reduces helpfulness. *Personality and Social Psychology Bulletin, 35*, 260–268.

50. Monroe, A. E. & Malle, B. F. (2010). From uncaused will to conscious choice: The need to study, not speculate about people's folk concept of free will. *Review of Philosophy and Psychology, 9*, 211–224.

51. Deci, E. L., & Ryan, R. M. (1985). *Intrinsic motivation and self-determination in human behavior*. New York: Plenum Press.

52. Deci, E. L., & Ryan, R. M. (2000). The "what" and "why" of goal pursuits: Human needs and the self-determination of behavior. *Psychological Inquiry, 11*, 227–268.

53. Ryan, R. M., & Deci, E. L. (2000). Self-determination theory and the facilitation of intrinsic motivation, social development, and well-being. *American Psychologist, 55*, 68–78.

54. deCharms, R. (1968). *Personal causation*. New York: Academic Press.

55. Deci, E. L. (1975). *Intrinsic motivation*. New York: Plenum Press.

56. Deci, E. L., Koestner, R., & Ryan, R. M. (1999). A meta-analytic review of experiments examining the effects of extrinsic rewards on intrinsic motivation. *Psychological Bulletin, 125*, 627–668.

57. Fisher, C. D. (1978). The effects of personal control, competence, and extrinsic reward systems on intrinsic motivation. *Organizational Behavior and Human Performance, 21*, 273–288.

58. Ryan, R. M. (1982). Control and information in the intrapersonal sphere: An extension of cognitive evaluation theory. *Journal of Personality and Social Psychology, 43*, 450–461.

59. Ryan, R. M., & Deci, E. L. (2000). Self-determination theory and the facilitation of intrinsic motivation, social development, and well-being. *American Psychologist, 55*, 68–78.

60. Amabile, T. M. (1996). *Creativity in context*. Boulder, CO: Westview Press.

61. Deci, E. L., Nezlek, J., & Sheinman, L. (1981). Characteristics of the rewarder and the intrinsic motivation of the rewardee. *Journal of Personality and Social Psychology, 40*, 1–10.

62. Deci, E. L., Koestner, R., & Ryan, R. M. (1999). A meta-analytic review of experiments examining the effects of extrinsic rewards on intrinsic motivation. *Psychological Bulletin, 125*, 627–668.

63. Flink, C., Boggiano, A. K., & Barrett, M. (1990). Controlling teaching strategies: Undermining children's self-determination and performance. *Journal of Personality and Social Psychology, 59*(5), 916–924.

64. Grolnick, W. S., & Ryan, R. M. (1987). Autonomy in children's learning: An experimental and individual differences investigation. *Journal of Personality and Social Psychology, 52*, 890–898.

65. Ryan, R. M., & Deci, E. L. (2000). Self-determination theory and the facilitation of intrinsic motivation, social development, and well-being. *American Psychologist, 55*, 68–78.

66. Ryan, R. M., & Grolnick, W. S. (1986). Origin and pawns in the classroom: Self-report and projective assessments of individual differences in children's perceptions. *Journal of Personality and Social Psychology, 50*, 550–558.

67. Utman, C. H. (1997). Performance effects of motivational state: A meta-analysis. *Personality and Social Psychology Review, 1*, 170–182.

68. Kasser, T., & Ryan, R. M. (2001). Be careful what you wish for: Optimal functioning and the relative attainment of intrinsic and extrinsic goals. In P. Schmuck & K. Sheldon (Eds.), *Life goals and well-being* (pp. 116–131). Göttingen: Hogrefe.

69. Sheldon, K. M., & Kasser, T. (1998). Pursuing personal goals: Skills enable progress but not all progress is beneficial. *Personality and Social Psychology Bulletin, 24*, 1319–1331.

70. Glass, D. C., Singer, J. E., & Friedman, L. N. (1969). Psychic cost of adaptation to an environmental stressor. *Journal of Personality and Social Psychology, 12*, 200–210. Retrieved from http://www.quotationspage.com/quote/34212.html

71. Oettingen, G., & Gollwitzer, P. M. (2001). Goal setting and goal striving. In A. Tesser & N. Schwarz (Eds.), *Blackwell handbook of social psychology: Intraindividual processes* (pp. 329–348). Oxford: Blackwell.

72. Locke, E. A., & Kristof, A. L. (1996). Volitional choices in the goal achievement process. In P. M. Gollwitzer & J. A. Bargh (Eds.), *The psychology of action: Linking cognition and motivation to behavior* (pp. 363–384). New York: Guilford Press.

73. Locke E. A., & Latham, G. P. (1990). *A theory of goal setting and task performance*. Englewood Cliffs, NJ: Prentice Hall.

74. Little, B. R. (1989). Personal projects analysis: Trivial pursuits, magnificent obsessions, and the search for coherence. In D. Buss & N. Cantor (Eds.), *Personality psychology: Recent trends and emerging directions* (pp. 15–31). New York: Springer Verlag.

75. Emmons, R. A. (1989). The personal striving approach to personality. In L. Pervin (Ed.), *Goal concepts and personality and social cognition* (pp. 87–126). Hillsdale, NJ: Erlbaum.

76. Little, B. R. (1989). Personal projects analysis: Trivial pursuits, magnificent obsessions, and the search for coherence. In D. Buss & N. Cantor (Eds.), *Personality psychology: Recent trends and emerging directions* (pp. 15–31). New York: Springer Verlag.

77. Tomasello, M., & Call, J. (1997). *Primate cognition*. New York: Oxford University Press.

78. Roberts, W. A. (2002). Are animals stuck in time? *Psychological Bulletin, 128*, 473–489.

79. Bonezzi, A., Brendl, C.M., & De Angelis, M. (2011). Stuck in the middle: The psychophysics of goal pursuit. *Psychological Science, 22*, 607–612.

80. Farrell, W. (1993). *The myth of male power*. New York: Berkley Books.

81. Kasser, T., & Ryan, R. M. (1993). A dark side of the American Dream: Correlates of financial success as a central life aspiration. *Journal of Personality and Social Psychology, 65*, 410–422.

82. Gollwitzer, P. M. (1996). The volitional benefits of planning. In P. M. Gollwitzer & J. A. Bargh (Eds.), *The psychology of action: Linking cognition and motivation to behavior* (pp. 287–312). New York: Guilford Press.

83. Locke, E. A., & Kristof, A. L. (1996). Volitional choices in the goal achievement process. In P. M. Gollwitzer & J. A. Bargh (Eds.), *The psychology of action: Linking cognition and motivation to behavior* (pp. 363–384). New York: Guilford Press.

84. Locke E. A., & Latham, G. P. (1990). *A theory of goal setting and task performance*. Englewood Cliffs, NJ: Prentice Hall.

85. Gollwitzer, P. M., & Kinney, R. F. (1989). Effects of deliberative and implemental mind-sets on the illusion of control. *Journal of Personality and Social Psychology, 56*, 531–542.

86. Taylor, S. E., & Gollwitzer, P. M. (1995). Effects of mindset on positive illusions. *Journal of Personality and Social Psychology, 69*, 213–226.

87. Gollwitzer, P. M. (1996). The volitional benefits of planning. In P. M. Gollwitzer & J. A. Bargh (Eds.), *The psychology of action: Linking cognition and motivation to behavior* (pp. 287–312). New York: Guilford Press.

88. Masicampo, E. J., & Baumeister, R. F. (2011). Consider it done! Plan making can eliminate the cognitive effects of unfulfilled goals. *Journal of Personality and Social Psychology*. Online publication doi: 10.1037/a0024192

89. Locke, E. A., & Kristof, A. L. (1996). Volitional choices in the goal achievement process. In P. M. Gollwitzer & J. A. Bargh (Eds.), *The psychology of action: Linking cognition and motivation to behavior* (pp. 363–384). New York: Guilford Press.

90. Locke E. A., & Latham, G. P. (1990). *A theory of goal setting and task performance*. Englewood Cliffs, NJ: Prentice Hall.

91. Bandura, A., & Schunk, D. H. (1981). Cultivating competence, self-efficacy, and intrinsic interest through proximal self-motivation. *Journal of Personality and Social Psychology, 41*, 586–598.

92. Bandura, A., & Schunk, D. H. (1981). Cultivating competence, self-efficacy, and intrinsic interest through proximal self-motivation. *Journal of Personality and Social Psychology, 41*, 586–598.

93. Shah, J. Y., Friedman, R., & Kruglanski, A. W. (2002). Forgetting all else: On the antecedents and consequences of goal shielding. *Journal of Personality and Social Psychology, 83*, 1261–1280.

94. Fitzsimons, G. M., & Bargh, J. A. (2003). Thinking of you: Nonconscious pursuit of interpersonal goals associated with relationship partners. *Journal of Personality and Social Psychology, 84*, 148–164.

95. Shah, J. Y. (2003). Automatic for the people: How representations of significant others implicitly affect goal pursuit. *Journal of Personality and Social Psychology, 84*, 661–681.

96. Shah, J. Y. (2003). Automatic for the people: How representations of significant others implicitly affect goal pursuit. *Journal of Personality and Social Psychology, 84*, 661–681.

97. Fitzsimons, G. M., & Shah, J. Y. (2008). How goal instrumentality shapes relationship evaluations. *Journal of Personality and Social Psychology, 95*, 319–337.

98. Gollwitzer, P. M. (1996). The volitional benefits of planning. In P. M. Gollwitzer & J. A. Bargh (Eds.), *The psychology of action: Linking cognition and motivation to behavior* (pp. 287–312). New York: Guilford Press.

99. Gollwitzer, P. M. (1996). The volitional benefits of planning. In P. M. Gollwitzer & J. A. Bargh (Eds.), *The psychology of action: Linking cognition and motivation to behavior* (pp. 287–312). New York: Guilford Press.

100. Kirschenbaum, D., Humphrey, L., & Malett, S. (1981). Specificity of planning in adult self-control: An applied investigation. *Journal of Personality and Social Psychology, 40*, 941–950.

101. Kirschenbaum, D., Malett, S., Humphrey, L., & Tomarken, A. (1982). Specificity of planning and maintenance of self-control: 1 year follow-up of a study improvement program. *Behavior Therapy, 13*, 232–240.

102. Kirschenbaum, D., Malett, S., Humphrey, L., & Tomarken, A. (1982). Specificity of planning and maintenance of self-control: 1 year follow-up of a study improvement program. *Behavior Therapy, 13*, 232–240.

103. Buehler, R., Griffin, D., & Ross, M. (1994). Exploring the "planning fallacy": Why people underestimate their task completion times. *Journal of Personality and Social Psychology, 67*, 366–381.

104. Buehler, R., Griffin, D., & Ross, M. (1994). Exploring the "planning fallacy": Why people underestimate their task completion times. *Journal of Personality and Social Psychology, 67*, 366–381.

105. Kahneman, D., & Tversky, A. (1979). Prospect theory: An analysis of decision under risk. *Econometrica, 47*, 263–291.

106. Buehler, R., Griffin, D., & Ross, M. (1994). Exploring the "planning fallacy": Why people underestimate their task completion times. *Journal of Personality and Social Psychology, 67*, 366–381.

107. Liberman, N., & Trope, Y. (1998). The role of feasibility and desirability considerations in near and distant future decisions: A test of temporal construal theory. *Journal of Personality and Social Psychology, 75*, 5–18.

108. Liberman, N., Sagristano, M. C., & Trope, Y. (2002). The effect of temporal perspective on level of construal. *Journal of Experimental Social Psychology, 38*, 524–534.

109. Baumeister, R. F., Stillwell, A. M., & Heatherton, T. F. (1994). Guilt: An interpersonal approach. *Psychological Bulletin, 115*, 243–267.

110. Mischel, W., Shoda, Y., & Peake, P. K. (1988). The nature of adolescent competencies predicted by preschool delay of gratification. *Journal of Personality and Social Psychology, 54*, 687–696.

111. Shoda, Y., Mischel, W., & Peake, P. K. (1990). Predicting adolescent cognitive and self-regulatory competencies from preschool delay of gratification: Identifying diagnostic conditions. *Developmental Psychology, 26*, 978–986.

112. Tangney, J. P., Baumeister, R. F., & Boone, A. L. (2004). High self-control predicts good adjustment, less pathology, better grades, and interpersonal success. *Journal of Personality, 72*, 271–322.

113. Olivola, C. Y., & de Neve, J. E. (2012). Going with your gut feelings lands you in the gutter: Decision making style in adolescence predicts financial well-being in adulthood. Manuscript submitted for publication. University of Warwick, United Kingdom.

114. Carver, C. S., & Scheier, M. F. (1981). *Attention and self-regulation: A control therapy approach to human behavior.* New York: Springer.

115. Carver, C. S., & Scheier, M. F. (1982). Control theory: A useful conceptual framework for personality-social, clinical and health psychology. *Psychological Bulletin, 92*, 111–135.

116. Carver, C. S., & Scheier, M. F. (1981). *Attention and self-regulation: A control therapy approach to human behavior.* New York: Springer.

117. Carver, C. S., & Scheier, M. F. (1982). Control theory: A useful conceptual framework for personality-social, clinical and health psychology. *Psychological Bulletin, 92*, 111–135.

118. Powers, W. T. (1973). *Behavior: The control of perception.* Chicago: Aldine.

119. Leon, G., & Chamberlain, K. (1973). Emotional arousal, eating patterns, and body image as differential factors associated with varying success in maintaining a weight loss. *Journal of Consulting and Clinical Psychology, 40*, 474.

120. Logue, A. W. (1991). *The psychology of eating and drinking: An introduction* (2nd ed.). New York: W. H. Freeman.

121. Polivy, J. (1976). Perception of calories and regulation of intake in restrained and unrestrained subjects. *Addictive Behaviors, 1*, 237–243.

122. Hull, J. G. (1981). A self-awareness model of the causes and effects of alcohol consumption. *Journal of Abnormal Psychology, 90*, 586–600.

123. Abraham, S. F., & Beumont, P. J. V. (1982). How patients describe bulimia or binge eating. *Psychological Medicine, 12*, 625–635.

124. Ashton, H., & Stepney, R. (1982). *Smoking: Psychology and pharmacology.* London: Tavistock.

125. Baumeister, R. F., Stillwell, A. M., & Heatherton, T. F. (1994). Guilt: An interpersonal approach. *Psychological Bulletin, 115*, 243–267.

126. Bushman, B. J., & Cooper, H. M. (1990). Effects of alcohol on human aggression: An integrative research review. *Psychological Bulletin, 107*, 341–354.

127. Steele, C. M., & Southwick, L. (1985). Alcohol and social behavior: I. The psychology of drunken excess. *Journal of Personality and Social Psychology, 48*, 18–34.

128. Baumeister, R. F., Bratslavsky, E., Muraven, M., & Tice, D. M. (1998). Ego depletion: Is the active self a limited resource? *Journal of Personality and Social Psychology, 74*, 1252–1265.

129. Baumeister, R. F., Bratslavsky, E., Muraven, M., & Tice, D. M. (1998). Ego depletion: Is the active self a limited resource? *Journal of Personality and Social Psychology, 74*, 1252–1265.

130. Baumeister, R. F., & Tierney, J. (2011). *Willpower: Rediscovering the greatest human strength.* New York: Penguin Press.

131. Baumeister, R. F. (2002). Ego depletion and self-control failure: An energy model of the self's executive function. *Self and Identity, 1*, 129–136.

132. Vohs, K. D., Baumeister, R. F., Schmeichel, B. J., Twenge, J. M., Nelson, N. M., & Tice, D. M. (2008). Making choices impairs subsequent self-control: A limited-resource account of decision making, self-regulation, and active initiative. *Journal of Personality and Social Psychology, 94*, 883–898. doi: 10.1037/0022-3514.94.5.883

133. Pocheptsova, A., Amir, O., Dhar, R., & Baumeister, R. F. (2009). Deciding without resources: Resource depletion and choice in context. *Journal of Marketing Research, 46*, 344–355. doi: 10.1509/jmkr.46.3.344

134. Levav, J., Heitmann, H., Herrmann, A., & Iyengar, S. S. (2010). Order in product customization decisions: Evidence from field experiments. *Journal of Political Economy, 118*, 274–299.

135. Danziger, S., Levav, J., & Avnaim-Pesso, L. (2011). Extraneous factors in judicial decisions. *PNAS, 108*, 6889–6892.

136. Wing, R. R., Tate, D. F., Gorin, A. A., Raynor, H. A., Fava, J. L., & Machan, J. (2007). "STOP regain": Are there negative effects of daily weighing? *Journal of Consulting and Clinical Psychology, 75*, 652–656.

137. Vohs, K. D. & Heatherton, T. F. (2000). Self-regulatory failure: A resource depletion approach. *Psychological Science, 11*, 249–254.

138. Wood, W. & Neal, D. (2007). A new look at habits and the habit-goal interface. *Psychological Review, 114*, 843–863.

139. Wood, W. & Neal, D. (2007). A new look at habits and the habit-goal interface. *Psychological Review, 114*, 843–863.

140. Wood, W., & Neal, D. T. (2009). The habitual consumer. *Journal of Consumer Psychology, 19*, 579–592.

141. Ouellette, J. A., & Wood, W. (1998). Habit and intention in everyday life: The multiple processes by which past behavior predicts future behavior. *Psychological Bulletin, 124*, 54–74.

142. Neal, D.T., Wood, W., & Drolet, A. (2013). How do people adhere to goals when willpower is low? The profits (and pitfalls) of strong habits. *Journal of Personality and Social Psychology, 104*, 959–975.

143. Neal, D. T., & Wood, W. (2007). Automaticity *in situ*: Direct context cuing of habits in daily life. In J. Bargh, P. Gollwitzer, & E. Morsella (Eds.), *Psychology of action (Vol. 2): Mechanisms of human action.* London: Oxford University Press.

144. Freud, S. (1964). *Beyond the pleasure principle* (J. Strachey, Trans.). New York: Norton. (Original work published 1920).

145. Horner, M. (1972). Toward an understanding of achievement related conflicts in women. *Journal of Social Issues, 28*, 157–176.

146. Hyland, M. E. (1989). There is no motive to avoid success: The compromise explanation for success-avoiding behavior. *Journal of Personality, 57*, 665–693.

147. Jones, E. E., & Berglas, S. (1978). Control of attributions about the self through self-handicapping strategies: The appeal of alcohol and the role of underachievement. *Personality and Social Psychology Bulletin, 4*, 200–206.

148. Mischel, W. (1996). From good intentions to willpower. In P. M. Gollwitzer & J. Bargh (Eds.), *The psychology of action: Linking cognition and motivation to behavior* (pp. 197–218). New York: Guilford Press.

149. Mischel, W., & Mendoza-Denton, R. (2002). Harnessing willpower and socio-emotional intelligence to enhance human agency and potential. In L. G. Aspinwall & U. M. Staudinger (Eds.), *A psychology of human strengths: Fundamental questions and future directions for a positive psychology* (pp. 245–256). Washington, DC: American Psychological Association.

150. Mischel, W., Shoda, Y., & Peake, P. K. (1988). The nature of adolescent competencies predicted by preschool delay of gratification. *Journal of Personality and Social Psychology, 54*, 687–696.

151. Shoda, Y., Mischel, W., & Peake, P. K. (1990). Predicting adolescent cognitive and self-regulatory competencies from preschool delay of gratification: Identifying diagnostic conditions. *Developmental Psychology, 26*, 978–986.

152. Gottfredson, M. R., & Hirschi, T. (1990). *A general theory of crime.* Stanford, CA: Stanford University Press.

153. Kidd, C., Palmeri, H., & Aslin, R.N. (2013). Rational snacking: Young children's decision-making on the marshmallow task is moderated by beliefs about environmental reliability. *Cognition, 126*, 109–114.

154. Ferrari, J. R., Johnson, J. L., & McCown, W. G. (1995). *Procrastination and task avoidance: Theory, research, and treatment.* New York: Plenum Press.

155. Tice, D. M., & Baumeister, R. F. (1997). Longitudinal study of procrastination, performance, stress, and health: The costs and benefits of dawdling. *Psychological Science, 8*, 454–458.

156. Ferrari, J. R. (2001). Procrastination as self-regulation failure of performance: Effects of cognitive load, self-awareness, and time limits on "working under pressure." *European Journal of Personality, 15,* 391–406.

157. Joiner, T. (2005). *Why people die by suicide.* Cambridge, MA: Harvard University Press.

158. Davis, P. A. (1983). *Suicidal adolescents.* Springfield, IL: C. C. Thomas.

159. Farberow, N. L. (1975). Cultural history of suicide. In N. L. Farberow (Ed.), *Suicide in different cultures* (pp. 1–16). Baltimore: University Park Press.

160. Hendin, H. (1982). *Suicide in America.* New York: Norton.

161. Maris, R. (1969). *Social forces in urban suicide.* Homewood, IL: Dorsey.

162. Maris, R. (1981). *Pathways to suicide: A survey of self-destructive behaviors.* Baltimore: Johns Hopkins University Press.

163. Rothberg, J. M., & Jones, F. D. (1987). Suicide in the U.S. Army: Epidemiological and periodic aspects. *Suicide and Life-Threatening Behavior, 17,* 119–132.

164. Baumeister, R. F. (1990). Suicide as escape from self. *Psychological Review, 97,* 90–113.

165. Gottschalk, L. A., & Gleser, G. C. (1960). An analysis of the verbal content of suicide notes. *British Journal of Medical Psychology, 33,* 195–204.

166. Hendin, H. (1982). *Suicide in America.* New York: Norton.

167. Henken, V. J. (1976). Banality reinvestigated: A computer-based content analysis of suicidal and forced-death documents. *Suicide and Life-Threatening Behavior, 6,* 36–43.

168. Shneidman, E. S. (1981). Suicide thoughts and reflections, 1960–1980. *Suicide and Life-Threatening Behavior, 11,* 197–360.

169. Joiner, T. (2005). *Why people die by suicide.* Cambridge, MA: Harvard University Press.

CHAPTER 5
Social Cognition

1. Iannelli, V. (2014, September 7). International measles outbreaks. About Health. Retrieved from http://pediatrics.about.com/od/measles/a/measles-outbreak.htm

2. Centers for Disease Control and Prevention (2014, May 29). Measles cases in the United States reach 20-year high. Retrieved from http://www.cdc.gov/media/releases/2014/p0529-measles.html

3. Iannelli, V. (2014, September 7). International measles outbreaks. About Health. Retrieved from http://pediatrics.about.com/od/measles/a/measles-outbreak.htm

4. Centers for Disease Control and Prevention (2014). Q&As about vaccination options for preventing measles, mumps, rubella, and varicella. Retrieved from http://www.cdc.gov/vaccines/vpd-vac/combo-vaccines/mmrv/vacopt-faqs-hcp.htm

5. Wakefield, A., Murch, S., Anthony, A. et al. (1998). Ileal-lymphoid-nodular hyperplasia, non-specific colitis, and pervasive developmental disorder in children. *Lancet, 351*(9103), 637–641. doi:10.1016/S0140-6736(97)11096-0

6. Rubin, D. B. (2008). Fanning the vaccine–autism link. *Neurology Today, 8*(15), 3. doi:10.1097/01.NT.0000335577.64245.34

7. Demicheli, V., Rivetti, A., Debalini, M. G., & Di Pietrantonj, C. (2012). Vaccines for measles, mumps and rubella in children. *Cochrane Database Systematic Reviews,* Issue 2. Art. No.: CD004407. doi:10.1002/14651858.CD004407.pub3

8. Jain, A., Marshall, J., Buikema, Bancroft, T., Kelly, J. P., & Newschaffer, C. J. (2015). Autism occurrence by MMR vaccine status among US children with older siblings with and without autism. *JAMA, 313*(15), 1534-1540. doi:10.1001/jama.2015.3077.

9. Doja, A., & Roberts, W. (2006). Immunizations and autism: A review of the literature. *Canadian Journal of Neurological Sciences, 33*(4), 341–346. PMID 17168158

10. Murch, S. H., Anthony, A., Casson, D. H. *et al.* (2004). Retraction of an interpretation. *Lancet, 363*(9411), 750. doi:10.1016/S0140-6736(04)15715-2

11. Boseley S (28 January 2010). Andrew Wakefield found "irresponsible" by GMC over MMR vaccine scare. *The Guardian* (London).

12. The Editors of the Lancet (February 2010). Retraction—Ileal-lymphoid-nodular hyperplasia, non-specific colitis, and pervasive developmental disorder in children. *Lancet, 375*(9713), 445. doi:10.1016/S0140-6736(10)60175-4

13. Stein, R. (2011, January 11). Wakefield tried to capitalize on autism-vaccine link, report says. *The Washington Post.* Retrieved from http://voices.washingtonpost.com/checkup/2011/01/wakefield_tried_to_capitalize.html.

14. Flaherty, D. K. (2011). The vaccine-autism connection: a public health crisis caused by unethical medical practices and fraudulent science. *Annals of Pharmacother, 45*(10), 1302–4. doi:10.1345/aph.1Q318

15. Parikh, R. (2011, January 20). Make anti-vaccine parents pay higher premiums. *CNN.* Retrieved from http://edition.cnn.com/2011/OPINION/01/20/parikh.childhood.immunizations/index.html?_s=PM:OPINION

16. Olson, S. (2014, July 30). Anti-vaccine mothers refuse vitamin K to help deficient babies just because it's an injection. *Medical Daily.* Retrieved from http://www.medicaldaily.com/anti-vaccine-mothers-refuse-vitamin-k-help-deficient-babies-just-because-its-injection-295808

17. Lewandowsky, S., Ecker, U. K. H., Seifert, C., Schwarz, N., & Cook, J. (2012). Misinformation and its correction: Continued influence and successful debiasing. *Psychological Science in the Public Interest, 13,* 106–131. doi: 10.1177/1529100612451018

18. Fiske, S. T., & Taylor, S. E. (1991). *Social cognition* (2nd ed.). New York: Random House.

19. Fiske, S. T., & Taylor, S. E. (1991). *Social cognition* (2nd ed.). New York: Random House.

20. Mercier, H., & Sperber, D. (2011). Why do humans reason? Arguments for an argumentative theory. *Behavioral and Brain Sciences, 34*(2), 57–74.

21. Baumeister, R. F., & Masicampo, E. J. (2010). Conscious thought is for facilitating social and cultural interactions: How mental simulations serve the animal-culture interface. *Psychological Review, 117,* 945–971.

22. Deacon, T. (1997). What makes the human brain different? *Annual Review of Anthropology, 26,* 337–357.

23. Heinz, S., Baron, G., & Frahm, H. (1988). Comparative size of brains and brain components. In H. D. Steklis & J. Erwin (Eds.), *Comparative Primate Biology: Vol. 4. Neurosciences.* New York: Wiley.

24. Macphail, E. (1982). *Brain and intelligence in vertebrates.* Oxford: Clarendon Press.

25. Wilson, T. D., Reinhard, D. A., Westgate, E. C., Gilbert, D. T., Ellerbeck, N., Hahn, C., Brown, C. L., & Shaked, A. (2014). Just think: The challenges of the disengaged mind. *Science, 345,* 75–77.

26. Fiske, S. T., & Taylor, S. E. (1984). *Social cognition.* New York: Random House.

27. Gilbert, D. T., Pelham, B. W., & Krull, D. S. (1988). On cognitive business: When person perceivers meet persons perceived. *Journal of Personality and Social Psychology, 54,* 733–740.

28. Stroop, J. R. (1935). Studies of interference in serial verbal reactions. *Journal of Experimental Psychology, 28,* 643–662.

29. Smith, J. D., Boomer, J., Zakrzewski, A. C., Roeder, J. L., Church, B. A., & Ashby, F. G. (2014). Deferred feedback sharply dissociates implicit and explicit category learning. *Psychological Science, 25*(2), 447–457. doi: 10.1177/0956797613509112

30. Mata, A., Ferreira, M. B., & Sherman, S. J. (2013). The metacognitive advantage of deliberative thinkers: A dual-process perspective on overconfidence. *Journal Of Personality And Social Psychology, 105*(3), 353-373. doi:10.1037/a0033640

31. Meyer, D. E., & Schvaneveldt, R. W. (1971). Facilitation in recognizing pairs of words: Evidence of a dependence between retrieval operations. *Journal of Experimental Psychology, 90,* 227–234.

32. Neely, J. H. (1991). Semantic priming effects in visual word recognition: A selective review of current findings and theories. In D. Besner & G. Humphreys (Eds.), *Basic processes in reading: Visual word recognition* (pp. 264–336). Hillsdale, NJ: Erlbaum.

33. Higgins, E. T., Rholes, W. S., & Jones, C. R. (1977). Category accessibility and impression formation. *Journal of Experimental Social Psychology, 13,* 141–154.

34. Bargh, J. A., Chen, M., & Burrows, L. (1996). Automaticity of social behavior: Direct effects of trait construct and stereotype activation on action. *Journal of Personality and Social Psychology, 71,* 230–244.

35. Hansen, J., Kutzner, F., & Wänke, M. (2013). Money and thinking: Reminders of money trigger abstract construal and shape consumer judgments. *Journal of Consumer Research, 39,* 1154–1166.

36. Epley, N., & Gneezy, A. (2007). The framing of financial windfalls and implications for public policy. *Journal of Socio-Economics, 36,* 36–47.

37. Epley, N., Mak, D., & Idson, L. C. (2006). Bonus or rebate? The impact of income framing on spending and saving. *Journal of Behavioral Decision Making, 19*(3), 213–227.

38. Rothman, A. J., Bartels, R. D., Wlaschin, J., & Salovey, P. (2006). The strategic use of gain- and loss-framed messages to promote healthy behavior: How theory can inform practice. *Journal of Communication, 56*(Suppl. 1), S202–S220.

39. Werle, C. O. C., Wansink, B., & Payne, C. R. (2014). Is it fun or exercise? The framing of physical activity biases subsequent snacking. *Marketing Letters.* doi: 10.1007/s11002-014-9301-6.

40. Wegner, D. M. (1994). Ironic processes of mental control. *Psychological Review, 101,* 34–52.

41. Biryukov, P. (1911). *Leo Tolstoy: His life and work.* New York: Charles Scribner's Sons.

42. Wegner, D. M. (1989). *White bears and other unwanted thoughts: Suppression, obsession, and the psychology of mental control.* New York: Viking/Penguin.

43. Wegner, D. M., Schneider, D. J., Carter, S. R., & White, T. L. (1987). Paradoxical effects of thought suppression. *Journal of Personality and Social Psychology, 53*(1), 5–13.

44. Wenzlaff, R. M., & Wegner D. M. (2000). Thought suppression. *Annual Review of Psychology, 51,* 59–91.

45. Toll, B. A., Sobell, M. B., Wagner, E. F., & Sobell, L. C. (2001). The relationship between thought suppression and smoking cessation. *Addictive Behaviors, 26,* 509–515.

46. Najmi, S., & Wegner, D. M. (2008). Thought suppression and psychopathology. In A. J. Elliot (Ed.), *Handbook of approach and avoidance motivation* (pp. 447–459). New York: Psychology Press.

47. Schmidt, R. E., & Gendolla, G. H. E. (2008). Dreaming of white bears: The return of the suppressed at sleep onset. *Consciousness and Cognition, 17*(3), 714–724.

48. Wegner, D. M., Wenzlaff, R. M., & Kozak, M. (2004). Dream rebound: The return of suppressed thoughts in dreams. *Psychological Science, 15,* 232–236.

49. Abramowitz, J. S., Tolin, D. F., & Street, G. P. (2001). Paradoxical effects of thought suppression: A meta-analysis of controlled studies. *Clinical Psychology Review, 21,* 683–705.

50. Lin, Y. J., & Wicker, F. W. (2007). A comparison of the effects of thought suppression, distraction and concentration. *Behaviour Research and Therapy, 45*(12), 2924–2937.

51. Dijksterhuis, A., & Nordgren, L. F. (2006). A theory of unconscious thought. *Perspectives on Psychological Science, 1,* 95–109.

52. Dijksterhuis, A., & Nordgren, L. F. (2006). A theory of unconscious thought. *Perspectives on Psychological Science, 1,* 95–109.

53. Gonzalez-Vallejo, C., Lassiter, G. D., Bellezza, F. S., & Lindberg, M. J. (2008). "Save angels perhaps": A critical examination of Unconscious Thought

Theory and the Deliberation-Without-Attention effect. *Review of General Psychology, 12*, 282–296.

54. DeWall, C. N., Baumeister, R. F., & Masicampo, E. J. (2008). Evidence that logical reasoning depends on conscious processing. *Consciousness and Cognition, 17*, 628–645.

55. Wilson, T. D. (2002). *Strangers to ourselves: Discovering the adaptive unconscious.* Cambridge, MA: Harvard University Press.

56. Herman, C. P., & Mack, D. (1975). Restrained and unrestrained eating. *Journal of Personality, 43*, 647–660.

57. Herman, C. P., & Mack, D. (1975). Restrained and unrestrained eating. *Journal of Personality, 43*, 647–660.

58. Knight, L. J., & Boland, F. J. (1989). Restrained eating: An experimental disentanglement of disinhibiting variables of perceived calories and food type. *Journal of Abnormal Psychology, 98*, 412–420.

59. Soetens, B., Braet, C., Dejonckheere, P., & Roets, A. (2006). When suppression backfires: The ironic effects of suppressing eating-related thoughts. *Journal of Health Psychology, 11*(5), 655–668.

60. Soetens, B., Braet, C., & Moens, E. (2008). Thought suppression in obese and non-obese restrained eaters: Piece of cake or forbidden fruit? *European Eating Disorders Review, 16*(1), 67–76.

61. Burger, J. M., Cooper, H. M., & Good, T. L. (1982). Teacher attributions of student performance: Effects of outcome. *Personality and Social Psychology Bulletin, 8*, 685–690.

62. Weiner, B. (1972). *Theories of motivation: From mechanism to cognition.* Chicago: Rand McNally.

63. Obach, M. S. (2003). A longitudinal-sequential study of perceived academic competence and motivational beliefs for learning among children in middle school. *Educational Psychology, 23*, 323–338.

64. Platt, C. W. (1988). Effects of causal attributions for success on first-term college performance: A covariance structure model. *Journal of Educational Psychology, 80*, 569–578.

65. Armbrister, R. C. (2002). A cross-cultural comparison of student social attributions. *Psychology in the Schools, 39*, 39–49.

66. Holloway, S. D., Kashiwagi, K., Hess, R. D., & Azuuma, H. (1986). Causal attributions by Japanese and American mothers and children about performance in mathematics. *International Journal of Psychology, 21*, 269–286.

67. Campbell, W. K., & Sedikides, C. (1999). Self-threat magnifies the self-serving bias: A meta-analytic integration. *Review of General Psychology, 3*, 23–43.

68. Zuckerman, M. (1979). Attribution of success and failure revisited, or: The motivational bias is alive and well in attribution theory. *Journal of Personality, 47*, 245–287.

69. Bradley, G. W. (1978). Self-serving biases in the attribution process: A reexamination of the fact or fiction question. *Journal of Personality and Social Psychology, 36*, 56–71.

70. Tetlock, P. E. (1980). Explaining teacher explanations for pupil performance: A test of the self-presentation position. *Social Psychology Quarterly, 43*, 283–290.

71. Ross, M., & Sicoiy, F. (1979). Egocentric biases in availability and attribution. *Journal of Personality and Social Psychology, 37*, 322–336.

72. Savitsky, K., Van Boven, L., Epley, N., & Wight, W. (2005). The unpacking effect in responsibility allocations for group tasks. *Journal of Experimental Social Psychology, 41*, 447–457.

73. Van Boven, L., & Epley, N. (2003). The unpacking effect in evaluative judgments: When the whole is less than the sum of its parts. *Journal of Experimental Social Psychology, 39*, 263–2.

74. Jones, E. E., & Nisbett, R. E. (1971). *The actor and the observer: Divergent perceptions of the causes of behavior.* New York: General Learning Press.

75. Jones, E. E., & Harris, V. A. (1967). The attribution of attitudes. *Journal of Experimental Social Psychology, 3*, 1–24.

76. Choi, I., & Nisbett, R. E. (1998). Situational salience and cultural differences in the correspondence bias and actor-observer bias. *Personality and Social Psychology Bulletin, 24*(9), 949–960.

77. Miyamoto, Y., & Kitayama, S. (2002). Cultural variation in correspondence bias: The critical role of attitude diagnosticity of socially constrained behavior. *Journal of Personality and Social Psychology, 83*(5), 1239–1248.

78. Masuda, T., & Kitayama, S. (2004). Perceiver-induced constraint and attitude attribution in Japan and the US: A case for the cultural dependence of the correspondence bias. *Journal of Experimental Social Psychology, 40*(3), 409–416.

79. Van Boven, L., Kamada, A., & Gilovich, T. (1999). The perceiver as perceived: Everyday intuitions about the correspondence bias. *Journal of Personality and Social Psychology, 77*(6), 1188–1199.

80. Zhou, X., He, L., Yang, Q., Lao, J., & Baumeister, R. F. (2012). Control deprivation and styles of thinking. *Journal of Personality and Social Psychology, 102*, 460–478. doi: 10.1037/a0026316

81. Malle, B. F. (2006). The actor-observer asymmetry in causal attribution: A (surprising) meta-analysis. *Psychological Bulletin, 132*, 895–919.

82. Malle, B. F., Knobe, J. M., & Nelson, S. E. (2007). Actor-observer asymmetries in explanations of behavior: New answers to an old question. *Journal of Personality and Social Psychology, 93*, 491–514.

83. Kruger, J., & Gilovich, T. (2004). Actions, intentions, and self-assessment: The road to self-enhancement is paved with good intentions. *Personality and Social Psychology Bulletin, 30*(3), 328–339.

84. Pronin, E., Berger, J., & Molouki, S. (2007). Alone in a crowd of sheep: Asymmetric perceptions of conformity and their roots in an introspection illusion. *Journal of Personality and Social Psychology, 92*, 585–595.

85. Pronin, E., Berger, J., & Molouki, S. (2007). Alone in a crowd of sheep: Asymmetric perceptions of conformity and their roots in an introspection illusion. *Journal of Personality and Social Psychology, 92*, 585–595.

86. Pronin, E., Berger, J., & Molouki, S. (2007). Alone in a crowd of sheep: Asymmetric perceptions of conformity and their roots in an introspection illusion. *Journal of Personality and Social Psychology, 92*, 585–595.

87. Malle, B. F. (2011). Time to give up the dogmas of attribution: An alternative theory of behavior explanation. *Advances of Experimental Social Psychology, 44*, 297–352.

88. http://www.quotationspage.com/search.php3?homesearch=Everything+should+be+made+as+simple+as+possible%2C+but+not+simpler&startsearch=Search

89. Fiske, S. T. (2004). *Social beings: A core motives approach to social psychology.* New York: Wiley.

90. Fischhoff, B., Lichtenstein, S., Slovic, P., Derby, S. L., & Keeney, R. L. (1981). *Acceptable risk.* New York: Cambridge University Press.

91. Report: Tobacco use kills 6M people a year. (2010, November 27). *CBS New Healthwatch.* Retrieved from http://www.cbsnews.com/stories/2009/08/26/health/main5266774.shtml

92. Doyle, A. C. (1974). *The memoirs of Sherlock Holmes.* London: J. Murray; Cape. (Original work published 1894)

93. Kahneman, D., & Tversky, A. (1982). The psychology of preferences. *Scientific American, 246*, 160–173.

94. Medvec, V. H., Madey, S. F., & Gilovich, T. (1995). When less is more: Counterfactual thinking and satisfaction among Olympic medalists. *Journal of Personality and Social Psychology, 69*, 603–610.

95. Slovic, P., & Lichtenstein, S. (1971). Comparison of Bayesian and regression approaches to the study of information processing in judgment. *Organizational Behavior and Human Performance, 6*, 649–744.

96. Tversky, A., & Kahneman, D. (1974) Judgment under uncertainty: Heuristics and biases. *Science, 185*, 1124–1131.

97. http://www.youtube.com/watch?v=PIsNt_7sah4

98. Laumann, E. O., Gagnon, J. H., Michael, R. T., & Michaels, S. (1994). *The social organization of sexuality: Sexual practices in the United States.* Chicago: University of Chicago Press.

99. Morokoff, P. J. (1986). Volunteer bias in the psychophysiological study of female sexuality. *Journal of Sex Research, 22*, 35–51.

100. Sawyer, D. (2004, October 21). American sex lives. *PrimeTime Live*, ABC television.

101. Janus, S. S., & Janus, C. L. (1993). *The Janus report on sexual behavior.* New York: Wiley.

102. Laumann, E. O., Gagnon, J. H., Michael, R. T., & Michaels, S. (1994). *The social organization of sexuality: Sexual practices in the United States.* Chicago: University of Chicago Press.

103. Laumann, E. O., Gagnon, J. H., Michael, R. T., & Michaels, S. (1994). *The social organization of sexuality: Sexual practices in the United States.* Chicago: University of Chicago Press.

104. Baumeister, R. F., & Vohs, K. D. (2004). Sexual economics: Sex as female resource for social exchange in heterosexual interactions. *Personality and Social Psychology Review, 8*(4), 339–363.

105. Buss, D. M., & Schmitt, D. P. (1993). Sexual strategies theory: An evolutionary perspective on human mating. *Psychological Review, 100*, 204–232.

106. Miller, L. C., & Fishkin, S. A. (1997). On the dynamics of human bonding and reproductive success: Seeking windows on the adapted-for-human environmental interface. In J. Simpson & D. Kenrick (Eds.), *Evolutionary social psychology* (pp. 197–235). Mahwah, NJ: Erlbaum.

107. Alexander, M. G., & Fisher, T. D. (2003). Truth and consequences: Using the bogus pipeline to examine sex differences in self-reported sexuality. *The Journal of Sex Research, 40*, 27–35.

108. Einon, D. (1994). Are men more promiscuous than women? *Ethology and Sociobiology, 15*(3), 131–143.

109. Phillis, D. E., & Gromko, M. H. (1985). Sex differences in sexual activity: Reality or illusion? *Journal of Sex Research, 21*, 437–443.

110. Phillis, D. E., & Gromko, M. H. (1985). Sex differences in sexual activity: Reality or illusion? *Journal of Sex Research, 21*, 437–443.

111. Brown, N. R., & Sinclair, R. C. (1999). Estimating number of lifetime sexual partners: Men and women do it differently. *Journal of Sex Research, 36*, 292–297.

112. Sinclair, R. C., & Brown, N. R. (1999, April–May). *Discrepant partner reports: Do women encode sexual experiences more deeply than men do?* Paper presented at the annual convention of the Midwestern Psychological Association, Chicago.

113. Wiederman, M. W. (1997). The truth must be in here somewhere: Examining the gender discrepancy in self-reported lifetime number of sex partners. *Journal of Sex Research, 34*, 375–386.

114. Sanders, S. A., & Reinisch, J. M. (1999). Would you say you "had sex" if ...? *Journal of the American Medical Association, 281*, 275–277.

115. Dunning, D. (1999). A newer look: Motivated social cognition and the schematic representation of social concepts. *Psychological Inquiry, 10*, 1–11.

116. Fiske, S. T., & Taylor, S. E. (1991). *Social cognition* (2nd ed.). New York: Random House.

117. Smith, D. (2004, June 20). Sign writer. *Observer.* Retrieved from http://observer.guardian.co.uk/comment/story/0,6903,1243121,00.html

118. Baggini, J. (2004). Bad moves: Confirmation bias. Retrieved from http://www.butterfliesandwheels.com/badmovesprint.php?num=42

119. http://books.google.com/books?id=FgAbAAAAYAAJ&pg=PA240&lpg=PA240&dq=%E2%80%9CIt+is+the+peculiar+and+perpetual+error+of+the+human+understanding+to+be+more+moved+and+excited+by+affirmatives+than+by+negatives.%E2%80%9D&source=bl&ots=gjQsBxs2Rg&sig=ECq3K_ih6WnhL6O4AoVeC8uWaoU&hl=en&ei=D8PeSfX1MJXxnQed6uS1CQ&sa=X&oi=book_result&ct=result&resnum=1

120. Rudski, J. M. (2002). Hindsight and confirmation biases in an exercise in telepathy. *Psychological Reports, 91*, 899–906.

121. Nickerson, R. S. (1998). Confirmation bias: A ubiquitous phenomenon in many guises. *Review of General Psychology, 2*, 175–220.

122. Mercier, H., & Sperber, D. (2011). Why do humans reason? Arguments for an argumentative theory. *Behavioral and Brain Sciences, 34*(2), 57–74.

123. Golding, S. L., & Rorer, L. G. (1972). Illusory correlation and subjective judgment. *Journal of Abnormal Psychology, 80*, 249–260.

124. Hamilton, D. L., & Gifford, R. K. (1976). Illusory correlation in interpersonal perception: A cognitive basis of stereotypic judgments. *Journal of Experimental Social Psychology, 12*, 392–407.

125. Risen, J. L., Gilovich, T., & Dunning, D. (2007). One-shot illusory correlations and stereotype formation. *Personality and Social Psychology Bulletin, 33*(11), 1492–1502.

126. Appelbaum, P., & Swanson, J. (2010). Gun laws and mental illness: How sensible are the current restrictions. *Psychiatric Services, 61*, 652-654. doi: 10.1176/appi.ps.61.7.652

127. Kahneman, D., Slovic, P., & Tversky, A. (Eds.). (1982). *Judgment under uncertainty: Heuristics and biases*. New York: Cambridge University Press.

128. Sundali, J., & Croson, R. (2006). Biases in casino betting: The hot hand and the gambler's fallacy. *Judgment and Decision Making, 1*(1), 1–12.

129. Krueger, J., & Clement, R. W. (1994). The truly false consensus effect: An ineradicable and egocentric bias in social perception. *Journal of Personality and Social Psychology, 67*, 596–610.

130. Marks, G., & Miller, N. (1987). Ten years of research on the false consensus effect: An empirical and theoretical review. *Psychological Bulletin, 102*, 72–90.

131. Ross, L., Greene, D. & House, P. (1977). The false consensus effect: An egocentric bias in social perception and attributional processes. *Journal of Experimental Social Psychology, 13*, 279–301.

132. Goel, S., Mason, W., & Watts, D. J. (2010). Real and perceived attitude agreement in social networks. *Journal of Social and Personality Psychology, 99*(4), 611–621.

133. Goethals, G. R., Messick, D. M., & Allison, S. T. (1991). The uniqueness bias: Studies of constructive social comparison. In J. Suls & T. A. Wills (Eds.), *Social comparison: Contemporary theory and research*. Hillsdale, NJ: Erlbaum.

134. Bosveld, W., Koomen, W., & Van der Pligt, J. (1996). Estimating group size: Effects of category membership, differential construal and selective exposure. *European Journal of Social Psychology, 26*, 523–535.

135. Dudley, R. T. (1999). Self-other judgments of paranormal and religious belief. *Journal of Social Behavior and Personality, 14*, 309–314.

136. Suls, J., Wan, C. K., & Sanders, G. S. (1988). False consensus and false uniqueness in estimating the prevalence of health-protective behaviors. *Journal of Applied Social Psychology, 18*, 66–79.

137. Anderson, C. A., Lepper, M. R., & Ross, L. (1980). The perseverance of social theories: The role of explanation in the persistence of discredited information. *Journal of Personality and Social Psychology, 39*, 1037–1049.

138. Lewandowsky, S., Ecker, U. K. H., Seifert, C., Schwarz, N., & Cook, J. (2012). Misinformation and its correction: Continued influence and successful debiasing. *Psychological Science in the Public Interest, 13*, 106–131. doi: 10.1177/1529100612451018

139. Ruscio, J. (2002). *Clear thinking with psychology: Separating sense from nonsense*. Pacific Grove, CA: Wadsworth.

140. Gilovich, T. (1991). *How we know what isn't so*. New York: Free Press.

141. Langer, E. J. (1975). The illusion of control. *Journal of Personality and Social Psychology, 32*, 311–328.

142. Langer, E. J., & Roth, J. (1975). Heads I win, tails it's chance: The illusion of control as a function of the sequence of outcomes in a purely chance task. *Journal of Personality and Social Psychology, 32*, 951–955.

143. Fenton-O'Creevy, M., Nicholson, N., Soane, E., & Willman, P. (2003). Trading on illusions: Unrealistic perceptions of control and trading performance. *Journal of Occupational and Organizational Psychology, 76*, 53–68.

144. Kahneman, D., & Tversky, A. (1982). The psychology of preferences. *Scientific American, 246*, 160–173.

145. Hofstadter, D. R. (1979). *Gödel, Escher, Bach: An eternal golden braid*. New York: Basic Books.

146. Kray, L. J., George, L., Liljenquist, K., Galinsky, A., Tetlock, P., & Roese, N. (2010). From what *might* have been to what *must* have been: Counterfactual thinking creates meaning. *Journal of Personality and Social Psychology, 98*, 106–118.

147. Krueger, J., Wirtz, D., & Miller, D. T. (2005). Counterfactual thinking and the first instinct fallacy. *Journal of Personality and Social Psychology, 88*, 725–735.

148. Brownstein, S. C., Wolf, I. K., & Green, S. W. (2000). *Barron's how to prepare for the GRE: Graduate Record Examination*. Hauppauge, NY: Barron's Education Series, p. 6.

149. Krueger, J., Wirtz, D., & Miller, D. T. (2005). Counterfactual thinking and the first instinct fallacy. *Journal of Personality and Social Psychology, 88*, 725–735.

150. Markman, K., Gavanski, I., Sherman, S., & McMullen, M. (1993). The mental simulation of better and worse possible worlds. *Journal of Experimental Social Psychology, 29*, 87–109.

151. McMullen, M. N., Markman, K. D., & Gavanski, I. (1995). Living in neither the best nor the worst of all possible worlds: Antecedents and consequences of upward and downward counterfactual thinking. In N. J. Roese & J. M. Olson (Eds.), *What might have been: The social psychology of counterfactual thinking* (pp. 133–167). Mahwah, NJ: Erlbaum.

152. Roese, N. J., & Olson, J. M. (1997). Counterfactual thinking: The intersection of affect and function. In M. P. Zanna (Ed.), *Advances in experimental social psychology* (Vol. 29, pp. 1–59). New York: Academic Press.

153. Taylor, S. E. (1983). Adjustment to threatening events: A theory of cognitive adaptation. *American Psychologist, 38*, 1161–1173.

154. McMullen, M. N., Markman K. D., & Gavanski, I. (1995). Living in neither the best nor the worst of all possible worlds: Antecedents and consequences of upward and downward counterfactual thinking. In N. J. Roese & J. M. Olson (Eds.), *What might have been: The social psychology of counterfactual thinking* (pp. 133–167). Mahwah, NJ: Erlbaum.

155. Roese, N. J., & Olson, J. M. (1997). Counterfactual thinking: The intersection of affect and function. In M. P. Zanna (Ed.), *Advances in experimental social psychology* (Vol. 29, pp. 1–59). New York: Academic Press.

156. Cosmides, L. (1989). The logic of social exchange: Has natural selection shaped how humans reason? Studies with the Wason selection task. *Cognition, 31*, 187–276.

157. Cosmides, L., & Tooby, J. (1992). Cognitive adaptations for social exchange. In J. Barkow, L. Cosmides, & J. Tooby (Eds.), *The adapted mind: Evolutionary psychology and the generation of culture* (pp. 163–228). Oxford: Oxford University Press.

158. Fiddick, L., Cosmides, L., & Tooby, J. (2000). No interpretation without representation: The role of domain-specific representations and inferences in the Wason selection task. *Cognition, 77*, 1–79.

159. Case, D. A., Fantino, E., & Goodie, A. S. (1999). Base-rate training without case cues reduces base-rate neglect. *Psychonomic Bulletin and Review, 6*(2), 319–327.

160. Lopes, L. L. (1987). Procedural debiasing. *Acta Psychologica, 64*, 167–185.

161. Williams, A. D. (1992). Bias and debiasing techniques in forensic psychology. *American Journal of Forensic Psychology, 10*, 19–26.

162. Hirt, E. R., Kardes, F. R., & Markman, K. D. (2004). Activating a mental simulation mind-set through generation of alternatives: Implications for *debiasing* in related and unrelated domains. *Journal of Experimental Social Psychology, 40*, 374–383.

163. Hirt, E. R., & Markman, K. D. (1995). Multiple explanation: A consider-an-alternative strategy for *debiasing* judgments. *Journal of Personality and Social Psychology, 69*, 1069–1086.

164. Sanna, L. J., & Schwarz, N. (2003). Using the hindsight bias: The role of accessibility experiences and (mis)attributions. *Journal of Experimental Social Psychology, 39*, 287–295.

165. Arkes, H. R. (1991). Costs and benefits of judgment errors: Implications for debiasing. *Psychological Bulletin, 110*, 486–498.

166. Williams, A. D. (1992). Bias and debiasing techniques in forensic psychology. *American Journal of Forensic Psychology, 10*, 19–26.

167. Arkes, H. R. (1991). Costs and benefits of judgment errors: Implications for debiasing. *Psychological Bulletin, 110*, 486–498.

168. Williams, A. D. (1992). Bias and debiasing techniques in forensic psychology. *American Journal of Forensic Psychology, 10*, 19–26.

169. Kray, L. J., & Galinsky, A. D. (2003). The debiasing effect of counterfactual mind-sets: Increasing the search for disconfirmatory information in group decisions. *Organizational Behavior and Human Decision Processes, 91*, 69–81.

170. Croskerry, P. (2003). The importance of cognitive errors in diagnosis and strategies to minimize them. *Academic Medicine, 78*, 775–780.

171. From "Cosmic Evolution – Epoch 7 – Cultural Evolution." Fig. 7.13 located at http://www.tufts.edu/as/wright_cenger/cosmic_evolution. Copyright © 2005 by Eric Chaison, Wright Center for Science Education. Reprinted by permission.

CHAPTER 6
Emotion and Affect

1. Tanner, A. (2003, November 26). Penis enlargement ads drive man to threaten torture. *Reuters News Service*. Retrieved from http://www.tribemagazine.com/board/tribe-main-forum/55009-penis-enlargement-ads-drive-man-threaten-torture.html

2. Brad Sucks. Retrieved from http://www.bradsucks.net/about/

3. Fehr, B., & Russell, J. A. (1984). Concept of emotion viewed from a prototype perspective. *Journal of Experimental Psychology: General, 113*, 464–486. Quote on p. 484.

4. Cacioppo, J. T., & Gardner, W. L. (1999). Emotion. *Annual Review of Psychology, 50*, 191–214.

5. Watson, D., & Clark, L. A. (1991). Self-versus peer ratings of specific emotional traits: Evidence of convergent and discriminant validity. *Journal of Personality and Social Psychology, 60*, 927–940.

6. Watson, D., & Clark, L. A. (1992). Affects separable and inseparable: On the hierarchical arrangement of the negative affects. *Journal of Personality and Social Psychology, 62*, 489–505.

7. Watson, D., & Tellegen, A. (1985). Toward a consensual structure of mood. *Psychological Bulletin, 98*, 219–235.

8. Gallagher, J. (2011). Babies can "hear" emotion as early as three months old. BBC News Health. June 30. Retrieved from http://www.bbc.co.uk/news/health-13962068

9. Baumeister, R. F., Bratslavsky, E., Finkenauer, C., & Vohs, K. D. (2001). Bad is stronger than good. *Review of General Psychology, 5*, 323–370.

10. Goleman, D. (1995, August 8). Brain may tag all perceptions with a value. *New York Times*, 1–10.

11. Bargh, J. A., Chaiken, S., Raymond, P., & Hymes, C. (1996). The automatic evaluation effect: Unconditional automatic attitude activation with a pronunciation task. *Journal of Experimental Social Psychology, 32*, 104–128.

12. James, W. (1884). What is an emotion? *Mind, 9*, 188–205.

13. James, W. (1890). *Principles of psychology* (p. 190). New York: Holt.

14. Izard, C. E. (1971). *The face of emotion*. New York: Appleton-Century-Crofts.

15. Izard, C. E. (1990). The substrates and functions of emotion feelings: William James and current emotion theory. *Personality and Social Psychology Bulletin, 16*, 626–635.

16. Tomkins, S. S. (1962). *Affect, imagery, consciousness: Vol. 1. The positive affects*. New York: Springer.

17. Strack, F., Martin, L., & Stepper, S. (1988). Inhibiting and facilitating conditions of the human smile: A nonobtrusive test of the facial feedback hypothesis. *Journal of Personality and Social Psychology, 54*, 768–777.

18. Neal, D., & Chartrand, T. L. (2011). Embodied emotion perception: Amplifying and dampening facial feedback modulates emotion perception accuracy. *Social Psychological and Personality Science, 2*, 673–678.

19. Schachter, S. (1964). The interaction of cognitive and physiological determinants of emotional state. In L. Berkowitz (Ed.), *Advances in experimental social psychology* (pp. 49–79). New York: Academic Press.

20. Schachter, S., & Singer, J. E. (1962). Cognitive, social, and physiological determinants of emotional state. *Psychological Review, 69*, 379–399.

21. Zillmann, D. (1979). *Hostility and aggression.* Hillsdale, NJ: Erlbaum.

22. Schachter, S., & Singer, J. E., (1962). Cognitive, social, and physiological determinants of emotional state. *Psychological Review, 69*, 379–399.

23. Chivers, M. L., Seto, M. C., Laan, E., Lalumière, M. L., & Grimbos, T. (2010). Agreement of genital and subjective measures of sexual arousal: A meta-analysis. *Archives of Sexual Behavior, 39*(1), 5–56.

24. Cohen, J. (1988). *Statistical power analysis for the behavioral sciences* (2nd ed.). New York: Academic Press.

25. Adams, H. E., Wright, L. W., Jr., & Lohr, B. A. (1996). Is homophobia associated with homosexual arousal? *Journal of Abnormal Psychology, 105*, 440–446.

26. Morokoff, P. J. (1985). Effects of sex guilt, repression, sexual "arousability," and sexual experience on female sexual arousal during erotica and fantasy. *Journal of Personality and Social Psychology, 49*, 177–187.

27. Dutton, D. G., & Aron, A. P. (1974). Some evidence for heightened sexual attraction under conditions of high anxiety. *Journal of Personality and Social Psychology, 30*, 510–517.

28. Marshall, G. D., & Zimbardo, P. G. (1979). Affective consequences of inadequately explained arousal. *Journal of Personality and Social Psychology, 37*, 970–988.

29. Maslach, C. (1979). Negative and emotional biasing of unexplained arousal. *Journal of Personality and Social Psychology, 37*, 953–969.

30. Zanna, M., Higgins, E., & Taves, P. (1976). Is dissonance phenomenologically aversive? *Journal of Experimental Social Psychology, 12*, 530–538.

31. Dutton, D. G., & Aron, A. P. (1974). Some evidence for heightened sexual attraction under conditions of high anxiety. *Journal of Personality and Social Psychology, 30*, 510–517.

32. Twenge, J. M., Campbell, W. K., & Foster, C. A. (2003). Parenthood and marital satisfaction: A meta-analytic review. *Journal of Marriage and Family, 65*, 574–583.

33. Baumeister, R. F. (1991). *Meanings of life*. New York: Guilford Press.

34. Baumeister, R. F. (1991). *Meanings of life*. New York: Guilford Press.

35. Campbell, A. (1981). *The sense of well-being in America*. New York: McGraw-Hill.

36. Hicken, M. (2013, August 14). Average cost to raise a kid: $241,080. *CNN Money*. Retrieved from http://money.cnn.com/2013/08/14/pf/cost-children/

37. Brickman, P., & Campbell, D. T. (1971). Hedonic relativism and planning the good society. In M. H. Apley (Ed.), *Adaptation-level theory: A symposium* (pp. 287–302). New York: Academic Press.

38. Brickman, P., Coates, D., & Janoff-Bulman, R. (1978). Lottery winners and accident victims: Is happiness

relative? *Journal of Personality and Social Psychology, 36*, 917–927.

39. Diener, E., Lucas, R. E., & Scollon, C. N. (2006). Beyond the hedonic treadmill: Revisions to the adaptation theory of well-being. *American Psychologist, 61*, 305–314.

40. Kahneman, D. (1999). Objective happiness. In D. Kahneman, E. Diener, & N. Schwartz (Eds.), *Well-being: The foundations of hedonic psychology* (pp. 3–25). New York: Russell Sage Foundation.

41. Kahneman, D., Knetsch, J. L., & Thaler, R. H. (1990). Experimental tests of the endowment effect and the Coase theorem. *Journal of Political Economy, 98*(6), 1325–1348.

42. Kahneman, D., Wakker, P. P., & Sarin, R. (1997). Back to Bentham? Explorations of experienced utility. *Quarterly Journal of Economics, 62*, 375–406.

43. Diener, E., Lucas, R. E., & Scollon, C. N. (2006). Beyond the hedonic treadmill: Revisions to the adaptation theory of well-being. *American Psychologist, 61*, 305–314.

44. Brickman, P., Coates, D., & Janoff-Bulman, R. (1978). Lottery winners and accident victims: Is happiness relative? *Journal of Personality and Social Psychology, 36*, 917–927.

45. Lucas, R. E. (2007). Long-term disability is associated with lasting changes in subjective well-being: Evidence from two nationally representative longitudinal studies. *Journal of Personality and Social Psychology, 92*(4), 717–730.

46. Costa, P. T., & McCrae, R. R. (1980). Influence of extraversion and neuroticism on subjective well-being: Happy and unhappy people. *Journal of Personality and Social Psychology, 38*, 668–678.

47. Costa, P. T., & McCrae, R. R. (1984). Personality as a lifelong determinant of wellbeing. In C. Z. Malatesta & C. E. Izard (Eds.), *Emotion in adult development* (pp. 141–157). Beverly Hills, CA: Sage.

48. Costa, P. T., McCrae, R. R., & Zonderman, A. B. (1987). Environmental and dispositional influences on well-being: Longitudinal follow-up of an American national sample. *British Journal of Psychology, 78*, 299–306.

49. Costa, P. T., McCrae, R. R., & Zonderman, A. B. (1987). Environmental and dispositional influences on well-being: Longitudinal follow-up of an American national sample. *British Journal of Psychology, 78*, 299–306.

50. Brown, K. W., & Ryan, R. M. (2003). The benefits of being present: Mindfulness and its role in psychological well-being. *Journal of Personality and Social Psychology, 84*, 822–848.

51. McCullough, M. E. (2008). *Beyond revenge: The evolution of the forgiveness instinct*. San Francisco: Jossey-Bass.

52. McCullough, M. E., Emmons, R. A., & Tsang, J. (2002). The grateful disposition: A conceptual and empirical topography. *Journal of Personality and Social Psychology, 82*, 112–127.

53. McCullough, M. E., Rachal, K. C., Sandage, S. J., Worthington, E. L., Brown, S. W., & Hight, T. L. (1998). Interpersonal forgiving in close relationships: II. Theoretical elaboration and measurement. *Journal of Personality and Social Psychology, 75*, 1586–1603.

54. Ryff, C. D. (1995). Psychological well-being in adult life. *Current Directions in Psychological Science, 4*, 99–104.

55. Sheldon, K. M., & Lyubomirsky, S. (2004). Achieving sustainable new happiness: Prospects, practices, and prescriptions. In P. A. Linley & S. Joseph (Eds.), *Positive psychology in practice* (pp. 127–145). Hoboken, NJ: Wiley.

56. Thrash, T. M., & Elliot, A. J. (2003). Inspiration as a psychological construct. *Journal of Personality and Social Psychology, 84*, 871–889.

57. Lyubomirsky, S. (2001). Why are some people happier than others? The role of cognitive and motivational processes in well-being. *American Psychologist, 56*, 239–249.

58. Danner, D., Snowdon, D., & Friesen, W. (2001). Positive emotions in early life and longevity: Findings from the Nun Study. *Journal of Personality and Social Psychology, 80*, 804–813.

59. Abel, E. L., & Kruger, M. L. (2010). Smile intensity in photographs predicts longevity. *Psychological Science, 21*(4), 542–544.

60. Alcock, I., White, M. P., Wheeler, B. W., Fleming, L. E., & Depledge, M. H. (2014). Longitudinal effects on mental health of moving to greener and less green urban areas. *Environmental Science & Technology, 48*(2), 1247–1255. doi: 10.1021/es403688w

61. Ryan, R. M., Weinstein, N., Bernstein, J., Brown, K. W., Mistretta, L., & Gagné, M. (2010). Vitalizing effects of being outdoors and in nature. *Journal of Environmental Psychology, 30* (2), 159–168. doi: 10.1016/j.jenvp.2009.10.009

62. For review, see Gruber, J., Mauss, I. B., & Tamir, M. (2011). A dark side of happiness? How, when, and why happiness is not always good. *Perspectives on Psychological Science, 6*, 222–233.

63. Luhmann, M., Lucas, R. E., Eid, M., & Diener, E. (2013). The prospective effect of life satisfaction on life events. *Social Psychological and Personality Science, 4*, 39–45.

64. Forgas, J. P., (2013). Don't worry, be sad! On the cognitive, motivational, and interpersonal benefits of negative mood. *Current Directions in Psychological Science, 22*, 225–232.

65. Schooler, J. W., Ariely, D., & Loewenstein, G. (2003). The pursuit and assessment of happiness may be self-defeating. In J. Carrillo & I. Brocas (Eds.), *The psychology of economic decisions* (pp. 41–70). Oxford, England: Oxford University Press.

66. Quoidbach, J., Gruber, J., Mikolajczak, M., Kogan, A., Kotsou, I., & Norton, M. I. (2014). Emodiversity and the emotional ecosystem. *Journal of Experimental Psychology: General.*

67. Larsen, R. J., & Diener, E. (1987). Affect intensity as an individual difference characteristic: A review. *Journal of Research in Personality, 21*, 1–39.

68. Sheldon, K. M. (1994). Emotionality differences between artists and scientists. *Journal of Research in Personality, 28*, 481–491.

69. Aries, P. (1962). *Centuries of childhood: A social history of family life* (Trans. R. Baldick). New York: Random House.

70. Stone, L. (1977). *The family, sex and marriage in England: 1500–1800*. London: Perennial.

71. Berkowitz, L. (1993). *Aggression: Its causes, consequences, and control*. New York: McGraw-Hill.

72. Peterson, C. K., & Harmon-Jones, E. (2012). Anger and testosterone: Evidence that situationally-induced anger relates to situationally-induced testosterone. *Emotion, 12*(5), 899-902. doi: 10.1037/a0025300

73. Carver, C. S., & Harmon-Jones, E. (2009). Anger is an approach-related affect: Evidence and implications. *Psychological Bulletin, 135*, 183–204.

74. Averill, J. R. (1982). *Anger and aggression: An essay on emotion*. New York: Springer-Verlag.

75. Tice, D. M., & Baumeister, R. F. (1993). Controlling anger: Self-induced emotion change. In D. M. Wegner & J. W. Pennebaker (Eds.), *Handbook of mental control* (pp. 393–409). Englewood Cliffs, NJ: Prentice-Hall.

76. Berkowitz, L. (1993). *Aggression: Its causes, consequences, and control*. New York: McGraw-Hill.

77. Van Dijk, E., Van Kleef, G. A., Steinel, W., & Van Beest, I. (2008). A social functional approach to emotions in bargaining: When communicating anger pays and when it backfires. *Journal of Personality and Social Psychology, 94*(4), 600–614.

78. Van Kleef, G. A., De Dreu, C. K. W., & Manstead, A. S. R. (2004a). The interpersonal effects of anger and happiness in negotiations. *Journal of Personality and Social Psychology, 86*(1), 57–76.

79. Van Kleef, G. A., De Dreu, C. K. W., & Manstead, A. S. R. (2004b). The interpersonal effects of emotions in negotiations: A motivated information processing approach. *Journal of Personality and Social Psychology, 87*(4), 510–528.

80. Tamir, M., Mitchell, C., & Gross, J. J. (2008). Hedonic and instrumental motives in anger regulation. *Psychological Science, 19*(4), 324–328.

81. Ellis, A. (1977). *How to live with—and without—anger*. New York: Reader's Digest Press.

82. Geen, R. G., & Quanty, M. B. (1977). The catharsis of aggression: An evaluation of a hypothesis. In L. Berkowitz (Ed.), *Advances in experimental social psychology* (Vol. 10, pp. 1–37). New York: Academic Press.

83. Lewis, W. A., & Bucher, A. M. (1992). Anger, catharsis, the reformulated frustration-aggression hypothesis, and health consequences. *Psychotherapy, 29,* 385–392.

84. Rosenman, R. H., & Chesney, M. A. (1982). Stress, Type A behavior and coronary heart disease. In L. Goldberger & S. Breznitz (Eds.), *Handbook of stress: Theoretical and clinical aspects* (pp. 547–565). New York: Free Press.

85. Miller, T. Q., Smith, T. W., Turner, C. W., Guijarro, M. L., & Hallet, A. J. (1996). A meta-analytic review of research on hostility and physical health. *Psychological Bulletin, 119,* 322–348.

86. Bushman, B. J., Baumeister, R. F., & Stack, A. D. (1999). Catharsis, aggression, and persuasive influence: Self-fulfilling or self-defeating prophecies? *Journal of Personality and Social Psychology, 76,* 367–376.

87. Bushman, B. J. (2002). Does venting anger feed or extinguish the flame? Catharsis, rumination, distraction, anger, and aggressive responding. *Personality and Social Psychology Bulletin, 28,* 724–731.

88. Zillmann, D. (1979). *Hostility and aggression.* Hillsdale, NJ: Erlbaum.

89. Baron, R. A. (1976). The reduction of human aggression: A field study of the influence of incompatible reactions. *Journal of Applied Social Psychology, 6,* 260–274.

90. Michaud, S. G., & Aynesworth, H. (2000). *Ted Bundy: Conversations with a killer.* Irving, TX: Authorlink. Quote on p. 320.

91. Michaud, S. G., & Aynesworth, H. (2000). *Ted Bundy: Conversations with a killer.* Irving, TX: Authorlink. Quote on p. 263.

92. Hare, R. D. (1998). *Without conscience: The disturbing world of the psychopaths among us.* New York: Guilford Press.

93. Cryder, C. E, Springer, S., & Morewedge, C. M. (2012), Guilty feelings, targeted actions. *Personality and Social Psychology Bulletin, 38*(5), 607–618. doi: 10.1177/0146167211435796

94. Tangney, J. P., & Dearing, R. L. (2002). *Shame and guilt.* New York: Guilford Press.

95. Baumeister, R. F., Stillwell, A. M., & Heatherton, T. F. (1994). Guilt: An interpersonal approach. *Psychological Bulletin, 115,* 243–267.

96. Tangney, J. P., & Dearing, R. L. (2002). *Shame and guilt.* New York: Guilford Press.

97. Tangney, J. P., & Fischer, K. W. (1995). *Self-conscious emotions: The psychology of shame, guilt, embarrassment, and pride.* New York: Guilford Press.

98. McMillen, D. L., & Austin, J. B. (1971). Effect of positive feedback on compliance following transgression. *Psychonomic Science, 24,* 59–61.

99. Cialdini, R. B., Darby, B. L., & Vincent, J. E. (1973). Transgression and altruism: A case for hedonism. *Journal of Experimental Social Psychology, 9,* 502–516.

100. Harris, M. B., Benson, S. M., & Hall, C. L. (1975). The effects of confession on altruism. *Journal of Social Psychology, 96,* 187–192.

101. Katzev, R., Edelsack, L., Reynolds, R., Steinmetz, G., Walker, T., & Wright, R. (1978). The effect of reprimanding transgressions on subsequent helping behavior: Two field experiments. *Personality and Social Psychology Bulletin, 4,* 326–329.

102. Goldsmith, K., Cho, E. K., & Dhar, R. (2012). When guilt begets pleasure: The positive effect of a negative emotion. *Journal of Marketing Research, 49,* 872–881.

103. Brockner, J., Greenberg, J., Brockner, A., Bortz, J., Davy, J., & Carter, C. (1986). Layoffs, equity theory, and work performance: Further evidence of the impact of survivor guilt. *Academy of Management Journal, 29,* 373–384.

104. Baumeister, R. F., Reis, H. T., & Delespaul, P. A. E. G. (1995). Subjective and experiential correlates of guilt in everyday life. *Personality and Social Psychology Bulletin, 21,* 1256–1268.

105. Nelissen, R. M. A. (2014). Relational utility as a moderator of guilt in social interactions. *Journal of Personality and Social Psychology, 106,* 257–271.

106. Baumeister, R. F., Stillwell, A. M., & Heatherton, T. F. (1994). Guilt: An interpersonal approach. *Psychological Bulletin, 115,* 243–267.

107. Matthew 27:24.

108. Haidt, J., & Joseph, C. (2008). The moral mind: How five sets of innate intuitions guide the development of many culture-specific virtues, and perhaps even modules. In P. Carruthers, S. Laurence, & S. Stich (Eds.), *The innate mind* (Vol. 3, pp. 367–392). New York: Oxford University Press.

109. Lee, S. W. S., & Schwarz, N. (2011). Wiping the slate clean: Psychological consequences of physical cleansing. *Current Directions in Psychological Science, 20*(5), 307–311.

110. Zhong, C. B., & Liljenquist, K. A. (2006). Washing away your sins: Threatened morality and physical cleansing. *Science, 313,* 1451–1452.

111. Xu, H., Bègue, L, & Bushman, B. J. (2014). Washing the guilt away: Effects of personal versus vicarious cleansing on guilty feelings and prosocial behavior. *Frontiers in Human neuroscience, 8,* 97. doi: 10.3389/fnhum.2014.00097

112. Hutcherson, C. A., & Gross, J. J. (2011). The moral emotions: A social-functionalist account of anger, disgust, and contempt. *Journal of Personality and Social Psychology, 100*(4), 719–737.

113. Curtis, V. (2011). Why disgust matters. *Philosophical Transactions of the Royal Society B, 366,* 3478–3490. Quote on p. 3486.

114. Curtis, V. (2011). Why disgust matters. *Philosophical Transactions of the Royal Society B, 366,* 3478–3490.

115. Skolnick, A., Bascom, K. L., & Wilson, D. T. (2013). Gender role expectations of disgust: Men are low and women are high. *Sex Roles, 69*(1–2), 72–88. doi: 10.1007/s11199-013-0279-y

116. Schaller, M. (2011). The behavioural immune system and the psychology of human sexuality. *Philosophical Transactions of the Royal Society B, 366,* 3418–3426.

117. Schaller, M. (2011). The behavioural immune system and the psychology of human sexuality. *Philosophical Transactions of the Royal Society B, 366,* 3418–3426.

118. Vartanian, L. R., Thomas, M. A., & Vanman, E. J. (2013). Disgust, contempt, and anger and the stereotypes of obese people. *Eating and Weight Disorders, 18*(4), 377–382. doi: 10.1007/s40519-013-0067-2

119. Taylor, K. (2007). Disgust is a factor in extreme prejudice. *British Journal of Social Psychology, 46*(3), 597–617.

120. Choma, B. L., Hodson, G., & Costello, K. (2012). Intergroup disgust sensitivity as a predictor of islamophobia: The modulating effect of fear. *Journal of Experimental Social Psychology, 48*(2), 499–506.

121. Ritter, R. S., & Preston, J. L. (2011). Gross gods and icky atheism: Disgust responses to rejected religious beliefs. *Journal of Experimental Social Psychology, 47*(6), 1225–1230.

122. Buckles, E. E., & Trapnell, P. D. (2013). Disgust facilitates outgroup dehumanization. *Group Processes & Intergroup Relations, 16*(6), 771–780. doi: 10.1177/1368430212471738

123. Chapman, H. A., & Anderson, A. K. (2013). Things Rank and Gross in Nature: A Review and Synthesis of Moral Disgust. *Psychological Bulletin, 139*(2), 300–327. doi: 10.1037/a0030964

124. Horberg, E. J., Oveis, C., Keltner, D., & Cohen, A. B. (2009). Disgust and the moralization of purity. *Journal of Personality and Social Psychology, 97*(6), 963–976.

125. Schnall, S., Haidt, J., Clore, G. L., & Jordan, A. H. (2008). Disgust as embodied moral judgment. *Personality and Social Psychology Bulletin, 34*(8), 1096–1109.

126. Damasio, A. R. (1994). *Descartes' error.* London: Picador.

127. Anderson, S. A., Russell, C. S., & Schumm, W. R. (1983). Perceived marital quality and family life-cycle categories: A further analysis. *Journal of Marriage and the Family, 45,* 127–139.

128. Baumeister, R. F., & Leary, M. R. (1995). The need to belong: Desire for interpersonal attachments as a fundamental human motivation. *Psychological Bulletin, 117,* 497–529.

129. Belsky, J. (1985). Exploring individual differences in marital change across the transition to parenthood: The role of violated expectations. *Journal of Marriage and the Family, 47,* 1037–1044.

130. Belsky, J., Lang, M. E., & Rovine, M. (1985). Stability and change in marriage across the transition to parenthood: A second study. *Journal of Marriage and the Family, 47,* 855–865.

131. Belsky, J., Spanier, G. B., & Rovine, M. (1983). Stability and change in marriage across the transition to parenthood. *Journal of Marriage and the Family, 45,* 567–577.

132. Bernard, J. (1982). *The future of marriage.* New Haven, CT: Yale University Press.

133. Campbell, A., Converse, P. E., & Rogers, W. L. (1976). *The quality of American life: Perceptions, evaluations, and satisfactions.* New York: Russell Sage.

134. Glenn, N. D., & McLanahan, S. (1982). Children and marital happiness: A further specification of the relationship. *Journal of Marriage and the Family, 44,* 63–72.

135. Glenn, N. D., & Weaver, C. N. (1978). A multi-variate multisurvey study of marital happiness. *Journal of Marriage and the Family, 40,* 269–282.

136. Ruble, D. N., Fleming, A. S., Hackel, L. S., & Stangor, C. (1988). Changes in the marital relationship during the transition to first time motherhood: Effects of violated expectations concerning division of household labor. *Journal of Personality and Social Psychology, 55,* 78–87.

137. Spanier, G. B., & Lewis, R. A. (1980). Marital quality: A review of the seventies. *Journal of Marriage and the Family, 42,* 825–839.

138. Twenge, J. M., Campbell, W. K., & Foster, C. A. (2003). Parenthood and marital satisfaction: A meta-analytic review. *Journal of Marriage and Family, 65,* 574–583.

139. Gable, S. L., & Reis, H. T. (2001). Appetitive and aversive social interaction. In J. Harvey (Ed.), *Close romantic relationships: Maintenance and enhancement* (pp. 169–194). Mahwah, NJ: Erlbaum.

140. Leary, M. R., & Springer, C. A. (2000). Hurt feelings: The neglected emotion. In R. Kowalski (Ed.), *Aversive behaviors and interpersonal transgression.* Washington, DC: American Psychological Association.

141. Coan, J. A., Schaefer, H. S., & Davidson, R. J. (2006). Lending a hand: Social regulation of the neural response to threat. *Psychological Science, 17*(12), 1032–1039.

142. Koole, S. L., Tjew A Sin, M., & Schneider, I. K. (2014). Embodied terror management: (Simulated) Interpersonal touch alleviates existential concerns among individuals with low self-esteem. *Psychological Science, 25*(1), 30–37. doi: 10.1177/0956797613483478

143. Hatfield, E., Cacioppo, J.T., & Rapson, R.L. (1993). Emotional contagion. *Current Directions in Psychological Science, 2,* 96–100.

144. Kramer, A. D. I., Guillory, J. E., & Hancock, J. T. (2014). Experimental evidence of massive-scale emotional contagion through social networks. *Proceedings of the National Academy of Science, 111,* 24–26.

145. Coviello, L., Sohn, Y., Kramer, A. D. I., Marlow, C., Franceschetti, M., Christakis, N. A., & Fowler, J. H. (2014). Detecting emotional contagion in massive social networks. PLOS ONE, 9(3), doi: 10.1371/journal.pone.0090315

146. Frijda, N. H. (1986). *The emotions*. New York: Cambridge University Press.

147. Frijda, N. H., Kuipers, P., & ter Schure, E. (1989). Relations among emotion, appraisal, and emotional action readiness. *Journal of Personality and Social Psychology, 57*, 212–228.

148. Frijda, N. H. (1986). *The emotions*. New York: Cambridge University Press.

149. Berkowitz, L. (1993). *Aggression: Its causes, consequences, and control*. New York: McGraw-Hill.

150. Gardner, M. P., Wansink, B., & Kim, J. (2014). Better moods for better eating?: How mood influences food choice. *Journal of Consumer Psychology, Vol 24*(3), Jul, 2014. pp. 320–335. doi: 10.1037/t01397-000

151. Agras, W. S., & Telch, C. F. (1998). The effects of caloric deprivation and negative affect on binge eating in obese binge-eating disordered women. *Behavior Therapy, 29*, 491–503.

152. Agras, W. S., & Telch, C. F. (1998). The effects of caloric deprivation and negative affect on binge eating in obese binge-eating disordered women. *Behavior Therapy, 29*, 491–503.

153. Telch, C. F., & Agras, W. S. (1996). Do emotional states influence binge eating in the obese? *International Journal of Eating Disorders, 20*, 271–279.

154. Johnson, W. G., Schlundt, D. G., Barclay, D. R., Carr-Nangle, R. E., & Engler, L. B. (1995). A naturalistic functional analysis of binge eating. *Behavior Therapy, 26*, 101–118.

155. Turner, S. A., Luszczynska, A., Warner, L., & Schwarzer, R. (2010). Emotional and uncontrolled eating styles and chocolate chip cookie consumption. A controlled trial of the effects of positive mood enhancement. *Appetite, 54*(1), 143–149.

156. Tice, D. M., Bratslavsky, E., & Baumeister, R. F. (2001). Emotional distress regulation takes precedence over impulse control: If you feel bad, do it! *Journal of Personality and Social Psychology, 80*, 53–67.

157. Handley, I. M., Lassiter, G. D., Nickell, E. F., & Herchenroeder, L. M. (2004). Affect and automatic mood maintenance. *Journal of Experimental Social Psychology, 40*, 106–112.

158. Cialdini, R. B., & Kenrick, D. T. (1976). Altruism as hedonism: A social development perspective on the relationship of negative mood state and helping. *Journal of Personality and Social Psychology, 34*, 907–914.

159. Hornstein, H. A. (1982). Promotive tension: Theory and research. In V. Derlega & J. Grzelak (Eds.), *Cooperation and helping behavior: Theories and research* (pp. 229–248). New York: Academic Press.

160. Lerner, M. J. (1982). The justice motive in human relations and economic model of man: A radical analysis of facts and fictions. In V. Derlega & J. Grzelak (Eds.), *Cooperation and helping behavior: Theories and research* (pp. 249–278). New York: Academic Press.

161. Reykowski, J. (1982). Motivation and prosocial behavior. In V. Derlega & J. Grzelak (Eds.), *Cooperation and helping behavior: Theories and research* (pp. 352–375). New York: Academic Press.

162. Manucia, G. K., Baumann, D. J., & Cialdini, R. B. (1984). Mood influences on helping: Direct effects or side effects? *Journal of Personality and Social Psychology, 46*, 357–364.

163. Van Dijk, W. W., & Zeelenberg, M. (2002). Investigating the appraisal patterns of regret and disappointment. *Motivation and Emotion, 26*, 321–331.

164. Damasio, A. R. (1994). *Descartes' error*. London: Picador.

165. Bechara, A., Damasio, H., Tranel, D., & Damasio, A. R. (1997). Deciding advantageously before knowing the advantageous strategy. *Science, 275*, 1293–1295.

166. Sakaki, M., Fryker, K., & Mather, M. (2014). Emotion strengthens high-priority memory traces but weakens low-priority memory traces. *Psychological Science, 25*, 387–395.

167. Roese, N. J., & Olson, J. M. (1997). Counterfactual thinking: The intersection of affect and function. In M. P. Zanna (Ed.), *Advances in experimental social psychology* (Vol. 29, pp. 1–59). New York: Academic Press.

168. Clore, G. L., Gasper, K., & Garvin, E. (2001). Affect as information. In J. P. Forgas (Ed.), *Handbook of affect and social cognition* (pp. 122–144). Mahwah, NJ: Erlbaum.

169. Schwarz, N., & Clore, G. L. (1983). Mood, misattribution, and judgments of well-being: Informative and directive functions of affective states. *Journal of Personality and Social Psychology, 45*, 513–523.

170. Niedenthal, P. M., Halberstadt, J. B., & Innes-Ker, A. H. (1999). Emotional response categorization. *Psychological Review, 106*, 337–361.

171. DeWall, C. N., Baumeister, R. F., Chester, D. S., & Bushman, B. J. (in press). How often does currently felt emotion predict social behavior and judgment? A meta-analytic test of two theories. *Emotion Review*. doi: 10.1177/1754073915572690. http://emr.sagepub.com/content/early/2015/03/16/1754073915572690.abstract.

172. Gilbert, D. T., Pinel, E. C., Wilson, T. D., Blumberg, S. J., & Wheatley, T. P. (1998). Immune neglect: A source of durability bias in affective forecasting. *Journal of Personality and Social Psychology, 75*, 617–638.

173. Buehler, R., & McFarland, C. (2001). Intensity bias in affective forecasting: The role of temporal focus. *Personality and Social Psychology Bulletin, 27*, 1480–1493.

174. Wilson, T. D., Wheatley, T., Meyers, J. M., Gilbert, D. T., & Axsom, D. (2000). Focalism: A source of durability bias in affective forecasting. *Journal of Personality and Social Psychology, 78*, 821–836.

175. Fiske, S. (2002, November/December). Forecasting the future. *Psychology Today*. Retrieved from http://www.psychologytoday.com/articles/pto-20021125-000001.html

176. Carlsmith, K. M., Wilson, T. D., & Gilbert, D. T. (2008). The paradoxical consequences of revenge. *Journal of Personality and Social Psychology, 95*(6), 1316–1324.

177. Nisbet, E. K., & Zelenski, J. M. (2011). Underestimating nearby nature: Affective forecasting errors obscure the happy path to sustainability. *Psychological Science, 22*(9), 1101–1106.

178. Mellers, B. A., Schwartz, A., Ho, K., & Ritov, I. (1997). Elation and disappointment: Emotional responses to risky options. *Psychological Science, 8*, 423–429.

179. Connolly, T. (2002). Regret in decision making. *Current Directions in Psychological Science, 11*, 212–216.

180. Barlow, D. H. (1988). *Anxiety and its disorders: The nature and treatment of anxiety and panic*. New York: Guilford Press.

181. Loewenstein, G. F., Weber, E. U., Hsee, C. K., & Welch, N. (2001). Risk as feelings. *Psychological Bulletin, 127*, 267–286.

182. Blanton, H., & Gerrard, M. (1997). Effect of sexual motivation on men's risk perception for sexually transmitted disease: There must be 50 ways to justify a lover. *Health Psychology, 16*, 374–379.

183. Lerner, J. S., Small, D. A., & Loewenstein, G. (2004). Heart strings and purse strings: Carryover effects of emotions on economic decisions. *Psychological Science, 15*(5), 337–341.

184. Rozin, P., Haidt, J., & McCauley, C. R. (1993). Disgust. In M. Lewis & J. M. Haviland (Eds.), *Handbook of emotions* (pp. 575–594). New York: Guilford Press.

185. Rozin, P., Haidt, J., & McCauley, C. R. (2009). Disgust: The body and soul emotion in the 21st century. In B. O. Olatunji & D. McKay (Eds.), *Disgust and its disorders: Theory, assessment, and treatment implications* (pp. 9–29). Washington, DC: American Psychological Association.

186. Gerrard, M., Gibbons, F. X., & McCoy, S. B. (1993). Emotional inhibition of effective contraception. *Anxiety, Stress & Coping: An International Journal, 6*, 73–88.

187. Okwumabua, J. O., & Duryea, E. J. (2003). Depressive symptoms and decision making among African American youth. *Journal of Adolescent Research, 18*, 436–453.

188. Fredrickson, B. L. (2003). The value of positive emotions. *American Scientist, 91*, 330–335.

189. Fredrickson, B. L. (1998). What good are positive emotions? *Review of General Psychology, 2*, 300–319.

190. Fredrickson, B. L. (2001). The role of positive emotions in positive psychology: The broaden-and-build theory of positive emotions. *American Psychologist, 56*, 218–226.

191. Fredrickson, B. L. (2003). The value of positive emotions. *American Scientist, 91*, 330–335.

192. Ellsworth, P. C., & Smith, C. A. (1988). Shades of joy: Patterns of appraisal differentiating pleasant emotions. *Cognition and Emotion, 2*, 301–331.

193. Frijda, N. H. (1986). *The emotions*. New York: Cambridge University Press.

194. Gable, S. L., Reis, H. T., & Elliot, A. J. (2000). Behavioral activation and inhibition in everyday life. *Journal of Personality and Social Psychology, 78*, 1135–1149.

195. David, J. P., Green, P. J., Martin, R., & Suls, J. (1997). Differential roles of neuroticism, extraversion, and event desirability for mood in daily life: An integrative model of top-down and bottom-up influences. *Journal of Personality and Social Psychology, 73*, 149–159.

196. Major, B., Zubek, J. M., Cooper, M. L., Cozzarelli, C., & Richards, C. (1997). Mixed messages: Implications of social conflict and social support within close relationships for adjustment to a stressful life event. *Journal of Personality and Social Psychology, 72*, 1349–1363.

197. Estrada, C. A., Isen, A. M., & Young, M. J. (1997). Positive affect facilitates integration of information and decreases anchoring in reasoning among physicians. *Organizational Behavior and Human Decision Processes, 72*, 117–135.

198. Isen, A. M. (2000). Positive affect and decision making. In M. Lewis & J. M. Haviland-Jones (Eds.), *Handbook of emotions* (2nd ed., pp. 417–435). New York: Guilford Press.

199. Erez, A., & Isen, A. M. (2002). The influence of positive affect on the components of expectancy motivation. *Journal of Applied Psychology, 87*, 1055–1067.

200. Nadler, R. T., Rabi, R., & Minda, J. P. (2010). Better mood and better performance: Learning rule-described categories is enhanced by positive mood. *Psychological Science, 21*(12), 1770–1776.

201. Isen, A. M., & Patrick, R. (1983). The effect of positive feelings and risk taking: When the chips are down. *Organizational Behavior and Human Performance, 31*, 194–202.

202. de Vries, M., Holland, R. W., Corneille, O., Rondeel, E., & Witteman, C. L. M. (2012). Mood effects on dominated choices: Positive mood induces departures from logical rules. *Journal of Behavioral Decision Making, 25*(1), 74–81.

203. Martin, E. A., & Kerns, J. G. (2011). The influence of positive mood on different aspects of cognitive control. *Cognition and Emotion, 25*(2), 265–279.

204. Biss, R. K., Hasher, L., & Thomas, R. C. (2010). Positive mood is associated with the implicit use of distraction. *Motivation and Emotion, 34*(1), 73–77.

205. Ekman, P., Friesen, W. V., O'Sullivan, M., Chan, A., Diacoyanni-Tarlatzis, I., Heider, K., et al. (1987). Universals and cultural differences in the judgments of facial expressions of emotion. *Journal of Personality and Social Psychology, 53*, 712–717.

206. Elfenbein, H. A., & Ambady, N. (2002). On the universality and cultural specificity of emotion recognition: A meta-analysis. *Psychological Bulletin, 128*, 203–235.

207. Larson, R. W., & Pleck, J. (1999). Hidden feelings: Emotionality in boys and men. In D. Bernstein (Ed.), *Nebraska Symposium on Motivation: Vol. 45. Gender and motivation* (pp. 25–74). Lincoln: University of Nebraska Press.

208. Larson, R. W., & Pleck, J. (1999). Hidden feelings: Emotionality in boys and men. In D. Bernstein (Ed.), *Nebraska Symposium on Motivation: Vol. 45. Gender and motivation* (pp. 25–74). Lincoln: University of Nebraska Press.

209. Larson, R. W., & Pleck, J. (1999). Hidden feelings: Emotionality in boys and men. In D. Bernstein (Ed.), *Nebraska Symposium on Motivation: Vol. 45. Gender and motivation* (pp. 25–74). Lincoln: University of Nebraska Press.

210. LaFrance, M., & Banaji, M. (1992). Toward a reconsideration of the gender-emotion relationship. In M. S. Clark (Ed.), *Emotion and social behavior: Review of personality and social psychology* (Vol. 14, pp. 178–201). Newbury Park, CA: Sage.

211. LaFrance, M., & Banaji, M. (1992). Toward a reconsideration of the gender-emotion relationship. In M. S. Clark (Ed.), *Emotion and social behavior: Review of personality and social psychology* (Vol. 14, pp. 178–201). Newbury Park, CA: Sage.

212. Goodenough, F. L. (1931). *Anger in young children.* Minneapolis: University of Minnesota Press.

213. Brody, L. R. (1996). Gender, emotional expression, and parent-child boundaries. In R. D. Kavanaugh, B. Zimmerberg, & S. Fein (Eds.), *Emotion: Interdisciplinary perspectives* (pp. 139–170). Mahwah, NJ: Erlbaum.

214. Buss, A. H. (1989). Temperaments as personality traits. In G. A. Kohnstamm, J. E. Bates, & M. Rothbart (Eds.), *Temperament in childhood* (pp. 49–58). Chichester, West Sussex, UK: Wiley.

215. Rothbart, M. K. (1989). Temperament and development. In G. A. Kohnstamm, J. E. Bates, & M. K. Rothbart (Eds.), *Temperament in childhood* (pp. 187–247). New York: Wiley.

216. Gottman, J. M. (1994). *What predicts divorce?* Hillsdale, NJ: Erlbaum.

217. Gottman, J. M. (1994). *What predicts divorce?* Hillsdale, NJ: Erlbaum.

218. Eisenberg, N., & Lennon, R. (1983). Sex differences in empathy and related capacities. *Psychological Bulletin, 94,* 100–131.

219. Ackerman, J. M., Griskevicius, V., & Li, N. P. (2011). Let's get serious: Communicating commitment in romantic relationships. *Journal of Personality and Social Psychology, 100*(6), 1079–1094.

220. Hill, C. T., Rubin, Z., & Peplau, L. A. (1976). Breakups before marriage: The end of 103 affairs. *Journal of Social Issues, 32,* 147–168.

221. Huston, T. L., Surra, C., Fitzgerald, N. M., & Cate, R. (1981). From courtship to marriage: Mate selection as an interpersonal process. In S. Duck & R. Gilmour (Eds.), *Personal relationships. 2: Developing personal relationships.* New York: Academic Press.

222. Kanin, E. J., Davidson, K. D., & Scheck, S. R. (1970). A research note on male-female differentials in the experience of heterosexual love. *Journal of Sex Research, 6,* 64–72.

223. Baumeister, R. F., Wotman, S. R., & Stillwell, A. M. (1993). Unrequited love: On heartbreak, anger, guilt, scriptlessness, and humiliation. *Journal of Personality and Social Psychology, 64,* 377–394.

224. Hill, C. T., Rubin, Z., & Peplau, L. A. (1976). Breakups before marriage: The end of 103 affairs. *Journal of Social Issues, 32,* 147–168.

225. Yerkes, R. M., & Dodson, J. D. (1908). The relation of strength of stimulus to rapidity of habit formation. *Journal of Comparative Neurology and Psychology, 18,* 459–482.

226. Easterbrook, J. A. (1959). The effect of emotion on the utilization and the organization of behavior. *Psychological Review, 66,* 183–201.

227. Chajut, E., & Algom, D. (2003). Selective attention improves under stress: Implications for theories of social cognition. *Journal of Personality and Social Psychology, 85,* 231–248.

228. Keinan, G. (1987). Decision making under stress: Scanning of alternatives under controllable and uncontrollable threats. *Journal of Personality and Social Psychology, 52,* 639–644.

229. Keinan, G., Friedland, N., & Ben-Porath, Y. (1987). Decision making under stress: Scanning of alternatives under physical threat. *Acta Psychologica, 64,* 219–228.

230. Salovey, P., & Mayer, J. D. (1990). Emotional intelligence. *Imagination, Cognition, and Personality, 9,* 185–211.

231. Mayer, J. D., & Salovey, P. (1997). What is emotional intelligence? In P. Salovey & D. Sluyter (Eds.), *Emotional development and emotional intelligence: Implications for educators* (pp. 3–31). New York: Basic Books.

232. Dunn, E. W., Brackett, M. A., Ashton-James, C., Schneiderman, E., & Salovey, P. (2007). On emotionally intelligent time travel: Individual differences in affective forecasting ability. *Personality and Social Psychology Bulletin, 33*(1), 85–93.

233. Hoerger, M., Chapman, B. P., Epstein, R. M., & Duberstein, P. R. (2012). Emotional intelligence: A theoretical framework for individual differences in affective forecasting. *Emotion, 12*(4), 716–725. doi: 10.1037/a0026724

234. Lopes, P. N., Brackett, M. A., Nezlek, J. B., Schütz, A., Sellin, I., & Salovey, P. (2004). Emotional intelligence and social interaction. *Personality and Social Psychology Bulletin, 30,* 1018–1034.

235. O'Boyle, E. H., Jr., Humphrey, R. H., Pollack, J. M., Hawver, T. H., & Story, P. A. (2011). The relation between emotional intelligence and job performance: A meta-analysis. *Journal of Organizational Behavior, 32*(5), 788–818.

236. Zhang, H.-H., & Wang, H. (2011). A meta-analysis of the relationship between individual emotional intelligence and workplace performance. *Acta Psychologica Sinica, 43*(2), 188–202.

237. Harms, P. D., & Credé, M. (2010). Emotional intelligence and transformational and transactional leadership: A meta-analysis. *Journal of Leadership & Organizational Studies, 17*(1), 5–17.

238. Martins, A.; Ramalho, N.; Morin, E. (2010). A comprehensive meta-analysis of the relationship between emotional intelligence and health. *Personality and Individual Differences, 49,* 554–564.

239. Peterson, K., Malouff, J., & Thorsteinsson, E. B. (2011). A meta-analytic investigation of emotional intelligence and alcohol involvement. *Substance Use & Misuse, 46*(14), 1726–1733.

240. Malouff, J. M., & Schutte, N. S. (2014). Trait emotional intelligence and romantic relationship satisfaction: A meta-analysis. *American Journal of Family Therapy, 42*(1), 53–66. doi: 10.1080/01926187.2012.748549

241. Perera, H. N., & DiGiacomo, M. (2013). The relationship of trait emotional intelligence with academic performance: A meta-analytic review. *Learning and Individual Differences, 28*(12), 20–33. doi: 10.1016/j.lindif.2013.08.002

242. Schlaerth, A., Ensari, N., & Christian, J. (2013). A meta-analytical review of the relationship between emotional intelligence and leaders' constructive conflict management. *Group Processes & Intergroup Relations, 16*(1), 126–136. doi: 10.1177/1368430212439907

243. Paulhus, D. L., & Williams, K. M. (2002). The dark triad of personality: Narcissism, Machiavellianism, and psychopathy. *Journal of Research in Personality, 36*(6) 556–563. doi: 10.1016/S0092-6566(02)00505-6

244. Nagler, U. K. J., Reiter, K. J., Furtner, M. R., & Rauthmann, J. F. (2014). Is there a "dark intelligence"? Emotional intelligence is used by dark personalities to emotionally manipulate others. *Personality and Individual Differences, 65*(7), 47–52. doi: 10.1016/j.paid.2014.01.025

245. Konrath, S., Corneille, O., Bushman, B. J., & Luminet, O. (2014). The relationship between narcissistic exploitativeness, dispositional empathy, and emotion recognition abilities. *Journal of Nonverbal Behavior, 38*(1), 129–143. doi: 10.1007/s10919-013-0164-y

246. Bradley, S. J. (1990). Affect regulation and psychopathology: Bridging the mind-body gap. *Canadian Journal of Psychiatry, 35,* 540–547.

247. Greenspan, S. I., & Porges, S. W. (1984). Psychopathology in infancy and early childhood: Clinical perspectives on the organization of sensory and affective-thematic experience. *Child Development, 55,* 49–70.

248. Van Praag, H. M. (1990). Two-tier diagnosing in psychiatry. *Psychiatry Research, 34,* 1–11.

249. Thayer, R. E., Newman, R., & McClain, T. M. (1994). Self-regulation of mood: Strategies for changing a bad mood, raising energy, and reducing tension. *Journal of Personality and Social Psychology, 67,* 910–925.

250. Cohen, J., & Andrade, E. B. (2004). Affect, intuition, and task-contingent affect regulation. *Journal of Consumer Research, 31,* 358–367.

251. Mick, D. G., & DeMoss, M. (1990). Self-gifts: Phenomenological insights from four contexts. *Journal of Consumer Research, 17,* 322–332.

252. Thayer, R. E., Newman, R., & McClain, T. M. (1994). Self-regulation of mood: Strategies for changing a bad mood, raising energy, and reducing tension. *Journal of Personality and Social Psychology, 67,* 910–925.

253. Rippere, V. (1977). "What's the thing to do when you're feeling depressed?" A pilot study. *Behaviour Research and Therapy, 15,* 185–191.

254. Bremner, R. H., Koole, S. L., & Bushman, B. J. (2011). "Pray for those who mistreat you": Effects of prayer on anger and aggression. *Personality and Social Psychology Bulletin, 37*(6), 830–837.

255. Mischkowski, D., Kross, E., & Bushman, B. J. (2012). Flies on the wall are less aggressive: Self-distanced reflection reduces angry feelings, aggressive thoughts, and aggressive behaviors. *Journal of Experimental Social Psychology, 48*(5), 1187–1191. doi: 10.1016/j.jesp.2012.03.012

256. Thayer, R. E., Newman, R., & McClain, T. M. (1994). Self-regulation of mood: Strategies for changing a bad mood, raising energy, and reducing tension. *Journal of Personality and Social Psychology, 67,* 910–925.

257. Bushman, B. J. (2002). Does venting anger feed or extinguish the flame? Catharsis, rumination, distraction, anger, and aggressive responding. *Personality and Social Psychology Bulletin, 28,* 724–731.

258. Tice, D. M., & Bratslavsky, E. (2000). Giving in to feel good: The place of emotion regulation in the context of general self-control. *Psychological Science, 11,* 149–159.

259. Erber, R., Wegner, D. M., & Therriault, N. (1996). On being cool and collected: Mood regulation in anticipation of social interaction. *Journal of Personality and Social Psychology, 70,* 757–766.

260. Erber, R., & Erber, M. W. (2000). The self-regulation of moods: Second thoughts on the importance of happiness in everyday life. *Psychological Science, 11,* 142–148.

261. Tamir, M., Mitchell, C., & Gross, J. J. (2008). Hedonic and instrumental motives in anger regulation. *Psychological Science, 19*(4), 324–328.

262. Larsen, R. J. (2000). Toward a science of mood regulation. *Psychological Inquiry, 11*(3), 129–141.

263. Thayer, R. E., Newman, R., & McClain, T. M. (1994). Self-regulation of mood: Strategies for changing a bad mood, raising energy, and reducing tension. *Journal of Personality and Social Psychology, 67,* 910–925.

264. Hyde, J. S. (2005). The gender similarities hypothesis. *American Psychologist, 60,* 581–592.

265. Nolen-Hoeksema, S. (1991). Responses to depression and their effects on the duration of depressive episodes. *Journal of Abnormal Psychology, 100,* 569–582.

266. Forster, J. L. & Jeffery, R. W. (1986). Gender differences related to weight history, eating patterns, efficacy expectations, self-esteem, and weight loss among participants in a weight reduction program. *Addictive Behaviors, 11,* 141–147.

267. Grunberg, N. E., & Straub, R. O. (1992). The role of gender and taste class in the effects of stress on eating. *Health Psychology, 11,* 97–100.

268. Berkowitz, A. D., & Perkins, H. W. (1987). Recent research on gender differences in collegiate alcohol use. *Journal of American College Health, 36,* 123–129.

269. Dube, K. C., Kumar, A., Kumar, N., & Gupta, S. P. (1978). Prevalence and pattern of drug use amongst college students. *Acta Psychiatrica Scandinavica, 57,* 336–356.

270. Engs, R. C., & Hanson, D. J. (1990). Gender differences in drinking patterns and problems among college students: A review of the literature. *Journal of Alcohol and Drug Education, 35,* 36–47.

271. Richman, J. A., & Flaherty, J. A. (1986). Sex differences in drinking among medical students: Patterns and psychosocial correlates. *Journal of Studies on Alcohol, 47,* 283–289.

272. Thayer, R. E., Newman, R., & McClain, T. M. (1994). Self-regulation of mood: Strategies for changing a bad mood, raising energy, and reducing tension. *Journal of Personality and Social Psychology, 67,* 910–925.

273. Larsen, R. J. (2000). Toward a science of mood regulation. *Psychological Inquiry, 11*(3), 129–141. Quote on p. 129.

274. Schachter, S., & Singer, J. E., (1962). Cognitive, social, and physiological determinants of emotional state. *Psychological Review, 69,* 379–399.

CHAPTER 7
Attitudes, Beliefs, and Consistency

1. Tabak, A. J. (2004). Hundreds register for new Facebook website, Facemash creator seeks new reputation with latest online project. Retrieved from http://www.thecrimson.com/article.aspx?ref=357292

2. Kirkpatrick, D. (2011). *The Facebook effect: The inside story of the company that is connecting the world.* New York: Simon & Schuster.

3. Kaplan, K. A. (2003). Facemash creator survives ad board. Retrieved from: http://www.thecrimson.com/article/2003/11/19/facemash-creator-survives-ad-board-the/

4. Fowler, G. A. (2012, October 4). Facebook: One billion and counting. *The Wall Street Journal.* Retrieved from http://online.wsj.com/news/articles/SB10000872396390443635404578036164027386112?mg=reno64-wsj&url=http%3A%2F%2Fonline.wsj.com%2Farticle%2FSB100008723963900443635404578036164027386112.html

5. Rosen, R. J. (2013, March 29). Facebook: 2.7 million people showed their support for marriage equality by changing their profile pictures. *The Atlantic.* Retrieved from http://www.theatlantic.com/technology/archive/2013/03/facebook-27-million-people-showed-their-support-for-marriage-equality-by-changing-their-profile-pictures/274497/

6. Watson, T. (2013, March 29). Did your Facebook just turn red? That's the color of our world changing. *Forbes.* Retrieved from http://www.forbes.com/sites/tomwatson/2013/03/27/did-your-facebook-just-turn-red-thats-the-color-of-our-world-changing/

7. Chokshi, N. (2013, July 2). State Department spent $630K to buy Facebook "likes." *National Journal.* Retrieved from http://m.nextgov.com/cio-briefing/2013/07/state-department-spent-630k-buy-facebook-likes/65999/

8. Willis, A. (2012, October 10). Vest inflates when you get a Facebook like. *Masahable.com* Retrieved from http://www.stuff.co.nz/technology/gadgets/7797712/Like-A-Hug-Vest-inflates-when-you-get-a-Facebook-like

9. Young, J. R. (2012). "Social-Media Blasphemy" Texas researcher adds "Enemy" feature to Facebook. Retrieved from http://chronicle.com/article/College-20-Social-Media/131300/

10. Ryan, T., & Xenos, S. (2011). Who uses Facebook? An investigation into the relationship between the Big Five, shyness, narcissism, loneliness, and Facebook usage. *Computers in Human Behavior, 27*(5), 1658–1664.

11. Orr, E. S., Sisic, M., Ross, C., Simmering, M. G., Arseneault, J. M., & Orr, R. R. (2009). The influence of shyness on the use of Facebook in an undergraduate sample. *CyberPsychology & Behavior, 12*(3), 337–340.

12. Sheldon, P. (2008). The relationship between unwillingness-to-communicate and students' Facebook use. *Journal of Media Psychology: Theories, Methods, and Applications, 20*(2), 67–75.

13. Indian, M., & Grieve, R. (2014). When Facebook is easier than face-to-face: Social support derived from Facebook in socially anxious individuals. *Personality and Individual Differences, 59*(3), 102–106. doi: 10.1016/j.paid.2013.11.016

14. Peluchette, J., & Karl, K. (2010). Examining students' intended image on Facebook: "What were they thinking?!" *Journal of Education for Business, 85*(1), 30–37.

15. Eaton. K. (2009). If you're applying for a job, censor your Facebook page. *Fast Company.* Retrieved from http://www.fastcompany.com/blog/kit-eaton/technomix/if-youre-applying-job-censor-your-facebook-page

16. Muchnik, L., Aral, S., & Taylor, S. J. (2013). Social influence bias: A randomized experiment. *Science, 341*(6146), 647–651.

17. Cannarella, J., & Spencer, J. A. (2014, January 17). Epidemiological modeling of online social network dynamics. Retrieved from http://arxiv.org/abs/1401.4208

18. Allport, G. (1935). Attitudes. In C. Murchinson (Ed.). *A Handbook of Social Psychology* (pp. 789–844). Worchester, MA: Clark University Press.

19. Eagly, A. H., & Chaiken, S. (1998). Attitude structure and function. In D. T. Gilbert, S. T. Fiske, & G. Lindzey (Eds.), *Handbook of social psychology* (4th ed., Vol. 1, pp. 269–322). New York: McGraw-Hill.

20. Wilson, T. D., Lindsey, S., & Schooler, T. Y. (2000). A model of dual attitudes. *Psychological Review, 107,* 101–126.

21. Hovland, C. I., Janis, I. L., & Kelley, H. H. (1953). *Communications and persuasion: Psychological studies in opinion change,* New Haven: Yale University Press.

22. Fazio, R. H., Jackson, J. R., Dunton, B. C., & Williams, C. J. (1995). Variability in automatic activation as an unobtrusive measure of racial attitudes: A bona fide pipeline? *Journal of Personality and Social Psychology, 69,* 1013–1027.

23. Fazio, R. H., & Olson, M. A. (2003). Implicit measures in social cognition research: Their meaning and use. *Annual Review of Psychology, 54,* 297–327.

24. Olson, M. A., & Fazio, R. H. (2009). Implicit and explicit measures of attitudes: The Perspective of the MODE model. In R. E. Petty, R. H. Fazio, & P. Briñol (Eds.), *Insights from the new implicit measures* (pp. 19–63). New York: Psychology Press.

25. Rhine, R. J., Hill, S. J., & Wandruff, S. E. (1967). Evaluative responses of preschool children. *Child Development, 38,* 1035–1042.

26. Baumeister, R. F., Bratslavsky, E., Finkenauer, C., & Vohs, K. D. (2001). Bad is stronger than good. *Review of General Psychology, 5,* 323–370.

27. Rozin, P., & Royzman, E. B. (2001). Negativity bias, negativity dominance, and contagion. *Personality and Social Psychology Review, 5,* 296–320.

28. Goleman, D. (1995, August 8). Brain may tag all perceptions with a value. *New York Times,* 1–10.

29. Bargh, J. A., Chaiken, S., Raymond, P., & Hymes, C. (1996). The automatic evaluation effect: Unconditional automatic attitude activation with a pronunciation task. *Journal of Experimental Social Psychology, 32,* 104–128.

30. Cited in Goleman, D. (1995, August 8). Brain may tag all perceptions with a value. *New York Times,* 1–10.

31. Fazio, R. H., Blascovich, J., & Driscoll, D. M. (1992). On the functional value of attitudes: The influence of accessible attitudes on the ease and quality of decision making. *Personality and Social Psychology Bulletin, 18,* 388–401.

32. Fazio, R. H., & Powell, M. C. (1997). On the value of knowing one's likes and dislikes: Attitude accessibility, stress, and health in college. *Psychological Science, 8,* 430–436.

33. Bornstein, R. F. (1989). Exposure and affect: Overview and meta-analysis of research, 1968–1987. *Psychological Bulletin, 106,* 265–289.

34. Zajonc, R. B. (1968). Attitudinal effects of mere exposure. *Journal of Personality and Social Psychology, 9*(2, Pt. 2), 1–27.

35. Zajonc, R. B. (1968). Attitudinal effects of mere exposure. *Journal of Personality and Social Psychology,* Monograph Supplement, 9, 1–27.

36. Zebrowitz, L. A., White, B., & Wieneke, K. (2008). Mere exposure and racial prejudice: Exposure to other-race faces increases liking for strangers of that race. *Social Cognition, 26*(3), 259–275.

37. Mita, T. H., Dermer, M., & Knight, J. (1977). Reversed facial images and the mere-exposure hypothesis. *Journal of Personality and Social Psychology, 35,* 597–601.

38. Harrison, A. A., & Fiscaro, S. A. (1974). Stimulus familiarity and alley illumination as determinants of approach response latencies of house crickets. *Perceptual and Motor Skills, 39,* 147–152.

39. Zajonc, R. B., Reimer, D. J., & Hausser, D. (1973). Imprinting and the development of object preference in chicks by mere repeated exposure. *Journal of Comparative Physiological Psychology, 83,* 434–440.

40. Harmon-Jones, E., & Allen, J. J. B. (2001). The role of affect in the mere exposure effect: Evidence from psychophysiological and individual differences approaches. *Personality and Social Psychology Bulletin, 27*(7), 889–898.

41. Cacioppo, J. T., & Petty, R. E. (1989). Effects of message repetition on argument processing, recall and persuasion. *Basic and Applied Social Psychology, 10,* 3–12.

42. Klinger, M. R., & Greenwald, A. G. (1994). Preferences need no inferences? The cognitive basis for unconscious emotional effects. In P. M. Niedenthal & S. Kitayama (Eds.), *The heart's eye: Emotional influences in perception and attention* (pp. 67–85). Orlando, FL: Academic Press.

43. Young, S. G., & Claypool, H. M. (2010). Mere exposure has differential effects on attention allocation to threatening and neutral stimuli. *Journal of Experimental Social Psychology, 46*(2), 424–427.

44. Crisp, R. J., Hutter, R. R. C., & Young, B. (2009). When mere exposure leads to less liking: The incremental threat effect in intergroup contexts. *British Journal of Psychology, 100*(1), 133–149.

45. Wells, G. L., & Petty, R. E. (1980). The effects of overt head movements on persuasion: Compatibility and incompatibility of responses. *Basic and Applied Social Psychology, 1,* 219–230.

46. Olson, M. A., & Fazio, R. H. (2001). Implicit attitude formation through classical conditioning. *Psychological Science, 12,* 413–417.

47. Staats, A. W., & Staats, C. K. (1958). Attitudes established by classical conditioning. *Journal of Abnormal and Social Psychology, 57,* 37–40.

48. Jonas, K., Eagly, A. H., & Stroebe, W. (1995). *Attitudes and persuasion.* In M. Argyle & A. M. Colman (Eds.), *Social psychology.* Harlow, UK: Longman.

49. Das, E., Bushman, B. J., Bezemer, M. D., Kerkhof, P., & Vermeulen, I. E. (2009). How terrorism news reports increase prejudice against outgroups: A Terror Management account. *Journal of Experimental Social Psychology, 45,* 453–459.

50. Albergotti, R., O'Connell, V., & Vranica, S. (2012, October 18). Lance Armstrong gets dumped: Nike, RadioShack, others distance themselves from cyclist amid drug scandal. *The Wall Street Journal.* Retrieved from http://online.wsj.com/news/articles/SB10000872396390444868204578062313532317222

51. Pendleton, M. (2014, September 9). Nike drops endorsement deal with Ray Rice. *FSS.* Retrieved from http://fullscalesports.com/2014/09/09/nike-drops-endorsement-deal-with-ray-rice/

52. Manfred, T. (2014, September 17). Nike drops Adrian Peterson. *Business Insider*. Retrieved from http://www.businessinsider.com/nike-drops-adrian-peterson-2014-9

53. Bostrom, R. N., Vlandis, J. W., & Rosenbaum, M. E. (1961). Grades as reinforcing contingencies and attitude change. *Journal of Educational Psychology, 52*(2), 112–115.

54. Bandura, A. (1977). *Social learning theory*. Englewood Cliffs, NJ: Prentice Hall.

55. Bandura, A., Ross, D., & Ross, S. A. (1961). Transmission of aggression through imitation of aggressive models. *Journal of Abnormal and Social Psychology, 63*, 575–582.

56. Bandura, A., Ross, D., & Ross, S. A. (1963). Vicarious reinforcement and imitative learning. *Journal of Abnormal and Social Psychology, 67*, 601–607.

57. Bandura, A. (1965). Influence of models' reinforcement contingencies on the acquisition of imitative responses. *Journal of Abnormal and Social Psychology, 66*, 575–582.

58. Bandura, A., Ross, D., & Ross, S. A. (1963). Vicarious reinforcement and imitative learning. *Journal of Abnormal and Social Psychology, 67*, 601–607.

59. Bandura, A. (1986). *Social foundations of thought and action: A social-cognitive theory*. Englewood Cliffs, NJ: Prentice-Hall.

60. Fiske, S. T. (2004). *Social beings: A core motives approach to social psychology*. New York: Wiley.

61. Miller, A. G., McHoskey, J. W., Bane, C. M., & Dowd, T. G. (1993). The attitude polarization phenomenon: Role of response measure, attitude extremity, and behavioral consequences of reported attitude change. *Journal of Personality and Social Psychology, 64*, 561–574.

62. Tesser, A. (1976). Attitude polarization as a function of thought and reality constraints. *Journal of Research in Personality, 10*, 183–194.

63. Wilson, T. D., Dunn, D. S., Kraft, D., & Lisle, D. J. (1989). Introspection, attitude change, and attitude-behavior consistency: The disruptive effects of explaining why we feel the way we do. In M. P. Zanna (Ed.), *Advances in experimental social psychology* (Vol. 22, pp. 287–343). San Diego: Academic Press.

64. Wilson, T. D., Hodges, S. D., & LaFleur, S. J. (1995). Effects of introspecting about reasons: Inferring attitudes from accessible thoughts. *Journal of Personality and Social Psychology, 69*, 16–28.

65. Miller, A. G., McHoskey, J. W., Bane, C. M., & Dowd, T. G. (1993). The attitude polarization phenomenon: Role of response measure, attitude extremity, and behavioral consequences of reported attitude change. *Journal of Personality and Social Psychology, 64*, 561–574.

66. Lord, C. G., Ross, L., & Lepper, M. R. (1979). Biased assimilation and attitude polarization: The effects of prior theories on subsequently considered evidence. *Journal of Personality and Social Psychology, 37*, 2098–2109.

67. Mackie, D., & Cooper, J. (1984). Attitude polarization: Effects of group membership. *Journal of Personality and Social Psychology, 46*, 575–585.

68. Aronson, E., & Mills, J. (1959). The effect of severity of initiation on liking for a group. *Journal of Abnormal and Social Psychology, 59*, 177–181.

69. Xygalatas, D., Mitkidis, P., Fischer, R., Reddish, P., Skewes, J., Geertz, A.W., Roepstorff, A., & Builbulia, J. (2013). Extreme rituals promote prosociality. *Psychological Science, 24*, 1602–1605.

70. Comer, R., & Laird, J. D. (1975). Choosing to suffer as a consequence of expecting to suffer: Why do people do it? *Journal of Personality and Social Psychology, 32*, 92–101.

71. Linder, D. E., Cooper, J., & Jones, E. E. (1967). Decision freedom as a determinant of the role of incentive magnitude in attitude change. *Journal of Personality and Social Psychology, 6*, 245–254.

72. Zanna, M. P., & Cooper, J. (1974). Dissonance and the pill: An attribution approach to studying the arousal properties of dissonance. *Journal of Personality and Social Psychology, 29*, 703–709.

73. Zanna, M., Higgins, E. & Taves, P. (1976). Is dissonance phenomenologically aversive? *Journal of Experimental Social Psychology, 12*, 530–538.

74. Knobloch-Westerwick, S. (2014). *Choice and preference in media use: Advances in selective exposure theory and research*. New York: Routledge.

75. Shin, C. (2011, March 22) Here are the 5 most liberal and conservative media Twitter feeds. *Business Insider*. Retrieved from http://www.businessinsider.com/twitter-political-leanings-conservative-liberal-oreilly-msnbc-katie-couric-sean-hannity-2011-3?op=1

76. Pariser, E. (2011). *The filter bubble: What the Internet is hiding from you*. New York: Penguin Press.

77. Kitayama, S., & Markus, H. R. (1999). Yin and Yang of the Japanese self: The cultural psychology of personality coherence. In D. Cervone (Ed.), *The coherence of personality: Social-cognitive bases of consistency, variability, and organization* (pp. 242302). New York: Guilford Press.

78. Heine, S. J., & Lehman, D. R. (1997). Culture, dissonance, and self-affirmation. *Personality and Social Psychology Bulletin, 23*, 389–400.

79. Hoshino-Browne, E., Zanna, A. S., Spencer, S. J., Zanna, M. P., Kitayama, S., & Lackenbauer, S. (2005). On the cultural guises of cognitive dissonance: The case of Easterners and Westerners. *Journal of Personality and Social Psychology, 89*, 294–310.

80. Kitayama, S., Snibbe, A. C., Markus, H. R., & Suzuki, T. (2004). Is there any "free" choice? Cognitive dissonance in two cultures. *Psychological Science, 15*, 527–533.

81. LaPiere, R. T. (1934). Attitudes vs. actions. *Social Forces, 13*, 230–237.

82. Wicker, A. W. (1969). Attitudes versus actions: The relationship of verbal and overt behavioral responses to attitude object. *Journal of Social Issues, 25*, 41–78.

83. Baumeister, R. F. (2000). Gender differences in erotic plasticity: The female sex drive as socially flexible and responsive. *Psychological Bulletin, 126*, 347–374.

84. Laumann, E. O., Gagnon, J. H., Michael, R. T., & Michaels, S. (1994). *The social organization of sexuality: Sexual practices in the United States*. Chicago: University of Chicago Press.

85. Antonovsky, H. F., Shoham, I., Kavenocki, S., Modan, B., & Lancet, M. (1978). Sexual attitude-behavior discrepancy among Israeli adolescent girls. *Journal of Sex Research, 14*, 260–272.

86. Christensen, H. T., & Carpenter, G. R. (1962). Value-behavior discrepancies regarding premarital coitus in three Western cultures. *American Sociological Review, 27*, 66–74.

87. Croake, J. W., & James, B. (1973). A four year comparison of premarital sexual attitudes. *Journal of Sex Research, 9*, 91–96.

88. Herold, E. S., & Mewhinney, D.-M. K. (1993). Gender differences in casual sex and AIDS prevention: A survey of dating bars. *Journal of Sex Research, 30*, 36–42.

89. Hansen, G. L. (1987). Extradyadic relations during courtship. *Journal of Sex Research, 23*, 382–390.

90. Beck, J. G., Bozman, A. W., & Qualtrough, T. (1991). The experience of sexual desire: Psychological correlates in a college sample. *Journal of Sex Research, 28*, 443–456.

91. O'Sullivan, L. F., & Allgeier, E. R. (1998). Feigning sexual desire: Consenting to unwanted sexual activity in heterosexual dating relationships. *Journal of Sex Research, 35*, 234–243.

92. Ajzen, I., & Fishbein, M. (1977). Attitude-behavior relations: A theoretical analysis and review of empirical research. *Psychological Bulletin, 84*, 888–918.

93. Rushton, J. P., Brainerd, C. J., & Pressley, M. (1983). Behavioral development and construct validity: The principle of aggregation. *Psychological Bulletin, 94*, 18–38.

94. Fazio, R. H., & Towles-Schwen, T. (1999). The MODE model of attitude-behavior processes. In S. Chaiken (Ed.), *Dual-process theories in social psychology* (pp. 97–116). New York: Guilford Press.

95. Ajzen, I. (2001). Nature and operation of attitudes. In T. Fiske, D. L. Schacter, & C. Zahn-Waxler (Eds.), *Annual review of psychology* (Vol. 52, pp. 27–58). Palo Alto, CA: Annual Reviews.

96. Fazio, R. H. (1990). Multiple processes by which attitudes guide behavior: The MODE model as an integrative frame work. In P. Zanna (Ed.), *Advances in experimental social psychology* (Vol. 23, pp. 75–109). San Diego: Academic Press.

97. Kraus, S. J. (1995). Attitudes and the prediction of behavior: A meta-analysis of the empirical literature. *Personality and Social Psychology Bulletin, 21*, 58–75.

98. Ajzen, I. (2012). The theory of planned behavior. In P. A. M. Lange, A. W. Kruglanski, & E. T. Higgins (Eds.), *Handbook of theories of social psychology* (Vol. 1, pp. 438–459). London, U.K.: Sage.

99. Armitage, C. J., & Conner, M. (2001). Efficacy of the theory of planned behaviour: A meta-analytic review. *British Journal of Social Psychology, 40*, 471–499.

100. Gilbert, D. T., Tafarodi, R. W., & Malone, P. S. (1993). You can't not believe everything you read. *Journal of Personality and Social Psychology, 65*, 221–233.

101. Gilbert, D. T. (1991). How mental systems believe. *American Psychologist, 46*, 107–119.

102. Gilbert, D. T. (1993). The assent of man: Mental representation and the control of belief. In D. Wegner & J. Pennebaker (Eds.), *Handbook of mental control* (pp. 57–87). Englewood Cliffs, NJ: Prentice-Hall.

103. Gilbert, D. T. (1991). How mental systems believe. *American Psychologist, 46*, 107–119.

104. Gilbert, D. T. (1991). How mental systems believe. *American Psychologist, 46*, 107–119.

105. Gilbert, D. T. (1993). The assent of man: Mental representation and the control of belief. In D. Wegner & J. Pennebaker (Eds.), *Handbook of mental control* (pp. 57–87). Englewood Cliffs, NJ: Prentice-Hall.

106. Ross, L., Lepper, M. R., & Hubbard, M. (1975). Perseverance in self-perception and social perception: Biased attributional processes in the debriefing paradigm. *Journal of Personality and Social Psychology, 32*, 880–892.

107. Anderson, C. A., Lepper, M. R., & Ross, L. (1980). The perseverance of social theories: The role of explanation in the persistence of discredited information. *Journal of Personality and Social Psychology, 39*, 1037–1049.

108. Anderson, C. A., & Sechler, E. S. (1986). Effects of explanation and counterexplanation on the development and use of social theories. *Journal of Personality and Social Psychology, 20*, 24–34.

109. Lord, C. G., Lepper, M. R., & Preston, E. (1984). Considering the opposite: A corrective strategy for social judgment. *Journal of Personality and Social Psychology, 47*, 1231–1243.

110. Janoff-Bulman, R. (1992). *Shattered assumptions: Towards a new psychology of trauma*. New York: Free Press.

111. Bulman, R. J., & Wortman, C. B. (1977). Attributions of blame and coping in the "real world": Severe accident victims react to their lot. *Journal of Personality and Social Psychology, 35*, 351–363.

112. Taylor, S. E. (1983). Adjustment to threatening events: A theory of cognitive adaptation. *American Psychologist, 38*, 1161–1173.

113. Wills, T. A. (1981). Downward comparison principles in social psychology. *Psychological Bulletin, 90*, 245–271.

114. Pargament, K. I. (1997). *The psychology of religion and coping. Theory, research, practice*. New York: Guilford Press.

115. Smith, T. B., McCullough, M. E., & Poll, J. (2003). Religiousness and depression: Evidence for a main effect and the moderating influence of stressful life events. *Psychological Bulletin, 129*, 614–636.

116. Frazier, P., Tashiro, T., Berman, M., Steger, M., & Long, J. (2004), Correlates of levels and patterns of positive life changes following sexual assault. *Journal of Consulting and Clinical Psychology, 72*, 19–30.

117. Bazargan, S., Sherkat, D. E., & Bazargan, M. (2004). Religion and alcohol use among African-American and Hispanic inner-city emergency care patients. *Journal for the Scientific Study of Religion, 43,* 419–428.

118. Burris, C. T., Harmon-Jones, E., & Tarpley, W. R. (1997). "By faith alone": Religious agitation and cognitive dissonance. *Basic and Applied Social Psychology, 19,* 17–31.

119. Knight, G. R. (1999). *A brief history of Seventh-Day Adventists.* Hagerstown, MD: Review & Herald.

120. 1 Thessalonians 4:17 (Bible).

121. Ravitz, J. (2011, March 23). Road trip to the end of the world. *CNN News.* Retrieved from: http://edition.cnn.com/2011/LIVING/03/06/judgment.day.caravan/index.html

122. Harold Camping False Prophet: Ministry Probably Doomed (2011). *International Business Times.* Retrieved from http://www.ibtimes.com/articles/149632/20110521/harold-camping-false-prophet-ministry-probably-doomed.htm

123. Suddath, C. (2011). It's the end of the world as we know it. *Time.* Retrieved from http://www.time.com/time/specials/packages/article/0,28804,2097462_2097456_2097489,00.html

124. Exline, J. J. (2002). Stumbling blocks on the religious road: Fractured relationships, nagging vices, and the inner struggle to believe. *Psychological Inquiry, 13,* 182–189.

125. Exline, J. J., & Rose, E. (2005). Religious and spiritual struggles. In R. F. Paloutzian & C. L. Park (Eds.), *Handbook of the psychology of religion* (pp. 315–330). New York: Guilford Press.

126. Exline, J. J., Park, C. L., Smyth, J. M., & Carey, M. P. (2011). Anger toward God: Social-cognitive predictors, prevalence, and links with adjustment to bereavement and cancer. *Journal of Personality and Social Psychology, 100*(1), 129–148.

127. Tobacyk, J., & Milford, G. (1983). Belief in paranormal phenomena: Assessment instrument development and implications for personality functioning. *Journal of Personality and Social Psychology, 44,* 1029–1037.

128. Tobacyk, J. J., & Downs, A. (1986). Personal construct threat and irrational beliefs as cognitive predictors of increases in musical performance anxiety. *Journal of Personality and Social Psychology, 51*(4), 779–782.

129. Thompson, M. P., Norris, F. H., & Hanacek, B. (1993). Age differences in the psychological consequences of Hurricane Hugo. *Psychology and Aging, 8,* 606–616.

130. Persons, J. B., & Rao, P. A. (1985). Longitudinal study of cognitions, life events, and depression in psychiatric inpatients. *Journal of Abnormal Psychology, 94,* 51–63.

131. Daly, M. J., & Burton, R. L. (1983). Self-esteem and irrational beliefs: An exploratory investigation with implications for counseling. *Journal of Counseling Psychology, 30,* 361–366.

132. Gilovich, T. (1983). Biased evaluation and persistence in gambling. *Journal of Social and Personal Psychology, 44,* 1110–1126.

133. Festinger, L., & Carlsmith, J. M. (1959). Cognitive consequences of forced compliance. *Journal of Abnormal and Social Psychology, 58,* 203–211.

CHAPTER 8
Social influence and Persuasion

1. Hall, J. R. (1987). *Gone from the promised land: Jonestown in American cultural history.* New Brunswick: Transaction Books.

2. Levi, K. (1982). *Violence and religious commitment: Implications of Jim Jones's Peoples Temple movement.* University Park: Pennsylvania State University Press.

3. Hall, J. R. (1987). *Gone from the promised land: Jonestown in American cultural history.* New Brunswick: Transaction Books.

4. Committee on Foreign Affairs. (1979). *The death of Representative Leo J. Ryan, Peoples Temple, and Jonestown: Understanding a tragedy.* U.S. House of Representatives, 96th Congress, First Session. Washington, DC: Government Printing Office.

5. Reston, J., Jr. (1981). *Our father who art in hell.* New York: Times Books.

6. Hall, J. R. (1987). *Gone from the promised land: Jonestown in American cultural history.* New Brunswick: Transaction Books.

7. Levi, K. (1982). *Violence and religious commitment: Implications of Jim Jones's Peoples Temple movement.* University Park: Pennsylvania State University Press.

8. Moore, R. (1986). *The Jonestown letters: Correspondence of the Moore Family 1970–1985.* Lewiston, NY: E. Mellen Press.

9. Hall, J. R. (1987). *Gone from the promised land: Jonestown in American cultural history.* New Brunswick: Transaction Books.

10. Moore, R. (1986). *The Jonestown letters: Correspondence of the Moore Family 1970–1985.* Lewiston, NY: E. Mellen Press.

11. Moore, R. (1986). *The Jonestown letters: Correspondence of the Moore Family 1970–1985.* Lewiston, NY: E. Mellen Press.

12. Hall, J. R. (1987). *Gone from the promised land: Jonestown in American cultural history.* New Brunswick: Transaction Books.

13. James R. Lewis (Ed.) (2006). *The Order of the Solar Temple: The temple of death.* Surrey, U.K.: Ashgate Publishing Company.

14. Balch, R. W., & Taylor, D. (2002). Making sense of the Heaven's Gate suicides. In D. G. Bromley & J. G. Melton (Eds.), *Cults, religion, and violence* (pp. 209–228). New York: Cambridge University Press.

15. Gleick, E. (1997). The marker we've been...waiting for. *Time, 149*(14).

16. CNN (1997, March 28). Some members of suicide cult castrated. Retrieved from http://edition.cnn.com/US/9703/28/mass.suicide.pm/

17. Lederer, E. M. (1997, April 2). Alien abduction insurance cancelled! Associated Press. Retrieved from http://www.artgomperz.com/newse/abd.html

18. Deutsch, M., & Gerard, H. B. (1955). A study of normative and informational social influences upon individual judgment. *Journal of Abnormal and Social Psychology, 51,* 629–636.

19. Asch, S. E. (1955, November). Opinions and social pressure. *Scientific American,* 31–35.

20. Asch, S. E. (1955, November). Opinions and social pressure. *Scientific American,* 31–35.

21. Asch, S. E. (1955, November). Opinions and social pressure. *Scientific American,* 31–35.

22. Schachter, S. (1951). Deviation, rejection, and communication. *Journal of Abnormal and Social Psychology, 46*(2), 190–207.

23. Tata, J., Anthony, T., Lin, H., Newman, B., Tang, S., Millson, M., & Suvakumar, K. (1996). Proportionate group size and rejection of the deviate: A meta-analytic integration. *Journal of Social Behavior and Personality, 11,* 739–752.

24. Tata, J., Anthony, T., Lin, H., Newman, B., Tang, S., Millson, M., & Suvakumar, K. (1996). Proportionate group size and rejection of the deviate: A meta-analytic integration. *Journal of Social Behavior and Personality, 11,* 739–752.

25. Sherif, M. (1935). A study of some social factors in perception. *Archives of Psychology* (Columbia University), No. 187, 60.

26. Rohrer, J. H., Baron, S. H., Hoffman, E. L., & Swander, D. V. (1954). The stability of autokinetic judgments. *Journal of Abnormal and Social Psychology, 49*(4, Pt. 1), 595–597.

27. Jacobs, R. C., & Campbell, D. T. (1961). The perpetuation of an arbitrary tradition through several generations of a laboratory microculture. *Journal of Abnormal and Social Psychology, 62,* 649–658.

28. Mercier, H., & Sperber, D. (2011). Why do humans reason? Arguments for an argumentative theory. *Behavioral and Brain Sciences, 34*(2), 57–74.

29. Cialdini, R. B. (2001). *Influence: Science and practice* (4th ed.). Boston: Allyn and Bacon.

30. Ornstein, R. (1991). *The evolution of consciousness: Of Darwin, Freud, and cranial fire: The origins of the way we think.* New York: Prentice Hall.

31. Freedman, J. L. & Fraser, S. C. (1966). Compliance without pressure: The foot-in-the-door technique. *Journal of Personality and Social Psychology, 4*(2), 195–202. doi: 10.1037/h0023552

32. Cialdini, R. B., Cacioppo, J. T., Bassett, R., & Miller, J. A. (1978). Low-ball procedure for producing compliance: Commitment then cost. *Journal of Personality and Social Psychology, 36,* 463–476.

33. Cialdini, R. B. (2001). *Influence: Science and practice* (4th ed.). Boston: Allyn and Bacon.

34. Cialdini, R. B. (2001). *Influence: Science and practice* (4th ed.). Boston: Allyn and Bacon.

35. Cialdini, R. B. (2001). *Influence: Science and practice* (4th ed.). Boston: Allyn and Bacon.

36. Cialdini, R. B., Eisenberg, N., Green, B. L., Rhoads, K., & Bator, R. (1998). Undermining the undermining effect of reward on sustained interest: When unnecessary conditions are sufficient. *Journal of Applied Social Psychology, 28,* 249–263.

37. Tybout, A. M., & Yalch, R. F. (1980). The effect of experience: A matter of salience? *Journal of Consumer Research, 6,* 406–413.

38. Cialdini, R. B., & Schroeder, D. A. (1976). Increasing compliance by legitimizing paltry contributions: When even a penny helps. *Journal of Personality and Social Psychology, 34*(4), 599–604.

39. Cialdini, R. B. (2001). *Influence: Science and practice* (4th ed.). Boston: Allyn and Bacon.

40. Myers, D. G. (2006). *Social psychology* (8th ed.). New York: McGraw Hill.

41. Cialdini, R. B. (2001). *Influence: Science and practice* (4th ed.). Boston: Allyn and Bacon.

42. Miller, R. L., Seligman, C., Clark, N. T., & Bush, M. (1976). Perceptual contrast versus reciprocal concession as mediators of induced compliance. *Journal of Behavioral Science, 7,* 401–409.

43. Schwarzwald, J., Raz, M., & Zvibel, M. (1979). The applicability of the door-in-the-face technique when established behavioral customs exist. *Journal of Applied Social Psychology, 9,* 576–586.

44. Cialdini, R. B., Vincent, J., Lewis, S., Catalan, J., Wheeler, D., & Darby, B. L. (1975). Reciprocal concessions procedure for inducing compliance: The door-in-the-face technique. *Journal of Personality and Social Psychology, 31,* 206–215.

45. Burger, J. M. (1986). Increasing compliance by improving the deal: The that's-not-all technique. *Journal of Personality and Social Psychology, 51,* 277–283.

46. Ecclesiastes 11:1 (Bible).

47. Cialdini, R. B. (2001). *Influence: Science and practice* (4th ed.). Boston: Allyn and Bacon.

48. Worchel, S., Lee, J., & Adewole, A. (1975). Effects of supply and demand on ratings of object value. *Journal of Personality and Social Psychology, 32,* 906–914.

49. Cialdini, R. B. (2001). *Influence: Science and practice* (4th ed.). Boston: Allyn and Bacon.

50. Santos, M. D., Leve, C., & Pratkanis, A. R. (1994). Hey buddy, can you spare seventeen cents? Mindful persuasion and the pique technique. *Journal of Applied Social Psychology, 24,* 755–764.

51. Glionna, J. M. (2013, January 30). New Aspen speed limit — 14 miles an hour? *Los Angeles Times.* Retrieved from http://articles.latimes.com/2013/jan/30/nation/la-na-nn-new-aspen-speed-limit-14-miles-an-hour-20130130

52. Davis, B. P., & Knowles, E. S. (1999). A disrupt-then-reframe technique of social influence. *Journal of Personality and Social Psychology, 76,* 192–199.

53. Mercier, H., & Sperber, D. (2011). Why do humans reason? Arguments for an argumentative theory. *Behavioral and Brain Sciences, 34*(02), 57–74.

54. *Why We Fight.* Retrieved from http://history.acusd.edu/gen/filmnotes/whywefight.html

55. Hovland, C., Lumsdaine, A., & Sheffield, F. (1949). *Experiments on mass communication: Studies in social psychology in World War II* (Vol. 3). Princeton, NJ: Princeton University Press.

56. Hovland, C. I., Janis, I. L., & Kelley, H. H. (1953). *Communication and persuasion.* New Haven: Yale University Press.

57. *Rhet.* I.3, 1358a37ff.
58. Hovland, C. I., & Weiss, W. (1951). The influence of source credibility on communication effectiveness. *Public Opinion Quarterly, 15,* 635–650.
59. Levine, J. M., & Valle, R. S. (1975). The convert as a credible communicator. *Social Behavior and Personality, 3,* 81–90.
60. Levine, J. M., & Valle, R. S. (1975). The convert as a credible communicator. *Social Behavior and Personality, 3,* 81–90.
61. Pratkanis, A. R., Greenwald, A. G., Leippe, M. R., & Baumgardner, M. H. (1988). In search of reliable persuasion effects: III. The sleeper effect is dead: Long live the sleeper effect. *Journal of Personality and Social Psychology, 54,* 203–218.
62. Jones, J. M. (2010). Nurses top honesty and ethics list for 11th year. Lobbyists, car salespeople, members of Congress get the lowest ratings. *Gallup Economy.* http://www.gallup.com/poll/145043/nurses-top-honesty-ethics-list-11-year.aspx
63. Public Policy Polling (2013, October 8). Americans like witches, the IRS, and even hemorrhoids better than Congress. Retrieved from http://www.publicpolicypolling.com/main/2013/10/americans-like-witches-the-irs-and-even-hemorrhoids-better-than-congress.html
64. Eagly, A. H., & Chaiken, S. (1998). Attitude structure and function. In D. T. Gilbert, S. T. Fiske, & G. Lindzey (Eds.), *Handbook of social psychology* (4th ed., Vol. 1, pp. 269–322). New York: McGraw-Hill.
65. Erickson, B., Lind, E. A., Johnson, B. C., & O'Barr, W. M. (1978). Speech style and impression formation in a court setting: The effects of "powerful" and "powerless" speech. *Journal of Experimental Social Psychology, 14,* 266–279.
66. Newcombe, D., & Arnkoff, D. B. (1979). Effects of speech style and sex of speaker on person perception. *Journal of Personality and Social Psychology, 37,* 1293–1303.
67. *Rhet.* II.1, 1378a6ff.
68. Miller, N., Maruyama, G., Beaber, R. J., & Valone, K. (1976). Speed of speech and persuasion. *Journal of Personality and Social Psychology, 34,* 615–624.
69. Smith, S. M., & Shaffer, D. R. (1991). Celerity and cajolery: Rapid speech may promote or inhibit persuasion through its impact on message elaboration. *Personality and Social Psychology Bulletin, 17,* 663–669.
70. Miller, N., Maruyama, G., Beaber, R. J., & Valone, K. (1976). Speed of speech and persuasion. *Journal of Personality and Social Psychology, 34,* 615–624.
71. Mackie, D. M., Worth L. T., & Asuncion, A. G. (1990). Processing of persuasive in-group messages. *Journal of Personality and Social Psychology, 58,* 812–822.
72. Budesheim, T. L., & DePaola, S. J. (1994). Beauty or the beast? The effects of appearance, personality and issue information on evaluations of political candidates. *Personality and Social Psychology Bulletin, 20,* 339–348.
73. Efran, M. G., & Patterson, E. W. J. (1974). Voters vote beautiful: The effects of physical appearance on a national election. *Canadian Journal of Behavioral Science, 6,* 352–356.
74. Hovland, C., Lumsdaine, A., & Sheffield, F. (1949). *Experiments on mass communication: Studies in social psychology in World War II* (Vol. 3). Princeton: Princeton University Press.
75. cp. *Rhet.* II.1, 1378a1ff.
76. Janis, I. L., Kaye, D., & Kirschner, P. (1965). Facilitating effects of "eating-while-reading" on responsiveness to persuasive communications. *Journal of Personality and Social Psychology, 1*(2), 181–186.
77. Unger, L. S. (1996). The potential for using humor in global advertising. *Humor, 9,* 143–168.
78. Duncan, C. P., & Nelson, J. E. (1985). Effects of humor in a radio advertising experiment. *Journal of Advertising, 14,* 33–40, 64.
79. Gruner, C. R. (1985). Advice to the beginning speaker on using humor: What the research tells us. *Communication Education, 34,* 142–147.

80. Cantor, J. R., & Venus, P. (1980). The effect of humor on recall of a radio advertisement. *Journal of Broadcasting, 24,* 13–22.
81. Janis, I. L. (1967). Effects of fear arousal on attitude change: Recent developments in theory and experimental research. *Advances in Experimental Social Psychology, 4,* 166–224.
82. Rogers, E. M. (1983). *Diffusion of innovations.* New York: Free Press.
83. De Hoog, N., Stroebe, W., & De Wit, J. B. F. (2007). The impact of vulnerability to and severity of a health risk on processing and acceptance of fear-arousing communications: A meta-analysis. *Review of General Psychology, 11*(3), 258–285.
84. Newman, A. (2001, February 4). Anti-smoking campaign: Rotten teeth and dead babies. *New York Times Magazine,* p. 16. Available at http://www.nytimes.com/
85. Hovland, C. I., Janis, I. L., & Kelley, H. H. (1953). *Communication and persuasion.* New Haven: Yale University Press.
86. Janis, I. L., & Feshbach, S. (1953). Effects of fear-arousing communications. *Journal of Abnormal and Social Psychology, 48,* 78–92.
87. Morris, K. A., & Swann, W. B., Jr. (1996). Denial and the AIDS crisis: Wishing away the threat of AIDS. In S. Oskamp & S. Thompson (Eds.), *Safer sex in the '90s* (pp. 57–79). New York: Sage.
88. Budesheim, T. L., Houston, D. A., & DePaola, S. J. (1996). The persuasiveness of in-group and out-group political messages: The case of negative political campaigning. *Journal of Personality and Social Psychology, 70,* 523–534.
89. Houston, D. A., Doan, K. A., & Roskos-Ewoldsen, D. (1999). Negative political advertising and choice conflict. *Journal of Experimental Psychology: Applied, 5,* 3–16.
90. Janiszewski, C., Noel, H., & Sawyer, A. G. (2003). A meta-analysis of the spacing effect in verbal learning: Implications for research on advertising repetition and consumer memory. *Journal of Consumer Research, 30,* 138–149.
91. Cacioppo, J. T., & Petty, R. E. (1989). Effects of message repetition on argument processing, recall and persuasion. *Basic and Applied Social Psychology, 10,* 3–12.
92. *Dictionary of Marketing Terms* (2004).
93. Parsley, A. (2009). 5 Things to Know About TV's Progressive Insurance Lady. *People.* Retrieved from http://www.people.com/people/article/0,,20301774,00.html
94. Falcone, L. B.(2009, October 7). Insurance pitchgirl a surprise TV hit: Going with the flo. *Boston Herald.* Retrieved from http://bostonherald.com/news_opinion/columnists/2009/10/insurance_pitchgirl_surprise_tv_hit
95. Pratkanis, A. R., & Aronson, E. (1992). *Age of propaganda: The everyday use and abuse of persuasion.* New York: Henry Holt.
96. Smith, G. F., & Dorfman, D. D. (1975). The effect of stimulus uncertainty on the relationship between frequency of exposure and liking. *Journal of Personality and Social Psychology, 31,* 150–155.
97. Hovland, C., Lumsdaine, A., & Sheffield, F. (1949). *Experiments on mass communication: Studies in social psychology in World War II* (Vol. 3). Princeton: Princeton University Press.
98. Hovland, C. I., & Weiss, W. (1951). The influence of source credibility on communication effectiveness. *Public Opinion Quarterly, 15,* 635–650.
99. McGuire, W. J. (1968). Personality and susceptibility to social influence. In E. F. Borgotta & W. W. Lambert (Eds.), *Handbook of personality theory and research* (pp. 1130–1187). Chicago: Rand McNally.
100. Rhodes, N., & Wood, W. (1992). Self-esteem and intelligence affect influenceability: The mediating role of message reception. *Psychological Bulletin, 111,* 156–171.
101. Cacioppo, J. T., & Petty, R. E. (1982). The need for cognition. *Journal of Personality and Social Psychology, 42,* 116–131. Quote from p. 116.

102. Ahlering, R. F. (1987). Need for cognition, attitudes, and the 1984 Presidential election. *Journal of Research in Personality, 21,* 100–102.
103. Cacioppo, J. T., & Petty, R. E. (1982). The need for cognition. *Journal of Personality and Social Psychology, 42,* 116–131. Quote from p. 116.
104. Snyder, M., & DeBono, K. G. (1985). Appeals to image and claims about quality: Understanding the psychology of advertising. *Journal of Personality and Social Psychology, 49,* 586–597.
105. Bushman, B. J. (1993). What's in a name? The moderating role of public self-consciousness on the relation between brand label and brand preference. *Journal of Applied Psychology, 78,* 857–861.
106. Hang-Pil, S., & Shavitt, S. (1994). Persuasion and culture: Advertising appeals in individualistic and collectivistic societies. *Journal of Experimental Social Psychology, 30,* 326–350.
107. Wang, C. L., Bristol, T., Mowen J. C., & Chakraborty, G. (2000). Alternative modes of self-construal: Dimensions of connectedness-separateness and advertising appeals to the cultural and gender-specific self. *Journal of Consumer Psychology, 9,* 107–115.
108. Walster, E., & Festinger, L. (1962). The effectiveness of "overheard" persuasive communication. *Journal of Abnormal and Social Psychology, 65,* 395–402.
109. Kardes, F. R. (1988). Spontaneous inference processes in advertising: The effects of conclusion omission and involvement on persuasion. *Journal of Consumer Research, 15,* 225–233.
110. Thinkexist.com. Retrieved from http://thinkexist.com/quotation/a_good_advertisement_is_one_which_sells_the/202773.html
111. Nelson, M. R. (2002). Recall of brand placements in computer/video games. *Journal of Advertising Research, 42,* 80–92.
112. Festinger, L., & Maccoby, N. (1964). On resistance to persuasive communications. *Journal of Abnormal and Social Psychology, 68,* 359–366.
113. Petty, R. E., & Cacioppo, J. T. (1986). *Communication and persuasion: Central and peripheral routes to attitude change.* New York: Springer-Verlag.
114. Eagly, A. H., & Chaiken, S. (1998). Attitude structure and function. In D. T. Gilbert, S. T. Fiske, & G. Lindzey (Eds.), *Handbook of social psychology* (4th ed., Vol. 1, pp. 269–322). New York: McGraw-Hill.
115. Apsler, R., & Sears, D. O. (1968). Warning, personal involvement, and attitude change. *Journal of Personality and Social Psychology, 9,* 162–168.
116. Blankenship, K. L., & Wegener, D. T. (2008). Opening the mind to close it: Considering a message in light of important values increases message processing and later resistance to change. *Journal of Personality and Social Psychology, 94*(2), 196–213.
117. Tsal, Y. (1984). *The role of attention in processing information from advertisements.* Unpublished manuscript, Cornell University, Ithaca, NY.
118. Cacioppo, J. T., & Petty, R. E. (1980). Sex differences in influenceability: Toward specifying the underlying processes. *Personality and Social Psychology Bulletin, 6*(4), 651–656.
119. Lord, C. G., Ross, L., & Lepper, M. R. (1979). Biased assimilation and attitude polarization: The effects of prior theories on subsequently considered evidence. *Journal of Personality and Social Psychology, 37,* 2098–2109.
120. Petty, R. E., & Cacioppo, J. T. (1979). Issue involvement can increase or decrease persuasion by enhancing message-relevant cognitive responses. *Journal of Personality and Social Psychology, 37,* 1915–1926.
121. McGuire, W. J. (1961). The effectiveness of supportive refutational defenses in immunizing and restoring beliefs against persuasion. *Sociometry, 24,* 184–197.
122. McGuire, W. J. (1964). Inducing resistance to persuasion: Some contemporary approaches. *Advances in Experimental Social Psychology, 1,* 191–229.

123. McGuire, W. J., & Papageorgis, D. (1961). The relative efficacy of various types of prior belief-defense in producing immunity against persuasion. *Journal of Abnormal Social Psychology, 62*, 327–337.

124. Papageorgis, D., & McGuire, W. J. (1961). The generality of immunity to persuasion produced by pre-exposure to weakened counterarguments. *Journal of Abnormal and Social Psychology, 62*, 475–481.

125. Perry, C. L., Killen, J., Slinkard, L. A., & McAlister, A. L. (1980). Peer teaching and smoking prevention among junior high students. *Adolescence, 15*, 277–281.

126. Chassin, L., Presson, C. C., Sherman, S. J., & Edwards, D. A. (1990). The natural history of cigarette smoking: Predicting young-adult smoking outcomes from adolescent smoking patterns. *Health Psychology, 9*, 701–716.

127. Falck, R., & Craig, R. (1988). Classroom-oriented primary prevention programming for drug abuse. *Journal of Psychoactive Drugs, 20*, 403–408.

128. Stanford, W. E. (1999, March–April). Dealing with student credit card debt. *About Campus*, 12–17. Quote on p. 13.

129. Compton, J. A., & Pfau, M. (2004). Use of inoculation to foster resistance to credit card marketing targeting college students. *Journal of Applied Communication Research, 32*(4), 343–364.

130. Tormala, Z. L., & Petty, R. E. (2002). What doesn't kill me makes me stronger: The effects of resisting persuasion on attitude certainty. *Journal of Personality and Social Psychology, 83*, 1298–1313.

131. Freedman, J. L., & Sears, D. O. (1965). Warning, distraction, and resistance to influence. *Journal of Personality and Social Psychology, 1*(3), 262–266.

132. Sesame Street breaks Iraqi POWs. (2003, May 20). Retrieved from http://news.bbc.co.uk/1/hi/world/middle_east/3042907.stm

133. Gilbert, D. T. (1991). How mental systems believe. *American Psychologist, 46*, 107–119.

134. Smith, S. M. and Shaffer, D. R. (1991). Celerity and cajolery: Rapid speech may promote or inhibit persuasion through its impact on message elaboration. *Personality and Social Psychology Bulletin, 17*, 663, 669. Reprinted by permission of Sage Publications.

CHAPTER 9
Prosocial Behavior: Doing What's Best for Others

1. Nowak, M., & Roch, S. (2006). Upstream reciprocity and the evolution of gratitude. *Proceedings of the Royal Society of London, Series B: Biological Sciences, 274*, 605–609.

2. Tran, C. (2014, August 6). All heave! Commuters work together to free with their bare hands man whose leg had become stuck between platform and train. *DailyMail*. Retrieved from http://www.dailymail.co.uk/news/article-2717511/Train-commuters-managed-free-man-leg-stuck-to.html

3. Fowler, J. H., & Christakis, N. A. (2010). Cooperative behavior cascades in human social networks. *PNAS, 107*(12), 5334–5338. doi: 10.1073/pnas.0913149107

4. Veenhoven, R. (2004). *World database of happiness: Continuous register of scientific research on subjective appreciation of life.* Retrieved from http://www.eur.nl/fsw/research/happiness

5. Lee, C. (1995). Prosocial organizational behaviors: The roles of workplace justice, achievement striving, and pay satisfaction. *Journal of Business and Psychology, 10*, 197–206.

6. Satow, K. L. (1975). Social approval and helping. *Journal of Experimental Social Psychology, 11*, 501–509.

7. Whatley, M. A., Webster, J. M., Smith, R. H., & Rhodes, A. (1999). The effect of a favor on public and private compliance: How internalized is the norm of reciprocity? *Basic and Applied Social Psychology, 21*, 251–259.

8. Triandis, H. C. (1978). Some universals of social behavior. *Personality and Social Psychology Bulletin, 4*, 1–16.

9. Kunz, P. R., & Woolcott, M. (1976). Season's greetings: From my status to yours. *Social Science Research, 5*, 269–278.

10. Ferriere, R. (1998, June 11). Help and you shall be helped. *Nature, 393*, 517–519.

11. Fisher, J. D., & Nadler, A. (1976). Effects of donor resources on recipient self-esteem and self-help. *Journal of Experimental Social Psychology, 12*(2), 139–150.

12. Dowd, J. J. (1975). Aging as exchange: A preface to theory. *Journal of Gerontology, 30*(5), 584–594.

13. McCullough, M. E., Kimeldorf, M. B., & Cohen, A. D. (2008). An adaptation for altruism? The social causes, social effects, and social evolution of gratitude. *Current Directions in Psychological Science, 17*(4), 281–285.

14. Biel, A., Eek, D., & Gaerling, T. (1999). The importance of fairness for cooperation public-goods dilemmas. In P. Juslin (Ed.), *Judgment and decision making: Neo-Brunswikian and process-tracing approaches* (pp. 245–259). Mahwah, NJ: Erlbaum.

15. Buss, D. M. (1999). *Evolutionary psychology: The new science of the mind.* New York: Allen & Bacon.

16. Allen, N. B., & Badcock, P. B. T. (2003). The social risk hypothesis of depressed mood: Evolutionary, psychosocial, and neurobiological perspectives. *Psychological Bulletin, 129*, 887–913.

17. Filiberti, A., Ripamonti, C., Totis, A., Ventafridda, V., De Conno, F., Contiero, P., & Tamburini, M. (2001). Characteristics of terminal cancer patients who committed suicide during a home palliative care program. *Journal of Pain and Symptom Management, 22*, 544–553.

18. Join Joiner, T., Pettit, J. W., Walker, R. L., Voelz, Z. R., Cruz, J., Rudd, M. D., & Lester, D. (2002). Perceived burdensomeness and suicidality: Two studies on the suicide notes of those attempting and those completing suicide. *Journal of Social & Clinical Psychology, 21*, 531–545.

19. Exline, J. J., & Lobel, M. (1999). The perils of outperformance: Sensitivity about being the target of a threatening upward comparison. *Psychological Bulletin, 125*, 307–337.

20. Muller, D., Bushman, B. J., Subra, B., & Ceaux, E. (2012). Are people more aggressive when they are worse off or better off than others? *Social Psychological and Personality Science, 3*(6), 754-759. DOI: 10.1177/1948550612436984

21. de Waal, F. B. M., & Davis, J. M. (2003). Capuchin cognitive ecology: Cooperation based on projected returns. *Neuropsychologia, 41*, 221–228.

22. Austin, W., McGinn, N. C., & Susmilch, C. (1980). Internal standards revisited: Effects of social comparisons and expectancies on judgments of fairness and satisfaction. *Journal of Experimental Social Psychology, 16*, 426–441.

23. Hassebrauck, M. (1986). Ratings of distress as a function of degree and kind of inequity. *Journal of Social Psychology, 126*, 269–270.

24. Berscheid, E., & Walster, E. (1967). When does a harm-doer compensate a victim? *Journal of Personality and Social Psychology, 6*, 433–441.

25. Hofmann, W., Wisneski, D.C., Brandt, M.J., & Skitka, L.J. (2014). Morality in everyday life. *Science, 345*, 1340–1343.

26. Ruedy, N.E., Moore, C., Gino, F., & Schweitzer, M.E. (2013). The cheater's high: The unexpected affective benefits of unethical behavior. *Journal of Personality and Social Psychology, 105*, 531–548.

27. Kouchaki, M., & Smith, I.H. (2014). The Morning Morality Effect: The influence of time of day on unethical behavior. *Psychological Science, 25*, 95–102.

28. Frimer, J.A., Schaefer, N.K., & Oakes, H. (2014). Moral actor, selfish agent. *Journal of Personality and Social Psychology, 106*, 790–802.

29. Haidt, J. (2001). The emotional dog and its rational tail: A social intuitionist approach to moral judgment. *Psychological Review, 108*, 814–834.

30. Haidt, J. (2007). The new synthesis in moral psychology. *Science, 316*, 998–1002.

31. Foot, P. (1967). The problem of abortion and the doctrine of double effect. *Oxford Review, 5*, 5–15.

32. Greene, J.D., Sommerville, R.B., Nystrom, L.E., Darley, J.M., Cohen, J.D. (2001). An fMRI investigation of emotional engagement in moral judgment. *Science, 293*, 2105–2108.

33. Knobe, J. (2003). Intentional action and side effects in ordinary language. *Analysis, 63*, 190–194.

34. Knobe, J. (2010). Person as scientist, person as moralist. *Behavioral and Brain Sciences, 33*, 315–329.

35. Graham, J., Haidt, J., & Nosek, B.A. (2009). Liberals and conservatives rely on different sets of moral foundations. *Journal of Personality and Social Psychology, 96*, 1029–1046.

36. Helzer, E.G., & Pizarro, D.A. (2011). Dirty liberals! Reminders of physical cleanliness influence moral and political attitudes. *Psychological Science, 22*, 517–522.

37. Axelrod. R. (1980). More effective choice in the prisoner's dilemma. *Journal of Conflict Resolution, 24*, 3–25.

38. Beggan, J. K., Messick, D. M., & Allison, S. T. (l988). Social values and egocentric bias: Two tests of the might over morality hypothesis. *Journal of Personality and Social Psychology, 55*, 606–611.

39. Liebrand, W. B. G., Wilke, H. A. M., & Wolters, F. J. M. (1986). Value orientation and conformity. A study using three types of social dilemma games. *Journal of Conflict Resolution, 30*, 77–97.

40. Kelley, H. H., & Stahelski, A. J. (1970). Social interaction basis of cooperators' and competitors' beliefs about others. *Journal of Personality and Social Psychology, 16*, 66–91.

41. Miller, D. T., & Holmes, J. G. (1975). The role of situational restrictiveness on self-fulfilling prophecies: A theoretical and empirical extension of Kelley and Stahelski's triangle hypothesis. *Journal of Personality & Social Psychology, 31*, 661–673.

42. Misra, S, & Kalro, A. (1979). Triangle effect and the connotative meaning of trust in prisoner's dilemma: A cross cultural study. International *Journal of Psychology, 14*, 255–263.

43. Green, L., Price, P. C., & Hamburger, M. E. (1995). Prisoner's dilemma and the pigeon: Control by immediate consequences. *Journal of the Experimental Analysis of Behavior, 64*, 1–17.

44. For excellent summary, see Tomasello, M. (2013) *A natural history of human thinking.* Cambridge, MA: Harvard University Press.

45. White, A. E., Kenrick, D. T., Li, Y. J., Mortensen, C. R., Neuberg, S.L., & Cohen, A. B. (2012). When nasty breeds nice: Threats of violence amplify agreeableness at national, individual, and situational levels. *Journal of Personality and Social Psychology, 103*, 622–634.

46. Fehr, E., & Gächter, S. (2002). Altruistic punishment in humans. *Nature, 415*, 137–140.

47. Mussweiler, T., & Ockenfels, A. (2013). Similarity increases altruistic punishment in humans. *PNAS*, early edition, http://www.pnas.org/cgi/doi/10.1073/pnas.1215443110.

48. Feinberg, M., Willer, R., Stellar, J., & Keltner, D. (2012). The virtues of gossip: Reputational information sharing as prosocial behavior. *Journal of Personality and Social Psychology, 102*, 1015–1030.

49. Khadjavi, M., & Lange, A. (2013). Prisoners and their dilemma. *Journal of Economic Behavior & Organization, 92*(8), 163–175. doi: 10.1016/j.jebo.2013.05.015

50. Wright R. (2000). *Non zero: The logic of human destiny.* New York: Pantheon.

51. Balliet, D., Li, N. P., Macfarlan, S. J., Van Vugt, M. (2011). Sex differences in cooperation: a meta-analytic review of social dilemmas. *Psychological Bulletin, 137*(6), 881–909.

52. http://www.apa.org/news/press/releases/2011/09/cooperate-equally.aspx

53. Benenson, J. F. (2014). *Warriors and worriers: The survival of the sexes.* Oxford, UK: Oxford University Press.

54. Vohs, K. D., Mead, N. L., & Goode, M. R. (2006, November). The psychological consequences of money. *Science, 314*(5802), 1154–1156.

55. 1 Timothy 6:10 (Bible).

56. Steinfatt, T. M. (1973). The Prisoner's Dilemma and a creative alternative game: The effects of communications under conditions of real reward. *Simulation and Games, 4,* 389–409.

57. Miller, J., Butts, C. T., & Rodes, D. (2002). Communication and cooperation. *Journal of Economic Behavior and Organization, 47,* 179–195.

58. Kiesler, S., Sproull, L., & Waters, K. (1996). A prisoner's dilemma experiment on cooperation with people and human-like computers. *Journal of Personality and Social Psychology, 70,* 47–65.

59. Exline, J. J., Worthington, E. L., Hill, P., & McCullough, M. E. (2003). Forgiveness and justice: A research agenda for social and personality psychology. *Personality and Social Psychology Review, 7,* 337–348.

60. McCullough, M. E., Pargament, K. I., & Thoresen, C. E. (Eds.) (2000). *Forgiveness: Theory, research, and practice.* New York: Guilford.

61. Finkel, E. J., Rusbult, C. E., Kumashiro, M., & Hannon, P. (2002). Dealing with betrayal in close relationships: Does commitment promote forgiveness? *Journal of Personality and Social Psychology, 82,* 956–974.

62. Fenell, D. (1993). Characteristics of long-term first marriages. *Journal of Mental Health Counseling, 15,* 446–460.

63. Fincham, F. D., Hall, J. H. & Beach, S. R. H. (2005). 'Til lack of forgiveness doth us part: Forgiveness in marriage. In E. L. Worthington (Ed.), *Handbook of forgiveness* (pp. 207–226). New York: Wiley.

64. Kachadourian, L. K., Fincham, F. D., & Davila, J. (2004). The tendency to forgive in dating and married couples: Association with attachment and relationship satisfaction. *Personal Relationships, 11,* 373–393.

65. Kachadourian, L. K., Fincham, F. D., & Davila, J. (2005). Attitudinal ambivalence, rumination and forgiveness of partner transgressions in marriage. *Personality and Social Psychology Bulletin, 31,* 334–342.

66. Paleari, G., Regalia, C., & Fincham, F. D. (2005). Marital quality, forgiveness, empathy, and rumination: A longitudinal analysis. *Personality and Social Psychology Bulletin, 31,* 368–378.

67. Coyle, C. T., & Enright, R. D. (1997). Forgiveness intervention with post-abortion men. *Journal of Consulting and Clinical Psychology, 65,* 1042–1046.

68. Freedman, S. R., & Enright, R. D. (1996). Forgiveness as an intervention goal with incest survivors. *Journal of Consulting and Clinical Psychology, 64,* 983–992.

69. Witvliet, C. V. O., Ludwig, T. E., & Van der Laan, K. L. (2001). Granting forgiveness or harboring grudges: Implications for emotion, physiology, and health. *Psychological Science, 121,* 117–123.

70. Kelln, B. R. C., & Ellard, J. H. (1999). An equity theory analysis of the impact of forgiveness and retribution on transgressor compliance. *Personality and Social Psychology Bulletin, 25,* 864–872; see also Wallace, H. M., Exline, J. J., & Baumeister, R. F. (2008). Interpersonal consequences of forgiveness: Does forgiveness deter or encourage repeat offenses? *Journal of Experimental Social Psychology, 44,* 453–460.

71. McNulty, J. K. (2011). The dark side of forgiveness: The tendency to forgive predicts continued psychological and physical aggression in marriage. *Personality and Social Psychology Bulletin, 37*(6), 770–783.

72. Fincham, F. D., Beach, S. R., & Davila, J. (2004). Forgiveness and conflict resolution in marriage. *Journal of Family Psychology, 18,* 72–81.

73. Kearns, J. N., & Fincham, F. D. (2005). Victim and perpetrator accounts of interpersonal transgressions: Self-serving or relationship-serving biases? *Personality and Social Psychology Bulletin, 31,* 321–333.

74. Hall, J. H., & Fincham, F.D. (2006). Relationship dissolution following infidelity: The roles of attributions and forgiveness. *Journal of Social and Clinical Psychology, 25,* 508–522.

75. Exline, J. J., Worthington, E. L., Hill, P., & McCullough, M. E. (2003). Forgiveness and justice: A research agenda for social and personality psychology. *Personality and Social Psychology Review, 7,* 337–348.

76. Exline, J. J., Worthington, E. L., Hill, P., & McCullough, M. E. (2003). Forgiveness and justice: A research agenda for social and personality psychology. *Personality and Social Psychology Review, 7,* 337–348.

77. Darby, B. W., & Schlenker, B. R. (1982). Children's reactions to apologies. *Journal of Personality and Social Psychology, 43,* 742–753.

78. Gonzales, M. H., Haugen, J. A., & Manning, D. J. (1994). Victims as "narrative critics": Factors influencing rejoinders and evaluative responses to offenders' accounts. *Personality and Social Psychology Bulletin, 20,* 691–704.

79. Exline, J. J., Baumeister, R. F., Zell, A. L., Kraft, A. J., & Witvliet, C. V. O. (2008). Not so innocent: Does seeing one's own capability for wrongdoing predict forgiveness? *Journal of Personality and Social Psychology, 94,* 495–515.

80. McCullough, M. E., Bono, G., & Root, L. M. (2007). Rumination, emotion, and forgiveness: Three longitudinal studies. *Journal of Personality and Social Psychology, 92,* 490–505.

81. Tsang, J.-A., McCullough, M. E., & Hoyt, W. T. (2005). Psychometric and rationalization accounts for the religion-forgiveness discrepancy. *Journal of Social Issues. 61,* 785–805.

82. Matthew 6:12 (Bible).

83. Pronk, T. M., Karremans, J. C., Overbeek, G., Vermulst, A. A., & Wigboldus, D. H. J. (2010). What it takes to forgive: When and why executive functioning facilitates forgiveness. *Journal of Personality and Social Psychology, 98*(1), 119–131.

84. Balliet, D., Li, N. P., & Joireman, J. (2011). Relating trait self-control and forgiveness within prosocials and proselfs: Compensatory versus synergistic models. *Journal of Personality and Social Psychology, 101*(5), 1090–1105.

85. Exline, J. J., Baumeister, R. F., Bushman, B. J., Campbell, W. K., & Finkel, E. J. (2004). Too proud to let go: Narcissistic entitlement as a barrier to forgiveness. *Journal of Personality and Social Psychology, 87,* 894–912.

86. Exline, J. J., & Zell, A. L. (2009). Empathy, self-affirmation, and forgiveness: The moderating roles of gender and entitlement. *Journal of Social and Clinical Psychology, 28*(9), 1071–1099.

87. Milgram, S. (1963). Behavioral study of obedience. *Journal of Abnormal and Social Psychology, 67,* 371–378.

88. Burger, J. M. (2009). Replicating Milgram: Would people still obey today? *American Psychologist, 64*(1), 1–11.

89. Bègue, L., Beauvois J-L., Courbet, D., Oberlé, D., Lepage, J., & Duke, A. A. (2015). Personality predicts obedience in a Milgram paradigm. *Journal of Personality, 83*(3), 299–306. doi: 10.1111/jopy.12104

90. Silfver, M., Helkama, K., Lönnqvist, J-E., & Verkasalo, M. (2008). The relation between value priorities and proneness to guilt, shame, and empathy. *Motivation and Emotion, 32*(2), 69–80.

91. Insko, C. A., Smith, R. H., Alicke, M. D., Wade, J., & Taylor, S. (1985). Conformity and group size: The concern with being right and the concern with being liked. *Personality and Social Psychology Bulletin, 11,* 41–50.

92. Munger, K., & Harris, S.J. (1989). Effects of an observer on handwashing in a public restroom. *Perceptual and Motor Skills, 69,* 733–734.

93. Guzmán, R. A., Rodríguez-Sickert, C., & Rowthorn, R. (2007). When in Rome, do as the Romans do: The coevolution of altruistic punishment, conformist learning, and cooperation. *Evolution and Human Behavior, 28*(2), 112–117.

94. Murray, D. R., Trudeau, R., & Schaller, M. (2011). On the origins of cultural differences in conformity: Four tests of the pathogen prevalence hypothesis. *Personality and Social Psychology Bulletin, 37*(3), 318–329.

95. Dunning, D., Anderson, J. E., Schlösser, T., Ehlebracht, D., & Fetchenhauer, D. (2014). Trust at zero acquaintance: More a matter of respect than expectation of reward. *Journal of Personality and Social Psychology, 107*(1), 122-141. doi: 10.1037/a0036673

96. Simpson, J. A. (2007). Foundations of interpersonal trust. In A. W. Kruglanski & E. T. Higgins (Eds.), *Social psychology: Handbook of basic principles* (2nd ed., pp. 587–607) New York: Guilford Press.

97. Miller, J. E., & Rempel, J. K. (2004) Trust and partner-enhancing attributions in close relationships. *Personality and Social Psychology Bulletin, 30,* 695–705.

98. Newman, E. J., Sanson, M., Miller, E. K., Quigley-McBride, A., Foster, J. L., Bernstein, D. M., & Garry, M. (2014). People with easier to pronounce names promote truthiness of claims. *PLOS ONE, 9*(2): e88671. doi: 10.1371/journal.pone.0088671. Retrieved from http://www.plosone.org/article/info%3Adoi%2F10.1371%2Fjournal.pone.0088671

99. Ariely, D., & Levav, J. (2000). Sequential choice in group settings: Taking the road less traveled and less enjoyed. *Journal of Consumer Research, 27,* 279–290.

100. Fetchenhauer, D., & Dunning, D. (2009). Do people trust too much or too little? *Journal of Economic Psychology, 30,* 263–276.

101. Righetti, F., & Finkenauer, C. (2011). If you are able to control yourself, I will trust you: The role of perceived self-control in interpersonal trust. *Journal of Personality and Social Psychology, 100,* 874–886.

102. Gervais, W. M., Shariff, A. F., & Norenzayan, A. (2011). Do you believe in atheists? Distrust is central to anti-atheist prejudice. *Journal of Personality and Social Psychology, 101,* 1189–1206.

103. Murray, S. L., Holmes, J. G., & Collins, N. L. (2006). Optimizing assurance: The risk regulation system in relationships. *Psychological Bulletin, 132,* 641–666.

104. Wieselquist, J., Rusbult, C. E., Foster, C. A., & Agnew, C. R. (1999). Commitment, pro-relationship behavior, and trust in close relationships. *Journal of Personality and Social Psychology, 77,* 942–966.

105. Rotenberg, K. J., Addis, N., Betts, L. R., Corrigan, A., Fox, C., Hobson, Z., Rennison, S., Trueman, M., & Boulton, M. J. (2010). The relation between trust beliefs and loneliness during early childhood, middle childhood, and adulthood. *Personality and Social Psychology Bulletin, 36,* 1086–1100.

106. Dawkins, R. (1976/1989). *The selfish gene.* New York: Oxford University Press.

107. Richard Dawkins, an original thinker who bashes orthodoxy. (2011, 19 September). *New York Times.* Retrieved from http://www.nytimes.com/2011/09/20/science/20dawkins.html?pagewanted=all

108. Darwin, C. (1859). *The origin of species by means of natural selection, or the preservation of favoured races in the struggle for life.* Reprinted from the 6th edition in New York, A. L. Burt Company, not dated.

109. Hamilton, W. D. (1964). The genetical evolution of social behaviour I and II. *Journal of Theoretical Biology, 7,* 1–16 and 17–52.

110. Burnstein, E., Crandall, C., & Kitayama, S. (1994). Some neo-Darwinian decision rules for altruism: Weighing cues for inclusive fitness as a function of the biological importance of the decision. *Journal of Personality and Social Psychology, 67,* 773–789.

111. Segal, N. L. (1984). Cooperation, competition and altruism within twin sets: A reappraisal. *Ethology and Sociobiology, 5,* 163–177.

112. Sime, J. D. (1983). Affiliative behavior during escape to building exits. *Journal of Environmental Psychology, 3,* 21–41.

113. Warneken, F., & Tomasello, M. (2006). Altruistic helping in human infants and young chimpanzees. *Science, 311,* 1301–1303.

114. Konrath, S., O'Brien, E., & Hsing, C. (2011). Changes in dispositional empathy in American college students over time: A meta-analysis. *Personality and Social Psychology Review, 15,* 180–198.

115. Bryner, J. (2010, May 28). Today's college students lack empathy. *LiveScience.* Retrieved from http://www.livescience.com/9918-today-college-students-lack-empathy.html

116. Anderson, C. A., Shibuya, A., Ihori, N., Swing, E. L., Bushman, B. J., Sakamoto, A., Rothstein, H. R., Saleem, M., & Barlett, C. P. (2010). Violent video game effects on aggression, empathy, and prosocial behavior in Eastern and Western countries: A meta-analytic review. *Psychological Bulletin, 136*(2), 151–173. doi: 10.1037/a0018251

117. Anderson, C. A., Shibuya, A., Ihori, N., Swing, E. L., Bushman, B. J., Sakamoto, A., Rothstein, H. R., Saleem, M., & Barlett, C. P. (2010). Violent video game effects on aggression, empathy, and prosocial behavior in Eastern and Western countries: A meta-analytic review. *Psychological Bulletin, 136*(2), 151–173. doi: 10.1037/a0018251

118. Greitemeyer, T., & Mügge, D. O. (2014). Video games do affect social outcomes: A meta-analytic review of the effects of violent and prosocial video game play. *Personality and Social Psychology Bulletin, 40*(5), 578–589. doi: 10.1177/0146167213520459

119. Batson, C. D., Batson, J. G., Slingsby, J. K., Harrell, K. L., Peekna, H. M., & Todd, R. M. (1991). Empathic joy and the empathy-altruism hypothesis. *Journal of Personality and Social Psychology, 61,* 413–426.

120. Batson, C. D., Duncan, B. D., Ackerman, P., Buckley, T., & Birch, K. (1981). Is empathic emotion a source of altruism motivation? *Journal of Personality and Social Psychology, 40,* 290–302.

121. Aknin, L. B., Barrington-Leigh, C. P., Dunn, E. W., Helliwell, J. F., Burns, J., Biswas-Diener, R., Kemerza, I., Nyende, P., Ashton-James, C. E., & Norton, M. I. (2013). Prosocial spending and well-being: Cross-cultural evidence for a psychological universal. *Journal of Personality and Social Psychology, 104,* 635–652.

122. Hepach, R., Vaish, A., & Tomasello, M. (2012). Young children are intrinsically motivated to see others helped. *Psychological Science, 23,* 967–972.

123. Baumeister, R. F. (2005). *The cultural animal: Human nature, meaning, and social life.* New York: Oxford University Press.

124. Peterson, C., & Seligman, M. E. P. (2004). *Character strengths and virtues.* New York: Oxford University Press.

125. Snyder, C. R., & Lopez, S. (Eds.) (2002). *Handbook of positive psychology.* New York: Oxford University Press.

126. "Junk DNA" defines differences between humans and chimps. (2011, October 25). *ScienceDaily.* Retrieved from http://www.sciencedaily.com/releases/2011/10/111025122615.htm

127. Silk, J. B., Brosnan, S. F., Vonk, J., Henrich, J., Povinelli, D. J., Richardson, A. S., Lambeth, S. P., Mascaro, J., & Schapiro, S. J. (2005, October 27). Chimpanzees are indifferent to the welfare of unrelated group members. *Nature, 437,* 1357–1359.

128. Cited in Robinson, P. (1995). *Schindler's List teaching guide.* Available at http://www.southerninstitute.info/holocaust_education/schind.html

129. Oliner, S. P., & Oliner, P. M. (1988). *The altruistic personality: Rescuers of Jews in Nazi Europe.* New York: The Free Press. Also see Midlarsky, E., Jones, S. F., & Corley, R. P. (2005). Personality correlates of heroic rescue during the holocaust. *Journal of Personality, 73,* 907–934.

130. Rushton, J. P., Fulker, D. W., Neale, M. C., Nias, D. K. B., & Eysenck, H. J. (1986). Altruism and aggression: The heritability of individual differences. *Journal of Personality and Social Psychology, 50,* 1192–1198.

131. Rushton, J. P., Chrisjohn, R. D., & Fekken, G. C. (1981). The altruistic personality and the Self-Report Altruism Scale. *Personality and Individual Differences, 2,* 293–302.

132. Rushton, J. P., Fulker, D. W., Neale, M. C., Nias, D. K. B., & Eysenck, H. J. (1986). Altruism and aggression: The heritability of individual differences. *Journal of Personality and Social Psychology, 50,* 1192–1198.

133. Emswiller, T., Deaux, K., & Willits, J. E. (1971). Similarity, sex, and requests for small favors. *Journal of Applied Social Psychology, 1,* 284–291.

134. Siem, B., & Stürmer, S. (2012). Cross-cultural volunteerism: Examining the effects of intercultural (dis)similarities on volunteers' motivations to support international students. *Basic and Applied Social Psychology, 34*(6), 544–557. doi: 10.1080/01973533.2012.727316

135. Eagly, A. H. & Crowley, M. (1986). Gender and helping behavior: A meta-analytic view of the social psychological literature. *Psychological Bulletin, 100,* 283–308.

136. Carnegie Hero Fund Commission. (2002). Requirements for a Carnegie Medal. Available at http://www.carnegiehero.org/nominate.php

137. Aries, E. J., & Johnson, F. L. (1983). Close friendship in adulthood: Conversational content between same-sex friends. *Sex Roles, 9,* 1183–1196.

138. Eisenberg, N., & Lennon, R. (1983). Sex differences in empathy and related capacities. *Psychological Bulletin, 94,* 100–131.

139. Hoffman, M. L. (1977). Sex differences in empathy and related behaviors. *Psychological Bulletin, 84,* 712–722.

140. Penner, L. A., Dertke, M. C., & Achenbach, C. J. (1973). The "flash" system: A field study of altruism. *Journal of Applied Social Psychology, 3,* 362–370.

141. Pomazal, R. J. & Clore, G. L. (1973). Helping on the highway: The effects of dependency and sex. *Journal of Applied Social Psychology, 3,* 150–164.

142. Harrell, W. A. (1978). Physical attractiveness, self-disclosure, and helping behavior. *Journal of Social Psychology, 104,* 15–17.

143. Benson, P. L., Karabenick, S. A., & Lerner, R. M. (1976). Pretty pleases: The effects of physical attractiveness, race, and sex on receiving help. *Journal of Experimental Social Psychology, 12,* 409–415.

144. Laumann, E. O., Gagnon, J. H., Michael, R. T., & Michaels, S. (1994). *The social organization of sexuality: Sexual practices in the United States.* Chicago: University of Chicago Press.

145. Couch, D., & Liamputtong, P. (2008). Online dating and mating: The use of the Internet to meet sexual partners. *Qualitative Health Research, 18*(2), 268–279.

146. Griscom, R. (2002, November). Why are online personals so hot? *Wired.* Retrieved from http://www.wired.com/wired/archive/10.11/view.html?pg=2

147. Maticka-Tyndale, E., Herold, E. S., & Mewhinney, D. (1998). Casual sex on spring break: Intentions and behaviors of Canadian students. *The Journal of Sex Research, 35,* 254–264.

148. Also see Baumeister, R. F., & Vohs, K. D. (2004). Sexual economics: Sex as female resource for social exchange in heterosexual interactions. *Personality and Social Psychology Review, 8*(4), 339–363.

149. West, S. G., & Brown, T. J. (1975). Physical attractiveness, the severity of the emergency and helping: A field experiment and interpersonal simulation. *Journal of Experimental Social Psychology, 11,* 531–538.

150. Hewstone, M. (1990). The "Ultimate Attribution Error"? A review of the literature on intergroup causal attribution. *European Journal of Social Psychology, 20,* 311–335.

151. Furnham, A. (2003). Belief in a just world: Research progress over the past decade. *Personality and Individual Differences, 34,* 795–817.

152. Lerner, M. J., & Miller, D. T. (1978). Just world research and the attribution process: Looking back and ahead. *Psychological Bulletin, 85,* 1030–1051.

153. Lerner, M. J., & Simmons, C. H. (1966). Observer's reaction to the "innocent victim": Compassion or rejection? *Journal of Personality and Social Psychology, 4,* 203–210.

154. Zuckerman, M. (1975). Belief in a just world and altruistic behavior. *Journal of Personality and Social Psychology, 31,* 972–997.

155. DePalma, M. T., Madey, S. F., Tillman, T. C., & Wheeler, J. (1999). Perceived patient responsibility and belief in a just world affect helping. *Basic and Applied Social Psychology, 21,* 131–137.

156. MacLean, M. J. & Chown, S. M. (1988). Just world beliefs and attitudes toward helping elderly people: A comparison of British and Canadian university students. *International Journal of Aging and Human Development, 26,* 249–260.

157. Zuckerman, M. (1975). Belief in a just world and altruistic behavior. *Journal of Personality and Social Psychology, 31,* 972–997.

158. Cunningham, M. R. (1979). Mood, and helping behavior: Quasi experiments with the Sunshine Samaritan. *Journal of Personality and Social Psychology 37,* 1947–1956.

159. Isen, A. M., & Levin, P. F. (1972). Effect of feeling good on helping: Cookies and kindness. *Journal of Personality and Social Psychology, 21,* 384–388.

160. Rosenhan, D. L., & White, G. M. (1967). Observation and rehearsal as determinants of prosocial behavior. *Journal of Personality and Social Psychology, 5,* 424–431.

161. Whitaker, J. L., & Bushman, B. J. (2012). "Remain calm. Be kind": Effects of relaxing video games on aggressive and prosocial behavior. *Social Psychological and Personality Science, 3*(1), 88–92. doi: 10.1177/1948550611409760

162. Manning, R., Levine, M., & Collins, A. (2007). The Kitty Genovese murder and the social psychology of helping: The parable of the 38 witnesses. *American Psychologist, 62,* 555–562.

163. Plötner, M., Over, H., Carpenter, M., and Tomasello, M. (2015, April). Young children show the bystander effect in helping situations. Psychological Science, 26, 499–506.

164. Latané, B., & Darley, J. (1968). Group inhibition of bystander intervention in emergencies. *Journal of Personality and Social Psychology, 10,* 215–221.

165. Shotland, R. L., & Straw, M. K. (1976). Bystander response to an assault: When a man attacks a woman. *Journal of Personality and Social Psychology, 34,* 990–999.

166. Darley, J. M., & Latané, B. (1968). Bystander intervention in emergencies: *Journal of Personality & Social Psychology, 8,* 377–383.

167. Cramer, R. E., McMaster, M. R., Bartell, P. A., & Dragna, M. (1988). Subject competence and minimization of the bystander effect. *Journal of Applied Social Psychology, 18,* 1133–1148.

168. Piliavin, I. M., Piliavin, J. A. & Rodin, J. (1975). Costs, diffusion, and the stigmatized victim. *Journal of Personality and Social Psychology, 32,* 429–438.

169. Darley, J. M. & Batson, C. D. (1973). From Jerusalem to Jericho: A study of situational and dispositional variables in helping behavior. *Journal of Personality and Social Psychology, 27,* 100–108.

170. Darley, J. M. & Batson, C. D. (1973). From Jerusalem to Jericho: A study of situational and dispositional variables in helping behavior. *Journal of Personality and Social Psychology, 27,* 100–108.

171. Cialdini, R. B. (1993) *Influence: Science and practice* (3rd ed.) (p. 113). New York: Harper-Collins.

172. Beaman, A. L., Barnes, P. J., & Klentz, B. (1978). Increasing helping rates through information dissemination: Teaching pays. *Personality and Social Psychology Bulletin, 4,* 406–411.

173. Rosenhan, D. L., & White, G. M. (1967). Observation and rehearsal as determinants of prosocial behavior. *Journal of Personality and Social Psychology, 5,* 424–431.

174. Hearold, S. (1986). A synthesis of 1043 effects of television on social behavior. In G. Comstock (Ed.), *Public communication and behavior* (pp. 65–133). New York: Academic Press.

175. Gentile, D. A., Anderson, C. A., Yukawa, S., Ihori, N., Saleem, M., Ming, L. K., Liau, A. K., Khoo, A., Bushman, B. J., Huesmann, L. R., & Sakamoto, A. (2009). The effects of prosocial video games on prosocial behaviors: International evidence from correlational, longitudinal, and experimental studies. *Personality and Social Psychology Bulletin, 35*(6), 752–763.

176. Greitemeyer, T. (2009). Effects of songs with prosocial lyrics on prosocial thoughts, affect, and behavior. *Journal of Experimental Social Psychology, 45*(1), 186–190.

177. Bureau of Labor Statistics (2014; February 25). Volunteering in the United States, 2013. Retrieved from http://www.bls.gov/news.release/volun.nr0.htm

178. McFarland, S., Webb, M., & Brown, D. (2012). All humanity is my ingroup: A measure and studies of identification with all humanity. *Journal of Personality and Social Psychology, 103*(5), 830–853. doi: 10.1037/a0028724

179. McFarland, S., Brown, D., & Webb, M.(2013). Identification with all humanity as a moral concept and psychological construct. *Current Directions in Psychological Science, 22*(3) 194–198. doi: 10.1177/0963721412471346

180. Veenhoven, R. (2004). *World database of happiness: Continuous register of scientific research on subjective appreciation of life.* Retrieved from http://www.eur.nl/fsw/research/happiness

181. Milgram, S. (1963). Behavioral study of obedience. *Journal of Abnormal and Social Psychology, 67,* 371–378.

182. Burnstein, et al. (1994). Some neo-Darwinian decision rules for altruism: Weighing cues for inclusive fitness as a function of the biological importance of the decision. *Journal of Personality and Social Psychology, 67,* 773–789. Copyright © 1994 by the American Psychological Association. Reprinted by permission.

183. Batson, C. D., Duncan, B. D., Ackerman, P., Buckley, T., & Birch, K. (1981). Is empathic emotion a source of altruism motivation? *Journal of Personality and Social Psychology, 40,* 290–302.

184. Latane, B. & Darley, J. (1970.) Group inhibition of bystander intervention in emergencies. *Journal of Personality and Social Psychology, 10,* 215–221. Copyright © 1968 by the American Psychological Association. Reprinted by permission.

CHAPTER 10
Aggression and Antisocial Behavior

1. Rwanda: How the genocide happened. (2004, December 18). *BBC News.* Retrieved from http://news.bbc.co.uk/2/hi/africa/1288230.stm

2. Timeline: Rwanda. (2008, August 8). *BBC News.* Retrieved from http://news.bbc.co.uk/2/hi/africa/1070329.stm

3. Smith, R. (2003, December 3). The impact of hate media in Rwanda. *BBC News.* Retrieved from http://news.bbc.co.uk/2/hi/africa/3257748.stm

4. De Brouwer, A.-M. (2005). *Supranational criminal prosecution of sexual violence: The ICC and the practice of the ICTY and the ICTR.* Mortsel, Belgium: Intersentia.

5. The triumph of evil. (1995). *PBS Frontline.* Retrieved from http://www.pbs.org/wgbh/pages/frontline/shows/evil

6. http://www.globalsecurity.org/military/world/war/congo.htm

7. Paul Rusesabagina. (2006, September 29). *BBC News.* Retrieved from http://news.bbc.co.uk/2/hi/programmes/hardtalk/5393104.stm

8. http://religion.blogs.cnn.com/2011/11/07/my-take-if-rwandans-can-forgive-killings-we-can-forgive-the-waitress/

9. Baumeister, R. F. (1997). *Evil: Inside human cruelty and violence.* New York: W. H. Freeman.

10. Tedeschi, J. T., & Felson, R. B. (1994). *Violence, aggression, and coercive actions.* Washington, DC: American Psychological Association.

11. Baron, R. A., & Richardson, D. R. (1994). *Human aggression* (2nd ed.). New York: Plenum Press.

12. Marcus-Newhall, A., Pedersen, W. C., Carlson, M., & Miller, N. (2000). Displaced aggression is alive and well: A meta-analytic review. *Journal of Personality and Social Psychology, 78,* 670–689.

13. Lagerspetz, K. M., Bjorkqvist, K., & Peltonen, T. (1988). Is indirect aggression typical of females? Gender differences in aggressiveness in 11- to 12-year-old children. *Aggressive Behavior, 14,* 403–414.

14. Buss, A. H. (1961). *The psychology of aggression.* New York: Wiley.

15. Dodge, K. A., & Coie, J. D. (1987). Social-information-processing factors in reactive and proactive aggression in children's peer groups. *Journal of Personality and Social Psychology, 53,* 1146–1158.

16. Feshbach, S. (1964). The function of aggression and the regulation of aggressive drive. *Psychological Review, 71,* 257–272.

17. Bushman, B. J., & Anderson, C. A. (2001). Is it time to pull the plug on the hostile versus instrumental aggression dichotomy? *Psychological Review, 108,* 273–279.

18. Olweus, D. (1978). *Aggression in the schools: Bullies and whipping boys.* Washington, DC: Hemisphere (Wiley).

19. American Psychiatric Association. (1994). *Diagnostic and statistical manual of mental disorders* (4th ed.). Washington, DC: Author.

20. Paik, H., & Comstock, G. (1994). The effects of television violence on antisocial behavior: A meta-analysis. *Communication Research, 21,* 516–546.

21. Tedeschi, J. T., & Felson, R. B. (1994). *Violence, aggression, and coercive actions.* Washington, DC: American Psychological Association.

22. Pinker, S. (2007, March 19). A history of violence. *New Republic, 236*(12), 18.

23. Pinker, S. (2007, March 19). A history of violence. *New Republic, 236*(12), 18.

24. Eisner, M. (2001). Modernization, self-control and lethal violence: The long-term dynamics of European homicide rates in theoretical perspective. *British Journal of Criminology, 41,* 618–638.

25. Gurr, T. R. (1981). Historical trends in violent crime: A critical review of the evidence. *Crime and Justice, 3,* 295.

26. Pinker, S. (2007, March 19). A history of violence. *New Republic, 236*(12), 18.

27. http://www.humansecuritybrief.info/

28. Pinker, S. (2007, March 19). A history of violence. *New Republic, 236*(12), 18.

29. Crossman, R. H. (1987). *The god that failed.* Washington, DC: Regnery Gateway. (Original work published 1949).

30. Darwin, C. (1948). *Origin of species.* New York: Modern Library. (Original work published 1871).

31. Freud, S. (1933/1950). Why war? In *Collected works of Sigmund Freud* (Vol. 16). London: Imagio.

32. Lorenz, K. (1966). *On aggression* (M. K. Wilson, Trans.) New York: Harcourt, Brace.

33. Berkowitz, L. (1993). *Aggression: Its causes, consequences, and control.* New York: McGraw-Hill.

34. Geen, R. G., & Quanty, M. B. (1977). The catharsis of aggression: An evaluation of a hypothesis. In L. Berkowitz (Ed.), *Advances in experimental social psychology* (Vol. 10, pp. 1–37). New York: Academic Press.

35. Scott, J. P. (1958). *Aggression.* Chicago: University of Chicago Press.

36. Lorenz, K. (1966). *On aggression* (M. K. Wilson, Trans.) New York: Harcourt, Brace.

37. Timbergen, N. (1952). The curious behavior of the Stickleback. *Scientific American, 187,* 22–26.

38. Hinde, R. A. (1970). *Animal behavior.* New York: McGraw-Hill.

39. Bandura, A. (1973). *Aggression: A social learning theory analysis.* Englewood Cliffs, NJ: Prentice-Hall.

40. Mischel, W. (1973). Toward a cognitive social learning reconceptualization of personality. *Psychological Review, 80,* 252–283.

41. Mischel, W., & Shoda, Y. (1995). A cognitive-affective system theory of personality: Reconceptualizing situations, dispositions, dynamics, and invariance in personality structure. *Psychological Review, 102,* 246–268.

42. Bandura, A., Ross, D., & Ross, S. A. (1961). Transmission of aggression through imitation of aggressive models. *Journal of Abnormal and Social Psychology, 63,* 575–582.

43. Bandura, A., Ross, D., & Ross, S. A. (1963). Vicarious reinforcement and initiative learning. *Journal of Abnormal and Social Psychology, 67,* 601–607.

44. Liebert, R., & Baron, R. (1972). Some immediate effects of televised violence on children's behavior. *Developmental Psychology, 6,* 469–475.

45. Alland, A., Jr. (1972). *The human imperative.* New York: Columbia University Press.

46. U.S. Federal Bureau of Investigation. (2012). *Uniform crime reports.* Washington, DC: U.S. Government Printing Office.

47. Dollard, J., Doob, L., Miller, N., Mowrer, O., & Sears, R. (1939). *Frustration and aggression.* New Haven, CT: Yale University Press.

48. Freud, S. (1961). *Mourning and melancholia* (standard ed.). London: Norton. (Original work published 1917).

49. Miller, N. E. (1941). The frustration-aggression hypothesis. *Psychological Review, 48,* 337–342.

50. Berkowitz, L. (1989). Frustration-aggression hypothesis: Examination and reformulation. *Psychological Bulletin, 106,* 59–73.

51. Xu, H., Bègue, L., & Bushman, B. J. (2014). Washing the guilt away: Effects of personal versus vicarious cleansing on guilty feelings and prosocial behavior. *Frontiers in Human Neuroscience, 8.* doi: 10.3389/fnhum.2014.00097

52. Tangney, J. P., Wagner, P., Fletcher, C., & Gramzow, R. (1992). Shamed into anger? The relation of shame and guilt to anger and self-reported aggression. *Journal of Personality and Social Psychology, 62*(4), 669–675. doi: 10.1037/0022-3514.62.4.669

53. Morris, W. N., & Reilly, N. P. (1987). Toward the self-regulation of mood: Theory and research. *Motivation and Emotion, 11,* 215–249.

54. Bushman, B. J., Baumeister, R. F., & Phillips, C. M. (2001). Do people aggress to improve their mood? Catharsis beliefs, affect regulation opportunity, and aggressive responding. *Journal of Personality and Social Psychology, 81,* 17–32.

55. Zillmann, D., Katcher, A. H., & Milavsky, B. (1972). Excitation transfer from physical exercise to subsequent aggressive behavior. *Journal of Experimental Social Psychology, 8,* 247–259.

56. Orobio de Castro, B., Veerman, J. W., Koops, W., Bosch, J. D., & Monshouwer, H. J. (2002). Hostile attribution of intent and aggressive behavior: A meta-analysis. *Child Development, 73,* 916–934.

57. Epps, J., & Kendall, P. C. (1995). Hostile attribution bias in adults. *Cognitive Therapy and Research, 19,* 159–178.

58. Dill, K. E., Anderson, C. A., Anderson, K. B., & Deuser, W. E. (1997). Effects of aggressive personality on social expectations and social perceptions. *Journal of Research in Personality, 31,* 272–292.

59. Bartholow, B. D., & Heinz, A. (2006). Alcohol and aggression without consumption: Alcohol cues, aggressive thoughts, and hostile perception bias. *Psychological Science, 17,* 30–37.

60. Dill, K. E., Anderson, C. A., Anderson, K. B., & Deuser, W. E. (1997). Effects of aggressive personality on social expectations and social perceptions. *Journal of Research in Personality, 31,* 272–292.

61. Bushman, B. J., & Anderson, C. A. (2002). Violent video games and hostile expectations: A test of the General Aggression Model. *Personality and Social Psychology Bulletin, 28,* 1679–1686.

62. Hasan, Y., Bègue, L., & Bushman, B. J. (2012). Viewing the world through "blood-red tinted glasses": The hostile expectation bias mediates the link between violent video game exposure and aggression. *Journal of Experimental Social Psychology, 48,* 953–956.

63. Hasan, Y., Bègue, L., & Bushman, B. J. (2012). Viewing the world through "blood-red tinted glasses": The hostile expectation bias mediates the link between violent video game exposure and aggression. *Journal of Experimental Social Psychology, 48,* 953–956.

64. Greitemeyer, T., & Osswald, S. (2009). Prosocial video games reduce aggressive cognitions. *Journal of Experimental Social Psychology, 45*(4), 896–900.

65. Penton-Voak I. S., Thomas, J., Gage, S. H., McMurran, M., McDonald, S., & Munafò M. R. (2013). Increasing recognition of happiness in ambiguous facial expressions reduces anger and aggressive behavior. *Psychological Science, 24*(5), 688–697. doi: 10.1177/0956797612459657

66. Tremblay, R. E. (2000). The development of aggressive behavior during childhood: What have we learned in the past century? *International Journal of Behavioral Development, 24*(2), 129–141.

67. U.S. Federal Bureau of Investigation. (2011). *Uniform crime reports.* Washington, DC: U.S. Government Printing Office.

68. Barry, D. (2000). Female or male? Take test. *Chicago Tribune.* Retrieved from http://news.google.com/new spapers?nid=1955&dat=20000702&id=Pw0iAAAAI BAJ&sjid=R6YFAAAAIBAJ&pg=1571,525620

69. Taylor, S. E., Klein, L. C., Lewis, B. P., Gruenewald, T. L., Gurung, R. A. R, & Updegraff, J. A. (2000). Biobehavioral responses to stress in females: Tend-and-befriend, not fight-or-flight. *Psychological Review, 107,* 441–429.

70. Taylor, S. E., Klein, L. C., Lewis, B. P., Gruenewald, T. L., Gurung, R. A. R, & Updegraff, J. A. (2000). Biobehavioral responses to stress in females: Tend-and-befriend, not fight-or-flight. *Psychological Review, 107,* 441–429.

71. Loeber, R., & Hay, D. (1997). Key issues in the development of aggression from childhood to early adulthood. *Annual Review of Psychology, 48,* 371–410.

72. Crick, N. R., & Grotpeter, J. K. (1995). Relational aggression, gender, and social-psychological adjustment. *Child Development, 66,* 710–722.

73. Vaillancourt, R. (2005). Indirect aggression among humans: Social construct or evolutionary adaption? In R. E. Tremblay, W. W. Hartup, & J. Archer (Eds.), *Developmental origins of aggression* (pp. 158–177). New York: Guilford Press.

74. Steffensmeier, D., & Allan, E. (1996). Gender and crime: Toward a gendered theory of female offending. *Annual Review of Sociology, 22,* 459–487.

75. Ainsworth, S. E., & Maner, J. K. (2012). Sex begets violence: Mating motives, social dominance, and physical aggression in men. *Journal of Personality and Social Psychology, 103,* 819–829.

76. Collins, R. L., Quigley, B., & Leonard, K. (2007). Women's physical aggression in bars: An event-based examination of precipitants and predictors of severity. *Aggressive Behavior, 33*(4), 304–313.

77. Bettencourt, B. A., & Miller, N. (1996). Gender differences in aggression as a function of provocation: A meta-analysis. *Psychological Bulletin, 119,* 422–447.

78. Archer, J. (2000). Sex differences in aggression between heterosexual partners: A meta-analytic review. *Psychological Bulletin, 126,* 651–680.

79. Straus, M. A. (1997). Physical assaults by women partners: A major social problem. In M. R. Walsh (Ed.), *Women, men and gender: Ongoing debates* (pp. 210–221). New Haven, CT: Yale University Press.

80. Crick, N. R., & Grotpeter, J. K. (1995). Relational aggression, gender, and social-psychological adjustment. *Child Development, 66,* 710–722.

81. Banny, A. M., Heilbron, N., Ames, A., & Prinstein, M. J. (2011). Relational benefits of relational aggression: Adaptive and maladaptive associations with adolescent friendship quality. *Developmental Psychology, 47*(4), 1153–1166.

82. Tedeschi, J. T., & Felson, R. B. (1994). *Violence, aggression, and coercive actions.* Washington, DC: American Psychological Association.

83. Dawkins, R. (1989). *The selfish gene.* New York: Oxford University Press. (Original work published 1976).

84. Tedeschi, J. T., & Felson, R. B. (1994). *Violence, aggression, and coercive actions.* Washington, DC: American Psychological Association.

85. Messick, D. M., Bloom, S., Boldizar, J. P., & Samuelson, C. D. (1985). Why we are fairer than others. *Journal of Experimental Social Psychology, 21,* 480–500.

86. Mikula, G., Petri, B., & Tanzer, N. (1989). What people regard as unjust: Types, structures and everyday experiences of injustice. *European Journal of Social Psychology, 20,* 133–149.

87. Pettiway, L. E. (1987). Arson for revenge: The role of environmental situation, age, sex, and race. *Journal of Quantitative Criminology, 3*(2), 169–184.

88. Wiehe, V. R. (1991). *Perilous rivalry: When siblings become abusive.* Lexington, MA: Heath/Lexington Books.

89. Zalar, R. W., Harris, R. B., Kyriacou, D. N., Anglin, D., & Minow, M. (2000). Domestic violence. *New England Journal of Medicine, 342,* 1450–1453.

90. Stanko, E. A. (2000). The day to count: Reflections on a methodology to raise awareness about the impact of domestic violence in the UK. *Caribbean Journal of Criminology & Social Psychology, 5*(1–2), 103–118.

91. Anderson, P. B., & Struckman-Johnson, C. (Eds.). (1998). *Sexually aggressive women: Current perspectives and controversies.* New York: Guilford Press.

92. Anderson, P. B., & Struckman-Johnson, C. (Eds.). (1998). *Sexually aggressive women: Current perspectives and controversies.* New York: Guilford Press.

93. Laumann, E. O., Gagnon, J. H., Michael, R. T., & Michaels, S. (1994). *The social organization of sexuality: Sexual practices in the United States.* Chicago: University of Chicago Press.

94. Meyer, C. B., & Taylor, S. E. (1986). Adjustment to rape. *Journal of Personality and Social Psychology, 50,* 1226–1234.

95. Rynd, N. (1988). Incidence of psychometric symptoms in rape victims. *Journal of Sex Research, 24,* 155–161.

96. Murnen, S. K., Perot, A., & Byrne, D. (1989). Coping with unwanted sexual activity: Normative responses, situational determinants, and individual differences. *Journal of Sex Research, 26,* 85–106.

97. O'Sullivan, L. F., Byers, E. S., & Finkelman, L. (1998). A comparison of male and female college students' experiences of sexual coercion. *Psychology of Women Quarterly, 22*(2), 177–195.

98. Koss, M. P. (1988). Hidden rape: Sexual aggression and victimization in the national sample of students in higher education. In M. A. Pirog-Good & J. E. Stets (Eds.), *Violence in dating relationships: Emerging social issues* (pp. 145–168). New York: Praeger.

99. Baumeister, R. F., Catanese, K. R., & Wallace, H. M. (2002). Conquest by force: A narcissistic reactance theory of rape and sexual coercion. *Review of General Psychology, 6,* 92–135.

100. Felson, R. B. (2002). *Violence and gender reexamined.* Washington, DC: American Psychological Association.

101. Bushman, B. J., Bonacci, A. M., Van Dijk, M., & Baumeister, R. F. (2003). Narcissism, sexual refusal, and sexual aggression: Testing a narcissistic reactance model of sexual coercion. *Journal of Personality and Social Psychology, 84,* 1027–1040.

102. Pitt, E. L. (2000). Domestic violence in gay and lesbian relationships. *Journal of the Gay and Lesbian Medical Association, 4,* 195–196.

103. Matud, M. P. (2005). The psychological impact of domestic violence on Spanish women. *Journal of Applied Social Psychology, 35*(11), 2310–2322.

104. Kunst, M., Bogaerts, S., & Winkel, F. W. (2010). Domestic violence and mental health in a Dutch community sample: The adverse role of loneliness. *Journal of Community & Applied Social Psychology, 20*(5), 419–425.

105. Finkel, E. J., DeWall, C. N., Slotter, E. B., McNulty, J. K., Pond, R. S., Jr., & Atkins, D. C. (2012). Using I³ theory to clarify when dispositional aggressiveness predicts intimate partner violence perpetration. *Journal of Personality and Social Psychology, 102*(3), 533–549.

106. Felson, R. B., & Messner, S. F. (2000). The control motive in intimate partner violence. *Social Psychology Quarterly, 63*(1), 86–94.

107. Ross, S. M. (1996). Risk of physical abuse to children of spouse abusing parents. *Child Abuse and Neglect, 20,* 589–598.

108. Caesar, P. L. (1988). Exposure to violence in the families-of-origin among wife-abusers and maritally nonviolent men. *Violence and Victims, 3,* 49–63.

109. Cappell, C., & Heiner, R. B. (1990). The intergenerational transmission of family aggression. *Journal of Family Violence, 5,* 135–152.

110. http://www.endcorporalpunishment.org

111. Berkowitz, L., & LePage, A. (1967). Weapons as aggression-eliciting stimuli. *Journal of Personality and Social Psychology, 7,* 202–207.

112. Carlson, M., Marcus-Newhall, A., & Miller, N. (1990). Effects of situational aggression cues: A quantitative review. *Journal of Personality and Social Psychology, 58,* 622–633.

113. Subra, B., Muller, D., Bègue, L., Bushman, B. J., & Delmas, F. (2010). Automatic effects of alcohol and weapon cues on aggressive thoughts and behaviors. *Personality and Social Psychology Bulletin, 36*(8), 1052–1057. doi: 10.1177/0146167210374725

114. Turner, C. W., Layton, J. F., & Simons, L. S. (1975). Naturalistic studies of aggressive behavior: Aggressive stimuli, victim visibility, and horn honking. *Journal of Personality and Social Psychology, 31,* 1098–1107.

115. Anderson, C. A., Benjamin, A. J., Jr., & Bartholow, B. D. (1998). Does the gun pull the trigger? Automatic priming effects of weapon pictures and weapon names. *Psychological Science, 9,* 308–314.

116. Hemenway, D., Vriniotis, M., & Miller, M. (2006). Is an armed society a polite society? Guns and road rage. *Accident Analysis and Prevention, 38*(4), 687–695.

117. Biggs, A. T., Brockmole, J. R., & Witt, J. K. (2013). Armed and attentive: Holding a weapon can bias attentional priorities during scene viewing. *Attention, Perception, & Psychophysics, 75*(8), 1715–1724.

118. Bushman, B. J., Jamieson, P. E., Weitz, I., & Romer, D. (2013). Gun violence trends in movies. *Pediatrics, 132*(6), 1014–1018. doi: 10.1542/peds.2013-1600

119. Apuzzo, M., & Schmidt, M. S. (2014, August 23). In Washington, Second Thoughts on Arming Police. *New York Times.* Retrieved from http://www.nytimes.com/2014/08/24/us/in-washington-second-thoughts-on-arming-police.html

120. Blanchette, I. (2006). Snakes, spiders, guns, and syringes: How specific are evolutionary constraints on the detection of threatening stimuli? *The Quarterly Journal of Experimental Psychology, 59*(8), 1484–1504.

121. Carlson, J. M., Fee, A. L., & Reinke, K. S. (2009). Backward masked snakes and guns modulate spatial attention. *Evolutionary Psychology, 7*(4), 534–544.

122. Fox, E., Griggs, L., & Mouchlianitis, E. (2007). The detection of fear-relevant stimuli: Are guns noticed as quickly as snakes? *Emotion, 7*(4), 691–696.

123. Diaz, J. H. (2004). The global epidemiology, syndromic classification, management, and prevention of spider bites. *American Journal of Tropical Medicine and Hygiene, 71*(2), 239–250.

124. http://historylist.wordpress.com/2008/05/29/human-deaths-in-the-us-caused-by-animals/

125. http://historylist.wordpress.com/2008/05/29/human-deaths-in-the-us-caused-by-animals/

126. Centers for Disease Control and Prevention (2104). Retrieved from http://www.cdc.gov/nchs/fastats/

127. Bushman, B. J., Newman, K., Calvert, S. L., Downey, G., Dredze, M., Gottfredson, M., Jablonski, N. G., Masten, A., Morrill, C., Neill, D. B., Romer, D., & Webster, D. (in press). Youth violence: What we know and what we need to know. *American Psychologist*.

128. Anderson, C. A., Shibuya, A., Ihori, N., Swing, E. L., Bushman, B. J., Sakamoto, A., Rothstein, H. R., Saleem, M., & Barlett, C. P. (2010). Violent video game effects on aggression, empathy, and prosocial behavior in Eastern and Western countries: A meta-analytic review. *Psychological Bulletin, 136*(2), 151–173. doi: 10.1037/a0018251

129. Greitemeyer, T., & Mügge, D. O. (2014). Video games do affect social outcomes: A meta-analytic review of the effects of violent and prosocial video game play. *Personality and Social Psychology Bulletin, 40*, 578–589. doi: 10.1177/0146167213520459

130. Bushman, B. J., & Huesmann, L. R. (2006). Short-term and long-term effects of violent media on aggression in children and adults. *Archives of Pediatrics & Adolescent Medicine, 160*(4), 348–352. doi: 10.1001/archpedi.160.4.348

131. Gentile, D. G., & Bushman, B. J. (2012). Reassessing media violence effects using a risk and resilience approach to understanding aggression. *Psychology of Popular Media Culture, 1*(3), 138–151. doi:10.1037/a0028481

132. Huesmann, L. R., Moise, J., Podolski, C. P., & Eron, L. D. (2003). Longitudinal relations between childhood exposure to media violence and adult aggression and violence: 1977–1992. *Developmental Psychology, 39*, 201–221.

133. Liptak, A. (2011, June 27). Justices reject ban on violent video games for children. *New York Times*. Retrieved from http://www.nytimes.com/2011/06/28/us/28scotus.html?pagewanted=all

134. Bushman, B. J., & Pollard-Sacks, D. (2014). Supreme Court decision on violent video games was based on the First Amendment, not scientific evidence. *American Psychologist, 69*(3), 306–307. doi: 10.1037/a0035509

135. Anderson, C. A., Shibuya, A., Ihori, N., Swing, E. L., Bushman, B.J., Sakamoto, A., Rothstein, H. R., & Saleem, M. (2010). Violent video game effects on aggression, empathy, and prosocial behavior in Eastern and Western countries. *Psychological Bulletin, 136*, 151–173.

136. Huesmann, L. R. (2010). Nailing the coffin shut on doubts that violent video games stimulate aggression—Comment on Anderson et al. (2010). *Psychological Bulletin, 136*(2), 179–181. For an alternative view, see Ferguson, C. J., & Kilburn, J. (2010). Much ado about nothing: The misestimation and overinterpretation of violent video game effects in Eastern and Western nations: Comment on Anderson et al. (2010). *Psychological Bulletin, 136*(2), 174–178, and response by Bushman, B. J., Rothstein, H. R., & Anderson, C. A. (2010). Much ado about something: Violent video game effects and a school of red herring—Reply to Ferguson and Kilburn (2010). *Psychological Bulletin, 136*(2), 182–187.

137. Greitemeyer, T., & Mügge, D. O. (2014). Video games do affect social outcomes: A meta-analytic review of the effects of violent and prosocial video game play. *Personality and Social Psychology Bulletin, 40*, 578–589. doi: 10.1177/0146167213520459

138. Yang, G. S., Huesmann, L. R., Bushman, B. J. (2014). Effects of playing a violent video game as male versus female avatar on subsequent aggression in male and female players. *Aggressive Behavior, 40*, 537–541. doi: 10.1002/ab.21551

139. Yang, G. S., Gibson, B., Lueke, A. K., Huesmann, L. R., Bushman, B. J. (2014). Effects of avatar race in violent video games on racial attitudes and aggression. *Social Psychological and Personality Science, 5*(6), 698–704. doi: 10.1177/1948550614528008.

140. Bushman, B. J., Gollwitzer, M., & Cruz, C. (2015). There is broad consensus: Media researchers agree that violent media increase aggression in children, and pediatricians and parents concur. *Psychology of Popular Media Culture, 4*(3), 200–214. DOI: 10.1037/ppm0000046

141. Donnerstein, E., & Berkowitz, L. (1981). Victim reactions in aggressive erotic films as a factor in violence against women. *Journal of Personality and Social Psychology, 41*, 710–724.

142. Malamuth, N. M., & Check, J. V. P. (1981). The effects of mass media exposure on acceptance of violence against women: A field experiment. *Journal of Research in Personality, 15*, 436–446.

143. Mullin, C. R., & Linz, D. (1995). Desensitization and resensitization to violence against women: Effects of exposure to sexually violent films on judgments of domestic violence victims. *Journal of Personality and Social Psychology, 69*, 449–459.

144. Anderson, C. A., Anderson, K. B., Dorr, N., DeNeve, K. M., & Flanagan, M. (2000). Temperature and aggression. In M. Zanna (Ed.), *Advances in experimental social psychology* (Vol. 32, pp. 63–133). New York: Academic Press.

145. Anderson, C. A., & Anderson, K. B. (1996). Violent crime rate studies in philosophical context: A destructive testing approach to heat and southern culture of violence effects. *Journal of Personality and Social Psychology, 70*, 740–756.

146. Anderson, C. A., Bushman, B. J., & Groom, R. W. (1997). Hot years and serious and deadly assault: Empirical tests of the heat hypothesis. *Journal of Personality and Social Psychology, 73*, 1213–1223.

147. Leffingwell, A. (1892). *Illegitimacy and the influence of the seasons upon conduct*. New York: Scribner's.

148. Gockel, C., Kolb, P. M., & Werth, L. (2014). Murder or not? Cold temperature makes criminals appear to be cold-blooded and warm temperature to be hot-headed. *PLoS ONE, 9*(4), e96231. doi:10.1371/journal.pone.0096231

149. Anderson, C. A., Bushman, B. J., & Groom, R. W. (1997). Hot years and serious and deadly assault: Empirical tests of the heat hypothesis. *Journal of Personality and Social Psychology, 73*(6), 1213–1223. doi: 10.1037//0022-3514.73.6.1213

150. Hsiang, S. M., Burke, M., & Miguel, E. (2013). Quantifying the influence of climate on human conflict. *Science, 341*(6151):1235367. doi: 10.1126/science.1235367

151. Gaur, S. D. (1988). Noise: Does it make you angry? *Indian Psychologist, 5*, 51–56.

152. Geen, R. G. (1978). Effects of attack and uncontrollable noise on aggression. *Journal of Research in Personality, 12*(1), 15–29.

153. Geen, R. G., & McCown, E. J. (1984). Effects of noise and attack on aggression and physiological arousal. *Motivation and Emotion, 8*, 231–241.

154. Rotton, J. (1979). The air pollution experience and physical aggression. *Journal of Applied Social Psychology, 9*, 397–412.

155. Jones, J. W., & Bogat, G. (1978). Air pollution and human aggression. *Psychological Reports, 43*(3, Pt. 1), 721–722.

156. Rotton, J., & Frey, J. (1985). Air pollution, weather, and violent crimes: Concomitant time-series analysis of archival data. *Journal of Personality and Social Psychology, 49*, 1207–1220.

157. Lipscomb, J. (2013, May 8). Flatulence leads to knife fight, arrest. *Naples Daily News*. Retrieved from http://www.naplesnews.com/tablet-showcase/courts-and-crime/fart-face-leads-knife-fight

158. Nijman, H. L. I., & Rector, G. (1999). Crowding and aggression on inpatient psychiatric wards. *Psychiatric Services, 50*(6), 830–831.

159. Lawrence, C., & Andrews, K. (2004). The influence of perceived prison crowding on male inmates' perception of aggressive events. *Aggressive Behavior, 30*(4), 273–283.

160. Sapolsky, R. M. (1998). *The trouble with testosterone: And other essays on the biology of the human predicament* (p. 150). New York: Scribner.

161. McGinnis, M. Y., Lumia, A., Breuer, M. E., & Possidente, B. (2002). Physical provocation potentiates aggression in male rats receiving anabolic androgenic steroids. *Hormones and Behavior, 41*, 101–110.

162. Archer, J. (1988). *The behavioral biology of aggression*. Cambridge: Cambridge University Press.

163. Gladue, B. A., Boechler, M., & McCaul, K. D. (1989). Hormonal responses to competition in human males. *Aggressive Behavior, 17*, 313–326.

164. Mazur, A., Susman, E. J., & Edelbrock, S. (1997). Sex differences in testosterone response to a video game contest. *Evolution and Human Behavior, 18*, 317–326.

165. McCaul, K. D., Gladue, B. A., & Joppa, M. (1992). Winning, losing, mood, and testosterone. *Hormones and Behavior, 26*, 486–504.

166. Moffitt, T., Brammer, G., Caspi, A., Fawcett, J., Raleigh, M., Yuwiler, A., & Silva, P. (1998). Whole blood serotonin relates to violence in an epidemiological study. *Biological Psychiatry, 43*, 446–457.

167. Goveas, J. S., Csernansky, J. G., & Coccaro, E. F. (2004). Platelet serotonin content correlates inversely with life history of aggression in personality-disordered subjects. *Psychiatry Research, 126*, 23–32.

168. Higley, J. D., Mehlman, P. T., Taub, D. M., Higley, S. B., Suomi, S. J., Vickers, J. H., & Linnoila, M. (1992). Cerebrospinal fluid mono-amine and adrenal correlates of aggression in free-ranging Rhesus monkeys. *Archives of General Psychiatry, 49*, 436–441.

169. Westergaard, G. C., Mehlman, P. T., Suomi, S. J., & Higley, J. D. (1999). CSF 5-HIAA and aggression in female macaque monkeys: Species and interindividual differences. *Psychopharmacology, 146*, 440–446.

170. Cleare, A. J., & Bond, A. J. (1995). The effect of tryptophan depletion and enhancement on subjective and behavioural aggression in normal male subjects. *Psychopharmacology, 118*, 72–81.

171. Marsh, D. M., Dougherty, D. M., Moeller, F. G., Swann, A. C., & Spiga, R. (2002). Laboratory-measured aggressive behavior of women: acute tryptophan depletion and augmentation. *Neuropsychopharmacology, 26*, 660–671.

172. Pihl, R. O., Young, S. N., Harden, P., Plotnick, S., Chamberlain, B., & Ervin, F. R. (1995). Acute effect of altered tryptophan levels and alcohol on aggression in normal human males. *Psychopharmacology, 119*, 353–360.

173. Berman, M. E., Tracy, J. I., & Coccaro, E. F. (1997). The serotonin hypothesis of aggression revisited. *Clinical Psychology Review, 17*, 651–665.

174. Keegan, J. (1993). *A history of warfare*. New York: Knopf.

175. Lipsey, M. W., Wilson, D. B., Cohen M. A., & Derzon, J. H. (1997). Is there a causal relationship between alcohol use and violence? A synthesis of the evidence. In M. Galanter (Ed.), *Recent developments in alcoholism: Vol. 13. Alcohol and violence: Epidemiology, neurobiology, psychology, and family issues* (pp. 245–282). New York: Plenum Press.

176. Lipsey, M. W., Wilson, D. B., Cohen M. A., & Derzon, J. H. (1997). Is there a causal relationship between alcohol use and violence? A synthesis of the evidence. In M. Galanter (Ed.), *Recent developments in alcoholism: Vol. 13. Alcohol and violence: Epidemiology, neurobiology, psychology, and family issues* (pp. 245–282). New York: Plenum Press.

177. Bushman, B. J., & Cooper, H. M. (1990). Effects of alcohol on human aggression: An integrative research review. *Psychological Bulletin, 107*, 341–354.

178. Ito, T. A., Miller, N., & Pollock, V. E. (1996). Alcohol and aggression: A meta-analysis on the moderating effects of inhibitory cues, triggering events, and self-focused attention. *Psychological Bulletin, 120*, 60–82.

179. Duke, A. A., & Giancola, P. R. (2013). Alcohol reverses religion's prosocial influence on aggression. *Journal for the Scientific Study of Religion, 52*(2), 279–292. doi: 10.1111/jssr.12029

180. Graham, K. (1980). Theories of intoxicated aggression. *Canadian Journal of Behavioral Science, 12*, 141–158.

181. Gailliot, M. T., & Baumeister, R. F. (2007). The physiology of willpower: Linking blood glucose to self-control. *Personality and Social Psychology Review, 11*(4), 303–327.

182. Badawy, A. A.-B. (2003). Alcohol and violence and the possible role of serotonin. *Criminal Behaviour and Mental Health, 13*(1), 31–44. doi: 10.1002/cbm

183. Steele, C. M., & Josephs, R. A. (1990). Alcohol myopia: Its prized and dangerous effects. *American Psychologist, 45*, 921–933.

184. Hull, J. G. (1981). A self-awareness model of the causes and effects of alcohol consumption. *Journal of Abnormal Psychology, 90*, 586–600.

185. Giancola, P. R. (2000). Executive functioning: A conceptual framework for alcohol-related aggression. *Experimental Clinical Psychopharmacology, 8*, 576–597.

186. Bushman, B. J. (1997). Effects of alcohol on human aggression: Validity of proposed explanations. In D. Fuller, R. Dietrich, & E. Gottheil (Eds.), *Recent developments in alcoholism: Alcohol and violence* (Vol. 13, pp. 227–243). New York: Plenum Press.

187. Shakur, S. (1993). *Monster: The autobiography of an L.A. gang member.* New York: Atlantic Monthly Press.

188. New studies show strong link between diet and behavior. (2004). Retrieved from http://www.kidscanlearn.net/artcri.htm

189. Gesch, B. C., Hammond, S. M., Hampson, S. E., Eves, A., & Crowder, M. J. (2002). Influence of supplementary vitamins, minerals and essential fatty acids on the antisocial behaviour of young adult prisoners: Randomised, placebo-controlled trial. *British Journal of Psychiatry, 181*, 22–28.

190. Benton, D. (2007). The impact of diet on anti-social, violent and criminal behaviour. *Neuroscience & Biobehavioral Reviews, 31*(5), 752–774.

191. *Merriam-Webster Dictionary,* http://www.merriam-webster.com/

192. Carr, J. E., & Tann, E. K. (1976). In search of the true Amok: Amok as viewed within Malay culture. *American Journal of Psychiatry, 133*(11), 1295–1299.

193. Gottfredson, M. R., & Hirschi, T. (1990). *A general theory of crime.* Stanford, CA: Stanford University Press. Also see DeWall, C. N., Finkel, E. J., & Denson, T. F. (2011). Self-control inhibits aggression. *Social and Personality Psychology Compass, 5*(7), 458–472.

194. Pratt, T. C., & Cullen, F. T. (2000). The empirical status of Gottfredson and Hirschi's general theory of crime: A meta-analysis. *Criminology, 38*, 931–964.

195. Henry, B., Caspi, A., Moffitt, T. E., & Silva, P. A. (1996). Temperamental and familial predictors of violent and nonviolent criminal convictions: Age 3 to age 18. *Developmental Psychology, 32*, 614–623.

196. Baumeister, R. F., Smart, L., & Boden, J. M. (1996). Relation of threatened egotism to violence and aggression: The dark side of high self-esteem. *Psychological Review, 103*, 5–33.

197. Morf, C. C., & Rhodewalt, F. (2001). Unraveling the paradoxes of narcissism: A dynamic self-regulatory processing model. *Psychological Inquiry, 12*, 177–196.

198. Raskin, R., & Terry, H. (1988). A principal-components analysis of the Narcissistic Personality Inventory and further evidence of its construct validation. *Journal of Personality and Social Psychology, 54*, 890–902.

199. Bushman, B. J., & Baumeister, R. F. (1998). Threatened egotism, narcissism, self-esteem, and direct and displaced aggression: Does self-love or self-hate lead to violence? *Journal of Personality and Social Psychology, 75*, 219–229.

200. Bushman, B. J., & Baumeister, R. F. (2002). Does self-love or self-hate lead to violence? *Journal of Research in Personality, 36*, 543–545.

201. Larson, M.J., Vaughn, M.G., Salas-Wright, C.P., & DeLisi, M. (2015). Narcissism, low self-control, and violence among a nationally representative sample. *Criminal Justice and Behavior, 42*(6), 644–661.

202. Bushman, B. J., & Baumeister, R. F. (1998). Threatened egotism, narcissism, self-esteem, and direct and displaced aggression: Does self-love or self-hate lead to violence? *Journal of Personality and Social Psychology, 75*, 219–229.

203. Day, D., & Ullom, H. H. (Eds.). (1947). *The autobiography of Sam Houston.* Norman: University of Oklahoma Press.

204. Cohen, D., & Nisbett, R. E. (1997). Field experiments examining the culture of honor: The role of institutions in perpetuating norms about violence. *Personality and Social Psychology Bulletin, 23*, 1188–1199.

205. Vandello, J. A., & Cohen, D. (2003). Male honor and female fidelity: Implicit cultural scripts that perpetuate domestic violence. *Journal of Personality and Social Psychology, 84*(5), 997–1010.

206. Cohen, D., & Nisbett, R. E. (1997). Field experiments examining the culture of honor: The role of institutions in perpetuating norms about violence. *Personality and Social Psychology Bulletin, 23*, 1188–1199.

207. Kelly, M. H. (1999). Regional naming patterns and the culture of honor. *Names, 47*, 3–20.

208. Campbell, J. K. (1965). Honour and the devil. In J. G. Peristiany (Ed.), *Honour and shame: The values of Mediterranean society* (pp. 112–175). London: Weidenfeld & Nicolson.

209. Edgerton, R. (1971). *The individual in cultural adaptation.* Berkeley: University of California Press.

210. Peristiany, J. G. (Ed.). (1965). *Honour and shame: The values of Mediterranean society.* London: Weidenfeld & Nicolson.

211. United Nations Population Fund. (2007/2008). A human rights and health priority. Retrieved October 17, 2008, from http://www.unfpa.org/swp/2000/english/ch03.html

212. William, I. M. (1993). *Humiliation: And other essays on honor, social discomfort, and violence.* Ithaca, NY: Cornell University Press.

213. http://www.emotionalcompetency.com/humiliation.htm

214. Atran, S. (2003). Genesis of suicide terrorism. *Science, 299*, 1534–1539.

215. Stern, J. (2004, June 6). Beneath bombast and bombs, a caldron of humiliation: Many seek to restore a dignity damaged by the new world order. *Los Angeles Times.*

216. Lindner, E. G. (2002). Healing the cycles of humiliation: How to attend to the emotional aspects of "unsolvable" conflicts and the use of "humiliation entrepreneurship." *Peace and Conflict: Journal of Peace Psychology, 8*, 125–138.

217. Serota, K. B., Levine, T. R., & Boster, F. J. (2010). The prevalence of lying in America: Three studies of self-reported lies. *Human Communication Research, 36*(1), 2–25.

218. Weiss, B., & Feldman, R. S. (2006). Looking good and lying to do it: Deception as an impression management strategy in job interviews. *Journal of Applied Social Psychology, 36*(4), 1070–1086.

219. Underwood, J. D. M., Kerlin, L., & Farrington-Flint, L. (2011). The lies we tell and what they say about us: Using behavioural characteristics to explain Facebook activity. *Computers in Human Behavior, 27*(5), 1621–1626.

220. Rowatt, W. C., Cunningham, M. R., & Druen, P. B. (1999). Lying to get a date: The effect of facial physical attractiveness on the willingness to deceive prospective dating partners. *Journal of Social and Personal Relationships, 16*(2), 209–223.

221. Toma, C. L., & Hancock, J. T. (2010). Looks and lies: The role of physical attractiveness in online dating self-presentation and deception. *Communication Research, 37*(3), 335–351.

222. Williams, S. S. (2001). Sexual lying among college students in close and casual relationships. *Journal of Applied Social Psychology, 31*(11), 2322–2338.

223. Cole, R. (2001). Lying to the one you love: The use of deception in romantic relationships. *Journal of Social and Personal Relationships, 18*(1), 107–129.

224. van 't Veer, A. E., Stel, M., & van Beest, I. (2014). Limited capacity to lie: Cognitive load interferes with being dishonest. *Judgment and Decision Making, 9*(3), 199–206. doi: 10.2139/ssrn.2351377

225. Ekman, P., & O'Sullivan, M. (1991). Who can catch a liar? *American Psychologist, 46*(9), 913–920.

226. Bond, C. F., Jr., & DePaulo, B. M. (2008). Individual differences in judging deception: Accuracy and bias. *Psychological Bulletin, 134*(4), 477–492.

227. Nysse-Carris, K. L., Bottoms, B. L., & Salerno, J. M. (2011). Experts' and novices' abilities to detect children's high-stakes lies of omission. *Psychology, Public Policy, and Law, 17*(1), 76–98.

228. Newman, M. L., Pennebaker, J. W., Berry, D. S., & Richards, J. M. (2003). Lying words: Predicting deception from linguistic styles. *Personality and Social Psychology Bulletin, 29*(5), 665–675.

229. Fields, D. A., & Kafai, Y. B. (2010). "Stealing from grandma" or generating cultural knowledge? Contestations and effects of cheating in a tween virtual world. *Games and Culture: A Journal of Interactive Media, 5*(1), 64–87.

230. Honour, J. W. (2004, July 8). The fight for fair play: Can athletes be held responsible for every substance they take? *Nature, 430*, 143–144.

231. Simkin, M. G., & McLeod, A. (2010). Why do college students cheat? *Journal of Business Ethics, 94*(3), 441–453.

232. Davis, S. F., Grover, C. A., Becker, A. H., & McGregor, L. N. (1992). Academic dishonesty: Prevalence, determinants, techniques, and punishments. *Teaching of Psychology, 19*, 16–20.

233. Bosch, T. (2012, August 20). Why would someone cheat on a free online class that doesn't count toward anything? *Slate.* Retrieved from http://www.slate.com/blogs/future_tense/2012/08/20/coursera_plagiarism_why_would_students_cheat_in_a_free_online_class_that_doesn_t_over_academic_credit_.html

234. Chait, J. (2013, April 2). Teachers cheating on tests: Not a big deal. *New York Magazine.* Retrieved from http://nymag.com/daily/intelligencer/2013/04/teachers-cheating-on-tests-not-a-big-deal.html

235. Park, C. (2003). In other (people's) words: Plagiarism by university students—literature and lessons. *Assessment and Evaluation in Higher Education, 28*, 471–488.

236. *Merriam-Webster Dictionary,* http://www.merriam-webster.com/

237. Altschuler, G. C. (2001, January 7). Battling the cheats. Retrieved October 17, 2004, from http://www.physics.ohio-state.edu/~wilkins/osu_and_ohio/essays/cheat-altschuler.html

238. Roberts, J. (2013, November 2). Three pages of Rand Paul's book were plagiarized from think tanks. *Reuters.* Retrieved from http://www.buzzfeed.com/andrewkaczynski/entire-section-of-rand-pauls-book-copied-verbatim-from-case#1m04yi5

239. Ruedy, N. E., Moore, C., Gino, F., & Schweitzer, M. E. (2013). The cheater's high: The unexpected affective benefits of unethical behavior. *Journal of Personality and Social Psychology, 105*(4), 531–548. doi: 10.1037/a0034231

240. Ruedy, N. E., Moore, C., Gino, F., & Schweitzer, M. E. (2013). The cheater's high: The unexpected affective benefits of unethical behavior. *Journal of Personality and Social Psychology, 105*(4), 531–548. doi: 10.1037/a0034231

241. Vohs, K. D., & Schooler, J. W. (2008). The value of believing in free will: Encouraging a belief in determinism increases cheating. *Psychological Science, 19*, 49–54.

242. Mead, N. L., Baumeister, R. F., Gino, F., Schweitzer, M. E., & Ariely, D. (2009). Too tired to tell the truth: Self-control resource depletion and dishonesty. *Journal of Experimental Social Psychology, 45*, 594–597. doi: 10.1016/j.jesp.2009.02.004

243. Gino, F., & Wiltermuth, S.S. (2014). Evil genius? How dishonesty can lead to greater creativity. *Psychological Science, 25*, 973–981.

244. Gino, F., & Ariely, D. (2012). The dark side of creativity: Original thinkers can be more dishonest. *Journal of Personality and Social Psychology, 102*, 445–459.

245. Shu, L. L., & Gino, F. (2012). Sweeping dishonesty under the rug: How unethical actions lead to forgetting of moral rules. *Journal of Personality and Social Psychology, 102*, 1164–1177.

246. 1 Timothy 6:10 (Bible).

247. Gino, F., & Mogilner, C. (2014). Time, money, and morality. *Psychological Science, 25*, 414–421.

248. Mazar, N., Amir, O., & Ariely, D. (2008). The dishonesty of honest people: A theory of self-concept maintenance. *Journal of Marketing Research, 45*, 633–644.

249. Yang, Q., Wu, X., Zhou, X., Mead, N. L., Vohs, K. D., & Baumeister, R. F. (2013). Diverging effects of clean versus dirty money on attitudes, values, and interpersonal behavior. *Journal of Personality and Social Psychology, 104*, 473–489.

250. Russakoff, R., & Goodman, M. (2011, July 14). Employee theft: Are you blind to it. *CBS Money Watch*. Retrieved from http://www.cbsnews.com/news/employee-theft-are-you-blind-to-it/

251. Umphress, E. E., Ren, L. R., Bingham, J. B., & Gogus, C. I. (2009). The influence of distributive justice on lying for and stealing from a supervisor. *Journal of Business Ethics, 86*, 507–518.

252. Umphress, E. E., Ren, L. R., Bingham, J. B., & Gogus, C. I. (2009). The influence of distributive justice on lying for and stealing from a supervisor. *Journal of Business Ethics, 86*(4), 507–518.

253. Henle, C. A., Reeve, C. L., & Pitts, V. E. (2010). Stealing time at work: Attitudes, social pressure, and perceived control as predictors of time theft. *Journal of Business Ethics, 94*(1), 53–67.

254. Shteir, R. (2011). *The steal: a cultural history of shoplifting.* New York: Penguin Press.

255. Hayes, R., & Downs, D. M. (2011). Controlling retail theft with CCTV domes, CCTV public view monitors, and protective containers: A randomized controlled trial. *Security Journal, 24*(3), 237–250.

256. Hagan, F. E. (2010). *Crime types and criminals.* Thousand Oaks, CA: Sage Publications.

257. Katz, J. (1988). *Seductions of crime: Moral and sensual attractions in doing evil.* New York: Basic Books.

258. Federal Trade Commission: Consumer information. Retrieved from http://www.consumer.ftc.gov/features/feature-0014-identity-theft

259. Federal Trade Commission: Consumer information. Retrieved from http://www.consumer.ftc.gov/features/feature-0014-identity-theft

260. U.S. Department of Justice. Identity theft and identity fraud. Retrieved from http://www.justice.gov/criminal/fraud/websites/idtheft.html

261. Eisenstein, E. M. (2008). Identity theft: An exploratory study with implications for marketers. *Journal of Business Research, 61*(11), 1160–1172.

262. Diener, E., Fraser, S. C., Beaman, A. L., & Kelem, R. T. (1976). Effects of deindividuation variables on stealing among Halloween trick-or-treaters. *Journal of Personality and Social Psychology, 33*(2), 178–183.

263. Hayes, R., & Downs, D. M. (2011). Controlling retail theft with CCTV domes, CCTV public view monitors, and protective containers: A randomized controlled trial. *Security Journal, 24*(3), 237–250.

264. Yap, A., Wazlawek, A. S., Lucas, B. J., Cuddy, A. J. C., & Carney, D. R. (2013).

265. The ergonomics of dishonesty: The effect of incidental posture on stealing, cheating, and traffic violations. *Psychological Science, 24*(11), 2281–2289. doi: 10.1177/0956797613492425

266. Gabbiadini, A., Riva, P., Andrighetto, L., Volpato, C., & Bushman, B. J. (2014). Moral disengagement moderates the effect of violent video games on self-control, cheating and aggression. *Social Psychological and Personality Science, 5*(4), 451–458. doi: 10.1177/1948550613509286

267. Krauss, R. M., Freedman, J. L., & Whitcup, M. (1978). Field and laboratory studies of littering. *Journal of Experimental Social Psychology, 14*, 109–122.

268. Reiter, S. M., & Samuel, W. (1980). Littering as a function of prior litter and the presence or absence of prohibitive signs. *Journal of Applied Social Psychology, 10*, 45–55.

269. Bator, R. J., Bryan, A. D., & Schultz, P. W. (2011). Who gives a hoot? Intercept surveys of litterers and disposers. *Environment and Behavior, 43*(3), 295–315.

270. http://articles.cnn.com/2011-07-01/us/texas.pride_1_texans-bumper-stickers-texas-department?_s=PM:US

271. Patel, V., Thomson, G. W., & Wilson, N. (2013). Cigarette butt littering in city streets: A new methodology for studying and results. *Tobacco Control: An International Journal, 22*(1), 59–62. doi: 10.1136/tobaccocontrol-2012-050529

272. Forsyth, A. J. M., & Davidson, N. (2010). The nature and extent of illegal drug and alcohol-related litter in Scottish social housing community: A photographic investigation. *Addiction Research & Theory, 18*(1), 71–83.

273. Cialdini, R. B., Reno, R. R., & Kallgren, C. A. (1990). A focus theory of normative conduct: Recycling the concept of norms to reduce littering in public places. *Journal of Personality and Social Psychology, 58*, 1015–1026.

274. Kallgren, C. A., Reno, R. R., & Cialdini, R. B. (2000). Littering can be reduced by anti-littering norms: A focus theory of normative conduct: When norms do and do not affect behavior. *Personality and Social Psychology Bulletin, 26*, 1002–1012.

275. Reno, R. R., Cialdini, R. B., & Kallgren, C. A. (1993). The trans-situational influence of social norms. *Journal of Personality and Social Psychology, 64*, 104–112.

276. Reich, J. W., & Robertson, J. L. (1979). Reactance and norm appeal in anti-littering messages. *Journal of Applied Social Psychology, 9*, 91–101.

277. Grasmick, H. G., Bursik, R. J., & Kinsey, K. A. (1991). Shame and embarrassment as deterrents to noncompliance with the law: The case of an antilittering campaign. *Environment and Behavior, 23*, 233–251.

278. Reams, M. A., Geaghan, J. P., & Gendron, R. C. (1996). The link between recycling and litter: A field study. *Environment and Behavior, 28*, 92–110.

279. Trinkaus, J. (1984). A bottle law: An informal look. *Perceptual and Motor Skills, 59*, 806.

280. Finnie, W. C. (1973). Field experiments and litter control. *Environment and Behavior, 5*, 123–143.

281. de Kort, Y. A. W., McCalley, L. T., & Midden, C. J. H. (2008). Persuasive trash cans: Activation of littering norms by design. *Environment and Behavior, 40*(6), 870–891.

282. Bandura, A., Ross, D., & Ross, S. A. (1961). Transmission of aggression through imitation of aggressive models. *Journal of Abnormal and Social Psychology, 63*, 575–582.

283. Zillmann, D., Katcher, A. H., & Milavsky, B. (1972). Excitation transfer from physical exercise to subsequent aggressive behavior. *Journal of Experimental Social Psychology, 8*, 247–259.

284. Huesmann, et al. (2003). Longitudinal relations between childhood exposure to media violence and adult aggression and violence: 1977–1992. *Developmental Psychology, 39*, 201–221. Copyright © 2003 by the American Psychological Association.

285. Diener, E., Fraser, S. C., Beaman, A. L., & Kelem, R. T. (1976). Effects of deindividuation variables on stealing among Halloween trick-or-treaters. *Journal of Personality and Social Psychology, 33*(2), 178–183.

CHAPTER 11
Interpersonal Attraction and Rejection

1. Shohat-Ophir, G., Kaun, K. R., Azanchi, R., & Heberlein, U. (2012). Sexual deprivation increases ethanol intake in *Drosophila*. *Science, 335*, 1351–1355.

2. Bowlby, J. (1969). *Attachment and loss: Vol. 1. Attachment.* New York: Basic Books.

3. Bowlby, J. (1973). *Attachment and loss: Vol. 2. Separation anxiety and anger.* New York: Basic Books.

4. Baumeister, R. F., & Leary, M. R. (1995). The need to belong: Desire for interpersonal attachments as a fundamental human motivation. *Psychological Bulletin, 117*, 497–529.

5. Jones, W. (1989, August). Address given at the annual convention of the American Psychological Association, New Orleans.

6. Dabbs, J. M. (2000). *Heroes, rogues, and lovers: Testosterone and behavior.* New York: McGraw-Hill.

7. Dabbs, J. M. (2000). *Heroes, rogues, and lovers: Testosterone and behavior.* New York: McGraw-Hill.

8. Roney, J. R., Mahler, S. V., & Maestripieri, D. (2003). Behavioral and hormonal responses of men to brief interactions with women. *Evolution and Human Behavior, 24*, 365–375.

9. Storey, A. E., Walsh, C. L., Quinton, R. L., & Wynne-Edward, K. E. (2000). Hormonal correlates of paternal responsiveness in new and expectant fathers. *Evolution and Human Behavior, 21*, 79–95.

10. Dabbs, J. M. (2000). *Heroes, rogues, and lovers: Testosterone and behavior.* New York: McGraw-Hill.

11. Van Goozen, S. H. M., Cohen-Kettenis, P. T., Gooren, L. J. G. M., Frijda, N. H., & Can de Poll, N. E. (1995). Gender differences in behaviour: Activating effects of cross-sex hormones. *Psychoneuroendocrinology, 20*, 343–363.

12. For a review, see Baumeister, R. F., Catanese, K. R., & Vohs, K. D. (2001). Is there a gender difference in strength of sex drive? Theoretical views, conceptual distinctions, and a review of relevant evidence. *Personality and Social Psychology Review, 5*, 242–273.

13. Worthman, C. M. (1999). Faster, farther, higher: Biology and the discourses on human sexuality. In D. Suggs & A. Miracle (Eds.), *Culture, biology, and sexuality* (pp. 64–75). Athens: University of Georgia Press.

14. McKenna, K. Y. A., & Bargh, J. A. (1998). Coming out in the age of the Internet: Identity "demarginalization" through virtual group participation. *Journal of Personality and Social Psychology, 75*, 681–694.

15. McKenna, K. Y. A., & Bargh, J. A. (1999). Causes and consequences of social interaction on the Internet: A conceptual framework. *Media Psychology, 1*, 249–269.

16. McKenna, K. Y. A., & Bargh, J. A. (2000). Plan 9 from Cyberspace: The implications of the Internet for personality and social psychology. *Personality and Social Psychology Review, 4*, 57–75.

17. Dunbar, R. I. M. (1998). The social brain hypothesis. *Evolutionary Anthropology, 6*, 178–190.

18. Ainsworth, M. D. (1989). Attachments beyond infancy. *American Psychologist, 44*, 709–716.

19. Axelrod, R., & Hamilton, W. D. (1981). The evolution of cooperation. *Science, 211*, 1390–1396.

20. Baumeister, R. F., & Leary, M. R. (1995). The need to belong: Desire for interpersonal attachments as a fundamental human motivation. *Psychological Bulletin, 117*, 497–529.

21. Bowlby, J. (1969). *Attachment and loss: Vol. 1. Attachment.* New York: Basic Books.

22. Buss, D. M. (1990). The evolution of anxiety and social exclusion. *Journal of Social and Clinical Psychology, 9*, 196–210.

23. Buss, D. M. (1991). Evolutionary personality psychology. *Annual Review of Psychology, 42*, 459–491.

24. Egan, G. (1970). *Encounter: Group processes for interpersonal growth.* Monterey, CA: Brooks/Cole.

25. Lacoursiere, R. B. (1980). *The life cycles of groups: Group developmental stage theory.* New York: Human Sciences Press.

26. Lieberman, M. A., Yalom, I. D., & Miles, M. B. (1973). *Encounter groups: First facts.* New York: Basic Books.

27. Baumeister, R. F., & Wotman, S. R. (1992). *Breaking hearts: The two sides of unrequited love.* New York: Guilford Press.

28. Baumeister, R. F., & Leary, M. R. (1995). The need to belong: Desire for interpersonal attachments as a fundamental human motivation. *Psychological Bulletin, 117*, 497–529.

29. Adler, P. (1980). On becoming a prostitute. In E. Muga (Ed.), *Studies in prostitution* (pp. 22–26). Nairobi: Kenya Literature Bureau.

30. McLeod, E. (1982). *Women working: Prostitution today.* London: Croom Helm.

31. Symanski, R. (1980). Prostitution in Nevada. In E. Muga (Ed.), *Studies in prostitution* (pp. 246–279). Nairobi: Kenya Literature Bureau.

32. Bunker, B. B., Zubek, J. M., Vanderslice, V. J., & Rice, R. W. (1992). Quality of life in dual-career families: Commuting versus single-residence couples. *Journal of Marriage and the Family, 54*, 399–407.

33. Gerstel, N., & Gross, H. (1982). Commuter marriages: A review. *Marriage and Family Review, 5*, 71–93.

34. Gerstel, N., & Gross, H. (1984). *Commuter marriage: A study of work and family.* New York: Guilford Press.

35. Govaerts, K., & Dixon, D. N. (1988). ... Until careers do us part: Vocational and marital satisfaction in the dual-career commuter marriage. *International Journal for the Advancement of Counseling, 11*, 265–281.

36. Harrison, A. A., & Connors, M. M. (1984). Groups in exotic environments. In L. Berkowitz (Ed.), *Advances in Experimental Social Psychology* (Vol. 18, pp. 49–87). New York: Academic Press.

37. Winfield, F. E. (1985). *Commuter marriage.* New York: Columbia University Press.

38. Caldwell, M. A., & Peplau, L. A. (1982). Sex differences in same-sex friendships. *Sex Roles, 8*, 721–732.

39. Wheeler, L., & Nezlek, J. (1977). Sex differences in social participation. *Journal of Personality and Social Psychology, 35*, 742–754.

40. Reis, H. T. (1990). The role of intimacy in interpersonal relations. *Journal of Social and Clinical Psychology, 9*, 15–30.

41. Wheeler, L., & Nezlek, J. (1977). Sex differences in social participation. *Journal of Personality and Social Psychology, 35*, 742–754.

42. Lynch, J. J. (1979). *The broken heart: The medical consequences of loneliness.* New York: Basic Books.

43. Bhatti, B., Derezotes, D., Kim, S., & Specht, H. (1989). The association between child maltreatment and self-esteem. In A. M. Mecca, N. J. Smelser, & J. Vasconcellos (Eds.), *The social importance of self-esteem* (pp. 24–71). Berkeley: University of California Press.

44. Cacioppo, J. T., Hawkley, L. C., Berntson, G. G., Ernst, J. M., Gibbs, A. C., Stickgold, R., et al. (2002). Lonely days invade the nights: Social modulation of sleep efficiency. *Psychological Science, 13*, 385–388.

45. Cacioppo, J. T., Hawkley, L. C., Crawford, L. E., Ernst, J. M., Burleson, M. H., Kowalewski, R. B., et al. (2002). Loneliness and health: Potential mechanisms. *Psychosomatic Medicine, 64*, 407–417.

46. DeLongis, A., Folkman, S., & Lazarus, R. S. (1988). The impact of daily stress on health and mood: Psychosocial and social resources as mediators. *Journal of Personality and Social Psychology, 54*, 486–495.

47. Goodwin, J. S., Hunt, W. C., Key, C. R., & Samet, J. M. (1987). The effect of marital status on stage, treatment, and survival of cancer patients. *Journal of the American Medical Association, 258*, 3125–3130.

48. Hawkley, L. C., Burleson, M. H., Berntson, G. G., & Cacioppo, J. T. (2003). Loneliness in everyday life: Cardiovascular activity, psychosocial context, and health behaviors. *Journal of Personality and Social Psychology, 85*, 105–120.

49. Herlitz, J., Wiklund, I., Caidahl, K., Hartford, M., Haglid, M., Karlsson, B. W., et al. (1998). The feeling of loneliness prior to coronary artery bypass grafting might be a predictor of short- and long-term postoperative mortality. *European Journal of Vascular and Endovascular Surgery, 16*, 120–125.

50. Kiecolt-Glaser, J. K., Fisher, L. D., Ogrocki, P., Stout, J. C., Speicher, C. E., & Glaser, R. (1987). Marital quality, marital disruption, and immune function. *Psychosomatic Medicine, 49*, 13–34.

51. Kiecolt-Glaser, J. K., Garner, W., Speicher, C., Penn, G. M., Holliday, J., & Glaser, R. (1984). Psychosocial modifiers of immunocompetence in medical students. *Psychosomatic Medicine, 46*, 7–14.

52. For review, see Uchino, B. N., Cacioppo, J. T., & Kiecolt-Glaser, J. K. (1996). The relationship between social support and physiological processes: A review with emphasis on underlying mechanisms and implications for health. *Psychological Bulletin, 119*, 488–531.

53. Cacioppo, J. T., & Hawkley, L. C. (2005). People thinking about people: The vicious cycle of being a social outcast in one's own mind. In K. D. Williams, J. P. Forgas, & W. von Hippel (Eds.), *The social outcast: Ostracism, social exclusion, rejection, and bullying* (pp. 91–108). New York: Psychology Press.

54. Lambert, N. M., Stillman, T. F., Hicks, J. A., Baumeister, R. F., Kamble, S., & Fincham, F. D. (2013). To belong is to matter: Sense of belonging enhances meaning in life. *Personality and Social Psychology Bulletin, 39*, 1418–1427.

55. Gardner, W. L., Pickett, C. L., & Knowles, M. (2005). Social snacking and shielding: Using social symbols, selves, and surrogates in the service of belonging needs. In K. D. Williams, J. P. Forgas, & W. von Hippel (Eds.), *The social outcast: Ostracism, social exclusion, rejection, and bullying* (pp. 227–242). New York: Psychology Press.

56. Gardner, W., Seeley, E., Gabriel, S., Pennington, G., Solomon, J., Ernst, J., et al. (2002). The role of "his" and "her" forms of interdependence in everyday life: Gender, belonging, and social experience. Unpublished manuscript, Northwestern University.

57. Jones, E. E. (1964). *Ingratiation.* New York: Irvington.

58. Byrne, D. (1971). *The attraction paradigm.* New York: Academic Press.

59. Green, G. (2005, December 9). Man dates gal on Internet for six months—and it turns out she's his mother! Retrieved from http://entertainment.tv.yahoo.com/news/wwn

60. Gangestad, S. W., & Snyder, M. (2000). Self-monitoring: Appraisal and reappraisal. *Psychological Bulletin, 126*, 530–555.

61. Lennox, R. D., & Wolfe, R. N. (1984). Revision of the self-monitoring scale. *Journal of Personality and Social Psychology, 46*, 1349–1364.

62. Snyder, M. (1974). Self monitoring of expressive behavior. *Journal of Personality and Social Psychology, 30*, 526–537.

63. Snyder, M., & Gangestad, S. (1986). On the nature of self-monitoring: Matters of assessment, matters of validity. *Journal of Personality and Social Psychology, 51*, 125–139.

64. Jensen, A. (1977). Genetic and behavioral effects of nonrandom mating. In C. Noble, R. Osborne, & N. Weyl (Eds.), *Human variation: Biogenetics of age, race, and sex.* New York: Academic Press.

65. Murstein, B. I., & Christy, P. (1976). Physical attractiveness and marriage adjustment in middle-aged couples. *Journal of Personality and Social Psychology, 34*, 537–542.

66. White, G. L. (1980). Physical attractiveness and courtship progress. *Journal of Personality and Social Psychology, 39*, 660–668.

67. Feingold, A. (1988). Matching for attractiveness in romantic partners and same-sex friends: A meta-analysis and theoretical critique. *Psychological Bulletin, 104*, 226–235.

68. McKillip, J., & Reidel, S. L. (1983). External validity of matching on physical attractiveness for same and opposite sex couples. *Journal of Applied Social Psychology, 13*, 328–337.

69. Walster, E., Aronson, V., Abrahams, D., & Rottmann, L. (1966). Importance of physical attractiveness in dating behavior. *Journal of Personality and Social Psychology, 4*, 508–516.

70. Fukuyama, F. (1999). *Trust.* New York: Free Press.

71. Rosenbaum, M. E. (1986). The repulsion hypothesis: On the nondevelopment of relationships. *Journal of Personality and Social Psychology, 51*, 1156–1166.

72. Norton, M. I., Frost, J. H., & Ariely, D. (2007). Less is more: The lure of ambiguity, or why familiarity breeds contempt. *Journal of Personality and Social Psychology, 92*, 97–105.

73. Jones, E. E., & Wortman, E. (1973). *Ingratiation: An attributional approach.* Morristown, NJ: General Learning Press.

74. Brehm, J. W., & Cole, A. H. (1966). Effect of a favor which reduces freedom. *Journal of Personality and Social Psychology, 3*, 420–426.

75. Jones, E. E., & Wortman, E. (1973). *Ingratiation: An attributional approach.* Morristown, NJ: General Learning Press.

76. Cialdini, R. B. (2001). *Influence: Science and practice* (4th ed.). Boston: Allyn and Bacon.

77. Cottrell, C. A., Neuberg, S. L., & Li, N. P. (2007). What do people desire in others? A sociofunctional perspective on the importance of different valued characteristics. *Journal of Personality and Social Psychology, 92*, 208–231.

78. Fiske, S. T., & Yamamoto, M. (2005). Coping with rejection: Core social motives, across cultures and individuals. In K. D. Williams, J. P. Forgas, & W. von Hippel (Eds.), *The social outcast: Ostracism, social exclusion, rejection, and bullying* (pp. 185–199). New York: Psychology Press.

79. Chartrand, T. L., & Bargh, J. A. (1999). The chameleon effect: The perception-behavior link and social interaction. *Journal of Personality and Social Psychology, 76*, 893–910.

80. Lakin, J. L., & Chartrand, T. L. (2005). Exclusion and nonconscious behavioral mimicry. In K. D. Williams, J. P. Forgas, & W. von Hippel (Eds.), *The social outcast: Ostracism, social exclusion, rejection, and bullying* (pp. 279–296). New York: Psychology Press.

81. Baumeister, R. F., Wotman, S. R., & Stillwell, A. M. (1993). Unrequited love: On heartbreak, anger, guilt, scriptlessness, and humiliation. *Journal of Personality and Social Psychology, 64*, 377–394.

82. Goodwin, G. P., Piazza, J., & Rozin, P. (2013). Moral character predominates in person perception and evaluation. *Journal of Personality and Social Psychology, 106*, 148–168.

83. Righetti, F., & Finkenauer, C. (2011). If you are able to control yourself, I will trust you: The role of perceived self-control in interpersonal trust. *Journal of Personality and Social Psychology, 100*, 874–886.

84. Shea, C. T., Davisson, E. K., & Fitzsimons, G. (2013). Riding other people's coattails: Individuals with low self-control value self-control in other people. *Psychological Science, 24*, 1031–1036.

85. Uhlmann, E. L., Pizarro, D. A., & Diermeier, D. (2015). A person-centered approach to moral judgment. *Perspectives on Psychological Science, 10*, 72–81.

86. Festinger, L., Schachter, S., & Back, K. W. (1950) *Social pressures in informal groups: A study of human factors in housing.* New York: Harper.

87. Latane, B., Eckman, J., & Joy, V. (1966). Shared stress and interpersonal attraction. *Journal of Experimental Social Psychology Supplement, 1*, 80–94.

88. Elder, G. H., Jr., & Clipp, E. C. (1988). Combat experience, comradeship, and psychological health. In J. P. Wilson, Z. Harel, & B. Kahana (Eds.), *Human adaptation to extreme stress: From the Holocaust to Vietnam* (pp. 131–156). New York: Plenum Press.

89. Barbee, A. P., Lawrence, T., & Cunningham, M. R. (1998). When a friend is in need: Feelings about seeking, giving, and receiving social support. In P. Anderson & L. Guerro (Eds.), *Handbook of communication and emotion* (pp. 282–298). New York: Academic Press.

90. Cunningham, M. R. (2009). Social allergies. In H. Reis & S. Sprecher (Eds.), *Handbook of human relationships.* Thousand Oaks, CA: Sage.

91. Cunningham, M. R., Barbee, A. P., & Druen, P. B. (1997). Social antigens and allergies: The development of hypersensitivity in close relationships. In R. Kowalski (Ed.), *Aversive interpersonal behaviors* (pp. 190–215). New York: Plenum Press.

92. Cunningham, M. R., Barbee, A. P., & Mandal, E. (2009). Hurtful behaviors in the workplace. In R. Kowalski (Ed.), *Feeling hurt in close relationships* (pp. 417–456). Cambridge: Cambridge University Press.

93. Eagly, A. H., Ashmore, R. D., Makhijani, M. G., & Longo, L. C. (1991). What is beautiful is good, but...: A meta-analytic review of the physical attractiveness stereotype. *Psychological Bulletin, 110*, 109–128.

94. Feingold, A. (1992). Gender differences in mate selection preferences: A test of the parental investment model. *Psychological Bulletin, 112*, 125–139.

95. Jackson, L. A., Hunter, J. E., & Hodge, C. N. (1995). Physical attractiveness and intellectual competence: A meta-analytic review. *Social Psychology Quarterly, 58*, 108–122.

96. Wheeler, L., & Kim, Y. (1997). What is beautiful is culturally good: The physical attractiveness stereotype has different content in collectivistic cultures. *Personality and Social Psychology Bulletin, 23*, 795–802.

97. Walster, E., Aronson, V., Abrahams, D., & Rottmann, L. (1966). Importance of physical attractiveness in dating behavior. *Journal of Personality and Social Psychology, 4*, 508–516.

98. Clifford, M., & Walster, E. (1973). The effect of physical attractiveness on teacher expectations. *Sociology of Education, 46*, 248–258.

99. Dion, K. (1973). Young children's stereotyping of facial attractiveness. *Developmental Psychology, 9*, 183–188.

100. Dion, K. K., Berscheid, E., & Walster, F. H. (1972). What is beautiful is good. *Journal of Personality and Social Psychology, 24*, 285–290.

101. Langlois, J. H., Roggman, L. A., Casey, R. J., & Ritter, J. M. (1987). Infant preferences for attractive faces: Rudiments of a stereotype? *Developmental Psychology, 23*, 363–369.

102. Cash, T. F., & Janda, L. H. (1984). The eye of the beholder. *Psychology Today, 18*, 46–52.

103. Mack, D., & Rainey, D. (1990). Female applicants' grooming and personnel selection. *Journal of Social Behavior and Personality, 5*, 399–407.

104. West, S. G., & Brown, T. J. (1975). Physical attractiveness, the severity of the emergency and helping: A field experiment and interpersonal simulation. *Journal of Experimental Social Psychology, 11*, 531–538.

105. Singh, D. (1993). Adaptive significance of female physical attractiveness: Role of waist-to-hip ratio. *Journal of Personality and Social Psychology, 65(2)*, 293–307.

106. Singh, D. (1995). Female judgment of male attractiveness and desirability for relationships: Role of waist-to-hip ratio and financial status. *Journal of Personality and Social Psychology, 69(6)*, 1089–1101.

107. Hitsch, G. J., Hortaçsu, A., & Ariely, D. (2006). What makes you click? Mate preferences and matching outcomes in online dating. MIT Sloan Research Paper No. 4603–06. Available at http://home.uchicago.edu/~hortacsu/onlinedating.pdf

108. Shepperd, J. A., & Strathman, A. J. (1989). Attractiveness and height: The role of stature in dating preference, frequency of dating, and perceptions of attractiveness. *Personality and Social Psychology Bulletin, 15(4)*, 617–627.

109. Grammer, K., Fink, B., Moller A. P., & Thornhill, R. (2003). Darwinian aesthetics: Sexual selection and the biology of beauty. *Biological Reviews, 78*, 385–407.

110. Garner, D. M., Garfinkel, P. E., Schwartz, D., & Thompson, M. (1980). Cultural expectations of thinness in women. *Psychological Reports, 47*, 483–491.

111. Buss, D. M. (1994). *The evolution of desire: Strategies of human mating*. New York: Basic Books.

112. Maner, J. K., Gailliot, M. T., & DeWall, C. N. (2007). Adaptive attentional attunement: Evidence for mating-related perceptual bias. *Evolution and Human Behavior, 28(1)*, 28–36.

113. Thornhill, R., & Gangestad, S. W. (1999). The scent of symmetry: A human sex pheromone that signals fitness? *Evolution and Human Behavior, 20*, 175–201.

114. Kant, I. (1924). *Critique of judgment*. Hamburg: Felix Meiner Verlag. (Original work published 1790).

115. Langlois, J. H., Roggman, L. A., Casey, R. J., & Ritter, J. M. (1987). Infant preferences for attractive faces: Rudiments of a stereotype? *Developmental Psychology, 23*, 363–369.

116. Nelson, L. D., & Morrison, E. L. (2005). The symptoms of resource scarcity: Judgments of food and finances impact preferences for potential partners. *Psychological Science, 16(2)*, 167–173.

117. Finkel, E. J., Eastwick, P. W., Karney, B. R., Reis, H. T., & Sprecher, S. (2012). Online dating: A critical analysis from the perspective of psychological science. *Psychological Science in the Public Interest, 13*, 3–66.

118. Toma, C. L., Hancock, J. T., & Ellison, N. B. (2008). Separating fact from fiction: An examination of deceptive self-presentation on online dating profiles. *Personality and Social Psychology Bulletin, 34*, 1023–1036.

119. Williams, K. D. (2001). *Ostracism: The power of silence*. New York: Guilford Press.

120. Williams, K. D. (2001). *Ostracism: The power of silence*. New York: Guilford Press.

121. Sommer, K. L., & Yoon, J. (2013). When silence is golden: Ostracism as resource conservation during aversive interactions. *Journal of Social and Personal Relationships, 30*, 901–918.

122. Williams, K. D. (2001). *Ostracism: The power of silence*. New York: Guilford Press.

123. Williams, K. D., & Zadro, L. (2005). Ostracism: The indiscriminate early detection system. In K. D. Williams, J. P. Forgas, & W. von Hippel (Eds.), *The social outcast: Ostracism, social exclusion, rejection, and bullying* (pp. 19–34). New York: Psychology Press.

124. Williams, K. D. (2001). *Ostracism: The power of silence*. New York: Guilford Press.

125. Williams, K. D., & Zadro, L. (2005). Ostracism: The indiscriminate early detection system. In K. D. Williams, J. P. Forgas, & W. von Hippel (Eds.), *The social outcast: Ostracism, social exclusion, rejection, and bullying* (pp. 19–34). New York: Psychology Press.

126. Romero-Canyas, R., & Downey, G. (2005). Rejection sensitivity as a predictor of affective and behavioral responses to interpersonal stress: A defensive motivational system. In K. D. Williams, J. P. Forgas, & W. von Hippel (Eds.), *The social outcast: Ostracism, social exclusion, rejection, and bullying* (pp. 131–154). New York: Psychology Press.

127. Sommer, K. L., & Rubin, Y. (2005). Maintaining self-esteem in the face of rejection. In K. D. Williams, J. P. Forgas, & W. von Hippel (Eds.), *The social outcast: Ostracism, social exclusion, rejection, and bullying* (pp. 171–184). New York: Psychology Press.

128. Leary, M. R., Springer, C., Negel, L., Ansell, E., & Evans, K. (1998). The causes, phenomenology, and consequences of hurt feelings. *Journal of Personality and Social Psychology, 74*, 1225–1237.

129. Leary, M. R. (2005). Varieties of interpersonal rejection. In K. D. Williams, J. P. Forgas, & W. von Hippel (Eds.), *The social outcast: Ostracism, social exclusion, rejection, and bullying* (pp. 35–54). New York: Psychology Press.

130. Twenge, J. M., Catanese, K. R., & Baumeister, R. F. (2002). Social exclusion causes self-defeating behavior. *Journal of Personality and Social Psychology, 83*, 606–615.

131. MacDonald, G., & Leary M. R. (2005). Why does social exclusion hurt? The relationship between social and physical pain. *Psychological Bulletin, 131*, 202–223.

132. Panksepp, J. (1998). *Affective neuroscience: The foundations of human and animal emotions*. London: Oxford University Press.

133. Panksepp, J., Herman, B. H., Conner, R., Bishop, P., & Scott, J. P. (1978). The biology of social attachments: Opiates alleviate separation distress. *Biological Psychiatry, 13*, 607–618.

134. Panksepp, J., Najam, N., & Soares, F. (1980). Morphine reduces social cohesion in rats. *Pharmacology, Biochemistry, and Behavior, 11*, 131–134.

135. Panksepp, J., Vilberg, T., Bean, N. J., Coy, D. H., & Kastin, A. J. (1978). Reduction of distress vocalization in chicks by opiate-like peptides. *Brain Research Bulletin, 3*, 663–667.

136. DeWall, C. N., & Baumeister, R. F. (2006). Alone but feeling no pain: Effects of social exclusion on physical pain tolerance and pain threshold, affective forecasting, and interpersonal empathy. *Journal of Personality and Social Psychology, 91*, 1–15.

137. Kross, E., Berman, M. G., Mischel, W., Smith, E. E., and Wager, T. D. (2011). Social rejection shares somatosensory representations with physical pain. *Proceedings of the National Academy of Sciences, 108*, 6270–6275.

138. DeWall, C. N., MacDonald, G., Webster, G. D., Masten, C., Baumeister, R. F., Powell, C., Combs, D., Schurtz, D. R., Stillman, T. F., Tice, D. M., & Eisenberger, N. I. (2010). Tylenol reduces social pain: Behavioral and neural evidence. *Psychological Science, 21*, 931–937.

139. Baumeister, R. F., Twenge, J. M., & Nuss, C. K. (2002). Effects of social exclusion on cognitive processes: Anticipated aloneness reduces intelligent thought. *Journal of Personality and Social Psychology, 83*, 817–827.

140. Baumeister, R. F., DeWall, C. N., Ciarocco, N. J., & Twenge, J. M. (2005). Social exclusion impairs self-regulation. *Journal of Personality and Social Psychology, 88*, 589–684.

141. Bargh, J. A., & Shaley, I. (2012). The substitutability of physical and social warmth in daily life. *Emotion, 12*, 154–162.

142. Blanchard, F. A., & Frost, R. O. (1983). Two factors of restraint: Concern for dieting and fluctuations. *Behavior Research and Therapy, 21*, 259–267.

143. Chiodo, J. (1987). Bulimia: An individual behavioral analysis. *Journal of Behavior Therapy and Experimental Psychiatry, 18*, 41–49.

144. Gross, J., & Rosen, J. C. (1988). Bulimia in adolescents: Prevalence and psychosocial correlates. *International Journal of Eating Disorders, 7*, 51–61.

145. Strober, M., & Humphrey, L. L. (1987). Familial contributions to the etiology and course of anorexia nervosa and bulimia. *Journal of Consulting and Clinical Psychology, 55*, 654–659.

146. Twenge, J. M., Catanese, K. R., & Baumeister, R. F. (2003). Social exclusion and the deconstructed state: Time perception, meaninglessness, lethargy, lack of emotion, and self-awareness. *Journal of Personality and Social Psychology, 85*, 409–423.

147. Baumeister, R. F., DeWall, C. N., Ciarocco, N. J., & Twenge, J. M. (2005). Social exclusion impairs self-regulation. *Journal of Personality and Social Psychology, 88*, 589–684.

148. Baumeister, R. F., DeWall, C. N., Ciarocco, N. J., & Twenge, J. M. (2005). Social exclusion impairs self-regulation. *Journal of Personality and Social Psychology, 88*, 589–684.

149. Maner, J. K., DeWall, C. N., Baumeister, R. F., & Schaller, M. (2007). Does social exclusion motivate interpersonal reconnection? Resolving the "porcupine problem." *Journal of Personality and Social Psychology, 92(1)*, 42–55.

150. Gardner, W. L., Pickett, C. L., & Brewer, M. B. (2000). Social exclusion and selective memory: How the need to belong influences memory for social events. *Personality and Social Psychology Bulletin, 26*, 486–496.

151. Gardner, W. L., Pickett, C. L., & Knowles, M. (2005). Social snacking and shielding: Using social

152. Kim, S. H., Vincent, L. C., & Goncalo, J. A. (2012). Outside advantage: Can social rejection fuel creative thought? *Journal of Experimental Psychology: General, 142,* 605–611.

153. Twenge, J. M., Baumeister, R. F., Tice, D. M., & Stucke, T. S. (2001). If you can't join them, beat them: Effects of social exclusion on aggressive behavior. *Journal of Personality and Social Psychology, 81,* 1058–1069.

154. Twenge, J. M., Ciarocco, N. J., Cuervo, D., Bartels, J. M., & Baumeister, R. F. (2004). Social exclusion reduces prosocial behavior. *Journal of Personality and Social Psychology, 92,* 56–66.

155. Twenge, J. M., Catanese, K. R., & Baumeister, R. F. (2002). Social exclusion causes self-defeating behavior. *Journal of Personality and Social Psychology, 83,* 606–615.

156. Gaertner, L., & Iuzzini, J. (2005). Rejection and entitativity: A synergistic model of mass violence. In K. D. Williams, J. P. Forgas, & W. von Hippel (Eds.), *The social outcast: Ostracism, social exclusion, rejection, and bullying* (pp. 307–320). New York: Psychology Press.

157. Leary, M. R., Kowalski, R. M., Smith, L., & Phillips, S. (2003). Teasing, rejection, and violence: Case studies of the school shootings. *Aggressive Behavior, 29,* 202–214.

158. Juvonen, J., & Gross, E. F. (2005). The rejected and the bullied: Lessons about social misfits from developmental psychology. In K. D. Williams, J. P. Forgas, & W. von Hippel (Eds.), *The social outcast: Ostracism, social exclusion, rejection, and bullying* (pp. 155–170). New York: Psychology Press.

159. Twenge, J. M., Baumeister, R. F., Tice, D. M., & Stucke, T. S. (2001). If you can't join them, beat them: Effects of social exclusion on aggressive behavior. *Journal of Personality and Social Psychology, 81,* 1058–1069.

160. Ouwerkerk, J. W., Kerr, N. L., Gallucci, M., & Van Lange, P. A. M. (2005). Avoiding the social death penalty: Ostracism and cooperation in social dilemmas. In K. D. Williams, J. P. Forgas, & W. von Hippel (Eds.), *The social outcast: Ostracism, social exclusion, rejection, and bullying* (pp. 321–332). New York: Psychology Press.

161. Williams, K. D., & Zadro, L. (2005). Ostracism: The indiscriminate early detection system. In K. D. Williams, J. P. Forgas, & W. von Hippel (Eds.), *The social outcast: Ostracism, social exclusion, rejection, and bullying* (pp. 19–34). New York: Psychology Press.

162. Lakin, J. L., & Chartrand, T. L. (2005). Exclusion and nonconscious behavioral mimicry. In K. D. Williams, J. P. Forgas, & W. von Hippel (Eds.), *The social outcast: Ostracism, social exclusion, rejection, and bullying* (pp. 279–296). New York: Psychology Press.

163. Cialdini, J. T., & Patrick, W. (2008). *Loneliness.* New York: Norton.

164. Wheeler, L., Reis, H., & Nezlek, J. B. (1983). Loneliness, social interaction, and sex roles. *Journal of Personality and Social Psychology, 45*(4), 943–953.

165. Cacioppo, J. T., & Hawkley, L. C. (2005). People thinking about people: The vicious cycle of being a social outcast in one's own mind. In K. D. Williams, J. P. Forgas, & W. von Hippel (Eds.), *The social outcast: Ostracism, social exclusion, rejection, and bullying* (pp. 91–108). New York: Psychology Press.

166. Pickett, C. L., & Gardner, W. L. (2005). The social monitoring system: Enhanced sensitivity to social cues and information as an adaptive response to social exclusion and belonging need. In K. D. Williams, J. P. Forgas, & W. von Hippel (Eds.), *The social outcast: Ostracism, social exclusion, rejection, and bullying* (pp. 213–226). New York: Psychology Press.

167. Peplau, L. A., & Perlman, D. (Eds.). (1982). *Loneliness: A sourcebook of current theory, research, and therapy.* New York: Wiley.

168. Russell, D., Peplau, L. A., & Cutrona, C. E. (1980). The revised UCLA Loneliness Scale: Concurrent and discriminant validity evidence. *Journal of Personality and Social Psychology, 39,* 472–480.

169. Cacioppo, J. T., Ernst, J. M., Burleson, M. H., McClintock, M. K., Malarkey, W. B., Hawkley, L. C., et al. (2000). Lonely traits and concomitant physiological processes: The MacArthur Social Neuroscience Studies. *International Journal of Psychophysiology, 35,* 143–154.

170. Gardner, W. L., Pickett, C. L., & Knowles, M. (2005). Social snacking and shielding: Using social symbols, selves, and surrogates in the service of belonging needs. In K. D. Williams, J. P. Forgas, & W. von Hippel (Eds.), *The social outcast: Ostracism, social exclusion, rejection, and bullying* (pp. 227–242). New York: Psychology Press.

171. Cacioppo, J. T., & Hawkley, L. C. (2005). People thinking about people: The vicious cycle of being a social outcast in one's own mind. In K. D. Williams, J. P. Forgas, & W. von Hippel (Eds.), *The social outcast: Ostracism, social exclusion, rejection, and bullying* (pp. 91–108). New York: Psychology Press.

172. Gardner, W., Seeley, E., Gabriel, S., Pennington, G., Solomon, J., Ernst, J., et al. (2002). The role of "his" and "her" forms of interdependence in everyday life: Gender, belonging, and social experience. Unpublished manuscript, Northwestern University.

173. Kanazawa, S. (2002). Bowling with our imaginary friends. *Evolution and Human Behavior, 23,* 167–171.

174. Gardner, W. L., Pickett, C. L., & Knowles, M. (2005). Social snacking and shielding: Using social symbols, selves, and surrogates in the service of belonging needs. In K. D. Williams, J. P. Forgas, & W. von Hippel (Eds.), *The social outcast: Ostracism, social exclusion, rejection, and bullying* (pp. 227–242). New York: Psychology Press.

175. Cacioppo, J. T., Hawkley, L. C., Berntson, G. G., Ernst, J. M., Gibbs, A. C., Stickgold, R., et al. (2002). Lonely days invade the nights: Social modulation of sleep efficiency. *Psychological Science, 13,* 385–388.

176. Cacioppo, J. T., Hawkley, L. C., Crawford, L. E., Ernst, J. M., Burleson, M. H., Kowalewski, R. B., et al. (2002). Loneliness and health: Potential mechanisms. *Psychosomatic Medicine, 64,* 407–417.

177. Cacioppo, J. T., & Hawkley, L. C. (2005). People thinking about people: The vicious cycle of being a social outcast in one's own mind. In K. D. Williams, J. P. Forgas, & W. von Hippel (Eds.), *The social outcast: Ostracism, social exclusion, rejection, and bullying* (pp. 91–108). New York: Psychology Press.

178. Cialdini, J. T., & Patrick, W. (2008). *Loneliness.* New York: Norton.

179. Juvonen, J., & Gross, E. F. (2005). The rejected and the bullied: Lessons about social misfits from developmental psychology. In K. D. Williams, J. P. Forgas, & W. von Hippel (Eds.), *The social outcast: Ostracism, social exclusion, rejection, and bullying* (pp. 155–170). New York: Psychology Press.

180. Wright, J. C., Giammarino, M., & Parad, H. W. (1986). Social status in small groups: Individual-group similarity and the social "misfit." *Journal of Personality and Social Psychology, 50,* 523–536.

181. Hogg, M. A. (2005). All animals are equal but some animals are more equal than others: Social identity and marginal membership. In K. D. Williams, J. P. Forgas, & W. von Hippel (Eds.), *The social outcast: Ostracism, social exclusion, rejection, and bullying* (pp. 243–262). New York: Psychology Press.

182. Marques, J. M., & Yzerbyt, V. Y. (1988). The black sheep effect: Judgmental extremity in inter- and intra-group situations. *European Journal of Social Psychology, 18,* 287–292.

183. Marques, J. M., Abrams, D., Páez, D., & Hogg, M. A. (2001). Social categorization, social identification, and rejection of deviant group members. In M. A. Hogg & R. S. Tindale (Eds.), *Blackwell handbook*

184. Marques, J. M., & Páez, D. (1994). The "black sheep effect": Social categorization, rejection of ingroup deviates and perception of group variability. *European Review of Social Psychology, 5,* 37–68.

185. Colman, A. M. (1982). *Game theory and experimental games: The study of strategic interaction.* Oxford: Pergamon Press.

186. Ouwerkerk, J. W., Kerr, N. L., Gallucci, M., & Van Lange, P. A. M. (2005). Avoiding the social death penalty: Ostracism and cooperation in social dilemmas. In K. D. Williams, J. P. Forgas, & W. von Hippel (Eds.), *The social outcast: Ostracism, social exclusion, rejection, and bullying* (pp. 321–332). New York: Psychology Press.

187. Ouwerkerk, J. W., Kerr, N. L., Gallucci, M., & Van Lange, P. A. M. (2005). Avoiding the social death penalty: Ostracism and cooperation in social dilemmas. In K. D. Williams, J. P. Forgas, & W. von Hippel (Eds.), *The social outcast: Ostracism, social exclusion, rejection, and bullying* (pp. 321–332). New York: Psychology Press.

188. Kerr, N. L., Rumble, A. C., Park, E. S, Ouwerkerk, J. W., Parks, C. D., Gallucci, M., & Van Lange, P. A. M. (2009). "How many bad apples does it take to spoil the whole barrel": Social exclusion and tolerance for bad apples. *Journal of Experimental Social Psychology, 45*(4), 603–613.

189. Fitness, J. (2005). Bye, bye, black sheep: The causes and consequences of rejection in family relationships. In K. D. Williams, J. P. Forgas, & W. von Hippel (Eds.), *The social outcast: Ostracism, social exclusion, rejection, and bullying* (pp. 263–277). New York: Psychology Press.

190. Folkes, V. S. (1982). Communicating the reasons for social rejection. *Journal of Personality and Social Psychology, 18,* 235–252.

191. Baumeister, R. F., & Wotman, S. R. (1992). *Breaking hearts: The two sides of unrequited love.* New York: Guilford Press.

192. Hill, C. A., Blakemore, J. E. O., & Drumm, P. (1997). Mutual and unrequited love in adolescence and adulthood. *Personal Relationships, 4*(1), 15–23.

193. Baumeister, R. F., & Wotman, S. R. (1992). *Breaking hearts: The two sides of unrequited love.* New York: Guilford Press.

194. Baumeister, R. F., Wotman, S. R., & Stillwell, A. M. (1993). Unrequited love: On heartbreak, anger, guilt, scriptlessness, and humiliation. *Journal of Personality and Social Psychology, 64,* 377–394.

195. Bjerregaard, B. (2000). An empirical study of stalking victimization. *Violence and Victims, 15,* 389–406.

196. Cupach, W. R., & Spitzberg, B. H. (2000). Obsessive relational intrusion: Incidence, perceived severity, and coping. *Violence and Victims, 15,* 357–372.

197. Davis, K. E., & Frieze, I. H. (2000). Research on stalking: What do we know and where do we go? *Violence and Victims, 15,* 473–487.

198. Tjaden, P., & Thoennes, N. (1998). *Stalking in America: Findings from the National Violence Against Women Survey* (NCJ Report no. 169592). Washington, DC: National Institute of Justice and Centers for Disease Control and Prevention.

199. White, G. L. (1980). Physical attractiveness and courtship progress. *Journal Personality and Social Psychology, 39,* 660–668. Copyright © 1980 by the American Psychological Association. Reprinted by permission.

CHAPTER 12
Close Relationships: Passion, Intimacy, and Sexuality

1. Reinisch, J. (1990). *The Kinsey Institute new report on sex: What you must know to be sexually literate.* Stuttgart: St. Martin's Press. (Quotation on p. 89).

2. Hegi, K. E., & Bergner, R. M. (2010). What is love? An empirically-based essentialist account. *Journal of Social and Personal Relationships, 27,* 620–636.

3. See Hatfield, E., & Rapson, R. L. (1987). Passionate love: New directions in research. In W. H. Jones & D. Perlman (Eds.), *Advances in personal relationships* (Vol. 1, pp. 109–139). Greenwich, CT: JAI Press.

4. Liebowitz, M. R. (1983). *The chemistry of love.* Boston: Little & Brown.

5. Walsh, A. (1991). The biological relationship between sex and love. *Free Inquiry, 11,* 20–24.

6. For example, de Rougemont, D. (1956). *Love in the Western world.* New York: Schoeken.

7. Jankowiak, W. (Ed.). (1995). *Romantic passion: A universal experience?* New York: Columbia University Press.

8. Stone, L. (1977). *The family, sex, and marriage in England 1500–1800.* London: Perennial.

9. For example, Acker, M., & Davis, M. H. (1992). Intimacy, passion and commitment in adult romantic relationships: A test of the triangular theory of love. *Journal of Social and Personality Relationships, 9,* 21–50.

10. Aron, A., Fisher, H., & Strong, G. (2006). Romantic love. In A. Vangelisti & D. Perlman (Eds.), *Cambridge handbook of personal relationships* (pp. 595–614). New York: Cambridge University Press.

11. Karney, B. R., & Bradbury, T. N. (1997). Neuroticism, marital interaction, and the trajectory of marital satisfaction. *Journal of Personality and Social Psychology, 72,* 1075–1092.

12. Blumstein, P., & Schwartz, P. (1983). *American couples: Money, work, and sex.* New York: Morrow.

13. Greenblat, C. (1983). The salience of sexuality in the early years of marriage. *Journal of Marriage and the Family, 45,* 277–288.

14. Griffitt, W. (1981). Sexual intimacy in aging marital partners. In J. Marsh & S. Kiesler (Eds.), *Aging: Stability and change in the family* (pp. 301–315). New York: Academic Press.

15. James, W. H. (1981). The honeymoon effect on marital coitus. *Journal of Sex Research, 17,* 114–123.

16. Laumann, E. O., Gagnon, J. H., Michael, R. T., & Michaels, S. (1994). *The social organization of sexuality: Sexual practices in the United States.* Chicago: University of Chicago Press.

17. Udry, J. R. (1980). Changes in the frequency of marital intercourse from panel data. *Archives of Sexual Behavior, 9,* 319–325.

18. James, W. H. (1981). The honeymoon effect on marital coitus. *Journal of Sex Research, 17,* 114–123.

19. Ard, B. N. (1977). Sex in lasting marriages: A longitudinal study. *Journal of Sex Research, 13,* 274–285.

20. Call, V., Sprecher, S., & Schwartz, P. (1995). The incidence and frequency of marital sex in a national sample. *Journal of Marriage and the Family, 57,* 639–650.

21. Laumann, E. O., Gagnon, J. H., Michael, R. T., & Michaels, S. (1994). *The social organization of sexuality: Sexual practices in the United States.* Chicago: University of Chicago Press.

22. Sternberg, R. J. (1986). A triangular theory of love. *Psychological Review, 93,* 119–135.

23. Acker, M., & Davis, M. H. (1992). Intimacy, passion and commitment in adult romantic relationships: A test of the triangular theory of love. *Journal of Social and Personality Relationships, 9,* 21–50.

24. Baumeister, R. F., & Bratslavsky, E. (1999). Passion, intimacy, and time: Passionate love as a function of change in intimacy. *Personality and Social Psychology Review, 3,* 49–67.

25. Spielmann, S. S., MacDonald, G., Maxwell, J. A., Joel, S., Peragine, D., Muise, A., & Impett, E. A. (2013). Settling for less out of fear of being single. *Journal of Personality and Social Psychology, 105,* 1049–1073.

26. Slotter, E. B., Finkel, E. J., DeWall, C. N., Pond, R. S., Lambert, N. M., Bodenhausen, G. V., & Fincham, F. D. (2011). Putting the brakes on aggression toward a romantic partner: The inhibitory influence of relationship commitment. *Journal of Personality and Social Psychology, 102,* 291–305.

27. Li, T., & Fung, H. H. (2012). How negative interactions affect relationship satisfaction: The paradoxical short-term and long-term effects of commitment. *Social Psychological and Personality Science, 4,* 274–281.

28. Francis, A. M., & Mialon, H. M. (2014). "A diamond is forever" and other fairy tales: The relationship between wedding expenses and marriage duration. Unpublished paper, Emory University, Atlanta, GA (Andrew.francis@emory.edu).

29. Meltzer, A. L,, & McNulty, J. K. (2013). "Tell me I'm sexy . . . and otherwise valuable": Body evaluation and relationship satisfaction. *Personal Relationships, 21,* 68–87.

30. Meltzer, A.L., McNulty, J.K., & Maner, J.K. (in press). Women like being valued for sex by their partner and engaging in frequent sex, as long as their partner is committed to a long-term relationship. *Archives of Sexual Behavior.*

31. Clark, M. S. (1984). Record keeping in two types of relationships. *Journal of Personality and Social Psychology, 47,* 549–557.

32. Clark, M. S., & Mills, J. (1979). Interpersonal attraction in exchange and communal relationships. *Journal of Personality and Social Psychology, 37,* 12–24.

33. Clark, M. S. (1984). Record keeping in two types of relationships. *Journal of Personality and Social Psychology, 47,* 549–557.

34. Clark, M. S., & Mills, J. (1979). Interpersonal attraction in exchange and communal relationships. *Journal of Personality and Social Psychology, 37,* 12–24.

35. Blumstein, P., & Schwartz, P. (1983). *American couples: Money, work, and sex.* New York: Morrow.

36. For example, Seabright, P. (2004). *The company of strangers: A natural history of economic life.* Princeton, NJ: Princeton University Press.

37. Clark, M. S., Ouellette, R., Powell, M., & Milberg, S. (1987). Recipients' mood, relationship type, and helping. *Journal of Personality and Social Psychology, 53,* 94–103.

38. Williamson, G. M., & Clark, M. S. (1989). Providing help and desired relationship type as determinants of changes in moods and self-evaluations. *Journal of Personality and Social Psychology, 56*(5), 722–734.

39. Clark, M. S., Ouellette, R., Powell, M., & Milberg, S. (1987). Recipients' mood, relationship type, and helping. *Journal of Personality and Social Psychology, 53,* 94–103.

40. Clark, M. S., Ouellette, R., Powell, M., & Milberg, S. (1987). Recipients' mood, relationship type, and helping. *Journal of Personality and Social Psychology, 53,* 94–103.

41. Clark, M. S., Mills, J., & Corcoran, D. (1989). Keeping track of needs and inputs of friends and strangers. *Personality and Social Psychology Bulletin, 15,* 533–542.

42. Bowlby, J. (1969). *Attachment and loss: Vol 1. Attachment.* New York: Basic Books.

43. Bartholomew, K., & Shaver, P. R. (1998). Measures of attachment: Do they converge? In J. A. Simpson & W. S. Rholes (Eds.), *Attachment theory and close relationships* (pp. 25–45). New York: Guilford Press.

44. Cooper, M. L., Shaver, P. R., & Collins, N. L. (1998). Attachment styles, emotion regulation, and adjustment in adolescence. *Journal of Personality and Social Psychology, 74,* 1380–1397.

45. Hazan, C., & Shaver, P. R. (1987). Romantic love conceptualized as an attachment process. *Journal of Personality and Social Psychology, 52,* 511–524.

46. Ainsworth, M. D. S., Blehar, M. C., Waters, E., & Wall, S. (1978). *Patterns of attachment: A psychological study of the strange situation.* Hillsdale, NJ: Erlbaum.

47. Edelstein, R. S., & Shaver, P. R. (2004). Avoidant attachment: Exploration of an oxymoron. In D. Mashek & A. Aron (Eds.), *Handbook of closeness and intimacy* (pp. 397–412). Mahwah, NJ: Erlbaum.

48. Bartholomew, K., & Horowitz, L. M. (1991). Attachment styles among young adults: A test of a four-category model. *Journal of Personality and Social Psychology, 61,* 226–244.

49. Brennan, K. A., Clark, C. L., & Shaver, P. R. (1998). Self-report measures of adult attachment. In J. A. Simpson & W. S. Rholes (Eds.), *Attachment theory and close relationships* (pp. 46–76). New York: Guilford Press.

50. Brennan, K. A., & Shaver, P. R. (1995). Dimensions of adult attachment, affect regulation, and romantic relationship functioning. *Personality and Social Psychology Bulletin, 21,* 267–283.

51. Collins, N. L., & Feeney, B. C. (2000). A safe haven: An attachment theory perspective on support-seeking and caregiving in adult romantic relationships. *Journal of Personality and Social Psychology, 58,* 644–663.

52. Edelstein, R. S., & Shaver, P. R. (2004). Avoidant attachment: Exploration of an oxymoron. In D. Mashek & A. Aron (Eds.), *Handbook of closeness and intimacy* (pp. 397–412). Mahwah, NJ: Erlbaum.

53. Collins, N. L., & Feeney, B. C. (2000). A safe haven: An attachment theory perspective on support-seeking and caregiving in adult romantic relationships. *Journal of Personality and Social Psychology, 58,* 644–663.

54. Collins, N. L., & Feeney, B. C. (2004). An attachment theory perspective on closeness and intimacy. In D. Mashek & A. Aron (Eds.), *Handbook of closeness and intimacy* (pp. 163–187). Mahwah, NJ: Erlbaum.

55. Bartholomew, K., & Horowitz, L. M. (1991). Attachment styles among young adults: A test of a four-category model. *Journal of Personality and Social Psychology, 61,* 226–244.

56. Collins, N. L., & Feeney, B. C. (2004). An attachment theory perspective on closeness and intimacy. In D. Mashek & A. Aron (Eds.), *Handbook of closeness and intimacy* (pp. 163–187). Mahwah, NJ: Erlbaum.

57. Collins, N. L., & Read, S. J. (1990). Adult attachment, working models and relationship quality in dating couples. *Journal of Personality and Social Psychology, 58,* 644–663.

58. Hazan, C., & Shaver, P. R. (1987). Romantic love conceptualized as an attachment process. *Journal of Personality and Social Psychology, 52,* 511–524.

59. Simpson, J. A. (1990). Influence of attachment styles on romantic relationships. *Journal of Personality and Social Psychology, 59,* 971–980.

60. Feeney, B. C., & Collins, N. L. (2001). Predictors of caregiving in adult intimate relationships. *Journal of Personality and Social Psychology, 80,* 972–994.

61. Feeney, J. A. (1996). Attachment, caregiving, and marital satisfaction. *Personal Relationships, 3,* 401–416.

62. Kunce, L. J., & Shaver, P. R. (1994). An attachment-theoretical approach to caregiving in romantic relationships. In K. Bartholomew & D. Perlman (Eds.), *Advances in personal relationships* (Vol. 5, pp. 205–237). London: Kingsley.

63. Bartholomew, K. (1990). Avoidance of intimacy: An attachment perspective. *Journal of Social and Personal Relationships, 7,* 147–178.

64. Collins, N. L., & Feeney, B. C. (2004). An attachment theory perspective on closeness and intimacy. In D. Mashek & A. Aron (Eds.), *Handbook of closeness and intimacy* (pp. 163–187). Mahwah, NJ: Erlbaum.

65. Baldwin, M. W. (1992). Relational schemas and the processing of social information. *Psychological Bulletin, 112,* 461–474.

66. Collins, N. L., & Feeney, B. C. (2004). An attachment theory perspective on closeness and intimacy. In D. Mashek & A. Aron (Eds.), *Handbook of closeness and intimacy* (pp. 163–187). Mahwah, NJ: Erlbaum.

67. Edelstein, R. S., & Shaver, P. R. (2004). Avoidant attachment: Exploration of an oxymoron. In D. Mashek & A. Aron (Eds.), *Handbook of closeness and intimacy* (pp. 397–412). Mahwah, NJ: Erlbaum.

68. Spangler, G., & Grossman, K. E. (1993). Biobehavioral organization in securely and insecurely attached infants. *Child Development, 64,* 1439–1450.

69. Sroufe, L. A., & Waters, E. (1977). Heart rate as a convergent measure in clinical and developmental research. *Merrill-Palmer Quarterly, 23,* 3–27.

70. Tidwell, M., Reis, H. T., & Shaver, P. R. (1996). Attachment styles, attractiveness, and emotions in social interactions: A diary study. *Journal of Personality and Social Psychology, 71*, 729–745.

71. Erikson, E. H. (1950). *Childhood and society.* New York: Norton.

72. Rogers, C. R. (1961). *On becoming a person.* Boston: Houghton Mifflin.

73. Maslow, A. H. (1968). *Toward a psychology of being.* New York: Van Nostrand.

74. Murray, S., Bellavia, G., Rose, P., & Griffin, D. (2003). Once hurt, twice hurtful: How perceived regard regulates daily marital interactions. *Journal of Personality and Social Psychology, 84*, 126–147.

75. Murray, S., Rose, P., Bellavia, G., Holmes, J., & Kusche, A. (2002). When rejection stings: How self-esteem constrains relationship enhancement processes. *Journal of Personality and Social Psychology, 83*, 556–573.

76. Rusbult, C. E., Morrow, G. D., & Johnson, D. J. (1987). Self-esteem and problem solving behavior in close relationships. *British Journal of Social Psychology, 26*, 293–303.

77. Sommer, K. L., Williams, K. D., Ciarocco, N. J., & Baumeister, R. F. (2001). When silence speaks louder than words: Explorations into the intra-psychic and interpersonal consequences of social ostracism. *Basic and Applied Social Psychology, 23*, 225–243.

78. Campbell, W. K., & Foster, C. A. (2002). Narcissism and commitment in romantic relationships: An investment model analysis. *Personality and Social Psychology Bulletin, 28*, 484–495.

79. Campbell, W. K. (1999). Narcissism and romantic attraction. *Journal of Personality and Social Psychology, 77*, 1254–1270.

80. Campbell, W. K., Reeder, G. D., Sedikides, C., & Elliot, A. J. (2000). Narcissism and comparative self-enhancement strategies. *Journal of Research in Personality, 34*, 329–347.

81. Farwell, L., & Wohlwend-Lloyd, R. (1998). Narcissistic processes: Optimistic expectations, favorable self-evaluations, and self-enhancing attributions. *Journal of Personality, 66*, 65–83.

82. Morf, C. C., & Rhodewalt, F. (2001). Unraveling the paradoxes of narcissism: A dynamic self-regulatory processing model. *Psychological Inquiry, 12*, 177–196.

83. Schütz, A. (2000). *Selbstwertgefühl: Zwischen Selbstakzeptanz und Arroganz.* Stuttgart: Kohlhammer.

84. Schütz, A. (2001). Self-esteem and interpersonal strategies. In J. P. Forgas, K. D. Williams, & L. Wheeler (Eds.), *The social mind: Cognitive and motivational aspects of interpersonal behavior* (pp. 157–176). New York: Cambridge University Press.

85. Schütz, A. (1999). It was your fault! Self-serving biases in autobiographical accounts of esteem threatening conflicts in married couples. *Journal of Social and Personal Relationships, 16*, 193–209.

86. Campbell, W. K., & Foster, C. A. (2002). Narcissism and commitment in romantic relationships: An investment model analysis. *Personality and Social Psychology Bulletin, 28*, 484–495.

87. Schütz, A. (1999). It was your fault! Self-serving biases in autobiographical accounts of esteem threatening conflicts in married couples. *Journal of Social and Personal Relationships, 16*, 193–209.

88. Miller, R. S. (1997). Inattentive and contented: Relationship commitment and attention to alternatives. *Journal of Personality and Social Psychology, 73*, 758–766.

89. Lydon, J. E., Menzies-Toman, D., Burton, K., & Bell, C. (2008). If-then contingencies and the differential effects of the availability of an attractive alternative on relationship maintenance for men and women. *Journal of Personality and Social Psychology, 95*, 50–65.

90. Meltzer, A. L., McNulty, J. K., Jackson, G. L., & Karney, B. R. (2014). Sex differences in the implications of partner physical attractiveness in the trajectory of marital satisfaction. *Journal of Personality and Social Psychology, 106*, 418–428.

91. Russell, V. M., McNulty, J. K., Baker, L. R., & Meltzer, A. L. (2014). The association between discontinuing hormonal contraceptives and wives' marital satisfaction depends on husbands' facial attractiveness. *PNAS, 111*, 17081–17086.

92. Sprecher, S. (1999). "I love you more today than yesterday": Romantic partners' perceptions of changes in love and related affect over time. *Journal of Personality and Social Psychology, 76*, 46–53.

93. Levenson, R. W., & Gottman, J. M. (1983). Marital interaction: Physiological linkage and affective exchange. *Journal of Personality and Social Psychology, 45*, 587–597.

94. Levenson, R. W., & Gottman, J. M. (1985). Physiological and affective predictors of change in marital satisfaction. *Journal of Personality and Social Psychology, 49*, 85–94.

95. Sprecher, S. (1999). "I love you more today than yesterday": Romantic partners' perceptions of changes in love and related affect over time. *Journal of Personality and Social Psychology, 76*, 46–53.

96. McNulty, J. K., Olson, M. A., Meltzer, A. L., & Shaffer, M. J. (2014). Though they may be unaware, newlyweds implicitly know whether their marriage will be satisfying. *Science, 342*, 1149–1120.

97. Baumeister, R. F., Stillwell, A. M., & Heatherton, T. F. (1995). Personal narratives about guilt: Role in action control and interpersonal relationships. *Basic and Applied Social Psychology, 17*, 173–198. doi: 10.1207/s15324834basp1701&2_10

98. Baumeister, R. F., Stillwell, A. M., & Heatherton, T. F. (1994). Guilt: An interpersonal approach. *Psychological Bulletin, 115*, 243–267. doi:10.1037/0033-2909.115.2.243

99. Overall, N. C., Girme, Y. U., Lemay, E. P., & Hammond, M. D. (2014). Attachment anxiety and reactions to relationship threat: The benefits and costs of inducing guilt in romantic partners. *Journal of Personality and Social Psychology, 106*, 235–256.

100. Rusbult, C. E. (1983). A longitudinal test of the investment model: The development (and deterioration) of satisfaction and commitment in heterosexual involvements. *Journal of Personality and Social Psychology, 45*, 101–117.

101. For example, Rusbult, C. E., & Martz, J. M. (1995). My relationship is better than—and not as bad as—yours is: The perception of superiority in close relationships. *Personality and Social Psychology Bulletin, 21*, 558–571.

102. Horowitz, A. V., White, H. R., & Howell-White, S. (1997). Becoming married and mental health: A longitudinal study of a cohort of young adults. *Journal of Marriage and the Family, 58*, 895–907.

103. Hu, Y., & Goldman, M. (1990). Mortality differentials by marital status: An international comparison. *Demography, 27*, 233–250.

104. See also Johnson, W., McGue, M., Krueger, R. F., & Bouchard, T. J. (2004). Marriage and personality: A genetic analysis. *Journal of Personality and Social Psychology, 86*, 285–294.

105. Coyne, J. C., & DeLongis, A. (1986). Going beyond social support: The role of social relationships in adaptation. *Journal of Consulting and Clinical Psychology, 54*, 454–460.

106. DeLongis, A., Folkman, S., & Lazarus, S. (1988). The impact of daily stress on health and mood: Psychological and social resources as mediators. *Journal of Personality and Social Psychology, 54*, 486–495.

107. Kiecolt-Glaser, J. K., Fisher, L. D., Ogrocki, P., Stout, J. C., Speicher, C. E., & Glaser, R. (1987). Marital quality, marital disruption, and immune function. *Psychosomatic Medicine, 49*, 13–34.

108. Myers, D. G. (1992). The secrets of happiness. *Psychology Today, 25*, 38–46.

109. Kiecolt-Glaser, J. K., & Newton, T. L. (2001). Marriage and health: His and hers. *Psychological Bulletin, 127*, 472–503.

110. Johnson, W., McGue, M., Krueger, R. F., & Bouchard, T. J. (2004). Marriage and personality: A genetic analysis. *Journal of Personality and Social Psychology, 86*, 285–294.

111. Bernard, J. (1982). *The future of marriage.* New Haven, CT: Yale University Press.

112. Holtzworth-Munroe, A., & Jacobson, N. S. (1985). Causal attributions of married couples: When do they search for causes? What do they conclude when they do? *Journal of Personality and Social Psychology, 48*, 1398–1412.

113. Luchies, L. B., Wieselquist, J., Rusbult, C. E., Kumasiro, M., Eastwick, P. W., Coolsen, M. K., & Finkel, E. J. (2013). Trust and biased memory of transgressions in romantic relationships. *Journal of Personality and Social Psychology, 104*, 673–694.

114. MacDonald, T. K., & Ross, M. (1999). Assessing the accuracy of predictions about dating relationships: How and why do lovers' predictions differ from those made by observers? *Personality and Social Psychology Bulletin, 25*, 1417–1429.

115. Vaughan, D. (1986). *Uncoupling: Turning points in intimate relationships.* New York: Oxford University Press.

116. Johnson, D. J., & Rusbult, C. E. (1989). Resisting temptation: Devaluation of alternative partners as a means of maintaining commitment in close relationships. *Journal of Personality and Social Psychology, 57*, 967–980.

117. Miller, R. S. (1997). Inattentive and contented: Relationship commitment and attention to alternatives. *Journal of Personality and Social Psychology, 73*, 758–766.

118. Simpson, J. A., Gangestad, S., & Lerma, M. (1990). Perception of physical attractiveness: Mechanisms involved in the maintenance of romantic relationships. *Journal of Personality and Social Psychology, 59*, 1192–1201.

119. For example, Swann, W. B., Jr. (1985). The self as architect of social reality. In B. Schlenker (Ed.), *The self and social life* (pp. 100–125). New York: McGraw-Hill.

120. Swann, W. B., Jr. (1987). Identity negotiation: Where two roads meet. *Journal of Personality and Social Psychology, 53*, 1038–1051.

121. Swann, W. B., De La Ronde, C., & Hixon, J. G. (1994). Authenticity and positivity strivings in marriage and courtship. *Journal of Personality and Social Psychology, 66*, 857–869.

122. Murray, S., Holmes, J. G., & Griffin, D. W. (1996). The benefits of positive illusions: Idealization and the construction of satisfaction in close relationships. *Journal of Personality and Social Psychology, 70*, 79–98.

123. Murray, S., & Holmes, J. G. (1993). See virtues in faults: Negativity and the transformation of interpersonal narratives in close relationships. *Journal of Personality and Social Psychology, 65*, 707–722.

124. Murray, S., & Holmes, J. G. (1994). Story-telling in close relationships: The construction of confidence. *Personality and Social Psychology Bulletin, 20*, 663–676.

125. Holmes, J. G. (2004, October). The power of positive thinking in close relationships. Paper presented at the Third International Positive Psychology Summit, Washington, DC.

126. Swann, W. B., Jr. (1998). The self and interpersonal relationships. Paper presented at the meeting of the Society of Experimental Social Psychologists, Lexington, KY.

127. Macfarlane, A. (1986). *Marriage and love in England: Modes of reproduction, 1300–1840.* New York: Basil Blackwell.

128. Shorter, E. (1975). *The making of the modern family.* New York: Basic Books.

129. Stone, L. (1977). *The family, sex, and marriage in England 1500–1800.* London: Perennial.

130. Diamond, L. M. (2003). What does sexual orientation orient? A biobehavioral model distinguishing romantic love and sexual desire. *Psychological Review, 110*, 173–192.

131. Diamond, L. M. (2004). Emerging perspectives on distinctions between romantic love and sexual desire. *Current Directions in Psychological Science, 13*, 116–119.

132. Diamond, L. M. (2003). An attachment perspective on female sexual fluidity. Paper presented at the Women's Sexualities Conference: Historical, Interdisciplinary, and International Perspectives, sponsored by the Kinsey Institute for Research in Sex, Gender, and Reproduction, Bloomington, IN.

133. DeLamater, J., & Hyde, J. S. (1998). Essentialism vs. social constructionism in the study of human sexuality. *Journal of Sex Research, 35,* 10–18.

134. Staples, R. (1973). *Black women in America: Sex, marriage, and family.* Chicago: Nelson-Hall.

135. For example, Kitzinger, C. (1987). *The social construction of lesbianism.* London: Sage.

136. Symons, D. (1979). *The evolution of human sexuality.* New York: Oxford University Press.

137. Symons, D. (1995). Beauty is in the adaptations of the beholder: The evolutionary psychology of human female sexual attractiveness. In P. R. Abramson & S. D. Pinkerton (Eds.), *Sexual nature/sexual culture* (pp. 80–118). Chicago: University of Chicago Press.

138. Buss, D. M. (1994). *The evolution of desire: Strategies of human mating.* New York: Basic Books.

139. Trivers, R. (1972). Parental investment and sexual selection. In B. Campbell (Ed.), *Sexual selection and the descent of man: 1871–1971* (pp. 136–179). Chicago: Aldine.

140. Symons, D. (1979). *The evolution of human sexuality.* New York: Oxford University Press.

141. Buss, D. M., & Schmitt, D. P. (1993). Sexual strategies theory: An evolutionary perspective on human mating. *Psychological Review, 100,* 204–232.

142. Buss, D. M., & Schmitt, D. P. (1993). Sexual strategies theory: An evolutionary perspective on human mating. *Psychological Review, 100,* 204–232.

143. Blau, P. N. (1964). *Exchange and power in social life.* New York: Wiley.

144. Homans, G. C. (1950). *The human group.* New York: Harcourt, Brace, & World.

145. Homans, G. C. (1961). *Social behavior: Its elementary forms.* New York: Harcourt, Brace, & World.

146. Sprecher, S. (1998). Social exchange theories and sexuality. *Journal of Sex Research, 35,* 32–43.

147. Baumeister, R. F., & Vohs, K. D. (2004). Sexual economics: Sex as female resource for social exchange in heterosexual interactions. *Personality and Social Psychology Review, 8*(4), 339–363.

148. Symons, D. (1979). *The evolution of human sexuality.* New York: Oxford University Press.

149. Regnerus, M. (2011). *Premarital sex in America: How young Americans meet, mate, and think about marrying.* New York: Oxford University Press.

150. Baumeister, R. F., Catanese, K. R., & Vohs, K. D. (2001). Is there a gender difference in strength of sex drive? Theoretical views, conceptual distinctions, and a review of relevant evidence. *Personality and Social Psychology Review, 5,* 242–273.

151. Conley, T. D., Moors, A. C., Matsick, J. L., Ziegler, A., & Valentine, B. A. (2011). Women, men, and the bedroom: Methodological and conceptual insights that narrow, reframe, and eliminate gender differences in sexuality. *Current Directions in Psychological Science, 20,* 296–300.

152. Schmitt, D. P., Jonason, P. K., Byerley, G. J., Flores, S. D., Illbeck, B. E., O'Leary, K. N., & Qudrat, A. (2012). A reexamination of sex differences in sexuality: New studies reveal old truths. *Current Directions in Psychological Science, 21,* 135–139.

153. Oliver, M. B., & Hyde, J. S. (1993). Gender differences in sexuality: A meta-analysis. *Psychological Bulletin, 114,* 29–51.

154. For example, Wilson, J., Kuehn, R., & Beach, F. (1963). Modifications in the sexual behavior of male rats produced by changing the stimulus female. *Journal of Comparative and Physiological Psychology, 56,* 636–644.

155. Francoeur, R. T., Perper, T., Scherzer, N. A., Sellmer, G. P., & Cornog, M. (1991). *A descriptive dictionary and atlas of sexology,* p. 130. New York: Greenwood Press.

156. Arndt, B. (2009). *The Sex Diaries.* Melbourne: Melbourne University Press.

157. Janus, S. S., & Janus, C. L. (1993). *The Janus report on sexual behavior.* New York: Wiley.

158. Baumeister, R. F. (2000). Gender differences in erotic plasticity: The female sex drive as socially flexible and responsive. *Psychological Bulletin, 126,* 347–374.

159. Diamond, L. M. (2008). *Sexual fluidity: Understanding women's love and desire.* Cambridge, MA: Harvard University Press.

160. For example, Kinsey, A. C., Pomeroy, W. B., Martin, C. E., & Gebhard, P. H. (1953). *Sexual behavior in the human female.* Philadelphia: Saunders.

161. For example, Savin-Williams, R. C. (1990). *Gay and lesbian youth: Expressions of identity.* New York: Hemisphere.

162. Whisman, V. (1996). *Queer by choice.* New York: Routledge.

163. Adams, C. G., & Turner, B. F. (1985). Reported change in sexuality from young adulthood to old age. *Journal of Sex Research, 21,* 126–141.

164. Ard, B. N. (1977). Sex in lasting marriages: A longitudinal study. *Journal of Sex Research, 13,* 274–285.

165. Adams, C. G., & Turner, B. F. (1985). Reported change in sexuality from young adulthood to old age. *Journal of Sex Research, 21,* 126–141.

166. Laumann, E. O., Gagnon, J. H., Michael, R. T., & Michaels, S. (1994). *The social organization of sexuality: Sexual practices in the United States.* Chicago: University of Chicago Press.

167. McCabe, P. (1987). Desired and experienced levels of premarital affection and sexual intercourse during dating. *Journal of Sex Research, 23,* 23–33.

168. Cohen, L. L., & Shotland, R. L. (1996). Timing of first sexual intercourse in a relationship: Expectations, experiences, and perceptions of others. *Journal of Sex Research, 33,* 291–299.

169. Pliner, P., & Chaiken, S. (1990). Eating, social motives, and self-presentation in women and men. *Journal of Experimental Social Psychology, 26,* 240–254.

170. Mori, D., Chaiken, S., & Pliner, P. (1987). "Eating lightly" and the self-presentation of femininity. *Journal of Personality and Social Psychology, 53,* 693–702.

171. Bell, A. P., & Weinberg, M. S. (1978). *Homosexualities: A study of diversity among men and women.* New York: Simon & Schuster.

172. Bem, D. J. (1996). Exotic becomes erotic: A developmental theory of sexual orientation. *Psychological Review, 103,* 320–335.

173. Bem, D. J. (1998). Is EBE theory supported by evidence? Is it androcentric? A reply to Peplau et al. (1998). *Psychological Review, 105,* 395–398.

174. Schachter, S. (1964). The interaction of cognitive and physiological determinants of emotional state. In L. Berkowitz (Ed.), *Advances in Experimental Social Psychology* (pp. 49–79). New York: Academic Press.

175. Bem, D. J. (1998). Is EBE theory supported by evidence? Is it androcentric? A reply to Peplau et al. (1998). *Psychological Review, 105,* 395–398.

176. Bailey, J. M., & Pillard, R. C. (1995). Genetics of human sexual orientation. *Annual Review of Sex Research, 6,* 126–150.

177. For example, Thompson, A. P. (1983). Extramarital sex: A review of the research literature. *Journal of Sex Research, 19,* 1–22.

178. Morokoff, P. J. (1986). Volunteer bias in the psychophysiological study of female sexuality. *Journal of Sex Research, 22,* 35–51.

179. Wiederman, M. W. (1993). Demographic and sexual characteristics of nonresponders to sexual experience items in a national survey. *Journal of Sex Research, 30,* 27–35.

180. Wiederman, M. W. (2004). Self-control and sexual behavior. In R. Baumeister & K. Vohs (Eds.), *Handbook of self-regulation* (pp. 537–552). New York: Guilford Press.

181. Laumann, E. O., Gagnon, J. H., Michael, R. T., & Michaels, S. (1994). *The social organization of sexuality: Sexual practices in the United States.* Chicago: University of Chicago Press.

182. Wiederman, M. W. (1997). The truth must be in here somewhere: Examining the gender discrepancy in self-reported lifetime number of sex partners. *Journal of Sex Research, 34,* 375–386.

183. For example, Thompson, A. P. (1983). Extramarital sex: A review of the research literature. *Journal of Sex Research, 19,* 1–22.

184. Abraham, C. (2002, December 14). Mommy's little secret. *The Globe and Mail* (Toronto), pp. F1, F6.

185. For example, Buss, D. M. (1994). *The evolution of desire: Strategies of human mating.* New York: Basic Books.

186. Abraham, C. (2002, December 14). Mommy's little secret. *The Globe and Mail* (Toronto), pp. F1, F6.

187. Abraham, C. (2002, December 14). Mommy's little secret. *The Globe and Mail* (Toronto), pp. F1, F6.

188. Laumann, E. O., Gagnon, J. H., Michael, R. T., & Michaels, S. (1994). *The social organization of sexuality: Sexual practices in the United States.* Chicago: University of Chicago Press.

189. Blumstein, P., & Schwartz, P. (1983). *American couples: Money, work, and sex.* New York: Morrow.

190. Wiederman, M. W. (1997). The truth must be in here somewhere: Examining the gender discrepancy in self-reported lifetime number of sex partners. *Journal of Sex Research, 34,* 375–386.

191. Spanier, G. P., & Margolis, R. L. (1983). Marital separation and extramarital sexual behavior. *Journal of Sex Research, 19,* 23–48.

192. Lawson, A. (1988). *Adultery: An analysis of love and betrayal.* New York: Basic Books.

193. Lawson, A. (1988). *Adultery: An analysis of love and betrayal.* New York: Basic Books.

194. Hansen, G. L. (1987). Extradyadic relations during courtship. *Journal of Sex Research, 23,* 382–390.

195. Shorter, E. (1975). *The making of the modern family.* New York: Basic Books.

196. Shorter, E. (1975). *The making of the modern family.* New York: Basic Books.

197. Shackelford, T. K. (2001). Self-esteem in marriage: An evolutionary psychological analysis. *Personality and Individual Differences, 30,* 371–390.

198. Pines, A., & Aronson, E. (1983). Antecedents, correlates, and consequences of sexual jealousy. *Journal of Personality, 51,* 108–136.

199. Mead, M. (1928). *Coming of age in Samoa: A psychological study of primitive youth for Western civilization.* New York: Morrow.

200. Reiss, I. L. (1986). *Journey into sexuality.* New York: Prentice Hall.

201. Reiss, I. L. (1986). A sociological journey into sexuality. *Journal of Marriage and the Family, 48,* 233–242.

202. Hupka, R. B. (1981). Cultural determinants of jealousy. *Alternative Lifestyles, 4,* 310–356.

203. Buunk, B. P. & Hupka, R. B. (1987). Cross-cultural differences in the elicitation of sexual jealousy. *Journal of Sex Research, 23,* 12–22.

204. Buss, D. M. (1994). *The evolution of desire: Strategies of human mating.* New York: Basic Books.

205. Abraham, C. (2002, December 14). Mommy's little secret. *The Globe and Mail* (Toronto), pp. F1, F6.

206. Buss, D. M., Larsen, R. J., Westen, D., & Semmelroth, J. (1992). Sex differences in jealousy: Evolution, physiology, and psychology. *Psychological Science, 3,* 251–255.

207. Buunk, B. P., Angleitner, A., Oubaid, V., & Buss, D. M. (1996). Sex differences in jealousy in evolutionary and cultural perspective: Tests from the Netherlands, Germany, and the United States. *Psychological Science, 7,* 1103–1116.

208. DeSteno, D. A., Bartlett, M. Y., Braverman, J., & Salovey, P. (2002). Sex differences in jealousy: Evolutionary mechanisms or artifact of measurement. *Journal of Personality and Social Psychology, 83,* 1103–1116.

209. Harris, C. R. (2000). Psychophysiological responses to imagined infidelity: The specific innate modular view of jealousy reconsidered. *Journal of Personality and Social Psychology, 75,* 1082–1091.

210. DeSteno, D. A., Bartlett, M. Y., Braverman, J., & Salovey, P. (2002). Sex differences in jealousy: Evolutionary mechanisms or artifact of measurement. *Journal of Personality and Social Psychology, 83,* 1103–1116.

211. Van den Bergh, B., Dewitte, S., & Warlop, L. (2008). Bikinis instigate generalized impatience in intertemporal choice. *Journal of Consumer Research, 35*(1), 85–97.

212. Wilson, M., & Daly M. (2003). Do pretty women inspire men to discount the future? Biology Letters. *Proceedings of the Royal Society, London. B (Suppl.).* doi: 10.1098/rsbl.2003.0134

213. Van den Bergh, B., Dewitte, S., & Warlop, L. (2008). Bikinis instigate generalized impatience in intertemporal choice. *Journal of Consumer Research, 35*(1), 85–97.

214. Roney, J. R. (2003). Effects of visual exposure to the opposite sex: Cognitive aspects of mate attraction in human males. *Personality and Social Psychology Bulletin, 29*(3), 393–404.

215. For example, Gondolf, E. W. (1985). *Men who batter: An integrated approach for stopping wife abuse.* Holmes Beach, CA: Learning Publications.

216. Renzetti, C. M. (1992). *Violent betrayal: Partner abuse in lesbian relationships.* Newbury Park, CA: Sage.

217. Blumstein, P., & Schwartz, P. (1983). *American couples: Money, work, and sex.* New York: Morrow.

218. Blumstein, P., & Schwartz, P. (1983). *American couples: Money, work, and sex.* New York: Morrow.

219. Seal, D. W. (1997). Interpartner concordance of self-reported sexual behavior among college dating couples. *Journal of Sex Research, 34,* 39–55.

220. Lawson, A. (1988). *Adultery: An analysis of love and betrayal.* New York: Basic Books.

221. DeSteno, D. A., & Salovey, P. (1996). Evolutionary origins of sex differences in jealousy? Questioning the "fitness" of the model. *Psychological Science, 7,* 367–372.

222. Salovey, P., & Rodin, J. (1991). Provoking jealousy and envy: Domain relevance and self-esteem threat. *Journal of Social and Clinical Psychology, 10,* 395–413.

223. Wiederman, M. W., & LaMar, L. (1998). "Not with him you don't!": Gender and emotional reactions to sexual infidelity during courtship. *Journal of Sex Research, 34,* 375–386.

224. Pines, A., & Aronson, E. (1983). Antecedents, correlates, and consequences of sexual jealousy. *Journal of Personality, 51,* 108–136.

225. Wicklund, R. A., & Gollwitzer, P. M. (1982). *Symbolic self-completion.* Hillsdale, NJ: Erlbaum.

226. Bailey, R. C., & Aunger, R. V. (1995). Sexuality, infertility and sexually transmitted disease among farmers and foragers in central Africa. In P. Abramson & S. Pinkerton (Eds.), *Sexual nature/sexual culture* (pp. 195–222). Chicago: University of Chicago Press.

227. For example, Ehrenreich, B. (1999, March 8). The real truth about the female. *Time, 153*(9), 57–91.

228. Oliver, M. B., & Hyde, J. S. (1993). Gender differences in sexuality: A meta-analysis. *Psychological Bulletin, 114,* 29–51.

229. King, K., Balswick, J. O., & Robinson, I. E. (1977). The continuing premarital sexual revolution among college females. *Journal of Marriage and the Family, 39,* 455–459.

230. Millhausen, R. R., & Herold, E. S. (1999). Does the sexual double standard still exist? Perceptions of university women. *Journal of Sex Research, 36,* 361–368.

231. Sprecher, S. (1989). Premarital sexual standards for different categories of individuals. *Journal of Sex Research, 19,* 23–48.

232. Smith, T. (1994). Attitudes toward sexual permissiveness: Trends, correlates, and behavioral connections. In A. S. Rossi (Ed.), *Sexuality across the life course* (pp. 63–97). Chicago: University of Chicago Press.

233. For a review, see Baumeister, R. F., & Twenge, J. M. (2002). Cultural suppression of female sexuality. *Review of General Psychology, 6,* 166–203.

234. Barash, D. P., & Lipton, J. E. (2002). *Myth of monogamy: Fidelity and infidelity in animals and people.* New York: W. H. Freeman.

235. Smuts, B. (1996). Male aggression against women: An evolutionary perspective. In D. Buss & N. Malamuth (Eds.), *Sex, power, conflict* (pp. 231–268). New York: Oxford University Press.

236. Dunbar, R. I. M. (1996). *Grooming, gossip, and the evolution of language.* Cambridge, MA: Harvard University Press.

237. James (1981). From James, W. H. (1981). The honeymoon effect on marital coitus. *Journal of Sex Research, 17,* 114–132. Copyright © 1981 Taylor & Francis Group, LLC. Reprinted by permission.

CHAPTER 13
Prejudice and Intergroup Relations

1. David, M. B. (2013, February 13). Deep racism: The forgotten history of human zoos. *Popular Resistance.* Retrieved from http://www.popularresistance.org/deep-racism-the-forgotten-history-of-human-zoos/

2. Mullan, B., & Marvin, G. (1998). *Zoo culture: The book about watching people watch animals* (2nd ed.). Urbana, IL: University of Illinois Press.

3. Harskamp, J., & Dijstelberge, P. (2012, April 12). The human zoo. Retrieved from http://abeautifulbook.wordpress.com/2012/04/21/the-human-zoo/

4. Mullan, B., & Marvin, G. (1998). *Zoo culture: The book about watching people watch animals* (2nd ed.). Urbana, IL: University of Illinois Press.

5. Harskamp, J., & Dijstelberge, P. (2012, April 12). The human zoo. Retrieved from http://abeautifulbook.wordpress.com/2012/04/21/the-human-zoo/

6. Cincinnati zoo and botanical garden. Retrieved from http://www.ohiohistorycentral.org/w/Cincinnati_Zoo_and_Botanical_Garden?rec=685

7. Missouri Historical Society. The *1904 World's Fair: Looking back at looking forward.* Retrieved from http://mohistory.org/Fair/WF/HTML/Overview/page3.html

8. Keller, M. (2006, August 6). The scandal at the zoo. *New York Times.* Retrieved from http://www.nytimes.com/2006/08/06/nyregion/thecity/06zoo.html?ex=1155009600&en=c2cc9b84edc068cd&ei=5087%0A

9. Political Blind Spot (2014, February 13). Through the 1950s, Africans and Native Americans were kept in zoos as exhibits. Retrieved from http://politicalblindspot.com/through-the-1950s-africans-and-native-americans-were-kept-in-zoos-as-exhibits/

10. Political Blind Spot (2014, February 13). Through the 1950s, Africans and Native Americans were kept in zoos as exhibits. Retrieved from http://politicalblindspot.com/through-the-1950s-africans-and-native-americans-were-kept-in-zoos-as-exhibits/

11. Hawley, C. (2005, June 9). German zoo scandal: "African Village" accused of putting humans on display. *Der Spiegel.* Retrieved from http://www.spiegel.de/international/german-zoo-scandal-african-village-accused-of-putting-humans-on-display-a-359799.html

12. Gaertner, S. L., & Dovidio, J. F. (1986). The aversive form of racism. In J. F. Dovidio & S. L. Gaertner (Eds.), *Prejudice, discrimination, and racism* (pp. 61–89). San Diego: Academic Press.

13. Word, C. O., Zanna, M. P., & Cooper, J. (1974). The nonverbal mediation of self-fulfilling prophecies in interracial interaction. *Journal of Experimental Social Psychology, 10,* 109–120.

14. Szymanski, S. (2000). A market test for discrimination in the English professional soccer leagues. *Journal of Political Economy, 108*(3), 590–603.

15. Richards, Z., & Hewstone, M. (2001). Subtyping and subgrouping: Processes for the prevention and promotion of stereotype change. *Personality and Social Psychology Review, 5,* 52–73.

16. Altermatt, T. W., & DeWall, C. N. (2003). Agency and virtue: Dimensions underlying subgroups of women. *Sex Roles, 49,* 631–641.

17. Stone, L. (1977). *The family, sex and marriage in England: 1500–1800.* London: Perennial.

18. Tracking the events in the wake of Michael Brown's shooting. *New York Times.* Retrieved from http://www.nytimes.com/interactive/2014/08/12/us/13police-shooting-of-black-teenager-michael-brown.html

19. Correll, J., Park, B., Judd, C. M., & Wittenbrink, B. (2002). The police officer's dilemma: Using ethnicity to disambiguate potentially threatening individuals. *Journal of Personality and Social Psychology, 86,* 1314–1329.

20. Greenwald, A. G., Oakes, M. A., & Hoffman, H. G. (2003). Targets of discrimination: Effects of race on responses to weapons holders. *Journal of Experimental Social Psychology, 39,* 399–340.

21. Payne, B. K. (2001). Prejudice and perception: The role of automatic and controlled processes in misperceiving a weapon. *Journal of Personality and Social Psychology, 81,* 181–192.

22. Plant, E. A., & Peruche, B. M. (2005). The consequences of race for police officers' responses to criminal suspects. *Psychological Science, 16,* 180–183.

23. Butz, D. A., Plant, E. A., & Doerr, C. (2007). Liberty and justice for all? The implications of exposure to the United States flag for intergroup relations. *Personality and Social Psychology Bulletin, 33,* 396–408.

24. Linville, P. W., & Jones, E. E. (1980). Polarized appraisals of outgroup members. *Journal of Personality and Social Psychology, 38,* 689–703.

25. Devine, P. G., & Malpass, R. S. (1985). Orienting strategies in differential face recognition. *Personality and Social Psychology Bulletin, 11*(1), 33–40.

26. Meissner, C. A., & Brigham, J. C. (2001). Thirty years of investigating the own-race bias in memory for faces: A meta-analytic review. *Psychology, Public Policy, and Law, 7,* 3–35.

27. Ackerman, J. M., Shapiro, J. R., Neuberg, S. L., Kenrick, D. T., Schaller, M., Becker, D. V., et al. (2006). They all look the same to me (unless they're angry): From out-group homogeneity to out-group heterogeneity. *Psychological Science, 17*(10), 836–840.

28. Levitt, S. D., & Dubner, S. J. (2005). *Freakonomics.* New York: Morrow HarperCollins.

29. DeSilver, D. (2013, June 7). World's Muslim population more widespread than you might think. Pew Research Center. Retrieved from http://www.pewresearch.org/fact-tank/2013/06/07/worlds-muslim-population-more-widespread-than-you-might-think/

30. Hendricks, N. J., Ortiz, C. W., Sugie, N., & Miller, J. (2007). Beyond the numbers: Hate crimes and cultural trauma within Arab American immigrant communities. *International Review of Victimology, 14*(1), 95–113.

31. Equal Opportunity Employment Commission. (2001). Muslim/Arab employment discrimination charges since 9/11. Retrieved from http://www.eeoc.gov/origin/z-stats.html

32. Malos, S. (2010). Post-9/11 backlash in the workplace: Employer liability for discrimination against Arab- and Muslim-Americans based on religion or national origin. *Employee Responsibilities and Rights Journal, 22*(4), 297–310.

33. Bushman, B. J., & Bonacci, A. M. (2004). You've got mail: Using e-mail to examine the effect of prejudiced attitudes on discrimination against Arabs. *Journal of Experimental Social Psychology, 40,* 753–759.

34. Milgram, S. (1977). *The individual in a social world.* New York: McGraw-Hill.

35. Stern, S. E., & Faber, J. E. (1997). The lost e-mail method: Milgram's lost-letter technique in the age of the Internet. *Behavior Research Methods, Instruments, and Computers, 29,* 260–263.

36. Ahmed, A. M. (2010). Muslim discrimination: Evidence from two lost-letter experiments. *Journal of Applied Social Psychology, 40*(4), 888–898.

37. Das, E., Bushman, B. J., Bezemer, M. D., Kerkhof, P., & Vermeulen, I. E. (2009). How terrorism news reports increase prejudice against outgroups: A terror management account. *Journal of Experimental Social Psychology, 45*, 453–459.

38. Sehgal, I. (2011, June 23). Media reacts to news that Norwegian terror suspect isn't Muslim. *Atlantic Wire*. Retrieved from http://www.theatlanticwire. com/global/2011/07/media-reacts-news-norwegian-terror-suspect-isnt-muslim/40322/

39. Gervais, W. M. & Norenzayan, A. (2013). Religion and the origins of anti-atheist prejudice. Chapter to appear in S. Clarke, R. Powell, & J. Savulescu (Eds.), *Intolerance and conflict: A scientific and conceptual investigation*. Oxford: Oxford University Press.

40. Winston, K. (2014, February 28). Student reverses course on secular club, citing threats. *Washington Post*. Retrieved from http://www.washingtonpost. com/national/religion/student-reverses-course-on-secular-club-citing-threats/2014/02/28/2555d50e-a0c1-11e3-878c-65222df220eb_story.html

41. Atheist must swear to God—or leave US Air Force (2014, September 10). Retrieved from http://news. yahoo.com/atheist-must-swear-god-leave-us-air-force-232153866.html

42. Gervais, W. M., Shariff, A. F., & Norenzayan, A. (2011). Do you believe in atheists? Distrust is central to anti-atheist prejudice. *Journal of Personality and Social Psychology, 101*, 1189–1206. doi: 10.1037/ a0025882

43. Psalms 14: 1 (Bible; King James version).

44. Pew Research Global Attitudes Project. (2014, March 13). Worldwide, many see belief in God as essential to morality. Retrieved from http://www.pewglobal. org/2014/03/13/worldwide-many-see-belief-in-god-as-essential-to-morality/

45. Lutz, A. (2013, May 3). Abercrombie & Fitch refuses to make clothes for large women *Business Insider*. Retrieved from http://www.businessinsider.com/ abercrombie-wants-thin-customers-2013-5

46. Cramer, P., & Steinwert, T. (1998). Thin is good, fat is bad: How early does it begin? *Journal of Applied Developmental Psychology, 19*, 429–451.

47. Kolata, G. (1992, November 22). The burdens of being overweight: Mistreatment and misconceptions. *New York Times*, A1.

48. Klaczynski, P., Daniel, D. B., & Keller, P. S. (2009). Appearance idealization, body esteem, causal attributions, and ethnic variations in the development of obesity stereotypes. *Journal of Applied Developmental Psychology, 30*(4), 537–551.

49. Centers for Disease Control. (2012). Overweight and obesity. Retrieved from http://www.cdc.gov/obesity/ data/trends.HTML

50. Harris, M. B., Harris, R. J., & Bochner, S. (1982). Fat, four-eyed and female: Stereotypes of obesity glasses and gender. *Journal of Applied Social Psychology, 12*, 503–516.

51. Hebl, M. R., & Heatherton, T. F. (1997). The stigma of obesity: The differences are black and white. *Personality and Social Psychology Bulletin, 24*, 417–426.

52. Larwood, L., & Gattiker, U. E. (1995). Rational bias and interorganizational power in the employment of management consultants. *Group and Organization Studies, 10*, 3–17.

53. Lerner, R. (1969). Some female stereotypes of male body build–behavior relations. *Perceptual and Motor Skills, 28*, 363–366.

54. Staffieri, J. (1967). A study of social stereotype of body image in children. *Journal of Personality and Social Psychology, 7*, 101–104.

55. Roehling, M. V., Roehling, P. V., & Odland, L. M. (2008). Investigating the validity of stereotypes about overweight employees: The relationship between body weight and normal personality traits. *Group and Organization Management, 33*(4), 392–424.

56. Tiggemann, M., & Rothblum, E. D. (1988). Gender differences in social consequences of perceived overweight in the United States and Australia. *Sex Roles, 18*, 75–86.

57. Hebl, M. R., & Mannix, L. M. (2003). The weight of obesity in evaluating others: A mere proximity effect. *Personality and Social Psychology Bulletin, 29*, 28–38.

58. Jones, D. (2004, April 9). Obesity can mean less pay. *USA Today*.

59. Hansson, L. M., Náslund, E., & Rasmussen, F. (2010). Perceived discrimination among men and women with normal weight and obesity. A population-based study from Sweden. *Scandinavian Journal of Public Health, 38*(6), 587–596.

60. Bejciy-Spring, S. M. (2008). R-E-S-P-E-C-T: A model for the sensitive treatment of the bariatric patient. *Bariatric Nursing and Surgical Patient Care, 3*(1), 47–56.

61. Miller, D. P., Spangler, J. G., Vitolins, M. Z., Davis, S. W., Ip, E. H., Marion, G. S., & Crandall, S. J. (2013). Are medical students aware of their anti-obesity bias? *Academic Medicine, 88*(7), 978–982. doi: 10.1097/ACM.0b013e318294f817

62. Palca, J. (2013, May 23). The weight of a med student's subconscious bias. *NPR*. Retrieved from http://www.npr.org/blogs/health/2013/05/23/ 186294402/the-weight-of-a-med-students-subconscious-bias

63. Clayson, D. E., & Klassen, M. L. (1989). Perception of attractiveness by obesity and hair color. *Perceptual and Motor Skills, 68*, 199–202.

64. DeJong, W. (1980). The stigma of obesity: The consequences of naive assumptions concerning the causes of physical deviance. *Journal of Health and Social Behavior, 21*(1), 75–87.

65. DeJong, W. (1993). Obesity as a characterological stigma: The issue of responsibility and judgments of task performance. *Psychological Reports, 73*, 963–970.

66. Crandall, C. S. (1994). Prejudice against fat people: Ideology and self-interest. *Journal of Personality and Social Psychology, 66*, 882–894.

67. King, B. J. (2013, June 6). The fat-shaming professor: A Twitter-fueled firestorm. *NPR*. Retrieved from http://www.npr.org/ blogs/13.7/2013/06/06/188891906/the-fat-shaming-professor-a-twitter-fueled-firestorm

68. Anderson, D. (2013, June 3). UNM Response to Tweet by Professor Geoffrey Miller. *UNM Newsroom*. Retrieved from http://news.unm.edu/news/unm-response-to-tweet-by-professor-geoffrey-miller

69. Burmeister, J. M., Kiefner, A. E., Carels, R. A., & Musher-Eizenman, D. R. (2013). Weight bias in graduate school admissions. *Obesity, 21*(5), 918–920. doi: 10.1002/oby.20171

70. Swami, V., & Monk, R. (2013). Weight bias against women in a university acceptance scenario. *Journal of General Psychology, 140*(1), 45–56. doi: 10.1080/00221309.2012.726288

71. Story Corps (2012, January 13). Threats and lies, and "Who I'm supposed to be." *NPR*. Retrieved from http://www.npr.org/2012/01/13/145099739/threats-and-lies-and-who-im-supposed-to-be

72. Wood, P. B., & Bartkowski, J. P. (2004). Attribution style and public policy attitudes toward gay rights. *Social Science Quarterly, 85*(1), 58–74.

73. American Psychological Association. (2008). Answers to your questions: For a better understanding of sexual orientation and homosexuality. Washington, DC: Author. Retrieved from http://www.apa.org/topics/sorientation.pdf

74. Payne, S. (2013, May 11). When did you choose to be straight? *Daily Kos*. Retrieved from http://www .dailykos.com/story/2013/05/11/1208457/-When-did-you-choose-to-be-straight

75. Tilcsik, A. (2011). Pride and prejudice: Employment discrimination against openly gay men in the United States. *American Journal of Sociology, 117*(2), 586–626.

76. Bahns, A. J., & Branscombe, N. R. (2011). Effects of legitimizing discrimination against homosexuals on gay bashing. *European Journal of Social Psychology, 41*(3), 388–396.

77. Schwartz, D. (2014, February 20). Arizona lawmakers pass bill to allow faith-based refusal of services. *Reuters*. Retrieved from http://www .reuters.com/article/2014/02/21/us-usa-gays-arizona-idUSBREA1K06M20140221

78. Santos, F. (2014, February 26). Arizona governor vetoes bill on refusal of service to gays. *New York Times*. Retrieved from http://www.nytimes. com/2014/02/27/us/Brewer-arizona-gay-service-bill. html?_r=0

79. Kerrigan, M. F. (2012). Transgender discrimination in the military: The new don't ask, don't tell. *Psychology, Public Policy, and Law, 18*(3), 500–518. doi: 10.1037/a0025771

80. Hendren, A., & Blank, H. (2009). Prejudiced behavior toward lesbians and gay men: A field experiment on everyday helping. *Social Psychology, 40*(4), 234–238.

81. Herek, G. M. (2000). The psychology of sexual prejudice. *Current Directions in Psychological Science, 9*, 19–22.

82. Bernat, J. A., Calhoun, K. S., Adams, H. E., & Zeichner, A. (2001). Homophobia and physical aggression toward homosexual and heterosexual individuals. *Journal of Abnormal Psychology, 110*, 179–187.

83. Parrott, D. J. (2009). Aggression toward gay men as gender role enforcement: Effects of male role norms, sexual prejudice, and masculine gender role stress. *Journal of Personality, 77*(4), 1137–1166.

84. Brown, M. J., & Groscup, J. L. (2009). Homophobia and acceptance of stereotypes about gays and lesbians. *Individual Differences Research, 7*(3), 159–167.

85. Owen, J. (2004, July 23). Homosexual activity among animals stirs debate. *National Geographic*. Retrieved from http://news.nationalgeographic.com/ news/2004/07/0722_040722_gayanimal.html

86. Herek, G. M., & Capitanio, J. P. (1996). "Some of my best friends": Intergroup contact, concealable stigma, and heterosexuals' attitudes toward gay men and lesbians. *Personality and Social Psychology Bulletin, 22*(4), 412–424.

87. Laumann, E. O., Gagnon, J. H., Michael, R. T., & Michaels, S. (1994). *The social organization of sexuality: Sexual practices in the United States*. Chicago: University of Chicago Press.

88. Whitley, B. E. (1988). Sex differences in heterosexuals' attitudes toward homosexuals: It depends upon what you ask. *Journal of Sex Research, 24*, 287–291.

89. Herek, G. M., & Capitanio, J. P. (1999). AIDS stigma and sexual prejudice. *American Behavioral Scientist, 42*, 1126–1143.

90. Whitley, B. E. (1988). Sex differences in heterosexuals' attitudes toward homosexuals: It depends upon what you ask. *Journal of Sex Research, 24*, 287–291.

91. Adams, H. E., Wright, L. W., Jr., & Lohr, B. A. (1996). Is homophobia associated with homosexual arousal? *Journal of Abnormal Psychology, 105*, 440–446.

92. Falomir-Pichastor, J. M., & Mugny, G. (2009). "I'm not gay ... I'm a real man!": Heterosexual men's gender self-esteem and sexual prejudice. *Personality and Social Psychology Bulletin, 35*(9), 1233–1243.

93. Buck, D. M., Plant, E. A., Ratcliff, J., Zielaskowski, K., & Boerner, P. (2013). Concern over the misidentification of sexual orientation: Social contagion and the avoidance of sexual minorities. *Journal of Personality and Social Psychology, 105*, 941–960.

94. Wood, P. B., & Bartkowski, J. P. (2004). Attribution style and public policy attitudes toward gay rights. *Social Science Quarterly, 85*(1), 58–74.

95. Olatunji, B. O. (2008). Disgust, scrupulosity and conservative attitudes about sex: Evidence for a mediational model of homophobia. *Journal of Research in Personality, 42*(5), 1364–1369.

96. Terrizzi, J. A., Jr., Shook, N. J., & Ventis, W. L. (2010). Disgust: A predictor of social conservatism and prejudicial attitudes toward homosexuals. *Personality and Individual Differences, 49*(6), 587–592.

97. Bos, H. M. W., Gartrell, N. K., Van Balen, F., Peyser, H., & Sandfort, T. G. M. (2008). Children in planned lesbian families: A cross-cultural comparison between the United States and the Netherlands. *American Journal of Orthopsychiatry, 78*(2), 211–219.

98. Pew Research Center (2014, February 23). *Gay marriage*. Retrieved from http://www.pewresearch.org/data-trend/domestic-issues/attitudes-on-gay-marriage/

99. Bronson, P., & Merryman, A. (2009, September 4). Even babies discriminate: A nurtureshock excerpt. *Newsweek*. Retrieved from http://www.newsweek.com/even-babies-discriminate-nurtureshock-excerpt-79233

100. Pinker, S. (2011). *The better angels of our nature: Why violence has declined*. New York: Viking Adult.

101. Billig, M., & Tajfel, H. (1973). Social categorization and similarity in intergroup behaviour. *European Journal of Social Psychology, 3*(1), 27–52.

102. Brewer, M. B. (1979). In-group bias in the minimal intergroup situation: A cognitive-motivational analysis. *Psychological Bulletin, 86*(2), 307–324.

103. Brewer, M. B., & Silver, M. (1978). Ingroup bias as a function of task characteristics. *European Journal of Social Psychology, 8*(3), 393–400.

104. Tajfel, H., & Billig, M. (1974). Familiarity and categorization in intergroup behavior. *Journal of Experimental Social Psychology, 10*(2), 159–170.

105. Tajfel, H., Billig, M. G., Bundy, R. P., & Flament, C. (1971). Social categorization and intergroup behaviour. *European Journal of Social Psychology, 1*(2), 149–178.

106. Locksley, A., Ortiz, V., & Hepburn, C. (1980). Social categorization and discriminatory behavior: Extinguishing the minimal intergroup discrimination effect. *Journal of Personality and Social Psychology, 39*(5), 773–783.

107. Pew Research Center (2014, February 23). *Gay marriage*. Retrieved from http://www.pewresearch.org/data-trend/domestic-issues/attitudes-on-gay-marriage/

108. Pew Research. (2014, June 19). Gay marriage around the world. Retrieved from http://www.pewforum.org/2013/12/19/gay-marriage-around-the-world-2013/

109. Sherif, M., & Sherif, C. W. (1953). *Groups in harmony and tension: An integration of studies of intergroup relations*. New York: Harper & Brothers.

110. Sherif, M. (1966) *In common predicament: Social psychology of intergroup conflict and cooperation*. Boston: Houghton-Mifflin.

111. Johnson, D. W., & Johnson, R. T. (1983). The socialization and achievement crises: Are cooperative learning experiences the solution? *Applied Social Psychology Annual, 4*, 119–164.

112. Johnson, D. W., & Johnson, R. T. (1983). The socialization and achievement crises: Are cooperative learning experiences the solution? *Applied Social Psychology Annual, 4*, 119–164.

113. Bonta, B. D. (1997). Cooperation and competition in peaceful societies. *Psychological Bulletin, 121*, 299–320.

114. Draper, P. (1976). Social and economic constraints on child life among the !Kung. In R. B. Lee & I. DeVore (Eds.), *Kalahari hunter-gatherers: Studies of the !Kung San and their neighbors* (pp. 199–217). Cambridge, MA: Harvard University Press.

115. Overing, J. (1986). Images of cannibalism, death and domination in a "non-violent" society. In D. Riches (Ed.), *The anthropology of violence* (pp. 86–101). Oxford: Blackwell.

116. Howell, S. (1989). "To be angry is not to be human, but to be fearful is": Chewong concepts of human nature. In S. Howell & R. Willis (Eds.), *Societies at peace: Anthropological perspectives* (pp. 45–59). London: Routledge.

117. Keir, G. (1966). The psychological assessment of the children from the island of Tristan da Cunha. In C. Banks & P. L. Broadhurst (Eds.), *Stephanos: Studies in psychology presented to Cyril Burt* (pp. 129–172). New York: Barnes & Noble.

118. Bonta, B. D. (1997). Cooperation and competition in peaceful societies. *Psychological Bulletin, 121*, 299–320.

119. Adhikary, A. K. (1984). *Society and world view of the Birhor: A nomadic hunting and gathering community of Orissa*. Calcutta: Anthropological Survey of India.

120. Willis, R. (1989). The "peace puzzle" in Ufipa. In S. Howell & R. Willis (Eds.), *Societies at peace: Anthropological perspectives* (pp. 133–145). London: Routledge.

121. McNeill, W. H. (1982). *The pursuit of power: Technology, armed force, and society since A.D. 1000*. Chicago: University of Chicago Press.

122. Waytz, A., Young, L.L., & Ginges, J. (2014). Motive attribution asymmetry for love vs. hate drives intractable conflict. *PNAS*, early edition.

123. Schopler, J., & Insko, C. A. (1992). The discontinuity effect in interpersonal and intergroup relations: Generality and mediation. *European Review of Social Psychology, 3*, 121–151.

124. Insko, C. A., Schopler, J., Hoyle, R. H., & Dardis, G. J. (1990). Individual-group discontinuity as a function of fear and greed. *Journal of Personality and Social Psychology, 58*, 68–79.

125. Schopler, J., Insko, C. A., Drigotas, S., & Graetz, K. A. (1993). Individual-group discontinuity: Further evidence for mediation by fear and greed. *Personality and Social Psychology Bulletin, 19*, 419–431.

126. Insko, C. A., Schopler, J., Pemberton, M. B., Wieselquist, J., McIlraith, S. A., Currey, D. P., et al. (1998). Long-term outcome maximization and the reduction of interindividual-intergroup discontinuity. *Journal of Personality and Social Psychology, 75*, 695–711.

127. Schopler, J., Insko, C. A., Drigotas, S. M., & Wieselquist, J. (1995). The role of identifiability in the reduction of interindividual-intergroup discontinuity. *Journal of Experimental Social Psychology, 31*, 553–574.

128. Allport, G. W. (1954) *The nature of prejudice*. Reading, MA: Addison-Wesley.

129. Pettigrew, T. F., & Tropp, L. R. (2005). Allport's intergroup contact hypothesis: Its history and influence. In J. F. Dovidio, P. Glick, & L. A. Rudman (Eds.), *On the nature of prejudice: Fifty years after Allport* (pp. 262–277). Malden, MA: Blackwell.

130. Pettigrew, T. F., & Tropp, L. R. (2006). A meta-analytic test of intergroup contact theory. *Journal of Personality and Social Psychology, 90*, 751–783.

131. Paolini, S., Harwood, J., & Rubin, M. (2010). Negative intergroup contact makes group memberships salient: Explaining why intergroup conflict endures. Personality and Social Psychology Bulletin 36(12) 1723–1738. doi: 10.1177/0146167210388667

132. Baumeister, R. F., Bratslavsky, E., Finkenauer, C., & Vohs, K. D. (2001). Bad is stronger than good. *Review of General Psychology, 5*(4), 323–370. doi: 10.1037//1089-2680.5.4.323

133. Barlow, F. K., Paolini, S., Pedersen, A., Hornsey, M. J., Radke, H. R. M., Harwood, J., Rubin, M., & Sibley, C. G. (2012). The contact caveat: Negative contact predicts increased prejudice more than positive contact predicts reduced prejudice. *Personality and Social Psychology Bulletin, 38*(12), 1629–1643. doi: 10.1177/0146167212457953

134. Pettigrew, T. F., & Tropp, L. R. (2008). How does intergroup contact reduce prejudice? Meta-analytic tests of three mediators. *European Journal of Social Psychology, 38*, 922–934.

135. Swart, H., Hewstone, M., Christ, O., & Voci, A. (2011). Affective mediators of intergroup contact: A three-wave longitudinal study in South Africa. *Journal of Personality and Social Psychology, 101*(6), 1221–1238.

136. Binder, J., Zagefka, H., Brown, R., Funke, F., Kessler, T., Mummendey, A., et al. (2009). Does contact reduce prejudice or does prejudice reduce contact? A longitudinal test of the contact hypothesis among majority and minority groups in three European countries. *Journal of Personality and Social Psychology, 96*(4), 843–856.

137. Hutchison, P., & Rosenthal, H. E. S. (2011). Prejudice against Muslims: Anxiety as a mediator between intergroup contact and attitudes, perceived group variability and behavioural intentions. *Ethnic and Racial Studies, 34*(1), 40–61.

138. Baunach, D. M., Burgess, E. O., & Muse, C. S. (2010). Southern (dis)comfort: Sexual prejudice and contact with gay men and lesbians in the south. *Sociological Spectrum, 30*(1), 30–64.

139. Mazziotta, A., Mummendey, A., & Wright, S. C. (2011). Vicarious intergroup contact effects: Applying social-cognitive theory to intergroup contact research. *Group Processes & Intergroup Relations, 14*(2), 255–274.

140. Crisp, R. J., Birtel, M. D., & Meleady, R. (2011). Mental simulations of social thought and action: Trivial tasks or tools for transforming social policy? *Current Directions in Psychological Science, 20*(4), 261–264.

141. Hewstone, M., & Swart, H. (2011). Fifty-odd years of inter-group contact: From hypothesis to integrated theory. *British Journal of Social Psychology, 50*(3), 374–386.

142. Sidanius, J., & Pratto, F. (1999). *Social dominance: An intergroup theory of social hierarchy and oppression*. New York: Cambridge University Press.

143. Jost, J. T., & Kay, A. C. (2005). Exposure to benevolent sexism and complementary gender stereotypes: Consequences for specific and diffuse forms of system justification. *Journal of Personality and Social Psychology, 88*, 498–509.

144. Allport, G. W. (1954) *The nature of prejudice*. Reading, MA: Addison-Wesley.

145. Macrae, C. N., Milne, A. B., & Bodenhausen, G. V. (1994). Stereotypes as energy-saving devices: A peek inside the cognitive toolbox. *Journal of Personality and Social Psychology, 66*, 37–47.

146. Bodenhausen, G. V. (1990). Stereotypes as judgmental heuristics: Evidence of circadian variations in discrimination. *Psychological Science, 1*, 319–322.

147. Fein, S., & Spencer, S. J. (1997). Prejudice as self-image maintenance: Affirming the self through derogating others. *Journal of Personality and Social Psychology, 73*, 31–44.

148. Swim, J. K. (1994). Perceived versus meta-analytic effect sizes: An assessment of the accuracy of gender stereotypes. *Journal of Personality and Social Psychology, 66*, 21–36.

149. Jussim, L., Cain, T. R., Crawford, J. T., Harber, K., & Cohen, F. (2009). The unbearable accuracy of stereotypes. In T. Nelson (Ed.), *Handbook of prejudice, stereotyping, and discrimination* (pp. 199–228). Mahwah, NJ: Erlbaum.

150. Judd, C., & Park, B. (1993). The assessment of accuracy of social stereotypes. *Psychological Review, 100*, 109–128.

151. Terracianno, A., et al. (2005). National character does not reflect mean personality trait levels in 49 cultures. *Science, 310*, 96–100.

152. Chan, W., McCrae, R. R., De Fruyt, F., Jussim, L., Löckenhoff, C. E., De Bolle, M., Costa, P. T., Jr., Sutin, A. R., Realo, A., Allik, J., Nakazato, K., Shimonaka, Y., Hřebíčková, M., Graf, S., Yik, M., Brunner-Sciarra, M., de Figueora, N. L., Schmidt, V., Ahn, C.-k., Ahn, H.-n., Aguilar-Vafaie, M. E., Siuta, J., Szmigielska, B., Cain, T. R., Crawford, J. T., Mastor, K. A., Rolland, J.-P., Nansubuga, F., Miramontez, D. R., Benet-Martínez, V., Rossier, J., Bratko, D., Marušić, I., Halberstadt, J., Yamaguchi, M., Knežević, G., Martin, T. A., Gheorghiu, M., Smith, P. B., Barbaranelli, C., Wang, L., Shakespeare-Finch, J., Lima, M. P., Klinkosz, W., Sekowski, A., Alcalay, L., Simonetti, F., Avdeyeva, T. V., Pramila, V. S., & Terracciano, A. (2012). Stereotypes of age differences in personality traits: Universal and accurate? *Journal of Personality and Social Psychology. 103*, 1050–1066. doi: 10.1037/a0029712

153. Jung, K., Shavitt, S., Viswanathan, M., & Hilbe, J. M. (2014). Female hurricanes are deadlier than male hurricanes. *PNAS, 111*, 8782–8787.

154. Jussim, L., Cain, T. R., Crawford, J. T., Harber, K., & Cohen, F. (2009). The unbearable accuracy of stereotypes. In T. Nelson (Ed.), *Handbook of prejudice, stereotyping, and discrimination* (pp. 199–228). Mahwah, NJ: Erlbaum.

155. Kunda, Z., & Thagard. P. (1996). Forming impressions from stereotypes, traits, and behaviors: A parallel-constraint-satisfaction theory. *Psychological Review, 103*, 284–308.

156. Glick, P., & Fiske, S. T. (1996). The Ambivalent Sexism Inventory: Differentiating hostile and benevolent sexism. *Journal of Personality and Social Psychology, 70*, 491–512.

157. Dardenne, B., Dumont, M., & Bollier, T. (2007). Insidious dangers of benevolent sexism: Consequences for women's performance. *Journal of Personality and Social Psychology, 93*, 764–779.

158. Moya, M., Glick, P., Expósito, F., de Lemus, S., & Hart, J. (2007). It's for your own good: Benevolent sexism and women's reactions to protectively justified restrictions. *Personality and Social Psychology Bulletin, 33*, 1421–1434.

159. Becker, J. C., & Wright, S. C. (2011). Yet another dark side of chivalry: Benevolent sexism undermines and hostile sexism motivates collective action for social change. *Journal of Personality and Social Psychology, 101*, 62–77.

160. Hamilton, D. L., Dugan, P. M., & Trolier, T. K. (1985). The formation of stereotypic beliefs: Further evidence for distinctiveness-based illusory correlations. *Journal of Personality and Social Psychology, 48*, 5–17.

161. Hamilton, D. L., & Gifford, R. K. (1976). Illusory correlation in interpersonal perception: A cognitive basis of stereotypic judgments. *Journal of Experimental Social Psychology, 12*, 392–407.

162. Hamilton, D. L., & Gifford, R. K. (1976). Illusory correlation in interpersonal perception: A cognitive basis of stereotypic judgments. *Journal of Experimental Social Psychology, 12*, 392–407.

163. Leviticus 16: 7–10 (Bible).

164. Rothschild, Z. K., Landau, M. J., Sullivan, D., & Keefer, L. A. (2012). A dual-motive model of scapegoating: Displacing blame to reduce guilt or increase control. *Journal of Personality and Social Psychology, 102*, 1148–1163.

165. Hovland, C. I., & Sears, R. (1940). Minor studies of aggression: Correlation of lynchings with economic conditions. *Journal of Psychology, 9*, 301–310.

166. Hepworth, J. T., & West, S. G. (1988). Lynchings and the economy: A time-series reanalysis of Hovland and Sears (1940). *Journal of Personality and Social Psychology, 55*, 239–247.

167. Sinclair, L., & Kunda, Z. (2000). Motivated stereotyping of women: She's fine if she praised me but incompetent if she criticized me. *Personality and Social Psychology Bulletin, 26*, 1329–1342.

168. Sinclair, L., & Kunda, Z. (1999). Reactions to a black professional: Motivated inhibition and activation of conflicting stereotypes. *Journal of Personality and Social Psychology, 77*, 885–904.

169. Kunda, Z., Davies, P. G., Adams, B. D., & Spencer, S. J. (2002). The dynamic time course of stereotype activation: Activation, dissipation, and resurrection. *Journal of Personality and Social Psychology, 82*, 283–299.

170. Maner, J. K., Kenrick, D. T., Neuberg, S. L., Becker, D. V., Robertson, T., Hofer, B., et al. (2005). Functional projection: How fundamental social motives can bias interpersonal perception. *Journal of Personality and Social Psychology, 88*, 63–78.

171. Darley, J. M., & Gross, P. H. (1983). A hypothesis-confirming bias in labeling effects. *Journal of Personality and Social Psychology, 44*(1), 20–33.

172. http://thinkexist.com/quotes/frederick_the_great/

173. Quoted by Krauthammer, C. (1997, June 29). Apology is not ours to give. *Cleveland Plain Dealer*, p. 2–E.

174. Fazio, R. H., Jackson, J. R., Dunton, B. C., & Williams, C. J. (1995). Variability in automatic activation as an unobtrusive measure of racial attitudes: A bona fide pipeline? *Journal of Personality and Social Psychology, 69*, 1013–1027.

175. Fazio, R. H., & Olson, M. A. (2003). Implicit measures in social cognition research: Their meaning and uses. *Annual Review of Psychology, 54*, 297–327.

176. Greenwald, A. G., McGhee, D. E., & Schwartz, J. K. L. (1998). Measuring individual differences in implicit cognition: The implicit association test. *Journal of Personality and Social Psychology, 74*, 1464–1480.

177. Payne, B. K. (2001). Prejudice and perception: The role of automatic and controlled processes in misperceiving a weapon. *Journal of Personality and Social Psychology, 81*, 181–192.

178. Rydell, R. J., & McConnell, A. R. (2006). Understanding implicit and explicit attitude change: A systems of reasoning analysis. *Journal of Personality and Social Psychology, 91*, 995–1008.

179. Ziegert, J. C., & Hanges, P. J. (2005). Employment discrimination: The role of implicit attitudes, motivation, and a climate for racial bias. *Journal of Applied Psychology, 90*, 553–562.

180. Payne, B. K., Govorun, O., & Arbuckle, N. L. (2008). Automatic attitudes and alcohol: Does implicit liking predict drinking? *Cognition and Emotion, 22*, 238–271.

181. Scherer, L. D., & Lambert, A. J. (2012). Implicit race bias revisited: On the utility of task context in assessing implicit attitude strength. *Journal of Experimental Social Psychology, 48*, 366–370.

182. Richeson, J. A., & Shelton, J. N. (2003). When prejudice doesn't pay: Effects of interracial contact on executive function. *Psychological Science, 14*, 287–290.

183. Richeson, J. A., Trawalter, S., & Shelton, J. N. (2005). African Americans' implicit racial attitudes and the depletion of executive function after interracial interactions. *Social Cognition, 23*, 336–352.

184. Devine, P. G. (1989). Stereotypes and prejudice: Their automatic and controlled components. *Journal of Personality and Social Psychology, 56*, 5–18.

185. Dutton, D. G., & Lake, R. A. (1973). Threat of own prejudice and reverse discrimination in interracial situations. *Journal of Personality and Social Psychology, 28*, 94–100.

186. Dutton, D. G. (1971). Reactions of restaurateurs to blacks and whites violating restaurant dress requirements. *Canadian Journal of Behavioural Science, 3*, 298–302.

187. Plant, E. A., & Devine, P. G. (1998). Internal and external motivation to respond without prejudice. *Journal of Personality and Social Psychology, 75*, 811–832.

188. Plant, E. A., & Devine, P. G. (2001). Responses to other-imposed pro-black pressure: Acceptance or backlash? *Journal of Experimental Social Psychology, 37*, 486–501.

189. Amodio, D. M., Harmon-Jones, E., & Devine, P. G. (2003). Individual differences in the activation and control of affective race bias as assessed by startle eyeblink response and self-report. *Journal of Personality and Social Psychology, 84*, 738–753.

190. Devine, P. G., Plant, E. A., Amodio, A. M., Harmon-Jones, E., & Vance, S. L. (2002). Exploring the relationship between implicit and explicit prejudice: The role of motivations to respond without prejudice. *Journal of Personality and Social Psychology, 82*, 835–848.

191. Binder, J., Zagefka, H., Brown, R., Funke, F., Kessler, T., Mummendey, A., et al. (2009). Does contact reduce prejudice or does prejudice reduce contact? A longitudinal test of the contact hypothesis among majority and minority groups in three European countries. *Journal of Personality and Social Psychology, 96*, 843–856.

192. Pettigrew, T. F., & Tropp, L. R. (2006). A meta-analytic test of intergroup contact theory. *Journal of Personality and Social Psychology, 90*, 751–783.

193. Shook, N. J., & Fazio, R. H. (2008). Interracial roommate relationships: An experimental field test of the contact hypothesis. *Psychological Science, 19*, 717–723.

194. Wright, S. C., Aron, A., McLaughlin-Volpe, T., & Ropp, S. A. (1997). The extended contact effect: Knowledge of cross-group friendships and prejudice. *Journal of Personality and Social Psychology, 73*, 73–90.

195. Dovidio, J. F., & Gaertner, S. L. (1999). Reducing prejudice: Combating intergroup biases. *Current Directions in Psychological Science, 8*, 101–105.

196. Bay-Hinitz, A. K., Peterson, R. F., & Quilitch, H. R. (1994). Cooperative games: A way to modify aggressive and cooperative behaviors in young children. *Journal of Applied Behavior Analysis, 27*, 435–446.

197. Aronson, E. (2000). *Nobody left to hate: Teaching compassion after Columbine.* New York: W. H. Freeman.

198. Aronson, E., Blaney, N., Stephin, C., Sikes, J., & Snapp, M. (1978). *The jigsaw classroom.* Beverly Hills, CA: Sage.

199. Aronson, E., & Patnoe, S. (1997). *The jigsaw classroom: Building cooperation in the classroom* (2nd ed.). New York: Addison Wesley Longman.

200. Aronson, E., & Osherow, N. (1980). Cooperation, prosocial behavior, and academic performance: Experiments in the desegregated classroom. *Applied Social Psychology Annual, 1*, 163–196.

201. Walker, I., & Crogan, M. (1998). Academic performance, prejudice, and the jigsaw classroom: New pieces to the puzzle. *Journal of Community and Applied Social Psychology, 8*, 381–393.

202. Walker, I., & Crogan, M. (1998). Academic performance, prejudice, and the jigsaw classroom: New pieces to the puzzle. *Journal of Community and Applied Social Psychology, 8*, 381–393.

203. Alebiosu, K. A. (2001). Cooperative learning and students' affective learning outcome in Nigerian chemistry classrooms. *IFE Psychologia, 9*, 135–142.

204. Maass, A., Cadinu, M., Guarnieri, G., & Grasselli, A. (2003). Sexual harassment under social identity threat: The computer harassment paradigm. *Journal of Personality and Social Psychology, 85*, 853–870.

205. Merton, R. K. (1948). The self-fulfilling prophecy. *Antioch Review*, pp. 193–210.

206. Merton, R. K. (1948). The self-fulfilling prophecy. *Antioch Review*, pp. 193–210.

207. Rosenthal, R., & Jacobson, L. (1968). *Pygmalion in the classroom: Teacher expectation and pupils' intellectual development.* New York: Rinehart and Winston.

208. Jussim, L., & Harber, K. D. (2005). Teacher expectations and self-fulfilling prophecies: Knowns and unknowns, resolved and unresolved controversies. *Personality and Social Psychology Review, 9*(2), 131–155.

209. Jussim, L., & Harber, K. D. (2005). Teacher expectations and self-fulfilling prophecies: Knowns and unknowns, resolved and unresolved controversies. *Personality and Social Psychology Review, 9*(2), 131–155.

210. Patterson, O. (1982). *Slavery and social death.* Cambridge, MA: Harvard University Press.

211. Crocker, J., & Major, B. (1989). Social stigma and self-esteem: The self-protective properties of stigma. *Psychological Review, 96*, 608–630.

212. Judd, C., & Park, B. (1993). The assessment of accuracy of social stereotypes. *Psychological Review, 100*, 109–128.

213. Twenge, J. M., & Crocker, J. (2002). Race and self-esteem: Meta-analyses comparing Whites, Blacks, Hispanics, Asians, and American Indians. *Psychological Bulletin, 128*, 371–408.

214. Crocker, J., & Major, B. (1989). Social stigma and self-esteem: The self-protective properties of stigma. *Psychological Review, 96*, 608–630.

215. Crocker, J., Voelkl, K., Testa, M., & Major, B. (1991). Social stigma: The affective consequences of attributional ambiguity. *Journal of Personality and Social Psychology, 60*, 218–228.

216. Sedlovskaya, A., Purdie-Vaughn, V., Eibach, R.P., LaFrance, M., Romero-Canyas, R., & Camp, N.P. (2013). Internalizing the closet: Concealment heightens the cognitive distinction between public and private selves. *Journal of Personality and Social Psychology, 104*, 695–715.

217. Bawer, B. (2012). *The victims' revolution: The rise of identity studies and the closing of the liberal mind.* New York: Broadside Books.

218. Cole, A.M. (2007). *The cult of true victimhood.* Palo Alto, CA: Stanford University Press.

219. Sommers, C. H. (2015). The media is making college rape culture worse. *The Daily Beast.* http://www.thedailybeast.com/articles/2015/01/23/the-media-is-making-college-rape-culture-worse.html

220. Wohl, M. J. A., & Branscombe, N. R. (2008). Remembering historical victimization: Collective guilt for current ingroup transgressions. *Journal of Personality and Social Psychology, 94,* 988–1006.

221. Steele, C. M., & Aronson, J. A. (1995). Stereotype threat and the intellectual test performance of African Americans. *Journal of Personality and Social Psychology, 69,* 797–811.

222. Benbow, C. P., Lubinski, D., Shea, D. L., & Eftekhari-Sanjani, H. (2000). Sex differences in mathematical reasoning ability: Their status 20 years later. *Psychological Science, 11,* 474–480.

223. Gottfredson, L. (Ed.). (1997). Intelligence and social policy, *Intelligence, 24,* 1–320.

224. Jencks, C., & Phillips, M. (Eds.). (1998). *The Black–White test score gap.* Washington, DC: Brookings Institution.

225. Spencer, S. J., Steele, C. M., & Quinn, D. M. (1999). Stereotype threat and women's math performance. *Journal of Experimental Social Psychology, 35,* 4–28.

226. Stone, J., & McWhinnie, C. (2008). Evidence that blatant versus subtle stereotype threat cues impact performance through dual processes. *Journal of Experimental Social Psychology, 44*(2), 445–452.

227. Wout, D., Danso, H., Jackson, J., & Spencer, S. (2008). The many faces of stereotype threat: Group- and self-threat. *Journal of Experimental Social Psychology, 44*(3), 792–799.

228. Aronson, J., Lustina, M. J., Good, C., Keough, K., Steele, C. M., & Brown, J. (1999). When white men can't do math: Necessary and sufficient factors in stereotype threat. *Journal of Experimental Social Psychology, 35,* 29–46.

229. Steele, C. M., & Aronson, J. A. (1995). Stereotype threat and the intellectual test performance of African Americans. *Journal of Personality and Social Psychology, 69,* 797–811.

230. Blascovich, J., Spencer, S. J., Quinn, D., & Steele, C. (2001). African Americans and high blood pressure: The role of stereotype threat. *Psychological Science, 12,* 225–229.

231. Sackett, P. R., Hardison, C. M., & Cullen, M. J. (2004). On interpreting stereotype threat as accounting for African American–White differences on cognitive tests. *American Psychologist, 59,* 7–13.

232. Sackett, P. R., Hardison, C. M., & Cullen, M. J. (2004b). On the value of correcting mischaracterizations of stereotype threat research. *American Psychologist, 59,* 48–49.

233. Steele, C. M., & Aronson, J. A. (2004). Stereotype threat does not live by Steele and Aronson (1995) alone. *American Psychologist, 59,* 47–55.

234. Nguyen, H.-H. D., & Ryan, A. M. (2008). Does stereotype threat affect test performance of minorities and women? A meta-analysis of experimental evidence. *Journal of Applied Psychology, 93*(6), 1314–1334.

235. Abrams, D., Crisp, R. J., Marques, S., Fagg, E., Bedford, L., & Provias, D. (2008). Threat inoculation: Experienced and imagined intergenerational contact prevents stereotype threat effects on older people's math performance. *Psychology and Aging, 23*(4), 934–939.

236. Brodish, A. B., & Devine, P. G. (2009). The role of performance-avoidance goals and worry in mediating the relationship between stereotype threat and performance. *Journal of Experimental Social Psychology, 45*(1), 180–185.

237. Johns, M., Inzlicht, M., & Schmader, T. (2008). Stereotype threat and executive resource depletion: Examining the influence of emotion regulation. *Journal of Experimental Psychology: General, 137*(4), 691–705.

238. Krendl, A. C., Richeson, J. A., Kelley, W. M., & Heatherton, T. F. (2008). The negative consequences of threat: A functional magnetic resonance imaging investigation of the neural mechanisms underlying women's underperformance in math. *Psychological Science, 19*(2), 168–175.

239. Abrams, D., Crisp, R. J., Marques, S., Fagg, E., Bedford, L., & Provias, D. (2008). Threat inoculation: Experienced and imagined intergenerational contact prevents stereotype threat effects on older people's math performance. *Psychology and Aging, 23*(4), 934–939.

240. Plant, E. A. (2004). Responses to interracial interactions over time. *Personality and Social Psychology Bulletin, 30,* 1458–1471.

241. Shelton, J. N. (2003). Interpersonal concerns in social encounters between majority and minority group members. *Group Processes and Intergroup Relations, 6,* 171–185.

242. All material in this section is taken from: Duarte, J. L., Crawford, J. T., Stern, C., Haidt, J., Jussim, L., & Tetlock, P. E. (in press/2015). Political diversity will improve social psychological science. *Behavioral and Brain Sciences.*

243. Ceci, S. J., Peters, D., & Plotkin, J. (1985). Human subjects review, personal values, and the regulation of social sciences research. *American Psychologist, 51,* 768–784.

244. From Plant, E. A., & Devine, P. G. (1998). Internal and external motivation to respond without prejudice. *Journal of Personality and Social Psychology, 75,* 811–832.

CHAPTER 14
Groups

1. Quotes – Henry Ford. Retrieved from http://quotes4all.net/henry%20ford:3.html

2. Gross, D. (1996). *Forbes greatest business stories of all time.* New York: Wiley.

3. Campbell, D. T. (1958). Common fate, similarity, and other indices of the status of aggregates of persons as social entities. *Behavioral Science, 3,* 14–25.

4. Lickel, B., Hamilton, D. L., Wieczorkowska, G., Lewis, A., Sherman, S. J., & Uhles, A. N. (2000). Varieties of groups and the perception of group entitativity. *Journal of Personality and Social Psychology, 78,* 223–246.

5. Laumann, E. O., Gagnon, J. H., Michael, R. T., & Michaels, S. (1994). *The social organization of sexuality: Sexual practices in the United States.* Chicago, IL: University of Chicago Press.

6. For a review, see Levine, J. M., & Moreland, R. L. (1998). Small groups. In D. Gilbert, S. Fiske, & G. Lindzey (Eds.), *Handbook of social psychology* (4th. ed., Vol. 2, pp. 415–469). Boston: McGraw-Hill.

7. Surowiecki, J. (2004). *The wisdom of crowds: Why the many are smarter than the few and how collective wisdom shapes business, economics, societies, and nations.* New York: Doubleday.

8. Page, S. E. (2008). *The difference: How the power of diversity creates better groups, firms, schools, and societies.* Princeton, NJ: Princeton University Press.

9. Levine, J. M., & Moreland, R. L. (1998). Small groups. In D. Gilbert, S. Fiske, & G. Lindzey (Eds.), *Handbook of social psychology* (4th. ed., Vol. 2, pp. 415–469). Boston: McGraw-Hill.

10. Mannix, E., & Neale, M.A. (2005). What differences make a difference? The promise and reality of diverse teams in organizations. *Psychological Science in the Public Interest, 6,* 31–55.

11. Hoyle, R. H., Pinkley, R. L., & Insko, C. A. (1989). Perceptions of social behavior: Evidence of differing expectations for interpersonal and intergroup interaction. *Personality and Social Psychology Bulletin, 15,* 365–376.

12. Baumeister, R. F. (2005). *The cultural animal: Human nature, meaning, and social life.* New York: Oxford University Press.

13. Diener, E., Fraser, S. C., Beaman, A. L., & Kelem, R. T. (1976). Effects of deindividuation variables on stealing among Halloween trick-or-treaters. *Journal of Personality and Social Psychology, 33,* 178–183.

14. Zimbardo, P. G. (1970). The human choice: Individuation, reason, and order versus deindividuation, impulse, and chaos. In W. J. Arnold & D. Levine (Eds.), *Nebraska Symposium on Motivation* (pp. 237–307). Lincoln: University of Nebraska Press.

15. Lerner, J. S., & Tetlock, P. E. (1999). Accounting for the effects of accountability. *Psychological Bulletin, 125,* 255–275.

16. Schopler, J., Insko, C. A., Drigotas, S. M., Wieselquist, J., Pemberton, M. B., & Cox, C. (1995). The role of identifiability in the reduction of interindividual-intergroup discontinuity. *Journal of Experimental Social Psychology, 31,* 553–574.

17. Cottrell, N. B., Wack, D. L., Sekerak, G. J, & Rittle, R. H. (1968). Social facilitation of dominant responses by the presence of an audience and the mere presence of others. *Journal of Personality and Social Psychology, 9,* 245–250.

18. Seta, C. E., & Seta, J. J. (1995). When audience presence is enjoyable: The influences of audience awareness of prior success on performance and task interest. *Basic and Applied Social Psychology, 16*(1–2), 95–108.

19. Beilock, S. L., & Carr, T. H. (2001). On the fragility of skilled performance: What governs choking under pressure? *Journal of Experimental Psychology: General, 130,* 701–725.

20. Butler, J. L., & Baumeister, R. F. (1998). The trouble with friendly faces: Skilled performance with a supportive audience. *Journal of Personality and Social Psychology, 75,* 1213–1230.

21. Wallace, H. M., & Baumeister, R. F. (2002). The performance of narcissists rises and falls with perceived opportunity for glory. *Journal of Personality and Social Psychology, 82,* 819–834.

22. Wright, E. F., & Jackson, W. (1991). The home-course disadvantage in golf championships: Further evidence for the undermining effect of supportive audiences on performance under pressure. *Journal of Sport Behavior, 14,* 51–60.

23. Wright, E. F., & Voyer, D. (1995). Supporting audiences and performance under pressure: The home-ice disadvantage in hockey championships. *Journal of Sport Behavior, 18,* 21–28.

24. For example, Spence, K. W. (1956). *Behavior theory and conditioning.* New Haven, CT: Yale University Press.

25. Zajonc, R. B. (1965). Social facilitation. *Science, 149,* 269–274.

26. Bond, C. F., & Titus, L. J. (1983). Social facilitation: A meta-analysis of 241 studies. *Psychological Bulletin, 94,* 265–292.

27. Zajonc, R. B., Heingartner, A., & Herman, E. M. (1969). Social enhancement and impairment of performance in the cockroach. *Journal of Personality and Social Psychology, 13,* 83–92.

28. Aiello, J. R., & Douthitt, E. A. (2001). Social facilitation: From Triplett to electronic performance monitoring. *Group Dynamics: Theory, Research, and Practice, 5,* 163–180.

29. Cottrell, N. B., Wack, D. L., Sekerak, G. J., & Rittle, R. H. (1968). Social facilitation of dominant responses by the presence of an audience and the mere presence of others. *Journal of Personality and Social Psychology, 9,* 245–250.

30. Wallace, H. M., & Baumeister, R. F. (2002). The performance of narcissists rises and falls with perceived opportunity for glory. *Journal of Personality and Social Psychology, 82,* 819–834.

31. Ringelmann, M. (1913). Recherches sur les moteurs animés: Travail de l'homme. *Annales de l'Institut National Argonomique,* 2e srie, tom 12, 1–40. Published in French, cited in Kravitz, D. A., & Martin, B. (1986). Ringelmann rediscovered: The original article. *Journal of Personality and Social Psychology, 50,* 936–941.

32. Latane, B., Williams, K., & Harkins, S. (1979). Many hands make light the work: The causes and consequences of social loafing. *Journal of Personality and Social Psychology, 37,* 822–832.

33. For example, Kerr, N. L., & Bruun, S. E. (1983). Dispensability of member effort and group motivation losses: Free-rider effects. *Journal of Personality and Social Psychology, 44,* 78–94.

34. Crandall, C. S. (1988). Social contagion of binge eating. *Journal of Personality and Social Psychology, 55,* 588–598.

35. Crandall, C. S. (1988). Social contagion of binge eating. *Journal of Personality and Social Psychology, 55,* 588–598.

36. Karau, S. J., & Williams, K. D. (1993). Social loafing: A meta-analytic review and theoretical integration. *Journal of Personality and Social Psychology, 65,* 681–706.

37. Kerr, N. L., & Bruun, S. E. (1981). Ringelmann revisited: Alternative explanations for the social loafing effect. *Personality and Social Psychology Bulletin, 7*(2), 224–231.

38. Williams, K., Harkins, S. G., & Latané, B. (1981). Identifiability as a deterrant to social loafing: Two cheering experiments. *Journal of Personality and Social Psychology, 40*(2), 303–311.

39. Karau, S. J., & Williams, K. D. (1993). Social loafing: A meta-analytic review and theoretical integration. *Journal of Personality and Social Psychology, 65,* 681–706.

40. Kerr, N. L. (1983). Motivation losses in small groups: A social dilemma analysis. *Journal of Personality and Social Psychology, 45,* 819–828.

41. Kerr, N. L., Rumble, A. C., Park, E. S., Ouwerkerk, J. W., Parks, C. D., Gallucci, M., & Van Lange, P. A. M. (2009). "How many bad apples does it take to spoil the whole barrel?" Social exclusion and tolerance for bad apples. *Journal of Experimental Social Psychology. 45*(4), 603–613. Retrieved from http://www.sciencedirect.com/science/article/pii/S0022103109000390

42. Kurzban, R., & Leary, M. R. (2001). Evolutionary origins of stigmatization: The functions of social exclusion. *Psychological Bulletin, 127,* 187–208.

43. See: Ouwerkerk, J. W., Van Lange, P. A., Gallucci, M., & Kerr, N. L. (2005). Avoiding the social death penalty: Ostracism and cooperation in social dilemmas. In K. D. Williams, J. P. Forgas, & W. von Hippel (Eds.), *The social outcast: Ostracism, social exclusion, rejection, and bullying* (pp. 321–332). New York: Psychology Press.

44. Kerr, N. L., & Bruun, S. E. (1983). Dispensability of member effort and group motivation losses: Free-rider effects. *Journal of Personality and Social Psychology, 44,* 78–94.

45. Fehr, E., & Gächter, S. (2002). Altruistic punishment in humans. *Nature, 415*(6868), 137–140.

46. Fehr, E., & Gächter, S. (2002). Altruistic punishment in humans. *Nature, 415*(6868), 137–140.

47. Diener, E., Fraser, S. C., Beaman, A. L., & Kelem, R. T. (1976). Effects of deindividuation variables on stealing among Halloween trick-or-treaters. *Journal of Personality and Social Psychology, 33*(2), 178–183.

48. Festinger, L., Pepitone, A., & Newcomb T. (1952). Some consequences of deindividuation in a group. *Journal of Abnormal and Social Psychology, 47,* 382–389.

49. Zimbardo, P. G. (1970). The human choice: Individuation, reason, and order versus deindividuation, impulse, and chaos. In W. J. Arnold & D. Levine (Eds.), *Nebraska Symposium on Motivation, 1969*(237–307). Lincoln: University of Nebraska Press.

50. Postmes, T., & Spears, R. (1998). Deindividuation and antinormative behavior: A meta-analysis. *Psychological Bulletin, 123,* 238–259.

51. Davies, J. B., Sandström, S., Shorrocks, A., & Wolff, E. N. (2008). The World Distribution of Household Wealth. UNU-WIDER. Retrieved from http://www.wider.unu.edu/publications/working-papers/discussion-papers/2008/en_GB/dp2008-03/

52. Hardin, G. (1968). The tragedy of the commons. *Science, 162,* 1243–1248.

53. For example, Brechner, K. C. (1977). An experimental analysis of social traps. *Journal of Experimental Social Psychology, 13,* 552–564.

54. Paulus, P. B., Dzindolet, M. T., Poletes, G., & Camacho, L. M. (1993). Perception of performance in group brainstorming: The illusion of group productivity. *Personality and Social Psychology Bulletin, 19,* 78–89.

55. Stroebe, W., Diehl, M., & Abakoumkin, G. (1992). The illusion of group effectivity. *Personality and Social Psychology Bulletin, 18,* 643–650.

56. Mullen, B., Johnson, C., & Salas, E. (1991). Productivity loss in brainstorming groups: A meta-analysis. *Basic and Applied Social Psychology, 12,* 3–23.

57. Mackay, C. (1932). *Extraordinary popular delusions and the madness of crowds.* New York: Farrar, Straus and Cudahy. (Original work published 1841).

58. Le Bon, G. (1908). *The crowd: A study of the popular mind.* London: T Fisher Unwin.

59. Surowiecki, J. (2004). *The wisdom of crowds: Why the many are smarter than the few and how collective wisdom shapes business, economics, societies, and nations.* New York: Doubleday.

60. Surowiecki, J. (2004). *The wisdom of crowds: Why the many are smarter than the few and how collective wisdom shapes business, economics, societies, and nations.* New York: Doubleday.

61. Surowiecki, J. (2004). *The wisdom of crowds: Why the many are smarter than the few and how collective wisdom shapes business, economics, societies, and nations.* New York: Doubleday. (Quotation on p. 11).

62. Davis-Stober, C.P., Budescu, D.V., Dana, J., & Broomell, S.B. (2014). When is a crowd wise? *Decision, 1,* 79–101.

63. Lorenz, J., Rauhut, H., Schweitzer, F., & Helbing, D. (2011). How social influence can undermine the wisdom of crowd effect. *PNAS (Proceedings of the National Academy of Sciences), 108,* 9020–9025.

64. Allen, N. J., & Hecht, T. D. (2004). The "romance of teams": Toward an understanding of its psychological underpinnings and implications. *Journal of Occupational and Organizational Psychology, 77,* 439–461.

65. Wegner, D. M. (1986). Transactive memory: A contemporary analysis of the group mind. In B. Mullen & G. R. Goethals (Eds.), *Theories of group behavior* (pp. 185–208). New York: Springer-Verlag.

66. Wegner, D. M., Giuliano, T., & Hertel, P. (1985). Cognitive interdependence in close relationships. In W. Ickes (Ed.), *Compatible and incompatible relationships* (pp. 253–276). New York: Springer-Verlag.

67. Hollingshead, A. B., & Brandon, D. P. (2003). Potential benefits of communication in transactive memory systems. *Human Communication Research, 29,* 607–615.

68. Hollingshead, A. B. (1998). Retrieval processes in transactive memory systems. *Journal of Personality and Social Psychology, 74,* 659–671.

69. Liang, D. W., Moreland, R. L., & Argote, L. (1995). Group versus individual training and group performance: The mediating role of transactive memory. *Personality and Social Psychology Bulletin, 21,* 384–393.

70. Moreland, R. L., Argote, L., & Krishnan, R. (1998). Training people to work in groups. In R. Tindale, L. Heath, J. Edwards, E. Posavac, F. Bryant, Y. Suarez-Balcazar, et al. (Eds.), *Theory and research on small groups* (pp. 37–60). New York: Plenum Press.

71. Janis, I. (1982). *Groupthink* (2nd ed.). Boston: Houghton Mifflin.

72. Janis, I. (1982). *Groupthink* (2nd ed.). Boston: Houghton Mifflin.

73. Stasser, G., & Titus, W. (1985). Pooling of unshared information in group decision making: Biased information sampling during discussion. *Journal of Personality and Social Psychology, 48,* 1467–1478.

74. Stasser, G., & Titus, W. (1987). Effects of information load and percentage of shared information on the dissemination of unshared information during group discussion. *Journal of Personality and Social Psychology, 53,* 81–93.

75. Stoner, J. A. F. (1961). *A comparison of individual and group decisions involving risk.* Unpublished master's thesis, Massachusetts Institute of Technology.

76. Wallach, M. A., Kogan, N., & Bem, D. J. (1962). Group influence on individual risk-taking. *Journal of Abnormal and Social Psychology, 65,* 75–86.

77. Moscovici, S., & Zavalloni, M. (1969). The group as a polarizer of attitudes. *Journal of Personality and Social Psychology, 12,* 125–135.

78. Joyce, W. F., Nohria, N., & Roberson, B. (2003). *What really works: The 4+2 formula for sustained business success.* New York: HarperBusiness.

79. Barrick, M. R., Day, D. V., Lord, R. G., & Alexander, R. A. (1991). Assessing the utility of executive leadership. *Leadership Quarterly, 2,* 9–22.

80. Collins, J. (2001). *Good to great.* New York: HarperCollins.

81. Collins, J. (2001). *Good to great.* New York: HarperCollins.

82. Hogan, R., & Kaiser, R. B. (2005). What we know about leadership. *Review of General Psychology, 9*(2), 169–180.

83. Kouzes, J. M., & Posner, B. Z. (2002). *The leadership challenge* (3rd ed.). San Francisco: Jossey-Bass.

84. Lord, R. G., Foti, R. J., & DeVader, C. L. (1984). A test of leadership categorization theory: Internal structure, information processing, and leadership perceptions. *Organizational Behavior and Human Performance, 34,* 343–378.

85. Schaumberg, R.L., & Flynn, F.J. (2012). Uneasy lies the head that wears the crown: The link between guilt proneness and leadership. *Journal of Personality and Social Psychology, 103,* 327–342.

86. Yukl, G. (2006). *Leadership in organizations.* Upper Saddle River, NJ: Prentice-Hall.

87. Brunell, A. B., Gentry, W. A., Campbell, W. K., Hoffman, B. J., Kuhnert, K. W., & DeMarree, K. G. (2008). Leadership emergence: The case of the narcissistic leader. *Personality and Social Psychology Bulletin, 34,* 1663–1676.

88. Ames, D. R., & Flynn, F. J. (2007). What breaks a leader: The curvilinear relation between assertiveness and leadership. *Journal of Personality and Social Psychology, 92,* 307–324.

89. Hogan, R., & Kaiser, R. B. (2005). What we know about leadership. *Review of General Psychology, 9*(2), 169–180.

90. DeVries, D., & Kaiser, R. B. (2003, November). Going sour in the suite. Paper presented at the Maximizing Executive Effectiveness workshop, Miami, FL.

91. Leslie, J. B., & Van Velsor, E. (1996). *A look at derailment today.* Greensboro, NC: Centre for Creative Leadership.

92. Mayer, J. D. (1993). The emotional madness of the dangerous leader. *Journal of Psychohistory, 20,* 331–348.

93. Mayer, J. D. (1993). The emotional madness of the dangerous leader. *Journal of Psychohistory, 20,* 331–348. (Quotation on p. 337).

94. Mayer, J. D. (1993). The emotional madness of the dangerous leader. *Journal of Psychohistory, 20,* 331–348.

95. Morgenthau, H. (1962). Love and power. *Commentary, 33,* 247–251.

96. Kipnis, D. (1972). Does power corrupt? *Journal of Personality and Social Psychology, 24,* 33–41.

97. Kipnis, D. (1976). *The powerholders.* Chicago: University of Chicago Press.

98. Kipnis, D. (1972). Does power corrupt? *Journal of Personality and Social Psychology, 24,* 33–41.

99. Park, S. H., Westphal, J. D., & Stern, I. (2011). Set up for a fall: The insidious effects of flattery and opinion conformity toward corporate leaders. *Administrative Science Quarterly, 56,* 2257–2302.
E40 | Endnotes

100. Abrams, D., de Moura, G., & Travaglino, G. (2013) A double standard when group members behave badly: Transgression credit to ingroup leaders. *Journal of Personality and Social Psychology, 105,* 799–815.

101. Lindskold, S., & Aronoff, J. R. (1980). Conciliatory strategies and relative power. *Journal of Experimental Social Psychology, 16,* 187–198.

102. Blader, S. L., & Chen, Y. (2012). Differentiating the effects of status and power: A justice perspective. *Journal of Personality and Social Psychology, 102,* 994–1014.

103. Keltner, D., Gruenfeld, D. H., & Anderson, C. (2003). Power, approach, and inhibition. *Psychological Review, 110,* 265–284.

104. Watson, D., & Clark, L. A. (1997). Extraversion and its positive emotional core. In R. Hogan, J. Johnson, & S. Briggs (Eds.), *Handbook of personality psychology* (pp. 767–793). New York: Academic Press.

105. Whitson, J. A., Liljenquist, K. A., Galinsky, A. D., Magee, J. C., Gruenfeld, D. H., & Cadena, B. (2013). The blind leading: Power reduces awareness of constraints. *Journal of Experimental Social Psychology, 49,* 579–582.

106. Guinote, A. (2008). Power and affordances: When the situation has more power over powerful than powerless individuals. *Journal of Personality and Social Psychology, 95,* 237–252.

107. Galinsky, A. D., Magee, J. C., Gruenfeld, D. H., Whitson, J. A., & Liljenquist, K. A. (2008). Power reduces the press of the situation: Implications for creativity, conformity, and dissonance. *Journal of Personality and Social Psychology, 95,* 1450–1466.

108. Keltner, D., Gruenfeld, D. H., & Anderson, C. (2003). Power, approach, and inhibition. *Psychological Review, 110,* 265–284.

109. Lerner, J. S., & Tetlock, P. E. (1999). Accounting for the effects of accountability. *Psychological Bulletin, 125,* 255–275.

110. Tetlock, P. E. (1992). The impact of accountability on judgment and choice: Toward a social contingency model. In M. P. Zanna (Ed.), *Advances in experimental social psychology* (Vol. 25, pp. 331–376). San Diego: Academic Press.

111. Bargh, J. A., Raymond, P., Pryor, J. B., & Strack, F. (1995). The attractiveness of the underling: An automatic power-sex association and its consequences for sexual harassment. *Journal of Personality and Social Psychology, 68,* 768–781.

112. Galinsky, A. D., Gruenfeld, D. H., & Magee, J. C. (2003). From power to action. *Journal of Personality and Social Psychology, 85,* 453–466.

113. Galinsky, A. D., Gruenfeld, D. H., & Magee, J. C. (2003). From power to action. *Journal of Personality and Social Psychology, 85,* 453–466.

114. Lee-Chai, A. Y., Chen, S., & Chartrand, T. L. (2001). From Moses to Marcos: Individual differences in the use and abuse of power. In A. Y. Lee-Chai & J. A. Bargh (Eds.), *The use and abuse of power: Multiple perspectives on the causes of corruption* (pp. 57–74). New York: Psychology Press.

115. Maner, J. K., & Mead, N. L. (2010). The essential tension between leadership and power: When leaders sacrifice group goals for the sake of self-interest. *Journal of Personality and Social Psychology, 99,* 482–497.

116. Mead, N. L., & Maner, J. K. (2012) On keeping your enemies close: Powerful leaders seek proximity to ingroup power threats. *Journal of Personality and Social Psychology, 102,* 576–591.

117. Erber, R., & Fiske, S. T. (1984). Outcome dependency and attention to inconsistent information. *Journal of Personality and Social Psychology, 47,* 709–726.

118. Lindskold, S., & Aronoff, J. R. (1980). Conciliatory strategies and relative power. *Journal of Experimental Social Psychology, 16,* 187–198.

119. Copeland, J. T. (1994). Prophecies of power: Motivational implications of social power for behavioral confirmation. *Journal of Personality and Social Psychology, 67,* 264–277.

120. Chen, E. S., & Tyler, T. R. (2001). Cloaking power: Legitimizing myths and the psychology of the advantaged. In A. Y. Lee-Chai & J. Bargh (Eds.), *The use and abuse of power: Multiple perspectives on the causes of corruption* (pp. 241–261). Philadelphia: Psychology Press.

121. Stillman, T. F., Baumeister, R. F., & DeWall, C. N. (2007). What's so funny about not having money? The effects of power on laughter. *Personality and Social Psychology Bulletin, 33,* 1547–1558.

122. Fraley, B., & Aron, A. (2004). The effect of a shared humorous experience on closeness in initial encounters. *Personal Relationships, 11,* 61–78.

123. Sprecher, S., & Regan, P. (2002). Liking some things (in some people) more than others: Partner preferences in romantic relationships and friendships. *Journal of Social and Personal Relationships, 19,* 463–481.

124. Zajonc, Heingartner, & Herman (1969). From Zajonc, R. B., Social enhancement and impairment of performance in the cockroach. *Journal of Personality and Social Psychology, 13*(2), 83–92.

125. David G. Myers, *Social Psychology* 9th ed., 2008.

MODULE A
Applying Social Psychology to Consumer Behavior

1. Frith, K. T., & Mueller, B. (2003). *Advertising and society: Global issues.* New York: Peter Lang.

2. Burgess, J. (2008) *"All your chocolate rain are belong to us?" Viral video, YouTube and the dynamics of participatory culture.* In UNSPECIFIED (Ed.), *Video vortex reader: Responses to YouTube.* Institute of Network Cultures, Amsterdam, pp. 101–109. Retrieved from http://eprints.qut.edu.au/18431/1/18431.pdf

3. Elliott, S. (2012). M&M's to Unveil New Speaking Role at Super Bowl. *New York Times.* Retrieved from http://www.nytimes.com/2012/01/17/business/media/mms-to-unveil-a-new-speaking-role-at-super-bowl.html?_r=1

4. Roberts, J. (2012, February 28). *How to begin analyzing social media.* Retrieved August 20, 2012, from http://www.collectiveintellect.com/blog/brand-tracker-super-bowl-2012.

5. Bishop, S. (2008, January 23). Don't bother with the "green" consumer. *Harvard Business Report.* Retrieved from http://www.hbrgreen.org/2008/01/dont_bother_with_the_green_con.html

6. Bruner, J. A., & Mason, J. L. (1968). The influence of driving time upon shopping center preference. *Journal of Marketing, 32*(2), 57–61.

7. Rhee, H., & Bell, D. R. (2002). The inter-store mobility of supermarket shoppers. *Journal of Retailing, 78,* 225–237.

8. Store of the month. (1976, October). *Progressive Grocer,* 104.

9. Babin, B. J., & Babin, L. (2001). Seeking something different? A model of schema typicality, consumer affect, purchase intentions and perceived shopping value. *Journal of Business Research, 54,* 89–96.

10. Milliman, R. E. (1982). Using background music to affect the behavior of supermarket shoppers. *Journal of Marketing, 46,* 86–91.

11. Areni, C. S., & Kim, D. (1993). The influence of background music on shopping behavior: Classical versus Top-Forty. In L. McAlister & M. L. Rothschild (Eds.), *Advances in consumer research* (pp. 336–340). Provo, UT: Association for Consumer Research.

12. Donovan, R., & Rossiter, J. (1982). Store atmosphere: An environmental psychology approach. *Journal of Retailing, 58,* 34–57.

13. Donovan, R., & Rossiter, J. (1982). Store atmosphere: An environmental psychology approach. *Journal of Retailing, 58,* 34–57.

14. Spangenberg, E. R., Crowley, A. E., & Henderson, P. W. (1996). Improving the store environment: Do olfactory cues affect evaluations and behaviors? *Journal of Marketing, 60,* 67–80.

15. Mitchell, D. J., Kahn, B. E., & Knasko, S. C. (1995). There's something in the air: Effects of congruent or incongruent ambient odor on consumer decision making. *Journal of Consumer Research, 22,* 229–238.

16. Steinmetz, K. (2012). Follow your nose: Food company launches 'smell-vertising' for potato ads. *Time NewsFeed.* Retrieved from http://newsfeed.time.com/2012/02/10/follow-your-nose-food-company-launches-smell-vertising-for-potato-ads/

17. Schifferstein, H. N. J., & Michaut, A. M. K. (2002). Effects of appropriate and inappropriate odors on product evaluation. *Perceptual and Motor Skills, 95,* 1199–1214.

18. Morrin, M., & Ratnewshwar, S. (2003). Does it make sense to use scents to enhance brand memory? *Journal of Marketing Research, 40,* 10–25.

19. Sommer, R. (1969). *Personal space: The behavioral basis of design.* Englewood Cliffs, NJ: Prentice-Hall.

20. Koernig, S. K. (2003). E-scapes: The electronic physical environment and service tangibility. *Psychology and Marketing, 20,* 151–167.

21. Yorkston, E., & Menon, G. (2004). A sound idea: Phonetic effects of brand names on consumer judgments. *Journal of Consumer Research, 31,* 43–51.

22. Chang, Y., Chen, R. C., Wahlqvist, M. L., & Lee, M. (2011). Frequent shopping by men and women increases survival in the older Taiwanese population. *Journal of Epidemial Community Health.* Retrieved from http://jech.bmj.com/content/early/2011/03/17/jech.2010.126698.abstract

23. New image. Retrieved from http://logos.wikia.com/wiki/Pepsi

24. Rosenthal, E. (2008, February 2). Motivated by a tax, Irish spurn plastic bags. *New York Times.* Retrieved from http://www.nytimes.com/2008/02/02/world/europe/02bags.html?_r=1&pagewanted=1

25. See http://www.campaignforrecycling.org/our_issues/plastic/plastic_bags/current_laws for a complete listing.

26. Sallie Mae. (2009). *How undergraduate students use credit cards: Sallie Mae's National Study of Usage Rates and Trends 2009.* Retrieved August 20, 2012, from http://static.mgnetwork.com/rtd/pdfs/20090830_iris.pdf

27. Jacobe, D. (2008, June 11). Nearly one-third of credit-card owners hold high balances. Retrieved from http://www.gallup.com/poll/107833/nearly-onethird-americans-hold-high-credit-balances.aspx

28. Prelec, D., & Simester, D. (2001). Always leave home without it. *Marketing Letters, 12,* 5–12.

29. Boddington, L., & Kemp, S. (1999). Student debt, attitudes towards debt, impulsive buying, and financial management. *New Zealand Journal of Psychology, 28,* 89–93.

30. Politano, J., & Lester, D. (1997). Self-destructiveness and credit card debt. *Psychological Reports, 81,* 634.

31. Lea, S. E. G., & Webley, P. (2006). Money as tool, money as drug: The biological psychology of a strong incentive. *Behavioral and Brain Sciences, 29,* 161–209.

32. Soman, D., & Cheema, A. (2002). The effect of credit on spending decisions: The role of the credit limit and credibility. *Marketing Science, 21,* 32–53.

33. Feinberg, R. (1986). Credit cards as spending facilitating stimuli: A conditioning interpretation. *Journal of Consumer Research, 3,* 348–356.

34. Beggan, J. K. (1992). On the social nature of nonsocial perception: The mere ownership effect. *Journal of Personality and Social Psychology, 62,* 229–237.

35. Iyengar, S. S., & Lepper, M. R. (2000). When choice is demotivating: Can one desire too much of a good thing? *Journal of Personality and Social Psychology, 79,* 995–1006.

36. Lee, B. K., & Lee, W. N. (2004). The effect of information overload on consumer choice quality in an on-line environment. *Psychology and Marketing, 21,* 159–183.

37. Macias, W. (2003). A beginning look at the effects of interactivity, product involvement, and web experience on comprehension: Brand web sites as interactive advertising. *Journal of Current Issues and Research in Advertising, 25,* 31–44.

38. Bagozzi, R. P., Wong, N., Abe, S., & Bergami, M. (2000). Cultural and situational contingencies and the theory of reasoned action: Application to fast food restaurant consumption. *Journal of Consumer Psychology, 9*, 97–106.

39. Cell phone or pheromone? New props for mating game. (2000, November 7). *New York Times.*

40. Right hand diamonds marketed to women as power sign. (2003, December 2). *Sacramento Bee.* Retrieved from http://www.sacbee.com/content/business/story/7887166p-8825882c.html

41. Newman, A. (May 26, 2010). With this ring, I thee what? *New York Times.* Retrieved February 18, 2012, from http://www.nytimes.com/2010/05/27/fashion/27rings.html?adxnnl=1&adxnnlx=1329596054-/Hwober8MpThtkMeSSX7pA

42. Solomon, S., Greenberg, J., & Pyszczynski, T. A. (2004). Lethal consumption: Death-denying materialism. In T. Kasser & A. D. Kanner (Eds.), *Psychology and consumer culture: The struggle for a good life in a materialistic world* (pp. 127–146). Washington, DC: American Psychological Association.

43. Kasser, T., & Sheldon, K. M. (2000). Of wealth and death: Materialism, mortality salience, and consumption behavior. *Psychological Science, 11,* 348–351.

44. Myers, D. G. (1993, July/August). Pursuing happiness. *Psychology Today,* pp. 32–35, 66–67.

45. Gould, S. J., & Weil, C. E. (1991). Gift-giving and gender self-concepts. *Gender Role, 24,* 617–637.

46. Wooten, D. B. (2000). Qualitative steps toward an expanded model of anxiety in gift-giving. *Journal of Consumer Research, 27,* 84–95.

47. Tse, A. C. B., & Yim, F. (2001). Factors affecting the choice of channels: Online vs. conventional. *Journal of International Consumer Marketing, 14,* 137–152.

48. McKinney, L. N. (2004). Internet shopping orientation segments: An exploration of differences in consumer behavior. *Family and Consumer Sciences Research Journal, 32,* 408–433.

49. Frith, K. T., & Mueller, B. (2003). *Advertising and society: Global issues.* New York: Peter Lang.

50. Some kids won't eat the middle of an Oreo. (1991, November 20). *Wall Street Journal,* p. B1.

51. Kwan, M. (2010). How many cell phones are in the US? Retrieved from http://cellphones.lovetoknow.com/how-many-cell-phones-are-us

52. CTIA.org. (2012). Background on CTIA's semiannual wireless industry survey. Retrieved from http://www.ctia.org/media/industry_info/index.cfm/AID/10323

53. Orville Redenbacher Company Website. Retrieved August 20, 2012, from http://www.orville.com/homemade-popcorn

54. DeAngelis, T. (2000). Is Internet addiction real? *Monitor on Psychology, 31.* Retrieved from http://www.apa.org/monitor/apr00/addiction.html

55. Lakin, A. (2009). Recyclable cars. *DriverSide.com.* Retrieved from http://www.driverside.com/auto-library/recyclable_cars-257

56. U.S. Census Bureau. (2009). New motor vehicle sales and car production. *The 2009 statistical abstract: National data book.* Retrieved from http://www.census.gov/compendia/statab/tables/09s1021.pdf

57. Consumer Electronics Association. (2008, April). *Market research report: Trends in CE reuse, recycle and removal.*

58. China's hi-tech toxics. (2002). *BBC News.* Retrieved from http://news.bbc.co.uk/hi/english/static/in_depth/world/2002/disposable_planet/waste/chinese_workshop

59. Sarrel, M. D. (2006, November 29). Recycling e-waste. *PCMag.com.* Retrieved from http://www.pcmag.com/article2/0,2817,2064151,00.asp

60. Roach, M. (2004). *Stiff: The curious lives of human cadavers.* New York: W. W. Norton.

61. Fetterman, M., & Hausen, B. (2006, November 19). Young people struggle to deal with kiss of debt. *USA Today.* Retrieved from http://www.usatoday.com/money/perfi/credit/2006-11-19-young-and-in-debt-cover_x.htm

MODULE B
Applying Social Psychology to Health

1. Gurung, R. A. R. (2014). *Health psychology* (3rd ed.). Belmont, CA: Cengage.

2. Centers for Disease Control. (2008). Alcohol-attributable deaths and years of potential life lost among American Indians and Alaska Natives—United States, 2001–2005. *Morbidity and Mortality Weekly Report,* 57(34); 938–941. Retrieved from http://www.cdc.gov/DataStatistics/

3. World Health Organization (2003). WHO definition of health. Preamble to the Constitution of the World Health Organization as adopted by the International Health Conference, New York, 19–22 June, 1946; signed on 22 July 1946 by the representatives of 61 States (Official Records of the World Health Organization, no. 2, p. 100) and entered into force on 7 April 1948. Retrieved from http://www.who.int/about/definition/en/print.html

4. Friedman, H., & Silver, R. (Eds.). (2007). *Foundations of health psychology.* New York: Oxford University Press.

5. Matarazzo, J. D. (1982). "Behavioral health" challenge to academic, scientific and professional psychology. *American Psychologist, 37*(1), 1–14.

6. Suls, J., Davidson, K., & Kaplan, R. (Eds.). 2010. *Handbook of health psychology and behavioral medicine.* New York: Guilford Press.

7. Gurung, R. A. R. (2012). Heath psychology. In D. S. Dunn (Ed.), *Oxford Bibliographies in Psychology.* New York: Oxford University Press.

8. Contrada, R., & Baum, A. (Eds.). (2011). *The handbook of stress science: Biology, psychology, and health.* New York: Springer.

9. Cannon, W. B. (1929). *Bodily changes in pain, hunger, fear and rage.* Oxford: Appleton.

10. Seyle, H. (1956). *The stress of life.* New York: McGraw-Hill.

11. Cannon, W. B. (1914). The interrelations of emotions as suggested by recent physiological researches. *American Journal of Physiology, 25,* 256–282.

12. Eiland, L., & McEwen, B. S. (2012). Early life stress followed by subsequent adult chronic stress potentiates anxiety and blunts hippocampal structural remodeling. *Hippocampus, 22*(1), 82–91. doi: 10.1002/hipo.20862

13. McEwen, B., & Lasley, E. 2007. Allostatic load: When protection gives way to damage. In A. Monat, R. S. Lazarus, G. Reevy, A. Monat, R. S. Lazarus, & G. Reevy (Eds.), *The Praeger handbook on stress and coping* (Vol. 1, pp. 99–109). Westport, CT: Praeger/Greenwood.

14. Lazarus, R. S. (1966). *Psychological stress and the coping process.* New York: McGraw-Hill.

15. Lazarus, R. S. (1991). Progress on a cognitive-motivational-relational theory of emotion. *American Psychologist, 46*(8), 819–834.

16. Langer, E. J., & Rodin, J. (1976). The effects of choice and enhanced personal responsibility for the aged: A field experiment in an institutional setting. *Journal of Personality and Social Psychology, 34*(2), 191–198.

17. Taylor, S. E., Klein, L. C., Lewis, B. P., Gruenewald, T. L., Gurung, R. A. R., & Udpegraff, J. A. (2000). Biobehavioral responses to stress in females: Tend-and-befriend, not fight-or-flight. *Psychological Review, 107*(3), 411–429.

18. Taylor, S. E., & Master, S. L. (2011). Social responses to stress: The tend-and-befriend model. In R. J. Contrada, A. Baum, R. J. Contrada, A. Baum (Eds.), *The handbook of stress science: Biology, psychology, and health* (pp. 101–109). New York: Springer.

19. Repetti, R. L. (1997). *The effects of daily job stress on parent behavior with preadolescents.* Paper presented at the biennial meeting of the Society for Research in Child Development, Washington, DC.

20. Somerfield, M. R., & McCrae, R. R. (2000). Stress and coping research: Methodological challenges, theoretical advances, and clinical applications. *American Psychologist, 55*(6), 620–625.

21. Carver, C. S., & Scheier, M. F. (1994). Situational coping and coping dispositions in a stressful transaction. *Journal of Social and Personality Psychology, 56,* 267–283.

22. Moos, R. H., & Schaefer, J. A. (1993). Coping resources and processes: Current concepts and measures. In L. Goldberger, & S. Breznitz (Eds.), *Handbook of stress: Theoretical and clinical aspects* (2nd ed., pp. 234–257). New York: Free Press.

23. Lazarus, R. S., & Launier, R. (1978). Stress-related transactions between person and environment. In L. A. Pervin & M. Lewis (Eds.), *Perspectives in interactional psychology* (pp. 287–322). New York: Plenum.

24. Tennen, H., Affleck, G., Armeli, S., & Carney, M. A. (2000). A daily process approach to coping: Linking theory, research, and practice. *American Psychologist, 55*(6), 626–636.

25. Dunkel-Schetter, C., & Bennett, T. L. (1990). Differentiating the cognitive and behavioral aspects of social support. In B. R. Sarason, & I. G. Sarason (Eds.), *Social support: An interactional view* (pp. 267–296). Oxford: John Wiley & Sons.

26. House, J. S., Umberson, D., & Landis, K. R. (1988). Structures and processes of social support. *Annual Review of Sociology, 14,* 293–318.

27. Lett, H. S., Blumenthal, J. A., Babyak, M. A., Catellier, D. J., Carney, R. M., Berkman, L. F., & … Schneiderman, N. (2008). Perceived social support predicts outcomes following myocardial infarction: A call for screening?: Response. *Health Psychology, 27*(1), 1–3. doi: 10.1037/0278-6133.27.1.1b

28. Sarason, B. R., Sarason, I. G., & Gurung, R. A. R. (2001). Close personal relationships and health outcomes: A key to the role of social support. In B. R. Sarason & S. Duck (Eds.), *Personal relationships. Implications for clinical and community psychology* (pp. 15–41). Chichester: Wiley.

29. Uchino, B. N., Cacioppo, J. T., & Kiecolt-Glaser, J. K. (1996). The relationship between social support and physiological processes: A review with emphasis on underlying mechanisms and implications for health. *Psychological Bulletin, 119*(3), 488–531.

30. Luckow, A., Reifman, A., & McIntosh, D. N. (1998). *Gender differences in coping: A meta-analysis.* Poster session presented at the 106th Annual Convention of the American Psychological Association, San Francisco.

31. Schachter, S. (1959). *The psychology of affiliation: Experimental studies of the sources of gregariousness.* Oxford: Stanford University Press.

32. Pouwelse, M., Bolman, C., Lodewijkx, H., & Spaa, M. (2011). Gender differences and social support: Mediators or moderators between peer victimization and depressive feelings. *Psychology in the Schools, 48*(8), 800–814. doi: 10.1002/pits.20589

33. Centers for Disease Control and Prevention. (2012). Vital signs. Retrieved from http://www.cdc.gov/tobacco/data_statistics/vital_signs/index.htm

34. Wills, T., Sargent, J., Stoolmiller, M., Gibbons, F., & Gerrard, M. (2008). Movie smoking exposure and smoking onset: A longitudinal study of mediation processes in a representative sample of U.S. adolescents. *Psychology of Addictive Behaviors, 22*(2), 269–277.

35. Sargent, J. D., Dalton, M. A., Heatherton, T. & Beach, M. (2003). Modifying exposure to smoking depicted in movies: A novel approach to preventing adolescent smoking. *Archives of Pediatrics and Adolescent Medicine, 157*(7), 643–648.

36. Sargent, J. D., Dalton, M. A., Beach M. L., Mott, L. A., Tickle, J. J., Ahrens, M. B., et al. (2002). Viewing tobacco use in movies: does it shape attitudes that mediate adolescent smoking? *American Journal of Preventive Medicine, 22*(3), 137–145.

37. Dal Cin, S., Gibson, B., Zanna, M., Shumate, R., & Fong, G. (2007). Smoking in movies, implicit associations of smoking with the self, and intentions to smoke. *Psychological Science, 18*(7), 559–563.

38. Dal Cin, S., Worth, K., Dalton, M., & Sargent, J. (2008). Youth exposure to alcohol use and brand appearances in popular contemporary movies. *Addiction, 103*(12), 1925–1932.

39. Dalton, M. A., Ahrens, M. B., Sargent, J. D., Mott, L. A., Beach, M. L., Tickle, J. J., et al. (2002). Relation between parental restrictions on movies and adolescent use of tobacco and alcohol. *Effective Clinical Practice, 5*(1), 1–10.

40. Hochbaum, G. M. (1958). *Public participation in medical screening programs: A sociopsychological study.* PHS publication no. 572. Washington, DC: Government Printing Office. Holder-Perkins & Wise.

41. Rosenstock, I. M. (1960). What research in motivation suggests for public health. *American Journal of Public Health, 50,* 295–301.

42. Kirscht, J. P. (1971). Social and psychological problems of surveys on health and illness. *Social Science and Medicine, 5*(6), 519–526.

43. Becker, M. H. (Ed.). (1974). The health belief model and personal health behavior. *Health Education Monographs, 2,* entire issue.

44. Skinner, B. F. (1938). *The behavior of organisms.* Englewood Cliffs, NJ: Appleton-Century-Crofts.

45. Rosenstock, I. M., Strecher, & Becker, M. H. (1988). The health belief model and HIV risk behavior change. In J. Peterson & R. DiClemente (Eds.), *Preventing AIDS: Theory and practice of behavior interventions* (pp. 5–24). New York: Plenum Press.

46. Fishbein, M., & Ajzen, I. (1975). *Belief, attitude, intention and behavior: An introduction to theory and research.* Boston: Addison-Wesley.

47. Ajzen, I. (1988). *Attitudes, personality, and behavior.* Homewood, IL: Dorsey Press.

48. Rogers, E. M. (1983). *Diffusion of innovations.* New York: Free Press.

49. Bandura, A. (1977). *Social learning theory.* Englewood Cliffs, NJ: Prentice Hall.

50. Prochaska, J. O., Wright, J. A., & Velicer, W. F. (2008). Evaluating theories of health behavior change: A hierarchy of criteria applied to the transtheoretical model. *Applied Psychology: An International Review, 57*(4), 561–588. doi: 10.1111/j.1464-0597.2008.00345.x

51. Prochaska, J. O., & Prochaska, J. M. (2010). Self-directed change: A transtheoretical model. In *Social psychological foundations of clinical psychology* (pp. 431–440). New York: Guilford Press.

52. Langer, G., Arnedt, C., & Sussman, D. (2004). A peek beneath the sheets. Retrieved from http://www.abcnews.go.com/Primetime/News

53. Gurung, R. A. R., Dunkel-Schetter, C., Collins, N., Rini, C., & Hobel. (2005). Psychosocial predictors of perceived prenatal stress. *Journal of Social and Clinical Psychology, 24,* 497–519

54. Hounton, S. H., Carabin, H., & Henderson, N. J. (2005). Towards an understanding of barriers to condom use in rural Benin using the Health Belief Model: A cross sectional survey. *BMC Public Health, 5,* 8.

55. Wayment H. A., Wyatt G. E., Tucker, M. B., Romero G. J., Carmona, J. V., Newcomb, M., et al. (2003). Predictors of risky and precautionary sexual behaviors among single and married white women. *Journal of Applied Social Psychology, 33,* 791–816.

56. Stone, J., Aronson, E., Crain, A. L., Winslow, M. P., & Fried, C. B. (1994). Inducing hypocrisy as a means of encouraging young adults to use condoms. *Personality and Social Psychology Bulletin, 20,* 116–128.

57. Prochaska, J. O., Redding, C. A., & Evers, K. E. (2002). The transtheoretical model and stages of change. In K. Glanz, B. K. Rimer, & F. M. Lewis (Eds.), *Health behavior and health education: Theory, research, and practice* (pp. 99–120). San Francisco: Jossey-Bass.

58. U. S. Department of Health and Human Services. (2000). Best practices for comprehensive tobacco control programs. Retrieved January 2012 from http://www.hsca.com/membersonly/USDHHSlink.htm

59. Snow, M. G., Prochaska, J. O., & Rossi, J. S. (1992). Stages of change for smoking cessation among former problem drinkers: A cross-sectional analysis. *Journal of Substance Abuse, 4*(2), 107–116.

60. Gibbons, F. X., & Gerrard, M. (1997). Health images and their effects on health behavior. In B. P. Buunk & F. X. Gibbons (Eds.), *Health, coping, and well-being: Perspectives from social comparison theory* (pp. 63–94). Mahwah, NJ: Erlbaum.

61. Dohnke, B., Steinhilber, A., & Fuchs, T. (2015). Adolescents' eating behaviour in general and in the peer context: Testing the prototype-willingness model. *Phychology & Health, 30*(4), 381–399. doi: 10.1080/08870446.2014.974604

62. Gibbons, F. X., Gerrard, M., & Lane, D. J. (2003). A social reaction model of adolescent health risk. In J. M. Suls & K. Wallston (Eds.), *Social psychological foundations of health and illness* (pp. 107–136). Oxford: Blackwell.

63. Gerrard, M., Gibbons, F., Houlihan, A., Stock, M., & Pomery, E. (2008). A dual-process approach to health risk decision making: The prototype willingness model. *Developmental Review, 28*(1), 29–61.

64. Hyde, M., & White, K. (2010). Are organ donation communication decisions reasoned or reactive? A test of the utility of an augmented theory of planned behaviour with the prototype/willingness model. *British Journal of Health Psychology, 15*(2), 435–452.

65. Rivis, A., Abraham, C., & Snook, S. (2011). Understanding young and older male drivers' willingness to drive while intoxicated: The predictive utility of constructs specified by the theory of planned behaviour and the prototype willingness model. *British Journal of Health Psychology, 16*(2), 445–456. doi: 10.1348/135910710X522662

66. Wagner, H. S., Ahlstrom, B., Redden, J. P., Vickers, Z., & Mann, T. (2014). The myth of comfort food. *Health Psychology, 33*(12), 1552–1557. doi: 10.1037/hea0000068

67. Olson, J. M., Roese, N. J., & Zanna, M. P. (1996). Expectancies. In E. T. Higgins, & A. W. Kruglanski (Eds.), *Social psychology: Handbook of basic principles* (pp. 211–239). New York: Guilford Press.

68. Stack, S. (2003). Media coverage as a risk factor in suicide. *Journal of Epidemiology and Community Health, 57*(4), 238–240.

69. Shavitt, S., Sanbonmatsu, D. M., Smittipatana, S., & Posavac, S. S. (1999). Broadening the conditions for illusory correlation formation: Implications for judging minority groups. *Basic and Applied Social Psychology, 21*(4), 263–279.

70. Fiske, S. T. (2004). *Social beings: A core motives approach to social psychology.* New York: Wiley.

71. Jones, E. E., Kannouse, D. E., Kelley, H. H., Nisbett, R. E., Valins, S., & Weiner, B. (Eds.). (1972). *Attribution: Perceiving the causes of behavior.* Morristown, NJ: General Learning Press.

72. Miller, S. M., & Diefenbach, M. A. (1998). The Cognitive-Social Health Information-Processing (C-SHIP) model: A theoretical framework for research in behavioral oncology. In D. S. Krantz, & A. Baum (Eds.), *Technology and methods in behavioral medicine* (pp. 219–244). Mahwah, NJ: Lawrence Erlbaum.

73. Gurung, R. A. R. (Ed.). (2014). *Multicultural approaches to health and wellness in America: Major issues and cultural groups.* Westport, CT: Praeger Publishers.

74. Padilla, A. M., & Ruiz, R. A. (1973). *Latino mental health: A review of literature.* Washington, DC: U.S. Government Printing Office.

75. Fadiman, A. (1997). *The spirit catches you and you fall down: A Hmong child, her American doctors, and the collusion of two cultures.* New York: Farrar, Straus and Giroux.

76. Schachter, S., & Singer, J. E., (1962). Cognitive, social, and physiological determinants of emotional state. *Psychological Review, 69,* 379–399.

77. Weber, K., Canuto, A., Giannakopoulos, P., Mouchian, A., Meiler-Mititelu, C., Meiler, A., & ... de Rivaupierre, A. (2015). Personality, psychosocial and health-related predictors of quality of life in old age. *Aging & Mental Health, 19*(2), 151–158. doi: 10.1080/13607863.2014.920295

78. Contrada, R. J., & Guyll, M. (2001). On who gets sick and why: The role of personality, stress, and disease. In A. Baum, T. A. Revenson, & J. E. Singer (Eds.), *Handbook of health psychology* (pp. 59–81). Hillsdale, NJ: Erlbaum.

79. Feldman, P. J., Cohen S., Gwaltney, J. M., Jr., Doyle, W. J., & Skoner, D. P. (1999). The impact of personality on the reporting of unfounded symptoms and illness. *Journal of Personality and Social Psychology, 77,* 370–378.

80. Leventhal, E. A., Hansell, S., Diefenbach, M., Leventhal, H., & Glass, D. C. (1996). Negative affect and self-report of physical symptoms: two longitudinal studies of older adults. *Health Psychology, 15,* 193–199.

81. Brown, K. W., & Moskowitz, D. S. (1997). Does unhappiness make you sick? The role of affect and neuroticism in the experience of common physical symptoms. *Journal of Personality and Social Psychology, 72*(4), 907–917.

82. Friedman, H. S., & Booth-Kewley, S. (1987). The "disease-prone personality": A meta-analytic view of the construct. *American Psychologist, 42,* 539–555.

83. Barsky, A. J. (1988). *Worried sick: Our troubled quest for wellness.* New York: Little Brown and Co.

84. Holder-Perkins, V., & Wise, T. N. (2001). Somatization disorder. In K. A. Phillips (Eds.), *Somatoform and factitious disorders* (pp. 1–26). Washington, DC: American Psychiatric Association.

MODULE C

Applying Social Psychology to the Workplace

1. Koughan, M. (1975, February 23). Arthur Friedman's outrage: Employees decide their pay. *Washington Post.*

2. Koughan, M. (1975, February 23). Arthur Friedman's outrage: Employees decide their pay. *Washington Post.*

3. Koughan, M. (1975, February 23). Arthur Friedman's outrage: Employees decide their pay. *Washington Post.*

4. The People History (2015). Money and inflation 1970s. Retrieved from http://www.thepeoplehistory.com/1970s.html

5. Koughan, M. (1975, February 23). Arthur Friedman's outrage: Employees decide their pay. *Washington Post.*

6. Ross, J. A. (2006, November). The reliability, validity, and utility of self-assessment. *Practical assessment, Research & Evaluation, 11*(10) [On-line]. Retrieved from http://pareonline.net/pdf/v11n10.pdf

7. Great Place to Work. (2015). Identifying best places to work: US and globally. Retrieved from http://www.greatplacetowork.com/best-companies

8. Fortune. (2015). Best companies 2014. Retrieved from http://fortune.com/best-companies/

9. Google. (2015). Life at Google. Retrieved from http://www.google.com/about/careers/lifeatgoogle/do-cool-things-that-matter.html

10. Google. (2012). Benefits. Retrieved from http://www.google.com/intl/en/jobs/lifeatgoogle/benefits/index.html

11. CBS News. (2011). Google job perks: Top 10 reasons we want to work there. Retrieved from http://www.cbsnews.com/news/google-job-perks-top-10-reasons-we-want-to-work-there/

12. Rucci, A. J. (2008). I-O psychology's "core purpose": Where science and practice meet. *The Industrial and Organizational Psychologist, 46*(1), 17–34.

13. Bureau of Labor Statistics (2015). American time use survey. Retrieved from http://www.bls.gov/tus/charts/

14. Swift, A. (2013, December 16). Honesty and ethics rating of clergy slides to new low. Gallup. Retrieved from http://www.gallup.com/poll/166298/honesty-ethics-rating-clergy-slides-new-low.aspx

15. Swift, A. (2013, December 16). Honesty and ethics rating of clergy slides to new low. Gallup. Retrieved from http://www.gallup.com/poll/166298/honesty-ethics-rating-clergy-slides-new-low.aspx

16. Jones, J. M. (2010). Nurses top honesty and ethics list for 11th year. Gallup Economy, December, 2010. Retrieved from http://www.gallup.com/poll/145043/nurses-top-honesty-ethics-list-11-year.aspx

17. Clark, R. E. (2003). Fostering the work motivation of individuals and teams. *Performance Improvement, 42*(3), 21–29.

18. Baard, P. P., Deci, E. L., & Ryan, R. M. (2004). Intrinsic need satisfaction: A motivational basis of performance and well-being in two work settings. *Journal of Applied Social Psychology, 34*(10), 2045–2068.

19. Peterson, N. G., Mumford, M. D., Borman, W. C., Jeanneret, P. R., & Fleishmann, E. A. (1999). *An occupational information system for the 21st century: The development of O*NET.* Washington, D.C.: American Psychological Association.

20. O*NET Resource Center. (2014). Production Database—O*NET 19.0. Retrieved from http://www.onetcenter.org/database.html

21. Aamodt, M. G. (2013). *Industrial/Organizational Psychology:* An Applied Approach. Belmont, CA: Wadsworth, Cengage Learning.

22. Gael, S. A. (1988). *The job analysis handbook for business, industry, and government* (Vols. 1 and 2). New York: Wiley.

23. Aamodt, M. G. (2013). *Industrial/Organizational Psychology: An Applied Approach.* Belmont, CA: Wadsworth, Cengage Learning.

24. Flanagan, J. C. (1954). The critical incident technique. *Psychological Bulletin, 51,* 327–358.

25. U.S. Equal Employment Opportunity Commission. (2012). Laws & guidance. Retrieved from http://www.eeoc.gov/laws/index.cfm

26. National Archives. (2012). Teaching with documents: The Civil Rights Act of 1964 and the Equal Employment Opportunity Commission. Retrieved from http://www.archives.gov/education/lessons/civil-rights-act/

27. Roy Rosenzweig Center for History and New Media. (2006, December). *An outline of the Anita Hill and Clarence Thomas controversy* [On-line]. Retrieved from http://chnm.gmu.edu/courses/122/hill/hillframe.htm

28. Roy Rosenzweig Center for History and New Media. (2006, December). *An outline of the Anita Hill and Clarence Thomas controversy* [On-line]. Retrieved from http://chnm.gmu.edu/courses/122/hill/hillframe.htm

29. Hanisch, K. A. (1996). An integrated framework for studying the outcomes of sexual harassment: Consequences for individuals and organizations. In M. S. Stockdale (Ed.), *Women and work: A research and policy series, volume 5: Sexual harassment in the workplace: Perspectives, frontiers, and response strategies* (pp. 174–199). Thousand Oaks, CA: Sage.

30. Knapp, D. E., & Kustis, G. A. (1996). The real "disclosure": Sexual harassment and the bottom line. In M. S. Stockdale (Ed.), *Women and work: A research and policy series, volume 5: Sexual harassment in the workplace: Perspectives, frontiers, and response strategies* (pp. 199–215). Thousand Oaks, CA: Sage.

31. Jablin, F. M. (1982). Organizational communication: An assimilation approach. In M. E. Rolff & C. R. Berger (Eds.), *Social cognition and communication* (pp. 255–286). Beverly Hills, CA: Sage.

32. Hanisch, K. A. (1995). Behavioral families and multiple causes: Matching the complexity of responses to the complexity of antecedents. *Current Directions in Psychological Science, 4*(5), 156–162.

33. Pogorzelski, S., & Harriott, J. (2007). Finding keepers: The Monster guide to hiring and holding the world's best employees. McGraw Hill: New York.

34. Sullivan, J. (2012). 10 compelling numbers that reveal the power of employee referrals. Retrieved from http://www.ere.net/2012/05/07/10-compelling-numbers-that-reveal-the-power-of-employee-referrals/

35. Sullivan, J. (2012). 10 compelling numbers that reveal the power of employee referrals. Retrieved from http://www.ere.net/2012/05/07/10-compelling-numbers-that-reveal-the-power-of-employee-referrals/

36. Zottoli, M. A., & Wanous, J. P. (2000). Recruitment source research: Current status and future directions. *Human Resource Management Review, 10,* 435–451.

37. McManus, M. A., & Baratta, J. E. (1992). *The relationship of recruiting source to performance and survival.* Paper presented at the annual meeting of the Society for Industrial and Organizational Psychology, Montreal, Canada.

38. Rupert, G. (1989). Employee referrals as a source of recruitment and job performance. *Proceedings of the 10th Annual Graduate Conference in Industrial/Organizational Psychology and Organizational Behavior.*

39. Aamodt, M. G., & Carr, K. (1988). Relationship between recruitment source and employee behavior. *Proceedings of the 12th Annual Meeting of the International Personnel Management Association Assessment Council,* 143–146.

40. Earnest, D. R., Allen, D. G., & Landis, R. S. (2011). Mechanisms linking realistic job previews with turnover: A meta-analytic path analysis. *Personnel Psychology, 64*(4), 865–897.

41. Raphael, T. (2010, June 22). Employee referral programs using more social media. Retrieved from http://www.ere.net/2010/06/22/employee-referral-programs-using-more-social-media/

42. Hargis, M. (2008). *Social networking sites dos and donts.* Retrieved from http://edition.cnn.com/2008/LIVING/worklife/11/05/cb.social.networking/index.html

43. Undercover Recruiter. (2015). How employers use social media to screen applicants. Retrieved from http://theundercoverrecruiter.com/infographic-how-recruiters-use-social-media-screen-applicants/

44. Cross-tab. (2010, January). Online reputation in a connected world. Retrieved from http://www.job-hunt.org/guides/DPD_Online-Reputation-Research_overview.pdf

45. Cross-tab. (2010, January). Online reputation in a connected world. Retrieved from http://www.job-hunt.org/guides/DPD_Online-Reputation-Research_overview.pdf

46. Cross-tab. (2010, January). Online reputation in a connected world. Retrieved from http://www.job-hunt.org/guides/DPD_Online-Reputation-Research_overview.pdf

47. Haefner, R. (2009, June 10). More employers screening candidates via social networking sites. Retrieved from http://www.careerbuilder.com/Article/CB-1337-Interview-Tips-More-Employers-Screening-Candidates-via-Social-Networking-Sites/

48. Finder, A. (2006, June 11). For some, online persona undermines a resume. *The New York Times.*

49. Cross-tab. (2010, January). Online reputation in a connected world. Retrieved from http://www.job-hunt.org/guides/DPD_Online-Reputation-Research_overview.pdf

50. Hargis, M. (2008). *Social networking sites dos and donts.* Retrieved from http://edition.cnn.com/2008/LIVING/worklife/11/05/cb.social.networking/index.html

51. The Believeau Law Group. (2012). Can companies use social media to screen job applicants? Retrieved from http://www.beliveaulaw.net/2012/02/can-companies-use-social-media-to-screen-job-applicants/

52. Waring, R. L., & Buchanan, F. R. (2010). Social networking web sites: The legal and ethical aspects of pre-employment screening and employee surveillance. *Journal of Human Resources Education, 4*(2), 14–23.

53. Salgado, J. F., Viswesvaran, C., & Ones, D. (2001). Predictors used for personnel selection: An overview of constructs, methods and techniques. In N. Anderson, D. S. Ones, H. K. Sinangil, & C. Viswesvaran, *Handbook of industrial, work and organizational psychology* (Vol. 1, pp. 166–199). Thousand Oaks, CA: Sage.

54. West Virginia Division of Personnel. (2004, September). Selection interviewing: Developing and administering structured behavioral interviews.

Retrieved from http://webcache.googleusercontent.com/search?q=cache:khtpGpmt7vwJ:www.state.wv.us/admin/personnel/emprel/toolbox/quiz/interviewing.pdf+&cd=1&hl=en&ct=clnk&gl=us

55. Arvey, R. D., & Campion, J. E. (1982). The employment interview: A summary and review of recent research. *Personnel Psychology, 35,* 281–322.

56. McDaniel, M. A., Whetzel, D. L., Schmidt, F. L., & Maurer, S. D. (1994). The validity of employment interviews: A comprehensive review and meta-analysis. *Journal of Applied Psychology, 79,* 599–616.

57. Huffcutt, A. I., & Arthur, W., Jr. (1994). Hunter and Hunter (1984) revisited: Interview validity for entry-level jobs. *Journal of Applied Psychology, 79,* 184–190.

58. Huffcutt, A. I., & Arthur, W., Jr. (1994). Hunter and Hunter (1984) revisited: Interview validity for entry-level jobs. *Journal of Applied Psychology, 79,* 184–190.

59. Schmidt, F. L., & Hunter, J. E. (1998). The validity and utility of selection methods in personnel psychology: Practical and theoretical implications of 85 years of research findings. *Psychological Bulletin, 124*(2), 262–274.

60. Hardison, C. M., Kim, D., & Sackett, P. R. (2005, April). *Meta-analysis of work sample criterion related validity: Revisiting anomalous findings.* Paper presented at the 20th annual conference of the Society for Industrial-Organizational Psychology, Los Angeles.

61. Ones, D. S., Viswesvaran, C., & Schmidt, F. L. (1993). Comprehensive meta-analysis of integrity test validities: Findings for personnel selection and theories of job performance. *Journal of Applied Psychology, 78*(4), 679–703.

62. Roth, P. L., BeVier, C. A., Switzer, F. S., & Schippmann, J. S. (1996). Meta-analyzing the relationship between grades and job performance. *Journal of Applied Psychology, 81*(5), 548–556.

63. Quinones, M. A., Ford, J. K., & Teachout, M. S. (1995). The relationship between work experience and job performance: A conceptual and meta-analytic review. *Personnel Psychology, 48*(4), 887–910.

64. Tett, R. P., Jackson, D. N., Rothstein, M., & Reddon, J. R. (1994). Meta-analysis of personality-job performance relations: A reply to Ones, Mount, Barrick, & Hunter (1994). *Personnel Psychology, 47*(1), 157–172.

65. Hunter, J. E., & Hunter, R. E. (1984). Validity and utility of alternative predictors of job performance. *Psychological Bulletin, 96*(1), 72–98.

66. Schmitt, N., Cortina, J. M., Ingerick, M. J., & Wiechmann, D. (2003). Personnel selection and employee performance. In W. C. Borman, D. R. Ilgen, & R. J. Klimoski (Eds.), *Handbook of psychology: Industrial and organizational psychology* (Vol. 12, pp. 77–105). New York: Wiley.

67. Jablin, F. M. (1982). Organizational communication: An assimilation approach. In M. E. Rolff & C. R. Berger (Eds.), *Social cognition and communication* (pp. 255–286). Beverly Hills, CA: Sage.

68. Crowley, M.C. (2015). How SAS became the world's best place to work. Fast Company. Retrieved from http://www.sas.com/en_us/careers/life-at-sas.html

69. SAS. (2015). Life at SAS. Retrieved from http://www.fastcompany.com/3004953/how-sas-became-worlds-best-place-work

70. Stewart, J.B. (2013, March 15). Looking for a lesson in Google's perks. Retrieved from http://www.nytimes.com/2013/03/16/business/at-google-a-place-to-work-and-play.html?pagewanted=all&_r=0

71. Sullivan, M. (2013, June 28). More proof office space design impacts productivity, focus and collaboration. Retrieved from http://www.officingtoday.com/2013/06/more-proof-office-space-design-impacts-productivity-focus-and-collaboration/

72. Gensler. (2013). 2013 U.S. workplace survey: Key findings. Retrieved from http://www.gensler.com/uploads/documents/2013_US_Workplace_Survey_07_15_2013.pdf

73. Gensler. (2013). 2013 U.S. workplace survey: Key findings. Retrieved from http://www.gensler.com/uploads/documents/2013_US_Workplace_Survey_07_15_2013.pdf

74. Van Horne, T. (2013, December 5). Workplace design impacts performance, employee engagement and innovation. Retrieved from http://www.canadaone.com/ezine/2013/workplace_design_impacts_performance.html

75. Sullivan, M. (2013, June 28). More proof office space design impacts productivity, focus and collaboration. Retrieved from http://www.officingtoday.com/2013/06/more-proof-office-space-design-impacts-productivity-focus-and-collaboration/

76. Lesiuk, T. (2005). The effect of music listening on work performance. *Psychology of Music, 33(2)*, 173-191.

77. Ciotti, G. (2015). How music affects your productivity. Sparring Mind. Retrieved from http://www.sparringmind.com/music-productivity/

78. Flanagin, A, J., & Waldeck, J. H. (2004). Technology use and organizational newcomer socialization. *Journal of Business Communication, 41(2)*, 137–165.

79. Allen, T. D., Lentz, E., & Day, R. (2006). Career success outcomes associated with mentoring others: A comparison of mentors and nonmentors. *Journal of Career Development, 32(3)*, 272–285.

80. Greenhaus, J. H. (2003). Career dynamics. In W. C. Borman, D. R. Ilgen, & R. J. Klimoski (Eds.), *Handbook of psychology: Industrial and organizational psychology* (Vol. 12, pp. 519–540). New York: Wiley.

81. Ragins, B. R., & Cotton, J. L. (1999). Mentor functions and outcomes: A comparison of men and women in formal and informal mentoring relationships. *Journal of Applied Psychology, 84(4)*, 529–550.

82. Denison, D. R. (1996). What is the difference between organizational culture and organizational climate? A native's point of view on a decade of paradigm wars. *The Academy of Management Review, 21(3)*, 619–654.

83. Denison, D. R. (1996). What is the difference between organizational culture and organizational climate? A native's point of view on a decade of paradigm wars. *The Academy of Management Review, 21(3)*, 619–654.

84. Ostroff, C., Kinicki, A. J., & Tamkins, M. M. (2003). Organizational culture and climate. In W. C. Borman, D. R. Ilgen, & R. J. Klimoski (Eds.), *Handbook of psychology: Industrial and organizational psychology* (Vol. 12, pp. 565–593). New York: Wiley.

85. SAS. (2015). Life at SAS. Retrieved from http://www.fastcompany.com/3004953/how-sas-became-worlds-best-place-work

86. Illuminant. (2011, January 17). Avoiding insult and injury when using color in China. Retrieved from http://www.illuminantpartners.com/2011/01/17/color/

87. Hare, A. P. (1962). *Handbook of small group research.* New York: The Free Press of Glencoe.

88. McGrath, J. E. (1966). *Small group research.* New York: Holt, Rinehart, & Winston.

89. Hill, G. W. (1982). Group versus individual performance: Are N + 1 heads better than one? *Psychological Bulletin, 91(3)*, 517–539.

90. Paulus, P. B. (2000). Groups, teams, and creativity: The creative potential of idea-generating groups. *Applied Psychology: An International Review, 49(2)*, 237–262.

91. Likert, R. (1967). *The human organization: Its management and value.* New York: McGraw-Hill.

92. Sagie, A. (1997). Leader direction and employee participation in decision making: Contradictory or compatible practices? *Applied Psychology: An International Review, 46(4)*, 387–452.

93. Lawler, E. E., Mohrman, S. A., & Ledford, G. E. (1995). *Creating high performance organizations: Practices and results of employee involvement and total quality management in Fortune 1000 companies.* San Francisco: Jossey-Bass.

94. Kozlowski, S. W., & Bell, B. S. (2003). Work groups and teams in organizations. In W. C. Borman, D. R. Ilgen, & R. J. Klimoski (Eds.), *Handbook of psychology: industrial and organizational psychology* (Vol. 12, pp. 333–375). New York: Wiley.

95. Aamodt, M. G. (2013). *Industrial/organizational psychology: An applied approach.* Belmont, CA: Wadsworth, Cengage Learning.

96. Mullen, B., Anthony, T., Salas, E., & Driskell, J. E. (1994). Group cohesiveness and quality of decision making: An integration of the groupthink hypothesis. *Small Group Research, 25(2)*, 189–204.

97. Beal, D. J., Cohen, R. R., Burke, M. J., & McLendon, C. L. (2003). Cohesion and performance in groups: A meta-analytic clarification of construct relations. *Journal of Applied Psychology, 88(6)*, 989–1004.

98. Brawley, L. R., Carron, A. V., & Widmeyer, W. N. (1993). The influence of the group and its cohesiveness on perceptions of group goal-related variables. *Journal of Sport and Exercise Psychology, 15(3)*, 245–260.

99. Aamodt, M. G. (2013). *Industrial/organizational psychology: An applied approach.* Belmont, CA: Wadsworth, Cengage Learning.

100. Forsyth, D. R. (2010). *Group dynamics* (5th ed.). Belmont, CA: Wadsworth.

101. Aamodt, M. G., Kimbrough, W. W., and Alexander, C. J. (1983). A preliminary investigation of the relationship between team racial heterogeneity and team performance in college basketball. *Journal of Sports Sciences, 1*, 131–133.

102. Mascio, C., Rainey, R., & Zinda, M. (2008, March). *Effect of group composition on group performance: Are slightly heterogeneous groups the answer to the homogeneity vs. heterogeneity puzzle?* Poster presentation at the annual Graduate Student Conference in Industrial-Organizational Psychology and Organizational Behavior (IOOB), Denver, CO.

103. Mello, J. A. (1993). Improving individual member accountability in small group settings. *Journal of Management Education, 17(2)*, 253–259.

104. Barfield, R. L. (2003). Students' perceptions of and satisfaction with group grades and the group experience in the college classroom. *Assessment and Evaluation in Higher Education, 28(4)*, 355–369.

105. Anderson, N., & Thomas, H. D. C. (1996). Work group socialization. In M. A. West (Ed.), *Handbook of work group psychology* (pp. 423–450). Chichester, UK: Wiley.

106. Manz, C. C. (1992). Self-leading work teams: Moving beyond self-management myths. *Human Relations, 45*, 1119–1140.

107. Cohen, S. G., & Ledford, G. E., Jr. (1994). The effectiveness of self-managing teams: A quasi-experiment. *Human Relations, 47*, 13–43.

108. Stewart, G. L., & Manz, C. C. (1995). Leadership for self-managing work teams: A typology and integrative model. *Human Relations, 48*, 347–370.

109. Kozlowski, S. W., & Bell, B. S. (2003). Work groups and teams in organizations. In W. C. Borman, D. R. Ilgen, & R. J. Klimoski (Eds.), *Handbook of psychology: Industrial and organizational psychology* (Vol. 12, pp. 333–375). New York: Wiley.

110. Kozlowski, S. W., Gully, S. M., McHugh, P. P., Salas, E., & Cannon-Bowers, J. A. (1996). A dynamic theory of leadership and team effectiveness: Developmental and task contingent leader roles. In G. R. Ferris (Ed.), *Research in personnel and human resource management* (Vol. 14, pp. 253–305). Greenwich, CT: JAI Press.

111. Katz, D., & Kahn, R. L. (1978). *The social psychology of organizations* (2nd ed.). New York: Wiley.

112. Bryman, A. S. (1996). The importance of context: Qualitative research and the study of leadership. *Leadership Quarterly, 7*, 353–370.

113. Kirkpatrick, S. A., & Locke, E. A. (1991). Leadership: Do traits matter? *Academy of Management Executive, 5*, 48–60.

114. Kaplan, R. E., Drath, W. H., & Kofodimos, J. R. (1991). *Beyond ambition: How driven managers can lead better and live better.* San Francisco: Jossey-Bass.

115. Northouse, P. G. (2004). *Leadership: Theory and practice.* Thousand Oaks, CA: Sage Publications.

116. Aamodt, M. G. (2013). *Industrial/organizational psychology: An applied approach.* Belmont, CA: Wadsworth, Cengage Learning.

117. Bass, B. M. (1990). From transactional to transformational leadership: Learning to share the vision. *Organizational Dynamics, 18(3)*, 19–31.

118. SAS. (2015). Life at SAS. Retrieved from http://www.fastcompany.com/3004953/how-sas-became-worlds-best-place-work

119. SAS. (2015). Jim Goodnight, Chief Executive Officer, SAS. Retrieved from http://www.sas.com/en_us/company-information/executive-bios/jim-goodnight.html

120. SAS. (2015). Life at SAS. Retrieved from http://www.fastcompany.com/3004953/how-sas-became-worlds-best-place-work

121. SAS. (2015). Life at SAS. Retrieved from http://www.fastcompany.com/3004953/how-sas-became-worlds-best-place-work

122. Avolio, B. J., Kahai, S. S., & Dodge, G. (2000). E-leading in organizations and it implications for theory, research and practice. *Leadership Quarterly, 11*, 615–670.

123. Lombardo, M. M., & Eichinger, R. W. (2000). High potentials as high learners. *Human Resource Management, 39(4)*, 321–329.

124. Lombardo, M. M., & Eichinger, R. W. (2000). High potentials as high learners. *Human Resource Management, 39(4)*, 321–329.

125. Ryan, J. R. (2009, February 27). Learning agility equals leadership success, *Bloomberg Businessweek*. Retrieved from http://www.businessweek.com/managing/content/feb2009/ca20090227_893956.htm

126. Fletcher, C., & Perry, E. L. (2001). Performance appraisal and feedback: A consideration of national culture and a review of contemporary research and future trends. In N. Anderson, D. S. Ones, H. K. Sinangil, & C. Viswesvaran, *Handbook of industrial, work and organizational psychology* (Vol. 1, pp. 127–144). Thousand Oaks, CA: Sage.

127. Aamodt, M. G. (2013). *Industrial/organizational psychology: An applied approach.* Belmont, CA: Wadsworth, Cengage Learning.

128. Sullivan, J. (2009, February 9). Employee furloughs can be a bad alternative to layoffs. Ere.net. Retrieved from http://www.ere.net/tags/furloughs

129. Tarquinio, M. (2009, January 27). Workforce planning research: How to strengthen your job in today's economy. Ere.net. Retrieved from http://www.ere.net/2009/01/27/workforce-planning-research-how-to-strengthen-your-job-in-today%e2%80%99s-economy

130. Hanisch, K. A. (1995). Behavioral families and multiple causes: Matching the complexity of responses to the complexity of antecedents. *Current Directions in Psychological Science, 4(5)*, 156–162.

131. Hackman, J. R., & Oldham, G. R. (1976). Motivation through the design of work: A test of a theory. *Organizational Behavior and Human Performance, 16(2)*, 250–279.

132. Cranny, C. J., Smith, P. C., & Stone, E. F. (1992). *Job satisfaction: How people feel about their jobs and how it affects their performance.* New York: Lexington Books.

133. Sullivan, M. (2013, June 28). More proof office space design impacts productivity, focus and collaboration. Retrieved from http://www.officingtoday.com/2013/06/more-proof-office-space-design-impacts-productivity-focus-and-collaboration

134. Adams, J. S. (1965). Inequity in social change. In L. Berkowitz (Ed.), *Advances in experimental social psychology* (Vol. 2, pp. 267–299). New York: Academic Press.

135. Meyer, J. P., & Allen, N. J. (1991). A three-component conceptualization of organizational commitment. *Human Resource Management Review, 1*, 61–89.

136. Meyer, J. P. & Herscovitch, L. (2001). Commitment in the workplace: Toward a general model. *Human Resource Management Review, 11*, 299–326.

137. Mueller, C. W., Boyer, E. M., Price, J. L. & Iverson, R. D. (1994). Employee attachment and non-coercive conditions of work: The case of dental hygienists. *Work and Occupations, 21*, 179–212.

138. Arthur, J. B. (1994). Effects of human resource systems on manufacturing performance and turnover. *Academy of Management Journal, 37,* 670–687.

139. Roskies, E., & Louis-Guerin, C. (1990). Job insecurity in managers: Antecedents and consequences. *Journal of Organizational Behavior, 11,* 345–359.

140. Meyer, J. P., Allen, N. J., & Smith, C. A. (1993). Commitments to organizations and occupations: Extension and test of a three component conceptualization. *Journal of Applied Psychology, 78,* 538–551.

141. Ellemers, N., de Gilder, D., & van den Heuvel, H. (1998). Career-oriented vs. team-oriented commitment and behavior at work. *Journal of Applied Psychology, 83,* 717–730.

142. Cooper-Hakim, A., & Viswesvaran, C. (2005). The construct of work commitment: Testing an integrative framework. *Journal of Applied Psychology, 131,* 241–259.

143. Greenberg J. (1990). Organizational justice: Yesterday, today and tomorrow. *Journal of Management 16,* 399–432.

144. Rupp, D. E., & Cropanzano, R. (2002). The mediating effects of social exchange relationships in predicting workplace outcomes from multifoci organizational justice. *Organizational Behavior and Human Decision Processes, 89,* 925–946.

145. Robbins, J. M., Ford, M.T., & Tetrick, L.E. (2012). Perceived unfairness and employee health: A meta-analytic integration. *Journal of Applied Psychology, 97(2),* 235–272.

146. Lam, S. S. K., Schaubroeck, J., & Aryee, S. (2002). Relationship between organizational justice and employee work outcomes: A cross-national study. *Journal of Organizational Behavior, 23,* 1–18.

147. Lam, S. S. K., Schaubroeck, J., & Aryee, S. (2002). Relationship between organizational justice and employee work outcomes: A cross-national study. *Journal of Organizational Behavior, 23,* 1–18.

148. Mills, H., Reiss, N., & Dombeck, M. (2008, Jun 30). Types of stressors (eustress vs. distress). Retrieved from http://www.mentalhelp.net/poc/view_doc.php?type=doc&id=15644

149. Sonnentag, S., & Frese, M. (2003). Stress in organizations. In W. C. Borman, D. R. Ilgen, & R. J. Klimoski (Eds.), *Handbook of psychology* (Vol. 12, pp. 453–491). Hoboken, NJ: John Wiley & Sons.

150. Robbins, J. M., Ford, M. T., & Tetrick, L. E. (2012). Perceived unfairness and employee health: A meta-analytic integration. *Journal of Applied Psychology, 97(2),* 235–272.

151. Chandola, T., Brunner, E., & Marmot, M. (2006). Chronic stress at work and the metabolic syndrome: Prospective study. *British Medical Journal.* [On-line]. Retrieved from http://www.bmj.com/content/early/2005/12/31/bmj.38693.435301.80

152. The American College Health Association. (2008). American College Health Association—National college health assessment spring 2007 reference group data report (abridged). *Journal of American College Health, 56(5),*469-479. Retrieved from http://www.acha-ncha.org/docs/JACH%20March%20 2008%20SP%2007%20Ref%20Grp.pdf

153. American Psychological Association (2015). How stress affects your health. Retrieved from http://www.apa.org/helpcenter/stress.aspx

154. Holmes, L. (2014, September 17). 5 ways stress wrecks your sleep (and what to do about it). Retrieved from http://www.huffingtonpost.com/2014/09/17/stress-and-sleep_n_5824506.html

155. WebMD (2015). Stress symptoms. Retrieved from http://www.webmd.com/balance/stress-management/stress-symptoms-effects_of-stress-on-the-body?page=2http://www.webmd.com/balance/stress-management/stress-symptoms-effects_of-stress-on-the-body?page=2

156. Aamodt, M. G. (2013). *Industrial/organizational psychology: An applied approach.* Belmont, CA: Wadsworth, Cengage Learning.

157. O'Connor, D. B., Jones, F., Conner, M., McMillan, B., & Ferguson, E. (2008). Effects of daily hassles and eating style on eating behavior. *Health Psychology, 27*(1), S20–S31.

158. O'Connor, D. B., Jones, F., Conner, M., McMillan, B., & Ferguson, E. (2008). Effects of daily hassles and eating style on eating behavior. *Health Psychology, 27*(1), S20–S31.

159. O'Connor, D. B., Jones, F., Conner, M., McMillan, B., & Ferguson, E. (2008). Effects of daily hassles and eating style on eating behavior. *Health Psychology, 27*(1), S20–S31.

160. Edelman, C., & Mandle, C. (2006). *Health promotion throughout the lifespan* (6th ed.). St. Louis: Mosby.

161. Eby, L. T., Casper, W. J., Lockwood, A., Bordeaux, C., & Brinley, A. (2005). Work and family research in IO/OB: Content analysis and review of the literature (1980–2002). *Journal of Vocational Behavior, 66,* 124–197.

162. Glasdoor. (2015). Maternity & paternity leave. Retrieved from http://www.glassdoor.com/Benefits/Google-Maternity-and-Paternity-Leave-US-BNFT23_E9079_N1.htm

163. Breaugh, J. A., & Frye, N. K. (2008). Work-family conflict: The importance of family-friendly employment practices and family-supportive supervisors. *Journal of Business Psychology, 22,* 345–353.

164. American Psychological Association (2015). Five tips to help manage stress. Retrieved from http://www.apa.org/helpcenter/manage-stress.aspx

165. Atkinson, T., Liem, R., & Liem, J. H. (1986). The social costs of unemployment: Implications for social support. *Journal of Health and Social Behavior, 27,* 317–331.

166. American Psychological Association (2015). Five tips to help manage stress. Retrieved from http://www.apa.org/helpcenter/manage-stress.aspx

167. Naylor, J. C., Pritchard, R. D., & Ilgen, D. R. (1980). *A theory of behavior in organizations.* New York: Academic Press.

168. Smith, C. A., Organ, D. W., & Near, J. P. (1983). Organizational citizenship behavior: Its nature and antecedents. *Journal of Applied Psychology, 68,* 653–663.

169. Witt, L. A., Kacmar, M., Carlson, D. S., & Zivnuska, S. (2002). Interactive effects of personality and organizational politics on contextual performance. *Journal of Organizational Behavior, 23,* 911–926.

170. Borman, W. C., Penner, L. A., Allen, T.D., & Motowidlo, S. J. (2001). Personality predictors of citizenship performance. *International Journal of Selection and Assessment, 9,* 52–69.

171. Heilman, M. E., & Chen, J. J. (2005). Same behavior, different consequences: Reactions to men's and women's altruistic citizenship behaviors. *Journal of Applied Psychology, 90,* 431–441.

172. Kidder, D. L., & Parks, J. M. (2001). The good soldier: Who is s(he)? *Journal of Organizational Behavior, 22,* 939–959.

173. Hanisch, K. A., Hulin, C. L., & Roznowski, M. A. (1998). The importance of individuals' repertoires of behaviors: The scientific appropriateness of studying multiple behaviors and general attitudes. *Journal of Organizational Behavior, 19,* 463–480.

174. Sackett, P. R., & DeVore, C. J. (2001). Counterproductive behaviors at work. In N. Anderson, D. S. Ones, H. K. Sinangil, & C. Viswesvaran, *Handbook of industrial, work and organizational psychology* (Vol. 1, pp. 145–165). Thousand Oaks, CA: Sage.

175. Hanisch, K. A., & Hulin, C. L. (1990). Job attitudes and organizational withdrawal: An examination of retirement and other voluntary withdrawal behaviors. *Journal of Vocational Behavior, 37*(1), 60–78.

176. Hanisch, K. A., & Hulin, C. L. (1991). General attitudes and organizational withdrawal: An evaluation of a causal model. *Journal of Vocational Behavior, 39,* 110–128.

177. Hanisch, K. A. (1995). Behavioral families and multiple causes: Matching the complexity of responses to the complexity of antecedents. *Current Directions in Psychological Science, 4*(5), 156–162.

178. Hanisch, K. A., & Hulin, C. L. (1990). Job attitudes and organizational withdrawal: An examination of retirement and other voluntary withdrawal behaviors. *Journal of Vocational Behavior, 37*(1), 60–78.

179. Sackett, P. R., & DeVore, C. J. (2001). Counterproductive behaviors at work. In N. Anderson, D. S. Ones, H. K. Sinangil, & C. Viswesvaran, *Handbook of industrial, work and organizational psychology* (Vol. 1, pp. 145–165). Thousand Oaks, CA: Sage.

180. LePine, J. A., Erez, A., & Johnston, D. E. (2002). The nature and dimensionality of organizational citizenship behavior: A critical review and a meta-analysis. *Journal of Applied Psychology, 87*(1), 52–65.

181. Dalal, R. S. (2006). A meta-analysis of the relationship between organizational citizenship behavior and counterproductive work behavior. *Journal of Applied Psychology, 90*(6), 1241–1255.

182. Hackett, R. D. (1989). Work attitudes and employee absenteeism: A synthesis of the literature. *Journal of Occupational Psychology, 62*(3), 235–248.

183. Hanisch, K. A., & Hulin, C. L. (1990). Job attitudes and organizational withdrawal: An examination of retirement and other voluntary withdrawal behaviors. *Journal of Vocational Behavior, 37*(1), 60–78.

184. Lennings, C. J. (1997). Police and occupationally related violence: A review. *Policing: An International Journal of Police Strategies and Management, 20*(3), 555–566.

185. Hanisch, K. A. (1999). Job loss and unemployment research from 1994–1998: A review and recommendations for research and intervention. *Journal of Vocational Behavior, 55*(2), 188–220.

186. Wanberg, C. R., Kammeyer-Mueller, J. D., & Shi, K. (2001). Job loss and the experience of unemployment: International research and perspectives. In N. Anderson, D. S. Ones, H. K. Sinangil, & C. Viswesvaran (Eds.), *Handbook of industrial, work and organizational psychology* (Vol. 2, pp. 253–269). Thousand Oaks, CA: Sage.

187. Smith, F. J. (1977). Work attitudes as a predictor of attendance on a specific day. *Journal of Applied Psychology, 62*(1), 16–19.

188. Schein, E. H. (1990). Organizational culture. *American Psychologist, 45*(2), 109–119.

MODULE D
Applying Social Psychology to Law

1. Cutler, B. L., & Kovera, M. B. (2010). *Evaluating eyewitness identification.* New York: Oxford University Press.

2. Wells, G. L. (1984). The psychology of lineup identifications. *Journal of Applied Social Psychology, 14,* 89–103.

3. Wells, G. L., & Olson, E. A. (2003). Eyewitness testimony. *Annual Review of Psychology, 54,* 277–295.

4. Shapiro, P. N., & Penrod, S. D. (1986). Metaanalysis of facial identification studies. *Psychological Bulletin, 100,* 139–156.

5. Pozzulo, J. D., & Lindsay, R. C. L. (1998). Identification accuracy of children versus adults: A meta-analysis. *Law and Human Behavior, 22,* 549–570.

6. Pozzulo, J. D., & Warren, K. L. (2003). Descriptions and identifications of strangers by youth and adult eyewitness. *Journal of Applied Psychology, 88,* 315–323.

7. Keast, A., Brewer, N., & Wells, G. L. (2007). Children's metacognitive judgments in an eyewitness identification task. *Journal of Experimental Child Psychology, 9,* 286–314.

8. Brewer, N., Keast, A., & Sauer, J. D. (2010). Children's eyewitness identification performance: Effects of a Not Sure response option and accuracy motivation. *Legal and Criminological Psychology, 15,* 261–277.

9. Meissner, C. A., & Brigham, J. C. (2001). Thirty years of investigating the own-race bias in memory for faces: A meta-analytic review. *Psychology, Public Policy, and Law, 7*, 3–35.

10. Behrman, B. W., & Davey, S. L. (2001). Eyewitness identification in actual criminal cases: An archival analysis. *Law and Human Behavior, 25*, 475–491.

11. Marcon, J. L., Susa, K. J., & Meissner, C. A. (2009). Assessing the influence of recollection and familiarity in memory for own- versus other-race faces. *Psychonomic Bulletin & Review, 16*, 99–103.

12. Susa, K. J., Meissner, C. A., & deHeer, H. (2010). Modeling the role of social-cognitive processes in the recognition of own- and other-race faces. *Social Cognition, 28*, 523–537.

13. Van Bavel, J. J., & Cunningham, W. A. (2012). A social identity approach to person memory: Group membership, collective identification, and social role shape attention and memory. *Personality and Social Psychology Bulletin, 38*, 1566–1578.

14. Light, L. L., Kayra-Stuart, F., & Hollander, S. (1979). Recognition memory for typical and unusual faces. *Journal of Experimental Psychology: Human Learning and Memory, 5*, 212–228.

15. Memon, A., Hope, L., & Bull, R. (2003). Exposure duration: Effects on eyewitness accuracy and confidence. *British Journal of Psychology, 94*, 339–354.

16. Deffenbacher, K. A., Bornstein, B. H., McGorty, E. K., & Penrod, S. D. (2008). Forgetting the once-seen face: Estimating the strength of an eyewitness's memory representation. *Journal of Experimental Psychology: Applied, 14*, 139–150.

17. Cutler, B. L., Penrod, S. D., & Martens, T. K. (1987). The reliability of eyewitness identification: The role of system and estimator variables. *Law and Human Behavior, 11*, 233–258.

18. Hockley, W. E., Hemsworth, D. H., & Consoli, A. (1999). Shades of the mirror effect: Recognition of faces with and without sunglasses. *Memory and Cognition, 27*, 128–138.

19. Mansour, J. K., Beaudry, J. L., Bertrand, M. I., Kalmet, N., Melsom, E. I., & Lindsay, R. C. L. (2012). Impact of disguise on identification decisions and confidence with simultaneous and sequential lineups. *Law and Human Behavior, 36*, 513–526.

20. Deffenbacher, K. A. (1994). Effects of arousal on everyday memory. *Human Performance, 7*, 141–161.

21. Safer, M. A., Christianson, S.-A., Autry, M. W., & Osterlund, K. (1998). Tunnel memory for traumatic events. *Applied Cognitive Psychology, 12*, 99–117.

22. Deffenbacher, K. A., Bornstein, B. H., Penrod, S. D., & McGorty, E. K. (2004). A meta-analytic review of the effects of high stress on eyewitness memory. *Law and Human Behavior, 28*, 687–706.

23. Morgan, C. A., III, Hazlett, G., Doran, A., Garrett, S., Hoyt, G., Thomas, P., Baranoski, M., & Southwick, S. M. (2004). Accuracy of eyewitness memory for persons encountered during exposure to highly intense stress. *International Journal of Law and Psychiatry, 27*, 265–279.

24. Valentine, T., & Mesout, J. (2009). Eyewitness identification under stress in the London Dungeon. *Applied Cognitive Psychology, 23*, 151–161.

25. Steblay, N. M. (1992). A meta-analytic review of the weapon focus effect. *Law & Human Behavior, 16*(4), 413–424.

26. Loftus, E. F., Loftus, G. R., & Messo, J. (1987). Some facts about "weapon focus." *Law and Human Behavior, 11*, 55–62.

27. Pickel, K. L. (1999). The influence of context on the "weapon focus" effect. *Law and Human Behavior, 23*, 299–311.

28. Pickel, K. L. (1998). Unusualness and threat as possible causes of "weapon focus." *Memory, 6*, 277–295.

29. Hope, L., & Wright, D. (2007). Beyond unusual? Examining the role of attention in the weapon focus effect. *Applied Cognitive Psychology, 21*, 951–961.

30. Davies, G. M., Smith, S., & Blincoe, C. (2008). A "weapon focus" effect in children. *Psychology, Crime, & Law, 14*, 19–28.

31. Neil v. Biggers, 409 U. S. 188 (1972).

32. Cutler, B. L., Penrod, S. D., & Martens, T. K. (1987). The reliability of eyewitness identification: The role of system and estimator variables. *Law and Human Behavior, 11*, 233–258.

33. Bothwell, R. K., Deffenbacher, K. A., & Brigham, J. C. (1987). Correlations of eyewitness accuracy and confidence: Optimality hypothesis revisited. *Journal of Applied Psychology, 72*, 691–695.

34. Sporer, S. L., Penrod, S. D., Read, J. D., & Cutler, B. L. (1995). Choosing, confidence, and accuracy: A meta-analysis of the confidence-accuracy relation in eyewitness identification studies. *Psychological Bulletin, 118*, 315–327.

35. Brewer, N., Keast, A., & Rishworth, A. (2002). The confidence-accuracy relationship in eyewitness identification: The effects of reflection and disconfirmation on correlation and calibration. *Journal of Experimental Psychology: Applied, 8*, 44–56.

36. Sauer, J., Brewer, N., Zweck, T., & Weber, N. (2010). The effect of retention interval on the confidence-accuracy relationship for eyewitness identification. *Law and Human Behavior, 34*, 337–347. doi: 10.1007/s10979-009-9192-x

37. Weber, N., Brewer, N., Wells, G. L., Semmler, C., & Keast, A. (2004). Eyewitness identification accuracy and response latency: The unruly 10–12-second rule. *Journal of Experimental Psychology: Applied, 10*, 139–147.

38. Dunning, D., & Stern, L. B. (1994). Distinguishing accurate from inaccurate identifications via inquiries about decision processes. *Journal of Personality and Social Psychology, 67*, 818–835.

39. Sauerland, M., & Sporer, S. L. (2009). Fast and confident: Postdicting eyewitness identification accuracy in a field study. *Journal of Experimental Psychology: Applied, 15*, 46–62.

40. Wells, G. L., & Luus, C. A. E. (1990). Police lineups as experiments: Social methodology as a framework for properly conducted lineups. *Personality and Social Psychology Bulletin, 16*, 106–117.

41. Wells, G. L., & Turtle, J. W. (1986). Eyewitness identification: The importance of lineup models. *Psychological Bulletin, 99*, 320–329.

42. Luus, C. A. E., & Wells, G. L. (1991). Eyewitness identification and the selection of distractors for lineups. *Law and Human Behavior, 15*, 43–57.

43. Clark, S. E., & Tunnicliff, J. L. (2001). Selecting lineup foils in eyewitness identification: Experimental control and real-world simulation. *Law and Human Behavior, 25*, 199–216.

44. Lindsay, R. C. L., & Wells, G. L. (1980). What price justice? Exploring the relationship between lineup fairness and identification accuracy. *Law and Human Behavior, 4*, 303–314.

45. Luus, C. A. E., & Wells, G. L. (1991). Eyewitness identification and the selection of distractors for lineups. *Law and Human Behavior, 15*, 43–57.

46. Fitzgerald, R. J., Price, H. L., Oriet, C., & Charman, S. D. (2013). The effect of suspect-filler similarity on eyewitness identification decisions: A meta-analysis. *Psychology, Public Policy, and Law, 19*, 151–164.

47. Charman, S. D., Wells, G. L., & Joy, S. W. (2011). The dud effect: Adding highly dissimilar fillers increases confidence in lineup identifications. *Law and Human Behavior, 35*, 479–500.

48. Steblay, N. M. (1997). Social influence in eyewitness recall: A meta-analytic review of lineup instruction effects. *Law and Human Behavior, 21*, 283–297.

49. Clark, S. E. (2005). A re-examination of the effects of biased lineup instructions in eyewitness identification. *Law and Human Behavior, 29*, 395–424.

50. Quinlivan, D. S., Neuschatz, J. S., Cutler, B. L., Wells, G. L., McClung, J., & Harker, D. L. (2012). Do pre-admonition suggestions moderate the effect of unbiased lineup instructions? *Legal and Criminological Psychology, 17*, 165–176.

51. Wells, G. L. (1984). The psychology of lineup identifications. *Journal of Applied Social Psychology, 14*, 89–103.

52. Lindsay, R. C. L., & Wells, G. L. (1985). Improving eyewitness identification from lineups: Simultaneous versus sequential lineup presentations. *Journal of Applied Psychology, 70*, 556–564.

53. Steblay, N. L., Dysart, J. E., & Wells, G. L. (2011). Seventy-two tests of the sequential lineup superiority effect: A meta-analysis and policy discussion. *Psychology, Public Policy, and Law, 17*, 99–139.

54. Lindsay, R. C. L., & Wells, G. L. (1985). Improving eyewitness identification from lineups: Simultaneous versus sequential lineup presentations. *Journal of Applied Psychology, 70*, 556–564.

55. Clark, S. E., Erickson, M. A., & Breneman, J. (2011). Probative value of absolute and relative judgments in eyewitness identification. *Law and Human Behavior, 35*, 364–380.

56. Meissner, C. A., Tredoux, C. G., Parker, J. F., & MacLin, O. H. (2005). Eyewitness decisions in simultaneous and sequential lineups: A dual-process signal detection theory analysis. *Memory & Cognition, 33*, 783–792.

57. Palmer, M. A., & Brewer, N. (2012). Sequential lineup presentation promotes less-biased criterion setting but does not improve discriminability. *Law and Human Behavior, 36*, 247–255.

58. McQuiston-Surrett, D. E., Malpass, R. S., & Tredoux, C. G. (2006). Sequential vs. simultaneous lineups: A review of methods, data, and theory. *Psychology, Public Policy and Law, 12*, 137–169.

59. Steblay, N. K., Dietrich, H. L., Ryan, S. L., Raczynski, J. L., & James, K. A. (2011). Sequential lineup laps and eyewitness accuracy. *Law and Human Behavior, 35*, 262–274.

60. Wells, G. L., Steblay, N. K., & Dysart, J. E. (2015). Double-blind photo lineups using actual eyewitnesses: An experimental test of a sequential versus simultaneous lineup procedure. *Law and Human Behavior, 39*, 1–14.

61. Rosenthal, R. (2002). Covert communication in classrooms, clinics, courtrooms, and cubicles. *American Psychologist, 57*, 839–849.

62. Clark, S. E., Brower, G. L., Rosenthal, R., Hicks, J. M., & Moreland, M. B. (2013). Lineup administrator influences on eyewitness identification and eyewitness confidence. *Journal of Applied Research in Memory and Cognition, 2*, 158–165.

63. Haw, R. M., & Fisher, R. P. (2004). Effects of administrator-witness contact on eyewitness identification accuracy. *Journal of Applied Psychology, 89*, 1106–1112.

64. Phillips, M., McAuliff, B. D., Kovera, M. B., & Cutler, B. L. (1999). Double-blind lineup administration as a safeguard against investigator bias. *Journal of Applied Psychology, 84*, 940–951.

65. Greathouse, S. M., & Kovera, M. B. (2009). Instruction bias and lineup presentation moderate the effects of administrator knowledge on eyewitness identification. *Law and Human Behavior, 33*, 70–82.

66. Greathouse, S. M., & Kovera, M. B. (2009). Instruction bias and lineup presentation moderate the effects of administrator knowledge on eyewitness identification. *Law and Human Behavior, 33*, 70–82.

67. Douglass, A. B., Smith, C., & Fraser-Thill, R. (2005). A problem with double-blind photospread procedures: Photospread administrators use one eyewitness's confidence to influence the identification of another eyewitness. *Law and Human Behavior, 29*, 543–562.

68. Garrioch, L., & Brimacombe, C. A. E. (2001). Lineup administrators' expectations: Their impact on eyewitness confidence. *Law and Human Behavior, 25*, 299–315.

69. Wells, G. L., & Bradfield, A. L. (1998). "Good, you identified the suspect": Feedback to eyewitnesses distorts their reports of the witnessing experience. *Journal of Applied Psychology, 83*, 360–376.

70. Wells, G. L., Olson, E. A., & Charman, S. D. (2003). Distorted retrospective eyewitness reports as functions of feedback and delay. *Journal of Experimental Psychology: Applied, 9*, 42–52.

71. Semmler, C., Brewer, N., & Wells, G. L. (2004). Effects of postidentification feedback on eyewitness identification and nonidentification confidence. *Journal of Applied Psychology, 89*, 334–346.

72. Neuschatz, J. S., Lawson, D. S., Fairless, A. H., Powers, R. A., Neuschatz, J. S., Goodsell, C. A., & Toglia, M. P. (2007). The mitigating effects of suspicion on post-identification feedback and on retrospective eyewitness memory. *Law and Human Behavior, 31*, 231–247.

73. Manson v. Braithwaite, 1977, 432 U.S. 98.

74. Steblay, N. K., Wells, G. L., & Douglass, A. B. (2014). The eyewitness post identification effect 15 years later: Theoretical and policy implications. *Psychology, Public Policy, and Law, 20*, 1–18.

75. Wells, G. L., & Quinlivan, D. S. (2009). Suggestive eyewitness identification procedures and the Supreme Court's reliability test in light of eyewitness science: 30 years later. *Law and Human Behavior, 33*, 1–24.

76. Wells, G. L., Small, M., Penrod, S., Malpass, R. S., Fulero, S. M., & Brimacombe, C. A. E. (1998). Eyewitness identification procedures: Recommendations for lineups and photospreads. *Law and Human Behavior, 22*, 603–647.

77. Clark, S. E. (2012). Costs and benefits of eyewitness identification reform: Psychological science and public policy. *Perspectives on Psychological Science, 7*, 238–259.

78. Wells, G. L., Steblay, N., & Dysart, J. E. (2012). Eyewitness identification reforms: Are suggestiveness-induced hits and guesses true hits? *Perspectives on Psychological Science, 7*, 264–271.

79. Thompson-Cannino, J., Cotton, R., & Torneo, E. (2009): *Picking Cotton: Our memoir of injustice and redemption*. New York: St. Martin's Press.

80. Death penalty for Troy Davis highlights problems with eyewitness accounts. (2011, September 22). *Star-Ledger Editorial Board*. Retrieved from http://blog.nj.com/njv_editorial_page/2011/09/death_penalty_for_troy_davis_h.html

81. Troy Davis execution fuels eyewitness ID debate. (2011, September 27). *Associated Press*. Retrieved from http://www.usatoday.com/news/nation/story/2011-09-27/troy-davis-eyewitness-testimony/50563754/1

82. Loftus, E. (1974). Reconstructing memory: The incredible eyewitness. *Psychology Today, 8*(7), 116–119.

83. Desmarais, S. L., & Read, J. D. (2011). After 30 years, what do we know about what jurors know? A meta-analytic review of lay knowledge regarding eyewitness factors. *Law and Human Behavior, 35*, 200–210.

84. Brigham, J. C., & Bothwell, R. K. (1983). The ability of prospective jurors to estimate the accuracy of eyewitness identification. *Law and Human Behavior, 7*, 19–30.

85. McAuliff, B. D., & Kovera, M. B. (2007). Estimating the effects of misleading information on witness accuracy: Can experts tell jurors something they don't already know? *Applied Cognitive Psychology, 21*, 849–870.

86. Abshire, J., & Bornstein, B. J. (2003). Juror sensitivity to the cross-race effect. *Law and Human Behavior, 27*, 471–480.

87. Bradfield, A., & McQuiston, D. E. (2004). When does evidence of eyewitness confidence inflation affect judgments in a criminal trial? *Law and Human Behavior, 28*, 369–387.

88. Douglass, A. B., Neuschatz, J. S., Imrich, J., & Wilkinson, M. (2010). Does post-identification feedback affect evaluations of eyewitness testimony and identification procedures? *Law and Human Behavior, 34*, 282–294.

89. Smalarz, L., & Wells, G. L. (2014). Post-identification feedback to eyewitnesses impairs evaluators' abilities to discriminate between accurate and mistaken testimony. *Law and Human Behavior, 38*, 194–202.

90. Cutler, B. L., Penrod, S. D., & Dexter, H. R. (1989). The eyewitness, the expert psychologist, and the jury. *Law and Human Behavior, 13*, 311–332.

91. Devenport, J. L., Stinson, V., Cutler, B. L., & Kravitz, D. A. (2002). How effective are the cross-examination and expert testimony safeguards? Jurors' perceptions of the suggestiveness and fairness of biased lineup procedures. *Journal of Applied Psychology, 87*, 1042–1054.

92. Devenport, J. L., & Cutler, B. L. (2004). Impact of defense-only and opposing eyewitness experts on juror judgments. *Law and Human Behavior, 28*, 569–576.

93. Leippe, M. R., Eisenstadt, D., Rauch, S. M., & Seib, H. M. (2004). Timing of eyewitness expert testimony, jurors' need for cognition, and case strength as determinants of trial verdicts. *Journal of Applied Psychology, 89*, 524–541.

94. Kressel, N. J., & Kressel, D. R. (2002). *Stack and sway*. Boulder, CO: Westview Press.

95. Davis, D., & Loftus, E. F. (2006). Psychologists in the forensic world. In S. I. Donaldson, D. E. Berger, & K. Pezdek (Eds.), *Applied psychology: New frontiers and rewarding careers* (pp. 171–200). Mahwah, NJ: Lawrence Erlbaum Associates.

96. Fulero, S. M., & Penrod, S. D. (1990a). Attorney jury selection folklore: What do they think and how can psychologists help? *Forensic Reports, 3*, 233–259.

97. Blue, L. A. (1991). Jury selection in a civil case. *Trial Lawyers Quarterly, 21*, 11–25.

98. Marques, J. M., Abrams, D., Páez, D., & Martinez-Taboada, C. (1998). The role of categorization and in-group norms in judgments of groups and their members. *Journal of Personality and Social Psychology, 75*, 976–988.

99. Culhane, S. E., Hosch, H. M., & Weaver, W. G. (2004). Crime victims serving as jurors: Is there bias present? *Law and Human Behavior, 28*, 649–659.

100. Taylor, T. S., & Hosch, H. M. (2004). An examination of jury verdicts for evidence of a similarity-leniency effect, an out-group punitiveness effect, or a black sheep effect. *Law and Human Behavior, 28*, 587–598.

101. Kerr, N. L., Hymes, R. W., Anderson, A. B., & Weathers, J. E. (1995). Defendant-juror similarity and mock juror judgments. *Law and Human Behavior, 19*, 545–567.

102. Otis, C. C., Greathouse, S. M., Kennard, J. B., & Kovera, M. B. (2014). Hypothesis testing in attorney-conducted voir dire. *Law and Human Behavior, 38*, 392–404.

103. Batson v. Kentucky, 106 S.Ct. 1712 (1986).

104. J.E.B. v. Alabama *ex rel.* T.B., 114 S.Ct. 1419 (1994).

105. Sommers, S. R., & Norton, M. I. (2007). Race-based judgments, race-neutral justifications: Experimental examination of peremptory use and the Batson challenge procedure. *Law and Human Behavior, 31*, 261–273.

106. Norton, M. I., Sommers, S. R., & Brauner, S. (2007). Bias in jury selection: Justifying prohibited peremptory challenges. *Journal of Behavioral Decision Making, 20*, 467–479. doi: 10.1002/bdm.571

107. Kovera, M. B., & Cutler, B. L. (2013). *Jury selection*. New York: Oxford University Press.

108. Wenger, A. A., & Bornstein, B. H. (2006). The effects of victim's substance use and relationship closeness on mock jurors' judgments in an acquaintance rape case. *Sex Roles, 54*, 547–555.

109. Quas, J. A., Bottoms, B. L., Haegerich, T. M., & Nysse-Carris, K. L. (2002). Effects of victim, defendant, and juror gender on decisions in child sexual assault cases. *Journal of Applied Social Psychology, 32*, 1993–2021.

110. Schuller, R. A., & Hastings, P. A. (1996). Trials of battered women who kill: The impact of alternative forms of expert evidence. *Law and Human Behavior, 20*, 167–187.

111. Bottoms, B. L., Kalder, A. K., Stevenson, M. C., Oudekerk, B. A., Wiley, T. R., & Perona, A. (2011). Gender differences in jurors' perceptions of infanticide involving disabled and non-disabled infant victims. *Child Abuse & Neglect, 35*, 127–141.

112. Bègue, L., & Bastounis, M. (2003). Two spheres of belief in justice: Extensive support for the bidimensional model of belief in a just world. *Journal of Personality, 71*, 435–463.

113. Narby, D. J., Cutler, B. L., & Moran, G. (1993). A meta-analysis of the association between authoritarianism and jurors' perceptions of defendant culpability. *Journal of Applied Psychology, 78*, 3442.

114. Kravitz, D. A., Cutler, B. L., & Brock, P. (1993). Reliability and validity of the original and revised Legal Attitudes Questionnaire. *Law and Human Behavior, 17*, 661–667.

115. Kovera, M. B., & Cutler, B. L. (2013). *Jury selection*. New York: Oxford University Press.

116. Moran, G., Cutler, B. L., & De Lisa, A. (1994). Attitudes toward tort reform, scientific jury selection, and juror bias: Verdict inclination in criminal and civil trials. *Law and Psychology Review, 18*, 309–328.

117. Crocker, C. B., & Kovera, M. B. (2010). The effects of rehabilitative voir dire on juror bias and decision making. *Law and Human Behavior, 34*, 212–226.

118. Moran, G., Cutler, B. L., & Loftus, E. F. (1990). Jury selection in major controlled substance trials: The need for extended voir dire. *Forensic Reports, 3*, 331–348.

119. O'Neil, K. M., Patry, M. W., & Penrod, S. D. (2004). Exploring the effects of attitudes toward the death penalty on capital sentencing verdicts. *Psychology, Public Policy, and Law, 10*, 443–470.

120. Moran, G., & Comfort, J. C. (1986). Neither "tentative nor fragmentary": Verdict preference of impaneled felony jurors as a function of attitude toward capital punishment. *Journal of Applied Psychology, 71*, 146–155.

121. Fitzgerald, R., & Ellsworth, P. C. (1984). Due process vs. crime control: Death qualification and jury attitudes. *Law and Human Behavior, 8*, 31–51.

122. Haney, C., Hurtado, A., & Vega, L. (1994). Modern death qualification: New data on its biasing effects. *Law and Human Behavior, 18*, 619–633.

123. Moran, G., & Comfort, J. C. (1986). Neither "tentative nor fragmentary": Verdict preference of impaneled felony jurors as a function of attitude toward capital punishment. *Journal of Applied Psychology, 71*, 146–155.

124. Cowan, C. L., Thompson, W. C., & Ellsworth, P. C. (1984). The effects of death qualification on jurors: Predisposition to convict and on the quality of deliberation. *Law and Human Behavior, 8*, 53–79.

125. Allen, M., Mabry, E., & McKelton, D. (1998). Impact of juror attitudes about the death penalty on juror evaluations of guilt and punishment: A meta-analysis. *Law and Human Behavior, 22*, 715–731.

126. Filkins, J. W., Smith, C. M., & Tindale, R. S. (1998). An evaluation of the biasing effects of death qualification: A meta-analytic/computer simulation approach. In R. S. Tindale et al. (Eds.), *Theory and research on small groups*. New York: Plenum Press.

127. Nietzel, M. T., McCarthy, D. M., & Kern, M. J. (1999). Juries: The current state of the empirical literature. In R. Roesch, S. D. Hart, & J. R. P. Ogloff (Eds.), *Psychology and law: The state of the discipline* (pp. 23–52). Dordrecht, Netherlands: Kluwer Academic Publishers.

128. Cowan, C. L., Thompson, W. C., & Ellsworth, P. C. (1984). The effects of death qualification on jurors: Predisposition to convict and on the quality of deliberation. *Law and Human Behavior, 8*, 53–79.

129. Steblay, N. M., Besirevic, J., Fulero, S. M., & Jimenez-Lorente, B. (1999). The effects of pretrial publicity on juror verdicts: A meta-analytic review. *Law and Human Behavior, 23*, 219–235.

130. Daftary-Kapur, T., Penros, S. D., O'Connor, M., & Wallace, B. (2014). Examining pretrial publicity in a shadow jury paradigm: Issues of slant, quantity, persistence and generalizability. *Law and Human Behavior, 38*, 462–477.

131. Dexter, H. R., Cutler, B. L., & Moran, G. (1992). A test of voir dire as a remedy for the prejudicial effects of pretrial publicity. *Journal of Applied Social Psychology, 22*, 819–832.

132. Crocker, C. B. (2010). *An investigation of the psychological processes involved in juror rehabilitation.* (Unpublished doctoral dissertation.) The City University of New York.

133. Ruva, C. L., McEvoy, C., & Bryant, J. B. (2007). Effects of pre-trial publicity and jury deliberation on juror bias and source memory errors. *Applied Cognitive Psychology, 21,* 45–67.

134. Ruva, C. L., & Guenther, C. C. (2014). From the shadows into the light: How pretrial publicity and deliberation affect mock jurors' decisions, impressions, and memory. *Law and Human Behavior.* Published online, December 15, 2014. doi: 10.1037/lhb0000117

135. Ruva, C. L., & LeVasseur, M. A. (2012). Behind closed doors: The effect of pretrial publicity on jury deliberations. *Psychology, Crime & Law, 18,* 431–452.

136. Steblay, N. M., Besirevic, J., Fulero, S. M., & Jimenez-Lorente, B. (1999). The effects of pretrial publicity on juror verdicts: A meta-analytic review. *Law and Human Behavior, 23,* 219–235.

137. Studebaker, C. A., Robbennolt, J. K., Pathak-Sharma, M. K., & Penrod, S. D. (2000). Assessing pretrial publicity effects: Integrating content analytic results. *Law and Human Behavior, 24,* 317–336.

138. Steblay, N. M., Besirevic, J., Fulero, S. M., & Jimenez-Lorente, B. (1999). The effects of pretrial publicity on juror verdicts: A meta-analytic review. *Law and Human Behavior, 23,* 219–235.

139. Blackstone, W. (1783). *Commentaries on the Laws of England* (9th ed., Vol. 4, p. 358). London: Strahan, Cadell & Prince.

140. Loftus, E. F., & Ketcham, K. (1994). *The myth of repressed memory.* New York: St. Martin's Press.

141. Alpert, J. L., Brown, L. S., & Courtois, C. A. (1998). Symptomatic clients and memories of childhood abuse: What the trauma and child sexual abuse literature tells us. *Psychology, Public Policy, and Law, 4,* 941–995.

142. Ornstein, P. A., Ceci, S. J., & Loftus, E. F. (1998). Adult recollections of childhood abuse: Cognitive and developmental perspectives. *Psychology, Public Policy, and Law, 7,* 1025–1051.

143. Ornstein, P. A., Ceci, S. J., & Loftus, E. F. (1998). Adult recollections of childhood abuse: Cognitive and developmental perspectives. *Psychology, Public Policy, and Law, 7,* 1025–1051.

MODULE E
Applying Social Psychology to the Environment

1. Viek, C., & Steg, L. (2007). Human behavior and environmental sustainability: problems, driving forces and research topics. *Journal of Social Issues, 63,* 1–19.

2. Kates, R. W., Clark, W. C., Corell, R., Hall, J. M., Jaeger, C. C., Lowe, I., McCarthy, J. J., Schellnhuber, H. J., Bolin, B., Dickson, N. M., Faucheux, S., Gallopin, G. C., Grubler, A., Huntley, B., Jager, J., Jodha, N. S., Kasperson, R. E., Mabogunje, A., Matson, P., Mooney, H., Moore, B., III, O'Riordan, T., & Svedin, U. (2001). Sustainability science. *Science, 292,* 641–642.

3. Nickerson, R. S. (2003). *Psychology and environmental change.* Mahway, NJ: Erlbaum.

4. Calhoun, J. B. (1962). Population density and social pathology, *Scientific American, 206,* 139–148.

5. Schwab, J., Nadeau, S. E., & Warheit, G. J. (1979). Crowding and mental health. *Pavlovian Journal of Biological Science, 14,* 226–233.

6. Saegert, S., MacIntosh, E., & West, S. (1975). Two studies of crowding in urban public spaces. *Environment and Behavior, 1,* 159–184.

7. Schmidt, C. (1969). Urban crime areas: Part I. *American Sociological Review, 25,* 527–542.

8. Evans, G. W., & Lepore, S. J. (1993). Household crowding and social support: A quasi-experimental analysis. *Journal of Personality and Social Psychology, 65,* 308–316.

9. Sundstrom, E. (1978). Crowding as a sequential process: Review of research on the effects of population density on humans. In A. Baum & Y. M. Epstein (Eds.), *Human response to crowding* (pp. 31–116). Hillsdale, NJ: Erlbaum.

10. Baum, A., & Paulus, P. B. (1987). Crowding. In D. Stokols & I. Altman (Eds.), *Handbook of environmental psychology* (Vol. 1, pp. 533–570). New York: Wiley-Interscience.

11. Benson, G. P., & Zieman, G. L. (1981). *The relationship of weather to children's behavior problems.* Unpublished manuscript, Colorado State University, Fort Collins, CO.

12. Bell, P. A., & Greene, T. C. (1982). Thermal stress: Physiological comfort, performance, and social effects of hot and cold environments. In G. W. Evans (Ed.), *Environmental stress* (pp. 75–105). London: Cambridge University Press.

13. Anderson, C. A., Bushman, B. J., & Groom, R. W. (1997). Hot years and serious and deadly assault: Empirical tests of the heat hypothesis. *Journal of Personality and Social Psychology, 73,* 1213–1223.

14. Fay, T. H. (Ed.). (1991). *Noise and health.* New York: New York Academy of Medicine.

15. Cohen, S., & Spacapan, S. (1984). The social psychology of noise. In D. M. Jones & A. J. Chapman (Eds.), *Noise and society* (pp. 221–245). New York: Wiley.

16. Matthews, K. E., & Canon, L. K. (1975). Environmental noise level as a determinant of helping behavior. *Journal of Personality and Social Psychology, 32,* 571–577.

17. Basner, M., Babisch, W., Davis, A., Brink, M., Clark, C., Janssen, S., & Stansfeld, S. (2014). Auditory and non-auditory effects of noise on health. *Lancet, 383,* 1325–1332.

18. Evans, G. W., Jacobs, S. V., Dooley, D., & Catalano, R. (1987). The interaction of stressful life events and chronic strains on community mental health. *American Journal of Community Psychology, 15,* 23–34.

19. Miller, P. V. (2002). The authority and limitation of polls. In J. Manza, F. L. Cook, & B. I. Page (Eds.), *Navigating public opinion* (pp. 221–231). New York: Oxford University Press.

20. Engelman, R., Halweil, B., & Nierenberg, D. (2002). Rethinking population, improving lives. In C. Flavin, H. French, & G. Gardner (Eds.), *State of the world 2002: A Worldwatch Institute report on progress toward a sustainable society* (p. 127). New York: Norton.

21. Quarantelli, E. L. (1998). *What is a disaster?* New York: Routledge.

22. Tichener, J. L., & Kapp, F. T. (1976). Family and character change at Buffalo Creek. *American Journal of Psychiatry, 33*(3), 295–299.

23. Helton, W. S., Head, J., & Kemp, S. (2011). Natural disaster induced cognitive disruption: Impacts on action slips. *Consciousness and Cognition, 20,* 1732–1737.

24. Hardin, G. (1968). The tragedy of the commons. *Science, 162,* 1243–1248.

25. Platt, J. (1973). Social traps. *American Psychologist, 28,* 641–651.

26. Martichuski, D. K., & Bell, P. A. (1991). Reward, punishment, privatization, and moral suasion in a commons dilemma. *Journal of Applied Social Psychology, 21,* 1356–1369.

27. Jorgenson, D. O., & Papciak, A. S. (1981). The effects of communication, resource feedback, and identifiability on behavior in a simulated commons. *Journal of Experimental Social Psychology, 17,* 373–385.

28. Kramer, R. M., & Brewer, M. B. (1984). Effects of group identity on resource use in a simulated commons dilemma. *Journal of Personality and Social Psychology, 46,* 1044–1057.

29. Ansari, S., Wijen, F., & Gray, B. (2013). Constructing a climate change logic: An institutional perspective on the "tragedy of the commons." *Organization Science, 24,* 1014–1040.

30. Union of Concerned Scientists. (1993). *World scientists warning to humanity.* Cambridge, MA: Union of Concerned Scientists.

31. Kates, R. W. (1994). Sustaining life on the earth. *Scientific American, 271*(4), 114–122.

32. Ehrenfeld, D. (1981). *The arrogance of humanism.* New York: Oxford University Press.

33. Clark, W. C. (1989). Managing planet earth. *Scientific American, 261*(3), 47–54.

34. Kraft, M. (2006). *Environmental policies and politics.* Englewood Cliffs, NJ: Prentice Hall.

35. Midden, C., Kaiser, F., & McCalley, T. (2007). Technology's four roles in understanding individuals' conservation of natural resources. *Journal of Social Issues, 63,* 155–174.

36. Sherrod, D. R. (1974). Crowding, perceived control, and behavioral aftereffects. *Journal of Applied Social Psychology, 4,* 171–186.

37. Schopler, J., & Stockdale, J. (1977). An interference analysis of crowding. *Environmental Psychology and Nonverbal Behavior, 1,* 81–88.

38. Paulus, P. B., & Matthews, R. (1980). Crowding, attribution, and task performance. *Basic and Applied Social Psychology, 1,* 3–13.

39. Saegert, S. (1978). High density environments: Their personal and social consequences. In A. Baum & Y. M. Epstein (Eds.), *Human response to crowding* (pp. 259–276). Hillsdale, NJ: Erlbaum.

40. Langer, E. J., & Saegert, S. (1977). Crowding and cognitive control. *Journal of Personality and Social Psychology, 35,* 175–182.

41. Novelli, D., Drury, J., Reicher, S., & Stott, C. (2013). Crowdedness mediates the effect of social identification on positive emotion in a crowd: A survey of two crowd events. *PLoS ONE, 8*(11), 1–7.

42. Hayduk, L. A. (1994). Personal space: Understanding the simplex model. *Journal of Nonverbal Behavior, 18,* 245–260.

43. Edwards, D. J. A. (1972). Approaching the unfamiliar: A study of human interaction distances. *Journal of Behavioral Sciences, 1,* 249–250.

44. Latta, R. M. (1978). Relation of status incongruous to personal space. *Personality and Social Psychology Bulletin, 4,* 143–146.

45. Kaya, N., & Erkip, F. E. (1999). Invasion of personal space under the condition of short-term crowding: A case study on an automatic teller machine. *Journal of Environmental Psychology, 19,* 183–189.

46. Aiello, J. R. (1987). Human spatial behavior. In D. Stokols & I. Altman (Eds.), *Handbook of environmental psychology* (Vol. 1, pp. 505–531). New York: Wiley.

47. Balogun, S. K. (1991). Personal space as affected by religions of the approaching and the approached people. *Indian Journal of Behaviour, 15,* 45–50.

48. Barrios, B. A., Corbitt, L. C., Estes, J. P., & Topping, J. S. (1976). Effect of social stigma on interpersonal distance. *The Psychological Record, 26,* 342–348.

49. Dean, L. M., Willis, F. N., & Hewitt, J. (1975). Initial interaction distance among individuals equal and unequal in military rank. *Journal of Personality and Social Psychology, 32,* 294–299.

50. Remland, M. S., Jones, T. S., & Brinkman, H. (1995). Interpersonal distance, body orientation, and touch: Effects of culture, gender, and age. *Journal of Social Psychology, 135,* 281–297.

51. Barnard, W. A., & Bell, P. A. (1982). An unobtrusive apparatus for measuring interpersonal distance. *Journal of General Psychology, 107,* 85–90.

52. Mulligan, R., Burmood, C., O'Hara, S., & Warren, C. (2004). Personal space preferences: The role of mortality salience and affiliation motivation. *Journal of Psychological Inquiry, 9*(1), 14–20.

53. Duke, M. P., & Wilson, J. (1973). The measurement of interpersonal distance in pre-school children. *Journal of Genetic Psychology, 123,* 361–362.

54. Hewitt, J., & Alqahtani, M. A. (2003). Differences between Saudi and U.S. students in reaction to same- and mixed-sex intimacy by others. *Journal of Social Psychology, 143,* 233–242.

55. Smith, R. J., & Knowles, E. S. (1979). Affective and cognitive mediators of reactions to spatial invasions. *Journal of Experimental Social Psychology, 15*, 437–452.

56. Murphy-Berman, V., & Berman, J. (1978). Importance of choice and sex invasions of personal space. *Personality and Social Psychology Bulletin, 4*, 424–428.

57. Evans, G. W., & Howard, H. R. B. (1972). A methodological investigation of personal space. In W. J. Mitchell (Ed.), *Environmental design: Research and practice*, Proceedings of EDRA3/AR8 Conference. University of California, Los Angeles, CA.

58. Konecni, V. J., Libuser, L., Morton, H., & Ebbesen, E. G. (1975). Effects of a violation of personal space on escape and helping response. *Journal of Experimental Social Psychology, 11*, 288–299.

59. Brown, B. (1987). Territoriality. In D. Stokols & I. Altman (Eds.), *Handbook of environmental psychology* (Vol. 1, pp. 505–531). New York: Wiley-Interscience.

60. Wortley, R., & McFarlane, M. (2011). The role of territoriality in crime prevention: A field experiment. *Security Journal, 24*, 149–156.

61. Harris, P. B., & Brown, B. B. (1996). The home and identity display: Interpreting resident territoriality from home exteriors. *Journal of Environmental Psychology, 16*, 187–203.

62. Childress, H. (2004). Teenagers, territories and the appropriation of space. *Childhood, 11*, 195–205.

63. Brown, B. B., & Werner, C. M. (1985). Social cohesiveness, territoriality, and holiday decorations: The influence of cul-de-sacs. *Environment and Behavior, 17*, 539–565.

64. Taylor, R. B., Gottfredson, S. D., & Brower, S. (1981). Territorial cognitions and social climate in urban neighborhoods. *Basic and Applied Social Psychology, 2*, 289–303.

65. Reinsch, J., & Spotanski, C. (2005). Human territoriality: The effects of status on personalization and demarcation. *Journal of Psychological Inquiry 10*(1), 16–21.

66. Miller, R. L. (1979). Middle class residents in ghetto housing: Attitudes & behavior. *Proceedings of the International Conference on Environmental Psychology, Guildford, England,* 75.

67. Kaya, N., & Weber, M. J. (2003). Cross-cultural differences in the perception of crowding and privacy regulation: American and Turkish students. *Journal of Environmental Psychology, 23*, 301–309.

68. Miller, R. L. (2013). Territoriality. In K. Keith (Ed.), *Encyclopedia of cross-cultural psychology* (pp. 1276–1278). New York, NY: Wiley-Blackwell.

69. Etherington, J. (2010). Nationalism, territoriality, and national territorial belonging. *Papers. Revista de Sociologia, 95*, 321–339.

70. DeScioli, P., & Wilson, B. J. (2011). The territorial foundations of human property. *Evolution and Human Behavior, 32*, 297–304.

71. Altman, I., Nelson, P. A., & Lett, E. E. (1972, Spring). The ecology of home environments. *Catalog of Selected Documents in Psychology* (No. 150).

72. Ley, D., & Cybriwsky, R. (1974). The spatial ecology of stripped cars. *Environment and Behavior, 6*, 53–68.

73. Martindale, D. A. (1971). Territorial dominance behavior in dyadic verbal interactions. *Proceedings of the Annual Convention of the American Psychological Association, 6*, 305–306.

74. Hall, E. T. (1976). *Beyond culture.* New York, NY: Anchor Books.

75. Sommers, P., & Moos, R. (1976). The weather and human behavior. In R. H. Moos (Ed.), *The human context: Environmental determinants of behavior* (pp. 73–107). New York: Wiley.

76. Sommers, P., & Moos, R. (1976). The weather and human behavior. In R. H. Moos (Ed.), *The human context: Environmental determinants of behavior* (pp. 73–107). New York: Wiley.

77. Hsiang, S. M., Burke, M., & Miquel, E. (2013). Quantifying the influence of climate on human conflict. *Science, 341*, 1212–1226.

78. Green, D. M., & Fidell, S. (1991). Variability in the criterion for reporting annoyance in community noise surveys. *Journal of the Acoustical Society of America, 89*, 234–243.

79. Szalma, J. L., & Hancock, P. A. (2011). Noise effects on human performance: A meta-analytic synthesis. *Psychological Bulletin, 137*, 682–707.

80. Basner, M., Babisch, W., Davis, A., Brink, M., Clark, C., Janssen, S., & Stansfeld, S. (2014). Auditory and non-auditory effects of noise on health. *Lancet, 383*, 1325–1332.

81. Glass, D. C., & Singer, J. E. (1972). *Urban stress: Experiments on noise and social stressors.* New York: Academic Press.

82. Evans, G. W., & Stecker, R. (2004). The motivational consequences of environmental stress. *Journal of Environmental Psychology, 24*, 143–165.

83. Basner, M., Babisch, W., Davis, A., Brink, M., Clark, C., Janssen, S., & Stansfeld, S. (2014). Auditory and non-auditory effects of noise on health. *Lancet, 383*, 1325–1332.

84. Cohen, S. (1978). Environmental load and the allocation of attention. In A. Baum, J. S. Singer, & S. Valins (Eds.), *Advances in environmental psychology* (Vol. 1, pp. 1–29). Hillsdale, NJ: Erlbaum.

85. Kenrick, D. T., & Johnson, G. A. (1979). Interpersonal attraction in aversive environments. A problem for the classical conditioning paradigm. *Journal of Personality and Social Psychology, 87*, 572–579.

86. Sundstrom, E., Town, J. P., Rice, R. W., Osborn, D. P., & Brill, M. (1994). Office noise, satisfaction, and performance. *Environment and Behavior, 26*, 195–222.

87. Staples, S. L. (1997). Public policy and environmental noise: Modeling exposure or understanding. *American Journal of Public Health, 87*, 2063–2067.

88. Basner, M., Babisch, W., Davis, A., Brink, M., Clark, C., Janssen, S., & Stansfeld, S. (2014). Auditory and non-auditory effects of noise on health. *Lancet, 383*, 1325–1332.

89. Anderson, J. O., Thundiyll, J. G., & Stobach, A. (2012). Clearing the air: A review of the effects of particulate matter air pollution on human health. *Journal of Medical Toxicology, 8*, 166–175.

90. Miller, G. T. (1990). *Living in the environment* (6th ed.). Belmont, CA: Wadsworth.

91. Guxens, M., & Sunyer, J. (2012). A review of epidemiological studies on neuropsychological effects of air pollution. *Swiss Medical Weekly, 141*, 1–7.

92. Holgate, S. T., Samet, J. M., Maynard, R. L., & Koren, H. S. (Eds.) (1999). *Air pollution and health.* San Diego: Academic Press.

93. Lewis, J., Baddeley, A. D., Bonham, K. G., & Lovett, D. (1970). Traffic pollution and mental efficiency. *Nature, 225*, 95–97.

94. Jacobs, S. V., Evans, G. W., Catalano, R., & Dooley, D. (1984). Air pollution and depressive symptomatology: Exploratory analyses of intervening psychosocial factors. *Population & Environment, 7*, 260–272.

95. Lundberg, A. (1996). Psychiatric aspects of air pollution. *Otolaryngology-Head and Neck Surgery, 114*(2), 227–231.

96. Brown, L. R. (1994). *State of the world 1994.* New York: Norton.

97. Schultz, P. W. (2011). Conservation means behavior. *Conservation Biology, 25*, 1080–1083.

98. Barker, M. R., Bailey, J. S., & Lee, N. (2004). The impact of verbal prompts on child safety-belt use in shopping carts. *Journal of Applied Behavior Analysis, 37*, 527–530.

99. Geller, E. S., Winett, R. A., & Everett, P. B. (1982). *Preserving the environment: Strategies for behavior change.* New York: Pergamon.

100. Finnie, W. C. (1973). Field experiments and litter control. *Environment and Behavior, 5*, 123–143.

101. Leonard-Barton, D. (1980, September). *The role of interpersonal communication networks in the diffusion of energy conserving practices and technologies.* Paper presented at the International Conference of Consumer Behavior and Energy Policy, Banff, Alberta, Canada.

102. Florin, P., & Wandersman, A. (1983). A psychosocial perspective on neighborhood conservation. In N. R. Feimer & E. S. Geller (Eds.), *Environmental psychology: Directions and perspectives.* New York: Praeger.

103. Kohlenberg, R. J., Phillips, T., & Proctor, W. (1976). A behavioral analysis of peaking in residential electricity energy consumption. *Journal of Applied Behavior Analysis, 9*, 13–18.

104. Goldstein, N. J., Cialdini, R. B., & Griskevicius, V. (2004). *A room with a viewpoint: Using norm-based appeals to motivate conservation behaviors in a hotel setting.* Paper presented at the annual meeting of the Society for Personality and Social Psychology, Austin, TX.

105. Abrahamse, W., Steg, L., Vlek, C., & Rothengatter, T. (2007). The effect of tailored information, goal setting, and tailored feedback on household energy use, energy-related behaviors, and behavioral antecedents. *Journal of Environmental Psychology, 27*, 265–276.

106. Baum, A., & Fleming, I. (1993). Implications of psychological research on stress and technological accidents. *American Psychologist, 48*, 665–672.

107. Drabek, T. E., & Stephenson, J. S. (1971). When disaster strikes. *Journal of Applied Social Psychology, 1*, 187–203.

108. Kotani, H., & Yokomatsu, M. (2013). Inheritance of local culture and disaster: Identity-formation-model approach. *Journal of Integrated Disaster Risk Management, 3*, 107–125.

109. Spielberg, W. E. (1986). Living with Indian Point: A study in investigating the relationship between stress, time distortion, ideology, coping style and expressed vulnerability of high school students in close residence to a nuclear power plant. *Dissertation Abstracts International, 47*(9–B), 3971–3972.

110. Stout-Wiegand, N., & Trent, R. B. (1984–1985). Comparison of students' and non-student residents' attitudes toward local energy developments: Environmentalism versus economic interest. *Journal of Environmental Education, 16*, 29–35.

111. Davis, I. (1978). *Shelter after disaster.* Oxford, UK: Oxford Polytechnic Press.

112. Parker, S. D., Brewer, M. B., & Spencer, J. R. (1980). Natural disaster, perceived control and attributions to fate. *Personality & Social Psychology Bulletin, 6*, 454–459.

113. Hansson, R. O., Noulles, D., & Bellovich, S. J. (1982). Knowledge warning and stress: A study of comparative roles in an urban floodplain. *Environment and Behavior, 14*, 171–185.

114. Archea, J. (1990). Two earthquakes: Three human conditions. In Y. Yoshitake, R. B. Bechtel, T. Takahashi, & M. Asai (Eds.), *Current issues in environment-behavior research.* Tokyo: University of Tokyo.

115. Weinrich, S., Hardin, S. B., & Johnson, M. (1990). Nurses respond to hurricane Hugo victims: Disaster stress. *Archives of Psychiatric Nursing, 4*, 195–205.

116. Fullerton, C. S., McCarroll, J. E., Ursano, R. S., & Wright, K. M. (1992). Psychological responses of rescue workers: Fire fighters and trauma. *American Journal of Orthopsychiatry, 62*, 371–378.

117. Chandrasekhar, D. (2010). Setting the stage: How policy institutions create the scope for participation in planning. *Journal of Disaster Research, 5*, 130–137.

118. American Planning Association-New York Metro Chapter. (2013). Getting back to business: Addressing the needs of Rockaway businesses impacted by Superstorm Sandy. Retrieved from http://www.nyplanning.org/docs/APANYM%20Business%20Recovery%20Report%20to%20RDRC.pdf.

119. Wang, P. S., Gruber, M. J., Powers, R. E., Schoenbaum, M., Speier, A. H., Wells, K. B., et al. (2007). Mental health service use among Hurricane Katrina survivors in the eight months after the disaster. *Psychiatric Services, 58*, 1403–1411.

120. Giannopoulou, I., Dikaiakou, A., Yule, W. (2006). Cognitive-behavioural group intervention for PTSD symptoms in children following the Athens 1999 earthquake: A pilot study. *Clinical Child Psychology and Psychiatry, 2011*, 543–553.

121. Lochman, J. E., Vernberg, E., Boxmeyer, C., & Powell, N. (2012, May). Tornado effects on children's behavioral, emotional and psychophysiological functioning and parents' depression. Paper to be presented in a symposium (R. Guadagno, Chair) at the Association of Psychological Science Annual Convention, Chicago, IL.

122. Doocy, S., Daniels, A., Dooling, S., & Gorokhovich, Y. (2013). The human impact of volcanoes: A historical review of events 1900–2009 and systematic literature review. *PLoS Currents, 16*, 5.

123. Doocy, S., Daniels, A., Murray, S., & Kirsch, T. D. (2013). The human impact of floods: A historical review of events 1980–2009 and systematic literature review. *PLoS Currents Disasters, 16*, doi: 10.1371/currents.dis.f4deb457904936b07c09daa98ee8171a

124. Bowler. R, Meqler, D., Huel. G., & Cone, J. (1994). Psychological, psychosocial, and psychophysiological sequelae in a community affected by a railroad chemical disaster. *Journal of Traumatic Stress, 7*, 601–624.

125. Bland, S. H., O'Leary, E. S., Farinaro, E., Jossa, F., & Trevisan, M. (1996). Long-term psychological effects of natural disasters. *Psychosomatic Medicine, 58*, 18–25.

126. Mardberg, B., Carlstedt, L., Stalberg-Carlstedt, B., & Shalit, B. (1987). Sex differences in perception of threat from the Chernobyl accident. *Perceptual & Motor Skills, 65*, 228.

127. Arochova, O., Kontrova, J., Lipkova, V., & Liska, J. (1988). Effect of toxic atmosphere emissions on cognitive performance by children. *Studia Psychologica, 30*, 101–114.

128. Solomon, S. D., & Canino, G. J. (1990). Appropriateness of the DSM-III-R criteria for Posttraumatic Stress Disorder. *Comprehensive Psychiatry, 31*, 227–237.

129. Escobar, J. I., Canino, G., Rubio-Stipec, M., & Bravo, M. (1992). Somatic symptoms after a natural disaster: A prospective study. *American Journal of Psychiatry, 149*, 965–967.

130. Adams, P. R., & Adams, G. R. (1984). Mount St. Helens ashfall: Evidence for a disaster stress reaction, *American Psychologist, 39*, 252–260.

131. Chen, X., Dai, K., & Parnell, A. (1992). Disaster tradition and change: Remarriage and family reconstruction in a post-earthquake community in the People's Republic of China. *Journal of Comparative Family Studies, 23*, 115–132.

132. Green, B. L., Grace, M. C., Vary, M. G., Krammer, T. L., Gleser, G. C., & Leonard, A. C. (1994). Children of disaster in the second decade: A 17-year follow-up of Buffalo Creek survivors. *Journal of the American Academy of Child and Adolescent Psychiatry, 33*, 71–79.

133. Thompson, M. P., Norris, F. H., & Hanacek, B. (1993). Age differences in the psychological consequences of Hurricane Hugo. *Psychology and Aging, 8*, 606–616.

134. Cialdini, R. B. (1989). Littering: When every litter bit hurts. In R. E. Rice & C. K. Atkin (Eds.), *Public communication campaigns* (2nd ed., pp. 221–223). London: Sage.

135. Purcell, A. H. (1981, February). The world's trashiest people: Will they clean up their act or throw away their future? *The Futurist, 2*, 51–59.

136. Tarrant, M. A., & Cordell, H. K. (1997). The effect of respondent characteristics on general environmental attitude-behavior correspondence. *Environment and Behavior, 29*, 618–637.

137. Carrus, G., Passafaro, P., & Bonnes, M. (2008). Emotions, habits and rational choices in ecological behaviours: The case of recycling and use of public transportation. *Journal of Environmental Psychology, 28*, 51–62.

138. Van Houten, R., & Nau, P. A. (1981). A comparison of the effects of posted feedback and increased police surveillance on highway speeding. *Journal of Applied Behavior Analysis, 14*, 261–271.

139. Seligman, C., & Darley, J. M. (1977). Feedback as a means of decreasing residential energy consumption. *Journal of Applied Psychology, 62*, 363–368.

140. Stern, P. C., & Oskamp, S. (1987). Managing scarce environmental resources. In D. Stokols & I. Altman (Eds.), *Handbook of environmental psychology* (Vol. 2, pp. 1043–1088). New York: Wiley.

141. Becker, L. J. (1978). The joint effect of feedback and goal setting on performance: A field study of residential energy conservation. *Journal of Applied Psychology, 63*, 228–233.

142. Siero, F. W., Bakker, A. B., Dekker, G. B., & Van Den Burg, M. T. C. (1996). Changing organizational energy consumption behavior through comparative feedback. *Journal of Environmental Psychology, 16*, 235–246.

143. Bamberg, S., & Moser, G. (2007). Twenty years after Hines, Hungerford, and Tomera: A new meta-analysis of psycho-social determinants of pro-environmental behaviour. *Journal of Environmental Psychology, 27*, 14–25.

144. Berenguer, J. (2010). The effect of empathy in environmental moral reasoning. *Environment and Behavior, 42*, 110–134.

145. Nisbet, E. K., Zelenski, J. M., & Murphy, S. A. (2009). The nature relatedness scale: Linking individuals' connection with nature, environmental concern, and behavior. *Environment and Behavior, 41*, 715–740.

146. Schwartz, S. H. (1977). Normative influences on altruism. *Advances in Experimental Social Psychology, 10*, 221–279.

147. Orbell, J. M., van de Kragt, A. J. C., & Dawes, R. M. (1988). Explaining discussion-induced comparison. *Journal of Personality and Social Psychology, 54*, 811–819.

148. Van Vugt, M., & Samuelson, C. (1999). The impact of personal metering in the management of a natural resource crisis: A social dilemma analysis. *Personality and Social Psychology Bulletin, 25*, 731–745.

149. Dickerson, C., Thibodeau, R., Aronson, E., & Miller, D. (1992). Using cognitive dissonance to encourage water conservation. *Journal of Applied Social Psychology, 22*, 841–854.

150. Clancy, B., & Milam, H. (2012). How psychological reactance modifies the effects of hypocrisy induction. *Journal of Psychological Inquiry, 17*, 36–39.

151. Hanley, N., Shogren, J., & White, B. (2007). *Environmental economics in theory and practice.* London, UK: Palgrave.

152. Hoerner, J. A., & Barrett, J. (2004, September). *Smarter, cleaner, stronger: Secure jobs, a clean environment, and less foreign oil.* Retrieved from http://www.rprogress.org/publications/2004/SmartCleanStrong_National.pdf

153. Thompson, S. C. G., & Stoutemyer, K. (1991). Water use as a commons dilemma: The effects of education that focuses on long-term consequences and individual action. *Environment and Behavior, 23*, 314–333.

154. De Young, R., Duncan, A., Frank, J., Gill, N., Rothman, S., Shenot, J., Shotkin, A., & Zweizig, M. (1993). Promoting source reduction behavior: The role of motivational behavior. *Environment and Behavior, 25*, 70–85.

References

Aamodt, M. G. (2013). *Industrial/Organizational Psychology: An Applied Approach*. Belmont, CA: Wadsworth, Cengage Learning.

Aamodt, M. G., & Carr, K. (1988). Relationship between recruitment source and employee behavior. *Proceedings of the 12th Annual Meeting of the International Personnel Management Association Assessment Council*, 143–146.

Aamodt, M. G., Kimbrough, W. W., and Alexander, C. J. (1983). A preliminary investigation of the relationship between team racial heterogeneity and team performance in college basketball. *Journal of Sports Sciences, 1*, 131–133.

Abel, E. L., & Kruger, M. L. (2010). Smile intensity in photographs predicts longevity. *Psychological Science, 21*(4), 542–544.

Aberson, C. L., Healy, M., & Romero, V. (2000). Ingroup bias and self-esteem: A meta-analysis. *Personality and Social Psychology Review, 4*, 157–173.

Abraham, C. (2002, December 14). Mommy's little secret. *The Globe and Mail* (Toronto), pp. F1, F6.

Abraham, S. F., & Beumont, P. J. V. (1982). How patients describe bulimia or binge eating. *Psychological Medicine, 12*, 625–635.

Abrahamse, W., Steg, L., Vlek, C., & Rothengatter, T. (2007). The effect of tailored information, goal setting, and tailored feedback on household energy use, energy-related behaviors, and behavioral antecedents. *Journal of Environmental Psychology, 27*, 265–276.

Abramowitz, J. S., Tolin, D. F., & Street, G. P. (2001). Paradoxical effects of thought suppression: A meta-analysis of controlled studies. *Clinical Psychology Review, 21*, 683–705.

Abrams, D., Crisp, R. J., Marques, S., Fagg, E., Bedford, L., & Provias, D. (2008). Threat inoculation: Experienced and imagined intergenerational contact prevents stereotype threat effects on older people's math performance. *Psychology and Aging, 23*(4), 934–939.

Abrams, D., de Moura, G., & Travaglino, G. (2013) A double standard when group members behave badly: Transgression credit to ingroup leaders. *Journal of Personality and Social Psychology, 105*, 799–815.

Abshire, J., & Bornstein, B. J. (2003). Juror sensitivity to the cross-race effect. *Law and Human Behavior, 27*, 471–480.

Acker, M., & Davis, M. H. (1992). Intimacy, passion and commitment in adult romantic relationships: A test of the triangular theory of love. *Journal of Social and Personality Relationships, 9*, 21–50.

Ackerman, J. M., Griskevicius, V., & Li, N. P. (2011). Let's get serious: Communicating commitment in romantic relationships. *Journal of Personality and Social Psychology, 100*(6), 1079–1094.

Ackerman, J. M., Shapiro, J. R., Neuberg, S. L., Kenrick, D. T., Schaller, M., Becker, D. V., et al. (2006). They all look the same to me (unless they're angry): From out-group homogeneity to out-group heterogeneity. *Psychological Science, 17*(10), 836–840.

Adams, C. G., & Turner, B. F. (1985). Reported change in sexuality from young adulthood to old age. *Journal of Sex Research, 21*, 126–141.

Adams, G. R., Ryan, B. A., Ketsetzis, M., & Keating, L. (2000). Rule compliance and peer sociability: A study of family process, parent-child school-focused interactions and children's classroom behavior. *Journal of Family Psychology, 14*, 237–250.

Adams, H. E., Wright, L. W., Jr., & Lohr, B. A. (1996). Is homophobia associated with homosexual arousal? *Journal of Abnormal Psychology, 105*, 440–446.

Adams, J. S. (1965). Inequity in social change. In L. Berkowitz (Ed.), *Advances in experimental social psychology* (Vol. 2, pp. 267–299). New York: Academic Press.

Adams, P. R., & Adams, G. R. (1984). Mount St. Helens ashfall: Evidence for a disaster stress reaction, *American Psychologist, 39*, 252–260.

Adhikary, A. K. (1984). *Society and world view of the Birhor: A nomadic hunting and gathering community of Orissa*. Calcutta: Anthropological Survey of India.

Adler, P. (1980). On becoming a prostitute. In E. Muga (Ed.), *Studies in prostitution* (pp. 22–26). Nairobi: Kenya Literature Bureau.

Agras, W. S., & Telch, C. F. (1998). The effects of caloric deprivation and negative affect on binge eating in obese binge-eating disordered women. *Behavior Therapy, 29*, 491–503.

Ahlering, R. F. (1987). Need for cognition, attitudes, and the 1984 Presidential election. *Journal of Research in Personality, 21*, 100–102.

Ahmed, A. M. (2010). Muslim discrimination: Evidence from two lost-letter experiments. *Journal of Applied Social Psychology, 40*(4), 888–898.

Aiello, J. R. (1987). Human spatial behavior. In D. Stokols & I. Altman (Eds.), *Handbook of environmental psychology* (Vol. 1, pp. 505–531). New York: Wiley.

Aiello, J. R., & Douthitt, E. A. (2001). Social facilitation: From Triplett to electronic performance monitoring. *Group Dynamics: Theory, Research, and Practice, 5*, 163–180.

Ainsworth, M. D. (1989). Attachments beyond infancy. *American Psychologist, 44*, 709–716.

Ainsworth, M. D. S., Blehar, M. C., Waters, E., & Wall, S. (1978). *Patterns of attachment: A psychological study of the strange situation*. Hillsdale, NJ: Erlbaum.

Ainsworth, S. E., & Maner, J. K. (2012). Sex begets violence: Mating motives, social dominance, and physical aggression in men. *Journal of Personality and Social Psychology, 103*, 819–829.

Ajzen, I. (1988). *Attitudes, personality, and behavior*. Homewood, IL: Dorsey Press.

Ajzen, I. (2001). Nature and operation of attitudes. In T. Fiske, D. L. Schacter, & C. Zahn-Waxler (Eds.), *Annual review of psychology* (Vol. 52, pp. 27–58). Palo Alto, CA: Annual Reviews.

Ajzen, I. (2012). The theory of planned behavior. In P. A. M. Lange, A. W. Kruglanski, & E. T. Higgins (Eds.), *Handbook of theories of social psychology* (Vol. 1, pp. 438–459). London, U.K.: Sage.

Ajzen, I., & Fishbein, M. (1977). Attitude-behavior relations: A theoretical analysis and review of empirical research. *Psychological Bulletin, 84*, 888–918.

Aknin, L. B., Barrington-Leigh, C. P., Dunn, E. W., Helliwell, J. F., Burns, J., Biswas-Diener, R., Kemerza, I., Nyende, P., Ashton-James, C. E., & Norton, M. I. (2013). Prosocial spending and well-being: Cross-cultural evidence for a psychological universal. *Journal of Personality and Social Psychology, 104*, 635–652.

Section 1.01 Albergotti, R., O'Connell, V., & Vranica, S. (2012, October 18). Lance Armstrong gets dumped: Nike, RadioShack, others distance themselves from cyclist amid drug scandal. *The Wall Street Journal*. Retrieved from http://online.wsj.com/news/articles/SB10000872396390444868204578062313532317222

Alcock, I., White, M. P., Wheeler, B. W., Fleming, L. E., & Depledge, M. H. (2014). Longitudinal effects on mental health of moving to greener and less green urban areas. *Environmental Science & Technology, 48*(2), 1247–1255. doi: 10.1021/es403688w

Alebiosu, K. A. (2001). Cooperative learning and students' affective learning outcome in Nigerian chemistry classrooms. *IFE Psychologia, 9*, 135–142.

Alexander, M. G., & Fisher, T. D. (2003). Truth and consequences: Using the bogus pipeline to examine sex differences in self-reported sexuality. *The Journal of Sex Research, 40*, 27–35.

Alland, A., Jr. (1972). *The human imperative*. New York: Columbia University Press.

Allen, M., Mabry, E., & McKelton, D. (1998). Impact of juror attitudes about the death penalty on juror evaluations of guilt and punishment: A meta-analysis. *Law and Human Behavior, 22*, 715–731.

Allen, N. B., & Badcock, P. B. T. (2003). The social risk hypothesis of depressed mood: Evolutionary, psychosocial, and neurobiological perspectives. *Psychological Bulletin, 129*, 887–913.

Allen, N. J., & Hecht, T. D. (2004). The "romance of teams": Toward an understanding of its psychological underpinnings and implications. *Journal of Occupational and Organizational Psychology, 77*, 439–461.

Allen, T. D., Lentz, E., & Day, R. (2006). Career success outcomes associated with mentoring others: A comparison of mentors and nonmentors. *Journal of Career Development, 32*(3), 272–285.

Alloy, L. B., & Abramson, L. Y. (1979). Judgment of contingency in depressed and nondepressed students: Sadder but wiser? *Journal of Experimental Psychology: General, 108*(4), 441–485.

Allport, F. H. (1924). *Social psychology*. Boston: Houghton Mifflin Company.

Allport, G. (1935). Attitudes. In C. Murchinson (Ed.). *A Handbook of Social Psychology* (pp. 789–844). Worchester, MA: Clark University Press.

Allport, G. W. (1954) *The nature of prejudice*. Reading, MA: Addison-Wesley.

Allport, G. W. (1954). The historical background of modern social psychology. In G. Lindzey (Ed.), *Handbook of social psychology* (Vol. 1, pp. 3–56). Cambridge, MA: Addison-Wesley.

Alpert, J. L., Brown, L. S., & Courtois, C. A. (1998). Symptomatic clients and memories of childhood abuse: What the trauma and child sexual abuse literature tells us. *Psychology, Public Policy, and Law, 4*, 941–995.

Altermatt, T. W., & DeWall, C. N. (2003). Agency and virtue: Dimensions underlying subgroups of women. *Sex Roles, 49*, 631–641.

Altman, I., Nelson, P. A., & Lett, E. E. (1972, Spring). The ecology of home environments. *Catalog of Selected Documents in Psychology* (No. 150).

Altschuler, G. C. (2001, January 7). Battling the cheats. Retrieved October 17, 2004, from http://www.physics.ohio-state.edu/~wilkins/osu_and_ohio/essays/cheat-altschuler.html

Amabile, T. M. (1996). *Creativity in context*. Boulder, CO: Westview Press.

American Planning Association-New York Metro Chapter. (2013). Getting back to business: Addressing the needs of Rockaway businesses impacted by Superstorm Sandy. Retrieved from http://www.nyplanning.org/docs/APANYM%20Business%20Recovery%20Report%20to%20RDRC.pdf

American Psychiatric Association. (1994). *Diagnostic and statistical manual of mental disorders* (4th ed.). Washington, DC: Author.

American Psychological Association (2015). Five tips to help manage stress. Retrieved from http://www.apa.org/helpcenter/manage-stress.aspx

American Psychological Association (2015). How stress affects your health. Retrieved from http://www.apa.org/helpcenter/stress.aspx

American Psychological Association. (2008). Answers to your questions: For a better understanding of sexual orientation and homosexuality. Washington, DC: Author. Retrieved from http://www.apa.org/topics/sorientation.pdf

Ames, D. R., & Flynn, F. J. (2007). What breaks a leader: The curvilinear relation between assertiveness and leadership. *Journal of Personality and Social Psychology, 92*, 307–324.

Amodio, D. M., Harmon-Jones, E., & Devine, P. G. (2003). Individual differences in the activation and control of affective race bias as assessed by startle eyeblink response and self-report. *Journal of Personality and Social Psychology, 84*, 738–753.

Anderson, C. A. (1983). Imagination and expectation: The effect of imagining behavioral scripts on personal intentions. *Journal of Personality and Social Psychology, 45*, 293–305.

Anderson, C. A., & Anderson, K. B. (1996). Violent crime rate studies in philosophical context: A destructive testing approach to heat and southern culture of violence effects. *Journal of Personality and Social Psychology, 70*, 740–756.

Anderson, C. A., & Dill, K. E. (2000). Video games and aggressive thoughts, feelings, and behavior in laboratory and real life. *Journal of Personality and Social Psychology, 78*(4), 772–790.

Anderson, C. A., & Sechler, E. S. (1986). Effects of explanation and counterexplanation on the development and use of social theories. *Journal of Personality and Social Psychology, 20*, 24–34.

Anderson, C. A., Anderson, K. B., Dorr, N., DeNeve, K. M., & Flanagan, M. (2000). Temperature and aggression. In M. Zanna (Ed.), *Advances in experimental social psychology* (Vol. 32, pp. 63–133). New York: Academic Press.

Anderson, C. A., Benjamin, A. J., Jr., & Bartholow, B. D. (1998). Does the gun pull the trigger? Automatic priming effects of weapon pictures and weapon names. *Psychological Science, 9*, 308–314.

Anderson, C. A., Bushman, B. J., & Groom, R. W. (1997). Hot years and serious and deadly assault: Empirical tests of the heat hypothesis. *Journal of Personality and Social Psychology, 73*, 1213–1223.

Anderson, C. A., Bushman, B. J., & Groom, R. W. (1997). Hot years and serious and deadly assault: Empirical tests of the heat hypothesis. *Journal of Personality and Social Psychology, 73*(6), 1213–1223. doi: 10.1037//0022-3514.73.6.1213

Anderson, C. A., Lepper, M. R., & Ross, L. (1980). The perseverance of social theories: The role of explanation in the persistence of discredited information. *Journal of Personality and Social Psychology, 39*, 1037–1049.

Anderson, C. A., Shibuya, A., Ihori, N., Swing, E. L., Bushman, B. J., Sakamoto, A., Rothstein, H. R., Saleem, M., & Barlett, C. P. (2010). Violent video game effects on aggression, empathy, and prosocial behavior in Eastern and Western countries: A meta-analytic review. *Psychological Bulletin, 136*(2), 151–173. doi: 10.1037/a0018251

Anderson, C. J. (2003). The psychology of doing nothing: Forms of decision avoidance result from reason and emotion. *Psychological Bulletin, 129*, 139–167.

Anderson, D. (2013, June 3). UNM Response to Tweet by Professor Geoffrey Miller. *UNM Newsroom*. Retrieved from http://news.unm.edu/news/unm-response-to-tweet-by-professor-geoffrey-miller

Anderson, J. O., Thundiyil, J. G., & Stobach, A. (2012). Clearing the air: A review of the effects of particulate matter air pollution on human health. *Journal of Medical Toxicology, 8*, 166–175.

Anderson, N., & Thomas, H. D. C. (1996). Work group socialization. In M. A. West (Ed.), *Handbook of work group psychology* (pp. 423–450). Chichester, UK: Wiley.

Anderson, P. B., & Struckman-Johnson, C. (Eds.). (1998). *Sexually aggressive women: Current perspectives and controversies.* New York: Guilford Press.

Anderson, S. A., Russell, C. S., & Schumm, W. R. (1983). Perceived marital quality and family life-cycle categories: A further analysis. *Journal of Marriage and the Family, 45*, 127–139.

Ansari, S., Wijen, F., & Gray, B. (2013). Constructing a climate change logic: An institutional perspective on the "tragedy of the commons." *Organization Science, 24*, 1014–1040.

Antonovsky, H. F., Shoham, I., Kavenocki, S., Modan, B., & Lancet, M. (1978). Sexual attitude-behavior discrepancy among Israeli adolescent girls. *Journal of Sex Research, 14*, 260–272.

Appelbaum, P., & Swanson, J. (2010). Gun laws and mental illness: How sensible are the current restrictions. *Psychiatric Services, 61*, 652-654. doi: 10.1176/appi.ps.61.7.652

Apsler, R., & Sears, D. O. (1968). Warning, personal involvement, and attitude change. *Journal of Personality and Social Psychology, 9*, 162–168.

Apuzzo, M., & Schmidt, M. S. (2014, August 23). In Washington, Second Thoughts on Arming Police. *New York Times*. Retrieved from http://www.nytimes.com/2014/08/24/us/in-washington-second-thoughts-on-arming-police.html

Archea, J. (1990). Two earthquakes: Three human conditions. In Y. Yoshitake, R. B. Bechtel, T. Takahashi, & M. Asai (Eds.), *Current issues in environment-behavior research*. Tokyo: University of Tokyo.

Archer, J. (1988). *The behavioral biology of aggression*. Cambridge: Cambridge University Press.

Archer, J. (2000). Sex differences in aggression between heterosexual partners: A meta-analytic review. *Psychological Bulletin, 126*, 651–680.

Ard, B. N. (1977). Sex in lasting marriages: A longitudinal study. *Journal of Sex Research, 13*, 274–285.

Areni, C. S., & Kim, D. (1993). The influence of background music on shopping behavior: Classical versus Top-Forty. In L. McAlister & M. L. Rothschild (Eds.), *Advances in consumer research* (pp. 336–340). Provo, UT: Association for Consumer Research.

Ariely, D., & Levav, J. (2000). Sequential choice in group settings: Taking the road less traveled and less enjoyed. *Journal of Consumer Research, 27*, 279–290.

Aries, E. J., & Johnson, F. L. (1983). Close friendship in adulthood: Conversational content between same-sex friends. *Sex Roles, 9*, 1183–1196.

Aries, P. (1962). *Centuries of childhood: A social history of family life* (Trans. R. Baldick). New York: Random House.

Arkes, H. R. (1991). Costs and benefits of judgment errors: Implications for debiasing. *Psychological Bulletin, 110*, 486–498.

Armbrister, R. C. (2002). A cross-cultural comparison of student social attributions. *Psychology in the Schools, 39*, 39–49.

Armitage, C. J., & Conner, M. (2001). Efficacy of the theory of planned behaviour: A meta-analytic review. *British Journal of Social Psychology, 40*, 471–499.

Arndt, B. (2009). *The Sex Diaries*. Melbourne: Melbourne University Press.

Arochova, O., Kontrova, J., Lipkova, V., & Liska, J. (1988). Effect of toxic atmosphere emissions on cognitive performance by children. *Studia Psychologica, 30*, 101–114.

Aron, A., Fisher, H., & Strong, G. (2006). Romantic love. In A. Vangelisti & D. Perlman (Eds.), *Cambridge handbook of personal relationships* (pp. 595–614). New York: Cambridge University Press.

Aronson, E. (2000). *Nobody left to hate: Teaching compassion after Columbine*. New York: W. H. Freeman.

Aronson, E. (2007). *The social animal*. New York: Worth.

Aronson, E., & Carlsmith, J. M. (1968). Experimentation in social psychology. In G. Lindzey & E. Aronson (Eds.), *Handbook of Social Psychology* (2nd ed., Vol. 2, pp. 1–79). Reading, MA: Addison-Wesley.

Aronson, E., & Mills, J. (1959). The effect of severity of initiation on liking for a group. *Journal of Abnormal and Social Psychology, 59*, 177–181.

Aronson, E., & Osherow, N. (1980). Cooperation, prosocial behavior, and academic performance: Experiments in the desegregated classroom. *Applied Social Psychology Annual, 1*, 163–196.

Aronson, E., & Patnoe, S. (1997). *The jigsaw classroom: Building cooperation in the classroom* (2nd ed.). New York: Addison Wesley Longman.

Aronson, E., Blaney, N., Stephin, C., Sikes, J., & Snapp, M. (1978). *The jigsaw classroom*. Beverly Hills, CA: Sage.

Aronson, J., Lustina, M. J., Good, C., Keough, K., Steele, C. M., & Brown, J. (1999). When white men can't do math: Necessary and sufficient factors in stereotype threat. *Journal of Experimental Social Psychology, 35*, 29–46.

Arthur, J. B. (1994). Effects of human resource systems on manufacturing performance and turnover. *Academy of Management Journal, 37*, 670–687.

Arvey, R. D., & Campion, J. E. (1982). The employment interview: A summary and review of recent research. *Personnel Psychology, 35*, 281–322.

Asch, S. E. (1955, November). Opinions and social pressure. *Scientific American*, 31–35.

Asch, S. E. (1956). Studies of independence and conformity: I. A minority of one against a unanimous majority. *Psychological Monographs, 70* (No. 416).

Ashton, H., & Stepney, R. (1982). *Smoking: Psychology and pharmacology*. London: Tavistock.

Associated Press (2013, May 7). Airman who led sex assault unit charged in groping. Retrieved from http://bigstory.ap.org/article/airman-who-led-sex-assault-unit-charged-groping

Associated Press. (2013, February 25). Homeless man to get more than $100,000 for good deed. Retrieved from http://www.thestar.com/news/world/2013/02/25/homeless_man_to_get_more_than_100000_for_good_deed.html

Atheist must swear to God—or leave US Air Force (2014, September 10). Retrieved from http://news.yahoo.com/atheist-must-swear-god-leave-us-air-force-232153866.html

Atkinson, T., Liem, R., & Liem, J. H. (1986). The social costs of unemployment: Implications for social support. *Journal of Health and Social Behavior, 27*, 317–331.

Atran, S. (2003). Genesis of suicide terrorism. *Science, 299*, 1534–1539.

Atthowe, J. M. (1960). Types of conflict and their resolution: A reinterpretation. *Journal of Experimental Psychology, 59*, 1–9.

Austin, W., McGinn, N. C., & Susmilch, C. (1980). Internal standards revisited: Effects of social comparisons and expectancies on judgments of fairness and satisfaction. *Journal of Experimental Social Psychology, 16*, 426–441.

Averill, J. R. (1982). *Anger and aggression: An essay on emotion*. New York: Springer-Verlag.

Avolio, B. J., Kahai, S. S., & Dodge, G. (2000). E-leading in organizations and it implications for theory, research and practice. *Leadership Quarterly, 11*, 615–670.

Axelrod, R., & Hamilton, W. D. (1981). The evolution of cooperation. *Science, 211*, 1390–1396.

Axelrod. R. (1980). More effective choice in the prisoner's dilemma. *Journal of Conflict Resolution, 24*, 3–25.

Baard, P. P., Deci, E. L., & Ryan, R. M. (2004). Intrinsic need satisfaction: A motivational basis of performance and well-being in two work settings. *Journal of Applied Social Psychology, 34*(10), 2045–2068.

Babin, B. J., & Babin, L. (2001). Seeking something different? A model of schema typicality, consumer affect, purchase intentions and perceived shopping value. *Journal of Business Research, 54*, 89–96.

Bachman, J. G., & O'Malley, P. M. (1977). Self-esteem in young men: A longitudinal analysis of the impact of educational and occupational attainment. *Journal of Personality and Social Psychology, 35*, 365–380.

Bachman, J. G., & O'Malley, P. M. (1986). Self-concepts, self-esteem, and educational experiences: The frog pond revisited (again). *Journal of Personality and Social Psychology, 50*, 35–46.

Backteman, G., & Magnusson, D. (1981). Longitudinal stability of personality characteristics. *Journal of Personality, 49*, 148–160.

Badawy, A. A.-B. (2003). Alcohol and violence and the possible role of serotonin. *Criminal Behaviour and Mental Health, 13*(1), 31–44. doi: 10.1002/cbm

Baggini, J. (2004). Bad moves: Confirmation bias. Retrieved from http://www.butterfliesandwheels.com/badmovesprint.php?num542

Bagozzi, R. P., Wong, N., Abe, S., & Bergami, M. (2000). Cultural and situational contingencies and the theory of reasoned action: Application to fast food restaurant consumption. *Journal of Consumer Psychology, 9*, 97–106.

Bahns, A. J., & Branscombe, N. R. (2011). Effects of legitimizing discrimination against homosexuals on gay bashing. *European Journal of Social Psychology, 41*(3), 388–396.

Bailey, J. M., & Pillard, R. C. (1995). Genetics of human sexual orientation. *Annual Review of Sex Research, 6*, 126–150.

Bailey, R. C., & Aunger, R. V. (1995). Sexuality, infertility and sexually transmitted disease among farmers and foragers in central Africa. In P. Abramson & S. Pinkerton (Eds.), *Sexual nature/sexual culture* (pp. 195–222). Chicago: University of Chicago Press.

Balch, R. W. & Taylor, D. (2002). Making sense of the Heaven's Gate suicides. In D. G. Bromley & J. G. Melton (Eds.), *Cults, religion, and violence* (pp. 209–228). New York: Cambridge University Press.

Baldwin, M. W. (1992). Relational schemas and the processing of social information. *Psychological Bulletin, 112*, 461–474.

Balliet, D., Li, N. P., & Joireman, J. (2011). Relating trait self-control and forgiveness within prosocials and proselfs: Compensatory versus synergistic models. *Journal of Personality and Social Psychology, 101*(5), 1090–1105.

Balliet, D., Li, N. P., Macfarlan, S. J., Van Vugt, M. (2011). Sex differences in cooperation: a meta-analytic review of social dilemmas. *Psychological Bulletin, 137*(6), 881–909.

Balogun, S. K. (1991). Personal space as affected by religions of the approaching and the approached people. *Indian Journal of Behaviour, 15*, 45–50.

Bamberg, S., & Moser, G. (2007). Twenty years after Hines, Hungerford, and Tomera: A new meta-analysis of psycho-social determinants of pro-environmental behaviour. *Journal of Environmental Psychology, 27*, 14–25.

Bandura, A. (1965). Influence of models' reinforcement contingencies on the acquisition of imitative responses. *Journal of Abnormal and Social Psychology, 66*, 575–582.

Bandura, A. (1973). *Aggression: A social learning theory analysis.* Englewood Cliffs, NJ: Prentice-Hall.

Bandura, A. (1977). *Social learning theory.* Englewood Cliffs, NJ: Prentice Hall.

Bandura, A. (1986). *Social foundations of thought and action: A social-cognitive theory.* Englewood Cliffs, NJ: Prentice-Hall.

Bandura, A., & Schunk, D. H. (1981). Cultivating competence, self-efficacy, and intrinsic interest through proximal self-motivation. *Journal of Personality and Social Psychology, 41*, 586–598.

Bandura, A., & Schunk, D. H. (1981). Cultivating competence, self-efficacy, and intrinsic interest through proximal self-motivation. *Journal of Personality and Social Psychology, 41*, 586–598.

Bandura, A., Ross, D., & Ross, S. A. (1961). Transmission of aggression through imitation of aggressive models. *Journal of Abnormal and Social Psychology, 63*, 575–582.

Bandura, A., Ross, D., & Ross, S. A. (1963). Vicarious reinforcement and imitative learning. *Journal of Abnormal and Social Psychology, 67*, 601–607.

Banny, A. M., Heilbron, N., Ames, A., & Prinstein, M. J. (2011). Relational benefits of relational aggression: Adaptive and maladaptive associations with adolescent friendship quality. *Developmental Psychology, 47*(4), 1153–1166.

Barash, D. P., & Lipton, J. E. (2002). *Myth of monogamy: Fidelity and infidelity in animals and people.* New York: W. H. Freeman.

Barbee, A. P., Lawrence, T., & Cunningham, M. R. (1998). When a friend is in need: Feelings about seeking, giving, and receiving social support. In P. Anderson & L. Guerro (Eds.), *Handbook of communication and emotion* (pp. 282–298). New York: Academic Press.

Barfield, R. L. (2003). Students' perceptions of and satisfaction with group grades and the group experience in the college classroom. *Assessment and Evaluation in Higher Education, 28*(4), 355–369.

Bargh, J. A. (1982). Attention and automaticity in the processing of self-relevant information. *Journal of Personality and Social Psychology, 43*, 425–436.

Bargh, J. A. (1994). The four horsemen of automaticity: Awareness, intention, efficiency, and control in social cognition. In R. S. Wyer, Jr., & T. K. Srull (Eds.), *Handbook of social cognition* (pp. 1–40). Hillsdale, NJ: Erlbaum.

Bargh, J. A., & Shaley, I. (2012). The substitutability of physical and social warmth in daily life. *Emotion, 12*, 154–162.

Bargh, J. A., Chaiken, S., Raymond, P., & Hymes, C. (1996). The automatic evaluation effect: Unconditional automatic attitude activation with a pronunciation task. *Journal of Experimental Social Psychology, 32*, 104–128.

Bargh, J. A., Chen, M., & Burrows, L. (1996). Automaticity of social behavior: Direct effects of trait construct and stereotype activation on action. *Journal of Personality and Social Psychology, 71*(2), 230–244.

Bargh, J. A., Gollwitzer, P. M., Lee-Chai, A., Barndollar, K., & Trötschel, R. (2001). The automated will: Nonconscious activation and pursuit of behavioral goals. *Journal of Personality and Social Psychology, 81*, 1014–1027.

Bargh, J. A., Raymond, P., Pryor, J. B., & Strack, F. (1995). The attractiveness of the underling: An automatic power-sex association and its consequences for sexual harassment. *Journal of Personality and Social Psychology, 68*, 768–781.

Barker, M. R., Bailey, J. S., & Lee, N. (2004). The impact of verbal prompts on child safety-belt use in shopping carts. *Journal of Applied Behavior Analysis, 37*, 527–530.

Barlow, D. H. (1988). *Anxiety and its disorders: The nature and treatment of anxiety and panic.* New York: Guilford Press.

Barlow, F. K., Paolini, S., Pedersen, A., Hornsey, M. J., Radke, H. R. M., Harwood, J., Rubin, M., & Sibley, C. G. (2012). The contact caveat: Negative contact predicts increased prejudice more than positive contact predicts reduced prejudice. *Personality and Social Psychology Bulletin, 38*(12), 1629–1643. doi: 10.1177/0146167212457953

Barnard, W. A., & Bell, P. A. (1982). An unobtrusive apparatus for measuring interpersonal distance. *Journal of General Psychology, 107*, 85–90.

Baron, R. A. (1976). The reduction of human aggression: A field study of the influence of incompatible reactions. *Journal of Applied Social Psychology, 6*, 260–274.

Baron, R. A., & Richardson, D. R. (1994). *Human aggression* (2nd ed.). New York: Plenum Press.

Barrick, M. R., Day, D. V., Lord, R. G., & Alexander, R. A. (1991). Assessing the utility of executive leadership. *Leadership Quarterly, 2*, 9–22.

Barrios, B. A., Corbitt, L. C., Estes, J. P., & Topping, J. S. (1976). Effect of social stigma on interpersonal distance. *The Psychological Record, 26*, 342–348.

Barry, D. (2000). Female or male? Take test. *Chicago Tribune.* Retrieved from http://news.google.com/newspapers?nid51955&dat520000702&id5Pw0iAAAAIBAJ&sjid5R6YFAAAAIBAJ&pg51571,525620

Barry, H., III, & Paxson, L. M. (1971). Infancy and early childhood: Cross-cultural codes II. *Ethnology, 10*, 466–508.

Barsky, A. J. (1988). *Worried sick: Our troubled quest for wellness.* New York: Little Brown and Co.

Bartholomew, K. (1990). Avoidance of intimacy: An attachment perspective. *Journal of Social and Personal Relationships, 7*, 147–178.

Bartholomew, K., & Horowitz, L. M. (1991). Attachment styles among young adults: A test of a four-category model. *Journal of Personality and Social Psychology, 61*, 226–244.

Bartholomew, K., & Shaver, P. R. (1998). Measures of attachment: Do they converge? In J. A. Simpson & W. S. Rholes (Eds.), *Attachment theory and close relationships* (pp. 25–45). New York: Guilford Press.

Bartholow, B. D., & Heinz, A. (2006). Alcohol and aggression without consumption: Alcohol cues, aggressive thoughts, and hostile perception bias. *Psychological Science, 17*, 30–37.

Basner, M., Babisch, W., Davis, A., Brink, M., Clark, C., Janssen, S., & Stansfeld, S. (2014). Auditory and non-auditory effects of noise on health. *Lancet, 383*, 1325–1332.

Bass, B. M. (1990). From transactional to transformational leadership: Learning to share the vision. *Organizational Dynamics, 18*(3), 19–31.

Bator, R. J., Bryan, A. D., & Schultz, P. W. (2011). Who gives a hoot? Intercept surveys of litterers and disposers. *Environment and Behavior, 43*(3), 295–315.

Batson v. Kentucky, 106 S.Ct. 1712 (1986).

Batson, C. D., Batson, J. G., Slingsby, J. K., Harrell, K. L., Peekna, H. M., & Todd, R. M. (1991). Empathic joy and the empathy-altruism hypothesis. *Journal of Personality and Social Psychology, 61*, 413–426.

Batson, C. D., Duncan, B. D., Ackerman, P., Buckley, T., & Birch, K. (1981). Is empathic emotion a source of altruism motivation? *Journal of Personality and Social Psychology, 40*, 290–302.

Battistich, V., Solomon, D., & Delucchi, K. (1993). Interaction processes and student outcomes in cooperative learning groups. *The Elementary School Journal, 94*, 19–32.

Baum, A., & Fleming, I. (1993). Implications of psychological research on stress and technological accidents. *American Psychologist, 48*, 665–672.

Baum, A., & Paulus, P. B. (1987). Crowding. In D. Stokols & I. Altman (Eds.), *Handbook of environmental psychology* (Vol. 1, pp. 533–570). New York: Wiley-Interscience.

Baumeister, R. F. (1982). A self-presentational view of social phenomena. *Psychological Bulletin, 91*, 3–26.

Baumeister, R. F. (1987). How the self became a problem: A psychological review of historical research. *Journal of Personality and Social Psychology, 52*, 163–176.

Baumeister, R. F. (1990). Suicide as escape from self. *Psychological Review, 97*, 90–113.

Baumeister, R. F. (1991). *Meanings of life.* New York: Guilford Press.

Baumeister, R. F. (1997). *Evil: Inside human cruelty and violence.* New York: W. H. Freeman.

Baumeister, R. F. (2000). Gender differences in erotic plasticity: The female sex drive as socially flexible and responsive. *Psychological Bulletin, 126*, 347–374.

Baumeister, R. F. (2002). Ego depletion and self-control failure: An energy model of the self's executive function. *Self and Identity, 1*, 129–136.

Baumeister, R. F. (2005). *The cultural animal: Human nature, meaning, and social life.* New York: Oxford University Press.

Baumeister, R. F., & Bratslavsky, E. (1999). Passion, intimacy, and time: Passionate love as a function of change in intimacy. *Personality and Social Psychology Review, 3*, 49–67.

Baumeister, R. F., & Cairns, K. J. (1992). Repression and self-presentation: When audiences interfere with self-deceptive strategies. *Journal of Personality and Social Psychology, 62*, 851–862.

Baumeister, R. F., & Jones, E. E. (1978). When self-presentation is constrained by the target's knowledge: Consistency and compensation. *Journal of Personality and Social Psychology, 36*, 608–618.

Baumeister, R. F., & Leary, M. R. (1995). The need to belong: Desire for interpersonal attachments as a fundamental human motivation. *Psychological Bulletin, 117*, 497–529.

Baumeister, R. F., & Masicampo, E. J. (2010). Conscious thought is for facilitating social and cultural interactions: How mental simulations serve the animal-culture interface. *Psychological Review, 117*, 945–971.

Baumeister, R. F., & Tice, D. M. (1984). Role of self-presentation and choice in cognitive dissonance under forced compliance: Necessary or sufficient causes? *Journal of Personality and Social Psychology, 46*, 5–13.

Baumeister, R. F., & Tierney, J. (2011). *Willpower: Rediscovering the greatest human strength.* New York: Penguin Press.

Baumeister, R. F., & Twenge, J. M. (2002). Cultural suppression of female sexuality. *Review of General Psychology, 6*, 166–203.

Baumeister, R. F., & Vohs, K. D. (2004). Sexual economics: Sex as female resource for social exchange in heterosexual interactions. *Personality and Social Psychology Review, 8*(4), 339–363.

Baumeister, R. F., & Wotman, S. R. (1992). *Breaking hearts: The two sides of unrequited love.* New York: Guilford Press.

Baumeister, R. F., Bratslavsky, E., Finkenauer, C., & Vohs, K. D. (2001). Bad is stronger than good. *Review of General Psychology, 5*, 323–370.

Baumeister, R. F., Bratslavsky, E., Finkenauer, C., & Vohs, K. D. (2001). Bad is stronger than good. *Review of General Psychology, 5*(4), 323–370. doi: 10.1037//1089-2680.5.4.323

Baumeister, R. F., Bratslavsky, E., Muraven, M., & Tice, D. M. (1998). Ego depletion: Is the active self a limited resource? *Journal of Personality and Social Psychology, 74*, 1252–1265.

Baumeister, R. F., Campbell, J. D., Krueger, J. I., & Vohs, K. D. (2003). Does high self-esteem cause better performance, interpersonal success, happiness, or healthier lifestyles? *Psychological Science in the Public Interest, 4*, 1–44.

Baumeister, R. F., Catanese, K. R., & Vohs, K. D. (2001). Is there a gender difference in strength of sex drive? Theoretical views, conceptual distinctions, and a review of relevant evidence. *Personality and Social Psychology Review, 5*, 242–273.

Baumeister, R. F., Catanese, K. R., & Wallace, H. M. (2002). Conquest by force: A narcissistic reactance theory of rape and sexual coercion. *Review of General Psychology, 6*, 92–135.

Baumeister, R. F., DeWall, C. N., Ciarocco, N. J., & Twenge, J. M. (2005). Social exclusion impairs self-regulation. *Journal of Personality and Social Psychology, 88*, 589–684.

Baumeister, R. F., Heatherton, T. F., & Tice, D. M. (1994). *Losing control: How and why people fail at self-regulation.* San Diego: Academic Press.

Baumeister, R. F., Hutton, D. G., & Tice, D. M. (1989). Cognitive processes during deliberate self-presentation: How self-presenters alter and misinterpret the behavior of their interaction partners. *Journal of Experimental Social Psychology, 25*, 59–78.

Baumeister, R. F., Masicampo, E. J., & DeWall, C. N. (2009). Prosocial benefits of feeling free: Disbelief in free will increases aggression and reduces helpfulness. *Personality and Social Psychology Bulletin, 35*, 260–268.

Baumeister, R. F., Masicampo, E. J., & Vohs, K. D. (2011). Do conscious thoughts cause behavior? *Annual Review of Psychology, 62*, 331–361.

Baumeister, R. F., Reis, H. T., & Delespaul, P. A. E. G. (1995). Subjective and experiential correlates of guilt in everyday life. *Personality and Social Psychology Bulletin, 21*, 1256–1268.

Baumeister, R. F., Smart, L., & Boden, J. M. (1996). Relation of threatened egotism to violence and aggression: The dark side of high self-esteem. *Psychological Review, 103*, 5–33.

Baumeister, R. F., Stillwell, A. M., & Heatherton, T. F. (1994). Guilt: An interpersonal approach. *Psychological Bulletin, 115*, 243–267. doi:10.1037/0033-2909.115.2.243

Baumeister, R. F., Stillwell, A. M., & Heatherton, T. F. (1995). Personal narratives about guilt: Role in action control and interpersonal relationships. *Basic and Applied Social Psychology, 17*, 173–198. doi: 10.1207/s15324834basp1701&2_10

Baumeister, R. F., Twenge, J. M., & Nuss, C. K. (2002). Effects of social exclusion on cognitive processes: Anticipated aloneness reduces intelligent thought. *Journal of Personality and Social Psychology, 83*, 817–827.

Baumeister, R. F., Wotman, S. R., & Stillwell, A. M. (1993). Unrequited love: On heartbreak, anger, guilt, scriptlessness, and humiliation. *Journal of Personality and Social Psychology, 64*, 377–394.

Baunach, D. M., Burgess, E. O., & Muse, C. S. (2010). Southern (dis)comfort: Sexual prejudice and contact with gay men and lesbians in the south. *Sociological Spectrum, 30*(1), 30–64.

Bawer, B. (2012). *The victims' revolution: The rise of identity studies and the closing of the liberal mind.* New York: Broadside Books.

Bay-Hinitz, A. K., Peterson, R. F., & Quilitch, H. R. (1994). Cooperative games: A way to modify aggressive and cooperative behaviors in young children. *Journal of Applied Behavior Analysis, 27*, 435–446.

Bazargan, S., Sherkat, D. E., & Bazargan, M. (2004). Religion and alcohol use among African-American and Hispanic inner-city emergency care patients. *Journal for the Scientific Study of Religion, 43*, 419–428.

Bazerman, M. H., Loewenstein, G. F., & White, S. B. (1992). Reversals of preference in allocation decisions: Judging an alternative versus choosing among alternatives. *Administrative Science Quarterly, 37*(2), 220–240.

Beal, D. J., Cohen, R. R., Burke, M. J., & McLendon, C. L. (2003). Cohesion and performance in groups: A meta-analytic clarification of construct relations. *Journal of Applied Psychology, 88*(6), 989–1004.

Beaman, A. L., Barnes, P. J., & Klentz, B. (1978). Increasing helping rates through information dissemination: Teaching pays. *Personality and Social Psychology Bulletin, 4*, 406–411.

Bechara, A., Damasio, H., Tranel, D., & Damasio, A. R. (1997). Deciding advantageously before knowing the advantageous strategy. *Science, 275*, 1293–1295.

Beck, A. T. (1976). *Cognitive therapy and the emotional disorders.* New York: Meridian.

Beck, A. T. (1988). *Cognitive therapy of depression: A personal reflection.* The Malcolm Millar Lecture in Psychotherapy. Aberdeen: Scottish Cultural Press.

Beck, A. T., & Burns, D. (1978). Cognitive therapy of depressed suicidal outpatients. In J. O. Cole, A. F. Schatzberg, & S. H. Frazier (Eds.), *Depression: Biology, psychodynamics, and treatment* (pp. 199–211). New York: Plenum Press.

Beck, J. G., Bozman, A. W., & Qualtrough, T. (1991). The experience of sexual desire: Psychological correlates in a college sample. *Journal of Sex Research, 28*, 443–456.

Becker, A. E., Burwell, R. A., Herzog, D. B., Hamburg, P., & Gilman, S. E. (2002). Eating behaviours and attitudes following prolonged exposure to television among ethnic Fijian adolescent girls. *British Journal of Psychiatry, 180*, 509–514.

Becker, J. C., & Wright, S. C. (2011). Yet another dark side of chivalry: Benevolent sexism undermines and hostile sexism motivates collective action for social change. *Journal of Personality and Social Psychology, 101*, 62–77.

Becker, L. J. (1978). The joint effect of feedback and goal setting on performance: A field study of residential energy conservation. *Journal of Applied Psychology, 63*, 228–233.

Becker, M. H. (Ed.). (1974). The health belief model and personal health behavior. *Health Education Monographs, 2*, entire issue.

Beggan, J. K. (1992). On the social nature of nonsocial perception: The mere ownership effect. *Journal of Personality and Social Psychology, 62*, 229–237.

Beggan, J. K., Messick, D. M., & Allison, S. T. (1988). Social values and egocentric bias: Two tests of the might over morality hypothesis. *Journal of Personality and Social Psychology, 55*, 606–611.

Bègue, L., & Bastounis, M. (2003). Two spheres of belief in justice: Extensive support for the bidimensional model of belief in a just world. *Journal of Personality, 71*, 435–463.

Bègue, L., Beauvois J-L., Courbet, D., Oberlé, D., Lepage, J., & Duke, A. A. (2015). Personality predicts obedience in a Milgram paradigm. *Journal of Personality, 83*(3), 299–306. doi: 10.1111/jopy.12104

Behrman, B. W., & Davey, S. L. (2001). Eyewitness identification in actual criminal cases: An archival analysis. *Law and Human Behavior, 25*, 475–491.

Beilock, S. L., & Carr, T. H. (2001). On the fragility of skilled performance: What governs choking under pressure? *Journal of Experimental Psychology: General, 130*, 701–725.

Bejciy-Spring, S. M. (2008). R-E-S-P-E-C-T: A model for the sensitive treatment of the bariatric patient. *Bariatric Nursing and Surgical Patient Care, 3*(1), 47–56.

Bell, A. P., & Weinberg, M. S. (1978). *Homosexualities: A study of diversity among men and women.* New York: Simon & Schuster.

Bell, P. A., & Greene, T. C. (1982). Thermal stress: Physiological comfort, performance, and social effects of hot and cold environments. In G. W. Evans (Ed.), *Environmental stress* (pp. 75–105). London: Cambridge University Press.

Belsky, J. (1985). Exploring individual differences in marital change across the transition to parenthood: The role of violated expectations. *Journal of Marriage and the Family, 47*, 1037–1044.

Belsky, J., Lang, M. E., & Rovine, M. (1985). Stability and change in marriage across the transition to parenthood: A second study. *Journal of Marriage and the Family, 47*, 855–865.

Belsky, J., Spanier, G. B., & Rovine, M. (1983). Stability and change in marriage across the transition to parenthood. *Journal of Marriage and the Family, 45*, 567–577.

Bem, D. J. (1965). An experimental analysis of self-persuasion. *Journal of Experimental Social Psychology, 1*, 199–218. Jones, E. E., & Gerard, H. B. (1967). *Foundations of social psychology.* New York: Wiley.

Bem, D. J. (1996). Exotic becomes erotic: A developmental theory of sexual orientation. *Psychological Review, 103*, 320–335.

Bem, D. J. (1998). Is EBE theory supported by evidence? Is it androcentric? A reply to Peplau et al. (1998). *Psychological Review, 105*, 395–398.

Benbow, C. P., Lubinski, D., Shea, D. L., & Eftekhari-Sanjani, H. (2000). Sex differences in mathematical reasoning ability: Their status 20 years later. *Psychological Science, 11*, 474–480.

Benenson, J. F. (2014). *Warriors and worriers: The survival of the sexes.* Oxford, UK: Oxford University Press.

Benson, G. P., & Zieman, G. L. (1981). *The relationship of weather to children's behavior problems.* Unpublished manuscript, Colorado State University, Fort Collins, CO.

Benson, P. L., Karabenick, S. A., & Lerner, R. M. (1976). Pretty pleases: The effects of physical attractiveness, race, and sex on receiving help. *Journal of Experimental Social Psychology, 12*, 409–415.

Benton, D. (2007). The impact of diet on anti-social, violent and criminal behaviour. *Neuroscience & Biobehavioral Reviews, 31*(5), 752–774.

Berenguer, J. (2010). The effect of empathy in environmental moral reasoning. *Environment and Behavior, 42*, 110–134.

Berglas, S., & Jones, E. E. (1978). Drug choice as a self-handicapping strategy in response to non-contingent success. *Journal of Personality and Social Psychology, 36*, 405–417.

Berglas, S. C., & Baumeister, R. F. (1993). *Your own worst enemy: Understanding the paradox of self-defeating behavior.* New York: Basic Books.

Berkowitz, A. D., & Perkins, H. W. (1987). Recent research on gender differences in collegiate alcohol use. *Journal of American College Health, 36*, 123–129.

Berkowitz, L. (1989). Frustration-aggression hypothesis: Examination and reformulation. *Psychological Bulletin, 106*, 59–73.

Berkowitz, L. (1993). *Aggression: Its causes, consequences, and control.* New York: McGraw-Hill.

Berkowitz, L., & Donnerstein, E. (1982). External validity is more than skin deep. *American Psychologist, 37*, 245–257.

Berkowitz, L., & LePage, A. (1967). Weapons as aggression-eliciting stimuli. *Journal of Personality and Social Psychology, 7*, 202–207.

Berman, M. E., Tracy, J. I., & Coccaro, E. F. (1997). The serotonin hypothesis of aggression revisited. *Clinical Psychology Review, 17*, 651–665.

Bernard, J. (1982). *The future of marriage.* New Haven, CT: Yale University Press.

Bernat, J. A., Calhoun, K. S., Adams, H. E., & Zeichner, A. (2001). Homophobia and physical aggression toward homosexual and heterosexual individuals. *Journal of Abnormal Psychology, 110*, 179–187.

Berscheid, E., & Walster, E. (1967). When does a harm-doer compensate a victim? *Journal of Personality and Social Psychology, 6*, 433–441.

Bettencourt, B. A., & Miller, N. (1996). Gender differences in aggression as a function of provocation: A meta-analysis. *Psychological Bulletin, 119*, 422–447.

Bhatti, B., Derezotes, D., Kim, S., & Specht, H. (1989). The association between child maltreatment and self-esteem. In A. M. Mecca, N. J. Smelser, & J. Vasconcellos (Eds.), *The social importance of self-esteem* (pp. 24–71). Berkeley: University of California Press.

Biddle, B. J., & Thomas, E. J. (1966). *Role theory: Concepts and research*. New York: Wiley.

Biel, A., Eek, D., & Gaerling, T. (1999). The importance of fairness for cooperation public-goods dilemmas. In P. Juslin (Ed.), *Judgment and decision making: Neo-Brunswikian and process-tracing approaches* (pp. 245–259). Mahwah, NJ: Erlbaum.

Biggs, A. T., Brockmole, J. R., & Witt, J. K. (2013). Armed and attentive: Holding a weapon can bias attentional priorities during scene viewing. *Attention, Perception, & Psychophysics, 75*(8), 1715–1724.

Billig, M., & Tajfel, H. (1973). Social categorization and similarity in intergroup behaviour. *European Journal of Social Psychology, 3*(1), 27–52.

Binder, J., Zagefka, H., Brown, R., Funke, F., Kessler, T., Mummendey, A., et al. (2009). Does contact reduce prejudice or does prejudice reduce contact? A longitudinal test of the contact hypothesis among majority and minority groups in three European countries. *Journal of Personality and Social Psychology, 96*(4), 843–856.

Biryukov, P. (1911). *Leo Tolstoy: His life and work*. New York: Charles Scribner's Sons.

Bishop, J. A., & Inderbitzen, H. M. (1995). Peer acceptance and friendship: An investigation of their relation to self-esteem. *Journal of Early Adolescence, 15*, 476–489.

Bishop, S. (2008, January 23). Don't bother with the "green" consumer. *Harvard Business Report*. Retrieved from http://www.hbrgreen.org/2008/01/dont_bother_with_the_green_con.html

Biss, R. K., Hasher, L., & Thomas, R. C. (2010). Positive mood is associated with the implicit use of distraction. *Motivation and Emotion, 34*(1), 73–77.

Bjerregaard, B. (2000). An empirical study of stalking victimization. *Violence and Victims, 15*, 389–406.

Blackstone, W. (1783). *Commentaries on the Laws of England* (9th ed., Vol. 4, p. 358). London: Strahan, Cadell & Prince.

Blackwell, B., & Hutchins, I. (1994). *Delights of the garden*. New York: Doubleday.

Blader, S. L., & Chen, Y. (2012). Differentiating the effects of status and power: A justice perspective. *Journal of Personality and Social Psychology, 102*, 994–1014.

Blanchard, F. A., & Frost, R. O. (1983). Two factors of restraint: Concern for dieting and fluctuations. *Behavior Research and Therapy, 21*, 259–267.

Blanchette, I. (2006). Snakes, spiders, guns, and syringes: How specific are evolutionary constraints on the detection of threatening stimuli? *The Quarterly Journal of Experimental Psychology, 59*(8), 1484–1504.

Bland, S. H., O'Leary, E. S., Farinaro, E., Jossa, F., & Trevisan, M. (1996). Long-term psychological effects of natural disasters. *Psychosomatic Medicine, 58*, 18–25.

Blankenship, K. L., & Wegener, D. T. (2008). Opening the mind to close it: Considering a message in light of important values increases message processing and later resistance to change. *Journal of Personality and Social Psychology, 94*(2), 196–213.

Blanton, H., & Gerrard, M. (1997). Effect of sexual motivation on men's risk perception for sexually transmitted disease: There must be 50 ways to justify a lover. *Health Psychology, 16*, 374–379.

Blascovich, J., Spencer, S. J., Quinn, D., & Steele, C. (2001). African Americans and high blood pressure: The role of stereotype threat. *Psychological Science, 12*, 225–229.

Blau, P. N. (1964). *Exchange and power in social life*. New York: Wiley.

Blue, L. A. (1991). Jury selection in a civil case. *Trial Lawyers Quarterly, 21*, 11–25.

Blumstein, P., & Schwartz, P. (1983). *American couples: Money, work, and sex*. New York: Morrow.

Boddington, L., & Kemp, S. (1999). Student debt, attitudes towards debt, impulsive buying, and financial management. *New Zealand Journal of Psychology, 28*, 89–93.

Bodenhausen, G. V. (1990). Stereotypes as judgmental heuristics: Evidence of circadian variations in discrimination. *Psychological Science, 1*, 319–322.

Bond, C. F., & Titus, L. J. (1983). Social facilitation: A meta-analysis of 241 studies. *Psychological Bulletin, 94*, 265–292.

Bond, C. F., Jr., & DePaulo, B. M. (2008). Individual differences in judging deception: Accuracy and bias. *Psychological Bulletin, 134*(4), 477–492.

Bond, R. A., & Smith, P. B. (1996). Culture and conformity: A meta-analysis of studies using Asch's (1952, 1956) line judgment task. *Psychological Bulletin, 119*, 111–137.

Bond, R., & Smith, P. B (1996). *Culture and conformity: A meta-analysis of studies using Asch's (1952b 1956) line judgment task*. Psychological Bulletin, 119 (1), 111–137.

Bonezzi, A., Brendl, C.M., & De Angelis, M. (2011). Stuck in the middle: The psychophysics of goal pursuit. *Psychological Science, 22*, 607–612.

Bonta, B. D. (1997). Cooperation and competition in peaceful societies. *Psychological Bulletin, 121*, 299–320.

Borman, W. C., Penner, L. A., Allen, T.D., & Motowidlo, S. J. (2001). Personality predictors of citizenship performance. *International Journal of Selection and Assessment, 9*, 52–69.

Bornstein, R. F. (1989). Exposure and affect: Overview and meta-analysis of research, 1968–1987. *Psychological Bulletin, 106*, 265–289.

Bos, H. M. W., Gartrell, N. K., Van Balen, F., Peyser, H., & Sandfort, T. G. M. (2008). Children in planned lesbian families: A cross-cultural comparison between the United States and the Netherlands. *American Journal of Orthopsychiatry, 78*(2), 211–219.

Bosch, T. (2012, August 20). Why would someone cheat on a free online class that doesn't count toward anything? *Slate*. Retrieved from http://www.slate.com/blogs/future_tense/2012/08/20/coursera_plagiarism_why_would_students_cheat_in_a_free_online_class_that_doesn_t_over_academic_credit_.html

Boseley S (28 January 2010). Andrew Wakefield found "irresponsible" by GMC over MMR vaccine scare. *The Guardian* (London).

Bostrom, R. N., Vlandis, J. W., & Rosenbaum, M. E. (1961). Grades as reinforcing contingencies and attitude change. *Journal of Educational Psychology, 52*(2), 112–115.

Bosveld, W., Koomen, W., & Van der Pligt, J. (1996). Estimating group size: Effects of category membership, differential construal and selective exposure. *European Journal of Social Psychology, 26*, 523–535.

Bothwell, R. K., Deffenbacher, K. A., & Brigham, J. C. (1987). Correlations of eyewitness accuracy and confidence: Optimality hypothesis revisited. *Journal of Applied Psychology, 72*, 691–695.

Botta, R. A. (2000). The mirror of television: A comparison of black and white adolescents' body image. *Journal of Communication, 50*, 144–159.

Bottoms, B. L., Kalder, A. K., Stevenson, M. C., Oudekerk, B. A., Wiley, T. R., & Perona, A. (2011). Gender differences in jurors' perceptions of infanticide involving disabled and non-disabled infant victims. *Child Abuse & Neglect, 35*, 127–141.

Bowlby, J. (1969). *Attachment and loss: Vol 1. Attachment*. New York: Basic Books.

Bowlby, J. (1973). *Attachment and loss: Vol. 2. Separation anxiety and anger*. New York: Basic Books.

Bowler. R, Meqler, D., Huel. G., & Cone, J. (1994). Psychological, psychosocial, and psychophysiological sequelae in a community affected by a railroad chemical disaster. *Journal of Traumatic Stress, 7*, 601–624.

Bowles, T. (1999). Focusing on time orientation to explain adolescent self concept and academic achievement: Part II. Testing a model. *Journal of Applied Health Behaviour, 1*, 1–8.

Boyd, R., & Richerson, P. J. (1985). *Culture and the evolutionary process*. Chicago: University of Chicago Press.

Boyd, R., & Richerson, P. J. (2005). *The origin and evolution of cultures*. New York: Oxford University Press

Brad Sucks. Retrieved from http://www.bradsucks.net/about/

Bradfield, A., & McQuiston, D. E. (2004). When does evidence of eyewitness confidence inflation affect judgments in a criminal trial? *Law and Human Behavior, 28*, 369–387.

Bradley, G. W. (1978). Self-serving biases in the attribution process: A reexamination of the fact or fiction question. *Journal of Personality and Social Psychology, 36*, 56–71.

Bradley, S. J. (1990). Affect regulation and psychopathology: Bridging the mind-body gap. *Canadian Journal of Psychiatry, 35*, 540–547.

Braginski, B. M., Braginski, D. D., & Ring, K. (1969). *Methods of madness: The mental hospital as a last resort*. New York: Holt, Rinehart & Winston.

Branden, N. (1994). *The six pillars of self-esteem*. New York: Bantam Books.

Brawley, L. R., Carron, A. V., & Widmeyer, W. N. (1993). The influence of the group and its cohesiveness on perceptions of group goal-related variables. *Journal of Sport and Exercise Psychology, 15*(3), 245–260.

Breaugh, J. A., & Frye, N. K. (2008). Work-family conflict: The importance of family-friendly employment practices and family-supportive supervisors. *Journal of Business Psychology, 22*, 345–353.

Brechner, K. C. (1977). An experimental analysis of social traps. *Journal of Experimental Social Psychology, 13*, 552–564.

Brehm, J. W. (1966). *A theory of psychological reactance*. New York: Academic Press.

Brehm, J. W. (1972). *Responses to loss of freedom: A theory of psychological reactance*. Morristown, NJ: General Learning Press.

Brehm, J. W., & Cole, A. H. (1966). Effect of a favor which reduces freedom. *Journal of Personality and Social Psychology, 3*, 420–426.

Brehm, S. S., & Brehm, J. W. (1981). *Psychological reactance*. New York: Wiley.

Bremner, R. H., Koole, S. L., & Bushman, B. J. (2011). "Pray for those who mistreat you": Effects of prayer on anger and aggression. *Personality and Social Psychology Bulletin, 37*(6), 830–837.

Brennan, K. A., & Shaver, P. R. (1995). Dimensions of adult attachment, affect regulation, and romantic relationship functioning. *Personality and Social Psychology Bulletin, 21*, 267–283.

Brennan, K. A., Clark, C. L., & Shaver, P. R. (1998). Self-report measures of adult attachment. In J. A. Simpson & W. S. Rholes (Eds.), *Attachment theory and close relationships* (pp. 46–76). New York: Guilford Press.

Brewer, M. B. (1979). In-group bias in the minimal intergroup situation: A cognitive-motivational analysis. *Psychological Bulletin, 86*(2), 307–324.

Brewer, M. B., & Silver, M. (1978). Ingroup bias as a function of task characteristics. *European Journal of Social Psychology, 8*(3), 393–400.

Brewer, N., Keast, A., & Rishworth, A. (2002). The confidence-accuracy relationship in eyewitness identification: The effects of reflection and disconfirmation on correlation and calibration. *Journal of Experimental Psychology: Applied, 8*, 44–56.

Brewer, N., Keast, A., & Sauer, J. D. (2010). Children's eyewitness identification performance: Effects of a Not Sure response option and accuracy motivation. *Legal and Criminological Psychology, 15*, 261–277.

Brickman, P., & Campbell, D. T. (1971). Hedonic relativism and planning the good society. In M. H. Apley (Ed.), *Adaptation-level theory: A symposium* (pp. 287–302). New York: Academic Press.

Brickman, P., Coates, D., & Janoff-Bulman, R. (1978). Lottery winners and accident victims: Is happiness relative? *Journal of Personality and Social Psychology, 36*, 917–927.

Brigham, J. C., & Bothwell, R. K. (1983). The ability of prospective jurors to estimate the accuracy of eyewitness identification. *Law and Human Behavior, 7*, 19–30.

Brockner, J. (1983). Low self-esteem and behavioral plasticity: Some implications. In L. Wheeler & P. Shaver (Eds.), *Review of personality and social psychology, Vol. 4* (pp. 237–271). Beverly Hills, CA: Sage.

Brockner, J., & Lloyd, K. (1986). Self-esteem and likability: Separating fact from fantasy. *Journal of Research in Personality, 20,* 496–508.

Brockner, J., Greenberg, J., Brockner, A., Bortz, J., Davy, J., & Carter, C. (1986). Layoffs, equity theory, and work performance: Further evidence of the impact of survivor guilt. *Academy of Management Journal, 29,* 373–384.

Brodish, A. B., & Devine, P. G. (2009). The role of performance-avoidance goals and worry in mediating the relationship between stereotype threat and performance. *Journal of Experimental Social Psychology, 45*(1), 180–185.

Brody, L. R. (1996). Gender, emotional expression, and parent-child boundaries. In R. D. Kavanaugh, B. Zimmerberg, & S. Fein (Eds.), *Emotion: Interdisciplinary perspectives* (pp. 139–170). Mahwah, NJ: Eribaum.

Bronson, P., & Merryman, A. (2009, September 4). Even babies discriminate: A nurtureshock excerpt. *Newsweek.* Retrieved from http://www.newsweek.com/even-babies-discriminate-nurtureshock-excerpt-79233

Brown, B. (1987). Territoriality. In D. Stokols & I. Altman (Eds.), *Handbook of environmental psychology* (Vol. 1, pp. 505–531). New York: Wiley-Interscience.

Brown, B. B., & Werner, C. M. (1985). Social cohesiveness, territoriality, and holiday decorations: The influence of cul-de-sacs. *Environment and Behavior, 17,* 539–565.

Brown, K. W., & Moskowitz, D. S. (1997). Does unhappiness make you sick? The role of affect and neuroticism in the experience of common physical symptoms. *Journal of Personality and Social Psychology, 72*(4), 907–917.

Brown, K. W., & Ryan, R. M. (2003). The benefits of being present: Mindfulness and its role in psychological well-being. *Journal of Personality and Social Psychology, 84,* 822–848.

Brown, L. R. (1994). *State of the world 1994.* New York: Norton.

Brown, M. J., & Groscup, J. L. (2009). Homophobia and acceptance of stereotypes about gays and lesbians. *Individual Differences Research, 7*(3), 159–167.

Brown, N. R., & Sinclair, R. C. (1999). Estimating number of lifetime sexual partners: Men and women do it differently. *Journal of Sex Research, 36,* 292–297.

Brownstein, S. C., Wolf, I. K., & Green, S. W. (2000). *Barron's how to prepare for the GRE: Graduate Record Examination.* Hauppauge, NY: Barron's Education Series, p. 6.

Brunell, A. B., Gentry, W. A., Campbell, W. K., Hoffman, B. J., Kuhnert, K. W., & DeMarree, K. G. (2008). Leadership emergence: The case of the narcissistic leader. *Personality and Social Psychology Bulletin, 34,* 1663–1676.

Bruner, J. A., & Mason, J. L. (1968). The influence of driving time upon shopping center preference. *Journal of Marketing, 32*(2), 57–61.

Bryan, C. J., Walton, G. M., Rogers, T., & Dweck, C. S. (2011). Motivating voter turnout by invoking the self. *PNAS, 108*(31), 12653–12656.

Bryman, A. S. (1996). The importance of context: Qualitative research and the study of leadership. *Leadership Quarterly, 7,* 353–370.

Bryner, J. (2010, May 28). Today's college students lack empathy. *LiveScience.* Retrieved from http://www.livescience.com/9918-today-college-students-lack-empathy.html

Buck, D. M., Plant, E. A., Ratcliff, J., Zielaskowski, K., & Boerner, P. (2013). Concern over the misidentification of sexual orientation: Social contagion and the avoidance of sexual minorities. *Journal of Personality and Social Psychology, 105,* 941–960.

Buckles, E. E., & Trapnell, P. D. (2013). Disgust facilitates outgroup dehumanization. *Group Processes & Intergroup Relations, 16*(6), 771–780. doi: 10.1177/1368430212471738

Budesheim, T. L., & DePaola, S. J. (1994). Beauty or the beast? The effects of appearance, personality and issue information on evaluations of political candidates. *Personality and Social Psychology Bulletin, 20,* 339–348.

Budesheim, T. L., Houston, D. A., & DePaola, S. J. (1996). The persuasiveness of in-group and out-group political messages: The case of negative political campaigning. *Journal of Personality and Social Psychology, 70,* 523–534.

Buehler, R., & McFarland, C. (2001). Intensity bias in affective forecasting: The role of temporal focus. *Personality and Social Psychology Bulletin, 27,* 1480–1493.

Buehler, R., Griffin, D., & Ross, M. (1994). Exploring the "planning fallacy": Why people underestimate their task completion times. *Journal of Personality and Social Psychology, 67,* 366–381.

Buhrmester, D., Furman, W., Wittenberg, M. T., & Reis, H. T. (1988). Five domains of interpersonal competence in peer relationships. *Journal of Personality and Social Psychology, 55,* 991–1008.

Bulman, R. J., & Wortman, C. B. (1977). Attributions of blame and coping in the "real world": Severe accident victims react to their lot. *Journal of Personality and Social Psychology, 35,* 351–363.

Bunker, B. B., Zubek, J. M., Vanderslice, V. J., & Rice, R. W. (1992). Quality of life in dual-career families: Commuting versus single-residence couples. *Journal of Marriage and the Family, 54,* 399–407.

Section 8.01 Bureau of Labor Statistics (2014; February 25). Volunteering in the United States, 2013. Retrieved from http://www.bls.gov/news.release/volun.nr0.htm

Bureau of Labor Statistics (2015). American time use survey. Retrieved from http://www.bls.gov/tus/charts/

Burger, J. M. (1986). Increasing compliance by improving the deal: The that's-not-all technique. *Journal of Personality and Social Psychology, 51,* 277–283.

Burger, J. M. (2009). Replicating Milgram: Would people still obey today? *American Psychologist, 64*(1), 1–11.

Burger, J. M., Cooper, H. M., & Good, T. L. (1982). Teacher attributions of student performance: Effects of outcome. *Personality and Social Psychology Bulletin, 8,* 685–690.

Burgess, J. (2008) *"All your chocolate rain are belong to us?" Viral video, YouTube and the dynamics of participatory culture.* In UNSPECIFIED (Ed.), *Video vortex reader: Responses to YouTube.* Institute of Network Cultures, Amsterdam, pp. 101–109. Retrieved from http://eprints.qut.edu.au/18431/1/18431.pdf

Burmeister, J. M., Kiefner, A. E., Carels, R. A., & Musher-Eizenman, D. R. (2013). Weight bias in graduate school admissions. *Obesity, 21*(5), 918–920. doi: 10.1002/oby.20171

Burnstein, E., Crandall, C., & Kitayama, S. (1994). Some neo-Darwinian decision rules for altruism: Weighing cues for inclusive fitness as a function of the biological importance of the decision. *Journal of Personality and Social Psychology, 67,* 773–789.

Burnstein, et al. (1994). Some neo-Darwinian decision rules for altruism: Weighing cues for inclusive fitness as a function of the biological importance of the decision. *Journal of Personality and Social Psychology, 67,* 773–789. Copyright © 1994 by the American Psychological Association. Reprinted by permission.

Burris, C. T., Harmon-Jones, E., & Tarpley, W. R. (1997). "By faith alone": Religious agitation and cognitive dissonance. *Basic and Applied Social Psychology, 19,* 17–31.

Bushman, B. J. (1993). What's in a name? The moderating role of public self-consciousness on the relation between brand label and brand preference. *Journal of Applied Psychology, 78,* 857–861.

Bushman, B. J. (1997). Effects of alcohol on human aggression: Validity of proposed explanations. In D. Fuller, R. Dietrich, & E. Gottheil (Eds.), *Recent developments in alcoholism: Alcohol and violence* (Vol. 13, pp. 227–243). New York: Plenum Press.

Bushman, B. J. (2002). Does venting anger feed or extinguish the flame? Catharsis, rumination, distraction, anger, and aggressive responding. *Personality and Social Psychology Bulletin, 28,* 724–731.

Bushman, B. J., & Anderson, C. A. (2001). Is it time to pull the plug on the hostile versus instrumental aggression dichotomy? *Psychological Review, 108,* 273–279.

Bushman, B. J., & Anderson, C. A. (2002). Violent video games and hostile expectations: A test of the General Aggression Model. *Personality and Social Psychology Bulletin, 28,* 1679–1686.

Bushman, B. J., & Baumeister, R. F. (1998). Threatened egotism, narcissism, self-esteem, and direct and displaced aggression: Does self-love or self-hate lead to violence? *Journal of Personality and Social Psychology, 75,* 219–229.

Bushman, B. J., & Baumeister, R. F. (2002). Does self-love or self-hate lead to violence. *Journal of Research in Personality, 36,* 543–545.

Bushman, B. J., & Bonacci, A. M. (2004). You've got mail: Using e-mail to examine the effect of prejudiced attitudes on discrimination against Arabs. *Journal of Experimental Social Psychology, 40,* 753–759.

Bushman, B. J., & Cantor, J. (2003). Media ratings for violence and sex: Implications for policy makers and parents. *American Psychologist, 58,* 130–141.

Bushman, B. J., & Cooper, H. M. (1990). Effects of alcohol on human aggression: An integrative research review. *Psychological Bulletin, 107,* 341–354.

Bushman, B. J., & Huesmann, L. R. (2006). Short-term and long-term effects of violent media on aggression in children and adults. *Archives of Pediatrics & Adolescent Medicine, 160*(4), 348–352. doi: 10.1001/archpedi.160.4.348

Bushman, B. J., & Pollard-Sacks, D. (2014). Supreme Court decision on violent video games was based on the First Amendment, not scientific evidence. *American Psychologist, 69*(3), 306–307. doi: 10.1037/a0035509

Bushman, B. J., Baumeister, R. F., & Phillips, C. M. (2001). Do people aggress to improve their mood? Catharsis beliefs, affect regulation opportunity, and aggressive responding. *Journal of Personality and Social Psychology, 81,* 17–32.

Bushman, B. J., Baumeister, R. F., & Stack, A. D. (1999). Catharsis, aggression, and persuasive influence: Self-fulfilling or self-defeating prophecies? *Journal of Personality and Social Psychology, 76,* 367–376.

Bushman, B. J., Bonacci, A. M., Van Dijk, M., & Baumeister, R. F. (2003). Narcissism, sexual refusal, and sexual aggression: Testing a narcissistic reactance model of sexual coercion. *Journal of Personality and Social Psychology, 84,* 1027–1040.

Bushman, B. J., Gollwitzer, M., & Cruz, C. (2015). There is broad consensus: Media researchers agree that violent media increase aggression in children, and pediatricians and parents concur. *Psychology of Popular Media Culture, 4*(3), 200–214. DOI: 10.1037/ppm0000046 .

Bushman, B. J., Jamieson, P. E., Weitz, I., & Romer, D. (2013). Gun violence trends in movies. *Pediatrics, 132*(6), 1014–1018. doi: 10.1542/peds.2013-1600

Bushman, B. J., Moeller, S. J., & Crocker, J. (2011). Sweets, sex, or self-esteem? Comparing the value of self-esteem boosts with other pleasant rewards. *Journal of Personality, 79*(5), 993–1012. doi: 10.1111/j.1467-6494.2011.00712.x

Bushman, B. J., Moeller, S. J., Konrath, S., & Crocker, J. (2012). Investigating the link between liking versus wanting self-esteem and depression in a nationally representative sample of American adults. *Journal of Personality, 80*(5), 1455-1471. doi: 10.1111/j.1467-6494.2012.00781.x.

Bushman, B. J., Moeller, S. J., Konrath, S., & Crocker, J. (2012). Investigating the link between liking versus wanting self-esteem and depression in a nationally representative sample of American adults. *Journal of Personality, 80*(5), 1455–1471. doi: 10.1111/j.1467-6494.2012.00781.x.

Bushman, B. J., Newman, K., Calvert, S. L., Downey, G., Dredze, M., Gottfredson, M., Jablonski, N. G., Masten, A., Morrill, C., Neill, D. B., Romer, D., & Webster, D. (in press). Youth violence: What we know and what we need to know. *American Psychologist.*

Buss, A. H. (1961). *The psychology of aggression*. New York: John Wiley.

Buss, A. H. (1989). Temperaments as personality traits. In G. A. Kohnstamm, J. E. Bates, & M. Rothbart (Eds.), *Temperament in childhood* (pp. 49–58). Chichester, West Sussex, UK: Wiley.

Buss, D. M. (1990). The evolution of anxiety and social exclusion. *Journal of Social and Clinical Psychology, 9*, 196–210.

Buss, D. M. (1991). Evolutionary personality psychology. *Annual Review of Psychology, 42*, 459–491.

Buss, D. M. (1994). *The evolution of desire: Strategies of human mating*. New York: Basic Books.

Buss, D. M. (1999). *Evolutionary psychology: The new science of the mind*. New York: Allen & Bacon.

Buss, D. M., & Schmitt, D. P. (1993). Sexual strategies theory: An evolutionary perspective on human mating. *Psychological Review, 100*, 204–232.

Buss, D. M., & Shackelford, T. K. (1997). From vigilance to violence: Mate retention tactics in married couples. *Journal of Personality and Social Psychology, 72*, 346–361.

Buss, D. M., Larsen, R. J., Westen, D., & Semmelroth, J. (1992). Sex differences in jealousy: Evolution, physiology, and psychology. *Psychological Science, 3*, 251–255.

Butler, J. L., & Baumeister, R. F. (1998). The trouble with friendly faces: Skilled performance with a supportive audience. *Journal of Personality and Social Psychology, 75*, 1213–1230.

Butz, D. A., Plant, E. A., & Doerr, C. (2007). Liberty and justice for all? The implications of exposure to the United States flag for intergroup relations. *Personality and Social Psychology Bulletin, 33*, 396–408.

Buunk, B. P. & Hupka, R. B. (1987). Cross-cultural differences in the elicitation of sexual jealousy. *Journal of Sex Research, 23*, 12–22.

Buunk, B. P., Angleitner, A., Oubaid, V., & Buss, D. M. (1996). Sex differences in jealousy in evolutionary and cultural perspective: Tests from the Netherlands, Germany, and the United States. *Psychological Science, 7*, 1103–1116.

Byrne, D. (1971). *The attraction paradigm*. New York: Academic Press.

Cacioppo, J. T., & Gardner, W. L. (1999). Emotion. *Annual Review of Psychology, 50*, 191–214.

Cacioppo, J. T., & Hawkley, L. C. (2005). People thinking about people: The vicious cycle of being a social outcast in one's own mind. In K. D. Williams, J. P. Forgas, & W. von Hippel (Eds.), *The social outcast: Ostracism, social exclusion, rejection, and bullying* (pp. 91–108). New York: Psychology Press.

Cacioppo, J. T., & Hawkley, L. C. (2005). People thinking about people: The vicious cycle of being a social outcast in one's own mind. In K. D. Williams, J. P. Forgas, & W. von Hippel (Eds.), *The social outcast: Ostracism, social exclusion, rejection, and bullying* (pp. 91–108). New York: Psychology Press.

Cacioppo, J. T., & Hawkley, L. C. (2005). People thinking about people: The vicious cycle of being a social outcast in one's own mind. In K. D. Williams, J. P. Forgas, & W. von Hippel (Eds.), *The social outcast: Ostracism, social exclusion, rejection, and bullying* (pp. 91–108). New York: Psychology Press.

Cacioppo, J. T., & Petty, R. E. (1980). Sex differences in influenceability: Toward specifying the underlying processes. *Personality and Social Psychology Bulletin, 6*(4), 651–656.

Cacioppo, J. T., & Petty, R. E. (1982). The need for cognition. *Journal of Personality and Social Psychology, 42*, 116–131. Quote from p. 116.

Cacioppo, J. T., & Petty, R. E. (1989). Effects of message repetition on argument processing, recall and persuasion. *Basic and Applied Social Psychology, 10*, 3–12.

Cacioppo, J. T., Ernst, J. M., Burleson, M. H., McClintock, M. K., Malarkey, W. B., Hawkley, L. C., et al. (2000). Lonely traits and concomitant physiological processes: The MacArthur Social Neuroscience Studies. *International Journal of Psychophysiology, 35*, 143–154.

Cacioppo, J. T., Hawkley, L. C., Berntson, G. G., Ernst, J. M., Gibbs, A. C., Stickgold, R., et al. (2002). Lonely days invade the nights: Social modulation of sleep efficiency. *Psychological Science, 13*, 385–388.

Cacioppo, J. T., Hawkley, L. C., Crawford, L. E., Ernst, J. M., Burleson, M. H., Kowalewski, R. B., et al. (2002). Loneliness and health: Potential mechanisms. *Psychosomatic Medicine, 64*, 407–417.

Caesar, P. L. (1988). Exposure to violence in the families-of-origin among wife-abusers and maritally nonviolent men. *Violence and Victims, 3*, 49–63.

Caldwell, M. A., & Peplau, L. A. (1982). Sex differences in same-sex friendships. *Sex Roles, 8*, 721–732.

Calhoun, J. B. (1962). Population density and social pathology, *Scientific American, 206*, 139–148.

Call, V., Sprecher, S., & Schwartz, P. (1995). The incidence and frequency of marital sex in a national sample. *Journal of Marriage and the Family, 57*, 639–650.

Cameron, J., Banko, K. M., & Pierce, W. D. (2001). Pervasive negative effects of rewards on intrinsic motivation: The myth continues. *The Behavior Analyst, 24*, 1–44.

Campbell, A. (1981). *The sense of well-being in America*. New York: McGraw-Hill.

Campbell, A., Converse, P. E., & Rogers, W. L. (1976). *The quality of American life: Perceptions, evaluations, and satisfactions*. New York: Russell Sage.

Campbell, D. T. (1958). Common fate, similarity, and other indices of the status of aggregates of persons as social entities. *Behavioral Science, 3*, 14–25.

Campbell, J. D. (1986). Similarity and uniqueness: The effects of attribute type, relevance, and individual differences in self-esteem and depression. *Journal of Personality and Social Psychology, 50*, 281–294.

Campbell, J. D. (1990). Self-esteem and clarity of the self-concept. *Journal of Personality and Social Psychology, 59*, 538–549.

Campbell, J. D., & Fehr, B. A. (1990). Self-esteem and perceptions of conveyed impressions: Is negative affectivity associated with greater realism? *Journal of Personality and Social Psychology, 58*, 122–133.

Campbell, J. D., Chew, B., & Scratchley, L. S. (1991). Cognitive and emotional reactions to daily events: The effects of self-esteem and self complexity. *Journal of Personality, 59*, 473–505.

Campbell, J. K. (1965). Honour and the devil. In J. G. Peristiany (Ed.), *Honour and shame: The values of Mediterranean society* (pp. 112–175). London: Weidenfeld & Nicolson.

Campbell, W. K. (1999). Narcissism and romantic attraction. *Journal of Personality and Social Psychology, 77*, 1254–1270.

Campbell, W. K. (2005). *When you love a man who loves himself*. Naperville, IL: Sourcebooks.

Campbell, W. K., & Foster, C. A. (2002). Narcissism and commitment in romantic relationships: An Investment Model analysis. *Personality and Social Psychology Bulletin, 28*, 484–495.

Campbell, W. K., & Sedikides, C. (1999). Self-threat magnifies the self-serving bias: A meta-analytic integration. *Review of General Psychology, 3*, 23–43.

Campbell, W. K., Foster, C. A., & Finkel, E. J. (2002). Does self-love lead to love for others? A story of narcissistic game playing. *Journal of Personality and Social Psychology, 83*, 340–354.

Campbell, W. K., Reeder, G. D., Sedikides, C., & Elliot, A. J. (2000). Narcissism and comparative self-enhancement strategies. *Journal of Research in Personality, 34*, 329–347.

Cannarella, J., & Spencer, J. A. (2014, January 17). Epidemiological modeling of online social network dynamics. Retrieved from http://arxiv.org/abs/1401.4208

Cannon, W. B. (1914). The interrelations of emotions as suggested by recent physiological researches. *American Journal of Physiology, 25*, 256–282.

Cannon, W. B. (1929). *Bodily changes in pain, hunger, fear and rage*. Oxford: Appleton.

Cantor, J. R., & Venus, P. (1980). The effect of humor on recall of a radio advertisement. *Journal of Broadcasting, 24*, 13–22.

Cappell, C., & Heiner, R. B. (1990). The intergenerational transmission of family aggression. *Journal of Family Violence, 5*, 135–152.

Caprariello, P. A. & Reis, H. T. (2013). To do, to have, or to share? Valuing experiences over material possessions depends on the involvement of others. *Journal of Personality and Social Psychology, 104*, 199–215.

Carlsmith, K. M., Wilson, T. D., & Gilbert, D. T. (2008). The paradoxical consequences of revenge. *Journal of Personality and Social Psychology, 95*(6), 1316–1324.

Carlson, J. M., Fee, A. L., & Reinke, K. S. (2009). Backward masked snakes and guns modulate spatial attention. *Evolutionary Psychology, 7*(4), 534–544.

Carlson, M., Marcus-Newhall, A., & Miller, N. (1990). Effects of situational aggression cues: A quantitative review. *Journal of Personality and Social Psychology, 58*, 622–633.

Carnegie Hero Fund Commission. (2002). Requirements for a Carnegie Medal. Available at http://www.carnegiehero.org/nominate.php

Carr, J. E., & Tann, E. K. (1976). In search of the true Amok: Amok as viewed within Malay culture. *American Journal of Psychiatry, 133*(11), 1295–1299.

Carroll, J. S. (1978). The effect of imagining an event on expectations for the event: An interpretation in terms of the availability heuristic. *Journal of Experimental Social Psychology, 14*, 88–96.

Carrus, G., Passafaro, P., & Bonnes, M. (2008). Emotions, habits and rational choices in ecological behaviours: The case of recycling and use of public transportation. *Journal of Environmental Psychology, 28*, 51–62.

Carver, C. S., & Harmon-Jones, E. (2009). Anger is an approach-related affect: Evidence and implications. *Psychological Bulletin, 135*, 183–204.

Carver, C. S., & Scheier, M. F. (1981). *Attention and self-regulation: A control therapy approach to human behavior*. New York: Springer Press.

Carver, C. S., & Scheier, M. F. (1982). Control theory: A useful conceptual framework for personality-social, clinical and health psychology. *Psychological Bulletin, 92*, 111–135.

Carver, C. S., & Scheier, M. F. (1990). Origins and functions of positive and negative affect: A control-process view. *Psychological Review, 97*, 19–35.

Carver, C. S., & Scheier, M. F. (1994). Situational coping and coping dispositions in a stressful transaction. *Journal of Social and Personality Psychology, 56*, 267–283.

Case, D. A., Fantino, E., & Goodie, A. S. (1999). Base-rate training without case cues reduces base-rate neglect. *Psychonomic Bulletin and Review, 6*(2), 319–327.

Cash, T. F., & Janda, L. H. (1984). The eye of the beholder. *Psychology Today, 18*, 46–52.

Caspi, A., & Roberts, B. W. (2001). Personality development across the life course: The argument for change and continuity. *Psychological Inquiry, 12*, 49–66.

CBS News. (2011). Google job perks: Top 10 reasons we want to work there. Retrieved from http://www.cbsnews.com/news/google-job-perks-top-10-reasons-we-want-to-work-there/

Ceci, S. J., Peters, D., & Plotkin, J. (1985). Human subjects review, personal values, and the regulation of social sciences research. *American Psychologist, 51*, 768–784.

Cell phone or pheromone? New props for mating game. (2000, November 7). *New York Times*.

Centers for Disease Control and Prevention (2014, May 29). Measles cases in the United States reach 20-year high. Retrieved from http://www.cdc.gov/media/releases/2014/p0529-measles.html

Centers for Disease Control and Prevention (2014). Q&As about vaccination options for preventing measles, mumps, rubella, and varicella. Retrieved from http://www.cdc.gov/vaccines/vpd-vac/combo-vaccines/mmrv/vacopt-faqs-hcp.htm

Centers for Disease Control and Prevention (2104). Retrieved from http://www.cdc.gov/nchs/fastats/

Centers for Disease Control and Prevention. (2012). Vital signs. Retrieved from http://www.cdc.gov/tobacco/data_statistics/vital_signs/index.htm

Centers for Disease Control. (2008). Alcohol-attributable deaths and years of potential life lost among American Indians and Alaska Natives—United States, 2001–2005. *Morbidity and Mortality Weekly Report, 57*(34); 938–941. Retrieved from http://www.cdc.gov/DataStatistics/

Centers for Disease Control. (2012). Overweight and obesity. Retrieved from http://www.cdc.gov/obesity/data/trends.HTML

Cesario, J., Plaks, J. E., & Higgins, E. T. (2006). Automatic social behavior as motivated preparation to interact. *Journal of Personality and Social Psychology, 90*, 893–910.

Chait, J. (2013, April 2). Teachers cheating on tests: Not a big deal. *New York Magazine*. Retrieved from http://nymag.com/daily/intelligencer/2013/04/teachers-cheating-on-tests-not-a-big-deal.html

Chajut, E., & Algom, D. (2003). Selective attention improves under stress: Implications for theories of social cognition. *Journal of Personality and Social Psychology, 85*, 231–248.

Chan, W., McCrae, R. R., De Fruyt, F., Jussim, L., Löckenhoff, C. E., De Bolle, M., Costa, P. T., Jr., Sutin, A. R., Realo, A., Allik, J., Nakazato, K., Shimonaka, Y., Hřebíčková, M., Graf, S., Yik, M., Brunner-Sciarra, M., de Figueora, N. L., Schmidt, V., Ahn, C.-k., Ahn, H.-n., Aguilar-Vafaie, M. E., Siuta, J., Szmigielska, B., Cain, T. R., Crawford, J. T., Mastor, K. A., Rolland, J.-P., Nansubuga, F., Miramontez, D. R., Benet-Martínez, V., Rossier, J., Bratko, D., Marušić, I., Halberstadt, J., Yamaguchi, M., Knežević, G., Martin, T. A., Gheorghiu, M., Smith, P. B., Barbaranelli, C., Wang, L., Shakespeare-Finch, J., Lima, M. P., Klinkosz, W., Sekowski, A., Alcalay, L., Simonetti, F., Avdeyeva, T. V., Pramila, V. S., & Terracciano, A. (2012). Stereotypes of age differences in personality traits: Universal and accurate? *Journal of Personality and Social Psychology. 103*, 1050–1066. doi: 10.1037/a0029712

Chandola, T., Brunner, E., & Marmot, M. (2006). Chronic stress at work and the metabolic syndrome: Prospective study. *British Medical Journal*. [On-line]. Retrieved from http://www.bmj.com/content/early/2005/12/31/bmj.38693.435301.80

Chandrasekhar, D. (2010). Setting the stage: How policy institutions create the scope for participation in planning. *Journal of Disaster Research, 5*, 130–137.

Chang, Y., Chen, R. C., Wahlqvist, M. L., & Lee, M. (2011). Frequent shopping by men and women increases survival in the older Taiwanese population. *Journal of Epidemial Community Health*. Retrieved from http://jech.bmj.com/content/early/2011/03/17/jech.2010.126698.abstract

Chapman, H. A., & Anderson, A. K. (2013). Things Rank and Gross in Nature: A Review and Synthesis of Moral Disgust. *Psychological Bulletin, 139*(2), 300–327. doi: 10.1037/a0030964

Charman, S. D., Wells, G. L., & Joy, S. W. (2011). The dud effect: Adding highly dissimilar fillers increases confidence in lineup identifications. *Law and Human Behavior, 35*, 479–500.

Chartrand, T. L., & Bargh, J. A. (1999). The chameleon effect: The perception-behavior link and social interaction. *Journal of Personality and Social Psychology, 76*, 893–910.

Chassin, L., Presson, C. C., Sherman, S. J., & Edwards, D. A. (1990). The natural history of cigarette smoking: Predicting young-adult smoking outcomes from adolescent smoking patterns. *Health Psychology, 9*, 701–716.

Chatard, A., & Selimbegovic, L. (2011). When self-destructive thoughts flash through the mind: Failure to meet standards affects the accessibility of suicide-related thoughts. *Journal of Personality and Social Psychology, 100*, 587–605.

Chen, E. S., & Tyler, T. R. (2001). Cloaking power: Legitimizing myths and the psychology of the advantaged. In A. Y. Lee-Chai & J. Bargh (Eds.), *The use and abuse of power: Multiple perspectives on the causes of corruption* (pp. 241–261). Philadelphia: Psychology Press.

Chen, X., Dai, K., & Parnell, A. (1992). Disaster tradition and change: Remarriage and family reconstruction in a post-earthquake community in the People's Republic of China. *Journal of Comparative Family Studies, 23*, 115–132.

Childress, H. (2004). Teenagers, territories and the appropriation of space. *Childhood, 11*, 195–205.

China's hi-tech toxics. (2002). *BBC News*. Retrieved from http://news.bbc.co.uk/hi/english/static/in_depth/world/2002/disposable_planet/waste/chinese_workshop

Chiodo, J. (1987). Bulimia: An individual behavioral analysis. *Journal of Behavior Therapy and Experimental Psychiatry, 18*, 41–49.

Chivers, M. L., Seto, M. C., Laan, E., Lalumière, M. L., & Grimbos, T. (2010). Agreement of genital and subjective measures of sexual arousal: A meta-analysis. *Archives of Sexual Behavior, 39*(1), 5–56.

Choi, I., & Nisbett, R. E. (1998). Situational salience and cultural differences in the correspondence bias and actor-observer bias. *Personality and Social Psychology Bulletin, 24*(9), 949–960.

Chokshi, N. (2013, July 2). State Department spent $630K to buy Facebook "likes." *National Journal*. Retrieved from http://m.nextgov.com/cio-briefing/2013/07/state-department-spent-630k-buy-facebook-likes/65999/

Choma, B. L., Hodson, G., & Costello, K. (2012). Intergroup disgust sensitivity as a predictor of islamophobia: The modulating effect of fear. *Journal of Experimental Social Psychology, 48*(2), 499–506.

Christensen, H. T., & Carpenter, G. R. (1962). Value-behavior discrepancies regarding premarital coitus in three Western cultures. *American Sociological Review, 27*, 66–74.

Cialdini, J. T., & Patrick, W. (2008). *Loneliness*. New York: Norton.

Cialdini, R. B. (1989). Littering: When every litter bit hurts. In R. E. Rice & C. K. Atkin (Eds.), *Public communication campaigns* (2nd ed., pp. 221–223). London: Sage.

Cialdini, R. B. (1993) *Influence: Science and practice* (3rd ed.) (p. 113). New York: Harper-Collins.

Cialdini, R. B. (2001). *Influence: Science and practice* (4th ed.). Boston: Allyn and Bacon.

Cialdini, R. B., & Kenrick, D. T. (1976). Altruism as hedonism: A social development perspective on the relationship of negative mood state and helping. *Journal of Personality and Social Psychology, 34*, 907–914.

Cialdini, R. B., & Schroeder, D. A. (1976). Increasing compliance by legitimizing paltry contributions: When even a penny helps. *Journal of Personality and Social Psychology, 34*(4), 599–604.

Cialdini, R. B., Cacioppo, J. T., Bassett, R., & Miller, J. A. (1978). Low-ball procedure for producing compliance: Commitment then cost. *Journal of Personality and Social Psychology, 36*, 463–476.

Cialdini, R. B., Darby, B. L., & Vincent, J. E. (1973). Transgression and altruism: A case for hedonism. *Journal of Experimental Social Psychology, 9*, 502–516.

Cialdini, R. B., Eisenberg, N., Green, B. L., Rhoads, K., & Bator, R. (1998). Undermining the undermining effect of reward on sustained interest: When unnecessary conditions are sufficient. *Journal of Applied Social Psychology, 28*, 249–263.

Cialdini, R. B., Reno, R. R., & Kallgren, C. A. (1990). A focus theory of normative conduct: Recycling the concept of norms to reduce littering in public places. *Journal of Personality and Social Psychology, 58*, 1015–1026.

Cialdini, R. B., Vincent, J., Lewis, S., Catalan, J., Wheeler, D., & Darby, B. L. (1975). Reciprocal concessions procedure for inducing compliance: The door-in-the-face technique. *Journal of Personality and Social Psychology, 31*, 206–215.

Cincinnati zoo and botanical garden. Retrieved from http://www.ohiohistorycentral.org/w/Cincinnati_Zoo_and_Botanical_Garden?rec5685

Ciotti, G. (2015). How music affects your productivity. Sparring Mind. Retrieved from http://www.sparringmind.com/music-productivity/

Clancy, B., & Milam, H. (2012). How psychological reactance modifies the effects of hypocrisy induction. *Journal of Psychological Inquiry, 17*, 36–39.

Clark, D. (1986). *The missing link*. New York: Humansphere.

Clark, D. A., Beck, A. T., & Brown, G. (1989). Cognitive mediation in general psychiatric outpatients: A test of the content specificity hypothesis. *Journal of Personality and Social Psychology, 56*, 958–964.

Clark, M. S. (1984). Record keeping in two types of relationships. *Journal of Personality and Social Psychology, 47*, 549–557.

Clark, M. S., & Mills, J. (1979). Interpersonal attraction in exchange and communal relationships. *Journal of Personality and Social Psychology, 37*, 12–24.

Clark, M. S., Mills, J., & Corcoran, D. (1989). Keeping track of needs and inputs of friends and strangers. *Personality and Social Psychology Bulletin, 15*, 533–542.

Clark, M. S., Ouellette, R., Powell, M., & Milberg, S. (1987). Recipients' mood, relationship type, and helping. *Journal of Personality and Social Psychology, 53*, 94–103.

Clark, R. E. (2003). Fostering the work motivation of individuals and teams. *Performance Improvement, 42*(3), 21–29.

Clark, S. E. (2005). A re-examination of the effects of biased lineup instructions in eyewitness identification. *Law and Human Behavior, 29*, 395–424.

Clark, S. E. (2012). Costs and benefits of eyewitness identification reform: Psychological science and public policy. *Perspectives on Psychological Science, 7*, 238–259.

Clark, S. E., & Tunnicliff, J. L. (2001). Selecting lineup foils in eyewitness identification: Experimental control and real-world simulation. *Law and Human Behavior, 25*, 199–216.

Clark, S. E., Brower, G. L., Rosenthal, R., Hicks, J. M., & Moreland, M. B. (2013). Lineup administrator influences on eyewitness identification and eyewitness confidence. *Journal of Applied Research in Memory and Cognition, 2*, 158–165.

Clark, S. E., Erickson, M. A., & Breneman, J. (2011). Probative value of absolute and relative judgments in eyewitness identification. *Law and Human Behavior, 35*, 364–380.

Clark, W. C. (1989). Managing planet earth. *Scientific American, 261*(3), 47–54.

Clayson, D. E., & Klassen, M. L. (1989). Perception of attractiveness by obesity and hair color. *Perceptual and Motor Skills, 68*, 199–202.

Cleare, A. J., & Bond, A. J. (1995). The effect of tryptophan depletion and enhancement on subjective and behavioural aggression in normal male subjects. *Psychopharmacology, 118*, 72–81.

Clifford, M., & Walster, E. (1973). The effect of physical attractiveness on teacher expectations. *Sociology of Education, 46*, 248–258.

Clore, G. L., Gasper, K., & Garvin, E. (2001). Affect as information. In J. P. Forgas (Ed.), *Handbook of affect and social cognition* (pp. 122–144). Mahwah, NJ: Erlbaum.

CNN (1997, March 28). Some members of suicide cult castrated. Retrieved from http://edition.cnn.com/US/9703/28/mass.suicide.pm/

CNN Poll: Support for legal marijuana soaring (2014, January 6). Retrieved from http://politicalticker.blogs.cnn.com/2014/01/06/cnn-poll-support-for-legal-marijuana-soaring/

Coan, J. A., Schaefer, H. S., & Davidson, R. J. (2006). Lending a hand: Social regulation of the neural response to threat. *Psychological Science, 17*(12), 1032–1039.

Cohen, D., & Nisbett, R. E. (1997). Field experiments examining the culture of honor: The role of institutions in perpetuating norms about violence. *Personality and Social Psychology Bulletin, 23*, 1188–1199.

Cohen, J. (1988). *Statistical power analysis for the behavioral sciences* (2nd ed.). New York: Academic Press.

Cohen, J., & Andrade, E. B. (2004). Affect, intuition, and task-contingent affect regulation. *Journal of Consumer Research, 31,* 358–367.

Cohen, L. L., & Shotland, R. L. (1996). Timing of first sexual intercourse in a relationship: Expectations, experiences, and perceptions of others. *Journal of Sex Research, 33,* 291–299.

Cohen, S. (1978). Environmental load and the allocation of attention. In A. Baum, J. S. Singer, & S. Valins (Eds.), *Advances in environmental psychology* (Vol. 1, pp. 1–29). Hillsdale, NJ: Erlbaum.

Cohen, S. G., & Ledford, G. E., Jr. (1994). The effectiveness of self-managing teams: A quasi-experiment. *Human Relations, 47,* 13–43.

Cohen, S., & Spacapan, S. (1984). The social psychology of noise. In D. M. Jones & A. J. Chapman (Eds.), *Noise and society* (pp. 221–245). New York: Wiley.

Colapinto, J. (2000). *As nature made him: The boy who was raised as a girl.* New York: HarperCollins.

Cole, A.M. (2007). *The cult of true victimhood.* Palo Alto, CA: Stanford University Press.

Cole, R. (2001). Lying to the one you love: The use of deception in romantic relationships. *Journal of Social and Personal Relationships, 18*(1), 107–129.

College Board. (1976–1977). *Student descriptive questionnaire.* Princeton, NJ: Educational Testing Service.

Collins, J. (2001). *Good to great.* New York: HarperCollins.

Collins, N. L., & Feeney, B. C. (2000). A safe haven: An attachment theory perspective on support-seeking and caregiving in adult romantic relationships. *Journal of Personality and Social Psychology, 58,* 644–663.

Collins, N. L., & Feeney, B. C. (2004). An attachment theory perspective on closeness and intimacy. In D. Mashek & A. Aron (Eds.), *Handbook of closeness and intimacy* (pp. 163–187). Mahwah, NJ: Erlbaum.

Collins, N. L., & Read, S. J. (1990). Adult attachment, working models and relationship quality in dating couples. *Journal of Personality and Social Psychology, 58,* 644–663.

Collins, R. L., Quigley, B., & Leonard, K. (2007). Women's physical aggression in bars: An event-based examination of precipitants and predictors of severity. *Aggressive Behavior, 33*(4), 304–313.

Colman, A. M. (1982). *Game theory and experimental games: The study of strategic interaction.* Oxford: Pergamon Press.

Colvin, C. R., Block, J., & Funder, D. C. (1995). Overly positive evaluations and personality: Negative implications for mental health. *Journal of Personality and Social Psychology, 68,* 1152–1162.

Comer, R., & Laird, J. D. (1975). Choosing to suffer as a consequence of expecting to suffer: Why do people do it? *Journal of Personality and Social Psychology, 32,* 92–101.

Committee on Foreign Affairs. (1979). *The death of Representative Leo J. Ryan, Peoples Temple, and Jonestown: Understanding a tragedy.* U.S. House of Representatives, 96th Congress, First Session. Washington, DC: Government Printing Office.

Compton, J. A., & Pfau, M. (2004). Use of inoculation to foster resistance to credit card marketing targeting college students. *Journal of Applied Communication Research, 32*(4), 343–364.

Conley, T. D., Moors, A. C., Matsick, J. L., Ziegler, A., & Valentine, B. A. (2011). Women, men, and the bedroom: Methodological and conceptual insights that narrow, reframe, and eliminate gender differences in sexuality. *Current Directions in Psychological Science, 20,* 296–300.

Connolly, T. (2002). Regret in decision making. *Current Directions in Psychological Science, 11,* 212–216.

Consumer Electronics Association. (2008, April). *Market research report: Trends in CE reuse, recycle and removal.*

Contrada, R. J., & Guyll, M. (2001). On who gets sick and why: The role of personality, stress, and disease. In A. Baum, T. A. Revenson, & J. E. Singer (Eds.), *Handbook of health psychology* (pp. 59–81). Hillsdale, NJ: Erlbaum.

Contrada, R., & Baum, A. (Eds.). (2011). *The handbook of stress science: Biology, psychology, and health.* New York: Springer.

Conway, M., & Ross, M. (1984). Getting what you want by revising what you had. *Journal of Personality and Social Psychology, 47,* 738–748.

Cook, T. D., & Campbell, D. T. (1979). *Quasi-experimentation* (pp. 37–94). Boston: Houghton Mifflin.

Cooley, C. H. (1902). *Human nature and the social order.* New York: Charles Scribner's Sons.

Cooper-Hakim, A., & Viswesvaran, C. (2005). The construct of work commitment: Testing an integrative framework. *Journal of Applied Psychology, 131,* 241–259.

Cooper, M. L., Shaver, P. R., & Collins, N. L. (1998). Attachment styles, emotion regulation, and adjustment in adolescence. *Journal of Personality and Social Psychology, 74,* 1380–1397.

Copeland, J. T. (1994). Prophecies of power: Motivational implications of social power for behavioral confirmation. *Journal of Personality and Social Psychology, 67,* 264–277.

Correll, J., Park, B., Judd, C. M., & Wittenbrink, B. (2002). The police officer's dilemma: Using ethnicity to disambiguate potentially threatening individuals. *Journal of Personality and Social Psychology, 86,* 1314–1329.

Cosmides, L. (1989). The logic of social exchange: Has natural selection shaped how humans reason? Studies with the Wason selection task. *Cognition, 31,* 187–276.

Cosmides, L., & Tooby, J. (1992). Cognitive adaptations for social exchange. In J. Barkow, L. Cosmides, & J. Tooby (Eds.), *The adapted mind: Evolutionary psychology and the generation of culture* (pp. 163–228). Oxford: Oxford University Press.

Costa, P. T., & McCrae, R. R. (1980). Influence of extraversion and neuroticism on subjective well-being: Happy and unhappy people. *Journal of Personality and Social Psychology, 38,* 668–678.

Costa, P. T., & McCrae, R. R. (1984). Personality as a lifelong determinant of wellbeing. In C. Z. Malatesta & C. E. Izard (Eds.), *Emotion in adult development* (pp. 141–157). Beverly Hills, CA: Sage.

Costa, P. T., McCrae, R. R., & Zonderman, A. B. (1987). Environmental and dispositional influences on well-being: Longitudinal follow-up of an American national sample. *British Journal of Psychology, 78,* 299–306.

Costa, P. T., McCrae, R. R., & Zonderman, A. B. (1987). Environmental and dispositional influences on well-being: Longitudinal follow-up of an American national sample. *British Journal of Psychology, 78,* 299–306.

Cottrell, C. A., Neuberg, S. L., & Li, N. P. (2007). What do people desire in others? A sociofunctional perspective on the importance of different valued characteristics. *Journal of Personality and Social Psychology, 92,* 208–231.

Cottrell, N. B., Wack, D. L., Sekerak, G. J., & Rittle, R. H. (1968). Social facilitation of dominant responses by the presence of an audience and the mere presence of others. *Journal of Personality and Social Psychology, 9,* 245–250.

Couch, D., & Liamputtong, P. (2008). Online dating and mating: The use of the Internet to meet sexual partners. *Qualitative Health Research, 18*(2), 268–279.

Coviello, L., Sohn, Y., Kramer, A. D. I., Marlow, C., Franceschetti, M., Christakis, N. A., & Fowler, J. H. (2014). Detecting emotional contagion in massive social networks. PLOS ONE, 9(3), doi: 10.1371/journal.pone.0090315

Cowan, C. L., Thompson, W. C., & Ellsworth, P. C. (1984). The effects of death qualification on jurors: Predisposition to convict and on the quality of deliberation. *Law and Human Behavior, 8,* 53–79.

Coyle, C. T., & Enright, R. D. (1997). Forgiveness intervention with post-abortion men. *Journal of Consulting and Clinical Psychology, 65,* 1042–1046.

Coyne, J. C., & DeLongis, A. (1986). Going beyond social support: The role of social relationships in adaptation. *Journal of Consulting and Clinical Psychology, 54,* 454–460.

cp. *Rhet.* II.1, 1378a1ff.

Cramer, P., & Steinwert, T. (1998). Thin is good, fat is bad: How early does it begin? *Journal of Applied Developmental Psychology, 19,* 429–451.

Cramer, R. E., McMaster, M. R., Bartell, P. A., & Dragna, M. (1988). Subject competence and minimization of the bystander effect. *Journal of Applied Social Psychology, 18,* 1133–1148.

Crandall, C. S. (1988). Social contagion of binge eating. *Journal of Personality and Social Psychology, 55,* 588–598.

Crandall, C. S. (1994). Prejudice against fat people: Ideology and self-interest. *Journal of Personality and Social Psychology, 66,* 882–894.

Cranny, C. J., Smith, P. C., & Stone, E. F. (1992). *Job satisfaction: How people feel about their jobs and how it affects their performance.* New York: Lexington Books.

Crary, W. G. (1966). Reactions to incongruent self-experiences. *Journal of Consulting Psychology, 30,* 246–252.

Crick, N. R., & Grotpeter, J. K. (1995). Relational aggression, gender, and social-psychological adjustment. *Child Development, 66,* 710–722.

Crisp, R. J., Birtel, M. D., & Meleady, R. (2011). Mental simulations of social thought and action: Trivial tasks or tools for transforming social policy? *Current Directions in Psychological Science, 20*(4), 261–264.

Crisp, R. J., Hutter, R. R. C., & Young, B. (2009). When mere exposure leads to less liking: The incremental threat effect in intergroup contexts. *British Journal of Psychology, 100*(1), 133–149.

Croake, J. W., & James, B. (1973). A four year comparison of premarital sexual attitudes. *Journal of Sex Research, 9,* 91–96.

Crocker, C. B. (2010). *An investigation of the psychological processes involved in juror rehabilitation.* (Unpublished doctoral dissertation.) The City University of New York.

Crocker, C. B., & Kovera, M. B. (2010). The effects of rehabilitative voir dire on juror bias and decision making. *Law and Human Behavior, 34,* 212–226.

Crocker, J., & Major, B. (1989). Social stigma and self-esteem: The self-protective properties of stigma. *Psychological Review, 96,* 608–630.

Crocker, J., & Park, L. E. (2004). The costly pursuit of self-esteem. *Psychological Bulletin, 130,* 392–414.

Crocker, J., & Schwartz, I. (1985). Prejudice and ingroup favoritism in a minimal intergroup situation: Effects of self-esteem. *Personality and Social Psychology Bulletin, 11,* 379–386.

Crocker, J., Sommers, S. R., & Luhtanen, R. K. (2002). Hopes dashed and dreams fulfilled: Contingencies of self-worth and admissions to graduate school. *Personality and Social Psychology Bulletin, 28,* 1275–1286.

Crocker, J., Voelkl, K., Testa, M., & Major, B. (1991). Social stigma: The affective consequences of attributional ambiguity. *Journal of Personality and Social Psychology, 60,* 218–228.

Croskerry, P. (2003). The importance of cognitive errors in diagnosis and strategies to minimize them. *Academic Medicine, 78,* 775–780.

Cross-tab. (2010, January). Online reputation in a connected world. Retrieved from http://www.job-hunt.org/guides/DPD_Online-Reputation-Research_overview.pdf

Crossman, R. H. (1987). *The god that failed.* Washington, DC: Regnery Gateway. (Original work published 1949).

Crowley, M.C. (2015). How SAS became the world's best place to work. Fast Company. Retrieved from http://www.sas.com/en_us/careers/life-at-sas.html

Cryder, C. E, Springer, S., & Morewedge, C. M. (2012), Guilty feelings, targeted actions. *Personality and Social Psychology Bulletin, 38*(5), 607–618. doi: 10.1177/0146167211435796

CTIA.org. (2012). Background on CTIA's semiannual wireless industry survey. Retrieved from http://www.ctia.org/media/industry_info/index.cfm/AID/10323

Culhane, S. E., Hosch, H. M., & Weaver, W. G. (2004). Crime victims serving as jurors: Is there bias present? *Law and Human Behavior, 28*, 649–659.

Cunningham, M. R. (1979). Mood, and helping behavior: Quasi experiments with the Sunshine Samaritan. *Journal of Personality and Social Psychology 37*, 1947–1956.

Cunningham, M. R. (2009). Social allergies. In H. Reis & S. Sprecher (Eds.), *Handbook of human relationships*. Thousand Oaks, CA: Sage.

Cunningham, M. R., Barbee, A. P., & Druen, P. B. (1997). Social antigens and allergies: The development of hypersensitivity in close relationships. In R. Kowalski (Ed.), *Aversive interpersonal behaviors* (pp. 190–215). New York: Plenum Press.

Cunningham, M. R., Barbee, A. P., & Mandal, E. (2009). Hurtful behaviors in the workplace. In R. Kowalski (Ed.), *Feeling hurt in close relationships* (pp. 417–456). Cambridge: Cambridge University Press.

Cupach, W. R., & Spitzberg, B. H. (2000). Obsessive relational intrusion: Incidence, perceived severity, and coping. *Violence and Victims, 15*, 357–372.

Curtis, V. (2011). Why disgust matters. *Philosophical Transactions of the Royal Society B, 366*, 3478–3490. Quote on p. 3486.

Cutler, B. L., & Kovera, M. B. (2010). *Evaluating eyewitness identification*. New York: Oxford University Press.

Cutler, B. L., Penrod, S. D., & Dexter, H. R. (1989). The eyewitness, the expert psychologist, and the jury. *Law and Human Behavior, 13*, 311–332.

Cutler, B. L., Penrod, S. D., & Martens, T. K. (1987). The reliability of eyewitness identification: The role of system and estimator variables. *Law and Human Behavior, 11*, 233–258.

Dabbs, J. M. (2000). *Heroes, rogues, and lovers: Testosterone and behavior*. New York: McGraw-Hill.

Daftary-Kapur, T., Penros, S. D., O'Connor, M., & Wallace, B. (2014). Examining pretrial publicity in a shadow jury paradigm: Issues of slant, quantity, persistence and generalizability. *Law and Human Behavior, 38*, 462–477.

Dal Cin, S., Gibson, B., Zanna, M., Shumate, R., & Fong, G. (2007). Smoking in movies, implicit associations of smoking with the self, and intentions to smoke. *Psychological Science, 18*(7), 559–563.

Dal Cin, S., Worth, K., Dalton, M., & Sargent, J. (2008). Youth exposure to alcohol use and brand appearances in popular contemporary movies. *Addiction, 103*(12), 1925–1932.

Dalal, R. S. (2006). A meta-analysis of the relationship between organizational citizenship behavior and counterproductive work behavior. *Journal of Applied Psychology, 90*(6), 1241–1255.

Dalton, M. A., Ahrens, M. B., Sargent, J. D., Mott, L. A., Beach, M. L., Tickle, J. J., et al. (2002). Relation between parental restrictions on movies and adolescent use of tobacco and alcohol. *Effective Clinical Practice, 5*(1), 1–10.

Daly, M. J., & Burton, R. L. (1983). Self-esteem and irrational beliefs: An exploratory investigation with implications for counseling. *Journal of Counseling Psychology, 30*, 361–366.

Damasio, A. R. (1994). *Descartes' error*. London: Picador.

Danner, D., Snowdon, D., & Friesen, W. (2001). Positive emotions in early life and longevity: Findings from the Nun Study. *Journal of Personality and Social Psychology, 80*, 804–813.

Danziger, S., Levav, J., & Avnaim-Pesso, L. (2011). Extraneous factors in judicial decisions. *PNAS, 108*, 6889–6892.

Darby, B. W., & Schlenker, B. R. (1982). Children's reactions to apologies. *Journal of Personality and Social Psychology, 43*, 742–753.

Dardenne, B., Dumont, M., & Bollier, T. (2007). Insidious dangers of benevolent sexism: Consequences for women's performance. *Journal of Personality and Social Psychology, 93*, 764–779.

Darley, J. M. & Batson, C. D. (1973). From Jerusalem to Jericho: A study of situational and dispositional variables in helping behavior. *Journal of Personality and Social Psychology, 27*, 100–108.

Darley, J. M. & Batson, C. D. (1973). From Jerusalem to Jericho: A study of situational and dispositional variables in helping behavior. *Journal of Personality and Social Psychology, 27*, 100–108.

Darley, J. M., & Gross, P. H. (1983). A hypothesis-confirming bias in labeling effects. *Journal of Personality and Social Psychology, 44*(1), 20–33.

Darley, J. M., & Latané, B. (1968). Bystander intervention in emergencies: *Journal of Personality & Social Psychology, 8*, 377–383.

Darwin, C. (1859). *The origin of species by means of natural selection, or the preservation of favoured races in the struggle for life*. Reprinted from the 6th edition in New York, A. L. Burt Company, not dated.

Darwin, C. (1948). *Origin of species*. New York: Modern Library. (Original work published 1871).

Das, E., Bushman, B. J., Bezemer, M. D., Kerkhof, P., & Vermeulen, I. E. (2009). How terrorism news reports increase prejudice against outgroups: A terror management account. *Journal of Experimental Social Psychology, 45*, 453–459.

David G. Myers, *Social Psychology* 9th ed., 2008.

David, J. P., Green, P. J., Martin, R., & Suls, J. (1997). Differential roles of neuroticism, extraversion, and event desirability for mood in daily life: An integrative model of top-down and bottom-up influences. *Journal of Personality and Social Psychology, 73*, 149–159.

David, M. B. (2013, February 13). Deep racism: The forgotten history of human zoos. *Popular Resistance*. Retrieved from http://www.popularresistance.org/deep-racism-the-forgotten-history-of-human-zoos/

Davies, G. (2002). *A history of money from ancient times to the present day*. Cardiff: University of Wales Press.

Davies, G. M., Smith, S., & Blincoe, C. (2008). A "weapon focus" effect in children. *Psychology, Crime, & Law, 14*, 19–28.

Davies, J. B., Sandström, S., Shorrocks, A., & Wolff, E. N. (2008). The World Distribution of Household Wealth. UNU-WIDER. Retrieved from http://www.wider.unu.edu/publications/working-papers/discussion-papers/2008/en_GB/dp2008-03/

Davis-Stober, C.P., Budescu, D.V., Dana, J., & Broomell, S.B. (2014). When is a crowd wise? *Decision, 1*, 79–101.

Davis, B. P., & Knowles, E. S. (1999). A disrupt-then-reframe technique of social influence. *Journal of Personality and Social Psychology, 76*, 192–199.

Davis, D., & Loftus, E. F. (2006). Psychologists in the forensic world. In S. I. Donaldson, D. E. Berger, & K. Pezdek (Eds.), *Applied psychology: New frontiers and rewarding careers* (pp. 171–200). Mahwah, NJ: Lawrence Erlbaum Associates.

Davis, I. (1978). *Shelter after disaster*. Oxford, UK: Oxford Polytechnic Press.

Davis, K. E., & Frieze, I. H. (2000). Research on stalking: What do we know and where do we go? *Violence and Victims, 15*, 473–487.

Davis, P. A. (1983). *Suicidal adolescents*. Springfield, IL: C. C. Thomas.

Davis, S. F., Grover, C. A., Becker, A. H., & McGregor, L. N. (1992). Academic dishonesty: Prevalence, determinants, techniques, and punishments. *Teaching of Psychology, 19*, 16–20.

Dawkins, R. (1976/1989). *The selfish gene*. New York: Oxford University Press.

Dawkins, R. (1989). *The selfish gene*. New York: Oxford University Press. (Original work published 1976).

Day, D., & Ullom, H. H. (Eds.). (1947). *The autobiography of Sam Houston*. Norman: University of Oklahoma Press.

De Brouwer, A.-M. (2005). *Supranational criminal prosecution of sexual violence: The ICC and the practice of the ICTY and the ICTR*. Mortsel, Belgium: Intersentia.

De Hoog, N., Stroebe, W., & De Wit, J. B. F. (2007). The impact of vulnerability to and severity of a health risk on processing and acceptance of fear-arousing communications: A meta-analysis. *Review of General Psychology, 11*(3), 258–285.

de Kort, Y. A. W., McCalley, L. T., & Midden, C. J. H. (2008). Persuasive trash cans: Activation of littering norms by design. *Environment and Behavior, 40*(6), 870–891.

de Rougemont, D. (1956). *Love in the Western world*. New York: Schoeken.

de Vries, M., Holland, R. W., Corneille, O., Rondeel, E., & Witteman, C. L. M. (2012). Mood effects on dominated choices: Positive mood induces departures from logical rules. *Journal of Behavioral Decision Making, 25*(1), 74–81.

de Waal, F. B. M. (2002). Evolutionary psychology: The wheat and the chaff. *Current Directions in Psychological Science, 11*, 187–191.

de Waal, F. B. M., & Davis, J. M. (2003). Capuchin cognitive ecology: Cooperation based on projected returns. *Neuropsychologia, 41*, 221–228.

De Young, R., Duncan, A., Frank, J., Gill, N., Rothman, S., Shenot, J., Shotkin, A., & Zweizig, M. (1993). Promoting source reduction behavior: The role of motivational behavior. *Environment and Behavior, 25*, 70–85.

Deacon, T. (1997). What makes the human brain different? *Annual Review of Anthropology, 26*, 337–357.

Dean, L. M., Willis, F. N., & Hewitt, J. (1975). Initial interaction distance among individuals equal and unequal in military rank. *Journal of Personality and Social Psychology, 32*, 294–299.

DeAngelis, T. (2000). Is Internet addiction real? *Monitor on Psychology, 31*. Retrieved from http://www.apa.org/monitor/apr00/addiction.html

Death penalty for Troy Davis highlights problems with eyewitness accounts. (2011, September 22). *Star-Ledger Editorial Board*. Retrieved from http://blog.nj.com/njv_editorial_page/2011/09/death_penalty_for_troy_davis_h.html

deCharms, R. (1968). *Personal causation*. New York: Academic Press.

Deci, E. L. (1971). The effects of externally mediated rewards on intrinsic motivation. *Journal of Personality and Social Psychology, 18*, 105–115.

Deci, E. L. (1975). *Intrinsic motivation*. New York: Plenum Press.

Deci, E. L., & Ryan, R. M. (1985). *Intrinsic motivation and self-determination in human behavior*. New York: Plenum Press.

Deci, E. L., & Ryan, R. M. (2000). The "what" and "why" of goal pursuits: Human needs and the self-determination of behavior. *Psychological Inquiry, 11*, 227–268.

Deci, E. L., Koestner, R., & Ryan, R. M. (1999). A meta-analytic review of experiments examining the effects of extrinsic rewards on intrinsic motivation. *Psychological Bulletin, 125*, 627–668.

Deci, E. L., Koestner, R., & Ryan, R. M. (1999). A meta-analytic review of experiments examining the effects of extrinsic rewards on intrinsic motivation. *Psychological Bulletin, 125*, 627–668.

Deci, E. L., Nezlek, J., & Sheinman, L. (1981). Characteristics of the rewarder and the intrinsic motivation of the rewardee. *Journal of Personality and Social Psychology, 40*, 1–10.

Deffenbacher, K. A. (1994). Effects of arousal on everyday memory. *Human Performance, 7*, 141–161.

Deffenbacher, K. A., Bornstein, B. H., McGorty, E. K., & Penrod, S. D. (2008). Forgetting the once-seen face: Estimating the strength of an eyewitness's memory representation. *Journal of Experimental Psychology: Applied, 14*, 139–150.

Deffenbacher, K. A., Bornstein, B. H., Penrod, S. D., & McGorty, E. K. (2004). A meta-analytic review of the effects of high stress on eyewitness memory. *Law and Human Behavior, 28*, 687–706.

DeJong, W. (1980). The stigma of obesity: The consequences of naive assumptions concerning the causes of physical deviance. *Journal of Health and Social Behavior, 21*(1), 75–87.

DeJong, W. (1993). Obesity as a characterological stigma: The issue of responsibility and judgments of task performance. *Psychological Reports, 73*, 963–970.

DeLamater, J., & Hyde, J. S. (1998). Essentialism vs. social constructionism in the study of human sexuality. *Journal of Sex Research, 35*, 10–18.

DeLongis, A., Folkman, S., & Lazarus, S. (1988). The impact of daily stress on health and mood: Psychosocial and social resources as mediators. *Journal of Personality and Social Psychology, 54*, 486–495.

DeMeis, J., & Stearns, E. (1992). Relationship of school entrance age to academic and social performance. *Journal of Educational Research, 86*, 21–27.

Demicheli, V., Rivetti, A., Debalini, M. G., & Di Pietrantonj, C. (2012). Vaccines for measles, mumps and rubella in children. *Cochrane Database Systematic Reviews*, Issue 2. Art. No.: CD004407. doi:10.1002/14651858.CD004407.pub3

Denison, D. R. (1996). What is the difference between organizational culture and organizational climate? A native's point of view on a decade of paradigm wars. *The Academy of Management Review, 21*(3), 619–654.

DePalma, M. T., Madey, S. F., Tillman, T. C., & Wheeler, J. (1999). Perceived patient responsibility and belief in a just world affect helping. *Basic and Applied Social Psychology, 21*, 131–137.

DeScioli, P., & Wilson, B. J. (2011). The territorial foundations of human property. *Evolution and Human Behavior, 32*, 297–304.

DeSilver, D. (2013, June 7). World's Muslim population more widespread than you might think. Pew Research Center. Retrieved from http://www.pewresearch.org/fact-tank/2013/06/07/worlds-muslim-population-more-widespread-than-you-might-think/

Desmarais, S. L., & Read, J. D. (2011). After 30 years, what do we know about what jurors know? A meta-analytic review of lay knowledge regarding eyewitness factors. *Law and Human Behavior, 35*, 200–210.

DeSteno, D. A., & Salovey, P. (1996). Evolutionary origins of sex differences in jealousy? Questioning the "fitness" of the model. *Psychological Science, 7*, 367–372.

DeSteno, D. A., Bartlett, M. Y., Braverman, J., & Salovey, P. (2002). Sex differences in jealousy: Evolutionary mechanisms or artifact of measurement. *Journal of Personality and Social Psychology, 83*, 1103–1116.

Deutsch, M., & Gerard, H. B. (1955). A study of normative and informational social influences upon individual judgment. *Journal of Abnormal and Social Psychology, 51*, 629–636.

Devenport, J. L., & Cutler, B. L. (2004). Impact of defense-only and opposing eyewitness experts on juror judgments. *Law and Human Behavior, 28*, 569–576.

Devenport, J. L., Stinson, V., Cutler, B. L., & Kravitz, D. A. (2002). How effective are the cross-examination and expert testimony safeguards? Jurors' perceptions of the suggestiveness and fairness of biased lineup procedures. *Journal of Applied Psychology, 87*, 1042–1054.

Devine, P. G. (1989). Stereotypes and prejudice: Their automatic and controlled components. *Journal of Personality and Social Psychology, 56*, 5–18.

Devine, P. G., & Malpass, R. S. (1985). Orienting strategies in differential face recognition. *Personality and Social Psychology Bulletin, 11*(1), 33–40.

Devine, P. G., Plant, E. A., Amodio, A. M., Harmon-Jones, E., & Vance, S. L. (2002). Exploring the relationship between implicit and explicit prejudice: The role of motivations to respond without prejudice. *Journal of Personality and Social Psychology, 82*, 835–848.

DeVries, D., & Kaiser, R. B. (2003, November). Going sour in the suite. Paper presented at the Maximizing Executive Effectiveness workshop, Miami, FL.

DeWall, C. N., & Baumeister, R. F. (2006). Alone but feeling no pain: Effects of social exclusion on physical pain tolerance and pain threshold, affective forecasting, and interpersonal empathy. *Journal of Personality and Social Psychology, 91*, 1–15.

DeWall, C. N., Baumeister, R. F., & Masicampo, E. J. (2008). Evidence that logical reasoning depends on conscious processing. *Consciousness and Cognition. 17*, 628–645.

DeWall, C. N., Baumeister, R. F., Chester, D. S., & Bushman, B. J. (in press). How often does currently felt emotion predict social behavior and judgment? A meta-analytic test of two theories. *Emotion Review.* doi: 10.1177/1754073915572690. http://emr.sagepub.com/content/early/2015/03/16/1754073915572690.abstract.

DeWall, C. N., MacDonald, G., Webster, G. D., Masten, C., Baumeister, R. F., Powell, C., Combs, D., Schurtz, D. R., Stillman, T. F., Tice, D. M., & Eisenberger, N. I. (2010). Tylenol reduces social pain: Behavioral and neural evidence. *Psychological Science, 21*, 931–937.

DeWall, C. N., Pond, R. S., Campbell, W. K., & Twenge, J. M. (2011). Tuning in to psychological change: Linguistic markers of psychological traits and emotions over time in popular U.S. song lyrics. *Psychology of Aesthetics, Creativity, and the Arts, 5*, 200–207.

Dexter, H. R., Cutler, B. L., & Moran, G. (1992). A test of voir dire as a remedy for the prejudicial effects of pretrial publicity. *Journal of Applied Social Psychology, 22*, 819–832.

Di Paula, A., & Campbell, J. D. (2002). Self-esteem and persistence in the face of failure. *Journal of Personality and Social Psychology, 83*, 711–724.

Diamond, L. M. (2003). An attachment perspective on female sexual fluidity. Paper presented at the Women's Sexualities Conference: Historical, Interdisciplinary, and International Perspectives, sponsored by the Kinsey Institute for Research in Sex, Gender, and Reproduction, Bloomington, IN.

Diamond, L. M. (2003). What does sexual orientation orient? A biobehavioral model distinguishing romantic love and sexual desire. *Psychological Review, 110*, 173–192.

Diamond, L. M. (2004). Emerging perspectives on distinctions between romantic love and sexual desire. *Current Directions in Psychological Science, 13*, 116–119.

Diamond, L. M. (2008). *Sexual fluidity: Understanding women's love and desire.* Cambridge, MA: Harvard University Press.

Diaz, J. H. (2004). The global epidemiology, syndromic classification, management, and prevention of spider bites. *American Journal of Tropical Medicine and Hygiene, 71*(2), 239–250.

Dickerson, C., Thibodeau, R., Aronson, E., & Miller, D. (1992). Using cognitive dissonance to encourage water conservation. *Journal of Applied Social Psychology, 22*, 841–854.

Dickinson, D. J., & Larsen, J. D. (1963). The effects of chronological age in months on school achievement. *Journal of Educational Research, 56*, 492–493.

Dictionary of Marketing Terms (2004).

Diener, E., & Diener, M. (1995). Cross-cultural correlates of life satisfaction and self-esteem. *Journal of Personality and Social Psychology, 68*, 653–663.

Diener, E., & Wallbom, M. (1976). Effects of self-awareness on antinormative behavior. *Journal of Research in Personality, 10*, 107–111.

Diener, E., Fraser, S. C., Beaman, A. L., & Kelem, R. T. (1976). Effects of deindividuation variables on stealing among Halloween trick-or-treaters. *Journal of Personality and Social Psychology, 33*(2), 178–183.

Diener, E., Lucas, R. E., & Scollon, C. N. (2006). Beyond the hedonic treadmill: Revisions to the adaptation theory of well-being. *American Psychologist, 61*, 305–314.

Diener, E., Wolsic, B., & Fujita, F. (1995). Physical attractiveness and subjective well-being. *Journal of Personality and Social Psychology, 69*, 120–129.

Dijksterhuis, A., & Nordgren, L. F. (2006). A theory of unconscious thought. *Perspectives on Psychological Science, 1*, 95–109.

Dill, K. E., Anderson, C. A., Anderson, K. B., & Deuser, W. E. (1997). Effects of aggressive personality on social expectations and social perceptions. *Journal of Research in Personality, 31*, 272–292.

Dion, J., & Mellor, B. (2004, August). Is sport really good for you? *EnRoute*, pp. 33–34.

Dion, K. (1973). Young children's stereotyping of facial attractiveness. *Developmental Psychology, 9*, 183–188.

Dion, K. K., Berscheid, E., & Walster, F. H. (1972). What is beautiful is good. *Journal of Personality and Social Psychology, 24*, 285–290.

Dodge, K. A., & Coie, J. D. (1987). Social-information-processing factors in reactive and proactive aggression in children's peer groups. *Journal of Personality and Social Psychology, 53*, 1146–1158.

Dohnke, B., Steinhilber, A., & Fuchs, T. (2015). Adolescents' eating behaviour in general and in the peer context: Testing the prototype-willingness model. *Phychology & Health, 30*(4), 381–399. doi: 10.1080/08870446.2014.974604

Doja, A., & Roberts, W. (2006). Immunizations and autism: A review of the literature. *Canadian Journal of Neurological Sciences, 33*(4), 341–346. PMID 17168158

Dollard, J., Doob, L., Miller, N., Mowrer, O., & Sears, R. (1939). *Frustration and aggression.* New Haven, CT: Yale University Press.

Donnerstein, E., & Berkowitz, L. (1981). Victim reactions in aggressive erotic films as a factor in violence against women. *Journal of Personality and Social Psychology, 41*, 710–724.

Donovan, R., & Rossiter, J. (1982). Store atmosphere: An environmental psychology approach. *Journal of Retailing, 58*, 34–57.

Donovan, R., & Rossiter, J. (1982). Store atmosphere: An environmental psychology approach. *Journal of Retailing, 58*, 34–57.

Doocy, S., Daniels, A., Dooling, S., & Gorokhovich, Y. (2013). The human impact of volcanoes: A historical review of events 1900–2009 and systematic literature review. *PLoS Currents, 16*, 5.

Doocy, S., Daniels, A., Murray, S., & Kirsch, T. D. (2013). The human impact of floods: A historical review of events 1980–2009 and systematic literature review. *PLoS Currents Disasters, 16*, doi: 10.1371/currents.dis.f4deb457904936b07c09daa98ee8171a

Douglass, A. B., Neuschatz, J. S., Imrich, J., & Wilkinson, M. (2010). Does post-identification feedback affect evaluations of eyewitness testimony and identification procedures? *Law and Human Behavior, 34*, 282–294.

Douglass, A. B., Smith, C., & Fraser-Thill, R. (2005). A problem with double-blind photospread procedures: Photospread administrators use one eyewitness's confidence to influence the identification of another eyewitness. *Law and Human Behavior, 29*, 543–562.

Dovidio, J. F., & Gaertner, S. L. (1999). Reducing prejudice: Combating intergroup biases. *Current Directions in Psychological Science, 8*, 101–105.

Dowd, J. J. (1975). Aging as exchange: A preface to theory. *Journal of Gerontology, 30*(5), 584–594.

Doyle, A. C. (1974). *The memoirs of Sherlock Holmes.* London: J. Murray; Cape. (Original work published 1894)

Drabek, T. E., & Stephenson, J. S. (1971). When disaster strikes. *Journal of Applied Social Psychology, 1*, 187–203.

Draper, P. (1976). Social and economic constraints on child life among the !Kung. In R. B. Lee & I. DeVore (Eds.), *Kalahari hunter-gatherers: Studies of the !Kung San and their neighbors* (pp. 199–217). Cambridge, MA: Harvard University Press.

Duarte, J. L., Crawford, J. T., Stern, C., Haidt, J., Jussim, L., & Tetlock, P. E. (in press/2015). Political diversity will improve social psychological science. *Behavioral and Brain Sciences.*

Dube, K. C., Kumar, A., Kumar, N., & Gupta, S. P. (1978). Prevalence and pattern of drug use amongst college students. *Acta Psychiatrica Scandinavica, 57*, 336–356.

Dudley, R. T. (1999). Self-other judgments of paranormal and religious belief. *Journal of Social Behavior and Personality, 14*, 309–314.

Duke, A. A., & Giancola, P. R. (2013). Alcohol reverses religion's prosocial influence on aggression. *Journal for the Scientific Study of Religion, 52*(2), 279–292. doi: 10.1111/jssr.12029

Duke, M. P., & Wilson, J. (1973). The measurement of interpersonal distance in pre-school children. *Journal of Genetic Psychology, 123*, 361–362.

Dunbar, R. I. M. (1993). Coevolution of neocortical size, group size, and language in humans. *Behavioral and Brain Sciences, 16*, 681–694.

Dunbar, R. I. M. (1996). *Grooming, gossip, and the evolution of language.* Cambridge, MA: Harvard University Press.

Dunbar, R. I. M. (1998). The social brain hypothesis. *Evolutionary Anthropology, 6*, 178–190.

Duncan, C. P., & Nelson, J. E. (1985). Effects of humor in a radio advertising experiment. *Journal of Advertising, 14*, 33–40, 64.

Dunkel-Schetter, C., & Bennett, T. L. (1990). Differentiating the cognitive and behavioral aspects of social support. In B. R. Sarason, & I. G. Sarason (Eds.), *Social support: An interactional view* (pp. 267–296). Oxford: John Wiley & Sons.

Dunn, E. W., Brackett, M. A., Ashton-James, C., Schneiderman, E., & Salovey, P. (2007). On emotionally intelligent time travel: Individual differences in affective forecasting ability. *Personality and Social Psychology Bulletin, 33*(1), 85–93.

Dunning, D. (1999). A newer look: Motivated social cognition and the schematic representation of social concepts. *Psychological Inquiry, 10*, 1–11.

Dunning, D., & McElwee, R. O. (1995). Idiosyncratic trait definitions: Implications for self-description and social judgment. *Journal of Personality and Social Psychology, 68*, 936–946.

Dunning, D., & Perretta, S. (2002). Automaticity and eyewitness accuracy: A 10-to-12 second rule for distinguishing accurate from inaccurate positive identifications. *Journal of Applied Psychology, 87*, 951–962.

Dunning, D., & Stern, L. B. (1994). Distinguishing accurate from inaccurate identifications via inquiries about decision processes. *Journal of Personality and Social Psychology, 67*, 818–835.

Dunning, D., Anderson, J. E., Schlösser, T., Ehlebracht, D., & Fetchenhauer, D. (2014). Trust at zero acquaintance: More a matter of respect than expectation of reward. *Journal of Personality and Social Psychology, 107*(1), 122-141. doi: 10.1037/a0036673

Dunning, D., Meyerowitz, J. A., & Holzberg, A. D. (1989). Ambiguity and self-evaluation: The role of idiosyncratic trait definitions in self-serving assessments of ability. *Journal of Personality and Social Psychology, 57*, 1082–1090.

Dunning, D., Perie, M., & Story, A. L. (1991). Self-serving prototypes of social categories. *Journal of Personality and Social Psychology, 61*, 957–968.

Dutton, D. G. (1971). Reactions of restaurateurs to blacks and whites violating restaurant dress requirements. *Canadian Journal of Behavioural Science, 3*, 298–302.

Dutton, D. G., & Aron, A. P. (1974). Some evidence for heightened sexual attraction under conditions of high anxiety. *Journal of Personality and Social Psychology, 30*, 510–517.

Dutton, D. G., & Lake, R. A. (1973). Threat of own prejudice and reverse discrimination in interracial situations. *Journal of Personality and Social Psychology, 28*, 94–100.

Duval, S., & Wicklund, R. (1972). *A theory of objective self-awareness.* New York: Academic Press.

Dweck, C. S. (1996). Implicit theories as organizers of goals and behavior. In P. Gollwitzer & J. Bargh (Eds.), *The psychology of action: Linking cognition and motivation to behavior* (pp. 69–91). New York: Guilford Press.

Dweck, C. S., & Leggett, E. L. (1988). A social-cognitive approach to motivation and personality. *Psychological Review, 95*, 256–273.

Eagly, A. H. & Crowley, M. (1986). Gender and helping behavior: A meta-analytic view of the social psychological literature. *Psychological Bulletin, 100*, 283–308.

Eagly, A. H., & Chaiken, S. (1998). Attitude structure and function. In D. T. Gilbert, S. T. Fiske, & G. Lindzey (Eds.), *Handbook of social psychology* (4th ed., Vol. 1, pp. 269–322). New York: McGraw-Hill.

Eagly, A. H., Ashmore, R. D., Makhijani, M. G., & Longo, L. C. (1991). What is beautiful is good, but . . . : A meta-analytic review of the physical attractiveness stereotype. *Psychological Bulletin, 110*, 109–128.

Earnest, D. R., Allen, D. G., & Landis, R. S. (2011). Mechanisms linking realistic job previews with turnover: A meta-analytic path analysis. *Personnel Psychology, 64*(4), 865–897.

Easterbrook, J. A. (1959). The effect of emotion on the utilization and the organization of behavior. *Psychological Review, 66*, 183–201.

Eaton. K. (2009). If you're applying for a job, censor your Facebook page. *Fast Company.* Retrieved from http://www.fastcompany.com/blog/kit-eaton/technomix/if-youre-applying-job-censor-your-facebook-page

Eby, L. T., Casper, W. J., Lockwood, A., Bordeaux, C., & Brinley, A. (2005). Work and family research in IO/OB: Content analysis and review of the literature (1980–2002). *Journal of Vocational Behavior, 66*, 124–197.

Ecclesiastes 11:1 (Bible).

Edelman, C., & Mandle, C. (2006). *Health promotion throughout the lifespan* (6th ed.). St. Louis: Mosby.

Edelstein, R. S., & Shaver, P. R. (2004). Avoidant attachment: Exploration of an oxymoron. In D. Mashek & A. Aron (Eds.), *Handbook of closeness and intimacy* (pp. 397–412). Mahwah, NJ: Erlbaum.

Edgerton, R. (1971). *The individual in cultural adaptation.* Berkeley: University of California Press.

Edwards, D. J. A. (1972). Approaching the unfamiliar: A study of human interaction distances. *Journal of Behavioral Sciences, 1*, 249–250.

Efran, M. G., & Patterson, E. W. J. (1974). Voters vote beautiful: The effects of physical appearance on a national election. *Canadian Journal of Behavioral Science, 6*, 352–356.

Egan, G. (1970). *Encounter: Group processes for interpersonal growth.* Monterey, CA: Brooks/Cole.

Ehrenfeld, D. (1981). *The arrogance of humanism.* New York: Oxford University Press.

Ehrenreich, B. (1999, March 8). The real truth about the female. *Time, 153*(9), 57–91.

Eiland, L., & McEwen, B. S. (2012). Early life stress followed by subsequent adult chronic stress potentiates anxiety and blunts hippocampal structural remodeling. *Hippocampus, 22*(1), 82–91. doi: 10.1002/hipo.20862

Einon, D. (1994). Are men more promiscuous than women? *Ethology and Sociobiology, 15*(3), 131–143.

Eisenberg, N., & Lennon, R. (1983). Sex differences in empathy and related capacities. *Psychological Bulletin, 94*, 100–131.

Eisenberg, N., & Lennon, R. (1983). Sex differences in empathy and related capacities. *Psychological Bulletin, 94*, 100–131.

Eisenstein, E. M. (2008). Identity theft: An exploratory study with implications for marketers. *Journal of Business Research, 61*(11), 1160–1172.

Eisner, M. (2001). Modernization, self-control and lethal violence: The long-term dynamics of European homicide rates in theoretical perspective. *British Journal of Criminology, 41*, 618–638.

Ekman, P., & O'Sullivan, M. (1991). Who can catch a liar? *American Psychologist, 46*(9), 913–920.

Ekman, P., Friesen, W. V., O'Sullivan, M., Chan, A., Diacoyanni-Tarlatzis, I., Heider, K., et al. (1987). Universals and cultural differences in the judgments of facial expressions of emotion. *Journal of Personality and Social Psychology, 53*, 712–717.

Elder, G. H., Jr., & Clipp, E. C. (1988). Combat experience, comradeship, and psychological health. In J. P. Wilson, Z. Harel, & B. Kahana (Eds.), *Human adaptation to extreme stress: From the Holocaust to Vietnam* (pp. 131–156). New York: Plenum Press.

Election polls—Accuracy record in presidential elections. Retrieved from http://www.gallup.com/poll/9442/election-polls-accuracy-record-presidential-elections.aspx

Elfenbein, H. A., & Ambady, N. (2002). On the universality and cultural specificity of emotion recognition: A meta-analysis. *Psychological Bulletin, 128*, 203–235.

Ellemers, N., de Gilder, D., & van den Heuvel, H. (1998). Career-oriented vs. team-oriented commitment and behavior at work. *Journal of Applied Psychology, 83*, 717–730.

Elliott, S. (2012). M&M's to Unveil New Speaking Role at Super Bowl. *New York Times.* Retrieved from http://www.nytimes.com/2012/01/17/business/media/mms-to-unveil-a-new-speaking-role-at-super-bowl.html?_r51

Ellis, A. (1977). *How to live with—and without—anger.* New York: Reader's Digest Press.

Ellsworth, P. C., & Smith, C. A. (1988). Shades of joy: Patterns of appraisal differentiating pleasant emotions. *Cognition and Emotion, 2*, 301–331.

Emmons, R. A. (1989). The personal striving approach to personality. In L. Pervin (Ed.), *Goal concepts and personality and social cognition* (pp. 87–126). Hillsdale, NJ: Erlbaum.

Emswiller, T., Deaux, K., & Willits, J. E. (1971). Similarity, sex, and requests for small favors. *Journal of Applied Social Psychology, 1*, 284–291.

Engelman, R., Halweil, B., & Nierenberg, D. (2002). Rethinking population, improving lives. In C. Flavin, H. French, & G. Gardner (Eds.), *State of the world 2002: A Worldwatch Institute report on progress toward a sustainable society* (p. 127). New York: Norton.

Engs, R. C., & Hanson, D. J. (1990). Gender differences in drinking patterns and problems among college students: A review of the literature. *Journal of Alcohol and Drug Education, 35*, 36–47.

Epley, N., & Gneezy, A. (2007). The framing of financial windfalls and implications for public policy. *Journal of Socio-Economics, 36*, 36–47.

Epley, N., & Huff, C. (1998). Suspicion, affective response, and educational benefit as a result of deception in psychology research. *Personality and Social Psychology Bulletin, 24*, 759–768.

Epley, N., Mak, D., & Idson, L. C. (2006). Bonus or rebate? The impact of income framing on spending and saving. *Journal of Behavioral Decision Making, 19*(3), 213–227.

Epps, J., & Kendall, P. C. (1995). Hostile attribution bias in adults. *Cognitive Therapy and Research, 19*, 159–178.

Epstein, S. (1979). The stability of behavior: I. On predicting most of the people much of the time. *Journal of Personality and Social Psychology, 37*, 1097–1126.

Equal Opportunity Employment Commission. (2001). Muslim/Arab employment discrimination charges since 9/11. Retrieved from http://www.eeoc.gov/origin/z-stats.html

Erber, R., & Erber, M. W. (2000). The self-regulation of moods: Second thoughts on the importance of happiness in everyday life. *Psychological Science, 11*, 142–148.

Erber, R., & Fiske, S. T. (1984). Outcome dependency and attention to inconsistent information. *Journal of Personality and Social Psychology, 47*, 709–726.

Erber, R., Wegner, D. M., & Therriault, N. (1996). On being cool and collected: Mood regulation in anticipation of social interaction. *Journal of Personality and Social Psychology, 70*, 757–766.

Erez, A., & Isen, A. M. (2002). The influence of positive affect on the components of expectancy motivation. *Journal of Applied Psychology, 87*, 1055–1067.

Erickson, B., Lind, E. A., Johnson, B. C., & O'Barr, W. M. (1978). Speech style and impression formation in a court setting: The effects of "powerful" and "powerless" speech. *Journal of Experimental Social Psychology, 14*, 266–279.

Erikson, E. H. (1950). *Childhood and society.* New York: Norton.

Eron, L. D., & Huesmann, L. R. (1990). The stability of aggressive behavior—even into the third generation. In M. Lewis & S. M. Miller (Eds.), *Handbook of developmental psychopathology* (pp. 147–156). New York: Plenum Press.

Escobar, J. I., Canino, G., Rubio-Stipec, M., & Bravo, M. (1992). Somatic symptoms after a natural disaster: A prospective study. *American Journal of Psychiatry, 149*, 965–967.

Estrada, C. A., Isen, A. M., & Young, M. J. (1997). Positive affect facilitates integration of information and decreases anchoring in reasoning among physicians. *Organizational Behavior and Human Decision Processes, 72,* 117–135.

Etherington, J. (2010). Nationalism, territoriality, and national territorial belonging. *Papers. Revista de Sociologia, 95,* 321–339.

Evans, G. W., & Howard, H. R. B. (1972). A methodological investigation of personal space. In W. J. Mitchell (Ed.), *Environmental design: Research and practice,* Proceedings of EDRA3/AR8 Conference. University of California, Los Angeles, CA.

Evans, G. W., & Lepore, S. J. (1993). Household crowding and social support: A quasi-experimental analysis. *Journal of Personality and Social Psychology, 65,* 308–316.

Evans, G. W., & Stecker, R. (2004). The motivational consequences of environmental stress. *Journal of Environmental Psychology, 24,* 143–165.

Evans, G. W., Jacobs, S. V., Dooley, D., & Catalano, R. (1987). The interaction of stressful life events and chronic strains on community mental health. *American Journal of Community Psychology, 15,* 23–34.

Exline, J. J. (2002). Stumbling blocks on the religious road: Fractured relationships, nagging vices, and the inner struggle to believe. *Psychological Inquiry, 13,* 182–189.

Exline, J. J., & Lobel, M. (1999). The perils of outperformance: Sensitivity about being the target of a threatening upward comparison. *Psychological Bulletin, 125,* 307–337.

Exline, J. J., & Rose, E. (2005). Religious and spiritual struggles. In R. F. Paloutzian & C. L. Park (Eds.), *Handbook of the psychology of religion* (pp. 315–330). New York: Guilford Press.

Exline, J. J., & Zell, A. L. (2009). Empathy, self-affirmation, and forgiveness: The moderating roles of gender and entitlement. *Journal of Social and Clinical Psychology, 28*(9), 1071–1099.

Exline, J. J., Baumeister, R. F., Bushman, B. J., Campbell, W. K., & Finkel, E. J. (2004). Too proud to let go: Narcissistic entitlement as a barrier to forgiveness. *Journal of Personality and Social Psychology, 87,* 894–912.

Exline, J. J., Baumeister, R. F., Zell, A. L., Kraft, A. J., & Witvliet, C. V. O. (2008). Not so innocent: Does seeing one's own capability for wrongdoing predict forgiveness? *Journal of Personality and Social Psychology, 94,* 495–515.

Exline, J. J., Park, C. L., Smyth, J. M., & Carey, M. P. (2011). Anger toward God: Social-cognitive predictors, prevalence, and links with adjustment to bereavement and cancer. *Journal of Personality and Social Psychology, 100*(1), 129–148.

Exline, J. J., Worthington, E. L., Hill, P., & McCullough, M. E. (2003). Forgiveness and justice: A research agenda for social and personality psychology. *Personality and Social Psychology Review, 7,* 337–348.

Fadiman, A. (1997). *The spirit catches you and you fall down: A Hmong child, her American doctors, and the collusion of two cultures.* New York: Farrar, Straus and Giroux.

Faith, heroics and bedtime snacks hailed at Columbine funerals. (1999, April 26). *CNN.* Retrieved from http://www.cnn.com/US/9904/26/school.shooting.funeral/

Falck, R., & Craig, R. (1988). Classroom-oriented primary prevention programming for drug abuse. *Journal of Psychoactive Drugs, 20,* 403–408.

Falcone, L. B.(2009, October 7). Insurance pitchgirl a surprise TV hit: Going with the flo. *Boston Herald.* Retrieved from http://bostonherald.com/news_opinion/columnists/2009/10/insurance_pitchgirl_surprise_tv_hit

Falomir-Pichastor, J. M., & Mugny, G. (2009). "I'm not gay . . . I'm a real man!": Heterosexual men's gender self-esteem and sexual prejudice. *Personality and Social Psychology Bulletin, 35*(9), 1233–1243.

Farberow, N. L. (1975). Cultural history of suicide. In N. L. Farberow (Ed.), *Suicide in different cultures* (pp. 1–16). Baltimore: University Park Press.

Farrell, W. (1993). *The myth of male power.* New York: Berkley Books.

Farwell, L., & Wohlwend-Lloyd, R. (1998). Narcissistic processes: Optimistic expectations, favorable self-evaluations, and self-enhancing attributions. *Journal of Personality, 66,* 65–83.

Fay, T. H. (Ed.). (1991). *Noise and health.* New York: New York Academy of Medicine.

Fazio, R. H. (1990). Multiple processes by which attitudes guide behavior: The MODE model as an integrative frame work. In P. Zanna (Ed.), *Advances in experimental social psychology* (Vol. 23, pp. 75–109). San Diego: Academic Press.

Fazio, R. H., & Olson, M. A. (2003). Implicit measures in social cognition research: Their meaning and use. *Annual Review of Psychology, 54,* 297–327.

Fazio, R. H., & Powell, M. C. (1997). On the value of knowing one's likes and dislikes: Attitude accessibility, stress, and health in college. *Psychological Science, 8,* 430–436.

Fazio, R. H., & Towles-Schwen, T. (1999). The MODE model of attitude-behavior processes. In S. Chaiken (Ed.), *Dual-process theories in social psychology* (pp. 97–116). New York: Guilford Press.

Fazio, R. H., Blascovich, J., & Driscoll, D. M. (1992). On the functional value of attitudes: The influence of accessible attitudes on the ease and quality of decision making. *Personality and Social Psychology Bulletin, 18,* 388–401.

Fazio, R. H., Effrein, E. A., & Falender, V. J. (1981). Self-perceptions following social interaction. *Journal of Personality and Social Psychology, 41,* 232–242.

Fazio, R. H., Jackson, J. R., Dunton, B. C., & Williams, C. J. (1995). Variability in automatic activation as an unobtrusive measure of racial attitudes: A bona fide pipeline? *Journal of Personality and Social Psychology, 69,* 1013–1027.

Federal Trade Commission: Consumer information. Retrieved from http://www.consumer.ftc.gov/features/feature-0014-identity-theft

Federal Trade Commission: Consumer information. Retrieved from http://www.consumer.ftc.gov/features/feature-0014-identity-theft

Feeney, B. C., & Collins, N. L. (2001). Predictors of caregiving in adult intimate relationships. *Journal of Personality and Social Psychology, 80,* 972–994.

Feeney, J. A. (1996). Attachment, caregiving, and marital satisfaction. *Personal Relationships, 3,* 401–416.

Fehr, B., & Russell, J. A. (1984). Concept of emotion viewed from a prototype perspective. *Journal of Experimental Psychology: General, 113,* 464–486. Quote on p. 484.

Fehr, E., & Gächter, S. (2002). Altruistic punishment in humans. *Nature, 415*(6868), 137–140.

Fein, S., & Spencer, S. J. (1997). Prejudice as self-image maintenance: Affirming the self through derogating others. *Journal of Personality and Social Psychology, 73,* 31–44.

Feinberg, M., Willer, R., Stellar, J., & Keltner, D. (2012). The virtues of gossip: Reputational information sharing as prosocial behavior. *Journal of Personality and Social Psychology, 102,* 1015–1030.

Feinberg, R. (1986). Credit cards as spending facilitating stimuli: A conditioning interpretation. *Journal of Consumer Research, 3,* 348–356.

Feingold, A. (1988). Matching for attractiveness in romantic partners and same-sex friends: A meta-analysis and theoretical critique. *Psychological Bulletin, 104,* 226–235.

Feingold, A. (1992). Gender differences in mate selection preferences: A test of the parental investment model. *Psychological Bulletin, 112,* 125–139.

Feldman, P. J., Cohen S., Gwaltney, J. M., Jr., Doyle, W. J., & Skoner, D. P. (1999). The impact of personality on the reporting of unfounded symptoms and illness. *Journal of Personality and Social Psychology, 77,* 370–378.

Felson, R. B. (2002). *Violence and gender reexamined.* Washington, DC: American Psychological Association.

Felson, R. B., & Messner, S. F. (2000). The control motive in intimate partner violence. *Social Psychology Quarterly, 63*(1), 86–94.

Fenell, D. (1993). Characteristics of long-term first marriages. *Journal of Mental Health Counseling, 15,* 446–460.

Fenigstein, A., Scheier, M. F., & Buss, A. H. (1975). Public and private self-consciousness: Assessment and theory. *Journal of Consulting and Clinical Psychology, 43,* 522–527.

Fenton-O'Creevy, M., Nicholson, N., Soane, E., & Willman, P. (2003). Trading on illusions: Unrealistic perceptions of control and trading performance. *Journal of Occupational and Organizational Psychology, 76,* 53–68.

Ferrari, J. R. (2001). Procrastination as self-regulation failure of performance: Effects of cognitive load, self-awareness, and time limits on "working under pressure." *European Journal of Personality, 15,* 391–406.

Ferrari, J. R., Johnson, J. L., & McCown, W. G. (1995). *Procrastination and task avoidance: Theory, research, and treatment.* New York: Plenum Press.

Ferriere, R. (1998, June 11). Help and you shall be helped. *Nature, 393,* 517–519.

Feshbach, S. (1964). The function of aggression and the regulation of aggressive drive. *Psychological Review, 71,* 257–272.

Festinger, L. (1954). A theory of social comparison processes. *Human Relations, 7,* 117–140.

Festinger, L., & Carlsmith, J. M. (1959). Cognitive consequences of forced compliance. *Journal of Abnormal and Social Psychology, 58,* 203–211.

Festinger, L., & Maccoby, N. (1964). On resistance to persuasive communications. *Journal of Abnormal and Social Psychology, 68,* 359–366.

Festinger, L., Pepitone, A., & Newcomb T. (1952). Some consequences of deindividuation in a group. *Journal of Abnormal and Social Psychology, 47,* 382–389.

Festinger, L., Schachter, S., & Back, K. W. (1950) *Social pressures in informal groups: A study of human factors in housing.* New York: Harper.

Fetchenhauer, D., & Dunning, D. (2009). Do people trust too much or too little? *Journal of Economic Psychology, 30,* 263–276.

Fetterman, M., & Hausen, B. (2006, November 19). Young people struggle to deal with kiss of debt. *USA Today.* Retrieved from http://www.usatoday.com/money/perfi/credit/2006-11-19-young-and-in-debt-cover_x.htm

Fiddick, L., Cosmides, L., & Tooby, J. (2000). No interpretation without representation: The role of domain-specific representations and inferences in the Wason selection task. *Cognition, 77,* 1–79.

Fields, D. A., & Kafai, Y. B. (2010). "Stealing from grandma" or generating cultural knowledge? Contestations and effects of cheating in a tween virtual world. *Games and Culture: A Journal of Interactive Media, 5*(1), 64–87.

Filiberti, A., Ripamonti, C., Totis, A., Ventafridda, V., De Conno, F., Contiero, P., & Tamburini, M. (2001). Characteristics of terminal cancer patients who committed suicide during a home palliative care program. *Journal of Pain and Symptom Management, 22,* 544–553.

Filkins, J. W., Smith, C. M., & Tindale, R. S. (1998). An evaluation of the biasing effects of death qualification: A meta-analytic/computer simulation approach. In R. S. Tindale et al. (Eds.), *Theory and research on small groups.* New York: Plenum Press.

Fincham, F. D., Beach, S. R., & Davila, J. (2004). Forgiveness and conflict resolution in marriage. *Journal of Family Psychology, 18,* 72–81.

Fincham, F. D., Hall, J. H. & Beach, S. R. H. (2005). 'Til lack of forgiveness doth us part: Forgiveness in marriage. In E. L. Worthington (Ed.), *Handbook of forgiveness* (pp. 207–226). New York: Wiley.

Fincher, C. L., Thornhill, R., Murray, D. R., & Schaller, M. (2008). Pathogen prevalence predicts human cross-cultural variability in individualism/collectivism. *Proceedings of the Royal Society B, 275,* 1279–1285.

Finder, A. (2006, June 11). For some, online persona undermines a resume. *The New York Times.*

Finkel, E. J., DeWall, C. N., Slotter, E. B., McNulty, J. K., Pond, R. S., Jr., & Atkins, D. C. (2012). Using I3 theory to clarify when dispositional aggressiveness predicts intimate partner violence perpetration. *Journal of Personality and Social Psychology, 102*(3), 533–549.

Finkel, E. J., Eastwick, P. W., Karney, B. R., Reis, H. T., & Sprecher, S. (2012). Online dating: A critical analysis from the perspective of psychological science. *Psychological Science in the Public Interest, 13,* 3–66.

Finkel, E. J., Rusbult, C. E., Kumashiro, M., & Hannon, P. (2002). Dealing with betrayal in close relationships: Does commitment promote forgiveness? *Journal of Personality and Social Psychology, 82,* 956–974.

Finnie, W. C. (1973). Field experiments and litter control. *Environment and Behavior, 5,* 123–143.

Fischhoff, B., Lichtenstein, S., Slovic, P., Derby, S. L., & Keeney, R. L. (1981). *Acceptable risk.* New York: Cambridge University Press.

Fishbein, M., & Ajzen, I. (1975). *Belief, attitude, intention and behavior: An introduction to theory and research.* Boston: Addison-Wesley.

Fisher, C. D. (1978). The effects of personal control, competence, and extrinsic reward systems on intrinsic motivation. *Organizational Behavior and Human Performance, 21,* 273–288.

Fisher, J. D., & Nadler, A. (1976). Effects of donor resources on recipient self-esteem and self-help. *Journal of Experimental Social Psychology, 12*(2), 139–150.

Fiske, S. (2002, November/December). Forecasting the future. *Psychology Today.* Retrieved from http://www.psychologytoday.com/articles/pto-20021125-000001.html

Fiske, S. T. (1992). Thinking is for doing: Portraits of social cognition from daguerreotype to laser-photo. *Journal of Personality and Social Psychology, 63,* 877–889.

Fiske, S. T. (2004). *Social beings: A core motives approach to social psychology.* New York: Wiley.

Fiske, S. T., & Taylor, S. E. (1984). *Social cognition.* New York: Random House.

Fiske, S. T., & Taylor, S. E. (1991). *Social cognition* (2nd ed.). New York: Random House.

Fiske, S. T., & Yamamoto, M. (2005). Coping with rejection: Core social motives, across cultures and individuals. In K. D. Williams, J. P. Forgas, & W. von Hippel (Eds.), *The social outcast: Ostracism, social exclusion, rejection, and bullying* (pp. 185–199). New York: Psychology Press.

Fitness, J. (2005). Bye, bye, black sheep: The causes and consequences of rejection in family relationships. In K. D. Williams, J. P. Forgas, & W. von Hippel (Eds.), *The social outcast: Ostracism, social exclusion, rejection, and bullying* (pp. 263–277). New York: Psychology Press.

Fitzgerald, R. J., Price, H. L., Oriet, C., & Charman, S. D. (2013). The effect of suspect-filler similarity on eyewitness identification decisions: A meta-analysis. *Psychology, Public Policy, and Law, 19,* 151–164.

Fitzgerald, R., & Ellsworth, P. C. (1984). Due process vs. crime control: Death qualification and jury attitudes. *Law and Human Behavior, 8,* 31–51.

Fitzsimons, G. M., & Bargh, J. A. (2003). Thinking of you: Nonconscious pursuit of interpersonal goals associated with relationship partners. *Journal of Personality and Social Psychology, 84,* 148–164.

Fitzsimons, G. M., & Shah, J. Y. (2008). How goal instrumentality shapes relationship evaluations. *Journal of Personality and Social Psychology, 95,* 319–337.

Flaherty, D. K. (2011). The vaccine-autism connection: a public health crisis caused by unethical medical practices and fraudulent science. *Annals of Pharmacother, 45*(10), 1302–4. doi:10.1345/aph.1Q318

Flanagan, J. C. (1954). The critical incident technique. *Psychological Bulletin, 51,* 327–358.

Flanagin, A, J., & Waldeck, J. H. (2004). Technology use and organizational newcomer socialization. *Journal of Business Communication, 41*(2), 137–165.

Fletcher, C., & Perry, E. L. (2001). Performance appraisal and feedback: A consideration of national culture and a review of contemporary research and future trends. In N. Anderson, D. S. Ones, H. K. Sinangil, & C. Viswesvaran, *Handbook of industrial, work and organizational psychology* (Vol. 1, pp. 127–144). Thousand Oaks, CA: Sage.

Flink, C., Boggiano, A. K., & Barrett, M. (1990). Controlling teaching strategies: Undermining children's

self-determination and performance. *Journal of Personality and Social Psychology, 59*(5), 916–924.

Florin, P., & Wandersman, A. (1983). A psychosocial perspective on neighborhood conservation. In N. R. Feimer & E. S. Geller (Eds.), *Environmental psychology: Directions and perspectives.* New York: Praeger.

Folkes, V. S. (1982). Communicating the reasons for social rejection. *Journal of Personality and Social Psychology, 18,* 235–252.

Foot, P. (1967). The problem of abortion and the doctrine of double effect. *Oxford Review, 5,* 5–15.

Forgas, J. P., (2013). Don't worry, be sad! On the cognitive, motivational, and interpersonal benefits of negative mood. *Current Directions in Psychological Science, 22,* 225–232.

Forster, J. L. & Jeffery, R. W. (1986). Gender differences related to weight history, eating patterns, efficacy expectations, self-esteem, and weight loss among participants in a weight reduction program. *Addictive Behaviors, 11,* 141–147.

Forsyth, A. J. M., & Davidson, N. (2010). The nature and extent of illegal drug and alcohol-related litter in Scottish social housing community: A photographic investigation. *Addiction Research & Theory, 18*(1), 71–83.

Forsyth, D. R. (2010). *Group dynamics* (5th ed.). Belmont, CA: Wadsworth.

Forsyth, D. R., & Kerr, N. A. (1999, August). *Are adaptive illusions adaptive?* Poster presented at the annual meeting of the American Psychological Association, Boston, MA.

Fortune. (2015). Best companies 2014. Retrieved from http://fortune.com/best-companies/

Fowler, G. A. (2012, October 4). Facebook: One billion and counting. *The Wall Street Journal.* Retrieved from http://online.wsj.com/news/articles/SB100008723 9639044363540457803616402738611?mg5reno64-wsj&url5http%3A%2F%2Fonline.wsj.com%2Farticle%2FSB100008723963904436354045780361640273861123.html

Fowler, J. H., & Christakis, N. A. (2010). Cooperative behavior cascades in human social networks. *PNAS, 107*(12), 5334–5338. doi: 10.1073/pnas.0913149107

Fox, E., Griggs, L., & Mouchlianitis, E. (2007). The detection of fear-relevant stimuli: Are guns noticed as quickly as snakes? *Emotion, 7*(4), 691–696.

Fraley, B., & Aron, A. (2004). The effect of a shared humorous experience on closeness in initial encounters. *Personal Relationships, 11,* 61–78.

Francis, A. M., & Mialon, H. M. (2014). "A diamond is forever" and other fairy tales: The relationship between wedding expenses and marriage duration. Unpublished paper, Emory University, Atlanta, GA (Andrew.francis@emory.edu).

Francoeur, R. T., Perper, T., Scherzer, N. A., Sellmer, G. P., & Cornog, M. (1991). *A descriptive dictionary and atlas of sexology,* p. 130. New York: Greenwood Press.

Frayser, S. G. (1985). *Varieties of sexual experience: An anthropological perspective on human sexuality.* New Haven, CT: HRAF Press.

Frazier, P., Tashiro, T., Berman, M., Steger, M., & Long, J. (2004), Correlates of levels and patterns of positive life changes following sexual assault. *Journal of Consulting and Clinical Psychology, 72,* 19–30.

Fredrickson, B. L. (1998). What good are positive emotions? *Review of General Psychology, 2,* 300–319.

Fredrickson, B. L. (2001). The role of positive emotions in positive psychology: The broaden-and-build theory of positive emotions. *American Psychologist, 56,* 218–226.

Fredrickson, B. L. (2003). The value of positive emotions. *American Scientist, 91,* 330–335.

Freedman, J. L. & Fraser, S. C. (1966). Compliance without pressure: The foot-in-the-door technique. *Journal of Personality and Social Psychology, 4*(2), 195–202. doi: 10.1037/h0023552

Freedman, J. L., & Sears, D. O. (1965). Warning, distraction, and resistance to influence. *Journal of Personality and Social Psychology, 1*(3), 262–266.

Freedman, S. R., & Enright, R. D. (1996). Forgiveness as an intervention goal with incest survivors. *Journal of Consulting and Clinical Psychology, 64,* 983–992.

Freud, S. (1933/1950). Why war? In *Collected works of Sigmund Freud* (Vol. 16). London: Imagio.

Freud, S. (1961). *Civilization and its discontents* (standard ed.). London: Norton. (Original work published 1930).

Freud, S. (1964). *Beyond the pleasure principle* (J. Strachey, Trans.). New York: Norton. (Original work published 1920).

Frey, R. G. (1983). *Rights, killing, and suffering: Moral vegetarianism and applied ethics.* Oxford: Blackwell.

Friedman, H. S., & Booth-Kewley, S. (1987). The "disease-prone personality": A meta-analytic view of the construct. *American Psychologist, 42,* 539–555.

Friedman, H., & Silver, R. (Eds.). (2007). *Foundations of health psychology.* New York: Oxford University Press.

Frijda, N. H. (1986). *The emotions.* New York: Cambridge University Press.

Frijda, N. H., Kuipers, P., & ter Schure, E. (1989). Relations among emotion, appraisal, and emotional action readiness. *Journal of Personality and Social Psychology, 57,* 212–228.

Frimer, J.A., Schaefer, N.K., & Oakes, H. (2014). Moral actor, selfish agent. *Journal of Personality and Social Psychology, 106,* 790–802.

Frith, K. T., & Mueller, B. (2003). *Advertising and society: Global issues.* New York: Peter Lang.

From "Cosmic Evolution – Epoch 7 – Cultural Evolution." Fig. 7.13 located at http://www.tufts.edu/as/wright_cenger/cosmic_evolution. Copyright © 2005 by Eric Chaison, Wright Center for Science Education. Reprinted by permission.

From Plant, E. A., & Devine, P. G. (1998). Internal and external motivation to respond without prejudice. *Journal of Personality and Social Psychology, 75,* 811–832.

Fukuyama, F. (1999). *Trust.* New York: Free Press.

Fulero, S. M., & Penrod, S. D. (1990a). Attorney jury selection folklore: What do they think and how can psychologists help? *Forensic Reports, 3,* 233–259.

Fullerton, C. S., McCarroll, J. E., Ursano, R. S., & Wright, K. M. (1992). Psychological responses of rescue workers: Fire fighters and trauma. *American Journal of Orthopsychiatry, 62,* 371–378.

Funder, D. C. (2001). Personality. *Annual Review of Psychology, 52,* 197–221.

Furnham, A. (2003). Belief in a just world: Research progress over the past decade. *Personality and Individual Differences, 34,* 795–817.

Gabbiadini, A., Riva, P., Andrighetto, L., Volpato, C., & Bushman, B. J. (2014). Moral disengagement moderates the effect of violent video games on self-control, cheating and aggression. *Social Psychological and Personality Science, 5*(4), 451–458. doi: 10.1177/1948550613509286

Gable, S. L., & Reis, H. T. (2001). Appetitive and aversive social interaction. In J. Harvey (Ed.), *Close romantic relationships: Maintenance and enhancement* (pp. 169–194). Mahwah, NJ: Erlbaum.

Gable, S. L., Reis, H. T., & Elliot, A. J. (2000). Behavioral activation and inhibition in everyday life. *Journal of Personality and Social Psychology, 78,* 1135–1149.

Gabriel, M. T., Critelli, J. W., & Ee, J. S. (1994). Narcissistic illusions in self-evaluations of intelligence and attractiveness. *Journal of Personality, 62,* 143–155.

Gael, S. A. (1988). *The job analysis handbook for business, industry, and government* (Vols. 1 and 2). New York: Wiley.

Gaertner, L., & Iuzzini, J. (2005). Rejection and entitativity: A synergistic model of mass violence. In K. D. Williams, J. P. Forgas, & W. von Hippel (Eds.), *The social outcast: Ostracism, social exclusion, rejection, and bullying* (pp. 307–320). New York: Psychology Press.

Gaertner, S. L., & Dovidio, J. F. (1986). The aversive form of racism. In J. F. Dovidio & S. L. Gaertner (Eds.), *Prejudice, discrimination, and racism* (pp. 61–89). San Diego: Academic Press.

Gailliot, M. T., & Baumeister, R. F. (2007). The physiology of willpower: Linking blood glucose to self-control. *Personality and Social Psychology Review, 11*(4), 303–327.

Galinsky, A. D., Gruenfeld, D. H., & Magee, J. C. (2003). From power to action. *Journal of Personality and Social Psychology, 85,* 453–466.

Galinsky, A. D., Magee, J. C., Gruenfeld, D. H., Whitson, J. A., & Liljenquist, K. A. (2008). Power reduces the press of the situation: Implications for creativity, conformity, and dissonance. *Journal of Personality and Social Psychology, 95,* 1450–1466.

Gallagher, J. (2011). Babies can "hear" emotion as early as three months old. BBC News Health. June 30. Retrieved from http://www.bbc.co.uk/news/health-13962068

Gangestad, S. W., & Snyder, M. (2000). Self-monitoring: Appraisal and reappraisal. *Psychological Bulletin, 126,* 530–555.

Gardner, M. P., Wansink, B., & Kim, J. (2014). Better moods for better eating?: How mood influences food choice. *Journal of Consumer Psychology, Vol 24*(3), Jul, 2014. pp. 320–335. doi: 10.1037/t01397-000

Gardner, W. L., Pickett, C. L., & Brewer, M. B. (2000). Social exclusion and selective memory: How the need to belong influences memory for social events. *Personality and Social Psychology Bulletin, 26,* 486–496.

Gardner, W. L., Pickett, C. L., & Knowles, M. (2005). Social snacking and shielding: Using social symbols, selves, and surrogates in the service of belonging needs. In K. D. Williams, J. P. Forgas, & W. von Hippel (Eds.), *The social outcast: Ostracism, social exclusion, rejection, and bullying* (pp. 227–242). New York: Psychology Press.

Gardner, W. L., Pickett, C. L., & Knowles, M. (2005). Social snacking and shielding: Using social symbols, selves, and surrogates in the service of belonging needs. In K. D. Williams, J. P. Forgas, & W. von Hippel (Eds.), *The social outcast: Ostracism, social exclusion, rejection, and bullying* (pp. 227–242). New York: Psychology Press.

Gardner, W., Seeley, E., Gabriel, S., Pennington, G., Solomon, J., Ernst, J., et al. (2002). The role of "his" and "her" forms of interdependence in everyday life: Gender, belonging, and social experience. Unpublished manuscript, Northwestern University.

Garner, D. M., Garfinkel, P. E., Schwartz, D., & Thompson, M. (1980). Cultural expectations of thinness in women. *Psychological Reports, 47,* 483–491.

Garrioch, L., & Brimacombe, C. A. E. (2001). Lineup administrators' expectations: Their impact on eyewitness confidence. *Law and Human Behavior, 25,* 299–315.

Gaur, S. D. (1988). Noise: Does it make you angry? *Indian Psychologist, 5,* 51–56.

Gazzaniga, M. S. (1998). *The mind's past.* Berkeley: University of California Press.

Gazzaniga, M. S. (2003, January). *The when, where, what, and why of conscious experience.* Paper presented at the 25th Annual National Institute on the Teaching of Psychology Convention, St. Petersburg Beach, FL.

Geen, R. G. (1978). Effects of attack and uncontrollable noise on aggression. *Journal of Research in Personality, 12*(1), 15–29.

Geen, R. G., & McCown, E. J. (1984). Effects of noise and attack on aggression and physiological arousal. *Motivation and Emotion, 8,* 231–241.

Geen, R. G., & Quanty, M. B. (1977). The catharsis of aggression: An evaluation of a hypothesis. In L. Berkowitz (Ed.), *Advances in experimental social psychology* (Vol. 10, pp. 1–37). New York: Academic Press.

Geller, E. S., Winett, R. A., & Everett, P. B. (1982). *Preserving the environment: Strategies for behavior change.* New York: Pergamon.

Gensler. (2013). 2013 U.S. workplace survey: Key findings. Retrieved from http://www.gensler.com/uploads/documents/2013_US_Workplace_Survey_07_15_2013.pdf

Gensler. (2013). 2013 U.S. workplace survey: Key findings. Retrieved from http://www.gensler.com/uploads/documents/2013_US_Workplace_Survey_07_15_2013.pdf

Gentile, D. A., Anderson, C. A., Yukawa, S., Ihori, N., Saleem, M., Ming, L. K., Liau, A. K., Khoo, A.,

Bushman, B. J., Huesmann, L. R., & Sakamoto, A. (2009). The effects of prosocial video games on prosocial behaviors: International evidence from correlational, longitudinal, and experimental studies. *Personality and Social Psychology Bulletin, 35*(6), 752–763.

Gentile, D. G., & Bushman, B. J. (2012). Reassessing media violence effects using a risk and resilience approach to understanding aggression. *Psychology of Popular Media Culture, 1*(3), 138–151. doi:10.1037/a0028481

George Santayana (1905) *Reason in Common Sense,* p. 284, volume 1 of *The Life of Reason.* (1905–1906) at Project Gutenberg https://en.wikiquote.org/wiki/George_Santayana

Gerrard, M., Gibbons, F. X., & McCoy, S. B. (1993). Emotional inhibition of effective contraception. *Anxiety, Stress & Coping: An International Journal, 6,* 73–88.

Gerrard, M., Gibbons, F., Houlihan, A., Stock, M., & Pomery, E. (2008). A dual-process approach to health risk decision making: The prototype willingness model. *Developmental Review, 28*(1), 29–61.

Gerstel, N., & Gross, H. (1982). Commuter marriages: A review. *Marriage and Family Review, 5,* 71–93.

Gerstel, N., & Gross, H. (1984). *Commuter marriage: A study of work and family.* New York: Guilford Press.

Gervais, W. M. & Norenzayan, A. (2013). Religion and the origins of anti-atheist prejudice. Chapter to appear in S. Clarke, R. Powell, & J. Savulescu (Eds.), *Intolerance and conflict: A scientific and conceptual investigation.* Oxford: Oxford University Press.

Gervais, W. M., Shariff, A. F., & Norenzayan, A. (2011). Do you believe in atheists? Distrust is central to anti-atheist prejudice. *Journal of Personality and Social Psychology, 101,* 1189–1206. doi: 10.1037/a0025882

Gesch, B. C., Hammond, S. M., Hampson, S. E., Eves, A., & Crowder, M. J. (2002). Influence of supplementary vitamins, minerals and essential fatty acids on the antisocial behaviour of young adult prisoners: Randomised, placebo-controlled trial. *British Journal of Psychiatry, 181,* 22–28.

Giancola, P. R. (2000). Executive functioning: A conceptual framework for alcohol-related aggression. *Experimental Clinical Psychopharmacology, 8,* 576–597.

Giannopoulou, I., Dikaiakou, A., Yule, W. (2006). Cognitive-behavioural group intervention for PTSD symptoms in children following the Athens 1999 earthquake: A pilot study. *Clinical Child Psychology and Psychiatry, 2011,* 543–553.

Gibbons, F. X., & Gerrard, M. (1997). Health images and their effects on health behavior. In B. P. Buunk & F. X. Gibbons (Eds.), *Health, coping, and well-being: Perspectives from social comparison theory* (pp. 63–94). Mahwah, NJ: Erlbaum.

Gibbons, F. X., Gerrard, M., & Lane, D. J. (2003). A social reaction model of adolescent health risk. In J. M. Suls & K. Wallston (Eds.), *Social psychological foundations of health and illness* (pp. 107–136). Oxford: Blackwell.

Gilbert, D. T. (1991). How mental systems believe. *American Psychologist, 46,* 107–119.

Gilbert, D. T. (1993). The assent of man: Mental representation and the control of belief. In D. Wegner & J. Pennebaker (Eds.), *Handbook of mental control* (pp. 57–87). Englewood Cliffs, NJ: Prentice-Hall.

Gilbert, D. T., Pelham, B. W., & Krull, D. S. (1988). On cognitive business: When person perceivers meet persons perceived. *Journal of Personality and Social Psychology, 54,* 733–740.

Gilbert, D. T., Pinel, E. C., Wilson, T. D., Blumberg, S. J., & Wheatley, T. P. (1998). Immune neglect: A source of durability bias in affective forecasting. *Journal of Personality and Social Psychology, 75,* 617–638.

Gilbert, D. T., Tafarodi, R. W., & Malone, P. S. (1993). You can't not believe everything you read. *Journal of Personality and Social Psychology, 65,* 221–233.

Gilovich, T. (1983). Biased evaluation and persistence in gambling. *Journal of Social and Personal Psychology, 44,* 1110–1126.

Gilovich, T. (1991). *How we know what isn't so.* New York: Free Press.

Gino, F., & Ariely, D. (2012). The dark side of creativity: Original thinkers can be more dishonest. *Journal of Personality and Social Psychology, 102,* 445–459.

Gino, F., & Mogilner, C. (2014). Time, money, and morality. *Psychological Science, 25,* 414–421.

Gino, F., & Wiltermuth, S.S. (2014). Evil genius? How dishonesty can lead to greater creativity. *Psychological Science, 25,* 973–981.

Gladue, B. A., Boechler, M., & McCaul, K. D. (1989). Hormonal responses to competition in human males. *Aggressive Behavior, 17,* 313–326.

Glasdoor. (2015). Maternity & paternity leave. Retrieved from http://www.glassdoor.com/Benefits/Google-Maternity-and-Paternity-Leave-US-BNFT23_E9079_N1.htm

Glass, D. C., & Singer, J. E. (1972). *Urban stress: Experiments on noise and social stressors.* New York: Academic Press.

Glass, D. C., Singer, J. E., & Friedman, L. N. (1969). Psychic cost of adaptation to an environmental stressor. *Journal of Personality and Social Psychology, 12,* 200–210. Retrieved from http://www.quotationspage.com/quote/34212.html

Gleick, E. (1997). The marker we've been...waiting for. *Time, 149*(14).

Glendenning, A., & Inglis, D. (1999). Smoking behaviour in youth: The problem of low self-esteem? *Journal of Adolescence, 22,* 673–682.

Glenn, N. D., & McLanahan, S. (1982). Children and marital happiness: A further specification of the relationship. *Journal of Marriage and the Family, 44,* 63–72.

Glenn, N. D., & Weaver, C. N. (1978). A multi-variate multisurvey study of marital happiness. *Journal of Marriage and the Family, 40,* 269–282.

Glick, P., & Fiske, S. T. (1996). The Ambivalent Sexism Inventory: Differentiating hostile and benevolent sexism. *Journal of Personality and Social Psychology, 70,* 491–512.

Glionna, J. M. (2013, January 30). New Aspen speed limit — 14 miles an hour? *Los Angeles Times.* Retrieved from http://articles.latimes.com/2013/jan/30/nation/la-na-nn-new-aspen-speed-limit-14-miles-an-hour-20130130

Gockel, C., Kolb, P. M., & Werth, L. (2014). Murder or not? Cold temperature makes criminals appear to be cold-blooded and warm temperature to be hot-headed. *PLoS ONE, 9*(4), e96231. doi:10.1371/journal.pone.0096231

Goel, S., Mason, W., & Watts, D. J. (2010). Real and perceived attitude agreement in social networks. *Journal of Social and Personality Psychology, 99*(4), 611–621.

Goethals, G. R., Messick, D. M., & Allison, S. T. (1991). The uniqueness bias: Studies of constructive social comparison. In J. Suls & T. A. Wills (Eds.), *Social comparison: Contemporary theory and research.* Hillsdale, NJ: Erlbaum.

Goffman, E. (1959). *The presentation of self in everyday life.* New York: Doubleday Anchor.

Golding, S. L., & Rorer, L. G. (1972). Illusory correlation and subjective judgment. *Journal of Abnormal Psychology, 80,* 249–260.

Goldsmith, K., Cho, E. K., & Dhar, R. (2012). When guilt begets pleasure: The positive effect of a negative emotion. *Journal of Marketing Research, 49,* 872–881.

Goldstein, N. J., Cialdini, R. B., & Griskevicius, V. (2004). *A room with a viewpoint: Using norm-based appeals to motivate conservation behaviors in a hotel setting.* Paper presented at the annual meeting of the Society for Personality and Social Psychology, Austin, TX.

Goleman, D. (1995, August 8). Brain may tag all perceptions with a value. *New York Times,* 1–10.

Gollwitzer, P. M. (1996). The volitional benefits of planning. In P. M. Gollwitzer & J. A. Bargh (Eds.), *The psychology of action: Linking cognition and motivation to behavior* (pp. 287–312). New York: Guilford Press.

Gollwitzer, P. M., & Kinney, R. F. (1989). Effects of deliberative and implemental mind-sets on the illusion of control. *Journal of Personality and Social Psychology, 56,* 531–542.

Gondolf, E. W. (1985). *Men who batter: An integrated approach for stopping wife abuse.* Holmes Beach, CA: Learning Publications.

Gonzales, M. H., Haugen, J. A., & Manning, D. J. (1994). Victims as "narrative critics": Factors influencing rejoinders and evaluative responses to offenders' accounts. *Personality and Social Psychology Bulletin, 20*, 691–704.

Gonzales, M., Pederson, J., Manning, D., & Wetter, D. (1990). Pardon my gaffe: Effects of sex, status, and consequence severity on accounts. *Journal of Personality and Social Psychology, 58*, 610–621.

Gonzalez-Vallejo, C., Lassiter, G. D., Bellezza, F. S., & Lindberg, M. J. (2008). "Save angels perhaps": A critical examination of Unconscious Thought Theory and the Deliberation-Without-Attention effect. *Review of General Psychology, 12*, 282–296.

Goodenough, F. L. (1931). *Anger in young children.* Minneapolis: University of Minnesota Press.

Goodwin, G. P., Piazza, J., & Rozin, P. (2013). Moral character predominates in person perception and evaluation. *Journal of Personality and Social Psychology, 106*, 148–168.

Goodwin, J. S., Hunt, W. C., Key, C. R., & Samet, J. M. (1987). The effect of marital status on stage, treatment, and survival of cancer patients. *Journal of the American Medical Association, 258*, 3125–3130.

Google. (2012). Benefits. Retrieved from http://www.google.com/intl/en/jobs/lifeatgoogle/benefits/index.html

Google. (2015). Life at Google. Retrieved from http://www.google.com/about/careers/lifeatgoogle/do-cool-things-that-matter.html

Gottfredson, L. (Ed.). (1997). Intelligence and social policy, *Intelligence, 24*, 1–320.

Gottfredson, M. R., & Hirschi, T. (1990). *A general theory of crime.* Stanford, CA: Stanford University Press. Also see DeWall, C. N., Finkel, E. J., & Denson, T. F. (2011). Self-control inhibits aggression. *Social and Personality Psychology Compass, 5*(7), 458–472.

Gottman, J. M. (1994). *What predicts divorce?* Hillsdale, NJ: Erlbaum.

Gottschalk, L. A., & Gleser, G. C. (1960). An analysis of the verbal content of suicide notes. *British Journal of Medical Psychology, 33*, 195–204.

Gould, S. J., & Weil, C. E. (1991). Gift-giving and gender self-concepts. *Gender Role, 24*, 617–637.

Govaerts, K., & Dixon, D. N. (1988). . . . Until careers do us part: Vocational and marital satisfaction in the dual-career commuter marriage. *International Journal for the Advancement of Counseling, 11*, 265–281.

Goveas, J. S., Csernansky, J. G., & Coccaro, E. F. (2004). Platelet serotonin content correlates inversely with life history of aggression in personality-disordered subjects. *Psychiatry Research, 126*, 23–32.

Graham, J., Haidt, J., & Nosek, B.A. (2009). Liberals and conservatives rely on different sets of moral foundations. *Journal of Personality and Social Psychology, 96*, 1029–1046.

Graham, K. (1980). Theories of intoxicated aggression. *Canadian Journal of Behavioral Science, 12*, 141–158.

Grammer, K., Fink, B., Moller A. P., & Thornhill, R. (2003). Darwinian aesthetics: Sexual selection and the biology of beauty. *Biological Reviews, 78*, 385–407.

Grasmick, H. G., Bursik, R. J., & Kinsey, K. A. (1991). Shame and embarrassment as deterrents to noncompliance with the law: The case of an antilittering campaign. *Environment and Behavior, 23*, 233–251.

Gray-Little, B., & Hafdahl, A. R. (2000). Factors influencing racial comparisons of self-esteem: A quantitative synthesis. *Psychological Bulletin, 126*, 26–54.

Great Place to Work. (2015). Identifying best places to work: US and globally. Retrieved from http://www.greatplacetowork.com/best-companies

Greathouse, S. M., & Kovera, M. B. (2009). Instruction bias and lineup presentation moderate the effects of administrator knowledge on eyewitness identification. *Law and Human Behavior, 33*, 70–82.

Greathouse, S. M., & Kovera, M. B. (2009). Instruction bias and lineup presentation moderate the effects of administrator knowledge on eyewitness identification. *Law and Human Behavior, 33*, 70–82.

Green, B. L., Grace, M. C., Vary, M. G., Krammer, T. L., Gleser, G. C., & Leonard, A. C. (1994). Children of disaster in the second decade: A 17-year follow-up of Buffalo Creek survivors. *Journal of the American Academy of Child and Adolescent Psychiatry, 33*, 71–79.

Green, D. M., & Fidell, S. (1991). Variability in the criterion for reporting annoyance in community noise surveys. *Journal of the Acoustical Society of America, 89*, 234–243.

Green, G. (2005, December 9). Man dates gal on Internet for six months—and it turns out she's his mother! Retrieved from http://entertainment.tv.yahoo.com/news/wwn

Green, L., Price, P. C., & Hamburger, M. E. (1995). Prisoner's dilemma and the pigeon: Control by immediate consequences. *Journal of the Experimental Analysis of Behavior, 64*, 1–17.

Greenberg J. (1990). Organizational justice: Yesterday, today and tomorrow. *Journal of Management 16*, 399–432.

Greenberg, J., & Musham, C. (1981). Avoiding and seeking self-focused attention. *Journal of Research in Personality, 15*, 191–200.

Greenberg, J., & Pyszczynski, J. (1985). Compensatory self-inflation: A response to the threat to self-regard of public failure. *Journal of Personality and Social Psychology, 49*, 273–280.

Greenberg, J., Solomon, S., & Pyszczynski, T. (1997). Terror management theory of self-esteem and cultural worldviews: Empirical assessments and conceptual refinements. In M. P. Zanna (Ed.), *Advances in experimental social psychology* (Vol. 29, pp. 61–139). San Diego: Academic Press.

Greenblat, C. (1983). The salience of sexuality in the early years of marriage. *Journal of Marriage and the Family, 45*, 277–288.

Greene, J.D., Sommerville, R.B., Nystrom, L.E., Darley, J.M., Cohen, J.D. (2001). An fMRI investigation of emotional engagement in moral judgment. *Science, 293*, 2105–2108.

Greenhaus, J. H. (2003). Career dynamics. In W. C. Borman, D. R. Ilgen, & R. J. Klimoski (Eds.), *Handbook of psychology: Industrial and organizational psychology* (Vol. 12, pp. 519–540). New York: Wiley.

Greenspan, S. I., & Porges, S. W. (1984). Psychopathology in infancy and early childhood: Clinical perspectives on the organization of sensory and affective-thematic experience. *Child Development, 55*, 49–70.

Greenwald, A. G., & Banaji, M. R. (1989). The self as a memory system: Powerful, but ordinary. *Journal of Personality and Social Psychology, 57*, 41–54.

Greenwald, A. G., McGhee, D. E., & Schwartz, J. K. L. (1998). Measuring individual differences in implicit cognition: The implicit association test. *Journal of Personality and Social Psychology, 74*, 1464–1480.

Greenwald, A. G., Oakes, M. A., & Hoffman, H. G. (2003). Targets of discrimination: Effects of race on responses to weapons holders. *Journal of Experimental Social Psychology, 39*, 399–340.

Gregory, L. W., Cialdini, R. B., & Carpenter, K. M. (1982). Self-relevant scenarios as mediator of likelihood estimates and compliance: Does imagining make it so? *Journal of Personality and Social Psychology, 43*, 89–99.

Greitemeyer, T. (2009). Effects of songs with prosocial lyrics on prosocial thoughts, affect, and behavior. *Journal of Experimental Social Psychology, 45*(1), 186–190.

Greitemeyer, T., & Mügge, D. O. (2014). Video games do affect social outcomes: A meta-analytic review of the effects of violent and prosocial video game play. *Personality and Social Psychology Bulletin, 40*(5), 578–589. doi: 10.1177/0146167213520459

Greitemeyer, T., & Osswald, S. (2009). Prosocial video games reduce aggressive cognitions. *Journal of Experimental Social Psychology, 45*(4), 896–900.

Griffitt, W. (1981). Sexual intimacy in aging marital partners. In J. Marsh & S. Kiesler (Eds.), *Aging: Stability and change in the family* (pp. 301–315). New York: Academic Press.

Griscom, R. (2002, November). Why are online personals so hot? *Wired.* Retrieved from http://www.wired.com/wired/archive/10.11/view.html?pg52

Griskevicius, V., Tybur, J. M., & Van den Bergh, B. (2010). Going green to be seen: Status, reputation, and conspicuous conservation. *Journal of Personality and Social Psychology, 98*, 392–404.

Grolnick, W. S., & Ryan, R. M. (1987). Autonomy in children's learning: An experimental and individual differences investigation. *Journal of Personality and Social Psychology, 52*, 890–898.

Grondin, S., Deshaies, P., & Nault, L. P. (1984). Trimestres de naissance et participation au hockey et au volleyball. *La Revue Quebecoise de l'Activité Physique, 2*, 97–103.

Gross, D. (1996). *Forbes greatest business stories of all time.* New York: Wiley.

Gross, J., & Rosen, J. C. (1988). Bulimia in adolescents: Prevalence and psychosocial correlates. *International Journal of Eating Disorders, 7*, 51–61.

Group for the Advancement of Psychiatry. (1957). *Methods of forceful indoctrination: Observations and interviews.* New York: Author.

Gruber, J., Mauss, I. B., & Tamir, M. (2011). A dark side of happiness? How, when, and why happiness is not always good. *Perspectives on Psychological Science, 6*, 222–233.

Grunberg, N. E., & Straub, R. O. (1992). The role of gender and taste class in the effects of stress on eating. *Health Psychology, 11*, 97–100.

Gruner, C. R. (1985). Advice to the beginning speaker on using humor: What the research tells us. *Communication Education, 34*, 142–147.

Guinote, A. (2008). Power and affordances: When the situation has more power over powerful than powerless individuals. *Journal of Personality and Social Psychology, 95*, 237–252.

Gurr, T. R. (1981). Historical trends in violent crime: A critical review of the evidence. *Crime and Justice, 3*, 295.

Gurung, R. A. R. (2012). Heath psychology. In D. S. Dunn (Ed.), *Oxford Bibliographies in Psychology.* New York: Oxford University Press.

Gurung, R. A. R. (2014). *Health psychology* (3rd ed.). Belmont, CA: Cengage.

Gurung, R. A. R. (Ed.). (2014). *Multicultural approaches to health and wellness in America: Major issues and cultural groups.* Westport, CT: Praeger Publishers.

Gurung, R. A. R., Dunkel-Schetter, C., Collins, N., Rini, C., & Hobel, C. (2005). Psychosocial predictors of perceived prenatal stress. *Journal of Social and Clinical Psychology, 24*, 497–519.

Guxens, M., & Sunyer, J. (2012). A review of epidemiological studies on neuropsychological effects of air pollution. *Swiss Medical Weekly, 141*, 1–7.

Guzmán, R. A., Rodríguez-Sickert, C., & Rowthorn, R. (2007). When in Rome, do as the Romans do: The coevolution of altruistic punishment, conformist learning, and cooperation. *Evolution and Human Behavior, 28*(2), 112–117.

Hackett, R. D. (1989). Work attitudes and employee absenteeism: A synthesis of the literature. *Journal of Occupational Psychology, 62*(3), 235–248.

Hackman, J. R., & Oldham, G. R. (1976). Motivation through the design of work: A test of a theory. *Organizational Behavior and Human Performance, 16*(2), 250–279.

Haefner, R. (2009, June 10). More employers screening candidates via social networking sites. Retrieved from http://www.careerbuilder.com/Article/CB-1337-Interview-Tips-More-Employers-Screening-Candidates-via-Social-Networking-Sites/

Hagan, F. E. (2010). *Crime types and criminals.* Thousand Oaks, CA: Sage Publications.

Haidt, J. (2001). The emotional dog and its rational tail: A social intuitionist approach to moral judgment. *Psychological Review, 108*, 814–834.

Haidt, J. (2007). The new synthesis in moral psychology. *Science, 316*, 998–1002.

Haidt, J., & Joseph, C. (2008). The moral mind: How five sets of innate intuitions guide the development of many culture-specific virtues, and perhaps even modules. In P. Carruthers, S. Laurence, & S. Stich (Eds.), *The innate mind* (Vol. 3, pp. 367–392). New York: Oxford University Press.

Hall, E. T. (1976). *Beyond culture*. New York, NY: Anchor Books.

Hall, J. H., & Fincham, F.D. (2006). Relationship dissolution following infidelity: The roles of attributions and forgiveness. *Journal of Social and Clinical Psychology, 25*, 508–522.

Hall, J. R. (1987). *Gone from the promised land: Jonestown in American cultural history*. New Brunswick: Transaction Books.

Hamilton, D. L., & Gifford, R. K. (1976). Illusory correlation in interpersonal perception: A cognitive basis of stereotypic judgments. *Journal of Experimental Social Psychology, 12*, 392–407.

Hamilton, D. L., Dugan, P. M., & Trolier, T. K. (1985). The formation of stereotypic beliefs: Further evidence for distinctiveness-based illusory correlations. *Journal of Personality and Social Psychology, 48*, 5–17.

Hamilton, W. D. (1964). The genetical evolution of social behaviour I and II. *Journal of Theoretical Biology, 7*, 1–16 and 17–52.

Handley, I. M., Lassiter, G. D., Nickell, E. F., & Herchenroeder, L. M. (2004). Affect and automatic mood maintenance. *Journal of Experimental Social Psychology, 40*, 106–112.

Haney, C., Hurtado, A., & Vega, L. (1994). Modern death qualification: New data on its biasing effects. *Law and Human Behavior, 18*, 619–633.

Hang-Pil, S., & Shavitt, S. (1994). Persuasion and culture: Advertising appeals in individualistic and collectivistic societies. *Journal of Experimental Social Psychology, 30*, 326–350.

Hanisch, K. A. (1995). Behavioral families and multiple causes: Matching the complexity of responses to the complexity of antecedents. *Current Directions in Psychological Science, 4*(5), 156–162.

Hanisch, K. A. (1996). An integrated framework for studying the outcomes of sexual harassment: Consequences for individuals and organizations. In M. S. Stockdale (Ed.), *Women and work: A research and policy series, volume 5: Sexual harassment in the workplace: Perspectives, frontiers, and response strategies* (pp. 174–199). Thousand Oaks, CA: Sage.

Hanisch, K. A. (1999). Job loss and unemployment research from 1994–1998: A review and recommendations for research and intervention. *Journal of Vocational Behavior, 55*(2), 188–220.

Hanisch, K. A., & Hulin, C. L. (1990). Job attitudes and organizational withdrawal: An examination of retirement and other voluntary withdrawal behaviors. *Journal of Vocational Behavior, 37*(1), 60–78.

Hanisch, K. A., & Hulin, C. L. (1991). General attitudes and organizational withdrawal: An evaluation of a causal model. *Journal of Vocational Behavior, 39*, 110–128.

Hanisch, K. A., Hulin, C. L., & Roznowski, M. A. (1998). The importance of individuals' repertoires of behaviors: The scientific appropriateness of studying multiple behaviors and general attitudes. *Journal of Organizational Behavior, 19*, 463–480.

Hanley, N., Shogren, J., & White, B. (2007). *Environmental economics in theory and practice*. London, UK: Palgrave.

Hansen, G. L. (1987). Extradyadic relations during courtship. *Journal of Sex Research, 23*, 382–390.

Hansen, J., Kutzner, F., & Wänke, M. (2013). Money and thinking: Reminders of money trigger abstract construal and shape consumer judgments. *Journal of Consumer Research, 39*, 1154–1166.

Hansson, L. M., Náslund, E., & Rasmussen, F. (2010). Perceived discrimination among men and women with normal weight and obesity. A population-based study from Sweden. *Scandinavian Journal of Public Health, 38*(6), 587–596.

Hansson, R. O., Noulles, D., & Bellovich, S. J. (1982). Knowledge warning and stress: A study of comparative roles in an urban floodplain. *Environment and Behavior, 14*, 171–185.

Hardin, G. (1968). The tragedy of the commons. *Science, 162*, 1243–1248.

Hardison, C. M., Kim, D., & Sackett, P. R. (2005, April). *Meta-analysis of work sample criterion related validity: Revisiting anomalous findings*. Paper presented at the 20th annual conference of the Society for Industrial-Organizational Psychology, Los Angeles.

Hare, A. P. (1962). *Handbook of small group research*. New York: The Free Press of Glencoe.

Hare, R. D. (1998). *Without conscience: The disturbing world of the psychopaths among us*. New York: Guilford Press.

Hargis, M. (2008). *Social networking sites dos and donts*. Retrieved from http://edition.cnn.com/2008/LIVING/worklife/11/05/cb.social.networking/index.html

Harmon-Jones, E., & Allen, J. J. B. (2001). The role of affect in the mere exposure effect: Evidence from psychophysiological and individual differences approaches. *Personality and Social Psychology Bulletin, 27*(7), 889–898.

Harms, P. D., & Credé, M. (2010). Emotional intelligence and transformational and transactional leadership: A meta-analysis. *Journal of Leadership & Organizational Studies, 17*(1), 5–17.

Harold Camping False Prophet: Ministry Probably Doomed (2011). *International Business Times*. Retrieved from http://www.ibtimes.com/articles/149632/20110521/harold-camping-false-prophet-ministry-probably-doomed.htm

Harrell, W. A. (1978). Physical attractiveness, self-disclosure, and helping behavior. *Journal of Social Psychology, 104*, 15–17.

Harris, C. R. (2000). Psychophysiological responses to imagined infidelity: The specific innate modular view of jealousy reconsidered. *Journal of Personality and Social Psychology, 75*, 1082–1091.

Harris, M. (1974). *Cows, pigs, wars, and witches: The riddles of culture*. New York: Random House.

Harris, M. (1977). *Cannibals and kings: The origins of culture*. New York: Random House.

Harris, M. B. (1974). Mediators between frustration and aggression in a field experiment. *Journal of Experimental Social Psychology, 10*(6), 561–571.

Harris, M. B. (1976). Instigators and inhibitors of aggression in a field experiment. *Journal of Social Psychology, 98*(1), 27–38.

Harris, M. B., Benson, S. M., & Hall, C. L. (1975). The effects of confession on altruism. *Journal of Social Psychology, 96*, 187–192.

Harris, M. B., Harris, R. J., & Bochner, S. (1982). Fat, four-eyed and female: Stereotypes of obesity glasses and gender. *Journal of Applied Social Psychology, 12*, 503–516.

Harris, P. B., & Brown, B. B. (1996). The home and identity display: Interpreting resident territoriality from home exteriors. *Journal of Environmental Psychology, 16*, 187–203.

Harrison, A. A., & Connors, M. M. (1984). Groups in exotic environments. In L. Berkowitz (Ed.), *Advances in Experimental Social Psychology* (Vol. 18, pp. 49–87). New York: Academic Press.

Harrison, K. (2000). The body electric: Thin-ideal media and eating disorders in adolescents. *Journal of Communication, 50*, 119–143.

Harrison, K. (2001). Ourselves, our bodies: Thin-ideal media, self-discrepancies, and eating disorder symptomatology in adolescents. *Journal of Social and Clinical Psychology, 20*, 289–323.

Harrison, K. (2003). Television viewers' ideal body proportions: The case of the curvaceously thin woman. *Sex Roles, 48*, 255–264.

Harskamp, J., & Dijstelberge, P. (2012, April 12). The human zoo. Retrieved from http://abeautifulbook.wordpress.com/2012/04/21/the-human-zoo/

Harter, S. (1993). Causes and consequences of low self-esteem in children and adolescents. In R. F. Baumeister (Ed.), *Self-esteem: The puzzle of low self-regard* (pp. 87–116). New York: Plenum Press.

Hasan, Y., Bègue, L., & Bushman, B. J. (2012). Viewing the world through "blood-red tinted glasses": The hostile expectation bias mediates the link between violent video game exposure and aggression. *Journal of Experimental Social Psychology, 48*, 953–956.

Haselton, M. G., & Buss, D. M. (2000). Error management theory: A new perspective on biases in cross-sex mind reading. *Journal of Personality and Social Psychology, 78*, 81–91.

Hassebrauck, M. (1986). Ratings of distress as a function of degree and kind of inequity. *Journal of Social Psychology, 126*, 269–270.

Hatfield, E., & Rapson, R. L. (1987). Passionate love: New directions in research. In W. H. Jones & D. Perlman (Eds.), *Advances in personal relationships* (Vol. 1, pp. 109–139). Greenwich, CT: JAI Press.

Hatfield, E., Cacioppo, J.T., & Rapson, R.L. (1993). Emotional contagion. *Current Directions in Psychological Science, 2*, 96–100.

Hauck, A., & Finch, A. (1993). The effect of relative age on achievement in middle school. *Psychology in the Schools, 30*, 74–79.

Haw, R. M., & Fisher, R. P. (2004). Effects of administrator-witness contact on eyewitness identification accuracy. *Journal of Applied Psychology, 89*, 1106–1112.

Hawkley, L. C., Burleson, M. H., Berntson, G. G., & Cacioppo, J. T. (2003). Loneliness in everyday life: Cardiovascular activity, psychosocial context, and health behaviors. *Journal of Personality and Social Psychology, 85*, 105–120.

Section 15.01 Hawley, C. (2005, June 9). German zoo scandal: "African Village" accused of putting humans on display. *Der Spiegel*. Retrieved from http://www.spiegel.de/international/german-zoo-scandal-african-village-accused-of-putting-humans-on-display-a-359799.html

Hayduk, L. A. (1994). Personal space: Understanding the simplex model. *Journal of Nonverbal Behavior, 18*, 245–260.

Hayes, R., & Downs, D. M. (2011). Controlling retail theft with CCTV domes, CCTV public view monitors, and protective containers: A randomized controlled trial. *Security Journal, 24*(3), 237–250.

Hazan, C., & Shaver, P. R. (1987). Romantic love conceptualized as an attachment process. *Journal of Personality and Social Psychology, 52*, 511–524.

Hearold, S. (1986). A synthesis of 1043 effects of television on social behavior. In G. Comstock (Ed.), *Public communication and behavior* (pp. 65–133). New York: Academic Press.

Heatherton, T. F., & Baumeister, R. F. (1991). Binge eating as escape from self-awareness. *Psychological Bulletin, 110*, 86–108.

Heatherton, T. F., & Nichols, P. A. (1994). Personal accounts of successful versus failed attempts at life change. *Personality and Social Psychology Bulletin, 20*, 664–675.

Heatherton, T. F., & Vohs, K. D. (2000). Interpersonal evaluations following threats to self: Role of self-esteem. *Journal of Personality and Social Psychology, 78*, 725–736.

Heatherton, T. F., personal communication, 1993.

Heatherton, T. F., Polivy, J., & Herman, C. P. (1989). Restraint and internal responsiveness: Effects of placebo manipulations of hunger state on eating. *Journal of Abnormal Psychology, 98*, 89–92.

Heatherton, T. F., Polivy, J., Herman, C. P., & Baumeister, R. F. (1993). Self-awareness, task failure and disinhibition: How attentional focus affects eating. *Journal of Personality, 61*, 49–61.

Hebl, M. R., & Heatherton, T. F. (1997). The stigma of obesity: The differences are black and white. *Personality and Social Psychology Bulletin, 24*, 417–426.

Hebl, M. R., & Mannix, L. M. (2003). The weight of obesity in evaluating others: A mere proximity effect. *Personality and Social Psychology Bulletin, 29*, 28–38.

Hee, K. H. (1993). *The tears of my soul*. New York: Morrow.

Hegi, K. E., & Bergner, R. M. (2010). What is love? An empirically-based essentialist account. *Journal of Social and Personal Relationships, 27*, 620–636.

Heider, F. (1958). *The psychology of interpersonal relations*. New York: John Wiley & Sons.

Heilman, M. E., & Chen, J. J. (2005). Same behavior, different consequences: Reactions to men's and women's altruistic citizenship behaviors. *Journal of Applied Psychology, 90*, 431–441.

Heine, S. J., & Lehman, D. R. (1997). Culture, dissonance, and self-affirmation. *Personality and Social Psychology Bulletin, 23,* 389–400.

Heine, S. J., Lehman, D. R., Markus, H. R., & Kitayama, S. (1999). Is there a universal need for positive self-regard? *Psychological Review, 106,* 766–794.

Heinz, S., Baron, G., & Frahm, H. (1988). Comparative size of brains and brain components. In H. D. Steklis & J. Erwin (Eds.), *Comparative Prim ate Biology: Vol. 4. Neurosciences.* New York: Wiley.

Helton, W. S., Head, J., & Kemp, S. (2011). Natural disaster-induced cognitive disruption: Impacts on action slips. *Consciousness and Cognition, 20,* 1732–1737.

Helzer, E.G., & Pizarro, D.A. (2011). Dirty liberals! Reminders of physical cleanliness influence moral and political attitudes. *Psychological Science, 22,* 517–522.

Hemenway, D., Vriniotis, M., & Miller, M. (2006). Is an armed society a polite society? Guns and road rage. *Accident Analysis and Prevention, 38*(4), 687–695.

Henderson, V., & Dweck, C. S. (1990). Achievement and motivation in adolescence: A new model and data. In S. Feldman & G. Elliott (Eds.), *At the threshold: The developing adolescent* (pp. 308–329). Cambridge, MA: Harvard University Press.

Hendin, H. (1982). *Suicide in America.* New York: Norton.

Hendren, A., & Blank, H. (2009). Prejudiced behavior toward lesbians and gay men: A field experiment on everyday helping. *Social Psychology, 40*(4), 234–238.

Hendricks, N. J., Ortiz, C. W., Sugie, N., & Miller, J. (2007). Beyond the numbers: Hate crimes and cultural trauma within Arab American immigrant communities. *International Review of Victimology, 14*(1), 95–113.

Henken, V. J. (1976). Banality reinvestigated: A computer-based content analysis of suicidal and forced-death documents. *Suicide and Life-Threatening Behavior, 6,* 36–43.

Henle, C. A., Reeve, C. L., & Pitts, V. E. (2010). Stealing time at work: Attitudes, social pressure, and perceived control as predictors of time theft. *Journal of Business Ethics, 94*(1), 53–67.

Henry, B., Caspi, A., Moffitt, T. E., & Silva, P. A. (1996). Temperamental and familial predictors of violent and nonviolent criminal convictions: Age 3 to age 18. *Developmental Psychology, 32,* 614–623.

Hepach, R., Vaish, A., & Tomasello, M. (2012). Young children are intrinsically motivated to see others helped. *Psychological Science, 23,* 967–972.

Hepworth, J. T., & West, S. G. (1988). Lynchings and the economy: A time-series reanalysis of Hovland and Sears (1940). *Journal of Personality and Social Psychology, 55,* 239–247.

Herdt, G. (1984). Ritualized homosexual behavior in the male cults of Melanesia, 1862–1983: An introduction. In G. Herdt (Ed.), *Ritualized homosexuality in Melanesia* (pp. 1–82). Berkeley: University of California Press.

Herek, G. M. (2000). The psychology of sexual prejudice. *Current Directions in Psychological Science, 9,* 19–22.

Herek, G. M., & Capitanio, J. P. (1996). "Some of my best friends": Intergroup contact, concealable stigma, and heterosexuals' attitudes toward gay men and lesbians. *Personality and Social Psychology Bulletin, 22*(4), 412–424.

Herek, G. M., & Capitanio, J. P. (1999). AIDS stigma and sexual prejudice. *American Behavioral Scientist, 42,* 1126–1143.

Herlitz, J., Wiklund, I., Caidahl, K., Hartford, M., Haglid, M., Karlsson, B. W., et al. (1998). The feeling of loneliness prior to coronary artery bypass grafting might be a predictor of short- and long-term postoperative mortality. *European Journal of Vascular and Endovascular Surgery, 16,* 120–125.

Herman, C. P., & Mack, D. (1975). Restrained and unrestrained eating. *Journal of Personality, 43,* 647–660.

Herold, E. S., & Mewhinney, D.-M K. (1993). Gender differences in casual sex and AIDS prevention: A survey of dating bars. *Journal of Sex Research, 30,* 36–42.

Hewitt, J., & Alqahtani, M. A. (2003). Differences between Saudi and U.S. students in reaction to same- and mixed-sex intimacy by others. *Journal of Social Psychology, 143,* 233–242.

Hewstone, M. (1990). The "Ultimate Attribution Error"? A review of the literature on intergroup causal attribution. *European Journal of Social Psychology, 20,* 311–335.

Hewstone, M., & Swart, H. (2011). Fifty-odd years of inter-group contact: From hypothesis to integrated theory. *British Journal of Social Psychology, 50*(3), 374–386.

Hicken, M. (2013, August 14). Average cost to raise a kid: $241,080. *CNN Money.*

Higgins, E. T., & Bargh, J. A. (1987). Social cognition and social perception. *Annual Review of Psychology, 38,* 369–425.

Higgins, E. T., Rholes, W. S., & Jones, C. R. (1977). Category accessibility and impression formation. *Journal of Experimental Social Psychology, 13,* 141–154.

Higley, J. D., Mehlman, P. T., Taub, D. M., Higley, S. B., Suomi, S. J., Vickers, J. H., & Linnoila, M. (1992). Cerebrospinal fluid mono-amine and adrenal correlates of aggression in free-ranging Rhesus monkeys. *Archives of General Psychiatry, 49,* 436–441.

Hill, C. A., Blakemore, J. E. O., & Drumm, P. (1997). Mutual and unrequited love in adolescence and adulthood. *Personal Relationships, 4*(1), 15–23.

Hill, C. T., Rubin, Z., & Peplau, L. A. (1976). Breakups before marriage: The end of 103 affairs. *Journal of Social Issues, 32,* 147–168.

Hill, G. W. (1982). Group versus individual performance: Are N 1 1 heads better than one? *Psychological Bulletin, 91*(3), 517–539.

Hilmert, C. J., Kulik, J. A., & Christenfeld, N. J. (2006). Positive and negative opinion modeling: The influence of another's similarity and dissimilarity. *Journal of Personality and Social Psychology, 90,* 440–452.

Hinde, R. A. (1970). *Animal behavior.* New York: McGraw-Hill.

Hirt, E. R., & Markman, K. D. (1995). Multiple explanation: A consider-an-alternative strategy for *debiasing* judgments. *Journal of Personality and Social Psychology, 69,* 1069–1086.

Hirt, E. R., & Sherman, S. J. (1985). The role of prior knowledge in explaining hypothetical events. *Journal of Experimental Social Psychology, 21,* 519–543.

Hirt, E. R., Deppe, R. K., & Gordon, L. J. (1991). Self-reported versus behavioral self-handicapping: Empirical evidence for a theoretical distinction. *Journal of Personality and Social Psychology, 61,* 981–991.

Hirt, E. R., Kardes, F. R., & Markman, K. D. (2004). Activating a mental simulation mind-set through generation of alternatives: Implications for *debiasing* in related and unrelated domains. *Journal of Experimental Social Psychology, 40,* 374–383.

Hitsch, G. J., Hortaçsu, A., & Ariely, D. (2006). What makes you click? Mate preferences and matching outcomes in online dating. MIT Sloan Research Paper No. 4603–06. Available at http://home .uchicago.edu/,hortacsu/onlinedating.pdf

Hochbaum, G. M. (1958). *Public participation in medical screening programs: A sociopsychological study.* PHS publication no. 572. Washington, DC: Government Printing Office. Holder-Perkins & Wise.

Hockley, W. E., Hemsworth, D. H., & Consoli, A. (1999). Shades of the mirror effect: Recognition of faces with and without sunglasses. *Memory and Cognition, 27,* 128–138.

Hoerger, M., Chapman, B. P., Epstein, R. M., & Duberstein, P. R. (2012). Emotional intelligence: A theoretical framework for individual differences in affective forecasting. *Emotion, 12*(4), 716–725. doi: 10.1037/a0026724

Hoerner, J. A., & Barrett, J. (2004, September). *Smarter, cleaner, stronger: Secure jobs, a clean environment, and less foreign oil.* Retrieved from http://www.rprogress. org/publications/2004/SmartCleanStrong_National. pdf

Hoff Sommers, C. (1994). *Who stole feminism: How women have betrayed women.* New York: Touchstone.

Hoffman, M. L. (1977). Sex differences in empathy and related behaviors. *Psychological Bulletin, 84,* 712–722.

Hofmann, W., Wisneski, D.C., Brandt, M.J., & Skitka, L.J. (2014). Morality in everyday life. *Science, 345,* 1340–1343.

Hofstadter, D. R. (1979), *Gödel, Escher, Bach: An eternal golden braid.* New York: Basic Books.

Hogan, R., & Kaiser, R. B. (2005). What we know about leadership. *Review of General Psychology, 9*(2), 169–180.

Hogg, M. A. (2005). All animals are equal but some animals are more equal than others: Social identity and marginal membership. In K. D. Williams, J. P. Forgas, & W. von Hippel (Eds.), *The social outcast: Ostracism, social exclusion, rejection, and bullying* (pp. 243–262). New York: Psychology Press.

Holder-Perkins, V., & Wise, T. N. (2001). Somatization disorder. In K. A. Phillips (Eds.), *Somatoform and factitious disorders* (pp. 1–26). Washington, DC: American Psychiatric Association.

Holgate, S. T., Samet, J. M., Maynard, R. L., & Koren, H. S. (Eds.) (1999). *Air pollution and health.* San Diego: Academic Press.

Hollingshead, A. B. (1998). Retrieval processes in transactive memory systems. *Journal of Personality and Social Psychology, 74,* 659–671.

Hollingshead, A. B., & Brandon, D. P. (2003). Potential benefits of communication in transactive memory systems. *Human Communication Research, 29,* 607–615.

Holloway, S. D., Kashiwagi, K., Hess, R. D., & Azuuma, H. (1986). Causal attributions by Japanese and American mothers and children about performance in mathematics. *International Journal of Psychology, 21,* 269–286.

Holmes, J. G. (2004, October). The power of positive thinking in close relationships. Paper presented at the Third International Positive Psychology Summit, Washington, DC.

Holmes, L. (2014, September 17). 5 ways stress wrecks your sleep (and what to do about it). Retrieved from http://www.huffingtonpost.com/2014/09/17/stress-and-sleep_n_5824506.html

Holtzworth-Munroe, A., & Jacobson, N. S. (1985). Causal attributions of married couples: When do they search for causes? What do they conclude when they do? *Journal of Personality and Social Psychology, 48,* 1398–1412.

Homans, G. C. (1950). *The human group.* New York: Harcourt, Brace, & World.

Homans, G. C. (1961). *Social behavior: Its elementary forms.* New York: Harcourt, Brace, & World.

Honour, J. W. (2004, July 8). The fight for fair play: Can athletes be held responsible for every substance they take? *Nature, 430,* 143–144.

Hope, L., & Wright, D. (2007). Beyond unusual? Examining the role of attention in the weapon focus effect. *Applied Cognitive Psychology, 21,* 951–961.

Horberg, E. J., Oveis, C., Keltner, D., & Cohen, A. B. (2009). Disgust and the moralization of purity. *Journal of Personality and Social Psychology, 97*(6), 963–976.

Horner, M. (1972). Toward an understanding of achievement related conflicts in women. *Journal of Social Issues, 28,* 157–176.

Hornstein, H. A. (1982). Promotive tension: Theory and research. In V. Derlega & J. Grzelak (Eds.), *Cooperation and helping behavior: Theories and research* (pp. 229–248). New York: Academic Press.

Horowitz, A. V., White, H. R., & Howell-White, S. (1997). Becoming married and mental health: A longitudinal study of a cohort of young adults. *Journal of Marriage and the Family, 58,* 895–907.

Hoshino-Browne, E., Zanna, A. S., Spencer, S. J., Zanna, M. P., Kitayama, S., & Lackenbauer, S. (2005). On the cultural guises of cognitive dissonance: The case of Easterners and Westerners. *Journal of Personality and Social Psychology, 89,* 294–310.

Hounton, S. H., Carabin, H., & Henderson, N. J. (2005). Towards an understanding of barriers to condom use in rural Benin using the Health Belief Model: A cross sectional survey. *BMC Public Health, 5,* 8.

House, J. S., Umberson, D., & Landis, K. R. (1988). Structures and processes of social support. *Annual Review of Sociology, 14*, 293–318.

Houston, D. A., Doan, K. A., & Roskos-Ewoldsen, D. (1999). Negative political advertising and choice conflict. *Journal of Experimental Psychology: Applied, 5*, 3–16.

Hovland, C. I., & Sears, R. (1940). Minor studies of aggression: Correlation of lynchings with economic conditions. *Journal of Psychology, 9*, 301–310.

Hovland, C. I., & Weiss, W. (1951). The influence of source credibility on communication effectiveness. *Public Opinion Quarterly, 15*, 635–650.

Hovland, C. I., Janis, I. L., & Kelley, H. H. (1953). *Communications and persuasion: Psychological studies in opinion change*, New Haven: Yale University Press.

Hovland, C., Lumsdaine, A., & Sheffield, F. (1949). *Experiments on mass communication: Studies in social psychology in World War II* (Vol. 3). Princeton, NJ: Princeton University Press.

Howell, S. (1989). "To be angry is not to be human, but to be fearful is": Chewong concepts of human nature. In S. Howell & R. Willis (Eds.), *Societies at peace: Anthropological perspectives* (pp. 45–59). London: Routledge.

Hoyle, R. H., Pinkley, R. L., & Insko, C. A. (1989). Perceptions of social behavior: Evidence of differing expectations for interpersonal and intergroup interaction. *Personality and Social Psychology Bulletin, 15*, 365–376.

Hsee, C. K. (1996). The evaluability hypothesis: An explanation for preference reversals between joint and separate evaluations of alternatives. *Organizational Behavior and Human Decision Processes, 67*(3), 247–257.

Hsee, C. K., & Zhang, J. (2004). Distinction bias: Misprediction and mischoice due to joint evaluation. *Journal of Personality and Social Psychology, 86*(5), 680–695.

Hsiang, S. M., Burke, M., & Miguel, E. (2013). Quantifying the influence of climate on human conflict. *Science, 341*(6151):1235367. doi: 10.1126/science.1235367

http://articles.cnn.com/2011-07-01/us/texas.pride_1_texans-bumper-stickers-texas-department?_s5PM:US

http://books.google.com/books?id5FgAbAAAAYAAJ&pg5PA240&lpg5PA240&dq5%E2%80%9CIt1is1the1peculiar1and1perpetual1error1of1the1human1understanding1to1be1more1moved1and1excited1by1affirmatives1than1by1negatives.%E2%80%9D&source5bl&ots5gjQsBxs2Rg&sig5ECq3K_ih6WnhL6O4AoVeC8uWaoU&hl5en&ei5D8PeSfX1MJXxnQed6uS1CQ&sa5X&oi5book_result&ct5result&resnum51

http://historylist.wordpress.com/2008/05/29/human-deaths-in-the-us-caused-by-animals/

http://religion.blogs.cnn.com/2011/11/07/my-take-if-rwandans-can-forgive-killings-we-can-forgive-the-waitress/

http://thinkexist.com/quotes/frederick_the_great/

http://www.apa.org/news/press/releases/2011/09/cooperate-equally.aspx

http://www.campaignforrecycling.org/our_issues/plastic/plastic_bags/current_laws for a complete listing.

http://www.emotionalcompetency.com/humiliation.htm

http://www.endcorporalpunishment.org

http://www.globalsecurity.org/military/world/war/congo.htm

http://www.humansecuritybrief.info/

http://www.quotationspage.com/search.php3?homesearch5Everything1should1be1made1as1simple1as1possible%2C1but1not1simpler&startsearch5Search

http://www.youtube.com/watch?v5PIsNt_7sah4

Hu, Y., & Goldman, M. (1990). Mortality differentials by marital status: An international comparison. *Demography, 27*, 233–250.

Huesmann, et al. (2003). Longitudinal relations between childhood exposure to media violence and adult aggression and violence: 1977–1992. *Developmental Psychology, 39*, 201–221. Copyright © 2003 by the American Psychological Association.

Huesmann, L. R. (2010). Nailing the coffin shut on doubts that violent video games stimulate aggression—Comment on Anderson et al. (2010). *Psychological Bulletin, 136*(2), 179–181. For an alternative view, see Ferguson, C. J., & Kilburn, J. (2010). Much ado about nothing: The misestimation and overinterpretation of violent video game effects in Eastern and Western nations: Comment on Anderson et al. (2010). *Psychological Bulletin, 136*(2), 174–178, and response by Bushman, B. J., Rothstein, H. R., & Anderson, C. A. (2010). Much ado about something: Violent video game effects and a school of red herring—Reply to Ferguson and Kilburn (2010). *Psychological Bulletin, 136*(2), 182–187.

Huesmann, L. R., Moise, J., Podolski, C. P., & Eron, L. D. (2003). Longitudinal relations between childhood exposure to media violence and adult aggression and violence: 1977–1992. *Developmental Psychology, 39*, 201–221.

Huffcutt, A. I., & Arthur, W., Jr. (1994). Hunter and Hunter (1984) revisited: Interview validity for entry-level jobs. *Journal of Applied Psychology, 79*, 184–190.

Hull, J. G. (1981). A self-awareness model of the causes and effects of alcohol consumption. *Journal of Abnormal Psychology, 90*, 586–600.

Hull, J. G., Levenson, R. W., Young, R. D., & Scher, K. J. (1983). Self-awareness-reducing effects of alcohol consumption. *Journal of Personality and Social Personality, 44*, 461–473.

Hunter, J. E., & Hunter, R. E. (1984). Validity and utility of alternative predictors of job performance. *Psychological Bulletin, 96*(1), 72–98.

Hupka, R. B. (1981). Cultural determinants of jealousy. *Alternative Lifestyles, 4*, 310–356.

Huston, T. L., Surra, C., Fitzgerald, N. M., & Cate, R. (1981). From courtship to marriage: Mate selection as an interpersonal process. In S. Duck & R. Gilmour (Eds.), *Personal relationships. 2: Developing personal relationships*. New York: Academic Press.

Hutcherson, C. A., & Gross, J. J. (2011). The moral emotions: A social-functionalist account of anger, disgust, and contempt. *Journal of Personality and Social Psychology, 100*(4), 719–737.

Hutchison, P., & Rosenthal, H. E. S. (2011). Prejudice against Muslims: Anxiety as a mediator between intergroup contact and attitudes, perceived group variability and behavioural intentions. *Ethnic and Racial Studies, 34*(1), 40–61.

Hyde, J. S. (2005). The gender similarities hypothesis. *American Psychologist, 60*, 581–592.

Hyde, M., & White, K. (2010). Are organ donation communication decisions reasoned or reactive? A test of the utility of an augmented theory of planned behaviour with the prototype/willingness model. *British Journal of Health Psychology, 15*(2), 435–452.

Hyland, M. E. (1989). There is no motive to avoid success: The compromise explanation for success-avoiding behavior. *Journal of Personality, 57*, 665–693.

Iannelli, V. (2014, September 7). International measles outbreaks. About Health. Retrieved from http://pediatrics.about.com/od/measles/a/measles-outbreak.htm

Illuminant. (2011, January 17). Avoiding insult and injury when using color in China. Retrieved from http://www.illuminantpartners.com/2011/01/17/color/

Indian, M., & Grieve, R. (2014). When Facebook is easier than face-to-face: Social support derived from Facebook in socially anxious individuals. *Personality and Individual Differences, 59*(3), 102–106. doi: 10.1016/j.paid.2013.11.016

Insko, C. A., Schopler, J., Hoyle, R. H., & Dardis, G. J. (1990). Individual-group discontinuity as a function of fear and greed. *Journal of Personality and Social Psychology, 58*, 68–79.

Insko, C. A., Schopler, J., Pemberton, M. B., Wieselquist, J., McIlraith, S. A., Currey, D. P., et al. (1998). Long-term outcome maximization and the reduction of interindividual-intergroup discontinuity. *Journal of Personality and Social Psychology, 75*, 695–711.

Insko, C. A., Smith, R. H., Alicke, M. D., Wade, J., & Taylor, S. (1985). Conformity and group size: The concern with being right and the concern with being liked. *Personality and Social Psychology Bulletin, 11*, 41–50.

Isen, A. M. (2000). Positive affect and decision making. In M. Lewis & J. M. Haviland-Jones (Eds.), *Handbook of emotions* (2nd ed., pp. 417–435). New York: Guilford Press.

Isen, A. M., & Levin, P. F. (1972). Effect of feeling good on helping: Cookies and kindness. *Journal of Personality and Social Psychology, 21*, 384–388.

Isen, A. M., & Patrick, R. (1983). The effect of positive feelings and risk taking: When the chips are down. *Organizational Behavior and Human Performance, 31*, 194–202.

Ito, T. A., Miller, N., & Pollock, V. E. (1996). Alcohol and aggression: A meta-analysis on the moderating effects of inhibitory cues, triggering events, and self-focused attention. *Psychological Bulletin, 120*, 60–82.

Iyengar, S. S., & Lepper, M. R. (2000). When choice is demotivating: Can one desire too much of a good thing? *Journal of Personality and Social Psychology, 79*, 995–1006.

Izard, C. E. (1971). *The face of emotion*. New York: Appleton-Century-Crofts.

Izard, C. E. (1990). The substrates and functions of emotion feelings: William James and current emotion theory. *Personality and Social Psychology Bulletin, 16*, 626–635.

J.E.B. v. Alabama *ex rel.* T.B., 114 S.Ct. 1419 (1994).

Jablin, F. M. (1982). Organizational communication: An assimilation approach. In M. E. Rolff & C. R. Berger (Eds.), *Social cognition and communication* (pp. 255–286). Beverly Hills, CA: Sage.

Jackson, L. A., Hunter, J. E., & Hodge, C. N. (1995). Physical attractiveness and intellectual competence: A meta-analytic review. *Social Psychology Quarterly, 58*, 108–122.

Jacobe, D. (2008, June 11). Nearly one-third of credit-card owners hold high balances. Retrieved from http://www.gallup.com/poll/107833/nearly-onethird-americans-hold-high-credit-balances.aspx

Jacobs, R. C., & Campbell, D. T. (1961). The perpetuation of an arbitrary tradition through several generations of a laboratory microculture. *Journal of Abnormal and Social Psychology, 62*, 649–658.

Jacobs, S. V., Evans, G. W., Catalano, R., & Dooley, D. (1984). Air pollution and depressive symptomatology: Exploratory analyses of intervening psychosocial factors. *Population & Environment, 7*, 260–272.

Jain, A., Marshall, J., Buikema, Bancroft, T., Kelly, J. P., & Newschaffer, C. J. (2015). Autism occurrence by MMR vaccine status among US children with older siblings with and without autism. *JAMA, 313*(15), 1534-1540. doi:10.1001/jama.2015.3077.

James (1981). From James, W. H. (1981). The honeymoon effect on marital coitus. *Journal of Sex Research, 17*, 114–132. Copyright © 1981 Taylor & Francis Group, LLC. Reprinted by permission.

James R. Lewis (Ed.) (2006). *The Order of the Solar Temple: The temple of death*. Surrey, U.K.: Ashgate Publishing Company.

James, W. (1884). What is an emotion? *Mind, 9*, 188–205.

James, W. (1890). *Principles of psychology* (p. 190). New York: Holt.

James, W. (1948). *Psychology*. Cleveland, OH: World Publishing. (Original work published 1892).

James, W. H. (1981). The honeymoon effect on marital coitus. *Journal of Sex Research, 17*, 114–123.

Janis, I. (1982). *Groupthink* (2nd ed.). Boston: Houghton Mifflin.

Janis, I. L. (1954). Personality correlates of susceptibility to persuasion. *Journal of Personality, 22*, 504–518.

Janis, I. L. (1967). Effects of fear arousal on attitude change: Recent developments in theory and experimental research. *Advances in Experimental Social Psychology, 4*, 166–224.

Janis, I. L., & Feshbach, S. (1953). Effects of fear-arousing communications. *Journal of Abnormal and Social Psychology, 48*, 78–92.

Janis, I. L., & Field, P. (1959). Sex differences and personality factors related to persuasibility. In C. Hovland & I. Janis (Eds.), *Personality and persuasibility* (pp. 55–68, 300–302). New Haven, CT: Yale University Press.

Janis, I. L., Kaye, D., & Kirschner, P. (1965). Facilitating effects of "eating-while-reading" on responsiveness to persuasive communications. *Journal of Personality and Social Psychology, 1*(2), 181–186.

Janiszewski, C., Noel, H., & Sawyer, A. G. (2003). A meta-analysis of the spacing effect in verbal learning: Implications for research on advertising repetition and consumer memory. *Journal of Consumer Research, 30*, 138–149.

Jankowiak, W. (Ed.). (1995). *Romantic passion: A universal experience?* New York: Columbia University Press.

Janoff-Bulman, R. (1992). *Shattered assumptions: Towards a new psychology of trauma.* New York: Free Press.

Janoff-Bulman, R., & Brickman, P. (1982). Expectations and what people learn from failure. In N. T. Feather (Ed.), *Expectations and actions: Expectancy-value models in psychology* (pp. 207–237). Hillsdale, NJ: Erlbaum.

Janus, S. S., & Janus, C. L. (1993). *The Janus report on sexual behavior.* New York: Wiley.

Jencks, C., & Phillips, M. (Eds.). (1998). *The Black–White test score gap.* Washington, DC: Brookings Institution.

Jensen, A. (1977). Genetic and behavioral effects of nonrandom mating. In C. Noble, R. Osborne, & N. Weyl (Eds.), *Human variation: Biogenetics of age, race, and sex.* New York: Academic Press.

Johns, M., Inzlicht, M., & Schmader, T. (2008). Stereotype threat and executive resource depletion: Examining the influence of emotion regulation. *Journal of Experimental Psychology: General, 137*(4), 691–705.

Johnson, D. J., & Rusbult, C. E. (1989). Resisting temptation: Devaluation of alternative partners as a means of maintaining commitment in close relationships. *Journal of Personality and Social Psychology, 57*, 967–980.

Johnson, D. W., & Johnson, R. T. (1983). The socialization and achievement crises: Are cooperative learning experiences the solution? *Applied Social Psychology Annual, 4*, 119–164.

Johnson, W. G., Schlundt, D. G., Barclay, D. R., Carr-Nangle, R. E., & Engler, L. B. (1995). A naturalistic functional analysis of binge eating. *Behavior Therapy, 26*, 101–118.

Johnson, W., McGue, M., Krueger, R. F., & Bouchard, T. J. (2004). Marriage and personality: A genetic analysis. *Journal of Personality and Social Psychology, 86*, 285–294.

Join Joiner, T., Pettit, J. W., Walker, R. L., Voelz, Z. R., Cruz, J., Rudd, M. D., & Lester, D. (2002). Perceived burdensomeness and suicidality: Two studies on the suicide notes of those attempting and those completing suicide. *Journal of Social & Clinical Psychology, 21*, 531–545.

Joiner, T. (2005). *Why people die by suicide.* Cambridge, MA: Harvard University Press.

Jonas, K., Eagly, A. H., & Stroebe, W. (1995). *Attitudes and persuasion.* In M. Argyle & A. M. Colman (Eds.), *Social psychology.* Harlow, UK: Longman.

Jones, D. (2004, April 9). Obesity can mean less pay. *USA Today.*

Jones, E. E. (1964). *Ingratiation.* New York: Irvington.

Jones, E. E., & Berglas, S. (1978). Control of attributions about the self through self-handicapping strategies: The appeal of alcohol and the role of underachievement. *Personality and Social Psychology Bulletin, 4*, 200–206.

Jones, E. E., & Gerard, H. B. (1967). *Foundations of social psychology.* New York: Wiley.

Jones, E. E., & Harris, V. A. (1967). The attribution of attitudes. *Journal of Experimental Social Psychology, 3*, 1–24.

Jones, E. E., & Nisbett, R. E. (1971). *The actor and the observer: Divergent perceptions of the causes of behavior.* New York: General Learning Press.

Jones, E. E., & Wortman, E. (1973). *Ingratiation: An attributional approach.* Morristown, NJ: General Learning Press.

Jones, E. E., Kannouse, D. E., Kelley, H. H., Nisbett, R. E., Valins, S., & Weiner, B. (Eds.). (1972). *Attribution: Perceiving the causes of behavior.* Morristown, NJ: General Learning Press.

Jones, E. E., Rhodewalt, F., Berglas, S., & Skelton, J. A. (1981). Effects of strategic self-presentation on subsequent self-esteem. *Journal of Personality and Social Psychology, 41*, 407–421.

http://www.gallup.com/poll/145043/nurses-top-honesty-ethics-list-11-year.aspx

Jones, J. M. (2010). Nurses top honesty and ethics list for 11th year. *Gallup Economy,* December, 2010. Retrieved from http://www.gallup.com/poll/145043/nurses-top-honesty-ethics-list-11-year.aspx

Jones, J. W., & Bogat, G. (1978). Air pollution and human aggression. *Psychological Reports, 43*(3, Pt. 1), 721–722.

Jones, W. (1989, August). Address given at the annual convention of the American Psychological Association, New Orleans.

Jorgenson, D. O., & Papciak, A. S. (1981). The effects of communication, resource feedback, and identifiability on behavior in a simulated commons. *Journal of Experimental Social Psychology, 17*, 373–385.

Jost, J. T., & Kay, A. C. (2005). Exposure to benevolent sexism and complementary gender stereotypes: Consequences for specific and diffuse forms of system justification. *Journal of Personality and Social Psychology, 88*, 498–509.

Joyce, W. F., Nohria, N., & Roberson, B. (2003). *What really works: The 4+2 formula for sustained business success.* New York: HarperBusiness.

Judd, C., & Park, B. (1993). The assessment of accuracy of social stereotypes. *Psychological Review, 100*, 109–128.

Jung, K., Shavitt, S., Viswanathan, M., & Hilbe, J. M. (2014). Female hurricanes are deadlier than male hurricanes. *PNAS, 111*, 8782–8787.

"Junk DNA" defines differences between humans and chimps. (2011, October 25). *ScienceDaily.* Retrieved from http://www.sciencedaily.com/releases/2011/10/111025122615.htm

Jussim, L., & Harber, K. D. (2005). Teacher expectations and self-fulfilling prophecies: Knowns and unknowns, resolved and unresolved controversies. *Personality and Social Psychology Review, 9*(2), 131–155.

Jussim, L., Cain, T. R., Crawford, J. T., Harber, K., & Cohen, F. (2009). The unbearable accuracy of stereotypes. In T. Nelson (Ed.), *Handbook of prejudice, stereotyping, and discrimination* (pp. 199–228). Mahwah, NJ: Erlbaum.

Jussim, L., HsiuJu, Y., & Aiello, J. R. (1995). Self-consistency, self-enhancement, and accuracy in reactions to feedback. *Journal of Experimental Social Psychology, 31*, 322–356.

Juvonen, J., & Gross, E. F. (2005). The rejected and the bullied: Lessons about social misfits from developmental psychology. In K. D. Williams, J. P. Forgas, & W. von Hippel (Eds.), *The social outcast: Ostracism, social exclusion, rejection, and bullying* (pp. 155–170). New York: Psychology Press.

Kachadourian, L. K., Fincham, F. D., & Davila, J. (2004). The tendency to forgive in dating and married couples: Association with attachment and relationship satisfaction. *Personal Relationships, 11*, 373–393.

Kachadourian, L. K., Fincham, F. D., & Davila, J. (2005). Attitudinal ambivalence, rumination and forgiveness of partner transgressions in marriage. *Personality and Social Psychology Bulletin, 31*, 334–342.

Kagan, J. (1981). *The second year: The emergence of self-awareness.* Cambridge, MA: Harvard University Press.

Kahneman, D. (1999). Objective happiness. In D. Kahneman, E. Diener, & N. Schwartz (Eds.), *Well-being: The foundations of hedonic psychology* (pp. 3–25). New York: Russell Sage Foundation.

Kahneman, D. (2011). *Thinking, fast and slow.* New York: Farrar, Straus, and Giroux.

Kahneman, D., & Frederick, S. (2002). Representativeness revisited: Attribute substitution in intuitive judgment. In T. Gilovich, D. Griffin, & D. Kahneman (Eds.), *Heuristics and biases* (pp. 49–81). New York: Cambridge University Press.

Kahneman, D., & Tversky, A. (1979). Prospect theory: An analysis of decision under risk. *Econometrica, 47*, 263–291.

Kahneman, D., & Tversky, A. (1982). The psychology of preferences. *Scientific American, 246*, 160–173.

Kahneman, D., & Tversky, A. (1984). Choices, values, and frames. *American Psychologist, 39*, 341–350.

Kahneman, D., Knetsch, J. L., & Thaler, R. H. (1990). Experimental tests of the endowment effect and the Coase theorem. *Journal of Political Economy, 98*(6), 1325–1348.

Kahneman, D., Slovic, P., & Tversky, A. (Eds.). (1982). *Judgment under uncertainty: Heuristics and biases.* New York: Cambridge University Press.

Kahneman, D., Wakker, P. P., & Sarin, R. (1997). Back to Bentham? Explorations of experienced utility. *Quarterly Journal of Economics, 62*, 375–406.

Kallgren, C. A., Reno, R. R., & Cialdini, R. B. (2000). Littering can be reduced by anti-littering norms: A focus theory of normative conduct: When norms do and do not affect behavior. *Personality and Social Psychology Bulletin, 26*, 1002–1012.

Kanazawa, S. (2002). Bowling with our imaginary friends. *Evolution and Human Behavior, 23*, 167–171.

Kanin, E. J., Davidson, K. D., & Scheck, S. R. (1970). A research note on male-female differentials in the experience of heterosexual love. *Journal of Sex Research, 6*, 64–72.

Kant, I. (1924). *Critique of judgment.* Hamburg: Felix Meiner Verlag. (Original work published 1790).

Kant, I. (1967). *Kritik der praktischen Vernunft* [Critique of practical reason]. Hamburg: Felix Meiner Verlag. (Original work published 1797).

Kaplan, K. A. (2003). Facemash creator survives ad board. Retrieved from: http://www.thecrimson.com/article/2003/11/19/facemash-creator-survives-ad-board-the/

Kaplan, R. E., Drath, W. H., & Kofodimos, J. R. (1991). *Beyond ambition: How driven managers can lead better and live better.* San Francisco: Jossey-Bass.

Karau, S. J., & Williams, K. D. (1993). Social loafing: A meta-analytic review and theoretical integration. *Journal of Personality and Social Psychology, 65*, 681–706.

Kardes, F. R. (1988). Spontaneous inference processes in advertising: The effects of conclusion omission and involvement on persuasion. *Journal of Consumer Research, 15*, 225–233.

Karney, B. R., & Bradbury, T. N. (1997). Neuroticism, marital interaction, and the trajectory of marital satisfaction. *Journal of Personality and Social Psychology, 72*, 1075–1092.

Kasser, T., & Ryan, R. M. (1993). A dark side of the American Dream: Correlates of financial success as a central life aspiration. *Journal of Personality and Social Psychology, 65*, 410–422.

Kasser, T., & Ryan, R. M. (2001). Be careful what you wish for: Optimal functioning and the relative attainment of intrinsic and extrinsic goals. In P. Schmuck & K. Sheldon (Eds.), *Life goals and well-being* (pp. 116–131). Göttingen: Hogrefe.

Kasser, T., & Sheldon, K. M. (2000). Of wealth and death: Materialism, mortality salience, and consumption behavior. *Psychological Science, 11*, 348–351.

Kates, R. W. (1994). Sustaining life on the earth. *Scientific American, 271*(4), 114–122.

Kates, R. W., Clark, W. C., Corell, R., Hall, J. M., Jaeger, C. C., Lowe, I., McCarthy, J. J., Schellnhuber, H. J., Bolin, B., Dickson, N. M., Faucheux, S., Gallopin, G. C., Grubler, A., Huntley, B., Jager, J., Jodha, N. S., Kasperson, R. E., Mabogunje, A., Matson, P., Mooney, H., Moore, B., III, O'Riordan, T., & Svedin, U. (2001). Sustainability science. *Science, 292*, 641–642.

Katz, D., & Kahn, R. L. (1978). *The social psychology of organizations* (2nd ed.). New York: Wiley.

Katz, J. (1988). *Seductions of crime: Moral and sensual attractions in doing evil.* New York: Basic Books.

Katzev, R., Edelsack, L., Reynolds, R., Steinmetz, G., Walker, T., & Wright, R. (1978). The effect of reprimanding transgressions on subsequent helping behavior: Two field experiments. *Personality and Social Psychology Bulletin, 4*, 326–329.

Kaya, N., & Erkip, F. E. (1999). Invasion of personal space under the condition of short-term crowding: A case study on an automatic teller machine. *Journal of Environmental Psychology, 19,* 183–189.

Kaya, N., & Weber, M. J. (2003). Cross-cultural differences in the perception of crowding and privacy regulation: American and Turkish students. *Journal of Environmental Psychology, 23,* 301–309.

Kearns, J. N., & Fincham, F. D. (2005). Victim and perpetrator accounts of interpersonal transgressions: Self-serving or relationship-serving biases? *Personality and Social Psychology Bulletin, 31,* 321–333.

Keast, A., Brewer, N., & Wells, G. L. (2007). Children's metacognitive judgments in an eyewitness identification task. *Journal of Experimental Child Psychology, 9,* 286–314.

Keefe, K., & Berndt, T. J. (1996). Relations of friendship quality to self-esteem in early adolescence. *Journal of Early Adolescence, 16,* 110–129.

Keegan, J. (1993). *A history of warfare.* New York: Knopf.

Keinan, G. (1987). Decision making under stress: Scanning of alternatives under controllable and uncontrollable threats. *Journal of Personality and Social Psychology, 52,* 639–644.

Keinan, G., Friedland, N., & Ben-Porath, Y. (1987). Decision making under stress: Scanning of alternatives under physical threat. *Acta Psychologica, 64,* 219–228.

Keir, G. (1966). The psychological assessment of the children from the island of Tristan da Cunha. In C. Banks & P. L. Broadhurst (Eds.), *Stephanos: Studies in psychology presented to Cyril Burt* (pp. 129–172). New York: Barnes & Noble.

Keller, M. (2006, August 6). The scandal at the zoo. *New York Times.* Retrieved from http://www.nytimes.com/2006/08/06/nyregion/thecity/06zoo.html?ex51155009600&en5c2cc9b84edc068cd&ei55087%0A

Kelley, H. H., & Stahelski, A. J. (1970). Social interaction basis of cooperators' and competitors' beliefs about others. *Journal of Personality and Social Psychology, 16,* 66–91.

Kelln, B. R. C., & Ellard, J. H. (1999). An equity theory analysis of the impact of forgiveness and retribution on transgressor compliance. *Personality and Social Psychology Bulletin, 25,* 864–872; see also Wallace, H. M., Exline, J. J., & Baumeister, R. F. (2008). Interpersonal consequences of forgiveness: Does forgiveness deter or encourage repeat offenses? *Journal of Experimental Social Psychology, 44,* 453–460.

Kelly, J. (2014). When these stuffed squirrels went on the auction block, bidders went nuts. Washington Post. Retrieved from http://www.washingtonpost.com/local/when-these-stuffed-squirrels-went-on-the-auction-block-bidders-went-nuts/2014/04/08/b792b472-be5e-11e3-b195-dd0c1174052c_story.html

Kelly, M. H. (1999). Regional naming patterns and the culture of honor. *Names, 47,* 3–20.

Keltner, D., Gruenfeld, D. H., & Anderson, C. (2003). Power, approach, and inhibition. *Psychological Review, 110,* 265–284.

Kenrick, D. T., & Johnson, G. A. (1979). Interpersonal attraction in aversive environments: A problem for the classical conditioning paradigm. *Journal of Personality and Social Psychology, 87,* 572–579.

Kerr, N. L. (1983). Motivation losses in small groups: A social dilemma analysis. *Journal of Personality and Social Psychology, 45,* 819–828.

Kerr, N. L., & Bruun, S. E. (1981). Ringelmann revisited: Alternative explanations for the social loafing effect. *Personality and Social Psychology Bulletin, 7(2),* 224–231.

Kerr, N. L., & Bruun, S. E. (1983). Dispensability of member effort and group motivation losses: Free-rider effects. *Journal of Personality and Social Psychology, 44,* 78–94.

Kerr, N. L., Hymes, R. W., Anderson, A. B., & Weathers, J. E. (1995). Defendant-juror similarity and mock juror judgments. *Law and Human Behavior, 19,* 545–567.

Kerr, N. L., Rumble, A. C., Park, E. S., Ouwerkerk, J. W., Parks, C. D., Gallucci, M., & Van Lange, P.

A. M. (2009). "How many bad apples does it take to spoil the whole barrel?" Social exclusion and tolerance for bad apples. *Journal of Experimental Social Psychology. 45(4),* 603–613. Retrieved from http://www.sciencedirect.com/science/article/pii/S0022103109000390

Kerrigan, M. F. (2012). Transgender discrimination in the military: The new don't ask, don't tell. *Psychology, Public Policy, and Law, 18(3),* 500–518. doi: 10.1037/a0025771

Khadjavi, M., & Lange, A. (2013). Prisoners and their dilemma. *Journal of Economic Behavior & Organization, 92(8),* 163–175. doi: 10.1016/j.jebo.2013.05.015

Kidd, C., Palmeri, H., & Aslin, R.N. (2013). Rational snacking: Young children's decision-making on the marshmallow task is moderated by beliefs about environmental reliability. *Cognition, 126,* 109–114.

Kidder, D. L., & Parks, J. M. (2001). The good soldier: Who is s(he)? *Journal of Organizational Behavior, 22,* 939–959.

Kiecolt-Glaser, J. K., & Newton, T. L. (2001). Marriage and health: His and hers. *Psychological Bulletin, 127,* 472–503.

Kiecolt-Glaser, J. K., Fisher, L. D., Ogrocki, P., Stout, J. C., Speicher, C. E., & Glaser, R. (1987). Marital quality, marital disruption, and immune function. *Psychosomatic Medicine, 49,* 13–34.

Kiecolt-Glaser, J. K., Garner, W., Speicher, C., Penn, G. M., Holliday, J., & Glaser, R. (1984). Psychosocial modifiers of immunocompetence in medical students. *Psychosomatic Medicine, 46,* 7–14.

Kiesler, S., Sproull, L., & Waters, K. (1996). A prisoner's dilemma experiment on cooperation with people and human-like computers. *Journal of Personality and Social Psychology, 70,* 47–65.

Kim, J., Glaser, P., & Smith, T. W. (2011). The polls—trends: Trends in surveys on surveys. *Public Opinion Quarterly, 75(1),* 165–191.

Kim, S. H., Vincent, L. C., & Goncalo, J. A. (2012). Outside advantage: Can social rejection fuel creative thought? *Journal of Experimental Psychology: General, 142,* 605–611.

Kim, Y.-H., Chiu, C., & Zou, Z. (2010). Know thyself: Misperceptions of actual performance undermine achievement motivation, future performance, and subjective well-being. *Journal of Personality and Social Psychology, 99,* 395–409.

King, B. J. (2013, June 6). The fat-shaming professor: A Twitter-fueled firestorm. *NPR.* Retrieved from http://www.npr.org/blogs/13.7/2013/06/06/188891906/the-fat-shaming-professor-a-twitter-fueled-firestorm

King, K., Balswick, J. O., & Robinson, I. E. (1977). The continuing premarital sexual revolution among college females. *Journal of Marriage and the Family, 39,* 455–459.

Kinsey, A. C., Pomeroy, W. B., Martin, C. E., & Gebhard, P. H. (1953). *Sexual behavior in the human female.* Philadelphia: Saunders.

Kipnis, D. (1972). Does power corrupt? *Journal of Personality and Social Psychology, 24,* 33–41.

Kipnis, D. (1976). *The powerholders.* Chicago: University of Chicago Press.

Kirkpatrick, D. (2011). *The Facebook effect: The inside story of the company that is connecting the world.* New York: Simon & Schuster.

Kirkpatrick, L. A., & Ellis, B. J. (2001). An evolutionary-psychological perspective on self-esteem: Multiple domains and multiple functions. In G. J. O. Fletcher & M. S. Clark (Eds.), *Blackwell handbook of social psychology: Vol. 2. Interpersonal processes* (pp. 411–436). Oxford: Blackwell.

Kirkpatrick, S. A., & Locke, E. A. (1991). Leadership: Do traits matter? *Academy of Management Executive, 5,* 48–60.

Kirschenbaum, D., Humphrey, L., & Malett, S. (1981). Specificity of planning in adult self-control: An applied investigation. *Journal of Personality and Social Psychology, 40,* 941–950.

Kirschenbaum, D., Malett, S., Humphrey, L., & Tomarken, A. (1982). Specificity of planning and maintenance of self-control: 1 year follow-up of a

study improvement program. *Behavior Therapy, 13,* 232–240.

Kirscht, J. P. (1971). Social and psychological problems of surveys on health and illness. *Social Science and Medicine, 5(6),* 519–526.

Kitayama, S., & Markus, H. R. (1999). Yin and Yang of the Japanese self: The cultural psychology of personality coherence. In D. Cervone (Ed.), *The coherence of personality: Social-cognitive bases of consistency, variability, and organization* (pp. 242302). New York: Guilford Press.

Kitayama, S., Snibbe, A. C., Markus, H. R., & Suzuki, T. (2004). Is there any "free" choice? Cognitive dissonance in two cultures. *Psychological Science, 15,* 527–533.

Kitzinger, C. (1987). *The social construction of lesbianism.* London: Sage.

Klaczynski, P., Daniel, D. B., & Keller, P. S. (2009). Appearance idealization, body esteem, causal attributions, and ethnic variations in the development of obesity stereotypes. *Journal of Applied Developmental Psychology, 30(4),* 537–551.

Klein, S. B., & Kihlstrom, J. F. (1986). Elaboration, organization, and the self-reference effect in memory. *Journal of Experimental Psychology: General, 115,* 26–39.

Kling, K. C., Hyde, J. S., Showers, C. J., & Buswell, B. N. (1999). Gender differences in self-esteem: A meta-analysis. *Psychological Bulletin, 125,* 470–500.

Klinger, M. R., & Greenwald, A. G. (1994). Preferences need no inferences? The cognitive basis for unconscious emotional effects. In P. M. Niedenthal & S. Kitayama (Eds.), *The heart's eye: Emotional influences in perception and attention* (pp. 67–85). Orlando, FL: Academic Press.

Knapp, D. E., & Kustis, G. A. (1996). The real "disclosure": Sexual harassment and the bottom line. In M. S. Stockdale (Ed.), *Women and work: A research and policy series, volume 5: Sexual harassment in the workplace: Perspectives, frontiers, and response strategies* (pp. 199–215). Thousand Oaks, CA: Sage.

Knight, G. R. (1999). *A brief history of Seventh-Day Adventists.* Hagerstown, MD: Review & Herald.

Knight, L. J., & Boland, F. J. (1989). Restrained eating: An experimental disentanglement of disinhibiting variables of perceived calories and food type. *Journal of Abnormal Psychology, 98,* 412–420.

Knobe, J. (2003). Intentional action and side effects in ordinary language. *Analysis, 63,* 190–194.

Knobe, J. (2010). Person as scientist, person as moralist. *Behavioral and Brain Sciences, 33,* 315–329.

Knobloch-Westerwick, S. (2014). *Choice and preference in media use: Advances in selective exposure theory and research.* New York: Routledge.

Koch, E. J., & Shepperd, J. A. (2008). Testing competence and acceptance explanations of self-esteem. *Self and Identity, 7,* 54–74.

Koernig, S. K. (2003). E-scapes: The electronic physical environment and service tangibility. *Psychology and Marketing, 20,* 151–167.

Kohlenberg, R. J., Phillips, T., & Proctor, W. (1976). A behavioral analysis of peaking in residential electricity energy consumption. *Journal of Applied Behavior Analysis, 9,* 13–18.

Koider, S., Andrillon, T., Barbosa, L. S., Goupil L., & Bekinschtein, T. A. (2014). Inducing task-relevant responses to speech in the sleeping brain. *Current Biology, 24,* 1–7.

Kolata, G. (1992, November 22). The burdens of being overweight: Mistreatment and misconceptions. *New York Times,* A1.

Kolditz, T., & Arkin, R. M. (1982). An impression management interpretation of the self-handicapping phenomenon. *Journal of Personality and Social Psychology, 43,* 492–502.

Konecni, V. J., Libuser, L., Morton, H., & Ebbesen, E. G. (1975). Effects of a violation of personal space on escape and helping response. *Journal of Experimental Social Psychology, 11,* 288–299.

Konrath, S., Corneille, O., Bushman, B. J., & Luminet, O. (2014). The relationship between narcissistic exploitativeness, dispositional empathy, and emotion recognition abilities. *Journal of Nonverbal Behavior, 38*(1), 129–143. doi: 10.1007/s10919-013-0164-y

Konrath, S., O'Brien, E., & Hsing, C. (2011). Changes in dispositional empathy in American college students over time: A meta-analysis. *Personality and Social Psychology Review, 15*, 180–198.

Koole, S. L., & Lakens, D. (2012). Rewarding replications: A sure and simple way to improve psychological science. *Perspectives in Psychological Science, 7*(6), 608–614. doi: 10.1177/1745691612462586

Koole, S. L., Tjew A Sin, M., & Schneider, I. K. (2014). Embodied terror management: (Simulated) Interpersonal touch alleviates existential concerns among individuals with low self-esteem. *Psychological Science, 25*(1), 30–37. doi: 10.1177/0956797613483478

Koss, M. P. (1988). Hidden rape: Sexual aggression and victimization in the national sample of students in higher education. In M. A. Pirog-Good & J. E. Stets (Eds.), *Violence in dating relationships: Emerging social issues* (pp. 145–168). New York: Praeger.

Kotani, H., & Yokomatsu, M. (2013). Inheritance of local culture and disaster: Identity-formation-model approach. *Journal of Integrated Disaster Risk Management, 3*, 107–125.

Kouchaki, M., & Smith, I.H. (2014). The Morning Morality Effect: The influence of time of day on unethical behavior. *Psychological Science, 25*, 95–102.

Koughan, M. (1975, February 23). Arthur Friedman's outrage: Employees decide their pay. *Washington Post*.

Kouzes, J. M., & Posner, B. Z. (2002). *The leadership challenge* (3rd ed.). San Francisco: Jossey-Bass.

Kovera, M. B., & Cutler, B. L. (2013). *Jury selection*. New York: Oxford University Press.

Kozlowski, S. W., & Bell, B. S. (2003). Work groups and teams in organizations. In W. C. Borman, D. R. Ilgen, & R. J. Klimoski (Eds.), *Handbook of psychology: industrial and organizational psychology* (Vol. 12, pp. 333–375). New York: Wiley.

Kozlowski, S. W., Gully, S. M., McHugh, P. P., Salas, E., & Cannon-Bowers, J. A. (1996). A dynamic theory of leadership and team effectiveness: Developmental and task contingent leader roles. In G. R. Ferris (Ed.), *Research in personnel and human resource management* (Vol. 14, pp. 253–305). Greenwich, CT: JAI Press.

Kraft, M. (2006). *Environmental policies and politics*. Englewood Cliffs, NJ: Prentice Hall.

Kramer, A. D. I., Guillory, J. E., & Hancock, J. T. (2014). Experimental evidence of massive-scale emotional contagion through social networks. *Proceedings of the National Academy of Science, 111*, 24–26.

Kramer, R. M., & Brewer, M. B. (1984). Effects of group identity on resource use in a simulated commons dilemma. *Journal of Personality and Social Psychology, 46*, 1044–1057.

Kraus, S. J. (1995). Attitudes and the prediction of behavior: A meta-analysis of the empirical literature. *Personality and Social Psychology Bulletin, 21*, 58–75.

Krauss, R. M., Freedman, J. L., & Whitcup, M. (1978). Field and laboratory studies of littering. *Journal of Experimental Social Psychology, 14*, 109–122.

Kravitz, D. A., Cutler, B. L., & Brock, P. (1993). Reliability and validity of the original and revised Legal Attitudes Questionnaire. *Law and Human Behavior, 17*, 661–667.

Kray, L. J., & Galinsky, A. D. (2003). The debiasing effect of counterfactual mind-sets: Increasing the search for disconfirmatory information in group decisions. *Organizational Behavior and Human Decision Processes, 91*, 69–81.

Kray, L. J., George, L., Liljenquist, K., Galinsky, A., Tetlock, P., & Roese, N. (2010). From what *might* have been to what *must* have been: Counterfactual thinking creates meaning. *Journal of Personality and Social Psychology, 98*, 106–118.

Krendl, A. C., Richeson, J. A., Kelley, W. M., & Heatherton, T. F. (2008). The negative consequences of threat: A functional magnetic resonance imaging investigation of the neural mechanisms underlying women's underperformance in math. *Psychological Science, 19*(2), 168–175.

Kressel, N. J., & Kressel, D. R. (2002). *Stack and sway*. Boulder, CO: Westview Press.

Kross, E., Berman, M. G., Mischel, W., Smith, E. E., and Wager, T. D. (2011). Social rejection shares somatosensory representations with physical pain. *Proceedings of the National Academy of Sciences, 108*, 6270–6275.

Krueger, J., & Clement, R. W. (1994). The truly false consensus effect: An ineradicable and egocentric bias in social perception. *Journal of Personality and Social Psychology, 67*, 596–610.

Krueger, J., Wirtz, D., & Miller, D. T. (2005). Counterfactual thinking and the first instinct fallacy. *Journal of Personality and Social Psychology, 88*, 725–735.

Kruger, J., & Gilovich, T. (2004). Actions, intentions, and self-assessment: The road to self-enhancement is paved with good intentions. *Personality and Social Psychology Bulletin, 30*(3), 328–339.

Kuiper, N. A., & Derry, P. A. (1982). Depressed and non-depressed content self-reference in mild depression. *Journal of Personality, 50*, 67–79.

Kunce, L. J., & Shaver, P. R. (1994). An attachment-theoretical approach to caregiving in romantic relationships. In K. Bartholomew & D. Perlman (Eds.), *Advances in personal relationships* (Vol. 5, pp. 205–237). London: Kingsley.

Kunda, Z. (1990). The case for motivated reasoning. *Psychological Bulletin, 108*, 480–498.

Kunda, Z., & Thagard. P. (1996). Forming impressions from stereotypes, traits, and behaviors: A parallel-constraint-satisfaction theory. *Psychological Review, 103*, 284–308.

Kunda, Z., Davies, P. G., Adams, B. D., & Spencer, S. J. (2002). The dynamic time course of stereotype activation: Activation, dissipation, and resurrection. *Journal of Personality and Social Psychology, 82*, 283–299.

Kunst, M., Bogaerts, S., & Winkel, F. W. (2010). Domestic violence and mental health in a Dutch community sample: The adverse role of loneliness. *Journal of Community & Applied Social Psychology, 20*(5), 419–425.

Kunz, P. R., & Woolcott, M. (1976). Season's greetings: From my status to yours. *Social Science Research, 5*, 269–278.

Kurzban, R., & Leary, M. R. (2001). Evolutionary origins of stigmatization: The functions of social exclusion. *Psychological Bulletin, 127*, 187–208.

Kwan, M. (2010). How many cell phones are in the US? Retrieved from http://cellphones.lovetoknow.com/how-many-cell-phones-are-us

Kwan, V. S., John, O., Robin, R., & Kuang, L. (2008). Conceptualizing and assessing self-enhancement bias: A componential approach. *Journal of Personality and Social Psychology, 94*, 1062–1077.

Lacoursiere, R. B. (1980). *The life cycles of groups: Group developmental stage theory*. New York: Human Sciences Press.

LaFrance, M., & Banaji, M. (1992). Toward a reconsideration of the gender-emotion relationship. In M. S. Clark (Ed.), *Emotion and social behavior: Review of personality and social psychology* (Vol. 14, pp. 178–201). Newbury Park, CA: Sage.

Lagerspetz, K. M., Bjorkqvist, K., & Peltonen, T. (1988). Is indirect aggression typical of females? Gender differences in aggressiveness in 11- to 12-year-old children. *Aggressive Behavior, 14*, 403–414.

Lakin, A. (2009). Recyclable cars. *DriverSide.com*. Retrieved from http://www.driverside.com/auto-library/recyclable_cars-257

Lakin, J. L., & Chartrand, T. L. (2005). Exclusion and nonconscious behavioral mimicry. In K. D. Williams, J. P. Forgas, & W. von Hippel (Eds.), *The social outcast: Ostracism, social exclusion, rejection, and bullying* (pp. 279–296). New York: Psychology Press.

Lam, S. S. K., Schaubroeck, J., & Aryee, S. (2002). Relationship between organizational justice and employee work outcomes: A cross-national study. *Journal of Organizational Behavior, 23*, 1–18.

Lambert, N. M., Stillman, T. F., Hicks, J. A., Baumeister, R. F., Kamble, S., & Fincham, F. D. (2013). To belong is to matter: Sense of belonging enhances meaning in life. *Personality and Social Psychology Bulletin, 39*, 1418–1427.

Langer, E. J. (1975). The illusion of control. *Journal of Personality and Social Psychology, 32*, 311–328.

Langer, E. J., & Rodin, J. (1976). The effects of choice and enhanced personal responsibility for the aged: A field experiment in an institutional setting. *Journal of Personality and Social Psychology, 34*(2), 191–198.

Langer, E. J., & Roth, J. (1975). Heads I win, tails it's chance: The illusion of control as a function of the sequence of outcomes in a purely chance task. *Journal of Personality and Social Psychology, 32*, 951–955.

Langer, E. J., & Saegert, S. (1977). Crowding and cognitive control. *Journal of Personality and Social Psychology, 35*, 175–182.

Langer, G., Arnedt, C., & Sussman, D. (2004). A peek beneath the sheets. Retrieved from http://www.abcnews.go.com/Primetime/News

Langer, L. M., & Tubman, J. G. (1997). Risky sexual behavior among substance-abusing adolescents: Psychosocial and contextual factors. *American Journal of Orthopsychiatry, 67*, 315–322.

Langlois, J. H., Roggman, L. A., Casey, R. J., & Ritter, J. M. (1987). Infant preferences for attractive faces: Rudiments of a stereotype? *Developmental Psychology, 23*, 363–369.

LaPiere, R. T. (1934). Attitudes vs. actions. *Social Forces, 13*, 230–237.

Larsen, R. J. (2000). Toward a science of mood regulation. *Psychological Inquiry, 11*(3), 129–141. Quote on p. 129.

Larsen, R. J., & Diener, E. (1987). Affect intensity as an individual difference characteristic: A review. *Journal of Research in Personality, 21*, 1–39.

Larson, M. J., Vaughn, M. G., Salas-Wright, C. P., & DeLisi, M. (2015). Narcissism, low self-control, and violence among a nationally representative sample. *Criminal Justice and Behavior, 42*(6), 644–661.

Larson, R. W., & Pleck, J. (1999). Hidden feelings: Emotionality in boys and men. In D. Bernstein (Ed.), *Nebraska Symposium on Motivation: Vol. 45. Gender and motivation* (pp. 25–74). Lincoln: University of Nebraska Press.

Larwood, L., & Gattiker, U. E. (1995). Rational bias and interorganizational power in the employment of management consultants. *Group and Organization Studies, 10*, 3–17.

Latané, B., & Darley, J. (1968). Group inhibition of bystander intervention in emergencies. *Journal of Personality and Social Psychology, 10*, 215–221.

Latane, B., Eckman, J., & Joy, V. (1966). Shared stress and interpersonal attraction. *Journal of Experimental Social Psychology Supplement, 1*, 80–94.

Latane, B., Williams, K., & Harkins, S. (1979). Many hands make light the work: The causes and consequences of social loafing. *Journal of Personality and Social Psychology, 37*, 822–832.

Latta, R. M. (1978). Relation of status incongruous to personal space. *Personality and Social Psychology Bulletin, 4*, 143–146.

Laumann, E. O., Gagnon, J. H., Michael, R. T., & Michaels, S. (1994). *The social organization of sexuality: Sexual practices in the United States*. Chicago: University of Chicago Press.

Lavine, H., Sweeney, D., & Wagner, S. H. (1999). Depicting women as sex objects in television advertising: Effects on body dissatisfaction. *Personality and Social Psychology Bulletin, 25*, 1049–1058.

Lawler, E. E., Mohrman, S. A., & Ledford, G. E. (1995). *Creating high performance organizations: Practices and results of employee involvement and total quality management in Fortune 1000 companies*. San Francisco: Jossey-Bass.

Lawrence, C., & Andrews, K. (2004). The influence of perceived prison crowding on male inmates' perception of aggressive events. *Aggressive Behavior, 30*(4), 273–283.

Lawson, A. (1988). *Adultery: An analysis of love and betrayal*. New York: Basic Books.

Lazarus, R. S. (1966). *Psychological stress and the coping process*. New York: McGraw-Hill.

Lazarus, R. S. (1991). Progress on a cognitive-motivational-relational theory of emotion. *American Psychologist, 46*(8), 819–834.

Lazarus, R. S., & Launier, R. (1978). Stress-related transactions between person and environment. In L. A. Pervin & M. Lewis (Eds.), *Perspectives in interactional psychology* (pp. 287–322). New York: Plenum.

Le Bon, G. (1908). *The crowd: A study of the popular mind*. London: T Fisher Unwin.

Lea, S. E. G., & Webley, P. (2006). Money as tool, money as drug: The biological psychology of a strong incentive. *Behavioral and Brain Sciences, 29*, 161–209.

Leary, M. R. (2005). Varieties of interpersonal rejection. In K. D. Williams, J. P. Forgas, & W. von Hippel (Eds.), *The social outcast: Ostracism, social exclusion, rejection, and bullying* (pp. 35–54). New York: Psychology Press.

Leary, M. R., & Baumeister, R. F. (2000). The nature and function of self-esteem: Sociometer theory. In M. Zanna (Ed.), *Advances in experimental social psychology* (Vol. 32, pp. 1–62). San Diego: Academic Press.

Leary, M. R., & Springer, C. A. (2000). Hurt feelings: The neglected emotion. In R. Kowalski (Ed.), *Aversive behaviors and interpersonal transgression*. Washington, DC: American Psychological Association.

Leary, M. R., Kowalski, R. M., Smith, L., & Phillips, S. (2003). Teasing, rejection, and violence: Case studies of the school shootings. *Aggressive Behavior, 29*, 202–214.

Leary, M. R., Springer, C., Negel, L., Ansell, E., & Evans, K. (1998). The causes, phenomenology, and consequences of hurt feelings. *Journal of Personality and Social Psychology, 74*, 1225–1237.

Leary, M. R., Tambor, E. S., Terdal, S. K., & Downs, D. L. (1995). Self-esteem as an interpersonal monitor: The sociometer hypothesis. *Journal of Personality Psychology, 68*, 518–530.

Leary, M. R., Tchividjian, L. R., & Kraxberger, B. E. (1994). Self-presentation can be hazardous to your health: Impression management and health risk. *Health Psychology, 13*, 461–470.

Section 20.01 Lederer, E. M. (1997, April 2). *Alien abduction insurance cancelled! Associated Press. Retrieved from http://www.artgomperz.com/newse/abd.html*

Lee-Chai, A. Y., Chen, S., & Chartrand, T. L. (2001). From Moses to Marcos: Individual differences in the use and abuse of power. In A. Y. Lee-Chai & J. A. Bargh (Eds.), *The use and abuse of power: Multiple perspectives on the causes of corruption* (pp. 57–74). New York: Psychology Press.

Lee, B. K., & Lee, W. N. (2004). The effect of information overload on consumer choice quality in an on-line environment. *Psychology and Marketing, 21*, 159–183.

Lee, C. (1995). Prosocial organizational behaviors: The roles of workplace justice, achievement striving, and pay satisfaction. *Journal of Business and Psychology, 10*, 197–206.

Lee, S. W. S., & Schwarz, N. (2011). Wiping the slate clean: Psychological consequences of physical cleansing. *Current Directions in Psychological Science, 20*(5), 307–311.

Leffingwell, A. (1892). *Illegitimacy and the influence of the seasons upon conduct*. New York: Scribner's.

Leippe, M. R., Eisenstadt, D., Rauch, S. M., & Seib, H. M. (2004). Timing of eyewitness expert testimony, jurors' need for cognition, and case strength as determinants of trial verdicts. *Journal of Applied Psychology, 89*, 524–541.

Lennings, C. J. (1997). Police and occupationally related violence: A review. *Policing: An International Journal of Police Strategies and Management, 20*(3), 555–566.

Lennox, R. D., & Wolfe, R. N. (1984). Revision of the self-monitoring scale. *Journal of Personality and Social Psychology, 46*, 1349–1364.

Leon, G., & Chamberlain, K. (1973). Emotional arousal, eating patterns, and body image as differential factors associated with varying success in maintaining

a weight loss. *Journal of Consulting and Clinical Psychology, 40*, 474.

Leonard-Barton, D. (1980, September). *The role of interpersonal communication networks in the diffusion of energy conserving practices and technologies*. Paper presented at the International Conference of Consumer Behavior and Energy Policy, Banff, Alberta, Canada.

LePine, J. A., Erez, A., & Johnston, D. E. (2002). The nature and dimensionality of organizational citizenship behavior: A critical review and a meta-analysis. *Journal of Applied Psychology, 87*(1), 52–65.

Lepper, M. P., Greene, D., & Nisbett, R. E. (1973). Undermining children's intrinsic interest with extrinsic reward: A test of the "overjustification" hypothesis. *Journal of Personality and Social Psychology, 28*, 129–137.

Lerner, J. S., & Tetlock, P. E. (1999). Accounting for the effects of accountability. *Psychological Bulletin, 125*, 255–275.

Lerner, J. S., Small, D. A., & Loewenstein, G. (2004). Heart strings and purse strings: Carryover effects of emotions on economic decisions. *Psychological Science, 15*(5), 337–341.

Lerner, M. J. (1982). The justice motive in human relations and economic model of man: A radical analysis of facts and fictions. In V. Derlega & J. Grzelak (Eds.), *Cooperation and helping behavior: Theories and research* (pp. 249–278). New York: Academic Press.

Lerner, M. J., & Miller, D. T. (1978). Just world research and the attribution process: Looking back and ahead. *Psychological Bulletin, 85*, 1030–1051.

Lerner, M. J., & Simmons, C. H. (1966). Observer's reaction to the "innocent victim": Compassion or rejection? *Journal of Personality and Social Psychology, 4*, 203–210.

Lerner, R. (1969). Some female stereotypes of male body build–behavior relations. *Perceptual and Motor Skills, 28*, 363–366.

Lesiuk, T. (2005). The effect of music listening on work performance. *Psychology of Music, 33*(2), 173-191.

Leslie, J. B., & Van Velsor, E. (1996). *A look at derailment today*. Greensboro, NC: Centre for Creative Leadership.

Lett, H. S., Blumenthal, J. A., Babyak, M. A., Catellier, D. J., Carney, R. M., Berkman, L. F., & . . . Schneiderman, N. (2008). Perceived social support predicts outcomes following myocardial infarction: A call for screening?: Response. *Health Psychology, 27*(1), 1–3. doi: 10.1037/0278-6133.27.1.1b

Leung, K., & Bond, M. H. (2004). Social axioms: A model for social beliefs in multicultural perspective. In M. Zanna (Ed.), *Advances in experimental social psychology* (Vol. 36, pp. 119–197). New York: Academic Press.

Levav, J., Heitmann, H., Herrmann, A., & Iyengar, S. S. (2010). Order in product customization decisions: Evidence from field experiments. *Journal of Political Economy, 118*, 274–299.

Levenson, R. W., & Gottman, J. M. (1983). Marital interaction: Physiological linkage and affective exchange. *Journal of Personality and Social Psychology, 45*, 587–597.

Levenson, R. W., & Gottman, J. M. (1985). Physiological and affective predictors of change in marital satisfaction. *Journal of Personality and Social Psychology, 49*, 85–94.

Leventhal, E. A., Hansell, S., Diefenbach, M., Leventhal, H., & Glass, D. C. (1996). Negative affect and self-report of physical symptoms: two longitudinal studies of older adults. *Health Psychology, 15*, 193–199.

Levi, K. (1982). *Violence and religious commitment: Implications of Jim Jones's Peoples Temple movement*. University Park: Pennsylvania State University Press.

Levine, J. M., & Moreland, R. L. (1998). Small groups. In D. Gilbert, S. Fiske, & G. Lindzey (Eds.), *Handbook of social psychology* (4th. ed., Vol. 2, pp. 415–469). Boston: McGraw-Hill.

Levine, J. M., & Valle, R. S. (1975). The convert as a credible communicator. *Social Behavior and Personality, 3*, 81–90.

Leviticus 16: 7–10 (Bible).

Levitt, S. D., & Dubner, S. J. (2005). *Freakonomics: A rogue economist explores the hidden side of everything*. New York: Morrow HarperCollins.

Lewandowsky, S., Ecker, U. K. H., Seifert, C., Schwarz, N., & Cook, J. (2012). Misinformation and its correction: Continued influence and successful debiasing. *Psychological Science in the Public Interest, 13*, 106–131. doi: 10.1177/1529100612451018

Lewin, K. (1936). *Principles of topological psychology*. New York: McGraw-Hill.

Lewin, K. (1951). *Field theory in social science: Selected theoretical papers* (D. Cartwright, Ed.). New York: Harper Torchbooks. Quote on p. 169.

Lewinsohn, P. M., Mischel, W., Chaplin, W., & Barton, R. (1980). Social competence and depression: The role of illusory self-perceptions. *Journal of Abnormal Psychology, 89*, 203–212.

Lewis, J., Baddeley, A. D., Bonham, K. G., & Lovett, D. (1970). Traffic pollution and mental efficiency. *Nature, 225*, 95–97.

Lewis, W. A., & Bucher, A. M. (1992). Anger, catharsis, the reformulated frustration-aggression hypothesis, and health consequences. *Psychotherapy, 29*, 385–392.

Ley, D., & Cybriwsky, R. (1974). The spatial ecology of stripped cars. *Environment and Behavior, 6*, 53–68.

Li, T., & Fung, H. H. (2012). How negative interactions affect relationship satisfaction: The paradoxical short-term and long-term effects of commitment. *Social Psychological and Personality Science, 4*, 274–281.

Liang, D. W., Moreland, R. L., & Argote, L. (1995). Group versus individual training and group performance: The mediating role of transactive memory. *Personality and Social Psychology Bulletin, 21*, 384–393.

Liberman, N., & Trope, Y. (1998). The role of feasibility and desirability considerations in near and distant future decisions: A test of temporal construal theory. *Journal of Personality and Social Psychology, 75*, 5–18.

Liberman, N., Sagristano, M. C., & Trope, Y. (2002). The effect of temporal perspective on level of construal. *Journal of Experimental Social Psychology, 38*, 524–534.

Lickel, B., Hamilton, D. L., Wieczorkowska, G., Lewis, A., Sherman, S. J., & Uhles, A. N. (2000). Varieties of groups and the perception of group entitativity. *Journal of Personality and Social Psychology, 78*, 223–246.

Lieberman, M. A., Yalom, I. D., & Miles, M. B. (1973). *Encounter groups: First facts*. New York: Basic Books.

Lieberman, M. D., Gaunt, R., Gilbert, D. T., & Trope, Y. (2002). Reflection and reflexion: A social cognitive neuroscience approach to attributional inference. *Advances in Experimental Social Psychology, 34*, 199–249.

Liebert, R., & Baron, R. (1972). Some immediate effects of televised violence on children's behavior. *Developmental Psychology, 6*, 469–475.

Liebowitz, M. R. (1983). *The chemistry of love*. Boston: Little & Brown.

Liebrand, W. B. G., Wilke, H. A. M., & Wolters, F. J. M. (1986). Value orientation and conformity. A study using three types of social dilemma games. *Journal of Conflict Resolution, 30*, 77–97.

Light, L. L., Kayra-Stuart, F., & Hollander, S. (1979). Recognition memory for typical and unusual faces. *Journal of Experimental Psychology: Human Learning and Memory, 5*, 212–228.

Likert, R. (1967). *The human organization: Its management and value*. New York: McGraw-Hill.

Lin, Y. J., & Wicker, F. W. (2007). A comparison of the effects of thought suppression, distraction and concentration. *Behaviour Research and Therapy, 45*(12), 2924–2937.

Linder, D. E., Cooper, J., & Jones, E. E. (1967). Decision freedom as a determinant of the role of incentive magnitude in attitude change. *Journal of Personality and Social Psychology, 6*, 245–254.

Lindner, E. G. (2002). Healing the cycles of humiliation: How to attend to the emotional aspects of "unsolvable" conflicts and the use of "humiliation entrepreneurship." *Peace and Conflict: Journal of Peace Psychology, 8*, 125–138.

Lindsay, R. C. L., & Wells, G. L. (1980). What price justice? Exploring the relationship between lineup fairness and identification accuracy. *Law and Human Behavior, 4*, 303–314.

Lindsay, R. C. L., & Wells, G. L. (1985). Improving eyewitness identification from lineups: Simultaneous versus sequential lineup presentations. *Journal of Applied Psychology, 70*, 556–564.

Lindskold, S., & Aronoff, J. R. (1980). Conciliatory strategies and relative power. *Journal of Experimental Social Psychology, 16*, 187–198.

Linville, P. W., & Jones, E. E. (1980). Polarized appraisals of outgroup members. *Journal of Personality and Social Psychology, 38*, 689–703.

Lipscomb, J. (2013, May 8). Flatulence leads to knife fight, arrest. *Naples Daily News*. Retrieved from http://www.naplesnews.com/tablet-showcase/courts-and-crime/fart-face-leads-knife-fight

Lipsey, M. W., Wilson, D. B., Cohen M. A., & Derzon, J. H. (1997). Is there a causal relationship between alcohol use and violence? A synthesis of the evidence. In M. Galanter (Ed.), *Recent developments in alcoholism: Vol. 13. Alcohol and violence: Epidemiology, neurobiology, psychology, and family issues* (pp. 245–282). New York: Plenum Press.

Liptak, A. (2011, June 27). Justices reject ban on violent video games for children. *New York Times*. Retrieved from http://www.nytimes.com/2011/06/28/us/28scotus.html?pagewanted5all

Litt, C. J. (1981). Children's attachment to transitional objects: A study of two pediatric populations. *American Journal of Orthopsychiatry, 51*, 131–139.

Little, B. R. (1989). Personal projects analysis: Trivial pursuits, magnificent obsessions, and the search for coherence. In D. Buss & N. Cantor (Eds.), *Personality psychology: Recent trends and emerging directions* (pp. 15–31). New York: Springer Verlag.

Lochman, J. E., Vernberg, E., Boxmeyer, C., & Powell, N. (2012, May). Tornado effects on children's behavioral, emotional and psychophysiological functioning and parents' depression. Paper to be presented in a symposium (R. Guadagno, Chair) at the Association of Psychological Science Annual Convention, Chicago, IL.

Locke E. A., & Latham, G. P. (1990). *A theory of goal setting and task performance*. Englewood Cliffs, NJ: Prentice Hall.

Locke, E. A., & Kristof, A. L. (1996). Volitional choices in the goal achievement process. In P. M. Gollwitzer & J. A. Bargh (Eds.), *The psychology of action: Linking cognition and motivation to behavior* (pp. 363–384). New York: Guilford Press.

Locksley, A., Ortiz, V., & Hepburn, C. (1980). Social categorization and discriminatory behavior: Extinguishing the minimal intergroup discrimination effect. *Journal of Personality and Social Psychology, 39*(5), 773–783.

Loeber, R., & Hay, D. (1997). Key issues in the development of aggression from childhood to early adulthood. *Annual Review of Psychology, 48*, 371–410.

Loersch, C., & Arbuckle, N.L. (2013). Unraveling the mystery of music: Music as an evolved group process. *Journal of Personality and Social Psychology, 105*, 777–798.

Loewenstein, G. F., Weber, E. U., Hsee, C. K., & Welch, N. (2001). Risk as feelings. *Psychological Bulletin, 127*, 267–286.

Loftus, E. (1974). Reconstructing memory: The incredible eyewitness. *Psychology Today, 8*(7), 116–119.

Loftus, E. F., & Ketcham, K. (1994). *The myth of repressed memory*. New York: St. Martin's Press.

Loftus, E. F., Loftus, G. R., & Messo, J. (1987). Some facts about "weapon focus." *Law and Human Behavior, 11*, 55–62.

Logue, A. W. (1991). *The psychology of eating and drinking: An introduction* (2nd ed.). New York: W. H. Freeman.

Lombardo, M. M., & Eichinger, R. W. (2000). High potentials as high learners. *Human Resource Management, 39*(4), 321–329.

Lopes, L. L. (1987). Procedural debiasing. *Acta Psychologica, 64*, 167–185.

Lopes, P. N., Brackett, M. A., Nezlek, J. B., Schütz, A., Sellin, I., & Salovey, P. (2004). Emotional intelligence and social interaction. *Personality and Social Psychology Bulletin, 30*, 1018–1034.

Lord, C. G., & Saenz, D. S. (1985). Memory deficits and memory surfeits: Differential cognitive consequences of tokenism for tokens and observers. *Journal of Personality and Social Psychology, 49*, 918–926.

Lord, C. G., Lepper, M. R., & Preston, E. (1984). Considering the opposite: A corrective strategy for social judgment. *Journal of Personality and Social Psychology, 47*, 1231–1243.

Lord, C. G., Ross, L., & Lepper, M. R. (1979). Biased assimilation and attitude polarization: The effects of prior theories on subsequently considered evidence. *Journal of Personality and Social Psychology, 37*, 2098–2109.

Lord, R. G., Foti, R. J., & DeVader, C. L. (1984). A test of leadership categorization theory: Internal structure, information processing, and leadership perceptions. *Organizational Behavior and Human Performance, 34*, 343–378.

Lorenz, J., Rauhut, H., Schweitzer, F., & Helbing, D. (2011). How social influence can undermine the wisdom of crowd effect. *PNAS (Proceedings of the National Academy of Sciences), 108*, 9020–9025.

Lorenz, K. (1966). *On aggression* (M. K. Wilson, Trans.) New York: Harcourt, Brace.

Lucas, R. E. (2007). Long-term disability is associated with lasting changes in subjective well-being: Evidence from two nationally representative longitudinal studies. *Journal of Personality and Social Psychology, 92*(4), 717–730.

Luce, M. F. (1998). Choosing to avoid: Coping with negatively emotion-laden consumer decisions. *Journal of Consumer Research, 24*, 409–433.

Luce, M. F., Bettman, J. R., & Payne, J. W. (1997). Choice processing in emotionally difficult decisions. *Journal of Experimental Psychology: Learning, Memory, and Cognition, 23*, 384–405.

Luce, M. F., Bettman, J. R., & Payne, J. W. (2001). *Emotional decisions: Tradeoff difficulty and coping in consumer choice*. Chicago: University of Chicago Press.

Luchies, L. B., Wieselquist, J., Rusbult, C. E., Kumasiro, M., Eastwick, P. W., Coolsen, M. K., & Finkel, E. J. (2013). Trust and biased memory of transgressions in romantic relationships. *Journal of Personality and Social Psychology, 104*, 673–694.

Luckow, A., Reifman, A., & McIntosh, D. N. (1998). *Gender differences in coping: A meta-analysis*. Poster session presented at the 106th Annual Convention of the American Psychological Association, San Francisco.

Luhmann, M., Lucas, R. E., Eid, M., & Diener, E. (2013). The prospective effect of life satisfaction on life events. *Social Psychological and Personality Science, 4*, 39–45.

Lundberg, A. (1996). Psychiatric aspects of air pollution. *Otolaryngology-Head and Neck Surgery, 114*(2), 227–231.

Lutz, A. (2013, May 3). Abercrombie & Fitch refuses to make clothes for large women *Business Insider*. Retrieved from http://www.businessinsider.com/abercrombie-wants-thin-customers-2013-5

Luus, C. A. E., & Wells, G. L. (1991). Eyewitness identification and the selection of distractors for lineups. *Law and Human Behavior, 15*, 43–57.

Lydon, J. E., Menzies-Toman, D., Burton, K., & Bell, C. (2008). If-then contingencies and the differential effects of the availability of an attractive alternative on relationship maintenance for men and women. *Journal of Personality and Social Psychology, 95*, 50–65.

Lynch, J. J. (1979). *The broken heart: The medical consequences of loneliness*. New York: Basic Books.

Lyubomirsky, S. (2001). Why are some people happier than others? The role of cognitive and motivational processes in well-being. *American Psychologist, 56*, 239–249.

Maass, A., Cadinu, M., Guarnieri, G., & Grasselli, A. (2003). Sexual harassment under social identity threat: The computer harassment paradigm. *Journal of Personality and Social Psychology, 85*, 853–870.

MacDonald, G., & Leary M. R. (2005). Why does social exclusion hurt? The relationship between social and physical pain. *Psychological Bulletin, 131*, 202–223.

MacDonald, T. K., & Ross, M. (1999). Assessing the accuracy of predictions about dating relationships: How and why do lovers' predictions differ from those made by observers? *Personality and Social Psychology Bulletin, 25*, 1417–1429.

Macfarlane, A. (1986). *Marriage and love in England: Modes of reproduction, 1300–1840*. New York: Basil Blackwell.

Macias, W. (2003). A beginning look at the effects of interactivity, product involvement, and web experience on comprehension: Brand web sites as interactive advertising. *Journal of Current Issues and Research in Advertising, 25*, 31–44.

Mack, D., & Rainey, D. (1990). Female applicants' grooming and personnel selection. *Journal of Social Behavior and Personality, 5*, 399–407.

Mackay, C. (1932). *Extraordinary popular delusions and the madness of crowds*. New York: Farrar, Straus and Cudahy. (Original work published 1841).

Mackie, D. M., Worth L. T., & Asuncion, A. G. (1990). Processing of persuasive in-group messages. *Journal of Personality and Social Psychology, 58*, 812–822.

Mackie, D., & Cooper, J. (1984). Attitude polarization: Effects of group membership. *Journal of Personality and Social Psychology, 46*, 575–585.

MacLean, M. J. & Chown, S. M. (1988). Just world beliefs and attitudes toward helping elderly people: A comparison of British and Canadian university students. *International Journal of Aging and Human Development, 26*, 249–260.

Macphail, E. (1982). *Brain and intelligence in vertebrates*. Oxford: Clarendon Press.

Macrae, C. N., Milne, A. B., & Bodenhausen, G. V. (1994). Stereotypes as energy-saving devices: A peek inside the cognitive toolbox. *Journal of Personality and Social Psychology, 66*, 37–47.

Maddux, C. D., Stacy, D., & Scott, M. (1981). School entry age in a group of gifted children. *Gifted Child Quarterly, 25*, 180–184.

Major, B., Zubek, J. M., Cooper, M. L., Cozzarelli, C., & Richards, C. (1997). Mixed messages: Implications of social conflict and social support within close relationships for adjustment to a stressful life event. *Journal of Personality and Social Psychology, 72*, 1349–1363.

Malamuth, N. M., & Check, J. V. P. (1981). The effects of mass media exposure on acceptance of violence against women: A field experiment. *Journal of Research in Personality, 15*, 436–446.

Malle, B. F. (2006). The actor-observer asymmetry in causal attribution: A (surprising) meta-analysis. *Psychological Bulletin, 132*, 895–919.

Malle, B. F. (2011). Time to give up the dogmas of attribution: An alternative theory of behavior explanation. *Advances of Experimental Social Psychology, 44*, 297–352.

Malle, B. F., Knobe, J. M., & Nelson, S. E. (2007). Actor-observer asymmetries in explanations of behavior: New answers to an old question. *Journal of Personality and Social Psychology, 93*, 491–514.

Malos, S. (2010). Post-9/11 backlash in the workplace: Employer liability for discrimination against Arab-and Muslim-Americans based on religion or national origin. *Employee Responsibilities and Rights Journal, 22*(4), 297–310.

Malouff, J. M., & Schutte, N. S. (2014). Trait emotional intelligence and romantic relationship satisfaction: A meta-analysis. *American Journal of Family Therapy, 42*(1), 53–66. doi: 10.1080/01926187.2012.748549

Maner, J. K., & Mead, N. L. (2010). The essential tension between leadership and power: When leaders sacrifice group goals for the sake of self-interest. *Journal of Personality and Social Psychology, 99*, 482–497.

Maner, J. K., DeWall, C. N., Baumeister, R. F., & Schaller, M. (2007). Does social exclusion motivate interpersonal reconnection? Resolving the "porcupine problem." *Journal of Personality and Social Psychology, 92*(1), 42–55.

Maner, J. K., Gailliot, M. T., & DeWall, C. N. (2007). Adaptive attentional attunement: Evidence for mating-related perceptual bias. *Evolution and Human Behavior, 28*(1), 28–36.

Maner, J. K., Kenrick, D. T., Neuberg, S. L., Becker, D. V., Robertson, T., Hofer, B., et al. (2005). Functional projection: How fundamental social motives can bias interpersonal perception. *Journal of Personality and Social Psychology, 88,* 63–78.

Manfred, T. (2014, September 17). Nike drops Adrian Peterson. *Business Insider.* Retrieved from http://www.businessinsider.com/nike-drops-adrian-peterson-2014-9

Manning, R., Levine, M., & Collins, A. (2007). The Kitty Genovese murder and the social psychology of helping: The parable of the 38 witnesses. *American Psychologist, 62,* 555–562.

Mannix, E., & Neale, M.A. (2005). What differences make a difference? The promise and reality of diverse teams in organizations. *Psychological Science in the Public Interest, 6,* 31–55.

Manson v. Braithwaite, 1977, 432 U.S. 98.

Mansour, J. K., Beaudry, J. L., Bertrand, M. I., Kalmet, N., Melsom, E. I., & Lindsay, R. C. L. (2012). Impact of disguise on identification decisions and confidence with simultaneous and sequential lineups. *Law and Human Behavior, 36,* 513–526.

Manucia, G. K., Baumann, D. J., & Cialdini, R. B. (1984). Mood influences on helping: Direct effects or side effects? *Journal of Personality and Social Psychology, 46,* 357–364.

Manz, C. C. (1992). Self-leading work teams: Moving beyond self-management myths. *Human Relations, 45,* 1119–1140.

Marcon, J. L., Susa, K. J., & Meissner, C. A. (2009). Assessing the influence of recollection and familiarity in memory for own- versus other-race faces. *Psychonomic Bulletin & Review, 16,* 99–103.

Marcus-Newhall, A., Pedersen, W. C., Carlson, M., & Miller, N. (2000). Displaced aggression is alive and well: A meta-analytic review. *Journal of Personality and Social Psychology, 78,* 670–689.

Mardberg, B., Carlstedt, L., Stalberg-Carlstedt, B., & Shalit, B. (1987). Sex differences in perception of threat from the Chernobyl accident. *Perceptual & Motor Skills, 65,* 228.

Maris, R. (1969). *Social forces in urban suicide.* Homewood, IL: Dorsey.

Maris, R. (1981). *Pathways to suicide: A survey of self-destructive behaviors.* Baltimore: Johns Hopkins University Press.

Markman, K., Gavanski, I., Sherman, S., & McMullen, M. (1993). The mental simulation of better and worse possible worlds. *Journal of Experimental Social Psychology, 29,* 87–109.

Marks, G. (1984). Thinking one's abilities are unique and one's opinions are common. *Personality and Social Psychology Bulletin, 10,* 203–208.

Marks, G., & Miller, N. (1987). Ten years of research on the false consensus effect: An empirical and theoretical review. *Psychological Bulletin, 102,* 72–90.

Markus, H. R., & Kitayama, S. (1991). Culture and the self: Implications for cognition, emotion, and motivation. *Psychological Review, 98,* 224–253. See also Triandis, H. C. (1989). The self and social behavior in differing cultural contexts. *Psychological Review, 96,* 506–520.

Markus, H. R., & Kitayama, S. (1991). Culture and the self: Implications for cognition, emotion, and motivation. *Psychological Review, 98,* 224–253. Copyright © 1991 by the American Psychological Association. Reprinted by permission.

Markus, H. R., & Kunda, Z. (1986). Stability and malleability in the self-concept in the perception of others. *Journal of Personality and Social Psychology, 51,* 858–866.

Marques, J. M., & Páez, D. (1994). The "black sheep effect": Social categorization, rejection of ingroup deviates and perception of group variability. *European Review of Social Psychology, 5,* 37–68.

Marques, J. M., & Yzerbyt, V. Y. (1988). The black sheep effect: Judgmental extremity in inter- and intra-group situations. *European Journal of Social Psychology, 18,* 287–292.

Marques, J. M., Abrams, D., Páez, D., & Hogg, M. A. (2001). Social categorization, social identification, and rejection of deviant group members. In M. A. Hogg & R. S. Tindale (Eds.), *Blackwell handbook of social psychology: Group processes* (pp. 400–424). Oxford: Blackwell.

Marques, J. M., Abrams, D., Páez, D., & Martinez-Taboada, C. (1998). The role of categorization and in-group norms in judgments of groups and their members. *Journal of Personality and Social Psychology, 75,* 976–988.

Marsh, D. M., Dougherty, D. M., Moeller, F. G., Swann, A. C., & Spiga, R. (2002). Laboratory-measured aggressive behavior of women: acute tryptophan depletion and augmentation. *Neuropsychopharmacology, 26,* 660–671.

Marshall, G. D., & Zimbardo, P. G. (1979). Affective consequences of inadequately explained arousal. *Journal of Personality and Social Psychology, 37,* 970–988.

Martichuski, D. K., & Bell, P. A. (1991). Reward, punishment, privatization, and moral suasion in a commons dilemma. *Journal of Applied Social Psychology, 21,* 1356–1369.

Martin, E. A., & Kerns, J. G. (2011). The influence of positive mood on different aspects of cognitive control. *Cognition and Emotion, 25*(2), 265–279.

Martindale, D. A. (1971). Territorial dominance behavior in dyadic verbal interactions. *Proceedings of the Annual Convention of the American Psychological Association, 6,* 305–306.

Martins, A.; Ramalho, N.; Morin, E. (2010). A comprehensive meta-analysis of the relationship between emotional intelligence and health. *Personality and Individual Differences, 49,* 554–564.

Maruyama, G., Rubin, R. A., & Kingsbury, G. G. (1981). Self-esteem and educational achievement: Independent constructs with a common cause? *Journal of Personality and Social Psychology, 40,* 962–975.

Mascio, C., Rainey, R., & Zinda, M. (2008, March). *Effect of group composition on group performance: Are slightly heterogeneous groups the answer to the homogeneity vs. heterogeneity puzzle?* Poster presentation at the annual Graduate Student Conference in Industrial-Organizational Psychology and Organizational Behavior (IOOB), Denver, CO.

Masicampo, E. J., & Baumeister, R. F. (2011). Consider it done! Plan making can eliminate the cognitive effects of unfulfilled goals. *Journal of Personality and Social Psychology.* Online publication doi: 10.1037/a0024192

Maslach, C. (1979). Negative and emotional biasing of unexplained arousal. *Journal of Personality and Social Psychology, 37,* 953–969.

Maslow, A. H. (1968). *Toward a psychology of being.* New York: Van Nostrand.

Masuda, T., & Kitayama, S. (2004). Perceiver-induced constraint and attitude attribution in Japan and the US: A case for the cultural dependence of the correspondence bias. *Journal of Experimental Social Psychology, 40*(3), 409–416.

Mata, A., Ferreira, M. B., & Sherman, S. J. (2013). The metacognitive advantage of deliberative thinkers: A dual-process perspective on overconfidence. *Journal Of Personality And Social Psychology, 105*(3), 353-373. doi:10.1037/a0033640

Matarazzo, J. D. (1982). "Behavioral health" challenge to academic, scientific and professional psychology. *American Psychologist, 37*(1), 1–14.

Maticka-Tyndale, E., Herold, E. S., & Mewhinney, D. (1998). Casual sex on spring break: Intentions and behaviors of Canadian students. *The Journal of Sex Research, 35,* 254–264.

Matthew 27:24.

Matthew 6:12 (Bible).

Matthews, K. E., & Canon, L. K. (1975). Environmental noise level as a determinant of helping behavior. *Journal of Personality and Social Psychology, 32,* 571–577.

Matud, M. P. (2005). The psychological impact of domestic violence on Spanish women. *Journal of Applied Social Psychology, 35*(11), 2310–2322.

Mayer, J. D. (1993). The emotional madness of the dangerous leader. *Journal of Psychohistory, 20,* 331–348. (Quotation on p. 337).

Mayer, J. D., & Salovey, P. (1997). What is emotional intelligence? In P. Salovey & D. Sluyter (Eds.), *Emotional development and emotional intelligence: Implications for educators* (pp. 3–31). New York: Basic Books.

Mazar, N., Amir, O., & Ariely, D. (2008). The dishonesty of honest people: A theory of self-concept maintenance. *Journal of Marketing Research, 45,* 633–644.

Mazur, A., Susman, E. J., & Edelbrock, S. (1997). Sex differences in testosterone response to a video game contest. *Evolution and Human Behavior, 18,* 317–326.

Mazziotta, A., Mummendey, A., & Wright, S. C. (2011). Vicarious intergroup contact effects: Applying social-cognitive theory to intergroup contact research. *Group Processes & Intergroup Relations, 14*(2), 255–274.

McAuliff, B. D., & Kovera, M. B. (2007). Estimating the effects of misleading information on witness accuracy: Can experts tell jurors something they don't already know? *Applied Cognitive Psychology, 21,* 849–870.

McCabe, P. (1987). Desired and experienced levels of premarital affection and sexual intercourse during dating. *Journal of Sex Research, 23,* 23–33.

McCaul, K. D., Gladue, B. A., & Joppa, M. (1992). Winning, losing, mood, and testosterone. *Hormones and Behavior, 26,* 486–504.

McCullough, M. E. (2008). *Beyond revenge: The evolution of the forgiveness instinct.* San Francisco: Jossey-Bass.

McCullough, M. E., Bono, G., & Root, L. M. (2007). Rumination, emotion, and forgiveness: Three longitudinal studies. *Journal of Personality and Social Psychology, 92,* 490–505.

McCullough, M. E., Emmons, R. A., & Tsang, J. (2002). The grateful disposition: A conceptual and empirical topography. *Journal of Personality and Social Psychology, 82,* 112–127.

McCullough, M. E., Kimeldorf, M. B., & Cohen, A. D. (2008). An adaptation for altruism? The social causes, social effects, and social evolution of gratitude. *Current Directions in Psychological Science, 17*(4), 281–285.

McCullough, M. E., Pargament, K. I., & Thoresen, C. E. (Eds.) (2000). *Forgiveness: Theory, research, and practice.* New York: Guilford.

McCullough, M. E., Rachal, K. C., Sandage, S. J., Worthington, E. L., Brown, S. W., & Hight, T. L. (1998). Interpersonal forgiving in close relationships: II. Theoretical elaboration and measurement. *Journal of Personality and Social Psychology, 75,* 1586–1603.

McDaniel, M. A., Whetzel, D. L., Schmidt, F. L., & Maurer, S. D. (1994). The validity of employment interviews: A comprehensive review and meta-analysis. *Journal of Applied Psychology, 79,* 599–616.

McDougall, William (1960. Original work published 1908). *An Introduction to Social Psychology* (23rd ed.). University Paperbacks. Imprint of Methuen & Co (London) and Barnes & Noble (New York), pp. xxi–xxii (Note: Preface to 23rd edition commences p. xxi, with date of this preface [October 1936] on p. xxii.)

McEwen, B., & Lasley, E. 2007. Allostatic load: When protection gives way to damage. In A. Monat, R. S. Lazarus, G. Reevy, A. Monat, R. S. Lazarus, & G. Reevy (Eds.), *The Praeger handbook on stress and coping* (Vol. 1, pp. 99–109). Westport, CT: Praeger/Greenwood.

McFarland, S., Brown, D., & Webb, M.(2013). Identification with all humanity as a moral concept and psychological construct. *Current Directions in Psychological Science, 22*(3) 194–198. doi: 10.1177/0963721412471346

McFarland, S., Webb, M., & Brown, D. (2012). All humanity is my ingroup: A measure and studies of identification with all humanity. *Journal of Personality and Social Psychology, 103*(5), 830–853. doi: 10.1037/a0028724

McFarlin, D. B. (1985). Persistence in the face of failure: The impact of self-esteem and contingency information. *Personality and Social Psychology Bulletin, 11,* 153–163.

McFarlin, D. B., & Blascovich, J. (1981). Effects of self-esteem and performance on future affective preferences and cognitive expectations. *Journal of Personality and Social Psychology, 40,* 521–531.

McFarlin, D. B., Baumeister, R. F., & Blascovich, J. (1984). On knowing when to quit: Task failure, self-esteem, advice, and nonproductive persistence. *Journal of Personality, 52,* 138–155.

McGee, R., & Williams, S. (2000). Does low self-esteem predict health compromising behaviours among adolescents? *Journal of Adolescence, 23,* 569–582.

McGinnis, M. Y., Lumia, A., Breuer, M. E., & Possidente, B. (2002). Physical provocation potentiates aggression in male rats receiving anabolic androgenic steroids. *Hormones and Behavior, 41,* 101–110.

McGrath, J. E. (1966). *Small group research.* New York: Holt, Rinehart, & Winston.

McGuire, W. J. (1961). The effectiveness of supportive refutational defenses in immunizing and restoring beliefs against persuasion. *Sociometry, 24,* 184–197.

McGuire, W. J. (1964). Inducing resistance to persuasion: Some contemporary approaches. *Advances in Experimental Social Psychology, 1,* 191–229.

McGuire, W. J. (1968). Personality and susceptibility to social influence. In E. F. Borgotta & W. W. Lambert (Eds.), *Handbook of personality theory and research* (pp. 1130–1187). Chicago: Rand McNally.

McGuire, W. J., & Papageorgis, D. (1961). The relative efficacy of various types of prior belief-defense in producing immunity against persuasion. *Journal of Abnormal Social Psychology, 62,* 327–337.

McGuire, W. J., McGuire, C. V., Child, P., & Fujioka, T. (1978). Salience of ethnicity in the spontaneous self-concept as a function of one's ethnic distinctiveness in the social environment. *Journal of Personality and Social Psychology, 36,* 511–520.

McGuire, W. J., McGuire, C. V., Child, P., & Winton, W. (1979). Effects of household gender composition on the salience of one's gender in the spontaneous self-concept. *Journal of Experimental Social Psychology, 15,* 77–90.

McKenna, K. Y. A., & Bargh, J. A. (1998). Coming out in the age of the Internet: Identity "demarginalization" through virtual group participation. *Journal of Personality and Social Psychology, 75,* 681–694.

McKenna, K. Y. A., & Bargh, J. A. (1999). Causes and consequences of social interaction on the Internet: A conceptual framework. *Media Psychology, 1,* 249–269.

McKenna, K. Y. A., & Bargh, J. A. (2000). Plan 9 from Cyberspace: The implications of the Internet for personality and social psychology. *Personality and Social Psychology Review, 4,* 57–75.

McKillip, J., & Reidel, S. L. (1983). External validity of matching on physical attractiveness for same and opposite sex couples. *Journal of Applied Social Psychology, 13,* 328–337.

McKinney, L. N. (2004). Internet shopping orientation segments: An exploration of differences in consumer behavior. *Family and Consumer Sciences Research Journal, 32,* 408–433.

McLeod, E. (1982). *Women working: Prostitution today.* London: Croom Helm.

McLeod, J. M., & Pan, Z. (2005). Concept explication and theory construction. In S. Dunwoody, L. B. Becker, D. M. McLeod, & G. M. Kosicki (Eds.), *The evolution of key mass communication concepts* (pp. 13–76). Creskill, NJ: Hampton Press.

McManus, M. A., & Baratta, J. E. (1992). *The relationship of recruiting source to performance and survival.* Paper presented at the annual meeting of the Society for Industrial and Organizational Psychology, Montreal, Canada.

McMillen, D. L., & Austin, J. B. (1971). Effect of positive feedback on compliance following transgression. *Psychonomic Science, 24,* 59–61.

McMullen, M. N., Markman, K. D., & Gavanski, I. (1995). Living in neither the best nor the worst of all possible worlds: Antecedents and consequences of upward and downward counterfactual thinking. In N. J. Roese & J. M. Olson (Eds.), *What might have been: The social psychology of counterfactual thinking* (pp. 133–167). Mahwah, NJ: Erlbaum.

McNeill, W. H. (1982). *The pursuit of power: Technology, armed force, and society since A.D. 1000.* Chicago: University of Chicago Press.

McNulty, J. K. (2011). The dark side of forgiveness: The tendency to forgive predicts continued psychological and physical aggression in marriage. *Personality and Social Psychology Bulletin, 37*(6), 770–783.

McNulty, J. K., Olson, M. A., Meltzer, A. L., & Shaffer, M. J. (2014). Though they may be unaware, newlyweds implicitly know whether their marriage will be satisfying. *Science, 342,* 1149–1120.

McQuiston-Surrett, D. E., Malpass, R. S., & Tredoux, C. G. (2006). Sequential vs. simultaneous lineups: A review of methods, data, and theory. *Psychology, Public Policy and Law, 12,* 137–169.

Mead, G. H. (1934). *Mind, self and society.* Chicago: University of Chicago Press.

Mead, M. (1928). *Coming of age in Samoa: A psychological study of primitive youth for Western civilization.* New York: Morrow.

Mead, N. L., & Maner, J. K. (2012) On keeping your enemies close: Powerful leaders seek proximity to in-group power threats. *Journal of Personality and Social Psychology, 102,* 576–591.

Mead, N. L., Baumeister, R. F., Gino, F., Schweitzer, M. E., & Ariely, D. (2009). Too tired to tell the truth: Self-control resource depletion and dishonesty. *Journal of Experimental Social Psychology, 45,* 594–597. doi: 10.1016/j.jesp.2009.02.004

Medvec, V. H., Madey, S. F., & Gilovich, T. (1995). When less is more: Counterfactual thinking and satisfaction among Olympic medalists. *Journal of Personality and Social Psychology, 69,* 603–610.

Meissner, C. A., & Brigham, J. C. (2001). Thirty years of investigating the own-race bias in memory for faces: A meta-analytic review. *Psychology, Public Policy, and Law, 7,* 3–35.

Meissner, C. A., Tredoux, C. G., Parker, J. F., & MacLin, O. H. (2005). Eyewitness decisions in simultaneous and sequential lineups: A dual-process signal detection theory analysis. *Memory & Cognition, 33,* 783–792.

Mellers, B. A., Schwartz, A., Ho, K., & Ritov, I. (1997). Elation and disappointment: Emotional responses to risky options. *Psychological Science, 8,* 423–429.

Mello, J. A. (1993). Improving individual member accountability in small group settings. *Journal of Management Education, 17*(2), 253–259.

Meltzer, A. L., & McNulty, J. K. (2013). "Tell me I'm sexy . . . and otherwise valuable": Body evaluation and relationship satisfaction. *Personal Relationships, 21,* 68–87.

Meltzer, A. L., McNulty, J. K., Jackson, G. L., & Karney, B. R. (2014). Sex differences in the implications of partner physical attractiveness in the trajectory of marital satisfaction. *Journal of Personality and Social Psychology, 106,* 418–428.

Meltzer, A.L., McNulty, J.K., & Maner, J.K. (in press). Women like being valued for sex by their partner and engaging in frequent sex, as long as their partner is committed to a long-term relationship. *Archives of Sexual Behavior.*

Memon, A., Hope, L., & Bull, R. (2003). Exposure duration: Effects on eyewitness accuracy and confidence. *British Journal of Psychology, 94,* 339–354.

Mercier, H., & Sperber, D. (2011). Why do humans reason? Arguments for an argumentative theory. *Behavioral and Brain Sciences, 34*(2), 57–74.

Merriam-Webster Dictionary, http://www.merriam-webster.com/

Merton, R. K. (1948). The self-fulfilling prophecy. *Antioch Review,* pp. 193–210.

Messick, D. M., Bloom, S., Boldizar, J. P., & Samuelson, C. D. (1985). Why we are fairer than others. *Journal of Experimental Social Psychology, 21,* 480–500.

Meyer, C. B., & Taylor, S. E. (1986). Adjustment to rape. *Journal of Personality and Social Psychology, 50,* 1226–1234.

Meyer, D. E., & Schvaneveldt, R. W. (1971). Facilitation in recognizing pairs of words: Evidence of a dependence between retrieval operations. *Journal of Experimental Psychology, 90,* 227–234.

Meyer, J. P., & Allen, N. J. (1991). A three-component conceptualization of organizational commitment. *Human Resource Management Review, 1,* 61–89.

Meyer, J. P. & Herscovitch, L. (2001). Commitment in the workplace: Toward a general model. *Human Resource Management Review, 11,* 299–326.

Meyer, J. P., Allen, N. J., & Smith, C. A. (1993). Commitments to organizations and occupations: Extension and test of a three component conceptualization. *Journal of Applied Psychology, 78,* 538–551.

Michaud, S. G., & Aynesworth, H. (2000). *Ted Bundy: Conversations with a killer.* Irving, TX: Authorlink. Quote on p. 320.

Mick, D. G., & DeMoss, M. (1990). Self-gifts: Phenomenological insights from four contexts. *Journal of Consumer Research, 17,* 322–332.

Midden, C., Kaiser, F., & McCalley, T. (2007). Technology's four roles in understanding individuals' conservation of natural resources. *Journal of Social Issues, 63,*155–174.

Middlemist, R. D., Knowles, E. S., & Matter, C. F. (1976). Personal space invasions in the lavatory: Suggestive evidence for arousal. *Journal of Personality and Social Psychology, 33*(5), 541–546.

Mikula, G., Petri, B., & Tanzer, N. (1989). What people regard as unjust: Types, structures and everyday experiences of injustice. *European Journal of Social Psychology, 20,* 133–149.

Milgram, S. (1963). Behavioral study of obedience. *Journal of Abnormal and Social Psychology, 67,* 371–378.

Milgram, S. (1973, December). The perils of obedience. *Harper's,* 62–66.

Milgram, S. (1974). *Obedience to authority; An experimental view.* New York: Harper and Row.

Milgram, S. (1977). *The individual in a social world.* New York: McGraw-Hill.

Miller, A. G., McHoskey, J. W., Bane, C. M., & Dowd, T. G. (1993). The attitude polarization phenomenon: Role of response measure, attitude extremity, and behavioral consequences of reported attitude change. *Journal of Personality and Social Psychology, 64,* 561–574.

Miller, C. T., & Downey, K. T. (1999). A meta-analysis of heavyweight and self-esteem. *Personality and Social Psychology Review, 3,* 68–84.

Miller, D. P., Spangler, J. G., Vitolins, M. Z., Davis, S. W., Ip, E. H., Marion, G. S., & Crandall, S. J. (2013). Are medical students aware of their anti-obesity bias? *Academic Medicine, 88*(7), 978–982. doi: 10.1097/ACM.0b013e318294f817

Miller, D. T., & Holmes, J. G. (1975). The role of situational restrictiveness on self-fulfilling prophecies: A theoretical and empirical extension of Kelley and Stahelski's triangle hypothesis. *Journal of Personality & Social Psychology, 31,* 661–673.

Miller, G. T. (1990). *Living in the environment* (6th ed.). Belmont, CA: Wadsworth.

Miller, J. E., & Rempel, J. K. (2004) Trust and partner-enhancing attributions in close relationships. *Personality and Social Psychology Bulletin, 30,* 695–705.

Miller, J., Butts, C. T., & Rodes, D. (2002). Communication and cooperation. *Journal of Economic Behavior and Organization, 47,* 179–195.

Miller, L. C., & Fishkin, S. A. (1997). On the dynamics of human bonding and reproductive success: Seeking windows on the adapted-for-human environmental interface. In J. Simpson & D. Kenrick (Eds.), *Evolutionary social psychology* (pp. 197–235). Mahwah, NJ: Erlbaum.

Miller, N. E. (1941). The frustration-aggression hypothesis. *Psychological Review, 48,* 337–342.

Miller, N., Maruyama, G., Beaber, R. J., & Valone, K. (1976). Speed of speech and persuasion. *Journal of Personality and Social Psychology, 34,* 615–624.

Miller, P. V. (2002). The authority and limitation of polls. In J. Manza, F. L. Cook, & B. I. Page (Eds.), *Navigating public opinion* (pp. 221–231). New York: Oxford University Press.

Miller, R. L. (1979). Middle class residents in ghetto housing: Attitudes & behavior. *Proceedings of the International Conference on Environmental Psychology, Guildford, England, 75*.

Miller, R. L. (2013). Territoriality. In K. Keith (Ed.), *Encyclopedia of cross-cultural psychology* (pp. 1276–1278). New York, NY: Wiley-Blackwell.

Miller, R. L., Seligman, C., Clark, N. T., & Bush, M. (1976). Perceptual contrast versus reciprocal concession as mediators of induced compliance. *Journal of Behavioral Science, 7,* 401–409.

Miller, R. S. (1997). Inattentive and contented: Relationship commitment and attention to alternatives. *Journal of Personality and Social Psychology, 73,* 758–766.

Miller, S. M., & Diefenbach, M. A. (1998). The Cognitive-Social Health Information-Processing (C-SHIP) model: A theoretical framework for research in behavioral oncology. In D. S. Krantz, & A. Baum (Eds.), *Technology and methods in behavioral medicine* (pp. 219–244). Mahwah, NJ: Lawrence Erlbaum.

Miller, T. Q., Smith, T. W., Turner, C. W., Guijarro, M. L., & Hallet, A. J. (1996). A meta-analytic review of research on hostility and physical health. *Psychological Bulletin, 119,* 322–348.

Millhausen, R. R., & Herold, E. S. (1999). Does the sexual double standard still exist? Perceptions of university women. *Journal of Sex Research, 36,* 361–368.

Milliman, R. E. (1982). Using background music to affect the behavior of supermarket shoppers. *Journal of Marketing, 46,* 86–91.

Mills, H., Reiss, N., & Dombeck, M. (2008, Jun 30). Types of stressors (eustress vs. distress). Retrieved from http://www.mentalhelp.net/poc/view_doc.php?type5doc&id515644

Mischel, W. (1973). Toward a cognitive social learning reconceptualization of personality. *Psychological Review, 80,* 252–283.

Mischel, W. (1974). Processes in delay of gratification. In L. Berkowitz (Ed.), *Advances in experimental social psychology* (Vol. 7, pp. 249–292). San Diego: Academic Press.

Mischel, W. (1996). From good intentions to willpower. In P. M. Gollwitzer & J. Bargh (Eds.), *The psychology of action: Linking cognition and motivation to behavior* (pp. 197–218). New York: Guilford Press.

Mischel, W., & Mendoza-Denton, R. (2002). Harnessing willpower and socio-emotional intelligence to enhance human agency and potential. In L. G. Aspinwall & U. M. Staudinger (Eds.), *A psychology of human strengths: Fundamental questions and future directions for a positive psychology* (pp. 245–256). Washington, DC: American Psychological Association.

Mischel, W., & Shoda, Y. (1995). A cognitive-affective system theory of personality: Reconceptualizing situations, dispositions, dynamics, and invariance in personality structure. *Psychological Review, 102,* 246–268.

Mischel, W., Ebbesen, E. B., & Zeiss, A. R. (1976). Determinants of selective memory about the self. *Journal of Consulting and Clinical Psychology, 44,* 92–103.

Mischel, W., Shoda, Y., & Peake, P. K. (1988). The nature of adolescent competencies predicted by preschool delay of gratification. *Journal of Personality and Social Psychology, 54,* 687–696.

Mischkowski, D., Kross, E., & Bushman, B. J. (2012). Flies on the wall are less aggressive: Self-distanced reflection reduces angry feelings, aggressive thoughts, and aggressive behaviors. *Journal of Experimental Social Psychology, 48(5),* 1187–1191. doi: 10.1016/j.jesp.2012.03.012

Misra, S, & Kalro, A. (1979). Triangle effect and the connotative meaning of trust in prisoner's dilemma: A cross cultural study. International *Journal of Psychology, 14,* 255–263.

Missouri Historical Society. The *1904 World's Fair: Looking back at looking forward*. Retrieved from http://mohistory.org/Fair/WF/HTML/Overview/page3.html

Mita, T. H., Dermer, M., & Knight, J. (1977). Reversed facial images and the mere-exposure hypothesis. *Journal of Personality and Social Psychology, 35,* 597–601.

Mitchell, D. J., Kahn, B. E., & Knasko, S. C. (1995). There's something in the air: Effects of congruent or incongruent ambient odor on consumer decision making. *Journal of Consumer Research, 22,* 229–238.

Miyamoto, Y., & Kitayama, S. (2002). Cultural variation in correspondence bias: The critical role of attitude diagnosticity of socially constrained behavior. *Journal of Personality and Social Psychology, 83(5),* 1239–1248.

Mochon, D. (2008, November). *Single option aversion: When the illusion of choices reduces deferral*. Paper presented at the annual meeting of the Society for Judgment and Decision Making, Chicago.

Moffitt, T., Brammer, G., Caspi, A., Fawcett, J., Raleigh, M., Yuwiler, A., & Silva, P. (1998). Whole blood serotonin relates to violence in an epidemiological study. *Biological Psychiatry, 43,* 446–457.

Monroe, A. E. & Malle, B. F. (2010). From uncaused will to conscious choice: The need to study, not speculate about people's folk concept of free will. *Review of Philosophy and Psychology, 9,* 211–224.

Moore, M. T., & Fresco, D. M. (2012). Depressive realism: A meta-analytic review. *Clinical Psychology Review, 32,* 496–509.

Moore, R. (1986). *The Jonestown letters: Correspondence of the Moore Family 1970–1985*. Lewiston, NY: E. Mellen Press.

Moos, R. H., & Schaefer, J. A. (1993). Coping resources and processes: Current concepts and measures. In L. Goldberger, & S. Breznitz (Eds.), *Handbook of stress: Theoretical and clinical aspects* (2nd ed., pp. 234–257). New York: Free Press.

Moran, G., & Comfort, J. C. (1986). Neither "tentative nor fragmentary": Verdict preference of impaneled felony jurors as a function of attitude toward capital punishment. *Journal of Applied Psychology, 71,* 146–155.

Moran, G., Cutler, B. L., & De Lisa, A. (1994). Attitudes toward tort reform, scientific jury selection, and juror bias: Verdict inclination in criminal and civil trials. *Law and Psychology Review, 18,* 309–328.

Moran, G., Cutler, B. L., & Loftus, E. F. (1990). Jury selection in major controlled substance trials: The need for extended voir dire. *Forensic Reports, 3,* 331–348.

Moreland, R. L., Argote, L., & Krishnan, R. (1998). Training people to work in groups. In R. Tindale, L. Heath, J. Edwards, E. Posavac, F. Bryant, Y. Suarez-Balcazar, et al. (Eds.), *Theory and research on small groups* (pp. 37–60). New York: Plenum Press.

Morf, C. C., & Rhodewalt, F. (2001). Unraveling the paradoxes of narcissism: A dynamic self-regulatory processing model. *Psychological Inquiry, 12,* 177–196.

Morgan, C. A., III, Hazlett, G., Doran, A., Garrett, S., Hoyt, G., Thomas, P., Baranoski, M., & Southwick, S. M. (2004). Accuracy of eyewitness memory for persons encountered during exposure to highly intense stress. *International Journal of Law and Psychiatry, 27,* 265–279.

Morgenthau, H. (1962). Love and power. *Commentary, 33,* 247–251.

Mori, D., Chaiken, S., & Pliner, P. (1987). "Eating lightly" and the self-presentation of femininity. *Journal of Personality and Social Psychology, 53,* 693–702.

Morokoff, P. J. (1985). Effects of sex guilt, repression, sexual "arousability," and sexual experience on female sexual arousal during erotica and fantasy. *Journal of Personality and Social Psychology, 49,* 177–187.

Morokoff, P. J. (1986). Volunteer bias in the psychophysiological study of female sexuality. *Journal of Sex Research, 22,* 35–51.

Morrin, M., & Ratnewshwar, S. (2003). Does it make sense to use scents to enhance brand memory? *Journal of Marketing Research, 40,* 10–25.

Morris, K. A., & Swann, W. B., Jr. (1996). Denial and the AIDS crisis: Wishing away the threat of AIDS. In S. Oskamp & S. Thompson (Eds.), *Safer sex in the '90s* (pp. 57–79). New York: Sage.

Morris, W. N., & Reilly, N. P. (1987). Toward the self-regulation of mood: Theory and research. *Motivation and Emotion, 11,* 215–249.

Moscovici, S., & Zavalloni, M. (1969). The group as a polarizer of attitudes. *Journal of Personality and Social Psychology, 12,* 125–135.

Moya, M., Glick, P., Expósito, F., de Lemus, S., & Hart, J. (2007). It's for your own good: Benevolent sexism and women's reactions to protectively justified restrictions. *Personality and Social Psychology Bulletin, 33,* 1421–1434.

Muchnik, L., Aral, S., & Taylor, S. J. (2013). Social influence bias: A randomized experiment. *Science, 341(6146),* 647–651.

Mueller, C. W., Boyer, E. M., Price, J. L. & Iverson, R. D. (1994). Employee attachment and non-coercive conditions of work: The case of dental hygienists. *Work and Occupations, 21,* 179–212.

Mullan, B., & Marvin, G. (1998). *Zoo culture: The book about watching people watch animals* (2nd ed.). Urbana, IL: University of Illinois Press.

Mullen, B., Anthony, T., Salas, E., & Driskell, J. E. (1994). Group cohesiveness and quality of decision making: An integration of the groupthink hypothesis. *Small Group Research, 25(2),* 189–204.

Mullen, B., Johnson, C., & Salas, E. (1991). Productivity loss in brainstorming groups: A meta-analysis. *Basic and Applied Social Psychology, 12,* 3–23.

Muller, D., Bushman, B. J., Subra, B., & Ceaux, E. (2012). Are people more aggressive when they are worse off or better off than others? *Social Psychological and Personality Science, 3(6),* 754-759. DOI: 10.1177/1948550612436984

Mulligan, R., Burmood, C., O'Hara, S., & Warren, C. (2004). Personal space preferences: The role of mortality salience and affiliation motivation. *Journal of Psychological Inquiry, 9(1),* 14–20.

Mullin, C. R., & Linz, D. (1995). Desensitization and resensitization to violence against women: Effects of exposure to sexually violent films on judgments of domestic violence victims. *Journal of Personality and Social Psychology, 69,* 449–459.

Munger, K., & Harris, S. J. (1989). Effects of an observer on handwashing in a public restroom. *Perceptual and Motor Skills, 69,* 733–734.

Murch, S. H., Anthony, A., Casson, D. H. *et al.* (2004). Retraction of an interpretation. *Lancet, 363(9411),* 750. doi:10.1016/S0140-6736(04)15715-2

Murnen, S. K., Perot, A., & Byrne, D. (1989). Coping with unwanted sexual activity: Normative responses, situational determinants, and individual differences. *Journal of Sex Research, 26,* 85–106.

Murphy-Berman, V., & Berman, J. (1978). Importance of choice and sex invasions of personal space. *Personality and Social Psychology Bulletin, 4,* 424–428.

Murray, D. R., Trudeau, R., & Schaller, M. (2011). On the origins of cultural differences in conformity: Four tests of the pathogen prevalence hypothesis. *Personality and Social Psychology Bulletin, 37,* 318–329.

Murray, S. L., Holmes, J. G., & Collins, N. L. (2006). Optimizing assurance: The risk regulation system in relationships. *Psychological Bulletin, 132,* 641–666.

Murray, S., & Holmes, J. G. (1993). See virtues in faults: Negativity and the transformation of interpersonal narratives in close relationships. *Journal of Personality and Social Psychology, 65,* 707–722.

Murray, S., & Holmes, J. G. (1994). Story-telling in close relationships: The construction of confidence. *Personality and Social Psychology Bulletin, 20,* 663–676.

Murray, S., Bellavia, G., Rose, P., & Griffin, D. (2003). Once hurt, twice hurtful: How perceived regard regulates daily marital interactions. *Journal of Personality and Social Psychology, 84,* 126–147.

Murray, S., Holmes, J. G., & Griffin, D. W. (1996). The benefits of positive illusions: Idealization and the construction of satisfaction in close relationships. *Journal of Personality and Social Psychology, 70,* 79–98.

Murray, S., Rose, P., Bellavia, G., Holmes, J., & Kusche, A. (2002). When rejection stings: How self-esteem constrains relationship enhancement processes. *Journal of Personality and Social Psychology, 83,* 556–573.

Murstein, B. I., & Christy, P. (1976). Physical attractiveness and marriage adjustment in middle-aged couples. *Journal of Personality and Social Psychology, 34,* 537–542.

Musch, J., & Grondin, S. (2001). Unequal competition as an impediment to personal development: A review of the relative age effect in sport. *Developmental Review, 21,* 147–167.

Mussweiler, T., & Ockenfels, A. (2013). Similarity increases altruistic punishment in humans. *PNAS,* early edition, http://www.pnas.org/cgi/doi/10.1073/pnas.1215443110.

Myers, D. G. (1992). The secrets of happiness. *Psychology Today, 25,* 38–46.

Myers, D. G. (1993, July/August). Pursuing happiness. *Psychology Today,* pp. 32–35, 66–67.

Myers, D. G. (2006). *Social psychology* (8th ed.). New York: McGraw Hill.

Nadler, R. T., Rabi, R., & Minda, J. P. (2010). Better mood and better performance: Learning rule-described categories is enhanced by positive mood. *Psychological Science, 21*(12), 1770–1776.

Nagler, U. K. J., Reiter, K. J., Furtner, M. R., & Rauthmann, J. F. (2014). Is there a "dark intelligence"? Emotional intelligence is used by dark personalities to emotionally manipulate others. *Personality and Individual Differences, 65*(7), 47–52. doi: 10.1016/j.paid.2014.01.025

Najmi, S., & Wegner, D. M. (2008). Thought suppression and psychopathology. In A. J. Elliot (Ed.), *Handbook of approach and avoidance motivation* (pp. 447–459). New York: Psychology Press.

Narby, D. J., Cutler, B. L., & Moran, G. (1993). A meta-analysis of the association between authoritarianism and jurors' perceptions of defendant culpability. *Journal of Applied Psychology, 78,* 3442.

National Archives. (2012). Teaching with documents: The Civil Rights Act of 1964 and the Equal Employment Opportunity Commission. Retrieved from http://www.archives.gov/education/lessons/civil-rights-act/

Naylor, J. C., Pritchard, R. D., & Ilgen, D. R. (1980). *A theory of behavior in organizations.* New York: Academic Press.

Neal, D. T., & Wood, W. (2007). Automaticity *in situ:* Direct context cuing of habits in daily life. In J. Bargh, P. Gollwitzer, & E. Morsella (Eds.), *Psychology of action (Vol. 2): Mechanisms of human action.* London: Oxford University Press.

Neal, D., & Chartrand, T. L. (2011). Embodied emotion perception: Amplifying and dampening facial feedback modulates emotion perception accuracy. *Social Psychological and Personality Science, 2,* 673–678.

Neal, D.T., Wood, W., & Drolet, A. (2013). How do people adhere to goals when willpower is low? The profits (and pitfalls) of strong habits. *Journal of Personality and Social Psychology, 104,* 959–975.

Neely, J. H. (1991). Semantic priming effects in visual word recognition: A selective review of current findings and theories. In D. Besner & G. Humphreys (Eds.), *Basic processes in reading: Visual word recognition* (pp. 264–336). Hillsdale, NJ: Erlbaum.

Neil v. Biggers, 409 U. S. 188 (1972).

Nelissen, R. M. A. (2014). Relational utility as a moderator of guilt in social interactions. *Journal of Personality and Social Psychology, 106,* 257–271.

Nelson, L. D., & Morrison, E. L. (2005). The symptoms of resource scarcity: Judgments of food and finances impact preferences for potential partners. *Psychological Science, 16*(2), 167–173.

Nelson, M. R. (2002). Recall of brand placements in computer/video games. *Journal of Advertising Research, 42,* 80–92.

Neuschatz, J. S., Lawson, D. S., Fairless, A. H., Powers, R. A., Neuschatz, J. S., Goodsell, C. A., & Toglia, M. P. (2007). The mitigating effects of suspicion on post-identification feedback and on retrospective eyewitness memory. *Law and Human Behavior, 31,* 231–247.

New image. Retrieved from http://logos.wikia.com/wiki/Pepsi

New studies show strong link between diet and behavior. (2004). Retrieved from http://www.kidscanlearn.net/artcri.htm

Newcombe, D., & Arnkoff, D. B. (1979). Effects of speech style and sex of speaker on person perception. *Journal of Personality and Social Psychology, 37,* 1293–1303.

Newman, A. (2001, February 4). Anti-smoking campaign: Rotten teeth and dead babies. *New York Times Magazine,* p. 16. Available at http://www.nytimes.com/

Newman, A. (May 26, 2010). With this ring, I thee what? *New York Times.* Retrieved February 18, 2012, from http://www.nytimes.com/2010/05/27/fashion/27rings.html?adxnnl51&adxnnlx51329596054-/Hwober8MpThtkMeSSX7pA

Newman, E. J., Sanson, M., Miller, E. K., Quigley-McBride, A., Foster, J. L., Bernstein, D. M., & Garry, M. (2014). People with easier to pronounce names promote truthiness of claims. *PLOS ONE, 9*(2): e88671. doi: 10.1371/journal.pone.0088671. Retrieved from http://www.plosone.org/article/info%3Adoi%2F10.1371%2Fjournal.pone.0088671

Newman, M. L., Pennebaker, J. W., Berry, D. S., & Richards, J. M. (2003). Lying words: Predicting deception from linguistic styles. *Personality and Social Psychology Bulletin, 29*(5), 665–675.

Nguyen, H.-H. D., & Ryan, A. M. (2008). Does stereotype threat affect test performance of minorities and women? A meta-analysis of experimental evidence. *Journal of Applied Psychology, 93*(6), 1314–1334.

Nickerson, R. S. (1998). Confirmation bias: A ubiquitous phenomenon in many guises. *Review of General Psychology, 2,* 175–220.

Nickerson, R. S. (2003). *Psychology and environmental change.* Mahway, NJ: Erlbaum.

Niedenthal, P. M., Halberstadt, J. B., & Innes-Ker, A. H. (1999). Emotional response categorization. *Psychological Review, 106,* 337–361.

Nietzel, M. T., McCarthy, D. M., & Kern, M. J. (1999). Juries: The current state of the empirical literature. In R. Roesch, S. D. Hart, & J. R. P. Ogloff (Eds.), *Psychology and law: The state of the discipline* (pp. 23–52). Dordrecht, Netherlands: Kluwer Academic Publishers.

Nijman, H. L. I., & Rector, G. (1999). Crowding and aggression on inpatient psychiatric wards. *Psychiatric Services, 50*(6), 830–831.

Nisbet, E. K., & Zelenski, J. M. (2011). Underestimating nearby nature: Affective forecasting errors obscure the happy path to sustainability. *Psychological Science, 22*(9), 1101–1106.

Nisbet, E. K., Zelenski, J. M., & Murphy, S. A. (2009). The nature relatedness scale: Linking individuals' connection with nature, environmental concern, and behavior. *Environment and Behavior, 41,* 715–740.

Nisbett, R. E., & Wilson, T. D. (1977). Telling more than we can know: Verbal reports on mental processes. *Psychological Review, 84,* 231–259.

Nolen-Hoeksema, S. (1991). Responses to depression and their effects on the duration of depressive episodes. *Journal of Abnormal Psychology, 100,* 569–582.

Northouse, P. G. (2004). *Leadership: Theory and practice.* Thousand Oaks, CA: Sage Publications.

Norton, M. I., Frost, J. H., & Ariely, D. (2007). Less is more: The lure of ambiguity, or why familiarity breeds contempt. *Journal of Personality and Social Psychology, 92,* 97–105.

Norton, M. I., Sommers, S. R., & Brauner, S. (2007). Bias in jury selection: Justifying prohibited peremptory challenges. *Journal of Behavioral Decision Making, 20,* 467–479. doi: 10.1002/bdm.571

Novelli, D., Drury, J., Reicher, S., & Stott, C. (2013). Crowdedness mediates the effect of social identification on positive emotion in a crowd: A survey of two crowd events. *PLoS ONE, 8*(11), 1–7.

Nowak, M., & Roch, S. (2006). Upstream reciprocity and the evolution of gratitude. *Proceedings of the Royal Society of London, Series B: Biological Sciences, 274,* 605–609.

Nysse-Carris, K. L., Bottoms, B. L., & Salerno, J. M. (2011). Experts' and novices' abilities to detect children's high-stakes lies of omission. *Psychology, Public Policy, and Law, 17*(1), 76–98.

O'Boyle, E. H., Jr., Humphrey, R. H., Pollack, J. M., Hawver, T. H., & Story, P. A. (2011). The relation between emotional intelligence and job performance: A meta-analysis. *Journal of Organizational Behavior, 32*(5), 788–818.

O'Brien, E. H., Anastasio, P. A., & Bushman, B. J. (2011). Time crawls when you're not having fun: Feeling entitled makes dull tasks drag on. *Personality and Social Psychology Bulletin, 37*(10), 1287–1296.

O'Connor, D. B., Jones, F., Conner, M., McMillan, B., & Ferguson, E. (2008). Effects of daily hassles and eating style on eating behavior. *Health Psychology, 27*(1), S20–S31.

O'Neil, K. M., Patry, M. W., & Penrod, S. D. (2004). Exploring the effects of attitudes toward the death penalty on capital sentencing verdicts. *Psychology, Public Policy, and Law, 10,* 443–470.

O'Sullivan, L. F., & Allgeier, E. R. (1998). Feigning sexual desire: Consenting to unwanted sexual activity in heterosexual dating relationships. *Journal of Sex Research, 35,* 234–243.

O'Sullivan, L. F., Byers, E. S., & Finkelman, L. (1998). A comparison of male and female college students' experiences of sexual coercion. *Psychology of Women Quarterly, 22*(2), 177–195.

O*NET Resource Center. (2014). Production Database—O*NET 19.0. Retrieved from http://www.onetcenter.org/database.html

Oakes, W. (1972). External validity and the use of real people as subjects. *American Psychologist, 27,* 959–962.

Obach, M. S. (2003). A longitudinal-sequential study of perceived academic competence and motivational beliefs for learning among children in middle school. *Educational Psychology, 23,* 323–338.

Oettingen, G., & Gollwitzer, P. M. (2001). Goal setting and goal striving. In A. Tesser & N. Schwarz (Eds.), *Blackwell handbook of social psychology: Intraindividual processes* (pp. 329–348). Oxford: Blackwell.

Okwumabua, J. O., & Duryea, E. J. (2003). Depressive symptoms and decision making among African American youth. *Journal of Adolescent Research, 18,* 436–453.

Olatunji, B. O. (2008). Disgust, scrupulosity and conservative attitudes about sex: Evidence for a mediational model of homophobia. *Journal of Research in Personality, 42*(5), 1364–1369.

Oliner, S. P., & Oliner, P. M. (1988). *The altruistic personality: Rescuers of Jews in Nazi Europe.* New York: The Free Press. Also see Midlarsky, E., Jones, S. F., & Corley, R. P. (2005). Personality correlates of heroic rescue during the holocaust. *Journal of Personality, 73,* 907–934.

Oliver, M. B., & Hyde, J. S. (1993). Gender differences in sexuality: A meta-analysis. *Psychological Bulletin, 114,* 29–51.

Olivola, C. Y., & de Neve, J. E. (2012). Going with your gut feelings lands you in the gutter: Decision making style in adolescence predicts financial well-being in adulthood. Manuscript submitted for publication. University of Warwick, United Kingdom.

Olson, J. M., Roese, N. J., & Zanna, M. P. (1996). Expectancies. In E. T. Higgins & A. W. Kruglanski (Eds.), *Social psychology: Handbook of basic principles* (pp. 211–239). New York: Guilford Press.

Olson, M. A., & Fazio, R. H. (2001). Implicit attitude formation through classical conditioning. *Psychological Science, 12,* 413–417.

Olson, M. A., & Fazio, R. H. (2009). Implicit and explicit measures of attitudes: The Perspective of the MODE model. In R. E. Petty, R. H. Fazio, & P. Briñol (Eds.), *Insights from the new implicit measures* (pp. 19–63). New York: Psychology Press.

Olson, S. (2014, July 30). Anti-vaccine mothers refuse vitamin K to help deficient babies just because it's an injection. *Medical Daily.* Retrieved from http://

www.medicaldaily.com/anti-vaccine-mothers-refuse-vitamin-k-help-deficient-babies-just-because-its-injection-295808

Olweus, D. (1978). *Aggression in the schools: Bullies and whipping boys.* Washington, DC: Hemisphere (Wiley).

Olweus, D. (1994). Bullying at school: Long-term outcomes for the victims and an effective school-based intervention program. In R. Huesmann (Ed.), *Aggressive behavior: Current perspectives* (pp. 97–130). New York: Plenum Press.

Ones, D. S., Viswesvaran, C., & Schmidt, F. L. (1993). Comprehensive meta-analysis of integrity test validities: Findings for personnel selection and theories of job performance. *Journal of Applied Psychology, 78*(4), 679–703.

Orbell, J. M., van de Kragt, A. J. C., & Dawes, R. M. (1988). Explaining discussion-induced comparison. *Journal of Personality and Social Psychology, 54,* 811–819.

Orne, M. T. (1962). On the social psychology of the psychological experiment: With particular reference to demand characteristics and their implications. *American Psychologist, 17*(11), 776–783.

Ornstein, P. A., Ceci, S. J., & Loftus, E. F. (1998). Adult recollections of childhood abuse: Cognitive and developmental perspectives. *Psychology, Public Policy, and Law, 7,* 1025–1051.

Ornstein, R. (1991). *The evolution of consciousness: Of Darwin, Freud, and cranial fire: The origins of the way we think.* New York: Prentice Hall.

Orobio de Castro, B., Veerman, J. W., Koops, W., Bosch, J. D., & Monshouwer, H. J. (2002). Hostile attribution of intent and aggressive behavior: A meta-analysis. *Child Development, 73,* 916–934.

Orr, E. S., Sisic, M., Ross, C., Simmering, M. G., Arseneault, J. M., & Orr, R. R. (2009). The influence of shyness on the use of Facebook in an undergraduate sample. *CyberPsychology & Behavior, 12*(3), 337–340.

Orth, U., Robins, R. W., & Widaman, K. F. (2012). Life-span development of self-esteem and its effects on important life outcomes. *Journal of Personality and Social Psychology, 102,* 1271–1288.

Orville Redenbacher Company Website. Retrieved August 20, 2012, from http://www.orville.com/homemade-popcorn

Ostroff, C., Kinicki, A. J., & Tamkins, M. M. (2003). Organizational culture and climate. In W. C. Borman, D. R. Ilgen, & R. J. Klimoski (Eds.), *Handbook of psychology: Industrial and organizational psychology* (Vol. 12, pp. 565–593). New York: Wiley.

Oswald, I., Taylor, A. M., & Treisman, M. (1960). Discriminative responses to stimulation during human sleep. *Brain, 83,* 440–453.

Otis, C. C., Greathouse, S. M., Kennard, J. B., & Kovera, M. B. (2014). Hypothesis testing in attorney-conducted voir dire. *Law and Human Behavior, 38,* 392–404.

Ottaviani, R., & Beck, A. T. (1987). Cognitive aspects of panic disorders. *Journal of Anxiety Disorders, 1,* 15–28.

Ouellette, J. A., & Wood, W. (1998). Habit and intention in everyday life: The multiple processes by which past behavior predicts future behavior. *Psychological Bulletin, 124,* 54–74.

Ouwerkerk, J. W., Kerr, N. L., Gallucci, M., & Van Lange, P. A. M. (2005). Avoiding the social death penalty: Ostracism and cooperation in social dilemmas. In K. D. Williams, J. P. Forgas, & W. von Hippel (Eds.), *The social outcast: Ostracism, social exclusion, rejection, and bullying* (pp. 321–332). New York: Psychology Press.

Ouwerkerk, J. W., Van Lange, P. A., Gallucci, M., & Kerr, N. L. (2005). Avoiding the social death penalty: Ostracism and cooperation in social dilemmas. In K. D. Williams, J. P. Forgas, & W. von Hippel (Eds.), *The social outcast: Ostracism, social exclusion, rejection, and bullying* (pp. 321–332). New York: Psychology Press.

Overall, N. C., Girme, Y. U., Lemay, E. P., & Hammond, M. D. (2014). Attachment anxiety and reactions to

relationship threat: The benefits and costs of inducing guilt in romantic partners. *Journal of Personality and Social Psychology, 106,* 235–256.

Overing, J. (1986). Images of cannibalism, death and domination in a "non-violent" society. In D. Riches (Ed.), *The anthropology of violence* (pp. 86–101). Oxford: Blackwell.

Owen, J. (2004, July 23). Homosexual activity among animals stirs debate. *National Geographic.* Retrieved from http://news.nationalgeographic.com/news/2004/07/0722_040722_gayanimal.html

Padilla, A. M., & Ruiz, R. A. (1973). *Latino mental health: A review of literature.* Washington, DC: U.S. Government Printing Office.

Page, S. E. (2008). *The difference: How the power of diversity creates better groups, firms, schools, and societies.* Princeton, NJ: Princeton University Press.

Paik, H., & Comstock, G. (1994). The effects of television violence on antisocial behavior: A meta-analysis. *Communication Research, 21,* 516–546.

Palca, J. (2013, May 23). The weight of a med student's subconscious bias. *NPR.* Retrieved from http://www.npr.org/blogs/health/2013/05/23/186294402/the-weight-of-a-med-students-subconscious-bias

Paleari, G., Regalia, C., & Fincham, F. D. (2005). Marital quality, forgiveness, empathy, and rumination: A longitudinal analysis. *Personality and Social Psychology Bulletin, 31,* 368–378.

Palmer, M. A., & Brewer, N. (2012). Sequential lineup presentation promotes less-biased criterion setting but does not improve discriminability. *Law and Human Behavior, 36,* 247– 255.

Panksepp, J. (1998). *Affective neuroscience: The foundations of human and animal emotions.* London: Oxford University Press.

Panksepp, J., Herman, B. H., Conner, R., Bishop, P., & Scott, J. P. (1978). The biology of social attachments: Opiates alleviate separation distress. *Biological Psychiatry, 13,* 607–618.

Panksepp, J., Najam, N., & Soares, F. (1980). Morphine reduces social cohesion in rats. *Pharmacology, Biochemistry, and Behavior, 11,* 131–134.

Panksepp, J., Vilberg, T., Bean, N. J., Coy, D. H., & Kastin, A. J. (1978). Reduction of distress vocalization in chicks by opiate-like peptides. *Brain Research Bulletin, 3,* 663–667.

Paolini, S., Harwood, J., & Rubin, M. (2010). Negative intergroup contact makes group memberships salient: Explaining why intergroup conflict endures. Personality and Social Psychology Bulletin 36(12) 1723–1738. doi: 10.1177/0146167210388667

Papageorgis, D., & McGuire, W. J. (1961). The generality of immunity to persuasion produced by pre-exposure to weakened counterarguments. *Journal of Abnormal and Social Psychology, 62,* 475–481.

Pargament, K. I. (1997). *The psychology of religion and coping. Theory, research, practice.* New York: Guilford Press.

Parikh, R. (2011, January 20). Make anti-vaccine parents pay higher premiums. *CNN.* Retrieved from http://edition.cnn.com/2011/OPINION/01/20/parikh.childhood.immunizations/index.html?_s5PM:OPINION

Pariser, E. (2011). *The filter bubble: What the Internet is hiding from you.* New York: Penguin Press.

Park, C. (2003). In other (people's) words: Plagiarism by university students—literature and lessons. *Assessment and Evaluation in Higher Education, 28,* 471–488.

Park, J. H., & Schaller, M. (2009). Parasites, minds and cultures. *The Psychologist, 22,* 942–945.

Park, S. H., Westphal, J. D., & Stern, I. (2011). Set up for a fall: The insidious effects of flattery and opinion conformity toward corporate leaders. *Administrative Science Quarterly, 56,* 2257–2302.

Parker, S. D., Brewer, M. B., & Spencer, J. R. (1980). Natural disaster, perceived control and attributions to fate. *Personality & Social Psychology Bulletin, 6,* 454–459.

Parrott, D. J. (2009). Aggression toward gay men as gender role enforcement: Effects of male role norms,

sexual prejudice, and masculine gender role stress. *Journal of Personality, 77*(4), 1137–1166.

Parsley, A. (2009). 5 Things to Know About TV's Progressive Insurance Lady. *People.* Retrieved from http://www.people.com/people/article/0,,20301774,00.html

Patel, V., Thomson, G. W., & Wilson, N. (2013). Cigarette butt littering in city streets: A new methodology for studying and results. *Tobacco Control: An International Journal, 22*(1), 59–62. doi: 10.1136/tobaccocontrol-2012-050529

Patterson, O. (1982). *Slavery and social death.* Cambridge, MA: Harvard University Press.

Paul Rusesabagina. (2006, September 29). *BBC News.* Retrieved from http://news.bbc.co.uk/2/hi/programmes/hardtalk/5393104.stm

Paul, C., Fitzjohn, J., Herbison, P., & Dickson, N. (2000). The determinants of sexual intercourse before age 16. *Journal of Adolescent Health, 27,* 136–147.

Paulhus, D. L., & Levitt, K. (1987). Desirable responding triggered by affect: Automatic egotism? *Journal of Personality and Social Psychology, 52,* 245–259.

Paulhus, D. L, & Williams, K. M. (2002). The dark triad of personality: Narcissism, Machiavellianism, and psychopathy. *Journal of Research in Personality, 36*(6) 556–563. doi: 10.1016/S0092-6566(02)00505-6

Paulus, P. B. (2000). Groups, teams, and creativity: The creative potential of idea-generating groups. *Applied Psychology: An International Review, 49*(2), 237–262.

Paulus, P. B., & Matthews, R. (1980). Crowding, attribution, and task performance. *Basic and Applied Social Psychology, 1,* 3–13.

Paulus, P. B., Dzindolet, M. T., Poletes, G., & Camacho, L. M. (1993). Perception of performance in group brainstorming: The illusion of group productivity. *Personality and Social Psychology Bulletin, 19,* 78–89.

Payne, B. K. (2001). Prejudice and perception: The role of automatic and controlled processes in misperceiving a weapon. *Journal of Personality and Social Psychology, 81,* 181–192.

Payne, B. K., Govorun, O., & Arbuckle, N. L. (2008). Automatic attitudes and alcohol: Does implicit liking predict drinking? *Cognition and Emotion, 22,* 238–271.

Section 25.01 Payne, S. (2013, May 11). When did you choose to be straight? *Daily Kos.* Retrieved from http://www.dailykos.com/story/2013/05/11/1208457/-When-did-you-choose-to-be-straight

Pedersen, W. C., Miller, L. C., Putcha-Bhagavatula, A. D., & Yang, Y. (2002). Evolved sex differences in the number of partners desired? The long and short of it. *Psychological Science, 13,* 157–161.

Peluchette, J., & Karl, K. (2010). Examining students' intended image on Facebook: "What were they thinking?!" *Journal of Education for Business, 85*(1), 30–37.

Pendleton, M. (2014, September 9). Nike drops endorsement deal with Ray Rice. *FSS.* Retrieved from http://fullscalesports.com/2014/09/09/nike-drops-endorsement-deal-with-ray-rice/

Penner, L. A., Dertke, M. C., & Achenbach, C. J. (1973). The "flash" system: A field study of altruism. *Journal of Applied Social Psychology, 3,* 362–370.

Penton-Voak I. S., Thomas, J., Gage, S. H., McMurran, M., McDonald, S., & Munafò M. R. (2013). Increasing recognition of happiness in ambiguous facial expressions reduces anger and aggressive behavior. *Psychological Science, 24*(5), 688–697. doi: 10.1177/0956797612459657

Peplau, L. A., & Perlman, D. (Eds.). (1982). *Loneliness: A sourcebook of current theory, research, and therapy.* New York: Wiley.

Perera, H. N., & DiGiacomo, M. (2013). The relationship of trait emotional intelligence with academic performance: A meta-analytic review. *Learning and Individual Differences, 28*(12), 20–33. doi: 10.1016/j.lindif.2013.08.002

Perez, R. C. (1973). The effect of experimentally induced failure, self-esteem and sex on cognitive differentiation. *Journal of Abnormal Psychology, 81,* 74–79.

Peristiany, J. G. (Ed.). (1965). *Honour and shame: The values of Mediterranean society.* London: Weidenfeld & Nicolson.

Perry, C. L., Killen, J., Slinkard, L. A., & McAlister, A. L. (1980). Peer teaching and smoking prevention among junior high students. *Adolescence, 15,* 277–281.

Persons, J. B., & Rao, P. A. (1985). Longitudinal study of cognitions, life events, and depression in psychiatric inpatients. *Journal of Abnormal Psychology, 94,* 51–63.

Peters, K., & Kashima, Y. (2007). From social talk to social action: Shaping the social triad with emotion sharing. *Journal of Personality and Social Psychology, 93,* 780–797.

Peterson, C. K., & Harmon-Jones, E. (2012). Anger and testosterone: Evidence that situationally-induced anger relates to situationally-induced testosterone. *Emotion,* 12(5), 899-902. doi: 10.1037/a0025300

Peterson, C., & Seligman, M. E. P. (2004). *Character strengths and virtues.* New York: Oxford University Press.

Peterson, K., Malouff, J., & Thorsteinsson, E. B. (2011). A meta-analytic investigation of emotional intelligence and alcohol involvement. *Substance Use & Misuse,* 46(14), 1726–1733.

Peterson, N. G., Mumford, M. D., Borman, W. C., Jeanneret, P. R., & Fleishmann, E. A. (1999). *An occupational information system for the 21st century: The development of O*NET.* Washington, D.C.: American Psychological Association.

Pettigrew, T. F., & Tropp, L. R. (2005). Allport's intergroup contact hypothesis: Its history and influence. In J. F. Dovidio, P. Glick, & L. A. Rudman (Eds.), *On the nature of prejudice: Fifty years after Allport* (pp. 262–277). Malden, MA: Blackwell.

Pettigrew, T. F., & Tropp, L. R. (2006). A meta-analytic test of intergroup contact theory. *Journal of Personality and Social Psychology, 90,* 751–783.

Pettigrew, T. F., & Tropp, L. R. (2008). How does intergroup contact reduce prejudice? Meta-analytic tests of three mediators. *European Journal of Social Psychology, 38,* 922–934.

Pettiway, L. E. (1987). Arson for revenge: The role of environmental situation, age, sex, and race. *Journal of Quantitative Criminology,* 3(2), 169–184.

Petty, R. E., & Cacioppo, J. T. (1979). Issue involvement can increase or decrease persuasion by enhancing message-relevant cognitive responses. *Journal of Personality and Social Psychology, 37,* 1915–1926.

Petty, R. E., & Cacioppo, J. T. (1986). *Communication and persuasion: Central and peripheral routes to attitude change.* New York: Springer-Verlag.

Pew Research Center (2014, February 23). *Gay marriage.* Retrieved from http://www.pewresearch.org/data-trend/domestic-issues/attitudes-on-gay-marriage/

Pew Research Global Attitudes Project. (2014, March 13). Worldwide, many see belief in God as essential to morality. Retrieved from http://www.pewglobal.org/2014/03/13/worldwide-many-see-belief-in-god-as-essential-to-morality/

Pew Research. (2014, June 19). Gay marriage around the world. Retrieved from http://www.pewforum.org/2013/12/19/gay-marriage-around-the-world-2013/

Phillips, M., McAuliff, B. D., Kovera, M. B., & Cutler, B. L. (1999). Double-blind lineup administration as a safeguard against investigator bias. *Journal of Applied Psychology, 84,* 940–951.

Phillis, D. E., & Gromko, M. H. (1985). Sex differences in sexual activity: Reality or illusion? *Journal of Sex Research, 21,* 437–443.

Pickel, K. L. (1998). Unusualness and threat as possible causes of "weapon focus." *Memory, 6,* 277–295.

Pickel, K. L. (1999). The influence of context on the "weapon focus" effect. *Law and Human Behavior, 23,* 299–311.

Pickett, C. L., & Gardner, W. L. (2005). The social monitoring system: Enhanced sensitivity to social cues and information as an adaptive response to social exclusion and belonging need. In K. D. Williams, J. P. Forgas, & W. von Hippel (Eds.), *The social outcast: Ostracism, social exclusion, rejection, and bullying* (pp. 213–226). New York: Psychology Press.

Pihl, R. O., Young, S. N., Harden, P., Plotnick, S., Chamberlain, B., & Ervin, F. R. (1995). Acute effect of altered tryptophan levels and alcohol on aggression in normal human males. *Psychopharmacology, 119,* 353–360.

Piliavin, I. M., Piliavin, J. A. & Rodin, J. (1975). Costs, diffusion, and the stigmatized victim. *Journal of Personality and Social Psychology, 32,* 429–438.

Pines, A., & Aronson, E. (1983). Antecedents, correlates, and consequences of sexual jealousy. *Journal of Personality, 51,* 108–136.

Pinker, S. (2007, March 19). A history of violence. *New Republic,* 236(12), 18.

Pinker, S. (2011). *The better angels of our nature: Why violence has declined.* New York: Viking Adult.

Pitt, E. L. (2000). Domestic violence in gay and lesbian relationships. *Journal of the Gay and Lesbian Medical Association, 4,* 195–196.

Plant, E. A. (2004). Responses to interracial interactions over time. *Personality and Social Psychology Bulletin, 30,* 1458–1471.

Plant, E. A., & Devine, P. G. (1998). Internal and external motivation to respond without prejudice. *Journal of Personality and Social Psychology, 75,* 811–832.

Plant, E. A., & Devine, P. G. (2001). Responses to other-imposed pro-black pressure: Acceptance or backlash? *Journal of Experimental Social Psychology, 37,* 486–501.

Plant, E. A., & Peruche, B. M. (2005). The consequences of race for police officers' responses to criminal suspects. *Psychological Science, 16,* 180–183.

Platt, C. W. (1988). Effects of causal attributions for success on first-term college performance: A covariance structure model. *Journal of Educational Psychology, 80,* 569–578.

Platt, J. (1973). Social traps. *American Psychologist, 28,* 641–651.

Pliner, P., & Chaiken, S. (1990). Eating, social motives, and self-presentation in women and men. *Journal of Experimental Social Psychology, 26,* 240–254.

Plötner, M., Over, H., Carpenter, M., and Tomasello. M. (2015, April). Young children show the bystander effect in helping situations. Psychological Science, 26, 499–506.

Pocheptsova, A., Amir, O., Dhar, R., & Baumeister, R. F. (2009). Deciding without resources: Resource depletion and choice in context. *Journal of Marketing Research, 46,* 344–355. doi: 10.1509/jmkr.46.3.344

Pogorzelski, S., & Harriott, J. (2007). Finding keepers: The Monster guide to hiring and holding the world's best employees. McGraw Hill: New York.

Politano, J., & Lester, D. (1997). Self-destructiveness and credit card debt. *Psychological Reports, 81,* 634.

Political Blind Spot (2014, February 13). Through the 1950s, Africans and Native Americans were kept in zoos as exhibits. Retrieved from http://politicalblindspot.com/through-the-1950s-africans-and-native-americans-were-kept-in-zoos-as-exhibits/

Polivy, J. (1976). Perception of calories and regulation of intake in restrained and unrestrained subjects. *Addictive Behaviors, 1,* 237–243.

Pomazal, R. J. & Clore, G. L. (1973). Helping on the highway: The effects of dependency and sex. *Journal of Applied Social Psychology, 3,* 150–164.

Postmes, T., & Spears, R. (1998). Deindividuation and antinormative behavior: A meta-analysis. *Psychological Bulletin, 123,* 238–259.

Pottebaum, S. M., Keith, T. Z., & Ehly, S. W. (1986). Is there a causal relation between self-concept and academic achievement? *Journal of Educational Research, 79,* 140–144.

Pouwelse, M., Bolman, C., Lodewijkx, H., & Spaa, M. (2011). Gender differences and social support: Mediators or moderators between peer victimization and depressive feelings. *Psychology in the Schools,* 48(8), 800–814. doi: 10.1002/pits.20589

Powell, J., Lewis, P.A., Roberts, N., Garcia-Finana, M., & Dunbar, R.I.M. (2012). Orbital prefrontal cortex volume predicts social network size: An imaging study of individual differences in humans. *Proceedings of the Royal Society B, 279,* 2157–2162.

Powers, W. T. (1973). *Behavior: The control of perception.* Chicago: Aldine.

Pozzulo, J. D., & Lindsay, R. C. L. (1998). Identification accuracy of children versus adults: A meta-analysis. *Law and Human Behavior, 22,* 549–570.

Pozzulo, J. D., & Warren, K. L. (2003). Descriptions and identifications of strangers by youth and adult eyewitness. *Journal of Applied Psychology, 88,* 315–323.

Pratkanis, A. R., & Aronson, E. (1992). *Age of propaganda: The everyday use and abuse of persuasion.* New York: Henry Holt.

Pratkanis, A. R., Greenwald, A. G., Leippe, M. R., & Baumgardner, M. H. (1988). In search of reliable persuasion effects: III. The sleeper effect is dead: Long live the sleeper effect. *Journal of Personality and Social Psychology, 54,* 203–218.

Pratt, T. C., & Cullen, F. T. (2000). The empirical status of Gottfredson and Hirschi's general theory of crime: A meta-analysis. *Criminology, 38,* 931–964.

Prelec, D., & Simester, D. (2001). Always leave home without it. *Marketing Letters, 12,* 5–12.

Prochaska, J. O., & Prochaska, J. M. (2010). Self-directed change: A transtheoretical model. In *Social psychological foundations of clinical psychology* (pp. 431–440). New York: Guilford Press.

Prochaska, J. O., Redding, C. A., & Evers, K. E. (2002). The transtheoretical model and stages of change. In K. Glanz, B. K. Rimer, & F. M. Lewis (Eds.), *Health behavior and health education: Theory, research, and practice* (pp. 99–120). San Francisco: Jossey-Bass.

Prochaska, J. O., Wright, J. A., & Velicer, W. F. (2008). Evaluating theories of health behavior change: A hierarchy of criteria applied to the transtheoretical model. *Applied Psychology: An International Review,* 57(4), 561–588. doi: 10.1111/j.1464-0597.2008.00345.x

Pronin, E., Berger, J., & Molouki, S. (2007). Alone in a crowd of sheep: Asymmetric perceptions of conformity and their roots in an introspection illusion. *Journal of Personality and Social Psychology, 92,* 585–595.

Pronk, T. M., Karremans, J. C., Overbeek, G., Vermulst, A. A., & Wigboldus, D. H. J. (2010). What it takes to forgive: When and why executive functioning facilitates forgiveness. *Journal of Personality and Social Psychology,* 98(1), 119–131.

Pryor, J. B., Gibbons, F. X., Wicklund, R. A., Fazio, R. H., & Hood, R. (1977). Self-focused attention and self-report validity. *Journal of Personality, 45,* 513–527.

Pryor, J. B., Reeder, G. D., Yeadon, C., & Hesson-McInnis, M. (2004). A dual-process model of reactions to perceived stigma. *Journal of Personality and Social Psychology, 87,* 436–452.

Psalms 14: 1 (Bible; King James version).

(a) Public Policy Polling (2013, October 8). Americans like witches, the IRS, and even hemorrhoids better than Congress. Retrieved from http://www.publicpolicypolling.com/main/2013/10/americans-like-witches-the-irs-and-even-hemorrhoids-better-than-congress.html

Purcell, A. H. (1981, February). The world's trashiest people: Will they clean up their act or throw away their future? *The Futurist, 2,* 51–59.

Pyszczynski, T., Greenberg, J., & Holt, K. (1985). Maintaining consistency between self-serving beliefs and available data: A bias in information processing. *Personality and Social Psychology Bulletin, 11,* 179–190.

Quarantelli, E. L. (1998). *What is a disaster?* New York: Routledge.

Quas, J. A., Bottoms, B. L., Haegerich, T. M., & Nysse-Carris, K. L. (2002). Effects of victim, defendant, and juror gender on decisions in child sexual assault cases. *Journal of Applied Social Psychology, 32,* 1993–2021.

Quinlivan, D. S., Neuschatz, J. S., Cutler, B. L., Wells, G. L., McClung, J., & Harker, D. L. (2012). Do pre-admonition suggestions moderate the effect of unbiased lineup instructions? *Legal and Criminological Psychology, 17,* 165–176.

Quinones, M. A., Ford, J. K., & Teachout, M. S. (1995). The relationship between work experience and job performance: A conceptual and meta-analytic review. *Personnel Psychology,* 48(4), 887–910.

Quoidbach, J., Gruber, J., Mikolajczak, M., Kogan, A., Kotsou, I., & Norton, M. I. (2014). Emodiversity and the emotional ecosystem. *Journal of Experimental Psychology: General.*

Quoted by Krauthammer, C. (1997, June 29). Apology is not ours to give. *Cleveland Plain Dealer*, p. 2–E.

Quotes – Henry Ford. Retrieved from http://quotes4all.net/henry%20ford:3.html

Ragins, B. R., & Cotton, J. L. (1999). Mentor functions and outcomes: A comparison of men and women in formal and informal mentoring relationships. *Journal of Applied Psychology, 84*(4), 529–550.

Raphael, T. (2010, June 22). Employee referral programs using more social media. Retrieved from http://www.ere.net/2010/06/22/employee-referral-programs-using-more-social-media/

Raskin, R., & Terry, H. (1988). A principal-components analysis of the Narcissistic Personality Inventory and further evidence of its construct validation. *Journal of Personality and Social Psychology, 54*, 890–902.

Ravitz, J. (2011, March 23). Road trip to the end of the world. *CNN News.* Retrieved from: http://edition.cnn.com/2011/LIVING/03/06/judgment.day.caravan/index.html

Reams, M. A., Geaghan, J. P., & Gendron, R. C. (1996). The link between recycling and litter: A field study. *Environment and Behavior, 28*, 92–110.

Regnerus, M. (2011). *Premarital sex in America: How young Americans meet, mate, and think about marrying.* New York: Oxford University Press.

Reich, J. W., & Robertson, J. L. (1979). Reactance and norm appeal in anti-littering messages. *Journal of Applied Social Psychology, 9*, 91–101.

Reinisch, J. (1990). *The Kinsey Institute new report on sex: What you must know to be sexually literate.* Stuttgart: St. Martin's Press. (Quotation on p. 89).

Reinsch, J., & Spotanski, C. (2005). Human territoriality: The effects of status on personalization and demarcation. *Journal of Psychological Inquiry 10*(1), 16–21.

Reis, H. T. (1990). The role of intimacy in interpersonal relations. *Journal of Social and Clinical Psychology, 9*, 15–30.

Reiss, I. L. (1986). A sociological journey into sexuality. *Journal of Marriage and the Family, 48*, 233–242.

Reiss, I. L. (1986). *Journey into sexuality.* New York: Prentice Hall.

Reiter, S. M., & Samuel, W. (1980). Littering as a function of prior litter and the presence or absence of prohibitive signs. *Journal of Applied Social Psychology, 10*, 45–55.

Remland, M. S., Jones, T. S., & Brinkman, H. (1995). Interpersonal distance, body orientation, and touch: Effects of culture, gender, and age. *Journal of Social Psychology, 135*, 281–297.

Reno, R. R., Cialdini, R. B., & Kallgren, C. A. (1993). The trans-situational influence of social norms. *Journal of Personality and Social Psychology, 64*, 104–112.

Renzetti, C. M. (1992). *Violent betrayal: Partner abuse in lesbian relationships.* Newbury Park, CA: Sage.

Repetti, R. L. (1997). *The effects of daily job stress on parent behavior with preadolescents.* Paper presented at the biennial meeting of the Society for Research in Child Development, Washington, DC.

Report: Tobacco use kills 6M people a year. (2010, November 27). *CBS New Healthwatch.* Retrieved from http://www.cbsnews.com/stories/2009/08/26/health/main5266774.shtml

Reston, J., Jr. (1981). *Our father who art in hell.* New York: Times Books.

Retrieved from http://money.cnn.com/2013/08/14/pf/cost-children/

Reykowski, J. (1982). Motivation and prosocial behavior. In V. Derlega & J. Grzelak (Eds.), *Cooperation and helping behavior: Theories and research* (pp. 352–375). New York: Academic Press.

Rhee, H., & Bell, D. R. (2002). The inter-store mobility of supermarket shoppers. *Journal of Retailing, 78*, 225–237.

Rhet. I.3, 1358a37ff.

Rhet. II.1, 1378a6ff.

Rhine, R. J., Hill, S. J., & Wandruff, S. E. (1967). Evaluative responses of preschool children. *Child Development, 38*, 1035–1042.

Rhodes, N., & Wood, W. (1992). Self-esteem and intelligence affect influenceability: The mediating role of message reception. *Psychological Bulletin, 111*, 156–171.

Rhodewalt, F., & Agustdottir, S. (1986). Effects of self-presentation on the phenomenal self. *Journal of Personality and Social Psychology, 50*, 47–55.

Richard Dawkins, an original thinker who bashes orthodoxy. (2011, 19 September). *New York Times.* Retrieved from http://www.nytimes.com/2011/09/20/science/20dawkins.html?pagewanted5all

Richards, Z., & Hewstone, M. (2001). Subtyping and subgrouping: Processes for the prevention and promotion of stereotype change. *Personality and Social Psychology Review, 5*, 52–73.

Richeson, J. A., & Shelton, J. N. (2003). When prejudice doesn't pay: Effects of interracial contact on executive function. *Psychological Science, 14*, 287–290.

Richeson, J. A., Trawalter, S., & Shelton, J. N. (2005). African Americans' implicit racial attitudes and the depletion of executive function after interracial interactions. *Social Cognition, 23*, 336–352.

Richman, J. A., & Flaherty, J. A. (1986). Sex differences in drinking among medical students: Patterns and psychosocial correlates. *Journal of Studies on Alcohol, 47*, 283–289.

Ridley, M. (1993). *The red queen: Sex and evolution in human nature.* New York: Penguin.

Ridley, M. (2004). *Evolution* (3rd ed.). Oxford: Blackwell Science.

Righetti, F., & Finkenauer, C. (2011). If you are able to control yourself, I will trust you: The role of perceived self-control in interpersonal trust. *Journal of Personality and Social Psychology, 100*, 874–886.

Right hand diamonds marketed to women as power sign. (2003, December 2). *Sacramento Bee.* Retrieved from http://www.sacbee.com/content/business/story/7887166p-8825882c.html

Ringelmann, M. (1913). Recherches sur les moteurs animés: Travail de l'homme. *Annales de l'Institut National Argonomique*, 2e srie, tom 12, 1–40. Published in French, cited in Kravitz, D. A., & Martin, B. (1986). Ringelmann rediscovered: The original article. *Journal of Personality and Social Psychology, 50*, 936–941.

Rippere, V. (1977). "What's the thing to do when you're feeling depressed?" A pilot study. *Behaviour Research and Therapy, 15*, 185–191.

Risen, J. L., Gilovich, T., & Dunning, D. (2007). One-shot illusory correlations and stereotype formation. *Personality and Social Psychology Bulletin, 33*(11), 1492–1502.

Ritson, J. (1802). *An essay on abstinence from animal food, as a moral duty.* London: Richard Phillips.

Ritter, R. S., & Preston, J. L. (2011). Gross gods and icky atheism: Disgust responses to rejected religious beliefs. *Journal of Experimental Social Psychology, 47*(6), 1225–1230.

Rivis, A., Abraham, C., & Snook, S. (2011). Understanding young and older male drivers' willingness to drive while intoxicated: The predictive utility of constructs specified by the theory of planned behaviour and the prototype willingness model. *British Journal of Health Psychology, 16*(2), 445–456. doi: 10.1348/135910710X522662

Roach, M. (2004). *Stiff: The curious lives of human cadavers.* New York: W. W. Norton.

Robbins, J. M., Ford, M. T., & Tetrick, L. E. (2012). Perceived unfairness and employee health: A meta-analytic integration. *Journal of Applied Psychology, 97*(2), 235–272.

Roberts, J. (2012, February 28). *How to begin analyzing social media.* Retrieved August 20, 2012, from http://www.collectiveintellect.com/blog/brand-tracker-super-bowl-2012.

Roberts, J. (2013, November 2). Three pages of Rand Paul's book were plagiarized from think tanks. *Reuters.* Retrieved from http://www.buzzfeed.com/andrewkaczynski/entire-section-of-rand-pauls-book-copied-verbatim-from-case#1m04yi5

Roberts, W. A. (2002). Are animals stuck in time? *Psychological Bulletin, 128*, 473–489.

Robinson, P. (1995). *Schindler's List teaching guide.* Available at http://www.southerninstitute.info/holocaust_education/schind.html

Roehling, M. V., Roehling, P. V., & Odland, L. M. (2008). Investigating the validity of stereotypes about overweight employees: The relationship between body weight and normal personality traits. *Group and Organization Management, 33*(4), 392–424.

Roese, N. J., & Olson, J. M. (1997). Counterfactual thinking: The intersection of affect and function. In M. P. Zanna (Ed.), *Advances in experimental social psychology* (Vol. 29, pp. 1–59). New York: Academic Press.

Rogers, C. R. (1961). *On becoming a person.* Boston: Houghton Mifflin.

Rogers, E. M. (1983). *Diffusion of innovations.* New York: Free Press.

Rogers, T. B., Kuiper, N. A., & Kirker, W. S. (1977). Self-reference and the encoding of personal information. *Journal of Personality and Social Psychology, 35*, 677–688.

Rogow, A. A, Carey, G. L., & Farrell, C. (1957). The significance of aphorisms in American culture. *Sociology and Social Research, 41*, 417–420.

Rohrer, J. H., Baron, S. H., Hoffman, E. L., & Swander, D. V. (1954). The stability of autokinetic judgments. *Journal of Abnormal and Social Psychology, 49*(4, Pt. 1), 595–597.

Romero-Canyas, R., & Downey, G. (2005). Rejection sensitivity as a predictor of affective and behavioral responses to interpersonal stress: A defensive motivational system. In K. D. Williams, J. P. Forgas, & W. von Hippel (Eds.), *The social outcast: Ostracism, social exclusion, rejection, and bullying* (pp. 131–154). New York: Psychology Press.

Roney, J. R. (2003). Effects of visual exposure to the opposite sex: Cognitive aspects of mate attraction in human males. *Personality and Social Psychology Bulletin, 29*(3), 393–404.

Roney, J. R., Mahler, S. V., & Maestripieri, D. (2003). Behavioral and hormonal responses of men to brief interactions with women. *Evolution and Human Behavior, 24*, 365–375.

Rosen, R. J. (2013, March 29). Facebook: 2.7 million people showed their support for marriage equality by changing their profile pictures. *The Atlantic.* Retrieved from http://www.theatlantic.com/technology/archive/2013/03/facebook-27-million-people-showed-their-support-for-marriage-equality-by-changing-their-profile-pictures/274497/

Rosenbaum, M. E. (1986). The repulsion hypothesis: On the nondevelopment of relationships. *Journal of Personality and Social Psychology, 51*, 1156–1166.

Rosenberg, M. (1979). *Conceiving the self.* New York: Basic Books.

Rosenberg, M., Schooler, C., & Schoenbach, C. (1989). Self-esteem and adolescent problems: Modeling reciprocal effects. *American Sociological Review, 54*, 1004–1018.

Rosenfeld, D. L., Folger, R., & Adelman, H. F. (1980). When rewards reflect competence: A qualification of the overjustification effect. *Journal of Personality and Social Psychology, 39*, 368–376.

Rosenhan, D. L., & White, G. M. (1967). Observation and rehearsal as determinants of prosocial behavior. *Journal of Personality and Social Psychology, 5*, 424–431.

Rosenman, R. H., & Chesney, M. A. (1982). Stress, Type A behavior and coronary heart disease. In L. Goldberger & S. Breznitz (Eds.), *Handbook of stress: Theoretical and clinical aspects* (pp. 547–565). New York: Free Press.

Rosenstock, I. M. (1960). What research in motivation suggests for public health. *American Journal of Public Health, 50*, 295–301.

Rosenstock, I. M., Strecher, & Becker, M. H. (1988). The health belief model and HIV risk behavior change. In J. Peterson & R. DiClemente (Eds.), *Preventing AIDS: Theory and practice of behavior interventions* (pp. 5–24). New York: Plenum Press.

Rosenthal, E. (2008, February 2). Motivated by a tax, Irish spurn plastic bags. *New York Times*. Retrieved from http://www.nytimes.com/2008/02/02/world/europe/02bags.html?_r51&pagewanted51

Rosenthal, R. (2002). Covert communication in classrooms, clinics, courtrooms, and cubicles. *American Psychologist, 57*, 839–849.

Rosenthal, R., & Jacobson, L. (1968). *Pygmalion in the classroom: Teacher expectation and pupils' intellectual development*. New York: Rinehart and Winston.

Roskies, E., & Louis-Guerin, C. (1990). Job insecurity in managers: Antecedents and consequences. *Journal of Organizational Behavior, 11*, 345–359.

Ross, Edward A. (1974. Original work published 1908). *Social Psychology*. New York: Arno Press.

Ross, J. A. (2006, November). The reliability, validity, and utility of self-assessment. *Practical assessment, Research & Evaluation, 11*(10) [On-line]. Retrieved from http://pareonline.net/pdf/v11n10.pdf

Ross, L., Greene, D. & House, P. (1977). The false consensus effect: An egocentric bias in social perception and attributional processes. *Journal of Experimental Social Psychology, 13*, 279–301.

Ross, L., Lepper, M. R., & Hubbard, M. (1975). Perseverance in self-perception and social perception: Biased attributional processes in the debriefing paradigm. *Journal of Personality and Social Psychology, 32*, 880–892.

Ross, M. (1989). The relation of implicit theories to the construction of personal histories. *Psychological Review, 96*, 341–357.

Ross, M., & Sicoiy, F. (1979). Egocentric biases in availability and attribution. *Journal of Personality and Social Psychology, 37*, 322–336.

Ross, S. M. (1996). Risk of physical abuse to children of spouse abusing parents. *Child Abuse and Neglect, 20*, 589–598.

Rotenberg, K. J., Addis, N., Betts, L. R., Corrigan, A., Fox, C., Hobson, Z., Rennison, S., Trueman, M., & Boulton, M. J. (2010). The relation between trust beliefs and loneliness during early childhood, middle childhood, and adulthood. *Personality and Social Psychology Bulletin, 36*, 1086–1100.

Roth, P. L., BeVier, C. A., Switzer, F. S., & Schippmann, J. S. (1996). Meta-analyzing the relationship between grades and job performance. *Journal of Applied Psychology, 81*(5), 548–556.

Rothbart, M. K. (1989). Temperament and development. In G. A. Kohnstamm, J. E. Bates, & M. K. Rothbart (Eds.), *Temperament in childhood* (pp. 187–247). New York: Wiley.

Rothberg, J. M., & Jones, F. D. (1987). Suicide in the U.S. Army: Epidemiological and periodic aspects. *Suicide and Life-Threatening Behavior, 17*, 119–132.

Rothman, A. J., Bartels, R. D., Wlaschin, J., & Salovey, P. (2006). The strategic use of gain- and loss-framed messages to promote healthy behavior: How theory can inform practice. *Journal of Communication, 56*(Suppl. 1), S202–S220.

Rothschild, Z. K., Landau, M. J., Sullivan, D., & Keefer, L. A. (2012). A dual-motive model of scapegoating: Displacing blame to reduce guilt or increase control. *Journal of Personality and Social Psychology, 102*, 1148–1163.

Rotton, J. (1979). The air pollution experience and physical aggression. *Journal of Applied Social Psychology, 9*, 397–412.

Rotton, J., & Frey, J. (1985). Air pollution, weather, and violent crimes: Concomitant time-series analysis of archival data. *Journal of Personality and Social Psychology, 49*, 1207–1220.

Rowatt, W. C., Cunningham, M. R., & Druen, P. B. (1999). Lying to get a date: The effect of facial physical attractiveness on the willingness to deceive prospective dating partners. *Journal of Social and Personal Relationships, 16*(2), 209–223.

Roy Rosenzweig Center for History and New Media. (2006, December). *An outline of the Anita Hill and Clarence Thomas controversy* [On-line]. Retrieved from http://chnm.gmu.edu/courses/122/hill/hillframe.htm

Rozin, P., & Royzman, E. B. (2001). Negativity bias, negativity dominance, and contagion. *Personality and Social Psychology Review, 5*, 296–320.

Rozin, P., Haidt, J., & McCauley, C. R. (1993). Disgust. In M. Lewis & J. M. Haviland (Eds.), *Handbook of emotions* (pp. 575–594). New York: Guilford Press.

Rozin, P., Haidt, J., & McCauley, C. R. (2009). Disgust: The body and soul emotion in the 21st century. In B. O. Olatunji & D. McKay (Eds.), *Disgust and its disorders: Theory, assessment, and treatment implications* (pp. 9–29). Washington, DC: American Psychological Association.

Rozin, P., Markwith, M., & McCauley, C. (1994). Sensitivity to indirect contacts with other persons: AIDS aversion as a composite of aversion to strangers, infection, moral taint, and misfortune. *Journal of Abnormal Psychology, 103*, 495–505.

Ruback, R. B. & Juieng, D. (1997). Territorial defense in parking lots: Retaliation against waiting drivers. *Journal of Applied Social Psychology, 27*, 821–834.

Rubin, D. B. (2008). Fanning the vaccine–autism link. *Neurology Today, 8*(15), 3. doi:10.1097/01.NT.0000335577.64245.34

Ruble, D. N., Fleming, A. S., Hackel, L. S., & Stangor, C. (1988). Changes in the marital relationship during the transition to first time motherhood: Effects of violated expectations concerning division of household labor. *Journal of Personality and Social Psychology, 55*, 78–87.

Rucci, A. J. (2008). I-O psychology's "core purpose": Where science and practice meet. *The Industrial and Organizational Psychologist, 46*(1), 17–34.

Rudski, J. M. (2002). Hindsight and confirmation biases in an exercise in telepathy. *Psychological Reports, 91*, 899–906.

Ruedy, N. E., Moore, C., Gino, F., & Schweitzer, M. E. (2013). The cheater's high: The unexpected affective benefits of unethical behavior. *Journal of Personality and Social Psychology, 105*(4), 531–548. doi: 10.1037/a0034231

Rupert, G. (1989). Employee referrals as a source of recruitment and job performance. *Proceedings of the 10th Annual Graduate Conference in Industrial/Organizational Psychology and Organizational Behavior.*

Rupp, D. E., & Cropanzano, R. (2002). The mediating effects of social exchange relationships in predicting workplace outcomes from multifoci organizational justice. *Organizational Behavior and Human Decision Processes, 89*, 925–946.

Rusbult, C. E. (1983). A longitudinal test of the investment model: The development (and deterioration) of satisfaction and commitment in heterosexual involvements. *Journal of Personality and Social Psychology, 45*, 101–117.

Rusbult, C. E., & Martz, J. M. (1995). My relationship is better than—and not as bad as—yours is: The perception of superiority in close relationships. *Personality and Social Psychology Bulletin, 21*, 558–571.

Rusbult, C. E., Morrow, G. D., & Johnson, D. J. (1987). Self-esteem and problem solving behavior in close relationships. *British Journal of Social Psychology, 26*, 293–303.

Ruscio, J. (2002). *Clear thinking with psychology: Separating sense from nonsense*. Pacific Grove, CA: Wadsworth.

Rushton, J. P., Brainerd, C. J., & Pressley, M. (1983). Behavioral development and construct validity: The principle of aggregation. *Psychological Bulletin, 94*, 18–38.

Rushton, J. P., Chrisjohn, R. D., & Fekken, G. C. (1981). The altruistic personality and the Self-Report Altruism Scale. *Personality and Individual Differences, 2*, 293–302.

Rushton, J. P., Fulker, D. W., Neale, M. C., Nias, D. K. B., & Eysenck, H. J. (1986). Altruism and aggression: The heritability of individual differences. *Journal of Personality and Social Psychology, 50*, 1192–1198.

Russakoff, R., & Goodman, M. (2011, July 14). Employee theft: Are you blind to it. *CBS Money Watch*. Retrieved from http://www.cbsnews.com/news/employee-theft-are-you-blind-to-it/

Russell, D., Peplau, L. A., & Cutrona, C. E. (1980). The revised UCLA Loneliness Scale: Concurrent and discriminant validity evidence. *Journal of Personality and Social Psychology, 39*, 472–480.

Russell, V. M., McNulty, J. K., Baker, L. R., & Meltzer, A. L. (2014). The association between discontinuing hormonal contraceptives and wives' marital satisfaction depends on husbands' facial attractiveness. *PNAS, 111*, 17081–17086.

Ruva, C. L., & Guenther, C. C. (2014). From the shadows into the light: How pretrial publicity and deliberation affect mock jurors' decisions, impressions, and memory. *Law and Human Behavior*. Published online, December 15, 2014. doi: 10.1037/lhb0000117

Ruva, C. L., & LeVasseur, M. A. (2012). Behind closed doors: The effect of pretrial publicity on jury deliberations. *Psychology, Crime & Law, 18*, 431–452.

Ruva, C. L., McEvoy, C., & Bryant, J. B. (2007). Effects of pre-trial publicity and jury deliberation on juror bias and source memory errors. *Applied Cognitive Psychology, 21*, 45–67.

Rwanda: How the genocide happened. (2004, December 18). *BBC News*. Retrieved from http://news.bbc.co.uk/2/hi/africa/1288230.stm

Ryan, J. R. (2009, February 27). Learning agility equals leadership success, *Bloomberg Businessweek*. Retrieved from http://www.businessweek.com/managing/content/feb2009/ca20090227_893956.htm

Ryan, R. M. (1982). Control and information in the intrapersonal sphere: An extension of cognitive evaluation theory. *Journal of Personality and Social Psychology, 43*, 450–461.

Ryan, R. M., & Deci, E. L. (2000). Self-determination theory and the facilitation of intrinsic motivation, social development, and well-being. *American Psychologist, 55*, 68–78.

Ryan, R. M., & Grolnick, W. S. (1986). Origin and pawns in the classroom: Self-report and projective assessments of individual differences in children's perceptions. *Journal of Personality and Social Psychology, 50*, 550–558.

Ryan, R. M., Weinstein, N., Bernstein, J., Brown, K. W., Mistretta, L., & Gagné, M. (2010). Vitalizing effects of being outdoors and in nature. *Journal of Environmental Psychology, 30* (2), 159–168. doi: 10.1016/j.jenvp.2009.10.009

Ryan, T., & Xenos, S. (2011). Who uses Facebook? An investigation into the relationship between the Big Five, shyness, narcissism, loneliness, and Facebook usage. *Computers in Human Behavior, 27*(5), 1658–1664.

Rydell, R. J., & McConnell, A. R. (2006). Understanding implicit and explicit attitude change: A systems of reasoning analysis. *Journal of Personality and Social Psychology, 91*, 995–1008.

Ryff, C. D. (1995). Psychological well-being in adult life. *Current Directions in Psychological Science, 4*, 99–104.

Rynd, N. (1988). Incidence of psychometric symptoms in rape victims. *Journal of Sex Research, 24*, 155–161.

Sackett, P. R., & DeVore, C. J. (2001). Counterproductive behaviors at work. In N. Anderson, D. S. Ones, H. K. Sinangil, & C. Viswesvaran, *Handbook of industrial, work and organizational psychology* (Vol. 1, pp. 145–165). Thousand Oaks, CA: Sage.

Sackett, P. R., Hardison, C. M., & Cullen, M. J. (2004). On interpreting stereotype threat as accounting for African American–White differences on cognitive tests. *American Psychologist, 59*, 7–13.

Sackett, P. R., Hardison, C. M., & Cullen, M. J. (2004b). On the value of correcting mischaracterizations of stereotype threat research. *American Psychologist, 59*, 48–49.

Saegert, S. (1978). High density environments: Their personal and social consequences. In A. Baum & Y. M. Epstein (Eds.), *Human response to crowding* (pp. 259–276). Hillsdale, NJ: Erlbaum.

Saegert, S., MacIntosh, E., & West, S. (1975). Two studies of crowding in urban public spaces. *Environment and Behavior, 1*, 159–184.

Safer, M. A., Christianson, S.-A., Autry, M. W., & Osterlund, K. (1998). Tunnel memory for traumatic events. *Applied Cognitive Psychology, 12*, 99–117.

Sagie, A. (1997). Leader direction and employee participation in decision making: Contradictory or compatible practices? *Applied Psychology: An International Review, 46*(4), 387–452.

Sakaki, M., Fryker, K., & Mather, M. (2014). Emotion strengthens high-priority memory traces but weakens low-priority memory traces. *Psychological Science, 25,* 387–395.

Salgado, J. F., Viswesvaran, C., & Ones, D. (2001). Predictors used for personnel selection: An overview of constructs, methods and techniques. In N. Anderson, D. S. Ones, H. K. Sinangil, & C. Viswesvaran, *Handbook of industrial, work and organizational psychology* (Vol. 1, pp. 166–199). Thousand Oaks, CA: Sage.

Sallie Mae. (2009). *How undergraduate students use credit cards: Sallie Mae's National Study of Usage Rates and Trends 2009.* Retrieved August 20, 2012, from http://static.mgnetwork.com/rtd/pdfs/20090830_iris.pdf

Salmivalli, C., Kaukiainen, A., Kaistaniemi, L., & Lagerspetz, K. M. J. (1999). Self-evaluated self-esteem, peer-evaluated self-esteem, and defensive egotism as predictors of adolescents' participation in bullying situations. *Personality and Social Psychology Bulletin, 25,* 1268–1278.

Salovey, P., & Mayer, J. D. (1990). Emotional intelligence. *Imagination, Cognition, and Personality, 9,* 185–211.

Salovey, P., & Rodin, J. (1991). Provoking jealousy and envy: Domain relevance and self-esteem threat. *Journal of Social and Clinical Psychology, 10,* 395–413.

Sandelands, L. E., Brockner, J., & Glynn, M. A. (1988). If at first you don't succeed, try, try again: Effects of persistence-performance contingencies, ego involvement, and self-esteem on task persistence. *Journal of Applied Psychology, 73,* 208–216.

Sanders, S. A., & Reinisch, J. M. (1999). Would you say you "had sex" if . . . ? *Journal of the American Medical Association, 281,* 275–277.

Sanna, L. J., & Schwarz, N. (2003). Using the hindsight bias: The role of accessibility experiences and (mis) attributions. *Journal of Experimental Social Psychology, 39,* 287–295.

Santos, F. (2014, February 26). Arizona governor vetoes bill on refusal of service to gays. *New York Times.* Retrieved from http://www.nytimes.com/2014/02/27/us/Brewer-arizona-gay-service-bill.html?_r50

Santos, M. D., Leve, C., & Pratkanis, A. R. (1994). Hey buddy, can you spare seventeen cents? Mindful persuasion and the pique technique. *Journal of Applied Social Psychology, 24,* 755–764.

Sapolsky, R. M. (1998). *The trouble with testosterone: And other essays on the biology of the human predicament* (p. 150). New York: Scribner.

Sarason, B. R., Sarason, I. G., & Gurung, R. A. R. (2001). Close personal relationships and health outcomes: A key to the role of social support. In B. R. Sarason & S. Duck (Eds.), *Personal relationships. Implications for clinical and community psychology* (pp. 15–41). Chichester: Wiley.

Sargent, J. D., Dalton, M. A., Beach M. L., Mott, L. A., Tickle, J. J., Ahrens, M. B., et al. (2002). Viewing tobacco use in movies: does it shape attitudes that mediate adolescent smoking? *American Journal of Preventive Medicine, 22*(3), 137–145.

Sargent, J. D., Dalton, M. A., Heatherton, T. & Beach, M. (2003). Modifying exposure to smoking depicted in movies: A novel approach to preventing adolescent smoking. *Archives of Pediatrics and Adolescent Medicine, 157*(7), 643–648.

Sarrel, M. D. (2006, November 29). Recycling e-waste. *PCMag.com.* Retrieved from http://www.pcmag.com/article2/0,2817,2064151,00.asp

SAS. (2015). Jim Goodnight, Chief Executive Officer, SAS. Retrieved from http://www.sas.com/en_us/company-information/executive-bios/jim-goodnight.html

SAS. (2015). Life at SAS. Retrieved from http://www.fastcompany.com/3004953/how-sas-became-worlds-best-place-work

Satow, K. L. (1975). Social approval and helping. *Journal of Experimental Social Psychology, 11,* 501–509.

Sauer, J., Brewer, N., Zweck, T., & Weber, N. (2010). The effect of retention interval on the confidence-accuracy relationship for eyewitness identification. *Law and Human Behavior, 34,* 337–347. doi: 10.1007/s10979-009-9192-x

Sauerland, M., & Sporer, S. L. (2009). Fast and confident: Postdicting eyewitness identification accuracy in a field study. *Journal of Experimental Psychology: Applied, 15,* 46–62.

Savin-Williams, R. C. (1990). *Gay and lesbian youth: Expressions of identity.* New York: Hemisphere.

Savitsky, K., Van Boven, L., Epley, N., & Wight, W. (2005). The unpacking effect in responsibility allocations for group tasks. *Journal of Experimental Social Psychology, 41,* 447–457.

Sawyer, D. (2004, October 21). American sex lives. *Prime-Time Live,* ABC television.

Schachter, S. (1951). Deviation, rejection, and communication. *Journal of Abnormal and Social Psychology, 46*(2), 190–207.

Schachter, S. (1959). *The psychology of affiliation: Experimental studies of the sources of gregariousness.* Oxford: Stanford University Press.

Schachter, S. (1964). The interaction of cognitive and physiological determinants of emotional state. In L. Berkowitz (Ed.), *Advances in experimental social psychology* (pp. 49–79). New York: Academic Press.

Schachter, S., & Singer, J. E. (1962). Cognitive, social, and physiological determinants of emotional state. *Psychological Review, 69,* 379–399.

Schaller, M. (2011). The behavioural immune system and the psychology of human sexuality. *Philosophical Transactions of the Royal Society B, 366,* 3418–3426.

Schaller, M., & Murray, D. R. (2008). Pathogens, personality, and culture: Disease prevalence predicts worldwide variability in sociosexuality, extraversion, and openness to experience. *Journal of Personality and Social Psychology, 95,* 212–221.

Schaumberg, R.L., & Flynn, F.J. (2012). Uneasy lies the head that wears the crown: The link between guilt proneness and leadership. *Journal of Personality and Social Psychology, 103,* 327–342.

Scheibehenne, B., Greifeneder, R., & Todd, P. M. (2008, November). *Can there ever be too many options? Reassessing the effect of choice overload.* Paper presented at the annual meeting of the Society for Judgment and Decision Making, Chicago.

Scheier, M. F., Fenigstein, A., & Buss, A. H. (1974). Self-awareness and physical aggression. *Journal of Experimental Social Psychology, 10,* 264–273.

Schein, E. H. (1990). Organizational culture. *American Psychologist, 45*(2), 109–119.

Scheirer, M. A., & Kraut, R. E. (1979). Increased educational achievement via self-concept change. *Review of Educational Research, 49,* 131–150.

Scherer, L. D., & Lambert, A. J. (2012). Implicit race bias revisited: On the utility of task context in assessing implicit attitude strength. *Journal of Experimental Social Psychology, 48,* 366–370.

Schifferstein, H. N. J., & Michaut, A. M. K. (2002). Effects of appropriate and inappropriate odors on product evaluation. *Perceptual and Motor Skills, 95,* 1199–1214.

Schlaerth, A., Ensari, N., & Christian, J. (2013). A meta-analytical review of the relationship between emotional intelligence and leaders' constructive conflict management. *Group Processes & Intergroup Relations, 16*(1), 126–136. doi: 10.1177/1368430212439907

Schlenker, B. R. (1975). Self-presentation: Managing the impression of consistency when reality interferes with self-enhancement. *Journal of Personality and Social Psychology, 32,* 1030–1037.

Schlenker, B. R. (1980). *Impression management: The self-concept, social identity, and interpersonal relations.* Monterey, CA: Brooks/Cole.

Schlenker, B. R., Dlugolecki, D. W., & Doherty, K. J. (1994). The impact of self-presentations on self-appraisals and behaviors: The power of public commitment. *Personality and Social Psychology Bulletin, 20,* 20–33.

Schmidt, C. (1969). Urban crime areas: Part I. *American Sociological Review, 25,* 527–542.

Schmidt, F. L., & Hunter, J. E. (1998). The validity and utility of selection methods in personnel psychology: Practical and theoretical implications of 85 years of research findings. *Psychological Bulletin, 124*(2), 262–274.

Schmidt, R. E., & Gendolla, G. H. E. (2008). Dreaming of white bears: The return of the suppressed at sleep onset. *Consciousness and Cognition, 17*(3), 714–724.

Schmitt, D. P. (2003). Universal sex differences in the desire for sexual variety: Tests from 52 nations, 6 continents, and 13 islands. *Journal of Personality and Social Psychology, 85,* 85–104.

Schmitt, D. P., Jonason, P. K., Byerley, G. J., Flores, S. D., Illbeck, B. E., O'Leary, K. N., & Qudrat, A. (2012). A reexamination of sex differences in sexuality: New studies reveal old truths. *Current Directions in Psychological Science, 21,* 135–139.

Schmitt, N., Cortina, J. M., Ingerick, M. J., & Wiechmann, D. (2003). Personnel selection and employee performance. In W. C. Borman, D. R. Ilgen, & R. J. Klimoski (Eds.), *Handbook of psychology: Industrial and organizational psychology* (Vol. 12, pp. 77–105). New York: Wiley.

Schnall, S., Haidt, J., Clore, G. L., & Jordan, A. H. (2008). Disgust as embodied moral judgment. *Personality and Social Psychology Bulletin, 34*(8), 1096–1109.

Schooler, J. W., Ariely, D., & Loewenstein, G. (2003). The pursuit and assessment of happiness may be self-defeating. In J. Carrillo & I. Brocas (Eds.), *The psychology of economic decisions* (pp. 41–70). Oxford, England: Oxford University Press.

Schopler, J., & Insko, C. A. (1992). The discontinuity effect in interpersonal and intergroup relations: Generality and mediation. *European Review of Social Psychology, 3,* 121–151.

Schopler, J., & Stockdale, J. (1977). An interference analysis of crowding. *Environmental Psychology and Nonverbal Behavior, 1,* 81–88.

Schopler, J., Insko, C. A., Drigotas, S. M., Wieselquist, J., Pemberton, M. B., & Cox, C. (1995). The role of identifiability in the reduction of interindividual-intergroup discontinuity. *Journal of Experimental Social Psychology, 31,* 553–574.

Schopler, J., Insko, C. A., Drigotas, S., & Graetz, K. A. (1993). Individual-group discontinuity: Further evidence for mediation by fear and greed. *Personality and Social Psychology Bulletin, 19,* 419–431.

Schuller, R. A., & Hastings, P. A. (1996). Trials of battered women who kill: The impact of alternative forms of expert evidence. *Law and Human Behavior, 20,* 167–187.

Schultz, P. W. (2011). Conservation means behavior. *Conservation Biology, 25,* 1080–1083.

Schuman, H., & Scott, J. (1987). Problems in the use of survey questions to measure public opinion. *Science, 236*(4804), 957–959.

Schütz, A. (1999). It was your fault! Self-serving biases in autobiographical accounts of esteem threatening conflicts in married couples. *Journal of Social and Personal Relationships, 16,* 193–209.

Schütz, A. (2000). *Selbstwertgefühl: Zwischen Selbstakzeptanz und Arroganz.* Stuttgart: Kohlhammer.

Schütz, A. (2001). Self-esteem and interpersonal strategies. In J. P. Forgas, K. D. Williams, & L. Wheeler (Eds.), *The social mind: Cognitive and motivational aspects of interpersonal behavior* (pp. 157–176). New York: Cambridge University Press.

Schwab, J., Nadeau, S. E., & Warheit, G. J. (1979). Crowding and mental health. *Pavlovian Journal of Biological Science, 14,* 226–233.

Schwartz, B. (2004, April). The tyranny of choice. *Scientific American,* 72–75.

Schwartz, D. (2014, February 20). Arizona lawmakers pass bill to allow faith-based refusal of services. *Reuters.* Retrieved from http://www.reuters.com/article/2014/02/21/us-usa-gays-arizona-idUSBREA1K06M20140221

Schwartz, S. H. (1977). Normative influences on altruism. *Advances in Experimental Social Psychology, 10,* 221–279.

Schwarz, N. (1999). Self-reports: How the questions shape the answers. *American Psychologist, 54*(2), 93-105. doi: 10.1037/0003-066X.54.2.93

Schwarz, N., & Clore, G. L. (1983). Mood, misattribution, and judgments of well-being: Informative and directive functions of affective states. *Journal of Personality and Social Psychology, 45,* 513–523.

Schwarzwald, J., Raz, M., & Zvibel, M. (1979). The applicability of the door-in-the-face technique when established behavioral customs exist. *Journal of Applied Social Psychology, 9,* 576–586.

Scott, J. P. (1958). *Aggression.* Chicago: University of Chicago Press.

Seabright, P. (2004). *The company of strangers: A natural history of economic life.* Princeton, NJ: Princeton University Press.

Seal, D. W. (1997). Interpartner concordance of self-reported sexual behavior among college dating couples. *Journal of Sex Research, 34,* 39–55.

Sears, D. O. (1986). College sophomores in the laboratory: Influences of a narrow data base on social psychology's view of human nature. *Journal of Personality and Social Psychology, 51,* 515–530.

Sedikides, C. (1993). Assessment, enhancement, and verification determinants of the self-evaluation process. *Journal of Personality and Social Psychology, 65,* 317–338.

Sedikides, C. S., & Gregg, A. P. (2008). Self-enhancement: Food for thought. *Perspectives on Psychological Science, 3,* 102–116.

Sedikides, C., Gaertner, L., & Toguchi, Y. (2003). Pancultural self-enhancement. *Journal of Personality and Social Psychology, 84,* 60–70.

Sedikides, C., Meek, R., Alicke, M. D., & Taylor, S. (2013). Behind bars but above the bar: Prisoners consider themselves more prosocial than non-prisoners. *British Journal of Social Psychology, 53,* 396–403.

Sedlovskaya, A., Purdie-Vaughn, V., Eibach, R.P., LaFrance, M., Romero-Canyas, R., & Camp, N.P. (2013). Internalizing the closet: Concealment heightens the cognitive distinction between public and private selves. *Journal of Personality and Social Psychology, 104,* 695–715.

Segal, N. L. (1984). Cooperation, competition and altruism within twin sets: A reappraisal. *Ethology and Sociobiology, 5,* 163–177.

Sehgal, I. (2011, June 23). Media reacts to news that Norwegian terror suspect isn't Muslim. *Atlantic Wire.* Retrieved from http://www.theatlanticwire.com/global/2011/07/media-reacts-news-norwegian-terror-suspect-isnt-muslim/40322/

Seligman, C., & Darley, J. M. (1977). Feedback as a means of decreasing residential energy consumption. *Journal of Applied Psychology, 62,* 363–368.

Semmler, C., Brewer, N., & Wells, G. L. (2004). Effects of postidentification feedback on eyewitness identification and nonidentification confidence. *Journal of Applied Psychology, 89,* 334–346.

Sennett, R. (1974). *The fall of public man.* New York: Random House.

Sentyrz, S. M., & Bushman, B. J. (1998). Mirror, mirror on the wall, who's the thinnest one of all? Effects of self-awareness on consumption of fatty, reduced-fat, and fat-free products. *Journal of Applied Psychology, 83,* 944–949.

Serota, K. B., Levine, T. R., & Boster, F. J. (2010). The prevalence of lying in America: Three studies of self-reported lies. *Human Communication Research, 36*(1), 2–25.

Sesame Street breaks Iraqi POWs. (2003, May 20). Retrieved from http://news.bbc.co.uk/1/hi/world/middle_east/3042907.stm

Seta, C. E., & Seta, J. J. (1995). When audience presence is enjoyable: The influences of audience awareness of prior success on performance and task interest. *Basic and Applied Social Psychology, 16*(1–2), 95–108.

Seyle, H. (1956). *The stress of life.* New York: McGraw-Hill.

Shackelford, T. K. (2001). Self-esteem in marriage: An evolutionary psychological analysis. *Personality and Individual Differences, 30,* 371–390.

Shah, J. Y. (2003). Automatic for the people: How representations of significant others implicitly affect goal pursuit. *Journal of Personality and Social Psychology, 84,* 661–681.

Shah, J. Y., Friedman, R., & Kruglanski, A. W. (2002). Forgetting all else: On the antecedents and consequences of goal shielding. *Journal of Personality and Social Psychology, 83,* 1261–1280.

Shakur, S. (1993). *Monster: The autobiography of an L.A. gang member.* New York: Atlantic Monthly Press.

Shapiro, P. N., & Penrod, S. D. (1986). Metaanalysis of facial identification studies. *Psychological Bulletin, 100,* 139–156.

Shavitt, S., Sanbonmatsu, D. M., Smittipatana, S., & Posavac, S. S. (1999). Broadening the conditions for illusory correlation formation: Implications for judging minority groups. *Basic and Applied Social Psychology, 21*(4), 263–279.

Shaw, B. F., & Beck, A. T. (1977). The treatment of depression with cognitive therapy. In A. Ellis & R. Grieger (Eds.), *Handbook of rational emotive therapy* (pp. 309–326). New York: Springer.

Shea, C. T., Davisson, E. K., & Fitzsimons, G. (2013). Riding other people's coattails: Individuals with low self-control value self-control in other people. *Psychological Science, 24,* 1031–1036.

Sheldon, K. M. (1994). Emotionality differences between artists and scientists. *Journal of Research in Personality, 28,* 481–491.

Sheldon, K. M., & Kasser, T. (1998). Pursuing personal goals: Skills enable progress but not all progress is beneficial. *Personality and Social Psychology Bulletin, 24,* 1319–1331.

Sheldon, K. M., & Lyubomirsky, S. (2004). Achieving sustainable new happiness: Prospects, practices, and prescriptions. In P. A. Linley & S. Joseph (Eds.), *Positive psychology in practice* (pp. 127–145). Hoboken, NJ: Wiley.

Sheldon, P. (2008). The relationship between unwillingness-to-communicate and students' Facebook use. *Journal of Media Psychology: Theories, Methods, and Applications, 20*(2), 67–75.

Shelton, J. N. (2003). Interpersonal concerns in social encounters between majority and minority group members. *Group Processes and Intergroup Relations, 6,* 171–185.

Shepperd, J. A., & Strathman, A. J. (1989). Attractiveness and height: The role of stature in dating preference, frequency of dating, and perceptions of attractiveness. *Personality and Social Psychology Bulletin, 15*(4), 617–627.

Sherif, M. (1935). A study of some social factors in perception. *Archives of Psychology* (Columbia University), No. 187, 60.

Sherif, M. (1966) *In common predicament: Social psychology of intergroup conflict and cooperation.* Boston: Houghton-Mifflin.

Sherif, M., & Sherif, C. W. (1953). *Groups in harmony and tension: An integration of studies of intergroup relations.* New York: Harper & Brothers.

Sherman, S. T., Zehner, K. S., Johnson, J., & Hirt, E. R. (1983). Social explanation: The role of timing, set, and recall on subjective likelihood estimates. *Journal of Personality and Social Psychology, 44,* 1127–1143.

Sherrod, D. R. (1974). Crowding, perceived control, and behavioral aftereffects. *Journal of Applied Social Psychology, 4,* 171–186.

Shin, C. (2011, March 22) Here are the 5 most liberal and conservative media Twitter feeds. *Business Insider.* Retrieved from http://www.businessinsider.com/twitter-political-leanings-conservative-liberal-oreilly-msnbc-katie-couric-sean-hannity-2011-3?op51

Shin, J., & Ariely, D. (2004). Keeping doors open: The effect of unavailability on incentives to keep options open. *Management Science, 50,* 575–586.

Shneidman, E. S. (1981). Suicide thoughts and reflections, 1960–1980. *Suicide and Life-Threatening Behavior, 11,* 197–360.

Shoda, Y., Mischel, W., & Peake, P. K. (1990). Predicting adolescent cognitive and self-regulatory competencies from preschool delay of gratification: Identifying diagnostic conditions. *Developmental Psychology, 26,* 978–986.

Shohat-Ophir, G., Kaun, K. R., Azanchi, R., & Heberlein, U. (2012). Sexual deprivation increases ethanol intake in *Drosophila. Science, 335,* 1351–1355.

Shook, N. J., & Fazio, R. H. (2008). Interracial roommate relationships: An experimental field test of the contact hypothesis. *Psychological Science, 19,* 717–723.

Shorter, E. (1975). *The making of the modern family.* New York: Basic Books.

Shotland, R. L., & Straw, M. K. (1976). Bystander response to an assault: When a man attacks a woman. *Journal of Personality and Social Psychology, 34,* 990–999.

Shrauger, J. S. (1975). Responses to evaluation as a function of initial self-perceptions. *Psychological Bulletin, 82,* 581–596.

Shrauger, J. S., & Shoeneman, T. J. (1979). Symbolic interactionist view of self-concept: Through the looking glass darkly. *Psychological Bulletin, 86,* 549–573.

Shrauger, J. S., & Sorman, P. B. (1977). Self-evaluations, initial success and failure, and improvement as determinants of persistence. *Journal of Consulting and Clinical Psychology, 45,* 784–795.

Shteir, R. (2011). *The steal: a cultural history of shoplifting.* New York: Penguin Press.

Shteynberg, G., & Apfelbaum, A. P. (2013). The power of shared experience: Simultaneous observation with similar others facilitates social learning. *Social Psychological and Personality Science, 4,* 738–744.

Shteynberg, G., Hirsh, J. B., Apfelbaum, E. P., Larsen, J. T., Galinsky, A. D., & Roese, N. J. (2014, August 25). Feeling more together: Group attention intensifies emotion. *Emotion.* Advance online publication. http://dx.doi.org/10.1037/a0037697

Shu, L. L., & Gino, F. (2012). Sweeping dishonesty under the rug: How unethical actions lead to forgetting of moral rules. *Journal of Personality and Social Psychology, 102,* 1164–1177.

Sidanius, J., & Pratto, F. (1999). *Social dominance: An intergroup theory of social hierarchy and oppression.* New York: Cambridge University Press.

Siem, B., & Stürmer, S. (2012). Cross-cultural volunteerism: Examining the effects of intercultural (dis)similarities on volunteers' motivations to support international students. *Basic and Applied Social Psychology, 34*(6), 544–557. doi: 10.1080/01973533.2012.727316

Siero, F. W., Bakker, A. B., Dekker, G. B., & Van Den Burg, M. T. C. (1996). Changing organizational energy consumption behavior through comparative feedback. *Journal of Environmental Psychology, 16,* 235–246.

Silfver, M., Helkama, K., Lönnqvist, J-E., & Verkasalo, M. (2008). The relation between value priorities and proneness to guilt, shame, and empathy. *Motivation and Emotion, 32*(2), 69–80.

Silk, J. B., Brosnan, S. F., Vonk, J., Henrich, J., Povinelli, D. J., Richardson, A. S., Lambeth, S. P., Mascaro, J., & Schapiro, S. J. (2005, October 27). Chimpanzees are indifferent to the welfare of unrelated group members. *Nature, 437,* 1357–1359.

Silvia, P. J., & Duval, T. S. (2001). Objective self-awareness theory: Recent progress and enduring problems. *Personality and Social Psychology Review, 5,* 230–241.

Sime, J. D. (1983). Affiliative behavior during escape to building exits. *Journal of Environmental Psychology, 3,* 21–41.

Simkin, M. G., & McLeod, A. (2010). Why do college students cheat? *Journal of Business Ethics, 94*(3), 441–453.

Simpson, J. A. (1990). Influence of attachment styles on romantic relationships. *Journal of Personality and Social Psychology, 59,* 971–980.

Simpson, J. A. (2007). Foundations of interpersonal trust. In A. W. Kruglanski & E. T. Higgins (Eds.), *Social psychology: Handbook of basic principles* (2nd ed., pp. 587–607) New York: Guilford Press.

Simpson, J. A., Gangestad, S., & Lerma, M. (1990). Perception of physical attractiveness: Mechanisms involved in the maintenance of romantic relationships. *Journal of Personality and Social Psychology, 59,* 1192–1201.

Sinclair, L., & Kunda, Z. (1999). Reactions to a black professional: Motivated inhibition and activation of conflicting stereotypes. *Journal of Personality and Social Psychology, 77,* 885–904.

Sinclair, L., & Kunda, Z. (2000). Motivated stereotyping of women: She's fine if she praised me but incompetent if she criticized me. *Personality and Social Psychology Bulletin, 26,* 1329–1342.

Sinclair, R. C., & Brown, N. R. (1999, April–May). *Discrepant partner reports: Do women encode sexual experiences more deeply than men do?* Paper presented at the annual convention of the Midwestern Psychological Association, Chicago.

Singh, D. (1993). Adaptive significance of female physical attractiveness: Role of waist-to-hip ratio. *Journal of Personality and Social Psychology, 65(2),* 293–307.

Singh, D. (1995). Female judgment of male attractiveness and desirability for relationships: Role of waist-to-hip ratio and financial status. *Journal of Personality and Social Psychology, 69(6),* 1089–1101.

Skaalvik, E. M., & Hagtvet, K. A. (1990). Academic achievement and self-concept: An analysis of causal predominance in a developmental perspective. *Journal of Personality and Social Psychology, 58,* 292–307.

Skinner, B. F. (1938). *The behavior of organisms.* Englewood Cliffs, NJ: Appleton-Century-Crofts.

Skolnick, A., Bascom, K. L., & Wilson, D. T. (2013). Gender role expectations of disgust: Men are low and women are high. *Sex Roles, 69(1–2),* 72–88. doi: 10.1007/s11199-013-0279-y

Slotter, E. B., Finkel, E. J., DeWall, C. N., Pond, R. S., Lambert, N. M., Bodenhausen, G. V., & Fincham, F. D. (2011). Putting the brakes on aggression toward a romantic partner: The inhibitory influence of relationship commitment. *Journal of Personality and Social Psychology, 102,* 291–305.

Slovic, P., & Lichtenstein, S. (1971). Comparison of Bayesian and regression approaches to the study of information processing in judgment. *Organizational Behavior and Human Performance, 6,* 649–744.

Smalarz, L., & Wells, G. L. (2014). Post-identification feedback to eyewitnesses impairs evaluators' abilities to discriminate between accurate and mistaken testimony. *Law and Human Behavior, 38,* 194–202.

Smith T. W., Snyder C. R., & Perkins S. C. (1983). The self-serving function of hypochondriacal complaints: Physical symptoms as self-handicapping strategies. *Journal of Personality and Social Psychology, 44,* 787–797.

Smith, C. A., Organ, D. W., & Near, J. P. (1983). Organizational citizenship behavior: Its nature and antecedents. *Journal of Applied Psychology, 68,* 653–663.

Smith, D. (2004, June 20). Sign writer. *Observer.* Retrieved from http://observer.guardian.co.uk/comment/story/0,6903,1243121,00.html

Smith, F. J. (1977). Work attitudes as a predictor of attendance on a specific day. *Journal of Applied Psychology, 62(1),* 16–19.

Smith, G. E., Gerrard, M., & Gibbons, F. X. (1997). Self-esteem and the relation between risk behavior and perceptions of vulnerability to unplanned pregnancy in college women. *Health Psychology, 16,* 137–146.

Smith, G. F., & Dorfman, D. D. (1975). The effect of stimulus uncertainty on the relationship between frequency of exposure and liking. *Journal of Personality and Social Psychology, 31,* 150–155.

Smith, G. H., & Engel, R. (1968). Influence of a female model on perceived characteristics of an automobile. *Proceedings of the Annual Convention of the American Psychological Association, 3,* 681–682.

Smith, J. D., Boomer, J., Zakrzewski, A. C., Roeder, J. L., Church, B. A., & Ashby, F. G. (2014). Deferred feedback sharply dissociates implicit and explicit category learning. *Psychological Science, 25(2),* 447–457. doi: 10.1177/0956797613509112

Smith, R. (2003, December 3). The impact of hate media in Rwanda. *BBC News.* Retrieved from http://news.bbc.co.uk/2/hi/africa/3257748.stm

Smith, R. J., & Knowles, E. S. (1979). Affective and cognitive mediators of reactions to spatial invasions. *Journal of Experimental Social Psychology, 15,* 437–452.

Smith, S. M. and Shaffer, D. R. (1991). Celerity and cajolery: Rapid speech may promote or inhibit persuasion through its impact on message elaboration. *Personality and Social Psychology Bulletin, 17,* 663, 669. Reprinted by permission of Sage Publications.

Smith, T. (1994). Attitudes toward sexual permissiveness: Trends, correlates, and behavioral connections. In A. S. Rossi (Ed.), *Sexuality across the life course* (pp. 63–97). Chicago: University of Chicago Press.

Smith, T. B., McCullough, M. E., & Poll, J. (2003). Religiousness and depression: Evidence for a main effect and the moderating influence of stressful life events. *Psychological Bulletin, 129,* 614–636.

Smuts, B. (1996). Male aggression against women: An evolutionary perspective. In D. Buss & N. Malamuth (Eds.), *Sex, power, conflict* (pp. 231–268). New York: Oxford University Press.

Snow, M. G., Prochaska, J. O., & Rossi, J. S. (1992). Stages of change for smoking cessation among former problem drinkers: A cross-sectional analysis. *Journal of Substance Abuse, 4(2),* 107–116.

Snyder, C. R., & Higgins, R. L. (1990). *Self-handicapping: The paradox that isn't.* Norwell, MA: Kluwer.

Snyder, C. R., & Lopez, S. (Eds.) (2002). *Handbook of positive psychology.* New York: Oxford University Press.

Snyder, M. (1974). Self monitoring of expressive behavior. *Journal of Personality and Social Psychology, 30,* 526–537.

Snyder, M., & DeBono, K. G. (1985). Appeals to image and claims about quality: Understanding the psychology of advertising. *Journal of Personality and Social Psychology, 49,* 586–597.

Snyder, M., & Gangestad, S. (1986). On the nature of self-monitoring: Matters of assessment, matters of validity. *Journal of Personality and Social Psychology, 51,* 125–139.

Soetens, B., Braet, C., & Moens, E. (2008). Thought suppression in obese and non-obese restrained eaters: Piece of cake or forbidden fruit? *European Eating Disorders Review, 16(1),* 67–76.

Soetens, B., Braet, C., Dejonckheere, P., & Roets, A. (2006). When suppression backfires: The ironic effects of suppressing eating-related thoughts. *Journal of Health Psychology, 11(5),* 655–668.

Solomon, S. D., & Canino, G. J. (1990). Appropriateness of the DSM-III-R criteria for Posttraumatic Stress Disorder. *Comprehensive Psychiatry, 31,* 227–237.

Solomon, S., Greenberg, J., & Pyszczynski, T. A. (2004). Lethal consumption: Death-denying materialism. In T. Kasser & A. D. Kanner (Eds.), *Psychology and consumer culture: The struggle for a good life in a materialistic world* (pp. 127–146). Washington, DC: American Psychological Association.

Soman, D., & Cheema, A. (2002). The effect of credit on spending decisions: The role of the credit limit and credibility. *Marketing Science, 21,* 32–53.

Some kids won't eat the middle of an Oreo. (1991, November 20). *Wall Street Journal,* p. B1.

Somerfield, M. R., & McCrae, R. R. (2000). Stress and coping research: Methodological challenges, theoretical advances, and clinical applications. *American Psychologist, 55(6),* 620–625.

Sommer, K. L., & Rubin, Y. (2005). Maintaining self-esteem in the face of rejection. In K. D. Williams, J. P. Forgas, & W. von Hippel (Eds.), *The social outcast: Ostracism, social exclusion, rejection, and bullying* (pp. 171–184). New York: Psychology Press.

Sommer, K. L., & Yoon, J. (2013). When silence is golden: Ostracism as resource conservation during aversive interactions. *Journal of Social and Personal Relationships, 30,* 901–918.

Sommer, K. L., Williams, K. D., Ciarocco, N. J., & Baumeister, R. F. (2001). When silence speaks louder than words: Explorations into the intra-psychic and interpersonal consequences of social ostracism. *Basic and Applied Social Psychology, 23,* 225–243.

Sommer, R. (1969). *Personal space: The behavioral basis of design.* Englewood Cliffs, NJ: Prentice-Hall.

Sommers, C. H. (2015). The media is making college rape culture worse. *The Daily Beast.* http://www.thedailybeast.com/articles/2015/01/23/the-media-is-making-college-rape-culture-worse.html

Sommers, P., & Moos, R. (1976). The weather and human behavior. In R. H. Moos (Ed.), *The human context: Environmental determinants of behavior* (pp. 73–107). New York: Wiley.

Sommers, S. R., & Norton, M. I. (2007). Race-based judgments, race-neutral justifications: Experimental examination of peremptory use and the Batson challenge procedure. *Law and Human Behavior, 31,* 261–273.

Sonnentag, S., & Frese, M. (2003). Stress in organizations. In W. C. Borman, D. R. Ilgen, & R. J. Klimoski (Eds.), *Handbook of psychology* (Vol. 12, pp. 453–491). Hoboken, NJ: John Wiley & Sons.

Spangenberg, E. R., Crowley, A. E., & Henderson, P. W. (1996). Improving the store environment: Do olfactory cues affect evaluations and behaviors? *Journal of Marketing, 60,* 67–80.

Spangler, G., & Grossman, K. E. (1993). Biobehavioral organization in securely and insecurely attached infants. *Child Development, 64,* 1439–1450.

Spanier, G. B., & Lewis, R. A. (1980). Marital quality: A review of the seventies. *Journal of Marriage and the Family, 42,* 825–839.

Spanier, G. P., & Margolis, R. L. (1983). Marital separation and extramarital sexual behavior. *Journal of Sex Research, 19,* 23–48.

Spence, K. W. (1956). *Behavior theory and conditioning.* New Haven, CT: Yale University Press.

Spencer, S. J., Steele, C. M., & Quinn, D. M. (1999). Stereotype threat and women's math performance. *Journal of Experimental Social Psychology, 35,* 4–28.

Spielberg, W. E. (1986). Living with Indian Point: A study in investigating the relationship between stress, time distortion, ideology, coping style and expressed vulnerability of high school students in close residence to a nuclear power plant. *Dissertation Abstracts International, 47(9–B),* 3971–3972.

Spielmann, S. S., MacDonald, G., Maxwell, J. A., Joel, S., Peragine, D., Muise, A., & Impett, E. A. (2013). Settling for less out of fear of being single. *Journal of Personality and Social Psychology, 105,* 1049–1073.

Sporer, S. L., Penrod, S. D., Read, J. D., & Cutler, B. L. (1995). Choosing, confidence, and accuracy: A meta-analysis of the confidence-accuracy relation in eyewitness identification studies. *Psychological Bulletin, 118,* 315–327.

Sprecher, S. (1989). Premarital sexual standards for different categories of individuals. *Journal of Sex Research, 19,* 23–48.

Sprecher, S. (1998). Social exchange theories and sexuality. *Journal of Sex Research, 35,* 32–43.

Sprecher, S. (1999). "I love you more today than yesterday": Romantic partners' perceptions of changes in love and related affect over time. *Journal of Personality and Social Psychology, 76,* 46–53.

Sprecher, S., & Regan, P. (2002). Liking some things (in some people) more than others: Partner preferences in romantic relationships and friendships. *Journal of Social and Personal Relationships, 19,* 463–481.

Sprecher, S., & Regan, P. C. (1996). College virgins: How men and women perceive their sexual status. *Journal of Sex Research, 33,* 3–15.

Sroufe, L. A., & Waters, E. (1977). Heart rate as a convergent measure in clinical and developmental research. *Merrill-Palmer Quarterly, 23,* 3–27.

Staats, A. W., & Staats, C. K. (1958). Attitudes established by classical conditioning. *Journal of Abnormal and Social Psychology, 57,* 37–40.

Stack, S. (2003). Media coverage as a risk factor in suicide. *Journal of Epidemiology and Community Health, 57(4),* 238–240.

Staffieri, J. (1967). A study of social stereotype of body image in children. *Journal of Personality and Social Psychology, 7,* 101–104.

Stanford, W. E. (1999, March–April). Dealing with student credit card debt. *About Campus,* 12–17. Quote on p. 13.

Stanko, E. A. (2000). The day to count: Reflections on a methodology to raise awareness about the impact of domestic violence in the UK. *Caribbean Journal of Criminology & Social Psychology, 5*(1–2), 103–118.

Staples, R. (1973). *Black women in America: Sex, marriage, and family.* Chicago: Nelson-Hall.

Staples, S. L. (1997). Public policy and environmental noise: Modeling exposure or understanding. *American Journal of Public Health, 87*, 2063–2067.

Stasser, G., & Titus, W. (1985). Pooling of unshared information in group decision making: Biased information sampling during discussion. *Journal of Personality and Social Psychology, 48*, 1467–1478.

Stasser, G., & Titus, W. (1987). Effects of information load and percentage of shared information on the dissemination of unshared information during group discussion. *Journal of Personality and Social Psychology, 53*, 81–93.

Steblay, N. K., Dietrich, H. L., Ryan, S. L., Raczynski, J. L., & James, K. A. (2011). Sequential lineup laps and eyewitness accuracy. *Law and Human Behavior, 35*, 262–274.

Steblay, N. K., Wells, G. L., & Douglass, A. B. (2014). The eyewitness post identification effect 15 years later: Theoretical and policy implications. *Psychology, Public Policy, and Law, 20*, 1–18.

Steblay, N. L., Dysart, J. E., & Wells, G. L. (2011). Seventy-two tests of the sequential lineup superiority effect: A meta-analysis and policy discussion. *Psychology, Public Policy, and Law, 17*, 99–139.

Steblay, N. M. (1992). A meta-analytic review of the weapon focus effect. *Law & Human Behavior, 16*(4), 413–424.

Steblay, N. M. (1997). Social influence in eyewitness recall: A meta-analytic review of lineup instruction effects. *Law and Human Behavior, 21*, 283–297.

Steblay, N. M., Besirevic, J., Fulero, S. M., & Jimenez-Lorente, B. (1999). The effects of pretrial publicity on juror verdicts: A meta-analytic review. *Law and Human Behavior, 23*, 219–235.

Steele, C. M., & Aronson, J. A. (1995). Stereotype threat and the intellectual test performance of African Americans. *Journal of Personality and Social Psychology, 69*, 797–811.

Steele, C. M., & Aronson, J. A. (2004). Stereotype threat does not live by Steele and Aronson (1995) alone. *American Psychologist, 59*, 47–55.

Steele, C. M., & Josephs, R. A. (1990). Alcohol myopia: Its prized and dangerous effects. *American Psychologist, 45*, 921–933.

Steele, C. M., & Southwick, L. (1985). Alcohol and social behavior: I. The psychology of drunken excess. *Journal of Personality and Social Psychology, 48*, 18–34.

Steffensmeier, D., & Allan, E. (1996). Gender and crime: Toward a gendered theory of female offending. *Annual Review of Sociology, 22*, 459–487.

Stein, R. (2011, January 11). Wakefield tried to capitalize on autism-vaccine link, report says. *The Washington Post.* Retrieved from http://voices.washingtonpost.com/checkup/2011/01/wakefield_tried_to_capitalize.html.

Steinfatt, T. M. (1973). The Prisoner's Dilemma and a creative alternative game: The effects of communications under conditions of real reward. *Simulation and Games, 4*, 389–409.

Steinmetz, K. (2012). Follow your nose: Food company launches 'smell-vertising' for potato ads. *Time NewsFeed.* Retrieved from http://newsfeed.time.com/2012/02/10/follow-your-nose-food-company-launches-smell-vertising-for-potato-ads/

Stephan, C. W. & Stephan, W. G. (1985). *Two Social Psychologies: An Integrative Approach.* Homewood, IL: Dorsey.

Stern, J. (2004, June 6). Beneath bombast and bombs, a caldron of humiliation: Many seek to restore a dignity damaged by the new world order. *Los Angeles Times.*

Stern, P. C., & Oskamp, S. (1987). Managing scarce environmental resources. In D. Stokols & I. Altman (Eds.), *Handbook of environmental psychology* (Vol. 2, pp. 1043–1088). New York: Wiley.

Stern, S. E., & Faber, J. E. (1997). The lost e-mail method: Milgram's lost-letter technique in the age of the Internet. *Behavior Research Methods, Instruments, and Computers, 29*, 260–263.

Sternberg, R. J. (1986). A triangular theory of love. *Psychological Review, 93*, 119–135.

Stewart, G. L., & Manz, C. C. (1995). Leadership for self-managing work teams: A typology and integrative model. *Human Relations, 48*, 347–370.

Stewart, J.B. (2013, March 15). Looking for a lesson in Google's perks. Retrieved from http://www.nytimes.com/2013/03/16/business/at-google-a-place-to-work-and-play.html?pagewanted5all&_r50

Stillman, T. F., Baumeister, R. F., & DeWall, C. N. (2007). What's so funny about not having money? The effects of power on laughter. *Personality and Social Psychology Bulletin, 33*, 1547–1558.

Stone, J., & McWhinnie, C. (2008). Evidence that blatant versus subtle stereotype threat cues impact performance through dual processes. *Journal of Experimental Social Psychology, 44*(2), 445–452.

Stone, J., Aronson, E., Crain, A. L., Winslow, M. P., & Fried, C. B. (1994). Inducing hypocricy as a means of encouraging young adults to use condoms. *Personality and Social Psychology Bulletin, 20*, 116–128.

Stone, L. (1977). *The family, sex and marriage in England: 1500–1800.* London: Perennial.

Stoner, J. A. F. (1961). *A comparison of individual and group decisions involving risk.* Unpublished master's thesis, Massachusetts Institute of Technology.

Store of the month. (1976, October). *Progressive Grocer,* 104.

Storey, A. E., Walsh, C. L., Quinton, R. L., & Wynne-Edward, K. E. (2000). Hormonal correlates of paternal responsiveness in new and expectant fathers. *Evolution and Human Behavior, 21*, 79–95.

Story Corps (2012, January 13). Threats and lies, and "Who I'm supposed to be." *NPR.* Retrieved from http://www.npr.org/2012/01/13/145099739/threats-and-lies-and-who-im-supposed-to-be

Stout-Wiegand, N., & Trent, R. B. (1984–1985). Comparison of students' and non-student residents' attitudes toward local energy developments: Environmentalism versus economic interest. *Journal of Environmental Education, 16*, 29–35.

Strack, F., & Deutsch, R. (2004). Reflective and impulsive determinants of social behavior. *Personality and Social Psychology Review, 8*(3), 220–247.

Strack, F., Martin, L., & Stepper, S. (1988). Inhibiting and facilitating conditions of the human smile: A nonobtrusive test of the facial feedback hypothesis. *Journal of Personality and Social Psychology, 54*, 768–777.

Straus, M. A. (1997). Physical assaults by women partners: A major social problem. In M. R. Walsh (Ed.), *Women, men and gender: Ongoing debates* (pp. 210–221). New Haven, CT: Yale University Press.

Strober, M., & Humphrey, L. L. (1987). Familial contributions to the etiology and course of anorexia nervosa and bulimia. *Journal of Consulting and Clinical Psychology, 55*, 654–659.

Stroebe, W., Diehl, M., & Abakoumkin, G. (1992). The illusion of group effectivity. *Personality and Social Psychology Bulletin, 18*, 643–650.

Stroop, J. R. (1935). Studies of interference in serial verbal reactions. *Journal of Experimental Psychology, 28*, 643–662.

Studebaker, C. A., Robbennolt, J. K., Pathak-Sharma, M. K., & Penrod, S. D. (2000). Assessing pretrial publicity effects: Integrating content analytic results. *Law and Human Behavior, 24*, 317–336.

Subra, B., Muller, D., Bègue, L., Bushman, B. J., & Delmas, F. (2010). Automatic effects of alcohol and weapon cues on aggressive thoughts and behaviors. *Personality and Social Psychology Bulletin, 36*(8), 1052–1057. doi: 10.1177/0146167210374725

Suddath, C. (2011). It's the end of the world as we know it. *Time.* Retrieved from http://www.time.com/time/specials/packages/article/0,28804,2097462_2097456_2097489,00.html

Sullivan, J. (2009, February 9). Employee furloughs can be a bad alternative to layoffs. Ere.net. Retrieved from http://www.ere.net/tags/furloughs

Sullivan, J. (2012). 10 compelling numbers that reveal the power of employee referrals. Retrieved from http://www.ere.net/2012/05/07/10-compelling-numbers-that-reveal-the-power-of-employee-referrals/

Sullivan, M. (2013, June 28). More proof office space design impacts productivity, focus and collaboration. Retrieved from http://www.officingtoday.com/2013/06/more-proof-office-space-design-impacts-productivity-focus-and-collaboration/

Suls, J., & Wan, C. K. (1987). In search of the false uniqueness phenomenon: Fear and estimates of social consensus. *Journal of Personality and Social Psychology, 52*, 211–217.

Suls, J., Davidson, K., & Kaplan, R. (Eds.). 2010. *Handbook of health psychology and behavioral medicine.* New York: Guilford Press.

Suls, J., Wan, C. K., & Sanders, G. S. (1988). False consensus and false uniqueness in estimating the prevalence of health-protective behaviors. *Journal of Applied Social Psychology, 18*, 66–79.

Sundali, J., & Croson, R. (2006). Biases in casino betting: The hot hand and the gambler's fallacy. *Judgment and Decision Making, 1*(1), 1–12.

Sundstrom, E. (1978). Crowding as a sequential process: Review of research on the effects of population density on humans. In A. Baum & Y. M. Epstein (Eds.), *Human response to crowding* (pp. 31–116). Hillsdale, NJ: Erlbaum.

Sundstrom, E., Town, J. P., Rice, R. W., Osborn, D. P., & Brill, M. (1994). Office noise, satisfaction, and performance. *Environment and Behavior, 26*, 195–222.

Surowiecki, J. (2004). *The wisdom of crowds: Why the many are smarter than the few and how collective wisdom shapes business, economics, societies, and nations.* New York: Doubleday. (Quotation on p. 11).

Susa, K. J., Meissner, C. A., & deHeer, H. (2010). Modeling the role of social-cognitive processes in the recognition of own- and other-race faces. *Social Cognition, 28*, 523–537.

Svenson, O. (1981). Are we less risky and more skillful than our fellow drivers? *Acta Psychologica, 47*, 143–51.

Swami, V., & Monk, R. (2013). Weight bias against women in a university acceptance scenario. *Journal of General Psychology, 140*(1), 45–56. doi: 10.1080/00221309.2012.726288

Swann, W. B., De La Ronde, C., & Hixon, J. G. (1994). Authenticity and positivity strivings in marriage and courtship. *Journal of Personality and Social Psychology, 66*, 857–869.

Swann, W. B., Jr. (1985). The self as architect of social reality. In B. Schlenker (Ed.), *The self and social life* (pp. 100–125). New York: McGraw-Hill.

Swann, W. B., Jr. (1987). Identity negotiation: Where two roads meet. *Journal of Personality and Social Psychology, 53*, 1038–1051.

Swann, W. B., Jr. (1998). The self and interpersonal relationships. Paper presented at the meeting of the Society of Experimental Social Psychologists, Lexington, KY.

Swann, W. B., Jr., Griffin, J. J., Predmore, S., & Gaines, B. (1987). The cognitive-affective crossfire: When self-consistency confronts self-enhancement. *Journal of Personality and Social Psychology, 52*, 881–889.

Swann, W. B., Jr., Hixon, J. G., Stein-Seroussi, A., & Gilbert, D. T. (1990). The fleeting gleam of praise: Cognitive processes underlying behavioral reactions to self-relevant feedback. *Journal of Personality and Social Psychology, 59*, 17–26.

Swann, W. B., Jr., Stein-Seroussi, A., & Giesler, R. B. (1992). Why people self-verify. *Journal of Personality and Social Psychology, 62*, 392–401.

Swart, H., Hewstone, M., Christ, O., & Voci, A. (2011). Affective mediators of intergroup contact: A three-wave longitudinal study in South Africa. *Journal of Personality and Social Psychology, 101*(6), 1221–1238.

Swift, A. (2013, December 16). Honesty and ethics rating of clergy slides to new low. Gallup. Retrieved from http://www.gallup.com/poll/166298/honesty-ethics-rating-clergy-slides-new-low.aspx

Swim, J. K. (1994). Perceived versus meta-analytic effect sizes: An assessment of the accuracy of gender stereotypes. *Journal of Personality and Social Psychology, 66*, 21–36.

Symanski, R. (1980). Prostitution in Nevada. In E. Muga (Ed.), *Studies in prostitution* (pp. 246–279). Nairobi: Kenya Literature Bureau.

Symons, C. S., & Johnson, B. T. (1997). The self-reference effect in memory: A meta-analysis. *Psychological Bulletin, 121*, 371–394.

Symons, D. (1979). *The evolution of human sexuality.* New York: Oxford University Press.

Symons, D. (1995). Beauty is in the adaptations of the beholder: The evolutionary psychology of human female sexual attractiveness. In P. R. Abramson & S. D. Pinkerton (Eds.), *Sexual nature/sexual culture* (pp. 80–118). Chicago: University of Chicago Press.

Szalma, J. L., & Hancock, P. A. (2011). Noise effects on human performance: A meta-analytic synthesis. *Psychological Bulletin, 137*, 682–707.

Szymanski, S. (2000). A market test for discrimination in the English professional soccer leagues. *Journal of Political Economy, 108*(3), 590–603.

Tabak, A. J. (2004). Hundreds register for new Facebook website, Facemash creator seeks new reputation with latest online project. Retrieved from http://www.thecrimson.com/article.aspx?ref5357292

Tajfel, H., & Billig, M. (1974). Familiarity and categorization in intergroup behavior. *Journal of Experimental Social Psychology, 10*(2), 159–170.

Tajfel, H., Billig, M. G., Bundy, R. P., & Flament, C. (1971). Social categorization and intergroup behaviour. *European Journal of Social Psychology, 1*(2), 149–178.

Tamir, D. I., & Mitchell, J. P. (2012). Disclosing information about the self is intrinsically rewarding. *PNAS, 109*, 8038–3043.

Tamir, M., Mitchell, C., & Gross, J. J. (2008). Hedonic and instrumental motives in anger regulation. *Psychological Science, 19*(4), 324–328.

Tangney, J. P., & Dearing, R. L. (2002). *Shame and guilt.* New York: Guilford Press.

Tangney, J. P., & Fischer, K. W. (1995). *Self-conscious emotions: The psychology of shame, guilt, embarrassment, and pride.* New York: Guilford Press.

Tangney, J. P., Baumeister, R. F., & Boone, A. L. (2004). High self-control predicts good adjustment, less pathology, better grades, and interpersonal success. *Journal of Personality, 72*, 271–322.

Tangney, J. P., Wagner, P., Fletcher, C., & Gramzow, R. (1992). Shamed into anger? The relation of shame and guilt to anger and self-reported aggression. *Journal of Personality and Social Psychology, 62*(4), 669–675. doi: 10.1037/0022-3514.62.4.669

Tannahill, R. (1980). *Sex in history.* London: Scarborough House.

Tanner, A. (2003, November 26). Penis enlargement ads drive man to threaten torture. *Reuters News Service.* Retrieved from http://www.tribemagazine.com/board/tribe-main-forum/55009-penis-enlargement-ads-drive-man-threaten-torture.html

Tansey, G., & D'Silva, J. (1999). *The meat business: Devouring a hungry planet.* New York: St. Martin's Press.

Tarquinio, M. (2009, January 27). Workforce planning research: How to strengthen your job in today's economy. Ere.net. Retrieved from http://www.ere.net/2009/01/27/workforce-planning-research-how-to-strengthen-your-job-in-today%e2%80%99s-economy

Tarrant, M. A., & Cordell, H. K. (1997). The effect of respondent characteristics on general environmental attitude-behavior correspondence. *Environment and Behavior, 29*, 618–637.

Tata, J., Anthony, T., Lin, H., Newman, B., Tang, S., Millson, M., & Suvakumar, K. (1996). Proportionate group size and rejection of the deviate: A meta-analytic integration. *Journal of Social Behavior and Personality, 11*, 739–752.

Taylor, K. (2007). Disgust is a factor in extreme prejudice. *British Journal of Social Psychology, 46*(3), 597–617.

Taylor, R. B., Gottfredson, S. D., & Brower, S. (1981). Territorial cognitions and social climate in urban neighborhoods. *Basic and Applied Social Psychology, 2*, 289–303.

Taylor, S. E. (1983). Adjustment to threatening events: A theory of cognitive adaptation. *American Psychologist, 38*, 1161–1173.

Taylor, S. E., & Brown, J. D. (1988). Illusion and well-being: A social psychological perspective on mental health. *Psychological Bulletin, 103*, 193–210.

Taylor, S. E., & Gollwitzer, P. M. (1995). Effects of mind-set on positive illusions. *Journal of Personality and Social Psychology, 69*, 213–226.

Taylor, S. E., & Master, S. L. (2011). Social responses to stress: The tend-and-befriend model. In R. J. Contrada, A. Baum, R. J. Contrada, A. Baum (Eds.), *The handbook of stress science: Biology, psychology, and health* (pp. 101–109). New York: Springer.

Taylor, S. E., & Pham, L. B. (1996). Mental simulation, motivation, and action. In P. M. Gollwitzer & J. A. Bargh (Eds.), *The psychology of action: Linking cognition and motivation to behavior* (pp. 219–235). New York: Guilford Press.

Taylor, S. E., Klein, L. C., Lewis, B. P., Gruenewald, T. L., Gurung, R. A. R, & Updegraff, J. A. (2000). Biobehavioral responses to stress in females: Tend-and-befriend, not fight-or-flight. *Psychological Review, 107*, 441–429.

Taylor, T. S., & Hosch, H. M. (2004). An examination of jury verdicts for evidence of a similarity-leniency effect, an out-group punitiveness effect, or a black sheep effect. *Law and Human Behavior, 28*, 587–598.

Tedeschi, J. T., & Felson, R. B. (1994). *Violence, aggression, and coercive actions.* Washington, DC: American Psychological Association.

Tedeschi, J. T., Schlenker, B. R., & Bonoma, T. V. (1971). Cognitive dissonance: Private ratiocination or public spectacle? *American Psychologist, 26*, 685–695.

Teigen, H. (1986). Old truths or fresh insights? A study of students' evaluations of proverbs. *British Journal of Social Psychology, 25*, 43–50.

Telch, C. F., & Agras, W. S. (1996). Do emotional states influence binge eating in the obese? *International Journal of Eating Disorders, 20*, 271–279.

Tennen, H., Affleck, G., Armeli, S., & Carney, M. A. (2000). A daily process approach to coping: Linking theory, research, and practice. *American Psychologist, 55*(6), 626–636.

Terracianno, A., et al. (2005). National character does not reflect mean personality trait levels in 49 cultures. *Science, 310*, 96–100.

Terrizzi, J. A., Jr., Shook, N. J., & Ventis, W. L. (2010). Disgust: A predictor of social conservatism and prejudicial attitudes toward homosexuals. *Personality and Individual Differences, 49*(6), 587–592.

Tesser, A. (1976). Attitude polarization as a function of thought and reality constraints. *Journal of Research in Personality, 10*, 183–194.

Tesser, A. (1988). Toward a self-evaluation maintenance model of social behavior. In L. Berkowitz (Ed.), *Advances in experimental social psychology* (Vol. 21, pp. 181–227). San Diego: Academic Press.

Tesser, A., & Rosen, S. (1975). The reluctance to transmit bad news. In L. Berkowitz (Ed.), *Advances in experimental social psychology* (Vol. 8, pp. 193–232). New York: Academic Press.

Tetlock, P. E. (1980). Explaining teacher explanations for pupil performance: A test of the self-presentation position. *Social Psychology Quarterly, 43*, 283–290.

Tetlock, P. E. (1981). Pre- to post-election shifts in presidential rhetoric: Impression management or cognitive adjustment? *Journal of Personality and Social Psychology, 41*, 207–212.

Tetlock, P. E. (1992). The impact of accountability on judgment and choice: Toward a social contingency model. In M. P. Zanna (Ed.), *Advances in experimental social psychology* (Vol. 25, pp. 331–376). San Diego: Academic Press.

Tetlock, P. E. (2000). Coping with trade-offs: Psychological constraints and political implications. In S. Lupia, M. McCubbins, & S. Popkin (Eds.), *Political reasoning and choice.* Berkeley: University of California Press.

Tett, R. P., Jackson, D. N., Rothstein, M., & Reddon, J. R. (1994). Meta-analysis of personality-job performance relations: A reply to Ones, Mount, Barrick, & Hunter (1994). *Personnel Psychology, 47*(1), 157–172.

Thayer, R. E., Newman, R., & McClain, T. M. (1994). Self-regulation of mood: Strategies for changing a bad mood, raising energy, and reducing tension. *Journal of Personality and Social Psychology, 67*, 910–925.

The American College Health Association. (2008). American College Health Association—National college health assessment spring 2007 reference group data report (abridged). *Journal of American College Health, 56*(5),469-479. Retrieved from http://www.acha-ncha.org/docs/JACH%20March%202008%20SP%2007%20Ref%20Grp.pdf

The Believeau Law Group. (2012). Can companies use social media to screen job applicants? Retrieved from http://www.beliveaulaw.net/2012/02/can-companies-use-social-media-to-screen-job-applicants/

The Editors of the Lancet (February 2010). Retraction—Ileal-lymphoid-nodular hyperplasia, non-specific colitis, and pervasive developmental disorder in children. *Lancet, 375*(9713), 445. doi:10.1016/S0140-6736(10)60175-4

The ergonomics of dishonesty: The effect of incidental posture on stealing, cheating, and traffic violations. *Psychological Science, 24*(11), 2281–2289. doi: 10.1177/0956797613492425

The Onion (2014, June 24). Report: Only predictor of happy marriage is if husband ever won wife big stuffed animal at amusement park. Retrieved from: http://www.theonion.com/articles/report-only-predictor-of-happy-marriage-is-if-husb,36353/

The People History (2015). Money and inflation 1970s. Retrieved from http://www.thepeoplehistory.com/1970s.html

The triumph of evil. (1995). *PBS Frontline.* Retrieved from http://www.pbs.org/wgbh/pages/frontline/shows/evil

1 Thessalonians 4:17 (Bible).

1 Timothy 6:10 (Bible).

Thinkexist.com. Retrieved from http://thinkexist.com/quotation/a_good_advertisement_is_one_which_sells_the/202773.html

Thomas, K. A., DeScioli, P., Haque, O. S., & Pinker, S. (2014). The psychology of coordination and common knowledge. *Journal of Personality and Social Psychology*, Advance online publication. http://dx.doi.org/10.1037/a0037037

Thompson-Cannino, J., Cotton, R., & Torneo, E. (2009): *Picking Cotton: Our memoir of injustice and redemption.* New York: St. Martin's Press.

Thompson, A. P. (1983). Extramarital sex: A review of the research literature. *Journal of Sex Research, 19*, 1–22.

Thompson, M. P., Norris, F. H., & Hanacek, B. (1993). Age differences in the psychological consequences of Hurricane Hugo. *Psychology and Aging, 8*, 606–616.

Thompson, S. C. G., & Stoutemyer, K. (1991). Water use as a commons dilemma: The effects of education that focuses on long-term consequences and individual action. *Environment and Behavior, 23*, 314–333.

Thornhill, R., & Gangestad, S. W. (1999). The scent of symmetry: A human sex pheromone that signals fitness? *Evolution and Human Behavior, 20*, 175–201.

Thrash, T. M., & Elliot, A. J. (2003). Inspiration as a psychological construct. *Journal of Personality and Social Psychology, 84*, 871–889.

Tice, D. M. (1991). Esteem protection or enhancement? Self-handicapping motives and attributions differ by trait self-esteem. *Journal of Personality and Social Psychology, 60*, 711–725.

Tice, D. M. (1992). Self-presentation and self-concept change: The looking-glass self is also a magnifying glass. *Journal of Personality and Social Psychology, 63*, 435–451.

Tice, D. M., & Baumeister, R. F. (1993). Controlling anger: Self-induced emotion change. In D. M. Wegner & J. W. Pennebaker (Eds.), *Handbook of mental control* (pp. 393–409). Englewood Cliffs, NJ: Prentice-Hall.

Tice, D. M., & Baumeister, R. F. (1997). Longitudinal study of procrastination, performance, stress, and health: The costs and benefits of dawdling. *Psychological Science, 8*, 454–458.

Tice, D. M., & Bratslavsky, E. (2000). Giving in to feel good: The place of emotion regulation in the context of general self-control. *Psychological Science, 11*, 149–159.

Tice, D. M., Bratslavsky, E., & Baumeister, R. F. (2001). Emotional distress regulation takes precedence over impulse control: If you feel bad, do it! *Journal of Personality and Social Psychology, 80*, 53–67.

Tice, D. M., Butler, J. L., Muraven, M. B., & Stillwell, A. M. (1995). When modesty prevails: Differential favorability of self-presentation to friends and strangers. *Journal of Personality and Social Psychology, 69*, 1120–1138.

Tichener, J. L., & Kapp, F. T. (1976). Family and character change at Buffalo Creek. *American Journal of Psychiatry, 33*(3), 295–299.

Tidwell, M., Reis, H. T., & Shaver, P. R. (1996). Attachment styles, attractiveness, and emotions in social interactions: A diary study. *Journal of Personality and Social Psychology, 71*, 729–745.

Tiggemann, M., & Pickering, A. S. (1996). Role of television in adolescent women's body dissatisfaction and drive for thinness. *International Journal of Eating Disorders, 20*, 199–220.

Tiggemann, M., & Rothblum, E. D. (1988). Gender differences in social consequences of perceived overweight in the United States and Australia. *Sex Roles, 18*, 75–86.

Tilcsik, A. (2011). Pride and prejudice: Employment discrimination against openly gay men in the United States. *American Journal of Sociology, 117*(2), 586–626.

Timbergen, N. (1952). The curious behavior of the Stickleback. *Scientific American, 187*, 22–26.

Timeline: Rwanda. (2008, August 8). *BBC News.* Retrieved from http://news.bbc.co.uk/2/hi/africa/1070329.stm

Tjaden, P., & Thoennes, N. (1998). *Stalking in America: Findings from the National Violence Against Women Survey* (NCJ Report no. 169592). Washington, DC: National Institute of Justice and Centers for Disease Control and Prevention.

Tobacyk, J. J., & Downs, A. (1986). Personal construct threat and irrational beliefs as cognitive predictors of increases in musical performance anxiety. *Journal of Personality and Social Psychology, 51*(4), 779–782.

Tobacyk, J., & Milford, G. (1983). Belief in paranormal phenomena: Assessment instrument development and implications for personality functioning. *Journal of Personality and Social Psychology, 44*, 1029–1037.

Toll, B. A., Sobell, M. B., Wagner, E. F., & Sobell, L. C. (2001). The relationship between thought suppression and smoking cessation. *Addictive Behaviors, 26*, 509–515.

Toma, C. L., & Hancock, J. T. (2010). Looks and lies: The role of physical attractiveness in online dating self-presentation and deception. *Communication Research, 37*(3), 335–351.

Toma, C. L., Hancock, J. T., & Ellison, N. B. (2008). Separating fact from fiction: An examination of deceptive self-presentation on online dating profiles. *Personality and Social Psychology Bulletin, 34*, 1023–1036.

Tomasello, M. (2013) *A natural history of human thinking.* Cambridge, MA: Harvard University Press.

Tomasello, M., & Call, J. (1997). *Primate cognition.* New York: Oxford University Press.

Tomkins, S. S. (1962). *Affect, imagery, consciousness: Vol. 1. The positive affects.* New York: Springer.

Tormala, Z. L., & Petty, R. E. (2002). What doesn't kill me makes me stronger: The effects of resisting persuasion on attitude certainty. *Journal of Personality and Social Psychology, 83*, 1298–1313.

Tracking the events in the wake of Michael Brown's shooting. *New York Times.* Retrieved from http://www.nytimes.com/interactive/2014/08/12/us/13police-shooting-of-black-teenager-michael-brown.html

Tran, C. (2014, August 6). All heave! Commuters work together to free with their bare hands man whose leg had become stuck between platform and train. *Daily-Mail.* Retrieved from http://www.dailymail.co.uk/news/article-2717511/Train-commuters-managed-free-man-leg-stuck-to.html

Tremblay, R. E. (2000). The development of aggressive behavior during childhood: What have we learned in the past century? *International Journal of Behavioral Development, 24*(2), 129–141.

Triandis, H. C. (1978). Some universals of social behavior. *Personality and Social Psychology Bulletin, 4*, 1–16.

Trinkaus, J. (1984). A bottle law: An informal look. *Perceptual and Motor Skills, 59*, 806.

Triplett, N. (1897). The dynamogenic factors in peacemaking and competition. *American Journal of Psychology, 9*, 507–533.

Trivers, R. (1972). Parental investment and sexual selection. In B. Campbell (Ed.), *Sexual selection and the descent of man: 1871–1971* (pp. 136–179). Chicago: Aldine.

Trope, Y. (1983). Self-assessment in achievement behavior. In J. Suls & A. Greenwald (Eds.), *Psychological perspectives on the self* (Vol. 2, pp. 93–121). Hillsdale, NJ: Erlbaum.

Trope, Y. (1986). Self-enhancement and self-assessment in achievement behavior. In R. Sorrentino & E. T. Higgins (Eds.), *Handbook of motivation and cognition* (Vol. 2, pp. 350–378). New York: Guilford Press.

Troy Davis execution fuels eyewitness ID debate. (2011, September 27). *Associated Press.* Retrieved from http://www.usatoday.com/news/nation/story/2011-09-27/troy-davis-eyewitness-testimony/50563754/1

Trzesniewski, K. H., Donnellan, M. B., & Robins, R. W. (2008). Is "Generation Me" really more narcissistic than previous generations? *Journal of Personality, 76*, 903–917.

Tsal, Y. (1984). *The role of attention in processing information from advertisements.* Unpublished manuscript, Cornell University, Ithaca, NY.

Tsang, J.-A., McCullough, M. E., & Hoyt, W. T. (2005). Psychometric and rationalization accounts for the religion-forgiveness discrepancy. *Journal of Social Issues. 61*, 785–805.

Tse, A. C. B., & Yim, F. (2001). Factors affecting the choice of channels: Online vs. conventional. *Journal of International Consumer Marketing, 14*, 137–152.

Tufekci, Z. (2008). Grooming, gossip, Facebook, and Myspace: What can we learn about these sites from those who won't assimilate? *Information, Communication & Society, 11*, 544–564.

Turnbull, S. (2003). *The Ottoman Empire 1326–1699.* New York: Routledge.

Turner, C. W., Layton, J. F., & Simons, L. S. (1975). Naturalistic studies of aggressive behavior: Aggressive stimuli, victim visibility, and horn honking. *Journal of Personality and Social Psychology, 31*, 1098–1107.

Turner, R. H. (1976). The real self: From institution to impulse. *American Journal of Sociology, 81*, 989–1016.

Turner, S. A., Luszczynska, A., Warner, L., & Schwarzer, R. (2010). Emotional and uncontrolled eating styles and chocolate chip cookie consumption. A controlled trial of the effects of positive mood enhancement. *Appetite, 54*(1), 143–149.

Tversky, A., & Kahneman, D. (1974) Judgment under uncertainty: Heuristics and biases. *Science, 185*, 1124–1131.

Tversky, A., & Kahneman, D. (1983). Extensional vs. intuitive reasoning: The conjunction fallacy in probability judgment. *Psychological Review, 91*, 293–3l5.

Twenge, J. M. (2006). *Generation me.* New York: Free Press.

Twenge, J. M., & Campbell, W. K. (2001). Age and birth cohort differences in self-esteem: A cross-temporal meta-analysis. *Personality and Social Psychology Review, 5*, 321–344.

Twenge, J. M., & Crocker, J. (2002). Race and self-esteem: Meta-analyses comparing Whites, Blacks, Hispanics, Asians, and American Indians. *Psychological Bulletin, 128*, 371–408.

Twenge, J. M., Baumeister, R. F., Tice, D. M., & Stucke, T. S. (2001). If you can't join them, beat them: Effects of social exclusion on aggressive behavior. *Journal of Personality and Social Psychology, 81*, 1058–1069.

Twenge, J. M., Campbell, W. K., & Foster, C. A. (2003). Parenthood and marital satisfaction: A meta-analytic review. *Journal of Marriage and Family, 65*, 574–583.

Twenge, J. M., Catanese, K. R., & Baumeister, R. F. (2002). Social exclusion causes self-defeating behavior. *Journal of Personality and Social Psychology, 83*, 606–615.

Twenge, J. M., Catanese, K. R., & Baumeister, R. F. (2003). Social exclusion and the deconstructed state: Time perception, meaninglessness, lethargy, lack of emotion, and self-awareness. *Journal of Personality and Social Psychology, 85*, 409–423.

Twenge, J. M., Ciarocco, N. J., Cuervo, D., Bartels, J. M., & Baumeister, R. F. (2004). Social exclusion reduces prosocial behavior. *Journal of Personality and Social Psychology, 92*, 56–66.

Twenge, J. M., Konrath, S., Foster, J. D., Campbell, W. K., & Bushman, B. J. (2008). Egos inflating over time: A cross-temporal meta-analysis of the Narcissistic Personality Inventory. *Journal of Personality, 76*, 875–901.

Twenge, J., & Crocker, J. (2002). Race, ethnicity, and self-esteem: Meta-analyses comparing whites, blacks, Hispanics, Asians, and Native Americans, including a commentary on Gray-Little and Hafdahl (2000). *Psychological Bulletin, 128*, 371–408.

Tybout, A. M., & Yalch, R. F. (1980). The effect of experience: A matter of salience? *Journal of Consumer Research, 6*, 406–413.

U. S. Department of Health and Human Services. (2000). Best practices for comprehensive tobacco control programs. Retrieved January 2012 from http://www.hsca.com/membersonly/USDHHSlink.htm

U.S. Census Bureau. (2009). New motor vehicle sales and car production. *The 2009 statistical abstract: National data book.* Retrieved from http://www.census.gov/compendia/statab/tables/09s1021.pdf

U.S. Department of Justice. Identity theft and identity fraud. Retrieved from http://www.justice.gov/criminal/fraud/websites/idtheft.html

U.S. Equal Employment Opportunity Commission. (2012). Laws & guidance. Retrieved from http://www.eeoc.gov/laws/index.cfm

U.S. Federal Bureau of Investigation. (2011). *Uniform crime reports.* Washington, DC: U.S. Government Printing Office.

U.S. Federal Bureau of Investigation. (2012). *Uniform crime reports.* Washington, DC: U.S. Government Printing Office.

Uchino, B. N., Cacioppo, J. T., & Kiecolt-Glaser, J. K. (1996). The relationship between social support and physiological processes: A review with emphasis on underlying mechanisms and implications for health. *Psychological Bulletin, 119*(3), 488–531.

Udry, J. R. (1980). Changes in the frequency of marital intercourse from panel data. *Archives of Sexual Behavior, 9*, 319–325.

Uhlmann, E. L., Pizarro, D. A., & Diermeier, D. (2015). A person-centered approach to moral judgment. *Perspectives on Psychological Science, 10*, 72–81.

Umphress, E. E., Ren, L. R., Bingham, J. B., & Gogus, C. I. (2009). The influence of distributive justice on lying for and stealing from a supervisor. *Journal of Business Ethics, 86*(4), 507–518.

Undercover Recruiter. (2015). How employers use social media to screen applicants. Retrieved from http://theundercoverrecruiter.com/infographic-how-recruiters-use-social-media-screen-applicants/

Underwood, J. D. M., Kerlin, L., & Farrington-Flint, L. (2011). The lies we tell and what they say about us: Using behavioural characteristics to explain Facebook activity. *Computers in Human Behavior, 27*(5), 1621–1626.

Unger, L. S. (1996). The potential for using humor in global advertising. *Humor, 9*, 143–168.

Union of Concerned Scientists. (1993). *World scientists warning to humanity*. Cambridge, MA: Union of Concerned Scientists.

United Nations Population Fund. (2007/2008). A human rights and health priority. Retrieved October 17, 2008, from http://www.unfpa.org/swp/2000/english/ch03.html

Utman, C. H. (1997). Performance effects of motivational state: A meta-analysis. *Personality and Social Psychology Review, 1*, 170–182.

Vaillancourt, R. (2005). Indirect aggression among humans: Social construct or evolutionary adaption? In R. E. Tremblay, W. W. Hartup, & J. Archer (Eds.), *Developmental origins of aggression* (pp. 158–177). New York: Guilford Press.

Valentine, T., & Mesout, J. (2009). Eyewitness identification under stress in the London Dungeon. *Applied Cognitive Psychology, 23*, 151–161.

van 't Veer, A. E., Stel, M., & van Beest, I. (2014). Limited capacity to lie: Cognitive load interferes with being dishonest. *Judgment and Decision Making, 9*(3), 199–206. doi: 10.2139/ssrn.2351377

Van Bavel, J. J., & Cunningham, W. A. (2012). A social identity approach to person memory: Group membership, collective identification, and social role shape attention and memory. *Personality and Social Psychology Bulletin, 38*, 1566–1578.

Van Beest, I., & Williams, K. D. (2006). When inclusion costs and ostracism pays, ostracism still hurts. *Journal of Personality and Social Psychology, 91*, 918–928.

Van Boven, L., & Epley, N. (2003). The unpacking effect in evaluative judgments: When the whole is less than the sum of its parts. *Journal of Experimental Social Psychology, 39*, 263–2.

Van Boven, L., & Gilovich, T. (2003). To do or to have? That is the question. *Journal of Personality and Social Psychology, 85*, 1193–1202.

Van Boven, L., Kamada, A., & Gilovich, T. (1999). The perceiver as perceived: Everyday intuitions about the correspondence bias. *Journal of Personality and Social Psychology, 77*(6), 1188–1199.

Van den Bergh, B., Dewitte, S., & Warlop, L. (2008). Bikinis instigate generalized impatience in intertemporal choice. *Journal of Consumer Research, 35*(1), 85–97.

Van der Wal, R.C., & van Dillen, L.F. (2013). Leaving a flat taste in your mouth: Task load reduces taste perception. *Psychological Science, 24*, 1277–1284.

Van Dijk, E., Van Kleef, G. A., Steinel, W., & Van Beest, I. (2008). A social functional approach to emotions in bargaining: When communicating anger pays and when it backfires. *Journal of Personality and Social Psychology, 94*(4), 600–614.

Van Dijk, W. W., & Zeelenberg, M. (2002). Investigating the appraisal patterns of regret and disappointment. *Motivation and Emotion, 26*, 321–331.

Van Goozen, S. H. M., Cohen-Kettenis, P. T., Gooren, L. J. G. M., Frijda, N. H., & Can de Poll, N. E. (1995). Gender differences in behaviour: Activating effects of cross-sex hormones. *Psychoneuroendocrinology, 20*, 343–363.

Van Horne, T. (2013, December 5). Workplace design impacts performance, employee engagement and innovation. Retrieved from http://www.canadaone.com/ezine/2013/workplace_design_impacts_performance.html

Van Houten, R., & Nau, P. A. (1981). A comparison of the effects of posted feedback and increased police surveillance on highway speeding. *Journal of Applied Behavior Analysis, 14*, 261–271.

Van Kleef, G. A., De Dreu, C. K. W., & Manstead, A. S. R. (2004a). The interpersonal effects of anger and happiness in negotiations. *Journal of Personality and Social Psychology, 86*(1), 57–76.

Van Kleef, G. A., De Dreu, C. K. W., & Manstead, A. S. R. (2004b). The interpersonal effects of emotions in negotiations: A motivated information processing approach. *Journal of Personality and Social Psychology, 87*(4), 510–528.

Van Praag, H. M. (1990). Two-tier diagnosing in psychiatry. *Psychiatry Research, 34*, 1–11.

Van Vugt, M., & Samuelson, C. (1999). The impact of personal metering in the management of a natural resource crisis: A social dilemma analysis. *Personality and Social Psychology Bulletin, 25*, 731–745.

Vandello, J. A., & Cohen, D. (2003). Male honor and female fidelity: Implicit cultural scripts that perpetuate domestic violence. *Journal of Personality and Social Psychology, 84*(5), 997–1010.

Vandello, J. A., Bosson, J. K., Cohen, D., Burnaford, R. M., & Weaver, J. R. (2008). Precarious manhood. *Journal of Personality and Social Psychology, 95*, 1325–1339.

Vartanian, L. R., Thomas, M. A., & Vanman, E. J. (2013). Disgust, contempt, and anger and the stereotypes of obese people. *Eating and Weight Disorders, 18*(4), 377–382. doi: 10.1007/s40519-013-0067-2

Vaughan, D. (1986). *Uncoupling: Turning points in intimate relationships*. New York: Oxford University Press.

Vazire, S. (2010). Who knows what about a person? The Self-Other Knowledge Asymmetry (SOKA) model. *Journal of Personality and Social Psychology, 98*, 281–300.

Veenhoven, R. (2004). *World database of happiness: Continuous register of scientific research on subjective appreciation of life*. Retrieved from http://www.eur.nl/fsw/research/happiness

Viek, C., & Steg, L. (2007). Human behavior and environmental sustainability: problems, driving forces and research topics. *Journal of Social Issues, 63*, 1–19.

Vohs, K. D. & Heatherton, T. F. (2000). Self-regulatory failure: A resource depletion approach. *Psychological Science, 11*, 249–254.

Vohs, K. D., & Schooler, J. W. (2008). The value of believing in free will: Encouraging a belief in determinism increases cheating. *Psychological Science, 19*, 49–54.

Vohs, K. D., Baumeister, R. F., Schmeichel, B. J., Twenge, J. M., Nelson, N. M., & Tice, D. M. (2008). Making choices impairs subsequent self-control: A limited-resource account of decision making, self-regulation, and active initiative. *Journal of Personality and Social Psychology, 94*, 883–898. doi: 10.1037/0022-3514.94.5.883

Vohs, K. D., Mead, N. L., & Goode, M. R. (2006, November). The psychological consequences of money. *Science, 314*(5802), 1154–1156.

Von Hippel, W., & Trivers, R. (2011). The evolution and psychology of self-deception. *Behavioral and Brain Sciences, 34*, 1–56.

Wagner, H. S., Ahlstrom, B., Redden, J. P., Vickers, Z., & Mann, T. (2014). The myth of comfort food. *Health Psychology, 33*(12), 1552–1557. doi: 10.1037/hea0000068

Wakefield, A., Murch, S., Anthony, A. et al. (1998). Ileal-lymphoid-nodular hyperplasia, non-specific colitis, and pervasive developmental disorder in children. *Lancet, 351*(9103), 637–641. doi:10.1016/S0140-6736(97)11096-0

Wakslak, C. J., Nussbaum, S., Liberman, N., & Trope, Y. (2008). Representations of the self in the near and distant future. *Journal of Personality and Social Psychology, 95*, 751–773.

Waldman, S. (1992, January 27). The tyranny of choice: Why the consumer revolution is ruining your life. *New Republic*, 22–25.

Walker, I., & Crogan, M. (1998). Academic performance, prejudice, and the jigsaw classroom: New pieces to the puzzle. *Journal of Community and Applied Social Psychology, 8*, 381–393.

Wallace, H. M., & Baumeister, R. F. (2002). The performance of narcissists rises and falls with perceived opportunity for glory. *Journal of Personality and Social Psychology, 82*, 819–834.

Wallach, M. A., Kogan, N., & Bem, D. J. (1962). Group influence on individual risk-taking. *Journal of Abnormal and Social Psychology, 65*, 75–86.

Walsh, A. (1991). Self-esteem and sexual behavior: Exploring gender differences. *Sex Roles, 25*, 441–450.

Walsh, A. (1991). The biological relationship between sex and love. *Free Inquiry, 11*, 20–24.

Walster, E., & Festinger, L. (1962). The effectiveness of "overheard" persuasive communication. *Journal of Abnormal and Social Psychology, 65*, 395–402.

Walster, E., Aronson, V., Abrahams, D., & Rottmann, L. (1966). Importance of physical attractiveness in dating behavior. *Journal of Personality and Social Psychology, 4*, 508–516.

Walters, K. S., & Portmess, L. (Eds.). (1999). *Ethical vegetarianism: From Pythagoras to Peter Singer*. Albany: State University of New York Press.

Walton, G. M., Cohen, G. L., Cwir, D., & Spencer, S. J. (2012). Mere belonging: The power of social connections. *Journal of Personality and Social Psychology, 102*, 513–532.

Wanberg, C. R., Kammeyer-Mueller, J. D., & Shi, K. (2001). Job loss and the experience of unemployment: International research and perspectives. In N. Anderson, D. S. Ones, H. K. Sinangil, & C. Viswesvaran (Eds.), *Handbook of industrial, work and organizational psychology* (Vol. 2, pp. 253–269). Thousand Oaks, CA: Sage.

Wang, C. L., Bristol, T., Mowen J. C., & Chakraborty, G. (2000). Alternative modes of self-construal: Dimensions of connectedness-separateness and advertising appeals to the cultural and gender-specific self. *Journal of Consumer Psychology, 9*, 107–115.

Wang, P. S., Gruber, M. J., Powers, R. E., Schoenbaum, M., Speier, A. H., Wells, K. B., et al. (2007). Mental health service use among Hurricane Katrina survivors in the eight months after the disaster. *Psychiatric Services, 58*, 1403–1411.

Waring, R. L., & Buchanan, F. R. (2010). Social networking web sites: The legal and ethical aspects of pre-employment screening and employee surveillance. *Journal of Human Resources Education, 4*(2), 14–23.

Warneken, F., & Tomasello, M. (2006). Altruistic helping in human infants and young chimpanzees. *Science, 311*, 1301–1303.

Watson, D., & Clark, L. A. (1991). Self-versus peer ratings of specific emotional traits: Evidence of convergent and discriminant validity. *Journal of Personality and Social Psychology, 60*, 927–940.

Watson, D., & Clark, L. A. (1992). Affects separable and inseparable: On the hierarchical arrangement of the negative affects. *Journal of Personality and Social Psychology, 62*, 489–505.

Watson, D., & Clark, L. A. (1997). Extraversion and its positive emotional core. In R. Hogan, J. Johnson, & S. Briggs (Eds.), *Handbook of personality psychology* (pp. 767–793). New York: Academic Press.

Watson, D., & Tellegen, A. (1985). Toward a consensual structure of mood. *Psychological Bulletin, 98*, 219–235.

Watson, T. (2013, March 29). Did your Facebook just turn red? That's the color of our world changing. *Forbes*. Retrieved from http://www.forbes.com/sites/tomwatson/2013/03/27/did-your-facebook-just-turn-red-thats-the-color-of-our-world-changing/

Wayment H. A., Wyatt G. E., Tucker, M. B., Romero G. J., Carmona, J. V., Newcomb, M., et al. (2003). Predictors of risky and precautionary sexual behaviors among single and married white women. *Journal of Applied Social Psychology, 33*, 791–816.

Waytz, A., Young, L.L., & Ginges, J. (2014). Motive attribution asymmetry for love vs. hate drives intractable conflict. *PNAS*, early edition.

Weary, G. (1980). Examination of affect and egotism as mediators of bias in causal attributions. *Journal of Personality and Social Psychology, 38*, 348–357.

Weber, K., Canuto, A., Giannakopoulos, P., Mouchian, A., Meiler-Mititelu, C., Meiler, A., & . . . de Rivaupierre, A. (2015). Personality, psychosocial and health-related predictors of quality of life in old age. *Aging & Mental Health, 19*(2), 151–158. doi: 10.1080/13607863.2014.920295

Weber, N., Brewer, N., Wells, G. L., Semmler, C., & Keast, A. (2004). Eyewitness identification accuracy and response latency: The unruly 10–12-second rule. *Journal of Experimental Psychology: Applied, 10*, 139–147.

WebMD (2015). Stress symptoms. Retrieved from http://www.webmd.com/balance/stress-management/stress-symptoms-effects_of-stress-on-the-body?page52http://www.webmd.com/balance/stress-management/stress-symptoms-effects_of-stress-on-the-body?page52

Wegner, D. M. (1986). Transactive memory: A contemporary analysis of the group mind. In B. Mullen & G. R. Goethals (Eds.), *Theories of group behavior* (pp. 185–208). New York: Springer-Verlag.

Wegner, D. M. (1989). *White bears and other unwanted thoughts: Suppression, obsession, and the psychology of mental control.* New York: Viking/Penguin.

Wegner, D. M. (1994). Ironic processes of mental control. *Psychological Review, 101,* 34–52.

Wegner, D. M. (2002). *The illusion of conscious will.* Cambridge, MA: MIT Press.

Wegner, D. M., Giuliano, T., & Hertel, P. (1985). Cognitive interdependence in close relationships. In W. Ickes (Ed.), *Compatible and incompatible relationships* (pp. 253–276). New York: Springer-Verlag.

Wegner, D. M., Schneider, D. J., Carter, S. R., & White, T. L. (1987). Paradoxical effects of thought suppression. *Journal of Personality and Social Psychology, 53*(1), 5–13.

Wegner, D. M., Wenzlaff, R. M., & Kozak, M. (2004). Dream rebound: The return of suppressed thoughts in dreams. *Psychological Science, 15,* 232–236.

Weiner, B. (1972). *Theories of motivation: From mechanism to cognition.* Chicago: Rand McNally.

Weinrich, S., Hardin, S. B., & Johnson, M. (1990). Nurses respond to hurricane Hugo victims: Disaster stress. *Archives of Psychiatric Nursing, 4,* 195–205.

Weintraub, K. J. (1978). *The value of the individual: Self and circumstance in autobiography.* Chicago: University of Chicago Press.

Weiss, B., & Feldman, R. S. (2006). Looking good and lying to do it: Deception as an impression management strategy in job interviews. *Journal of Applied Social Psychology, 36*(4), 1070–1086.

Wells, G. L. (1984). The psychology of lineup identifications. *Journal of Applied Social Psychology, 14,* 89–103.

Wells, G. L., & Bradfield, A. L. (1998). "Good, you identified the suspect": Feedback to eyewitnesses distorts their reports of the witnessing experience. *Journal of Applied Psychology, 83,* 360–376.

Wells, G. L., & Luus, C. A. E. (1990). Police lineups as experiments: Social methodology as a framework for properly conducted lineups. *Personality and Social Psychology Bulletin, 16,* 106–117.

Wells, G. L., & Olson, E. A. (2003). Eyewitness testimony. *Annual Review of Psychology, 54,* 277–295.

Wells, G. L., & Petty, R. E. (1980). The effects of overt head movements on persuasion: Compatibility and incompatibility of responses. *Basic and Applied Social Psychology, 1,* 219–230.

Wells, G. L., & Quinlivan, D. S. (2009). Suggestive eyewitness identification procedures and the Supreme Court's reliability test in light of eyewitness science: 30 years later. *Law and Human Behavior, 33,* 1–24.

Wells, G. L., & Turtle, J. W. (1986). Eyewitness identification: The importance of lineup models. *Psychological Bulletin, 99,* 320–329.

Wells, G. L., & Windschitl, P. D. (1999). Stimulus sampling and social psychological experimentation. *Personality and Social Psychology Bulletin, 25,* 1115–1125.

Wells, G. L., Olson, E. A., & Charman, S. D. (2003). Distorted retrospective eyewitness reports as functions of feedback and delay. *Journal of Experimental Psychology: Applied, 9,* 42–52.

Wells, G. L., Small, M., Penrod, S., Malpass, R. S., Fulero, S. M., & Brimacombe, C. A. E. (1998). Eyewitness identification procedures: Recommendations for lineups and photospreads. *Law and Human Behavior, 22,* 603–647.

Wells, G. L., Steblay, N. K., & Dysart, J. E. (2015). Double-blind photo lineups using actual eyewitnesses: An experimental test of a sequential versus simultaneous lineup procedure. *Law and Human Behavior, 39,* 1–14.

Wells, G. L., Steblay, N., & Dysart, J. E. (2012). Eyewitness identification reforms: Are suggestiveness-induced hits and guesses true hits? *Perspectives on Psychological Science, 7,* 264–271.

Wenger, A. A., & Bornstein, B. H. (2006). The effects of victim's substance use and relationship closeness on mock jurors' judgments in an acquaintance rape case. *Sex Roles, 54,* 547–555.

Wenzlaff, R. M., & Wegner D. M. (2000). Thought suppression. *Annual Review of Psychology, 51,* 59–91.

Werle, C. O. C., Wansink, B., & Payne, C. R. (2014). Is it fun or exercise? The framing of physical activity biases subsequent snacking. *Marketing Letters.* doi: 10.1007/s11002-014-9301-6.

West Virginia Division of Personnel. (2004, September). Selection interviewing: Developing and administering structured behavioral interviews. Retrieved from http://webcache.googleusercontent.com/search?q5cache:khtpGpmt7vwJ:www.state.wv.us/admin/personnel/emprel/toolbox/quiz/interviewing.pdf1&cd51&hl5en&ct5clnk&gl5us

West, S. G., & Brown, T. J. (1975). Physical attractiveness, the severity of the emergency and helping: A field experiment and interpersonal simulation. *Journal of Experimental Social Psychology, 11,* 531–538.

Westergaard, G. C., Mehlman, P. T., Suomi, S. J., & Higley, J. D. (1999). CSF 5-HIAA and aggression in female macaque monkeys: Species and interindividual differences. *Psychopharmacology, 146,* 440–446.

Whatley, M. A., Webster, J. M., Smith, R. H., & Rhodes, A. (1999). The effect of a favor on public and private compliance: How internalized is the norm of reciprocity? *Basic and Applied Social Psychology, 21,* 251–259.

Wheeler, L., & Kim, Y. (1997). What is beautiful is culturally good: The physical attractiveness stereotype has different content in collectivistic cultures. *Personality and Social Psychology Bulletin, 23,* 795–802.

Wheeler, L., & Nezlek, J. (1977). Sex differences in social participation. *Journal of Personality and Social Psychology, 35,* 742–754.

Wheeler, L., Reis, H., & Nezlek, J. B. (1983). Loneliness, social interaction, and sex roles. *Journal of Personality and Social Psychology, 45*(4), 943–953.

Whisman, V. (1996). *Queer by choice.* New York: Routledge.

Whitaker, J. L., & Bushman, B. J. (2012). "Remain calm. Be kind": Effects of relaxing video games on aggressive and prosocial behavior. *Social Psychological and Personality Science, 3*(1), 88–92. doi: 10.1177/1948550611409760

White, A. E., Kenrick, D. T., Li, Y. J., Mortensen, C. R., Neuberg, S.L., & Cohen, A. B. (2012). When nasty breeds nice: Threats of violence amplify agreeableness at national, individual, and situational levels. *Journal of Personality and Social Psychology, 103,* 622–634.

White, C. M., Reisen, N., & Hoffrage, U. (2008, November). *Choice deferral can arise from absolute evaluation or relative comparison.* Paper presented at the annual meeting of the Society for Judgment and Decision Making, Chicago.

White, G. L. (1980). Physical attractiveness and courtship progress. *Journal Personality and Social Psychology, 39,* 660–668. Copyright © 1980 by the American Psychological Association. Reprinted by permission.

Whitley, B. E. (1988). Sex differences in heterosexuals' attitudes toward homosexuals: It depends upon what you ask. *Journal of Sex Research, 24,* 287–291.

Whitson, J. A., Liljenquist, K. A., Galinsky, A. D., Magee, J. C., Gruenfeld, D. H., & Cadena, B. (2013). The blind leading: Power reduces awareness of constraints. *Journal of Experimental Social Psychology, 49,* 579–582.

Why We Fight. Retrieved from http://history.acusd.edu/gen/filmnotes/whywefight.html

Wicker, A. W. (1969). Attitudes versus actions: The relationship of verbal and overt behavioral responses to attitude object. *Journal of Social Issues, 25,* 41–78.

Wicklund, R. A. (1974). *Freedom and reactance.* Potomac, MD: Erlbaum.

Wicklund, R. A., & Gollwitzer, P. M. (1982). *Symbolic self-completion.* Hillsdale, NJ: Erlbaum.

Wiederman, M. W. (1993). Demographic and sexual characteristics of nonresponders to sexual experience items in a national survey. *Journal of Sex Research, 30,* 27–35.

Wiederman, M. W. (1997). The truth must be in here somewhere: Examining the gender discrepancy in self-reported lifetime number of sex partners. *Journal of Sex Research, 34,* 375–386.

Wiederman, M. W. (2004). Self-control and sexual behavior. In R. Baumeister & K. Vohs (Eds.), *Handbook of self-regulation* (pp. 537–552). New York: Guilford Press.

Wiederman, M. W., & LaMar, L. (1998). "Not with him you don't!": Gender and emotional reactions to sexual infidelity during courtship. *Journal of Sex Research, 34,* 375–386.

Wiehe, V. R. (1991). *Perilous rivalry: When siblings become abusive.* Lexington, MA: Heath/Lexington Books.

Wieselquist, J., Rusbult, C. E., Foster, C. A., & Agnew, C. R. (1999). Commitment, pro-relationship behavior, and trust in close relationships. *Journal of Personality and Social Psychology, 77,* 942–966.

William, I. M. (1993). *Humiliation: And other essays on honor, social discomfort, and violence.* Ithaca, NY: Cornell University Press.

Williams, A. D. (1992). Bias and debiasing techniques in forensic psychology. *American Journal of Forensic Psychology, 10,* 19–26.

Williams, K. D. (2001). *Ostracism: The power of silence.* New York: Guilford Press.

Williams, K. D., & Zadro, L. (2005). Ostracism: The indiscriminate early detection system. In K. D. Williams, J. P. Forgas, & W. von Hippel (Eds.), *The social outcast: Ostracism, social exclusion, rejection, and bullying* (pp. 19–34). New York: Psychology Press.

Williams, K., Harkins, S. G., & Latané, B. (1981). Identifiability as a deterrant to social loafing: Two cheering experiments. *Journal of Personality and Social Psychology, 40*(2), 303–311.

Williams, S. S. (2001). Sexual lying among college students in close and casual relationships. *Journal of Applied Social Psychology, 31*(11), 2322–2338.

Williamson, G. M., & Clark, M. S. (1989). Providing help and desired relationship type as determinants of changes in moods and self-evaluations. *Journal of Personality and Social Psychology, 56*(5), 722–734.

Willis, A. (2012, October 10). Vest inflates when you get a Facebook like. *Masahable.com* Retrieved from http://www.stuff.co.nz/technology/gadgets/7797712/Like-A-Hug-Vest-inflates-when-you-get-a-Facebook-like

Willis, R. (1989). The "peace puzzle" in Ufipa. In S. Howell & R. Willis (Eds.), *Societies at peace: Anthropological perspectives* (pp. 133–145). London: Routledge.

Wills, T. A. (1981). Downward comparison principles in social psychology. *Psychological Bulletin, 90,* 245–271.

Wills, T., Sargent, J., Stoolmiller, M., Gibbons, F., & Gerrard, M. (2008). Movie smoking exposure and smoking onset: A longitudinal study of mediation processes in a representative sample of U.S. adolescents. *Psychology of Addictive Behaviors, 22*(2), 269–277.

Wilson, J., Kuehn, R., & Beach, F. (1963). Modifications in the sexual behavior of male rats produced by changing the stimulus female. *Journal of Comparative and Physiological Psychology, 56,* 636–644.

Wilson, M., & Daly M. (2003). Do pretty women inspire men to discount the future? Biology Letters. *Proceedings of the Royal Society, London. B (Suppl.).* doi: 10.1098/rsbl.2003.0134

Wilson, T. D. (2002). *Strangers to ourselves: Discovering the adaptive unconscious.* Cambridge, MA: Harvard University Press.

Wilson, T. D., Dunn, D. S., Kraft, D., & Lisle, D. J. (1989). Introspection, attitude change, and attitude-behavior consistency: The disruptive effects of explaining why we feel the way we do. In M. P. Zanna (Ed.), *Advances in experimental social psychology* (Vol. 22, pp. 287–343). San Diego: Academic Press.

Wilson, T. D., Hodges, S. D., & LaFleur, S. J. (1995). Effects of introspecting about reasons: Inferring attitudes from accessible thoughts. *Journal of Personality and Social Psychology, 69,* 16–28.

Wilson, T. D., Lindsey, S., & Schooler, T. Y. (2000). A model of dual attitudes. *Psychological Review, 107,* 101–126.

Wilson, T. D., Reinhard, D. A., Westgate, E. C., Gilbert, D. T., Ellerbeck, N., Hahn, C., Brown, C. L., & Shaked, A. (2014). Just think: The challenges of the disengaged mind. *Science, 345,* 75–77.

Wilson, T. D., Wheatley, T., Meyers, J. M., Gilbert, D. T., & Axsom, D. (2000). Focalism: A source of durability bias in affective forecasting. *Journal of Personality and Social Psychology, 78,* 821–836.

Winfield, F. E. (1985). *Commuter marriage.* New York: Columbia University Press.

Wing, R. R., Tate, D. F., Gorin, A. A., Raynor, H. A., Fava, J. L., & Machan, J. (2007). "STOP regain": Are there negative effects of daily weighing? *Journal of Consulting and Clinical Psychology, 75,* 652–656.

Winston, K. (2014, February 28). Student reverses course on secular club, citing threats. *Washington Post.* Retrieved from http://www.washingtonpost.com/national/religion/student-reverses-course-on-secular-club-citing-threats/2014/02/28/2555d50e-a0c1-11e3-878c-65222df220eb_story.html

Witt, L. A., Kacmar, M., Carlson, D. S., & Zivnuska, S. (2002). Interactive effects of personality and organizational politics on contextual performance. *Journal of Organizational Behavior, 23,* 911–926.

Witvliet, C. V. O., Ludwig, T. E., & Van der Laan, K. L. (2001). Granting forgiveness or harboring grudges: Implications for emotion, physiology, and health. *Psychological Science, 121,* 117–123.

Wohl, M. J. A., & Branscombe, N. R. (2008). Remembering historical victimization: Collective guilt for current ingroup transgressions. *Journal of Personality and Social Psychology, 94,* 988–1006.

Wood, P. B., & Bartkowski, J. P. (2004). Attribution style and public policy attitudes toward gay rights. *Social Science Quarterly, 85*(1), 58–74.

Wood, W. & Neal, D. (2007). A new look at habits and the habit-goal interface. *Psychological Review, 114,* 843–863.

Wood, W., & Neal, D. T. (2009). The habitual consumer. *Journal of Consumer Psychology, 19,* 579–592.

Wooten, D. B. (2000). Qualitative steps toward an expanded model of anxiety in gift-giving. *Journal of Consumer Research, 27,* 84–95.

Worchel, S., Lee, J., & Adewole, A. (1975). Effects of supply and demand on ratings of object value. *Journal of Personality and Social Psychology, 32,* 906–914.

Word, C. O., Zanna, M. P., & Cooper, J. (1974). The nonverbal mediation of self-fulfilling prophecies in interracial interaction. *Journal of Experimental Social Psychology, 10,* 109–120.

World Health Organization (2003). WHO definition of health. Preamble to the Constitution of the World Health Organization as adopted by the International Health Conference, New York, 19–22 June, 1946; signed on 22 July 1946 by the representatives of 61 States (Official Records of the World Health Organization, no. 2, p. 100) and entered into force on 7 April 1948. Retrieved from http://www.who.int/about/definition/en/print.html

Worthman, C. M. (1999). Faster, farther, higher: Biology and the discourses on human sexuality. In D. Suggs & A. Miracle (Eds.), *Culture, biology, and sexuality* (pp. 64–75). Athens: University of Georgia Press.

Wortley, R., & McFarlane, M. (2011). The role of territoriality in crime prevention: A field experiment. *Security Journal, 24,* 149–156.

Wortman, C. B., & Brehm, J. W. (1975). Responses to uncontrollable outcomes: An integration of reactance theory and the learned helplessness model. In L. Berkowitz (Ed.), *Advances in experimental social psychology* (Vol. 8, pp. 277–336). New York: Academic Press.

Wout, D., Danso, H., Jackson, J., & Spencer, S. (2008). The many faces of stereotype threat: Group- and self-threat. *Journal of Experimental Social Psychology, 44*(3), 792–799.

Wright R. (2000). *Non zero: The logic of human destiny.* New York: Pantheon.

Wright, E. F., & Jackson, W. (1991). The home-course disadvantage in golf championships: Further evidence for the undermining effect of supportive audiences on performance under pressure. *Journal of Sport Behavior, 14,* 51–60.

Wright, E. F., & Voyer, D. (1995). Supporting audiences and performance under pressure: The home-ice disadvantage in hockey championships. *Journal of Sport Behavior, 18,* 21–28.

Wright, J. C., Giammarino, M., & Parad, H. W. (1986). Social status in small groups: Individual-group similarity and the social "misfit." *Journal of Personality and Social Psychology, 50,* 523–536.

Wright, S. C., Aron, A., McLaughlin-Volpe, T., & Ropp, S. A. (1997). The extended contact effect: Knowledge of cross-group friendships and prejudice. *Journal of Personality and Social Psychology, 73,* 73–90.

Wrzesniewski, A., Schwartz, B., Cong, X., Kane, M., Omar, A., & Kolditz, T. (2014). Multiple types of motives don't multiply the motivation of West Point cadets. *PNAS, 111,* 10990–10995.

Wyer, R. S., & Frey, D. (1983). The effects of feedback about self and others on the cognitive processing of feedback-relevant information. *Journal of Experimental Social Psychology, 19,* 540–559.

Wylie, R. C. (1979). *The self-concept: Vol. 2. Theory and research on selected topics.* Lincoln: University of Nebraska Press.

Wynder, E. L., & Graham, E. A. (1950). Tobacco smoking as a possible etiological factor in bronchiogenic carcinoma. *Journal of the American Medical Association, 143,* 329–336.

Xu, H., Bègue, L, & Bushman, B. J. (2014). Washing the guilt away: Effects of personal versus vicarious cleansing on guilty feelings and prosocial behavior. *Frontiers in Human neuroscience, 8,* 97. doi: 10.3389/fnhum.2014.00097

Xygalatas, D., Mitkidis, P., Fischer, R., Reddish, P., Skewes, J., Geertz, A.W., Roepstorff, A., & Builbulia, J. (2013). Extreme rituals promote prosociality. *Psychological Science, 24,* 1602–1605.

Yang, G. S., Gibson, B., Lueke, A. K., Huesmann, L. R., Bushman, B. J. (2014). Effects of avatar race in violent video games on racial attitudes and aggression. *Social Psychological and Personality Science, 5*(6), 698–704. doi: 10.1177/1948550614528008.

Yang, G. S., Huesmann, L. R., Bushman, B. J. (2014). Effects of playing a violent video game as male versus female avatar on subsequent aggression in male and female players. *Aggressive Behavior, 40,* 537–541. doi: 10.1002/ab.21551

Yang, Q., Wu, X., Zhou, X., Mead, N. L., Vohs, K. D., & Baumeister, R. F. (2013). Diverging effects of clean versus dirty money on attitudes, values, and interpersonal behavior. *Journal of Personality and Social Psychology, 104,* 473–489.

Yap, A., Wazlawek, A. S., Lucas, B. J., Cuddy, A. J. C., & Carney, D. R. (2013).

Yerkes, R. M., & Dodson, J. D. (1908). The relation of strength of stimulus to rapidity of habit formation. *Journal of Comparative Neurology and Psychology, 18,* 459–482.

Yorkston, E., & Menon, G. (2004). A sound idea: Phonetic effects of brand names on consumer judgments. *Journal of Consumer Research, 31,* 43–51.

Young, J. R. (2012). "Social-Media Blasphemy" Texas researcher adds "Enemy" feature to Facebook. Retrieved from http://chronicle.com/article/College-20-Social-Media/131300/

Young, S. G., & Claypool, H. M. (2010). Mere exposure has differential effects on attention allocation to threatening and neutral stimuli. *Journal of Experimental Social Psychology, 46*(2), 424–427.

Yukl, G. (2006). *Leadership in organizations.* Upper Saddle River, NJ: Prentice-Hall.

Zajonc, Heingartner, & Herman (1969). From Zajonc, R. B., Social enhancement and impairment of performance in the cockroach. *Journal of Personality and Social Psychology, 13*(2), 83–92.

Zajonc, R. B. (1965). Social facilitation. *Science, 149,* 269–274.

Zajonc, R. B. (1968). Attitudinal effects of mere exposure. *Journal of Personality and Social Psychology, Monograph Supplement, 9*(2, Pt. 2), 1–27.

Zajonc, R. B., Heingartner, A., & Herman, E. M. (1969). Social enhancement and impairment of performance in the cockroach. *Journal of Personality and Social Psychology, 13,* 83–92.

Zajonc, R. B., Reimer, D. J., & Hausser, D. (1973). Imprinting and the development of object preference in chicks by mere repeated exposure. *Journal of Comparative Physiological Psychology, 83,* 434–440.

Zalar, R. W., Harris, R. B., Kyriacou, D. N., Anglin, D., & Minow, M. (2000). Domestic violence. *New England Journal of Medicine, 342,* 1450–1453.

Zanna, M. P., & Cooper, J. (1974). Dissonance and the pill: An attribution approach to studying the arousal properties of dissonance. *Journal of Personality and Social Psychology, 29,* 703–709.

Zanna, M., Higgins, E. & Taves, P. (1976). Is dissonance phenomenologically aversive? *Journal of Experimental Social Psychology, 12,* 530–538.

Zebrowitz, L. A., White, B., & Wieneke, K. (2008). Mere exposure and racial prejudice: Exposure to other-race faces increases liking for strangers of that race. *Social Cognition, 26*(3), 259–275.

Zhang, H.-H., & Wang, H. (2011). A meta-analysis of the relationship between individual emotional intelligence and workplace performance. *Acta Psychologica Sinica, 43*(2), 188–202.

Zhao, W., & Dweck, C. S. (1994). *Implicit theories and vulnerability to depression-like responses.* Unpublished manuscript, Columbia University, New York. Cited in Dweck, C. S. (1996). Implicit theories as organizers of goals and behavior. In P. Gollwitzer & J. Bargh (Eds.), *The psychology of action: Linking cognition and motivation to behavior* (pp. 69–91). New York: Guilford Press.

Zhong, C. B., & Liljenquist, K. A. (2006). Washing away your sins: Threatened morality and physical cleansing. *Science, 313,* 1451–1452.

Zhou, X., He, L., Yang, Q., Lao, J., & Baumeister, R. F. (2012). Control deprivation and styles of thinking. *Journal of Personality and Social Psychology, 102,* 460–478. doi: 10.1037/a0026316

Ziegert, J. C., & Hanges, P. J. (2005). Employment discrimination: The role of implicit attitudes, motivation, and a climate for racial bias. *Journal of Applied Psychology, 90,* 553–562.

Zillmann, D. (1979). *Hostility and aggression.* Hillsdale, NJ: Erlbaum.

Zillmann, D., Katcher, A. H., & Milavsky, B. (1972). Excitation transfer from physical exercise to subsequent aggressive behavior. *Journal of Experimental Social Psychology, 8,* 247–259.

Zimbardo, P. G. (1970). The human choice: Individuation, reason, and order versus deindividuation, impulse, and chaos. In W. J. Arnold & D. Levine (Eds.), *Nebraska Symposium on Motivation* (pp. 237–307). Lincoln: University of Nebraska Press.

Zottoli, M. A., & Wanous, J. P. (2000). Recruitment source research: Current status and future directions. *Human Resource Management Review, 10,* 435–451.

Zuckerman, M. (1975). Belief in a just world and altruistic behavior. *Journal of Personality and Social Psychology, 31,* 972–997.

Zuckerman, M. (1979). Attribution of success and failure revisited, or: The motivational bias is alive and well in attribution theory. *Journal of Personality, 47,* 245–287.

Brandon, D. P., 509n67
Brandt, M.J., 298n25
Branscombe, N. R., 459n76, 484n220
Bratslavsky, E., 134n128, 134n129, 187n9, 209n156, 221n258, 233n26, 410n24, 466n132
Brauner, S., D16n106
Braverman, J., 438n208, 438n210
Bravo, M., E16n129
Brawley, L. R., C17n98
Breaugh, J. A., C25n163
Brechner, K. C., 505n52
Brehm, J. W., 21n33, 120n31, 120n32, 120n33, 120n35, 120n36, 121n37, 380n74
Brehm, S. S., 120n33, 121n37
Bremner, R. H., 220n254
Brendl, C.M., 125n79
Breneman, J., D9n55
Brennan, K. A., 414n49, 414n50
Breuer, M. E., 353n161
Brewer, M. B., 392n150, 462n102, 462n103, E3n28, E15n112
Brewer, N., D4n7, D4n8, D6n35, D6n36, D6n37, D9n57, D10n71
Brickman, P., 100n234, 196n37, 196n38, 196n44
Brigham, J. C., 452n26, D4n9, D6n33, D12n84
Brill, M., E11n86
Brimacombe, C. A. E., D10n68, D11n76
Brink, M., E4n17, E10n80, E11n83, E11n88
Brinkman, H., E6n50
Bristol, T., 279n107
Brock, P., D16n114
Brockmole, J. R., 350n117
Brockner, A., 203n103
Brockner, J., 96n191, 97n199, 100n237, 203n103
Brodish, A. B., 485n236
Brody, L. R., 216n213
Bronson, P., 461n99
Broomell, S.B., 508n62
Brosnan, S. F., 316n127
Brower, G. L., D10n62
Brower, S., E8n64
Brown, B., E7n59
Brown, B. B., E7n61, E8n63
Brown, C. L., 150n25
Brown, D., 326n178, 326n179
Brown, G., 94n143
Brown, J., 485n227
Brown, J. D., 94n149
Brown, K. W., 197n50, 198n61, B16n81
Brown, L. R., E12n96
Brown, L. S., D19n141
Brown, M. J., 459n84
Brown, N. R., 170n114, 170n115
Brown, R., 467n136, 479n191
Brown, S. W., 197n53
Brown, T. J., 318n149, 384n104
Brownstein, S. C., 176n151
Brunell, A. B., 514n87
Bruner, J. A., A5n6
Brunner, E., C24n151
Bruun, S. E., 501n33, 502n37, 503n44

Bryan, A. D., 364n269
Bryan, C. J., 105n264
Bryant, J. B., D18n133
Bryman, A. S., C18n112
Bryner, J., 313n115
Buchanan, F. R., C11n52
Bucher, A. M., 201n83
Buck, D. M., 460n93
Buckles, E. E., 205n122
Buckley, T., 313n120
Budescu, D.V., 508n62
Budesheim, T. L., 274n72, 277n88
Buehler, R., 129n103, 130n104, 130n106, 212n173
Buhrmester, D., 96n192
Buikema, 148n8
Builbulia, J., 241n69
Bull, R., D5n15
Bulman, R. J., 249n111
Bundy, R. P., 462n105
Bunker, B. B., 376n32
Burger, J. M., 160n62, 265n45, 307n88
Burgess, E. O., 467n138
Burgess, J., A4n2
Burke, M., 353n150, E10n77
Burleson, M. H., 377n45, 377n48, 394n169, 395n176
Burmeister, J. M., 457n69
Burmood, C., E7n52
Burnaford, R. M., 45n40, 45n41
Burns, D., 94n142
Burns, J., 314n121
Burnstein, E., 312n110
Burris, C. T., 251n118
Burrows, L., 7n13, 155n34
Bursik, R. J., 365n277
Burton, K., 418n89
Burton, R. L., 252n131
Burwell, R. A., 74n18
Bush, M., 266n42
Bushman, B. J., 7n14, 27n50, 75n27, 93n127, 93n128, 99n214, 99n219, 99n220, 99n221, 121n38, 121n40, 134n126, 201n86, 201n87, 204n111, 211n171, 219n245, 220n254, 220n255, 221n257, 236n49, 278n105, 297n20, 306n85, 313n116, 313n117, 319n161, 325n175, 335n17, 342n51, 342n54, 344n61, 344n62, 344n63, 348n101, 350n113, 350n118, 351n127, 352n130, 352n131, 352n134, 352n135, 352n138, 352n139, 352n140, 353n146, 353n149, 354n177, 354n186, 358n199, 358n200, 358n202, 364n266, 454n33, 455n37, E3n13
Buss, A. H., 15n23, 74n15, 75n29, 216n214, 335n14
Buss, D. M., 38n5, 100n224, 119n21, 170n108, 297n15, 376n22, 376n23, 386n111, 426n138, 427n141, 427n142, 434n185, 437n204, 438n206, 438n207
Buswell, B. N., 93n134
Butler, J. L., 106n270, 500n20
Butts, C. T., 304n57

Butz, D. A., 452n23
Buunk, B. P., 437n203, 438n207
Byerley, G. J., 429n152
Byers, E. S., 348n97
Byrne, D., 348n96, 378n58

C

Cacioppo, J. T., 187n4, 208n143, 235n41, 264n32, 277n91, 278n101, 278n103, 280n113, 281n118, 281n120, 377n44, 377n45, 377n48, 377n52, 377n53, 394n165, 394n169, 394n171, 395n175, 395n176, 395n177, B8n29
Cadinu, M., 481n204
Caesar, P. L., 349n108
Caidahl, K., 377n49
Cain, T. R., 470n149, 471n154
Cairns, K. J., 95n158, 103n252
Caldwell, M. A., 376n38
Calhoun, J. B., E3n4
Calhoun, K. S., 459n82
Call, J., 125n77
Call, V., 408n20
Calvert, S. L., 351n127
Camacho, L. M., 507n54
Cameron, J., 82n59, 83n63, 83n65
Campbell, A., 195n35, 207n133
Campbell, D. T., 16n27, 20n31, 196n37, 261n27, 494n3
Campbell, J. D., 93n123, 93n125, 96n165, 96n179, 96n189, 96n193, 96n198, 100n238
Campbell, J. K., 359n208
Campbell, W. K., 93n130, 99n214, 99n217, 100n225, 100n226, 100n227, 100n229, 161n68, 195n32, 207n138, 306n85, 416n78, 416n79, 416n80, 417n86, 514n87
Campion, J. E., C12n55
Can de Poll, N. E., 375n11
Canino, G., E16n129Canino, G. J., E16n128
Cannarella, J., 213n17
Cannon, W. B., B3n9, B4n11
Cannon-Bowers, J. A., C18n110
Canon, L. K., E4n16
Cantor, J., 121n38, 275n80
Canuto, A., B16n77
Capitanio, J. P., 460n86, 460n89
Cappell, C., 349n109
Caprariello, P. A., 44n23
Carabin, H., B12n54
Carels, R. A., 457n69
Carey, G. L., 13n20
Carey, M. P., 252n126
Carlsmith, J. M., 22n36
Carlsmith, K. M., 212n176
Carlson, D. S., C26n169
Carlson, J. M., 351n121
Carlson, M., 334n12, 350n112
Carlstedt, L., E16n126
Carney, D. R., 364n264, B8n24
Carpenter, G. R., 245n86
Carpenter, K. M., 115n8
Carpenter, M., 320n163
Carr, J. E., 356n192

Carr, K., C9n39
Carr, T. H., 500n19
Carr-Nangle, R. E., 209n154
Carroll, J. S., 115n7
Carron, A. V., C17n98
Carrus, G., E18n137
Carter, C., 203n103
Carter, S. R., 157n43
Carver, C. S., 74n16, 76n37, 76n38, 132n114, 133n115, 133n116, 133n117, 200n73, B8n21
Case, D. A., 179n162
Casey, R. J., 384n101, 386n115
Cash, T. F., 384n102
Casper, W. J., C24n161
Caspi, A., 89n110, 354n166, 356n195
Casson, D. H., 148n10
Catalan, J., 266n44
Catalano, R., E4n18, E12n94
Catanese, K. R., 121n39, 348n99, 375n12, 390n130, 391n146, 392n155, 429n150
Cate, R., 216n221
Ceaux, E., 297n20
Ceci, S. J., 487n243, D19n142, D19n143
Cesario, J., 56n78
Chaiken, S., 188n11, 232n19, 233n29, 273n64, 280n114, 432n169, 432n170
Chait, J., 362n234
Chajut, E., 218n227
Chakraborty, G., 279n107
Chamberlain, B., 354n172
Chamberlain, K., 133n119
Chan, A., 215n205
Chan, W., 470n152
Chandola, T., C24n151
Chandrasekhar, D., E16n117
Chang, Y., A7n22
Chaplin, W., 94n148
Chapman, B. P., 219n233
Chapman, H. A., 205n123
Charman, S. D., D8n46, D8n47, D10n70
Chartrand, T. L., 190n18, 380n79, 381n80, 393n162, 521n114
Chassin, L., 283n126
Chatard, A., 76n36
Check, J. V. P., 352n142
Cheema, A., A11n32
Chen, E. S., 522n120
Chen, J. J., C26n171
Chen, M., 7n13, 155n34
Chen, R. C., A7n22
Chen, S., 521n114
Chen, X., E16n131
Chen, Y., 518n102
Chesney, M. A., 201n84
Chester, D. S., 211n171
Chew, B., 93n125
Child, P., 83n68, 83n69
Childress, H., E7n62
Chiodo, J., 391n143
Chiu, C., 85n79, 86n80
Chivers, M. L., 191n123
Cho, E. K., 203n102
Choi, I., 162n77
Chokshi, N., 231n7

Choma, B. L., 205n120
Chown, S. M., 318n156
Chrisjohn, R. D., 316n131
Christ, O., 466n135
Christakis, N. A., 208n145, 293n3
Christenfeld, N. J., 62n101
Christensen, H. T., 245n86
Christian, J., 219n242
Christianson, S.-A., D5n21
Christy, P., 379n65
Church, B. A., 152n29
Cialdini, J. T., 394n163, 395n178
Cialdini, R. B., 115n8, 203n99,
    209n158, 263n29, 264n32,
    264n33, 264n34, 265n35,
    265n36, 265n38, 266n39,
    266n41, 266n44, 268n47,
    269n49, 324n171, 365n273,
    365n274, 365n275, 380n76,
    E13n104, E17n134
Ciarocco, N. J., 391n140, 391n147,
    391n148, 392n154, 416n77
Ciotti, G., C15n77
Clancy, B., E19n150
Clark, C. L., 414n49
Clark, C., E4n17, E10n80, E11n83,
    E11n88
Clark, D., 72n10
Clark, D. A., 94n143
Clark, L. A., 187n5, 187n6, 518n104
Clark, M. S., 412n31, 412n32, 412n33,
    412n34, 413n37, 413n38, 413n39,
    413n40, 413n41
Clark, N. T., 266n42
Clark, R. E., C5n17
Clark, S. E., D8n43, D8n49, D9n55,
    D10n62, D11n77
Clark, W. C., E2n2, E4n33
Claypool, H. M., 235n43
Clayson, D. E., 57n63, 457n63
Cleare, A. J., 354n170
Clement, R. W., 174n132
Clifford, M., 384n98
Clipp, E. C., 382n88
Clore, G. L., 205n125, 211n168,
    211n169, 317n141
Coan, J. A., 207n141
Coates, D., 196n38, 196n44
Coccaro, E. F., 354n167, 354n173
Cohen M. A., 354n175, 354n176
Cohen S., B16n79
Cohen, A. B., 205n124, 302n45
Cohen, A. D., 296n13
Cohen, D., 45n40, 45n41, 359n204,
    359n205, 359n206
Cohen, G. L., 55n77
Cohen, J., 22n40, 191n24, 220n250
Cohen, J.D., 299n32
Cohen, L. L., 430n168
Cohen, R. R., C17n97
Cohen, S., E4n15, E11n84
Cohen, S. G., C18n107
Cohen-Kettenis, P. T., 375n11
Coie, J. D., 335n15
Colapinto, J., 34n1, 34n2
Cole, A. H., 380n74, 484n218
Cole, R., 361n223
Collins, A., 319n162
Collins, J., 513n80, 513n81

Collins, N., B12n53
Collins, N. L., 311n103, 414n44,
    414n51, 415n53, 415n54, 415n56,
    415n57, 415n60, 415n64, 415n66
Collins, R. L., 346n76
Colman, A. M., 396n185
Colvin, C. R., 96n197
Combs, D., 391n138
Comer, R., 242n70
Comfort, J. C., D17n120, D17n123
Compton, J. A., 284n129
Comstock, G., 335n20
Cone, J., E16n124
Cong, X., 83n67
Conley, T. D., 429n151
Conner, M., 247n99, C25n157,
    C25n158,C 25n159
Conner, R., 390n133
Connolly, T., 213n179
Connors, M. M., 376n36
Consoli, A., D5n18
Contiero, P., 297n17
Contrada, R. J., B3n8, B16n78
Converse, P. E., 207n133
Conway, M., 91n120
Cook, J., 149n17, 175n141
Cook, T. D., 16n27, 20n31
Cooley, C. H., 78n42
Cooper, H. M., 134n126, 160n62,
    354n177
Cooper, J., 238n67, 242n71, 243n72,
    449n13
Cooper, M. L., 214n196, 414n43
Cooper-Hakim, A., C23n142
Copeland, J. T., 521n119
Corbitt, L. C., E6n48
Corcoran, D., 413n41
Cordell, H. K., E17n136
Corell, R., E2n2
Corneille, O., 214n202, 219n245
Cornog, M., 429n155
Correll, J., 452n19
Corrigan, A., 311n105
Cortina, J. M., C13n66
Cosmides, L., 178n159, 178n160,
    178n161
Costa, P. T., 196n46, 196n47,
    196n48, 196n49, 470n152
Costello, K., 205n120
Cotton, J. L., C14n81
Cotton, R., C12n79, D12n79
Cottrell, C. A., 380n77
Cottrell, N. B., 500n17, 501n29
Couch, D., 317n145
Courbet, D., 308n89
Courtois, C. A., D19n141
Coviello, L., 208n145
Cowan, C. L., D17n124, D17n128
Coy, D. H., 390n135
Coyle, C. T., 305n67
Coyne, J. C., 420n105
Cozzarelli, C., 214n196
Craig, R., 283n127
Crain, A. L., B12n56
Cramer, P., 457n46
Cramer, R. E., 322n167
Crandall, C. S., 457n66, 502n34,
    502n35
Crandall, C., 312n110

Cranny, C. J., C22n132
Crary, W. G., 95n159
Crawford, J. T., 470n149, 471n154,
    487n242
Crawford, L. E., 377n45, 395n176
Credé, M., 219n237
Crick, N. R., 345n72, 346n80
Crisp, R. J., 235n44, 467n140,
    485n235, 486n239
Critelli, J. W., 96n172, 96n175
Croake, J. W., 245n87
Crocker, C. B., D16n117, D18n132
Crocker, J., 93n127, 93n128, 93n135,
    93n137, 93n138, 95n162, 100n223,
    100n240, 101n241, 101n243,
    482n211, 482n214, 483n215
Crogan, M., 480n201, 480n202
Cropanzano, R., C23n144
Croskerry, P., 179n173
Croson, R., 173n131
Crossman, R. H., 338n29
Crowder, M. J., 355n189
Crowley, A. E., A7n14
Crowley, M., 316n135
Crowley, M.C., C15n68
Cruz, C., 352n140
Cryder, C. E., 202n93
Csernansky, J. G., 354n167
Cuddy, A. J. C., 364n264
Cuervo, D., 392n154
Culhane, S. E., D15n99
Cullen, F. T., 356n194
Cullen, M. J., 485n231, 485n232
Cunningham, M. R., 318n158,
    360n220, 383n89, 383n90,
    383n91, 383n92
Cunningham, W. A., D5n13
Cupach, W. R., 398n196
Curtis, V., 204n113, 204n114
Cutler, B. L., D3n11, D5n17,D6n32,
    D6n34, D8n50, D10n64,
    D13n90, D13n91, D13n92,
    D16n107, D16n113, D16n114,
    D16n115, D16n116, D16n118,
    D18n131
Cutrona, C. E., 394n168
Cwir, D., 55n77
Cybriwsky, R., E8n72

D

D'Silva, J., 44n27
Dabbs, J. M., 374n7, 375n10
Daftary-Kapur, T., D17n130
Dai, K., E16n131
Dal Cin, S., B10n37, B10n38
Dalal, R. S., C27n181
Dalton, M. A., B9n35, B10n36,
    B10n39
Dalton, M., B10n38
Daly M., 119n22, 439n212
Daly, M. J., 252n131
Damasio, A. R., 207n126, 210n164,
    210n165
Damasio, H., 210n165
Dana, J., 508n62
Daniel, D. B., 457n48
Daniels, A., E16n122, E16n123
Danner, D., 197n58
Danso, H., 485n227

Danziger, S., 136n135
Darby, B. L., 203n99, 266n44
Darby, B. W., 306n77
Dardenne, B., 471n157
Dardis, G. J., 466n124
Darley, J., 320n164
Darley, J. M., 299n32, 322n166,
    323n169, 324n170, 474n171,
    E18n139
Darwin, C., 312n108, 338n30
Das, E., 236n49, 455n37
Davey, S. L., D5n10
David G., 512n125
David, J. P., 214n195
David, M. B., 448n1
Davidson, K. D., 216n222, B3n6
Davidson, N., 365n272
Davidson, R. J., 207n141
Davies, G., 43n18
Davies, G. M., D6n30
Davies, J. B., 505n51
Davies, P. G., 474n169
Davila, J., 305n64, 305n65, 305n72
Davis, A., E4n17, E10n80, E11n83,
    E11n88
Davis, B. P., 269n52
Davis, D., D14n95
Davis, I., E15n111
Davis, J. M., 297n21
Davis, K. E., 398n197
Davis, M. H., 407n9, 410n23
Davis, P. A., 141n158
Davis, S. F., 361n232
Davis, S. W., 457n61
Davisson, E. K., 382n84
Davis-Stober, C.P., 508n62
Davy, J., 203n103
Dawes, R. M., E19n147
Dawkins, R., 312n106, 347n83
Day, D., 358n203
Day, D. V., 513n79
Day, R., C14n79
De Angelis, M., 125n79
De Bolle, M., 470n152
De Brouwer, A.-M., 333n4
De Conno, F., 297n17
De Dreu, C. K. W., 201n78, 201n79
De Fruyt, F., 470n152
de Gilder, D., C23n141
De Hoog, N., 275n83
de Kort, Y. A. W., 365n281
De La Ronde, C., 424n121
de Lemus, S., 471n158
De Lisa, A., D16n116
de Moura, G., 518n100
de Neve, J. E., 132n113
de Rougemont, D., 406n6
de Vries, M., 214n202
de Waal, F. B. M., 36n4, 40n13,
    297n21
De Wit, J. B. F., 275n83
De Young, R., E19n154
Deacon, T., 150n22
Dean, L. M., E6n49
DeAngelis, T., A19n54
Dearing, R. L., 58n85, 202n94,
    203n96
Deaux, K., 316n133
Debalini, M. G., 148n7

DeBono, K. G., 278n104
deCharms, R., 123n54
Deci, E. L., 82n57, 82n58, 82n60,
    83n62, 83n66, 123n51, 123n52,
    123n53, 123n55, 123n56, 123n59,
    124n61, 124n62, 24n65, C5n18
Deffenbacher, K. A., D5n16, D5n20,
    D5n22, D6n33
deHeer, H., D5n12
Dejonckheere, P., 159n59
DeJong, W., 457n64, 457n65
Dekker, G. B., E18n142
DeLamater, J., 426n133
Delespaul, P. A. E. G., 58n84,
    204n104
DeLisi, M., 358n201
Delmas, F., 350n113
DeLongis, A., 377n46, 420n105,
    420n106
Delucchi, K., 96n188
DeMarree, K. G., 514n87
DeMeis, J., 45n39
Demicheli, V., 148n7
DeMoss, M., 220n251
DeNeve, K. M., 353n144
Denison, D. R., C14n82, C14n83
DePalma, M. T., 318n155
DePaola, S. J., 274n72, 277n88
DePaulo, B. M., 361n226
Depledge, M. H., 198n60
Deppe, R. K., 86n86
Derby, S. L., 165n92
Derezotes, D., 377n43
Dermer, M., 235n37
Derry, P. A., 95n160
Dertke, M. C., 317n140
Derzon, J. H., 354n175, 354n176
DeScioli, P., 42n17, E8n70
Deshaies, P., 44n29
DeSilver, D., 454n29
Desmarais, S. L., D12n83
DeSteno, D. A., 438n208, 438n210,
    440n221
Deuser, W. E., 343n58, 344n60
Deutsch, M., 260n18
Deutsch, R., 51n59, 54n74
DeVader, C. L., 513n84
Devenport, J. L., D13n91, D13n92
Devine, P. G., 452n25, 477n184,
    478n187, 479n188, 479n189,
    479n190, 485n236, 479n244
DeVore, C. J., C26n174, C26n179
DeVries, D., 515n90
DeWall, C. N., 53n71, 99n217,
    123n49, 158n54, 211n171, 349n105,
    386n112, 390n136, 391n138,
    391n140, 391n147, 391n148,
    392n149, 411n26, 450n16,
    522n121
Dewitte, S., 439n211, 439n213
Dexter, H. R., D13n90, D18n131
Dhar, R., 136n133, 203n102
Di Paula, A., 100n238
Di Pietrantonj, C., 148n7
Diacoyanni-Tarlatzis, I., 215n205
Diamond, L. M., 425n130, 425n131,
    426n132, 430n159
Diaz, J. H., 351n123
Dickerson, C., E19n149

Dickinson, D. J., 45n36
Dickson, N., 97n202
Dickson, N. M., E2n2
Diefenbach, M., B16n80
Diefenbach, M. A., B16n72
Diehl, M., 507n55
Diener, E., 75n26, 96n174, 97n208,
    196n39, 196n43, 198n63,
    199n67, 364n262, 498n13,
    504n47
Diener, M., 97n208
Diermeier, D., 382n85
Dietrich, H. L., D9n59
DiGiacomo, M., 219n241
Dijksterhuis, A., 158n51, 158n52
Dikaiakou, A., E16n120
Dill, K. E., 22n39, 343n58, 344n60
Dion, J., 59n90
Dion, K., 384n99, 384n100
Dixon, D. N., 376n35
Dlugolecki, D. W., 91n118
Doan, K. A., 277n89
Dodge, G., C19n122
Dodge, K. A., 335n15
Dodson, J. D., 217n225
Doerr, C., 452n23
Doherty, K. J., 91n118
Dohnke, B., B13n61
Doja, A., 148n9
Dollard, J., 15n24, 342n47
Dombeck, M., C24n148
Donnellan, M. B., 99n215
Donnerstein, E., 22n37, 352n141
Donovan, R., A6n12, A7n13
Doob, L., 15n24, 342n47
Doocy, S., E16n122, E16n123
Dooley, D., E4n18, E12n94
Dooling, S., E16n122
Doran, A., D5n23
Dorfman, D. D., 277n96
Dorr, N., 353n144
Dougherty, D. M., 354n171
Douglass, A. B., D10n67, D10n74,
    D13n88
Douthitt, E. A., 501n28
Dovidio, J. F., 449n12, 479n195
Dowd, J. J., 238n65, 296n12
Dowd, T. G., 238n61
Downey, G., 351n127, 390n126
Downey, K. T., 96n176
Downs, A., 252n128
Downs, D. L., 98n210
Downs, D. M., 363n255, 364n263
Doyle, A. C., 165n94
Doyle, W. J., B16n79
Drabek, T. E., E15n107
Dragna, M., 322n167
Draper, P., 465n114
Drath, W. H., C18n114
Dredze, M., 351n127
Drigotas, S. M., 466n125, 466n127,
    500n16
Driscoll, D. M., 234n31
Driskell, J. E., C17n96
Drolet, A., 137n142
Druen, P. B., 360n220, 383n91
Drumm, P., 397n192
Drury, J., E6n41
Duarte, J. L., 487n242

Dube, K. C., 222n269
Duberstein, P. R. 219n233
Dubner, S. D., 43n21
Dubner, S. J., 453n28
Dudley, R. T., 174n138
Dugan, P. M., 472n160
Duke, A. A., 308n89, 354n179
Duke, M. P., E7n53
Dumont, M., 471n157
Dunbar, R. I. M., 39n9, 39n10,
    39n11, 375n17, 443n236
Duncan, A., E19n154
Duncan, B. D., 313n120
Duncan, C. P., 275n78
Dunkel-Schetter, C., B8n25, B12n53
Dunn, D. S., 238n63
Dunn, E. W., 219n232, 314n121
Dunning, D., 96n168, 96n169,
    96n170, 96n171, 170n118,
    172n128, 309n95, 311n100, D6n38
Dunton, B. C., 232n22, 476n174
Duryea, E. J., 213n187
Dutton, D. G., 192n27, 193n31,
    477n185, 477n186
Duval, S., 74n14
Duval, T. S., 75n25
Dweck, C. S., 121n42, 121n43,
    121n44, 122n45, 122n46
Dysart, J. E., D9n53, D9n60, D11n78
Dzindolet, M. T., 507n54

E

Eagly, A. H., 232n19, 236n48,
    273n64, 280n114, 316n135,
    383n93
Earnest, D. R., C9n40
Easterbrook, J. A., 217n226
Eastwick, P. W., 385n117, 422n113
Eaton. K., 213n15
Ebbesen, E. B., 95n161
Ebbesen, E. G., E7n58
Eby, L. T., C24n161
Ecker, U. K. H., 149n17, 175n141
Eckman, J., 382n87
Edelbrock, S., 353n164
Edelman, C., C25n160
Edelsack, L., 203n101
Edelstein, R. S., 414n47, 414n52,
    415n67
Edgerton, R., 359n209
Edwards, D. A., 283n126
Edwards, D. J. A., E6n43
Ee, J. S., 96n172, 96n175
Eek, D., 296n14
Effrein, E. A., 90n116
Efran, M. G., 274n73
Eftekhari-Sanjani, H., 484n222
Egan, G., 376n24
Ehly, S. W., 96n182
Ehrenfeld, D., E4n32
Ehrenreich, B., 441n227
Eibach, R.P., 483n216
Eichinger, R. W., C19n123, C19n124
Eid, M., 198n63
Eiland, L., B6n12
Einon, D., 170n111
Eisenberg, N., 216n218, 265n36,
    316n138
Eisenberg, N. I., 391n138

Eisenstadt, D., D13n93
Eisenstein, E. M., 363n261
Eisner, M., 335n24
Ekman, P., 215n205, 361n225
Elder, G. H., 382n88
Elfenbein, H. A., 215n206
Ellard, J. H., 305n70
Ellerbeck, N., 150n25
Elliot, A. J., 197n56, 214n194
Elliott, S., A5n3
Ellis, A., 201n81
Ellis, B. J., 84n72
Ellison, N. B., 387n118
Ellsworth, P. C., 214n192, D17n121,
    D17n124, D17n128
Emmons, R. A., 125n75, 197n52
Emswiller, T., 316n133
Engel, R., 80n49
Engelman, R., E4n20
Engler, L. B., 209n154
Engs, R. C., 222n270
Enright, R. D., 305n67, 305n68
Ensari, N., 219n242
Epley, N., 19n30, 156n36, 156n37,
    161n73, 161n74
Epps, J., 343n57
Epstein, R. M., 219n233
Epstein, S., 89n111
Erber, M. W., 221n260
Erber, R., 221n259, 221n260, 521n117
Erez, A., 214n199, C27n180
Erickson, B., 273n65
Erickson, M. A., D9n55
Erikson, E. H., 416n71
Erkip, F. E., E6n45
Ernst, J., 377n56, 395n172
Ernst, J. M., 377n44, 377n45,
    394n169, 395n175, 395n176
Eron, L. D., 89n112, 352n132
Ervin, F. R., 354n172
Escobar, J. I., E16n129
Estes, J. P., E6n48
Estrada, C. A., 214n197
Etherington, J., E8n69
Evans, G. W., E3n8, E4n18, E7n57,
    E11n82, E12n94
Evans, K., 390n128
Everett, P. B., E12n99
Evers, K. E., B13n57
Eves, A., 355n189
Exline, J. J., 252n124, 252n125,
    252n126, 297n19, 304n59,
    306n75, 306n76, 306n79,
    306n85, 306n86
Expósito, F., 471n158
Eysenck, H. J., 316n130, 316n132

F

Faber, J. E., 454n35
Fadiman, A., B16n75
Fagg, E., 485n235, 485n239
Fairless, A. H., D10n72
Falck, R., 283n127
Falcone, L. B., 277n94
Falender, V. J., 90n116
Falomir-Pichastor, J. M., 460n92
Fantino, E., 179n162
Farberow, N. L., 141n159
Farinaro, E., E16n125

Farrell, C., 13n20
Farrell, W., 125n80
Farrington-Flint, L., 360n219
Farwell, L., 416n81
Faucheux, S., E2n2
Fava, J. L., 136n136
Fawcett, J., 354n166
Fay, T. H., E4n14
Fazio, R. H., 75n31, 90n116, 232n22, 232n23, 232n24, 234n31, 234n32, 235n46, 246n94, 246n96, 476n174, 476n175, 479n193
Fee, A. L., 351n121
Feeney, B. C., 414n51, 415n53, 415n54, 415n56, 415n60, 415n64, 415n66
Feeney, J. A., 415n61
Fehr, B., 187n3
Fehr, B. A., 96n193
Fehr, E., 302n46, 503n45, 503n46
Fein, S., 468n147
Feinberg, M., 302n48
Feinberg, R., A11n33
Feingold, A., 379n67, 383n94
Fekken, G. C., 316n131
Feldman, P. J., B16n79
Feldman, R. S., 360n218
Felson, R. B., 334n10, 335n21, 347n82, 347n84, 348n100, 349n106
Fenell, D., 304n62
Fenigstein, A., 74n15, 75n29
Fenton-O'Creevy, M., 176n146
Ferrari, J. R., 140n154, 141n156
Ferreira, M. B., 153n30
Ferriere, R., 296n10
Feshbach, S., 276n86, 335n16
Festinger, L., 80n52, 279n108, 279n112, 382n86, 504n48
Fetchenhauer, D., 311n100
Fetterman, M., A22n61
Fiddick, L., 178n161
Fidell, S., E10n78
Field, P., 97n201
Fields, D. A., 361n229
Filiberti, A., 297n17
Filkins, J. W., D17n126
Finch, A., 45n37
Fincham, F. D., 304n63, 305n64, 305n65, 305n66, 305n72, 306n73, 306n74, 377n54, 411n26
Fincher, C. L., 47n45
Finder, A., C11n48
Fink, B., 384n109
Finkel, E. J., 100n228, 304n61, 306n85, 349n105, 385n117, 411n26, 422n113
Finkelman, L., 348n97
Finkenauer, C., 187n9, 233n26, 311n101, 382n83, 466n132
Finnie, W. C., 365n280, E12n100
Fiscaro, S. A., 235n38
Fischer, K. W., 203n97
Fischer, R., 241n69
Fischhoff, B., 165n92
Fishbein, M., 246n92, B11n46
Fisher, C. D., 123n57
Fisher, H., 407n10
Fisher, J. D., 296n11

Fisher, L. D., 377n50, 420n107
Fisher, R. P., D10n63
Fisher, T. D., 170n110
Fishkin, S. A., 170n109
Fiske, S., 212n175
Fiske, S. T., 115n3, 149n18, 149n19, 151n26, 164n91, 237n60, 238n61, 380n78, 471n156, 521n117, B16n70
Fitness, J., 397n189
Fitzgerald, N. M., 216n221
Fitzgerald, R., D17n121
Fitzgerald, R. J., D8n46
Fitzjohn, J., 97n202
Fitzsimons, G., 382n84
Fitzsimons, G. M., 128n94, 128n97
Flaherty, D. K., 148n14
Flaherty, J. A., 222n271
Flament, C., 462n105
Flanagan, J. C., C7n24
Flanagan, M., 353n144
Flanagin, A, J., C14n78
Fleishmann, E. A., C5n19
Fleming, A. S., 207n136
Fleming, I., E14n106
Fleming, L. E., 198n60
Fletcher, C., 342n52, C19n126
Flink, C., 124n63
Flores, S. D., 429n152
Florin, P., E13n102
Flynn, F. J., 513n85, 514n88
Folger, R., 83n64
Folkes, V. S., 397n190
Folkman, S., 377n46, 420n106
Fong, G., B10n37
Foot, P., 299n31
Ford, J. K., C12n63
Ford, M. T., C23n145, C24n150
Forgas, J. P., 198n64
Forster, J. L., 222n266
Forsyth, A. J. M., 365n272
Forsyth, D. R., 96n180, C17n100
Foster, C. A., 100n227, 195n32, 207n138, 311n104, 416n78, 417n86
Foster, J. D., 99n214
Foster, J. L., 310n98
Foti, R. J., 513n84
Fowler, G. A., 230n4
Fowler, J. H., 208n145, 293n3
Fox, C., 311n105
Fox, E., 351n122
Frahm, H., 150n23
Fraley, B., 522n122
Franceschetti, M., 208n145
Francis, A. M., 411n28
Francoeur, R. T., 429n155
Frank, J., E19n154
Fraser, S. C., 364n262, 498n13, 504n47
Fraser-Thill, R., D10n67
Frayser, S. G., 46n33
Frazier, P., 251n116
Frederick, S., 53n72
Frederickson, B. L., 214n188, 214n189, 214n190, 214n191
Freedman, J. L., 263n31, 284n131, 364n267
Freedman, S. R., 305n68
Fresco, D. M., 94n146

Frese, M., C24n149
Freud, S., 57n80, 138n144, 339n31, 342n48
Frey, D., 95n157
Frey, J., 353n156
Frey, R. G., 44n25
Fried, C. B., B12n56
Friedland, N., 218n229
Friedman, H. S., B16n82
Friedman, H., B3n4
Friedman, L. N., 124n70
Friedman, R., 128n93
Friesen, W., 197n58
Friesen, W. V., 215n205
Frieze, I. H., 398n197
Frijda, N. H., 208n146, 208n147, 208n148, 214n193, 375n11
Frimer, J.A., 299n28
Frith, K. T., A4n1, A17n49
Frost, J. H., 379n72
Frost, R. O., 77n40, 391n142
Frye, N. K., C25n163
Fryker, K., 210n166
Fuchs, T., B13n61
Fujioka, T., 83n68
Fujita, F., 96n174
Fukuyama, F., 379n70
Fulero, S. M., D11n76, D15n96, D17n129, D18n136, D18n138
Fulker, D. W., 316n130, 316n132
Fullerton, C. S., E15n116
Funder, D. C., 9n17, 96n197
Fung, H. H., 411n27
Funke, F., 467n136, 479n191
Furman, W., 96n192
Furnham, A., 318n151
Furtner, M. R., 219n244

G

Gabbiadini, A., 364n266
Gable, S. L., 207n139, 214n194
Gabriel, M. T., 96n172, 96n175
Gabriel, S., 376n56, 395n172
Gáchter, S., 302n46, 503n45, 503n46
Gael, S. A., C7n22
Gaerling, T., 296n14
Gaertner, L., 106n272, 393n156
Gaertner, S. L., 449n12, 479n195
Gage, S. H., 344n65
Gagne, M., 198n61
Gagnon, J. H., 170n101, 170n105, 170n106, 245n84, 317n144, 348n93, 407n16, 409n21, 430n166, 434n181, 434n188, 460n87, 495n5
Gailliot, M. T., 354n181, 386n112
Gaines, B., 86n85
Galinsky, A. D., 42n15, 179n172, 519n105, 519n107, 520n112, 520n113
Galinsky, A., 176n149
Gallagher, J., 187n8
Gallopin, G. C., E2n2
Gallucci, M., 393n160, 396n186, 397n187, 397n188, 503n41, 503n43
Gangestad, S., 379n63, 423n118
Gangestad, S. W., 379n60, 386n113

Garcia-Finana, M., 39n11
Gardner, M. P., 209n150
Gardner, W. L., 187n4, 377n55, 392n150, 392n151, 394n166, 394n170, 395n174
Gardner, W., 377n56, 395n172
Garfinkel, P. E., 385n110
Garner, D. M., 385n110
Garner, W., 377n51
Garrett, S., D5n23
Garrioch, L., D10n68
Garry, M., 310n98
Gartrell, N. K., 459n97
Garvin, E., 211n168
Gasper, K., 211n168
Gattiker, U. E., 457n52
Gaunt, R., 52n67, 52n69
Gaur, S. D., 353n151
Gavanski, I., 176n153, 176n154
Gazzaniga, M. S., 52n60, 52n61
Geaghan, J. P., 365n278
Gebhard, P. H., 430n160
Geen, R. G., 201n82, 339n34, 353n152, 353n153
Geertz, A.W., 241n69
Geller, E. S., E12n99
Gendolla, G. H. E., 157n47
Gendron, R. C., 365n278
Gentile, D. A., 325n175
Gentile, D. G., 352n131
Gentry, W. A., 514n87
George, L., 176n149
Gerard, H. B., 82n55, 260n18
Gerrard, M., 75n30, 97n207, 213n182, 213n186, B9n34, B13n60, B14n62, B14n63
Gerstel, N., 376n33, 376n34
Gervais, W. M., 311n102, 455n39, 455n42
Gesch, B. C., 355n189
Giammarino, M., 396n180
Giancola, P. R., 354n179, 354n185
Giannopoulou, I., E16n120
Gibbons, F., B9n34, B14n63
Gibbons, F. X., 75n30, 75n31, 97n207, 213n186, B13n60, B14n62
Gibbs, A. C., 377n44, 395n175
Gibson, B., 352n139
Giesler, R. B., 87n96
Gifford, R. K., 171n127, 472n161, 472n162
Gilbert, D. T., 52n67, 52n69, 87n95, 150n25, 151n27, 211n172, 212n174, 212n176, 247n100, 248n101, 248n102, 248n103, 248n104, 248n105, 285n133
Gill, N., E19n154
Gilovich, T., 44n22, 93n133, 162n80, 163n84, 166n96, 172n28, 175n143, 252n132
Ginges, J., 464n122
Gino, F., 299n26, 362n239, 362n240, 362n242, 362n243, 362n244, 362n245, 363n247
Girme, Y. U., 419n99
Giuliano, T., 509n66
Gladue, B. A., 353n163, 353n165
Glaser, P., 25n46

Glaser, R., 377n50, 377n51, 420n107
Glass, D. C., 124n70, B16n80, E10n81
Gleick, E., 259n15
Glendenning, A., 96n194
Glenn, N. D., 207n134, 207n135
Gleser, G. C., E16n132
Glick, P., 471n156, 471n158
Glionna, J. M., 261n51
Glynn, M. A., 100n237
Gneezy, A., 156n36
Gockel, C., 353n148
Goel, S., 174n135
Goethals, G. R., 174n136
Goffman, E., 71n8, 73n13, 102n246, 103n258
Gogus, C. I., 363n251, 363n252
Golding, S. L., 171n126
Goldman, M., 420n103
Goldsmith, K., 203n102
Goldstein, N. J., E13n104
Goleman, D., 188n10, 233n28, 233n30
Gollwitzer, M., 352n140
Gollwitzer, P. M., 94n150, 94n151, 105n262, 105n263, 125n71, 126n82, 126n85, 126n86, 126n87, 129n98, 129n99, 440n225
Goncalo, J. A., 392n152
Gondolf, E. W., 438n215
Gonzales, M., 95n152
Gonzales, M. H., 306n78
Gonzalez-Vallejo, C., 158n53
Good, C., 485n227
Good, T. L., 160n62
Goode, M. R., 305n54
Goodenough, F. L., 216n212
Goodie, A. S., 179n162
Goodman, M., 363n250
Goodsell, C. A., D10n72
Goodwin, G. P., 382n82
Goodwin, J. S., 377n47
Gooren, L. J. G. M., 375n11
Gordon, L. J., 86n86
Gorin, A. A., 136n136
Gorokhovich, Y., E16n122
Gottfredson, L. 484n223
Gottfredson, M. R., 140n152, 356n193
Gottfredson, M., 351n127
Gottfredson, S. D., E8n64
Gottman, J. M., 216n216, 216n217, 418n93, 418n94
Gottschalk, L. A., 142n165
Gould, S. J., A15n45
Goupil L., 51n57
Govaerts, K., 376n35
Goveas, J. S., 354n167
Govorun, O., 476n180
Grace, M. C., E16n132
Graetz, K. A., 466n125
Graham, E. A., 22n38
Graham, J., 300n35
Graham, K., 354n180
Grammer, K., 384n109
Gramzow, R., 342n52
Grasmick, H. G., 365n277
Grasselli, A., 481n204
Gray, B., E3n29

Gray-Little, B., 93n136
Greathouse, S. M., D10n65, D10n66, D15n102
Green, B. L., 265n36, E16n132
Green, D. M., E10n78
Green, G., 378n59
Green, L., 302n43
Green, P. J., 214n195
Green, S. W., 176n151
Greenberg, J., 75n32, 95n156, 98n212, 103n254, 203n103, A14n42, C23n143
Greenblat, C., 407n13
Greene, D., 83n61, 174n134
Greene, J.D., 299n32
Greene, T. C., E3n12
Greenhaus, J. H., C14n80
Greenspan, S. I., 220n247
Greenwald, A. G., 88n99, 235n42, 273n61, 452n20, 476n176
Gregg, A. P., 85n75
Gregory, L. W., 115n8
Greifeneder, R., 120n28
Greitemeyer, T., 313n118, 325n176, 344n64, 352n129, 352n137
Grieve, R., 231n13
Griffin, D., 129n103, 130n104, 130n106, 416n74
Griffin, D. W., 424n122
Griffin, J. J., 86n85
Griffitt, W., 407n14
Griggs, L., 351n122
Grimbos, T., 191n23
Griscom, R., 317n146
Griskevicius, V., 106n265, 216n219, E13n104
Grolnick, W. S., 124n64, 124n66
Gromko, M. H., 170n112, 170n113
Grondin, S., 44n29, 45n30, 45n35
Groom, R. W., 353n146, 353n149, E3n13
Groscup, J. L., 459n84
Gross, D., 493n2
Gross, E. F., 393n158, 395n179
Gross, H., 376n33, 376n34
Gross, J. J., 201n80, 204n112, 221n261
Gross, J., 391n144
Gross, P. H., 474n171
Grotpeter, J. K., 345n72, 346n80
Grover, C. A., 361n232
Gruber, J., 198n62, 199n66
Gruber, M. J., 415n68
Grubler, A., E2n2
Gruenewald, T. L., 345n69, 345n70, B7n17
Gruenfeld, D. H., 518n103, 519n105, 519n107, 519n108, 520n112, 520n113
Grunberg, N. E., 222n267
Gruner, C. R., 275n79
Guarnieri, G., 481n204
Guenther, C. C., D18n134
Guijarro, M. L., 201n85
Guillory, J. E., 208n144
Guinote, A., 519n106
Gully, S. M., C18n110
Gupta, S. P., 222n269
Gurr, T. R., 335n25

Gurung, R. A. R., 345n69, 345n70, B2n1, B3n7, B8n28, B12n53, B16n73
Guxens, M., E11n91
Guyll, M., B16n78
Guzmán, R. A., 309n93
Gwaltney, J. M., B16n79

H

Hackel, L. S., 207n136
Hackett, R. D., C27n182
Hackman, J. R., C22n131
Haefner, R., C11n47
Hafdahl, A. R., 93n136
Hagan, F. E., 363n256
Haglid, M., 377n49
Hagtvet, K. A., 96n185
Hahn, C., 150n25
Haidt, J., 204n108, 205n125, 213n184, 213n185, 299n29, 299n30, 300n35, 487n242
Halberstadt, J. B., 211n170
Hall, C. L., 203n100
Hall, E. T., E9n74
Hall, J. H., 304n63, 306n74
Hall, J. M., E2n2
Hall, J. R., 258n1, 258n3, 258n6, 258n9, 259n12
Hallet, A. J., 201n85
Halweil, B., E4n20
Hamburger, M. E., 302n43
Hamilton, D. L., 171n127, 472n160, 472n161, 472n162, 494n4
Hamilton, W. D., 312n109, 376n19
Hammond, M. D., 419n99
Hammond, S. M., 355n189
Hampson, S. E., 355n189
Hanacek, B., 252n129, E16n133
Hancock, J. T., 208n144, 361n221, 387n118
Hancock, P. A., E10n79
Handley, I. M., 209n157
Haney, C., D17n122
Hanges, P. J., 476n179
Hang-Pil, S., 279n106
Hanisch, K. A., C8n29, C8n32, C20n130, C26n173, C26n175, C26n176, C26n177, C26n178, C27n183, C27n185
Hanley, N., E19n151
Hannon, P., 304n61
Hansell, S., B16n80
Hansen, G. L., 245n89, 436n194
Hansen, J., 156n35
Hanson, D. J., 222n270
Hansson, L. M., 457n59
Hansson, R. O., E15n113
Haque, O. S., 42n17
Harber, K. D., 470n149, 471n154, 481n208, 481n209
Harden, P., 354n172
Hardin, G., 505n52, E3n24
Hardin, S. B., E15n115
Hardison, C. M., 485n231, 485n232, C12n60
Hare, A. P., C17n87
Hare, R. D., 202n92
Hargis, M., C10n42, C11n50
Harkins, S., 501n32

Harkins, S. G., 502n38
Harmon-Jones, E., 199n72, 200n73, 235n40, 251n118, 479n189, 479n190
Harms, P. D., 219n237
Harrell, K. L., 313n119
Harrell, W. A., 317n142
Harriott, J., C8n33
Harris, C. R., 438n209
Harris, M., 46n42, 46n43
Harris, M. B., 16n25, 16n26, 21n35, 203n100, 457n50
Harris, P. B., E7n61
Harris, R. B., 347n89
Harris, R. J., 457n50
Harris, S. J., 103n255, 309n92
Harris, V. A., 162n76
Harrison, A. A., 235n38, 376n36
Harrison, K., 74n20, 74n21, 74n22
Harskamp, J., 448n3, 448n5
Harter, S., 90n113
Hartford, M., 377n49
Harwood, J., 466n131, 466n133
Hasan, Y., 344n62, 344n63
Haselton, M. G., 119n21
Hasher, L., 214n204
Hassebrauck, M., 298n23
Hastings, P. A., D16n110
Hatfield, E., 208n143, 406n3
Hauck, A., 45n37
Haugen, J. A., 306n78
Hausen, B., A22n61
Hausser, D., 235n39
Haw, R. M., D10n63
Hawkley, L. C., 377n44, 377n45, 377n48, 377n53, 394n165, 394n169, 394n171, 395n175, 395n176, 395n177
Hawley, C., 449n11
Hawver, T. H., 219n235
Hay, D., 345n71
Hayduk, L. A., E6n42
Hayes, R., 363n255, 364n263
Hazan, C., 414n45, 415n58
Hazlett, G., D5n23
He, L., 163n81
Head, J., E4n23
Healy, M., 100n222
Hearold, S., 325n174
Heatherton, T., B9n35
Heatherton, T. F., 57n81, 75n28, 77n39, 77n41, 90n115, 96n196, 103n256, 131n109, 134n125, 203n95, 204n106, 419n97, 419n98, 457n51, 485n238
Heberlein, U., 373n1
Hebl, M. R., 457n51, 457n57
Hecht, T. D., 509n64
Hee, K. H., 114n1
Hegi, K. E., 406n2
Heider, F., 160n61, 163n89, 168n99
Heider, K., 215n205
Heilbron, N., 346n81
Heilman, M. E., C26n171
Heine, S. J., 106n271, 121n41, 243n78
Heiner, R. B., 349n109
Heingartner, A., 501n27, 501n124
Heinz, A., 343n59
Heinz, S., 150n23

Heitmann, H., 136n134
Helbing, D., 508n63
Helkama, K., 309n90
Helliwell, J. F., 314n121
Helton, W. S., E4n23
Helzer, E.G., 300n36
Hemenway, D., 350n116
Hemsworth, D. H., D5n18
Henderson, N. J., B12n54
Henderson, P. W., A7n14
Henderson, V., 121n44
Hendin, H., 141n160, 142n166
Hendren, A., 459n80
Hendricks, N. J., 454n30
Henken, V. J., 142n167
Henle, C. A., 363n253
Henrich, J., 316n127
Henry, B., 356n195
Hepach, R., 314n122
Hepburn, C., 462n106
Hepworth, J. T., 473n166
Herbison, P., 97n202
Herchenroeder, L. M., 209n157
Herdt, G., 46n34
Herek, G. M., 459n81, 460n86, 460n89
Herlitz, J., 377n49
Herman, B. H., 390n133
Herman, C. P., 75n28, 77n41, 159n56, 159n57
Herman, E. M., 501n27
Herold, E. S., 245n88, 317n147, 441n230
Herrmann, A., 136n134
Herscovitch, L., C22n136
Hertel, P., 509n66
Herzog, D. B., 74n18
Hess, R. D., 161n67
Hesson-McInnis, M., 58n87
Hewitt, J., E6n49, E7n54
Hewstone, M., 318n150, 450n15, 466n135, 467n141
Hicken, M., 195n36
Hicks, J. A., 377n54
Hicks, J. M., D10n62, 471n153
Higgins, E., 193n30, 243n73
Higgins, E. T., 56n78, 88n102, 155n33
Higgins, R. L., 86n89
Hight, T. L., 197n53
Higley, J. D., 354n168, 354n169
Higley, S. B., 354n168
Hill, C. A., 397n192
Hill, C. T., 216n220, 216n224
Hill, G. W., C17n89
Hill, P., 304n59, 306n75, 306n76
Hill, S. J., 233n25
Hilmert, C. J., 62n101
Hinde, R. A., 339n38
Hirschi, T., 140n152, 356n193
Hirsh, J. B., 42n15
Hirt, E. R., 86n86, 115n9, 115n10, 179n165, 179n166
Hitsch, G. J., 384n107
Hixon, J. G., 87n95, 424n121
Ho, K., 212n178
Hobson, Z., 311n105
Hochbaum, G. M., B10n40
Hockley, W. E., D5n18

Hodge, C. N., 383n95
Hodges, S. D., 238n64
Hodson, G., 205n120
Hoerger, M., 219n233
Hoerner, J. A., E19n152
Hoff Sommers, C., 12n19
Hoffman, B. J., 514n87
Hoffman, E. L., 261n26
Hoffman, H. G., 452n20
Hoffman, M. L., 316n139
Hoffrage, U., 120n30
Hofmann, W., 298n25
Hofstadter, D. R., 176n148
Hogan, R., 513n82, 515n89
Hogg, M. A., 396n181, 396n183
Holder-Perkins, V., B16n84
Holgate, S. T., E11n92
Holland, R. W., 214n202
Hollander, S., D5n14
Holliday, J., 377n51
Hollingshead, A. B., 509n67, 509n68
Holloway, S. D., 161n67
Holmes, J. G., 301n41, 311n103, 424n122, 424n123, 424n124, 424n125
Holmes, J., 416n75
Holmes, L., C24n154
Holt, K., 95n156
Holtzworth-Munroe, A., 421n112
Holzberg, A. D., 96n169
Homans, G. C., 428n144, 428n145
Honour, J. W., 361n230
Hood, R., 75n31
Hope, L., D5n15, D6n29
Horberg, E. J., 205n124
Horner, M., 139n145
Hornsey, M. J., 466n133
Hornstein, H. A., 209n159
Horowitz, A. V., 420n102
Horowitz, L. M., 414n48, 415n55
Hortaçsu, A., 384n107
Hosch, H. M., D15n99, D15n100
Hoshino-Browne, E., 243n79
Houlihan, A., B14n63
Hounton, S. H., B12n54
House, J. S., B8n26
House, P., 174n134
Houston, D. A., 277n88, 277n89
Hovland, C. I., 232n21, 271n56, 271n58, 276n85, 278n98, 474n165
Hovland, C., 271n55, 275n74, 278n97
Howard, H. R. B., E7n57
Howell, S., 465n116
Howell-White, S., 420n102
Hoyle, R. H., 466n124, 495n11
Hoyt, G., E5n23
Hoyt, W. T., 306n81
Hsee, C. K., 117n14, 117n16, 213n181
Hsiang, S. M., 353n150, E10n77
Hsing, C., 312n114
HsiuJu, Y., 86n82
Hu, Y., 420n103
Hubbard, M., 248n106
Huel. G., E16n124
Huesmann, L. R., 89n112, 325n175, 352n130, 352n132, 352n136, 352n138, 352n139

Huff, C., 19n30
Huffcutt, A. I., C12n57, C12n58
Hulin, C. L., C26n173, C26n175, C26n176, C26n178, C27n183
Hull, J. G., 76n33, 76n34, 133n122, 354n184
Humphrey, L. L., 391n145
Humphrey, L., 129n100, 129n101, 129n102
Humphrey, R. H., 219n235
Hunt, W. C., 377n47
Hunter, J. E., 383n95, C12n59, C12n65
Hunter, R. E., C12n65
Huntley, B., E2n2
Hupka, R. B., 437n202, 437n203
Hurtado, A., D17n122
Huston, T. L., 216n221
Hutcherson, C. A., 204n112
Hutchins, I., 44n24
Hutchison, P., 467n137
Hutter, R. R. C., 235n44
Hutton, D. G., 93n124
Hyde, J. S., 93n134, 222n264, 426n133, 429n153, 441n228
Hyde, M., B14n64
Hyland, M. E., 139n146
Hymes, C., 188n11, 233n29
Hymes, R. W., D15n101

I

Iannelli, V., 148n1, 148n3
Idson, L. C., 156n37
Ihori, N., 27n50, 313n116, 313n117, 352n128, 352n135
Ilgen, D. R., C26n167
Illbeck, B. E., 429n152
Imrich, J., D13n88
Inderbitzen, H. M., 96n190
Indian, M., 231n13
Ingerick, M. J., C13n66
Inglis, D., 96n194
Innes-Ker, A. H., 211n170
Insko, C. A., 309n91, 466n123, 466n124, 466n125, 466n126, 466n127, 495n11, 500n16
Inzlicht, M., 485n237
Isen, A. M., 214n197, 214n128, 214n199, 214n201, 318n159
Ito, T. A., 354n178
Iuzzini, J., 393n156
Iverson, R. D., C23n137
Iyengar, S. S., 120n26, 136n134, A12n35
Izard, C. E., 189n14, 189n15

J

Jablin, F. M., C8n31, C14n67
Jablonski, N. G., 351n127
Jackson, D. N., C12n64
Jackson, J. R., 232n22, 476n174
Jackson, J., 485n227
Jackson, L. A., 383n95
Jackson, W., 500n22
Jacobe, A., A11n27
Jacobs, R. C., 261n27
Jacobs, S. V., E4n18, E12n94
Jacobson, L., 481n207
Jacobson, N. S. 421n112

Jaeger, C. C., E2n2
Jager, J., E2n2
Jain, A., 148n8
James, B., 245n87
James, K. A., D9n59
James, R. L., 259n13
James, W., 70n2, 115n2, 188n12, 188n13
James, W. H., 407n15, 408n18, 408n237
Jamieson, P. E., 350n118
Janda, L. H., 384n102
Janis, I., 509n71, 509n72
Janis, I. L., 97n200, 97n201, 232n21, 271n56, 275n76, 275n81, 276n85, 276n86
Janiszewski, C., 277n90
Janoff-Bulman, R., 100n234, 196n38, 196n44, 249n110
Janssen, S., E4n17, E10n80, E11n83, E11n88
Janus, C. L., 170n104, 430n137
Janus, S. S., 170n104, 430n137
Jeanneret, P. R., C5n19
Jeffery, R. W., 222n266
Jensen, A., 379n64
Jimenez-Lorente, B., D17n129, D18n136, D18n138
Jodha, N. S., E2n2
Joel, S., 411n25
John, O., 86n81
Johns, M., 485n237
Johnson, B. C., 273n65
Johnson, B. T., 88n102
Johnson, C., 507n56
Johnson, D. J., 416n76, 423n116
Johnson, D. W., 464n111, 464n112
Johnson, F. L., 316n137
Johnson, G. A., E11n85
Johnson, J. L., 140n154
Johnson, J., 115n10
Johnson, M., E15n115
Johnson, R. T., 464n111, 464n112
Johnson, W. G., 209n154
Johnson, W., 420n104, 421n110
Johnston, D. E., C27n180
Join Joiner, T., 297n18
Joiner, T., 34n3, 141n157, 142n169
Joireman, J., 306n84
Jonas, K., 236n48
Jonason, P. K., 429n152
Jones, C. R., 155n33
Jones, D., 457n58
Jones, E. E., 82n55, 86n87, 87n92, 89n106, 89n108, 103n253, 139n147, 162n75, 162n76, 242n71, 378n57, 380n73, 380n75, 452n24, B16n71
Jones, F. D., 141n163
Jones, F., C25n157, C25n158, C25n159
Jones, J. M., 273n62, C5n16
Jones, J. W., 353n155
Jones, T. S., E6n50
Jones, W., 373n5
Joppa, M., 353n165
Jordan, A. H., 205n125
Jorgenson, D. O., E3n27
Joseph, C., 204n108
Josephs, R. A., 354n183

Jossa, F., E16n125
Jost, J. T., 467n143
Joy, S. W., D8n47
Joy, V., 382n87
Joyce, W. F., 513n78
Judd, C., 470n150, 482n212
Judd, C. M., 452n19
Juieng, D., 21n34
Jung, K., 471n153
Jussim, L., 86n82, 470n149, 470n152, 471n154, 481n208, 482n209, 487n242
Juvonen, J., 393n158, 395n179

K

Kachadourian, L. K., 305n64, 305n65
Kacmar, M., C26n169
Kafai, Y. B., 361n229
Kagan, J., 74n17
Kahai, S. S., C19n122
Kahn, B. E., A7n15
Kahn, R. L., C18n111
Kahneman, D., 53n72, 53n73, 88n103, 116n13, 118n20, 130n105, 166n95, 166n98, 172n130, 176n147, 196n40, 196n41, 196n42
Kaiser, F., E5n35
Kaiser, R. B., 513n82, 515n89, 515n90
Kaistaniemi, L., 100n231
Kalder, A. K., D16n111
Kallgren, C. A., 365n273, 365n274, 365n275
Kalmet, N., D5n19
Kalro, A., 301n42
Kamada, A., 162n80
Kamble, S., 377n54
Kammeyer-Mueller, J. D., C27n186
Kanazawa, S., 395n173
Kane, M., 83n67
Kanin, E. J., 216n222
Kannouse, D. E., B16n71
Kant, I., 122n47, 386n114
Kaplan, K. A., 230n3
Kaplan, R. E., B3n6, C18n114
Kapp, F. T., E4n22
Karabenick, S. A., 317n143
Karau, S. J., 502n36, 502n39
Kardes, F. R., 179n165, 279n109
Karl, K., 213n14
Karlsson, B. W., 377n49
Karney, B. R., 385n117, 407n11
Karremans, J. C., 306n83
Kashima, Y., 55n76
Kashiwagi, K., 161n67
Kasperson, R. E., E2n2
Kasser, T., 124n68, 124n69, 126n81, A14n43
Kastin, A. J., 390n135
Katcher, A. H., 343n55
Kates, R. W., E2n2, E4n31
Katz, D., C18n111
Katz, J., 363n257
Katzev, R., 203n101
Kaukiainen, A., 100n231
Kaun, K. R., 373n1
Kavenocki, S., 245n85
Kay, A. C., 467n143

Kaya, N., E6n45, E8n67
Kaye, D., 275n76
Kayra-Stuart, F., D5n14
Kearns, J. N., 306n73
Keast, A., D4n7, D4n8, D6n35, D6n37
Keating, L., 96n187
Keefe, K., 96n195
Keefer, L. A., 474n164
Keegan, J., 354n174
Keeney, R. L., 165n92
Keinan, G., 218n228, 218n229
Keir, G., 465n117
Keith, T. Z., 96n182
Kelem, R. T., 364n262, 498n13, 504n47
Keller, M., 449n8
Keller, P. S., 457n48
Kelley, H. H., 232n21, 271n56, 276n85, 301n40, B16n71
Kelley, W. M., 485n238
Kelln, B. R. C., 305n70
Kelly, J., 2n1
Kelly, J. P., 148n8
Kelly, M. H., 359n207
Keltner, D., 205n124, 302n48, 518n103, 519n108
Kemerza, I., 314n121
Kemp, S., A11n29, E4n23
Kendall, P. C., 343n57
Kennard, J. B., D15n102
Kenrick, D. T., 209n158, 302n45, 452n27, 474n170, E11n85
Keough, K., 485n227
Kerkhof, P., 236n49, 455n37
Kerlin, L., 360n219
Kern, M. J., D17n127
Kerns, J. G., 214n203
Kerr, N. A., 96n180
Kerr, N. L., 393n160, 396n186, 397n187, 397n188, 501n33, 502n37, 503n40, 503n41, 503n43, 503n44, D15n101
Kerrigan, M. F., 459n79
Kessler, T., 467n136, 479n191
Ketcham, K., D19n140
Ketsetzis, M., 96n187
Key, C. R., 377n47
Khadjavi, M., 303n49
Khoo, A., 325n175
Kidd, C., 140n153
Kidder, D. L., C26n172
Kiecolt-Glaser, J. K., 377n50, 377n51, 377n52, 420n107, 420n109, B8n29
Kiefner, A. E., 457n69
Kiesler, S., 304n58
Kihlstrom, J. F., 88n101
Killen, J., 283n125
Kim, D., A6n11, C12n60
Kim, J., 25n46, 209n150
Kim, S. H., 392n152
Kim, S., 377n43
Kim, Y., 383n96
Kim, Y.-H., 85n79, 86n80
Kimeldorf, M. B., 296n13
King, B. J., 456n67
King, K., 441n229
Kingsbury, G. G., 96n181

Kinicki, A. J., C14n84
Kinney, R. F., 94n150, 126n85
Kinsey, A. C., 430n160
Kinsey, K. A., 365n277
Kipnis, D., 517n96, 517n97, 518n98
Kirker, W. S., 88n97, 88n98
Kirkpatrick, D., 230n2
Kirkpatrick, L. A., 84n72
Kirkpatrick, S. A., C18n113
Kirsch, T. D., E16n123
Kirschenbaum, D., 129n100, 129n101, 129n102
Kirschner, P., 275n76
Kirscht, J. P., B1on42
Kitayama, S., 72n9, 106n271, 121n41, 162n78, 162n79, 243n77, 243n79, 243n80, 312n110
Kitzinger, C., 426n135
Klaczynski, P., 457n48
Klassen, M. L., 457n63
Klein, L. C., 345n69, 345n70, B7n17
Klein, S. B., 88n101
Klentz, B., 325n172
Kling, K. C., 93n134
Klinger, M. R., 235n42
Knapp, D. E., C8n30
Knasko, S. C., A7n15
Knetsch, J. L., 88n103, 196n41
Knight, G. R., 251n119
Knight, J., 235n37
Knight, L. J., 159n58
Knobe, J., 300n33, 300n34
Knobe, J. M., 163n83
Knobloch-Westerwick, S., 243n74
Knowles, E. S., 18n28, 269n52, E7n55
Knowles, M., 377n55, 392n151, 394n170, 395n174
Koch, E. J., 98n213
Koernig, S. K., A7n20
Koestner, R., 82n58, 83n62, 83n66, 123n56, 124n62
Kofodimos, J. R., C18n114
Kogan, A., 199n66
Kogan, N., 511n76
Kohlenberg, R. J., E13n103
Koider, S., 51n57
Kolata, G., 457n47
Kolb, P. M., 353n148
Kolditz, T., 83n67, 86n90
Konecni, V. J., E7n58
Konrath, S., 93n128, 99n214, 219n245, 312n114
Kontrova, J., E16n127
Koole, S. L., 26n47, 207n142, 220n254
Koomen, W., 174n137
Koops, W., 343n56
Koren, H. S., E11n92
Koss, M. P., 348n98
Kotani, H., E15n108
Kotsou, I., 199n66
Kouchaki, M., 299n27
Koughan, M., C2n1, C2n2, C2n3, C2n5
Kouzes, J. M., 513n83
Kovera, M. B., D3n1, D10n64, D10n65, D10n66, D12n85, D15n102, D16n107, D16n115, D16n117

Kowalewski, R. B., 377n45, 395n176
Kowalski, R. M., 393n157
Kozak, M., 157n48
Kozlowski, S. W., C17n94, C18n109, C18n110
Kraft, A. J., 306n79
Kraft, D., 238n63
Kraft, M., E4n34
Kramer, A. D. I., 208n144, 208n145
Kramer, R. M., E3n28
Krammer, T. L., E16n132
Kraus, S. J., 246n97
Krauss, R. M., 364n267
Kraut, R. E., 96n184
Kravitz, D. A., D13n91, D16n114
Kraxberger, B. E., 106n273
Kray, L. J., 176n149, 179n172
Krendl, A. C., 485n238
Kressel, D. R., D14n94
Kressel, N. J., D14n94
Krishnan, R., 509n70
Kristof, A. L., 125n72, 126n83, 127n89
Kross, E., 220n255, 390n137
Krueger, J., 174n132, 176n150, 176n152
Krueger, J. I., 96n179, 96n189, 96n198
Krueger, R. F., 420n104
Kruger, J., 163n84
Kruger, M. L., 197n59
Kruglanski, A. W., 128n93
Krull, D. S., 151n27
Kuang, L., 86n81
Kuehn, R., 429n154
Kuhnert, K. W., 514n87
Kuiper, N. A., 88n97, 88n98, 95n160
Kuipers, P., 208n147
Kulik, J. A., 62n101
Kumar, A., 222n269
Kumar, N., 222n269
Kumashiro, M., 304n61, 422n113
Kunce, L. J., 415n62
Kunda, Z., 82n56, 95n155, 471n155, 473n167, 473n168, 474n169
Kunst, M., 349n104
Kunz, P. R., 296n8
Kurzban, R., 503n42
Kustis, G. A., C8n30
Kutzner, F., 156n35
Kwan, M., A17n51
Kwan, V. S., 86n81
Kyriacou, D. N., 347n89

L

Laan, E., 191n23
Lackenbauer, S., 243n79
Lacoursiere, R. B., 376n25
LaFleur, S. J., 238n64
LaFrance, M., 216n210, 216n211, 483n216
Lagerspetz, K. M., 334n13
Lagerspetz, K. M. J., 100n231
Laird, J. D., 242n70
Lake, R. A., 477n185
Lakens, D., 26n47
Lakin, A., A21n155

Mandal, E., 383n92
Mandle, C., C25n160
Maner, J. K., 346n75, 386n112, 392n149, 411n30, 474n170, 521n115, 521n116
Manfred, T., 236n52
Mann, T., B14n66
Manning, D., 95n152
Manning, D. J. 306n78
Manning, R., 319n162
Mannix, E., 496n10
Mannix, L. M., 457n57
Mansour, J. K., D5n19
Manstead, A. S. R., 201n78, 201n79
Manucia, G. K., 209n162
Manz, C. C., C18n106, C18n108
Marcon, J. L., D5n11
Marcus-Newhall, A., 334n12, 350n112
Mardberg, B., E16n126
Margolis, R. L., 435n191
Maris, R., 141n161, 141n162
Markman, K., 176n153
Markman, K. D., 176n154, 179n165, 179n166
Marks, G., 96n166, 174n133
Markus, H. R., 72n9, 82n56, 106n271, 121n41, 243n77, 243n80
Markwith, M., 58n86
Marlow, C., 208n145
Marmot, M., C24n151
Marques, J. M., 396n182, 396n183, 396n184, D15n98
Marques, S., 485n235, 485n239
Marsh, D. M., 354n171
Marshall, G. D., 192n28
Marshall, J., 148n8
Martens, T. K., D5n17, D6n32
Martichuski, D. K., E3n26
Martin, C. E., 430n160
Martin, E. A., 214n203
Martin, L., 189n17
Martin, R., 214n195
Martindale, D. A., E8n73
Martinez-Taboada, C., D15n98
Martins, A., 219n238
Martz, J. M., 420n101
Maruyama, G., 96n181, 274n68, 274n70
Marvin, G., 448n2, 448n4
Mascaro, J., 316n127
Mascio, C., C17n102
Masicampo, E. J., 53n71, 54n75, 115n4, 123n49, 126n88, 150n21, 158n54
Maslach, C., 92n29
Maslow, A. H., 416n73
Mason, J. L., A5n6
Mason, W., 174n135
Masten, A., 351n127
Masten, C., 391n138
Master, S. L., B7n18
Masuda, T., 162n79
Mata, A., 153n30
Matarazzo, J. D., B3n5
Mather, M., 210n166
Maticka-Tyndale, E., 317n147
Matsick, J. L., 429n151
Matson, P., E2n2
Matter, C. F., 18n28

Matthews, K. E., E4n16
Matthews, R., E6n38
Matud, M. P., 349n103
Mauss, I. B., 198n62
Maxwell, J. A., 411n25
Mayer, J. D., 219n230, 219n231, 516n92, 516n93, 516n94
Maynard, R. L., E11n92
Mazar, N., 363n248
Mazur, A., 353n164
Mazziotta, A., 467n139
McAlister, A. L., 283n125
McAuliff, B. D., D10n64, D12n85
McCabe, P., 431n167
McCalley, L. T., 365n281
McCalley, T., E5n35
McCarroll, J. E., E15n116
McCarthy, D. M., D17n127
McCarthy, J. J., E2n2
McCaul, K. D., 353n163, 353n165
McCauley, C., 58n86
McCauley, C. R., 213n184, 213n185
McClain, T. M., 220n249, 220n252, 221n256, 222n263, 222n272
McClintock, M. K., 394n169
McConnell, A. R., 476n178
McCown, E. J., 353n153
McCown, W. G., 140n154
McCoy, S. B., 213n186
McCrae, R. R., 196n46, 196n47, 196n48, 196n49, 470n152, B8n20
McCullough, M. E., 197n51, 197n52, 197n53, 251n115, 296n13, 304n59, 304n60, 306n75, 306n76, 306n80, 306n81
McDaniel, M. A., C12n56
McElwee, R. O., 96n168
McEvoy, C., D18n133
McEwen, B., B6n13
McEwen, B. S., B6n12
McFarland, C., 212n173
McFarland, S., 326n178, 326n179
McFarlane, M., E7n60
McFarlin, D. B., 86n83, 92n122, 100n235, 100n236, 100n239
McGee, R., 97n204
McGhee, D. E., 476n176
McGinn, N. C., 298n22
McGinnis, M. Y., 353n161
McGorty, E. K., D5n16, D5n22
McGrath, J. E., C17n88
McGregor, L. N., 361n232
McGue, M., 420n104
McGuire, C. V., 83n68, 83n69
McGuire, W. J., 83n68, 83n69, 278n99, 283n121, 283n122, 283n123, 283n124
McHoskey, J. W., 238n61, 238n65
McHugh, P. P., C18n110
McIntosh, D. N., B8n30
McKelton, D., D17n125
McKillip, J., 379n68
McKinney, L. N., A16n48
McLanahan, S., 207n134
McLaughlin-Volpe, T., 479n194
McLendon, C. L., C17n97
McLeod, A., 361n231
McLeod, E., 376n30

McLeod, J. M., 15n22
McManus, M. A., C9n37
McMaster, M. R., 322n167
McMillan, B., C25n157, C25n158, C25n159
McMillen, D. L., 203n98
McMullen, M., 176n153
McMullen, M. N., 176n154
McNeill, W. H., 465n121
McNulty, J. K., 305n71, 349n105, 411n29, 411n30, 418n90, 418n91, 419n96
McQuiston, D. E., D13n87
McQuiston-Surrett, D. E., D9n58
McWhinnie, C., 485n226
Mead, G. H., 73n12, 78n43
Mead, M., 437n199
Mead, N. L., 305n54, 362n242, 363n249, 521n115, 521n116
Medvec, V. H., 166n96
Meek, R., 93n139
Mehlman, P. T., 354n168, 354n169
Meissner, C. A., 452n26, D4n9, D5n11, D5n12, D9n56
Meleady, R., 467n140
Mellers, B. A., 212n178
Mello, J. A., C17n103
Mellor, B., 59n90
Melsom, E. I.,D5n19
Meltzer, A. L., 411n29, 411n30, 418n90, 418n91, 419n96
Memon, A., D5n15
Mendoza-Denton, R., 140n149
Menon, G., A7n21
Menzies-Toman, D., 418n89
Meqler, D., E16n124
Mercier, H., 150n20, 171n125, 263n28, 270n53
Merryman, A., 461n99
Merton, R. K., 481n205, 481n206
Mesout, J., D5n24
Messick, D. M., 174n136, 301n38, 347n85
Messner, S. F., 349n106
Messo, J., D6n26
Mewhinney, D., 317n147
Mewhinney, D.-M. K., 245n88
Meyer, C. B., 348n94
Meyer, D. E., 155n31
Meyer, J. P., C22n135, C22n136, C23n140
Meyerowitz, J. A., 96n169
Meyers, J. M., 212n174
Mialon, H. M., 411n28
Michael, R. T., 170n101, 170n105, 170n106, 245n84, 317n144, 348n93, 407n16, 409n21, 430n166, 434n181, 434n188, 460n87, 495n5
Michaels, S., 170n105, 170n106, 245n84, 348n93, 407n16, 409n21, 430n166, 434n181, 434n188, 460n87, 495n5
Michaud, S. G., 202n90, 202n91
Michaut, A. M. K., A7n17
Mick, D. G., 220n251
Midden, C. J. H., 365n281
Midden, C., E5n35
Middlemist, R. D., 18n28

Miguel, E., 353n150
Mikolajczak, M., 199n66
Mikula, G., 347n86
Milam, H., E19n150
Milavsky, B., 343n55
Milberg, S., 413n37, 413n39, 413n40
Miles, M. B., 376n26
Milford, G., 252n127
Milgram, S., 5n11, 5n12, 306n87, 327n181, 454n34
Miller, A. G., 238n65
Miller, C. T., 96n176
Miller, D., E19n149
Miller, D. P., 457n61
Miller, D. T., 176n150, 176n152, 301n41, 318n152
Miller, E. K., 310n98
Miller, G. T., E11n90
Miller, J., 304n57, 454n30
Miller, J. A., 264n32
Miller, J. E., 310n97
Miller, L. C., 46n31, 170n109
Miller, M., 350n116
Miller, N., 15n24, 174n133, 274n68, 274n70, 334n12, 342n47, 346n77, 350n112, 354n178
Miller, N. E., 342n49
Miller, P. V., E4n19
Miller, R. L., 266n42, E8n66, E8n68
Miller, R. S., 418n88, 423n117
Miller, S. M., B16n72
Miller, T. Q., 201n85
Millhausen, R. R., 441n230
Milliman, R. E., A6n10
Mills, H., C24n148
Mills, J., 239n68, 412n32, 412n34, 413n41
Millson, M., 261n23, 261n24
Milne, A. B., 467n145
Minda, J. P., 214n200
Ming, L. K., 325n175
Minow, M., 347n89
Miquel, E., E10n77
Mischel, W., 58n88, 58n89, 94n148, 95n161, 132n110, 132n111, 139n148, 140n149, 140n150, 140n151, 339n40, 339n41, 390n137
Mischkowski, D., 220n255
Misra, S, 301n42
Mistretta, L., 198n61
Mita, T. H., 235n37
Mitchell, C., 201n80, 221n261
Mitchell, D. J., A7n15
Mitchell, J. P. 102n248
Mitkidis, P., 241n69
Miyamoto, Y., 162n78
Mochon, D., 120n29
Modan, B., 245n85
Moeller, F. G., 354n171
Moeller, S. J., 93n127, 93n128
Moens, E., 159n60
Moffitt, T. E., 356n195
Moffitt, T., 354n166
Mogilner, C., 363n247
Mohrman, S. A., C17n93
Moise, J., 352n132
Moller A. P., 384n109
Molouki, S., 163n85, 163n86, 163n87

Monk, R., 457n70
Monroe, A. E., 123n50
Mooney, H., E2n2
Moore, B., E2n2
Monshouwer, H. J., 343n56
Moore, C., 299n26, 362n239, 362n240
Moore, M. T., 94n146
Moore, R., 258n8, 258n10, 258n11
Moors, A. C., 429n151
Moos, R., E10n75, E10n76
Moos, R. H., B8n22
Moran, G., D16n113, D16n116, D16n118, D17n120, D17n123, D18n131
Moreland, M. B., D10n62
Moreland, R. L., 496n6, 496n9, 509n69, 509n70
Morewedge, C. M., 202n93
Morf, C. C., 99n218, 358n197, 416n82
Morgan, C. A., D5n23
Morgenthau, H., 517n95
Mori, D., 432n170
Morin, E., 219n238
Morokoff, P. J., 170n102, 191n26, 434n178
Morrill, C., 351n127
Morrin, M., A7n18
Morris, K. A., 276n87
Morris, W. N., 342n53
Morrison, E. L., 386n116
Morrow, G. D., 416n76
Mortensen, C. R., 302n45
Morton, H., E7n58
Moscovici, S., 511n77
Moser, G., E18n143
Moskowitz, D. S., B16n81
Motowidlo, S. J., C26n170
Mott, L. A., B10n36, B10n39
Mouchlianitis, E., 351n122
Mowen J. C., 279n107
Mowrer, O., 15n24, 342n47
Moya, M., 471n158
Muchnik, L., 213n16
Mueller, B., 507n56, A4n1, A17n49
Mügge, D. O., 313n118, 352n129, 352n137
Mugny, G., 460n92
Mullan, B., 448n2, 448n4, C17n96
Muller, D., 297n20, 350n113
Mulligan, R., E7n52
Mullin, C. R., 352n143
Mumford, M. D., C5n19
Mummendey, A., 467n136, 467n139, 479n191
Munger, K., 103n255, 309n92
Muraven, M., 134n128, 134n129
Muraven, M. B., 106n270
Murch, S. H., 148n10
Murch, S., 148n5
Murnen, S. K., 348n96
Murphy, S. A., E19n145
Murphy-Berman, V., E7n56
Murray, D. R., 47n44, 47n45, 47n47, 47n48, 309n94
Murray, S. L., 311n103
Murray, S., 416n74, 416n75, 424n122, 424n123, 424n124, E16n123

Murstein, B. I., 379n65
Musch, J., 45n30, 45n35
Muse, C. S., 467n138
Musham, C., 75n32
Musher-Eizenman, D. R., 457n69
Mussweiler, T., 302n47
Myers, D. G., 266n40, 420n108, 512n125, A14n44

N

Nadeau, S. E., E3n5
Nadler, A., 296n11
Nadler, R. T., 214n200
Nagler, U. K. J., 219n244
Najam, N., 390n134
Najmi, S., 157n46
Narby, D. J., D16n113
Náslund, E., 457n59
Nau, P. A., E18n138
Nault, L. P., 44n29
Naylor, J. C., C26n167
Neal, D., 137n139, 190n18
Neal, D. T., 137n140, 137n142, 137n143
Neale, M. C., 316n130, 316n132
Neale, M.A., 496n10
Near, J. P., C26n168
Neely, J. H., 155n32
Negel, L., 390n128
Neill, D. B., 351n127
Nelissen, R. M. A., 204n105
Nelson, J. E., 275n78
Nelson, L. D., 386n116
Nelson, M. R., 279n111
Nelson, N. M., 136n132
Nelson, P. A., E8n71
Nelson, S. E., 163n83
Neuberg, S. L., 302n45, 380n77, 452n27, 474n170
Neuschatz, J. S., D8n50, D10n72, D13n88
Newcomb T., 504n48
Newcombe, D., 273n66
Newman, A., 275n84, A14n41
Newman, B., 261n23, 261n24
Newman, E. J., 310n98
Newman, K., 351n127
Newman, M. L., 361n228
Newman, M., 220n249, 220n252, 221n256, 222n263, 222n272
Newschaffer, C. J., 148n8
Newton, T. L., 420n109
Nezlek, J., 376n39, 377n41
Nezlek, J. B., 219n234, 394n164
Nezlek, J., 124n61
Nguyen, H.-H. D., 485n234
Nias, D. K. B., 316n130, 316n132
Nichols, P. A., 90n115
Nicholson, N., 176n146
Nickell, E. F., 209n157
Nickerson, R. S., 171n124, E2n3
Niedenthal, P. M., 211n170
Nierenberg, D., E4n20
Nietzel, M. T., D17n127
Nijman, H. L. I., 353n158
Nisbet, E. K., 212n177, E19n145
Nisbett, R. E., 79n47, 80n48, 80n50, 83n61, 89n108, 162n75, 162n77, 359n204, 359n206, B16n71

Noel, H., 277n90
Nohria, N., 513n78
Nolen-Hoeksema, S., 222n265
Nordgren, L. F., 158n51, 158n52
Norenzayan, A., 311n102, 455n39, 455n42
Norris, F. H., 252n129, E16n133
Northouse, P. G., C18n115
Norton, M. I., 199n66, 314n121, 379n72, D16n105, D16n106
Nosek, B.A., 300n35
Noulles, D., E15n113
Novelli, D., E6n41
Nowak, M., 292n1
Nuss, C. K., 391n139
Nussbaum, S., 84n71
Nyende, P., 314n121
Nysse-Carris, K. L., 361n227
Nystrom, L.E., 299n32

O

O'Barr, W. M., 273n65
O'Boyle, E. H., 219n235
O'Brien, E. H., 7n14
O'Brien, E., 312n114
O'Connell, V., 236n50
O'Connor, D. B., C25n157, C25n158, C25n159
O'Connor, M., D17n130
O'Hara, S., E7n52
O'Leary, E. S., 429n152, E16n125
O'Malley, P. M., 96n177, 96n178
Omar, A., 83n67
O'Neil, K. M., D17n119
O'Sullivan, L. F., 245n91, 348n97
O'Sullivan, M., 215n205, 361n225
Oakes, H., 299n28
Oakes, M. A., 452n20
Oakes, W., 27n48
Obach, M. S., 161n64
Oberlé, D., 308n89
Ockenfels, A., 302n47
Odland, L. M., 457n55
Oettingen, G., 125n71
Ogrocki, P., 377n50, 420n107
Okwumabua, J. O., 213n187
Olatunji, B. O., 459n95
Oldham, G. R., C22n131
Oliner, P. M., 316n129
Oliner, S. P., 316n129
Oliver, M. B., 429n153, 441n228
Olivola, C. Y., 132n113
Olson, E. A., D4n3, D10n70
Olson, J. M., 176n155, 210n167, B15n67
Olson, M. A., 232n23, 232n24, 235n46, 419n96, 476n175
Olson, S., 149n16
Olweus, D., 100n230, 335n18
Ones, D., C11n53
Ones, D. S., C12n61
Orbell, J. M., E19n147
Organ, D. W., C26n168
Oriet, C., D8n46
O'Riordan, T., E2n2
Orne, M. T., 19n29
Ornstein, P. A., D19n142, D19n143
Ornstein, R., 263n30
Orobio de Castro, B., 343n56

Orr, E. S., 231n11
Orr, R. R., 231n11
Orth, U., 98n209
Ortiz, C. W., 454n30
Ortiz, V., 462n106
Osborn, D. P., E11n86
Osherow, N., 480n200
Oskamp, S., E18n140
Osswald, S., 344n64
Osterlund, K., D5n21
Ostroff, C., C14n84
Oswald, I., 51n58
Otis, C. C., D15n102
Ottaviani, R., 94n144
Oubaid, V., 438n207
Oudekerk, B. A., D16n111
Ouellette, J. A., 137n141
Ouellette, R., 413n37, 413n39, 413n40
Ouwerkerk, J. W., 393n160, 396n186, 397n187, 397n188, 503n41, 503n43
Oveis, C., 205n124
Over, H., 320n163
Overall, N. C., 419n99
Overbeek, G., 306n83
Overing, J., 465n115
Owen, J., 460n85

P

Padilla, A. M., B16n74
Páez, D., 396n183, 396n184, D15n98
Page, S. E., 496n8
Paik, H., 335n20
Palca, J., 457n62
Paleari, G., 305n66
Palmer, M. A., D9n57
Palmeri, H., 140n153
Pan, Z., 15n22
Panksepp, J., 390n132, 390n133, 390n134, 390n135
Paolini, S., 466n131, 466n133
Papageorgis, D., 283n123, 283n124
Papciak, A. S., E3n27
Parad, H. W., 396n180
Pargament, K. I., 251n114, 304n60
Parikh, R., 149n15
Pariser, E., 243n76
Park, B., 452n19, 470n150, 482n212
Park, C., 362n235
Park, C. L., 252n126
Park, E. S., 397n188, 503n41
Park, J. H., 47n46
Park, L. E., 100n240, 101n241
Park, S. H., 518n99
Parker, J. F., D9n56
Parker, S. D., E15n112
Parks, C. D., 397n188
Parks, J. M., C26n172
Parnell, A., E16n131
Parrott, D. J., 459n83
Parsley, A., 277n93
Passafaro, P., E18n137
Patel, V., 365n271
Pathak-Sharma, M. K., D18n137
Patnoe, S., 480n199
Patrick, R., 214n201
Patrick, W., 394n163, 395n178
Patry, M. W., D17n119
Patterson, E. W. J., 274n73

Patterson, O., 482n210
Paul, C., 97n202
Paulhus, D. L, 87n94, 106n269, 219n243
Paulus, P. B., 507n54, C17n90, E3n10, E6n38
Paxson, L. M., 49n55
Payne, B. K., 452n21, 476n177, 476n180
Payne, C. R., 156n39
Payne, J. W., 60n93, 60n94
Payne, S., 458n74
Peake, P. K., 132n110, 132n111, 140n150, 140n151
Pedersen, A., 466n133
Pedersen, W. C., 46n31, 334n12
Pederson, J., 95n152
Peekna, H. M., 313n119
Pelham, B. W., 151n27
Peltonen, T., 334n13
Peluchette, J., 213n14
Pemberton, M. B., 466n126
Pendleton, M., 236n51
Penn, G. M., 377n51
Pennebaker, J. W., 361n228
Penner, L. A., 317n140, C26n170
Pennington, G., 377n56, 395n172
Penrod, S. D., D4n4, D5n16, D5n17, D5n22, D6n32, D6n34, D11n76, D13n90, D15n96, D17n119, D18n137
Penrod, S., D11n76
Penros, S. D., D17n130
Penton-Voak I. S., 344n65
Pepitone, A., 504n48
Peplau, L. A., 216n220, 216n224, 376n38, 394n167, 394n168
Peragine, D., 411n25
Perera, H. N., 219n241
Perez, R. C., 100n232
Perie, M., 96n170
Peristiany, J. G., 359n210
Perkins S. C., 86n88
Perkins, H. W., 222n268
Perlman, D., 394n167
Perona, A., D16n111
Perot, A., 348n96
Perper, T., 429n155
Perretta, S., 96n171
Perry, C. L., 283n125
Perry, E. L., C19n126
Persons, J. B., 252n130
Peruche, B. M., 452n22
Peters, D., 487n243
Peters, K., 55n76
Peterson, C. K., 199n72
Peterson, C., 315n124
Peterson, K., 219n239
Peterson, N. G., C5n19
Peterson, R. F., 480n196
Petri, B., 347n86
Pettigrew, T. F., 466n129, 466n130, 466n134, 479n192
Pettit, J. W., 297n18
Pettiway, L. E., 347n87
Petty, R. E., 235n41, 235n45, 277n91, 278n101, 278n103, 280n113, 281n118, 281n120, 284n130
Peyser, H., 459n97

Pfau, M., 284n129
Pham, L. B., 116n11
Phillips, C. M., 342n54
Phillips, M., 484n224, D10n64
Phillips, S., 393n157
Phillips, T., E13n103
Phillis, D. E., 170n112, 170n113
Piazza, J., 382n82
Pickel, K. L., D6n27, D6n28
Pickering, A. S., 74n24
Pickett, C. L., 377n55, 392n150, 392n151, 394n166, 394n170, 395n174
Pierce, W. D., 82n59, 83n63, 83n65
Pihl, R. O., 354n172
Piliavin, I. M., 323n168
Piliavin, J. A., 323n168
Pillard, R. C., 433n176
Pinel, E. C., 211n172
Pines, A., 437n198, 440n224
Pinker, S., 42n17, 335n22, 335n23, 335n26, 336n28, 461n100
Pinkley, R. L., 495n11
Pitt, E. L., 348n102
Pitts, V. E., 363n253
Pizarro, D. A., 300n36, 382n85
Plaks, J. E., 56n78
Plant, E. A., 452n22, 452n23, 460n93, 478n187, 479n188, 479n190, 486n240, 479n244
Platt, C. W., 161n65
Platt, J., E3n125
Pleck, J., 216n207, 216n208, 216n209
Pliner, P., 432n169, 432n170
Plotkin, J., 487n243
Plötner, M., 320n163
Plotnick, S., 354n172
Pocheptsova, A., 136n133
Podolski, C. P., 352n132
Pogorzelski, S., C8n33
Poletes, G., 507n54
Politano, J., A11n30
Polivy, J., 75n28, 77n41, 133n121
Poll, J., 251n115
Pollack, J. M., 219n235
Pollard-Sacks, D., 352n134
Pollock, V. E., 354n178
Pomazal, R. J., 317n141
Pomeroy, W. B., 430n160
Pomery, E., B14n63
Pond, R. S., 99n217, 349n105, 411n26
Porges, S. W., 220n247
Portmess, L., 44n28
Posavac, S. S., B15n69
Posner, B. Z., 513n83
Postmes, T., 504n50
Pottebaum, S. M., 96n182
Pouwelse, M., B8n31
Povinelli, D. J., 316n127
Powell, C., 391n138
Powell, J., 39n11
Powell, M., 413n37, 413n39, 413n40
Powell, M. C., 234n132
Powell, N., E16n121
Powers, R. A., D10n72
Powers, R. E., E16n119
Powers, W. T., 133n118

Pozzulo, J. D., D4n5, D4n6
Pratkanis, A. R., 269n50, 273n61, 277n95
Pratt, T. C., 356n194
Pratto, F., 467n142
Predmore, S., 86n85
Prelec, D., A11n28
Pressley, M., 246n93
Presson, C. C., 283n126
Preston, E., 249n109
Preston, J. L., 205n121
Price, H. L., D8n46
Price, J. L., C23n137
Price, P. C., 302n43
Prinstein, M. J., 346n81
Pritchard, R. D., C26n167
Prochaska, J. M., B11n51
Prochaska, J. O., B11n50, B11n51, B13n57, B13n59
Proctor, W., E13n103
Pronin, E., 163n85, 163n86, 163n87
Pronk, T. M., 306n83
Provias, D., 485n235, 485n239
Pryor, J. B., 58n87, 75n31, 520n111
Purcell, A. H., E17n135
Purdie-Vaughn, V., 483n216
Putcha-Bhagavatula, A. D., 46n31
Pyszczynski, J., 103n254
Pyszczynski, T., 95n156, 98n212
Pyszczynski, T. A., A14n42

Q

Qualtrough, T., 245n90
Quanty, M. B., 201n82, 339n34
Quarantelli, E. L., E4n21
Quas, J. A., D16n109
Quigley, B., 346n76
Quigley-McBride, A., 310n98
Quilitch, H. R., 480n196
Quinlivan, D. S., D8n50, D11n75
Quinn, D. M., 485n225
Quinn, D., 485n230
Quinones, M. A., C12n63
Quinton, R. L., 375n9
Quoidbach, J., 199n66

R

Rabi, R., 214n200
Rachal, K. C., 197n53
Raczynski, J. L., D9n59
Radke, H. R. M., 466n133
Ragins, B. R., C14n81
Rainey, D., 384n103
Rainey, R., C17n102
Raleigh, M., 354n166
Ramalho, N., 219n238
Rao, P. A., 252n130
Raphael, T., C10n41
Rapson, R. L., 208n143, 406n3
Raskin, R., 358n198
Rasmussen, F., 457n59
Ratcliff, J., 460n93
Ratnewshwar, S., A7n18
Rauch, S. M., D13n93
Rauhut, H., 508n63
Rauthmann, J. F., 219n244
Ravitz, J., 252n121
Raymond, P., 188n11, 233n29, 520n111

Raynor, H. A., 136n136
Raz, M., 266n43
Read, J. D., D6n33, D12n83
Read, S. J., 415n57
Reams, M. A., 365n278
Rector, G., 353n158
Redden, J. P., B14n66
Redding, C. A., B13n57
Reddish, P., 241n69
Reddon, J. R., C12n64
Reeder, G. D., 58n87, 416n80
Reeve, C. L., 363n253
Regalia, C., 305n66
Regan, P., 522n123
Regan, P. C., 97n205
Regnerus, M., 428n149
Reich, J. W., 365n276
Reicher, S., E6n41
Reidel, S. L., 379n68
Reifman, A., B8n30
Reilly, N. P., 342n53
Reimer, D. J., 235n39
Reinhard, D. A., 150n25
Reinisch, J., 405n1
Reinisch, J. M., 170n117
Reinke, K. S., 351n121
Reinsch, J., E8n65
Reis, H. T., 44n23, 58n84, 96n192, 204n104, 207n139, 214n194, 377n40, 385n117, 416n70
Reis, H., 394n164
Reisen, N., 120n30
Reiss, I. L., 437n200, 437n201
Reiss, N., C24n148
Reiter, K. J., 219n244
Reiter, S. M., 364n268
Remland, M. S., E6n50
Rempel, J. K., 310n97
Ren, L. R., 363n251, 363n252
Rennison, S., 311n105
Reno, R. R., 365n273, 365n274, 365n275
Renzetti, C. M., 438n216
Repetti, R. L., B7n19
Reston, J., 258n5
Reykowski, J., 209n161
Reynolds, R., 203n101
Rhee, H., A5n7
Rhine, R. J., 233n25
Rhoads, K., 265n36
Rhodes, N., 278n100
Rhodewalt, F., 89n106, 89n107, 99n218, 358n197, 416n82
Rholes, W. S., 155n33
Rice, R. W., 376n32, E11n86
Richards, C., 214n196
Richards, J. M., 361n228
Richards, Z., 450n15
Richardson, A. S., 316n127
Richardson, D. R., 334n11
Richerson, P. J., 41n14, 47n49, 47n50, 47n53
Richeson, J. A., 476n182, 476n183, 485n238
Richman, J. A., 222n271
Ridley, M., 57n82, 57n83
Righetti, F., 311n101, 382n83
Ring, K., 103n257
Ringelmann, M., 3n5, 501n31

Rini, C., B12n53
Ripamonti, C., 297n17
Rippere, V., 220n253
Risen, J. L., 172n28
Rishworth, A., D6n35
Ritov, I., 212n178
Ritson, J., 44n26
Ritter, J. M., 384n101, 386n115
Ritter, R. S., 205n121
Rittle, R. H., 500n17, 501n29
Riva, P., 364n266
Rivetti, A., 148n7
Rivis, A., B14n65
Roach, M., A21n60
Robbennolt, J. K., D18n137
Robbins, J. M., C23n145, C24n150
Roberson, B., 513n78
Roberts, B. W., 89n110
Roberts, J., 362n238, A5n4
Roberts, N., 39n11
Roberts, W., 148n9
Roberts, W. A., 59n91, 125n78
Robertson, J. L., 365n276, 474n170
Robin, R., 86n81
Robins, R. W., 98n209, 99n215
Robinson, I. E., 441n229
Robinson, P., 316n128
Roch, S., 292n1
Rodes, D., 304n57
Rodin, J., 323n168, 440n222, B7n16
Rodríguez-Sickert, C., 309n93
Roeder, J. L., 152n129
Roehling, M. V., 457n55
Roehling, P. V., 457n55
Roepstorff, A., 241n69
Roese, N., 176n149
Roese, N. J., 42n15, 176n155, 210n167, B15n67
Roets, A., 159n59
Rogers, C. R., 416n72
Rogers, E. M., 275n82, B11n48
Rogers, T. B., 88n97, 88n98
Rogers, W. L., 207n133
Roggman, L. A., 384n101, 386n115
Rogow, A. A, 13n20
Rohrer, J. H., 261n26
Romer, D., 350n118, 351n127
Romero, V., 100n222
Romero-Canyas, R., 390n126, 483n216
Rondeel, E., 214n202
Roney, J. R., 375n8, 439n214
Root, L. M., 306n80
Ropp, S. A., 479n194
Rorer, L. G., 171n126
Rose, P., 416n74, 416n75
Rosen, J. C., 391n144
Rosen, R. J., 230n5
Rosen, S., 79n45
Rosenbaum, M. E., 236n53, 379n71
Rosenberg, M., 79n46, 96n183
Rosenfeld, D. L., 83n64
Rosenhan, D. L., 319n160, 325n173
Rosenman, R. H., 201n84
Rosenstock, I. M., B10n41, B11n45
Rosenthal, E., A10n24
Rosenthal, H. E. S., 467n137
Rosenthal, R., 481n207, D10n61, D10n62

Roskies, E., C23n139
Roskos-Ewoldsen, D., 277n89
Ross, C., 231n11
Ross, D., 237n55, 237n56, 237n58, 339n42, 339n43
Ross, E. A., 4n7
Ross, J. A., C2n6
Ross, L., 174n134, 175n140, 238n66, 248n106, 248n107, 281n119
Ross, M., 91n119, 91n120, 91n121, 129n103, 130n104, 130n106, 161n72, 422n114
Ross, S. A., 237n55, 237n56, 237n58, 339n42, 339n43
Ross, S. M., 349n107
Rossi, J. S., B13n59
Rossiter, J., A6n12, A7n13
Rotenberg, K. J., 311n105
Roth, J., 175n145
Roth, P. L., C12n62
Rothbart, M. K., 216n215
Rothberg, J. M., 141n163
Rothblum, E. D., 457n56
Rothengatter, T., E13n105
Rothman, A. J., 156n38
Rothman, S., E19n154
Rothschild, Z. K., 474n164
Rothstein, H. R., 27n50, 313n116, 313n117, 352n135
Rothstein, M., C12n64
Rottmann, L., 379n69, 384n97
Rotton, J., 353n154, 353n156
Rovine, M., 207n130, 207n131
Rowatt, W. C., 360n220
Rowthorn, R., 309n93
Royzman, E. B., 233n27
Rozin, P., 58n86, 213n184, 213n185, 233n27, 382n82
Roznowski, M. A., C26n173
Ruback, R. B., 21n34
Rubin, D. B., 148n6
Rubin, M., 466n131, 466n133
Rubin, R. A., 96n181
Rubin, Y., 390n127
Rubin, Z., 216n220, 216n224
Rubio-Stipec, M., E16n129
Ruble, D. N., 207n136
Rudd, M. D., 297n18
Rudski, J. M., 171n123
Ruedy, N. E., 299n26, 362n239, 362n240
Ruiz, R. A., B16n74
Rumble, A. C., 397n188, 503n41
Rupert, G., C9n38
Rupp, D. E., C23n144
Rusbult, C. E., 304n61, 311n104, 416n76, 419n100, 420n101, 422n113, 423n116
Ruscio, J., 175n142
Rushton, J. P., 246n93, 316n130, 316n131, 316n132
Russakoff, R., 363n250
Russell, C. S., 207n127
Russell, D., 394n168
Russell, J. A., 187n3
Russell, V. M., 418n91
Ruva, C. L., D18n133, D18n134, D18n135
Ryan, A. M., 485n234, C5n18

Ryan, B. A., 96n187
Ryan, J. R., C19n125
Ryan, R. M., 82n58, 83n62, 83n66, 123n51, 123n52, 123n53, 123n56, 123n58, 123n59, 124n62, 124n64, 124n65, 124n66, 124n68, 126n81, 197n50, 198n61
Ryan, S. L., D9n59
Ryan, T., 231n10
Rydell, R. J., 476n178
Ryff, C. D., 197n54
Rynd, N., 348n95

S

Sackett, P. R., 485n231, 485n232, C12n60, C26n174, C26n179
Saegert, S., E3n6, E6n39, E6n40
Saenz, D. S., 84n70
Safer, M. A., D5n21
Sagie, A., C17n92
Sagristano, M. C., 131n108
Sakaki, M., 210n166
Sakamoto, A., 27n50, 313n116, 313n117, 325n175, 352n135
Salas, E., 507n56, C17n96, C18n110
Salas-Wright, C. P., 358n201
Saleem, M., 27n50, 313n116, 313n117, 325n175, 352n128, 352n135
Salerno, J. M., 361n227
Salgado, J. F., C11n53
Salmivalli, C., 100n231
Salovey, P., 156n38, 219n230, 219n231, 219n232, 219n234, 438n208, 438n210, 440n221, 440n222
Samet, J. M., 377n47, E11n92
Samuel, W., 364n268
Samuelson, C., E19n148
Samuelson, C. D., 347n85
Sanbonmatsu, D. M., B15n69
Sandage, S. J., 197n53
Sandelands, L. E., 100n237
Sanders, G. S., 174n139
Sanders, S. A., 170n117
Sandfort, T. G. M., 459n97
Sandström, S., 505n51
Sanna, L. J., 179n167
Sanson, M., 310n98
Santayana, G., 8n15
Santos, F., 459n78
Santos, M. D., 269n50
Sapolsky, R. M., 353n160
Sarason, B. R., B8n28
Sarason, I. G., B8n28
Sargent, J. B9n34, B10n38, B10n39
Sargent, J. D., B9n35, B10n36
Sarin, R., 196n42
Sarrel, M. D., A21n59
Satow, K. L., 295n6
Sauer, J., D6n36
Sauer, J. D., D4n8
Sauerland, M., D7n39
Savin-Williams, R. C., 430n161
Savitsky, K., 161n73
Sawyer, A. G., 277n90
Sawyer, D., 170n103
Schachter, S., 190n19, 190n20, 191n22, 223n274, 261n22, 382n86, 433n174, B8n31, B16n76

Schaefer, H. S., 207n141
Schaefer, J. A., B8n22
Schaefer, N.K., 299n28
Schaller, M., 47n44, 47n45, 47n46, 47n47, 47n48, 205n116, 205n117, 309n94, 392n149, 452n27
Schapiro, S. J., 316n127
Schaubroeck, J., C23n146, C24n147
Schaumberg, R.L., 514n85
Scheck, S. R., 216n222
Scheibehenne, B., 120n28
Scheier, M. A., 96n184
Scheier, M. F., 74n15, 74n16, 75n29, 76n37, 76n38, 132n114, 133n115, 133n116, 133n117, B8n21
Schein, E. H., C29n188
Schellnhuber, H. J., E2n2
Scher, K. J., 76n34
Scherer, L. D., 476n181
Scherzer, N. A., 429n155
Schifferstein, H. N. J., A7n17
Schippmann, J. S., C12n62
Schlaerth, A., 219n242
Schlenker, B. R., 91n118, 102n247, 103n251, 103n259, 104n260, 106n266, 106n267, 106n268, 306n77
Schlösser, T., 309n95
Schlundt, D. G., 209n154
Schmader, T., 485n237
Schmeichel, B. J., 136n132
Schmidt, C., E3n7
Schmidt, F. L., C12n56, C12n59, C12n61
Schmidt, M. S., 350n119
Schmidt, R. E., 157n47
Schmitt, D. P., 38n8, 170n108, 427n141, 427n142, 429n152
Schmitt, N., C13n66
Schnall, S., 205n125
Schneider, D. J., 157n43
Schneider, I. K., 207n142
Schneiderman, E., 219n232, B8n27
Schoenbach, C., 96n183
Schoenbaum, M., E16n119
Schooler, C., 96n183
Schooler, J., 123n48
Schooler, J. W., 198n65, 362n241
Schooler, T. Y., 232n20
Schopler, J., 466n123, 466n124, 466n125, 466n126, 466n127, 500n16, E5n37
Schroeder, D. A., 265n138
Schuller, R. A., D16n110
Schultz, P. W., 364n269, E12n97
Schuman, H., 25n44
Schumm, W. R., 207n127
Schunk, D. H., 127n91, 127n92
Schurtz, D. R., 391n138
Schutte, N. S., 219n240
Schütz, A., 219n234, 416n83, 416n84, 416n85, 417n87
Schvaneveldt, R. W., 155n31
Schwab, J., E3n5
Schwartz, A., 212n178
Schwartz, B., 83n67, 120n27
Schwartz, D., 385n110, 459n77
Schwartz, I., 100n223
Schwartz, J. K. L., 476n176

Schwartz, P., 407n12, 408n20, 413n35, 435n189, 439n217, 439n218
Schwartz, S. H., E19n146
Schwarz, N., 25n45, 149n17, 175n141, 179n167, 204n109, 211n169
Schwarzer, R., 209n155
Schwarzwald, J., 266n43
Schweitzer, F., 508n63
Schweitzer, M. E., 299n26, 362n239, 362n240, 362n242
Scollon, C. N., 196n39, 196n43
Scott, J., 25n44
Scott, J. P., 339n35, 390n133
Scott, M., 45n38
Scratchley, L. S., 93n125
Seabright, P., 413n36
Seal, D. W., 439n219
Sears, D. O., 27n49, 280n115, 284n131
Sears, R., 15n24, 342n47, 473n165
Sechler, E. S., 115n6, 249n108
Sedikides, C., 85n78, 93n139, 106n272, 161n68, 416n80
Sedikides, C. S., 85n75
Sedlovskaya, A., 483n216
Seeley, E., 377n56, 395n172
Segal, N. L., 312n111
Sehgal, I., 455n38
Seib, H. M., D13n93
Seifert, C., 149n17, 175n141
Sekerak, G. J., 500n17, 501n29
Seligman, C., 266n42, E18n139
Seligman, M. E. P., 315n124
Selimbegovic, L., 76n36
Sellin, I., 219n234
Sellmer, G. P., 429n155
Semmelroth, J., 438n206
Semmler, C., D6n37, D10n71
Sennett, R., 70n3
Sentyrz, S. M., 75n27
Serota, K. B., 360n217
Seta, C. E., 500n18
Seta, J. J., 500n18
Seto, M. C., 191n23
Seyle, H., B3n10
Shackelford, T. K., 100n224, 437n197
Shaffer, D. R., 274n69
Shaffer, M. J., 419n96
Shah, J. Y., 128n93, 128n95, 128n96, 128n97
Shaked, A., 150n25
Shakur, S., 355n187
Shaley, I., 391n141
Shalit, B., E16n126
Shapiro, J. R., 452n27
Shapiro, P. N., D4n4
Shariff, A. F., 311n102, 455n42
Shaver, P. R., 414n43, 414n44, 414n45, 414n47, 414n49, 414n50, 414n52, 415n58, 415n62, 415n67, 416n70
Shavitt, S., 279n106, 471n153, B15n69
Shaw, B. F., 94n145
Shea, C. T., 382n84
Shea, D. L., 484n222
Sheffield, F., 271n55, 275n74, 278n97

Sheinman, L., 124n61
Sheldon, K. M., 124n69, 197n55, 199n68, A14n43
Sheldon, P., 231n12
Shelton, J. N., 476n182, 476n183, 486n241
Shenot, J., E19n154
Shepperd, J. A., 98n213, 384n108
Sherif, C. W., 462n109
Sherif, M., 261n25, 462n109, 464n110
Sherkat, D. E., 251n117
Sherman, S., 176n153
Sherman, S. J., 115n9, 153n30, 283n126, 494n4
Sherman, S. T., 115n10
Sherrod, D. R., E5n36
Shi, K., C27n186
Shibuya, A., 27n50, 313n116, 313n117, 352n128, 352n135
Shin, C., 243n75
Shin, J., 119n23
Shneidman, E. S., 142n168
Shoda, Y., 132n110, 132n111, 140n150, 140n151, 339n41
Shoeneman, T. J., 78n44
Shogren, J., E19n151
Shoham, I., 245n85
Shohat-Ophir, G., 373n1
Shook, N. J., 459n96, 479n193
Shorrocks, A., 505n51
Shorter, E., 425n128, 436n195, 436n196
Shotkin, A., E19n154
Shotland, R. L., 321n165, 430n168
Showers, C. J., 93n134
Shrauger, J. S., 78n44, 86n84, 100n233
Shteir, R., 363n254
Shteynberg, G., 42n15, 42n16
Shu, L. L., 362n245
Shumate, R., B10n37
Sibley, C. G., 466n133
Sicoiy, F., 161n72
Sidanius, J., 467n142
Siem, B., 316n134
Siero, F. W., E18n142
Sikes, J., 480n198
Silfver, M., 309n90
Silk, J. B., 316n127
Silva, P., 354n166
Silva, P. A., 356n195
Silver, M., 462n103
Silver, R., B3n4
Silvia, P. J., 75n25
Sime, J. D., 312n112
Simester, D., A11n28
Simkin, M. G., 361n231
Simmering, M. G., 231n11
Simmons, C. H., 318n153
Simons, L. S., 350n114
Simpson, J. A., 310n96, 415n59, 423n118
Sinclair, L., 473n167, 473n168
Sinclair, R. C., 170n114, 170n115
Singer, J. E., 124n70, 190n20, 191n22, 223n274, B16n76
Singh, D., 384n105, 384n106
Sisic, M., 231n11

Skaalvik, E. M., 96n185
Skelton, J. A., 89n106
Skewes, J., 241n69
Skinner, B. F., B10n44
Skitka, L.J., 298n25
Skolnick, A., 205n115
Skoner, D. P., B16n79
Slingsby, J. K., 313n119
Slinkard, L. A., 283n125
Slotter, E. B., 349n105, 411n26
Slovic, P., 165n92, 166n97, 172n130
Smalarz, L., D13n89
Small, D. A., 213n183
Small, M., D11n76
Smart, L., 357n196
Smith, C., D10n67
Smith, C. A., 214n192, C23n140, C26n168
Smith, C. M., D17n126
Smith, D., 171n120
Smith, E. E., 390n137
Smith, F. J., C27n187
Smith, G. E., 75n30, 97n207
Smith, G. F., 277n96
Smith, G. H., 80n49
Smith, I.H., 299n27
Smith, J. D., 152n29
Smith, L., 393n157
Smith, P. B., 27n51, 62n100
Smith, P. C., C22n132
Smith, R., 332n3
Smith, R. H., 309n91
Smith, R. J., E7n55
Smith, S. M., 274n69
Smith, S., D6n30
Smith, T., 441n232
Smith, T. B., 251n115
Smith, T. W., 25n46, 86n88, 201n85
Smittipatana, S., B15n69
Smuts, B., 443n235
Smyth, J. M., 252n126
Snapp, M., 480n198
Snibbe, A. C., 243n80
Snook, S., B14n65
Snow, M. G., B13n59
Snowdon, D., 197n58
Snyder, C. R., 86n88, 86n89, 315n125
Snyder, M., 278n104, 379n60, 379n62, 379n63
Soane, E., 176n146
Soares, F., 390n134
Sobell, L. C., 157n45
Sobell, M. B., 157n45
Soetens, B., 159n59, 159n60
Sohn, Y., 208n145
Solomon, D., 96n188, 98n212
Solomon, J., 377n56, 395n172
Solomon, S. D., E16n128
Solomon, S., A14n42
Soman, D., A11n32
Somerfield, M. R., B8n20
Sommer, K. L., 390n121, 390n127, 416n77
Sommer, R., A7n19
Sommers, C. H., 484n219
Sommers, P., E10n75, E10n76
Sommers, S. R., 101n243, D16n105, D16n106

Sommerville, R.B., 299n32
Sonnentag, S., C24n149
Sorman, P. B., 100n233
Southwick, L., 134n127
Southwick, S. M., E5n23
Spacapan, S., E4n15
Spangenberg, E. R., A7n14
Spangler, G., 415n68
Spangler, J. G., 457n61
Spanier, G. B., 207n131, 207n137
Spanier, G. P., 435n191
Spears, R., 504n50
Specht, H., 377n43
Speicher, C. E., 377n50, 420n107
Speicher, C., 377n51
Speier, A. H., E16n116
Spence, K. W., 500n24
Spencer, J. A., 213n17
Spencer, J. R., E15n112
Spencer, S., 485n227
Spencer, S. J., 55n77, 243n79, 468n147, 474n169, 485n225, 485n230
Sperber, D., 150n20, 171n125, 263n28, 270n53
Spielberg, W. E., E15n109
Spielmann, S. S., 411n25
Spiga, R., 354n171
Spitzberg, B. H., 398n196
Sporer, S. L., D6n34, D7n39
Spotanski, C., E8n65
Sprecher, S., 97n205, 385n117, 408n20, 418n92, 418n95, 428n146, 441n231, 522n123
Springer, C. A., 207n140
Springer, C., 390n128
Springer, S., 202n93
Sproull, L., 304n58
Sroufe, L. A., 415n69
Staats, A. W., 236n47
Staats, C. K., 236n47
Stack, A. D., 201n86
Stack, S., B15n68
Stacy, D., 45n38
Staffieri, J., 457n54
Stahelski, A. J., 301n40
Stalberg-Carlstedt, B., E16n126
Stanford, W. E., 284n128
Stangor, C., 207n136
Stanko, E. A., 347n90
Stansfeld, S., E4n17, E10n80, E11n83, E11n88
Staples, R., 426n134
Staples, S. L., E11n87
Stasser, G., 511n73, 511n74
Stearns, E., 45n39
Steblay, N., D11n78
Steblay, N. K., D9n59, D9n60, D10n74
Steblay, N. L., D9n53
Steblay, N. M., D6n25, D8n48, D17n129, D18n136, D18n138
Stecker, R., E11n82
Steele, C., 485n230
Steele, C. M., 134n127, 354n183, 484n221, 485n225, 485n227, 485n228, 485n233
Steffensmeier, D., 346n74

Steg, L., E2n11, E14n105
Steger, M., 251n116
Stein, R., 148n13
Steinel, W., 201n77
Steinfatt, T. M., 304n56
Steinhilber, A., B13n61
Steinmetz, G., 203n101
Steinmetz, K., A7n16
Stein-Seroussi, A., 87n95, 87n96
Steinwert, T., 457n46
Stel, M., 361n224
Stellar, J., 302n48
Stephan, C. W., 8n16
Stephan, W. G., 8n16
Stephenson, J. S., E15n107
Stephin, C., 480n198
Stepney, R., 134n124
Stepper, S., 189n17
Stern, C., 487n242
Stern, I., 518n99
Stern, J., 359n215
Stern, L. B., D6n38
Stern, P. C., E18n140
Stern, S. E., 454n35
Sternberg, R. J., 408n22
Stevenson, M. C., D16n111
Stewart, G. L., C18n108
Stewart, J.B., C15n70
Stickgold, R., 377n44, 395n175
Stillman, T. F., 377n54, 391n138, 522n121
Stillwell, A. M., 106n270, 131n109, 134n125, 203n95, 204n106, 216n223, 381n81, 397n194, 419n97, 419n98
Stinson, V., D13n91
Stobach, A., E11n89
Stock, M., B14n63
Stockdale, J., E5n37
Stone, E. F., C22n132
Stone, J., 70n4, 485n226, B12n56
Stone, L., 199n70, 407n8, 425n129, 451n17
Stoner, J. A. F., 511n75
Stoolmiller, M., B9n34
Storey, A. E., 375n9
Story, A. L., 96n170
Story, P. A., 219n235
Stott, C., E6n41
Stout, J. C., 377n50, 420n107
Stoutemyer, K., E19n153
Stout-Wiegand, N., E15n110
Strack, F., 51n59, 54n74, 189n17, 520n111
Strathman, A. J., 384n108
Straub, R. O., 222n267
Straus, M. A., 346n79
Straw, M. K., 321n165
Street, G. P., 157n49
Strober, M., 391n145
Stroebe, W., 236n48, 275n83, 507n55
Strong, G., 407n10
Stroop, J. R., 152n28
Struckman-Johnson, C., 348n91, 348n92
Stucke, T. S., 392n153, 393n159
Studebaker, C. A., D18n137
Stürmer, S., 316n134
Subra, B., 297n20, 350n113

Suddath, C., 252n123
Sugie, N., 454n30
Sullivan, D., 474n164
Sullivan, J., C9n34, C9n35, C20n128
Sullivan, M., C22n133
Suls, J., 96n167, 174n139, 214n195, B3n6
Sundali, J., 173n131
Sundstrom, E., E3n9, E11n86
Sunyer, J., E11n91
Suomi, S. J., 354n168, 354n169
Surowiecki, J., 496n7, 507n59, 507n60, 508n61
Surra, C., 216n221
Susa, K. J., D5n11, D5n12
Susman, E. J., 353n164
Susmilch, C., 298n22
Sussman, D., B12n52
Suvakumar, K., 261n23, 261n24
Suzuki, T., 243n80
Svedin, U., E2n2
Svenson, O., 93n131
Swami, V., 457n70
Swander, D. V., 261n26
Swann, A. C., 354n171
Swann, W. B., 85n76, 85n77, 86n85, 87n95, 87n96, 276n87, 424n119, 424n120, 424n121, 424n126
Swanson, J., 172n129
Swart, H., 466n135, 467n141
Sweeney, D., 74n23
Swift, A., C5n14, C5n15
Swim, J. K., 470n148
Swing, E. L., 27n50, 313n116, 313n117, 352n128, 352n135
Switzer, F. S., C12n62
Symanski, R., 376n31
Symons, C. S., 88n102, 426n136, 426n137
Symons, D., 38n6, 427n140, 428n148
Szalma, J. L., E10n79
Szymanski, S., 450n14

T

Tabak, A. J., 230n1
Tafarodi, R. W., 247n100
Tajfel, H., 462n101, 462n104, 462n105
Tambor, E. S., 98n210
Tamburini, M., 297n17
Tamir, D. I., 102n249
Tamir, M., 198n62, 201n80, 221n261
Tamkins, M. M., C14n84
Tang, S., 261n23, 261n24
Tangney, J. P., 58n85, 132n112, 202n94, 203n96, 203n97, 342n52
Tann, E. K., 356n192
Tannahill, R., 46n32
Tanner, A., 186n1
Tansey, G., 44n27
Tanzer, N., 347n86
Tarpley, W. R., 251n118
Tarquinio, M., C20n129
Tarrant, M. A., E17n136
Tashiro, T., 251n116
Tata, J., 261n23, 261n24
Tate, D. F., 136n136

Taub, D. M., 354n168
Taves, P., 193n30, 243n73
Taylor, A. M., 51n58
Taylor, D., 259n14
Taylor, K., 205n119
Taylor, R. B., E8n64
Taylor, S., 93n139, 309n91
Taylor, S. E., 94n149, 94n151, 95n163, 116n11, 126n86, 149n18, 149n19, 151n26, 176n156, 250n112, 345n69, 345n70, 348n94, B7n17, B7n18
Taylor, S. J., 213n16
Taylor, T. S., D15n100
Tchividjian, L. R., 106n273
Teachout, M. S., C12n63
Tedeschi, J. T., 103n251, 334n10, 335n21, 347n82, 347n84
Teigen, H., 13n21
Telch, C. F., 209n151, 209n152, 209n153
Tellegen, A., 187n7
Tennen, H., B8n24
ter Schure, E., 208n147
Terdal, S. K., 98n210
Terracianno, A., 470n151, 470n152
Terrizzi, J. A., 459n96
Terry, H., 358n198
Tesser, A., 79n45, 81n53, 101n242, 238n62
Tetlock, P., 176n149
Tetlock, P. E., 60n95, 60n96, 161n71, 487n242, 500n15, 519n109, 519n110
Tetrick, L. E., C23n145, C24n150
Tett, R. P., C12n64
Thagard, P., 471n155
Thaler, R. H., 88n103, 196n41
Thayer, R. E., 220n249, 220n252, 221n256, 221n263, 222n272
Therriault, N., 221n259
Thibodeau, R., E19n149
Thoennes, N., 398n198
Thomas, E. J., 73n11
Thomas, H. D. C., C18n105
Thomas, J., 344n65
Thomas, K. A., 42n17
Thomas, M. A., 205n118
Thomas, P., E5n23
Thomas, R. C., 214n204
Thompson, A. P., 434n177, 434n183
Thompson, M., 385n110
Thompson, M. P., 252n129, E16n133
Thompson, S. C. G., E19n153
Thompson, W. C., D17n124, D17n128
Thompson-Cannino, J., D12n79
Thomson, G. W., 365n271
Thornhill, R., 47n45, 384n109, 386n113
Thoresen, C. E., 304n60
Thorsteinsson, E. B., 219n239
Thrash, T. M., 197n56
Thundiyill, J. G., E11n89
Tice, D. M., 57n81, 87n91, 91n117, 93n124, 103n250, 106n270, 134n128, 134n129, 136n132, 141n155, 200n75, 209n156, 221n258, 391n138, 392n153, 393n159

Tichener, J. L., E4n22
Tickle, J. J., B10n36, B10n39
Tidwell, M., 416n70
Tierney, J., 135n130
Tiggemann, M., 74n24, 457n56
Tilcsik, A., 458n75
Tillman, T. C., 318n155
Timbergen, N., 339n37
Tindale, R. S., D17n126
Titus, L. J., 500n26
Titus, W., 511n73, 511n74
Tjaden, P., 398n198
Tjew A Sin, M., 207n142
Tobacyk, J. J., 252n128
Tobacyk, J., 252n127
Todd, P. M., 120n28
Todd, R. M., 313n119
Toglia, M. P., D10n72
Toguchi, Y., 106n272
Tolin, D. F., 157n49
Toll, B. A., 157n45
Toma, C. L., 361n221, 387n118
Tomarken, A., 129n101, 129n102
Tomasello, M., 125n77, 312n113, 314n122, 320n163
Tomkins, S. S., 189n16
Tooby, J., 178n160, 178n161
Topping, J. S., E6n48
Tormala, Z. L., 284n130
Torneo, E., D12n79
Totis, A., 297n17
Towles-Schwen, T., 246n94
Town, J. P., E11n86
Tracy, J. I., 354n173
Tranel, D., 210n165
Trapnell, P. D., 205n122
Travaglino, G., 518n100
Trawalter, S., 476n183
Tredoux, C. G., D9n56, D9n58
Treisman, M., 51n58
Tremblay, R. E., 345n66
Trent, R. B., E15n110
Trevisan, M., E16n125
Triandis, H. C., 296n8
Trinkaus, J., 365n279
Triplett, N., 4n7
Trivers, R., 38n7, 102n244, 427n139
Trolier, T. K., 472n160
Trope, Y., 52n67, 52n69, 84n71, 85n73, 85n74, 130n107, 131n108
Tropp, L. R., 466n129, 466n130, 466n134, 479n192
Trudeau, R., 47n44, 309n94
Trueman, M., 311n105
Trzesniewski, K. H., 99n215
Tsal, Y., 281n117
Tsang, J., 197n52
Tsang, J.-A., 306n81
Tse, A. C. B., A16n47
Tubman, J. G., 97n203
Tucker, M. B., B12n55
Tufekci, Z., 102n248
Tunnicliff, J. L., D7n43
Turnbull, S, 68n1
Turner, B. F., 430n163, 430n165
Turner, C. W., 201n85, 350n114
Turner, R. H., 71n7
Turner, S. A., 209n155
Turtle, J. W., D7n41

misattribution of, 190–193
performance and, 217–218
pleasant vs. unpleasant states, 193
Schachter–Singer theory of emotion, 190
sexual arousal, 191, 213, 433
shopping, A7
social facilitation theory, 500
Arsenic, E11
Arson, 347
Asian Americans
selfhood, 72
As Nature Made Him (Colapinto), 34
Assembly lines, 493
Assertiveness, 514
Association for Psychological Science, 385
Assumptive worlds, 249
Atheists, 311, 455–456
Athletics. *See* Sports
Attachment, 413–416, 425
Attachment theory, 414–416
Attention
alcohol use impact, 354
emotional arousal and, 217
heat and, E3
self-esteem and, 95
social influence techniques based on
capturing or disrupting, 269–270
Attitude polarization, 237–238
Attitudes, 229–247
accessibility of, 246
Allport's work, 4
as behavior predictor, 244–247
beliefs vs., 232
change through persuasion, 280–282
consistency, 239–244
defined, 232
dual model of, 232
environmental issues, E17–E18
formation of, 234–237
inoculation of, 283–284
polarization of, 237–238
reasons for, 232–234
summary, 254–255
at work, C21–C25, C27–C28
Attitudes at work, C21–C25, C27–C28
Attraction, 379–387
defined, 372
importance of, 373
online dating, 385–387
summary, 399–400
theories of, 378–385
Attractiveness
helpfulness and, 317–318
persuasion and, 274
of spouses, 379
what is beautiful is good effect, 383
Attributions and attribution theory
action explanations, 163
actor/observer bias, 161–163
challenges of, 163
defined, 160
history of, 5
illness symptoms, B16
importance of, 160
racism, 483
romantic rejection, 397
self-serving bias, 483
success and failure explanations,
160–161

Audience, 278–280
Audience inhibition, 323
Australian Aborigines, E9
Authoritarian personality, D16
Authority, obedience to, 306–309
Autokinetic effect, 261
Automatic affect, 187–188, 193, 208
Automatic attitudes, 232
Automatic egotism, 87, 106
Automatic system
cognitive errors, 178–179
conscious override of, 54, 58, 87,
476–479
defined, 51
vs. deliberate system, 51–53
goals hierarchies and, 127, 128
habits, 138
mental shortcuts (*See* Heuristics)
power, 519
prejudice, 476–477
thinking, 151–153, 155
Automobile industry, 592, A2
Autonomy, 123
Availability heuristic, 165, 174
Average Joe, 372, 381
Aversive racism, 449
Avoidant attachment, 414, 415–416
Awareness, 152. *See also* Self-awareness

B

Babies, 187, 381. *See also* Children
Bad apple effect, 396, 503, 505
Bait-and-switch technique, 264
Baseball players, 197
Base rate fallacy, 172–173
Basic research, 12
Beauty, 383–385. *See also* Attractiveness
Behavior. *See also* Choices and actions
antisocial behavior (*See* Antisocial behavior)
attitudes as predictor of, 244–247
choices (*See* Choices and actions)
consumer behavior (*See* Consumer behavior)
defined, 6
emotional causes, 208–210
environmental issues, E17–E18
Lewin's work, 4
from nature, 56–57
prosocial behavior (*See* Prosocial behavior)
rejection and, 392–393
risky behavior (*See* Risky behavior)
self-awareness and, 75
self-defeating behavior, 138–142
self-presentation, 101–103
sexual behavior (*See* Sexuality and sexual
behavior)
at work, C26–C27
Behavioral intentions, 246–247
Behaviorism, 5, 115, 236
Belief in a just world, 318
Belief perseverance, 248–249
Beliefs
attitudes vs., 232
coping and, 249–251
defined, 232
doubting vs., 247–248
health belief model, B10–B11
irrational beliefs, 252
in just world, 318
perseverance of, 248–249

religious beliefs, 251–252
summary, 255
Belongingness, 207–208, 373–376, 517
Benefits, employee, C1–C3, C24–C25
Benevolent sexism, 471
Betty Crocker, A8
Between-subjects design, 15
BFOQ (bona fide occupational qualifications), C8
Biases and errors
actor/observer bias, 161–163
attitude polarization, 238
automatic system's role in, 178–179
base rate fallacy, 172–173
confirmation bias, 171, 474, B15
correspondence bias, 162
counterfactual thinking, 166, 176–177
debate over, 168–169
false consensus effect, 174
false uniqueness effect, 174
fundamental attribution error, 162, 319
gambler's fallacy, 173
hostile cognitive biases, 343–344
illusion of control, 175–176
illusory correlations, 171, B15
liberal bias, 487
omission bias, 120
optimistic bias, 130
outgroup homogeneity bias, 452
own-race bias, D5
reduction strategies, 178–179
self-serving bias, 95, 161, 472, 483
statistical regression, 175
status quo bias, 119
summary, 177
theory perseverance, 174–175
Big 5, 577
Binge eating, 77, 133–135, 502
Biological psychology, 8
Biology, influence of, 5
Biopsychosocial approach to health, B9
Birthdays, 44–45
Bisexuality, 433, 439
Black people. *See* African Americans
Black sheep hypothesis, D15
Blame
aggression and, 348
coping and, 250
for natural disasters, E16
rape victims, 348
scapegoat theory, 472–473
of victims, 318
Blank lineups, D8
Bobo doll study, 339
Body odor, 386
Body shape, 385
Body weight, 385
Bona fide occupational qualifications (BFOQ), C8
Boomerang effect, 284
Bosses, 515–516
Brain
aggression and, 353–354
computer comparison, 63
duplex mind, 50–54
sexual arousal, 191
size of, 39
Brainstorming, 506–508
Brainwashing, 90, 248
Brand loyalty, A8
Broaden-and-build theory, 214

Asch's research, 62, 261–262
criticism of, 294–295
defined, 309
as groupthink indication, 510
restaurant diners, 310
Confounding, 20
Conscious emotion, 187–188
Conscious override, 54, 58, 87, 476–479
Conscious system, 51
Conscious thought, 51–54, 158. *See also* Deliberate system
Consent forms, 19
Conservation, E12–E14, E18
Conservatism, 459
Consistency
social influence techniques based on, 263–266
theories of, 239–244
Consistency motive, 85, 86
Conspicuous consumption, A13–A14
Constructs, 15
Construct validity of the cause, 16
Construct validity of the effect, 16
Consumer behavior, A1–A23
cell phones, A17–A19
consumption process, A9
dark side of, A19–A20
decision making, A2–A9
e-commerce, A5, A12–A13, A16–A17
post-consumption process, A20–A21
purchase making, A10–A15
Consumer Reports, 169
Consumer segments, e-commerce, A16
Consumption process, A9
Contact hypothesis, 466–467, 479
Contemplation stage of transtheoretical model, B12, B13
Continuance (trials), D18
Continuance commitment, C22
Control
in cognitive appraisal model, B7
domestic violence and, 349
illusion of, 175–176
over female sexuality, 441–442
panic button effect, 124
rejection and, 391
thinking, 152–153
Controls, experimental, 22
Convert communicators, 272
Convictions, wrongful, D2–D3
Coolidge effect, 429
Cooperation
after rejection, 393
vs. competition, 465
defined, 464
reciprocity basis, 301–304
Coping
attachment styles and, 414
beliefs and, 249–251
defined, 249, B8
with natural disasters, E16
Corporations. *See* Work and workplace
Correct identification, D3
Correct rejection, D3
Correlation, 22
Correlational approach, 22–23
Correlation coefficient (r), 22
Correlations, illusory, 171, B15
Correspondence bias, 162

Corruption, 517–518
Counterfactual thinking, 166, 176–177
Counterproductive behaviors, C26–C27
Counterregulation, 159
Credibility, source, 271–273
Credit cards, 283, A11
Crimes
eyewitness memory, D3–D13
hate crimes, 476
hot temperatures and, 352–353
self-control and, 356–357
theft, 363–364, A20
violent crimes, 335 (*See also* Rape)
Crisis situations, 262
Critical Incident Technique (CIT), C7
Criticism, 79, 103, 516
Crowding, 353, E2, E5–E6
Cues
lying detection, 361
prompts, E12
rejection and, 392
social interaction and, 55–56
Cults, 259, 263
Cultural animals. *See also* Humans as cultural animals
advantages of, 63, 64
defined, 40
vs. social animals, 47–48
Cultural groups, 496
Cultural relativity, 27
Culture and cultural differences
advantages of, 63
advertising preferences, 278–279
aggression, 56, 338–341, 356–360
alcohol use, 354
anger, 200
attraction, 379
attributions, B16
vs. being social, 47–48
competition vs. cooperation, 465
conformity, 309
conscious override importance, 54
consistency, 243–244
defined, 41–43
differences in people, 49–50
domestic violence, 349
duplex mind, 50–54
eating habits, 44, 57
emotions, 215
gender roles, 46
goal setting, 125–127
groups, 496
happiness, 195
homosexuality and, 431–433
ideal body weight, 385
information, 43–44
intergroup relationships, 487–488
Internet comparison, 63
jealousy, 437
love, 406–407
meaning learned through, 115
money, 42–43
nature and, 36, 44–47
organizational culture, C14–C16
people first theory, 61–63
personal space, E6–E7
persuasion, 278–279
physical attractiveness, 383
praxis, 42–43

prejudice, 462, 480–481
role differentiation, 498
self, 71–72
self-control from, 56–57
selfishness vs. social conscience, 57–58
sexual behavior, 46, 57, 426–427, 428, 430, 440–442
sleep, 49
smoking, B2
social acceptance, 54–55
social system, 42
standards, 132
summary of, 64–65
territoriality, E8–E9
tradeoffs, 58–60
violence, 356–360
Culture of honor, 358–360
Curiosity, 10–11, 85
Cyberbullying, 335

D

Date rape, 348
Dating
attractiveness of partner and, 383
break-ups, 418, 422–423
eating, 431
infidelity, 436
interracial dating, 453
number of dates before sex, 431
online dating, 385–387
view of partner, 424
Death and dying
awareness of and purchasing decisions, A14
behavioral risks, B9
beliefs about, 37
from cancer, B2
from disease, 377
donating body to science, A21
fear of, E7
by guns, 351
instinct (thanatos), 339
suicide (*See* Suicide)
Death penalty, 238, D17
Death qualification, D17
Debiasing, 179
Debriefing, 19
Debt, consumer, A11
Deception studies, 19
Decision avoidance, 119, 129–130
Decision fatigue, 136–137
Decision-making. *See* Choices and actions
Defense mechanisms, 414
Deindividuation, 364, 498, 504
Delay of gratification, 140
Deliberate attitudes, 232
Deliberate system
vs. automatic system, 52–53
conscious override by, 54, 58, 87, 476–479
defined, 51
goals hierarchies and, 127–128
power, 519
thinking, 151–153
Demand characteristics, 19, D7
Demographics, D16
Density of population, 353, E5–E6
Dependent variables, 16, 20
Depression
air pollution and, E12
crowding and, E3

gender differences, 222
helpfulness and, 209
irrational beliefs and, 252
powerlessness and, 518
rejection and, 390
self-esteem and, 94
Descriptive norms, 365
Devaluation of others, 516
Developmental psychology, 9
Deviance, 395–397
Diets and dieting. *See also* Eating
counterregulation, 159
self-awareness and, 77
self-presentation influence, 103
self-regulation, 135
Diffusion of responsibility, 322
Direct aggression, 334
Disasters, natural, E4, E14–E16
Disbelief, 248
Disconnection from others, 516
Discontinuity effect, 466
Discounting, 118, 119
Discrimination
against Arab Americans, 454–455
as behavioral component of intergroup
relations, 450
defined, 449
employment, 454–455, 458–459,
C7–C8
against homosexuals, 458–459
reverse discrimination, 478
in sports, 450
Disease. *See* Illness
Disgust, 57, 204–205, 459–460
Dismissing avoidant attachment, 415
Displaced aggression, 334
Dispute resolution, 48
Disrupt-then-reframe technique, 269–270
Dissimilarities, 379
Dissonance. *See* Cognitive dissonance theory
Distal goals, 127
Distraction
good moods and, 214
as obstacle to helping, 320
in persuasion, 279–280
in social facilitation, 501
Distress-maintaining style of attribution, 421
Diversity, 379, 495
Division of labor, 47
Divorce, 435, A14
DNA testing, 434, 438, 441, D12
Dogs, 61
Domestic violence
culture of honor and, 359
defined, 347
rejection as cause of, 398
risk of, 347–349
victim's reasons for staying with abuser,
376, 420
Dominant responses, 500, A7
Donations, 265, 293
Door-in-the-face technique, 266–267
Double-blind testing, D10
Double standard, 441–442
Doubting, 247
Downward counterfactuals, 176
Downward social comparison, 81, 250
Driving, 264
Drug use, 59, 354–355

Dual attitudes, 232
Duplex mind, 50–54
automatic system (*See* Automatic system)
beliefs, 248
biases and errors, 169
consistency, 244
defined, 51
deliberate system (*See* Deliberate system)
goal hierarchies, 127
persuasion, 280
power, 519
prejudice, 476–477
self-knowledge and, 87
thinking, 151
Dyads, 494

E

Eating. *See also* Diets and dieting
comfort foods, B14
counterregulation, 159
cultural influences, 44, 57
on dates, 432
disgusting foods, 242
emotional eating, 222
habits, 137
loneliness and, 395
mood and, 209
rejection and, 390, 391
in restaurants, 310
self-awareness and, 74, 77
stress and, C25
vegetarianism, 44
violence and, 355
Eating disorders
binge eating, 77, 133, 502
deaths from, 12
rejection and, 390
self-awareness and, 77
TV's impact, 74
EBE (exotic becomes erotic), 433
E-commerce, A5, A12–A13, A16–A17
Economics, 8, 428, E19. *See also* Money
e-cycling, A21
Education. *See also* Academic performance
college education, 59
environmental education, E19
jigsaw classroom, 480
sexual behavior and, 430
of spouses, 379
Efficiency, in thinking, 152–153
Effort, 152–153, 161
Effort justification, 239–241
Egoistic helping, 313–315
Egotism. *See* Selfishness
Elaboration likelihood model (ELM), 280
Elderly
disaster response, E16
shopping behavior, A7
Election polls, 24
Electronics, e-cycling of, A21
ELM (elaboration likelihood model), 280
e-mail, 186
Embodied attitudes, 235
Emergencies
helping in (*See* Prosocial behavior)
natural disasters, E4, E14–E16
Emodiversity, 198–199
Emotional disregard for others, 516
Emotional infidelity, 438

Emotional intelligence (EI or EQ), 218–219
Emotional persuasive messages, 275
Emotions and affect, 184–225
anger (*See* Anger)
arousal (*See* Arousal)
belongingness, 207–208
chronic negative affect, B16
control of, 220–222
cultural differences, 215
defined, 187
disgust, 57, 204–205
fear (*See* Fear)
guilt (*See* Guilt)
happiness (*See* Happiness)
helping behavior and, 318–319
intelligence, 218–219
mood (*See* Mood)
power and, 518
purchasing decisions, A2
reactance, 21
reasons for, 207–214
regulation of, 220–224
rejection and, 390–391
sadness, 209 (*See also* Depression)
self-esteem and, 93, 98
shame, 202
social functions, 55
social information and, 208
of suicidal people, 141
summary, 224–225
theories of, 188–190, 433
uniqueness to human beings, 223–224
Empathy, 312–315
Empathy–altruism hypothesis, 313–314
Employees and employment. *See* Work and
workplace
Endowment effect, 88–89
Energy conservation, E12–E14, E18
Energy sources, E4
England
attachment of children during WWII
separations from family, 413–414
murder rates, 335
Entity theorists, 121
Environment. *See also* Environmental problems;
Nature
aggression impact, 352–353
consumer behavior influences, A6–A8
of workplace, C19, C28
Environmentally-conscious products, 105, A2, A5
Environmental problems, E1–E22
attitude and behavioral changes, E17–E18
barriers to solving, E4–E5
costs and benefits of protection, E20
environmental quality, E9–E12
natural disasters, E4, E14–E16
overpopulation, E4, E5–E9
overview of, E2–E4
scarcity of natural resources, E12–E14
types of, E2–E4
Environmental protection, E20
Environmental psychology, A6
EQ (emotional intelligence), 218–219
Equality, 297, 513
Equity, 296–297
Eros, 339
Erotic plasticity, 430
Error, margin of, 24–25
Error management theory, 119

A General Theory of Crime (Gottfredson & Hirschi), 356
Genetic factors, 421, 426, 433. *See also* Nature
Genocide, in Rwanda, 332–334, 342
Genovese murder, 319–320
Geo-targeting, A16
Gifts and gift giving, A15, C16
Glamour, 25
Globalization, A17, C16
Global warming, 353
Goals
    defined, 125
    vs. habits, 137–138
    hierarchy, 127–128
    management of multiple goals, 128–129
    pursuit of, 125–127
    reaching, 129–130, 196
    self-awareness and, 76
    setting, 125–127
    superordinate goals, 463, 480
Goal shielding, 128–129
Gone With the Wind, 432
Good looks. *See* Attractiveness
Good Samaritan parable, 323
Google, C2–C3, C24
Gratification, delay of, 140
Gratitude, 197, 296
Greed
    commons dilemma, 505–506, 520
    discontinuity effect, 466
    private ownership and, 505
Green products, 105, A5
Group norms, 261
Group polarization effect, 511–512
Groups, 492–525
    actions of, 499–505
    attitude polarization, 238
    conformity, 309
    defined, 494
    diversity in, 496
    expulsion from, 397
    ingroup members, 326, 452, 462
    intergroup relations (*See* Intergroup relations)
    leadership, 513–517, 522–524, C18–C19
    membership in and loneliness, 395
    need to belong and, 377
    obedience, 294, 306–308
    outgroup members, 452
    power, 517–522
    reasons for, 494–495
    rejection in, 396
    roles, 497–499
    summary, 524–525
    thinking of, 506–512
    unity of, 494
    in workplace, 376, C17–C18
Group selection, 57
Groupthink, 508, 509–510
Guilt
    from being overbenefited, 298
    benefits of, 202–203
    defined, 202
    effects of, 202–203
    forgiveness and, 305
    littering and, 364–365
    of rejecters, 398
    relationships and, 58, 203–204
    self-blame and, 250
    vs. shame, 202

    survivor guilt, 203
    washing away, 204
Gullibility, 248
Guns, 350–351

H

Habits, 137–138
Halo effect, 274
Handicapping of self, 86–87, 139. *See also* Self handicapping
Hand washing, 103, 204, 309
Happiness, 194–199
    in close relationships, 207, 421–423
    defined, 194
    marriage and, 420
    physical attractiveness and, 383
    roots of, 194–196, 197
    rule of law and, 295
    in Siberian prison camp, 194
    strategy for, 197–198
Harm appraisals, B6
Harvard Business Review, A5
Hate crimes, 476
Head scarves, 454
Health, B1–B19
    anger impact, 201
    attitudes and, 234
    bad habits, B2
    cancer, 250–251, B2
    convert communicators of messages, 272
    crowding and, E3
    defined, B2
    disgust reaction and, 205
    domestic violence risks, 347
    environmental concerns, E9–E12
    framing of messages about, 156
    happiness impact, 197
    illness, B15–B17
    improvement approaches, B9–B14
    loneliness impact, 395
    self-esteem impact, 101
    self-presentation and, 107
    social connectiveness and, 377
    stress (*See* Stress)
Health belief model, B10–B11
Health psychology, B3
Healthy behaviors, B9–B14
Hearing, 61–62
Heart disease, 201
Heat, 352–353, E3, E10
Hedonic treadmill, 196
Height, 384, 449
Helping. *See also* Prosocial behavior
    bystander effect, 319–333
    contagious, 293
    defined, 294
    increasing, 324–326
    likeliness of, 316–319
    reasons for, 311–315
Helplessness, rejection and, 390
Herd instinct, 375
Heroic acts, 316
Heuristic processing, 280
Heuristics, 164–167
    anchoring and adjustment, 166–167
    availability heuristic, 165
    defined, 164
    representativeness heuristic, 164–165
    scarcity heuristic, 268

    simulation heuristic, 166
    stereotypes as, 467–468, 470
Heuristic/systematic model, 280
Hierarchy of goals, 127–128
High-context cultures, E8
High-empathy people, 313
Higher purpose, belief in, 251
Hiring process, C6–C12. *See also* Work and workplace
History
    of social psychology, 3–5
    as social science, 8
Hit (correct identification), D3
HIV/AIDS, 276, 361, 434, B12
Hmong Americans, attributions of, B16
Hoarding, A14
Holocaust
    humiliation as root of, 360
    rescues of Jews during, 316
    social psychology studies based on, 5
Homeostasis, B4
Homicides, 335
Homophobia, 459
Homosexuality
    attitudes toward, 245
    biological basis for, 425
    domestic violence, 348
    gender differences, 430
    intimacy, 425
    prejudice, 457–461
    prejudice reduction methods, 467
    sexual behavior, 431–433
Honesty, 382, 423–425
Honor, culture of, 358–360
Honor killings, 359
Hoover Institution Task Force on National Security and Law, 359
Hormones, 353–354, 374–375
Hostile aggression, 335
Hostile attribution bias, 343
Hostile expectation bias, 344
Hostile perception bias, 343
Hostile sexism, 471
Hostile work environment, C9
Hot hand, 173
Hot temperatures, 352–353, E3, E10
Hourglass figures, 385
Hours of work, C5
Humans as cultural animals
    antisocial behavior, 366
    attitudes, 253
    attraction, 399
    choice and actions, 143
    close relationships, 443
    consumer behavior, A22–A23
    culture, 63
    emotions, 223–224
    environmental problems, E21
    groups, 523–524
    health, B18
    intergroup relations, 487–488
    laws, D20
    prosocial behavior, 327
    rejection, 399
    self, 108–109
    social cognition, 179–180
    social influence, 286
    work and workplace, C29
Human zoos, 448–449

Humiliation, 359, 436–437
Humility, 106, 513
Humor, 220, 222, 275
Hunger, 56. *See also* Eating
Hurricanes, E14–E15
Hurt feelings, 390
Hydraulic model of aggression, 339
Hypochondriacs, B16
Hypocrisy, 103
Hypocrisy induction, E19
Hypothesis, 14, 15

I

Idealization, 423–425
Ideas, 42, 56
Identity, 105–106, 494–495, 498
Identity theft, 363
Ifaluk people, 465
Ignorance, 466–467
Illness. *See also* Mental illness
    attributions and, B16
    behavior and attitudes in cultures with more
        disease, 47
    cancer, 250–251, B2
    confirmation bias, B15–B16
    heart disease, 201
    loneliness and, 377
    personality and, B16–B17
Illusion of control, 175–176
Illusions, 94, 126
Illusory correlations, 171–172, B15
Imagination, 116
Imitation, 236–237
Implicit attitudes, 476–477
Implicit personality theories, D15
Impressions, 104–106
Impulses, 57–58
Impulsive system. *See* Automatic system
Incorrect rejection, D3
Incremental theorists, 121
Independent self-construal, 72
Independent variables, 15, 19–20
Indirect aggression, 334
Individual good–collective bad trap, E3
Individualism, 47, 106
Industrial and organizational (I/O) psychology,
    C3–C5, C22
Inequality, 505, 522
Infants, 216, 381. *See also* Children
Infidelity, 433–440
Influence. *See* Social influence
Information, reliance on other people for, 61–63
Informational influence, 261–262
Information processing, self and, 88–91
Ingratiation, 378, 380
Ingroup favoritism, 462
Ingroup members, 325, 452
Inhibition orientation to power, 519–521
Initiative, 96, 100
Injunctive norms, 365
Inner processes serving interpersonal relations
        theory
    choices and actions, 115, 123
    defined, 55–56
    emotions, 193
    forgiveness, 306
    prejudice and stereotyping, 472–474
    self-awareness, 74
    self-esteem, 98

Inoculation of attitudes, 283–284
Instinct
    defined, 339
    first instinct fallacy, 176
    herd instinct, 375
    theories of, 338–339
Institutional Review Board (IRB), 19
Instrumental aggression, 335
Instrumental conditioning, 236
Intelligence
    of audience, 278
    emotional intelligence, 218–219
    of groups, 506–508
    physical attractiveness and, 383
    rejection and, 392
    self-fulfilling prophecies, 481
    sex partner choice and, 427–428
    of spouses, 379
    stereotype threat and, 484–485
    stereotyping and, 474
Intentions, behavioral, 246–247
Interdependent self-construal, 72
Intergroup relations, 448–489
    ABCs of, 449–452
    discrimination (*See* Discrimination)
    prejudice (*See* Prejudice)
    stereotypes (*See* Stereotypes)
    summary, 488–489
Internalization, 91
Internal Motivation to Respond Without
      Prejudice, 478–479
Internal validity, 20
Internet
    addiction to, A4, A19
    e-commerce, A5, A12–A13, A16–A18
    employers' searching potential job
        candidates, C10
    online dating, 385–387
    plagiarism, 362
    sex for sale on, A4
    social connections, 374
    social media (*See* Social media)
Interpersonal self, 70
Interpretation, 321
Interracial dating, 453
Interventions, B9
Interviews, C12
Intimacy
    attachment and, 414–415
    defined, 409
    sexuality and, 426 (*See also* Sexuality and
        sexual behavior)
    in Sternberg's triangle of love, 409, 410
Intimate-partner violence. *See* Domestic
      violence
Intrinsic motivation, 82, 123–124
Introspection, 79–80
Introversion, 9
Intuition, 13, 53
Inverted U-shaped relationship, 275
Investment model, 419
Invulnerability, 510
I/O (industrial and organizational) psychology,
    C3–C5, C22
iPhone, A17
IQ testing, 481. *See also* Intelligence
IRB (Institutional Review Board), 19
Ironic processes, 157
Irrational behavior, 138–142

Irrational beliefs, 252
Islam. *See* Muslims

J

Jains, 465
James-Lange Theory of Emotion, 188–190
Japan
    athletes, 121
    modesty, 106
    selfhood, 72–73
    sleeping arrangements, 49
Jealousy, 436–440
Jews and Judaism, 470, 473. *See also* Holocaust
Jigsaw classroom, 480
Job analysis, C7
Job interviews, C11–C12
Jobs. *See also* Work and workplace
    most respected, C4
    types of, C5
Job satisfaction, C21–C22, C23, C27–C28
Job withdrawal, C26–C27
Jonestown, 258–259
Judgments, 468, 470–471
Junk food, 355
Juries
    eyewitness testimony, D12–D14
    selection of, D16–D17
Justice, 294, C23–C24
Just world, belief in, 318

K

Kin selection, 312
Knowledge
    cultural animals' sharing of, 47
    of lineup administrators, D10–D11
    persuasion and, 281
    of self (*See* Self-knowledge)
Knowledge structures, 153
!Kung people, 465

L

Labeling technique, 265
Laboratory experiments, 21–22
Language, 43
Lateral cycling, A20–A21
Laughter, 522
Law, D1–D21
    eyewitness memory, D3–D13
    jury selection, D14–D16
    pretrial publicity, D17–D18
    rule of law, 294
    tradeoffs, 60
    wrongful convictions, D2–D3, D19
Law of least effort, 467
Lead, E11
Leadership, 513–517, 522–524, C18–C19
Learned helplessness, 122, E10
Learning
    aggression, 339–340
    animals vs. humans, 62
    emotions and, 210–211
    social learning theory, 236–237, 339, 461
Legal system. *See* Law
Legitimizing myths, 522
Lesbian, gay, bisexual, and transgendered (LGBT),
      prejudice against, 458–460. *See also*
      Homosexuality
Liberal bias, 487
Life, prolonging, 37

Life satisfaction, 194
Likability, of sources, 273–274
Like-a-hug vest, 231
Liking, 380–382. *See also* Attraction
Limited-number technique, 268
Lineups, D3, D7–D11
Literary Digest poll, 24
Littering, 364–365
Living situation, loneliness and, 394
Location, of store, A6–A8
Loneliness
    defined, 394–395
    health impact, 377, 395
    of powerful people, 517
    studies of, 373–374
    trust and, 311
Long-distance relationships, 376
Long-term goals, 127
Long-term relationships, 417–425
Looking-glass self, 78–79, 90
Loss-framed appeals, 156
Lost letter study, 454–455
Lotteries, 118, 196
Love
    across time, 407–408
    biological basis for, 425
    companionate love (*See*
        Companionate love)
    culture and, 406–407
    defined, 405–406
    gender differences, 216
    lying for, 360–361
    passionate love (*See* Passionate love)
    of self, 416–417
    sex separated from, 430
    Sternberg's triangle, 408–411
    unrequited love, 381, 397–398
Low-ball technique, 264
Low-context cultures, E8–E9
Low-empathy people, 313
Lying, 360–361, 389
Lynching, 473

M

Maintenance stage of transtheoretical model,
    B12, B13
Malay culture, 356
Manhood, 45, 384
Margin of error, 24–25
Market failure, E20
Marriage
    commuter marriages, 376
    companionate vs. passionate love as basis for,
        407–408
    forgiveness in, 304–305
    happiness and, 420
    infidelity, 433–440
    loneliness in, 398
    long-distance relationships, 376
    of Prince Charles and Princess Diana,
        404–405, 408
    remarriages, E16
    self and, 71
    sexual behavior in, 407–408, 409,
        429–430
    similarity of couple's characteristics, 379
    in Victorian period, 424
    view of spouse, 424
Mass action, 47

Mass media. *See also* Social media; Television
    aggression and, 332–333, 351–352
    dissonance theory and, 243
    framing of stories, 156
    packaging and selling of consumers to
        advertisers, A4
    prejudice against Muslims, 455
    Rwanda genocide role, 332–334
Mass murders, 337
Matching hypothesis, 379
Match-to-culprit description, D7
Match-to-suspect strategy, D7
Mathematics, 484–485
McDonald's, A17
Meaning, 115, 123, 125
Measles, mumps, and rubella (MMR) vaccine,
    148–149
Measurement validity, 25
Media. *See* Mass media
Memory
    of eyewitnesses, D3–D13
    heat and, E3
    mood and, 214
    priming, 155
    recovered memory, D19
    self-esteem and, 95
    self-knowledge and, 91
    transactive memory, 509
Men. *See also* Gender and gender differences
    brain size, 40
    disgust reaction, 205
    emotional expression, 215–216
    emotion control strategies, 222
    goal setting, 125–126
    micturation delay study, 18
    self-esteem, 93
    sexual arousal, 191
    testosterone and aggression, 353
Menstrual periods, 91
Mental illness
    affect regulation problems, 220
    aggression in psychiatric wards, 353
    depression (*See* Depression)
    leaders with, 516
    passionate love as, 407
    self-presentation, 103
Mental shortcuts. *See* Heuristics
Mentoring, C14
Mere exposure effect, 234–235, 382–383
Messages
    one-sided vs. two-sided messages,
        275–277
    overheard messages, 279
    reason vs. emotion, 275
    repetition, 277
Meta-analysis, 23, D4
Meta-cognition, 179
Methodology, 13–21
    accumulated common wisdom, 13–14
    cognitive psychology influences, 9
    common wisdom, 13–14
    research design, 17–21
    scientific method, 7, 14
    scientific theories, 15–16
    theories, 15–16
Mexican Americans, attributions of, B16
Mexico, sleep patterns in, 49
Micturation delay study, 18
Milgram experiments, 306–309

Military
    eyewitness memory, D5
    homosexuals in, 459
    morale of soldiers, 270
    tactics to break prisoner's resistance, 284
Millerite Movement, 251
Mimicking, 380, 393
Minimal group effect, 462
Minorities. *See* Race and ethnicity
Mirrors, and self-awareness, 74, 75
Misattribution of arousal, 190–193
Misattributions, B16
Miscarriage of justice, D2
Missing hero trap, E3
Mistaken identification, D3
MMR (Measles, mumps, and rubella) vaccine,
    148–149
Mob violence, 504
Modeling, 325, 339
Modesty, 87, 106, 513
Money
    charitable donations, 268
    cultural significance, 42–43
    decision-making impact, 117
    emotional decisions, 213
    happiness and, 196
    laughter and, 522
    manhood and, 384
    motivation for making, 82
    physical attractiveness and, 384
    prosocial behavior and, 305
    questionable behavior for, 240
    saying things you don't mean for, 240
    self-sufficiency and, 305
    sexual attraction based on, 439
    social acceptance and, 62
    sports teams, 450
    thinking about, 156
Monitoring, 133–134, 278, 379
Mood
    aggression and, 342–343
    defined, 187
    eating and, 209
    good mood benefits, 214
    helping behavior and, 318–319
    persuasion receptivity and, 275
    regulation of, 220–222
Moral inclusion, 326
Moral intuitions, 299
Morality
    environmental issues, E18–E19
    inclusion of others in ingroup, 325–326
    prosocial behavior and, 298–300
    religious principles, 57
    sexuality, 441–442
    in small vs. large groups, 58
Moral judgment, 299
Moral reasoning, 299, E18–E19
Moral superiority, 510
Moral traits, 382
Morning morality effect, 299
Motivation
    for aggression, 334
    guilt as, 203
    for helping, 313–315
    for prejudice avoidance, 478–479
    self-determination theory, 123–124
    self-perception and, 82–83
Movies, smoking depicted in, B9–B10

Multiple goals, 128–129
Mundane realism, 22
Murder rates, 337
Music
    affect regulation strategy, 220
    consumer behavior effects, A6
    military use to break prisoner's resistance, 284
    prosocial behavior modeling, 325
Muslims
    humiliation as contributor to terrorism, 359
    Islamic law, 396
    personal space, E7
    prejudice against, 454–455
    prejudice reduction methods, 467
Mutations, 38
MyPlate, B14

N

Narcissism
    aggression and, 99, 358
    close relationships and, 416–417
    defined, 99–100
    forgiveness, 306
    inflated self-knowledge and, 85
    lack of evaluation apprehension, 501
    leadership and, 513
Narcissists, 501
National Health and Social Life Survey, 409, 434
National Violence Against Women Survey, 398
Natural disasters, E4, E14–E16
Natural resources, scarcity of, E12–E14
Natural selection, 37
Nature
    aggression, 340–341
    behavior from, 56–57
    culture and, 36, 44–47
    defined, 36
    eating habits, 44
    evolution, 36–38
    homosexuality and, 431–433
    prejudice and, 462
    sexuality and, 430–431
    social behavior and, 35–40
    summary of, 63–64
Nature–nurture debate
    children raised as different gender, 34–35
    consistency drive, 243–244
    criticisms of, 36, 341
    summary of, 64–65
Nazi Germany. See also Holocaust
    deindividuation in, 498
    Eichmann trial, 4
    scapegoating of Jews, 473
    stereotypes of Jews, 470
Need for cognition, 278, 280
Need to belong, 373–377, 415, 509
Negative attitude change, 284
Negative emotions or affect, 187, 213–214, 342–343. See also Anger; Fear
Negative political campaigns, 276
Negotiation, 201
Nervous system, B5
Netherlands, prejudice against Muslims, 462
Netnography, A3
Networks, 42
Neuroscience, 5, 8
Neuroticism, B16
Neurotransmitters, 353–354, 406
Neutral stimulus, 235

Night and Fog, 214
1984 (Orwell), 509
Noise, 353, A7, E10–E11
Nonconformity, 47
Nonexperimental studies, 22–24
Nonprejudiced people, mental processes of, 477
Nonverbal communication, E6
Non-zero-sum game, 304
Normative commitment, C22
Normative influence, 260–261
Norms
    aggression and, 356
    about anger, 200
    defined, 296, 365
    of fairness, 294, 296–298
    group norms, 261
    of reciprocity (See Reciprocity)
    subjective norms, 247
Norway, mass murder in, 455
Numbness, 390
Nun studies, 197

O

Obedience, 294–295, 306–309
Obesity, 456, 457
Objective predictors of happiness, 194–196, 197
Observational learning, 236–237
OCBs (organizational citizenship behaviors), C26, C27
Occupational Information Network (O*NET), C5
Occupy movements, 505
Odors, aggression and, 353
Oil drilling, 11, 60
O.J. Simpson trial, D14–D15
Oklahoma City bombing, D18
Olfactory sense, A7
Omission bias, 120
One Day in the Life of Ivan Denisovich (Solzhenitzyn), 194
One-person trap, E3
One-shot illusory correlation, 172
One-sided messages, 275–277
O*NET (Occupational Information Network), C5
Online activities, generally. See Internet
Online dating, 385, 387
Online shopping, A5, A12–A13, A16–A17
Online virtual memorials, A3
Open marriages, 435
Operant conditioning, 236, 239
Operational definitions, 16
Opposites attract, 378
Opposite theory, 249
Optimism
    happiness and, 197
    over-optimism, 94, 131
Options, 118
Organizational citizenship behaviors (OCBs), C26, C27
Organizational climate, 583
Organizational commitment, C22–C23, C27
Organizational culture, C14–C16
Organizational justice, C23–C24
Organizational socialization, C14
Organizational withdrawal, C26–C27
Ostracism, 388–389
Outback Steakhouse, 310
Outgroup homogeneity bias, 452
Outgroup members, 452
Outlook, 197

Outperformers, 297
Overbenefited, 297
Overconsumption, A14–A15
Overheard messages, 279
Overjustification effect, 82–83
Overpopulation, E4, E5–E9
Overweight people, 456, 457
Ownership, A13
Own-race bias, D5
Ozone, E11

P

Pain, 5, 390, 391
The Painted Bird (Kosinski), 496
Panic button effect, 124
Paranoid, 439
Para-sympathetic nervous system (PNS), B5
Parents and parenting
    Affect Intensity Measure and, 199
    attachment, 413–416
    discipline, 349
    emotional bonds, 199
    happiness of, 195
    kin selection, 312
    sleeping arrangements, 49
Passion, 408, 408
Passionate love. See also Close relationships
    across time, 407–408
    vs. companionate love, 406
    cultural differences, 406–407
    defined, 406
    Sternberg's triangle of love theory, 410
    view of lover, 423–424
Paternity tests, 434, 438, 441
Paternity uncertainty, 441
Pay it Forward, 292–293
PEA (phenylethylamine), 406, 408
Peer pressure, 97
People first theory
    description of, 61–63
    self-awareness, 76
    self-knowledge, 86
    social comparison, 80
Perceived behavioral control, 247
Perceived support, B8
Perceptions, 343
Peremptory challenges, D15
Performance
    CEOs' impact on, 513
    emotional arousal and, 217–218
    emotional intelligence and, 219
    rejection and, 396
    of teams, 508–509
    transactive memory and, 509
Performance reviews, C19–C20
Peripheral cues, 281
Peripheral route, 280
Persistence, 100, 126, 513
Personality
    employee selection factors, C12
    happiness and, 196
    health and, B16–B17
    helpfulness, 316
    jury selection, D16
Personality psychology, 9
Personalization, E8
Personal projects. See Goals
Personal relevance, 280
Personal space, E6–E7

Persuasion, 270–286
  audience, 278–280
  defined, 270–271
  eyewitness memory, D11–D13
  messages, 275–277
  models of, 280–282
  resistance to, 282–285
  sources, 271–274
Pets, 395. *See also* Animals
Phenomenal self, 82
Phenylethylamine (PEA), 406, 408
Philosophy, 11
Phobias, 459
Physical aggression, 334. *See also* Aggression
Physical attractiveness. *See* Attractiveness
Physiological psychology, 8
Piaroa people, 465
Pique technique, 269, 270
Plagiarism, 362
Planned behavior theory, 246–247, B11
Planning, 129–131, C20
Planning fallacy, 130
Plastic bags, A10
Plasticity, erotic, 430
Plausibility vs. favorability tradeoff, 106
Pluralistic ignorance, 262, 321
PNS (para-sympathetic nervous system), B5
Point of purchase perceptions,
    A11–A15
Polarization
  attitudes, 237–238
  of group, 511–512
Political issues and attitudes
  American beliefs and practices, 41
  campaigns, 275–277
  polling, 24
  of social psychologists, 12–13
  stereotypes, 470
  tradeoffs, 60
Political science, 8
Pollution, E4, E11–E12
Polychronic activity, A18
Polygraphs (lie detector), 361
Poor people, laughter and, 522
Popularity, 384, 502
Population, 24, E2, E5–E9
Positive affect or emotions, 187, 214. *See also*
    Happiness
Positive illusions, 94–95, 126
Positive psychology movement, 197
Possessiveness, 436–440
Post-consumption process, A20–A21
Post-decision dissonance, 242
Post-traumatic stress disorder (PTSD), E16
Power, 517–522
Praise, 380
Praxis, 42
Prayer, 220
Precarious manhood, 45
Precontemplation stage of transtheoretical model,
    B11–B13
Predictability, in cognitive appraisal model, B7
Predictions, 211–212
Pregnancy
  evolutionary theory and, 427–428,
    437–438
  of prison inmates, 60
  self-esteem and unplanned pregnancy, 97
Prehistoric societies, 335

Prejudice
  as affective component of intergroup
    relations, 450
  in America, 475–476, 477
  against atheists, 455–456
  competition and, 462–466
  consequences of, 451
  contact hypothesis, 466–467
  content of, 470–471
  defined, 449
  disgust reaction, 205
  explanations for, 461–469
  against homosexuals, 457–460
  impact of, 480–486
  inner processes behind, 472–474
  against Muslims, 454–455
  against obese people, 456, 457
  racial prejudice (*See* Racism)
  rationalizations for, 467
  reduction of, 475–480
  self-esteem and, 100, 468
  socialization role, 461
  societal objections to, 451
  true self and, 70
  types of, 453–460
Premarital sex, 441–442
Preoccupied attachment, 415
Preparation stage of transtheoretical model, B12, B13
Presence of others, social facilitation theory,
    500–501
Pretrial publicity, D17–D18
Pride, wounded pride theory, 357–358
Primary appraisals, B6
Primary territories, E8
Prime the pump, 155
Priming, 155–156
The Prince of Tides (Conroy), 392
Prisoner's dilemma, 301, 302, 303–304, 518
Prisons and prisoners, 60, 355, 375
Private acceptance, 262
Private ownerships, 505
Private self-awareness, 74
Private settings, 295–296
Privileged access, 79, 81
Proactive aggression, 335
Procrastination, 141
Product, human beings as, A19–A20
Product misuse, A19
Product placement, 279
Promiscuity, rejection and, 390. *See also* Sexuality
    and sexual behavior
Prompts, E12
Propinquity effect, 382–383
Prosocial behavior, 290–327
  bystander effect, 319–333
  in communal relationships, 413
  conformity, 309
  cooperation, 301–304
  defined, 294–298
  depression and, 208
  fairness, 295, 296–298
  forgiveness, 304–306
  human uniqueness, 47–48
  increasing, 324–326
  likeliness of, 316–319
  morality, 298–300
  obedience, 306–309
  organizational citizenship behaviors,
    C26, C27

personal space and, E7
physical attractiveness and, 384
reasons for, 311–315
reciprocity, 296
summary, 328–329
trust, 309–311
Prostitutes, 376
Prototype-willingness model, B13–B14
Proximal goals, 128
Psyche, 35–36
Psychoanalysis, 5, 6
Psychological reactance, 21, 268, 365
Psychology, 8–9
PTSD (post-traumatic stress disorder), E16
Public awareness, 440
Public compliance, 262
Public image, concern for, 278
Public opinion polls, 25
Public self, 70
Public self-awareness, 74
Public self-consciousness, 77
Public settings, and prosocial behavior, 295–296,
    324–325
Public territories, E8
Punishment
  of children, 349
  power and, 519
  of social loafers, 503–504
Purity, 204
Purpose, in life, 251

Q

Quasi-experiments, 19
Quid pro quo, C9

R

Race and ethnicity
  peremptory challenges based on, D16
  phenomenal self, 82–83
  research issues, 18–19
  scapegoat theory, 473
  self-esteem, 93
  social psychology impact, 6
Racism
  conscious override, 476
  defined, 449
  problem of, 452
  in sports, 450
Radio, A4
Random assignment, 18, 20, 21
Random sample, 24
Rape
  chastity belts, 437
  criminal convictions, D16
  defined, 348
  media portrayals, 352
  in Rwanda, 333
Rationalization, 467
Reactance, 21, 365
Reactance theory, 120–121
Reactive aggression, 335
Realism, 22
Realistic conflict theory, 464
Reality shows, 372, 381
Real self, 70–71
Reason, 54, 275
Received support, B8
Receptivity, 79, 278
Reciprocity

of animals, 297
cooperation, 301
defined, 296
energy conservation promotion, E14
in exchange relationships, 412
liking and, 380–382
lying in romantic relationships, 361
social influence techniques based on, 266–268
Recovered memory, D19
Recruitment of employees, C8–C11
Recycling, 365, A21
Referrals, employee, C9
Reflective system. *See* Deliberate system
Reframing, 221
Regression to the mean, 175
Regret, 120, 177, 212
Reinforcement theory, 380
Rejection, 388–399
defined, 372
for deviation from group norms, 261
effects of, 390–393
loneliness from, 394–395
ostracism, 388–389
reasons for, 395–397
Rejection sensitivity, 390
Relational aggression, 346
Relationship-enhancing style of attribution, 421–422
Relationship orientation, 514
Relationships
attraction (*See* Attraction)
belongingness, 207–208, 373–376
close relationships (*See* Close relationships)
emotions in, 207
exchange relationships, 412–413
forgiveness, 304–306
friendship (*See* Friendship)
guilt's role in, 203–204
happiness and, 195
loneliness and, 394–395
lying in, 361
narcissists, 99–100
self-esteem and, 100–101
self-presentation, 106
social allergy effect, 383
Relative age effect, 45
Relativity, cultural, 27
Relevance, and persuasion impact, 280
Reliability, 25–26, C11
Relief workers, E15
Religion
affect regulation, 220
atheists, 311, 455
beliefs, 251–252
brainwashing, 248
false uniqueness effect, 174
forgiveness, 306
happiness and, 197
laws and moral principles, 57
reciprocation and, 268
self-presentation and, 106
sexual behavior and, 430
Remarriage, E16
Renewable energy, E20
Repetition, 277
Repetition with variation, 277
Replication, 26
Representativeness heuristic, 164–165

Reproduction
evolution and, 38, 39, 297, 427
as feature of life, 38
Research, 17–24
cultural influences, 49
ethical issues, 18–19
experimental studies (*See* Experimental studies)
nonexperimental studies, 22–24
Resistance to social influence, 282–285
Responsibility, diffusion of, 321–322
Restaurants, 309
Retail stores, A5–A6
Retail theft, 363
Retaliation, 347
Revenge, 212, 347
Reverse discrimination, 478, 487
Reverse double standard, 441
Reverse psychology, 120
Rewards
aggression and, 347
attraction and, 380
overjustification effect, 82–83
power and, 519
Rhetoric (Aristotle), 271, 275
Risk-as-feelings hypothesis, 213
Risk aversion, 116
Risky behavior
of adolescents, B13–B14
good mood impact, 214
self-presentation impact, 106–107
sexual arousal and, 213–214
testosterone and, 374
Risky shift, 511–512
Robber's Cave study, 462–464
Roles, 72–74, 497–499
Romantic love. *See* Passionate love
Romantic Passion: A Universal Experience? (Jankowiak), 407
Romantic Period, 406
Romantic relationships. *See* Close relationships
Royal family, 405
Rule breaking, 396–397
Rule of law, 295
Rules, in exchange vs. communal relationships, 413
Running amok, 356
Russian roulette, 118
Rwanda genocide, 332–334, 342

S

Sadness, 209. *See also* Depression
Safe sex practices, 276, B12
Salience, 472
Samoans, 437
Samples and sampling, college students, 26–27
Scapegoat theory, 472–473
Scarcity
of natural resources, E12–E14
social influence techniques based on, 268–269
Scare tactics, for persuasion, 275–276
Schachter–Singer theory of emotion, 190, 433
Schemas, 153–154
Schools. *See* Education
Scientific method, 7, 14
Scripts, 154
Secondary appraisals, B6
Secondary territories, E8

Second-hand stores, A20–A21
Secure attachment, 414, 415
Selective confirmation, 424
Selective exposure, 243
Self, 66–110
acceptance of, 417
awareness of (*See* Self-awareness)
blame of, 250
censorship of, 510
control of (*See* Self-control)
correction of, 26
creation of, 70–74
defined, 69
esteem of (*See* Self-esteem)
fluctuating images of, 82–84
functions of, 69–70
handicapping of, 86–87, 139
information processing and, 88–92
knowledge of (*See* Self-knowledge)
presentation of (*See* Self-presentation)
study of, 5
summary of, 109–110
uniqueness to human beings, 108–109
Self-acceptance, 417
Self-actualization, 416
Self-awareness
aggression and, 20–21
alcohol use impact, 354
avoidance of, 75
behavior and, 75
defined, 74
deindividuation and, 498
escaping, 75–76
reasons for, 76
standards, 74–75
suicide and, 76, 142
theory of, 75
types of, 74
Self-blame, 250
Self-censorship, 510
Self-concept. *See* Self-knowledge
Self-concept confusion, 92
Self-consciousness, 278
Self-construal, 72
Self-control. *See also* Self-regulation
aggression and, 356–357
culture and, 56–57
forgiveness and, 306
trust and, 311
Self-correction, 26
Self-deception strategies, 94, 95, 102
Self-defeating behavior, 138–141
Self-defeating prophecies, 484
Self-destructive behavior, 138–141
Self-determination theory, 123–124
Self-efficacy, B11
Self-enhancement motive, 85–86, 106
Self-esteem
aggression and, 357
benefits of, 96–98
changes in, 90
close relationships and, 416–417, 424
defined, 92–94
depression and, 94
high, 99–100
illness and, B17
importance of, 96–97
negative aspects of, 99
prejudice and, 100, 468, 482–483